THE BIG FAT BOOK OF EGYPTIAN ARABIC VERBS

MATTHEW ALDRICH
WITH
YOMNA ADLY

Revised 2021

ISBN: 978-0985816094

website: www.lingualism.com
email: contact@lingualism.com

TABLE OF CONTENTS

INTRODUCTION

This book is designed as a learning tool for advanced beginner and intermediate learners of Egyptian Colloquial Arabic (ECA). It contains conjugation tables for 264 of the most common verbs used by Egyptians in their everyday speech. Each table appears on a left-facing page, while the opposing, right-facing page gives several example sentences demonstrating the verb in various contexts. All of the examples were written by a native speaker from Cairo and *then* translated into English. Care was given to provide a variety of forms for each verb (different persons, numbers, tenses, negative forms, etc.) in the examples, following which are notes shedding more light on the verb's meaning and usage.

All of the Arabic in this book appears in both Arabic script and its phonemic transcription. The Arabic is written with tashkeel (voweling) so that each word's pronunciation is clear. The phonemic transcription provides an even more accurate representation of the sounds of ECA, which cannot always be represented by the Arabic script. It can also be helpful for learners who are not yet completely comfortable with Arabic script.

I would like to thank Yomna Adly for her tremendous help throughout this project. Not only did Yomna write the example sentences, but she also answered numerous questions I had about verb forms and usage and checked the accuracy of the conjugation tables, offering invaluable feedback along the way. Of course, any remaining mistakes are my own. I would also like to thank Mohamed Maged and Heba Salah Ali for providing the excellent audio recordings that accompany this book on MP3.

FREE ACCOMPANYING AUDIO

You can download or stream the accompanying audio tracks from our website, where you can also find other resources.

www.lingualism.com/bfb

HOW TO USE THIS BOOK

The Big Fat Book of Egyptian Verbs is *not* an introduction to ECA verbs. To best make use of this book, you should have some Arabic under your belt, whether that be ECA or MSA (Modern Standard Arabic). It is assumed that you already have at least a basic understanding of verb conjugation in Arabic and the use of tenses. But fear not, very brief reviews are provided in the glossary on page vi. A review of the sounds of ECA and the phonemic transcription is found in the Pronunciation section starting on page iii. For more in-depth coverage of verb tenses, see Lingualism's book **Egyptian Colloquial Arabic Verbs: Conjugation Tables and Grammar**, which lays out the system by which all ECA verbs can be grouped.

This book contains 264 'key' verbs, numbered for easy reference. They are ordered alphabetically according to the Arabic script, with the exception of the first two tables. Verb 1 is كان *kān* 'be', which is arguably the most important and common verb in Arabic and is used to form compound tenses. Verb 2 is actually not a verb at all, but three common structures (pseudo-verbs) which are used with the verb كان *kān* 'be' and translate 'have'.

Next to each verb's number (on the left margin of the left-facing page), you will see the base form of the Arabic verb (that is, the masculine third-person singular perfect tense form) with a common English translation. A verb often has many possible translations, and these are given after the examples on the right-facing page.

THE CONJUGATION TABLES

Take a look at any of the conjugation tables in this book as you read the following paragraph:

In ECA, there are eight persons (labeled on the left side of each table) and, therefore, eight conjugations for each tense of a verb. (Strictly speaking, some of these should be called *moods,* not tenses, but for simplicity's sake, we'll call them all *tenses.*) The four tenses of ECA are the perfect, the (bare) imperfect, the bi-imperfect, and the future. You will see each of these labels along the right side of each table. The four tenses and the imperative have both affirmative and negative forms. The affirmative forms are listed on the left half of the table, while the negative forms are on the right. At the bottom of the table, you can see the participle forms. Not all verbs have both active and passive participles. Finally, on the left edge of the table, you will see the verbal noun(s). (Explanations for all of these terms can be found in the Glossary on page vi.)

Take a look on page 1 to see an English translation example of a table, which will help you understand the organization of the conjugation tables better.

THE RIGHT-FACING PAGE

Several example sentences are given on the right-facing page. Each example is numbered for easy reference. Try to find the key verb in each example and match it to its place on the conjugation table. Notice if the verb's pronunciation is affected by neighboring words or suffixes. (See Pronunciation: Sound Changes)Take time to analyze the sentence and notice how the verb is used in relation to other words. Does it take a direct object? Does a preposition follow it? Does it seem to have just one meaning or several distinct meanings? Can you spot collocations? Some of these questions will be answered for you in the notes.

Below the example sentences, you will see English translations for the verb. Synonyms are separated by commas, while semicolons separate different meanings. If a verb requires a preposition before its object, you will also see this here in parentheses. Note that a verb may require a preposition in one meaning but not in another.

Preceding the translations, you will see square brackets. These contain references to the verb's corresponding table as presented in the book *Egyptian Colloquial Arabic Verbs: Conjugation Tables and Grammar.* In brief, Arabic verbs can be grouped into a few dozen conjugation patterns. If you compare two verbs in this book that have the same reference number in brackets, you will see that their conjugations are identical. Only the radicals (consonants) are different. The book *Egyptian Colloquial Arabic Verbs: Conjugation Tables and Grammar* focuses on the underlying organization of the verb system in Egyptian Arabic.

Under the line of translations, there may be bullet-pointed notes highlighting interesting points about the verb, its forms, and its uses in some of the examples. It is beyond the scope of this book to gloss the vocabulary found in the examples or explain the grammar. But hopefully, you can work out the individual meaning of most unknown words by comparing a sentence to its English translation.

Finally, if the key verb can be found in examples on other pages in the book, these are referenced at the bottom of the page.

THE MP3S

You can download or stream the audio tracks from our website. Each key verb has its own MP3 file, labeled by the table number it corresponds to. First, you will hear the base form of the verb in the perfect tense followed by the imperfect tense, and then any common verbal nouns, as shown in the book. The example sentences follow, in the order they appear on the page. You are encouraged to pause the audio at any time to repeat the sentences after the native speaker(s).

THE INDEX

At the back of the book, starting on page 534, you can find an English-Arabic index. Note that the numbers in the index reference the table numbers of verbs and not page numbers.

PRONUNCIATION

Egyptian Colloquial Arabic is a spoken dialect with no official status or rules of orthography. Egyptians tend to borrow spelling conventions from MSA with some accommodations to account for ECA pronunciation. Arabic script, however, is ill-suited to show the actual pronunciation of ECA and the sound changes that occur when words are inflected. Even if you are comfortable with Arabic script, it is advised that you pay close attention to the phonemic transcription to determine the exact pronunciation of words and phrases.

CONSONANTS

The following sounds are also found in English and should pose no difficulties for learners:

			examples
b	ب	[b] as in **b**ed	*bána* بنَى *(build)*
d	د	[d̪] as in **d**og, but with the tongue touching the back of the upper teeth	*dáras* درس *(study)*
f	ف	[f] as in **f**our	*fāz* فاز *(win)*
g	ج	[g] as in **g**as	*gíri* جِري *(run)*
h	ه	[h] as in **h**ouse	*hágam* هجم *(attack)*
k	ك	[k] as in **k**id	*kal* كل *(eat)*
l	ل	[l] a light ***l*** as in **l**ove; but in the word الله [ɫ] a dark, velarized ***l*** as in ye**ll**.	*líbis* لِبس *(get dressed)*
m	م	[m] as in **m**oon	*māt* مات *(die)*
n	ن	[n] as in **n**ice	*nísi* نِسي *(forget)*
s	س ث	[s] as in **s**un	*sāb* ساب *(leave)*
š	ش	[š] as in **sh**ow	*šakk* شكّ *(doubt)*
t	ت	[t̪] as in **t**ie, but with the tongue touching the back of the upper teeth	*taff* تفّ *(spit)*
w	و	[w] as in **w**ord	*wárra* وَرّى *(show)*
y	ي	[j] as in **y**es	*yíktib* يِكْتِب *(he writes)*
z	ز ذ	[z] as in **z**oo	*zār* زار *(visit)*
ž	ج	[ʒ] as in plea**s**ure and bei**g**e; used in foreign borrowings and sometimes written چ to distinguish it from ج [g].	*žim* جيم *(gym)*
v	ف	[v] (sometimes spelled ڤ) and [p] (پ) appear in some	*seven ap* سفن اپ *(7 Up)*
p	ب	foreign borrowings, but may also be pronounced [f] and [b], respectively, by many speakers	

The following sounds have no equivalent in English and require special attention. However, some exist in other languages you may be familiar with.

r	ر	[r] tapped (flapped) as in the Spanish ca**r**a, or the Scottish pronunciation of t**r**ee	*ráma* رمى *(throw)*
ɣ	غ	[ɣ] very similar to a guttural ***r*** as in the French Pa**r**is, or the German **r**ot	*ɣāb* غاب *(be absent)*
x	خ	[x] as in the German do**ch**, Spanish ro**j**o, or Scottish lo**ch**	*xad* خد *(take)*
q	ق	[q] like ***k*** but further back, almost in the throat, with the tongue touching the uvula	*qād* قاد *(lead)*
ḥ	ح	[ħ] like a strong, breathy ***h***, as if you were trying to fog up a window	*ḥáfar* حفر *(dig)*

3	ع	[ʕ] a voiced glottal stop, as if you had opened your mouth under water and constricted your throat to prevent choking and then released the constriction with a sigh	*3írif* عِرِف *(know)*
ʔ	ء ق	[ʔ] an unvoiced glottal stop, as [ʕ] above, but with a wispy, unvoiced sigh; or more simply put, like the constriction separating the vowels in uh-oh	*ʔíbil* قِبِل *(accept)* *ʔá3lan* أعْلن *(announce)*

The following sounds also have no equivalent in English but are emphatic versions of otherwise familiar sounds. An emphatic consonant is produced by pulling the tongue back toward the pharynx (throat), spreading the sides of the tongue wide as if you wanted to bite down on both sides of your tongue, and producing a good puff of air from the lungs.

ḍ	ض	[dˤ] emphatic ***d***	*ḍárab* ضرب *(hit)*
ṣ	ص	[sˤ] emphatic ***s***	*ṣamm* صمّ *(memorize)*
ṭ	ط	[tˤ] emphatic ***t***	*ṭáwa* طوَى *(fold)*
ẓ	ظ	[zˤ] emphatic ***z***	*ẓann* ظنّ *(believe)*

VOWELS

			<u>*examples*</u>
a	ـَ	[æ] normally as in c**a**t (but with the jaw not quite as lowered as in English); [a] as in st**o**ck when in the same syllable with ***ħ*** or ***3*** (with the tongue lower than [æ]); usually [ɑ] as in f**a**ther (but shorter) when in the same word as ***q, ḍ, ṣ, ṭ, ẓ*** or, in most cases, ***r***	*kátab* كتب *(write)* *ma-bá3š* مباعْش *(he didn't sell)* *ḍárab* ضرب *(hit)* *ɣáṣab* غصب *(force)*
ā	ـا	[æ:] / [a:] / [ɑ:] as with ***a*** above but longer	*nām* نام *(sleep)* *gā3* جاع *(get hungry)* *qād* قاد *(lead)*
ē	ـيْ	[e:] as in pl**ay** (but without the glide to [j])	*malēt* مليْت *(I filled)*
^{ə}		[ə] as in tick**e**t. In ECA, ^{ə} is inserted to avoid three adjacent consonants.	*kúnt*^{ə} *hína* كُنْت هنا *(I was here)*
i	ـِ	[ɪ] as in k**i**d; [ɛ] as in b**e**d when in the same syllable with ***ħ*** or ***3***; when in the same word as ***q, ḍ, ṣ, ṭ,*** or ***ẓ***, [ɨ] with the tongue pulled back a bit	*3ílim* علِم *(know)* *biyíħsib* بيِحْسِب *(he calculates)* *itẓāhir* اِتْظاهِر *(protest)*
ī	ـي	[i:] as in sk**i**; [ɛ:] and [ɨ:] as with **i** above (but longer)	*biygīb* بيْجيب *(he brings)* *biybī3* بيْبيع *(he sells)* *3āqib* عاقِب *(punish)*
ō	ـوْ	[o:] as with **o** above but longer	*nōm* نوْم *(sleep)*
u	ـُ	[ʊ] as in b**oo**k; [o] as in kn**ow** (but shorter and without the glide to [w]) when in the same syllable with ***ħ*** or ***3***	*yúṭlub* يُطْلُب *(he orders)* *inbā3u* اِنْباعوا *(they sold)*
ū	ـو	[u:] as in m**oo**n; [o:] as in kn**ow** (but without the glide to [w]) when in the same syllable with ***ħ*** or ***3***	*bitšūf* بِتْشوف *(you see)* *maba3ūš* مباعوش *(they didn't sell)*

SOUND CHANGES

A lot of the changes which occur in conjugated ECA verbs are due to the rules of syllable structure and stress. The rules are summarized here using phonemic transcription only, as the Arabic script does not reflect these changes.

Vowel Shortening: When a suffix beginning in a consonant is added immediately after a syllable containing a long vowel, or when a suffix causes the stressed syllable to move, the long vowel is shortened. This is because a long vowel can only exist in a stressed syllable and cannot be followed by two consonants.

bagīb + ha = bagībha → ***bagíbha***	I bring it
ma + nām + š = ma-nāmš → ***ma-námš***	he didn't sleep
sāfir + t = sāfírt → ***safírt***	you traveled
nisīt + ni = nisītni → ***nisítni***	you forgot me

A long **ē** is shortened to **i**.

ma + ђabbēt + š = ma-ђabbētš → ***ma-ђabbítš***	I didn't love

Vowel Lengthening: A final vowel is lengthened when certain suffixes are added to a word ending in a short vowel.

ma + ráma + š = ma-rámaš → ***ma-ramāš***	he didn't throw
3ámalu + u = 3ámaluu → ***3amalū***	they did it
nísi + t = nísit → ***nisīt***	you forgot

Vowel Elision: A short, unstressed **i** (or **u**) is elided (that is, omitted) from a word when its omission would not result in a series of three adjacent consonants, in other words, when the vowel is both preceded and followed by a single consonant only. This does not happen in a final syllable, and it only happens in the first syllable if the preceding word ends in a vowel.

Vowel omission occurs when ***-it*** (the third person feminine singular ***(híyya)*** suffix of the perfect tense) or ***-u*** (the third person plural ***(húmma)*** suffix of the perfect tense) is added to a sound measure I verb containing **i**:

šírib + it = šíribit → ***šírbit***	she drank

Notice that the elision may create two adjacent consonants following a long vowel, in which case the long vowel must be shortened. In the second example, it is the feminine form of an active participle in which elision occurs.

sāfir + it = sāfirit → *sāfrit* → ***sáfrit***	she traveled
kātib + a = kātiba → *kātba* → ***kátba***	writing

Elision can also take place with the addition of a prefix. That is, the **i** of the imperfect prefixes ***ni-***, ***ti-***, and ***yi-*** is elided when the imperfect prefix ***bi-***, the negative prefix ***ma-***, or the future prefix ***ha-*** is added, as long as the elision would not result in three adjacent consonants.

ha + nifákkar = hanifákkar → ***hanfákkar***	we'll think
ma + yisāfir + š = ma-yisāfirš → ***ma-ysafírš***	he doesn't travel
bi + yitárgim = biyitárgim → ***biytárgim***	he translates
ha + tiʔūl = hatiʔūl → ***hatʔūl***	you'll speak
bi + tiђíbb = bitiђíbb → ***bitђíbb***	she loves

An originally long vowel is normally not elided, even after it has become short because of a shift in stress. An exception occurs in the following verb:

ma + tīgi + š = ma-tīgiš → *ma-tigīš* → ***ma-tgīš*** she doesn't come

Elision can occur in the first syllable of a word if the preceding word ends in a vowel, as long as this would not result in three adjacent consonants (as in the second example below).

híyya bitúskun → ***híyya btúskun***	she lives
húwwa biyɧíbb → ***húwwa biyɧíbb***	he loves

Vowel Insertion (Epenthesis): A short vowel is inserted when a suffix or a following word would create a situation with three adjacent consonants. ***i*** is inserted between two consonants and the negative suffix **-š** or indirect object pronouns. Direct object pronouns may take ***a**, **i***, or ***u***.

ma + ʔúlt + š = ma-ʔúltš → ***ma-ʔúltiš***	I didn't say
gibt + li = gibtli → ***gibtíli***	you brought (to) me
šuft + ni = šúftni → ***šuftíni***	you saw me
šuft + ha = šúftha → ***šuftáha***	I saw her
šuft + ku = šúftku → ***šuftúku***	I saw you (pl.)

Vowel insertion can also occur between word boundaries. When a word ends in two consonants and the next word begins with a consonant, **ə** is inserted to avoid three adjacent consonants.

biyɧíbb bint → ***biyɧíbbᵊ bint***	He loves a girl.
ʔúlt ʔē → ***ʔúltᵊ ʔē***	What did you say?

Once **ə** is inserted, the vowel of the first syllable of the following word may be a candidate for elision.

kúntᵊ mišīt → ***kúntᵊ mšīt***	I had walked
kúntᵊ bitúskun → ***kúntᵊ btúskun***	you were living

Consonant Assimilation: A voiced consonant immediately preceding an unvoiced consonant tends to become unvoiced. The table below shows such consonants in pairs—voiced consonants in the left column and their voiceless counterparts on the right. The change is not reflected in writing, either in Arabic script or the phonemic transcription used in this book.

voiced	voiceless	
b	**p**	*b* → *p:* ***katábt*** */katápt/*
d	**t**	*d* → *t:* ***rafádku*** */rafátku/*
ḑ	**ţ**	*ḑ* → *ţ:* ***ma-faraḑš*** */-raţš/*
v	**f**	-
g	**k**	*g* → *k:* ***nahágti*** */nahákti/*
ɣ	**x**	*ɣ* → *x:* ***balláɣt*** */ balláxt/*
z	**s**	*z* → *s:* ***ɧagázt*** */ɧagást/*
ẓ	**ṣ**	*ẓ* → *ṣ:* ***ɧafaẓt*** */ɧafaṣt/*

The reverse is also true, so that a voiceless consonant followed by a voiced consonant may become voiced. Listen for such sound changes in the accompanying MP3s.

The prefix ***it-*** of many verbs is not only affected by the following consonant's voicing, but, in relaxed speech, it may be totally assimilated by a following ***d, ḍ, g, k, s, ṣ, š, ṭ, z,*** or ***ẓ***.

itdāra →/iddāra/	be hidden
itḍárr →/iḍḍárr/	be damaged
itgámma3 →/idgámma3 / →/iggámma3 /	come together
itkátab →/ikkátab/	be written
itsállim →/issállim/	receive
itṣāɦib →/iṣṣāɦib/	become friends
itšárab →/iššárab/	be drunk
itṭábax →/iṭṭábax/	cook
itzáɦlaʔ →/idzáɦlaʔ/→/izzáɦlaʔ/	slip
itẓábaṭ →/idẓábaṭ/ →/iẓẓábaṭ/	be adjusted

Vowel Assimilation: Two vowels cannot occur together. When the addition of a prefix or preceding word would result in such a case, one vowel is assimilated into the other. As seen in the last example below, this also applies across word boundaries in some cases.

ma- + itkátab + š = ma-itkátabš → ***ma-tkatábš***	it wasn't written
ma- + áktib + š = ma-áktibš → ***ma-ktíbš***	I don't write
ha- + áktib = haáktib → ***háktib***	I will write
yi- + istáxdim = yiistáxdim → ***yistáxdim***	he uses
ána + istaxdímt = ána istaxdímt → ***ána staxdímt***	I used

Vowel assimilation also occurs with the final vowel a verb ends in ***a*** or ***u***. Thi vowel is dropped when a suffix beginning with a vowel is added.

yímši + -u = yímšiu → ***yímšu***	they walk
tínsa + -i = tínsai → ***tínsi***	you (f.) forget
ráma + -u = rámau → ***rámu***	they threw
mála + -it = málait → ***málit***	she filled

When ***-it*** and ***-u*** are added to a verb ending in ***i,*** the ***i*** changes into a ***y***.

nísi + -it = nísiit → ***nísyit***	she forgot
míši + -u = míšiu → ***míšyu***	they walked

GLOSSARY

active participle: In English, the active participle (commonly known as the present participle) ends in -ing. It can be used as an adjective, as in *the singing bird* or *the book is interesting.* In ECA, active participles are also used as quasi-verbs, often corresponding to the present perfect (*I have eaten*) or present continuous (*I am going*) of English. An active participle agrees with its subject in gender or number but is otherwise unconjugated.

affirmative: This is simply a verb that is grammatically not negative. *I like* and *I dislike* are affirmative verbs, while *I don't like* and *I don't dislike* are negative verbs.

auxiliary: An auxiliary is a conjugated verb or participle that precedes an imperfect verb. This corresponds to verbs that precede an infinitive or gerund in English: *I <u>might</u> come. / I <u>need</u> to go. / I <u>like</u> drawing.*

bi-imperfect: The bi-imperfect tense is formed by adding the prefix بِـ *bi-* to the imperfect tense. It is essentially the present tense of ECA, translating as the present simple (*I write*) or the present continuous (*I am writing*) of English. It can express a repeated (habitual) action or an ongoing (continuous) action.

collocation: A collocation is a combination of two or more words that are commonly found together. Collocations can be adjectives with nouns (*fast car, cold day*), verbs with nouns (*quit a job, play soccer*), etc. By comparison, combinations like *cold car, fast day, and quit soccer* are far less common, and *play a job* hardly makes sense.

ditransitive: A ditransitive verb takes two direct objects. English and Arabic are similar in their use of ditransitive verbs. In the example *give me the pen*, the verb *give* has two objects *me* and *the pen.* By comparison, the verb *explain* is not ditransitive. You cannot say *explain me it.* Instead, you have to use a preposition before one of the objects: *explain it to me.*

future: The future tense in Arabic is formed with the prefix هـ *ha-*. (Note that it can also be written and pronounced حـ *ħa*.) هعْمِل *há3mil*, for example, can be translated as *I will do, I'm going to do,* or *I'm doing* in English.

imperative: The imperative is the command form used to give an order: *Do! / Don't do!*

imperfect: The imperfect tense of ECA is comparable to the subjunctive of MSA. It is most commonly used after certain conjunctions, and also after auxiliaries and other verbs. It would be used to translate the following underlined words: *I'm studying <u>in order to pass</u> the test. / I want <u>to go</u>. / I can <u>swim</u>. / I have <u>to try</u> / I like <u>drawing</u>.*

intransitive: An intransitive verb cannot take a direct object. (See **transitive**)

invariable: If an adjective is invariable, it remains in the masculine form, not taking the feminine suffix ـه *-a* or plural suffix ـين *-īn*. An invariable verb remains in the masculine third-person form.

negative: A negative verb is formed in ECA with the prefix-suffix combo مـ......ـش *ma-...-š* or the word مِش *miš* (also pronounced مُش *muš*). In English, this is done using the word *not,* in various forms such as *didn't, don't, doesn't,* and *won't.*

participle: Participles are the *adjective* forms of verbs. (See **active participle** and **passive participle**.)

passive participle: Passive participles are derived from verbs but are used as adjectives. In English, this may be referred to as the *past participle* and is formed with -ed or may be irregular: *cooked, written, done.*

perfect: The perfect tense is the past tense of ECA. It is usually translated with the past simple of English (*I did*) or the present perfect (*I have done*).

transitive: A transitive verb takes, or at least can take, a direct object. If the object requires a preposition, the verb is not considered transitive. For example, *see* is transitive: *I see <u>it</u>.* But *go* is intransitive because you cannot *go something,* although you can *go <u>to</u> something.*

verbal noun: A verbal noun is also known as a gerund, and in Arabic grammars, as *maṣdar*. The English gerund always ends in -ing. However, in Arabic it may take many different forms. It always expresses an action (the act of __ing), rather than a tangible object. The verbal noun is, as the name implies, a noun form derived from a verb. As such, it can be the subject or object of a verb: *<u>Cooking</u> is fun. / I'm interested in <u>learning</u> more about that.*

EXAMPLE TABLE

This is an English translation example to help you understand the organization of a conjugation table.

0 to write

	affirmative	negative	
I	I wrote	I didn't write	perfect
we	we wrote	we didn't write	
you (m.)	you wrote	you didn't write	
you (f.)	you wrote	you didn't write	
you (pl.)	you wrote	you didn't write	
he (it)	he wrote	he didn't write	
she (it/they)	she wrote	she didn't write	
they	they wrote	they didn't write	
I	I write	I don't write	imperfect
we	we write	we don't write	
you (m.)	you write	you don't write	
you (f.)	you write	you don't write	
you (pl.)	you write	you don't write	
he (it)	he writes	he doesn't write	
she (it/they)	she writes	she doesn't write	
they	they write	they don't write	
I	I write	I don't write	bi-imperfect
we	we write	we don't write	
you (m.)	you write	you don't write	
you (f.)	you write	you don't write	
you (pl.)	you write	you don't write	
he (it)	he writes	he doesn't write	
she (it/they)	she writes	she doesn't write	
they	they write	they don't write	
I	I will write	I won't write	future
we	we will write	we won't write	
you (m.)	you will write	you won't write	
you (f.)	you will write	you won't write	
you (pl.)	you will write	you won't write	
he (it)	he will write	he won't write	
she (it/they)	she will write	she won't write	
they	they will write	they won't write	
you (m.)	write!	don't write!	imperative
you (f.)	write!	don't write!	
you (pl.)	write!	don't write!	

	active	passive	
masculine	writing	written	participles
feminine	writing	written	
plural	writing	written	

verbal noun: (the act of) writing

Note that the tenses can be translated in more than one way. See the Glossary for details on the tenses.

THE VERBS

1 to be *kān* كان

verbal noun: *kōn* كَوْن

	affirmative		negative		
ána	*kunt*	كُنْت	*ma-kúntiš*	مَكُنْتِش	**perfect**
íḥna	*kúnna*	كُنّا	*ma-kunnāš*	مَكُنّاش	
ínta	*kunt*	كُنْت	*ma-kúntiš*	مَكُنْتِش	
ínti	*kúnti*	كُنْتي	*ma-kuntīš*	مَكُنْتيش	
íntu	*kúntu*	كُنْتوا	*ma-kuntūš*	مَكُنْتوش	
húwwa	*kān*	كان	*ma-kánš*	مَكانْش	
híyya	*kānit*	كانِت	*ma-kanítš*	مَكانِتْش	
húmma	*kānu*	كانوا	*ma-kanūš*	مَكانوش	
ána	*akūn*	أكون	*ma-kúnš*	مَكونْش	**imperfect**
íḥna	*nikūn*	نِكون	*ma-nkúnš*	مَنْكونْش	
ínta	*tikūn*	تِكون	*ma-tkúnš*	مَتْكونْش	
ínti	*tikūni*	تِكوني	*ma-tkunīš*	مَتْكونيش	
íntu	*tikūnu*	تِكونوا	*ma-tkunūš*	مَتْكونوش	
húwwa	*yikūn*	يِكون	*ma-ykúnš*	مَيْكونْش	
híyya	*tikūn*	تِكون	*ma-tkúnš*	مَتْكونْش	
húmma	*yikūnu*	يِكونوا	*ma-ykunūš*	مَيْكونوش	
ána	*bakūn*	بَكون	*ma-bakúnš*	مَبَكونْش	**bi-imperfect**
íḥna	*binkūn*	بِنْكون	*ma-binkúnš*	مَبِنْكونْش	
ínta	*bitkūn*	بِتْكون	*ma-bitkúnš*	مَبِتْكونْش	
ínti	*bitkūni*	بِتْكوني	*ma-bitkunīš*	مَبِتْكونيش	
íntu	*bitkūnu*	بِتْكونوا	*ma-bitkunūš*	مَبِتْكونوش	
húwwa	*biykūn*	بِيْكون	*ma-biykúnš*	مَبِيْكونْش	
híyya	*bitkūn*	بِتْكون	*ma-bitkúnš*	مَبِتْكونْش	
húmma	*biykūnu*	بِيْكونوا	*ma-biykunūš*	مَبِيْكونوش	
ána	*hakūn*	هَكون	*miš hakūn*	مِش هَكون	**future**
íḥna	*hankūn*	هَنْكون	*miš hankūn*	مِش هَنْكون	
ínta	*hatkūn*	هَتْكون	*miš hatkūn*	مِش هَتْكون	
ínti	*hatkūni*	هَتْكوني	*miš hatkūni*	مِش هَتْكوني	
íntu	*hatkūnu*	هَتْكونوا	*miš hatkūnu*	مِش هَتْكونوا	
húwwa	*haykūn*	هَيْكون	*miš haykūn*	مِش هَيْكون	
híyya	*hatkūn*	هَتْكون	*miš hatkūn*	مِش هَتْكون	
húmma	*haykūnu*	هَيْكونوا	*miš haykūnu*	مِش هَيْكونوا	
ínta	*xallīk*	خَلّيك	*ma-tbaʔāš*	مَتْبَقاش	**imperative**
ínti	*xallīki*	خَلّيكي	*ma-tbaʔīš*	مَتْبَقيش	
íntu	*xallīku(m)*	خَلّيكو / خَلّيكُم	*ma-tbaʔūš*	مَتْبَقوش	

	active		passive		
masculine	—	—	—	—	**participles**
feminine	—	—	—	—	
plural	—	—	—	—	

①

أنا كُنْت أطْوَل واحْدة في فصْلي في اِبْتِدائي.

ána kuntᵊ ʔáṭwal wáħda f fáṣli f ibtidāʔi.

I was the tallest in my class in elementary school.

②

أحْمد مكانْش فاهِم وَلا كِلْمة مِن الرّاجِل الألْماني بسّ فِضِل يِبْتِسِم و يْهِزّ راسُه.

áħmad ma-kánšᵊ fāhim wála kílma min irrāgil ilʔalmāni bassᵊ fíḍil yibtísim wi yhízzᵊ rāsu.

Ahmed couldn't understand a word the German man said, but he kept smiling and nodding his head.

③

سُميّة بِتْكون مبْسوطة لمّا جوْزْها بِيْفاجِئْها بِوَرْد.

sumáyya bitkūn mabsūṭa lámma gúzha biyfagíʔha bi-wárd.

Sumaya becomes happy when her husband surprises her with flowers.

④

إنْتو هتْكونوا فيْن النّهارْده بِاللّيْل؟

íntu hatkūnu fēn innahárda bi-llēl?

Where will you guys be tonight?

⑤

كوْنك مِتْضايِق مَيِسْمحْلكْش تِعلّي صوْتك عليْنا بِالطّريقة دي.

kōnak mitḍāyiʔ ma-yismaħlákšᵊ ti3álli ṣōtak 3alēna bi-ṭṭarīʔa di.

Being angry doesn't make it okay for you to raise your voice at us like that.

⑥

خلّيك صبور و كُلّ شيْء هَيِتْحلّ.

xallīk ṣabūr wi kullᵊ šēʔ hayitħáll.

Be patient, and everything will sort itself out.

⑦

فُكّها بقى و متْبقاش رِخِم.

fukkáha báʔa wi ma-tbaʔāš ríxim.

Cheer up! Don´t be so glum.

❖ [1h1] **to be (am, is, are; was, were); to become**

- Although this verb is generally omitted in the present tense (➲ 27.7, 54.3, 156.4), it is commonly found in the imperfect after auxiliaries and conjunctions. (➲ 9.2, 28.3, 34.1) The bi-imperfect forms are used in compound tenses and to express habitual states or occurrences. (➲ 1.3, 12.3, 183.6)
- There is no imperative form based on this verb. You may expect a form such as كون *kūn*, but this is not in common use. Instead, the verb خلّى *xálla* (to cause/make) with a pronoun suffix can be used to express the affirmative imperative, literally 'make yourself...'. (➲ 1.6) The negative imperative is borrowed from the synonymous verb بقى *báʔa*. (➲ 1.7)
- This verb has neither an active nor passive participle.
- In relaxed speech, كُتّ *kutt* may be heard instead of كُنْت *kunt* and كات *kāt* for كانِت *kānit*. (➲ 73.1)

➲ This verb is so common that it appears in over one hundred example sentences throughout this book. It would not be practical to cross-reference so many examples here. So, keep an eye out for it. You'll be seeing it around a lot.

2 to have عنْدـ لِـ معَـ

	affirmative		negative		
ána	3ándi	عَنْدي	ma-3andīš	مَعَنْديش	3and-
íḫna	3andína	عَنْدِنا	ma-3andināš	مَعَنْدِناش	
ínta	3ándak	عَنْدَك	ma-3andákš	مَعَنْدَكْش	
ínti	3ándik	عَنْدِك	ma-3andikīš	مَعَنْدِكيش	
íntu	3andúku	عَنْدُكو	ma-3andukūš	مَعَنْدُكوش	
húwwa	3ándu	عَنْدُه	ma-3andūš	مَعَنْدوش	
híyya	3andáha	عَنْدَها	ma-3andahāš	مَعَنْدَهاش	
húmma	3andúhum	عَنْدُهُم	ma-3anduhúmš	مَعَنْدُهُمْش	
ána	líyya	لِيّا	ma-līš	مَليش	li-
íḫna	līna / lína	لينا	ma-lnāš	مَلْناش	
ínta	līk / lak	ليك / لَك	ma-lákš	مَلَكْش	
ínti	līki / líki	ليكي	ma-lkīš	مَلْكيش	
íntu	līku / líku	ليكو	ma-lkūš	مَلْكوش	
húwwa	lī / lu(h)	ليه / لُه	ma-lūš	مَلوش	
híyya	līha / láha	ليها / لَها	ma-lhāš	مَلْهاش	
húmma	līhum / líhum	ليهُم	ma-lhúmš	مَلْهُمْش	
ána	ma-3āya	مَعايَ	ma-(m)3īš	مَمْعيش / مَعيش	ma3a-
íḫna	ma-3āna	مَعانا	ma-(m)3anāš	مَمْعَناش / مَعَناش	
ínta	ma-3āk	مَعاك	ma-(m)3ákš	مَمْعَكْش / مَعَكْش	
ínti	ma-3āki	مَعاكي	ma-(m)3akīš	مَمْعَكيش / مَعَكيش	
íntu	ma-3āku	مَعاكو	ma-(m)3akūš	مَمْعَكوش / مَعَكوش	
húwwa	ma-3ā(h)	مَعاه	ma-(m)3ahūš	مَمْعَهوش / مَعَهوش	
híyya	ma-3āha	مَعاها	ma-(m)3ahāš	مَمْعَهاش / مَعَهاش	
húmma	ma-3āhum	مَعاهُم	ma-(m)3ahúmš	مَمْعَهُمْش / مَعَهُمْش	

①

كان عنْدي قُطّة إسْمها ميزّو و دِلْوَقْتي عنْدي سُلْحِفة إسْمها فِلْفِل.

kān 3ándi ʔúṭṭa ʔismáha mízzu wi dilwáʔti 3ándi sulḫífa ʔismáha fílfil.

I used to have a cat called Mezzo, and now I have a turtle called Felfel.

②

إنْتَ ليك كام إيد عشان تِسوق و تاكُل و تْرُدّ عَ الموْبايْل في نفس الوَقْت؟

ínta līk kam ʔīd 3ašān tisūʔ wi tākul wi trúddᵊ 3a -lmubáyl fi nafs ilwáʔt?

How many hands do you have that you can drive, eat, and talk on the phone at the same time?

③

أ: هتِتْفرّجي على الماتْش معانا؟

ب: لأ، مليش في الكّوْرة خالِص.

A: *hatitfarrági 3ála -lmatšᵊ ma3āna?*

B: *laʔ, ma-līš fi -kkōra xāliṣ.*

A: Are you going to watch the match with us?

B: No, I'm not interested in soccer at all.

④

معاك عشرة جِنيْهْ سلف؟

ma3āk 3ášara ginēh sálaf?

Can you lend me ten pounds?
[lit. Do you have ten pounds on you to lend?]

⑤

القاهِرة ليها جمال خاصّ بِاللّيْل.

ilqāhíra līha gamāl xaṣṣᵊ bi-llēl.

Cairo has a special beauty at night.

⑥

معنْديش مانع تِـروح الحفْلة، بسّ تْكون في البيْت قبْل ١٢.

ma-3andīš māni3 tirūḥ ilḥáfla, bassᵊ tkūn fi -lbēt ʔabl itnāšar.

I don't have any objection if you go to the party, but you should be home before 12.

⑦

عنْدك خِطط النّهارْده؟

3ándak xíṭaṭ innahárda?

Do you have plans for today?

⑧

هَيِبْقى عنْدِك ٦ سْنين الشّهْر الجايّ، و هعْمِلّك حفْلة كْبيرة.

hayíbʔa 3ándik sittᵊ snīn iššáhr ilgáyy, wi ha3míllak ḥáfla kbīra.

You'll be six next month, and I'll throw you a big party.

⑨

معاكْش وَلّاعة؟

ma-3ákšᵊ wallā3a?

Don't you have a lighter?

⑩

لمّا يِبْقى معاك مِلْيوْن جِنيْهْ إبْقى دوّر على ڤيلّا تِشْتِـريها.

lámma yíbʔa ma3āk milyōn ginēh ʔibʔa dáwwar 3ála vílla tištirīha.

When you have a million pounds, look for a villa to buy.

❖ **to have, possess**

- عنْد لِـ معَ are not actually verbs at all. They are prepositions with pronoun suffixes that usually translate as the verb 'have' in English.
- The most common of the three is عنْد, your *go-to* translation of 'have' if the subject is human. (➲ 2.1, 2.6, 2.7) It is also used in an idiom expressing 'be __ years old', literally 'have __ years'. (➲ 2.8)
- معَ specifically expresses 'have on oneself', literally 'with one'. (➲ 2.4, 2.9, 2.10)
- لِـ is used when the object is a body part or a relative (➲ 2.2), or when the subject is inanimate. (➲2.5) It can also be used idiomatically. (➲ 2.3)
- These prepositions do not precede nouns when they express 'have'. Instead, the noun subject is followed by the preposition with a pronoun suffix. (➲ 2.5)
- The masculine third-person singular form of the verb كان *kān* 'be' is used to express various tenses. (➲ 2.1) The verb بقى *báʔa* 'become' is also sometimes used. (➲ 2.8, 2.10)
- The audio for this verb begins: كان عنْدُه / كان معاهْ / كان لُهْ *kān 3ándu / kān ma3āh / kān luh*.

➲ عنْد 39.4, 40.2, 51.7, 90.4, 93.3, 103.5 105.1, 106.3, 117.1, 123.2, 161.2, 178.3, 195.5, 199.3, 227.3
معَ 39.1, 81.5, 169.3
لِـ 101.4

3 to begin *ibtáda* اِبْتَدَى

		affirmative		negative	
perfect	ána	*ibtadēt*	اِبْتَديْت	*ma-btadítš*	مَبْتَديْتْش
	íḥna	*ibtadēna*	اِبْتَديْنا	*ma-btadināš*	مَبْتَديناش
	ínta	*ibtadēt*	اِبْتَديْت	*ma-btadítš*	مَبْتَديْتْش
	ínti	*ibtadēti*	اِبْتَديْتي	*ma-btaditīš*	مَبْتَديتيش
	íntu	*ibtadētu*	اِبْتَديْتوا	*ma-btaditūš*	مَبْتَديتوش
	húwwa	*ibtáda*	اِبْتَدَى	*ma-btadāš*	مَبْتَداش
	híyya	*ibtádit*	اِبْتَدِت	*ma-btadítš*	مَبْتَدِتْش
	húmma	*ibtádu*	اِبْتَدوا	*ma-btadūš*	مَبْتَدوش
imperfect	ána	*abtídi*	أَبْتِدي	*ma-btidīš*	مَبْتِديش
	íḥna	*nibtídi*	نِبْتِدي	*ma-nibtidīš*	مَنِبْتِديش
	ínta	*tibtídi*	تِبْتِدي	*ma-tibtidīš*	مَتِبْتِديش
	ínti	*tibtídi*	تِبْتِدي	*ma-tibtidīš*	مَتِبْتِديش
	íntu	*tibtídu*	تِبْتِدوا	*ma-tibtidūš*	مَتِبْتِدوش
	húwwa	*yibtídi*	يِبْتِدي	*ma-yibtidīš*	مَيِبْتِديش
	híyya	*tibtídi*	تِبْتِدي	*ma-tibtidīš*	مَتِبْتِديش
	húmma	*yibtídu*	يِبْتِدوا	*ma-yibtidūš*	مَيِبْتِدوش
bi-imperfect	ána	*babtídi*	بَبْتِدي	*ma-babtidīš*	مَبَبْتِديش
	íḥna	*binibtídi*	بِنِبْتِدي	*ma-bnibtidīš*	مَبْنِبْتِديش
	ínta	*bitibtídi*	بِتِبْتِدي	*ma-btibtidīš*	مَبْتِبْتِديش
	ínti	*bitibtídi*	بِتِبْتِدي	*ma-btibtidīš*	مَبْتِبْتِديش
	íntu	*bitibtídu*	بِتِبْتِدوا	*ma-btibtidūš*	مَبْتِبْتِدوش
	húwwa	*biyibtídi*	بِيِبْتِدي	*ma-byibtidīš*	مَبْيِبْتِديش
	híyya	*bitibtídi*	بِتِبْتِدي	*ma-btibtidīš*	مَبْتِبْتِديش
	húmma	*biyibtídu*	بِيِبْتِدوا	*ma-byibtidūš*	مَبْيِبْتِدوش
future	ána	*habtídi*	هَبْتِدي	*miš habtídi*	مِش هَبْتِدي
	íḥna	*hanibtídi*	هَنِبْتِدي	*miš hanibtídi*	مِش هَنِبْتِدي
	ínta	*hatibtídi*	هَتِبْتِدي	*miš hatibtídi*	مِش هَتِبْتِدي
	ínti	*hatibtídi*	هَتِبْتِدي	*miš hatibtídi*	مِش هَتِبْتِدي
	íntu	*hatibtídu*	هَتِبْتِدوا	*miš hatibtídu*	مِش هَتِبْتِدوا
	húwwa	*hayibtídi*	هَيِبْتِدي	*miš hayibtídi*	مِش هَيِبْتِدي
	híyya	*hatibtídi*	هَتِبْتِدي	*miš hatibtídi*	مِش هَتِبْتِدي
	húmma	*hayibtídu*	هَيِبْتِدوا	*miš hayibtídu*	مِش هَيِبْتِدوا
imperative	ínta	*ibtídi*	اِبْتِدي	*ma-tibtidīš*	مَتِبْتِديش
	ínti	*ibtídi*	اِبْتِدي	*ma-tibtidīš*	مَتِبْتِديش
	íntu	*ibtídu*	اِبْتِدوا	*ma-tibtidūš*	مَتِبْتِدوش

		active		passive	
participles	masculine	*mibtídi*	مِبْتِدي	*mibtídi*	مِبْتِدي
	feminine	*mibtidíyya*	مِبْتِدِيَّة	*mibtidíyya*	مِبْتِدِيَّة
	plural	*mibtidiyīn*	مِبْتِدِيين	*mibtidiyīn*	مِبْتِدِيين

verbal noun: *bidāya* بِدايَة

①

لِسّه مبْتديْتْش رْجيم رغْم إنيّ واخْدة قرار مِن أوِّل السّنة.

líssa ma-btadítšᵊ ržīm raɣm ínni wáxda qarār min áwwil issána.

I still haven't started my diet, even though I decided to at the beginning of the year.

②

إنْتَ هتِبْتِدي امْتِحانات يوْم أيْه؟

ínta hatibtídi -mtiħanāt yōm ʔē?

When will you start your exams?

③

لَوْ مبْتديناش نِتْحرّك حالاً، مِش هنِوْصل في معادْنا.

law ma-btadināš nitħárrak ħālan, miš haníwṣal fi ma3ádna.

If we don't start moving now, we won't arrive in time.

④

هُمّا بِيِبْتِدوا الحفْلة السّاعة كام؟

húmma biyibtídu -lħáfla -ssā3a kām?

When do they begin the performance?

⑤

الموْضوع ده اِبْتدى مِن زمان بسّ هُمّا مكانوش عايْزين حدّ يِعْرف.

ilmawḍū3 dah ibtáda min zaman, bassᵊ húmma ma-kanūš 3ayzīn ħaddᵊ yí3raf.

This issue started long ago, but they didn't want anyone to know.

⑥

مِبْتِدِيّين حَياتْهُم مِن الصِّفْر معَ بعْض، ربِّنا يِبارِكْلُهُم.

mibtidiyyīn ħayáthum min iṣṣífrᵊ má3a ba3ḍ, rabbína yibariklúhum.

They are beginning their life together from scratch, God bless them.

❖ [8d] **to begin, start**

- This verb can be transitive (➲ 3.1, 3.2, 3.4, 3.6) or intransitive (➲ 3.5).
- It can also be followed by an imperfect verb. (➲ 3.3)
- Compare with بدأ *báda?*. (➲ 56)

➲ 6.2, 41.4, 92.1, 104.6, 178.6

4 to smile *ibtásam* اِبْتَسَم

	affirmative		negative		
ána	*ibtasámt*	اِبْتَسَمْت	*ma-btasámtiš*	مَبْتَسَمْتِش	**perfect**
íḫna	*ibtasámna*	اِبْتَسَمْنا	*ma-btasamnāš*	مَبْتَسَمْناش	
ínta	*ibtasámt*	اِبْتَسَمْت	*ma-btasámtiš*	مَبْتَسَمْتِش	
ínti	*ibtasámti*	اِبْتَسَمْتي	*ma-btasamtīš*	مَبْتَسَمْتيش	
íntu	*ibtasámtu*	اِبْتَسَمْتوا	*ma-btasamtūš*	مَبْتَسَمْتوش	
húwwa	*ibtásam*	اِبْتَسَم	*ma-btasámš*	مَبْتَسَمْش	
híyya	*ibtásamit*	اِبْتَسَمِت	*ma-btasamítš*	مَبْتَسَمِتْش	
húmma	*ibtásamu*	اِبْتَسَموا	*ma-btasamūš*	مَبْتَسَموش	
ána	*abtísim*	أَبْتِسِم	*ma-btisímš*	مَبْتِسِمْش	**imperfect**
íḫna	*nibtísim*	نِبْتِسِم	*ma-nibtisímš*	مَنِبْتِسِمْش	
ínta	*tibtísim*	تِبْتِسِم	*ma-tibtisímš*	مَتِبْتِسِمْش	
ínti	*tibtísmi*	تِبْتِسْمي	*ma-tibtismīš*	مَتِبْتِسْميش	
íntu	*tibtísmu*	تِبْتِسْموا	*ma-tibtismūš*	مَتِبْتِسْموش	
húwwa	*yibtísim*	يِبْتِسِم	*ma-yibtisímš*	مَيِبْتِسِمْش	
híyya	*tibtísim*	تِبْتِسِم	*ma-tibtisímš*	مَتِبْتِسِمْش	
húmma	*yibtísmu*	يِبْتِسْموا	*ma-yibtismūš*	مَيِبْتِسْموش	
ána	*babtísim*	بَبْتِسِم	*ma-babtisímš*	مَبَبْتِسِمْش	**bi-imperfect**
íḫna	*binibtísim*	بِنِبْتِسِم	*ma-bnibtisímš*	مَبْنِبْتِسِمْش	
ínta	*bitibtísim*	بِتِبْتِسِم	*ma-btibtisímš*	مَبْتِبْتِسِمْش	
ínti	*bitibtísmi*	بِتِبْتِسْمي	*ma-btibtismīš*	مَبْتِبْتِسْميش	
íntu	*bitibtísmu*	بِتِبْتِسْموا	*ma-btibtismūš*	مَبْتِبْتِسْموش	
húwwa	*biyibtísim*	بِيِبْتِسِم	*ma-byibtisímš*	مَبْيِبْتِسِمْش	
híyya	*bitibtísim*	بِتِبْتِسِم	*ma-btibtisímš*	مَبْتِبْتِسِمْش	
húmma	*biyibtísmu*	بِيِبْتِسْموا	*ma-byibtismūš*	مَبْيِبْتِسْموش	
ána	*habtísim*	هَبْتِسِم	*miš habtísim*	مِش هَبْتِسِم	**future**
íḫna	*hanibtísim*	هَنِبْتِسِم	*miš hanibtísim*	مِش هَنِبْتِسِم	
ínta	*hatibtísim*	هَتِبْتِسِم	*miš hatibtísim*	مِش هَتِبْتِسِم	
ínti	*hatibtísmi*	هَتِبْتِسْمي	*miš hatibtísmi*	مِش هَتِبْتِسْمي	
íntu	*hatibtísmu*	هَتِبْتِسْموا	*miš hatibtísmu*	مِش هَتِبْتِسْموا	
húwwa	*hayibtísim*	هَيِبْتِسِم	*miš hayibtísim*	مِش هَيِبْتِسِم	
híyya	*hatibtísim*	هَتِبْتِسِم	*miš hatibtísim*	مِش هَتِبْتِسِم	
húmma	*hayibtísmu*	هَيِبْتِسْموا	*miš hayibtísmu*	مِش هَيِبْتِسْموا	
ínta	*ibtísim*	اِبْتِسِم	*ma-tibtisímš*	مَتِبْتِسِمْش	**imperative**
ínti	*ibtísmi*	اِبْتِسْمي	*ma-tibtismīš*	مَتِبْتِسْميش	
íntu	*ibtísmu*	اِبْتِسْموا	*ma-tibtismūš*	مَتِبْتِسْموش	

	active		passive		
masculine	*mubtásim*	مُبْتَسِم	–	–	**participles**
feminine	*mubtásma*	مُبْتَسْمَة	–	–	
plural	*mubtasmīn*	مُبْتَسْمين	–	–	

verbal noun: *ibtisām* اِبْتِسام

①

اِبْتسمِت مرام بِخجل لمّا خطيبْها باس إيدَيْها.

ibtásamit marām bi-xágal lámma xaţíbha bās ʔidēha.

Maram smiled bashfully when
her fiancé kissed her hands.

②

خِدْمِةْ العُملا لازِم يِبْتِسْموا لِلْجُمْهور مهْما كانوا مُرْهقين.

xídmit il3úmala lāzim yibtísmu li-lgumhūr máhma kānu murhaqīn.

Employees in customer service should
smile at people even if they are tired.

③

أ: **أيْه أكْتر حاجة بِتْخلّيكي تِبْتِسْمي؟**

ب: **لمّا بشوف اِبْتِسامِةْ طِفْل صُغيرّ.**

A: *ʔē áktar ḫāga bitxallīki tibtísmi?*

B: *lámma bašūf ibtisāmit ţiflᵊ şuɣáyyar.*

A: What makes you smile?

B: When I see a baby's smile.

④

اِبْتِسِم لِحدّ متِعْرفوش و هتْشوف قدّ أيْه هَيِفْرح.

ibtisim li-ḫáddᵘ ma-ti3rafūš wi hatšūf addᵊ ʔē hayífraḫ.

Smile at someone you don't know, and
you'll see how happy they will be.

⑤

عمّ جمال مُبْتسِم على طول. بِيِدّينا دفْعِةْ تفاؤُل.

3ammᵊ gamāl mubtásim 3ála ţūl. biyiddīna dáf3it tafāʔul.

Uncle Gamal is always smiling. He
gives us a boost of optimism.

⑥

عامِر مبْيِبْتِسِمْش أبداً. دايْماً مُعْترِض و مِش عاجْبُه الكلام.

3āmir ma-byibtisímš ábadan. dáyman mu3táriḍ wi miš 3ágbu -lkalām.

Amer never smiles. He's always objecting
and not happy with anything you say.

❖ [8s1] **to smile (at** لِـ *li-*)

➲ 1.2

5 to allow ʔatāḥ أتاح

verbal noun: *itāḥa* إتاحة

perfect

	affirmative		negative	
ána	ʔatáḥt	أتَحْت	ma-ʔatáḥtiš	مَأتَحْتِش
íḥna	ʔatáḥna	أتَحْنا	ma-ʔatáḥnāš	مَأتَحْناش
ínta	ʔatáḥt	أتَحْت	ma-ʔatáḥtiš	مَأتَحْتِش
ínti	ʔatáḥti	أتَحْتي	ma-ʔataḥtīš	مَأتَحْتيش
íntu	ʔatáḥtu	أتَحْتوا	ma-ʔataḥtūš	مَأتَحْتوش
húwwa	ʔatāḥ	أتاح	ma-ʔatāḥš	مَأتاحْش
híyya	ʔatāḥit	أتاحِت	ma-ʔataḥítš	مَأتاحِتْش
húmma	ʔatāḥu	أتاحوا	ma-ʔataḥūš	مَأتاحوش

imperfect

	affirmative		negative	
ána	atīḥ	أتيح	ma-tíḥš	مَتيحْش
íḥna	nutīḥ	نُتيح	ma-ntíḥš	مَنْتيحْش
ínta	tutīḥ	تُتيح	ma-ttíḥš	مَتْتيحْش
ínti	tutīḥi	تُتيحي	ma-ttiḥīš	مَتْتيحيش
íntu	tutīḥu	تُتيحوا	ma-ttiḥūš	مَتْتيحوش
húwwa	yutīḥ	يُتيح	ma-ytíḥš	مَيْتيحْش
híyya	tutīḥ	تُتيح	ma-ttíḥš	مَتْتيحْش
húmma	yutīḥu	يُتيحوا	ma-ytiḥūš	مَيْتيحوش

bi-imperfect

	affirmative		negative	
ána	batīḥ	بَتيح	ma-batíḥš	مَبَتيحْش
íḥna	bintīḥ	بِنْتيح	ma-bintíḥš	مَبِنْتيحْش
ínta	bittīḥ	بِتْتيح	ma-bittíḥš	مَبِتْتيحْش
ínti	bittīḥi	بِتْتيحي	ma-bittiḥīš	مَبِتْتيحيش
íntu	bittīḥu	بِتْتيحوا	ma-bittiḥūš	مَبِتْتيحوش
húwwa	biytīḥ	بِيْتيح	ma-biytíḥš	مَبِيْتيحْش
híyya	bittīḥ	بِتْتيح	ma-bittíḥš	مَبِتْتيحْش
húmma	biytīḥu	بِيْتيحوا	ma-biytiḥūš	مَبِيْتيحوش

future

	affirmative		negative	
ána	hatīḥ	هَتيح	miš hatīḥ	مِش هَتيح
íḥna	hantīḥ	هَنْتيح	miš hantīḥ	مِش هَنْتيح
ínta	hattīḥ	هَتْتيح	miš hattīḥ	مِش هَتْتيح
ínti	hattīḥi	هَتْتيحي	miš hattīḥi	مِش هَتْتيحي
íntu	hattīḥu	هَتْتيحوا	miš hattīḥu	مِش هَتْتيحوا
húwwa	haytīḥ	هَيْتيح	miš haytīḥ	مِش هَيْتيح
híyya	hattīḥ	هَتْتيح	miš hattīḥ	مِش هَتْتيح
húmma	haytīḥu	هَيْتيحوا	miš haytīḥu	مِش هَيْتيحوا

imperative

	affirmative		negative	
ínta	tīḥ	تيح	ma-ttíḥš	مَتْتيحْش
ínti	tīḥi	تيحي	ma-ttiḥīš	مَتْتيحيش
íntu	tīḥu	تيحوا	ma-ttiḥūš	مَتْتيحوش

participles

	active		passive	
masculine	mutīḥ	مُتيح	mutāḥ	مُتاح
feminine	mutīḥa	مُتيحَة	mutāḥa	مُتاحَة
plural	mutiḥīn	مُتيحين	mutaḥīn	مُتاحين

①
البنات أتاحولْنا نِتْكلِّم معاهُم بِحُرّية و نِسْمع قِصصْهُم.

ilbanāt ʔataḫúlna nitkállim ma3āhum bi-ḫurríyya wi nísma3 qiṣáṣhum.

The girls let us speak with them freely and hear their stories.

②
في النّادي بِيُتاح لِلشّباب مُمارْسِةْ هِوايّات و رِياضات كِتير.

fi -nnādi biyutāḫ li-ššabāb mumársit hiwayyāt wi riyaḍāt kitīr.

In the club, youth have the opportunity to do lots of hobbies and activities.

③
النُّسْخة الجِديدة مِن الكِتاب هتُتاح لِلجُّمْهور مِن بُكْره.

innúsxa -lgidīda min ilkitāb hatutāḫ li-ggumhūr min búkra.

Tomorrow the new edition of the book will be released [lit. allowed] to the public.

④
الأطْفال في المناطِق الفقيرة مِش مُتاحْلُهُم أنْواع كِتير مِن التّرْفِيهْ المُفيد.

ilʔaṭfāl fi -lmanāṭiʔ ilfaʔīra miš mutaḫlúhum anwā3 kitīr min ittarfīh ilmufīd.

Children in poor areas aren’t given [lit. allowed] many kinds of useful entertainment.

⑤
بحاوِل أتيح لِأوْلادي مُمارْسِةْ أنْشِطة حَياتية كْتير مِن صُغْرُهُم.

baḫāwil atīḫ li-awlādi mumársit anšíṭa ḫayatíyya ktīr min ṣuɣrúhum.

I try to let my kids have a lot of life experiences from the time they are little.

⑥
دِراسْتُه برّه أتاحِتْلُه فُرْصِةْ تكْوين صداقات مِن بِلاد كِتير.

dirástu bárra ʔataḫítlu fúrṣit takwīn ṣadaqāt min bilād kitīr.

Studying abroad allowed him [gave him the opportunity] to make friends from many countries.

⑦
إصابْتي مبِتْتيحْليش أشارِك في البُطولات.

iṣábti ma-bittiḫlīš ašārik fi -lbuṭulāt.

My injury prevents me from participating in the championships.

❖ [4h] **to allow, let** (لِ *li-*)

- This verb takes an indirect object. When the indirect object is a pronoun, it is suffixed to the verb and affects which syllable is stressed.
- The direct object is the thing which is allowed. (➲ 6.4, 6.5, 6.6)
- It can also be followed by an imperfect verb, translating ‘allow __ to (do)...’ (➲ 6.1, 6.7)
- The passive forms (أُتيح *ʔutīḫ*, يُتاح *yutāḫ* ‘be allowed’) are common. (➲ 6.2, 6.3, 6.4)
- Notice the variation of translations, including ‘prevent’ when negative. (➲ 6.7)
- Although theoretically possible, the imperative تيح is rarely used in practice. Instead, the idiom أتاحْلُه فُرْصِةْ... *atáḫlu fúrṣit...* ‘allow someone the opportunity to...’ in the imperative would be اِدّيلُه فُرْصِةْ *iddīlu fúrṣit...* ‘Give him the opportunity to...!’
- Compare with سمح *sámaḫ*. (➲ 142)

6 to be late *itʔáxxar* اِتّأخّر ١٣ 13

verbal nouns: *taʔáxxur* تأخُّر - *taʔxīr* تأخير

	affirmative		negative		
ána	*itʔaxxárt*	اِتّأخّرْت	*ma-tʔaxxártiš*	مَتْأخّرْتِش	perfect
íḥna	*itʔaxxárna*	اِتّأخّرْنا	*ma-tʔaxxarnāš*	مَتْأخّرْناش	
ínta	*itʔaxxárt*	اِتّأخّرْت	*ma-tʔaxxártiš*	مَتْأخّرْتِش	
ínti	*itʔaxxárti*	اِتّأخّرْتي	*ma-tʔaxxartīš*	مَتْأخّرْتيش	
íntu	*itʔaxxártu*	اِتّأخّرْتوا	*ma-tʔaxxartūš*	مَتْأخّرْتوش	
húwwa	*itʔáxxar*	اِتّأخّر	*ma-tʔaxxárš*	مَتْأخّرْش	
híyya	*itʔaxxárit*	اِتّأخّرِت	*ma-tʔaxxarítš*	مَتْأخّرِتْش	
húmma	*itʔaxxáru*	اِتّأخّروا	*ma-tʔaxxarūš*	مَتْأخّروش	
ána	*atʔáxxar*	أتّأخّر	*ma-tʔaxxárš*	مَتْأخّرْش	imperfect
íḥna	*nitʔáxxar*	نِتّأخّر	*ma-nitʔaxxárš*	مَنِتْأخّرْش	
ínta	*titʔáxxar*	تِتّأخّر	*ma-titʔaxxárš*	مَتِتْأخّرْش	
ínti	*titʔaxxári*	تِتّأخّري	*ma-titʔaxxarīš*	مَتِتْأخّريش	
íntu	*titʔaxxáru*	تِتّأخّروا	*ma-titʔaxxarūš*	مَتِتْأخّروش	
húwwa	*yitʔáxxar*	يِتّأخّر	*ma-yitʔaxxárš*	مَيِتْأخّرْش	
híyya	*titʔáxxar*	تِتّأخّر	*ma-titʔaxxárš*	مَتِتْأخّرْش	
húmma	*yitʔaxxáru*	يِتّأخّروا	*ma-yitʔaxxarūš*	مَيِتْأخّروش	
ána	*batʔáxxar*	بَتْأخّر	*ma-batʔaxxárš*	مَبَتْأخّرْش	bi-imperfect
íḥna	*binitʔáxxar*	بِنِتْأخّر	*ma-bnitʔaxxárš*	مَبْنِتْأخّرْش	
ínta	*bititʔáxxar*	بِتِتْأخّر	*ma-btitʔaxxárš*	مَبْتِتْأخّرْش	
ínti	*bititʔaxxári*	بِتِتْأخّري	*ma-btitʔaxxarīš*	مَبْتِتْأخّريش	
íntu	*bititʔaxxáru*	بِتِتْأخّروا	*ma-btitʔaxxarūš*	مَبْتِتْأخّروش	
húwwa	*biyitʔáxxar*	بِيِتْأخّر	*ma-byitʔaxxárš*	مَبْيِتْأخّرْش	
híyya	*bititʔáxxar*	بِتِتْأخّر	*ma-btitʔaxxárš*	مَبْتِتْأخّرْش	
húmma	*biyitʔaxxáru*	بِيِتْأخّروا	*ma-byitʔaxxarūš*	مَبْيِتْأخّروش	
ána	*hatʔáxxar*	هَتْأخّر	*miš hatʔáxxar*	مِش هَتْأخّر	future
íḥna	*hanitʔáxxar*	هَنِتْأخّر	*miš hanitʔáxxar*	مِش هَنِتْأخّر	
ínta	*hatitʔáxxar*	هَتِتْأخّر	*miš hatitʔáxxar*	مِش هَتِتْأخّر	
ínti	*hatitʔaxxári*	هَتِتْأخّري	*miš hatitʔaxxári*	مِش هَتِتْأخّري	
íntu	*hatitʔaxxáru*	هَتِتْأخّروا	*miš hatitʔaxxáru*	مِش هَتِتْأخّروا	
húwwa	*hayitʔáxxar*	هَيِتْأخّر	*miš hayitʔáxxar*	مِش هَيِتْأخّر	
híyya	*hatitʔáxxar*	هَتِتْأخّر	*miš hatitʔáxxar*	مِش هَتِتْأخّر	
húmma	*hayitʔaxxáru*	هَيِتْأخّروا	*miš hayitʔaxxáru*	مِش هَيِتْأخّروا	
ínta	*itʔáxxar*	اِتّأخّر	*ma-titʔaxxárš*	مَتِتْأخّرْش	imperative
ínti	*itʔaxxári*	اِتّأخّري	*ma-titʔaxxarīš*	مَتِتْأخّريش	
íntu	*itʔaxxáru*	اِتّأخّروا	*ma-titʔaxxarūš*	مَتِتْأخّروش	

	active		passive		
masculine	*mitʔáxxar*	مِتْأخّر	–	–	participles
feminine	*mitʔaxxára*	مِتْأخّرة	–	–	
plural	*mitʔaxxarīn*	مِتْأخّرين	–	–	

①

إحْنا اتْأخّرْنا أوي و كِده هتْفوتْنا الرِّحْلة.

íḫna -tʔaxxárna ʔáwi wi kída hatfútna -rríḫla.

We're too late, so we're going to miss the flight.

②

إنّك تِبْتِدي مِتْأخّر أفْضل مِن إنّك متِبْتِديش خالِص.

ínnak tibtídi mitʔáxxar ʔáfḍal min ínnak ma-tibtidīš xāliṣ.

Beginning late is better than not beginning at all.

③

أ: آجي المُحاضْرة السّاعة كام؟

ب: متِتْأخّريش عن تِسْعة و نُصّ.

A: āgi -lmuḫáḍra -ssā3a kām?

B: ma-titʔaxxarīš 3an tís3a w nuṣṣ.

A: When is the lecture?

B: Don't be any later than 9:30.

④

مبْيِتْأخّرْش عن شُغْله أبداً. مُلْتزِم جِدّاً حتّى و هُوَّ مِش مبْسوط في الشُّغْل.

ma-byitʔaxxárš^ə 3an šúɣlu ʔábadan. multázim gíddan ḫátta w húwwa miš mabsūṭ fi -ššuɣl.

He is never late for work. He is so disciplined even when he's not happy at work.

⑤

يِتْأخّر أوْ مَيِتْأخّرْش، إحْنا كِده كِده هنِبْدأ في معادْنا.

yitʔáxxar aw ma-yitʔaxxárš, íḫna kída kída haníbdaʔ fi mi3ádna.

Whether or not he's late, we'll start on time anyway.

❖ [5s2] **to be late** (**for** عن *3an*)

➲ 15.5, 45.7, 51.7, 61.7, 74.1, 75.1, 96.1, 103.3, 123.7, 155.1, 187.5, 201.2, 231.6, 260.1, 261.5

7 to be sure itʔákkid اِتأكّد

ءكد

verbal nouns: taʔákkud تأكُّد - taʔkīd تأكيد

perfect

	affirmative		negative	
ána	itʔakkídt	اِتأكّدْت	ma-tʔakkídtiš	مَتأكّدْتِش
íḥna	itʔakkídna	اِتأكّدْنا	ma-tʔakkidnāš	مَتأكّدْناش
ínta	itʔakkídt	اِتأكّدْت	ma-tʔakkídtiš	مَتأكّدْتِش
ínti	itʔakkídti	اِتأكّدْتي	ma-tʔakkidtīš	مَتأكّدْتيش
íntu	itʔakkídtu	اِتأكّدْتوا	ma-tʔakkidtūš	مَتأكّدْتوش
húwwa	itʔákkid	اِتأكّد	ma-tʔakkídš	مَتأكّدْش
híyya	itʔakkídit	اِتأكّدِت	ma-tʔakkidítš	مَتأكّدِتْش
húmma	itʔakkídu	اِتأكّدوا	ma-tʔakkidūš	مَتأكّدوش

imperfect

	affirmative		negative	
ána	atʔákkid	أتأكّد	ma-tʔakkídš	مَتأكّدْش
íḥna	nitʔákkid	نِتأكّد	ma-nitʔakkídš	مَنِتأكّدْش
ínta	titʔákkid	تِتأكّد	ma-titʔakkídš	مَتِتأكّدْش
ínti	titʔakkídi	تِتأكّدي	ma-titʔakkidīš	مَتِتأكّديش
íntu	titʔakkídu	تِتأكّدوا	ma-titʔakkidūš	مَتِتأكّدوش
húwwa	yitʔákkid	يِتأكّد	ma-yitʔakkídš	مَيِتأكّدْش
híyya	titʔákkid	تِتأكّد	ma-titʔakkídš	مَتِتأكّدْش
húmma	yitʔakkídu	يِتأكّدوا	ma-yitʔakkidūš	مَيِتأكّدوش

bi-imperfect

	affirmative		negative	
ána	batʔákkid	بَتأكّد	ma-batʔakkídš	مَبَتأكّدْش
íḥna	binitʔákkid	بِنِتأكّد	ma-bnitʔakkídš	مَبْنِتأكّدْش
ínta	bititʔákkid	بِتِتأكّد	ma-btitʔakkídš	مَبْتِتأكّدْش
ínti	bititʔakkídi	بِتِتأكّدي	ma-btitʔakkidīš	مَبْتِتأكّديش
íntu	bititʔakkídu	بِتِتأكّدوا	ma-btitʔakkidūš	مَبْتِتأكّدوش
húwwa	biyitʔákkid	بِيِتأكّد	ma-byitʔakkídš	مَبْيِتأكّدْش
híyya	bititʔákkid	بِتِتأكّد	ma-btitʔakkídš	مَبْتِتأكّدْش
húmma	biyitʔakkídu	بِيِتأكّدوا	ma-byitʔakkidūš	مَبْيِتأكّدوش

future

	affirmative		negative	
ána	hatʔákkid	هَتأكّد	miš hatʔákkid	مِش هَتأكّد
íḥna	hanitʔákkid	هَنِتأكّد	miš hanitʔákkid	مِش هَنِتأكّد
ínta	hatitʔákkid	هَتِتأكّد	miš hatitʔákkid	مِش هَتِتأكّد
ínti	hatitʔakkídi	هَتِتأكّدي	miš hatitʔakkídi	مِش هَتِتأكّدي
íntu	hatitʔakkídu	هَتِتأكّدوا	miš hatitʔakkídu	مِش هَتِتأكّدوا
húwwa	hayitʔákkid	هَيِتأكّد	miš hayitʔákkid	مِش هَيِتأكّد
híyya	hatitʔákkid	هَتِتأكّد	miš hatitʔákkid	مِش هَتِتأكّد
húmma	hayitʔakkídu	هَيِتأكّدوا	miš hayitʔakkídu	مِش هَيِتأكّدوا

imperative

	affirmative		negative	
ínta	itʔákkid	اِتأكّد	ma-titʔakkídš	مَتِتأكّدْش
ínti	itʔakkídi	اِتأكّدي	ma-titʔakkidīš	مَتِتأكّديش
íntu	itʔakkídu	اِتأكّدوا	ma-titʔakkidūš	مَتِتأكّدوش

participles

	active		passive	
masculine	mutaʔákkid	مُتأكّد	—	—
feminine	mutaʔakkída	مُتأكّدة	—	—
plural	mutaʔakkidīn	مُتأكّدين	—	—

①

أ: إنْتو اتْأكّدْتوا مِن حجْز الفُنْدُق وَلّا لِسّه؟

ب: اِتّصلْنا بيهُم و اِتْأكّدْنا.

A: íntu -tʔakkídtu min ḥagz ilfúnduʔ wálla líssa?

B: ittaṣálna bīhum w itʔakkídna.

A: Did you confirm the hotel reservation?

B: Yes, we called them and confirmed it.

②

لمّا أتْأكّد إنّك مبْتِكْدِبْش عليّا تانى، هتِرجع ثِقتي فيك.

lámm- atʔákkid ínnak ma-btikdíbšᵊ 3aláyya tāni, hatírga3 tíqati fīk.

When I am sure that you are not lying

to me again, I'll trust you again.

③

الحاجات بِتْبوظ عنْدُكو عشان مبْتِتْأكّدوش مِن تاريخ الصّلاحية قبْل الشِّرا.

ilḥagāt bitbūẓ 3andúku 3ašān ma-btitʔakkidūš min tarīx iṣṣalaḥíyya ʔabl iššíra.

Your stuff goes bad because you don't check

the expiration date before buying it.

④

شهْد هتِتْأكّد إنُّه ده الشّخْص المُناسِب ليها و بعْديْن تِوافِق إنّها تِتْجوِّزُه.

šahdᵊ hatitʔákkid ínnu da -ššáxṣ ilmunāsib līha wi ba3dēn tiwāfiʔ innáha titgawwízu.

Shahd will make sure he's the right person

for her, and then she will agree to marry him.

⑤

و اِتْأكّدوا بِتْسيبوا وِلادْكو معَ مين علشان مَيِتْعرّضوش لإِساءة.

w itʔakkídu bitsību wiládku má3a mīn 3alašān ma-yit3arraḍūš li-isāʔa.

Be careful about who you leave your kids with so that they

don't get abused [lit. be exposed to wrongdoing].

⑥

أنا مُتأكّده إني شُفْت حدّ بيِتْحرّك. هُوَّ البيْت ده مسْكون وَلّا أيْه؟

ána mutaʔakkída ʔínni šuftᵊ ḥaddᵊ biyitḥárrak. húwwa -lbēt da maskūn wálla ʔē?

I'm sure I saw something move. Is this house haunted or something?

❖ [5s1] **to be certain, be sure (that** إنّ *inn*; **about** مِن *min*)**; to verify, confirm, check** (مِن *min*)

- The participle can also be pronounced مِتْأكّد *mitʔákkid.*

➲ 37.4, 102.5, 115.2, 171.8, 174.5, 174.6

8 to get together *itgámma3* اِتْجَمَّع

	affirmative		negative		
ána	*itgammá3t*	اِتْجَمَّعْت	*ma-tgammá3tiš*	مَتْجَمَّعْتِش	perfect
íḫna	*itgammá3na*	اِتْجَمَّعْنا	*ma-tgamma3nāš*	مَتْجَمَّعْناش	
ínta	*itgammá3t*	اِتْجَمَّعْت	*ma-tgammá3tiš*	مَتْجَمَّعْتِش	
ínti	*itgammá3ti*	اِتْجَمَّعْتي	*ma-tgamma3tīš*	مَتْجَمَّعْتيش	
íntu	*itgammá3tu*	اِتْجَمَّعْتوا	*ma-tgamma3tūš*	مَتْجَمَّعْتوش	
húwwa	*itgámma3*	اِتْجَمَّع	*ma-tgammá3š*	مَتْجَمَّعْش	
híyya	*itgammá3it*	اِتْجَمَّعِت	*ma-tgamma3ítš*	مَتْجَمَّعِتْش	
húmma	*itgammá3u*	اِتْجَمَّعوا	*ma-tgamma3ūš*	مَتْجَمَّعوش	
ána	*atgámma3*	أتْجَمَّع	*ma-tgammá3š*	مَتْجَمَّعْش	imperfect
íḫna	*nitgámma3*	نِتْجَمَّع	*ma-nitgammá3š*	مَنِتْجَمَّعْش	
ínta	*titgámma3*	تِتْجَمَّع	*ma-titgammá3š*	مَتِتْجَمَّعْش	
ínti	*titgammá3i*	تِتْجَمَّعي	*ma-titgamma3īš*	مَتِتْجَمَّعيش	
íntu	*titgammá3u*	تِتْجَمَّعوا	*ma-titgamma3ūš*	مَتِتْجَمَّعوش	
húwwa	*yitgámma3*	يِتْجَمَّع	*ma-yitgammá3š*	مَيِتْجَمَّعْش	
híyya	*titgámma3*	تِتْجَمَّع	*ma-titgammá3š*	مَتِتْجَمَّعْش	
húmma	*yitgammá3u*	يِتْجَمَّعوا	*ma-yitgamma3ūš*	مَيِتْجَمَّعوش	
ána	*batgámma3*	بَتْجَمَّع	*ma-batgammá3š*	مَبَتْجَمَّعْش	bi-imperfect
íḫna	*binitgámma3*	بِنِتْجَمَّع	*ma-bnitgammá3š*	مَبْنِتْجَمَّعْش	
ínta	*bititgámma3*	بِتِتْجَمَّع	*ma-btitgammá3š*	مَبْتِتْجَمَّعْش	
ínti	*bititgammá3i*	بِتِتْجَمَّعي	*ma-btitgamma3īš*	مَبْتِتْجَمَّعيش	
íntu	*bititgammá3u*	بِتِتْجَمَّعوا	*ma-btitgamma3ūš*	مَبْتِتْجَمَّعوش	
húwwa	*biyitgámma3*	بِيِتْجَمَّع	*ma-byitgammá3š*	مَبْيِتْجَمَّعْش	
híyya	*bititgámma3*	بِتِتْجَمَّع	*ma-btitgammá3š*	مَبْتِتْجَمَّعْش	
húmma	*biyitgammá3u*	بِيِتْجَمَّعوا	*ma-byitgamma3ūš*	مَبْيِتْجَمَّعوش	
ána	*hatgámma3*	هَتْجَمَّع	*miš hatgámma3*	مِش هَتْجَمَّع	future
íḫna	*hanitgámma3*	هَنِتْجَمَّع	*miš hanitgámma3*	مِش هَنِتْجَمَّع	
ínta	*hatitgámma3*	هَتِتْجَمَّع	*miš hatitgámma3*	مِش هَتِتْجَمَّع	
ínti	*hatitgammá3i*	هَتِتْجَمَّعي	*miš hatitgammá3i*	مِش هَتِتْجَمَّعي	
íntu	*hatitgammá3u*	هَتِتْجَمَّعوا	*miš hatitgammá3u*	مِش هَتِتْجَمَّعوا	
húwwa	*hayitgámma3*	هَيِتْجَمَّع	*miš hayitgámma3*	مِش هَيِتْجَمَّع	
híyya	*hatitgámma3*	هَتِتْجَمَّع	*miš hatitgámma3*	مِش هَتِتْجَمَّع	
húmma	*hayitgammá3u*	هَيِتْجَمَّعوا	*miš hayitgammá3u*	مِش هَيِتْجَمَّعوا	
ínta	*itgámma3*	اِتْجَمَّع	*ma-titgammá3š*	مَتِتْجَمَّعْش	imperative
ínti	*itgammá3i*	اِتْجَمَّعي	*ma-titgamma3īš*	مَتِتْجَمَّعيش	
íntu	*itgammá3u*	اِتْجَمَّعوا	*ma-titgamma3ūš*	مَتِتْجَمَّعوش	

	active		passive		
masculine	*mitgámma3*	مِتْجَمَّع	–	–	participles
feminine	*mitgammá3a*	مِتْجَمَّعَة	–	–	
plural	*mitgamma3īn*	مِتْجَمَّعين	–	–	

verbal noun: *tagámmu3* تَجَمُّع

①

لمّا اتْجمّعْنا في الكُلّية بعْد عشر سِنين لقيْنا شكْلِنا اتْغيرّ خالِص.

lámma -tgammá3na fi -kkullíyya ba3d[ə] 3ášar sinīn la?ēna šaklína -tɣáyyar xāliṣ.

When we got together at our college ten years later,
we found that we had changed a lot.

②

مرْوَة بِتِتْجمّع معَ عيلِتْها كُلّ جُمْعة و مِش بِيْفوِّتوا مرّة.

márwah bititgámma3 má3a 3ilítha kull[ə] gúm3a wi miš biyfawwítu márra.

Marwa gets together with her family every Friday
without fail [lit. and they don't miss it once].

③

لمّا إخْواتي بِيِتْجمّعوا كُلُّهُم، مبِنْبطّلْش ضِحْك.

lámma ?ixwāti biyitgammá3u kullúhum, ma-binbaṭṭálš[ə] diḫk.

When all my siblings get together,
we don't stop laughing.

④

هنِتْجمّع تاني عَ الفِطار في رمضان؟

hanitgámma3 tāni 3a -lfiṭār fi ramaḍān?

Shall we come together again for
iftar [breaking fast] during Ramadan?

⑤

اِتْجمّعوا معَ بعْض أكْتر مِن كِده علشان تِحافْظوا على ترابُط العيْلة.

itgammá3u má3a ba3ḍ áktar min kída 3alašān tiḫáfẓu 3ála tarābuṭ il3ēla.

Get together more often to maintain family bonds.

⑥

ما شاء الله عليْكو، مِتْجمّعين عنْد النّبي.

ma šā? allāh 3alēku, mitgamma3īn 3and innábi.

It was lovely getting together. I hope we can do it again.
[lit. May you gather at the prophet's.]

⑦

أنا و صُحابي مبْنِتْجمّعْش كِتير مِن ساعِةْ ما اتْخرّجْنا.

ána wi ṣuḫābi ma-bnitgammá3š[ə] kitīr min sā3it ma -txarrágna.

My friends and I haven't gotten together
a lot since we graduated.

❖ [5s2] **to get together, gather, assemble; to be collected**

➲ 106.1

9 to get married *itgáwwiz* اِتْجَوِّز

verbal noun: *gawāz* جَواز

	affirmative		negative		
ána	*itgawwízt*	اِتْجَوِّزْت	*ma-tgawwíztiš*	مَتْجَوِّزْتِش	**perfect**
íḫna	*itgawwízna*	اِتْجَوِّزْنا	*ma-tgawwiznāš*	مَتْجَوِّزْناش	
ínta	*itgawwízt*	اِتْجَوِّزْت	*ma-tgawwíztiš*	مَتْجَوِّزْتِش	
ínti	*itgawwízti*	اِتْجَوِّزْتي	*ma-tgawwiztīš*	مَتْجَوِّزْتيش	
íntu	*itgawwíztu*	اِتْجَوِّزْتوا	*ma-tgawwiztūš*	مَتْجَوِّزْتوش	
húwwa	*itgáwwiz*	اِتْجَوِّز	*ma-tgawwízš*	مَتْجَوِّزْش	
híyya	*itgawwízit*	اِتْجَوِّزِت	*ma-tgawwizítš*	مَتْجَوِّزِتْش	
húmma	*itgawwízu*	اِتْجَوِّزوا	*ma-tgawwizūš*	مَتْجَوِّزوش	
ána	*atgáwwiz*	أَتْجَوِّز	*ma-tgawwízš*	مَتْجَوِّزْش	**imperfect**
íḫna	*nitgáwwiz*	نِتْجَوِّز	*ma-nitgawwízš*	مَنِتْجَوِّزْش	
ínta	*titgáwwiz*	تِتْجَوِّز	*ma-titgawwízš*	مَتِتْجَوِّزْش	
ínti	*titgawwízi*	تِتْجَوِّزي	*ma-titgawwizīš*	مَتِتْجَوِّزيش	
íntu	*titgawwízu*	تِتْجَوِّزوا	*ma-titgawwizūš*	مَتِتْجَوِّزوش	
húwwa	*yitgáwwiz*	يِتْجَوِّز	*ma-yitgawwízš*	مَيِتْجَوِّزْش	
híyya	*titgáwwiz*	تِتْجَوِّز	*ma-titgawwízš*	مَتِتْجَوِّزْش	
húmma	*yitgawwízu*	يِتْجَوِّزوا	*ma-yitgawwizūš*	مَيِتْجَوِّزوش	
ána	*batgáwwiz*	بَتْجَوِّز	*ma-batgawwízš*	مَبَتْجَوِّزْش	**bi-imperfect**
íḫna	*binitgáwwiz*	بِنِتْجَوِّز	*ma-bnitgawwízš*	مَبْنِتْجَوِّزْش	
ínta	*bititgáwwiz*	بِتِتْجَوِّز	*ma-btitgawwízš*	مَبْتِتْجَوِّزْش	
ínti	*bititgawwízi*	بِتِتْجَوِّزي	*ma-btitgawwizīš*	مَبْتِتْجَوِّزيش	
íntu	*bititgawwízu*	بِتِتْجَوِّزوا	*ma-btitgawwizūš*	مَبْتِتْجَوِّزوش	
húwwa	*biyitgáwwiz*	بِيِتْجَوِّز	*ma-byitgawwízš*	مَبْيِتْجَوِّزْش	
híyya	*bititgáwwiz*	بِتِتْجَوِّز	*ma-btitgawwízš*	مَبْتِتْجَوِّزْش	
húmma	*biyitgawwízu*	بِيِتْجَوِّزوا	*ma-byitgawwizūš*	مَبْيِتْجَوِّزوش	
ána	*hatgáwwiz*	هَتْجَوِّز	*miš hatgáwwiz*	مِش هَتْجَوِّز	**future**
íḫna	*hanitgáwwiz*	هَنِتْجَوِّز	*miš hanitgáwwiz*	مِش هَنِتْجَوِّز	
ínta	*hatitgáwwiz*	هَتِتْجَوِّز	*miš hatitgáwwiz*	مِش هَتِتْجَوِّز	
ínti	*hatitgawwízi*	هَتِتْجَوِّزي	*miš hatitgawwízi*	مِش هَتِتْجَوِّزي	
íntu	*hatitgawwízu*	هَتِتْجَوِّزوا	*miš hatitgawwízu*	مِش هَتِتْجَوِّزوا	
húwwa	*hayitgáwwiz*	هَيِتْجَوِّز	*miš hayitgáwwiz*	مِش هَيِتْجَوِّز	
híyya	*hatitgáwwiz*	هَتِتْجَوِّز	*miš hatitgáwwiz*	مِش هَتِتْجَوِّز	
húmma	*hayitgawwízu*	هَيِتْجَوِّزوا	*miš hayitgawwízu*	مِش هَيِتْجَوِّزوا	
ínta	*itgáwwiz*	اِتْجَوِّز	*ma-titgawwízš*	مَتْجَوِّزْش	**imperative**
ínti	*itgawwízi*	اِتْجَوِّزي	*ma-titgawwizīš*	مَتْجَوِّزيش	
íntu	*itgawwízu*	اِتْجَوِّزوا	*ma-titgawwizūš*	مَتْجَوِّزوش	

	active		passive		
masculine	*mitgáwwiz*	مِتْجَوِّز	–	–	**participles**
feminine	*mitgawwíza*	مِتْجَوِّزَة	–	–	
plural	*mitgawwizīn*	مِتْجَوِّزين	–	–	

①

مايا اتْجوِّزِت علاء بعْد قِصّةْ حُبّ طَويلة.

māya -tgawwízit 3alāʔ ba3dᵊ qíṣṣit ɧubbᵊ ṭawīla.

Maya married Alaa after a long love story.

②

مِش هتْجوِّز أيّ حدّ و خلاص،. لازِم أكون مُقْتنِعة و بحِبُّه.

miš hatgáwwiz ayyᵊ ɧaddᵊ wi xalāṣ. lāzim akūn muqtáni3a wi baɧíbbu.

I won't marry anyone unless I am convinced and in love with him.

③

البنات في المناطِق الرّيفية بْيِتْجوِّزوا في سِنّ صُغيرّ أوي.

ilbanāt fi -lmanāṭiʔ irrifíyya byitgawwízu fi sinnᵊ ṣuɣáyyar áwi.

Girls in rural areas get married at a very young age.

④

ما تِتْجوِّزوا بقى و تْخلّصونا! بقالْكُم كام سنة مخْطوبين؟

ma titgawwízu báʔa wi txallaṣūna! baʔálkum kam sána maxṭubīn?

Do us a favor and get married already! You've been engaged for how many years now??

⑤

أتْجوِّز أوْ متْجوِّزْش ، ده شيْء يِخُصِّني لِوَحْدي.

atgáwwiz aw ma-tgawwízš, da šēʔ yixuṣṣíni li-wáɧdi.

It's my own business whether I get married or not.

❖ [5s1] **to get married (to)**

➲ 7.4, 26.6, 45.2, 130.2, 135.4, 140.1, 172.2, 256.1

10 to move itḫárrak اِتْحَرَّك

verbal nouns: taḫárruk تَحَرُّك - ḫáraka حَرَكَة

perfect

	affirmative		negative	
ána	itḫarrákt	اِتْحَرَّكْت	ma-tḫarráktiš	مَتْحَرَّكْتِش
íḫna	itḫarrákna	اِتْحَرَّكْنا	ma-tḫarraknāš	مَتْحَرَّكْناش
ínta	itḫarrákt	اِتْحَرَّكْت	ma-tḫarráktiš	مَتْحَرَّكْتِش
ínti	itḫarrákti	اِتْحَرَّكْتي	ma-tḫarraktīš	مَتْحَرَّكْتيش
íntu	itḫarráktu	اِتْحَرَّكْتوا	ma-tḫarraktūš	مَتْحَرَّكْتوش
húwwa	itḫárrak	اِتْحَرَّك	ma-tḫarrákš	مَتْحَرَّكْش
híyya	itḫarrákit	اِتْحَرَّكِت	ma-tḫarrakítš	مَتْحَرَّكِتْش
húmma	itḫarráku	اِتْحَرَّكوا	ma-tḫarrakūš	مَتْحَرَّكوش

imperfect

	affirmative		negative	
ána	atḫárrak	أَتْحَرَّك	ma-tḫarrákš	مَتْحَرَّكْش
íḫna	nitḫárrak	نِتْحَرَّك	ma-nitḫarrákš	مَنِتْحَرَّكْش
ínta	titḫárrak	تِتْحَرَّك	ma-titḫarrákš	مَتِتْحَرَّكْش
ínti	titḫarráki	تِتْحَرَّكي	ma-titḫarrakīš	مَتِتْحَرَّكيش
íntu	titḫarráku	تِتْحَرَّكوا	ma-titḫarrakūš	مَتِتْحَرَّكوش
húwwa	yitḫárrak	يِتْحَرَّك	ma-yitḫarrákš	مَيِتْحَرَّكْش
híyya	titḫárrak	تِتْحَرَّك	ma-titḫarrákš	مَتِتْحَرَّكْش
húmma	yitḫarráku	يِتْحَرَّكوا	ma-yitḫarrakūš	مَيِتْحَرَّكوش

bi-imperfect

	affirmative		negative	
ána	batḫárrak	بَتْحَرَّك	ma-batḫarrákš	مَبَتْحَرَّكْش
íḫna	binitḫárrak	بِنِتْحَرَّك	ma-bnitḫarrákš	مَبْنِتْحَرَّكْش
ínta	bititḫárrak	بِتِتْحَرَّك	ma-btitḫarrákš	مَبْتِتْحَرَّكْش
ínti	bititḫarráki	بِتِتْحَرَّكي	ma-btitḫarrakīš	مَبْتِتْحَرَّكيش
íntu	bititḫarráku	بِتِتْحَرَّكوا	ma-btitḫarrakūš	مَبْتِتْحَرَّكوش
húwwa	biyitḫárrak	بِيِتْحَرَّك	ma-byitḫarrákš	مَبْيِتْحَرَّكْش
híyya	bititḫárrak	بِتِتْحَرَّك	ma-btitḫarrákš	مَبْتِتْحَرَّكْش
húmma	biyitḫarráku	بِيِتْحَرَّكوا	ma-byitḫarrakūš	مَبْيِتْحَرَّكوش

future

	affirmative		negative	
ána	hatḫárrak	هَتْحَرَّك	miš hatḫárrak	مِش هَتْحَرَّك
íḫna	hanitḫárrak	هَنِتْحَرَّك	miš hanitḫárrak	مِش هَنِتْحَرَّك
ínta	hatitḫárrak	هَتِتْحَرَّك	miš hatitḫárrak	مِش هَتِتْحَرَّك
ínti	hatitḫarráki	هَتِتْحَرَّكي	miš hatitḫarráki	مِش هَتِتْحَرَّكي
íntu	hatitḫarráku	هَتِتْحَرَّكوا	miš hatitḫarráku	مِش هَتِتْحَرَّكوا
húwwa	hayitḫárrak	هَيِتْحَرَّك	miš hayitḫárrak	مِش هَيِتْحَرَّك
híyya	hatitḫárrak	هَتِتْحَرَّك	miš hatitḫárrak	مِش هَتِتْحَرَّك
húmma	hayitḫarráku	هَيِتْحَرَّكوا	miš hayitḫarráku	مِش هَيِتْحَرَّكوا

imperative

	affirmative		negative	
ínta	itḫárrak	اِتْحَرَّك	ma-titḫarrákš	مَتِتْحَرَّكْش
ínti	itḫarráki	اِتْحَرَّكي	ma-titḫarrakīš	مَتِتْحَرَّكيش
íntu	itḫarráku	اِتْحَرَّكوا	ma-titḫarrakūš	مَتِتْحَرَّكوش

participles

	active		passive	
masculine	mitḫárrak	مِتْحَرَّك	—	—
feminine	mitḫarráka	مِتْحَرَّكَة	—	—
plural	mitḫarrakīn	مِتْحَرَّكين	—	—

①

صلّينا الفجْر و اِتْحرّكْنا على إسْكِنْدِرية على طول علشان نِوْصل قبْل الضُّهْر.

ṣallēna -lfágr, w itḫarrákna 3ála -skindiríyya 3ála ṭūl 3alašān níwṣal ʔabl iḍḍúhr.

We prayed at dawn then immediately set off for Alexandria in order to arrive before noon.

②

مِش هَيِتْحرّك مِن مكانُه طول ما الماتْش شغّال.

miš hayitḫárrak min makānu ṭūl ma -lmátšᵊ šaɣɣāl.

He won't move from where he is as long as the [soccer] match is still going.

③

مِن ساعِةْ الحادْثة و هِيَّ مبْتِتْحرّكْش غيْر بِالعُكّاز.

min sā3it ilḫádsa w híyya ma-btitḫarrákšᵊ ɣēr bi-l3ukkāz.

Since the accident, she can't get around without crutches.

④

لَوْ بِتْحِبّها، اِتْحرّك بِسُرْعة قبْل ما تْروح مِن إيدك.

law bitḫibbáha, itḫárrak bi-súr3a ʔáblᵊ ma trūḫ min īdak.

If you love her, move fast before you lose her [lit. goes from your hands].

⑤

أنا شُفْتُهُم و هُمّا مِتْحرّكين ناحْيِةْ الباب. كانوا هَيِخْطفوا الوَلد و يِهْربوا.

ána šuftúhum wi húmma mitḫarrakīn náḫyit ilbāb. kānu hayixṭáfu -lwálad wi yihrábu.

I saw them moving toward the door. They were going to kidnap the boy and get away.

⑥

القُطّة متْحرّكِتْش مِن مكانْها بقالْها تلات ساعات. هِيَّ لِسّه عايْشة؟

ilʔúṭṭa ma-tḫarrakítšᵊ min makánha baʔálha tálat sa3āt. híyya líssa 3áyša?

The cat hasn't moved in three hours. Is it still alive?

❖ [5s2] **to move, make a movement**

- This is an intransitive verb. The transitive verb is حرّك *ḫárrak*. (➲ 79)
- 'move' as in ´change residences´ is عزّل *3ázzil*. (➲ 178)

➲ 3.3, 7.6, 81.4, 100.8, 173.6, 174.6, 245.5

11 to improve itḫássin اِتْحَسِّن

	affirmative		negative		
ána	itḫassínt	اِتْحَسِّنْت	ma-tḫassíntiš	مَتْحَسِّنْتِش	perfect
íḫna	itḫassínna	اِتْحَسِّنّا	ma-tḫassinnāš	مَتْحَسِّنّاش	
ínta	itḫassínt	اِتْحَسِّنْت	ma-tḫassíntiš	مَتْحَسِّنْتِش	
ínti	itḫassínti	اِتْحَسِّنْتي	ma-tḫassintīš	مَتْحَسِّنْتيش	
íntu	itḫassíntu	اِتْحَسِّنْتوا	ma-tḫassintūš	مَتْحَسِّنْتوش	
húwwa	itḫássin	اِتْحَسِّن	ma-tḫassínš	مَتْحَسِّنْش	
híyya	itḫassínit	اِتْحَسِّنِت	ma-tḫassinítš	مَتْحَسِّنِتْش	
húmma	itḫassínu	اِتْحَسِّنوا	ma-tḫassinūš	مَتْحَسِّنوش	
ána	atḫássin	أتْحَسِّن	ma-tḫassínš	مَتْحَسِّنْش	imperfect
íḫna	nitḫássin	نِتْحَسِّن	ma-nitḫassínš	مَنِتْحَسِّنْش	
ínta	titḫássin	تِتْحَسِّن	ma-titḫassínš	مَتِتْحَسِّنْش	
ínti	titḫassíni	تِتْحَسِّني	ma-titḫassinīš	مَتِتْحَسِّنيش	
íntu	titḫassínu	تِتْحَسِّنوا	ma-titḫassinūš	مَتِتْحَسِّنوش	
húwwa	yitḫássin	يِتْحَسِّن	ma-yitḫassínš	مَيِتْحَسِّنْش	
híyya	titḫássin	تِتْحَسِّن	ma-titḫassínš	مَتِتْحَسِّنْش	
húmma	yitḫassínu	يِتْحَسِّنوا	ma-yitḫassinūš	مَيِتْحَسِّنوش	
ána	batḫássin	بَتْحَسِّن	ma-batḫassínš	مَبَتْحَسِّنْش	bi-imperfect
íḫna	binitḫássin	بِنِتْحَسِّن	ma-bnitḫassínš	مَبْنِتْحَسِّنْش	
ínta	bititḫássin	بِتِتْحَسِّن	ma-btitḫassínš	مَبْتِتْحَسِّنْش	
ínti	bititḫassíni	بِتِتْحَسِّني	ma-btitḫassinīš	مَبْتِتْحَسِّنيش	
íntu	bititḫassínu	بِتِتْحَسِّنوا	ma-btitḫassinūš	مَبْتِتْحَسِّنوش	
húwwa	biyitḫássin	بِيِتْحَسِّن	ma-byitḫassínš	مَبْيِتْحَسِّنْش	
híyya	bititḫássin	بِتِتْحَسِّن	ma-btitḫassínš	مَبْتِتْحَسِّنْش	
húmma	biyitḫassínu	بِيِتْحَسِّنوا	ma-byitḫassinūš	مَبْيِتْحَسِّنوش	
ána	hatḫássin	هَتْحَسِّن	miš hatḫássin	مِش هَتْحَسِّن	future
íḫna	hanitḫássin	هَنِتْحَسِّن	miš hanitḫássin	مِش هَنِتْحَسِّن	
ínta	hatitḫássin	هَتِتْحَسِّن	miš hatitḫássin	مِش هَتِتْحَسِّن	
ínti	hatitḫassíni	هَتِتْحَسِّني	miš hatitḫassíni	مِش هَتِتْحَسِّني	
íntu	hatitḫassínu	هَتِتْحَسِّنوا	miš hatitḫassínu	مِش هَتِتْحَسِّنوا	
húwwa	hayitḫássin	هَيِتْحَسِّن	miš hayitḫássin	مِش هَيِتْحَسِّن	
híyya	hatitḫássin	هَتِتْحَسِّن	miš hatitḫássin	مِش هَتِتْحَسِّن	
húmma	hayitḫassínu	هَيِتْحَسِّنوا	miš hayitḫassínu	مِش هَيِتْحَسِّنوا	
ínta	itḫássin	اِتْحَسِّن	ma-titḫassínš	مَتِتْحَسِّنْش	imperative
ínti	itḫassíni	اِتْحَسِّني	ma-titḫassinīš	مَتِتْحَسِّنيش	
íntu	itḫassínu	اِتْحَسِّنوا	ma-titḫassinūš	مَتِتْحَسِّنوش	

	active		passive		
masculine	mitḫássin	مِتْحَسِّن	–	–	participles
feminine	mitḫassína	مِتْحَسِّنَة	–	–	
plural	mitḫassinīn	مِتْحَسِّنين	–	–	

verbal noun: taḫássun تَحَسُّن

①

سارة اتْحسِّنت في الإنْجِليزي أوي بعْد ما سافْرِت أمْريكا.

sāra -tḫassínit fi -lʔingilīzi ʔáwi ba3dᵊ ma sáfrit amrīka.

Sara's English improved a lot after she went to America.

②

عُمْرِك ما هتِتْحسِّني في الطّبْخ و إنْتي مبْتُدْخُليش المطْبخ خالِص.

3úmrik ma hatitḫassíni fi -ṭṭabxᵊ w ínti ma-btudxulīš ilmáṭbax xāliṣ.

Your cooking won't improve if you never set foot in the kitchen.

③

أ: مُعاذ اِتْحسِّن وَلّا لِسّه؟

ب: حالْتُه اتْحسِّنِت شُوَيّة و بعْديْن تِعِب تاني.

A: mu3āz itḫássin wálla líssa?

B: ḫáltu -tḫassínit šuwáyya wi ba3dēn tí3ib tāni.

A: Is Moaz better now?

B: Well, he got a bit better, then he got sick again.

④

شكْلك مِتْحسِّن أوي. مِن يوْميْن وِشّك كان مُرْهق خالِص.

šáklak mitḫássin áwi. min yumēn wíššak kān múrhaq xāliṣ.

You look better. A couple of days ago,
your face looked so tired.

⑤

درجاتْهُم مبْتِتْحسِّنْش علشان مِش بيْذاكْروا.

daragáthum ma-btitḫassínšᵊ 3alašān miš biyzákru.

Their grades don't improve
because they don't study.

❖ [5s1] **to improve, get better**

➲ 186.5

12 to fight *itxāniʔ* اِتْخانِق

	affirmative		negative		
ána	*itxaníʔt*	اِتْخانِقْت	*ma-txaníʔtiš*	مَتْخانِقْتِش	**perfect**
íḫna	*itxaníʔna*	اِتْخانِقْنا	*ma-txaniʔnāš*	مَتْخانِقْناش	
ínta	*itxaníʔt*	اِتْخانِقْت	*ma-txaníʔtiš*	مَتْخانِقْتِش	
ínti	*itxaníʔti*	اِتْخانِقْتي	*ma-txaniʔtīš*	مَتْخانِقْتيش	
íntu	*itxaníʔtu*	اِتْخانِقْتوا	*ma-txaniʔtūš*	مَتْخانِقْتوش	
húwwa	*itxāniʔ*	اِتْخانِق	*ma-txaníʔš*	مَتْخانِقْش	
híyya	*itxánʔit*	اِتْخانْقِت	*ma-txanʔítš*	مَتْخانْقِتْش	
húmma	*itxánʔu*	اِتْخانْقوا	*ma-txanʔūš*	مَتْخانْقوش	
ána	*atxāniʔ*	أتْخانِق	*ma-txaníʔš*	مَتْخانِقْش	**imperfect**
íḫna	*nitxāniʔ*	نِتْخانِق	*ma-nitxaníʔš*	مَنِتْخانِقْش	
ínta	*titxāniʔ*	تِتْخانِق	*ma-titxaníʔš*	مَتِتْخانِقْش	
ínti	*titxánʔi*	تِتْخانْقي	*ma-titxanʔīš*	مَتِتْخانْقيش	
íntu	*titxánʔu*	تِتْخانْقوا	*ma-titxanʔūš*	مَتِتْخانْقوش	
húwwa	*yitxāniʔ*	يِتْخانِق	*ma-yitxaníʔš*	مَيِتْخانِقْش	
híyya	*titxāniʔ*	تِتْخانِق	*ma-titxaníʔš*	مَتِتْخانِقْش	
húmma	*yitxánʔu*	يِتْخانْقوا	*ma-yitxanʔūš*	مَيِتْخانْقوش	
ána	*batxāniʔ*	بَتْخانِق	*ma-batxaníʔš*	مَبَتْخانِقْش	**bi-imperfect**
íḫna	*bibitxāniʔ*	بِنِتْخانِق	*ma-bbitxaníʔš*	مَبِنِتْخانِقْش	
ínta	*bititxāniʔ*	بِتِتْخانِق	*ma-btitxaníʔš*	مَبْتِتْخانِقْش	
ínti	*bititxánʔi*	بِتِتْخانْقي	*ma-btitxanʔīš*	مَبْتِتْخانْقيش	
íntu	*bititxánʔu*	بِتِتْخانْقوا	*ma-btitxanʔūš*	مَبْتِتْخانْقوش	
húwwa	*biyitxāniʔ*	بِيِتْخانِق	*ma-byitxaníʔš*	مَبْيِتْخانِقْش	
híyya	*bititxāniʔ*	بِتِتْخانِق	*ma-btitxaníʔš*	مَبْتِتْخانِقْش	
húmma	*biyitxánʔu*	بِيِتْخانْقوا	*ma-byitxanʔūš*	مَبْيِتْخانْقوش	
ána	*hatxāniʔ*	هَتْخانِق	*miš hatxāniʔ*	مِش هَتْخانِق	**future**
íḫna	*hanitxāniʔ*	هَنِتْخانِق	*miš hanitxāniʔ*	مِش هَنِتْخانِق	
ínta	*hatitxāniʔ*	هَتِتْخانِق	*miš hatitxāniʔ*	مِش هَتِتْخانِق	
ínti	*hatitxánʔi*	هَتِتْخانْقي	*miš hatitxánʔi*	مِش هَتِتْخانْقي	
íntu	*hatitxánʔu*	هَتِتْخانْقوا	*miš hatitxánʔu*	مِش هَتِتْخانْقوا	
húwwa	*hayitxāniʔ*	هَيِتْخانِق	*miš hayitxāniʔ*	مِش هَيِتْخانِق	
híyya	*hatitxāniʔ*	هَتِتْخانِق	*miš hatitxāniʔ*	مِش هَتِتْخانِق	
húmma	*hayitxánʔu*	هَيِتْخانْقوا	*miš hayitxánʔu*	مِش هَيِتْخانْقوا	
ínta	*itxāniʔ*	اِتْخانِق	*ma-titxaníʔš*	مَتِتْخانِقْش	**imperative**
ínti	*itxánʔi*	اِتْخانْقي	*ma-titxanʔīš*	مَتِتْخانْقيش	
íntu	*itxánʔu*	اِتْخانْقوا	*ma-titxanʔūš*	مَتِتْخانْقوش	

	active		passive		
masculine	*mitxāniʔ*	مِتْخانِق	–	–	**participles**
feminine	*mitxánʔa*	مِتْخانْقة	–	–	
plural	*mitxanʔīn*	مِتْخانْقين	–	–	

verbal nouns: *xināʔ* خِناق - *xināʔa* خِناقة

①

وِلاد عمّي اتْخانْقوا إمْبارِح خِناقة كْبيرة عَ الواتْساب.

wilād 3ámmi -txán?u ?imbāriḥ xinā?a kbīra 3a -lwatsāp.

My cousins had a big argument on
WhatsApp [messaging app] yesterday.

②

أ: إنْتو اتْخانِقْتوا معَ بعْض؟

ب: أه، و مِتْخاصْمين.

A: íntu -txaní?tu má3a ba3ḍ?
B: āh, wi mitxaṣmīn.

A: Did you have a fight with each other?
B: Yes, and now we're on bad terms.

③

لمّا واحِد بِيْكون عصبي بِيْقولوا ده بِيْتْخانِق معَ دِبّان وِشُّه.

lámma wāḥid biykūn 3áṣabi biy?ūlu da byitxāni? má3a dibbān wíššu.

If someone is upset, people say, "He is
fighting the flies in front of him."

④

نُهى أكيد هتِتْخانِق معَ مها لمّا تِعْرف اللي عملِتُه.

núha ?akīd hatitxāni? má3a máha lámma ti3raf ílli 3amalítu.

Noha will quarrel with Maha for sure when she finds out what she did.

⑤

شادي شكْلُه مِتْخانِق معَ مْراتُه. دوْل متْكلِّموش وَلا كِلْمة مِن ساعِةْ ما وِصْلوا.

šādi šáklu mitxāni? má3a mrātu. dōl ma-tkallimūš wálla kílma min sā3it ma wíṣlu.

It seems Shady has had a quarrel with his wife.
They haven't spoken a word since they arrived.

⑥

إمْبارِح اِتْنيْن اِتْخانْقوا في الشّارِع و عوّروا بعْض. الإسْعاف و البوليس جُم.

imbāriḥ itnēn itxán?u fi -ššāri3 wi 3awwáru ba3ḍ. il?is3āf w ilbulīs gum.

Two people had a fight in the street yesterday and injured
each other. An ambulance and the police came.

⑦

متِتْخانْقوش قُدّام وِلادْكو.

ma-titxan?ūš ?uddām wiládku.

Don't fight in front of your kids.

❖ [6s] **to fight; to argue, quarrel (with** معَ *má3a*)

- As with the English verb 'fight', this verb can refer to a physical fight or a verbal argument, depending on the context.

➲ 41.6, 71.3

13 to graduate *itxárrag* اِتْخَرَّج

verbal noun: *taxárrug* تَخَرُّج

perfect

	affirmative		negative	
ána	*itxarrágt*	اِتْخَرَّجْت	*ma-txarrágtiš*	مَتْخَرَّجْتِش
íḫna	*itxarrágna*	اِتْخَرَّجْنا	*ma-txarragnāš*	مَتْخَرَّجْناش
ínta	*itxarrágt*	اِتْخَرَّجْت	*ma-txarrágtiš*	مَتْخَرَّجْتِش
ínti	*itxarrágti*	اِتْخَرَّجْتي	*ma-txarragtīš*	مَتْخَرَّجْتيش
íntu	*itxarrágtu*	اِتْخَرَّجْتوا	*ma-txarragtūš*	مَتْخَرَّجْتوش
húwwa	*itxárrag*	اِتْخَرَّج	*ma-txarrágš*	مَتْخَرَّجْش
híyya	*itxarrágit*	اِتْخَرَّجِت	*ma-txarragítš*	مَتْخَرَّجِتْش
húmma	*itxarrágu*	اِتْخَرَّجوا	*ma-txarragūš*	مَتْخَرَّجوش

imperfect

	affirmative		negative	
ána	*atxárrag*	أَتْخَرَّج	*ma-txarrágš*	مَتْخَرَّجْش
íḫna	*nitxárrag*	نِتْخَرَّج	*ma-nitxarrágš*	مَنِتْخَرَّجْش
ínta	*titxárrag*	تِتْخَرَّج	*ma-titxarrágš*	مَتِتْخَرَّجْش
ínti	*titxarrági*	تِتْخَرَّجي	*ma-titxarragīš*	مَتِتْخَرَّجيش
íntu	*titxarrágu*	تِتْخَرَّجوا	*ma-titxarragūš*	مَتِتْخَرَّجوش
húwwa	*yitxárrag*	يِتْخَرَّج	*ma-yitxarrágš*	مَيِتْخَرَّجْش
híyya	*titxárrag*	تِتْخَرَّج	*ma-titxarrágš*	مَتِتْخَرَّجْش
húmma	*yitxarrágu*	يِتْخَرَّجوا	*ma-yitxarragūš*	مَيِتْخَرَّجوش

bi-imperfect

	affirmative		negative	
ána	*batxárrag*	بَتْخَرَّج	*ma-batxarrágš*	مَبَتْخَرَّجْش
íḫna	*binitxárrag*	بِنِتْخَرَّج	*ma-bnitxarrágš*	مَبْنِتْخَرَّجْش
ínta	*bititxárrag*	بِتِتْخَرَّج	*ma-btitxarrágš*	مَبْتِتْخَرَّجْش
ínti	*bititxarrági*	بِتِتْخَرَّجي	*ma-btitxarragīš*	مَبْتِتْخَرَّجيش
íntu	*bititxarrágu*	بِتِتْخَرَّجوا	*ma-btitxarragūš*	مَبْتِتْخَرَّجوش
húwwa	*biyitxárrag*	بِيِتْخَرَّج	*ma-byitxarrágš*	مَبْيِتْخَرَّجْش
híyya	*bititxárrag*	بِتِتْخَرَّج	*ma-btitxarrágš*	مَبْتِتْخَرَّجْش
húmma	*biyitxarrágu*	بِيِتْخَرَّجوا	*ma-byitxarragūš*	مَبْيِتْخَرَّجوش

future

	affirmative		negative	
ána	*hatxárrag*	هَتْخَرَّج	*miš hatxárrag*	مِش هَتْخَرَّج
íḫna	*hanitxárrag*	هَنِتْخَرَّج	*miš hanitxárrag*	مِش هَنِتْخَرَّج
ínta	*hatitxárrag*	هَتِتْخَرَّج	*miš hatitxárrag*	مِش هَتِتْخَرَّج
ínti	*hatitxarrági*	هَتِتْخَرَّجي	*miš hatitxarrági*	مِش هَتِتْخَرَّجي
íntu	*hatitxarrágu*	هَتِتْخَرَّجوا	*miš hatitxarrágu*	مِش هَتِتْخَرَّجوا
húwwa	*hayitxárrag*	هَيِتْخَرَّج	*miš hayitxárrag*	مِش هَيِتْخَرَّج
híyya	*hatitxárrag*	هَتِتْخَرَّج	*miš hatitxárrag*	مِش هَتِتْخَرَّج
húmma	*hayitxarrágu*	هَيِتْخَرَّجوا	*miš hayitxarrágu*	مِش هَيِتْخَرَّجوا

imperative

	affirmative		negative	
ínta	*itxárrag*	اِتْخَرَّج	*ma-titxarrágš*	مَتِتْخَرَّجْش
ínti	*itxarrági*	اِتْخَرَّجي	*ma-titxarragīš*	مَتِتْخَرَّجيش
íntu	*itxarrágu*	اِتْخَرَّجوا	*ma-titxarragūš*	مَتِتْخَرَّجوش

participles

	active		passive	
masculine	*mitxárrag*	مِتْخَرَّج	–	–
feminine	*mitxarrága*	مِتْخَرَّجَة	–	–
plural	*mitxarragīn*	مِتْخَرَّجين	–	–

①

أ: صفاء اِتْخرّجِت مِن الجامْعة في مايو و اشْتغلِت في يولْيَة.

ب: ياه، لقِت شُغْل بِالسُّرْعة دي؟

A: ṣafāʔ itxarrágit min ilgám3a f māyu w ištáɣalit fi yúlya.
B: yā, láʔit šuɣlᵊ bi-ssúr3a di?

A: Safaa graduated from college in May and found a job in July.
B: Oh, she found a job that soon?

②

إحْنا نِتْخرّج الأوّل و بعْديْن نِبْقى نْدوّر على مِنْحة نْكمِّل بيها دِراسِتْنا برّه.

íḫna nitxárrag ilʔáwwil wi ba3dēn níbʔa ndáwwar 3ála mínḫa nkámmil bīha dirasítna bárra.

First, we graduate, and then we search for a scholarship to continue studying abroad.

③

إنْتَ مبْتِتْخرّجْش ليْه؟ ما تْركِّز في دْراسْتك، خلّيك تِخْلص.

ínta ma-btitxarrágšᵊ lē? ma trákkiz fi drástak, xallīk tíxlaṣ.

Why don't you graduate? Focus on your studies and get it done.

④

نُصّ دُفْعِتْنا مِش هَيِتْخرّجوا السّنة دي علشان درجاتْهُم وِحْشة أوي و هَيْعيدوا السّنة.

nuṣṣᵊ duf3ítna miš hayitxarrágu -ssanādi 3ašān daragáthum wíḫša ʔáwi wi hay3īdu -ssána.

Half of our class will not graduate this year because their grades aren't good enough, and they'll repeat the year.

⑤

متِتْخرّجْش مِن ثانَوي إلّا و إنْتَ مِحدِّد هدفك في المرْحلة اللي بعْدها.

ma-titxarrágšᵊ min sānawi ílla w ínta miḫáddid hádafak fi -lmarḫála ʔílli ba3dáha.

Don't graduate from high school without having set your goals for the next stage [of life].

⑥

أخويا مِتْخرّج مِن هنْدسِةْ بِتْروْل، بسّ بِيْموت في العربِيّات، عايِز يِشْتغل في الميكانيكا.

axūya mitxárrag min handásit bitrōl, bassᵊ biymūt fi -l3arabiyyāt, 3āyiz yištáɣal fi -lmikanīka.

My brother has a degree in [lit. graduated from] petroleum engineering, but he loves cars and wants to work in mechanics.

❖ [5s2] **to graduate (from** مِن *min*)

➲ 8.7, 26.6, 253.1

14 to imagine *itxáyyil* اِتْخَيِّل

	affirmative		negative		
ána	*itxayyílt*	اِتْخَيِّلْت	*ma-txayyíltiš*	مَتْخَيِّلْتِش	perfect
íḥna	*itxayyílna*	اِتْخَيِّلْنا	*ma-txayyilnāš*	مَتْخَيِّلْناش	
ínta	*itxayyílt*	اِتْخَيِّلْت	*ma-txayyíltiš*	مَتْخَيِّلْتِش	
ínti	*itxayyílti*	اِتْخَيِّلْتي	*ma-txayyiltīš*	مَتْخَيِّلْتيش	
íntu	*itxayyíltu*	اِتْخَيِّلْتوا	*ma-txayyiltūš*	مَتْخَيِّلْتوش	
húwwa	*itxáyyil*	اِتْخَيِّل	*ma-txayyílš*	مَتْخَيِّلْش	
híyya	*itxayyílit*	اِتْخَيِّلِت	*ma-txayyilítš*	مَتْخَيِّلِتْش	
húmma	*itxayyílu*	اِتْخَيِّلوا	*ma-txayyilūš*	مَتْخَيِّلوش	
ána	*atxáyyil*	أتْخَيِّل	*ma-txayyílš*	مَتْخَيِّلْش	imperfect
íḥna	*nitxáyyil*	نِتْخَيِّل	*ma-nitxayyílš*	مَنِتْخَيِّلْش	
ínta	*titxáyyil*	تِتْخَيِّل	*ma-titxayyílš*	مَتِتْخَيِّلْش	
ínti	*titxayyíli*	تِتْخَيِّلي	*ma-titxayyilīš*	مَتِتْخَيِّليش	
íntu	*titxayyílu*	تِتْخَيِّلوا	*ma-titxayyilūš*	مَتِتْخَيِّلوش	
húwwa	*yitxáyyil*	يِتْخَيِّل	*ma-yitxayyílš*	مَيِتْخَيِّلْش	
híyya	*titxáyyil*	تِتْخَيِّل	*ma-titxayyílš*	مَتِتْخَيِّلْش	
húmma	*yitxayyílu*	يِتْخَيِّلوا	*ma-yitxayyilūš*	مَيِتْخَيِّلوش	
ána	*batxáyyil*	بَتْخَيِّل	*ma-batxayyílš*	مَبَتْخَيِّلْش	bi-imperfect
íḥna	*binitxáyyil*	بِنِتْخَيِّل	*ma-bnitxayyílš*	مَبْنِتْخَيِّلْش	
ínta	*bititxáyyil*	بِتِتْخَيِّل	*ma-btitxayyílš*	مَبْتِتْخَيِّلْش	
ínti	*bititxayyíli*	بِتِتْخَيِّلي	*ma-btitxayyilīš*	مَبْتِتْخَيِّليش	
íntu	*bititxayyílu*	بِتِتْخَيِّلوا	*ma-btitxayyilūš*	مَبْتِتْخَيِّلوش	
húwwa	*biyitxáyyil*	بِيِتْخَيِّل	*ma-byitxayyílš*	مَبْيِتْخَيِّلْش	
híyya	*bititxáyyil*	بِتِتْخَيِّل	*ma-btitxayyílš*	مَبْتِتْخَيِّلْش	
húmma	*biyitxayyílu*	بِيِتْخَيِّلوا	*ma-byitxayyilūš*	مَبْيِتْخَيِّلوش	
ána	*hatxáyyil*	هَتْخَيِّل	*miš hatxáyyil*	مِش هَتْخَيِّل	future
íḥna	*hanitxáyyil*	هَنِتْخَيِّل	*miš hanitxáyyil*	مِش هَنِتْخَيِّل	
ínta	*hatitxáyyil*	هَتِتْخَيِّل	*miš hatitxáyyil*	مِش هَتِتْخَيِّل	
ínti	*hatitxayyíli*	هَتِتْخَيِّلي	*miš hatitxayyíli*	مِش هَتِتْخَيِّلي	
íntu	*hatitxayyílu*	هَتِتْخَيِّلوا	*miš hatitxayyílu*	مِش هَتِتْخَيِّلوا	
húwwa	*hayitxáyyil*	هَيِتْخَيِّل	*miš hayitxáyyil*	مِش هَيِتْخَيِّل	
híyya	*hatitxáyyil*	هَتِتْخَيِّل	*miš hatitxáyyil*	مِش هَتِتْخَيِّل	
húmma	*hayitxayyílu*	هَيِتْخَيِّلوا	*miš hayitxayyílu*	مِش هَيِتْخَيِّلوا	
ínta	*itxáyyil / taxáyyal*	اِتْخَيِّل / تَخَيَّل	*ma-titxayyílš*	مَتِتْخَيِّلْش	imperative
ínti	*itxayyíli / taxayyáli*	اِتْخَيِّلي / تَخَيَّلي	*ma-titxayyilīš*	مَتِتْخَيِّليش	
íntu	*itxayyílu / taxayyálu*	اِتْخَيِّلوا / تَخَيَّلوا	*ma-titxayyilūš*	مَتِتْخَيِّلوش	

	active		passive		
masculine	*mitxáyyil*	مِتْخَيِّل	–	–	participles
feminine	*mitxayyíla*	مِتْخَيِّلَة	–	–	
plural	*mitxayyilīn*	مِتْخَيِّلين	–	–	

verbal nouns: *taxáyyul* تَخَيُّل - *xayāl* خَيَال

①

متْخيِّلْتِش أبداً إنّك تِطْلع زيُّهم.

ma-txayyíltiš ábadan ínnak títla3 zayyúhum.

I would never have imagined
that you'd turn out like them.

②

شيرين مِش قادْرة تِتْخيِّل نفْسها مِن غيْر جَواز.

širīn miš ʔádra titxáyyil nafsáha min ɣēr gawāz.

Sherien can't imagine herself not being married.

③

العِيال الصُّغيرّة بِيِتْخيِّلوا حاجات غريبة جِدّاً.

il3iyāl iṣṣuɣayyára biyitxayyílu ħagāt ɣarība gíddan.

Young children can imagine very strange things.

④

هتْغمّض عيْنك و هتِتْخيِّل إنّك في مكان بِتْحِبُّه.

hatɣámmaḍ 3ēnak wi hatitxáyyil ínnak fi makān bitħíbbu.

You will close your eyes and imagine
yourself in a place that you like.

⑤

متِتْخيِّلْش أنا فرْحان قدّ أيْه إني شُفْتك.

ma-titxayyílš, ána farħān addᵊ ʔē ínni šúftak.

You can't imagine how happy I am to see you.

⑥

تخيّل إنّ عمْرو دِياب عدّى الخمْسين.

taxáyyal innᵊ 3ámrᵊ diyāb 3ádda -lxamsīn.

Imagine, Amr Diab [Egyptian pop star] is over 50 years old now.

⑦

اِتْخيِّل نفْسك بعْد خمس سِنين. هتْكون فيْن و بِتِعْمِل أيْه؟

itxáyyil náfsak ba3dᵊ xámas sinīn. hatkūn fēn wi bití3mil ʔē?

Imagine yourself in five years. Where will
you be, and what will you be doing?

❖ [5s1] **to imagine** (**that** إنّ *inn*)

- This verb has an alternative affirmative imperative borrowed from Modern Standard Arabic. (➲ 14.6)

15 to connect ittáṣal اِتّصل [13]

verbal noun: ittiṣāl اِتّصال

	affirmative		negative		
ána	ittaṣált	اِتّصَلْت	ma-ttaṣáltiš	مَتّصَلْتِش	perfect
íḫna	ittaṣálna	اِتّصَلْنا	ma-ttaṣalnāš	مَتّصَلْناش	
ínta	ittaṣált	اِتّصَلْت	ma-ttaṣáltiš	مَتّصَلْتِش	
ínti	ittaṣálti	اِتّصَلْتي	ma-ttaṣaltīš	مَتّصَلْتيش	
íntu	ittaṣáltu	اِتّصَلْتوا	ma-ttaṣaltūš	مَتّصَلْتوش	
húwwa	ittáṣal	اِتّصَل	ma-ttaṣálš	مَتّصَلْش	
híyya	ittáṣalit	اِتّصَلِت	ma-ttaṣalítš	مَتّصَلِتْش	
húmma	ittáṣalu	اِتّصَلوا	ma-ttaṣalūš	مَتّصَلوش	
ána	attíṣil	أتّصِل	ma-ttiṣílš	مَتّصِلْش	imperfect
íḫna	nittíṣil	نِتّصِل	ma-nittiṣílš	مَنِتّصِلْش	
ínta	tittíṣil	تِتّصِل	ma-tittiṣílš	مَتِتّصِلْش	
ínti	tittíṣli	تِتّصْلي	ma-tittiṣlīš	مَتِتّصْليش	
íntu	tittíṣlu	تِتّصْلوا	ma-tittiṣlūš	مَتِتّصْلوش	
húwwa	yittíṣil	يِتّصِل	ma-yittiṣílš	مَيِتّصِلْش	
híyya	tittíṣil	تِتّصِل	ma-tittiṣílš	مَتِتّصِلْش	
húmma	yittíṣlu	يِتّصْلوا	ma-yittiṣlūš	مَيِتّصْلوش	
ána	battíṣil	بَتّصِل	ma-battiṣílš	مَبَتّصِلْش	bi-imperfect
íḫna	binittíṣil	بِنِتّصِل	ma-bnittiṣílš	مَبْنِتّصِلْش	
ínta	bitittíṣil	بِتِتّصِل	ma-btittiṣílš	مَبْتِتّصِلْش	
ínti	bitittíṣli	بِتِتّصْلي	ma-btittiṣlīš	مَبْتِتّصْليش	
íntu	bitittíṣlu	بِتِتّصْلوا	ma-btittiṣlūš	مَبْتِتّصْلوش	
húwwa	biyittíṣil	بِيِتّصِل	ma-byittiṣílš	مَبْيِتّصِلْش	
híyya	bitittíṣil	بِتِتّصِل	ma-btittiṣílš	مَبْتِتّصِلْش	
húmma	biyittíṣlu	بِيِتّصْلوا	ma-byittiṣlūš	مَبْيِتّصْلوش	
ána	hattíṣil	هَتّصِل	miš hattíṣil	مِش هَتّصِل	future
íḫna	hanittíṣil	هَنِتّصِل	miš hanittíṣil	مِش هَنِتّصِل	
ínta	hatittíṣil	هَتِتّصِل	miš hatittíṣil	مِش هَتِتّصِل	
ínti	hatittíṣli	هَتِتّصْلي	miš hatittíṣmi	مِش هَتِتّصْمي	
íntu	hatittíṣlu	هَتِتّصْلوا	miš hatittíṣlu	مِش هَتِتّصْلوا	
húwwa	hayittíṣil	هَيِتّصِل	miš hayittíṣil	مِش هَيِتّصِل	
híyya	hatittíṣil	هَتِتّصِل	miš hatittíṣil	مِش هَتِتّصِل	
húmma	hayittíṣlu	هَيِتّصْلوا	miš hayittíṣlu	مِش هَيِتّصْلوا	
ínta	ittíṣil	اِتّصِل	ma-tittiṣílš	مَتِتّصِلْش	imperative
ínti	ittíṣli	اِتّصْلي	ma-tittiṣlīš	مَتِتّصْليش	
íntu	ittíṣlu	اِتّصْلوا	ma-tittiṣlūš	مَتِتّصْلوش	

	active		passive		
masculine	mittíṣil	مِتّصِل	–	–	participles
feminine	mittíṣla	مِتّصْلة	–	–	
plural	mittiṣlīn	مِتّصْلين	–	–	

①

لمّا ماما تِعْبِت، اِتّصلْنا بِالإسْعاف ييجوا يِلْحقونا.

lámma māma tí3bit, ittaṣálna bi-lʔis3āf yīgu yilħaʔūna.

When our mom fell ill, we called the ambulance to come to our rescue.

②

متِتّصْليش بِخطيبِك كُلّ عشر دقايِق. اِتْقلّي شْوَيّة و سيبيه هُوَّ يْكلِّمِك.

ma-tittiṣlīš bi-xaṭībik kullᵊ 3ášar daʔāyiʔ. itʔálli šwáyya wi sibī húwwa ykallímik.

Don't call your fiancé every ten minutes. Be tough and make him call you.

③

علشان مبتِّصِلْش بِخالْتي في المُناسبات، أهيْ دِلْوَقْتي زعْلانة مِنّي.

3alašān ma-battiṣílšᵊ bi-xálti fi -lmunasabāt, ahé dilwáʔti za3lāna mínni.

Because I don't call my aunt on special occasions, she's mad at me now.

④

الشّاري مِش هَيِتّصِل بيك. هُوَّ معجبِتوش الشّقّة.

iššāri miš hayittíṣil bīk. húwwa ma-3agabitūš iššáʔʔa.

The buyer won't call you. He didn't like the apartment.

⑤

اِتِّصِل بِاخوك و قولُّه ميتْأخّرْش علشان يِلْحق الفرح مِن أوِّلُه.

ittíṣil bi-axūk wi ʔúllu ma-yitʔaxxáršᵊ 3alašān yílħaʔ ilfáraħ min awwílu.

Call your brother and tell him not to be late, so he makes it on time for the beginning of the wedding.

⑥

مين اللي مِتّصِل بينا بِاللّيْل كِده؟ رُدّي بِسُرْعة لتْكون حاجة خطيرة.

mīn ílli mittíṣil bīna bi-llēl kída? rúddi bi-súr3a la-tkūn ħāga xaṭīra.

Who's calling us so late? Quick, answer it in case it's an emergency.

⑦

طول ما أنا مِتّصِل بِالوايْ فايْ، جِهازي عمّال يِنزِّل تحْديثات لِلبرامِج.

ṭūl m- ána mittíṣil bi-lwāy fāy, gihāzi 3ammāl yinázzil taħdisāt li-lbarāmig.

As long as I'm connected to wifi, my cell phone is downloading updates for its programs.

❖ [8s1] **to call, phone (بِ** *bi-*); **to be connected (to بِ** *bi-*)

- This verb's actual meaning is 'be connected' (➲15.7). In Arabic, when you say 'call (by phone)', you are literally saying 'be connected (by phone)', and this is the modern meaning it is most commonly used for.

➲ 7.1, 119.1, 119.4, 171.3, 197.5

16 to handle *it3āmil* اِتْعامِل

verbal nouns: *ta3āmul* تَعامُل - *mu3āmla* مُعامْلَة

	affirmative		negative		
ána	*it3amílt*	اِتْعامِلْت	*ma-t3amíltiš*	مَتْعامِلْتِش	**perfect**
íḥna	*it3amílna*	اِتْعامِلْنا	*ma-t3amilnāš*	مَتْعامِلْناش	
ínta	*it3amílt*	اِتْعامِلْت	*ma-tit3amíltiš*	مَتْعامِلْتِش	
ínti	*it3amílti*	اِتْعامِلْتي	*ma-tit3amiltīš*	مَتْعامِلْتيش	
íntu	*it3amíltu*	اِتْعامِلْتوا	*ma-tit3amiltūš*	مَتْعامِلْتوش	
húwwa	*it3āmil*	اِتْعامِل	*ma-yit3amílš*	مَتْعامِلْش	
híyya	*it3ámlit*	اِتْعامْلِت	*ma-tit3amlítš*	مَتْعامْلِتْش	
húmma	*it3ámlu*	اِتْعامْلوا	*ma-yit3amlūš*	مَتْعامْلوش	
ána	*at3āmil*	أَتْعامِل	*ma-t3amílš*	مَتْعامِلْش	**imperfect**
íḥna	*nit3āmil*	نِتْعامِل	*ma-nit3amílš*	مَنِتْعامِلْش	
ínta	*tit3āmil*	تِتْعامِل	*ma-tit3amílš*	مَتِتْعامِلْش	
ínti	*tit3ámli*	تِتْعامْلي	*ma-tit3amlīš*	مَتِتْعامْليش	
íntu	*tit3ámlu*	تِتْعامْلوا	*ma-tit3amlūš*	مَتِتْعامْلوش	
húwwa	*yit3āmil*	يِتْعامِل	*ma-yit3amílš*	مَيِتْعامِلْش	
híyya	*tit3āmil*	تِتْعامِل	*ma-tit3amílš*	مَتِتْعامِلْش	
húmma	*yit3ámlu*	يِتْعامْلوا	*ma-yit3amlūš*	مَيِتْعامْلوش	
ána	*bat3āmil*	بَتْعامِل	*ma-bat3amílš*	مَبَتْعامِلْش	**bi-imperfect**
íḥna	*binit3āmil*	بِنِتْعامِل	*ma-bnit3amílš*	مَبْنِتْعامِلْش	
ínta	*bitit3āmil*	بِتِتْعامِل	*ma-btit3amílš*	مَبْتِتْعامِلْش	
ínti	*bitit3ámli*	بِتِتْعامْلي	*ma-btit3amlīš*	مَبْتِتْعامْليش	
íntu	*bitit3ámlu*	بِتِتْعامْلوا	*ma-btit3amlūš*	مَبْتِتْعامْلوش	
húwwa	*biyit3āmil*	بِيِتْعامِل	*ma-byit3amílš*	مَبْيِتْعامِلْش	
híyya	*bitit3āmil*	بِتِتْعامِل	*ma-btit3amílš*	مَبْتِتْعامِلْش	
húmma	*biyit3ámlu*	بِيِتْعامْلوا	*ma-byit3amlūš*	مَبْيِتْعامْلوش	
ána	*hat3āmil*	هَتْعامِل	*miš hat3āmil*	مِش هَتْعامِل	**future**
íḥna	*hanit3āmil*	هَنِتْعامِل	*miš hanit3āmil*	مِش هَنِتْعامِل	
ínta	*hatit3āmil*	هَتِتْعامِل	*miš hatit3āmil*	مِش هَتِتْعامِل	
ínti	*hatit3ámli*	هَتِتْعامْلي	*miš hatit3ámli*	مِش هَتِتْعامْلي	
íntu	*hatit3ámlu*	هَتِتْعامْلوا	*miš hatit3ámlu*	مِش هَتِتْعامْلوا	
húwwa	*hayit3āmil*	هَيِتْعامِل	*miš hayit3āmil*	مِش هَيِتْعامِل	
híyya	*hatit3āmil*	هَتِتْعامِل	*miš hatit3āmil*	مِش هَتِتْعامِل	
húmma	*hayit3ámlu*	هَيِتْعامْلوا	*miš hayit3ámlu*	مِش هَيِتْعامْلوا	
ínta	*it3āmil*	اِتْعامِل	*ma-tit3amílš*	مَتِتْعامِلْش	**imperative**
ínti	*it3ámli*	اِتْعامْلي	*ma-tit3amlīš*	مَتِتْعامْليش	
íntu	*it3ámlu*	اِتْعامْلوا	*ma-tit3amlūš*	مَتِتْعامْلوش	

	active		passive		
masculine	*mit3āmil*	مِتْعامِل	–	–	**participles**
feminine	*mit3ámla*	مِتْعامْلَة	–	–	
plural	*mit3amlīn*	مِتْعامْلين	–	–	

①

البيّاع اِتْعامِل معانا بْطريقة وِحْشة فا اشْتكيناهْ لِلمُدير.

ilbayyā3 it3āmil ma3āna b-ṭarīʔa wíḥša fa -štakināh li-lmudīr.

The salesman treated us badly, so we complained to the manager.

②

المفْروض يِتْعامْلوا معَ بعْض أحْسن مِن كِده.

ilmafrūḍ yit3ámlu má3a ba3ḍ áḥsan min kída.

They should deal with each other in a better way.

③

مبْيِتْعامِلْش معَ أطْفال أبداً. علشان كِده مِش بِيِسْتحْمِل دَوْشِتْهُم.

ma-byit3āmilšᵊ má3a ʔaṭfāl ábadan. 3alašān kída miš biyistáḥmil dawšíthum.

He never deals with kids. That's why he can't put up with their noise.

④

هتِتْعامِل معَ أنْهي بنْك لمّا تْسافِر؟

hatit3āmil má3a ʔánhi bankᵊ lámma tsāfir?

Which bank will you deal with when you're abroad?

⑤

متِتْعامْلوش معَ الحَيَوانات بِقسْوة.

ma-tit3amlūš má3a -lḥayawanāt bi-qáswa.

Don't treat animals cruelly.

⑥

مِتْعامِل معَ مرضُه بْشجاعة. أنا مُعْجب بيه.

mit3āmil má3a máraḍu b-šagā3a. ána mú3gab bī.

He is dealing with his illness bravely. I admire him.

❖ [6s] **to handle, deal with, treat** (معَ *má3a*)

➲ 21.1, 88.3

17 to get to know *it3árraf* اِتْعَرَّف

verbal nouns: *ta3árruf* تَعَرُّف - *ma3rifa* مَعْرِفة

	affirmative		negative		
ána	*it3arráft*	اِتْعَرَّفْت	*ma-t3arráftiš*	مَتْعَرَّفْتِش	perfect
íḫna	*it3arráfna*	اِتْعَرَّفْنا	*ma-t3arrafnāš*	مَتْعَرَّفْناش	
ínta	*it3arráft*	اِتْعَرَّفْت	*ma-t3arráftiš*	مَتْعَرَّفْتِش	
ínti	*it3arráfti*	اِتْعَرَّفْتي	*ma-t3arraftīš*	مَتْعَرَّفْتيش	
íntu	*it3arráftu*	اِتْعَرَّفْتوا	*ma-t3arraftūš*	مَتْعَرَّفْتوش	
húwwa	*it3árraf*	اِتْعَرَّف	*ma-t3arráfš*	مَتْعَرَّفْش	
híyya	*it3arráfit*	اِتْعَرَّفِت	*ma-t3arrafítš*	مَتْعَرَّفِتْش	
húmma	*it3arráfu*	اِتْعَرَّفوا	*ma-t3arrafūš*	مَتْعَرَّفوش	
ána	*at3árraf*	أَتْعَرَّف	*ma-t3arráfš*	مَتْعَرَّفْش	imperfect
íḫna	*nit3árraf*	نِتْعَرَّف	*ma-nit3arráfš*	مَنِتْعَرَّفْش	
ínta	*tit3árraf*	تِتْعَرَّف	*ma-tit3arráfš*	مَتِتْعَرَّفْش	
ínti	*tit3arráfi*	تِتْعَرَّفي	*ma-tit3arrafīš*	مَتِتْعَرَّفيش	
íntu	*tit3arráfu*	تِتْعَرَّفوا	*ma-tit3arrafūš*	مَتِتْعَرَّفوش	
húwwa	*yit3árraf*	يِتْعَرَّف	*ma-yit3arráfš*	مَيِتْعَرَّفْش	
híyya	*tit3árraf*	تِتْعَرَّف	*ma-tit3arráfš*	مَتِتْعَرَّفْش	
húmma	*yit3arráfu*	يِتْعَرَّفوا	*ma-yit3arrafūš*	مَيِتْعَرَّفوش	
ána	*bat3árraf*	بَتْعَرَّف	*ma-bat3arráfš*	مَبَتْعَرَّفْش	bi-imperfect
íḫna	*binit3árraf*	بِنِتْعَرَّف	*ma-bnit3arráfš*	مَبْنِتْعَرَّفْش	
ínta	*bitit3árraf*	بِتِتْعَرَّف	*ma-btit3arráfš*	مَبْتِتْعَرَّفْش	
ínti	*bitit3arráfi*	بِتِتْعَرَّفي	*ma-btit3arrafīš*	مَبْتِتْعَرَّفيش	
íntu	*bitit3arráfu*	بِتِتْعَرَّفوا	*ma-btit3arrafūš*	مَبْتِتْعَرَّفوش	
húwwa	*biyit3árraf*	بِيِتْعَرَّف	*ma-byit3arráfš*	مَبْيِتْعَرَّفْش	
híyya	*bitit3árraf*	بِتِتْعَرَّف	*ma-btit3arráfš*	مَبْتِتْعَرَّفْش	
húmma	*biyit3arráfu*	بِيِتْعَرَّفوا	*ma-byit3arrafūš*	مَبْيِتْعَرَّفوش	
ána	*hat3árraf*	هَتْعَرَّف	*miš hat3árraf*	مِش هَتْعَرَّف	future
íḫna	*hanit3árraf*	هَنِتْعَرَّف	*miš hanit3árraf*	مِش هَنِتْعَرَّف	
ínta	*hatit3árraf*	هَتِتْعَرَّف	*miš hatit3árraf*	مِش هَتِتْعَرَّف	
ínti	*hatit3arráfi*	هَتِتْعَرَّفي	*miš hatit3arráfi*	مِش هَتِتْعَرَّفي	
íntu	*hatit3arráfu*	هَتِتْعَرَّفوا	*miš hatit3arráfu*	مِش هَتِتْعَرَّفوا	
húwwa	*hayit3árraf*	هَيِتْعَرَّف	*miš hayit3árraf*	مِش هَيِتْعَرَّف	
híyya	*hatit3árraf*	هَتِتْعَرَّف	*miš hatit3árraf*	مِش هَتِتْعَرَّف	
húmma	*hayit3arráfu*	هَيِتْعَرَّفوا	*miš hayit3arráfu*	مِش هَيِتْعَرَّفوا	
ínta	*it3árraf*	اِتْعَرَّف	*ma-tit3arráfš*	مَتِتْعَرَّفْش	imperative
ínti	*it3arráfi*	اِتْعَرَّفي	*ma-tit3arrafīš*	مَتِتْعَرَّفيش	
íntu	*it3arráfu*	اِتْعَرَّفوا	*ma-tit3arrafūš*	مَتِتْعَرَّفوش	

	active		passive		
masculine	*mit3árraf*	مِتْعَرَّف	—	—	participles
feminine	*mit3arráfa*	مِتْعَرَّفَة	—	—	
plural	*mit3arrafīn*	مِتْعَرَّفين	—	—	

①

ابْتِسام اِتْعرّفِت على جوْزْها في الجامْعة.

ibtisām it3arráfit 3ála gúzha fi -lgám3a.

Ebtesam met her husband at college.

②

حاوِل تِتْعرّف على البِنْت دي.

ḥāwil tit3árraf 3ála -lbintᵊ di.

Try to meet that girl.

③

رُقَيّة مبْتِتْعرّفْش على النّاس بِسْهولة.

ruʔáyya ma-btit3arráfšᵊ 3ála -nnās bi-shūla.

Roqaya doesn't get to know people easily.

④

لمّا هتِتْعرّفي على عُيوبِك و مُميِّزاتِك هتِنْجحي في إدارِةْ نفْسِك صحّ.

lámma hatit3arráfi 3ála 3uyūbik wi mumayyizātik hatingáḥi fi idārit náfsik ṣaḥḥ.

When you know your weaknesses and strengths,
you'll do better at managing yourself.

⑤

اِتْعرّف على النّاس. معْرِفِةْ النّاس كُنوز.

it3árraf 3ála -nnās. ma3rífit innās kunūz.

Get to know people. Knowing
people is a treasure.

❖ [5s2] **to get to know, meet** (على *3ála*)

- Compare with ➲ 176.1, 179.1, 186.1.

➲ 77.6, 106.2

18 to have dinner *it3ášša* اِتْعَشّى

	affirmative		negative		
ána	*it3aššēt*	اِتْعَشّيْت	*ma-t3aššítš*	مَتْعَشّيْتْش	**perfect**
íḥna	*it3aššēna*	اِتْعَشّيْنا	*ma-t3aššināš*	مَتْعَشّيناش	
ínta	*it3aššēt*	اِتْعَشّيْت	*ma-t3aššítš*	مَتْعَشّيْتْش	
ínti	*it3aššēti*	اِتْعَشّيْتي	*ma-t3aššitīš*	مَتْعَشّيتيش	
íntu	*it3aššētu*	اِتْعَشّيْتوا	*ma-t3aššitūš*	مَتْعَشّيتوش	
húwwa	*it3ášša*	اِتْعَشّى	*ma-t3aššāš*	مَتْعَشّاش	
híyya	*it3áššit*	اِتْعَشّت	*ma-t3aššítš*	مَتْعَشّتْش	
húmma	*it3áššu*	اِتْعَشّوا	*ma-t3aššūš*	مَتْعَشّوش	
ána	*at3ášša*	أتْعَشّى	*ma-t3aššāš*	مَتْعَشّاش	**imperfect**
íḥna	*nit3ášša*	نِتْعَشّى	*ma-nit3aššāš*	مَنِتْعَشّاش	
ínta	*tit3ášša*	تِتْعَشّى	*ma-tit3aššāš*	مَتِتْعَشّاش	
ínti	*tit3ášši*	تِتْعَشّي	*ma-tit3aššīš*	مَتِتْعَشّيش	
íntu	*tit3áššu*	تِتْعَشّوا	*ma-tit3aššūš*	مَتِتْعَشّوش	
húwwa	*yit3ášša*	يِتْعَشّى	*ma-yit3aššāš*	مَيِتْعَشّاش	
híyya	*tit3ášša*	تِتْعَشّى	*ma-tit3aššāš*	مَتِتْعَشّاش	
húmma	*yit3áššu*	يِتْعَشّوا	*ma-yit3aššūš*	مَيِتْعَشّوش	
ána	*bat3ášša*	بَتْعَشّى	*ma-bat3aššāš*	مَبَتْعَشّاش	**bi-imperfect**
íḥna	*binit3ášša*	بِنِتْعَشّى	*ma-bnit3aššāš*	مَبْنِتْعَشّاش	
ínta	*bitit3ášša*	بِتِتْعَشّى	*ma-btit3aššāš*	مَبْتِتْعَشّاش	
ínti	*bitit3ášši*	بِتِتْعَشّي	*ma-btit3aššīš*	مَبْتِتْعَشّيش	
íntu	*bitit3áššu*	بِتِتْعَشّوا	*ma-btit3aššūš*	مَبْتِتْعَشّوش	
húwwa	*biyit3ášša*	بِيِتْعَشّى	*ma-byit3aššāš*	مَبْيِتْعَشّاش	
híyya	*bitit3ášša*	بِتِتْعَشّى	*ma-btit3aššāš*	مَبْتِتْعَشّاش	
húmma	*biyit3áššu*	بِيِتْعَشّوا	*ma-byit3aššūš*	مَبْيِتْعَشّوش	
ána	*hat3ášša*	هَتْعَشّى	*miš hat3ášša*	مِش هَتْعَشّى	**future**
íḥna	*hanit3ášša*	هَنِتْعَشّى	*miš hanit3ášša*	مِش هَنِتْعَشّى	
ínta	*hatit3ášša*	هَتِتْعَشّى	*miš hatit3ášša*	مِش هَتِتْعَشّى	
ínti	*hatit3ášši*	هَتِتْعَشّي	*miš hatit3ášši*	مِش هَتِتْعَشّي	
íntu	*hatit3áššu*	هَتِتْعَشّوا	*miš hatit3áššu*	مِش هَتِتْعَشّوا	
húwwa	*hayit3ášša*	هَيِتْعَشّى	*miš hayit3ášša*	مِش هَيِتْعَشّى	
híyya	*hatit3ášša*	هَتِتْعَشّى	*miš hatit3ášša*	مِش هَتِتْعَشّى	
húmma	*hayit3áššu*	هَيِتْعَشّوا	*miš hayit3áššu*	مِش هَيِتْعَشّوا	
ínta	*it3ášša*	اِتْعَشّى	*ma-tit3aššāš*	مَتِتْعَشّاش	**imperative**
ínti	*it3ášši*	اِتْعَشّي	*ma-tit3aššīš*	مَتِتْعَشّيش	
íntu	*it3áššu*	اِتْعَشّوا	*ma-tit3aššūš*	مَتِتْعَشّوش	

	active		passive		
masculine	*mit3ášši*	مِتْعَشّي	–	–	**participles**
feminine	*mit3aššíyya*	مِتْعَشّيّة	–	–	
plural	*mit3aššiyīn*	مِتْعَشّيين	–	–	

verbal noun: *3áša* عَشا

①

مْتعشّيتْش إمْبارِح و قايِم مِ النّوْم جعان جِدّاً.

ma-t3aššítš imbāriḫ wi ʔāyim mi -nnōm ga3ān gíddan.

I didn't have dinner yesterday, so I woke up feeling so hungry.

②

أيْه رأْيك نِتْعشّى معَ بعْض النّهارْده؟

ʔē ráʔyak nit3ášša má3a ba3ḍ innahárda?

What do you say to having dinner together tonight?

③

بيِتْعشّوا معَ بعْض على ضوْء الشُّموع كُلّ يوْم بقالْهُم أرْبعين سنة.

biyit3áššu má3a ba3ḍ[ə] 3ála ḍōʔ iššumū3 kull[ə] yōm baʔálhum arba3īn sána.

They've had dinner together by candlelight every day for 40 years.

④

مِش هتِتْعشّوا وَلّا أيْه؟

miš hatit3áššu wálla ʔē?

Aren't you going to eat dinner?

⑤

اِتْعشّى خفيف عشان متِتْخنْش.

it3áššа xafīf 3ašān ma-titxánš.

Have a light dinner, so you don't get fat.

⑥

مِتْعشّيين إمْبارِح فتّة قبْل النّوْم. كانِت تِقيلة أوي.

mit3aššiyīn imbāriḫ fátta ʔabl innōm. kānit tiʔīla ʔáwi.

We ate fattah yesterday before
going to bed. It was so heavy.

❖ [5d] **to have dinner**

- This verb is often intransitive, but can take an object, in which case it can translate 'have __ for dinner' or simply 'eat'. (➲ 18.6)

➲ 27.5, 146.1, 175.3, 238.5

19 to learn *it3állim* اِتْعَلِّم

verbal noun: *ta3állum* تَعَلُّم

		affirmative		negative		
ána	*it3allímt*	اِتْعَلِّمْت	*ma-t3allímtiš*	مَتْعَلِّمْتِش		perfect
íḫna	*it3allímna*	اِتْعَلِّمْنا	*ma-t3allimnāš*	مَتْعَلِّمْناش		
ínta	*it3allímt*	اِتْعَلِّمْت	*ma-t3allímtiš*	مَتْعَلِّمْتِش		
ínti	*it3allímti*	اِتْعَلِّمْتي	*ma-t3allimtīš*	مَتْعَلِّمْتيش		
íntu	*it3allímtu*	اِتْعَلِّمْتوا	*ma-t3allimtūš*	مَتْعَلِّمْتوش		
húwwa	*it3állim*	اِتْعَلِّم	*ma-t3allímš*	مَتْعَلِّمْش		
híyya	*it3allímit*	اِتْعَلِّمِت	*ma-t3allimítš*	مَتْعَلِّمِتْش		
húmma	*it3allímu*	اِتْعَلِّموا	*ma-t3allimūš*	مَتْعَلِّموش		
ána	*at3állim*	أتْعَلِّم	*ma-t3allímš*	مَتْعَلِّمْش		imperfect
íḫna	*nit3állim*	نِتْعَلِّم	*ma-nit3allímš*	مَنِتْعَلِّمْش		
ínta	*tit3állim*	تِتْعَلِّم	*ma-tit3allímš*	مَتِتْعَلِّمْش		
ínti	*tit3allími*	تِتْعَلِّمي	*ma-tit3allimīš*	مَتِتْعَلِّميش		
íntu	*tit3allímu*	تِتْعَلِّموا	*ma-tit3allimūš*	مَتِتْعَلِّموش		
húwwa	*yit3állim*	يِتْعَلِّم	*ma-yit3allímš*	مَيِتْعَلِّمْش		
híyya	*tit3állim*	تِتْعَلِّم	*ma-tit3allímš*	مَتِتْعَلِّمْش		
húmma	*yit3allímu*	يِتْعَلِّموا	*ma-yit3allimūš*	مَيِتْعَلِّموش		
ána	*bat3állim*	بَتْعَلِّم	*ma-bat3allímš*	مَبَتْعَلِّمْش		bi-imperfect
íḫna	*binit3állim*	بِنِتْعَلِّم	*ma-bnit3allímš*	مَبْنِتْعَلِّمْش		
ínta	*bitit3állim*	بِتِتْعَلِّم	*ma-btit3allímš*	مَبْتِتْعَلِّمْش		
ínti	*bitit3allími*	بِتِتْعَلِّمي	*ma-btit3allimīš*	مَبْتِتْعَلِّميش		
íntu	*bitit3allímu*	بِتِتْعَلِّموا	*ma-btit3allimūš*	مَبْتِتْعَلِّموش		
húwwa	*biyit3állim*	بِيِتْعَلِّم	*ma-byit3allímš*	مَبْيِتْعَلِّمْش		
híyya	*bitit3állim*	بِتِتْعَلِّم	*ma-btit3allímš*	مَبْتِتْعَلِّمْش		
húmma	*biyit3allímu*	بِيِتْعَلِّموا	*ma-byit3allimūš*	مَبْيِتْعَلِّموش		
ána	*hat3állim*	هَتْعَلِّم	*miš hat3állim*	مِش هَتْعَلِّم		future
íḫna	*hanit3állim*	هَنِتْعَلِّم	*miš hanit3állim*	مِش هَنِتْعَلِّم		
ínta	*hatit3állim*	هَتِتْعَلِّم	*miš hatit3állim*	مِش هَتِتْعَلِّم		
ínti	*hatit3allími*	هَتِتْعَلِّمي	*miš hatit3allími*	مِش هَتِتْعَلِّمي		
íntu	*hatit3allímu*	هَتِتْعَلِّموا	*miš hatit3allímu*	مِش هَتِتْعَلِّموا		
húwwa	*hayit3állim*	هَيِتْعَلِّم	*miš hayit3állim*	مِش هَيِتْعَلِّم		
híyya	*hatit3állim*	هَتِتْعَلِّم	*miš hatit3állim*	مِش هَتِتْعَلِّم		
húmma	*hayit3allímu*	هَيِتْعَلِّموا	*miš hayit3allímu*	مِش هَيِتْعَلِّموا		
ínta	*it3állim*	اِتْعَلِّم	*ma-tit3allímš*	مَتِتْعَلِّمْش		imperative
ínti	*it3allími*	اِتْعَلِّمي	*ma-tit3allimīš*	مَتِتْعَلِّميش		
íntu	*it3allímu*	اِتْعَلِّموا	*ma-tit3allimūš*	مَتِتْعَلِّموش		

	active		passive		
masculine	*mit3állim*	مِتْعَلِّم	*mit3állim*	مِتْعَلِّم	participles
feminine	*mit3allíma*	مِتْعَلِّمَة	*mit3allíma*	مِتْعَلِّمَة	
plural	*mit3allimīn*	مِتْعَلِّمين	*mit3allimīn*	مِتْعَلِّمين	

①

اِتْعلِّمْت مِن الدُّنْيا كْتير.

it3allímtᵊ min iddúnya ktīr.

I've learned a lot from life.

②

يِتْعلِّم إزّاي و هُوَّ مِش لاقي ياكُل؟

yit3állim izzāy wi húwwa miš lāʔi yākul?

How can he afford to study when he's so poor [lit. he can't find (anything) to eat)]?

③

شَيْماء بِتِتْعلِّم فرنْساوي عشان تِساعِد إبْنها في واجِباتُه.

šaymāʔ bitit3állim faransāwi 3ašān tisā3id ibnáha f wagibātu.

Shimaa is studying French to help her son with his homework.

④

هَيِتْعلِّم جُغْرافْيا في سنة تانْيَة.

hayit3állim guɣráfya fi sána tánya.

He will study geography in second grade.

⑤

اِتْعلِّم مِن أخْطاءك و متِتْكرّرْهاش.

it3állim min axṭāʔak wi ma-titkarrarhāš.

Learn from your mistakes, and don't repeat them.

⑥

هُوَّ مِتْعلِّم برّه، بسّ عايِز يِعْمِل هِنا مشْروع يِفيد البلد.

húwwa mit3állim bárra, bassᵊ 3āyiz yí3mil hína mašrū3 yifīd ilbálad.

He studied abroad, but he wants to undertake a project here to help his country.

⑦

برْضُه مبتْعلِّمْش مِن أخْطائي و برْجع أكرّرْها و أنْدم.

bárḍu ma-bat3allímšᵊ min axṭāʔi wi bárga3 akarrárha w ándam.

I don't learn from my mistakes, and I keep repeating them and regretting it.

❖ [5s1] **to learn; to study**

➲ 20.6, 26.2, 107.7, 193.1, 215.6, 245.5

20 to get used to *it3áwwid* اِتْعَوِّد

verbal noun: *ta3áwwud* تَعَوُّد

		affirmative		negative	
perfect	ána	*it3awwídt*	اِتْعَوِّدْت	*ma-t3awwídtiš*	مَتْعَوِّدْتِش
	íḫna	*it3awwídna*	اِتْعَوِّدْنا	*ma-t3awwidnāš*	مَتْعَوِّدْناش
	ínta	*it3awwídt*	اِتْعَوِّدْت	*ma-t3awwídtiš*	مَتْعَوِّدْتِش
	ínti	*it3awwídti*	اِتْعَوِّدْتي	*ma-t3awwidtīš*	مَتْعَوِّدْتيش
	íntu	*it3awwídtu*	اِتْعَوِّدْتوا	*ma-t3awwidtūš*	مَتْعَوِّدْتوش
	húwwa	*it3áwwid*	اِتْعَوِّد	*ma-t3awwídš*	مَتْعَوِّدْش
	híyya	*it3awwídit*	اِتْعَوِّدِت	*ma-t3awwidítš*	مَتْعَوِّدِتْش
	húmma	*it3awwídu*	اِتْعَوِّدوا	*ma-t3awwidūš*	مَتْعَوِّدوش
imperfect	ána	*at3áwwid*	أَتْعَوِّد	*ma-t3awwídš*	مَتْعَوِّدْش
	íḫna	*nit3áwwid*	نِتْعَوِّد	*ma-nit3awwídš*	مَنِتْعَوِّدْش
	ínta	*tit3áwwid*	تِتْعَوِّد	*ma-tit3awwídš*	مَتِتْعَوِّدْش
	ínti	*tit3awwídi*	تِتْعَوِّدي	*ma-tit3awwidīš*	مَتِتْعَوِّديش
	íntu	*tit3awwídu*	تِتْعَوِّدوا	*ma-tit3awwidūš*	مَتِتْعَوِّدوش
	húwwa	*yit3áwwid*	يِتْعَوِّد	*ma-yit3awwídš*	مَيِتْعَوِّدْش
	híyya	*tit3áwwid*	تِتْعَوِّد	*ma-tit3awwídš*	مَتِتْعَوِّدْش
	húmma	*yit3awwídu*	يِتْعَوِّدوا	*ma-yit3awwidūš*	مَيِتْعَوِّدوش
bi-imperfect	ána	*bat3áwwid*	بَتْعَوِّد	*ma-bat3awwídš*	مَبَتْعَوِّدْش
	íḫna	*binit3áwwid*	بِنِتْعَوِّد	*ma-bnit3awwídš*	مَبْنِتْعَوِّدْش
	ínta	*bitit3áwwid*	بِتِتْعَوِّد	*ma-btit3awwídš*	مَبْتِتْعَوِّدْش
	ínti	*bitit3awwídi*	بِتِتْعَوِّدي	*ma-btit3awwidīš*	مَبْتِتْعَوِّديش
	íntu	*bitit3awwídu*	بِتِتْعَوِّدوا	*ma-btit3awwidūš*	مَبْتِتْعَوِّدوش
	húwwa	*biyit3áwwid*	بِيِتْعَوِّد	*ma-byit3awwídš*	مَبْيِتْعَوِّدْش
	híyya	*bitit3áwwid*	بِتِتْعَوِّد	*ma-btit3awwídš*	مَبْتِتْعَوِّدْش
	húmma	*biyit3awwídu*	بِيِتْعَوِّدوا	*ma-byit3awwidūš*	مَبْيِتْعَوِّدوش
future	ána	*hat3áwwid*	هَتْعَوِّد	*miš hat3áwwid*	مِش هَتْعَوِّد
	íḫna	*hanit3áwwid*	هَنِتْعَوِّد	*miš hanit3áwwid*	مِش هَنِتْعَوِّد
	ínta	*hatit3áwwid*	هَتِتْعَوِّد	*miš hatit3áwwid*	مِش هَتِتْعَوِّد
	ínti	*hatit3awwídi*	هَتِتْعَوِّدي	*miš hatit3awwídi*	مِش هَتِتْعَوِّدي
	íntu	*hatit3awwídu*	هَتِتْعَوِّدوا	*miš hatit3awwídu*	مِش هَتِتْعَوِّدوا
	húwwa	*hayit3áwwid*	هَيِتْعَوِّد	*miš hayit3áwwid*	مِش هَيِتْعَوِّد
	híyya	*hatit3áwwid*	هَتِتْعَوِّد	*miš hatit3áwwid*	مِش هَتِتْعَوِّد
	húmma	*hayit3awwídu*	هَيِتْعَوِّدوا	*miš hayit3awwídu*	مِش هَيِتْعَوِّدوا
imperative	ínta	*it3áwwid*	اِتْعَوِّد	*ma-tit3awwídš*	مَتِتْعَوِّدْش
	ínti	*it3awwídi*	اِتْعَوِّدي	*ma-tit3awwidīš*	مَتِتْعَوِّديش
	íntu	*it3awwídu*	اِتْعَوِّدوا	*ma-tit3awwidūš*	مَتِتْعَوِّدوش

		active		passive	
participles	masculine	*mit3áwwid*	مِتْعَوِّد	–	–
	feminine	*mit3awwída*	مِتْعَوِّدَة	–	–
	plural	*mit3awwidīn*	مِتْعَوِّدين	–	–

①

رِحاب اِتْعوِّدِت تِصْحى بدْري تِلْعب تمارين قبْل الشُّغْل.

riĥāb it3awwídit tíṣĥa bádri tíl3ab tamarīn ʔabl iššúɣl.

Rehab made it a habit to get up early and do aerobics before work.

②

الوَلد لازِم يِتْعوِّد يِدْخُل الحمّام لِوَحْدُه.

ilwálad lāzim yit3áwwid yídxul ilĥammām li-wáĥdu.

The boy should get used to using the bathroom by himself.

③

كُلّ يوْم بتْعوِّد أكْتر على وُجود هِبة في البيْت. شكْلي مِش هقْدر أسْتغْنى عنْها.

kull[ə] yōm bat3áwwid áktar 3ála wugūd híba fi -lbēt. šákli miš háʔdar astáɣna 3ánha.

Every day I get more used to Heba's presence at home. I don't think I'll be able to get along without her.

④

اللي يْعيش في القاهِرة هَيِتْعوِّد على الزّحْمة.

ílli y3īš fi -lqāhíra hayit3áwwid 3ála -zzáĥma.

Anyone who lives in Cairo will get used to the crowds.

⑤

اِتْعوِّدي تْنامي بدْري. هتْلاقي الهالات تحْت عيْنِك راحِت.

it3awwídi tnāmi bádri. hatlāʔi -lhalāt taĥt[ə] 3ēnik rāĥit.

Make a habit of going to bed early, and you'll find that the circles under your eyes go away.

⑥

مليكة متْعوِّدِتْش تُطْبُخ. هتِتْعلِّم لمّا تِعيش لِوَحْدها.

malīka ma-t3awwidítš[ə] túṭbux. hatit3állim lámma ti3īš li-waĥdáha.

Malika isn't used to cooking. She'll learn when she lives alone.

❖ [5s1] **to get used to, become accustomed to** (على *3ála*)**; to make a habit of, be in the habit of**

- This verb can be followed by an imperfect verb.

➲ 66.4, 152.2, 155.3, 167.9, 218.2

21 to become annoyed *ityāẓ* اِتْغاظ

verbal noun: *yēẓ* غيظ

perfect

	affirmative		negative	
ána	*ityáẓt*	اِتْغَظْت	*ma-tyáẓtiš*	مَتْغَظْتِش
íḫna	*ityáẓna*	اِتْغَظْنا	*ma-tyaẓnāš*	مَتْغَظْناش
ínta	*ityáẓt*	اِتْغَظْت	*ma-tyáẓtiš*	مَتْغَظْتِش
ínti	*ityáẓti*	اِتْغَظْتي	*ma-tyaẓtīš*	مَتْغَظْتيش
íntu	*ityáẓtu*	اِتْغَظْتوا	*ma-tyaẓtūš*	مَتْغَظْتوش
húwwa	*ityāẓ*	اِتْغاظ	*ma-tyáẓš*	مَتْغاظْش
híyya	*ityāẓit*	اِتْغاظِت	*ma-tyaẓítš*	مَتْغاظِتْش
húmma	*ityāẓu*	اِتْغاظوا	*ma-tyaẓūš*	مَتْغاظوش

imperfect

	affirmative		negative	
ána	*atyāẓ*	أَتْغاظ	*ma-tyáẓš*	مَتْغاظْش
íḫna	*nityāẓ*	نِتْغاظ	*ma-nityáẓš*	مَنِتْغاظْش
ínta	*tityāẓ*	تِتْغاظ	*ma-tityáẓš*	مَتِتْغاظْش
ínti	*tityāẓi*	تِتْغاظي	*ma-tityaẓīš*	مَتِتْغاظيش
íntu	*tityāẓu*	تِتْغاظوا	*ma-tityaẓūš*	مَتِتْغاظوش
húwwa	*yityāẓ*	يِتْغاظ	*ma-yityáẓš*	مَيِتْغاظْش
híyya	*tityāẓ*	تِتْغاظ	*ma-tityáẓš*	مَتِتْغاظْش
húmma	*yityāẓu*	يِتْغاظوا	*ma-yityaẓūš*	مَيِتْغاظوش

bi-imperfect

	affirmative		negative	
ána	*batyāẓ*	بَتْغاظ	*ma-batyáẓš*	مَبَتْغاظْش
íḫna	*binityāẓ*	بِنِتْغاظ	*ma-bnityáẓš*	مَبْنِتْغاظْش
ínta	*bitityāẓ*	بِتِتْغاظ	*ma-btityáẓš*	مَبْتِتْغاظْش
ínti	*bitityāẓi*	بِتِتْغاظي	*ma-btityaẓīš*	مَبْتِتْغاظيش
íntu	*bitityāẓu*	بِتِتْغاظوا	*ma-btityaẓūš*	مَبْتِتْغاظوش
húwwa	*biyityāẓ*	بِيِتْغاظ	*ma-byityáẓš*	مَبْيِتْغاظْش
híyya	*bitityāẓ*	بِتِتْغاظ	*ma-btityáẓš*	مَبْتِتْغاظْش
húmma	*biyityāẓu*	بِيِتْغاظوا	*ma-byityaẓūš*	مَبْيِتْغاظوش

future

	affirmative		negative	
ána	*hatyāẓ*	هَتْغاظ	*miš hatyāẓ*	مِش هَتْغاظ
íḫna	*hanityāẓ*	هَنِتْغاظ	*miš hanityāẓ*	مِش هَنِتْغاظ
ínta	*hatityāẓ*	هَتِتْغاظ	*miš hatityāẓ*	مِش هَتِتْغاظ
ínti	*hatityāẓi*	هَتِتْغاظي	*miš hatityāẓi*	مِش هَتِتْغاظي
íntu	*hatityāẓu*	هَتِتْغاظوا	*miš hatityāẓu*	مِش هَتِتْغاظوا
húwwa	*hayityāẓ*	هَيِتْغاظ	*miš hayityāẓ*	مِش هَيِتْغاظ
híyya	*hatityāẓ*	هَتِتْغاظ	*miš hatityāẓ*	مِش هَتِتْغاظ
húmma	*hayityāẓu*	هَيِتْغاظوا	*miš hayityāẓu*	مِش هَيِتْغاظوا

imperative

	affirmative		negative	
ínta	*ityāẓ*	اِتْغاظ	*ma-tityáẓš*	مَتِتْغاظْش
ínti	*ityāẓi*	اِتْغاظي	*ma-tityaẓīš*	مَتِتْغاظيش
íntu	*ityāẓu*	اِتْغاظوا	*ma-tityaẓūš*	مَتِتْغاظوش

participles

	active		passive	
masculine	—	—	*mityāẓ*	مِتْغاظ
feminine	—	—	*mityāẓa*	مِتْغاظَة
plural	—	—	*mityaẓīn*	مِتْغاظين

①

أنا اِتْغاظْت مِن تصرُّفه أوي، و مِش هتْعامِل معاه تاني.

ána -tɣázṭᵊ min taṣarrúfu ʔáwi, wi miš hat3āmil ma3ā tāni.

I was very annoyed by his behavior,
and I won't deal with him again.

②

لازِم يِتْغاظ مِنِّك و إنْتي كُلّ ما يِكلِّمك في حاجة مترْدّيش.

lāzim yitɣāẓ mínnik w ínti kullᵊ ma yikallímak fi ɧāga ma-truddīš.

He should be annoyed by you. Every time he talks to you
about something, you don't respond.

③

مبتْغاظْش مِن حاجة أكْتر مِن اللي بيِرمي زِبالة مِن شِبّاك عربيتُه.

ma-batɣáẓšᵊ min ɧāga ʔáktar min ílli biyírmi zibāla min šibbāk 3arabītu.

Nothing annoys me more than someone
throwing garbage from their car window.

④

هتِتْغاظوا لمّا تْشوفوا البِرنامِج ده و مدى هَيافْتُه.

hatitɣāẓu lámma tšūfu -lbirnāmig da wi máda hayáftu.

You'll be annoyed when you watch
this show and how silly it is.

⑤

أنا جايّة أقولّك إنّي رايْحة الرِّحْلة و إنْتي لأ. يَلّا اتْغاظي!

ána gáyy- aʔúllak ínni ráyɧa -rríɧla w ínti laʔ. yálla -tɣāẓi!

I came to tell you that I'm going on the trip
and you're not. Come on, be annoyed!

⑥

هِيَّ على طول مِتْغاظه مِن بِنْت عمّها، أصْلها أحْلى مِنْها.

híyya 3ála ṭūl mitɣāẓa min bintᵊ 3ammáha, aṣláha ʔáɧla mínha.

She is always annoyed by her cousin
because she is prettier.

❖ [7h1] **to be annoyed (by** مِن *min*)

22 to have lunch itɣádda اِتْغَدّى

غ د ي

13

	affirmative		negative		
ána	itɣaddēt	اِتْغَدّيْت	ma-tɣaddítš	مَتْغَدّيْتْش	perfect
íḥna	itɣaddēna	اِتْغَدّيْنا	ma-tɣaddinâš	مَتْغَدّيناش	
ínta	itɣaddēt	اِتْغَدّيْت	ma-tɣaddítš	مَتْغَدّيْتْش	
ínti	itɣaddēti	اِتْغَدّيْتي	ma-tɣadditīš	مَتْغَدّيتيش	
íntu	itɣaddētu	اِتْغَدّيْتوا	ma-tɣadditūš	مَتْغَدّيتوش	
húwwa	itɣádda	اِتْغَدّى	ma-tɣaddāš	مَتْغَدّاش	
híyya	itɣáddit	اِتْغَدّت	ma-tɣaddítš	مَتْغَدّتْش	
húmma	itɣáddu	اِتْغَدّوا	ma-tɣaddūš	مَتْغَدّوش	
ána	atɣádda	أَتْغَدّى	ma-tɣaddāš	مَتْغَدّاش	imperfect
íḥna	nitɣádda	نِتْغَدّى	ma-nitɣaddāš	مَنِتْغَدّاش	
ínta	titɣádda	تِتْغَدّى	ma-titɣaddāš	مَتِتْغَدّاش	
ínti	titɣáddi	تِتْغَدّي	ma-titɣaddīš	مَتِتْغَدّيش	
íntu	titɣáddu	تِتْغَدّوا	ma-titɣaddūš	مَتِتْغَدّوش	
húwwa	yitɣádda	يِتْغَدّى	ma-yitɣaddāš	مَيِتْغَدّاش	
híyya	titɣádda	تِتْغَدّى	ma-titɣaddāš	مَتِتْغَدّاش	
húmma	yitɣáddu	يِتْغَدّوا	ma-yitɣaddūš	مَيِتْغَدّوش	
ána	batɣádda	بَتْغَدّى	ma-batɣaddāš	مَبَتْغَدّاش	bi-imperfect
íḥna	binitɣádda	بِنِتْغَدّى	ma-bnitɣaddāš	مَبْنِتْغَدّاش	
ínta	bititɣádda	بِتِتْغَدّى	ma-btitɣaddāš	مَبْتِتْغَدّاش	
ínti	bititɣáddi	بِتِتْغَدّي	ma-btitɣaddīš	مَبْتِتْغَدّيش	
íntu	bititɣáddu	بِتِتْغَدّوا	ma-btitɣaddūš	مَبْتِتْغَدّوش	
húwwa	biyitɣádda	بِيِتْغَدّى	ma-byitɣaddāš	مَبْيِتْغَدّاش	
híyya	bititɣádda	بِتِتْغَدّى	ma-btitɣaddāš	مَبْتِتْغَدّاش	
húmma	biyitɣáddu	بِيِتْغَدّوا	ma-byitɣaddūš	مَبْيِتْغَدّوش	
ána	hatɣádda	هَتْغَدّى	miš hatɣádda	مِش هَتْغَدّى	future
íḥna	hanitɣádda	هَنِتْغَدّى	miš hanitɣádda	مِش هَنِتْغَدّى	
ínta	hatitɣádda	هَتِتْغَدّى	miš hatitɣádda	مِش هَتِتْغَدّى	
ínti	hatitɣáddi	هَتِتْغَدّي	miš hatitɣáddi	مِش هَتِتْغَدّي	
íntu	hatitɣáddu	هَتِتْغَدّوا	miš hatitɣáddu	مِش هَتِتْغَدّوا	
húwwa	hayitɣádda	هَيِتْغَدّى	miš hayitɣádda	مِش هَيِتْغَدّى	
híyya	hatitɣádda	هَتِتْغَدّى	miš hatitɣádda	مِش هَتِتْغَدّى	
húmma	hayitɣáddu	هَيِتْغَدّوا	miš hayitɣáddu	مِش هَيِتْغَدّوا	
ínta	itɣádda	اِتْغَدّى	ma-titɣaddāš	مَتِتْغَدّاش	imperative
ínti	itɣáddi	اِتْغَدّي	ma-titɣaddīš	مَتِتْغَدّيش	
íntu	itɣáddu	اِتْغَدّوا	ma-titɣaddūš	مَتِتْغَدّوش	

	active		passive		
masculine	mitɣáddi	مِتْغَدّي	–	–	participles
feminine	mitɣaddíyya	مِتْغَدّيَّة	–	–	
plural	mitɣaddiyīn	مِتْغَدّيين	–	–	

verbal noun: *ɣáda* غدا

①

إمْبارِح اِتْغدّيْنا معَ صُحابْنا في المطْعم إيّاه. كان يوْم جميل أوي.

imbāriḫ ityaddēna má3a ṣuḫábna fi -lmáṭ3am iyyā. kān yōm gamīl áwi.

Yesterday we had lunch with our friends in that restaurant. It was a lovely day.

②

تِتْغدّى فْراخ وَلّا سمك؟

tityádda frāx wálla sámak?

Do you want chicken or fish for lunch?

③

هُمّا بِيِتْغدّوا سمك؟ غريبة، مكُنْتِش أعْرف إنُّهُم بِيْحِبّوه.

húmma biyityáddu sámak? yarība, ma-kúntiš á3raf innúhum biyḫibbū.

Are they eating fish for lunch? Strange, I didn't know they liked it.

④

هنِتْغدّى أيْه النّهارْده؟ قولولي بْسُرْعة عشان ألْحق أعْمِل الأكْل.

hanityadda ʔē innahárda? ʔulūli b-súr3a 3ašān álḫaʔ á3mil ilʔákl.

What shall we have for lunch today? Tell me fast. I want to start cooking.

⑤

اِتْغدّوا بْسُرْعة عشان عايْزين نِنْزِل.

ityáddu b-súr3a 3ašān 3ayzīn nínzil.

Finish your lunch fast. We want to go out.

⑥

أنا مِتْغدّي سمك مشْوي بسّ أيْه يجنِّن!

ána mityáddi sámak máświ bass[ə] ʔē yigánnin!

I had grilled fish for lunch. It was amazing!

⑦

اِسْتنّى، متِتْغدّاش . أنا عازِمْكو برّه.

istánna, ma-tityaddāš. ána 3azímku bárra.

Wait, don't eat your lunch. I'll take you out to eat.

❖ [5d] **to have lunch**

- This verb is often intransitive, but can take an object, in which case it can translate 'have __ for lunch' or simply 'eat'. (➲ 22.2, 22.3, 22.4, 22.6)

➲ 197.1, 248.1

23 to change itɣáyyar اِتْغَيّر

13

verbal noun: taɣáyyur تَغَيُّر

	affirmative		negative		
ána	itɣayyárt	اِتْغَيّرْت	ma-tɣayyártiš	مَتْغَيّرْتِش	perfect
íḥna	itɣayyárna	اِتْغَيّرْنا	ma-tɣayyarnāš	مَتْغَيّرْناش	
ínta	itɣayyárt	اِتْغَيّرْت	ma-tɣayyártiš	مَتْغَيّرْتِش	
ínti	itɣayyárti	اِتْغَيّرْتي	ma-tɣayyartīš	مَتْغَيّرْتيش	
íntu	itɣayyártu	اِتْغَيّرْتوا	ma-tɣayyartūš	مَتْغَيّرْتوش	
húwwa	itɣáyyar	اِتْغَيّر	ma-tɣayyárš	مَتْغَيّرْش	
híyya	itɣayyárit	اِتْغَيّرِت	ma-tɣayyarítš	مَتْغَيّرِتْش	
húmma	itɣayyáru	اِتْغَيّروا	ma-tɣayyarūš	مَتْغَيّروش	
ána	atɣáyyar	أَتْغَيّر	ma-tɣayyárš	مَتْغَيّرْش	imperfect
íḥna	nitɣáyyar	نِتْغَيّر	ma-nitɣayyárš	مَنِتْغَيّرْش	
ínta	titɣáyyar	تِتْغَيّر	ma-titɣayyárš	مَتِتْغَيّرْش	
ínti	titɣayyári	تِتْغَيّري	ma-titɣayyarīš	مَتِتْغَيّريش	
íntu	titɣayyáru	تِتْغَيّروا	ma-titɣayyarūš	مَتِتْغَيّروش	
húwwa	yitɣáyyar	يِتْغَيّر	ma-yitɣayyárš	مَيِتْغَيّرْش	
híyya	titɣáyyar	تِتْغَيّر	ma-titɣayyárš	مَتِتْغَيّرْش	
húmma	yitɣayyáru	يِتْغَيّروا	ma-yitɣayyarūš	مَيِتْغَيّروش	
ána	batɣáyyar	بَتْغَيّر	ma-batɣayyárš	مَبَتْغَيّرْش	bi-imperfect
íḥna	binitɣáyyar	بِنِتْغَيّر	ma-bnitɣayyárš	مَبْنِتْغَيّرْش	
ínta	bititɣáyyar	بِتِتْغَيّر	ma-btitɣayyárš	مَبْتِتْغَيّرْش	
ínti	bititɣayyári	بِتِتْغَيّري	ma-btitɣayyarīš	مَبْتِتْغَيّريش	
íntu	bititɣayyáru	بِتِتْغَيّروا	ma-btitɣayyarūš	مَبْتِتْغَيّروش	
húwwa	biyitɣáyyar	بِيِتْغَيّر	ma-byitɣayyárš	مَبْيِتْغَيّرْش	
híyya	bititɣáyyar	بِتِتْغَيّر	ma-btitɣayyárš	مَبْتِتْغَيّرْش	
húmma	biyitɣayyáru	بِيِتْغَيّروا	ma-byitɣayyarūš	مَبْيِتْغَيّروش	
ána	hatɣáyyar	هَتْغَيّر	miš hatɣáyyar	مِش هَتْغَيّر	future
íḥna	hanitɣáyyar	هَنِتْغَيّر	miš hanitɣáyyar	مِش هَنِتْغَيّر	
ínta	hatitɣáyyar	هَتِتْغَيّر	miš hatitɣáyyar	مِش هَتِتْغَيّر	
ínti	hatitɣayyári	هَتِتْغَيّري	miš hatitɣayyári	مِش هَتِتْغَيّري	
íntu	hatitɣayyáru	هَتِتْغَيّروا	miš hatitɣayyáru	مِش هَتِتْغَيّروا	
húwwa	hayitɣáyyar	هَيِتْغَيّر	miš hayitɣáyyar	مِش هَيِتْغَيّر	
híyya	hatitɣáyyar	هَتِتْغَيّر	miš hatitɣáyyar	مِش هَتِتْغَيّر	
húmma	hayitɣayyáru	هَيِتْغَيّروا	miš hayitɣayyáru	مِش هَيِتْغَيّروا	
ínta	itɣáyyar	اِتْغَيّر	ma-titɣayyárš	مَتِتْغَيّرْش	imperative
ínti	itɣayyári	اِتْغَيّري	ma-titɣayyarīš	مَتِتْغَيّريش	
íntu	itɣayyáru	اِتْغَيّروا	ma-titɣayyarūš	مَتِتْغَيّروش	

	active		passive		
masculine	mitɣáyyar	مِتْغَيّر	–	–	participles
feminine	mitɣayyára	مِتْغَيّرة	–	–	
plural	mitɣayyarīn	مِتْغَيّرين	–	–	

①

أمينة اتْغيّرِت خالِص بعْد الجَواز. بقِت أحْلى كْتير.

amīna -tɣayyárit xāliṣ ba3d ilgawāz. báʔit áḥla ktīr.

Amina completely changed after getting married. She became prettier.

②

فِلْتر البنْزين لازِم يِتْغيّر كُلّ مُدّة.

fíltar ilbanzīn lāzim yitɣáyyar kullᵊ múdda.

The fuel filter should be changed every so often.

③

الأصيل مبْيِتْغيّرْش مهْما شاف مِ النّاس.

ilʔaṣīl ma-byitɣayyáršᵊ máhma šāf mi -nnās.

Good people don't change, however bad they are treated by other people.

④

هيِتْغيّر رأْيُكو لمّا تِسْمعوة بِيْغنّي. هتْحِبّوه.

hayitɣáyyar raʔyúku lámma tisma3ū biyɣánni. hatḥibbū.

You'll change your mind when you hear him singing. You'll love him.

⑤

اِتْغيّري شْوَيّة، اِهْتمّي بِنفْسِك، هتْلاقي جوْزِك رِجِع يِهْتمّ بيكي أكْتر.

itɣayyári šwáyya, ihtámmi bi-náfsik, hatlāʔi gōzik rígi3 yihtámmᵊ bīki ʔáktar.

Change a bit, take care of yourself, and you'll find that your husband will go back to being more interested in you.

⑥

النّاس بقِت مِتْغيّرة . مبقاش فيه وِدّ زيّ زمان.

innās báʔit mitɣayyára. ma-baʔāš fī widdᵊ zayyᵊ zamān.

People are different now [lit. have changed]. There is no amiability like in the past.

❖ [5s2] **to change, be changed**

- This is an intransitive verb. The transitive verb is غيّر *ɣáyyar*. (➲ 186)

➲ 8.1, 216.3

24 to view *itfárrag* اِتْفَرّج

perfect

	affirmative		negative	
ána	*itfarrágt*	اِتْفَرّجْت	*ma-tfarrágtiš*	مَتْفَرّجْتِش
íḫna	*itfarrágna*	اِتْفَرّجْنا	*ma-tfarragnāš*	مَتْفَرّجْناش
ínta	*itfarrágt*	اِتْفَرّجْت	*ma-tfarrágtiš*	مَتْفَرّجْتِش
ínti	*itfarrágti*	اِتْفَرّجْتي	*ma-tfarragtīš*	مَتْفَرّجْتيش
íntu	*itfarrágtu*	اِتْفَرّجْتوا	*ma-tfarragtūš*	مَتْفَرّجْتوش
húwwa	*itfárrag*	اِتْفَرّج	*ma-tfarrágš*	مَتْفَرّجْش
híyya	*itfarrágit*	اِتْفَرّجِت	*ma-tfarragítš*	مَتْفَرّجِتْش
húmma	*itfarrágu*	اِتْفَرّجوا	*ma-tfarragūš*	مَتْفَرّجوش

imperfect

ána	*atfárrag*	أتْفَرّج	*ma-tfarrágš*	مَتْفَرّجْش
íḫna	*nitfárrag*	نِتْفَرّج	*ma-nitfarrágš*	مَنِتْفَرّجْش
ínta	*titfárrag*	تِتْفَرّج	*ma-titfarrágš*	مَتِتْفَرّجْش
ínti	*titfarrági*	تِتْفَرّجي	*ma-titfarragīš*	مَتِتْفَرّجيش
íntu	*titfarrágu*	تِتْفَرّجوا	*ma-titfarragūš*	مَتِتْفَرّجوش
húwwa	*yitfárrag*	يِتْفَرّج	*ma-yitfarrágš*	مَيِتْفَرّجْش
híyya	*titfárrag*	تِتْفَرّج	*ma-titfarrágš*	مَتِتْفَرّجْش
húmma	*yitfarrágu*	يِتْفَرّجوا	*ma-yitfarragūš*	مَيِتْفَرّجوش

bi-imperfect

ána	*batfárrag*	بَتْفَرّج	*ma-batfarrágš*	مَبَتْفَرّجْش
íḫna	*binitfárrag*	بِنِتْفَرّج	*ma-bnitfarrágš*	مَبْنِتْفَرّجْش
ínta	*bititfárrag*	بِتِتْفَرّج	*ma-btitfarrágš*	مَبْتِتْفَرّجْش
ínti	*bititfarrági*	بِتِتْفَرّجي	*ma-btitfarragīš*	مَبْتِتْفَرّجيش
íntu	*bititfarrágu*	بِتِتْفَرّجوا	*ma-btitfarragūš*	مَبْتِتْفَرّجوش
húwwa	*biyitfárrag*	بِيِتْفَرّج	*ma-byitfarrágš*	مَبْيِتْفَرّجْش
híyya	*bititfárrag*	بِتِتْفَرّج	*ma-btitfarrágš*	مَبْتِتْفَرّجْش
húmma	*biyitfarrágu*	بِيِتْفَرّجوا	*ma-byitfarragūš*	مَبْيِتْفَرّجوش

future

ána	*hatfárrag*	هَتْفَرّج	*miš hatfárrag*	مِش هَتْفَرّج
íḫna	*hanitfárrag*	هَنِتْفَرّج	*miš hanitfárrag*	مِش هَنِتْفَرّج
ínta	*hatitfárrag*	هَتِتْفَرّج	*miš hatitfárrag*	مِش هَتِتْفَرّج
ínti	*hatitfarrági*	هَتِتْفَرّجي	*miš hatitfarrági*	مِش هَتِتْفَرّجي
íntu	*hatitfarrágu*	هَتِتْفَرّجوا	*miš hatitfarrágu*	مِش هَتِتْفَرّجوا
húwwa	*hayitfárrag*	هَيِتْفَرّج	*miš hayitfárrag*	مِش هَيِتْفَرّج
híyya	*hatitfárrag*	هَتِتْفَرّج	*miš hatitfárrag*	مِش هَتِتْفَرّج
húmma	*hayitfarrágu*	هَيِتْفَرّجوا	*miš hayitfarrágu*	مِش هَيِتْفَرّجوا

imperative

ínta	*itfárrag*	اِتْفَرّج	*ma-titfarrágš*	مَتِتْفَرّجْش
ínti	*itfarrági*	اِتْفَرّجي	*ma-titfarragīš*	مَتِتْفَرّجيش
íntu	*itfarrágu*	اِتْفَرّجوا	*ma-titfarragūš*	مَتِتْفَرّجوش

participles

	active		passive	
masculine	*mitfárrag*	مِتْفَرّج	–	–
feminine	*mitfarrága*	مِتْفَرّجة	–	–
plural	*mitfarragīn*	مِتْفَرّجين	–	–

verbal noun: *fúrga* فُرْجة

①

الوِلاد اِتْفرّجوا عَ البِرنامِج و قاموا يِقلِّدوا الحركات الخطيرة اللي فيه.

ilwilād itfarrágu 3a -lbirnāmig wi ʔāmu yiʔallídu -lħarakāt ilxaṭīra -lli fī.

After watching the show, the kids began to imitate the dangerous moves they had seen in it.

②

لمّا تِتْفرّجوا على العفْش في المناصْرة هتْلاقوا حاجات حِلْوَة و رِخيصة.

lámma titfarrágu 3ála -l3afšᵊ fi -lmanáṣra hatlāʔu ħagāt ħílwa w rixīṣa.

Whenever you go to see the furniture in Manasra, you'll find nice, cheap stuff.

③

اِبْتِهال مبْتِتْفرّجْش عَ التِّليفِزْيوْن خالِص. بِتْشوف إنُّه بِيْضيّع وَقْتها.

ibtihāl ma-btitfarrágšᵊ 3a -ttilivizyōn xāliṣ. bitšūf ínnu biyḍáyya3 waʔtáha.

Ebtihal doesn't watch TV ever. She sees it as a waste of time.

④

أ: هنِتْفرّج عَ الماتْش فيْن؟

ب: في القهْوَة أكيد.

A: hanitfárrag 3a -lmatšᵊ fēn?

B: fi -lʔáhwa ʔakīd.

A: Where shall we watch the match?

B: At the coffee shop, of course!

⑤

اِتْفرّجي على حفْلةْ التّنورة. هتِعْجِبِك أوي.

itfarrági 3ála ħáflit ittanūra. hati3gíbik áwi.

Watch the Tannora show. You'll really like it.

⑥

مِتْفرّجين عَ الحلْقة دي مرِّتيْن قبْل كِده. حفظْناها خلاص.

mitfarragīn 3a -lħálʔa di marritēn ʔablᵊ kída. ħafaẓnāha xalāṣ.

We have seen this episode twice before. We have it memorized.

❖ [5s2] **to view, watch, see** (على *3ála*)

➲ 2.3, 45.3, 100.1, 100.9, 103.6, 193.2

25 to be broken *itkásar* 

verbal noun: *kasr* كسر

	affirmative		negative		
ána	*itkasárt*	اِتْكَسَرْت	*ma-tkasártiš*	مَتْكَسَرْتِش	**perfect**
íḫna	*itkasárna*	اِتْكَسَرْنا	*ma-tkasarnāš*	مَتْكَسَرْناش	
ínta	*itkasárt*	اِتْكَسَرْت	*ma-tkasártiš*	مَتْكَسَرْتِش	
ínti	*itkasárti*	اِتْكَسَرْتي	*ma-tkasartīš*	مَتْكَسَرْتيش	
íntu	*itkasártu*	اِتْكَسَرْتوا	*ma-tkasartūš*	مَتْكَسَرْتوش	
húwwa	*itkásar*	اِتْكَسَر	*ma-tkasárš*	مَتْكَسَرْش	
híyya	*itkásarit*	اِتْكَسَرِت	*ma-tkasarítš*	مَتْكَسَرِتْش	
húmma	*itkásaru*	اِتْكَسَروا	*ma-tkasarūš*	مَتْكَسَروش	
ána	*atkísir*	أَتْكِسِر	*ma-tkisírš*	مَتْكِسِرْش	**imperfect**
íḫna	*nitkísir*	نِتْكِسِر	*ma-nitkisírš*	مَنِتْكِسِرْش	
ínta	*titkísir*	تِتْكِسِر	*ma-titkisírš*	مَتِتْكِسِرْش	
ínti	*titkísri*	تِتْكِسْري	*ma-titkisrīš*	مَتِتْكِسْريش	
íntu	*titkísru*	تِتْكِسْروا	*ma-titkisrūš*	مَتِتْكِسْروش	
húwwa	*yitkísir*	يِتْكِسِر	*ma-yitkisírš*	مَيِتْكِسِرْش	
híyya	*titkísir*	تِتْكِسِر	*ma-titkisírš*	مَتِتْكِسِرْش	
húmma	*yitkísru*	يِتْكِسْروا	*ma-yitkisrūš*	مَيِتْكِسْروش	
ána	*batkísir*	بَتْكِسِر	*ma-batkisírš*	مَبَتْكِسِرْش	**bi-imperfect**
íḫna	*binitkísir*	بِنِتْكِسِر	*ma-bnitkisírš*	مَبْنِتْكِسِرْش	
ínta	*bititkísir*	بِتِتْكِسِر	*ma-btitkisírš*	مَبْتِتْكِسِرْش	
ínti	*bititkísri*	بِتِتْكِسْري	*ma-btitkisrīš*	مَبْتِتْكِسْريش	
íntu	*bititkísru*	بِتِتْكِسْروا	*ma-btitkisrūš*	مَبْتِتْكِسْروش	
húwwa	*biyitkísir*	بِيِتْكِسِر	*ma-byitkisírš*	مَبْيِتْكِسِرْش	
híyya	*bititkísir*	بِتِتْكِسِر	*ma-btitkisírš*	مَبْتِتْكِسِرْش	
húmma	*biyitkísru*	بِيِتْكِسْروا	*ma-byitkisrūš*	مَبْيِتْكِسْروش	
ána	*hatkísir*	هَتْكِسِر	*miš hatkísir*	مِش هَتْكِسِر	**future**
íḫna	*hanitkísir*	هَنِتْكِسِر	*miš hanitkísir*	مِش هَنِتْكِسِر	
ínta	*hatitkísir*	هَتِتْكِسِر	*miš hatitkísir*	مِش هَتِتْكِسِر	
ínti	*hatitkísri*	هَتِتْكِسْري	*miš hatitkísri*	مِش هَتِتْكِسْري	
íntu	*hatitkísru*	هَتِتْكِسْروا	*miš hatitkísru*	مِش هَتِتْكِسْروا	
húwwa	*hayitkísir*	هَيِتْكِسِر	*miš hayitkísir*	مِش هَيِتْكِسِر	
híyya	*hatitkísir*	هَتِتْكِسِر	*miš hatitkísir*	مِش هَتِتْكِسِر	
húmma	*hayitkísru*	هَيِتْكِسْروا	*miš hayitkísru*	مِش هَيِتْكِسْروا	
ínta	*itkísir*	اِتْكِسِر	*ma-titkisírš*	مَتِتْكِسِرْش	**imperative**
ínti	*itkísri*	اِتْكِسْري	*ma-titkisrīš*	مَتِتْكِسْريش	
íntu	*itkísru*	اِتْكِسْروا	*ma-titkisrūš*	مَتِتْكِسْروش	

	active		passive		
masculine	—	—	*maksūr*	مَكْسور	**participles**
feminine	—	—	*maksūra*	مَكْسورَة	
plural	—	—	*maksurīn*	مَكْسورين	

①

الفازة بْتاعِةْ جِدّتي اِتْكسرِت مِنّي. زعْلانة أوي عليْها.

ilvāza btā3it giddíti itkásarit mínni. za3lāna ʔáwi 3alēha.

I broke my grandmother's vase.
I'm really upset about it.

②

بخاف أشيل العِيال الصُّغيرّة لتِتْكِسِر مِنّي.

baxāf ašīl il3iyāl iṣṣuɣayyára la-titkísir mínni.

I feel afraid to hold young babies.
I'm afraid I'll break them.

③

مجْدي بِيْحافِظ على حاجْتُه. مبْتِتْكِسِرْش مِنُّه.

mágdi biyḥāfiẓ 3ála ḥágtu. ma-btitkisírš[ə] mínnu.

Magdi takes good care of his things.
They don't get broken.

④

قلْبك هَيِتْكِسِر لَوْ فِضِلْتي مِصدّقة الرّاجِل ده.

ʔálbak hayitkísir law fiḍílti miṣaddáʔa -rrāgil da.

Your heart will be broken if you
keep believing that man.

⑤

اِتْكِسِر و قوم تاني. إوْعى تِسْتسْلِم.

itkísir wi ʔūm tāni. íw3a tistáslim.

When you get broken, stand
up again. Don't give up.

❖ [7s1] **to break, be broken**

- This is an intransitive verb. It is the passive of the transitive verb is كسر *kásar*. (➲ 222)
- If the preposition مِن *min*, literally 'be broken by' is used, the English translation will have the transitive verb 'break' and an object. (➲ 25.1, 25.2, 25.3)
- Keep in mind that most verbs can be used figuratively in Arabic, just as they can in English. (➲ 25.5)

➲ 252.1

26 to speak *itkállim* اِتْكَلِّم

ك - ل - م

	affirmative		negative		
ána	*itkallímt*	اِتْكَلِّمْت	*ma-tkallímtiš*	مَتْكَلِّمْتِش	perfect
íḫna	*itkallímna*	اِتْكَلِّمْنا	*ma-tkallimnāš*	مَتْكَلِّمْناش	
ínta	*itkallímt*	اِتْكَلِّمْت	*ma-tkallímtiš*	مَتْكَلِّمْتِش	
ínti	*itkallímti*	اِتْكَلِّمْتي	*ma-tkallimtīš*	مَتْكَلِّمْتيش	
íntu	*itkallímtu*	اِتْكَلِّمْتوا	*ma-tkallimtūš*	مَتْكَلِّمْتوش	
húwwa	*itkállim*	اِتْكَلِّم	*ma-tkallímš*	مَتْكَلِّمْش	
híyya	*itkallímit*	اِتْكَلِّمِت	*ma-tkallimítš*	مَتْكَلِّمِتْش	
húmma	*itkallímu*	اِتْكَلِّموا	*ma-tkallimūš*	مَتْكَلِّموش	
ána	*atkállim*	أتْكَلِّم	*ma-tkallímš*	مَتْكَلِّمْش	imperfect
íḫna	*nitkállim*	نِتْكَلِّم	*ma-nitkallímš*	مَنِتْكَلِّمْش	
ínta	*titkállim*	تِتْكَلِّم	*ma-titkallímš*	مَتِتْكَلِّمْش	
ínti	*titkallími*	تِتْكَلِّمي	*ma-titkallimīš*	مَتِتْكَلِّميش	
íntu	*titkallímu*	تِتْكَلِّموا	*ma-titkallimūš*	مَتِتْكَلِّموش	
húwwa	*yitkállim*	يِتْكَلِّم	*ma-yitkallímš*	مَيِتْكَلِّمْش	
híyya	*titkállim*	تِتْكَلِّم	*ma-titkallímš*	مَتِتْكَلِّمْش	
húmma	*yitkallímu*	يِتْكَلِّموا	*ma-yitkallimūš*	مَيِتْكَلِّموش	
ána	*batkállim*	بَتْكَلِّم	*ma-batkallímš*	مَبَتْكَلِّمْش	bi-imperfect
íḫna	*binitkállim*	بِنِتْكَلِّم	*ma-bnitkallímš*	مَبْنِتْكَلِّمْش	
ínta	*bititkállim*	بِتِتْكَلِّم	*ma-btitkallímš*	مَبْتِتْكَلِّمْش	
ínti	*bititkallími*	بِتِتْكَلِّمي	*ma-btitkallimīš*	مَبْتِتْكَلِّميش	
íntu	*bititkallímu*	بِتِتْكَلِّموا	*ma-btitkallimūš*	مَبْتِتْكَلِّموش	
húwwa	*biyitkállim*	بِيِتْكَلِّم	*ma-byitkallímš*	مَبْيِتْكَلِّمْش	
híyya	*bititkállim*	بِتِتْكَلِّم	*ma-btitkallímš*	مَبْتِتْكَلِّمْش	
húmma	*biyitkallímu*	بِيِتْكَلِّموا	*ma-byitkallimūš*	مَبْيِتْكَلِّموش	
ána	*hatkállim*	هَتْكَلِّم	*miš hatkállim*	مِش هَتْكَلِّم	future
íḫna	*hanitkállim*	هَنِتْكَلِّم	*miš hanitkállim*	مِش هَنِتْكَلِّم	
ínta	*hatitkállim*	هَتِتْكَلِّم	*miš hatitkállim*	مِش هَتِتْكَلِّم	
ínti	*hatitkallími*	هَتِتْكَلِّمي	*miš hatitkallími*	مِش هَتِتْكَلِّمي	
íntu	*hatitkallímu*	هَتِتْكَلِّموا	*miš hatitkallímu*	مِش هَتِتْكَلِّموا	
húwwa	*hayitkállim*	هَيِتْكَلِّم	*miš hayitkállim*	مِش هَيِتْكَلِّم	
híyya	*hatitkállim*	هَتِتْكَلِّم	*miš hatitkállim*	مِش هَتِتْكَلِّم	
húmma	*hayitkallímu*	هَيِتْكَلِّموا	*miš hayitkallímu*	مِش هَيِتْكَلِّموا	
ínta	*itkállim*	اِتْكَلِّم	*ma-titkallímš*	مَتِتْكَلِّمْش	imperative
ínti	*itkallími*	اِتْكَلِّمي	*ma-titkallimīš*	مَتِتْكَلِّميش	
íntu	*itkallímu*	اِتْكَلِّموا	*ma-titkallimūš*	مَتِتْكَلِّموش	

	active		passive		
masculine	*mitkállim*	مِتْكَلِّم	–	–	participles
feminine	*mitkallíma*	مِتْكَلِّمَة	–	–	
plural	*mitkallimīn*	مِتْكَلِّمين	–	–	

verbal noun: *kalām* كَلام

①

أنا و أخوك اِتْكلِّمْنا إمْبارِح مُدّة طَويلة و أقْنعْته مَيِشْتِريش الموْتوْسيكْل.

ána w axūk itkallímna -mbāriḫ múdda ṭawīla w aʔnáʒtu ma-yištirīš ilmutusíkl.

Your brother and I talked for a long time yesterday, and I convinced him not to buy the motorcycle.

②

هَيِتْعلِّم أسْباني علشان يِتْكلِّم معَ صاحْبِته بِطلاقة.

hayit3állim asbāni 3alašān yitkállim má3a ṣaḫbítu bi-ṭalāqa.

He'll learn Spanish so he can talk to his girlfriend fluently.

③

المصْرِيين بيِتْكلِّموا بِلهْجات كِتير، لِدرجِةْ إنُّه مُمْكِن اِتْنيْن مصْرِيين يِفْهموا بعْض بِصُعوبة.

ilmaṣriyīn biyitkallímu bi-lahgāt kitīr, li-dáragit ínnu múmkin itnēn maṣriyīn yifhámu ba3ḍ^a bi-ṣu3ūba.

Egyptians speak many dialects, so that two Egyptians may find it difficult to understand each other.

④

أ: هتِتْكلِّم في المُؤْتمر عن أيْه؟

ب: عن التّنْمية المُسْتدامة.

A: hatitkállim fi -lmuʔtámar 3an ʔē?

B: 3an ittanmíyya -lmustadāma.

A: What are you going to talk about at the conference?

B: About sustainable development.

⑤

اِتْكلِّم كُوَيِّس عن النّاس، علشان النّاس تثِق فيك.

itkállim kuwáyyis 3an innās, 3alašān innās tásiq fīk.

Speak well of people so that they will trust you.

⑥

إبْن عمّها مِتْكلِّم عليْها، بسّ مِسْتنِّيين تِتْخرّج و يِتْجوِّزوا على طول.

ibn^a 3ammáha mitkállim 3alēha, bass^a mistanniyīn titxárrag wi yitgawwízu 3ála ṭūl.

Her cousin wants to marry her, but they're waiting for her to graduate, and then they'll get married immediately.

⑦

مبتْكلِّمْش فرنْساوي كُوَيِّس.

ma-batkallímš^a faransāwi kuwáyyis.

I don't speak French well.

❖ [5s1] **to speak, talk** (**about** في *fi* / عن *3an*)

- This verb is generally intransitive. The exception is when the object is a language. (➲ 26.2, 26.6)
- Compare with the transitive verb كلِّم *kállim*. (➲ 224)
- The expression مِتْكلِّم على *mitkállim 3ála* means 'be engaged', 'committed', or 'promised' to someone. (➲26.5)

➲ 5.1, 12.5, 58.5, 169.5, 211.9, 247.1

27 to take a walk *itmášša* اِتْمَشّى

verbal nouns: *tamšíyya* تَمْشِيَة - *mašy* مَشْي

	affirmative		negative		
ána	*itmaššēt*	اِتْمَشّيْت	*ma-tmaššítš*	مَتْمَشّيْتْش	perfect
íḥna	*itmaššēna*	اِتْمَشّيْنا	*ma-tmaššināš*	مَتْمَشّيناش	
ínta	*itmaššēt*	اِتْمَشّيْت	*ma-tmaššítš*	مَتْمَشّيْتْش	
ínti	*itmaššēti*	اِتْمَشّيْتي	*ma-tmaššitīš*	مَتْمَشّيتيش	
íntu	*itmaššētu*	اِتْمَشّيْتوا	*ma-tmaššitūš*	مَتْمَشّيتوش	
húwwa	*itmášša*	اِتْمَشّى	*ma-tmaššāš*	مَتْمَشّاش	
híyya	*itmáššit*	اِتْمَشّت	*ma-tmaššítš*	مَتْمَشّتْش	
húmma	*itmáššu*	اِتْمَشّوا	*ma-tmaššūš*	مَتْمَشّوش	
ána	*atmášša*	أتْمَشّى	*ma-tmaššāš*	مَتْمَشّاش	imperfect
íḥna	*nitmášša*	نِتْمَشّى	*ma-nitmaššāš*	مَنِتْمَشّاش	
ínta	*titmášša*	تِتْمَشّى	*ma-titmaššāš*	مَتِتْمَشّاش	
ínti	*titmášši*	تِتْمَشّي	*ma-titmaššīš*	مَتِتْمَشّيش	
íntu	*titmáššu*	تِتْمَشّوا	*ma-titmaššūš*	مَتِتْمَشّوش	
húwwa	*yitmášša*	يِتْمَشّى	*ma-yitmaššāš*	مَيِتْمَشّاش	
híyya	*titmášša*	تِتْمَشّى	*ma-titmaššāš*	مَتِتْمَشّاش	
húmma	*yitmáššu*	يِتْمَشّوا	*ma-yitmaššūš*	مَيِتْمَشّوش	
ána	*batmášša*	بَتْمَشّى	*ma-batmaššāš*	مَبَتْمَشّاش	bi-imperfect
íḥna	*binitmášša*	بِنِتْمَشّى	*ma-bnitmaššāš*	مَبْنِتْمَشّاش	
ínta	*bititmášša*	بِتِتْمَشّى	*ma-btitmaššāš*	مَبْتِتْمَشّاش	
ínti	*bititmášši*	بِتِتْمَشّي	*ma-btitmaššīš*	مَبْتِتْمَشّيش	
íntu	*bititmáššu*	بِتِتْمَشّوا	*ma-btitmaššūš*	مَبْتِتْمَشّوش	
húwwa	*biyitmášša*	بِيِتْمَشّى	*ma-byitmaššāš*	مَبْيِتْمَشّاش	
híyya	*bititmášša*	بِتِتْمَشّى	*ma-btitmaššāš*	مَبْتِتْمَشّاش	
húmma	*biyitmáššu*	بِيِتْمَشّوا	*ma-byitmaššūš*	مَبْيِتْمَشّوش	
ána	*hatmášša*	هَتْمَشّى	*miš hatmášša*	مِش هَتْمَشّى	future
íḥna	*hanitmášša*	هَنِتْمَشّى	*miš hanitmášša*	مِش هَنِتْمَشّى	
ínta	*hatitmášša*	هَتِتْمَشّى	*miš hatitmášša*	مِش هَتِتْمَشّى	
ínti	*hatitmášši*	هَتِتْمَشّي	*miš hatitmášši*	مِش هَتِتْمَشّي	
íntu	*hatitmáššu*	هَتِتْمَشّوا	*miš hatitmáššu*	مِش هَتِتْمَشّوا	
húwwa	*hayitmášša*	هَيِتْمَشّى	*miš hayitmášša*	مِش هَيِتْمَشّى	
híyya	*hatitmášša*	هَتِتْمَشّى	*miš hatitmášša*	مِش هَتِتْمَشّى	
húmma	*hayitmáššu*	هَيِتْمَشّوا	*miš hayitmáššu*	مِش هَيِتْمَشّوا	
ínta	*itmášša*	اِتْمَشّى	*ma-titmaššāš*	مَتِتْمَشّاش	imperative
ínti	*itmášši*	اِتْمَشّي	*ma-titmaššīš*	مَتِتْمَشّيش	
íntu	*itmáššu*	اِتْمَشّوا	*ma-titmaššūš*	مَتِتْمَشّوش	

	active		passive		
masculine	*mitmášši*	مِتْمَشّي	–	–	participles
feminine	*mitmaššíyya*	مِتْمَشّيَّة	–	–	
plural	*mitmaššiyīn*	مِتْمَشّيين	–	–	

①

لمّا كُنْت في الغرْدقة اِتْمشّيْت عَ البحْر كْتير.

lámma kuntᵊ fi -lɣardáʔa, itmaššēt 3a -lbaḫrᵊ ktīr.

When I was in Hurghada, I walked along the sea a lot.

②

بِنْحِبّ نِتْمشّى عَ الكورْنيش بِاللّيْل.

binḫíbbᵊ nitmašša 3a -lkurnīš bi-llēl.

We love going for a walk along the corniche [waterfront] at night.

③

جارْنا و مْراتُه كُلّ يوْم بِيِتْمشّوا ماسْكين إيديْن بعْض، و عُمْرُهم سبْعين سنة!

gárna wi mrātu kullᵊ yōm biyitmáššu maskīn idēn ba3ḍ, wi 3umrúhum sab3īn sána!

Every day our neighbor goes for a walk with his wife holding hands. They are 70 years old!

④

أ: هتِتْمشّوا لِحدّ المحلّ وَلّا هتاخْدوا العربية؟

ب: هنِتْمشّى. الجَوّ حِلْو أوي.

A: hatitmáššu li-ḫadd ilmaḫállᵊ wálla hatáxdu -l3arabíyya?
B: hanitmášša. ilgáwwᵊ ḫilwᵊ ʔáwi.

A: Are you walking or taking the car to the store?
B: We'll walk. The weather is lovely.

⑤

المثل بِيْقول: اِتْعشّى و اِتْمشّى.

ilmásal biyʔūl: it3ášša w itmášša.

The common saying is: Have dinner, then take a walk.

⑥

مِتْمشّية حِتّةْ تمْشية. خدْت كورْنيش الزّمالِك مِن السّاقْيَة لِحدّ الأوبْرا.

mitmaššíyya ḫíttit tamšíyya. xadtᵊ kurnīš izzamālik min issáʔya li-ḫadd ilʔúbra.

I had a lovely walk. I walked along the Zamalek corniche from Sakia to the Opera.

⑦

بفضّل منِتْمشّاش اللّيْلة دي. أنا تعْبان.

bafáḍḍal ma-nitmaššāš illilādi. ána ta3bān.

I'd rather we not go for a walk this evening. I'm tired.

❖ [5d] **to go for a walk, take a stroll**

- Compare with مِشى *míši*. (➲ 238)

➲ 175.1

28 to wish *itmánna* اِتْمَنّى

	affirmative		negative		
ána	*itmannēt*	اِتْمَنّيْت	*ma-tmannítš*	مَتْمَنّيْتْش	perfect
íḫna	*itmannēna*	اِتْمَنّيْنا	*ma-tmanninā̆š*	مَتْمَنّيْناش	
ínta	*itmannēt*	اِتْمَنّيْت	*ma-tmannítš*	مَتْمَنّيْتْش	
ínti	*itmannēti*	اِتْمَنّيْتي	*ma-tmannitīš*	مَتْمَنّيْتيش	
íntu	*itmannētu*	اِتْمَنّيْتوا	*ma-tmannitūš*	مَتْمَنّيْتوش	
húwwa	*itmánna*	اِتْمَنّى	*ma-tmannāš*	مَتْمَنّاش	
híyya	*itmánnit*	اِتْمَنّْت	*ma-tmannítš*	مَتْمَنّْتْش	
húmma	*itmánnu*	اِتْمَنّوا	*ma-tmannūš*	مَتْمَنّوش	
ána	*atmánna*	أتْمَنّى	*ma-tmannāš*	مَتْمَنّاش	imperfect
íḫna	*nitmánna*	نِتْمَنّى	*ma-nitmannāš*	مَنْتْمَنّاش	
ínta	*titmánna*	تِتْمَنّى	*ma-titmannāš*	مَتْتْمَنّاش	
ínti	*titmánni*	تِتْمَنّي	*ma-titmannīš*	مَتْتْمَنّيش	
íntu	*titmánnu*	تِتْمَنّوا	*ma-titmannūš*	مَتْتْمَنّوش	
húwwa	*yitmánna*	يِتْمَنّى	*ma-yitmannāš*	مَيْتْمَنّاش	
híyya	*titmánna*	تِتْمَنّى	*ma-titmannāš*	مَتْتْمَنّاش	
húmma	*yitmánnu*	يِتْمَنّوا	*ma-yitmannūš*	مَيْتْمَنّوش	
ána	*batmánna*	بَتْمَنّى	*ma-batmannāš*	مَبَتْمَنّاش	bi-imperfect
íḫna	*binitmánna*	بِنِتْمَنّى	*ma-bnitmannāš*	مَبْنِتْمَنّاش	
ínta	*bititmánna*	بِتِتْمَنّى	*ma-btitmannāš*	مَبْتِتْمَنّاش	
ínti	*bititmánni*	بِتِتْمَنّي	*ma-btitmannīš*	مَبْتِتْمَنّيش	
íntu	*bititmánnu*	بِتِتْمَنّوا	*ma-btitmannūš*	مَبْتِتْمَنّوش	
húwwa	*biyitmánna*	بِيِتْمَنّى	*ma-byitmannāš*	مَبْيِتْمَنّاش	
híyya	*bititmánna*	بِتِتْمَنّى	*ma-btitmannāš*	مَبْتِتْمَنّاش	
húmma	*biyitmánnu*	بِيِتْمَنّوا	*ma-byitmannūš*	مَبْيِتْمَنّوش	
ána	*hatmánna*	هَتْمَنّى	*miš hatmánna*	مِش هَتْمَنّى	future
íḫna	*hanitmánna*	هَنِتْمَنّى	*miš hanitmánna*	مِش هَنِتْمَنّى	
ínta	*hatitmánna*	هَتِتْمَنّى	*miš hatitmánna*	مِش هَتِتْمَنّى	
ínti	*hatitmánni*	هَتِتْمَنّي	*miš hatitmánni*	مِش هَتِتْمَنّي	
íntu	*hatitmánnu*	هَتِتْمَنّوا	*miš hatitmánnu*	مِش هَتِتْمَنّوا	
húwwa	*hayitmánna*	هَيِتْمَنّى	*miš hayitmánna*	مِش هَيِتْمَنّى	
híyya	*hatitmánna*	هَتِتْمَنّى	*miš hatitmánna*	مِش هَتِتْمَنّى	
húmma	*hayitmánnu*	هَيِتْمَنّوا	*miš hayitmánnu*	مِش هَيِتْمَنّوا	
ínta	*itmánna*	اِتْمَنّى	*ma-titmannāš*	مَتْتْمَنّاش	imperative
ínti	*itmánni*	اِتْمَنّي	*ma-titmannīš*	مَتْتْمَنّيش	
íntu	*itmánnu*	اِتْمَنّوا	*ma-titmannūš*	مَتْتْمَنّوش	

	active		passive		
masculine	*mitmánni*	مِتْمَنّي	–	–	participles
feminine	*mitmanníyya*	مِتْمَنّيّة	–	–	
plural	*mitmanniyīn*	مِتْعَنّيين	–	–	

verbal noun: *tamánni* تَمَنّي

①

اِتْمَنّيْت طول عُمْري أكون نِجْمة.

itmannēt ṭūl 3úmri ʔakūn nígma.

I've wanted to become
a star all my life.

②

مَوَدّة كُلّ ما تِتْمنّى حاجة، أهْلها مَيْجيبوهُلْهاش.

mawádda kullᵊ ma titmánna ḥāga, ahláha ma-ygibuhulhāš.

Mawada's parents don't give her
everything she wishes for.

③

سامِر بيِتْمنّى يْكون رائِد فضاء.

sāmir biyitmánna ykūn rāʔid faḍāʔ.

Samer hopes to become an astronaut.

④

إنْتَ لِسّه هتِتْمنّى ؟ قوم حقّق اللي إنْتَ عايْزُه بإيدك.

ínta líssa hatitmánna? ʔūm ḥáʔʔaʔ íll- ínta 3áyzu bi-īdak.

Are you just going to keep wishing?
Achieve what you want by yourself.

⑤

متِتْمنّاش بِصوْت عالي. لازِم تِقولْها في سِرّك.

ma-titmannāš bi-ṣōt 3āli. lāzim tiʔúlha fi sírrak.

Don't say your wish out loud.
Keep it in your mind.

⑥

ألْف مبْروك! أنا بتْمنّالك التّوْفيق في المرْحلة الجايّة.

alfᵊ mabrūk! ána batmannālak ittawfīʔ fi -lmarḥála -lgáyya.

Congratulations! I wish you success
in what's next to come!

❖ [5d] **to wish, hope, want**

- This verb can be intransitive (➲ 28.4, 28.5) or transitive (➲ 28.2, 28.6).
- It can be followed by an imperfect verb (➲ 28.1, 28.3,).

➲ 152.1

29 to jump around *itnáttat* اِتْنَطّ 13

no verbal noun

perfect

	affirmative		negative	
ána	*itnaṭṭáṭt*	اِتْنَطَّطْت	*ma-tnaṭṭáṭtiš*	مَتْنَطَّطْتِش
íḫna	*itnaṭṭáṭna*	اِتْنَطَّطْنا	*ma-tnaṭṭaṭnāš*	مَتْنَطَّطْناش
ínta	*itnaṭṭáṭt*	اِتْنَطَّطْت	*ma-tnaṭṭáṭtiš*	مَتْنَطَّطْتِش
ínti	*itnaṭṭáṭti*	اِتْنَطَّطْتي	*ma-tnaṭṭaṭtīš*	مَتْنَطَّطْتيش
íntu	*itnaṭṭáṭtu*	اِتْنَطَّطْتوا	*ma-tnaṭṭaṭtūš*	مَتْنَطَّطْتوش
húwwa	*itnáṭṭaṭ*	اِتْنَطَّط	*ma-tnaṭṭáṭš*	مَتْنَطَّطْش
híyya	*itnaṭṭáṭit*	اِتْنَطَّطِت	*ma-tnaṭṭaṭítš*	مَتْنَطَّطِتْش
húmma	*itnaṭṭáṭu*	اِتْنَطَّطوا	*ma-tnaṭṭaṭūš*	مَتْنَطَّطوش

imperfect

	affirmative		negative	
ána	*atnáṭṭaṭ*	أَتْنَطَّط	*ma-tnaṭṭáṭš*	مَتْنَطَّطْش
íḫna	*nitnáṭṭaṭ*	نِتْنَطَّط	*ma-nitnaṭṭáṭš*	مَنِتْنَطَّطْش
ínta	*titnáṭṭaṭ*	تِتْنَطَّط	*ma-titnaṭṭáṭš*	مَتِتْنَطَّطْش
ínti	*titnaṭṭáṭi*	تِتْنَطَّطي	*ma-titnaṭṭaṭīš*	مَتِتْنَطَّطيش
íntu	*titnaṭṭáṭu*	تِتْنَطَّطوا	*ma-titnaṭṭaṭūš*	مَتِتْنَطَّطوش
húwwa	*yitnáṭṭaṭ*	يِتْنَطَّط	*ma-yitnaṭṭáṭš*	مَيِتْنَطَّطْش
híyya	*titnáṭṭaṭ*	تِتْنَطَّط	*ma-titnaṭṭáṭš*	مَتِتْنَطَّطْش
húmma	*yitnaṭṭáṭu*	يِتْنَطَّطوا	*ma-yitnaṭṭaṭūš*	مَيِتْنَطَّطوش

bi-imperfect

	affirmative		negative	
ána	*batnáṭṭaṭ*	بَتْنَطَّط	*ma-batnaṭṭáṭš*	مَبَتْنَطَّطْش
íḫna	*binitnáṭṭaṭ*	بِنِتْنَطَّط	*ma-bnitnaṭṭáṭš*	مَبْنِتْنَطَّطْش
ínta	*bititnáṭṭaṭ*	بِتِتْنَطَّط	*ma-btitnaṭṭáṭš*	مَبْتِتْنَطَّطْش
ínti	*bititnaṭṭáṭi*	بِتِتْنَطَّطي	*ma-btitnaṭṭaṭīš*	مَبْتِتْنَطَّطيش
íntu	*bititnaṭṭáṭu*	بِتِتْنَطَّطوا	*ma-btitnaṭṭaṭūš*	مَبْتِتْنَطَّطوش
húwwa	*biyitnáṭṭaṭ*	بِيِتْنَطَّط	*ma-byitnaṭṭáṭš*	مَبْيِتْنَطَّطْش
híyya	*bititnáṭṭaṭ*	بِتِتْنَطَّط	*ma-btitnaṭṭáṭš*	مَبْتِتْنَطَّطْش
húmma	*biyitnaṭṭáṭu*	بِيِتْنَطَّطوا	*ma-byitnaṭṭaṭūš*	مَبْيِتْنَطَّطوش

future

	affirmative		negative	
ána	*hatnáṭṭaṭ*	هَتْنَطَّط	*miš hatnáṭṭaṭ*	مِش هَتْنَطَّط
íḫna	*hanitnáṭṭaṭ*	هَنِتْنَطَّط	*miš hanitnáṭṭaṭ*	مِش هَنِتْنَطَّط
ínta	*hatitnáṭṭaṭ*	هَتِتْنَطَّط	*miš hatitnáṭṭaṭ*	مِش هَتِتْنَطَّط
ínti	*hatitnaṭṭáṭi*	هَتِتْنَطَّطي	*miš hatitnaṭṭáṭi*	مِش هَتِتْنَطَّطي
íntu	*hatitnaṭṭáṭu*	هَتِتْنَطَّطوا	*miš hatitnaṭṭáṭu*	مِش هَتِتْنَطَّطوا
húwwa	*hayitnáṭṭaṭ*	هَيِتْنَطَّط	*miš hayitnáṭṭaṭ*	مِش هَيِتْنَطَّط
híyya	*hatitnáṭṭaṭ*	هَتِتْنَطَّط	*miš hatitnáṭṭaṭ*	مِش هَتِتْنَطَّط
húmma	*hayitnaṭṭáṭu*	هَيِتْنَطَّطوا	*miš hayitnaṭṭáṭu*	مِش هَيِتْنَطَّطوا

imperative

	affirmative		negative	
ínta	*itnáṭṭaṭ*	اِتْنَطَّط	*ma-titnaṭṭáṭš*	مَتِتْنَطَّطْش
ínti	*itnaṭṭáṭi*	اِتْنَطَّطي	*ma-titnaṭṭaṭīš*	مَتِتْنَطَّطيش
íntu	*itnaṭṭáṭu*	اِتْنَطَّطوا	*ma-titnaṭṭaṭūš*	مَتِتْنَطَّطوش

participles

	active		passive	
masculine	*mitnáṭṭaṭ*	مِتْنَطَّط	–	–
feminine	*mitnaṭṭáṭa*	مِتْنَطَّطَة	–	–
plural	*mitnaṭṭaṭīn*	مِتْنَطَّطين	–	–

①

عربيتي باظِت و إضْطرّيْت اِتّنطّط في المُواصْلات.

3arabīti bāẓit w iḍṭarrēt atnáṭṭaṭ fi -lmuwaṣlāt.

My car broke down, so I had to take [lit. jump on] public transportation.

②

إبْني لازِم يِتْنطّط أوِّل ما يْشوفْني.

íbni lāzim yitnáṭṭaṭ áwwil ma yšúfni.

My son always jumps up and down when he sees me.

③

متِقْلقيش. إبْني هادي. مبْيِتْنطّطْش.

ma-tiʔlaʔīš. íbni hādi. ma-byitnaṭṭáṭš.

Don't worry. My son is quiet. He doesn't make a mess.

④

هتِتْنطّط بيِنْ الكُلِّيّات لِحدّ إمْتى يابْني؟

hatitnáṭṭaṭ bēn ilkulliyyāt li-ḥadd ímta ya -bni?

How long are you going to keep jumping back and forth between faculties [i.e. departments of study]?

⑤

متِتْنطّطْش عَ الكنبة. هتِكْسرْها.

ma-titnaṭṭáṭšᵊ 3a -lkánaba. hatiksárha.

Don't keep jumping on the sofa. You'll break it.

❖ [5s2] **to jump around, be hyper**

- Compare with نطّ *naṭṭ*. (➲ 252)

30 to be born *itwálad* اتْوَلَد

	affirmative		negative		
ána	*itwaládt*	اتْوَلَدْت	*ma-twaládtiš*	مَتْوَلَدْتِش	**perfect**
íḥna	*itwaládna*	اتْوَلَدْنا	*ma-twaladnāš*	مَتْوَلَدْناش	
ínta	*itwaládt*	اتْوَلَدْت	*ma-twaládtiš*	مَتْوَلَدْتِش	
ínti	*itwaládti*	اتْوَلَدْتي	*ma-twaladtīš*	مَتْوَلَدْتيش	
íntu	*itwaládtu*	اتْوَلَدْتوا	*ma-twaladtūš*	مَتْوَلَدْتوش	
húwwa	*itwálad*	اتْوَلَد	*ma-twaládš*	مَتْوَلَدْش	
híyya	*itwáladit*	اتْوَلَدِت	*ma-twaladítš*	مَتْوَلَدِتْش	
húmma	*itwáladu*	اتْوَلَدوا	*ma-twaladūš*	مَتْوَلَدوش	
ána	*atwílid*	أتْوِلِد	*ma-twilídš*	مَتْوِلِدْش	**imperfect**
íḥna	*nitwílid*	نِتْوِلِد	*ma-nitwilídš*	مَنِتْوِلِدْش	
ínta	*titwílid*	تِتْوِلِد	*ma-titwilídš*	مَتِتْوِلِدْش	
ínti	*titwíldi*	تِتْوِلْدي	*ma-titwildīš*	مَتِتْوِلْديش	
íntu	*titwíldu*	تِتْوِلْدوا	*ma-titwildūš*	مَتِتْوِلْدوش	
húwwa	*yitwílid*	يِتْوِلِد	*ma-yitwilídš*	مَيِتْوِلِدْش	
híyya	*titwílid*	تِتْوِلِد	*ma-titwilídš*	مَتِتْوِلِدْش	
húmma	*yitwíldu*	يِتْوِلْدوا	*ma-yitwildūš*	مَيِتْوِلْدوش	
ána	*batwílid*	بَتْوِلِد	*ma-batwilídš*	مَبَتْوِلِدْش	**bi-imperfect**
íḥna	*binitwílid*	بِنِتْوِلِد	*ma-bnitwilídš*	مَبْنِتْوِلِدْش	
ínta	*bititwílid*	بِتِتْوِلِد	*ma-btitwilídš*	مَبْتِتْوِلِدْش	
ínti	*bititwíldi*	بِتِتْوِلْدي	*ma-btitwildīš*	مَبْتِتْوِلْديش	
íntu	*bititwíldu*	بِتِتْوِلْدوا	*ma-btitwildūš*	مَبْتِتْوِلْدوش	
húwwa	*biyitwílid*	بِيِتْوِلِد	*ma-byitwilídš*	مَبْيِتْوِلِدْش	
híyya	*bititwílid*	بِتِتْوِلِد	*ma-btitwilídš*	مَبْتِتْوِلِدْش	
húmma	*biyitwíldu*	بِيِتْوِلْدوا	*ma-byitwildūš*	مَبْيِتْوِلْدوش	
ána	*hatwílid*	هَتْوِلِد	*miš hatwílid*	مِش هَتْوِلِد	**future**
íḥna	*hanitwílid*	هَنِتْوِلِد	*miš hanitwílid*	مِش هَنِتْوِلِد	
ínta	*hatitwílid*	هَتِتْوِلِد	*miš hatitwílid*	مِش هَتِتْوِلِد	
ínti	*hatitwíldi*	هَتِتْوِلْدي	*miš hatitwíldi*	مِش هَتِتْوِلْدي	
íntu	*hatitwíldu*	هَتِتْوِلْدوا	*miš hatitwíldu*	مِش هَتِتْوِلْدوا	
húwwa	*hayitwílid*	هَيِتْوِلِد	*miš hayitwílid*	مِش هَيِتْوِلِد	
híyya	*hatitwílid*	هَتِتْوِلِد	*miš hatitwílid*	مِش هَتِتْوِلِد	
húmma	*hayitwíldu*	هَيِتْوِلْدوا	*miš hayitwíldu*	مِش هَيِتْوِلْدوا	
ínta	–	–	–	–	**imperative**
ínti	–	–	–	–	
íntu	–	–	–	–	

	active		passive		
masculine	–	–	*mawlūd*	مَوْلود	**participles**
feminine	–	–	*mawlūda*	مَوْلودَة	
plural	–	–	*mawludīn*	مَوْلودين	

verbal noun: *wilāda* ولادة

①

وِلادي الاِتْنين اِتْوَلدوا في أغُسْطُس.

wilādi -lʔitnēn itwáladu fi ʔaɣústus.

Both of my sons were born in August.

②

المُمرِّضات بِيْوَعّوا الحَوامِل علشان أطْفالْهُم يِتْولْدوا أصِحّاء.

ilmumarraḍāt biywá33u -lħawāmil 3alašān aṭfálhum yitwíldu ʔaṣiħħāʔ.

Nurses educate pregnant women so
that their babies are born healthy.

③

اللي بِيْروح يِحِجّ، ده بْيِتْوِلِد مِن جِديد.

ílli biyrūħ yiħígg, da byitwílid min gidīd.

He who goes on hajj is born once again.

④

آلاء حامِل في وَلد. هَيِتْوِلِد الشّهْر الجايّ.

alāʔ ħāmil fi wálad. hayitwílid iššáhr ilgáyy.

Alaa will have a boy. He'll be born next month.

⑤

بِنْتي مَوْلودة في السّابِع. قعدِت شهْر في الحضانة.

bínti mawlūda fi -ssābi3. ʔá3adit šahrᵊ fi -lħaḍāna.

My daughter was born two months premature
[lit. in the seventh month]. She was put in a
neonatal unit [lit. nursery] for a month.

⑥

أنا ليْه متْوَلَدْتِش في القاهِرة؟

ána lē ma-twaládtiš fi -lqāhíra?

Why couldn't I have been born in Cairo?

❖ [7s1] **to be born**

- There is logically no imperative of this verb.

➲ 233.1

31 to need *iḫtāg* اِحْتاج

	affirmative		negative		
ána	*iḫtágt*	اِحْتَجْت	*ma-ḫtágtiš*	مَحْتَجْتِش	perfect
íḫna	*iḫtágna*	اِحْتَجْنا	*ma-ḫtagnāš*	مَحْتَجْناش	
ínta	*iḫtágt*	اِحْتَجْت	*ma-ḫtágtiš*	مَحْتَجْتِش	
ínti	*iḫtágti*	اِحْتَجْتي	*ma-ḫtagtīš*	مَحْتَجْتيش	
íntu	*iḫtágtu*	اِحْتَجْتوا	*ma-ḫtagtūš*	مَحْتَجْتوش	
húwwa	*iḫtāg*	اِحْتاج	*ma-ḫtágš*	مَحْتاجْش	
híyya	*iḫtāgit*	اِحْتاجِت	*ma-ḫtagítš*	مَحْتاجِتْش	
húmma	*iḫtāgu*	اِحْتاجوا	*ma-ḫtagūš*	مَحْتاجوش	
ána	*aḫtāg*	أَحْتاج	*ma-ḫtágš*	مَحْتاجْش	imperfect
íḫna	*niḫtāg*	نِحْتاج	*ma-niḫtágš*	مَنِحْتاجْش	
ínta	*tiḫtāg*	تِحْتاج	*ma-tiḫtágš*	مَتِحْتاجْش	
ínti	*tiḫtāgi*	تِحْتاجي	*ma-tiḫtagīš*	مَتِحْتاجيش	
íntu	*tiḫtāgu*	تِحْتاجوا	*ma-tiḫtagūš*	مَتِحْتاجوش	
húwwa	*yiḫtāg*	يِحْتاج	*ma-yiḫtágš*	مَيِحْتاجْش	
híyya	*tiḫtāg*	تِحْتاج	*ma-tiḫtágš*	مَتِحْتاجْش	
húmma	*yiḫtāgu*	يِحْتاجوا	*ma-yiḫtagūš*	مَيِحْتاجوش	
ána	*baḫtāg*	بَحْتاج	*ma-baḫtágš*	مَبَحْتاجْش	bi-imperfect
íḫna	*biniḫtāg*	بِنِحْتاج	*ma-bniḫtágš*	مَبْنِحْتاجْش	
ínta	*bitiḫtāg*	بِتِحْتاج	*ma-btiḫtágš*	مَبْتِحْتاجْش	
ínti	*bitiḫtāgi*	بِتِحْتاجي	*ma-btiḫtagīš*	مَبْتِحْتاجيش	
íntu	*bitiḫtāgu*	بِتِحْتاجوا	*ma-btiḫtagūš*	مَبْتِحْتاجوش	
húwwa	*biyiḫtāg*	بِيِحْتاج	*ma-byiḫtágš*	مَبْيِحْتاجْش	
híyya	*bitiḫtāg*	بِتِحْتاج	*ma-btiḫtágš*	مَبْتِحْتاجْش	
húmma	*biyiḫtāgu*	بِيِحْتاجوا	*ma-byiḫtagūš*	مَبْيِحْتاجوش	
ána	*haḫtāg*	هَحْتاج	*miš haḫtāg*	مِش هَحْتاج	future
íḫna	*haniḫtāg*	هَنِحْتاج	*miš haniḫtāg*	مِش هَنِحْتاج	
ínta	*hatiḫtāg*	هَتِحْتاج	*miš hatiḫtāg*	مِش هَتِحْتاج	
ínti	*hatiḫtāgi*	هَتِحْتاجي	*miš hatiḫtāgi*	مِش هَتِحْتاجي	
íntu	*hatiḫtāgu*	هَتِحْتاجوا	*miš hatiḫtāgu*	مِش هَتِحْتاجوا	
húwwa	*hayiḫtāg*	هَيِحْتاج	*miš hayiḫtāg*	مِش هَيِحْتاج	
híyya	*hatiḫtāg*	هَتِحْتاج	*miš hatiḫtāg*	مِش هَتِحْتاج	
húmma	*hayiḫtāgu*	هَيِحْتاجوا	*miš hayiḫtāgu*	مِش هَيِحْتاجوا	
ínta	*iḫtāg*	اِحْتاج	*ma-tiḫtágš*	مَتِحْتاجْش	imperative
ínti	*iḫtāgi*	اِحْتاجي	*ma-tiḫtagīš*	مَتِحْتاجيش	
íntu	*iḫtāgu*	اِحْتاجوا	*ma-tiḫtagūš*	مَتِحْتاجوش	

	active		passive		
masculine	*miḫtāg*	مِحْتاج	–	–	participles
feminine	*miḫtāga*	مِحْتاجَة	–	–	
plural	*miḫtagīn*	مِحْتاجين	–	–	

verbal nouns: *iḫtiyāg* إِحْتِياج - *ḫāga* حاجَة

①

أحْمد اِحْتاج ٣ شُهور عشان يِتْأقْلِم معَ شُغْلُه الجِديد.

áħmad iħtāg tálat šuhūr 3ašān yitʔáqlim má3a šúɣlu -lgidīd.

It took Ahmed [lit. Ahmed needed] three months to get used to his new job.

②

اللّحْمة تِحْتاج ساعْتينْ عَ النّار عشان تِسْتَوي.

illáħma tiħtāg sa3tēn 3a -nnār 3ašān tistáwi.

The beef needs to be cooked for two hours to be done.

③

في الصّيْف بِنِحْتاج نِشْرب سَوايِل كِتير.

fi -ṣṣēf biniħtāg níšrab sawāyil kitīr.

We need to drink plenty of drinks in the summer.

④

مِش هَيِحْتاجوا يْروحوا السِّفارة. أنا هروح بُكْره أخلّصْلُهُم الوَرق.

miš hayiħtāgu yrūħu -ssifāra. ána harūħ búkra -xallaṣlúhum ilwáraʔ.

They won't need to go to the embassy. I'll finish up the papers for them.

⑤

مِحْتاجه آخُد شهْر أجازة و أروح مكان بِعيد.

miħtāg- āxud šahr agāza w arūħ makān bi3īd.

I need to take a month off and go somewhere far away.

⑥

مِش مِحْتاج فِلوس كِتير عشان أكون سعيد.

miš miħtāg filūs kitīr 3ašān akūn sa3īd.

I don't need a lot of money to be happy.

❖ [8h] **to need**

- This verb can be transitive (➲ 31.1, 31.2, 31.6) or followed by an imperfect verb (➲ 31.3, 31.4, 31.5).

➲ 39.3, 77.5, 100.6, 145.2, 249.2

32 to respect iḫtáram اِحْتَرَم

verbal noun: iḫtirām اِحْتِرام

		affirmative		negative	
perfect	ána	iḫtarámt	اِحْتَرَمْت	ma-ḫtarámtiš	مَحْتَرَمْتِش
	íḫna	iḫtarámna	اِحْتَرَمْنا	ma-ḫtaramnāš	مَحْتَرَمْناش
	ínta	iḫtarámt	اِحْتَرَمْت	ma-ḫtarámtiš	مَحْتَرَمْتِش
	ínti	iḫtarámti	اِحْتَرَمْتي	ma-ḫtaramtīš	مَحْتَرَمْتيش
	íntu	iḫtarámtu	اِحْتَرَمْتوا	ma-ḫtaramtūš	مَحْتَرَمْتوش
	húwwa	iḫtáram	اِحْتَرَم	ma-ḫtarámš	مَحْتَرَمْش
	híyya	iḫtáramit	اِحْتَرَمِت	ma-ḫtaramítš	مَحْتَرَمِتْش
	húmma	iḫtáramu	اِحْتَرَموا	ma-ḫtaramūš	مَحْتَرَموش
imperfect	ána	aḫtírim	أَحْتِرِم	ma-ḫtirímš	مَحْتِرِمْش
	íḫna	niḫtírim	نِحْتِرِم	ma-niḫtirímš	مَنِحْتِرِمْش
	ínta	tiḫtírim	تِحْتِرِم	ma-tiḫtirímš	مَتِحْتِرِمْش
	ínti	tiḫtírmi	تِحْتِرْمي	ma-tiḫtirmīš	مَتِحْتِرْميش
	íntu	tiḫtírmu	تِحْتِرْموا	ma-tiḫtirmūš	مَتِحْتِرْموش
	húwwa	yiḫtírim	يِحْتِرِم	ma-yiḫtirímš	مَيِحْتِرِمْش
	híyya	tiḫtírim	تِحْتِرِم	ma-tiḫtirímš	مَتِحْتِرِمْش
	húmma	yiḫtírmu	يِحْتِرْموا	ma-yiḫtirmūš	مَيِحْتِرْموش
bi-imperfect	ána	baḫtírim	بَحْتِرِم	ma-baḫtirímš	مَبَحْتِرِمْش
	íḫna	biniḫtírim	بِنِحْتِرِم	ma-bniḫtirímš	مَبْنِحْتِرِمْش
	ínta	bitiḫtírim	بِتِحْتِرِم	ma-btiḫtirímš	مَبْتِحْتِرِمْش
	ínti	bitiḫtírmi	بِتِحْتِرْمي	ma-btiḫtirmīš	مَبْتِحْتِرْميش
	íntu	bitiḫtírmu	بِتِحْتِرْموا	ma-btiḫtirmūš	مَبْتِحْتِرْموش
	húwwa	biyiḫtírim	بِيِحْتِرِم	ma-byiḫtirímš	مَبْيِحْتِرِمْش
	híyya	bitiḫtírim	بِتِحْتِرِم	ma-btiḫtirímš	مَبْتِحْتِرِمْش
	húmma	biyiḫtírmu	بِيِحْتِرْموا	ma-byiḫtirmūš	مَبْيِحْتِرْموش
future	ána	haḫtírim	هَحْتِرِم	miš haḫtírim	مِش هَحْتِرِم
	íḫna	haniḫtírim	هَنِحْتِرِم	miš haniḫtírim	مِش هَنِحْتِرِم
	ínta	hatiḫtírim	هَتِحْتِرِم	miš hatiḫtírim	مِش هَتِحْتِرِم
	ínti	hatiḫtírmi	هَتِحْتِرْمي	miš hatiḫtírmi	مِش هَتِحْتِرْمي
	íntu	hatiḫtírmu	هَتِحْتِرْموا	miš hatiḫtírmu	مِش هَتِحْتِرْموا
	húwwa	hayiḫtírim	هَيِحْتِرِم	miš hayiḫtírim	مِش هَيِحْتِرِم
	híyya	hatiḫtírim	هَتِحْتِرِم	miš hatiḫtírim	مِش هَتِحْتِرِم
	húmma	hayiḫtírmu	هَيِحْتِرْموا	miš hayiḫtírmu	مِش هَيِحْتِرْموا
imperative	ínta	iḫtírim	اِحْتِرِم	ma-tiḫtirímš	مَتِحْتِرِمْش
	ínti	iḫtírmi	اِحْتِرْمي	ma-tiḫtirmīš	مَتِحْتِرْميش
	íntu	iḫtírmu	اِحْتِرْموا	ma-tiḫtirmūš	مَتِحْتِرْموش

		active		passive	
participles	masculine	miḫtírim	مِحْتِرِم	muḫtáram	مُحْتَرَم
	feminine	miḫtírma	مِحْتِرْمَة	muḫtárama	مُحْتَرَمَة
	plural	miḫtirmīn	مِحْتِرْمين	muḫtaramīn	مُحْتَرَمين

①

مَحْترمْناش الرّاجِل خالِص لمّا علّى صوْتُه على أُمُّه.

ma-ħtaramnāš irrāgil xāliṣ lámma 3álla ṣōtu 3ála ʔúmmu.

We didn't respect the man after he raised his voice at his mother.

②

لازِم تِحْتِـرِم اللي أكْبر مِنّك.

lāzim tiħtírim ílli ʔákbar mínnak.

You should respect those older than you.

③

الوِلاد بِيِحْتِـرْموا كابْتِن محْمود أوي. بِالنِّسْبالْهُم مثل أعْلى.

ilwilād biyiħtírmu kábtin maħmūd áwi. bi-nnisbálhum másal á3la.

The kids respect captain Mahmoud so much. They look at him as a role model.

④

إنْتَ مِش هتِحْتِـرِم نفْسك إلّا أمّا أهزّأك.

ínta miš hatiħtírim náfsak ílla ʔámma -hazzáʔak.

You won't behave unless I teach you a lesson.

⑤

اِحْتِـرْموا قَواعِد المُرور.

iħtírmu qawā3id ilmurūr.

Respect the traffic rules.

❖ [8s1] **to respect**

➲ 58.2, 93.6

33 to celebrate iħtáfal اِحْتَفَل

verbal noun: *iħtifāl* اِحْتِفال

perfect

	affirmative		negative	
ána	*iħtafált*	اِحْتَفَلْت	*ma-ħtafáltiš*	مَحْتَفَلْتِش
íħna	*iħtafálna*	اِحْتَفَلْنا	*ma-ħtafalnāš*	مَحْتَفَلْناش
ínta	*iħtafált*	اِحْتَفَلْت	*ma-ħtafáltiš*	مَحْتَفَلْتِش
ínti	*iħtafálti*	اِحْتَفَلْتي	*ma-ħtafaltīš*	مَحْتَفَلْتيش
íntu	*iħtafáltu*	اِحْتَفَلْتوا	*ma-ħtafaltūš*	مَحْتَفَلْتوش
húwwa	*iħtáfal*	اِحْتَفَل	*ma-ħtafálš*	مَحْتَفَلْش
híyya	*iħtáfalit*	اِحْتَفَلِت	*ma-ħtafalítš*	مَحْتَفَلِتْش
húmma	*iħtáfalu*	اِحْتَفَلوا	*ma-ħtafalūš*	مَحْتَفَلوش

imperfect

	affirmative		negative	
ána	*aħtífil*	أَحْتِفِل	*ma-ħtifílš*	مَحْتِفِلْش
íħna	*niħtífil*	نِحْتِفِل	*ma-niħtifílš*	مَنِحْتِفِلْش
ínta	*tiħtífil*	تِحْتِفِل	*ma-tiħtifílš*	مَتِحْتِفِلْش
ínti	*tiħtífli*	تِحْتِفْلي	*ma-tiħtiflīš*	مَتِحْتِفْليش
íntu	*tiħtíflu*	تِحْتِفْلوا	*ma-tiħtiflūš*	مَتِحْتِفْلوش
húwwa	*yiħtífil*	يِحْتِفِل	*ma-yiħtifílš*	مَيِحْتِفِلْش
híyya	*tiħtífil*	تِحْتِفِل	*ma-tiħtifílš*	مَتِحْتِفِلْش
húmma	*yiħtíflu*	يِحْتِفْلوا	*ma-yiħtiflūš*	مَيِحْتِفْلوش

bi-imperfect

	affirmative		negative	
ána	*baħtífil*	بَحْتِفِل	*ma-baħtifílš*	مَبَحْتِفِلْش
íħna	*biniħtífil*	بِنِحْتِفِل	*ma-bniħtifílš*	مَبْنِحْتِفِلْش
ínta	*bitiħtífil*	بِتِحْتِفِل	*ma-ħtiħtifílš*	مَبْتِحْتِفِلْش
ínti	*bitiħtífli*	بِتِحْتِفْلي	*ma-ħtiħtiflīš*	مَبْتِحْتِفْليش
íntu	*bitiħtíflu*	بِتِحْتِفْلوا	*ma-ħtiħtiflūš*	مَبْتِحْتِفْلوش
húwwa	*biyiħtífil*	بِيِحْتِفِل	*ma-byiħtifílš*	مَبْيِحْتِفِلْش
híyya	*bitiħtífil*	بِتِحْتِفِل	*ma-ħtiħtifílš*	مَبْتِحْتِفِلْش
húmma	*biyiħtíflu*	بِيِحْتِفْلوا	*ma-byiħtiflūš*	مَبْيِحْتِفْلوش

future

	affirmative		negative	
ána	*haħtífil*	هَحْتِفِل	*miš haħtífil*	مِش هَحْتِفِل
íħna	*haniħtífil*	هَنِحْتِفِل	*miš haniħtífil*	مِش هَنِحْتِفِل
ínta	*hatiħtífil*	هَتِحْتِفِل	*miš hatiħtífil*	مِش هَتِحْتِفِل
ínti	*hatiħtífli*	هَتِحْتِفْلي	*miš hatiħtífli*	مِش هَتِحْتِفْلي
íntu	*hatiħtíflu*	هَتِحْتِفْلوا	*miš hatiħtíflu*	مِش هَتِحْتِفْلوا
húwwa	*hayiħtífil*	هَيِحْتِفِل	*miš hayiħtífil*	مِش هَيِحْتِفِل
híyya	*hatiħtífil*	هَتِحْتِفِل	*miš hatiħtífil*	مِش هَتِحْتِفِل
húmma	*hayiħtíflu*	هَيِحْتِفْلوا	*miš hayiħtíflu*	مِش هَيِحْتِفْلوا

imperative

	affirmative		negative	
ínta	*iħtífil*	اِحْتِفِل	*ma-tiħtifílš*	مَتِحْتِفِلْش
ínti	*iħtífli*	اِحْتِفْلي	*ma-tiħtiflīš*	مَتِحْتِفْليش
íntu	*iħtíflu*	اِحْتِفْلوا	*ma-tiħtiflūš*	مَتِحْتِفْلوش

participles

	active		passive	
masculine	*miħtífil*	مِحْتِفِل	–	–
feminine	*miħtífla*	مِحْتِفْلَة	–	–
plural	*miħtiflīn*	مِحْتِفْلين	–	–

①

اِحْتفلْنا إمْبارِح بِعيد الفِطْر و كلْنا كمِّيِّة كحْك رهيبة.

iḫtafálna -mbāriḫ bi-3īd ilfíṭr, wi kálna kammíyyit kaḫkᵊ rahība.

We celebrated Eid el-Fitr yesterday, and we ate a huge amount of kahk [cookies].

②

أُمْنية عملِت تحْضيرات كِتير عشان تِحْتِفِل بِذِكْرى جَوازْها.

umníyya 3ámalit taḫḍirāt kitīr 3ašān tiḫtífil bi-zíkra gawázha.

Omnia made lots of preparations to celebrate her wedding anniversary.

③

مبحْتِفِلْش عادةً بِعيد ميلادى، بسّ أصْحابي بِيْفاجْئوني بِحفْلة ساعات.

ma-baḫtifílšᵊ 3ādatan bi-3īd milādi, bass aṣḫābi biyfag?ūni bi-ḫáfla sa3āt.

I don't usually celebrate my birthday, but sometimes my friends throw me a surprise party.

④

النّاس هتِحْتِفِل بِعيد الفِطْر كمان إسْبوع.

innās hatiḫtífil bi-3īd ilfíṭrᵊ kamān isbū3.

People will celebrate Eid al-Fitr in a week.

⑤

اِحْتِفِل بِخْطوبْتك في النّادي. المكان هِناك حِلْو أوي.

iḫtífil bi-xṭúbtak fi -nnādi. ilmakān hinā̄k ḫilw áwi.

Celebrate your engagement in the [country] club. That place is very nice.

⑥

فرْحانين أوي، أصْلُهُم لِسّه مِحْتِفْلين بِنجاحْهُم.

farḫanīn áwi, aṣlúhum líssa miḫtiflīn bi-nagáḫhum.

They are very happy because they have just celebrated their success.

❖ [8s1] **to celebrate** (بِـ *bi-*)

➲ 42.1

34 to choose *ixtār* اِخْتار

	affirmative		negative		
ána	*ixtárt*	اِخْترْت	*ma-xtártiš*	مَخْترْتِش	perfect
íḫna	*ixtárna*	اِخْترْنا	*ma-xtarnāš*	مَخْترْناش	
ínta	*ixtárt*	اِخْترْت	*ma-xtártiš*	مَخْترْتِش	
ínti	*ixtárti*	اِخْترْتي	*ma-xtartīš*	مَخْترْتيش	
íntu	*ixtártu*	اِخْترْتوا	*ma-xtartūš*	مَخْترْتوش	
húwwa	*ixtār*	اِخْتار	*ma-xtárš*	مَخْتارْش	
híyya	*ixtārit*	اِخْتارِت	*ma-xtarítš*	مَخْتارِتْش	
húmma	*ixtāru*	اِخْتاروا	*ma-xtarūš*	مَخْتاروش	
ána	*axtār*	أخْتار	*ma-xtárš*	مَخْتارْش	imperfect
íḫna	*nixtār*	نِخْتار	*ma-nixtárš*	مَنِخْتارْش	
ínta	*tixtār*	تِخْتار	*ma-tixtárš*	مَتِخْتارْش	
ínti	*tixtāri*	تِخْتاري	*ma-tixtarīš*	مَتِخْتاريش	
íntu	*tixtāru*	تِخْتاروا	*ma-tixtarūš*	مَتِخْتاروش	
húwwa	*yixtār*	يِخْتار	*ma-yixtárš*	مَيِخْتارْش	
híyya	*tixtār*	تِخْتار	*ma-tixtárš*	مَتِخْتارْش	
húmma	*yixtāru*	يِخْتاروا	*ma-yixtarūš*	مَيِخْتاروش	
ána	*baxtār*	بَخْتار	*ma-baxtárš*	مَبَخْتارْش	bi-imperfect
íḫna	*binixtār*	بِنِخْتار	*ma-bnixtárš*	مَبْنِخْتارْش	
ínta	*bitixtār*	بِتِخْتار	*ma-btixtárš*	مَبْتِخْتارْش	
ínti	*bitixtāri*	بِتِخْتاري	*ma-btixtarīš*	مَبْتِخْتاريش	
íntu	*bitixtāru*	بِتِخْتاروا	*ma-btixtarūš*	مَبْتِخْتاروش	
húwwa	*biyixtār*	بِيِخْتار	*ma-byixtárš*	مَبْيِخْتارْش	
híyya	*bitixtār*	بِتِخْتار	*ma-btixtárš*	مَبْتِخْتارْش	
húmma	*biyixtāru*	بِيِخْتاروا	*ma-byixtarūš*	مَبْيِخْتاروش	
ána	*haxtār*	هَخْتار	*miš haxtār*	مِش هَخْتار	future
íḫna	*hanixtār*	هَنِخْتار	*miš hanixtār*	مِش هَنِخْتار	
ínta	*hatixtār*	هَتِخْتار	*miš hatixtār*	مِش هَتِخْتار	
ínti	*hatixtāri*	هَتِخْتاري	*miš hatixtāri*	مِش هَتِخْتاري	
íntu	*hatixtāru*	هَتِخْتاروا	*miš hatixtāru*	مِش هَتِخْتاروا	
húwwa	*hayixtār*	هَيِخْتار	*miš hayixtār*	مِش هَيِخْتار	
híyya	*hatixtār*	هَتِخْتار	*miš hatixtār*	مِش هَتِخْتار	
húmma	*hayixtāru*	هَيِخْتاروا	*miš hayixtāru*	مِش هَيِخْتاروا	
ínta	*ixtār*	اِخْتار	*ma-tixtárš*	مَتِخْتارْش	imperative
ínti	*ixtāri*	اِخْتاري	*ma-tixtarīš*	مَتِخْتاريش	
íntu	*ixtāru*	اِخْتاروا	*ma-tixtarūš*	مَتِخْتاروش	

	active		passive		
masculine	*mixtār*	مِخْتار	*muxtār*	مُخْتار	participles
feminine	*mixtāra*	مِخْتارَة	*muxtāra*	مُخْتارَة	
plural	*mixtarīn*	مِخْتارين	*muxtarīn*	مُخْتارين	

verbal noun: *ixtiyār* اِخْتِيار

①

اِخْترْت أسْكُن في الهرم عشان أكون قُريِّبة مِن شُغْلي.

ixtárt áskun fi -lháram 3ašān akūn ʔurayyíba min šúɣli.

I chose to live on Haram [Street] in order to be close to my work.

②

سيبوني أخْتار الكُلّية اللي بحِبّها عشان أنْجح فيها.

sibūni ʔaxtār ilkullíyya -lli baħibbáha 3ašān ángaħ fīha.

Let me choose the faculty [department of study] that I like so I can succeed in it.

③

هِنْد بِتْحِبّ اللّوْن الأحْمر أوي. دي بْتِخْتار كُلّ حاجاتْها بِاللّوْن ده.

hindᵊ bitħíbb illōn ilʔáħmar áwi. di btixtār kullᵊ ħagátha bi-llōn da.

Hend likes red. She chooses everything in that color.

④

هخْتار الاِسْتِثْمار في العقارات بدل البورْصة. العقارات أأْمن.

haxtār ilʔistismār fi -l3aqarāt bádal ilbúrṣa. il3aqarāt áʔman.

I'll choose [to invest in] real estate instead of the stock market. Real estate is safer.

⑤

اِخْتار شِريك حَياتك بِعِنايَة لإِنُّه هَيْكون سبب كِبير في سعادْتك أوْ تعاسْتك باقي حَياتك.

ixtār širīk ħayātak bi-3ināya li-ínnu haykūn sábab kibīr fi sa3ádtak aw ta3ástak bāʔi ħayātak.

Choose your life partner carefully. They will be the reason for your happiness or sadness for the rest of your life.

⑥

أُخْتي اللي مُخْتاره الفُسْتان ده. أنا بثِق في ذوقْها.

úxti -lli muxtāra -lfustān da. ána básiq fi zúʔha.

My sister's the one who picked this dress out. I trust her taste.

⑦

إحْنا لِسّه مخْترْناش إسْم لِلبيْبي.

íħna líssa ma-xtarnāš ismᵊ li-lbēbi.

We still haven't chosen a name for the baby.

❖ [8h] **to choose, pick**

- This verb is transitive.
- It can also be followed by an imperfect verb. (➲ 34.1)

35 to give ídda إدّى 13

	affirmative		negative		
ána	iddēt	إدّيْت	ma-ddítš	مَدّيتْش	perfect
íḫna	iddēna	إدّيْنا	ma-ddināš	مَدّيناش	
ínta	iddēt	إدّيْت	ma-ddítš	مَدّيتْش	
ínti	iddēti	إدّيْتي	ma-dditīš	مَدّيتيش	
íntu	iddētu	إدّيْتوا	ma-dditūš	مَدّيتوش	
húwwa	ídda	إدّى	ma-ddāš	مَدّاش	
híyya	íddit	إدّت	ma-ddítš	مَدّتْش	
húmma	íddu	إدّوا	ma-ddūš	مَدّوش	
ána	áddi	أدّي	ma-ddīš	مَدّيش	imperfect
íḫna	níddi	نِدّي	ma-niddīš	مَنِدّيش	
ínta	tíddi	تِدّي	ma-tiddīš	مَتِدّيش	
ínti	tíddi	تِدّي	ma-tiddīš	مَتِدّيش	
íntu	tíddu	تِدّوا	ma-tiddūš	مَتِدّوش	
húwwa	yíddi	يِدّي	ma-yiddīš	مَيِدّيش	
híyya	tíddi	تِدّي	ma-tiddīš	مَتِدّيش	
húmma	yíddu	يِدّوا	ma-yiddūš	مَيِدّوش	
ána	báddi	بَدّي	ma-baddīš	مَبَدّيش	bi-imperfect
íḫna	biníddi	بِنِدّي	ma-bniddīš	مَبْنِدّيش	
ínta	bitíddi	بِتِدّي	ma-btiddīš	مَبْتِدّيش	
ínti	bitíddi	بِتِدّي	ma-btiddīš	مَبْتِدّيش	
íntu	bitíddu	بِتِدّوا	ma-btiddūš	مَبْتِدّوش	
húwwa	biyíddi	بِيِدّي	ma-byiddīš	مَبْيِدّيش	
híyya	bitíddi	بِتِدّي	ma-btiddīš	مَبْتِدّيش	
húmma	biyíddu	بِيِدّوا	ma-byiddūš	مَبْيِدّوش	
ána	háddi	هَدّي	miš háddi	مِش هَدّي	future
íḫna	haníddi	هَنِدّي	miš haníddi	مِش هَنِدّي	
ínta	hatíddi	هَتِدّي	miš hatíddi	مِش هَتِدّي	
ínti	hatíddi	هَتِدّي	miš hatíddi	مِش هَتِدّي	
íntu	hatíddu	هَتِدّوا	miš hatíddu	مِش هَتِدّوا	
húwwa	hayíddi	هَيِدّي	miš hayíddi	مِش هَيِدّي	
híyya	hatíddi	هَتِدّي	miš hatíddi	مِش هَتِدّي	
húmma	hayíddu	هَيِدّوا	miš hayíddu	مِش هَيِدّوا	
ínta	íddi	إدّي	ma-tiddīš	مَتِدّيش	imperative
ínti	íddi	إدّي	ma-tiddīš	مَتِدّيش	
íntu	íddu	إدّوا	ma-tiddūš	مَتِدّوش	

	active		passive		
masculine	míddi	مِدّي	–	–	participles
feminine	middíyya	مِدّيّة	–	–	
plural	middiyīn	مِدّيين	–	–	

no verbal noun

①

الميس إدِّتْني صِفر في الاِمْتِحان عشان اِفْتكرِتْني بِغِشّ.

ilmīs iddítni ṣifrᵊ fi -lʔimtiḫān 3ašān iftakarítni bi-ɣíšš.

The teacher gave me zero on the exam;
she thought I was cheating.

②

إبْني الصُّغيرّ بِيْحِبّ يِدّي أخوة مِن أيّ حاجة معاه.

íbni -ṣṣuɣáyyar biyḫíbbᵊ yíddi ʔaxū min ayyᵊ ḫāga ma3ā.

My younger son likes to share with his brother.

③

مبدّيش فِلوس لِلشّحّاتين في الشّارِع. بفضّل أدّيها لِجمْعِيّات مَوْثوقة.

ma-baddīš filūs li-ššaḫḫatīn fi -ššāri3. bafáḍḍal addīha li-gam3iyyāt mawsūqa.

I don't give money to beggars on the street.
I prefer to donate to trusted organizations.

④

الحُكومة هتِدّينا عِلاوَة على مُرتّباتْنا أوّل شهْر سبْعة.

ilḫukūma hatiddīna 3ilāwa 3ála murattabátna ʔáwwil šahrᵊ sáb3a.

The government will give us a raise in
our salaries on the first of July.

⑤

إدّيْنا حقِّنا في الوِرْث بدل ما نِرْفع عليْك قضية.

iddēna ḫaʔʔína fi -lwirsᵊ bádal ma nírfa3 3alēk ʔaḍíyya.

Give us our share of the inheritance,
or else we will sue you.

⑥

أنا لِسّه مِدِّيّاك فِلوس إمْبارِح. لِحِقْت خلّصْتها؟

ána líssa middiyyāk filūs imbāriḫ. liḫíʔtᵊ xallaṣtáha?

I just gave you money yesterday. You
managed to spend it all already?

❖ [i2] **to give (to** لِ *li-*)

- This verb takes two objects, direct and indirect. An indirect object noun takes the preposition لِ *li-* (➲ 35.3).
- If the indirect object is a pronoun, it appears as a (direct) object pronoun suffix on the verb. (➲ 35.1, 31.4, 31.5, 31.6)
- Note that some idiomatic expressions may not follow the rules above. (➲ 35.2)

➲ 93.2, 205.5

36 to relax *irtāḫ* ارْتاح

	affirmative		negative		
ána	*irtáḫt*	اِرْتَحْت	*ma-rtáḫtiš*	مَرْتَحْتِش	perfect
íḫna	*irtáḫna*	اِرْتَحْنا	*ma-rtaḫnāš*	مَرْتَحْناش	
ínta	*irtáḫt*	اِرْتَحْت	*ma-rtáḫtiš*	مَرْتَحْتِش	
ínti	*irtáḫti*	اِرْتَحْتي	*ma-rtaḫtīš*	مَرْتَحْتيش	
íntu	*irtáḫtu*	اِرْتَحْتوا	*ma-rtaḫtūš*	مَرْتَحْتوش	
húwwa	*irtāḫ*	اِرْتاح	*ma-rtáḫš*	مَرْتاحْش	
híyya	*irtāḫit*	اِرْتاحِت	*ma-rtaḫítš*	مَرْتاحِتْش	
húmma	*irtāḫu*	اِرْتاحوا	*ma-rtaḫūš*	مَرْتاحوش	
ána	*artāḫ*	أَرْتاح	*ma-rtáḫš*	مَرْتاحْش	imperfect
íḫna	*nirtāḫ*	نِرْتاح	*ma-nirtáḫš*	مَنِرْتاحْش	
ínta	*tirtāḫ*	تِرْتاح	*ma-tirtáḫš*	مَتِرْتاحْش	
ínti	*tirtāḫi*	تِرْتاحي	*ma-tirtaḫīš*	مَتِرْتاحيش	
íntu	*tirtāḫu*	تِرْتاحوا	*ma-tirtaḫūš*	مَتِرْتاحوش	
húwwa	*yirtāḫ*	يِرْتاح	*ma-yirtáḫš*	مَيِرْتاحْش	
híyya	*tirtāḫ*	تِرْتاح	*ma-tirtáḫš*	مَتِرْتاحْش	
húmma	*yirtāḫu*	يِرْتاحوا	*ma-yirtaḫūš*	مَيِرْتاحوش	
ána	*bartāḫ*	بَرْتاح	*ma-bartáḫš*	مَبَرْتاحْش	bi-imperfect
íḫna	*binirtāḫ*	بِنِرْتاح	*ma-bnirtáḫš*	مَبْنِرْتاحْش	
ínta	*bitirtāḫ*	بِتِرْتاح	*ma-btirtáḫš*	مَبْتِرْتاحْش	
ínti	*bitirtāḫi*	بِتِرْتاحي	*ma-btirtaḫīš*	مَبْتِرْتاحيش	
íntu	*bitirtāḫu*	بِتِرْتاحوا	*ma-btirtaḫūš*	مَبْتِرْتاحوش	
húwwa	*biyirtāḫ*	بِيِرْتاح	*ma-byirtáḫš*	مَبْيِرْتاحْش	
híyya	*bitirtāḫ*	بِتِرْتاح	*ma-btirtáḫš*	مَبْتِرْتاحْش	
húmma	*biyirtāḫu*	بِيِرْتاحوا	*ma-byirtaḫūš*	مَبْيِرْتاحوش	
ána	*hartāḫ*	هَرْتاح	*miš hartāḫ*	مِش هَرْتاح	future
íḫna	*hanirtāḫ*	هَنِرْتاح	*miš hanirtāḫ*	مِش هَنِرْتاح	
ínta	*hatirtāḫ*	هَتِرْتاح	*miš hatirtāḫ*	مِش هَتِرْتاح	
ínti	*hatirtāḫi*	هَتِرْتاحي	*miš hatirtāḫi*	مِش هَتِرْتاحي	
íntu	*hatirtāḫu*	هَتِرْتاحوا	*miš hatirtāḫu*	مِش هَتِرْتاحوا	
húwwa	*hayirtāḫ*	هَيِرْتاح	*miš hayirtāḫ*	مِش هَيِرْتاح	
híyya	*hatirtāḫ*	هَتِرْتاح	*miš hatirtāḫ*	مِش هَتِرْتاح	
húmma	*hayirtāḫu*	هَيِرْتاحوا	*miš hayirtāḫu*	مِش هَيِرْتاحوا	
ínta	*irtāḫ*	اِرْتاح	*ma-tirtáḫš*	مَتِرْتاحْش	imperative
ínti	*irtāḫi*	اِرْتاحي	*ma-tirtaḫīš*	مَتِرْتاحيش	
íntu	*irtāḫu*	اِرْتاحوا	*ma-tirtaḫūš*	مَتِرْتاحوش	

	active		passive		
masculine	*mirtāḫ*	مِرْتاح	–	–	participles
feminine	*mirtāḫa*	مِرْتاحَة	–	–	
plural	*mirtaḫīn*	مِرْتاحين	–	–	

verbal nouns: *irtiyāḫ* اِرْتِياح - *rāḫa* راحَة

①

عبْد الله ارْتاح في شُغْلُه الجِديد مِن أوِّل ما راح.

3abdálla -rtāḫ fi šúɣlu -lgidīd min áwwil ma rāḫ.

Abdullah felt comfortable at his new job ever since he arrived.

②

إحْساس جميل لمّا الواحِد يِـرتاح بعْد تعب.

iḫsās gamīl lámma -lwāḫid yirtāḫ ba3dᵊ tá3ab.

It's a nice feeling when you rest after working hard.

③

أحْمد بِيِـرتاح في الكلام معَ شُروق. بِيِعْتبِـرها أعزّ أصْدِقاؤُه.

áḫmad biyirtāḫ fi -lkalām má3a šurūʔ. biyi3tibírha ʔa3ázz aṣdiqāʔu.

Ahmed feels comfortable talking to Shorouk. He considers her his best friend.

④

مِن كُتْر تعبْها مِن المرض، الواحِد بِيْقول هتِـرتاح لمّا تمْوت.

min kutrᵊ ta3ábha min ilmáraḍ, ilwāḫid biyʔūl hatirtāḫ lámma tmūt.

Because she is suffering a lot in her illness, they say she'll be relieved by death.

⑤

اِرْتاحي شْوَيّة. إنْتي واقْفة في المطْبخ مِ الصُّبْح.

irtāḫi šwáyya. ínti wáʔfa fi -lmáṭbax mi -ṣṣubḫ.

Relax a little. You've been standing in the kitchen since morning.

⑥

أنا مِش مِرْتاح لِلرّاجِل ده، شكْلُه مُريب.

ána miš mirtāḫ li-rrāgil da, šáklu murīb.

I don't feel comfortable with this man. He looks suspicious.

⑦

مرْتحْتِش في البيْت مِن يوْم ما رْجِعْت مِ السّفر.

ma-rtáḫtiš fi -lbēt min yōm ma rgi3tᵊ mi -ssáfar.

I haven't relaxed at home since I got back from traveling.

❖ [8h] **to relax, rest; feel comfortable, feel relieved**

➲ 201.5, 208.3, 221.5

37 to endure istáħmil اِسْتَحْمِل

verbal nouns: taħámmul تَحَمُّل - iħtimāl اِحْتِمال

	affirmative		negative		
ána	istaħmílt	اِسْتَحْمِلْت	ma-staħmíltiš	مَسْتَحْمِلْتِش	perfect
íħna	istaħmílna	اِسْتَحْمِلْنا	ma-staħmilnāš	مَسْتَحْمِلْناش	
ínta	istaħmílt	اِسْتَحْمِلْت	ma-staħmíltiš	مَسْتَحْمِلْتِش	
ínti	istaħmílti	اِسْتَحْمِلْتي	ma-staħmiltīš	مَسْتَحْمِلْتيش	
íntu	istaħmíltu	اِسْتَحْمِلْتوا	ma-staħmiltūš	مَسْتَحْمِلْتوش	
húwwa	istáħmil	اِسْتَحْمِل	ma-staħmílš	مَسْتَحْمِلْش	
híyya	istaħmílit	اِسْتَحْمِلِت	ma-staħmilítš	مَسْتَحْمِلِتْش	
húmma	istaħmílu	اِسْتَحْمِلوا	ma-staħmilūš	مَسْتَحْمِلوش	
ána	astáħmil	أَسْتَحْمِل	ma-staħmílš	مَسْتَحْمِلْش	imperfect
íħna	nistáħmil	نِسْتَحْمِل	ma-nistaħmílš	مَنِسْتَحْمِلْش	
ínta	tistáħmil	تِسْتَحْمِل	ma-tistaħmílš	مَتِسْتَحْمِلْش	
ínti	tistaħmíli	تِسْتَحْمِلي	ma-tistaħmilīš	مَتِسْتَحْمِليش	
íntu	tistaħmílu	تِسْتَحْمِلوا	ma-tistaħmilūš	مَتِسْتَحْمِلوش	
húwwa	yistáħmil	يِسْتَحْمِل	ma-yistaħmílš	مَيِسْتَحْمِلْش	
híyya	tistáħmil	تِسْتَحْمِل	ma-tistaħmílš	مَتِسْتَحْمِلْش	
húmma	yistaħmílu	يِسْتَحْمِلوا	ma-yistaħmilūš	مَيِسْتَحْمِلوش	
ána	bastáħmil	بَسْتَحْمِل	ma-bastaħmílš	مَبَسْتَحْمِلْش	bi-imperfect
íħna	binistáħmil	بِنِسْتَحْمِل	ma-bnistaħmílš	مَبْنِسْتَحْمِلْش	
ínta	bitistáħmil	بِتِسْتَحْمِل	ma-btistaħmílš	مَبْتِسْتَحْمِلْش	
ínti	bitistaħmíli	بِتِسْتَحْمِلي	ma-btistaħmilīš	مَبْتِسْتَحْمِليش	
íntu	bitistaħmílu	بِتِسْتَحْمِلوا	ma-btistaħmilūš	مَبْتِسْتَحْمِلوش	
húwwa	biyistáħmil	بِيِسْتَحْمِل	ma-byistaħmílš	مَبْيِسْتَحْمِلْش	
híyya	bitistáħmil	بِتِسْتَحْمِل	ma-btistaħmílš	مَبْتِسْتَحْمِلْش	
húmma	biyistaħmílu	بِيِسْتَحْمِلوا	ma-byistaħmilūš	مَبْيِسْتَحْمِلوش	
ána	hastáħmil	هَسْتَحْمِل	miš hastáħmil	مِش هَسْتَحْمِل	future
íħna	hanistáħmil	هَنِسْتَحْمِل	miš hanistáħmil	مِش هَنِسْتَحْمِل	
ínta	hatistáħmil	هَتِسْتَحْمِل	miš hatistáħmil	مِش هَتِسْتَحْمِل	
ínti	hatistaħmíli	هَتِسْتَحْمِلي	miš hatistaħmíli	مِش هَتِسْتَحْمِلي	
íntu	hatistaħmílu	هَتِسْتَحْمِلوا	miš hatistaħmílu	مِش هَتِسْتَحْمِلوا	
húwwa	hayistáħmil	هَيِسْتَحْمِل	miš hayistáħmil	مِش هَيِسْتَحْمِل	
híyya	hatistáħmil	هَتِسْتَحْمِل	miš hatistáħmil	مِش هَتِسْتَحْمِل	
húmma	hayistaħmílu	هَيِسْتَحْمِلوا	miš hayistaħmílu	مِش هَيِسْتَحْمِلوا	
ínta	istáħmil	اِسْتَحْمِل	ma-tistaħmílš	مَتِسْتَحْمِلْش	imperative
ínti	istaħmíli	اِسْتَحْمِلي	ma-tistaħmilīš	مَتِسْتَحْمِليش	
íntu	istaħmílu	اِسْتَحْمِلوا	ma-tistaħmilūš	مَتِسْتَحْمِلوش	

	active		passive		
masculine	mistáħmil	مِسْتَحْمِل	muħtámal	مُحْتَمَل	participles
feminine	mistaħmíla	مِسْتَحْمِلَة	muħtamála	مُحْتَمَلَة	
plural	mistaħmilīn	مِسْتَحْمِلين	muħtamalīn	مُحْتَمَلين	

①

ناريمان اِسْتحْمِلِت خطيبْها كْتير قبْل ما تْسيبُه.

narimān istaḫmílit xaṭíbha ktīr ʔablᵊ ma tsību.

Nariman put up with her fiancé for a long time before she left him.

②

يا ربّ ساعِدْنا نِسْتحْمِل الحرّ في رمضان.

ya rabb, sa3ídna nistáḫmil ilḫárrᵊ f ramaḍān.

Please, God, help us endure the hot weather during Ramadan.

③

أميرة مبْتِسْتحْمِلْش الحرّ. في الصّيْف بِتِفْضل في السّاحِل.

amīra ma-btistaḫmílš ilḫárr. fi -ṣṣēf bitífḍal fi -ssāḫil.

Amira can't stand the heat. She stays on the coast all summer.

④

أنا مُتأكِّدة إِنُّه مِش هَيِسْتحْمِل العيْشة برّه لِوَحْدُه.

ána muta?akkída ?ínnu miš hayistáḫmil il3ēša bárra li-wáḫdu.

I'm sure he won't be able to stand living abroad alone.

⑤

متِسْتحْمِلْش النّاس السّخيفة. إدّيهُم على دْماغْهُم علشان يِبطّلوا.

ma-tistaḫmílš innās issaxīfa. iddīhum 3ála dmáyhum 3alašān yibaṭṭálu.

Don't put up with idiotic people. Just kick their butts, and they will stop.

⑥

طلّقْني. أنا مِسْتحْمِلاك بقالي كْتير و خلاص مِش قادْرة.

ṭallá?ni. ána mistaḫmilāk ba?āli ktīr wi xalāṣ miš ?ádra.

I want a divorce! I've put up with you for too long, and I can't anymore.

❖ [10s1] **to put up with, endure, stand, bear**

- The verbal nouns are borrowed from synonymous verbs.
- The passive participle is borrowed from the synonymous verb اِحْتمل *iḫtámal*.

➲ 16.3, 171.2

38 to bathe *istaħámma* اِسْتَحَمَّى

	affirmative		negative		
ána	*istaħammēt*	اِسْتَحَمّيْت	*ma-staħammítš*	مَسْتَحَمّيْتْش	perfect
íħna	*istaħammēna*	اِسْتَحَمّيْنا	*ma-staħamminā́š*	مَسْتَحَمّيناش	
ínta	*istaħammēt*	اِسْتَحَمّيْت	*ma-staħammítš*	مَسْتَحَمّيْتْش	
ínti	*istaħammēti*	اِسْتَحَمّيْتي	*ma-staħammitī́š*	مَسْتَحَمّيتيش	
íntu	*istaħammētu*	اِسْتَحَمّيْتوا	*ma-staħammitū́š*	مَسْتَحَمّيتوش	
húwwa	*istaħámma*	اِسْتَحَمَّى	*ma-staħammā́š*	مَسْتَحَمّاش	
híyya	*istaħámmit*	اِسْتَحَمِّت	*ma-staħammítš*	مَسْتَحَمِّتْش	
húmma	*istaħámmu*	اِسْتَحَمّوا	*ma-staħammū́š*	مَسْتَحَمّوش	
ána	*astaħámma*	أَسْتَحَمَّى	*ma-staħammā́š*	مَسْتَحَمّاش	imperfect
íħna	*nistaħámma*	نِسْتَحَمَّى	*ma-nistaħammā́š*	مَنِسْتَحَمّاش	
ínta	*tistaħámma*	تِسْتَحَمَّى	*ma-tistaħammā́š*	مَتِسْتَحَمّاش	
ínti	*tistaħámmi*	تِسْتَحَمّي	*ma-tistaħammī́š*	مَتِسْتَحَمّيش	
íntu	*tistaħámmu*	تِسْتَحَمّوا	*ma-tistaħammū́š*	مَتِسْتَحَمّوش	
húwwa	*yistaħámma*	يِسْتَحَمَّى	*ma-yistaħammā́š*	مَيِسْتَحَمّاش	
híyya	*tistaħámma*	تِسْتَحَمَّى	*ma-tistaħammā́š*	مَتِسْتَحَمّاش	
húmma	*yistaħámmu*	يِسْتَحَمّوا	*ma-yistaħammū́š*	مَيِسْتَحَمّوش	
ána	*bastaħámma*	بَسْتَحَمَّى	*ma-bastaħammā́š*	مَبَسْتَحَمّاش	bi-imperfect
íħna	*binistaħámma*	بِنِسْتَحَمَّى	*ma-bnistaħammā́š*	مَبْنِسْتَحَمّاش	
ínta	*bitistaħámma*	بِتِسْتَحَمَّى	*ma-btistaħammā́š*	مَبْتِسْتَحَمّاش	
ínti	*bitistaħámmi*	بِتِسْتَحَمّي	*ma-btistaħammī́š*	مَبْتِسْتَحَمّيش	
íntu	*bitistaħámmu*	بِتِسْتَحَمّوا	*ma-btistaħammū́š*	مَبْتِسْتَحَمّوش	
húwwa	*biyistaħámma*	بِيِسْتَحَمَّى	*ma-byistaħammā́š*	مَبْيِسْتَحَمّاش	
híyya	*bitistaħámma*	بِتِسْتَحَمَّى	*ma-btistaħammā́š*	مَبْتِسْتَحَمّاش	
húmma	*biyistaħámmu*	بِيِسْتَحَمّوا	*ma-byistaħammū́š*	مَبْيِسْتَحَمّوش	
ána	*hastaħámma*	هَسْتَحَمَّى	*miš hastaħámma*	مِش هَسْتَحَمَّى	future
íħna	*hanistaħámma*	هَنِسْتَحَمَّى	*miš hanistaħámma*	مِش هَنِسْتَحَمَّى	
ínta	*hatistaħámma*	هَتِسْتَحَمَّى	*miš hatistaħámma*	مِش هَتِسْتَحَمَّى	
ínti	*hatistaħámmi*	هَتِسْتَحَمّي	*miš hatistaħámmi*	مِش هَتِسْتَحَمّي	
íntu	*hatistaħámmu*	هَتِسْتَحَمّوا	*miš hatistaħámmu*	مِش هَتِسْتَحَمّوا	
húwwa	*hayistaħámma*	هَيِسْتَحَمَّى	*miš hayistaħámma*	مِش هَيِسْتَحَمَّى	
híyya	*hatistaħámma*	هَتِسْتَحَمَّى	*miš hatistaħámma*	مِش هَتِسْتَحَمَّى	
húmma	*hayistaħámmu*	هَيِسْتَحَمّوا	*miš hayistaħámmu*	مِش هَيِسْتَحَمّوا	
ínta	*istaħámma*	اِسْتَحَمَّى	*ma-tistaħammā́š*	مَتِسْتَحَمّاش	imperative
ínti	*istaħámmi*	اِسْتَحَمّي	*ma-tistaħammī́š*	مَتِسْتَحَمّيش	
íntu	*istaħámmu*	اِسْتَحَمّوا	*ma-tistaħammū́š*	مَتِسْتَحَمّوش	

	active		passive		
masculine	*mistaħámmi*	مِسْتَحَمّي	–	–	participles
feminine	*mistaħammíyya*	مِسْتَحَمّيّة	–	–	
plural	*mistaħammiyīn*	مِسْتَحَمّيين	–	–	

verbal noun: *ħúma* حُما

①

اِسْتحمّيْت مِن عشر دقايِق و دِلْوَقْتي بخُرّ عرق.

istaħammēt min 3ášar daʔāyiʔ wi dilwáʔti baxúrrᵊ 3áraʔ.

I took a shower ten minutes ago,
and now I'm sweating.

②

في الصّيْف، بحِبّ أسْتحمّى كْتير.

fi -ṣṣēf, baħíbb astaħamma ktīr.

In the summer, I like to shower a lot.

③

نُهى بْتِسْتحمّى أوِّل ما تِطْلع مِ البحْر. الميّة المالْحة و الشّمْس بِيِحْرقوا جِلْدها.

núha btistaħámma ʔáwwil ma tíṭla3 mi -lbaħr. ilmáyya -lmálħa w iššámsᵊ biyiħráʔu gildáha.

Noha takes a shower as soon as she comes out of
the sea. The salty water and sun burn her skin.

④

شكْلُه مسْتحمّاش بقالُه كْتير.

šáklu ma-staħammāš baʔālu ktīr.

He looks like he hasn't
bathed in a long time.

⑤

اِسْتحمّى الصُّبْح بمِيّة ساقْعة عشان تِنشّطك.

istaħámma -ṣṣubħᵊ bi-máyya sáʔ3a 3ašān tinaššáṭak.

In the morning, take a cold
shower to energize yourself.

⑥

اِبْعِد عن التُّراب ده يا وَلد. إنْتَ لِسّه مِسْتحمّي.

íb3id 3an itturāb da ya wálad. ínta líssa mistaħámmi.

Stay away from the dust, boy.
You just took a bath.

❖ [10.2d] **to bathe, take a bath, take a shower**

- This verb can be synonymous with خد دُشّ *xad dušš*. (➲ 98.6, 201.5)

➲ 226.6

39 to use *istáxdim* اِسْتَخْدِم

	affirmative		negative		
ána	*istaxdímt*	اِسْتَخْدِمْت	*ma-staxdímtiš*	مَسْتَخْدِمْتِش	**perfect**
íḫna	*istaxdímna*	اِسْتَخْدِمْنا	*ma-staxdimnāš*	مَسْتَخْدِمْناش	
ínta	*istaxdímt*	اِسْتَخْدِمْت	*ma-staxdímtiš*	مَسْتَخْدِمْتِش	
ínti	*istaxdímti*	اِسْتَخْدِمْتي	*ma-staxdimtīš*	مَسْتَخْدِمْتيش	
íntu	*istaxdímtu*	اِسْتَخْدِمْتوا	*ma-staxdimtūš*	مَسْتَخْدِمْتوش	
húwwa	*istáxdim*	اِسْتَخْدِم	*ma-staxdímš*	مَسْتَخْدِمْش	
híyya	*istaxdímit*	اِسْتَخْدِمِت	*ma-staxdimítš*	مَسْتَخْدِمِتْش	
húmma	*istaxdímu*	اِسْتَخْدِموا	*ma-staxdimūš*	مَسْتَخْدِموش	
ána	*astáxdim*	أَسْتَخْدِم	*ma-staxdímš*	مَسْتَخْدِمْش	**imperfect**
íḫna	*nistáxdim*	نِسْتَخْدِم	*ma-nistaxdímš*	مَنِسْتَخْدِمْش	
ínta	*tistáxdim*	تِسْتَخْدِم	*ma-tistaxdímš*	مَتِسْتَخْدِمْش	
ínti	*tistaxdími*	تِسْتَخْدِمي	*ma-tistaxdimīš*	مَتِسْتَخْدِميش	
íntu	*tistaxdímu*	تِسْتَخْدِموا	*ma-tistaxdimūš*	مَتِسْتَخْدِموش	
húwwa	*yistáxdim*	يِسْتَخْدِم	*ma-yistaxdímš*	مَيِسْتَخْدِمْش	
híyya	*tistáxdim*	تِسْتَخْدِم	*ma-tistaxdímš*	مَتِسْتَخْدِمْش	
húmma	*yistaxdímu*	يِسْتَخْدِموا	*ma-yistaxdimūš*	مَيِسْتَخْدِموش	
ána	*bastáxdim*	بَسْتَخْدِم	*ma-bastaxdímš*	مَبَسْتَخْدِمْش	**bi-imperfect**
íḫna	*binistáxdim*	بِنِسْتَخْدِم	*ma-bnistaxdímš*	مَبْنِسْتَخْدِمْش	
ínta	*bitistáxdim*	بِتِسْتَخْدِم	*ma-btistaxdímš*	مَبْتِسْتَخْدِمْش	
ínti	*bitistaxdími*	بِتِسْتَخْدِمي	*ma-btistaxdimīš*	مَبْتِسْتَخْدِميش	
íntu	*bitistaxdímu*	بِتِسْتَخْدِموا	*ma-btistaxdimūš*	مَبْتِسْتَخْدِموش	
húwwa	*biyistáxdim*	بِيِسْتَخْدِم	*ma-byistaxdímš*	مَبْيِسْتَخْدِمْش	
híyya	*bitistáxdim*	بِتِسْتَخْدِم	*ma-btistaxdímš*	مَبْتِسْتَخْدِمْش	
húmma	*biyistaxdímu*	بِيِسْتَخْدِموا	*ma-byistaxdimūš*	مَبْيِسْتَخْدِموش	
ána	*hastáxdim*	هَسْتَخْدِم	*miš hastáxdim*	مِش هَسْتَخْدِم	**future**
íḫna	*hanistáxdim*	هَنِسْتَخْدِم	*miš hanistáxdim*	مِش هَنِسْتَخْدِم	
ínta	*hatistáxdim*	هَتِسْتَخْدِم	*miš hatistáxdim*	مِش هَتِسْتَخْدِم	
ínti	*hatistaxdími*	هَتِسْتَخْدِمي	*miš hatistaxdími*	مِش هَتِسْتَخْدِمي	
íntu	*hatistaxdímu*	هَتِسْتَخْدِموا	*miš hatistaxdímu*	مِش هَتِسْتَخْدِموا	
húwwa	*hayistáxdim*	هَيِسْتَخْدِم	*miš hayistáxdim*	مِش هَيِسْتَخْدِم	
híyya	*hatistáxdim*	هَتِسْتَخْدِم	*miš hatistáxdim*	مِش هَتِسْتَخْدِم	
húmma	*hayistaxdímu*	هَيِسْتَخْدِموا	*miš hayistaxdímu*	مِش هَيِسْتَخْدِموا	
ínta	*istáxdim*	اِسْتَخْدِم	*ma-tistaxdímš*	مَتِسْتَخْدِمْش	**imperative**
ínti	*istaxdími*	اِسْتَخْدِمي	*ma-tistaxdimīš*	مَتِسْتَخْدِميش	
íntu	*istaxdímu*	اِسْتَخْدِموا	*ma-tistaxdimūš*	مَتِسْتَخْدِموش	
	active		**passive**		
masculine	*mistáxdim*	مِسْتَخْدِم	*mustáxdam*	مُسْتَخْدَم	**participles**
feminine	*mistaxdíma*	مِسْتَخْدِمَة	*mustaxdáma*	مُسْتَخْدَمَة	
plural	*mistaxdimīn*	مِسْتَخْدِمين	*mustaxdamīn*	مُسْتَخْدَمين	

verbal noun: *istixdām* إِسْتِخْدام

①

اِسْتخْدِمْت كارْت الفيزا بْتاعي عشان أدْفع الحِساب. مكانْش معايا كاش.

istaxdímtᵊ kart ilvīza btā3i 3ašān ádfa3 ilḩisāb. ma-kánšᵊ ma3āya kāš.

I used my Visa card to pay the bill. I didn't have cash on me.

②

وَجيهْ دايْماً يِسْتخْدِم سِحْرُه عشان يِكْسب.

wagīh dáyman yistáxdim síḩru 3ašān yíksab.

Wagih always uses his charm to win.

③

بسْتخْدِم الزّبادي بدل المايونيْز، عشان مِحْتاجة أخِسّ.

bastáxdim izzabādi bádal ilmayunēz, 3ašān miḩtāga ʔaxíss.

I use yogurt instead of mayonnaise
because I need to lose some weight.

④

هسْتخْدِم شامْبو طِبّي لِشعْري عشان عنْدي قِشْرة.

hastáxdim šámbu ţíbbi li-šá3ri 3ašān 3ándi ʔíšra.

I will use a medical shampoo for
my hair since I have dandruff.

⑤

اِسْتخْدِموا الألات الحاسْبة في الحِسابات المُعقّدة بسّ.

istaxdímu -lʔalāt ilḩásba fi -lḩisabāt ilmu3aqqáda bass.

Use calculators for complex equations only.

⑥

إنْتَ مِسْتخْدِم أنْهي بِرنامِج في رسْم البوْسْتر ده؟

ínta mistáxdim ánhi biranāmig fi rasm ilbústar da?

Which program did you use to draw this poster?

⑦

ليْه متِسْتخْدِمْش قلم رُصاص بدل القلم الجافّ؟

lē ma-tistaxdímšᵊ ʔálam ruşāş bádal ilʔálam ilgáff?

Why don't you use a pencil instead of a pen?

❖ [10s1] **to use**

- This verb is synonymous with اِسْتعْمِل *istá3mil.* (➲ 40)

➲ 217.6

40 to use istá3mil اِسْتَعْمِل

	affirmative		negative		
ána	ista3mílt	اِسْتَعْمِلْت	ma-sta3míltiš	مَسْتَعْمِلْتِش	perfect
íḫna	ista3mílna	اِسْتَعْمِلْنا	ma-sta3milnāš	مَسْتَعْمِلْناش	
ínta	ista3mílt	اِسْتَعْمِلْت	ma-sta3míltiš	مَسْتَعْمِلْتِش	
ínti	ista3mílti	اِسْتَعْمِلْتي	ma-sta3miltīš	مَسْتَعْمِلْتيش	
íntu	ista3míltu	اِسْتَعْمِلْتوا	ma-sta3miltūš	مَسْتَعْمِلْتوش	
húwwa	istá3mil	اِسْتَعْمِل	ma-sta3mílš	مَسْتَعْمِلْش	
híyya	ista3mílit	اِسْتَعْمِلِت	ma-sta3milítš	مَسْتَعْمِلِتْش	
húmma	ista3mílu	اِسْتَعْمِلوا	ma-sta3milūš	مَسْتَعْمِلوش	
ána	astá3mil	أَسْتَعْمِل	ma-sta3mílš	مَسْتَعْمِلْش	imperfect
íḫna	nistá3mil	نِسْتَعْمِل	ma-nista3mílš	مَنِسْتَعْمِلْش	
ínta	tistá3mil	تِسْتَعْمِل	ma-tista3mílš	مَتِسْتَعْمِلْش	
ínti	tista3míli	تِسْتَعْمِلي	ma-tista3milīš	مَتِسْتَعْمِليش	
íntu	tista3mílu	تِسْتَعْمِلوا	ma-tista3milūš	مَتِسْتَعْمِلوش	
húwwa	yistá3mil	يِسْتَعْمِل	ma-yista3mílš	مَيِسْتَعْمِلْش	
híyya	tistá3mil	تِسْتَعْمِل	ma-tista3mílš	مَتِسْتَعْمِلْش	
húmma	yista3mílu	يِسْتَعْمِلوا	ma-yista3milūš	مَيِسْتَعْمِلوش	
ána	bastá3mil	بَسْتَعْمِل	ma-basta3mílš	مَبَسْتَعْمِلْش	bi-imperfect
íḫna	binistá3mil	بِنِسْتَعْمِل	ma-bnista3mílš	مَبْنِسْتَعْمِلْش	
ínta	bitistá3mil	بِتِسْتَعْمِل	ma-btista3mílš	مَبْتِسْتَعْمِلْش	
ínti	bitista3míli	بِتِسْتَعْمِلي	ma-btista3milīš	مَبْتِسْتَعْمِليش	
íntu	bitista3mílu	بِتِسْتَعْمِلوا	ma-btista3milūš	مَبْتِسْتَعْمِلوش	
húwwa	biyistá3mil	بِيِسْتَعْمِل	ma-byista3mílš	مَبْيِسْتَعْمِلْش	
híyya	bitistá3mil	بِتِسْتَعْمِل	ma-btista3mílš	مَبْتِسْتَعْمِلْش	
húmma	biyista3mílu	بِيِسْتَعْمِلوا	ma-byista3milūš	مَبْيِسْتَعْمِلوش	
ána	hastá3mil	هَسْتَعْمِل	miš hastá3mil	مِش هَسْتَعْمِل	future
íḫna	hanistá3mil	هَنِسْتَعْمِل	miš hanistá3mil	مِش هَنِسْتَعْمِل	
ínta	hatistá3mil	هَتِسْتَعْمِل	miš hatistá3mil	مِش هَتِسْتَعْمِل	
ínti	hatista3míli	هَتِسْتَعْمِلي	miš hatista3míli	مِش هَتِسْتَعْمِلي	
íntu	hatista3mílu	هَتِسْتَعْمِلوا	miš hatista3mílu	مِش هَتِسْتَعْمِلوا	
húwwa	hayistá3mil	هَيِسْتَعْمِل	miš hayistá3mil	مِش هَيِسْتَعْمِل	
híyya	hatistá3mil	هَتِسْتَعْمِل	miš hatistá3mil	مِش هَتِسْتَعْمِل	
húmma	hayista3mílu	هَيِسْتَعْمِلوا	miš hayista3mílu	مِش هَيِسْتَعْمِلوا	
ínta	istá3mil	اِسْتَعْمِل	ma-tista3mílš	مَتِسْتَعْمِلْش	imperative
ínti	ista3míli	اِسْتَعْمِلي	ma-tista3milīš	مَتِسْتَعْمِليش	
íntu	ista3mílu	اِسْتَعْمِلوا	ma-tista3milūš	مَتِسْتَعْمِلوش	

	active		passive		
masculine	mistá3mil	مِسْتَعْمِل	mustá3mal	مُسْتَعْمَل	participles
feminine	mista3míla	مِسْتَعْمِلَة	musta3mála	مُسْتَعْمَلَة	
plural	mista3milīn	مِسْتَعْمِلين	musta3malīn	مُسْتَعْمَلين	

verbal noun: isti3māl اِسْتِعْمال

①

محمّد اِسْتعْمِل ذكاؤُه عشان يُخْرُج مِ المُشْكِلة الصّعْبة دي.

maђámmad istá3mil zakāʔu 3ašān yúxrug mi -lmuškíla -ṣṣá3ba di.

Mohamed used his brain to get out of that difficult problem.

②

مُمْكِن أسْتعْمِل الصّلْصة عَ المكروْنة لَوْ معنْديش طماطِم.

múmkin astá3mil iṣṣálṣa 3a -lmakarōna law ma-3andīš ṭamāṭim.

I can use sauce for the pasta if I don't have tomatoes.

③

قُليِّلين النّاس اللي لِسّه بِيِسْتعْمِلوا التِّليفوْن الأرْضي في القاهِرة.

ʔulayyilīn innās ílli líssa biyista3mílu -ttilifōn ilʔárḍi fi -lqāhíra.

There aren't many people who still use a landline in Cairo.

④

هَيِسْتعْمِلوا الجِنيْه الوَرق تاني.

haysta3mílu -lginēh ilwáraʔ tāni.

They will use the paper pound again.

⑤

اِسْتعْمِلي الكِتاب بِتاعي. أنا خلّصْت مُذاكْرة فيه.

ista3míli -lkitāb bitā3i. ána xalláṣtᵊ muzákra fī.

Use my book. I finished studying it.

⑥

هشْتِـري عربية مُسْتعْملة . أنا معيش فِلوس أجيب واحْدة جْديدة.

haštíri 3arabíyya musta3mála. ána ma-3īš filūs agīb wáђda gdīda.

I'm going to buy a used car. I don't have money to get a new one.

⑦

أنا مِسْتعْمِلْتِش الجزْمة دي وَلا مرّة. مِش مُريحاني.

ána mista3míltiš ilgázma di wála márra. miš muriђāni.

I haven't worn [lit. used] this pair of shoes even once. They're not comfortable for me.

❖ [10s1] **to use**

- This verb is synonymous with اِسْتخْدِم *istáxdim.* (➲ 39)

➲ 55.5

41 to do without *istáɣna* اِسْتَغْنَى

verbal nouns: *istíɣna* اِسْتِغْنا - *ɣína* غِنا

	affirmative		negative		
ána	*istaɣnēt*	اِسْتَغْنيْت	*ma-staɣnítš*	مَسْتَغْنيتْش	perfect
íḫna	*istaɣnēna*	اِسْتَغْنيْنا	*ma-staɣninā̄š*	مَسْتَغْنيناش	
ínta	*istaɣnēt*	اِسْتَغْنيْت	*ma-staɣnítš*	مَسْتَغْنيتْش	
ínti	*istaɣnēti*	اِسْتَغْنيْتي	*ma-staɣnitīš*	مَسْتَغْنيتيش	
íntu	*istaɣnētu*	اِسْتَغْنيْتوا	*ma-staɣnitūš*	مَسْتَغْنيتوش	
húwwa	*istáɣna*	اِسْتَغْنَى	*ma-staɣnāš*	مَسْتَغْناش	
híyya	*istáɣnit*	اِسْتَغْنِت	*ma-staɣnítš*	مَسْتَغْنِتْش	
húmma	*istáɣnu*	اِسْتَغْنوا	*ma-staɣnūš*	مَسْتَغْنوش	
ána	*astáɣna*	أَسْتَغْنَى	*ma-staɣnāš*	مَسْتَغْناش	imperfect
íḫna	*nistáɣna*	نِسْتَغْنَى	*ma-nistaɣnāš*	مَنِسْتَغْناش	
ínta	*tistáɣna*	تِسْتَغْنَى	*ma-tistaɣnāš*	مَتِسْتَغْناش	
ínti	*tistáɣni*	تِسْتَغْني	*ma-tistaɣnīš*	مَتِسْتَغْنيش	
íntu	*tistáɣnu*	تِسْتَغْنوا	*ma-tistaɣnūš*	مَتِسْتَغْنوش	
húwwa	*yistáɣna*	يِسْتَغْنَى	*ma-yistaɣnāš*	مَيِسْتَغْناش	
híyya	*tistáɣna*	تِسْتَغْنَى	*ma-tistaɣnāš*	مَتِسْتَغْناش	
húmma	*yistáɣnu*	يِسْتَغْنوا	*ma-yistaɣnūš*	مَيِسْتَغْنوش	
ána	*bastáɣna*	بَسْتَغْنَى	*ma-bastaɣnāš*	مَبَسْتَغْناش	bi-imperfect
íḫna	*binistáɣna*	بِنِسْتَغْنَى	*ma-bnistaɣnāš*	مَبْنِسْتَغْناش	
ínta	*bitistáɣna*	بِتِسْتَغْنَى	*ma-btistaɣnāš*	مَبْتِسْتَغْناش	
ínti	*bitistáɣni*	بِتِسْتَغْني	*ma-btistaɣnīš*	مَبْتِسْتَغْنيش	
íntu	*bitistáɣnu*	بِتِسْتَغْنوا	*ma-btistaɣnūš*	مَبْتِسْتَغْنوش	
húwwa	*biyistáɣna*	بِيِسْتَغْنَى	*ma-byistaɣnāš*	مَبْيِسْتَغْناش	
híyya	*bitistáɣna*	بِتِسْتَغْنَى	*ma-btistaɣnāš*	مَبْتِسْتَغْناش	
húmma	*biyistáɣnu*	بِيِسْتَغْنوا	*ma-byistaɣnūš*	مَبْيِسْتَغْنوش	
ána	*hastáɣna*	هَسْتَغْنَى	*miš hastáɣna*	مِش هَسْتَغْنَى	future
íḫna	*hanistáɣna*	هَنِسْتَغْنَى	*miš hanistáɣna*	مِش هَنِسْتَغْنَى	
ínta	*hatistáɣna*	هَتِسْتَغْنَى	*miš hatistáɣna*	مِش هَتِسْتَغْنَى	
ínti	*hatistáɣni*	هَتِسْتَغْني	*miš hatistáɣni*	مِش هَتِسْتَغْني	
íntu	*hatistáɣnu*	هَتِسْتَغْنوا	*miš hatistáɣnu*	مِش هَتِسْتَغْنوا	
húwwa	*hayistáɣna*	هَيِسْتَغْنَى	*miš hayistáɣna*	مِش هَيِسْتَغْنَى	
híyya	*hatistáɣna*	هَتِسْتَغْنَى	*miš hatistáɣna*	مِش هَتِسْتَغْنَى	
húmma	*hayistáɣnu*	هَيِسْتَغْنوا	*miš hayistáɣnu*	مِش هَيِسْتَغْنوا	
ínta	*istáɣna*	اِسْتَغْنَى	*ma-tistaɣnāš*	مَتِسْتَغْناش	imperative
ínti	*istáɣni*	اِسْتَغْني	*ma-tistaɣnīš*	مَتِسْتَغْنيش	
íntu	*istáɣnu*	اِسْتَغْنوا	*ma-tistaɣnūš*	مَتِسْتَغْنوش	

	active		passive		
masculine	*mistáɣni*	مِسْتَغْني	–	–	participles
feminine	*mistaɣníyya*	مِسْتَغْنيَّة	–	–	
plural	*mistaɣniyīn*	مِسْتَغْنيين	–	–	

①

أ: عايْزة حاجة يا ماما؟

ب: مسْتغْناش عنّك يا حبيبي.

A: 3áyza ḫāga ya māma?

B: ma-staɣnāš 3ánnak ya ḫabībi.

A: Do you need anything, mom?

B: No, thank you, honey.

②

مقْدرْش أسْتغْنى عن الكُتُب. القِرايَة عِشْقي.

ma-ʔdárš astáɣna 3an ilkútub. ilʔirāya 3íšʔi.

I can't live without books. Reading is my passion!

③

بسْتغْني عن السُّكّر في المشْروبات و بحُطّ بدالُه عسل نحْل.

bastáɣna 3an issúkkar fi -lmašrubāt wi baḫúṭṭ[ə] badālu 3ásal naḫl.

I've given up sugar and instead put honey in my drinks.

④

شريف هَيِسْتغْني عن عربيتُه، عشان عايِز الفِلوس يِبْتِدي مشْروع.

šarīf hayistáɣna 3an 3arabītu, 3ašān 3āyiz ilfilūs yibtídi mašrū3.

Sharif will give up his car. He needs the money to start a venture.

⑤

اللي يِسْتغْني عنّك، إسْتغْنى عنُّه.

ílli yistáɣna 3ánnak, istáɣna 3ánnu.

Whoever can live without you, you can live without, too.

⑥

هُمّا رايْحين يِتْخانْقوا معَ الفِتِوّات دوْل؟ هُمّا مِسْتغْنِيين عن عُمْرُهُم وَلّا أيْه؟

húmma rayḫīn yitxánʔu má3a -lfitiwwāt dōl? húmma mistaɣniyīn 3an 3umrúhum wálla ʔē?

Are they going to fight with these bullies? Are they suicidal or what?

❖ [10d1] **to do without, get by without, be able to live without** (عن *3an*)

- The idiom مسْتغْناش عنّك *ma-staɣnāš 3ánnak* (lit. I can't do without you.) is used to show appreciation for an offer of help. (➲ 41.1)
- The idiom مِسْتغْني عن عُمْرُه *mistáɣni 3an 3úmru* (lit. to do without one's life) means 'take a big risk'.

➲ 20.3

42 to receive istálam اِسْتَلَم

verbal nouns: *istilām* اِسْتِلام - *tasállum* تَسَلُّم

	affirmative		negative		
ána	*istalámt*	اِسْتَلَمْت	*ma-stalámtiš*	مَسْتَلَمْتِش	**perfect**
íḥna	*istalámna*	اِسْتَلَمْنا	*ma-stalamnāš*	مَسْتَلَمْناش	
ínta	*istalámt*	اِسْتَلَمْت	*ma-stalámtiš*	مَسْتَلَمْتِش	
ínti	*istalámti*	اِسْتَلَمْتي	*ma-stalamtīš*	مَسْتَلَمْتيش	
íntu	*istalámtu*	اِسْتَلَمْتوا	*ma-stalamtūš*	مَسْتَلَمْتوش	
húwwa	*istálam*	اِسْتَلَم	*ma-stalámš*	مَسْتَلَمْش	
híyya	*istálamit*	اِسْتَلَمِت	*ma-stalamítš*	مَسْتَلَمِتْش	
húmma	*istálamu*	اِسْتَلَموا	*ma-stalamūš*	مَسْتَلَموش	
ána	*astílim*	أَسْتِلِم	*ma-stilímš*	مَسْتِلِمْش	**imperfect**
íḥna	*nistílim*	نِسْتِلِم	*ma-nistilímš*	مَنِسْتِلِمْش	
ínta	*tistílim*	تِسْتِلِم	*ma-tistilímš*	مَتِسْتِلِمْش	
ínti	*tistílmi*	تِسْتِلْمي	*ma-tistilmīš*	مَتِسْتِلْميش	
íntu	*tistílmu*	تِسْتِلْموا	*ma-tistilmūš*	مَتِسْتِلْموش	
húwwa	*yistílim*	يِسْتِلِم	*ma-yistilímš*	مَيِسْتِلِمْش	
híyya	*tistílim*	تِسْتِلِم	*ma-tistilímš*	مَتِسْتِلِمْش	
húmma	*yistílmu*	يِسْتِلْموا	*ma-yistilmūš*	مَيِسْتِلْموش	
ána	*bastílim*	بَسْتِلِم	*ma-bastilímš*	مَبَسْتِلِمْش	**bi-imperfect**
íḥna	*binistílim*	بِنِسْتِلِم	*ma-bnistilímš*	مَبْنِسْتِلِمْش	
ínta	*bitistílim*	بِتِسْتِلِم	*ma-btistilímš*	مَبْتِسْتِلِمْش	
ínti	*bitistílmi*	بِتِسْتِلْمي	*ma-btistilmīš*	مَبْتِسْتِلْميش	
íntu	*bitistílmu*	بِتِسْتِلْموا	*ma-btistilmūš*	مَبْتِسْتِلْموش	
húwwa	*biyistílim*	بِيِسْتِلِم	*ma-byistilímš*	مَبْيِسْتِلِمْش	
híyya	*bitistílim*	بِتِسْتِلِم	*ma-btistilímš*	مَبْتِسْتِلِمْش	
húmma	*biyistílmu*	بِيِسْتِلْموا	*ma-byistilmūš*	مَبْيِسْتِلْموش	
ána	*hastílim*	هَسْتِلِم	*miš hastílim*	مِش هَسْتِلِم	**future**
íḥna	*hanistílim*	هَنِسْتِلِم	*miš hanistílim*	مِش هَنِسْتِلِم	
ínta	*hatistílim*	هَتِسْتِلِم	*miš hatistílim*	مِش هَتِسْتِلِم	
ínti	*hatistílmi*	هَتِسْتِلْمي	*miš hatistílmi*	مِش هَتِسْتِلْمي	
íntu	*hatistílmu*	هَتِسْتِلْموا	*miš hatistílmu*	مِش هَتِسْتِلْموا	
húwwa	*hayistílim*	هَيِسْتِلِم	*miš hayistílim*	مِش هَيِسْتِلِم	
híyya	*hatistílim*	هَتِسْتِلِم	*miš hatistílim*	مِش هَتِسْتِلِم	
húmma	*hayistílmu*	هَيِسْتِلْموا	*miš hayistílmu*	مِش هَيِسْتِلْموا	
ínta	*istílim*	اِسْتِلِم	*ma-tistilímš*	مَتِسْتِلِمْش	**imperative**
ínti	*istílmi*	اِسْتِلْمي	*ma-tistilmīš*	مَتِسْتِلْميش	
íntu	*istílmu*	اِسْتِلْموا	*ma-tistilmūš*	مَتِسْتِلْموش	

	active		passive		
masculine	*mistílim*	مِسْتِلِم	*mustálam*	مُسْتَلَم	**participles**
feminine	*mistílma*	مِسْتِلْمَة	*mustálama*	مُسْتَلَمَة	
plural	*mistilmīn*	مِسْتِلْمين	*mustalamīn*	مُسْتَلَمين	

①

الوِلاد اِسْتلموا الشّهادات مِن هِنا و نِزْلوا يِحْتِفْلوا على طول.

ilwilād istálamu -ššahadāt min hína wi nízlu yiħtíflu 3āla ţūl.

The boys received their diplomas and
went right out to celebrate.

②

رُحْنا نِسْتِلِم الجَوازات عشان نِجهِّز نفْسِنا لِلسّفر.

rúħna nistílim ilgawazāt 3ašān nigáhhiz nafsína li-ssáfar.

We went to get our passports
in preparation for traveling.

③

بِنِسْتِلِم نتايِج التّحاليل مِن المعْمل ده في نفْس اليوْم.

binistílim natāyig ittaħalīl min ilmá3mal da fi nafs ilyōm.

We receive same-day test results from that laboratory.

④

هسْتِلِم الفُسْتان يوْم الفرح الصُّبْح.

hastílim ilfustān yōm ilfáraħ iṣṣúbħ.

I will receive the dress on the
morning of the wedding day.

⑤

اِسْتِلْموا وَرقْكو مِن شِبّاك ٤.

istílmu wará?ku min šibbāk arbá3a.

Get your papers from window no. 4.

⑥

لِسّه مِسْتِلْمين العربية الجِديدة. تيجوا ناخُدْها فُسْحة؟

líssa mistilmīn il3arabíyya -lgidīda. tīgu naxúdha fúsħa?

We just got the new car. Shall we take it for a ride?

⑦

أشْرف مسْتلمْش شهادْتُه لِحدّ دِلْوَقْتي.

ášraf ma-stalámšᵊ šahádtu li-ħaddᵊ dilwá?ti.

Ashraf still hasn't received his certificate.

❖ [8s1] **to receive, obtain, get**

➲ 174.1

43 to enjoy *istámta3* اِسْتَمْتَع

verbal nouns: *istimtā3* اِسْتِمْتاع - *mút3a* مُتْعة

	affirmative		negative		
ána	*istamtá3t*	اِسْتَمْتَعْت	*ma-stamtá3tiš*	مَسْتَمْتَعْتِش	**perfect**
íḥna	*istamtá3na*	اِسْتَمْتَعْنا	*ma-stamta3nāš*	مَسْتَمْتَعْناش	
ínta	*istamtá3t*	اِسْتَمْتَعْت	*ma-stamtá3tiš*	مَسْتَمْتَعْتِش	
ínti	*istamtá3ti*	اِسْتَمْتَعْتي	*ma-stamta3tīš*	مَسْتَمْتَعْتيش	
íntu	*istamtá3tu*	اِسْتَمْتَعْتوا	*ma-stamta3tūš*	مَسْتَمْتَعْتوش	
húwwa	*istámta3*	اِسْتَمْتَع	*ma-stamtá3š*	مَسْتَمْتَعْش	
híyya	*istamtá3it*	اِسْتَمْتَعِت	*ma-stamta3ítš*	مَسْتَمْتَعِتْش	
húmma	*istamtá3u*	اِسْتَمْتَعوا	*ma-stamta3ūš*	مَسْتَمْتَعوش	
ána	*astámti3*	أَسْتَمْتِع	*ma-stamtí3š*	مَسْتَمْتِعْش	**imperfect**
íḥna	*nistámti3*	نِسْتَمْتِع	*ma-nistamtí3š*	مَنِسْتَمْتِعْش	
ínta	*tistámti3*	تِسْتَمْتِع	*ma-tistamtí3š*	مَتِسْتَمْتِعْش	
ínti	*tistamtí3i*	تِسْتَمْتِعي	*ma-tistamti3īš*	مَتِسْتَمْتِعيش	
íntu	*tistamtí3u*	تِسْتَمْتِعوا	*ma-tistamti3ūš*	مَتِسْتَمْتِعوش	
húwwa	*yistámti3*	يِسْتَمْتِع	*ma-yistamtí3š*	مَيِسْتَمْتِعْش	
híyya	*tistámti3*	تِسْتَمْتِع	*ma-tistamtí3š*	مَتِسْتَمْتِعْش	
húmma	*yistamtí3u*	يِسْتَمْتِعوا	*ma-yistamti3ūš*	مَيِسْتَمْتِعوش	
ána	*bastámti3*	بَسْتَمْتِع	*ma-bastamtí3š*	مَبَسْتَمْتِعْش	**bi-imperfect**
íḥna	*binistámti3*	بِنِسْتَمْتِع	*ma-bnistamtí3š*	مَبْنِسْتَمْتِعْش	
ínta	*bitistámti3*	بِتِسْتَمْتِع	*ma-btistamtí3š*	مَبْتِسْتَمْتِعْش	
ínti	*bitistamtí3i*	بِتِسْتَمْتِعي	*ma-btistamti3īš*	مَبْتِسْتَمْتِعيش	
íntu	*bitistamtí3u*	بِتِسْتَمْتِعوا	*ma-btistamti3ūš*	مَبْتِسْتَمْتِعوش	
húwwa	*biyistámti3*	بِيِسْتَمْتِع	*ma-byistamtí3š*	مَبْيِسْتَمْتِعْش	
híyya	*bitistámti3*	بِتِسْتَمْتِع	*ma-btistamtí3š*	مَبْتِسْتَمْتِعْش	
húmma	*biyistamtí3u*	بِيِسْتَمْتِعوا	*ma-byistamti3ūš*	مَبْيِسْتَمْتِعوش	
ána	*hastámti3*	هَسْتَمْتِع	*miš hastámti3*	مِش هَسْتَمْتِع	**future**
íḥna	*hanistámti3*	هَنِسْتَمْتِع	*miš hanistámti3*	مِش هَنِسْتَمْتِع	
ínta	*hatistámti3*	هَتِسْتَمْتِع	*miš hatistámti3*	مِش هَتِسْتَمْتِع	
ínti	*hatistamtí3i*	هَتِسْتَمْتِعي	*miš hatistamtí3i*	مِش هَتِسْتَمْتِعي	
íntu	*hatistamtí3u*	هَتِسْتَمْتِعوا	*miš hatistamtí3u*	مِش هَتِسْتَمْتِعوا	
húwwa	*hayistámti3*	هَيِسْتَمْتِع	*miš hayistámti3*	مِش هَيِسْتَمْتِع	
híyya	*hatistámti3*	هَتِسْتَمْتِع	*miš hatistámti3*	مِش هَتِسْتَمْتِع	
húmma	*hayistamtí3u*	هَيِسْتَمْتِعوا	*miš hayistamtí3u*	مِش هَيِسْتَمْتِعوا	
ínta	*istámti3*	اِسْتَمْتِع	*ma-tistamtí3š*	مَتِسْتَمْتِعْش	**imperative**
ínti	*istamtí3i*	اِسْتَمْتِعي	*ma-tistamti3īš*	مَتِسْتَمْتِعيش	
íntu	*istamtí3u*	اِسْتَمْتِعوا	*ma-tistamti3ūš*	مَتِسْتَمْتِعوش	

	active		passive		
masculine	*mistámti3*	مِسْتَمْتِع	—	—	**participles**
feminine	*mistamtí3a*	مِسْتَمْتِعَة	—	—	
plural	*mistamti3īn*	مِسْتَمْتِعين	—	—	

①

العيْلة كُلّها اِسْتمْتعِت بِـرِحْلِةْ الغرْدقة جِدّاً.

il3ēla kulláha -stamtá3it bi-ríђlit ilɣardáʔa gíddan.

The whole family enjoyed the trip to Hurghada so much.

②

وَدّيْت الوِلاد لِماما و قِدِرْت أَسْتمْتِع بِيوْم أجازة لِوَحْدي.

waddēt ilwilād li-māma wi ʔidírt astámti3 bi-yōm agāza li-wáђdi.

I took the kids to my mom's and enjoyed a day off by myself.

③

بسْتمْتِع جِدّاً بِقِرايْةْ القُرآن.

bastámti3 gíddan bi-ʔiráyt ilqurʔān.

I really enjoy reading the Quran.

④

هَيْقضّوا شهْر في الشّرْق الأقْصى. أكيد هَيِسْتمْتِعوا جِدّاً.

hayʔáḍḍu šahrᵊ fi -ššarʔ ilʔáqṣa. akīd hayistamtí3u gíddan.

They're going to spend a month in the Far East. I'm sure they'll have a good time.

⑤

اِسْتمْتِعوا بِشبابْكو قبْل ما تِنْدموا.

istamtí3u bi-šabábku ʔablᵊ ma tindámu.

Enjoy your youth before it's too late [lit. you regret].

⑥

أنا مُسْتمْتِع بِالايْس كْريم ده بِشكْل.

ána mustámti3 bi-lʔáys krīm da bi-šákl.

I'm enjoying this ice cream so much.

⑦

مبسْتمْتِعْش بِقِرايِةْ شِعْر زيّ ما إنْتَ بِتِسْتمْتِع.

ma-bastamtí3šᵊ bi-ʔirāyit ši3rᵊ zayyᵊ ma -nta bitistámti3.

I don't enjoy reading poetry as you do.

❖ [10s1] **to enjoy (بِـ *bi-*); to enjoy oneself, have a good time**

- The object of this verb takes the preposition بِـ *bi-*. The object can be a noun, pronoun, or verbal noun (➲ 43.3, 43.6).
- There may be no object at all. (➲ 43.4)

➲ 127.2.

44 to continue istamárr اِسْتَمَرّ

	affirmative		negative		
ána	istamarrēt	اِسْتَمَرّيْت	ma-stamarrítš	مَسْتَمَرّيْتْش	perfect
íḥna	istamarrēna	اِسْتَمَرّيْنا	ma-stamarrināš	مَسْتَمَرّيناش	
ínta	istamarrēt	اِسْتَمَرّيْت	ma-stamarrítš	مَسْتَمَرّيْتْش	
ínti	istamarrēti	اِسْتَمَرّيْتي	ma-stamarritīš	مَسْتَمَرّيتيش	
íntu	istamarrētu	اِسْتَمَرّيْتوا	ma-stamarritūš	مَسْتَمَرّيتوش	
húwwa	istamárr	اِسْتَمَرّ	ma-stamárriš	مَسْتَمَرّش	
híyya	istamárrit	اِسْتَمَرّت	ma-stamárritš	مَسْتَمَرّتْش	
húmma	istamárru	اِسْتَمَرّوا	ma-stamarrūš	مَسْتَمَرّوش	
ána	astamírr	أَسْتَمِرّ	ma-stamírriš	مَسْتَمِرّش	imperfect
íḥna	nistamírr	نِسْتَمِرّ	ma-nistamírriš	مَنِسْتَمِرّش	
ínta	tistamírr	تِسْتَمِرّ	ma-tistamírriš	مَتِسْتَمِرّش	
ínti	tistamírri	تِسْتَمِرّي	ma-tistamirrīš	مَتِسْتَمِرّيش	
íntu	tistamírru	تِسْتَمِرّوا	ma-tistamirrūš	مَتِسْتَمِرّوش	
húwwa	yistamírr	يِسْتَمِرّ	ma-yistamírriš	مَيِسْتَمِرّش	
híyya	tistamírr	تِسْتَمِرّ	ma-tistamírriš	مَتِسْتَمِرّش	
húmma	yistamírru	يِسْتَمِرّوا	ma-yistamirrūš	مَيِسْتَمِرّوش	
ána	bastamírr	بَسْتَمِرّ	ma-bastamírriš	مَبَسْتَمِرّش	bi-imperfect
íḥna	binistamírr	بِنِسْتَمِرّ	ma-bnistamírriš	مَبْنِسْتَمِرّش	
ínta	bitistamírr	بِتِسْتَمِرّ	ma-btistamírriš	مَبْتِسْتَمِرّش	
ínti	bitistamírri	بِتِسْتَمِرّي	ma-btistamirrīš	مَبْتِسْتَمِرّيش	
íntu	bitistamírru	بِتِسْتَمِرّوا	ma-btistamirrūš	مَبْتِسْتَمِرّوش	
húwwa	biyistamírr	بِيِسْتَمِرّ	ma-byistamírriš	مَبْيِسْتَمِرّش	
híyya	bitistamírr	بِتِسْتَمِرّ	ma-btistamírriš	مَبْتِسْتَمِرّش	
húmma	biyistamírru	بِيِسْتَمِرّوا	ma-byistamirrūš	مَبْيِسْتَمِرّوش	
ána	hastamírr	هَسْتَمِرّ	miš hastamírr	مِش هَسْتَمِرّ	future
íḥna	hanistamírr	هَنِسْتَمِرّ	miš hanistamírr	مِش هَنِسْتَمِرّ	
ínta	hatistamírr	هَتِسْتَمِرّ	miš hatistamírr	مِش هَتِسْتَمِرّ	
ínti	hatistamírri	هَتِسْتَمِرّي	miš hatistamírri	مِش هَتِسْتَمِرّي	
íntu	hatistamírru	هَتِسْتَمِرّوا	miš hatistamírru	مِش هَتِسْتَمِرّوا	
húwwa	hayistamírr	هَيِسْتَمِرّ	miš hayistamírr	مِش هَيِسْتَمِرّ	
híyya	hatistamírr	هَتِسْتَمِرّ	miš hatistamírr	مِش هَتِسْتَمِرّ	
húmma	hayistamírru	هَيِسْتَمِرّوا	miš hayistamírru	مِش هَيِسْتَمِرّوا	
ínta	istamírr	اِسْتَمِرّ	ma-tistamírriš	مَتِسْتَمِرّش	imperative
ínti	istamírri	اِسْتَمِرّي	ma-tistamirrīš	مَتِسْتَمِرّيش	
íntu	istamírru	اِسْتَمِرّوا	ma-tistamirrūš	مَتِسْتَمِرّوش	

	active		passive		
masculine	mustamírr	مُسْتَمِرّ	—	—	participles
feminine	mustamírra	مُسْتَمِرّة	—	—	
plural	mustamirrīn	مُسْتَمِرّين	—	—	

verbal noun: *istimrār* اِسْتِمْرار

①

الحرْب العالمية التّانْيَة اِسْتمرِّت حَوالي سِتّ سْنين.

ilħárb il3alamíyya -ttánya -stamárrit ħawāli sitt^ə snīn.

The Second World War lasted for nearly six years.

②

عايْزين نِسْتمِرّ في المُذاكْرة لِحدّ ما نِلِمّ المنْهج كُلُّه.

3ayzīn nistamírr^ə fi -lmuzákra li-ħadd^ə ma nilímm ilmánhag kúllu.

We should keep studying until we
get through the whole curriculum.

③

التّخْفيضات بِتِسْتمِرّ طول مُدِّةْ الصّيْف.

ittaxfiḍāt bitistamírr^ə ṭūl múddit iṣṣēf.

Sales go on all summer.

④

هَيِسْتمِرّوا في تحْسين خدماتْهُم لِحدّ ما يِبْقوا أفْضل مطْعم في مصْر.

hayistamírru f taħsīn xadamáthum li-ħadd^ə ma yíbʔu ʔáfḍal máṭ3am fi maṣr.

They'll continue improving their services until they
become the best restaurant in Egypt.

⑤

اِسْتمِرّ في المُحاوْلة. إوْعى تِيْأس أبداً.

istamírr^ə fi -lmuħáwla. íw3a tíyʔas ábadan.

Keep trying. Never give up.

⑥

الشُّغْل مِسْتمِرّ في العيد. إحْنا مبْناخُدْش أجازة أبداً.

iššúɣl^ə mistamírr^ə fi -l3īd. íħna ma-bnaxúdš agāza ʔábadan.

We work during the holiday. We never take time off.

⑦

جَوازْهُم مسْتمرِّش أكْتر مِن تلات شُهور لِلاسف.

gawázhum ma-stamárriš áktar min tálat šuhūr li-lʔásaf.

Unfortunately, their marriage didn't
last for more than three months.

❖ [10g1] **to continue (في *fi*); last; keep __ing**

- The object of this verb can be a verbal noun preceded by the preposition في *fi*. (➲ 44.2, 44.4, 44.5)

➲ 47.4, 76.6, 77.3, 221.4

45 to wait *istánna* اِسْتَنّى

verbal noun: *intiẓār* اِنْتِظار

		affirmative		negative	
perfect	ána	*istannēt*	اِسْتَنّيْت	*ma-stannítš*	مَسْتَنّيْتْش
	íħna	*istannēna*	اِسْتَنّيْنا	*ma-stanninā̆š*	مَسْتَنّيناش
	ínta	*istannēt*	اِسْتَنّيْت	*ma-stannítš*	مَسْتَنّيْتْش
	ínti	*istannēti*	اِسْتَنّيْتي	*ma-stannitīš*	مَسْتَنّيتيش
	íntu	*istannētu*	اِسْتَنّيْتوا	*ma-stannitūš*	مَسْتَنّيتوش
	húwwa	*istánna*	اِسْتَنّى	*ma-stannā̆š*	مَسْتَنّاش
	híyya	*istánnit*	اِسْتَنّت	*ma-stannítš*	مَسْتَنّتْش
	húmma	*istánnu*	اِسْتَنّوا	*ma-stannū̆š*	مَسْتَنّوش
imperfect	ána	*astánna*	أسْتَنّى	*ma-stannā̆š*	مَسْتَنّاش
	íħna	*nistánna*	نِسْتَنّى	*ma-nistannā̆š*	مَنِسْتَنّاش
	ínta	*tistánna*	تِسْتَنّى	*ma-tistannā̆š*	مَتِسْتَنّاش
	ínti	*tistánni*	تِسْتَنّي	*ma-tistannī̆š*	مَتِسْتَنّيش
	íntu	*tistánnu*	تِسْتَنّوا	*ma-tistannū̆š*	مَتِسْتَنّوش
	húwwa	*yistánna*	يِسْتَنّى	*ma-yistannā̆š*	مَيِسْتَنّاش
	híyya	*tistánna*	تِسْتَنّى	*ma-tistannā̆š*	مَتِسْتَنّاش
	húmma	*yistánnu*	يِسْتَنّوا	*ma-yistannū̆š*	مَيِسْتَنّوش
bi-imperfect	ána	*bastánna*	بَسْتَنّى	*ma-bastannā̆š*	مَبَسْتَنّاش
	íħna	*binistánna*	بِنِسْتَنّى	*ma-bnistannā̆š*	مَبْنِسْتَنّاش
	ínta	*bitistánna*	بِتِسْتَنّى	*ma-btistannā̆š*	مَبْتِسْتَنّاش
	ínti	*bitistánni*	بِتِسْتَنّي	*ma-btistannī̆š*	مَبْتِسْتَنّيش
	íntu	*bitistánnu*	بِتِسْتَنّوا	*ma-btistannū̆š*	مَبْتِسْتَنّوش
	húwwa	*biyistánna*	بِيِسْتَنّى	*ma-byistannā̆š*	مَبْيِسْتَنّاش
	híyya	*bitistánna*	بِتِسْتَنّى	*ma-btistannā̆š*	مَبْتِسْتَنّاش
	húmma	*biyistánnu*	بِيِسْتَنّوا	*ma-byistannū̆š*	مَبْيِسْتَنّوش
future	ána	*hastánna*	هَسْتَنّى	*miš hastánna*	مِش هَسْتَنّى
	íħna	*hanistánna*	هَنِسْتَنّى	*miš hanistánna*	مِش هَنِسْتَنّى
	ínta	*hatistánna*	هَتِسْتَنّى	*miš hatistánna*	مِش هَتِسْتَنّى
	ínti	*hatistánni*	هَتِسْتَنّي	*miš hatistánni*	مِش هَتِسْتَنّي
	íntu	*hatistánnu*	هَتِسْتَنّوا	*miš hatistánnu*	مِش هَتِسْتَنّوا
	húwwa	*hayistánna*	هَيِسْتَنّى	*miš hayistánna*	مِش هَيِسْتَنّى
	híyya	*hatistánna*	هَتِسْتَنّى	*miš hatistánna*	مِش هَتِسْتَنّى
	húmma	*hayistánnu*	هَيِسْتَنّوا	*miš hayistánnu*	مِش هَيِسْتَنّوا
imperative	ínta	*istánna*	اِسْتَنّى	*ma-tistannā̆š*	مَتِسْتَنّاش
	ínti	*istánni*	اِسْتَنّي	*ma-tistannī̆š*	مَتِسْتَنّيش
	íntu	*istánnu*	اِسْتَنّوا	*ma-tistannū̆š*	مَتِسْتَنّوش

participles		active		passive	
	masculine	*mistánni*	مِسْتَنّي	–	–
	feminine	*mistanníyya*	مِسْتَنّيَّة	–	–
	plural	*mistanniyīn*	مِسْتَنّيين	–	–

①

اِسْتنّيْت المُوَظّف كِتير عشان أدْفع الفِلوس في السِّفارة.

istannēt ilmuwáẓẓaf kitīr 3ašān ádfa3 ilfilūs fi -ssifāra.

I had to wait so long for the employee in order to pay the money at the embassy.

②

مُمْكِن أسْتنّى العُمْر كُلُّه بسّ مِش هتْجوِّز غيرْها.

múmkin astánna -l3umrᵊ kúllu bassᵊ miš hatgáwwiz ɣírha.

I may wait my whole life just to marry her.

③

بسْتنّى كاس العالم كُلّ أرْبع سِنين عشان أتْفرّج عَ الكوْرة الحِلْوَة.

bastánna kās il3ālam kull árba3 sinīn 3ašān atfárrag 3a -lkōra -lḫílwa.

I wait for the World Cup every four years to watch the great matches.

④

هنِسْتنّاكو عَ الغدا بُكْره.

hanistannāku 3a -lɣáda búkra.

We'll wait for you tomorrow for lunch.

⑤

اِسْتنّوني . أنا نازِل معاكو.

istannūni. ána nāzil ma3āku.

Wait for me. I'm coming with you.

⑥

مِسْتنّيين بقالْنا ساعْتيْن و المُوَظّف المسْئول لِسّه مجاش.

mistanniyīn baʔálna sa3tēn w ilmuwáẓẓaf ilmasʔūl líssa ma-gāš.

We've been waiting for two hours, and the employee in charge still hasn't arrived.

⑦

متِسْتنّونيش لَوْ اِتْأخّرْت. أنا هحصّلْكو بعْديْن.

ma-tistannunīš law itʔaxxárt. ána haḫaṣṣálku ba3dēn.

Don't wait for me if I'm late. I'll catch up with you later.

❖ [10.2i] **to wait (for)**

- This verb is transitive, taking an object without any preposition, unlike the English verb 'wait', which requires the preposition 'for' before an object.
- The verbal noun is borrowed from MSA.

➲ 22.7, 26.6, 61.4, 94.3, 99.6, 126.5, 168.1, 260.4

46 to buy ištára اِشْتَرَى

	affirmative		negative		
ána	ištarēt	اِشْتَرَيْت	ma-štarítš	مَشْتَرَيْتْش	**perfect**
íḫna	ištarēna	اِشْتَرَيْنا	ma-štarināš	مَشْتَرَيناش	
ínta	ištarēt	اِشْتَرَيْت	ma-štarítš	مَشْتَرَيْتْش	
ínti	ištarēti	اِشْتَرَيْتي	ma-štaritīš	مَشْتَرَيتيش	
íntu	ištarētu	اِشْتَرَيْتوا	ma-štaritūš	مَشْتَرَيتوش	
húwwa	ištára	اِشْتَرَى	ma-štarāš	مَشْتَرَاش	
híyya	ištárit	اِشْتَرِت	ma-štarítš	مَشْتَرِتْش	
húmma	ištáru	اِشْتَروا	ma-štarūš	مَشْتَروش	
ána	aštíri	أَشْتِري	ma-štirīš	مَشْتِريش	**imperfect**
íḫna	ništíri	نِشْتِري	ma-ništirīš	مَنِشْتِريش	
ínta	tištíri	تِشْتِري	ma-tištirīš	مَتِشْتِريش	
ínti	tištíri	تِشْتِري	ma-tištirīš	مَتِشْتِريش	
íntu	tištíru	تِشْتِروا	ma-tištirūš	مَتِشْتِروش	
húwwa	yištíri	يِشْتِري	ma-yištirīš	مَيِشْتِريش	
híyya	tištíri	تِشْتِري	ma-tištirīš	مَتِشْتِريش	
húmma	yištíru	يِشْتِروا	ma-yištirūš	مَيِشْتِروش	
ána	baštíri	بَشْتِري	ma-baštirīš	مَبَشْتِريش	**bi-imperfect**
íḫna	biništíri	بِنِشْتِري	ma-bništirīš	مَبْنِشْتِريش	
ínta	bitištíri	بِتِشْتِري	ma-btištirīš	مَبْتِشْتِريش	
ínti	bitištíri	بِتِشْتِري	ma-btištirīš	مَبْتِشْتِريش	
íntu	bitištíru	بِتِشْتِروا	ma-btištirūš	مَبْتِشْتِروش	
húwwa	biyištíri	بِيِشْتِري	ma-byištirīš	مَبْيِشْتِريش	
híyya	bitištíri	بِتِشْتِري	ma-btištirīš	مَبْتِشْتِريش	
húmma	biyištíru	بِيِشْتِروا	ma-byištirūš	مَبْيِشْتِروش	
ána	haštíri	هَشْتِري	miš haštíri	مِش هَشْتِري	**future**
íḫna	haništíri	هَنِشْتِري	miš haništíri	مِش هَنِشْتِري	
ínta	hatištíri	هَتِشْتِري	miš hatištíri	مِش هَتِشْتِري	
ínti	hatištíri	هَتِشْتِري	miš hatištíri	مِش هَتِشْتِري	
íntu	hatištíru	هَتِشْتِروا	miš hatištíru	مِش هَتِشْتِروا	
húwwa	hayištíri	هَيِشْتِري	miš hayištíri	مِش هَيِشْتِري	
híyya	hatištíri	هَتِشْتِري	miš hatištíri	مِش هَتِشْتِري	
húmma	hayištíru	هَيِشْتِروا	miš hayištíru	مِش هَيِشْتِروا	
ínta	ištíri	اِشْتِري	ma-tištirīš	مَتِشْتِريش	**imperative**
ínti	ištíri	اِشْتِري	ma-tištirīš	مَتِشْتِريش	
íntu	ištíru	اِشْتِروا	ma-tištirūš	مَتِشْتِروش	

	active		passive	
masculine	šāri / mištíri	شاري / مِشْتِرى	–	– **participles**
feminine	šárya / mištírya	شارْيَة / مِشْتِريَة	–	–
plural	šaryīn / mištiryīn	شارْيين / مِشْتِريين	–	–

verbal noun: šíra شِرا

①

اِشْترِيْنا فراوْلة مِن سوق الجُمْلة و خزِّنّاها في الفْريزِر. بعْمِل مِنْها عصير كُلّ يوْم.

ištarēna faráwla min sūʔ ilgúmla wi xazzinnāha fi -lfrīzir. bá3mil mínha 3aṣīr kullᵊ yōm.

We bought strawberries from the wholesale market and put them in the freezer. I make juice from them every day.

②

بِنْروح نِشْتِـرِي القُماش مِ الأزْهر. بِيْكون أحْلى و أرْخص.

binrūḥ ništíri -lʔumāš mi -lʔázhar. biykūn áḥla w árxaṣ.

We [usually] go to Al-Azhar to buy fabric. It's better [quality] and less expensive.

③

بِنِشْتِـرِي طلباتْنا عادةً مِن كارْفور.

biništíri ṭalabátna 3ādatan min karfūr.

We usually buy our provisions [groceries and household items] from Carrefour.

④

هشْتِـرِي بوكيْهْ وَرْد و أروح أصالِح مِراتي.

haštíri bukēh wardᵊ w arūḥ aṣāliḥ mirāti.

I'll buy a bouquet of flowers and go make up with my wife.

⑤

اِشْتِـرولي معاكو عيْش و إِنْتو جايِّين.

ištirūli ma3āku 3ēš w íntu gayyīn.

Buy me bread on your way here.

⑥

الخلّاط مِش راضي يِشْتغل؟ ده إحْنا لِسّه مِشْتِـرِيِينُه!

ilxallāṭ miš rāḍi yištáɣal? da -ḥna líssa mištiriyīnu!

The blender won't work? But we just bought it!

⑦

مبشْتِـرِيش أيّ حاجة مِن المحلّ اللي عَ النّاصْيَة. صاحِب المحلّ مرّة عامِلْني وِحِش أوي.

ma-baštirīš ayyᵊ ḥāga min ilmaḥáll ílli 3a -nnáṣya. ṣāḥib ilmaḥállᵊ márra 3amílni wíḥiš áwi.

I don't buy anything from the corner shop. The owner was so rude to me once.

❖ [8d] **to buy**

➲ 2.10, 26.1, 40.6, 115.1, 227.5, 230.2

47 to work *ištáɣal* اِشْتَغَل

	affirmative		negative		
ána	*ištaɣált*	اِشْتَغَلْت	*ma-štaɣáltiš*	مَشْتَغَلْتِش	**perfect**
íḥna	*ištaɣálna*	اِشْتَغَلْنا	*ma-štaɣalnāš*	مَشْتَغَلْناش	
ínta	*ištaɣált*	اِشْتَغَلْت	*ma-štaɣáltiš*	مَشْتَغَلْتِش	
ínti	*ištaɣálti*	اِشْتَغَلْتي	*ma-štaɣaltīš*	مَشْتَغَلْتيش	
íntu	*ištaɣáltu*	اِشْتَغَلْتوا	*ma-štaɣaltūš*	مَشْتَغَلْتوش	
húwwa	*ištáɣal*	اِشْتَغَل	*ma-štaɣálš*	مَشْتَغَلْش	
híyya	*ištáɣalit*	اِشْتَغَلِت	*ma-štaɣalítš*	مَشْتَغَلِتْش	
húmma	*ištáɣalu*	اِشْتَغَلوا	*ma-štaɣalūš*	مَشْتَغَلوش	
ána	*aštáɣal*	أَشْتَغَل	*ma-štaɣálš*	مَشْتَغَلْش	**imperfect**
íḥna	*ništáɣal*	نِشْتَغَل	*ma-ništaɣálš*	مَنِشْتَغَلْش	
ínta	*tištáɣal*	تِشْتَغَل	*ma-tištaɣálš*	مَتِشْتَغَلْش	
ínti	*tištáɣali*	تِشْتَغَلي	*ma-tištaɣalīš*	مَتِشْتَغَليش	
íntu	*tištáɣalu*	تِشْتَغَلوا	*ma-tištaɣalūš*	مَتِشْتَغَلوش	
húwwa	*yištáɣal*	يِشْتَغَل	*ma-yištaɣálš*	مَيِشْتَغَلْش	
híyya	*tištáɣal*	تِشْتَغَل	*ma-tištaɣálš*	مَتِشْتَغَلْش	
húmma	*yištáɣalu*	يِشْتَغَلوا	*ma-yištaɣalūš*	مَيِشْتَغَلوش	
ána	*baštáɣal*	بَشْتَغَل	*ma-baštaɣálš*	مَبَشْتَغَلْش	**bi-imperfect**
íḥna	*biništáɣal*	بِنِشْتَغَل	*ma-bništaɣálš*	مَبْنِشْتَغَلْش	
ínta	*bitištáɣal*	بِتِشْتَغَل	*ma-btištaɣálš*	مَبْتِشْتَغَلْش	
ínti	*bitištáɣali*	بِتِشْتَغَلي	*ma-btištaɣalīš*	مَبْتِشْتَغَليش	
íntu	*bitištáɣalu*	بِتِشْتَغَلوا	*ma-btištaɣalūš*	مَبْتِشْتَغَلوش	
húwwa	*biyištáɣal*	بِيِشْتَغَل	*ma-byištaɣálš*	مَبْيِشْتَغَلْش	
híyya	*bitištáɣal*	بِتِشْتَغَل	*ma-btištaɣálš*	مَبْتِشْتَغَلْش	
húmma	*biyištáɣalu*	بِيِشْتَغَلوا	*ma-byištaɣalūš*	مَبْيِشْتَغَلوش	
ána	*haštáɣal*	هَشْتَغَل	*miš haštáɣal*	مِش هَشْتَغَل	**future**
íḥna	*haništáɣal*	هَنِشْتَغَل	*miš haništáɣal*	مِش هَنِشْتَغَل	
ínta	*hatištáɣal*	هَتِشْتَغَل	*miš hatištáɣal*	مِش هَتِشْتَغَل	
ínti	*hatištáɣali*	هَتِشْتَغَلي	*miš hatištáɣali*	مِش هَتِشْتَغَلي	
íntu	*hatištáɣalu*	هَتِشْتَغَلوا	*miš hatištáɣalu*	مِش هَتِشْتَغَلوا	
húwwa	*hayištáɣal*	هَيِشْتَغَل	*miš hayištáɣal*	مِش هَيِشْتَغَل	
híyya	*hatištáɣal*	هَتِشْتَغَل	*miš hatištáɣal*	مِش هَتِشْتَغَل	
húmma	*hayištáɣalu*	هَيِشْتَغَلوا	*miš hayištáɣalu*	مِش هَيِشْتَغَلوا	
ínta	*ištáɣal*	اِشْتَغَل	*ma-tištaɣálš*	مَتِشْتَغَلْش	**imperative**
ínti	*ištáɣali*	اِشْتَغَلي	*ma-tištaɣalīš*	مَتِشْتَغَليش	
íntu	*ištáɣalu*	اِشْتَغَلوا	*ma-tištaɣalūš*	مَتِشْتَغَلوش	

	active		passive		
masculine	*šaɣɣāl / mištáɣál*	شَغّال / مِشْتَغَل	–	–	**participles**
feminine	*šaɣɣāla / mištáɣala*	شَغّالَة / مِشْتَغَلَة	–	–	
plural	*šaɣɣalīn / mištaɣalīn*	شَغّالين / مِشْتَغَلين	–	–	

verbal nouns: *šuɣl* شُغْل - *ištiɣāl* اِشْتِغال

①

مُراد اِشْتغل حاجات كِتير جنْب دِراسْتُه عشان يِقْدر يِكمِّلْها.

murād ištáɣal ɧagāt kitīr gambᵊ dirástu 3ašān yíʔdar yikammílha.

Murad did many jobs besides his studies in order to pay for them.

②

عشان يِشْتغل برّه لازِم يِمْتِحِن أَيْلتْس الأوِّل.

3ašān yištáɣal bárra lāzim yimtíɧin áylats ilʔáwwil.

In order to work abroad, he should pass the IELTS first.

③

ماما بْتِشْتغل كُروشيْه حِلْو أوي. هتِعْمِلّي كُلّ مفارِش البيْت.

māma btištáɣal kurušēh ɧilw áwi. hati3mílli kullᵊ mafāriš ilbēt.

My mom does beautiful crochet work. She'll
make me all the tablecloths and bedspreads.

④

هتِشْتغل معانا شهْر و لَوْ أثْبتّ كفاءة هتِسْتمِرّ.

hatištáɣal ma3āna šahrᵊ wi law asbáttᵊ kafāʔa hatistamírr.

You'll work with us for a month, and if you
prove your competence, you'll continue.

⑤

اِشْتغلي على نفْسِك أكْتر و هتْلاقي الفرْق في شخْصِيِّتِك و شكْلِك.

ištáɣali 3ála náfsik áktar wi hatlāʔi -lfarʔᵊ fi šaxṣiyyítik wi šáklik.

Work on yourself more, and you'll see the difference
in your personality and appearance.

⑥

أحْمد شغّال شُغْلانة حِلْوَة، مُرتّبْها كِبير و مُسْتقْبِلْها كُوَيِّس.

áɧmadᵊ šaɣɣāl šuɣlāna ɧílwa, murattábha kibīr wi mustaʔbílha kuwáyyis.

Ahmed has a good job with a high salary and a good future.

⑦

أغْلب النّاس مبْتِشْتغلْش في أجازْة العيد.

áɣlab innās ma-btištaɣálšᵊ fi ʔagázt il3īd.

Most people don't work on the Eid holiday.

⑧

أنا بشْتغل مُدرِّس.

ána baštáɣal mudárris.

I work as a teacher.

❖ [8s2] **to work; to do**

- This verb can be intransitive or transitive. Notice that no preposition equivalent to 'as' is needed. (➲ 47.8)
- This verb also covers, as does the verb 'work' in English, the meaning 'function correctly. (➲ 46.6, 261.6)

➲ 13.1, 13.6, 65.3, 113.7, 127.3

48 to insist ʔaṣárr أصرّ ص ر ر

	affirmative		negative		
ána	ʔaṣarrēt	أَصَرّيْت	ma-ʔaṣarrítš	مَأَصَرّيْتْش	perfect
íḥna	ʔaṣarrēna	أَصَرّيْنا	ma-ʔaṣarrināš	مَأَصَرّيناش	
ínta	ʔaṣarrēt	أَصَرّيْت	ma-ʔaṣarrítš	مَأَصَرّيْتْش	
ínti	ʔaṣarrēti	أَصَرّيْتي	ma-ʔaṣarritīš	مَأَصَرّيتيش	
íntu	ʔaṣarrētu	أَصَرّيْتوا	ma-ʔaṣarritūš	مَأَصَرّيتوش	
húwwa	ʔaṣárr	أَصَرّ	ma-ʔaṣárriš	مَأَصَرِّش	
híyya	ʔaṣárrit	أَصَرِّت	ma-ʔaṣarrítš	مَأَصَرِّتْش	
húmma	ʔaṣárru	أَصَرّوا	ma-ʔaṣarrūš	مَأَصَرّوش	
ána	aṣírr	أصِرّ	ma-ṣírriš	مَصِرِّش	imperfect
íḥna	niṣírr	نِصِرّ	ma-nṣírriš	مَنصِرِّش	
ínta	tiṣírr	تِصِرّ	ma-tṣírriš	مَتْصِرِّش	
ínti	tiṣírri	تِصِرّي	ma-tṣirrīš	مَتْصِرّيش	
íntu	tiṣírru	تِصِرّوا	ma-tṣirrūš	مَتْصِرّوش	
húwwa	yiṣírr	يِصِرّ	ma-yṣírriš	مَيْصِرِّش	
híyya	tiṣírr	تِصِرّ	ma-tṣírriš	مَتْصِرِّش	
húmma	yiṣírru	يِصِرّوا	ma-yṣirrūš	مَيْصِرّوش	
ána	baṣírr	بَصِرّ	ma-baṣírriš	مَبَصِرِّش	bi-imperfect
íḥna	binṣírr	بِنْصِرّ	ma-binṣírriš	مَبِنْصِرِّش	
ínta	bitṣírr	بِتْصِرّ	ma-bitṣírriš	مَبِتْصِرِّش	
ínti	bitṣírri	بِتْصِرّي	ma-bitṣirrīš	مَبِتْصِرّيش	
íntu	bitṣírru	بِتْصِرّوا	ma-bitṣirrūš	مَبِتْصِرّوش	
húwwa	biyṣírr	بِيْصِرّ	ma-biyṣírriš	مَبِيْصِرِّش	
híyya	bitṣírr	بِتْصِرّ	ma-bitṣírriš	مَبِتْصِرِّش	
húmma	biyṣírru	بِيْصِرّوا	ma-biyṣirrūš	مَبِيْصِرّوش	
ána	haṣírr	هَصِرّ	miš haṣírr	مِش هَصِرّ	future
íḥna	hanṣírr	هَنْصِرّ	miš hanṣírr	مِش هَنْصِرّ	
ínta	hatṣírr	هَتْصِرّ	miš hatṣírr	مِش هَتْصِرّ	
ínti	hatṣírri	هَتْصِرّي	miš hatṣírri	مِش هَتْصِرّي	
íntu	hatṣírru	هَتْصِرّوا	miš hatṣírru	مِش هَتْصِرّوا	
húwwa	hayṣírr	هَيْصِرّ	miš hayṣírr	مِش هَيْصِرّ	
híyya	hatṣírr	هَتْصِرّ	miš hatṣírr	مِش هَتْصِرّ	
húmma	hayṣírru	هَيْصِرّوا	miš hayṣírru	مِش هَيْصِرّوا	
ínta	ṣírr	صِرّ	ma-tṣírriš	مَتْصِرِّش	imperative
ínti	ṣírri	صِرّي	ma-tṣirrīš	مَتْصِرّيش	
íntu	iṣírru	صِرّوا	ma-tṣirrūš	مَتْصِرّوش	

	active		passive		
masculine	muṣírr	مُصِرّ	–	–	participles
feminine	muṣírra	مُصِرّة	–	–	
plural	muṣirrīn	مُصِرّين	–	–	

verbal noun: iṣrār إصرار

①

داليا أصرّت تِنْزِل الشُّغْل و هِيَّ تعْبانة.

dálya ʔaṣárrit tínzil iššúɣlᵊ wi híyya ta3bāna.

Dalia insisted on going to work even when she was tired.

②

لازِم تِصِرّ على مَوْقِفك لِحدّ ما تاخُد حقّك.

lāzim tiṣírrᵊ 3ála mawqífak li-ḥáddᵊ ma tāxud ḥáʔʔak.

You must take a stance until you achieve your rights.

③

مبِتْصِرّيش على رأْيك ليْه؟ المَوْضوع أصْلاً يِخُصّك.

ma-bitṣirrīš 3ála ráʔyik lē? ilmawḍū3 áṣlan yixúṣṣik.

Why don't you insist on your opinion?
The whole issue is yours anyway.

④

لمّا هتْصِرّ على السّفر، هَيِعْرفوا إنّك جادّ، مِش رايِح تِلْعب.

lámma hatṣírrᵊ 3ála -ssáfar, hayi3ráfu ʔínnak gadd, miš rāyiḥ tíl3ab.

When you insist on traveling, they'll know that
you're serious and not going for fun.

⑤

متْصِرّش على مَوْقِفك و إنْتَ عارِف إنُّه غلط.

ma-tṣírriš 3ála mawqífak w ínta 3ārif ínnu ɣálaṭ.

Don't insist on your position when you're wrong.

❖ [4g] **to insist** (**on** على *3ála*)

- This verb can be followed by a verb in the imperfect. (➲ 48.1)

➲ 77.1

49 to consider i3tábar اِعْتَبَر

	affirmative		negative		
ána	i3tabárt	اِعْتَبَرْت	ma-3tabártiš	مَعْتَبَرْتِش	perfect
íḥna	i3tabárna	اِعْتَبَرْنا	ma-3tabarnāš	مَعْتَبَرْناش	
ínta	i3tabárt	اِعْتَبَرْت	ma-3tabártiš	مَعْتَبَرْتِش	
ínti	i3tabárti	اِعْتَبَرْتي	ma-3tabartīš	مَعْتَبَرْتيش	
íntu	i3tabártu	اِعْتَبَرْتوا	ma-3tabartūš	مَعْتَبَرْتوش	
húwwa	i3tábar	اِعْتَبَر	ma-3tabárš	مَعْتَبَرْش	
híyya	i3tábarit	اِعْتَبَرِت	ma-3tabarítš	مَعْتَبَرِتْش	
húmma	i3tábaru	اِعْتَبَروا	ma-3tabarūš	مَعْتَبَروش	
ána	a3tíbir	أَعْتِبِر	ma-3tibírš	مَعْتِبِرْش	imperfect
íḥna	ni3tíbir	نِعْتِبِر	ma-ni3tibírš	مَنِعْتِبِرْش	
ínta	ti3tíbir	تِعْتِبِر	ma-ti3tibírš	مَتِعْتِبِرْش	
ínti	ti3tíbri	تِعْتِبْري	ma-ti3tibrīš	مَتِعْتِبْريش	
íntu	ti3tíbru	تِعْتِبْروا	ma-ti3tibrūš	مَتِعْتِبْروش	
húwwa	yi3tíbir	يِعْتِبِر	ma-yi3tibírš	مَيِعْتِبِرْش	
híyya	ti3tíbir	تِعْتِبِر	ma-ti3tibírš	مَتِعْتِبِرْش	
húmma	yi3tíbru	يِعْتِبْروا	ma-yi3tibrūš	مَيِعْتِبْروش	
ána	ba3tíbir	بَعْتِبِر	ma-ba3tibírš	مَبَعْتِبِرْش	bi-imperfect
íḥna	bini3tíbir	بِنِعْتِبِر	ma-bni3tibírš	مَبْنِعْتِبِرْش	
ínta	biti3tíbir	بِتِعْتِبِر	ma-3ti3tibírš	مَبْتِعْتِبِرْش	
ínti	biti3tíbri	بِتِعْتِبْري	ma-3ti3tibrīš	مَبْتِعْتِبْريش	
íntu	biti3tíbru	بِتِعْتِبْروا	ma-3ti3tibrūš	مَبْتِعْتِبْروش	
húwwa	biyi3tíbir	بِيِعْتِبِر	ma-byi3tibírš	مَبْيِعْتِبِرْش	
híyya	biti3tíbir	بِتِعْتِبِر	ma-3ti3tibírš	مَبْتِعْتِبِرْش	
húmma	biyi3tíbru	بِيِعْتِبْروا	ma-byi3tibrūš	مَبْيِعْتِبْروش	
ána	ha3tíbir	هَعْتِبِر	miš ha3tíbir	مِش هَعْتِبِر	future
íḥna	hani3tíbir	هَنِعْتِبِر	miš hani3tíbir	مِش هَنِعْتِبِر	
ínta	hati3tíbir	هَتِعْتِبِر	miš hati3tíbir	مِش هَتِعْتِبِر	
ínti	hati3tíbri	هَتِعْتِبْري	miš hati3tíbri	مِش هَتِعْتِبْري	
íntu	hati3tíbru	هَتِعْتِبْروا	miš hati3tíbru	مِش هَتِعْتِبْروا	
húwwa	hayi3tíbir	هَيِعْتِبِر	miš hayi3tíbir	مِش هَيِعْتِبِر	
híyya	hati3tíbir	هَتِعْتِبِر	miš hati3tíbir	مِش هَتِعْتِبِر	
húmma	hayi3tíbru	هَيِعْتِبْروا	miš hayi3tíbru	مِش هَيِعْتِبْروا	
ínta	i3tíbir	اِعْتِبِر	ma-ti3tibírš	مَتِعْتِبِرْش	imperative
ínti	i3tíbri	اِعْتِبْري	ma-ti3tibrīš	مَتِعْتِبْريش	
íntu	i3tíbru	اِعْتِبْروا	ma-ti3tibrūš	مَتِعْتِبْروش	

	active		passive		
masculine	mu3tábir	مُعْتَبِر	mu3tábar	مُعْتَبَر	participles
feminine	mu3tábra	مُعْتَبْرَة	mu3tábara	مُعْتَبَرَة	
plural	mu3tabrīn	مُعْتَبْرين	mu3tábarīn	مُعْتَبَرين	

verbal noun: i3tibār اِعْتِبار

①

سلْوَى اعْتبرِت أبوها مات لمّا اتْسجن في قضِيِّةْ إخْتِلاس.

sálwa -3tábarit abūha māt lámma -tságan fi ʔaḍíyyit ixtilās.

Salwa considered her father dead [lit. to have died] after he was jailed for embezzlement.

②

نِقْدر نِعْتبِـر الجَوّ في مصْر جَوّ لطيف صيْف و شِتا.

níʔdar ni3tíbir ilgáwwᵊ f maṣrᵊ gawwᵊ laṭīf ṣēf wi šíta.

We can consider the weather in Egypt nice in the summer and winter.

③

يُعْتبر شهْر أغُسْطس أحرّ شهْر في السّنة.

yu3tábar šahr aɣúsṭas aḥárrᵊ šahrᵊ fi -ssána.

August is considered the hottest month of the year.

④

تُعْتبر أسْوان مِن أجْمل المُدُن المصْرية.

tu3tábar aswān min ágmal ilmúdun ilmaṣríyya.

Aswan is considered one of the most beautiful cities in Egypt.

⑤

اِعْتبِرْيها أُخْتِك الصُّغيرّة. سامْحيها و علِّميها الصّحّ.

i3tibrīha ʔúxtik iṣṣuɣayyára. samḥīha wi 3allimīha -ṣṣaḥḥ.

Think of her as your little sister. Forgive her and teach her the right thing.

⑥

أنا مُعْتبِـرك إبْني و عشان كِده بنْصحك.

ána mu3tábirak íbni wi 3ašān kída banṣáḥak.

I consider you my son. That's why I give you advice.

⑦

إحْنا مبْنِعْتبِرْكْش غريب. إنْتَ زيّ إبْننا.

íḥna ma-bni3tibrákšᵊ ɣarīb. ínta zayy ibnína.

We don't consider you an outsider. You're like a son to us.

❖ [8s1] **to consider, think of __ as**

- This verb is ditransitive, taking a direct object followed by a second direct object, as does the verb 'consider' in English.
- The second direct object may be replaced by an adjective or even a verb (➲ 49.1).
- It is often used in the passive. Notice the voweling: يُعْتبر *yu3tábar* 'is considered' vs. يِعْتبِـر *yi3tíbir*. (➲ 49.3, 49.4)

➲ 36.3

50 to remember *iftákar* اِفْتَكَر

verbal noun: *tazákkur* تذكُّر

	affirmative		negative		
ána	*iftakárt*	اِفْتَكَرْت	*ma-ftakártiš*	مَفْتَكَرْتِش	**perfect**
íḫna	*iftakárna*	اِفْتَكَرْنا	*ma-ftakarnāš*	مَفْتَكَرْناش	
ínta	*iftakárt*	اِفْتَكَرْت	*ma-ftakártiš*	مَفْتَكَرْتِش	
ínti	*iftakárti*	اِفْتَكَرْتي	*ma-ftakartīš*	مَفْتَكَرْتيش	
íntu	*iftakártu*	اِفْتَكَرْتوا	*ma-ftakartūš*	مَفْتَكَرْتوش	
húwwa	*iftákar*	اِفْتَكَر	*ma-ftakárš*	مَفْتَكَرْش	
híyya	*iftákarit*	اِفْتَكَرِت	*ma-ftakarítš*	مَفْتَكَرِتْش	
húmma	*iftákaru*	اِفْتَكَروا	*ma-ftakarūš*	مَفْتَكَروش	
ána	*aftíkir*	أَفْتِكِر	*ma-ftikírš*	مَفْتِكِرْش	**imperfect**
íḫna	*niftíkir*	نِفْتِكِر	*ma-niftikírš*	مَنِفْتِكِرْش	
ínta	*tiftíkir*	تِفْتِكِر	*ma-tiftikírš*	مَتِفْتِكِرْش	
ínti	*tiftíkri*	تِفْتِكْري	*ma-tiftikrīš*	مَتِفْتِكْريش	
íntu	*tiftíkru*	تِفْتِكْروا	*ma-tiftikrūš*	مَتِفْتِكْروش	
húwwa	*yiftíkir*	يِفْتِكِر	*ma-yiftikírš*	مَيِفْتِكِرْش	
híyya	*tiftíkir*	تِفْتِكِر	*ma-tiftikírš*	مَتِفْتِكِرْش	
húmma	*yiftíkru*	يِفْتِكْروا	*ma-yiftikrūš*	مَيِفْتِكْروش	
ána	*baftíkir*	بَفْتِكِر	*ma-baftikírš*	مَبَفْتِكِرْش	**bi-imperfect**
íḫna	*biniftíkir*	بِنِفْتِكِر	*ma-bniftikírš*	مَبْنِفْتِكِرْش	
ínta	*bitiftíkir*	بِتِفْتِكِر	*ma-btiftikírš*	مَبْتِفْتِكِرْش	
ínti	*bitiftíkri*	بِتِفْتِكْري	*ma-btiftikrīš*	مَبْتِفْتِكْريش	
íntu	*bitiftíkru*	بِتِفْتِكْروا	*ma-btiftikrūš*	مَبْتِفْتِكْروش	
húwwa	*biyiftíkir*	بِيِفْتِكِر	*ma-byiftikírš*	مَبْيِفْتِكِرْش	
híyya	*bitiftíkir*	بِتِفْتِكِر	*ma-btiftikírš*	مَبْتِفْتِكِرْش	
húmma	*biyiftíkru*	بِيِفْتِكْروا	*ma-byiftikrūš*	مَبْيِفْتِكْروش	
ána	*haftíkir*	هَفْتِكِر	*miš haftíkir*	مِش هَفْتِكِر	**future**
íḫna	*haniftíkir*	هَنِفْتِكِر	*miš haniftíkir*	مِش هَنِفْتِكِر	
ínta	*hatiftíkir*	هَتِفْتِكِر	*miš hatiftíkir*	مِش هَتِفْتِكِر	
ínti	*hatiftíkri*	هَتِفْتِكْري	*miš hatiftíkri*	مِش هَتِفْتِكْري	
íntu	*hatiftíkru*	هَتِفْتِكْروا	*miš hatiftíkru*	مِش هَتِفْتِكْروا	
húwwa	*hayiftíkir*	هَيِفْتِكِر	*miš hayiftíkir*	مِش هَيِفْتِكِر	
híyya	*hatiftíkir*	هَتِفْتِكِر	*miš hatiftíkir*	مِش هَتِفْتِكِر	
húmma	*hayiftíkru*	هَيِفْتِكْروا	*miš hayiftíkru*	مِش هَيِفْتِكْروا	
ínta	*iftíkir*	اِفْتِكِر	*ma-tiftikírš*	مَتِفْتِكِرْش	**imperative**
ínti	*iftíkri*	اِفْتِكْري	*ma-tiftikrīš*	مَتِفْتِكْريش	
íntu	*iftíkru*	اِفْتِكْروا	*ma-tiftikrūš*	مَتِفْتِكْروش	

	active		passive		
masculine	*fākir*	فاكِر	–	–	**participles**
feminine	*fákra*	فاكْرَة	–	–	
plural	*fakrīn*	فاكْرين	–	–	

①

لمّا سألوني عن أجْمل يوْم في حَياتي، اِفْتكرْت يوْم جَوازي.

lámma saʔalūni 3an ágmal yōm fi ḫayāti, iftakártᵊ yōm gawāzi.

When they asked me what the best day of my life was, I thought of my wedding day.

②

أفْتِكِر إنّ تصرُّفك ده مِش مُناسِب في المكان ده.

aftíkir innᵊ taṣarrúfak da miš munāsib fi -lmakān da.

I think your behavior is inappropriate for this place.

③

دايْماً بفْتِكِر إنيّ ناسْيَة تِليفوْني بعْد ما بنْزِل.

dáyman baftíkir ínni násya tilifōni ba3dᵊ ma bánzil.

I always think that I forgot to take my cell phone after I've left the house.

④

هفْتِكِر الوَصْفة و أملّيهالِك.

haftíkir ilwáṣfa w amallihālik.

I'll [try to] remember the recipe and tell you.

⑤

اِفْتِكْري أرْجوكى، حطّيْتي المفاتيح فيْن؟

iftíkri ʔargūki, ḫaṭṭēti -lmafatīḫ fēn?

Please, think. Where did you put the keys?

⑥

عَلى ما أفْتِكِر ، بيتْهُم كان تاني عِمارة عَ الشِّمال.

3ála ma -ftíkir, bíthum kān tāni 3imāra 3a -ššimāl.

As far as I recall, their house was the second building on the left.

⑦

متِفْتِكْريش شكْل الرّاجِل اللي خطف الشّنْطة؟

ma-tiftikrīš šakl irrāgil ílli xáṭaf iššánṭa?

Can't you remember how the man who took your bag looks like?

❖ [8s1] **to think (that** إنّ *inn***); to remember, recall**

- Compare with فكّر *fákkar*. (➲ 195)
- The verbal noun is borrowed from MSA.
- The active participle is borrowed, modeled after that of a [1s] verb.

➲ 35.1, 91.6, 195.7

51 to discover *iktášaf* اِكْتَشَف

verbal noun: *iktišāf* اِكْتِشاف

	affirmative		negative		
ána	*iktašáft*	اِكْتَشَفْت	*ma-ktašáftiš*	مَكْتَشَفْتِش	**perfect**
íḥna	*iktašáfna*	اِكْتَشَفْنا	*ma-ktašafnāš*	مَكْتَشَفْناش	
ínta	*iktašáft*	اِكْتَشَفْت	*ma-ktašáftiš*	مَكْتَشَفْتِش	
ínti	*iktašáfti*	اِكْتَشَفْتي	*ma-ktašaftīš*	مَكْتَشَفْتيش	
íntu	*iktašáftu*	اِكْتَشَفْتوا	*ma-ktašaftūš*	مَكْتَشَفْتوش	
húwwa	*iktášaf*	اِكْتَشَف	*ma-ktašáfš*	مَكْتَشَفْش	
híyya	*iktášafit*	اِكْتَشَفِت	*ma-ktašafítš*	مَكْتَشَفِتْش	
húmma	*iktášafu*	اِكْتَشَفوا	*ma-ktašafūš*	مَكْتَشَفوش	
ána	*aktíšif*	أكْتِشِف	*ma-ktišífš*	مَكْتِشِفْش	**imperfect**
íḥna	*niktíšif*	نِكْتِشِف	*ma-niktišífš*	مَنِكْتِشِفْش	
ínta	*tiktíšif*	تِكْتِشِف	*ma-tiktišífš*	مَتِكْتِشِفْش	
ínti	*tiktíšfi*	تِكْتِشْفي	*ma-tiktišfīš*	مَتِكْتِشْفيش	
íntu	*tiktíšfu*	تِكْتِشْفوا	*ma-tiktišfūš*	مَتِكْتِشْفوش	
húwwa	*yiktíšif*	يِكْتِشِف	*ma-yiktišífš*	مَيِكْتِشِفْش	
híyya	*tiktíšif*	تِكْتِشِف	*ma-tiktišífš*	مَتِكْتِشِفْش	
húmma	*yiktíšfu*	يِكْتِشْفوا	*ma-yiktišfūš*	مَيِكْتِشْفوش	
ána	*baktíšif*	بَكْتِشِف	*ma-baktišífš*	مَبَكْتِشِفْش	**bi-imperfect**
íḥna	*biniktíšif*	بِنِكْتِشِف	*ma-bniktišífš*	مَبْنِكْتِشِفْش	
ínta	*bitiktíšif*	بِتِكْتِشِف	*ma-btiktišífš*	مَبْتِكْتِشِفْش	
ínti	*bitiktíšfi*	بِتِكْتِشْفي	*ma-btiktišfīš*	مَبْتِكْتِشْفيش	
íntu	*bitiktíšfu*	بِتِكْتِشْفوا	*ma-btiktišfūš*	مَبْتِكْتِشْفوش	
húwwa	*biyiktíšif*	بِيِكْتِشِف	*ma-byiktišífš*	مَبْيِكْتِشِفْش	
híyya	*bitiktíšif*	بِتِكْتِشِف	*ma-btiktišífš*	مَبْتِكْتِشِفْش	
húmma	*biyiktíšfu*	بِيِكْتِشْفوا	*ma-byiktišfūš*	مَبْيِكْتِشْفوش	
ána	*haktíšif*	هَكْتِشِف	*miš haktíšif*	مِش هَكْتِشِف	**future**
íḥna	*haniktíšif*	هَنِكْتِشِف	*miš haniktíšif*	مِش هَنِكْتِشِف	
ínta	*hatiktíšif*	هَتِكْتِشِف	*miš hatiktíšif*	مِش هَتِكْتِشِف	
ínti	*hatiktíšfi*	هَتِكْتِشْفي	*miš hatiktíšfi*	مِش هَتِكْتِشْفي	
íntu	*hatiktíšfu*	هَتِكْتِشْفوا	*miš hatiktíšfu*	مِش هَتِكْتِشْفوا	
húwwa	*hayiktíšif*	هَيِكْتِشِف	*miš hayiktíšif*	مِش هَيِكْتِشِف	
híyya	*hatiktíšif*	هَتِكْتِشِف	*miš hatiktíšif*	مِش هَتِكْتِشِف	
húmma	*hayiktíšfu*	هَيِكْتِشْفوا	*miš hayiktíšfu*	مِش هَيِكْتِشْفوا	
ínta	*iktíšif*	اِكْتِشِف	*ma-tiktišífš*	مَتِكْتِشِفْش	**imperative**
ínti	*iktíšfi*	اِكْتِشْفي	*ma-tiktišfīš*	مَتِكْتِشْفيش	
íntu	*iktíšfu*	اِكْتِشْفوا	*ma-tiktišfūš*	مَتِكْتِشْفوش	

	active		passive		
masculine	*miktíšif*	مِكْتِشِف	*muktášaf*	مُكْتَشَف	**participles**
feminine	*miktíšfa*	مِكْتِشْفَة	*muktášafa*	مُكْتَشَفَة	
plural	*miktišfīn*	مِكْتِشْفين	*muktášafīn*	مُكْتَشَفين	

①

نْيوتُن اِكْتشف الجاذْبية لمّا التُّفاحة وِقْعِت على راسُه.

nyūtun iktášaf ilgazbíyya lámma -ttufāћa wíʔ3it 3ála rāsu.

Newton discovered gravity when
an apple fell on his head.

②

بحاوِل أكْتِشِف سِرّ حُبّ النّاس لِلحلَوِيّات في رمضان و خُصوصاً الكُنافة.

baћāwil aktíšif sirrᵊ ћubb innās li-lћalawiyyāt fi ramaḍān wi xuṣūṣan ilkunāfa.

I'm trying to figure out why people love desserts
during Ramadan, especially konafa.

③

كُلّ ما تِعْرف واحِد بِتِكْتِشِف إنُّه بِيْخونْها.

kullᵊ ma tí3raf wāћid bitiktíšif ínnu biyxúnha.

Every time she gets to know someone,
she finds out that he is a cheater.

④

هتِكْتِشِف حاجات جميلة لَوْ دقّقْت النّظر في الطّبيعة حَواليْك.

hatiktíšif ћagāt gamīla law daʔʔáʔt innáẓar fi -ṭṭabī3a ћawalēk.

You'll discover beautiful things when you look
closely at the nature surrounding you.

⑤

اِكْتِشِف مَواهِب طِفْلك مِن صُغْرُه. هتْفيدُه جِدّاً.

iktíšif mawāhib ṭíflak min ṣúɣru. hatfīdu gíddan.

Discover the gifts in your kid at a young
age. This will really benefit him.

⑥

إحْنا لِسّه مِكْتِشْفين حالاً إنّ الوَزير رفض الطّلب بِتاعْنا.

íћna líssa miktišfīn ћālan inn ilwazīr ráfaḍ iṭṭálab bitá3na.

We just found out that the minister refused our request.

⑦

مكْتشفْناش إنّ ماما عنْدها سرطان غيْر بعْد ما حالِتْها اتْأخّرِت أوي.

ma-ktašafnāš innᵊ māma 3andáha saraṭān ɣēr ba3dᵊ ma ћalítha -tʔaxxárit áwi.

We didn't discover mom had cancer until it was too late.

❖ [8s1] **to discover, find out, figure out** (**that** إنّ *inn*)

➲ 63.5, 199.2

52 to be interested *ihtámm* اِهْتَمّ

verbal noun: *ihtimām* اِهْتِمام

	affirmative		negative		
ána	*ihtammēt*	اِهْتَمّيْت	*ma-htammítš*	مَهْتَمّيتْش	**perfect**
íḥna	*ihtammēna*	اِهْتَمّيْنا	*ma-htamminā́š*	مَهْتَمّيناش	
ínta	*ihtammēt*	اِهْتَمّيْت	*ma-htammítš*	مَهْتَمّيتْش	
ínti	*ihtammēti*	اِهْتَمّيْتي	*ma-htammitī́š*	مَهْتَمّيتيش	
íntu	*ihtammētu*	اِهْتَمّيْتوا	*ma-htammitū́š*	مَهْتَمّيتوش	
húwwa	*ihtámm*	اِهْتَمّ	*ma-htámmiš*	مَهْتَمّش	
híyya	*ihtámmit*	اِهْتَمّت	*ma-htammítš*	مَهْتَمّتْش	
húmma	*ihtámmu*	اِهْتَمّوا	*ma-htammū́š*	مَهْتَمّوش	
ána	*ahtámm*	أهْتَمّ	*ma-htámmiš*	مَهْتَمّش	**imperfect**
íḥna	*nihtámm*	نِهْتَمّ	*ma-nihtámmiš*	مَنِهْتَمّش	
ínta	*tihtámm*	تِهْتَمّ	*ma-tihtámmiš*	مَتِهْتَمّش	
ínti	*tihtámmi*	تِهْتَمّي	*ma-tihtammī́š*	مَتِهْتَمّيش	
íntu	*tihtámmu*	تِهْتَمّوا	*ma-tihtammū́š*	مَتِهْتَمّوش	
húwwa	*yihtámm*	يِهْتَمّ	*ma-yihtámmiš*	مَيِهْتَمّش	
híyya	*tihtámm*	تِهْتَمّ	*ma-tihtámmiš*	مَتِهْتَمّش	
húmma	*yihtámmu*	يِهْتَمّوا	*ma-yihtammū́š*	مَيِهْتَمّوش	
ána	*bahtámm*	بَهْتَمّ	*ma-bahtámmiš*	مَبَهْتَمّش	**bi-imperfect**
íḥna	*binihtámm*	بِنِهْتَمّ	*ma-bnihtámmiš*	مَبْنِهْتَمّش	
ínta	*bitihtámm*	بِتِهْتَمّ	*ma-btihtámmiš*	مَبْتِهْتَمّش	
ínti	*bitihtámmi*	بِتِهْتَمّي	*ma-btihtammī́š*	مَبْتِهْتَمّيش	
íntu	*bitihtámmu*	بِتِهْتَمّوا	*ma-btihtammū́š*	مَبْتِهْتَمّوش	
húwwa	*biyihtámm*	بِيِهْتَمّ	*ma-byihtámmiš*	مَبْيِهْتَمّش	
híyya	*bitihtámm*	بِتِهْتَمّ	*ma-btihtámmiš*	مَبْتِهْتَمّش	
húmma	*biyihtámmu*	بِيِهْتَمّوا	*ma-byihtammū́š*	مَبْيِهْتَمّوش	
ána	*hahtámm*	هَهْتَمّ	*miš hahtámm*	مِش هَهْتَمّ	**future**
íḥna	*hanihtámm*	هَنِهْتَمّ	*miš hanihtámm*	مِش هَنِهْتَمّ	
ínta	*hatihtámm*	هَتِهْتَمّ	*miš hatihtámm*	مِش هَتِهْتَمّ	
ínti	*hatihtámmi*	هَتِهْتَمّي	*miš hatihtámmi*	مِش هَتِهْتَمّي	
íntu	*hatihtámmu*	هَتِهْتَمّوا	*miš hatihtámmu*	مِش هَتِهْتَمّوا	
húwwa	*hayihtámm*	هَيِهْتَمّ	*miš hayihtámm*	مِش هَيِهْتَمّ	
híyya	*hatihtámm*	هَتِهْتَمّ	*miš hatihtámm*	مِش هَتِهْتَمّ	
húmma	*hayihtámmu*	هَيِهْتَمّوا	*miš hayihtámmu*	مِش هَيِهْتَمّوا	
ínta	*ihtámm*	اِهْتَمّ	*ma-tihtámmiš*	مَتِهْتَمّش	**imperative**
ínti	*ihtámmi*	اِهْتَمّي	*ma-tihtammī́š*	مَتِهْتَمّيش	
íntu	*ihtámmu*	اِهْتَمّوا	*ma-tihtammū́š*	مَتِهْتَمّوش	

	active		passive		
masculine	*muhtámm*	مُهْتَمّ	—	—	**participles**
feminine	*muhtámma*	مُهْتَمّة	—	—	
plural	*muhtammīn*	مُهْتَمّين	—	—	

①
اِهْتمّيْت بِالرّسْم مِن صُغْري و اِتْمنّيْت طول عُمْري أكون فنانة.

ihtammēt bi-rrásmᵊ min ṣúɣri w itmannēt ṭūl 3úmri ʔakūn fanāna.

I've been interested in drawing ever since I was little.
I've wanted to become an artist all my life.

②
بحِبّ أهْتمّ بِالزّرْع، أصْل وْجوده في البيْت مُبْهِج.

baḥíbb ahtámmᵊ bi-zzár3, aṣlᵊ wgūdu fi -lbēt múbhig.

I like taking care of plants, as having
them in the house is delightful.

③
خالي و مْراته بِيِهْتمّوا بِبعْض كإِنُّهُم لِسّه مخْطوبين.

xāli wi mrātu biyihtámmu bi-bá3ḍᵊ ka-innúhum líssa maxṭubīn.

My uncle and his wife take care of each
other as if they were still engaged.

④
ههْتمّ بِالمُذاكْرة لَوْ المَوادّ مُسلّية، إنّما دي مُمِلّة جِدّاً.

hahtámmᵊ bi-lmuzákra law ilmawáddᵊ musallíyya, innáma di mumílla gíddan.

I'd be interested in studying if the subjects
were interesting, but they are so boring

⑤
اِهْتمّ بِشُغْلك زيّ ما إنْتَ مُهْتمّ بِالعربِيّات كِده و إنْتَ تِفْلح.

ihtámmᵊ bi-šúɣlak zayyᵊ ma -nta muhtámmᵊ bi-l3arabiyyāt kída w ínta tíflaḥ.

Take an interest in your work as you do in cars, and you'll succeed.

⑥
كلِّمْني عن إخْتِراعك أكْتر. أنا مُهْتمّ بيه أوي.

kallímni 3an ixtirā3ak áktar. ána muhtámmᵊ bī ʔáwi.

Tell me more about your invention.
I'm really interested in it.

⑦
مهْتمّيناش نِسْأل على أيّ تفاصيل بعْد ما عِرِفْنا السِّعْر.

ma-htamminā̆š nísʔal 3ála ʔayyᵊ tafaṣīl ba3dᵊ ma 3irífna -ssi3r.

We weren't interested in asking about
any details after we learned the price.

❖ [8g] **to be interested (in** بِ *bi-*)**; take care (of** بِ *bi-*)

➲ 23.5

53 to spend the night *bāt* باتْ

verbal nouns: *bayāt* بَيات - *biyāt* بِيات

		affirmative		negative	
perfect	ána	*bitt*	بِتّ	*ma-bíttiš*	مَبِتِّش
	íḫna	*bítna*	بِتْنا	*ma-bitbāš*	مَبِتْناش
	ínta	*bitt*	بِتّ	*ma-bíttiš*	مَبِتِّش
	ínti	*bítti*	بِتّي	*ma-bittīš*	مَبِتّيش
	íntu	*bíttu*	بِتّوا	*ma-bittūš*	مَبِتّوش
	húwwa	*bāt*	بات	*ma-bátš*	مَباتْش
	híyya	*bātit*	باتِت	*ma-batítš*	مَباتِتْش
	húmma	*bātu*	باتوا	*ma-batūš*	مَباتوش
imperfect	ána	*abāt*	أبات	*ma-bátš*	مَباتْش
	íḫna	*nibāt*	نِبات	*ma-nbátš*	مَنْباتْش
	ínta	*tibāt*	تِبات	*ma-tbátš*	مَتْباتْش
	ínti	*tibāti*	تِباتي	*ma-tbatīš*	مَتْباتيش
	íntu	*tibātu*	تِباتوا	*ma-tbatūš*	مَتْباتوش
	húwwa	*yibāt*	يِبات	*ma-ybátš*	مَيْباتْش
	híyya	*tibāt*	تِبات	*ma-tbátš*	مَتْباتْش
	húmma	*yibātu*	يِباتوا	*ma-ybatūš*	مَيْباتوش
bi-imperfect	ána	*babāt*	بَبات	*ma-babátš*	مَبَباتْش
	íḫna	*binbāt*	بِنْبات	*ma-binbátš*	مَبِنْباتْش
	ínta	*bitbāt*	بِتْبات	*ma-bitbátš*	مَبِتْباتْش
	ínti	*bitbāti*	بِتْباتي	*ma-bitbatīš*	مَبِتْباتيش
	íntu	*bitbātu*	بِتْباتوا	*ma-bitbatūš*	مَبِتْباتوش
	húwwa	*biybāt*	بِيْبات	*ma-biybátš*	مَبِيْباتْش
	híyya	*bitbāt*	بِتْبات	*ma-bitbátš*	مَبِتْباتْش
	húmma	*biybātu*	بِيْباتوا	*ma-biybatūš*	مَبِيْباتوش
future	ána	*habāt*	هَبات	*miš habāt*	مِش هَبات
	íḫna	*hanbāt*	هَنْبات	*miš hanbāt*	مِش هَنْبات
	ínta	*hatbāt*	هَتْبات	*miš hatbāt*	مِش هَتْبات
	ínti	*hatbāti*	هَتْباتي	*miš hatbāti*	مِش هَتْباتي
	íntu	*hatbātu*	هَتْباتوا	*miš hatbātu*	مِش هَتْباتوا
	húwwa	*haybāt*	هَيْبات	*miš haybāt*	مِش هَيْبات
	híyya	*hatbāt*	هَتْبات	*miš hatbāt*	مِش هَتْبات
	húmma	*haybātu*	هَيْباتوا	*miš haybātu*	مِش هَيْباتوا
imperative	ínta	*bāt*	بات	*ma-tbátš*	مَتْباتْش
	ínti	*bāti*	باتي	*ma-tbatīš*	مَتْباتيش
	íntu	*bātu*	باتوا	*ma-tbatūš*	مَتْباتوش

		active		passive	
participles	masculine	*bāyit*	بايِت	–	–
	feminine	*báyta*	بايْتَة	–	–
	plural	*baytīn*	بايْتين	–	–

①

حمْزة بات عنْد جِدُّه يومينْ. كانوا مبْسوطين هُمّا الاِتْنينْ.

ɧámza bāt 3andᵊ gíddu yumēn. kānu mabsuṭīn húmma -lʔitnēn.

Hamza spent two nights with his grandpa.
Both of them enjoyed it.

②

لمّا أجي أبات عنْدك، هلاعْبك كوتْشينة لِحدّ الصُّبْح.

lámm- ági ʔabāt 3ándak, halá3bak kutšīna li-ɧadd iṣṣúbɧ.

When I come to spend the night with you,
I'll play cards with you all night.

③

أخويا بِيْبات في شُغْله كْتير.

axūya biybāt fi šúɣlu kitīr.

My brother stays overnight at his work a lot.

④

هبات عنْد ماما بُكْره. أحْمد هَيْبات في الشُّغْل.

habāt 3andᵊ māma búkra. áɧmad haybāt fi -ššuɣl.

Tomorrow, I'll stay the night at mom's. Ahmed will be at work.

⑤

باتي في بيْتِك مهْما حصل بيْنِك و بيْن جوْزِك. السِّتّ متْسيبْش بيتْها أبداً.

bāti fi bētik máhma ɧáṣal bēnik wi bēn gōzik. issíttᵊ ma-tsíbšᵊ bítha ʔábadan.

Stay in your home whatever happens between you and your
husband. A woman should never abandon her home.

⑥

سافْرِت الغرْدقة و بايْته هِناك أُسْبوع.

sáfrit ilɣardáʔa wi báyta hināk ʔusbū3.

She's gone to Hurghada and is staying
[lit. overnighting] there for a week.

⑦

المُتور لمّا بات في مكانُه صحّ، العربية مشْيِت زيّ الفُلّ.

ilmutūr lámma bāt fi makānu ṣaɧɧ, il3arabíyya mášyit zayy ilfúll.

When the motor was fit into its proper place, the car ran perfectly.

⑧

متْبيتْش في الشُّغْل. أنا هسْتنّاك.

ma-tbítšᵊ fi -ššuɣl. ána hastannāk.

Don't stay at work all night. I'll be waiting for you.

❖ [1h3] **to spend the night, stay overnight, sleep over; to fit correctly**

- This verb's main meaning is 'stay overnight', and usually implies one is sleeping there, but can also refer to simply spending the whole night somewhere, for example, working. (➲ 53.3, 53.8)
- A lesser-used meaning is 'fit correctly'. (➲ 53.7)

54 to kiss *bās* باس

	affirmative		negative		
ána	*bust*	بُسْت	*ma-bústiš*	مَبُسْتِش	perfect
íḥna	*búsna*	بُسْنا	*ma-busnāš*	مَبُسْناش	
ínta	*bust*	بُسْت	*ma-bústiš*	مَبُسْتِش	
ínti	*bústi*	بُسْتي	*ma-bustīš*	مَبُسْتيش	
íntu	*bústu*	بُسْتوا	*ma-bustūš*	مَبُسْتوش	
húwwa	*bās*	باس	*ma-básš*	مَباسْش	
híyya	*bāsit*	باسِت	*ma-basítš*	مَباسْتِش	
húmma	*bāsu*	باسوا	*ma-basūš*	مَباسوش	
ána	*abūs*	أبوس	*ma-búsš*	مَبوسْش	imperfect
íḥna	*nibūs*	نِبوس	*ma-nbúsš*	مَنْبوسْش	
ínta	*tibūs*	تِبوس	*ma-tbúsš*	مَتْبوسْش	
ínti	*tibūsi*	تِبوسي	*ma-tbusīš*	مَتْبوسيش	
íntu	*tibūsu*	تِبوسوا	*ma-tbusūš*	مَتْبوسوش	
húwwa	*yibūs*	يِبوس	*ma-ybúsš*	مَيْبوسْش	
híyya	*tibūs*	تِبوس	*ma-tbúsš*	مَتْبوسْش	
húmma	*yibūsu*	يِبوسوا	*ma-ybusūš*	مَيْبوسوش	
ána	*babūs*	بَبوس	*ma-babúsš*	مَبَبوسْش	bi-imperfect
íḥna	*binbūs*	بِنْبوس	*ma-binbúsš*	مَبِنْبوسْش	
ínta	*bitbūs*	بِتْبوس	*ma-bitbúsš*	مَبِتْبوسْش	
ínti	*bitbūsi*	بِتْبوسي	*ma-bitbusīš*	مَبِتْبوسيش	
íntu	*bitbūsu*	بِتْبوسوا	*ma-bitbusūš*	مَبِتْبوسوش	
húwwa	*biybūs*	بِيْبوس	*ma-biybúsš*	مَبِيْبوسْش	
híyya	*bitbūs*	بِتْبوس	*ma-bitbúsš*	مَبِتْبوسْش	
húmma	*biybūsu*	بِيْبوسوا	*ma-biybusūš*	مَبِيْبوسوش	
ána	*habūs*	هَبوس	*miš habūs*	مِش هَبوس	future
íḥna	*hanbūs*	هَنْبوس	*miš hanbūs*	مِش هَنْبوس	
ínta	*hatbūs*	هَتْبوس	*miš hatbūs*	مِش هَتْبوس	
ínti	*hatbūsi*	هَتْبوسي	*miš hatbūsi*	مِش هَتْبوسي	
íntu	*hatbūsu*	هَتْبوسوا	*miš hatbūsu*	مِش هَتْبوسوا	
húwwa	*haybūs*	هَيْبوس	*miš haybūs*	مِش هَيْبوس	
híyya	*hatbūs*	هَتْبوس	*miš hatbūs*	مِش هَتْبوس	
húmma	*haybūsu*	هَيْبوسوا	*miš haybūsu*	مِش هَيْبوسوا	
ínta	*būs*	بوس	*ma-tbúsš*	مَتْبوسْش	imperative
ínti	*būsi*	بوسي	*ma-tbusīš*	مَتْبوسيش	
íntu	*būsu*	بوسوا	*ma-tbusūš*	مَتْبوسوش	

	active		passive		
masculine	*bāyis*	بايِس	*mitbās*	مِتْباس	participles
feminine	*báysa*	بايْسَة	*mitbāsa*	مِتْباسَة	
plural	*baysīn*	بايْسين	*mitbasīn*	مِتْباسين	

verbal noun: *bōs* بوْس

①

الوَلد باس أخوه الصُّغيرّ أوِّل ما صِحي.

ilwálad bās axū -ṣṣuɣáyyar áwwil ma ṣíḥi.

The boy kissed his little brother when he woke up.

②

لمّا أبوسِك في الفرح هتِتْكِسْفي؟

lámm- abūsik fi -lfáraḥ hatitkísfi?

When I kiss you at the wedding [ceremony], will you be embarrassed?

③

ببوس الوَلد ده كُلّ شْوَيّة. ده عسل أوي.

babūs ilwálad da kullᵊ šwáyya. da 3ásal áwi.

I kiss this boy every so often. He's so cute.

④

هَيْبوسْها دِلْوَقْتي. المُصوِّر هَياخُدْلُهُم صورة.

haybúsha dilwáʔti. ilmuṣáwwir hayaxudlúhum ṣūra.

He will kiss her now, so the photographer can get a picture of them.

⑤

بوس إيدك وِشّ و ضهْر إنّ المَوْضوع ده خِلِص.

būs īdak wiššᵊ wi ḍahr inn ilmawḍū3 da xíliṣ.

Be glad [lit. Kiss your hand, face, and back] that this issue has reached an end.

⑥

بَبوس إيدي وِشّ و ضهْر كُلّ يوْم عشان ربِّنا رزقْني بيكو.

babūs īdi wiššᵊ wi ḍahrᵊ kullᵊ yōm 3ašān rabbína razáʔni bīku.

I feel glad daily that God gave me both of you.

⑦

العريس مباسْش العروسة قُدّام المُصوِّر. مبيْحِبِّش الحركات دي.

il3arīs ma-bássš il3arūsa ʔuddām ilmuṣáwwir. ma-biyḥíbbiš ilḥarakāt di.

The groom didn't kiss the bride in front of the photographer. He doesn't like things like that.

❖ [1h1] **to kiss**

➲ 4.1

55 to sell *bā3* باع

verbal noun: *bē3* بيْع

	affirmative		negative		
ána	*bi3t*	بِعْت	*ma-bí3tiš*	مَبِعْتِش	perfect
íḫna	*bí3na*	بِعْنا	*ma-bi3nāš*	مَبِعْناش	
ínta	*bi3t*	بِعْت	*ma-bí3tiš*	مَبِعْتِش	
ínti	*bí3ti*	بِعْتي	*ma-bi3tīš*	مَبِعْتيش	
íntu	*bí3tu*	بِعْتوا	*ma-bi3tūš*	مَبِعْتوش	
húwwa	*bā3*	باع	*ma-bá3š*	مَباعْش	
híyya	*bā3it*	باعِت	*ma-ba3ítš*	مَباعِتْش	
húmma	*bā3u*	باعوا	*ma-ba3ūš*	مَباعوش	

ána	*abī3*	أبيع	*ma-bí3š*	مَبيعْش	imperfect
íḫna	*nibī3*	نِبيع	*ma-nbí3š*	مَنْبيعْش	
ínta	*tibī3*	تِبيع	*ma-tbí3š*	مَتْبيعْش	
ínti	*tibī3i*	تِبيعي	*ma-tbi3īš*	مَتْبيعيش	
íntu	*tibī3u*	تِبيعوا	*ma-tbi3ūš*	مَتْبيعوش	
húwwa	*yibī3*	يِبيع	*ma-ybí3š*	مَيْبيعْش	
híyya	*tibī3*	تِبيع	*ma-tbí3š*	مَتْبيعْش	
húmma	*yibī3u*	يِبيعوا	*ma-ybi3ūš*	مَيْبيعوش	

ána	*babī3*	بَبيع	*ma-babí3š*	مَبَبيعْش	bi-imperfect
íḫna	*binbī3*	بِنْبيع	*ma-binbí3š*	مَبِنْبيعْش	
ínta	*bitbī3*	بِتْبيع	*ma-bitbí3š*	مَبِتْبيعْش	
ínti	*bitbī3i*	بِتْبيعي	*ma-bitbi3īš*	مَبِتْبيعيش	
íntu	*bitbī3u*	بِتْبيعوا	*ma-bitbi3ūš*	مَبِتْبيعوش	
húwwa	*biybī3*	بِيْبيع	*ma-biybí3š*	مَبِيْبيعْش	
híyya	*bitbī3*	بِتْبيع	*ma-bitbí3š*	مَبِتْبيعْش	
húmma	*biybī3u*	بِيْبيعوا	*ma-biybi3ūš*	مَبِيْبيعوش	

ána	*habī3*	هَبيع	*miš habī3*	مِش هَبيع	future
íḫna	*hanbī3*	هَنْبيع	*miš hanbī3*	مِش هَنْبيع	
ínta	*hatbī3*	هَتْبيع	*miš hatbī3*	مِش هَتْبيع	
ínti	*hatbī3i*	هَتْبيعي	*miš hatbī3i*	مِش هَتْبيعي	
íntu	*hatbī3u*	هَتْبيعوا	*miš hatbī3u*	مِش هَتْبيعوا	
húwwa	*haybī3*	هَيْبيع	*miš haybī3*	مِش هَيْبيع	
híyya	*hatbī3*	هَتْبيع	*miš hatbī3*	مِش هَتْبيع	
húmma	*haybī3u*	هَيْبيعوا	*miš haybī3u*	مِش هَيْبيعوا	

ínta	*bī3*	بيع	*ma-tbí3š*	مَتْبيعْش	imperative
ínti	*bī3i*	بيعي	*ma-tbi3īš*	مَتْبيعيش	
íntu	*bī3u*	بيعوا	*ma-tbi3ūš*	مَتْبيعوش	

	active		passive		
masculine	*bāyi3*	بايِع	*mitbā3*	مِتْباع	participles
feminine	*báy3a*	بايْعَة	*mitbā3a*	مِتْباعَة	
plural	*bay3īn*	بايْعين	*mitba3īn*	مِتْباعين	

①

الكِتاب مِن أوِّل ما نِزِل باع خمْسين الْف نُسْخة.

ilkitāb min áwwil ma nízil bā3 xamsīn alf[ə] núsxa.

The book has sold 50,000 copies
since it was released.

②

جَواز بِنْتها خلّاها تِبيع دهبْها عشان تِعْرف تِجهِّز البِنْت.

gawāz bintáha xallāha tibī3 dahábha 3ašān tí3raf tigáhhiz ilbínt.

For her daughter's marriage, she had to sell
her jewelry in order to prepare for it.

③

بِيْبيعوا حاجات حِلْوَة أوي في المحلّ ده.

biybī3u ḫagāt ḫílwa ʔáwi fi -lmaḫáll[ə] da.

They sell very good stuff at this shop.

④

هبيع عربيتي بُكْره. عايِز أجيب واحْدة جْديدة.

habī3 3arabīti búkra. 3āyiz agīb wáḫda gdīda.

I'll sell my car tomorrow. I want to buy a new one.

⑤

بيع حاجْتك المُسْتعْملة عَ النّت.

bī3 ḫágtak ilmusta3mála 3a -nnat.

Sell your used stuff on the internet.

⑥

آسْفة يافنْدِم، القُطْعة دي مِتْباعة.

ásfa yafándim, ilqíṭ3a di mitbā3a.

Sorry sir, this piece is sold.

⑦

المحلّ ده مبِيْبيعْش فضّة. مُتخصّص في الدّهب بسّ.

ilmaḫáll[ə] da ma-biybí3š[ə] fáḍḍa. mutaxáṣṣaṣ fi -ddáhab bass.

This shop doesn't sell silver. It just specializes in gold.

❖ [1h2] **to sell**

➲ 117.1

56 to begin bádaʔ بَدَأ

verbal nouns: *badʔ* بَدْء - *bidāya* بِدايَة

	affirmative		negative		
ána	badáʔt	بَدَأْت	ma-badáʔtiš	مَبَدَأْتِش	**perfect**
íḥna	badáʔna	بَدَأْنا	ma-badaʔnāš	مَبَدَأْناش	
ínta	badáʔt	بَدَأْت	ma-badáʔtiš	مَبَدَأْتِش	
ínti	badáʔti	بَدَأْتي	ma-badaʔtīš	مَبَدَأْتيش	
íntu	badáʔtu	بَدَأْتوا	ma-badaʔtūš	مَبَدَأْتوش	
húwwa	bádaʔ	بَدَأ	ma-badáʔš	مَبَدَأْش	
híyya	bádaʔit	بَدَأِت	ma-badaʔítš	مَبَدَأِتْش	
húmma	bádaʔu	بَدَأوا	ma-badaʔūš	مَبَدَأوش	
ána	ábdaʔ	أَبْدَأ	ma-bdáʔš	مَبْدَأْش	**imperfect**
íḥna	níbdaʔ	نِبْدَأ	ma-nibdáʔš	مَنِبْدَأْش	
ínta	tíbdaʔ	تِبْدَأ	ma-tibdáʔš	مَتِبْدَأْش	
ínti	tibdáʔi	تِبْدَأي	ma-tibdaʔīš	مَتِبْدَأيش	
íntu	tibdáʔu	تِبْدَأوا	ma-tibdaʔūš	مَتِبْدَأوش	
húwwa	yíbdaʔ	يِبْدَأ	ma-yibdáʔš	مَيِبْدَأْش	
híyya	tíbdaʔ	تِبْدَأ	ma-tibdáʔš	مَتِبْدَأْش	
húmma	yibdáʔu	يِبْدَأوا	ma-yibdaʔūš	مَيِبْدَأوش	
ána	bábdaʔ	بَبْدَأ	ma-babdáʔš	مَبَبْدَأْش	**bi-imperfect**
íḥna	biníbdaʔ	بِنِبْدَأ	ma-bnibdáʔš	مَبْنِبْدَأْش	
ínta	bitíbdaʔ	بِتِبْدَأ	ma-btibdáʔš	مَبْتِبْدَأْش	
ínti	bitibdáʔi	بِتِبْدَأي	ma-btibdaʔīš	مَبْتِبْدَأيش	
íntu	bitibdáʔu	بِتِبْدَأوا	ma-btibdaʔūš	مَبْتِبْدَأوش	
húwwa	biyíbdaʔ	بِيِبْدَأ	ma-byibdáʔš	مَبْيِبْدَأْش	
híyya	bitíbdaʔ	بِتِبْدَأ	ma-btibdáʔš	مَبْتِبْدَأْش	
húmma	biyibdáʔu	بِيِبْدَأوا	ma-byibdaʔūš	مَبْيِبْدَأوش	
ána	hábdaʔ	هَبْدَأ	miš hábdaʔ	مِش هَبْدَأ	**future**
íḥna	haníbdaʔ	هَنِبْدَأ	miš haníbdaʔ	مِش هَنِبْدَأ	
ínta	hatíbdaʔ	هَتِبْدَأ	miš hatíbdaʔ	مِش هَتِبْدَأ	
ínti	hatibdáʔi	هَتِبْدَأي	miš hatibdáʔi	مِش هَتِبْدَأي	
íntu	hatibdáʔu	هَتِبْدَأوا	miš hatibdáʔu	مِش هَتِبْدَأوا	
húwwa	hayíbdaʔ	هَيِبْدَأ	miš hayíbdaʔ	مِش هَيِبْدَأ	
híyya	hatíbdaʔ	هَتِبْدَأ	miš hatíbdaʔ	مِش هَتِبْدَأ	
húmma	hayibdáʔu	هَيِبْدَأوا	miš hayibdáʔu	مِش هَيِبْدَأوا	
ínta	íbdaʔ	اِبْدَأ	ma-tibdáʔš	مَتِبْدَأْش	**imperative**
ínti	ibdáʔi	اِبْدَأي	ma-tibdaʔīš	مَتِبْدَأيش	
íntu	ibdáʔu	اِبْدَأوا	ma-tibdaʔūš	مَتِبْدَأوش	

	active		passive		
masculine	bādiʔ / bādi	بادِئ / بادي	–	–	**participles**
feminine	bádʔa / bádya	بادْأة / بادْيَة	–	–	
plural	badʔīn / badyīn	بادْئين / بادْيين	–	–	

①

الماراثون بدأ السّاعة ٨ الصُّبْح و خِلِص على ١٢ الضُّهْر.

ilmarasōn báda? issā3a tamánya -ṣṣúbḫᵊ wi xíliṣ 3ála -tnāšar iḍḍúhr.

The marathon started at 8 a.m. and ended around 12 p.m.

②

لمّا يِبْدأ المُسلْسل صحّيني.

lámma yíbda? ilmusálsal ṣaḫḫīni.

When the TV show comes on, wake me up.

③

أنا ببْدأ تمْريني بِالمشْي و بخْتِمُه بِالسّاوْنا.

ána bábda? tamrīni bi-lmášyᵊ wi baxtímu bi-ssáwna.

I begin my training with a walk and finish with the sauna.

④

هبْدأ الرِّجيم بُكْره.

hábda? irrižīm búkra.

I'll start my diet tomorrow.

⑤

اِبْدأ كِبير، هتِفْضل كِبير.

íbda? kibīr, hatífḍal kibīr.

Start big, stay big.

⑥

مبدأْتِش مُذاكْرة لِحدّ دِلْوَقْتي. مِش عارْفة هعْمِل أيْه في الاِمْتِحان؟

ma-badá?tiš muzákra li-ḫáddᵊ dilwá?ti. miš 3árfa há3mil ?ē fi -l?imtiḫān?

I haven't started studying yet. I don't
know what I'll do on the exam.

❖ [1s1] **to begin, start**

- This verb can be transitive (➲ 56.3, 56.4, 56.6) or intransitive (➲ 56.1, 56.2, 56.5).
- Compare with اِبْتَدَى *ibtáda*. (➲ 3)

➲ 6.5, 191.2, 201.1, 225.2

57 to look *baṣṣ* بص 3 1

	affirmative		negative		
ána	baṣṣēt	بَصّيْت	ma-baṣṣítš	مَبَصّيْتْش	perfect
íḥna	baṣṣēna	بَصّيْنا	ma-baṣṣināš	مَبَصّيناش	
ínta	baṣṣēt	بَصّيْت	ma-baṣṣítš	مَبَصّيْتْش	
ínti	baṣṣēti	بَصّيْتي	ma-baṣṣitīš	مَبَصّيتيش	
íntu	baṣṣētu	بَصّيْتوا	ma-baṣṣitūš	مَبَصّيتوش	
húwwa	baṣṣ	بَصّ	ma-báṣṣiš	مَبَصّش	
híyya	báṣṣit	بَصّت	ma-baṣṣítš	مَبَصّتْش	
húmma	báṣṣu	بَصّوا	ma-baṣṣūš	مَبَصّوش	
ána	abúṣṣ	أبُصّ	ma-búṣṣiš	مَبُصّش	imperfect
íḥna	nibúṣṣ	نِبُصّ	ma-nbúṣṣiš	مَنْبُصّش	
ínta	tibúṣṣ	تِبُصّ	ma-tbúṣṣiš	مَتْبُصّش	
ínti	tibúṣṣi	تِبُصّي	ma-tbuṣṣīš	مَتْبُصّيش	
íntu	tibúṣṣu	تِبُصّوا	ma-tbuṣṣūš	مَتْبُصّوش	
húwwa	yibúṣṣ	يِبُصّ	ma-ybúṣṣiš	مَيْبُصّش	
híyya	tibúṣṣ	تِبُصّ	ma-tbúṣṣiš	مَتْبُصّش	
húmma	yibúṣṣu	يِبُصّوا	ma-ybuṣṣūš	مَيْبُصّوش	
ána	babúṣṣ	بَبُصّ	ma-babúṣṣiš	مَبَبُصّش	bi-imperfect
íḥna	binbúṣṣ	بِنْبُصّ	ma-binbúṣṣiš	مَبِنْبُصّش	
ínta	bitbúṣṣ	بِتْبُصّ	ma-bitbúṣṣiš	مَبِتْبُصّش	
ínti	bitbúṣṣi	بِتْبُصّي	ma-bitbuṣṣīš	مَبِتْبُصّيش	
íntu	bitbúṣṣu	بِتْبُصّوا	ma-bitbuṣṣūš	مَبِتْبُصّوش	
húwwa	biybúṣṣ	بِيْبُصّ	ma-biybúṣṣiš	مَبِيْبُصّش	
híyya	bitbúṣṣ	بِتْبُصّ	ma-bitbúṣṣiš	مَبِتْبُصّش	
húmma	biybúṣṣu	بِيْبُصّوا	ma-biybuṣṣūš	مَبِيْبُصّوش	
ána	habúṣṣ	هَبُصّ	miš habúṣṣ	مِش هَبُصّ	future
íḥna	hanbúṣṣ	هَنْبُصّ	miš hanbúṣṣ	مِش هَنْبُصّ	
ínta	hatbúṣṣ	هَتْبُصّ	miš hatbúṣṣ	مِش هَتْبُصّ	
ínti	hatbúṣṣi	هَتْبُصّي	miš hatbúṣṣi	مِش هَتْبُصّي	
íntu	hatbúṣṣu	هَتْبُصّوا	miš hatbúṣṣu	مِش هَتْبُصّوا	
húwwa	haybúṣṣ	هَيْبُصّ	miš haybúṣṣ	مِش هَيْبُصّ	
híyya	hatbúṣṣ	هَتْبُصّ	miš hatbúṣṣ	مِش هَتْبُصّ	
húmma	haybúṣṣu	هَيْبُصّوا	miš haybúṣṣu	مِش هَيْبُصّوا	
ínta	buṣṣ	بُصّ	ma-tbúṣṣiš	مَتْبُصّش	imperative
ínti	búṣṣi	بُصّي	ma-tbuṣṣīš	مَتْبُصّيش	
íntu	búṣṣu	بُصّوا	ma-tbuṣṣūš	مَتْبُصّوش	

	active		passive		
masculine	bāṣiṣ	باصِص	mabṣūṣ	مَبْصوص	participles
feminine	báṣṣa	باصّة	mabṣūṣa	مَبْصوصَة	
plural	baṣṣīn	باصّين	mabṣuṣīn	مَبْصوصين	

verbal noun: *baṣṣ* بَصّ

①

سِمِعْنا صوْت عالي، بصّيْنا فوْق لقيْنا طيّارات نفّاثة مْعدّية.

simí3na ṣōt 3āli, baṣṣēna fō? la?ēna ṭayyarāt naffāsa m3addíyya.

We heard a loud noise, looked up, and
saw jet airplanes passing over.

②

بحِبّ أبُصّ عَ الأطْفال و هُمّا نايْمين، كإنُّهُم ملايْكة.

baḫíbb abúṣṣᵊ 3a -l?aṭfāl wi húmma naymīn, ka-innúhum maláyka.

I love looking at babies sleeping like the angels they are.

③

الشّابّ ده بِيْبُصِّلِك كُلّ شْوَيّة. شكْلُه مُعْجب بيكي.

iššábbᵊ da biybuṣṣílik kullᵊ šwáyya. šáklu mú3gab bīki.

The guy keeps looking at you. He seems to like you.

④

اِنْدهْلي لمّا تِوْصل تحْت البيْت، و أنا هبُصِّلك مِن الشِّبّاك.

indáhli lámma tíwṣal taḫt ilbēt, w ána habuṣṣílak min iššibbāk.

Give me a shout when you are in front of the house,
and I'll look at you from the window.

⑤

اِنْزِلي بُصّي على اللِّبْس في وِسْط البلد، هتْلاقي حاجات حِلْوَة.

inzíli búṣṣi 3ála -llibsᵊ f wisṭ ilbálad, hatlā?i ḫagāt ḫílwa.

You'll find nice things if you go downtown to look at clothes.

⑥

خبّي الهدية دي، لتْشوفْها بِنْت خالْتِك و تِبُصِّلِك فيها.

xábbi -lhadíyya di, la-tšúfha bintᵊ xáltik wi tibuṣṣílik fīha.

Hide this gift, or else your niece will see it and be envious.

⑦

متْبُصِّليش مِن فوْق لِتحْت. كُلِّنا وِلاد ناس.

ma-tbuṣṣilīš min fō? li-taḫt. kullína wilād nās.

Don't look at me disparagingly. We are all equal.

❖ [1g2] **to look** (**at** لِـ *li-*, على *3ála*)

- This verb can take a indirect object pronoun (with لِـ *li-*) (➲ 57.3, 57.4, 57.7), or a noun object with the preposition على *3ála* (➲ 57.2, 57.5).
- It is used idiomatically. (➲ 57.6)

➲ 175.2, 227.3, 231.9, 262.3

58 to stop báṭṭal بطّل 13

	affirmative		negative		
ána	baṭṭált	بَطّلْت	ma-baṭṭáltiš	مَبَطّلْتِش	perfect
íḫna	baṭṭálna	بَطّلْنا	ma-baṭṭalnāš	مَبَطّلْناش	
ínta	baṭṭált	بَطّلْت	ma-baṭṭáltiš	مَبَطّلْتِش	
ínti	baṭṭálti	بَطّلْتي	ma-baṭṭaltīš	مَبَطّلْتيش	
íntu	baṭṭáltu	بَطّلْتوا	ma-baṭṭaltūš	مَبَطّلْتوش	
húwwa	báṭṭal	بَطّل	ma-baṭṭálš	مَبَطّلْش	
híyya	baṭṭálit	بَطّلِت	ma-baṭṭalítš	مَبَطّلِتْش	
húmma	baṭṭálu	بَطّلوا	ma-baṭṭalūš	مَبَطّلوش	
ána	abáṭṭal	أبطّل	ma-baṭṭálš	مَبَطّلْش	imperfect
íḫna	nibáṭṭal	نِبَطّل	ma-nbaṭṭálš	مَنْبَطّلْش	
ínta	tibáṭṭal	تِبَطّل	ma-tbaṭṭálš	مَتْبَطّلْش	
ínti	tibaṭṭáli	تِبَطّلي	ma-tbaṭṭalīš	مَتْبَطّليش	
íntu	tibaṭṭálu	تِبَطّلوا	ma-tbaṭṭalūš	مَتْبَطّلوش	
húwwa	yibáṭṭal	يِبَطّل	ma-ybaṭṭálš	مَيْبَطّلْش	
híyya	tibáṭṭal	تِبَطّل	ma-tbaṭṭálš	مَتْبَطّلْش	
húmma	yibaṭṭálu	يِبَطّلوا	ma-ybaṭṭalūš	مَيْبَطّلوش	
ána	babáṭṭal	بَبَطّل	ma-babaṭṭálš	مَبَبَطّلْش	bi-imperfect
íḫna	binbáṭṭal	بِنْبَطّل	ma-binbaṭṭálš	مَبِنْبَطّلْش	
ínta	bitbáṭṭal	بِتْبَطّل	ma-bitbaṭṭálš	مَبِتْبَطّلْش	
ínti	bitbaṭṭáli	بِتْبَطّلي	ma-bitbaṭṭalīš	مَبِتْبَطّليش	
íntu	bitbaṭṭálu	بِتْبَطّلوا	ma-bitbaṭṭalūš	مَبِتْبَطّلوش	
húwwa	biybáṭṭal	بِيْبَطّل	ma-biybaṭṭálš	مَبِيْبَطّلْش	
híyya	bitbáṭṭal	بِتْبَطّل	ma-bitbaṭṭálš	مَبِتْبَطّلْش	
húmma	biybaṭṭálu	بِيْبَطّلوا	ma-biybaṭṭalūš	مَبِيْبَطّلوش	
ána	habáṭṭal	هَبَطّل	miš habáṭṭal	مِش هَبَطّل	future
íḫna	hanbáṭṭal	هَنْبَطّل	miš hanbáṭṭal	مِش هَنْبَطّل	
ínta	hatbáṭṭal	هَتْبَطّل	miš hatbáṭṭal	مِش هَتْبَطّل	
ínti	hatbaṭṭáli	هَتْبَطّلي	miš hatbaṭṭáli	مِش هَتْبَطّلي	
íntu	hatbaṭṭálu	هَتْبَطّلوا	miš hatbaṭṭálu	مِش هَتْبَطّلوا	
húwwa	haybáṭṭal	هَيْبَطّل	miš haybáṭṭal	مِش هَيْبَطّل	
híyya	hatbáṭṭal	هَتْبَطّل	miš hatbáṭṭal	مِش هَتْبَطّل	
húmma	haybaṭṭálu	هَيْبَطّلوا	miš haybaṭṭálu	مِش هَيْبَطّلوا	
ínta	báṭṭal	بَطّل	ma-tbaṭṭálš	مَتْبَطّلْش	imperative
ínti	baṭṭáli	بَطّلي	ma-tbaṭṭalīš	مَتْبَطّليش	
íntu	baṭṭálu	بَطّلوا	ma-tbaṭṭalūš	مَتْبَطّلوش	

	active		passive		
masculine	mibáṭṭal	مِبَطّل	mitbáṭṭal	مِتْبَطّل	participles
feminine	mibaṭṭála	مِبَطّلة	mitbaṭṭála	مِتْبَطّلة	
plural	mibaṭṭalīn	مِبَطّلين	mitbaṭṭalīn	مِتْبَطّلين	

verbal noun: tabṭīl تبْطيل

①

بطّلْت تدْخين مِن خمس سِنين، لمّا جالي مشاكِل صِحّية.

baṭṭált^ə tadxīn min xámas sinīn, lámma gāli mašākil ṣiḫḫíyya.

I stopped smoking five years ago when
I started having health problems.

②

مِش تِبطّل بصْبصة لِلبنات بقى و تِحْتِرِم سِنّك!

miš tibáṭṭal baṣbáṣa li-lbanāt báʔa wi tiḫtírim sínnak!

Won't you stop ogling girls?! Act your age!

③

لمّا غيرّْت البطارية، بقيْت ببطّل العربية و أرْجع أدوّرْها تاني بِسْهولة.

lámma ɣayyárt ilbaṭaríyya, baʔēt babáṭṭal il3arabíyya w árga3 adawwárha tāni bi-shūla.

After I changed the battery, it became easier
to switch off the car and start it up again.

④

محْمود هَيْبطّل كسل و هَيْروح يِشْتِرِك في نشاط تطوُّعي.

maḫmūd haybáṭṭal kásal wi hayrūḫ yištírik fi našāṭ taṭawwú3i.

Mahmoud will stop being lazy and
will go do some volunteer work.

⑤

بطّلي هِزار بقى و اِتْكلِّمي جدّ شْوَيّة.

baṭṭáli hizār báʔa w itkallími gadd^ə šwáyya.

Stop joking and talk seriously for a while.

⑥

أنا مْبطّل سُكّرِيّات و نِشَوِيّات بقالي شهْر.

ána mbáṭṭál sukkariyyāt wi nišawiyyāt baʔāli šahr.

I've given up sugar and starches for a month.

⑦

أنا مبطّلْتِش تفْكير فيك طول اللّيْل.

ána ma-baṭṭáltiš tafkīr fīk ṭūl illēl.

I didn't stop thinking about you all night.

❖ [2s2] **to stop, quit, give up; to turn off** (an engine)

- This verb can take a noun (➲ 58.6) or a verbal noun as its object.

➲ 8.3, 37.5, 101.3, 131.2, 147.5, 151.3, 176.7, 216.5, 242.2, 246.2, 250.2

59 to send bá3at بَعَت

verbal noun: ba3t بَعْت

	affirmative		negative		
ána	ba3átt	بَعَتّ	ma-ba3áttiš	مَبَعَتِّش	perfect
íḫna	ba3átna	بَعَتْنا	ma-ba3atnāš	مَبَعَتْناش	
ínta	ba3átt	بَعَتّ	ma-ba3áttiš	مَبَعَتِّش	
ínti	ba3átti	بَعَتّي	ma-ba3attīš	مَبَعَتّيش	
íntu	ba3áttu	بَعَتّوا	ma-ba3attūš	مَبَعَتّوش	
húwwa	bá3at	بَعَت	ma-ba3átš	مَبَعَتْش	
híyya	bá3atit	بَعَتِت	ma-ba3atítš	مَبَعَتِتْش	
húmma	bá3atu	بَعَتوا	ma-ba3atūš	مَبَعَتوش	
ána	áb3at	أَبْعَت	ma-t3átš	مَبْعَتْش	imperfect
íḫna	níb3at	نِبْعَت	ma-nib3átš	مَنِبْعَتْش	
ínta	tíb3at	تِبْعَت	ma-tib3átš	مَتِبْعَتْش	
ínti	tib3áti	تِبْعَتي	ma-tib3atīš	مَتِبْعَتيش	
íntu	tib3átu	تِبْعَتوا	ma-tib3atūš	مَتِبْعَتوش	
húwwa	yíb3at	يِبْعَت	ma-yib3átš	مَيِبْعَتْش	
híyya	tíb3at	تِبْعَت	ma-tib3átš	مَتِبْعَتْش	
húmma	yib3átu	يِبْعَتوا	ma-yib3atūš	مَيِبْعَتوش	
ána	báb3at	بَبْعَت	ma-bab3átš	مَبَبْعَتْش	bi-imperfect
íḫna	biníb3at	بِنِبْعَت	ma-bnib3átš	مَبْنِبْعَتْش	
ínta	bitíb3at	بِتِبْعَت	ma-btib3átš	مَبْتِبْعَتْش	
ínti	bitib3áti	بِتِبْعَتي	ma-btib3atīš	مَبْتِبْعَتيش	
íntu	bitib3átu	بِتِبْعَتوا	ma-btib3atūš	مَبْتِبْعَتوش	
húwwa	biyíb3at	بِيِبْعَت	ma-byib3átš	مَبْيِبْعَتْش	
híyya	bitíb3at	بِتِبْعَت	ma-btib3átš	مَبْتِبْعَتْش	
húmma	biyib3átu	بِيِبْعَتوا	ma-byib3atūš	مَبْيِبْعَتوش	
ána	háb3at	هَبْعَت	miš háb3at	مِش هَبْعَت	future
íḫna	haníb3at	هَنِبْعَت	miš haníb3at	مِش هَنِبْعَت	
ínta	hatíb3at	هَتِبْعَت	miš hatíb3at	مِش هَتِبْعَت	
ínti	hatib3áti	هَتِبْعَتي	miš hatib3áti	مِش هَتِبْعَتي	
íntu	hatib3átu	هَتِبْعَتوا	miš hatib3átu	مِش هَتِبْعَتوا	
húwwa	hayíb3at	هَيِبْعَت	miš hayíb3at	مِش هَيِبْعَت	
híyya	hatíb3at	هَتِبْعَت	miš hatíb3at	مِش هَتِبْعَت	
húmma	hayib3átu	هَيِبْعَتوا	miš hayib3átu	مِش هَيِبْعَتوا	
ínta	íb3at	اِبْعَت	ma-tib3átš	مَتِبْعَتْش	imperative
ínti	ib3áti	اِبْعَتي	ma-tib3atīš	مَتِبْعَتيش	
íntu	ib3átu	اِبْعَتوا	ma-tib3atūš	مَتِبْعَتوش	

	active		passive		
masculine	bā3it	باعِت	mab3ūt	مَبْعوت	participles
feminine	bá3ta	باعْتَة	mab3ūta	مَبْعوتَة	
plural	ba3tīn	باعْتين	mab3utīn	مَبْعوتين	

①

بعتّي الإيميْل لِلعميل وَلّا لِسّه؟

ba3átti -lʔīmēl li-l3amīl wálla líssa?

Did you send the email to the client yet?

②

جارْنا كُلّ يوْم يِبْعت بوكيْه وَرد لِمْراته، رومانْسي أوي!

gárna kullᵊ yōm yíb3at bukēh wárad li-mrātu, rumánsi ʔáwi!

Our neighbor sends a bouquet of flowers
to his wife every day. So romantic!

③

ماما بِتِبْعت كحْك لِكُلّ جاراتْنا في العيد.

māma bitíb3at kaħkᵊ li-kullᵊ garátna fi -l3īd.

My mom sends kahk to all our lady neighbors at Eid.

④

محمّد هَيِبْعتْلك الفِلوس على رصيدك.

maħámmad hayib3átlak ilfilūs 3ála raṣīdak.

Mohamed will send you the money to your bank account.

⑤

اِبْعتوا بَياناتْكو على مَوْقِعْنا الإلِكْتْروْنى، و هنرُدّ عليْكُم خِلال يوْميْن.

ib3átu bayanátku 3ála mawqí3na -lʔiliktrōni, wi hanrúddᵊ 3alēkum xilāl yumēn.

Send your info to our website, and we'll reply within two days.

⑥

الأكْل مبْعوتْلِنا بارِد. مَيِنْفعْش كِده.

ilʔáklᵊ mab3utlína bārid. ma-yinfá3šᵊ kída.

The meal was delivered cold. This is unacceptable.

⑦

إنْتَ مبعتّش الإيميْل لِحدّ دِلْوَقْتي؟

ínta ma-ba3áttiš ilʔīmēl li-ħaddᵊ dilwáʔti?

You still haven't sent the email?

❖ [1s1] **to send**

➲ 171.3, 213.4, 258.5

60 to stay away *bí3id* بِعِد

		affirmative		negative		
ána	*bi3ídt*	بِعِدْت	*ma-b3ídtiš*	مَبْعِدْتِش	**perfect**
íḫna	*bi3ídna*	بِعِدْنا	*ma-b3idnāš*	مَبْعِدْناش	
ínta	*bi3ídt*	بِعِدْت	*ma-b3ídtiš*	مَبْعِدْتِش	
ínti	*bi3ídti*	بِعِدْتي	*ma-b3idtīš*	مَبْعِدْتيش	
íntu	*bi3ídtu*	بِعِدْتوا	*ma-b3idtūš*	مَبْعِدْتوش	
húwwa	*bí3id*	بِعِد	*ma-b3ídš*	مَبْعِدْش	
híyya	*bí3dit*	بِعْدِت	*ma-bi3dítš*	مَبِعْدِتْش	
húmma	*bí3du*	بِعْدوا	*ma-bi3dūš*	مَبِعْدوش	
ána	*áb3ad*	أَبْعَد	*ma-b3ádš*	مَبْعَدْش	**imperfect**
íḫna	*níb3ad*	نِبْعَد	*ma-nib3ádš*	مَنِبْعَدْش	
ínta	*tíb3ad*	تِبْعَد	*ma-tib3ádš*	مَتِبْعَدْش	
ínti	*tib3ádi*	تِبْعَدي	*ma-tib3adīš*	مَتِبْعَديش	
íntu	*tib3ádu*	تِبْعَدوا	*ma-tib3adūš*	مَتِبْعَدوش	
húwwa	*yíb3ad*	يِبْعَد	*ma-yib3ádš*	مَيِبْعَدْش	
híyya	*tíb3ad*	تِبْعَد	*ma-tib3ádš*	مَتِبْعَدْش	
húmma	*yib3ádu*	يِبْعَدوا	*ma-yib3adūš*	مَيِبْعَدوش	
ána	*báb3ad*	بَبْعَد	*ma-bab3ádš*	مَبَبْعَدْش	**bi-imperfect**
íḫna	*biníb3ad*	بِنِبْعَد	*ma-bnib3ádš*	مَبْنِبْعَدْش	
ínta	*bitíb3ad*	بِتِبْعَد	*ma-btib3ádš*	مَبْتِبْعَدْش	
ínti	*bitib3ádi*	بِتِبْعَدي	*ma-btib3adīš*	مَبْتِبْعَديش	
íntu	*bitib3ádu*	بِتِبْعَدوا	*ma-btib3adūš*	مَبْتِبْعَدوش	
húwwa	*biyíb3ad*	بِيِبْعَد	*ma-byib3ádš*	مَبْيِبْعَدْش	
híyya	*bitíb3ad*	بِتِبْعَد	*ma-btib3ádš*	مَبْتِبْعَدْش	
húmma	*biyib3ádu*	بِيِبْعَدوا	*ma-byib3adūš*	مَبْيِبْعَدوش	
ána	*háb3ad*	هَبْعَد	*miš háb3ad*	مِش هَبْعَد	**future**
íḫna	*haníb3ad*	هَنِبْعَد	*miš haníb3ad*	مِش هَنِبْعَد	
ínta	*hatíb3ad*	هَتِبْعَد	*miš hatíb3ad*	مِش هَتِبْعَد	
ínti	*hatib3ádi*	هَتِبْعَدي	*miš hatib3ádi*	مِش هَتِبْعَدي	
íntu	*hatib3ádu*	هَتِبْعَدوا	*miš hatib3ádu*	مِش هَتِبْعَدوا	
húwwa	*hayíb3ad*	هَيِبْعَد	*miš hayíb3ad*	مِش هَيِبْعَد	
híyya	*hatíb3ad*	هَتِبْعَد	*miš hatíb3ad*	مِش هَتِبْعَد	
húmma	*hayib3ádu*	هَيِبْعَدوا	*miš hayib3ádu*	مِش هَيِبْعَدوا	
ínta	*íb3ad*	اِبْعَد	*ma-tib3ádš*	مَتِبْعَدْش	**imperative**
ínti	*ib3ádi*	اِبْعَدي	*ma-tib3adīš*	مَتِبْعَديش	
íntu	*ib3ádu*	اِبْعَدوا	*ma-tib3adūš*	مَتِبْعَدوش	

	active		passive		
masculine	*bā3id*	باعِد	*mab3ūd*	مَبْعود	**participles**
feminine	*bá3da*	باعْدَة	*mab3ūda*	مَبْعودَة	
plural	*ba3dīn*	باعْدين	*mab3udīn*	مَبْعودين	

verbal noun: *bu3d* بُعْد

①

ماهيتاب بِعْدِت عن شِلِّةْ البنات اللي كانِت مِصاحْباهُم، لمّا لقِت نفْسها هتِفْشل في دْراسِتْها.

mahitāb bí3dit 3an šíllit ilbanāt ílli kānit miṣaɦbāhum, lámma láʔit nafsáha hatífšal fi drasítha.

Mahitab distanced herself from the group of girls she was friends with when she found herself failing in her studies.

②

مِش جايّة معاكو. مِش هقْدر أبْعد عن الوِلاد.

miš gáyya ma3āku. miš háʔdar áb3ad 3an ilwilād.

I'm not going with you. I can't be away from my kids.

③

أُكْتوبر بِتِبْعد عن الهرم مسافةْ رُبْع ساعة بِالعربية.

uktūbar bitíb3ad 3an ilháram masāfit rub3ᵊ sā3a bi-l3arabíyya.

October City is a quarter-hour away from Haram street by car.

④

هتِبْعدوا أوي عنِّنا لمّا تُسْكُنوا في العُبور.

hatib3ádu ʔáwi 3annína lámma tuskúnu fi -l3ubūr.

You'll be so far from us when you move to Obour City.

⑤

المثل بِيْقول: اِبْعد عن الشّر و غنّيلُه.

ilmásal biyʔūl: íb3ad 3an iššár wi ɣannīlu.

A proverb goes: Stay away from evil and maintain your peace [lit. sing for it].

⑥

متِبْعدْش عنّي يا حبيبى، عشان متْتوهْش.

ma-tib3ádšᵊ 3ánni ya ɦabībi, 3ašān ma-ttúhš.

(mother to child:) Don't go far, dear. I don't want you to get lost.

❖ [1s4] **to be away, distance oneself (from** عن *3an*)

➲ 38.6

61 to become báʔa بقى

	affirmative		negative		
ána	baʔēt	بَقيْت	ma-baʔítš	مَبَقيتْش	perfect
íḥna	baʔēna	بَقيْنا	ma-baʔināš	مَبَقيناش	
ínta	baʔēt	بَقيْت	ma-baʔítš	مَبَقيتْش	
ínti	baʔēti	بَقيْتي	ma-baʔitīš	مَبَقيتيش	
íntu	baʔētu	بَقيْتوا	ma-baʔitūš	مَبَقيتوش	
húwwa	báʔa	بَقَى	ma-baʔāš	مَبَقاش	
híyya	báʔit	بَقِت	ma-baʔítš	مَبَقِتْش	
húmma	báʔu	بَقوا	ma-baʔūš	مَبَقوش	

ána	ábʔa	أَبْقَى	ma-bʔāš	مَبْقاش	imperfect
íḥna	níbʔa	نِبْقَى	ma-nibʔāš	مَنِبْقاش	
ínta	tíbʔa	تِبْقَى	ma-tibʔāš	مَتِبْقاش	
ínti	tíbʔi	تِبْقي	ma-tibʔīš	مَتِبْقيش	
íntu	tíbʔu	تِبْقوا	ma-tibʔūš	مَتِبْقوش	
húwwa	yíbʔa	يِبْقَى	ma-yibʔāš	مَيِبْقاش	
híyya	tíbʔa	تِبْقَى	ma-tibʔāš	مَتِبْقاش	
húmma	yíbʔu	يِبْقوا	ma-yibʔūš	مَيِبْقوش	

ána	bábʔa	بَبْقَى	ma-babʔāš	مَبَبْقاش	bi-imperfect
íḥna	biníbʔa	بِنِبْقَى	ma-bnibʔāš	مَبْنِبْقاش	
ínta	bitíbʔa	بِتِبْقَى	ma-btibʔāš	مَبْتِبْقاش	
ínti	bitíbʔi	بِتِبْقي	ma-btibʔīš	مَبْتِبْقيش	
íntu	bitíbʔu	بِتِبْقوا	ma-btibʔūš	مَبْتِبْقوش	
húwwa	biyíbʔa	بِيِبْقَى	ma-byibʔāš	مَبْيِبْقاش	
híyya	bitíbʔa	بِتِبْقَى	ma-btibʔāš	مَبْتِبْقاش	
húmma	biyíbʔu	بِيِبْقوا	ma-byibʔūš	مَبْيِبْقوش	

ána	hábʔa	هَبْقَى	miš hábʔa	مِش هَبْقَى	future
íḥna	haníbʔa	هَنِبْقَى	miš haníbʔa	مِش هَنِبْقَى	
ínta	hatíbʔa	هَتِبْقَى	miš hatíbʔa	مِش هَتِبْقَى	
ínti	hatíbʔi	هَتِبْقي	miš hatíbʔi	مِش هَتِبْقي	
íntu	hatíbʔu	هَتِبْقوا	miš hatíbʔu	مِش هَتِبْقوا	
húwwa	hayíbʔa	هَيِبْقَى	miš hayíbʔa	مِش هَيِبْقَى	
híyya	hatíbʔa	هَتِبْقَى	miš hatíbʔa	مِش هَتِبْقَى	
húmma	hayíbʔu	هَيِبْقوا	miš hayíbʔu	مِش هَيِبْقوا	

ínta	íbʔa	اِبْقَى	ma-tibʔāš	مَتِبْقاش	imperative
ínti	íbʔi	اِبْقي	ma-tibʔīš	مَتِبْقيش	
íntu	íbʔu	اِبْقوا	ma-tibʔūš	مَتِبْقوش	

no verbal noun

	active		passive		
masculine	—	—	—	—	participles
feminine	—	—	—	—	
plural	—	—	—	—	

①

شعْبان بقى عصبي جِدّاً بعْد الحادْثة اللي حصلِتْله.

ša3bān báʔa 3áṣabi gíddan ba3d ilħádsa -lli ħaṣalítlu.

Sha'ban became so nervous after the accident he had.

③

تورْتِةْ الفَواكِهْ حِلْوَة بسّ بِتِبْقي أحْلى لَوْ شُكولاتة.

túrtit ilfawākih ħílwa bass^ə bitíbʔa ʔáħla law šukulāta.

Fruit cake is good, but it's better if it's with chocolate.

②

محْمود يِبْقى إبْن عمِّتي و أحْمد إبْن أُخْتي.

maħmūd yíbʔa ʔibn^ə 3ammíti w áħmad ʔibn úxti.

Mahmoud is my cousin, and Ahmed is my nephew.

④

هتِبْقوا تِعدّوا علِيْنا بقى، هنِسْتنّاكو.

hatíbʔu ti3áddu 3alēna báʔa, hanistannāku.

You'll pass by us. We'll be waiting for you.

⑤

محمّد لمّا سافِر لِوَحْدُه اِعْتمد على نفْسُه و بقى يِعْمِل أكْل حِلْو.

maħámmad lámma sāfir li-wáħdu, i3támad 3ála náfsu wi báʔa yí3mil akl^ə ħilw.

When Mohamed was living abroad alone, he had to be independent, and now he can make tasty food.

⑥

إبْني مبقاش يِعْمِل على نفْسُه مِن سِنّ سنة و نُصّ.

íbni ma-baʔāš yí3mil 3ála náfsu min sinn^ə sána wi nuṣṣ.

My son stopped wetting himself when he was a year and a half old.

⑧

أنا مبقيتْش أحِبّ الفُرْجة عَ التِّليفِزْيوْن.

ána ma-baʔítš aħíbb ilfúrga 3a -ttilivizyōn.

I don't like watching TV anymore.

⑦

الوَلد باباه اتْأخّر عليْه و بقي لْوَحْدُه في المدْرسة.

ilwálad babāh itʔáxxar 3alēh wi báʔa l-wáħdu fi -lmadrása.

The boy was alone [the only one still] at school when his father was late [picking him up].

❖ [1d1] **to become; to be**

- This verb can be synonymous with كان *kān* and show a state, translating 'be' (am, is, are, was, were). (➲ 61.2, 61.3)
- It can show a change of state, often translating 'become'. (➲ 61.1, 61.7)
- It can be followed by an imperfect verb, expressing a change or beginning. (➲ 61.4, 61.5)
- When negative, this 'change' translates 'stop doing' 'not to do anymore'. (➲ 61.6, 61.8)

➲ 1.7, 2.8, 2.10, 13.2, 23.1, 23.6, 44.4, 58.3, 83.5, 91.3, 98.2, 124.5, 137.6, 158.5, 171.8, 176.2, 176.7, 178.2, 180.1, 216.4, 236.4, 244.6, 250.3, 263.3

62 to build bána بنى

perfect

	affirmative		negative	
ána	banēt	بَنيْت	ma-banítš	مَبَنيْتْش
íḫna	banēna	بَنيْنا	ma-baninā̄š	مَبَنيناش
ínta	banēt	بَنيْت	ma-banítš	مَبَنيْتْش
ínti	banēti	بَنيْتي	ma-banitīš	مَبَنيتيش
íntu	banētu	بَنيْتوا	ma-banitūš	مَبَنيتوش
húwwa	bána	بَنَى	ma-banāš	مَبَناش
híyya	bánit	بَنِت	ma-banítš	مَبَنِتْش
húmma	bánu	بَنوا	ma-banūš	مَبَنوش

imperfect

	affirmative		negative	
ána	ábni	أَبْني	ma-bnīš	مَبْنيش
íḫna	níbni	نِبْني	ma-nibnīš	مَنِبْنيش
ínta	tíbni	تِبْني	ma-tibnīš	مَتِبْنيش
ínti	tíbni	تِبْني	ma-tibnīš	مَتِبْنيش
íntu	tíbnu	تِبْنوا	ma-tibnūš	مَتِبْنوش
húwwa	yíbni	يِبْني	ma-yibnīš	مَيِبْنيش
híyya	tíbni	تِبْني	ma-tibnīš	مَتِبْنيش
húmma	yíbnu	يِبْنوا	ma-yibnūš	مَيِبْنوش

bi-imperfect

	affirmative		negative	
ána	bábni	بَبْني	ma-babnīš	مَبَبْنيش
íḫna	biníbni	بِنِبْني	ma-bnibnīš	مَبْنِبْنيش
ínta	bitíbni	بِتِبْني	ma-btibnīš	مَبْتِبْنيش
ínti	bitíbni	بِتِبْني	ma-btibnīš	مَبْتِبْنيش
íntu	bitíbnu	بِتِبْنوا	ma-btibnūš	مَبْتِبْنوش
húwwa	biyíbni	بِيِبْني	ma-byibnīš	مَبْيِبْنيش
híyya	bitíbni	بِتِبْني	ma-btibnīš	مَبْتِبْنيش
húmma	biyíbnu	بِيِبْنوا	ma-byibnūš	مَبْيِبْنوش

future

	affirmative		negative	
ána	hábni	هَبْني	miš hábni	مِش هَبْني
íḫna	haníbni	هَنِبْني	miš haníbni	مِش هَنِبْني
ínta	hatíbni	هَتِبْني	miš hatíbni	مِش هَتِبْني
ínti	hatíbni	هَتِبْني	miš hatíbni	مِش هَتِبْني
íntu	hatíbnu	هَتِبْنوا	miš hatíbnu	مِش هَتِبْنوا
húwwa	hayíbni	هَيِبْني	miš hayíbni	مِش هَيِبْني
híyya	hatíbni	هَتِبْني	miš hatíbni	مِش هَتِبْني
húmma	hayíbnu	هَيِبْنوا	miš hayíbnu	مِش هَيِبْنوا

imperative

	affirmative		negative	
ínta	íbni	اِبْني	ma-tibnīš	مَتِبْنيش
ínti	íbni	اِبْني	ma-tibnīš	مَتِبْنيش
íntu	íbnu	اِبْنوا	ma-tibnūš	مَتِبْنوش

participles

	active		passive	
masculine	bāni	باني	mábni	مَبْني
feminine	bánya	بانْيَة	mabníyya	مَبْنِيَّة
plural	banyīn	بانْيين	mabniyīn	مَبْنِيين

verbal nouns: *búna* بُنا - *bināʔ* بِناء

①

أنا بنيْت المصْنع ده بإيدي طوبة طوبة.

ána banēt ilmáṣna3 da bi-īdi ṭūba ṭūba.

I built this factory brick by brick with my own hands.

②

لمّا أبْني فيلّتي الخاصّة هعْمِل فيها بِسين.

lámma ʔábni villíti -lxáṣṣa há3mil fīha pisīn.

When I build my own house, I'll put a swimming pool in it.

③

إنْتَ بْتِبْني كُلّ يوْم ثِقِةْ العُملا فيك.

ínta btíbni kullᵊ yōm tíqit il3úmala fīk.

You are building your client's trust in you on a daily basis.

④

إنْتَ هتِبْني فيلّتك الجِديدة فينْ؟

ínta hatíbni villítak ilgidīda fēn?

Where are you going to build your new villa?

⑤

اِبْني إبْنك و لأ تِبْنيلوش.

íbni íbnak wi la tibnilūš.

Build your son, not build for him.

⑥

البيْت ده مبْني بمَواد طبيعية مِن البيئة المُحيطة بِالموْقِع.

ilbēt da mábni b-mawáddᵊ ṭabi3íyya min ilbīʔa -lmuḥīṭa bi-lmáwqi3.

This house was built with natural materials from the surrounding environment.

⑦

متِبْنيش سعادْتك على تعاسِةْ غيرْك.

ma-tibnīš sa3ádtak 3ála ta3āsit ɣērak.

Don't build your happiness on others' misery.

❖ [1d2] **to build**

63 to follow *tābi3* تابع

verbal noun: *mutáb3a* مُتابْعة

	affirmative		negative		
ána	*tabí3t*	تابِعْت	*ma-tabí3tiš*	مَتابِعْتِش	**perfect**
íḥna	*tabí3na*	تابِعْنا	*ma-tabi3nāš*	مَتابِعْناش	
ínta	*tabí3t*	تابِعْت	*ma-tabí3tiš*	مَتابِعْتِش	
ínti	*tabí3ti*	تابِعْتي	*ma-tabi3tīš*	مَتابِعْتيش	
íntu	*tabí3tu*	تابِعْتوا	*ma-tabi3tūš*	مَتابِعْتوش	
húwwa	*tābi3*	تابِع	*ma-tabí3š*	مَتابِعْش	
híyya	*táb3it*	تابْعِت	*ma-tab3íts̆*	مَتابْعِتْش	
húmma	*táb3u*	تابْعوا	*ma-tab3ūš*	مَتابْعوش	

	affirmative		negative		
ána	*atābi3*	أتابِع	*ma-tabí3š*	مَتابِعْش	**imperfect**
íḥna	*nitābi3*	نِتابِع	*ma-ntabí3š*	مَنْتابِعْش	
ínta	*titābi3*	تِتابِع	*ma-ttabí3š*	مَتْتابِعْش	
ínti	*titáb3i*	تِتابْعي	*ma-ttab3īš*	مَتْتابْعيش	
íntu	*titáb3u*	تِتابْعوا	*ma-ttab3ūš*	مَتْتابْعوش	
húwwa	*yitābi3*	يِتابِع	*ma-ytabí3š*	مَيْتابِعْش	
híyya	*titābi3*	تِتابِع	*ma-ttabí3š*	مَتْتابِعْش	
húmma	*yitáb3u*	يِتابْعوا	*ma-ytab3ūš*	مَيْتابْعوش	

	affirmative		negative		
ána	*batābi3*	بَتابِع	*ma-batabí3š*	مَبَتابِعْش	**bi-imperfect**
íḥna	*bintābi3*	بِنْتابِع	*ma-bintabí3š*	مَبِنْتابِعْش	
ínta	*bittābi3*	بِتْتابِع	*ma-bittabí3š*	مَبِتْتابِعْش	
ínti	*bittáb3i*	بِتْتابْعي	*ma-bittab3īš*	مَبِتْتابْعيش	
íntu	*bittáb3u*	بِتْتابْعوا	*ma-bittab3ūš*	مَبِتْتابْعوش	
húwwa	*biytābi3*	بِيْتابِع	*ma-biytabí3š*	مَبِيْتابِعْش	
híyya	*bittābi3*	بِتْتابِع	*ma-bittabí3š*	مَبِتْتابِعْش	
húmma	*biytáb3u*	بِيْتابْعوا	*ma-biytab3ūš*	مَبِيْتابْعوش	

	affirmative		negative		
ána	*hatābi3*	هَتابِع	*miš hatābi3*	مِش هَتابِع	**future**
íḥna	*hantābi3*	هَنْتابِع	*miš hantābi3*	مِش هَنْتابِع	
ínta	*hattābi3*	هَتْتابِع	*miš hattābi3*	مِش هَتْتابِع	
ínti	*hattáb3i*	هَتْتابْعي	*miš hattáb3i*	مِش هَتْتابْعي	
íntu	*hattáb3u*	هَتْتابْعوا	*miš hattáb3u*	مِش هَتْتابْعوا	
húwwa	*haytābi3*	هَيْتابِع	*miš haytābi3*	مِش هَيْتابِع	
híyya	*hattābi3*	هَتْتابِع	*miš hattābi3*	مِش هَتْتابِع	
húmma	*haytáb3u*	هَيْتابْعوا	*miš haytáb3u*	مِش هَيْتابْعوا	

	affirmative		negative		
ínta	*tābi3*	تابِع	*ma-ttabí3š*	مَتْتابِعْش	**imperative**
ínti	*táb3i*	تابْعي	*ma-ttab3īš*	مَتْتابْعيش	
íntu	*táb3u*	تابْعوا	*ma-ttab3ūš*	مَتْتابْعوش	

	active		passive		
masculine	*mitābi3*	مِتابِع	*mittābi3*	مِتّابِع	**participles**
feminine	*mitáb3a*	مِتابْعَة	*mittáb3a*	مِتّابْعَة	
plural	*mitab3īn*	مِتابْعين	*mittab3īn*	مِتّابْعين	

①

تابِعْت المُسلْسل لِحدّ أخْرُه، بسّ معجبِتْنيش النِّهايَة.

tabí3t ilmusálsal li-ħadd^ə ʔāxru, bass^ə ma-3agabitnīš innihāya.

I watched the series until the end,
but I didn't like the finale.

②

لازِم أتابِع الصّنايعية بِنفْسي وَ إلّا هَيْبوّظوا الشُّغْل.

lāzim atābi3 iṣṣanay3íyya bináfsi wa ʔílla haybawwáẓu -ššuɣl.

I must supervise the workers myself
or else they'll ruin the job.

③

بتابِع مقالات الرّاجِل ده. رأْيُه على طول في الجوْن.

batābi3 maqalāt irrāgil da. ráʔyu 3ála ṭūl fi -lgōn.

I follow this man's articles. His opinion is always right.

④

اِتْطمِنّى، هتابِع أنا الوِلاد لِحدّ ما تِـرجعي.

itṭamínni, hatābi3 ána -lwilād li-ħadd^ə ma tirgá3i.

Don't worry. I'll take care of the
kids until you get back.

⑤

تابْعوا نمُوّ أوْلادْكو بِعنايَة، عشان تِكْتِشْفوا أيّ مُشْكِلة في أوِّلْها.

táb3u numúww awládku bi-3ināya, 3ašān tiktíšfu ʔayy^ə muškíla fi ʔawwílha.

Track your children's growth carefully so that you
can discover any problem from the beginning.

⑥

إحْنا مِتابْعين الحالة معَ دُكْتور مُخّ و أعْصاب كِبير.

íħna mitab3īn ilħāla má3a duktūr muxx^ə w a3ṣāb kibīr.

We are following up with a famous neurologist.

⑦

أنا متابِعْتِش مِ الأوِّل. مُمْكِن تِدّيني مُلخّص اللي فاتْني؟

ána ma-tabí3tiš mi -lʔáwwil. múmkin tiddīni muláxxaṣílli fátni?

I haven't been following [it] since it began. Would
you give me a summary of what I missed?

❖ [6s] **to follow, follow up on, keep up with**

- The passive participle might also be written مِتْتابِع.

64 to get lost *tāh* تاهْ

	affirmative		negative		
ána	*tuht*	تُهْت	*ma-túhtiš*	مَتُهْتِش	perfect
íḫna	*túhna*	تُهْنا	*ma-tuhnāš*	مَتُهْناش	
ínta	*tuht*	تُهْت	*ma-túhtiš*	مَتُهْتِش	
ínti	*túhti*	تُهْتي	*ma-tuhtīš*	مَتُهْتيش	
íntu	*túhtu*	تُهْتوا	*ma-tuhtūš*	مَتُهْتوش	
húwwa	*tāh*	تاهْ	*ma-táhš*	مَتاهْش	
híyya	*tāhit*	تاهِت	*ma-tahítš*	مَتاهْتِش	
húmma	*tāhu*	تاهوا	*ma-tahūš*	مَتاهوش	
ána	*atūh*	أتوهْ	*ma-túhš*	مَتوهْش	imperfect
íḫna	*nitūh*	نِتوهْ	*ma-ntúhš*	مَنْتوهْش	
ínta	*titūh*	تِتوهْ	*ma-ttúhš*	مَتْتوهْش	
ínti	*titūhi*	تِتوهي	*ma-ttuhīš*	مَتْتوهيش	
íntu	*titūhu*	تِتوهوا	*ma-ttuhūš*	مَتْتوهوش	
húwwa	*yitūh*	يِتوهْ	*ma-ytúhš*	مَيْتوهْش	
híyya	*titūh*	تِتوهْ	*ma-ttúhš*	مَتْتوهْش	
húmma	*yitūhu*	يِتوهوا	*ma-ytuhūš*	مَيْتوهوش	
ána	*batūh*	بَتوهْ	*ma-batúhš*	مَبَتوهْش	bi-imperfect
íḫna	*bintūh*	بِنْتوهْ	*ma-bintúhš*	مَبِنْتوهْش	
ínta	*bittūh*	بِتْتوهْ	*ma-bittúhš*	مَبِتْتوهْش	
ínti	*bittūhi*	بِتْتوهي	*ma-bittuhīš*	مَبِتْتوهيش	
íntu	*bittūhu*	بِتْتوهوا	*ma-bittuhūš*	مَبِتْتوهوش	
húwwa	*biytūh*	بِيْتوهْ	*ma-biytúhš*	مَبِيْتوهْش	
híyya	*bittūh*	بِتْتوهْ	*ma-bittúhš*	مَبِتْتوهْش	
húmma	*biytūhu*	بِيْتوهوا	*ma-biytuhūš*	مَبِيْتوهوش	
ána	*hatūh*	هَتوهْ	*miš hatūh*	مِش هَتوهْ	future
íḫna	*hantūh*	هَنْتوهْ	*miš hantūh*	مِش هَنْتوهْ	
ínta	*hattūh*	هَتْتوهْ	*miš hattūh*	مِش هَتْتوهْ	
ínti	*hattūhi*	هَتْتوهي	*miš hattūhi*	مِش هَتْتوهي	
íntu	*hattūhu*	هَتْتوهوا	*miš hattūhu*	مِش هَتْتوهوا	
húwwa	*haytūh*	هَيْتوهْ	*miš haytūh*	مِش هَيْتوهْ	
híyya	*hattūh*	هَتْتوهْ	*miš hattūh*	مِش هَتْتوهْ	
húmma	*haytūhu*	هَيْتوهوا	*miš haytūhu*	مِش هَيْتوهوا	
ínta	*tūh*	توهْ	*ma-ttúhš*	مَتْتوهْش	imperative
ínti	*tūhi*	توهي	*ma-ttuhīš*	مَتْتوهيش	
íntu	*tūhu*	توهوا	*ma-ttuhūš*	مَتْتوهوش	

	active		passive		
masculine	*tāyih*	تايِه	–	–	participles
feminine	*táyha*	تايْهَة	–	–	
plural	*tayhīn*	تايْهين	–	–	

verbal noun: *tawahān* تَوَهان

①

تُهْت مرّتينْ و أنا صُغيرّة و لِسّه فاكْرة إحْساسي بِالخوْف ساعِتْها كان عامِل إزّاي.

tuht[ə] marritēn w ána ṣuɣayyára wi líssa fákra ʔiḫsāsi bi-lxōf sa3ítha kān 3āmil izzāy.

I got lost twice when I was young, and I still remember the fear I felt then.

②

إزّاي تِتوهْ مِنّي حاجة زيّ دي؟

izzāy titūh mínni ḫāga zayy[ə] di?

How could I forget something like this?

③

جِدّي بقى بِيْتوهْ مِنّي و أنا بكلِّمُه. الظّاهِر داخِل على ألْزْهايْمر.

gíddi báʔa biytūh mínni w ána bakallímu. iẓẓāhir dāxil 3ála ʔalzháymar.

My grandpa can't concentrate when I talk to him. I think it's symptomatic of Alzheimer's.

④

إبْني كان هَيْتوهْ مِنّي مرّة بسّ الحمْدُ لِلّه لِحِقْناه بْسُرْعة.

íbni kān haytūh mínni márra bass ilḫámdu li-llāh liḫiʔnā b-súr3a.

My son nearly went missing, but we quickly found him.

⑤

توهوا شْوَيّة مِن مشاغِلْكو و سيبوا نفْسُكو معَ أيّ مُغامْرة جْديدة.

tūhu šwáyya min mašayílku wi sību nafsúku má3a ʔayy[ə] muɣámra gdīda.

Forget your troubles, and take yourself away on a new adventure.

⑥

الحمْدُ لِله، أنا مبتوهْش بِسْهولة. بعْرف أحدِّد الاِتّجاهات كُوَيِّس.

ilḫámdu li-llāh, ána ma-batúhš[ə] bi-shūla. bá3raf aḫáddid ilʔittagahāt kuwáyyis.

Thank God I don't get lost easily. I'm pretty good with directions.

❖ [1h1] **to get lost, go missing (from** مِن *min*); **to forget** (مِن *min*)

65 to tire tá3ab تَعَب

perfect	affirmative			negative	
ána	ta3ábt	تَعَبْت	ma-ta3ábtiš	مَتَعَبْتِش
íḫna	ta3ábna	تَعَبْنا	ma-ta3abnāš	مَتَعَبْناش
ínta	ta3ábt	تَعَبْت	ma-ta3ábtiš	مَتَعَبْتِش
ínti	ta3ábti	تَعَبْتي	ma-ta3abtīš	مَتَعَبْتيش
íntu	ta3ábtu	تَعَبْتوا	ma-ta3abtūš	مَتَعَبْتوش
húwwa	tá3ab	تَعَب	ma-ta3ábš	مَتَعَبْش
híyya	tá3abit	تَعَبِت	ma-ta3abítš	مَتَعَبِتْش
húmma	tá3abu	تَعَبوا	ma-ta3abūš	مَتَعَبوش

imperfect				
ána	át3ib	أتْعِب	ma-t3íbš	مَتْعِبْش
íḫna	nít3ib	نِتْعِب	ma-nit3íbš	مَنِتْعِبْش
ínta	tít3ib	تِتْعِب	ma-tit3íbš	مَتِتْعِبْش
ínti	tit3íbi	تِتْعِبي	ma-tit3ibīš	مَتِتْعِبيش
íntu	tit3íbu	تِتْعِبوا	ma-tit3ibūš	مَتِتْعِبوش
húwwa	yít3ib	يِتْعِب	ma-yit3íbš	مَيِتْعِبْش
híyya	tít3ib	تِتْعِب	ma-tit3íbš	مَتِتْعِبْش
húmma	yit3íbu	يِتْعِبوا	ma-yit3ibūš	مَيِتْعِبوش

bi-imperfect				
ána	bát3ib	بَتْعِب	ma-bat3íbš	مَبَتْعِبْش
íḫna	binít3ib	بِنِتْعِب	ma-bnit3íbš	مَبْنِتْعِبْش
ínta	bitít3ib	بِتِتْعِب	ma-btit3íbš	مَبْتِتْعِبْش
ínti	bitit3íbi	بِتِتْعِبي	ma-btit3ibīš	مَبْتِتْعِبيش
íntu	bitit3íbu	بِتِتْعِبوا	ma-btit3ibūš	مَبْتِتْعِبوش
húwwa	biyít3ib	بِيِتْعِب	ma-byit3íbš	مَبْيِتْعِبْش
híyya	bitít3ib	بِتِتْعِب	ma-btit3íbš	مَبْتِتْعِبْش
húmma	biyit3íbu	بِيِتْعِبوا	ma-byit3ibūš	مَبْيِتْعِبوش

future				
ána	hát3ib	هَتْعِب	miš hát3ib	مِش هَتْعِب
íḫna	hanít3ib	هَنِتْعِب	miš hanít3ib	مِش هَنِتْعِب
ínta	hatít3ib	هَتِتْعِب	miš hatít3ib	مِش هَتِتْعِب
ínti	hatit3íbi	هَتِتْعِبي	miš hatit3íbi	مِش هَتِتْعِبي
íntu	hatit3íbu	هَتِتْعِبوا	miš hatit3íbu	مِش هَتِتْعِبوا
húwwa	hayít3ib	هَيِتْعِب	miš hayít3ib	مِش هَيِتْعِب
híyya	hatít3ib	هَتِتْعِب	miš hatít3ib	مِش هَتِتْعِب
húmma	hayit3íbu	هَيِتْعِبوا	miš hayit3íbu	مِش هَيِتْعِبوا

imperative				
ínta	ít3ib	اِتْعِب	ma-tit3íbš	مَتِتْعِبْش
ínti	it3íbi	اِتْعِبي	ma-tit3ibīš	مَتِتْعِبيش
íntu	it3íbu	اِتْعِبوا	ma-tit3ibūš	مَتِتْعِبوش

participles	active		passive	
masculine	tā3ib	تاعِب	mat3ūb	مَتْعوب
feminine	tá3ba	تاعْبَة	mat3ūba	مَتْعوبَة
plural	ta3bīn	تاعْبين	mat3ubīn	مَتْعوبين

verbal noun: tá3ab تَعَب

①

تعبْتِني معاك يابْني. إنْتَ عايِز أيْه بِالظّبْط؟

ta3abtíni ma3āk ya -bni. ínta 3āyiz ʔē bi-zzabṭ?

You've worn me out, son. What exactly do you want?

②

بابا مُنْزعِج مِن قعْدِةْ البيْت، أصْلُه مبِيْحِبِّش يِتْعِب حدّ معاه.

bāba munzá3ig min ʔá3dit ilbēt, áṣlu ma-biyḫíbbiš yít3ib ḫaddᵊ ma3ā.

My dad isn't comfortable having to stay at home, but he doesn't like troubling anyone.

③

سارة مبْتِتْعِبْش أهْلها .بِتِدْرِس و بْتِشْتغل.

sāra ma-btit3íbš ahláha. bitídris wi btištáɣal.

Sara isn't any trouble for her parents. She studies and works.

④

هتِتْعِبوا نفْسُكو عَ الفاضي في المِشْوار ده.

hatit3íbu nafsúku 3a -lfāḍi fi -lmišwār da.

You'll wear yourself out for nothing doing that errand.

⑤

متِتْعِبْش أبوك أكْتر مِن كِده. اِعْتِمِد على نفْسك بقى.

ma-tit3íbš abūk áktar min kída. i3tímid 3ála náfsak báʔa.

Don't trouble your father any further. Do it on your own.

⑥

إنْتَ تاعِبْني معاك كِده على طول؟ يابْني اِسْمع كلامي مرّة.

ínta ta3íbni ma3āk kída 3ála ṭūl? ya -bni ísma3 kalāmi márra.

Do you always have to make me tired? Obey me for once, son.

❖ [1s2] **to tire, wear out, make tired; to trouble, inconvenience**

➲ 247.4

66 to get tired tí3ib تِعِب

	affirmative		negative		
ána	ti3íbt	تِعِبْت	ma-t3íbtiš	مَتْعِبْتِش	perfect
íḫna	ti3íbna	تِعِبْنا	ma-t3ibnāš	مَتْعِبْناش	
ínta	ti3íbt	تِعِبْت	ma-t3íbtiš	مَتْعِبْتِش	
ínti	ti3íbti	تِعِبْتي	ma-t3ibtīš	مَتْعِبْتيش	
íntu	ti3íbtu	تِعِبْتوا	ma-t3ibtūš	مَتْعِبْتوش	
húwwa	tí3ib	تِعِب	ma-t3íbš	مَتْعِبْش	
híyya	tí3bit	تِعْبِت	ma-ti3bítš	مَتِعْبِتْش	
húmma	tí3bu	تِعْبوا	ma-ti3būš	مَتِعْبوش	
ána	át3ab	أتْعَب	ma-t3ábš	مَتْعَبْش	imperfect
íḫna	nít3ab	نِتْعَب	ma-nit3ábš	مَنِتْعَبْش	
ínta	tít3ab	تِتْعَب	ma-tit3ábš	مَتِتْعَبْش	
ínti	tit3ábi	تِتْعَبي	ma-tit3abīš	مَتِتْعَبيش	
íntu	tit3ábu	تِتْعَبوا	ma-tit3abūš	مَتِتْعَبوش	
húwwa	yít3ab	يِتْعَب	ma-yit3ábš	مَيِتْعَبْش	
híyya	tít3ab	تِتْعَب	ma-tit3ábš	مَتِتْعَبْش	
húmma	yit3ábu	يِتْعَبوا	ma-yit3abūš	مَيِتْعَبوش	
ána	bát3ab	بَتْعَب	ma-bat3ábš	مَبَتْعَبْش	bi-imperfect
íḫna	binít3ab	بِنِتْعَب	ma-bnit3ábš	مَبْنِتْعَبْش	
ínta	bitít3ab	بِتِتْعَب	ma-btit3ábš	مَبْتِتْعَبْش	
ínti	bitit3ábi	بِتِتْعَبي	ma-btit3abīš	مَبْتِتْعَبيش	
íntu	bitit3ábu	بِتِتْعَبوا	ma-btit3abūš	مَبْتِتْعَبوش	
húwwa	biyít3ab	بِيِتْعَب	ma-byit3ábš	مَبْيِتْعَبْش	
híyya	bitít3ab	بِتِتْعَب	ma-btit3ábš	مَبْتِتْعَبْش	
húmma	biyit3ábu	بِيِتْعَبوا	ma-byit3abūš	مَبْيِتْعَبوش	
ána	hát3ab	هَتْعَب	miš hát3ab	مِش هَتْعَب	future
íḫna	hanít3ab	هَنِتْعَب	miš hanít3ab	مِش هَنِتْعَب	
ínta	hatít3ab	هَتِتْعَب	miš hatít3ab	مِش هَتِتْعَب	
ínti	hatit3ábi	هَتِتْعَبي	miš hatit3ábi	مِش هَتِتْعَبي	
íntu	hatit3ábu	هَتِتْعَبوا	miš hatit3ábu	مِش هَتِتْعَبوا	
húwwa	hayít3ab	هَيِتْعَب	miš hayít3ab	مِش هَيِتْعَب	
híyya	hatít3ab	هَتِتْعَب	miš hatít3ab	مِش هَتِتْعَب	
húmma	hayit3ábu	هَيِتْعَبوا	miš hayit3ábu	مِش هَيِتْعَبوا	
ínta	ít3ab	اِتْعَب	ma-tit3ábš	مَتِتْعَبْش	imperative
ínti	it3ábi	اِتْعَبي	ma-tit3abīš	مَتِتْعَبيش	
íntu	it3ábu	اِتْعَبوا	ma-tit3abūš	مَتِتْعَبوش	

	active		passive		
masculine	ta3bān	تَعْبان	–	–	participles
feminine	ta3bāna	تَعْبانَة	–	–	
plural	ta3banīn	تَعْبانين	–	–	

verbal noun: tá3ab تَعَب

①

فية ناس تِعْبِت مِن مُحاوْلِةْ إصْلاح أحْوال المُجْتمع بِلا نتيجة.

fī nās tí3bit min muḫáwit iṣlāḫ aḫwāl ilmugtáma3 bi-la natīga.

Some people are tired of trying to fix society's problems to no avail.

②

لمّا تِتْعب قولّي و أنا هكمِّل سِواقة.

lámma tít3ab ʔúlli w ána hakámmil siwāʔa.

When you're tired, tell me, and I'll drive.

③

خديجة بْتِتْعب مِن شُغْل البيْت. قرّرِت تِجيب واحْدة تْساعِدْها.

xadīga btít3ab min šuɣl ilbēt. qarrárit tigīb wáḫda tsa3ídha.

Khadiga gets tired from housework, so she's decided to get someone to help her.

④

نِسْرين هتِتْعب في الرِّحْلة دي. هِيَّ مِش مِتْعوِّدة عَ السّفر الطّويل.

nisrīn hatít3ab fi -rríḫla di. híyya miš mit3awwída 3a -ssáfar iṭṭawīl.

Nisreen will get tired on this trip. She's not used to long trips.

⑤

اِتْعبوا في تربِيِّةْ وِلادْكو، و هتْلاقوا النّتيجة قُدّام.

it3ábu f tarabíyyit wiládku, wi hatlāʔu -nnatīga ʔuddām.

Put effort into disciplining your children, and you'll reap the benefit of it later.

⑥

أنا متْعِبْتِش في المِشْوار ده. خلّصْت و رْجِعْت بْسُرْعة.

ána ma-t3íbtiš fi -lmišwār da. xalláṣtᵊ wi rgí3tᵊ b-súr3a.

I didn't get tired of running that errand. I finished it and went back quickly.

❖ [1s4] **to become tired; to get sick, fall ill; to trouble oneself, suffer**

➲ 11.3, 15.1, 27.7, 36.2, 36.4, 48.1, 73.7, 113.6, 126.4, 135.1, 173.5, 210.2, 243.1

67 to complete tamm تمّ 1 3

	affirmative		negative		
ána	tammēt	تمّيْت	ma-tammítš	مَتَمّيتْش	perfect
íḫna	tammēna	تمّيْنا	ma-tamminā̌š	مَتَمّيناش	
ínta	tammēt	تمّيْت	ma-tammítš	مَتَمّيتْش	
ínti	tammēti	تمّيْتي	ma-tammitīš	مَتَمّيتيش	
íntu	tammētu	تمّيْتوا	ma-tammitūš	مَتَمّيتوش	
húwwa	tamm	تَمّ	ma-támmiš	مَتَمّش	
híyya	támmit	تمّت	ma-tammítš	مَتَمّتْش	
húmma	támmu	تمّوا	ma-tammūš	مَتَمّوش	
ána	atímm	أتِمّ	ma-tímmiš	مَتِمّش	imperfect
íḫna	nitímm	نِتِمّ	ma-ntímmiš	مَنْتِمّش	
ínta	titímm	تِتِمّ	ma-ttímmiš	مَتْتِمّش	
ínti	titímmi	تِتِمّي	ma-ttimmīš	مَتْتِمّيش	
íntu	titímmu	تِتِمّوا	ma-ttimmūš	مَتْتِمّوش	
húwwa	yitímm	يِتِمّ	ma-ytímmiš	مَيْتِمّش	
híyya	titímm	تِتِمّ	ma-ttímmiš	مَتْتِمّش	
húmma	yitímmu	يِتِمّوا	ma-ytimmūš	مَيْتِمّوش	
ána	batímm	بَتِمّ	ma-batímmiš	مَبَتِمّش	bi-imperfect
íḫna	bintímm	بِنْتِمّ	ma-bintímmiš	مَبِنْتِمّش	
ínta	bittímm	بِتْتِمّ	ma-bittímmiš	مَبِتْتِمّش	
ínti	bittímmi	بِتْتِمّي	ma-bittimmīš	مَبِتْتِمّيش	
íntu	bittímmu	بِتْتِمّوا	ma-bittimmūš	مَبِتْتِمّوش	
húwwa	biytímm	بِيْتِمّ	ma-biytímmiš	مَبِيْتِمّش	
híyya	bittímm	بِتْتِمّ	ma-bittímmiš	مَبِتْتِمّش	
húmma	biytímmu	بِيْتِمّوا	ma-biytimmūš	مَبِيْتِمّوش	
ána	hatímm	هَتِمّ	miš hatímm	مِش هَتِمّ	future
íḫna	hantímm	هَنْتِمّ	miš hantímm	مِش هَنْتِمّ	
ínta	hattímm	هَتْتِمّ	miš hattímm	مِش هَتْتِمّ	
ínti	hattímmi	هَتْتِمّي	miš hattímmi	مِش هَتْتِمّي	
íntu	hattímmu	هَتْتِمّوا	miš hattímmu	مِش هَتْتِمّوا	
húwwa	haytímm	هَيْتِمّ	miš haytímm	مِش هَيْتِمّ	
híyya	hattímm	هَتْتِمّ	miš hattímm	مِش هَتْتِمّ	
húmma	haytímmu	هَيْتِمّوا	miš haytímmu	مِش هَيْتِمّوا	
ínta	timm	تِمّ	ma-ttímmiš	مَتْتِمّش	imperative
ínti	tímmi	تِمّي	ma-ttimmīš	مَتْتِمّيش	
íntu	tímmu	تِمّوا	ma-ttimmūš	مَتْتِمّوش	
	active		**passive**		
masculine	tāmim	تامِم	–	–	participles
feminine	támma	تامّة	–	–	
plural	tammīn	تامّين	–	–	

verbal nouns: tamām تَمام - itmām إتْمام

①

إنْتَ لِسّه متمّيتْش ٣٠ سنة؟

ínta líssa ma-tammítš talatīn sána?

You haven't turned 30 yet?

②

لمّا حمْزة يْتِمّ سبْع سْنين هعْمِلُه حفْلة حِلْوَة.

lámma ɧámza ytímmᵊ sab3ᵊ snīn ha3mílu ɧáfla ɧílwa.

When Hamza turns seven, I'll throw him a nice party.

③

حُسام مبِيْتِمِّش صفْقة أبداً. كُلّ مرّة يِلْغيها.

ɧusām ma-biytímmiš şáfqa ʔábadan. kullᵊ márra yilɣīha.

Hossam never completes a deal. Each time he cancels it.

④

حاتِم هَيْتِمّ بُكْره ٢١.

ɧātim haytímmᵊ búkra wāɧid w 3išrīn.

Tomorrow Hatem will turn 21.

⑤

تِمّ ١٦ و أنا أجيبْلك موتوسيكْل.

timm sittāšar w ána ʔagíblak mutusíkl.

Turn 16 [first], and I'll get you a motorcycle.

⑥

مبْروك يا حبيبْتي. ربِّنا يِتِمِّلك على خيْر.

mabrūk ya ɧabíbti. rabbína yitimmílak 3ála xēr.

Congratulations, dear! God completes it finely for you.

❖ [1g3] **to complete**

- This verb literally means 'complete', but it is most commonly used with age, translating 'turn __ years old'.

68 to bring *gāb* جاب

	affirmative		negative		
ána	gibt	جِبْت	ma-gíbtiš	مَجِبْتِش	perfect
íḫna	gíbna	جِبْنا	ma-gibnāš	مَجِبْناش	
ínta	gibt	جِبْت	ma-gíbtiš	مَجِبْتِش	
ínti	gíbti	جِبْتي	ma-gibtīš	مَجِبْتيش	
íntu	gíbtu	جِبْتوا	ma-gibtūš	مَجِبْتوش	
húwwa	gāb	جاب	ma-gábš	مَجابْش	
híyya	gābit	جابِت	ma-gabítš	مَجابِتْش	
húmma	gābu	جابوا	ma-gabūš	مَجابوش	

ána	agīb	أجيب	ma-gíbš	مَجيبْش	imperfect
íḫna	nigīb	نِجيب	ma-ngíbš	مَنْجيبْش	
ínta	tigīb	تِجيب	ma-tgíbš	مَتْجيبْش	
ínti	tigībi	تِجيبي	ma-tgibīš	مَتْجيبيش	
íntu	tigību	تِجيبوا	ma-tgibūš	مَتْجيبوش	
húwwa	yigīb	يِجيب	ma-ygíbš	مَيْجيبْش	
híyya	tigīb	تِجيب	ma-tgíbš	مَتْجيبْش	
húmma	yigību	يِجيبوا	ma-ygibūš	مَيْجيبوش	

ána	bagīb	بَجيب	ma-bagíbš	مَبَجيبْش	bi-imperfect
íḫna	bingīb	بِنْجيب	ma-bingíbš	مَبِنْجيبْش	
ínta	bitgīb	بِتْجيب	ma-bitgíbš	مَبِتْجيبْش	
ínti	bitgībi	بِتْجيبي	ma-bitgibīš	مَبِتْجيبيش	
íntu	bitgību	بِتْجيبوا	ma-bitgibūš	مَبِتْجيبوش	
húwwa	biygīb	بِيْجيب	ma-biygíbš	مَبِيْجيبْش	
híyya	bitgīb	بِتْجيب	ma-bitgíbš	مَبِتْجيبْش	
húmma	biygību	بِيْجيبوا	ma-biygibūš	مَبِيْجيبوش	

ána	hagīb	هَجيب	miš hagīb	مِش هَجيب	future
íḫna	hangīb	هَنْجيب	miš hangīb	مِش هَنْجيب	
ínta	hatgīb	هَتْجيب	miš hatgīb	مِش هَتْجيب	
ínti	hatgībi	هَتْجيبي	miš hatgībi	مِش هَتْجيبي	
íntu	hatgību	هَتْجيبوا	miš hatgību	مِش هَتْجيبوا	
húwwa	haygīb	هَيْجيب	miš haygīb	مِش هَيْجيب	
híyya	hatgīb	هَتْجيب	miš hatgīb	مِش هَتْجيب	
húmma	haygību	هَيْجيبوا	miš haygību	مِش هَيْجيبوا	

ínta	gīb / hāt	جيب / هات	ma-tgíbš	مَتْجيبْش	imperative
ínti	gībi / hāti	جيبي / هاتي	ma-tgibīš	مَتْجيبيش	
íntu	gību / hātu	جيبوا / هاتوا	ma-tgibūš	مَتْجيبوش	

	active		passive		
masculine	gāyib	جايِب	mitgāb	مِتْجاب	participles
feminine	gáyba	جايْبَة	mitgāba	مِتْجابَة	
plural	gaybīn	جايْبين	mitgabīn	مِتْجابين	

verbal noun: *gayabān* جَيَبان

①

جِبْت النّتيجة النّهارْده. ناجِح بِاِمْتِياز الحمْدُ لِله.

gibt innatīga -nnahárda. nāgiḫ biymtiyāz, ilḫámdu li-llāh.

I got my result [grade/score] today.
Thank God I passed with an A.

②

تِجيب عِرْقِسوس ليْه؟ محدِّش فينا بِيْحِبُّه.

tigīb 3irʔisūs lē? ma-ḫáddiš fīna biyḫíbbu.

Why did you buy licorice juice? None of us likes it.

③

لِبْسك دايْماً شيك أوي. إِنْتَ بِتْجيب قُمْصانك مِنيْن؟

libsak dáyman šīk áwi. ínta bitgīb ʔumṣānak minēn?

Your clothes are always stylish. Where do you buy your shirts?

④

هتْجيبي الوَلد مِن الحضانة السّاعة كام؟

hatgībi -lwálad min ilḫaḍāna -ssā3a kām?

When will you pick up the boy from preschool?

⑤

جيب معاك لِبّ و سوداني.

gīb ma3āk libbᵃ w sudāni.

Bring some seeds and peanuts with you.

⑥

فِكْري راح لِمْراتُه و جابْلها خاتِم ألْماظ عشان يِصالِحْها.

fíkri rāḫ li-mrātu wi gabláha xātim almāẓ 3ašān yiṣalíḫha.

Fekry went to his wife and brought her
a diamond ring to make up with her.

⑦

تيتو شغّال على تاكْس، بِيْجيبْلُه ٣٠٠ جِنيْهْ في اليوْم.

tītu šaɣɣāl 3ála taks, biygíblu tultumíyya ginēh fi -lyōm.

Tito drives a taxi, which brings him 300 pounds a day.

⑧

مجِبْتِليش معاك عيْش. طب، هعْمِلْكو سنْدِوِتْشات بِإيْه؟

ma-gibtilīš ma3āk 3ēš. ṭab, ha3mílku sandiwitšāt bi-ʔē?

You didn't get me any bread. What am I
going to make you sandwiches with?

❖ [1h2] **to bring; to get; to buy**

- This verb has a common alternative affirmative imperative. (➲ 167.11)

➲ 28.2, 40.6, 55.4, 67.5, 73.4, 84.5, 90.3, 152.4, 160.4, 161.3, 190.2, 204.4, 221.1, 225.5, 250.5

69 to answer gāwib جاوِب

verbal noun: migáwba مِجاوْبة

	affirmative		negative		
ána	gawíbt	جاوِبْت	ma-gawíbtiš	مَجاوِبْتِش	perfect
íḥna	gawíbna	جاوِبْنا	ma-gawibnāš	مَجاوِبْناش	
ínta	gawíbt	جاوِبْت	ma-gawíbtiš	مَجاوِبْتِش	
ínti	gawíbti	جاوِبْتي	ma-gawibtīš	مَجاوِبْتيش	
íntu	gawíbtu	جاوِبْتوا	ma-gawibtūš	مَجاوِبْتوش	
húwwa	gāwib	جاوِب	ma-gawíbš	مَجاوِبْش	
híyya	gáwbit	جاوْبِت	ma-gawbítš	مَجاوْبِتْش	
húmma	gáwbu	جاوْبوا	ma-gawbūš	مَجاوْبوش	
ána	agāwib	أجاوِب	ma-gawíbš	مَجاوِبْش	imperfect
íḥna	nigāwib	نِجاوِب	ma-ngawíbš	مَنْجاوِبْش	
ínta	tigāwib	تِجاوِب	ma-tgawíbš	مَتْجاوِبْش	
ínti	tigáwbi	تِجاوْبي	ma-tgawbīš	مَتْجاوْبيش	
íntu	tigáwbu	تِجاوْبوا	ma-tgawbūš	مَتْجاوْبوش	
húwwa	yigāwib	يِجاوِب	ma-ygawíbš	مَيْجاوِبْش	
híyya	tigāwib	تِجاوِب	ma-tgawíbš	مَتْجاوِبْش	
húmma	yigáwbu	يِجاوْبوا	ma-ygawbūš	مَيْجاوْبوش	
ána	bagāwib	بَجاوِب	ma-bagawíbš	مَبَجاوِبْش	bi-imperfect
íḥna	bingāwib	بِنْجاوِب	ma-bingawíbš	مَبِنْجاوِبْش	
ínta	bitgāwib	بِتْجاوِب	ma-bitgawíbš	مَبِتْجاوِبْش	
ínti	bitgáwbi	بِتْجاوْبي	ma-bitgawbīš	مَبِتْجاوْبيش	
íntu	bitgáwbu	بِتْجاوْبوا	ma-bitgawbūš	مَبِتْجاوْبوش	
húwwa	biygāwib	بِيْجاوِب	ma-biygawíbš	مَبِيْجاوِبْش	
híyya	bitgāwib	بِتْجاوِب	ma-bitgawíbš	مَبِتْجاوِبْش	
húmma	biygáwbu	بِيْجاوْبوا	ma-biygawbūš	مَبِيْجاوْبوش	
ána	hagāwib	هَجاوِب	miš hagāwib	مِش هَجاوِب	future
íḥna	hangāwib	هَنْجاوِب	miš hangāwib	مِش هَنْجاوِب	
ínta	hatgāwib	هَتْجاوِب	miš hatgāwib	مِش هَتْجاوِب	
ínti	hatgáwbi	هَتْجاوْبي	miš hatgáwbi	مِش هَتْجاوْبي	
íntu	hatgáwbu	هَتْجاوْبوا	miš hatgáwbu	مِش هَتْجاوْبوا	
húwwa	haygāwib	هَيْجاوِب	miš haygāwib	مِش هَيْجاوِب	
híyya	hatgāwib	هَتْجاوِب	miš hatgāwib	مِش هَتْجاوِب	
húmma	haygáwbu	هَيْجاوْبوا	miš haygáwbu	مِش هَيْجاوْبوا	
ínta	gāwib	جاوِب	ma-tgawíbš	مَتْجاوِبْش	imperative
ínti	gáwbi	جاوْبي	ma-tgawbīš	مَتْجاوْبيش	
íntu	gáwbu	جاوْبوا	ma-tgawbūš	مَتْجاوْبوش	

	active		passive		
masculine	migāwib	مِجاوِب	mitgāwib	مِتْجاوِب	participles
feminine	migáwba	مِجاوْبَة	mitgáwba	مِتْجاوْبَة	
plural	migawbīn	مِجاوْبين	mitgawbīn	مِتْجاوْبين	

①

جاوِبْت على خمس أسْئِلة مِن السِّتّة. السُّؤال الأخير كان اِخْتِياري.

gawíbtᵊ 3ála xámas asʔíla min issítta. issuʔāl ilʔaxīr kān ixtiyāri.

I answered five questions out of six. The last one was optional.

②

حاوِل تِجاوِب عَ الدُّكْتور إجابات واضْحة عشان يِعْرف يِعالْجك.

ɧāwil tigāwib 3a -dduktūr igabāt wáďɧa 3ašān yí3raf yi3álgak.

Try to answer the doctor with clear answers so that he can treat you.

③

هِيَّ بِتْجاوِب كِده إزّاي على أيّ سُؤال؟ دي مَوْسوعة!

híyya bitgāwib kída -zzāy 3ála ʔayyᵊ suʔāl? di mawsū3a!

How does she answer any question like that? She's an encyclopedia!

④

أ: هتْجاوْبي المُسابْقة إمْتى؟

ب: لازِم النّهارْده، عشان بُكْره آخِر معاد لِلتّقْديم.

A: *hatgáwbi -lmusábʔa ʔímta?*

B: *lāzim innahárda, 3ašān búkra āxir mi3ād li-ttaʔdīm.*

A: When will you answer the quiz?

B: It must be today, as tomorrow is the last day to submit it.

⑤

كُنْت بِتِعْمِل أيْه عنْد هِنْد في شقِّتْها؟ جاوِبْني حالاً.

kuntᵊ bití3mil ʔē 3andᵊ hindᵊ fi šaʔʔítha? gawíbni ɧālan.

What were you doing at Hend's place? Answer me right now.

⑥

متْجاوْبيش الأسْئِلْة السّخيفة. تِجاهْليها بسّ.

ma-tgawbīš ilʔasʔía -ssaxīfa. tigahlīha bass.

Don't answer silly questions. Just ignore them.

❖ [3s] **to answer** (على *3ála*)

- This verb usually takes a preposition but may also take a direct object. (➲ 69.4)

➲ 121.6, 134.2

70 to try out gárrab جَرَّب

verbal nouns: tagrīb تَجْرِيب - tagrúba تَجْرُبَة

	affirmative		negative		
ána	garrábt	جَرَّبْت	ma-garrábtiš	مَجَرَّبْتِش	perfect
íḫna	garrábna	جَرَّبْنا	ma-garrabnāš	مَجَرَّبْناش	
ínta	garrábt	جَرَّبْت	ma-garrábtiš	مَجَرَّبْتِش	
ínti	garrábti	جَرَّبْتي	ma-garrabtīš	مَجَرَّبْتيش	
íntu	garrábtu	جَرَّبْتوا	ma-garrabtūš	مَجَرَّبْتوش	
húwwa	gárrab	جَرَّب	ma-garrábš	مَجَرَّبْش	
híyya	garrábit	جَرَّبِت	ma-garrabítš	مَجَرَّبِتْش	
húmma	garrábu	جَرَّبوا	ma-garrabūš	مَجَرَّبوش	
ána	agárrab	أَجَرَّب	ma-garrábš	مَجَرَّبْش	imperfect
íḫna	nigárrab	نِجَرَّب	ma-ngarrábš	مَنْجَرَّبْش	
ínta	tigárrab	تِجَرَّب	ma-tgarrábš	مَتْجَرَّبْش	
ínti	tigarrábi	تِجَرَّبي	ma-tgarrabīš	مَتْجَرَّبيش	
íntu	tigarrábu	تِجَرَّبوا	ma-tgarrabūš	مَتْجَرَّبوش	
húwwa	yigárrab	يِجَرَّب	ma-ygarrábš	مَيْجَرَّبْش	
híyya	tigárrab	تِجَرَّب	ma-tgarrábš	مَتْجَرَّبْش	
húmma	yigarrábu	يِجَرَّبوا	ma-ygarrabūš	مَيْجَرَّبوش	
ána	bagárrab	بَجَرَّب	ma-bagarrábš	مَبَجَرَّبْش	bi-imperfect
íḫna	bingárrab	بِنْجَرَّب	ma-bingarrábš	مَبِنْجَرَّبْش	
ínta	bitgárrab	بِتْجَرَّب	ma-bitgarrábš	مَبِتْجَرَّبْش	
ínti	bitgarrábi	بِتْجَرَّبي	ma-bitgarrabīš	مَبِتْجَرَّبيش	
íntu	bitgarrábu	بِتْجَرَّبوا	ma-bitgarrabūš	مَبِتْجَرَّبوش	
húwwa	biygárrab	بِيْجَرَّب	ma-biygarrábš	مَبِيْجَرَّبْش	
híyya	bitgárrab	بِتْجَرَّب	ma-bitgarrábš	مَبِتْجَرَّبْش	
húmma	biygarrábu	بِيْجَرَّبوا	ma-biygarrabūš	مَبِيْجَرَّبوش	
ána	hagárrab	هَجَرَّب	miš hagárrab	مِش هَجَرَّب	future
íḫna	hangárrab	هَنْجَرَّب	miš hangárrab	مِش هَنْجَرَّب	
ínta	hatgárrab	هَتْجَرَّب	miš hatgárrab	مِش هَتْجَرَّب	
ínti	hatgarrábi	هَتْجَرَّبي	miš hatgarrábi	مِش هَتْجَرَّبي	
íntu	hatgarrábu	هَتْجَرَّبوا	miš hatgarrábu	مِش هَتْجَرَّبوا	
húwwa	haygárrab	هَيْجَرَّب	miš haygárrab	مِش هَيْجَرَّب	
híyya	hatgárrab	هَتْجَرَّب	miš hatgárrab	مِش هَتْجَرَّب	
húmma	haygarrábu	هَيْجَرَّبوا	miš haygarrábu	مِش هَيْجَرَّبوا	
ínta	gárrab	جَرَّب	ma-tgarrábš	مَتْجَرَّبْش	imperative
ínti	garrábi	جَرَّبي	ma-tgarrabīš	مَتْجَرَّبيش	
íntu	garrábu	جَرَّبوا	ma-tgarrabūš	مَتْجَرَّبوش	

	active		passive		
masculine	migárrab	مِجَرَّب	mitgárrab	مِتْجَرَّب	participles
feminine	migarrába	مِجَرَّبَة	mitgarrába	مِتْجَرَّبَة	
plural	migarrabīn	مِجَرَّبين	mitgarrabīn	مِتْجَرَّبين	

①

جرّبْت كُلّ حاجة عشان أعالِج تقصُّف الشّعْر بسّ مفيش نتيجة.

garrábtᵊ kullᵊ ḫāga 3ašān a3ālig taʔáṣṣuf iššá3rᵊ bassᵊ ma-fīš natīga.

I've tried everything to treat my split ends, but nothing worked.

②

أكْمَل بِيْحِبّ يِجرّب أيّ أكْلة يِشوفْها و أيّ مطْعم يِسْمع عنُّه.

ákmal biyḫíbbᵊ yigárrab ayy ákla yišúfha w ayyᵊ máṭ3am yísma3 3ánnu.

Akmal likes to try any food he sees and any restaurant he hears about.

③

رُؤى لمّا بِتِدْخُل محلّ بِتْجرّب كُلّ اللِّبْس اللي فيه.

rúʔa lámma bitídxul maḫállᵊ bitgárrab kull illíbs ílli fī.

Roaa tries on everything whenever she goes into a shop.

④

متْجرّبوش الحاجات دي لِوَحْدُكو في البيْت.

ma-tgarrabūš ilḫagāt di li-waḫdúku fi -lbēt.

Don't try these things alone at home.

⑤

جرّبوا كُلّ حاجة و سافْروا كُلّ حِتّة و متِنْدموش على حاجة لمّا تِكْبروا.

garrábu kullᵊ ḫāga wi sáfru kullᵊ ḫitta wi ma-tindamūš 3ála ḫāga lámma tikbáru.

Try everything, travel everywhere, and don't regret anything when you're old.

❖ [2s2] **to try (out)**

- Compare with حاوِل *ḫāwil*. (➲ 77)
- The verbal noun can also be pronounced *tagríba*.

➲ 142.3, 145.5, 211.3

71 to happen *gára* جَرَى

no verbal noun

		affirmative		negative	
perfect		gára	جَرَى	ma-garāš	مَجَراش
	ána	garāli	جَرالي	ma-garalīš	مَجَراليش
	íḥna	garálna	جَرالْنا	ma-garalnāš	مَجَرالْناش
	ínta	garālak	جَرالَك	ma-garalákš	مَجَرالَكْش
	ínti	garālik	جَرالِك	ma-garalkīš	مَجَرالْكيش
	íntu	garálku	جَرالْكو	ma-garalkūš	مَجَرالْكوش
	húwwa	garālu	جَرالُه	ma-garalūš	مَجَرالوش
	híyya	garálha	جَرالْها	ma-garalhāš	مَجَرالْهاش
	húmma	garálhum	جَرالْهُم	ma-garalhúmš	مَجَرالْهُمْش
imperfect		yígra	يِجْرَى	ma-yigrāš	مَيِجْراش
	ána	yigrāli	يِجْرالي	ma-yigralīš	مَيِجْراليش
	íḥna	yigrálna	يِجْرالْنا	ma-yigralnāš	مَيِجْرالْناش
	ínta	yigrālak	يِجْرالَك	ma-yigralákš	مَيِجْرالَكْش
	ínti	yigrālik	يِجْرالِك	ma-yigralkīš	مَيِجْرالْكيش
	íntu	yigrálku	يِجْرالْكو	ma-yigralkūš	مَيِجْرالْكوش
	húwwa	yigrālu	يِجْرالُه	ma-yigralūš	مَيِجْرالوش
	híyya	yigrálha	يِجْرالْها	ma-yigralhāš	مَيِجْرالْهاش
	húmma	yigrálhum	يِجْرالْهُم	ma-yigralhúmš	مَيِجْرالْهُمْش
bi-imperfect		biyígra	بِيِجْرَى	ma-byigrāš	مَبْيِجْراش
	ána	biyigrāli	بِيِجْرالي	ma-byigralīš	مَبْيِجْراليش
	íḥna	biyigrálna	بِيِجْرالْنا	ma-byigralnāš	مَبْيِجْرالْناش
	ínta	biyigrālak	بِيِجْرالَك	ma-byigralákš	مَبْيِجْرالَكْش
	ínti	biyigrālik	بِيِجْرالِك	ma-byigralkīš	مَبْيِجْرالْكيش
	íntu	biyigrálku	بِيِجْرالْكو	ma-byigralkūš	مَبْيِجْرالْكوش
	húwwa	biyigrālu	بِيِجْرالُه	ma-byigralūš	مَبْيِجْرالوش
	híyya	biyigrálha	بِيِجْرالْها	ma-byigralhāš	مَبْيِجْرالْهاش
	húmma	biyigrálhum	بِيِجْرالْهُم	ma-byigralhúmš	مَبْيِجْرالْهُمْش
future		hayígra	هَيِجْرَى	miš hayígra	مِش هَيِجْرَى
	ána	hayigrāli	هَيِجْرالي	miš hayigrāli	مِش هَيِجْرالي
	íḥna	hayigrálna	هَيِجْرالْنا	miš hayigrálna	مِش هَيِجْرالْنا
	ínta	hayigrālak	هَيِجْرالَك	miš hayigrālak	مِش هَيِجْرالَك
	ínti	hayigrālik	هَيِجْرالِك	miš hayigrālik	مِش هَيِجْرالِك
	íntu	hayigrálku	هَيِجْرالْكو	miš hayigrálku	مِش هَيِجْرالْكو
	húwwa	hayigrālu	هَيِجْرالُه	miš hayigrālu	مِش هَيِجْرالُه
	híyya	hayigrálha	هَيِجْرالْها	miš hayigrálha	مِش هَيِجْرالْها
	húmma	hayigrálhum	هَيِجْرالْهُم	miš hayigrálhum	مِش هَيِجْرالْهُم

	gāri	جاري	active participle
ána	garīli	جاريلي	
íḫna	garílna	جاريلْنا	
ínta	garīlak	جاريلَك	
ínti	garīlik	جاريلِك	
íntu	garílku	جاريلْكو	
húwwa	garīlu	جاريله	
híyya	garílha	جاريلْها	
húmma	garílhum	جاريلْهُم	

①

جرالْكو حاجة لمّا خبطْتوا في العربية اللي قُدّامْكو؟

garálku ḫāga lámma xabáṭṭu fi -l3arabíyya -lli ʔuddámku?

Did anything happen to you when you hit the car in front of you?

②

أنا هغيب مِ الشُّغْل النّهارْده، و اللي يِجْرى يِجْرى.

ána hayīb mi -ššuɣl innahárda, w ílli yígra yígra.

I'll take today off from work, and whatever happens, happens.

③

إنْتي بيِجْرالِك أيْه لمّا بِتْشوفي عِماد؟ مفيش مرّة متِتْخانْقوش.

ínti biyigrālik ʔē lámma bitšūfi 3imād? ma-fīš márra ma-titxanʔūš.

What happens each time you see Emad? Every time you have a fight.

④

مِش هَيِجْرالك حاجة لَوْ مرّة شِلْت الكُبّايَة اللي شْرِبْت فيها!

miš hayigrālak ḫāga law márra šilt ilkubbāya -lli šribtᵊ fīha!

Nothing bad will happen if, for once, you put the glass back after drinking!

⑤

أنا سْمِعْت عن المُشْكِلة اللي حصلِت في شِرِكِتْها. أرْجو مَيْكونْش جرالْها حاجة وِحْشة.

ána smi3tᵊ 3an ilmuškíla -lli ḫáṣalit fi širkítha. árgu ma-ykúnšᵊ garálha ḫāga wíḫša.

I heard about the problem in her company. I hope nothing bad happened to her.

⑥

اِتْطمِنّوا. أنا كْوَيِّس. مجراليش حاجة.

itṭamínnu. ána kwáyyis. ma-garalīš ḫāga.

Calm down. I'm okay. Nothing happened to me.

❖ [1d1] **to happen (to** لِ *li-*)

- This verb is invariable (only found in the masculine third-person). Because of this, the verb's table has been set up a bit differently. Each section starts with the verb without a suffix, followed by forms for each person as an indirect object, 'happened to me', 'happened to you', etc.
- Compare with حصل *ḫáṣal*. (➲83)

➲ 169.4

72 to run *gíri* جِري

	affirmative		negative		
ána	*girīt*	جريت	*ma-grítš*	مَجْريتْش	**perfect**
íḫna	*girīna*	جرينا	*ma-grināš*	مَجْريناش	
ínta	*girīt*	جريت	*ma-grítš*	مَجْريتْش	
ínti	*girīti*	جريتي	*ma-gritīš*	مَجْريتيش	
íntu	*girītu*	جريتوا	*ma-gritūš*	مَجْريتوش	
húwwa	*gíri*	جري	*ma-grīš*	مَجْريش	
híyya	*gíryit*	جِرْيِت	*ma-giryítš*	مَجِرْيِتْش	
húmma	*gíryu*	جِرْيوا	*ma-giryūš*	مَجِرْيوش	

ána	*ágri*	أَجْري	*ma-grīš*	مَجْريش	**imperfect**
íḫna	*nígri*	نِجْري	*ma-nigrīš*	مَنِجْريش	
ínta	*tígri*	تِجْري	*ma-tigrīš*	مَتِجْريش	
ínti	*tígri*	تِجْري	*ma-tigrīš*	مَتِجْريش	
íntu	*tígru*	تِجْروا	*ma-tigrūš*	مَتِجْروش	
húwwa	*yígri*	يِجْري	*ma-yigrīš*	مَيِجْريش	
híyya	*tígri*	تِجْري	*ma-tigrīš*	مَتِجْريش	
húmma	*yígru*	يِجْروا	*ma-yigrūš*	مَيِجْروش	

ána	*bágri*	بَجْري	*ma-bagrīš*	مَبَجْريش	**bi-imperfect**
íḫna	*binígri*	بِنِجْري	*ma-bnigrīš*	مَبْنِجْريش	
ínta	*bitígri*	بِتِجْري	*ma-btigrīš*	مَبْتِجْريش	
ínti	*bitígri*	بِتِجْري	*ma-btigrīš*	مَبْتِجْريش	
íntu	*bitígru*	بِتِجْروا	*ma-btigrūš*	مَبْتِجْروش	
húwwa	*biyígri*	بِيِجْري	*ma-byigrīš*	مَبْيِجْريش	
híyya	*bitígri*	بِتِجْري	*ma-btigrīš*	مَبْتِجْريش	
húmma	*biyígru*	بِيِجْروا	*ma-byigrūš*	مَبْيِجْروش	

ána	*hágri*	هَجْري	*miš hágri*	مِش هَجْري	**future**
íḫna	*hanígri*	هَنِجْري	*miš hanígri*	مِش هَنِجْري	
ínta	*hatígri*	هَتِجْري	*miš hatígri*	مِش هَتِجْري	
ínti	*hatígri*	هَتِجْري	*miš hatígri*	مِش هَتِجْري	
íntu	*hatígru*	هَتِجْروا	*miš hatígru*	مِش هَتِجْروا	
húwwa	*hayígri*	هَيِجْري	*miš hayígri*	مِش هَيِجْري	
híyya	*hatígri*	هَتِجْري	*miš hatígri*	مِش هَتِجْري	
húmma	*hayígru*	هَيِجْروا	*miš hayígru*	مِش هَيِجْروا	

ínta	*ígri*	اِجْري	*ma-tigrīš*	مَتِجْريش	**imperative**
ínti	*ígri*	اِجْري	*ma-tigrīš*	مَتِجْريش	
íntu	*ígru*	اِجْروا	*ma-tigrūš*	مَتِجْروش	

	active		passive		
masculine	*gāri*	جاري	–	–	**participles**
feminine	*gárya*	جارْيَة	–	–	
plural	*garyīn*	جارْيين	–	–	

verbal noun: *gary* جَرْي

①

جِري لِمُدِّةْ ٤ ساعات مُتَواصْلة في الماراثوْن الأخير، و طِلِع في المرْكز التّاني.

gíri li-múddit árba3 sa3āt mutawáṣla fi -lmárason il?axīr, wi ṭíli3 fi -lmárkaz ittāni.

He ran for four hours straight in the last marathon and came in second.

②

بحِبّ أجْري كُلّ يوْم الصُّبْح نُصّ ساعة.

baḫíbb ágri kullᵊ yōm iṣṣúbḫᵊ nuṣṣᵊ sā3a.

I like to run for half an hour every morning.

③

مبجْريش ورا حدّ. اللي عايزْني يْيجيني.

ma-bagrīš wára ḫadd. ílli 3ayízni ygīni.

I don't chase after anyone. Whoever needs me should come to me.

④

لازِم تِروح الفَيوم و تْشوف منْظر الميّة بْتِجْري في شلّال وادي الرّيان.

lāzim tirūḫ ilfayūm wi tšūf mánẓar ilmáyya btígri fi šallāl wādi -rrayān.

You should go to Fayoum and see the running water at Wadi El Rayan falls.

⑤

اِجْري وَرا حِلْمك و متْسيبوش مهْما حصل.

ígri wára ḫílmak wi ma-tsibūš máhma ḫáṣal.

Pursue your dream and never let it go no matter what happens.

❖ [1d5] **to run; to pursue, chase (after)** (وَرا *wára*)

➲ 72.3, 73.7, 92.1, 111.1, 188.2

73 to come *gih* جِهْ

verbal noun: *migíyy* مَجِي

	affirmative		negative		
ána	*gēt (gīt)*	جيْت (جيت)	*ma-gítš*	مَجيتْش	**perfect**
íḥna	*gēna (gīna)*	جيْنا (جينا)	*ma-gināš*	مَجيناش	
ínta	*gēt (gīt)*	جيْت (جيت)	*ma-gítš*	مَجيتْش	
ínti	*gēti (gīti)*	جيْتي (جيتي)	*ma-gitīš*	مَجيتيش	
íntu	*gētu (gītu)*	جيْتوا (جيتوا)	*ma-gitūš*	مَجيتوش	
húwwa	*gih (gā-)*	جِهْ (جا-)	*ma-gāš*	مَجاش	
híyya	*gat*	جَت	*ma-gátš*	مَجَتْش	
húmma	*gum (gū-)*	جُم (جو-)	*ma-gūš*	مَجوش	
ána	*āgi*	آجي	*ma-gīš*	مَجيش	**imperfect**
íḥna	*nīgi*	نيجي	*ma-ngīš*	مَنْجيش	
ínta	*tīgi*	تيجي	*ma-tgīš*	مَتْجيش	
ínti	*tīgi*	تيجي	*ma-tgīš*	مَتْجيش	
íntu	*tīgu*	تيجوا	*ma-tgūš*	مَتْجوش	
húwwa	*yīgi*	ييجي	*ma-ygīš*	مَيْجيش	
híyya	*tīgi*	تيجي	*ma-tgīš*	مَتْجيش	
húmma	*yīgu*	ييجوا	*ma-ygūš*	مَيْجوش	
ána	*bāgi*	باجي	*ma-bagīš*	مَباجيش	**bi-imperfect**
íḥna	*binīgi*	بِنيجي	*ma-bingīš*	مَبِنْجيش	
ínta	*bitīgi*	بِتيجي	*ma-bitgīš*	مَبِتْجيش	
ínti	*bitīgi*	بِتيجي	*ma-bitgīš*	مَبِتْجيش	
íntu	*bitīgu*	بِتيجوا	*ma-bitgūš*	مَبِتْجوش	
húwwa	*biyīgi*	بِييجي	*ma-biygīš*	مَبِيْجيش	
híyya	*bitīgi*	بِتيجي	*ma-bitgīš*	مَبِتْجيش	
húmma	*biyīgu*	بِييجوا	*ma-biygūš*	مَبِيْجوش	
ána	*hāgi*	هاجي	*miš hāgi*	مِش هَاجي	**future**
íḥna	*hanīgi*	هَنيجي	*miš hanīgi*	مِش هَنيجي	
ínta	*hatīgi*	هَتيجي	*miš hatīgi*	مِش هَتيجي	
ínti	*hatīgi*	هَتيجي	*miš hatīgi*	مِش هَتيجي	
íntu	*hatīgu*	هَتيجوا	*miš hatīgu*	مِش هَتيجوا	
húwwa	*hayīgi*	هَييجي	*miš hayīgi*	مِش هَييجي	
híyya	*hatīgi*	هَتيجي	*miš hatīgi*	مِش هَتيجي	
húmma	*hayīgu*	هَييجوا	*miš hayīgu*	مِش هَييجوا	
ínta	*ta3āla*	تَعالى	*ma-tgīš*	مَتْجيش	**imperative**
ínti	*ta3āli*	تَعالي	*ma-tgīš*	مَتْجيش	
íntu	*ta3ālu*	تَعالوا	*ma-tgūš*	مَتْجوش	

	active		passive		
masculine	*gayy*	جايّ	–	–	**participles**
feminine	*gáyya*	جايّة	–	–	
plural	*gayyīn*	جايّين	–	–	

①

هِيَّ أميرة جتْلْكو وَلّا لِسّه؟ أصْلها كات قايْلالي إنّها هتْعدّي عليْكو.

híyya ʔamīra gatlúku wálla líssa? aṣláha kāt ʔaylāli innáha hat3áddi 3alēku.

Did Amira come to you yet? Because she was telling me she would drop by to see you.

②

خالو دايْماً ييجي يِفْطر معانا أوِّل يوْم رمضان.

xālu dáyman yīgi yíftar ma3āna ʔáwwil yōm ramaḍān.

My uncle always comes and breaks the fast with us on the first day of Ramadan.

③

باجي على نفْسي كْتير عشان المرْكِب تِمْشي بسّ خايْفة في يوْم أنْفِجِر في الكُلّ.

bāgi 3ála náfsi ktīr 3ašān ilmárkib tímši bass[ə] xáyfa fi yōm anfígir fi -lkull.

I usually just let things go in order to keep the peace, but I'm afraid I'll lose it one day and blow up at everyone.

④

هاجيلْكو بُكْره و نْروح نِجيب عبودي مِن المطار سَوا.

hagílku búkra wi nirūḥ nigīb 3abūdi min ilmaṭār sáwa.

I'll come by tomorrow, and we'll go pick up Aboudy from the airport together.

⑤

تيجي نْروح مرْسى مطْروح في العيد. المكان هِناك تُحْفة.

tīgi nrūḥ mársa maṭrūḥ fi -l3īd. ilmakān hinād túḥfa.

Let's go to Marsa Matrouh at Eid [on the holiday]. It's wonderful there.

⑥

كان فيه أُغْنية بحِبّها زمان بِتْقول: جاني الأسْمر جاني.

kān fī uɣníyya baḥibbáha zamān bitʔūl: gāni -lʔásmar gāni.

There was a song I liked long ago that goes, "The dark boy came to me."

⑦

الوِلاد لمّا أبوهُم تِعِب جوله جرْي.

ilwilād lámma ʔabūhum tí3ib gūlu gary.

When their father fell ill, all of his children came at once to his side.

⑧

الضُّيوف قالوا جايّين ٨ بسّ جُم على ١٠، حتّى معْتذروش.

iḍḍuyūf ʔālu gayyīn tamánya bass[ə] gum 3ála 3ášara, ḥátta ma-3tazarūš.

The guests said they'd come at 8, but they came around 10 o'clock and didn't even apologize.

⑨

إنْتَ جايّ الرِّحْلة وَلّا مِش جايّ ؟ لازِم تِقولي النّهارْده.

ínta gayy irríɦla wálla miš gayy? lāzim tiʔūli -nnahárda.

Are you coming on the trip or not? You need to tell me today.

⑩

كُلّ اللي جِهْ المُحاضْرة دي هَياخُد درجِةْ أعْمال السّنة كامْلة.

kull ílli gih ilmuɦáḍra di hayāxud dáragit a3māl issána kámla.

All who attended this lecture will receive an A for the year.

⑪

الوِلاد مبْسوطين أوي عشان جينا النّادي.

ilwilād mabsuṭīn ʔáwi 3ašān gīna -nnādi.

The kids are so happy that we came to the [country] club.

⑫

بعْد ما وْقِفْنا طابور طَويل، المُوَظّف مجاش.

ba3dᵊ ma wʔífna ṭabūr ṭawīl, ilmuwáẓẓaf ma-gāš.

After we stood in a long line, the employee didn't show up.

⑬

متْجيش بُكْره العِيادة. هتْكون زحْمة أوي.

ma-tgīš búkra -l3iyāda. hatkūn záɦma ʔáwi.

Don't come to the clinic tomorrow. It'll be too crowded.

⑭

مجيناش الحفْلة، عشان راحِت علیْنا نوْمة.

ma-gināš ilɦáfla, 3ašān rāɦit 3alēna nōma.

We didn't come to the party because we overslept.

⑮

تعالى معايا. عايْزك في مِشْوار.

ta3āla ma3āya. 3áyzak fi mišwār.

Come with me. I want you to come along on an errand.

⑯

تعالي نْروح نِتْبرّع بِالدّمّ.

ta3āli nrūɦ nitbárra3 bi-ddámm.

Let's go donate our blood.

❖ [i1] **to come (to** لِ *li*-)

- The affirmative first- and second-person perfect forms can be pronounced with *ē* or *ī*. (➲ 73.11)
- The masculine third-person singular and third-person plural perfect forms have special forms (جا *gā*- and جو *gū*-, respectively) used when a suffix is added. The suffix may be an object pronoun (➲ 73.6, 73.7) or the negative suffix ـش -*š* (➲ 73.12).
- In Egyptian Arabic, a long vowel can be shortened, but is usually not elided. An exception occurs in the imperfect (and bi-imperfect) forms of this verb. The *ī* elides in the negative forms. (➲ 73.13)
- Notice that the affirmative imperative forms are unrelated to the actual verb. (➲ 73.15, 73.16) The negative imperative forms, however, are formed regularly. (➲ 73.13)
- This verb takes a direct object when it is a place (➲ 73.13, 73.14), but the preposition لِ *li*- before object pronouns. The exception is the first-person singular pronoun suffix, which is ـني -*ni* instead of ـلي -*li*. (➲ 73.6)
- A affirmative second-person imperfect or imperative form of this verb can be followed by a first-person plural imperfect verb to express a proposal, translating 'let's'. (➲ 73.5, 73.16)

➲ 12.5, 58.1, 95.1, 101.5, 109.6

74 to get ready *gíhiz* جِهِز

verbal noun: *gahazān* جَهَزان

	affirmative		negative		
ána	*gihízt*	جِهِزْت	*ma-ghíztiš*	مَجْهِزْتِش	perfect
íḫna	*gihízna*	جِهِزْنا	*ma-ghiznāš*	مَجْهِزْناش	
ínta	*gihízt*	جِهِزْت	*ma-ghíztiš*	مَجْهِزْتِش	
ínti	*gihízti*	جِهِزْتي	*ma-ghiztīš*	مَجْهِزْتيش	
íntu	*gihíztu*	جِهِزْتوا	*ma-ghiztūš*	مَجْهِزْتوش	
húwwa	*gíhiz*	جِهِز	*ma-ghízš*	مَجْهِزْش	
híyya	*gíhzit*	جِهْزِت	*ma-gihzítš*	مَجِهْزِتْش	
húmma	*gíhzu*	جِهْزوا	*ma-gihzūš*	مَجِهْزوش	
ána	*ágh az*	أَجْهَز	*ma-gházš*	مَجْهَزْش	imperfect
íḫna	*níghaz*	نِجْهَز	*ma-nigházš*	مَنِجْهَزْش	
ínta	*tíghaz*	تِجْهَز	*ma-tigházš*	مَتِجْهَزْش	
ínti	*tigházi*	تِجْهَزي	*ma-tighazīš*	مَتِجْهَزيش	
íntu	*tigházu*	تِجْهَزوا	*ma-tighazūš*	مَتِجْهَزوش	
húwwa	*yíghaz*	يِجْهَز	*ma-yigházš*	مَيِجْهَزْش	
híyya	*tíghaz*	تِجْهَز	*ma-tigházš*	مَتِجْهَزْش	
húmma	*yigházu*	يِجْهَزوا	*ma-yighazūš*	مَيِجْهَزوش	
ána	*bághaz*	بَجْهَز	*ma-bagházš*	مَبَجْهَزْش	bi-imperfect
íḫna	*biníghaz*	بِنِجْهَز	*ma-bnigházš*	مَبْنِجْهَزْش	
ínta	*bitíghaz*	بِتِجْهَز	*ma-btigházš*	مَبْتِجْهَزْش	
ínti	*bitighází*	بِتِجْهَزي	*ma-btighazīš*	مَبْتِجْهَزيش	
íntu	*bitigházu*	بِتِجْهَزوا	*ma-btighazūš*	مَبْتِجْهَزوش	
húwwa	*biyíghaz*	بِيِجْهَز	*ma-byigházš*	مَبْيِجْهَزْش	
híyya	*bitíghaz*	بِتِجْهَز	*ma-btigházš*	مَبْتِجْهَزْش	
húmma	*biyigházu*	بِيِجْهَزوا	*ma-byighazūš*	مَبْيِجْهَزوش	
ána	*hághaz*	هَجْهَز	*miš hághaz*	مِش هَجْهَز	future
íḫna	*haníghaz*	هَنِجْهَز	*miš haníghaz*	مِش هَنِجْهَز	
ínta	*hatíghaz*	هَتِجْهَز	*miš hatíghaz*	مِش هَتِجْهَز	
ínti	*hatighází*	هَتِجْهَزي	*miš hatighází*	مِش هَتِجْهَزي	
íntu	*hatigházu*	هَتِجْهَزوا	*miš hatigházu*	مِش هَتِجْهَزوا	
húwwa	*hayíghaz*	هَيِجْهَز	*miš hayíghaz*	مِش هَيِجْهَز	
híyya	*hatíghaz*	هَتِجْهَز	*miš hatíghaz*	مِش هَتِجْهَز	
húmma	*hayigházu*	هَيِجْهَزوا	*miš hayigházu*	مِش هَيِجْهَزوا	
ínta	*íghaz*	اِجْهَز	*ma-tigházš*	مَتِجْهَزْش	imperative
ínti	*igházi*	اِجْهَزي	*ma-tighazīš*	مَتِجْهَزيش	
íntu	*igházu*	اِجْهَزوا	*ma-tighazūš*	مَتِجْهَزوش	

	active		passive		
masculine	*gāhiz*	جاهِز	–	–	participles
feminine	*gáhza*	جاهْزَة	–	–	
plural	*gahzīn*	جاهْزين	–	–	

①

لمّا صْحيت مِتْأخّر، جِهِزْت و نْزِلْت في خمس دقايِق.

lámma ṣḫīt mitʔáxxar, gihíztᵊ wi nziltᵊ f xámas daʔāyiʔ.

When I woke up late, I got ready
and went out in five minutes.

②

لازِم يِجْهز قبْل كُلّ مُحاضْرة، رغْم إنُّه أُسْتاذ كِبير.

lāzim yíghaz ʔablᵊ kullᵊ muḫáḍra, raɣm ínnu ustāz kibīr.

He has to prepare before every lecture,
even though he is a great professor.

③

الغدا بيِجْهز . غيرّوا هُدومْكو على ما أغْرِف.

ilɣáda biyíghaz. ɣayyáru hudúmku 3ála m- áɣrif.

Lunch is being prepared. Change your
clothes by the time I dish it out.

④

هتِجْهزي إمْتى؟ الحفْلة خلاص كمان ساعْتينْ.

hatigházi ímta? ilḫáfla xalāṣ kamān sa3tēn.

When are you going to get ready? The
party starts in just a couple of hours.

⑤

اِجْهزوا بْسُرْعة. الضُّيوف عَ السِّلِّم.

igházu b-súr3a. iḍḍuyūf 3a -ssíllim.

Get ready fast. The guests are
coming up the stairs.

⑥

مجْهِزْتوش لِحدّ دِلْوَقْتي ليْه؟ أنا هنْزِل و أسيبْكو.

ma-ghiztūš li-ḫaddᵊ dilwáʔti lē? ána hánzil w asíbku.

Why haven't you gotten ready
yet? I'll go without you.

❖ [1s4] **to get ready, be prepared**

75 to prepare gáhhiz جهّز

verbal noun: taghīz تجهيز

	affirmative		negative		
ána	gahhízt	جهّزت	ma-gahhíztiš	مجهّزتش	perfect
íḫna	gahhízna	جهّزنا	ma-gahhiznāš	مجهّزناش	
ínta	gahhízt	جهّزت	ma-gahhíztiš	مجهّزتش	
ínti	gahhízti	جهّزتي	ma-gahhiztīš	مجهّزتيش	
íntu	gahhíztu	جهّزتوا	ma-gahhiztūš	مجهّزتوش	
húwwa	gáhhiz	جهّز	ma-gahhízš	مجهّزش	
híyya	gahhízit	جهّزت	ma-gahhizítš	مجهّزتش	
húmma	gahhízu	جهّزوا	ma-gahhizūš	مجهّزوش	
ána	agáhhiz	أجهّز	ma-gahhízš	مجهّزش	imperfect
íḫna	nigáhhiz	نجهّز	ma-ngahhízš	منجهّزش	
ínta	tigáhhiz	تجهّز	ma-tgahhízš	متجهّزش	
ínti	tigahhízi	تجهّزي	ma-tgahhizīš	متجهّزيش	
íntu	tigahhízu	تجهّزوا	ma-tgahhizūš	متجهّزوش	
húwwa	yigáhhiz	يجهّز	ma-ygahhízš	ميجهّزش	
híyya	tigáhhiz	تجهّز	ma-tgahhízš	متجهّزش	
húmma	yigahhízu	يجهّزوا	ma-ygahhizūš	ميجهّزوش	
ána	bagáhhiz	بجهّز	ma-bagahhízš	مبجهّزش	bi-imperfect
íḫna	bingáhhiz	بنجهّز	ma-bingahhízš	مبنجهّزش	
ínta	bitgáhhiz	بتجهّز	ma-bitgahhízš	مبتجهّزش	
ínti	bitgahhízi	بتجهّزي	ma-bitgahhizīš	مبتجهّزيش	
íntu	bitgahhízu	بتجهّزوا	ma-bitgahhizūš	مبتجهّزوش	
húwwa	biygáhhiz	بيجهّز	ma-biygahhízš	مبيجهّزش	
híyya	bitgáhhiz	بتجهّز	ma-bitgahhízš	مبتجهّزش	
húmma	biygahhízu	بيجهّزوا	ma-biygahhizūš	مبيجهّزوش	
ána	hagáhhiz	هجهّز	miš hagáhhiz	مش هجهّز	future
íḫna	hangáhhiz	هنجهّز	miš hangáhhiz	مش هنجهّز	
ínta	hatgáhhiz	هتجهّز	miš hatgáhhiz	مش هتجهّز	
ínti	hatgahhízi	هتجهّزي	miš hatgahhízi	مش هتجهّزي	
íntu	hatgahhízu	هتجهّزوا	miš hatgahhízu	مش هتجهّزوا	
húwwa	haygáhhiz	هيجهّز	miš haygáhhiz	مش هيجهّز	
híyya	hatgáhhiz	هتجهّز	miš hatgáhhiz	مش هتجهّز	
húmma	haygahhízu	هيجهّزوا	miš haygahhízu	مش هيجهّزوا	
ínta	gáhhiz	جهّز	ma-tgahhízš	متجهّزش	imperative
ínti	gahhízi	جهّزي	ma-tgahhizīš	متجهّزيش	
íntu	gahhízu	جهّزوا	ma-tgahhizūš	متجهّزوش	

	active		passive		
masculine	migáhhiz	مجهّز	mitgáhhiz	متجهّز	participles
feminine	migahhíza	مجهّزة	mitgahhíza	متجهّزة	
plural	migahhizīn	مجهّزين	mitgahhizīn	متجهّزين	

①
جهِّزْتوا شُنطْكو وَلّا لِسّه؟ هتِتْأخّروا على معاد الطّيّارة.

gahhíztu šunáṭku wálla líssa? hatitʔaxxáru 3ála mi3ād iṭṭayyāra.

Did you pack [lit. prepare] your bags yet?
You're going to be late for the flight.

②
لازِم تِجهِّزي نفْسِك لِلفرح مِن بدْري عشان متْكونيش مُتوَتِّرة.

lāzim tigahhízi náfsik li-lfáraḥ min bádri 3ašān ma-tkunīš mutawattíra.

You must get ready for the wedding
early so as not to get anxious.

③
بجهِّز الفِطار. اِلْبِسوا على ما أخلّص.

bagáhhiz ilfiṭār. ilbísu 3ála m- axállaṣ.

I'm preparing breakfast. Get dressed
by the time it's ready.

④
هتْجهِّزوا الكحْك إمْتى؟ ده العيد خلاص باقيلُه يوْميْن.

hatgahhízu -lkaḥk ímta? da -l3īd xalāṣ baʔīlu yumēn.

When are you going to make kahk?
There are only two days of Eid left.

⑤
باعوا اللي وَراهُم و اللي قُدّامْهُم عشان يِجهِّزوا بِنْتُهُم.

bā3u -lli warāhum w ílli ʔuddámhum 3ašān yigahhízu bintúhum.

They spent everything they had in order to
prepare for their daughter's marriage.

⑥
مِجهِّزين فقرات حِلْوَة أوي في الحفْلة. لازِم تيجوا كُلُّكو.

migahhizīn faqarāt ḥílwa ʔáwi fi -lḥáfla. lāzim tīgu kullúku.

We've prepared very nice activities
for the party. You must all come.

⑦
لِسّه مجهِّزْتِش الغدا. خُدْلك أيّ تصْبيرة.

líssa ma-gahhíztiš ilɣáda. xúdlak ayy^{ə} taṣbīra.

I haven't fixed [lit. prepared]
lunch yet. Have a snack.

❖ [2s1] **to prepare, make ready**

➲ 44.2, 55.2

76 to pay attention *ḥāfiẓ* حافِظ

verbal nouns: *muḥáfẓa* مُحافْظة - *ḥifāẓ* حِفاظ

	affirmative		negative		
ána	*ḥafíẓt*	حافِظْت	*ma-ḥafíẓtiš*	مَحافِظْتِش	perfect
íḥna	*ḥafíẓna*	حافِظْنا	*ma-ḥafiẓnāš*	مَحافِظْناش	
ínta	*ḥafíẓt*	حافِظْت	*ma-ḥafíẓtiš*	مَحافِظْتِش	
ínti	*ḥafíẓti*	حافِظْتي	*ma-ḥafiẓtīš*	مَحافِظْتيش	
íntu	*ḥafíẓtu*	حافِظْتوا	*ma-ḥafiẓtūš*	مَحافِظْتوش	
húwwa	*ḥāfiẓ*	حافِظ	*ma-ḥafíẓš*	مَحافِظْش	
híyya	*ḥáfẓit*	حافْظِت	*ma-ḥafẓítš*	مَحافْظِتْش	
húmma	*ḥáfẓu*	حافْظوا	*ma-ḥafẓūš*	مَحافْظوش	
ána	*aḥāfiẓ*	أحافِظ	*ma-ḥafíẓš*	مَحافِظْش	imperfect
íḥna	*niḥāfiẓ*	نِحافِظ	*ma-nḥafíẓš*	مَنْحافِظْش	
ínta	*tiḥāfiẓ*	تِحافِظ	*ma-tḥafíẓš*	مَتْحافِظْش	
ínti	*tiḥáfẓi*	تِحافْظي	*ma-tḥafẓīš*	مَتْحافْظيش	
íntu	*tiḥáfẓu*	تِحافْظوا	*ma-tḥafẓūš*	مَتْحافْظوش	
húwwa	*yiḥāfiẓ*	يِحافِظ	*ma-yḥafíẓš*	مَيْحافِظْش	
híyya	*tiḥāfiẓ*	تِحافِظ	*ma-tḥafíẓš*	مَتْحافِظْش	
húmma	*yiḥáfẓu*	يِحافْظوا	*ma-yḥafẓūš*	مَيْحافْظوش	
ána	*baḥāfiẓ*	بَحافِظ	*ma-baḥafíẓš*	مَبَحافِظْش	bi-imperfect
íḥna	*binḥāfiẓ*	بِنْحافِظ	*ma-binḥafíẓš*	مَبِنْحافِظْش	
ínta	*bitḥāfiẓ*	بِتْحافِظ	*ma-bitḥafíẓš*	مَبِتْحافِظْش	
ínti	*bitḥáfẓi*	بِتْحافْظي	*ma-bitḥafẓīš*	مَبِتْحافْظيش	
íntu	*bitḥáfẓu*	بِتْحافْظوا	*ma-bitḥafẓūš*	مَبِتْحافْظوش	
húwwa	*biyḥāfiẓ*	بِيْحافِظ	*ma-biyḥafíẓš*	مَبِيْحافِظْش	
híyya	*bitḥāfiẓ*	بِتْحافِظ	*ma-bitḥafíẓš*	مَبِتْحافِظْش	
húmma	*biyḥáfẓu*	بِيْحافْظوا	*ma-biyḥafẓūš*	مَبِيْحافْظوش	
ána	*haḥāfiẓ*	هَحافِظ	*miš haḥāfiẓ*	مِش هَحافِظ	future
íḥna	*hanḥāfiẓ*	هَنْحافِظ	*miš hanḥāfiẓ*	مِش هَنْحافِظ	
ínta	*hatḥāfiẓ*	هَتْحافِظ	*miš hatḥāfiẓ*	مِش هَتْحافِظ	
ínti	*hatḥáfẓi*	هَتْحافْظي	*miš hatḥáfẓi*	مِش هَتْحافْظي	
íntu	*hatḥáfẓu*	هَتْحافْظوا	*miš hatḥáfẓu*	مِش هَتْحافْظوا	
húwwa	*hayḥāfiẓ*	هَيْحافِظ	*miš hayḥāfiẓ*	مِش هَيْحافِظ	
híyya	*hatḥāfiẓ*	هَتْحافِظ	*miš hatḥāfiẓ*	مِش هَتْحافِظ	
húmma	*hayḥáfẓu*	هَيْحافْظوا	*miš hayḥáfẓu*	مِش هَيْحافْظوا	
ínta	*ḥāfiẓ*	حافِظ	*ma-tḥafíẓš*	مَتْحافِظْش	imperative
ínti	*ḥáfẓi*	حافْظي	*ma-tḥafẓīš*	مَتْحافْظيش	
íntu	*ḥáfẓu*	حافْظوا	*ma-tḥafẓūš*	مَتْحافْظوش	

	active		passive		
masculine	*miḥāfiẓ*	مِحافِظ	*mitḥāfiẓ*	مِتْحافِظ	participles
feminine	*miḥáfẓa*	مِحافْظَة	*mitḥáfẓa*	مِتْحافْظَة	
plural	*miḥafẓīn*	مِحافْظين	*mitḥafẓīn*	مِتْحافْظين	

①

عيلْتي حافْظِت على التُّحفة دي مِن جيل لِجيل لِحدّ ما وَصلِتْني.

3ílti ɧáfẓit 3ála -ttúɧafa di min gīl li-gīl li-ɧaddᵊ ma waṣalítni.

My family kept this antique from generation to generation until it reached me.

②

لمْياء بِتِعْرف تِحافِظ على هُدوءْها في أصْعب المَواقِف.

lamyā? bití3raf tiɧāfiẓ 3ála hudú?ha fi ?áṣ3ab ilmawāqif.

Lamia knows how to stay calm [lit. hold onto her calmness] even in the most difficult situations.

③

عمْرو بِيْحافِظ على صِحِّتُه جامِد: مفيش سجايِر، مُنْتظِم في الجيم و أكْلُه صِحّي.

3ámrᵊ biyɧāfiẓ 3ála ṣiɧɧítu gāmid: ma-fīš sagāyir, muntáẓim fi -lžīm w áklu ṣíɧɧi.

Amr takes very good care of his health: no smoking, goes to the gym regularly, and eats healthy.

④

هتْحافْظوا عَ النِّظام في القاعة وَلّا هتُخْرُجوا برّه؟

hatɧáfẓu 3a -nniẓām fi -lqā3a wálla hatuxrúgu bárra?

(teacher to rowdy students:) Are you going to keep order in the [lecture] hall or go out?

⑤

حافِظ على أكْل عيْشك. متِعْمِلْش مشاكِل معَ الزّبايِن.

ɧāfiẓ 3ála ?aklᵊ 3ēšak. ma-ti3mílšᵊ mašākil má3a -zzabāyin.

Hold onto your job. Don't make trouble with customers.

⑥

لَوْ اِسْتمرّيْتوا متْحافْظوش على البيئة، هتِتْسببوا في كَوارِث قُدّام.

law istamarrētu ma-tɧafẓūš 3ála -lbī?a, hatitsábbabu fi kawāris ?uddām.

If you continue to not maintain the environment, you'll cause disasters afterward.

❖ [3s] **to take care of, maintain, protect; to keep, hold onto**

- Compare with حفظ *ɧáfaẓ*. (➲ 86)

➲ 8.5, 25.3, 79.5, 108.5, 162.5, 173.3, 204.2

77 to try ɧāwil حاول

	affirmative		negative		
ána	ɧawílt	حاولْت	ma-ɧawíltiš	مَحاولْتِش	perfect
íɧna	ɧawílna	حاولْنا	ma-ɧawilnāš	مَحاولْناش	
ínta	ɧawílt	حاولْت	ma-ɧawíltiš	مَحاولْتِش	
ínti	ɧawílti	حاولْتي	ma-ɧawiltīš	مَحاولْتيش	
íntu	ɧawíltu	حاولْتوا	ma-ɧawiltūš	مَحاولْتوش	
húwwa	ɧāwil	حاول	ma-ɧawílš	مَحاولْش	
híyya	ɧáwlit	حاوْلِت	ma-ɧawlítš	مَحاوْلِتْش	
húmma	ɧáwlu	حاوْلوا	ma-ɧawlūš	مَحاوْلوش	
ána	aɧāwil	أحاوِل	ma-ɧawílš	مَحاوِلْش	imperfect
íɧna	niɧāwil	نِحاوِل	ma-nɧawílš	مَنْحاوِلْش	
ínta	tiɧāwil	تِحاوِل	ma-tɧawílš	مَتْحاوِلْش	
ínti	tiɧáwli	تِحاوْلي	ma-tɧawlīš	مَتْحاوْليش	
íntu	tiɧáwlu	تِحاوْلوا	ma-tɧawlūš	مَتْحاوْلوش	
húwwa	yiɧāwil	يِحاوِل	ma-yɧawílš	مَيْحاوِلْش	
híyya	tiɧāwil	تِحاوِل	ma-tɧawílš	مَتْحاوِلْش	
húmma	yiɧáwlu	يِحاوْلوا	ma-yɧawlūš	مَيْحاوْلوش	
ána	baɧāwil	بَحاوِل	ma-baɧawílš	مَبَحاوِلْش	bi-imperfect
íɧna	binɧāwil	بِنْحاوِل	ma-binɧawílš	مَبِنْحاوِلْش	
ínta	bitɧāwil	بِتْحاوِل	ma-bitɧawílš	مَبِتْحاوِلْش	
ínti	bitɧáwli	بِتْحاوْلي	ma-bitɧawlīš	مَبِتْحاوْليش	
íntu	bitɧáwlu	بِتْحاوْلوا	ma-bitɧawlūš	مَبِتْحاوْلوش	
húwwa	biyɧāwil	بِيْحاوِل	ma-biyɧawílš	مَبِيْحاوِلْش	
híyya	bitɧāwil	بِتْحاوِل	ma-bitɧawílš	مَبِتْحاوِلْش	
húmma	biyɧáwlu	بِيْحاوْلوا	ma-biyɧawlūš	مَبِيْحاوْلوش	
ána	haɧāwil	هَحاوِل	miš haɧāwil	مِش هَحاوِل	future
íɧna	hanɧāwil	هَنْحاوِل	miš hanɧāwil	مِش هَنْحاوِل	
ínta	hatɧāwil	هَتْحاوِل	miš hatɧāwil	مِش هَتْحاوِل	
ínti	hatɧáwli	هَتْحاوْلي	miš hatɧáwli	مِش هَتْحاوْلي	
íntu	hatɧáwlu	هَتْحاوْلوا	miš hatɧáwlu	مِش هَتْحاوْلوا	
húwwa	hayɧāwil	هَيْحاوِل	miš hayɧāwil	مِش هَيْحاوِل	
híyya	hatɧāwil	هَتْحاوِل	miš hatɧāwil	مِش هَتْحاوِل	
húmma	hayɧáwlu	هَيْحاوْلوا	miš hayɧáwlu	مِش هَيْحاوْلوا	
ínta	ɧāwil	حاوِل	ma-tɧawílš	مَتْحاوِلْش	imperative
ínti	ɧáwli	حاوْلي	ma-tɧawlīš	مَتْحاوْليش	
íntu	ɧáwlu	حاوْلوا	ma-tɧawlūš	مَتْحاوْلوش	

	active		passive		
masculine	miɧāwil	مِحاوِل	–	–	participles
feminine	miɧáwla	مِحاوْلَة	–	–	
plural	miɧawlīn	مِحاوْلين	–	–	

verbal noun: *muɧáwla* مُحاوْلَة

①

حاوِلْت كْتير أقْنِعه يِفْضل في الشُّغْل بسّ هُوَّ أصرّ يمْشي.

ḫawílt^ə ktīr aqní3u yífḍal fi -ššuɣl^ə bass^ə húwwa ʔaṣárr^ə yímši.

I tried a lot to convince him to stay at work, but he insisted on leaving.

②

إنّها تْحاوِل تِكمِّل تعْليمْها في السِّنّ ده، ده شيْء كُوَيِّس.

innáha tḫāwil tikámmil ta3límha fi -ssinn^ə da, da šēʔ kuwáyyis.

It's a good thing that she's trying to continue her education at this age.

③

الإعْلام بيْحاوِل بِاسْتِمْرار يمْلي دْماغْنا بِافْكار مِش مُفيدة لينا.

ilʔi3lām biyḫāwil bi-stimrār yímli dmáɣna bi-afkār miš mufīda līna.

The media is constantly trying to fill our heads with useless nonsense.

④

مها هتْحاوِل تِخلّص المشْروع في الوَقْت المُحدّد. هِيَّ قالِت كِده.

máha hatḫāwil tixállaṣ ilmašrū3 fi -lwaʔt ilmuḫáddad. híyya ʔālit kída.

Maha will try to finish the project by the deadline. That's what she said.

⑤

حاوْلوا كْتير و متِزْهقوش. هُوَّ العمل الحُرّ مِحْتاج مُثابْرة.

ḫáwlu ktīr wi ma-tizhaʔūš. húwwa -l3ámal ilḫúrr^ə miḫtāg musábra.

Try hard, and don't give up. Entrepreneurship requires perseverance.

⑥

آثِر محاوِلْش أبداً يِتْعرّف على حلا رغْم إنُّه مُعْجب بيها.

āsir ma-ḫawílš ábadan yit3árraf 3ála ḫála raɣm ínnu mú3gab bīha.

Ather never tried to meet Hala, even though he likes her.

❖ [3s] **to try, attempt**

- This verb is often followed by an imperfect verb.
- Compare with جرّب *gárrab.* (➲ 70)

➲ 5.5, 17.2, 44.5, 51.2, 66.1, 69.2, 81.3, 87.2, 97.2, 100.5, 118.2, 156.1, 158.1, 164.2, 182.6, 192.2, 193.1, 195.2, 199.2, 220.2, 231.5, 238.2, 240.2, 250.2, 261.7

78 to like ḫabb حَبّ 3

	affirmative		negative		
ána	ḫabbēt	حَبّيت	ma-ḫabbítš	مَحَبّيتْش	perfect
íḫna	ḫabbēna	حَبّينا	ma-ḫabbināš	مَحَبّيناش	
ínta	ḫabbēt	حَبّيت	ma-ḫabbítš	مَحَبّيتْش	
ínti	ḫabbēti	حَبّيتي	ma-ḫabbitīš	مَحَبّيتيش	
íntu	ḫabbētu	حَبّيتوا	ma-ḫabbitūš	مَحَبّيتوش	
húwwa	ḫabb	حَبّ	ma-ḫábbiš	مَحَبّش	
híyya	ḫábbit	حَبّت	ma-ḫabbítš	مَحَبّتْش	
húmma	ḫábbu	حَبّوا	ma-ḫabbūš	مَحَبّوش	
ána	aḫíbb	أحِبّ	ma-ḫíbbiš	مَحِبّش	imperfect
íḫna	niḫíbb	نِحِبّ	ma-nḫíbbiš	مَنْحِبّش	
ínta	tiḫíbb	تِحِبّ	ma-tḫíbbiš	مَتْحِبّش	
ínti	tiḫíbbi	تِحِبّي	ma-tḫibbīš	مَتْحِبّيش	
íntu	tiḫíbbu	تِحِبّوا	ma-tḫibbūš	مَتْحِبّوش	
húwwa	yiḫíbb	يِحِبّ	ma-yḫíbbiš	مَيْحِبّش	
híyya	tiḫíbb	تِحِبّ	ma-tḫíbbiš	مَتْحِبّش	
húmma	yiḫíbbu	يِحِبّوا	ma-yḫibbūš	مَيْحِبّوش	
ána	baḫíbb	بَحِبّ	ma-baḫíbbiš	مَبَحِبّش	bi-imperfect
íḫna	binḫíbb	بِنْحِبّ	ma-binḫíbbiš	مَبِنْحِبّش	
ínta	bitḫíbb	بِتْحِبّ	ma-bitḫíbbiš	مَبِتْحِبّش	
ínti	bitḫíbbi	بِتْحِبّي	ma-bitḫibbīš	مَبِتْحِبّيش	
íntu	bitḫíbbu	بِتْحِبّوا	ma-bitḫibbūš	مَبِتْحِبّوش	
húwwa	biyḫíbb	بِيْحِبّ	ma-biyḫíbbiš	مَبِيْحِبّش	
híyya	bitḫíbb	بِتْحِبّ	ma-bitḫíbbiš	مَبِتْحِبّش	
húmma	biyḫíbbu	بِيْحِبّوا	ma-biyḫibbūš	مَبِيْحِبّوش	
ána	haḫíbb	هَحِبّ	miš haḫíbb	مِش هَحِبّ	future
íḫna	hanḫíbb	هَنْحِبّ	miš hanḫíbb	مِش هَنْحِبّ	
ínta	hatḫíbb	هَتْحِبّ	miš hatḫíbb	مِش هَتْحِبّ	
ínti	hatḫíbbi	هَتْحِبّي	miš hatḫíbbi	مِش هَتْحِبّي	
íntu	hatḫíbbu	هَتْحِبّوا	miš hatḫíbbu	مِش هَتْحِبّوا	
húwwa	hayḫíbb	هَيْحِبّ	miš hayḫíbb	مِش هَيْحِبّ	
híyya	hatḫíbb	هَتْحِبّ	miš hatḫíbb	مِش هَتْحِبّ	
húmma	hayḫíbbu	هَيْحِبّوا	miš hayḫíbbu	مِش هَيْحِبّوا	
ínta	ḫibb	حِبّ	ma-tḫíbbiš	مَتْحِبّش	imperative
ínti	ḫíbbi	حِبّي	ma-tḫibbīš	مَتْحِبّيش	
íntu	ḫíbbu	حِبّوا	ma-tḫibbūš	مَتْحِبّوش	

	active		passive		
masculine	ḫābib	حابِب	maḫbūb	مَحْبوب	participles
feminine	ḫábba	حابّة	maḫbūba	مَحْبوبة	
plural	ḫabbīn	حابّين	maḫbubīn	مَحْبوبين	

verbal noun: ḫubb حُبّ

①

حبّيْت أسْوان مِن أوّل مرّة زُرْتها فيها.

ḫabbēt aswān min áwwil márra zurtáha fīha.

I've loved Aswan since the first time I went there.

②

المثل بِيْقول: القُطّ مَيْحِبِّش إلّا خنّاقُه.

ilmásal biyʔūl: ilʔúṭṭᵊ ma-yḫíbbiš ílla xannāʔu.

As the saying goes, "The cat doesn't like anyone except its strangler."

③

سلْمان بِيْحِبّ الزّبادي جِدّاً. تلاجْتُه على طول ملْيانة زبادي.

salmān biyḫibb izzabādi gíddan. talágtu 3ála ṭūl malyāna zabādi.

Salman likes yogurt a lot. His fridge is always full of it.

④

نورا هتْحِبُّه لَوْ أظْهرْلها اِهْتِمامُه.

nūra hatḫíbbu law aẓharláha ʔihtimāmu.

Nora would love him if he showed an interest in her.

⑤

حِبّوا شُغْلُكو عشان تِبْدعوا فيه.

ḫíbbu šuɣlúku 3ašān tibdá3u fī.

Love your work in order to be innovative in it.

⑥

أبويا مبِيْحِبِّش يُطْلُب حاجة مِن حدّ.

abūya ma-biyḫíbbiš yúṭlub ḫāga min ḫadd.

My dad doesn't like to request anything from anyone.

⑦

مبحِبِّش الجِبْنة الحادْقة. بِتوْجعْلي لِساني.

ma-baḫíbbiš ilgíbna -lḫádʔa. bitiwgá3li lisāni.

I don't like salty cheese. It hurts my tongue.

⑧

بحِبّ أحْلق عنْد مُصْطفي. بِيِعْرف يِظبّطْلي شعْري.

baḫíbb áḫlaʔ 3andᵊ muṣṭáfa. biyí3raf yiẓabbáṭli šá3ri.

I like to get my hair cut at Mustafa's. He knows just how to cut my hair.

⑨

هاني محْبوب جِدّاً وِسْط زمايْلُه، أصْلُه خدوم أوي و دمُّه خفيف.

hāni maḫbūb giddan wisṭᵊ zamáylu, áṣlu xadūm ʔáwi wi dámmu xafīf.

Hany is very popular among his colleagues since he's so helpful and funny.

❖ [1g3] **to like; to love**

- This verb can be followed by an imperfect verb. (➲ 78.6, 78.8)
- Compare with عِشِق *3íšiʔ*. (➲ 180)

➲ This verb can be found in over 70 example sentences throughout the book, including 9.1, 14.4, 22.3, 35.2, 51.2, 57.2, 78.1, 101.2, 107.5, 108.6, 122.4, 143.2, 166.1, 175.4, 189.2, 217.2, 228.1, 262.1

79 to move ḫárrak حَرّك

verbal noun: *taḫrīk* تحْريك

	affirmative		negative		
ána	ḫarrákt	حَرّكْت	ma-ḫarráktiš	مَحَرّكْتِش	**perfect**
íḫna	ḫarrákna	حَرّكْنا	ma-ḫarraknāš	مَحَرّكْناش	
ínta	ḫarrákt	حَرّكْت	ma-ḫarráktiš	مَحَرّكْتِش	
ínti	ḫarrákti	حَرّكْتي	ma-ḫarraktīš	مَحَرّكْتيش	
íntu	ḫarráktu	حَرّكْتوا	ma-ḫarraktūš	مَحَرّكْتوش	
húwwa	ḫárrak	حَرّك	ma-ḫarrákš	مَحَرّكْش	
híyya	ḫarrákit	حَرّكِت	ma-ḫarrakítš	مَحَرّكِتْش	
húmma	ḫarráku	حَرّكوا	ma-ḫarrakūš	مَحَرّكوش	
ána	aḫárrak	أحَرّك	ma-ḫarrákš	مَحَرّكْش	**imperfect**
íḫna	niḫárrak	نِحَرّك	ma-nḫarrákš	مَنْحَرّكْش	
ínta	tiḫárrak	تِحَرّك	ma-tḫarrákš	مَتْحَرّكْش	
ínti	tiḫarráki	تِحَرّكي	ma-tḫarrakīš	مَتْحَرّكيش	
íntu	tiḫarráku	تِحَرّكوا	ma-tḫarrakūš	مَتْحَرّكوش	
húwwa	yiḫárrak	يِحَرّك	ma-yḫarrákš	مَيْحَرّكْش	
híyya	tiḫárrak	تِحَرّك	ma-tḫarrákš	مَتْحَرّكْش	
húmma	yiḫarráku	يِحَرّكوا	ma-yḫarrakūš	مَيْحَرّكوش	
ána	baḫárrak	بَحَرّك	ma-baḫarrákš	مَبَحَرّكْش	**bi-imperfect**
íḫna	binḫárrak	بِنْحَرّك	ma-binḫarrákš	مَبِنْحَرّكْش	
ínta	bitḫárrak	بِتْحَرّك	ma-bitḫarrákš	مَبِتْحَرّكْش	
ínti	bitḫarráki	بِتْحَرّكي	ma-bitḫarrakīš	مَبِتْحَرّكيش	
íntu	bitḫarráku	بِتْحَرّكوا	ma-bitḫarrakūš	مَبِتْحَرّكوش	
húwwa	biyḫárrak	بِيْحَرّك	ma-biyḫarrákš	مَبِيْحَرّكْش	
híyya	bitḫárrak	بِتْحَرّك	ma-bitḫarrákš	مَبِتْحَرّكْش	
húmma	biyḫarráku	بِيْحَرّكوا	ma-biyḫarrakūš	مَبِيْحَرّكوش	
ána	haḫárrak	هَحَرّك	miš haḫárrak	مِش هَحَرّك	**future**
íḫna	hanḫárrak	هَنْحَرّك	miš hanḫárrak	مِش هَنْحَرّك	
ínta	hatḫárrak	هَتْحَرّك	miš hatḫárrak	مِش هَتْحَرّك	
ínti	hatḫarráki	هَتْحَرّكي	miš hatḫarráki	مِش هَتْحَرّكي	
íntu	hatḫarráku	هَتْحَرّكوا	miš hatḫarráku	مِش هَتْحَرّكوا	
húwwa	hayḫárrak	هَيْحَرّك	miš hayḫárrak	مِش هَيْحَرّك	
híyya	hatḫárrak	هَتْحَرّك	miš hatḫárrak	مِش هَتْحَرّك	
húmma	hayḫarráku	هَيْحَرّكوا	miš hayḫarráku	مِش هَيْحَرّكوا	
ínta	ḫárrak	حَرّك	ma-tḫarrákš	مَتْحَرّكْش	**imperative**
ínti	ḫarráki	حَرّكي	ma-tḫarrakīš	مَتْحَرّكيش	
íntu	ḫarráku	حَرّكوا	ma-tḫarrakūš	مَتْحَرّكوش	

	active		passive		
masculine	miḫárrak	مِحَرّك	mitḫárrak	مِتْحَرّك	**participles**
feminine	miḫarráka	مِحَرّكة	mitḫarráka	مِتْحَرّكة	
plural	miḫarrakīn	مِحَرّكين	mitḫarrakīn	مِتْحَرّكين	

①

مين اللي حرّك الوَرق ده مِن على مكْتبي؟

mīn ílli ḫárrak ilwára? da min 3ála maktábi?

Who moved those files from my desk?

②

مِن فضْلك تِحرّك عربيتك شُوَيّة عشان أرْكِن.

min fáḍlak tiḫárrak 3arabītak šuwáyya 3ašān árkin.

Please, move your car a little bit so I can park.

③

الرّاجِل ده بيْحرّك إيدُه بِعصْبية طول المُقابْلة. شكْلُه مُتَوَتِر أوي.

irrāgil da biyḫárrak īdu bi-3aṣbíyya ṭūl ilmu?ábla. šáklu mutawáttir áwi.

This man kept moving his hand nervously during the interview. He seemed quite nervous.

④

إنْتي مِش هتْحرّكي الدّولاب ده مِن هِنا؟ كِبير أوي عَ المكان هِنا.

ínti miš hatḫarráki -ddulāb da min hína? kibīr ?áwi 3a -lmakān hína.

Won't you move this cupboard from here? Its' too big for the space.

⑤

حرّكوا أجْسامْكو عشان تِحافْظوا على لِياقْتْكو.

ḫarráku ?agsámku 3ašān tiḫáfẓu 3ála liyaqítku.

Move your body to stay fit.

❖ [2s2] **to move**

- This verb is transitive. Compare with اِتْحرّك *itḫárrak*. (➲ 10)

80 to feel ɧass حَسّ

	affirmative		negative		
ána	ɧassēt	حَسّيْت	ma-ɧassítš	مَحَسّيْتْش	perfect
íɧna	ɧassēna	حَسّيْنا	ma-ɧassināš	مَحَسّيناش	
ínta	ɧassēt	حَسّيْت	ma-ɧassítš	مَحَسّيْتْش	
ínti	ɧassēti	حَسّيْتي	ma-ɧassitīš	مَحَسّيتيش	
íntu	ɧassētu	حَسّيْتوا	ma-ɧassitūš	مَحَسّيتوش	
húwwa	ɧass	حَسّ	ma-ɧássiš	مَحَسِّش	
híyya	ɧássit	حَسِّت	ma-ɧassítš	مَحَسّتْش	
húmma	ɧássu	حَسّوا	ma-ɧassūš	مَحَسّوش	

ána	aɧíss	أحِسّ	ma-ɧissiš	مَحِسِّش	imperfect
íɧna	niɧíss	نِحِسّ	ma-nɧissiš	مَنْحِسِّش	
ínta	tiɧíss	تِحِسّ	ma-tɧissiš	مَتْحِسِّش	
ínti	tiɧíssi	تِحِسّي	ma-tɧissīš	مَتْحِسّيش	
íntu	tiɧíssu	تِحِسّوا	ma-tɧissūš	مَتْحِسّوش	
húwwa	yiɧíss	يِحِسّ	ma-yɧissiš	مَيْحِسِّش	
híyya	tiɧíss	تِحِسّ	ma-tɧissiš	مَتْحِسِّش	
húmma	yiɧíssu	يِحِسّوا	ma-yɧissūš	مَيْحِسّوش	

ána	baɧíss	بَحِسّ	ma-baɧissiš	مَبَحِسِّش	bi-imperfect
íɧna	binɧíss	بِنْحِسّ	ma-binɧíssiš	مَبِنْحِسِّش	
ínta	bitɧíss	بِتْحِسّ	ma-bitɧíssiš	مَبِتْحِسِّش	
ínti	bitɧíssi	بِتْحِسّي	ma-bitɧissīš	مَبِتْحِسّيش	
íntu	bitɧíssu	بِتْحِسّوا	ma-bitɧissūš	مَبِتْحِسّوش	
húwwa	biyɧíss	بِيْحِسّ	ma-biyɧíssiš	مَبِيْحِسِّش	
híyya	bitɧíss	بِتْحِسّ	ma-bitɧíssiš	مَبِتْحِسِّش	
húmma	biyɧíssu	بِيْحِسّوا	ma-biyɧissūš	مَبِيْحِسّوش	

ána	haɧíss	هَحِسّ	miš haɧíss	مِش هَحِسّ	future
íɧna	hanɧíss	هَنْحِسّ	miš hanɧíss	مِش هَنْحِسّ	
ínta	hatɧíss	هَتْحِسّ	miš hatɧíss	مِش هَتْحِسّ	
ínti	hatɧíssi	هَتْحِسّي	miš hatɧíssi	مِش هَتْحِسّي	
íntu	hatɧíssu	هَتْحِسّوا	miš hatɧíssu	مِش هَتْحِسّوا	
húwwa	hayɧíss	هَيْحِسّ	miš hayɧíss	مِش هَيْحِسّ	
híyya	hatɧíss	هَتْحِسّ	miš hatɧíss	مِش هَتْحِسّ	
húmma	hayɧíssu	هَيْحِسّوا	miš hayɧíssu	مِش هَيْحِسّوا	

ínta	ɧiss	حِسّ	ma-tɧíssiš	مَتْحِسِّش	imperative
ínti	ɧíssi	حِسّي	ma-tɧissīš	مَتْحِسّيش	
íntu	ɧíssu	حِسّوا	ma-tɧissūš	مَتْحِسّوش	

	active		passive		
masculine	ɧāsis	حاسِس	maɧsūs	مَحْسوس	participles
feminine	ɧássa	حاسّة	maɧsūsa	مَحْسوسَة	
plural	ɧassīn	حاسّين	maɧsusīn	مَحْسوسين	

verbal noun: iɧsās إحْساس

①

حسّيْت بِالفخْر لمّا أبْني طِلِع في المرْكز الأوّل في بْطولْة الكاراتيْه.

ḥassēt bi-lfáxrᵊ lámma -bni ṭíli3 fi -lmárkaz ilʔáwwil fi bṭult ilkaratēh.

I felt proud [lit. felt with pride] when my son took first place in the karate championship.

②

إنّك تِحِسّ بِالاِنْتِماء، ده مِن أرْقى الأحاسيس عنْد الإِنْسان.

ínnak tiḥíssᵊ bi-lʔintimāʔ, da min árqa -lʔaḥasīs 3and ilʔinsān.

A feeling of belonging is one of the greatest feelings for human beings.

③

إنْتَ بِتْحِسّ بِأيْه بِالظّبْط؟ اِوْصِفْلي كُويِّس عشان أعْرف أعالْجك.

ínta bitḥíssᵊ bi-ʔē bi-ẓẓábṭ? iwṣífli kuwáyyis 3ašān á3raf a3álgak.

(doctor to patient:) What exactly do you feel? Tell me in detail, so I can treat you.

④

بعْد العملية هتْحِسّي بِتنْميل مكان الجرْح.

ba3d il3amalíyya hatḥíssi bi-tanmīl makān ilgárḥ.

After the surgery, you'll feel some numbness where the wound is.

⑤

حِسّوا بِالنّاس اللي مِش لاقْيَة لُقْمة. بلاش تِرموا أكْلُكو و اِتْبرّعوا بيه.

ḥíssu bi-nnās ílli miš láʔya lúʔma. balāš tírmu ʔaklúku w itbarrá3u bī.

Feel for those who go hungry. Don't throw away your food. Donate it.

⑥

مبحِسِّش بِرمضان غيْر لمّا أشوف الزّينة في الشّارِع.

ma-baḥíssiš bi-ramaḍān ɣēr lámma ʔašūf izzīna fi -ššāri3.

I don't feel it's Ramadan unless I've seen the decorations in the streets.

❖ [1g3] **to feel** (بِـ *bi-*)

- Whereas the English verb 'feel' can be followed by an adjective, in Arabic this verb is followed by the preposition بِـ *bi-* and a noun. (➲ 80.1)

➲ 87.5, 143.5, 159.5, 173.5, 244.5

81 to calculate ḫásab حَسَب

	affirmative		negative		
ána	ḫasábt	حَسَبْت	ma-ḫasábtiš	مَحَسَبْتِش	perfect
íḫna	ḫasábna	حَسَبْنا	ma-ḫasabnāš	مَحَسَبْناش	
ínta	ḫasábt	حَسَبْت	ma-ḫasábtiš	مَحَسَبْتِش	
ínti	ḫasábti	حَسَبْتي	ma-ḫasabtīš	مَحَسَبْتيش	
íntu	ḫasábtu	حَسَبْتوا	ma-ḫasabtūš	مَحَسَبْتوش	
húwwa	ḫásab	حَسَب	ma-ḫasábš	مَحَسَبْش	
híyya	ḫásabit	حَسَبِت	ma-ḫasabítš	مَحَسَبِتْش	
húmma	ḫásabu	حَسَبوا	ma-ḫasabūš	مَحَسَبوش	

ána	áḫsib	أَحْسِب	ma-ḫsíbš	مَحْسِبْش	imperfect
íḫna	níḫsib	نِحْسِب	ma-niḫsíbš	مَنِحْسِبْش	
ínta	tíḫsib	تِحْسِب	ma-tiḫsíbš	مَتِحْسِبْش	
ínti	tiḫsíbi	تِحْسِبي	ma-tiḫsibīš	مَتِحْسِبيش	
íntu	tiḫsíbu	تِحْسِبوا	ma-tiḫsibūš	مَتِحْسِبوش	
húwwa	yíḫsib	يِحْسِب	ma-yiḫsíbš	مَيِحْسِبْش	
híyya	tíḫsib	تِحْسِب	ma-tiḫsíbš	مَتِحْسِبْش	
húmma	yiḫsíbu	يِحْسِبوا	ma-yiḫsibūš	مَيِحْسِبوش	

ána	báḫsib	بَحْسِب	ma-baḫsíbš	مَبَحْسِبْش	bi-imperfect
íḫna	biníḫsib	بِنِحْسِب	ma-bniḫsíbš	مَبْنِحْسِبْش	
ínta	bitíḫsib	بِتِحْسِب	ma-btiḫsíbš	مَبْتِحْسِبْش	
ínti	bitiḫsíbi	بِتِحْسِبي	ma-btiḫsibīš	مَبْتِحْسِبيش	
íntu	bitiḫsíbu	بِتِحْسِبوا	ma-btiḫsibūš	مَبْتِحْسِبوش	
húwwa	biyíḫsib	بِيِحْسِب	ma-byiḫsíbš	مَبْيِحْسِبْش	
híyya	bitíḫsib	بِتِحْسِب	ma-btiḫsíbš	مَبْتِحْسِبْش	
húmma	biyiḫsíbu	بِيِحْسِبوا	ma-byiḫsibūš	مَبْيِحْسِبوش	

ána	háḫsib	هَحْسِب	miš háḫsib	مِش هَحْسِب	future
íḫna	haníḫsib	هَنِحْسِب	miš haníḫsib	مِش هَنِحْسِب	
ínta	hatíḫsib	هَتِحْسِب	miš hatíḫsib	مِش هَتِحْسِب	
ínti	hatiḫsíbi	هَتِحْسِبي	miš hatiḫsíbi	مِش هَتِحْسِبي	
íntu	hatiḫsíbu	هَتِحْسِبوا	miš hatiḫsíbu	مِش هَتِحْسِبوا	
húwwa	hayíḫsib	هَيِحْسِب	miš hayíḫsib	مِش هَيِحْسِب	
híyya	hatíḫsib	هَتِحْسِب	miš hatíḫsib	مِش هَتِحْسِب	
húmma	hayiḫsíbu	هَيِحْسِبوا	miš hayiḫsíbu	مِش هَيِحْسِبوا	

ínta	íḫsib	اِحْسِب	ma-tiḫsíbš	مَتِحْسِبْش	imperative
ínti	iḫsíbi	اِحْسِبي	ma-tiḫsibīš	مَتِحْسِبيش	
íntu	iḫsíbu	اِحْسِبوا	ma-tiḫsibūš	مَتِحْسِبوش	

	active		passive		
masculine	ḫāsib	حاسِب	maḫsūb	مَحْسوب	participles
feminine	ḫásba	حاسْبَة	maḫsūba	مَحْسوبَة	
plural	ḫasbīn	حاسْبين	maḫsubīn	مَحْسوبين	

verbal noun: ḫisāb حِساب

①

مِتْوَلّي حسب تكاليف تشْطيب الشّقّة، طِلْعِت أكْتر مِن إمْكانِيّاته.

mitwálli ḫásab takalīf tašṭīb iššáʔʔa, ṭíl3it áktar min imkaniyyātu.

When Mitwally calculated the expenses of finishing the apartment, he found it to be more than he could afford.

②

شاهيناز بِتْفضّل تِحْسِب مصاريف البيْت بِالأُسْبوع مِش بِالشّهْر.

šahināz bitfáḍḍal tíḫsib maṣarīf ilbēt bi-lʔisbū3 miš bi-ššahr.

Shahinaz prefers to calculate the household expenses weekly, not monthly.

③

بِتِحْسِبي المسْألة دي إزّاي؟ أنا حاولْت كْتير، مِش عارْفة.

bitiḫsíbi -lmasʔála di -zzāy? ána ḫawíltᵊ ktīr, miš 3árfa.

How do you calculate this problem? I tried a lot, but I don't know how.

④

هتِحْسِبوا المسافة مِن أوِّل ما تِتْحرّكوا لِحدّ ما تِوْصلوا عشان نِعْرف قدّ أيْه المِشْوار ده.

hatiḫsíbu -lmasāfa min áwwil ma titḫarráku li-ḫaddᵊ ma tiwṣálu 3ašān ní3raf add ʔē -lmišwār da.

You'll calculate the distance from the time you start until when you arrive, so we know how long that trip is.

⑤

اِحْسِبي سِعْر اللي الحاجات اللي هناخُدْها عشان أشوف معايا فِلوس تِكفّي وَلّا لأ.

iḫsíbi si3r ílli -lḫagāt ílli hanaxúdha 3ašān ašūf ma3āya filūs tikáffi wálla laʔ.

Calculate the price of what we're buying, so I can see if I have enough money or not.

⑥

كُنْت بحْسِب إنِّك لِسّه في ثانَوى، أصْل شكْلِك صُغيرّة.

kuntᵊ báḫsib ínnik líssa fi sānawi, aṣlᵊ šáklik ṣuɣayyára.

I thought you were still in high school because you look so young.

⑦

متِحْسِبوش يا بنات إنّ الجَواز راحة.

ma-tiḫsibūš ya banāt inn ilgawāz rāḫa.

"Girls, don't think that marriage is easy." (line from an old song)

❖ [1s2] **to calculate; to think, believe**

82 to stuff ḫáša حَشَى

	affirmative		negative		
ána	ḫašēt	حَشيْت	ma-ḫašítš	مَحَشيْتْش	perfect
íḫna	ḫašēna	حَشيْنا	ma-ḫašināš	مَحَشيناش	
ínta	ḫašēt	حَشيْت	ma-ḫašítš	مَحَشيْتْش	
ínti	ḫašēti	حَشيْتي	ma-ḫašitīš	مَحَشيتيش	
íntu	ḫašētu	حَشيْتوا	ma-ḫašitūš	مَحَشيتوش	
húwwa	ḫáša	حَشَى	ma-ḫašāš	مَحَشاش	
híyya	ḫášit	حَشِت	ma-ḫašítš	مَحَشِتْش	
húmma	ḫášu	حَشوا	ma-ḫašūš	مَحَشوش	
ána	áḫši	أحْشي	ma-ḫšīš	مَحْشيش	imperfect
íḫna	níḫši	نِحْشي	ma-niḫšīš	مَنِحْشيش	
ínta	tíḫši	تِحْشي	ma-tiḫšīš	مَتِحْشيش	
ínti	tíḫši	تِحْشي	ma-tiḫšīš	مَتِحْشيش	
íntu	tíḫšu	تِحْشوا	ma-tiḫšūš	مَتِحْشوش	
húwwa	yíḫši	يِحْشي	ma-yiḫšīš	مَيِحْشيش	
híyya	tíḫši	تِحْشي	ma-tiḫšīš	مَتِحْشيش	
húmma	yíḫšu	يِحْشوا	ma-yiḫšūš	مَيِحْشوش	
ána	báḫši	بَحْشي	ma-baḫšīš	مَبَحْشيش	bi-imperfect
íḫna	biníḫši	بِنِحْشي	ma-bniḫšīš	مَبْنِحْشيش	
ínta	bitíḫši	بِتِحْشي	ma-btiḫšīš	مَبْتِحْشيش	
ínti	bitíḫši	بِتِحْشي	ma-btiḫšīš	مَبْتِحْشيش	
íntu	bitíḫšu	بِتِحْشوا	ma-btiḫšūš	مَبْتِحْشوش	
húwwa	biyíḫši	بِيِحْشي	ma-byiḫšīš	مَبْيِحْشيش	
híyya	bitíḫši	بِتِحْشي	ma-btiḫšīš	مَبْتِحْشيش	
húmma	biyíḫšu	بِيِحْشوا	ma-byiḫšūš	مَبْيِحْشوش	
ána	háḫši	هَحْشي	miš háḫši	مِش هَحْشي	future
íḫna	haníḫši	هَنِحْشي	miš haníḫši	مِش هَنِحْشي	
ínta	hatíḫši	هَتِحْشي	miš hatíḫši	مِش هَتِحْشي	
ínti	hatíḫši	هَتِحْشي	miš hatíḫši	مِش هَتِحْشي	
íntu	hatíḫšu	هَتِحْشوا	miš hatíḫšu	مِش هَتِحْشوا	
húwwa	hayíḫši	هَيِحْشي	miš hayíḫši	مِش هَيِحْشي	
híyya	hatíḫši	هَتِحْشي	miš hatíḫši	مِش هَتِحْشي	
húmma	hayíḫšu	هَيِحْشوا	miš hayíḫšu	مِش هَيِحْشوا	
ínta	íḫši	اِحْشي	ma-tiḫšīš	مَتِحْشيش	imperative
ínti	íḫši	اِحْشي	ma-tiḫšīš	مَتِحْشيش	
íntu	íḫšu	اِحْشوا	ma-tiḫšūš	مَتِحْشوش	

	active		passive		
masculine	ḫāši	حاشي	máḫši	مَحْشي	participles
feminine	ḫášya	حاشْيَة	maḫšíyya	مَحْشِيَّة	
plural	ḫašyīn	حاشْيين	maḫšiyīn	مَحْشِيين	

verbal noun: ḫašw حَشْو - ḫašy حَشْي

①

إمْبارِح رُحْت لْدُكْتور السِّنان، بسّ محشاليش حاجة.

imbāriḫ ruḫtᵊ l-duktūr issinān, bassᵊ ma-ḫašalīš ḫāga.

I went to the dentist yesterday, but he didn't fill any [of my teeth].

②

أُمّي بِتْحِبّ أوي تِحْشي الكوْسة.

úmmi bitḫíbbᵊ ʔáwi tíḫši -lkōsa.

My mom likes to stuff zucchini.

③

إحْنا بْنِحْشي دِماغْنا طول السّنة عشان نِفضّيها في الاِمْتِحان.

íḫna bníḫši dimáɣna ṭūl issána 3ašān nifaḍḍīha fi -lʔimtiḫān.

We fill our heads all year to empty them in the exam.

④

جارِتْنا هتِحْشي وَرق عِنب و إحْنا نازْلين نِساعِدْها.

garítna hatíḫši wáraʔ 3ínab w íḫna nazlīn nisa3ídha.

Our neighbor is stuffing grape leaves, and we're going to help her.

⑤

متِحْشيش دِماغك أفْكار ملْهاش أيّ لزْمة.

ma-tiḫšīš dimāɣak afkār ma-lhāš ayyᵊ lázma.

Don't fill your brain with nonsense.

❖ [1d2] **to stuff, fill**

- This verb can be ditransitive. (➲ 82.5)

83 to happen ḫáṣal حَصَل

	affirmative		negative		
ána	—	—	—	—	perfect
íḫna	—	—	—	—	
ínta	—	—	—	—	
ínti	—	—	—	—	
íntu	—	—	—	—	
húwwa	ḫáṣal	حَصَل	ma-ḫaṣálš	مَحَصَلْش	
híyya	ḫáṣalit	حَصَلِت	ma-ḫaṣalítš	مَحَصَلِتْش	
húmma	ḫáṣalu	حَصَلوا	ma-ḫaṣalūš	مَحَصَلوش	
ána	—	—	—	—	imperfect
íḫna	—	—	—	—	
ínta	—	—	—	—	
ínti	—	—	—	—	
íntu	—	—	—	—	
húwwa	yíḫṣal	يِحْصَل	ma-yiḫṣálš	مَيِحْصَلْش	
híyya	tíḫṣal	تِحْصَل	ma-tiḫṣálš	مَتِحْصَلْش	
húmma	yiḫṣálu	يِحْصَلوا	ma-yiḫṣalūš	مَيِحْصَلوش	
ána	—	—	—	—	bi-imperfect
íḫna	—	—	—	—	
ínta	—	—	—	—	
ínti	—	—	—	—	
íntu	—	—	—	—	
húwwa	biyíḫṣal	بِيِحْصَل	ma-byiḫṣálš	مَبْيِحْصَلْش	
híyya	bitíḫṣal	بِتِحْصَل	ma-btiḫṣálš	مَبْتِحْصَلْش	
húmma	biyiḫṣálu	بِيِحْصَلوا	ma-byiḫṣalūš	مَبْيِحْصَلوش	
ána	—	—	—	—	future
íḫna	—	—	—	—	
ínta	—	—	—	—	
ínti	—	—	—	—	
íntu	—	—	—	—	
húwwa	hayíḫṣal	هَيِحْصَل	miš hayíḫṣal	مِش هَيِحْصَل	
híyya	hatíḫṣal	هَتِحْصَل	miš hatíḫṣal	مِش هَتِحْصَل	
húmma	hayiḫṣálu	هَيِحْصَلوا	miš hayiḫṣálu	مِش هَيِحْصَلوا	
ínta	—	—	—	—	imperative
ínti	—	—	—	—	
íntu	—	—	—	—	

	active		passive		
masculine	ḫāṣil	حاصِل	—	—	participles
feminine	ḫáṣla	حاصْلَة	—	—	
plural	ḫaṣlīn	حاصْلين	—	—	

verbal noun: ḫuṣūl حصول

①

أحْمد حصلِتْله حادْثة كْبيرة مِن سنتينْ. مِن ساعِتْها بِيِكْرَه السِّواقة.

áħmad ħaṣalítlu ħádsa kbīra min sanatēn. min sa3ítha biyíkrah issiwāʔa.

Ahmed got in a big accident two years ago.
Ever since then, he's hated driving.

②

كِفايَة بقى! مِش عارْفة أيْه مُمْكِن يِحْصل أسْوَء مِن كِده.

kifāya báʔa! miš 3árfa ʔē múmkin yíħṣal áswaʔ min kída.

Enough! What could possibly happen worse than this?

③

أ: هِيَّ الأعْراض دي بْتِحْصلّك كِتير؟

ب: كُلّ ما أتْعصّب بِتِحْصلّي.

A: híyya -lʔa3rāḍ di btiħṣállak kitīr?
B: kull^ə m- at3íṣib bitiħṣálli.

A: Do you have these symptoms
[lit. happen to you] a lot?
B: Every time I get nervous.

④

هَيِحْصل أيْه يعْني لَوْ زوِّدولْنا مُرتّباتْنا؟ ده حقّنا!

hayíħṣal ʔē yá3ni law zawwidúlna murattabátna? da ħaʔʔína!

What's going to happen if they raise
our salaries? It's our right!

⑤

نجْلاء حاصِلّها حاجة غريبة. مبقِتْش عايْزة تْشوف وَلّا تْكلِّم حدّ.

naglāʔ ħaṣilláha ħāga ɣarība. ma-baʔítš^ə 3áyza tšūf wálla tkállim ħadd.

Something strange is happening with Naglaa. She
doesn't want to see or talk to anyone.

⑥

متْخافيش، محصلْش حاجة لِلوِلاد. كُلِّنا كْوَيِّسين.

ma-txafīš, ma-ħaṣálš^ə ħāga li-lwilād. kullína kwayyisīn.

Don't panic. Nothing happened
to the kids. We're all okay.

❖ [1s1] **to happen (to** لِ *li-*)

- This verb logically only appears in the third person, and can be masculine, feminine, or plural, according to its subject (➲ 83.1, 83.3), or remain masculine singular even with a feminine subject (➲ 83.6, 205.6). Compare this to the synonym جرى *gára,* which is invariably masculine. (➲ 71)

➲ 53.5, 72.5, 89.5, 203.4, 205.6

84 to attend ḥáḍar حَضَر

perfect

	affirmative		negative	
ána	ḥaḍárt	حَضَرْت	ma-ḥaḍártiš	مَحَضَرْتِش
íḥna	ḥaḍárna	حَضَرْنا	ma-ḥaḍarnāš	مَحَضَرْناش
ínta	ḥaḍárt	حَضَرْت	ma-ḥaḍártiš	مَحَضَرْتِش
ínti	ḥaḍárti	حَضَرْتي	ma-ḥaḍartīš	مَحَضَرْتيش
íntu	ḥaḍártu	حَضَرْتوا	ma-ḥaḍartūš	مَحَضَرْتوش
húwwa	ḥáḍar	حَضَر	ma-ḥaḍárš	مَحَضَرْش
híyya	ḥáḍarit	حَضَرِت	ma-ḥaḍarítš	مَحَضَرِتْش
húmma	ḥáḍaru	حَضَروا	ma-ḥaḍarūš	مَحَضَروش

imperfect

	affirmative		negative	
ána	áḥḍar	أحْضَر	ma-ḥḍárš	مَحْضَرْش
íḥna	níḥḍar	نِحْضَر	ma-niḥḍárš	مَنِحْضَرْش
ínta	tíḥḍar	تِحْضَر	ma-tiḥḍárš	مَتِحْضَرْش
ínti	tiḥḍári	تِحْضَري	ma-tiḥḍarīš	مَتِحْضَريش
íntu	tiḥḍáru	تِحْضَروا	ma-tiḥḍarūš	مَتِحْضَروش
húwwa	yíḥḍar	يِحْضَر	ma-yiḥḍárš	مَيِحْضَرْش
híyya	tíḥḍar	تِحْضَر	ma-tiḥḍárš	مَتِحْضَرْش
húmma	yiḥḍáru	يِحْضَروا	ma-yiḥḍarūš	مَيِحْضَروش

bi-imperfect

	affirmative		negative	
ána	báḥḍar	بَحْضَر	ma-baḥḍárš	مَبَحْضَرْش
íḥna	biníḥḍar	بِنِحْضَر	ma-bniḥḍárš	مَبْنِحْضَرْش
ínta	bitíḥḍar	بِتِحْضَر	ma-btiḥḍárš	مَبْتِحْضَرْش
ínti	bitiḥḍári	بِتِحْضَري	ma-btiḥḍarīš	مَبْتِحْضَريش
íntu	bitiḥḍáru	بِتِحْضَروا	ma-btiḥḍarūš	مَبْتِحْضَروش
húwwa	biyíḥḍar	بِيِحْضَر	ma-byiḥḍárš	مَبْيِحْضَرْش
híyya	bitíḥḍar	بِتِحْضَر	ma-btiḥḍárš	مَبْتِحْضَرْش
húmma	biyiḥḍáru	بِيِحْضَروا	ma-byiḥḍarūš	مَبْيِحْضَروش

future

	affirmative		negative	
ána	háḥḍar	هَحْضَر	miš háḥḍar	مِش هَحْضَر
íḥna	haníḥḍar	هَنِحْضَر	miš haníḥḍar	مِش هَنِحْضَر
ínta	hatíḥḍar	هَتِحْضَر	miš hatíḥḍar	مِش هَتِحْضَر
ínti	hatiḥḍári	هَتِحْضَري	miš hatiḥḍári	مِش هَتِحْضَري
íntu	hatiḥḍáru	هَتِحْضَروا	miš hatiḥḍáru	مِش هَتِحْضَروا
húwwa	hayíḥḍar	هَيِحْضَر	miš hayíḥḍar	مِش هَيِحْضَر
híyya	hatíḥḍar	هَتِحْضَر	miš hatíḥḍar	مِش هَتِحْضَر
húmma	hayiḥḍáru	هَيِحْضَروا	miš hayiḥḍáru	مِش هَيِحْضَروا

imperative

	affirmative		negative	
ínta	íḥḍar	اِحْضَر	ma-tiḥḍárš	مَتِحْضَرْش
ínti	iḥḍári	اِحْضَري	ma-tiḥḍarīš	مَتِحْضَريش
íntu	iḥḍáru	اِحْضَروا	ma-tiḥḍarūš	مَتِحْضَروش

participles

	active		passive	
masculine	ḥāḍir	حاضِر	maḥḍūr	مَحْضور
feminine	ḥáḍra	حاضْرَة	maḥḍūra	مَحْضورَة
plural	ḥaḍrīn	حاضْرين	maḥḍurīn	مَحْضورين

verbal noun: ḥuḍūr حُضور

①

حضرْنا إمْبارِح حِتِّةْ حفْلة، تِجنِّن!

ḫaḍárna -mbāriḫ ḫíttit ḫáfla, tigánnin!

We attended a marvelous
party yesterday!

②

لازِم أحْضر كُلّ المُحاضْرات وَلّا مِش هعْرف أحِلّ في الامْتِحان.

lāzim áḫḍar kull ilmuḫaḍrāt wálla miš há3raf aḫíllᵊ fi -lʔimtiḫān.

I should attend all the lectures, or
I won't be able to pass the exam.

③

نُهى بْتِحْضر دُروس زومْبا. بِتْحِبّ الرّقْص.

núha btíḫḍar durūs zúmba. bitḫíbb irráʔṣ.

Noha takes Zumba lessons.
She likes dancing.

④

شريف هَيِحْضر النّدْوَة، أصْلُه بِيْحِبّ الرّاجِل ده أوي.

šarīf hayíḫḍar innádwa, áṣlu biyḫibb irrāgil da ʔáwi.

Sherif will attend the seminar, as
he really likes that guy.

⑤

يابْني احْضر مُحاضْراتك، خلّيك تِجيب تقْدير السّنة دي.

ya -bni íḫḍar muḫaḍrātak, xallīk tigīb taʔdīr issanādi.

Son, go to your classes, so you
can get good grades this year.

⑥

مايْكل محضرْش وَلّا مُحاضْرة مِن أوِّل السّنة.

māykal ma-ḫaḍáršᵊ wálla muḫáḍra min áwwil issána.

Michel hasn't gone to a single lecture since
the beginning of the [school] year.

❖ [1s1] **to attend**

➲ 160.3, 179.1

85 to put ḫaṭṭ حَطّ

	affirmative		negative		
ána	ḫaṭṭēt	حَطّيْت	ma-ḫaṭṭítš	مَحَطّيْتْش	perfect
íḫna	ḫaṭṭēna	حَطّيْنا	ma-ḫaṭṭinā̆š	مَحَطّيناش	
ínta	ḫaṭṭēt	حَطّيْت	ma-ḫaṭṭítš	مَحَطّيْتْش	
ínti	ḫaṭṭēti	حَطّيْتي	ma-ḫaṭṭitīš	مَحَطّيتيش	
íntu	ḫaṭṭētu	حَطّيْتوا	ma-ḫaṭṭitūš	مَحَطّيتوش	
húwwa	ḫaṭṭ	حَطّ	ma-ḫáṭṭiš	مَحَطّش	
híyya	ḫáṭṭit	حَطّت	ma-ḫaṭṭítš	مَحَطّتْش	
húmma	ḫáṭṭu	حَطّوا	ma-ḫaṭṭūš	مَحَطّوش	

	affirmative		negative		
ána	aḫúṭṭ	أحُطّ	ma-ḫúṭṭiš	مَحُطّش	imperfect
íḫna	niḫúṭṭ	نِحُطّ	ma-nḫúṭṭiš	مَنْحُطّش	
ínta	tiḫúṭṭ	تِحُطّ	ma-tḫúṭṭiš	مَتْحُطّش	
ínti	tiḫúṭṭi	تِحُطّي	ma-tḫuṭṭīš	مَتْحُطّيش	
íntu	tiḫúṭṭu	تِحُطّوا	ma-tḫuṭṭūš	مَتْحُطّوش	
húwwa	yiḫúṭṭ	يِحُطّ	ma-yḫúṭṭiš	مَيْحُطّش	
híyya	tiḫúṭṭ	تِحُطّ	ma-tḫúṭṭiš	مَتْحُطّش	
húmma	yiḫúṭṭu	يِحُطّوا	ma-yḫuṭṭūš	مَيْحُطّوش	

	affirmative		negative		
ána	baḫúṭṭ	بَحُطّ	ma-baḫúṭṭiš	مَبَحُطّش	bi-imperfect
íḫna	binḫúṭṭ	بِنْحُطّ	ma-binḫúṭṭiš	مَبِنْحُطّش	
ínta	bitḫúṭṭ	بِتْحُطّ	ma-bitḫúṭṭiš	مَبِتْحُطّش	
ínti	bitḫúṭṭi	بِتْحُطّي	ma-bitḫuṭṭīš	مَبِتْحُطّيش	
íntu	bitḫúṭṭu	بِتْحُطّوا	ma-bitḫuṭṭūš	مَبِتْحُطّوش	
húwwa	biyḫúṭṭ	بِيْحُطّ	ma-biyḫúṭṭiš	مَبِيْحُطّش	
híyya	bitḫúṭṭ	بِتْحُطّ	ma-bitḫúṭṭiš	مَبِتْحُطّش	
húmma	biyḫúṭṭu	بِيْحُطّوا	ma-biyḫuṭṭūš	مَبِيْحُطّوش	

	affirmative		negative		
ána	haḫúṭṭ	هَحُطّ	miš haḫúṭṭ	مِش هَحُطّ	future
íḫna	hanḫúṭṭ	هَنْحُطّ	miš hanḫúṭṭ	مِش هَنْحُطّ	
ínta	hatḫúṭṭ	هَتْحُطّ	miš hatḫúṭṭ	مِش هَتْحُطّ	
ínti	hatḫúṭṭi	هَتْحُطّي	miš hatḫúṭṭi	مِش هَتْحُطّي	
íntu	hatḫúṭṭu	هَتْحُطّوا	miš hatḫúṭṭu	مِش هَتْحُطّوا	
húwwa	hayḫúṭṭ	هَيْحُطّ	miš hayḫúṭṭ	مِش هَيْحُطّ	
híyya	hatḫúṭṭ	هَتْحُطّ	miš hatḫúṭṭ	مِش هَتْحُطّ	
húmma	hayḫúṭṭu	هَيْحُطّوا	miš hayḫúṭṭu	مِش هَيْحُطّوا	

	affirmative		negative		
ínta	ḫuṭṭ	حُطّ	ma-tḫúṭṭiš	مَتْحُطّش	imperative
ínti	ḫúṭṭi	حُطّي	ma-tḫuṭṭīš	مَتْحُطّيش	
íntu	ḫúṭṭu	حُطّوا	ma-tḫuṭṭūš	مَتْحُطّوش	

	active		passive		
masculine	ḫāṭiṭ	حاطِط	maḫṭūṭ	مَحْطوط	participles
feminine	ḫáṭṭa	حاطّة	maḫṭūṭa	مَحْطوطَة	
plural	ḫaṭṭīn	حاطّين	maḫṭuṭīn	مَحْطوطين	

verbal nouns: ḫaṭaṭān حَطَطان - ḫaṭṭ حَطّ

①

إنْتَ كِده حطّيْت إيدك على أوِّل الخيْط.

ínta kída ḫaṭṭēt īdak 3ála ʔáwwil ilxēṭ.

Now you've put your
hand on the first clue.

②

مارْيان بِتْحِبّ تِحُطّ مكْياج تِقيل حتّى و هِيَّ نازْلة الصُّبْح.

maryān bitḫíbbᵊ tiḫúṭṭᵊ makyāž tiʔīl ḫátta wi híyya názla -ṣṣúbḫ.

Marian likes putting on heavy makeup,
even when she goes out in the morning.

③

مَيادة بِتْحُطّ أكْل لِلكِلاب اللي قُدّام بيتْها كُلّ يوْم.

mayāda bitḫúṭṭ aklᵊ li-lkilāb ílli ʔuddām bítha kullᵊ yōm.

Mayada puts food out for the dogs
in front of her house every day.

④

هتْحُطّي شطّة في الأكْل وَلّا مِش بِتْحِبّيها؟

hatḫúṭṭi šáṭṭa fi -lʔaklᵊ wálla miš bitḫibbīha?

Do you put hot pepper in the
food, or don't you like it?

⑤

حُطّ نفْسك مكاني. كُنْت هتِعْمِل أيْه في الموْقِف ده؟

ḫuṭṭᵊ náfsak makāni. kuntᵊ hatí3mil ʔē fi -lmáwqif da?

Put yourself in my shoes. What
would you do in this situation?

⑥

إنْتَ يابْني، متْحُطِّش صُباعك في الكهْربا.

ínta ya -bni, ma-tḫúṭṭiš ṣubā3ak fi -lkahrába.

Young man, don't put your finger
in the electrical outlet.

❖ [1g2] **to put, set, place**

➲ 41.3, 50.5, 148.5, 167.5

86 to keep ḥáfaẓ حَفَظ

	affirmative		negative		
ána	ḥafáẓt	حَفَظْت	ma-ḥafáẓtiš	مَحَفَظْتِش	perfect
íḥna	ḥafáẓna	حَفَظْنا	ma-ḥafaẓnāš	مَحَفَظْناش	perfect
ínta	ḥafáẓt	حَفَظْت	ma-ḥafáẓtiš	مَحَفَظْتِش	perfect
ínti	ḥafáẓti	حَفَظْتي	ma-ḥafaẓtīš	مَحَفَظْتيش	perfect
íntu	ḥafáẓtu	حَفَظْتوا	ma-ḥafaẓtūš	مَحَفَظْتوش	perfect
húwwa	ḥáfaẓ	حَفَظ	ma-ḥafáẓš	مَحَفَظْش	perfect
híyya	ḥáfaẓit	حَفَظِت	ma-ḥafaẓítš	مَحَفَظِتْش	perfect
húmma	ḥáfaẓu	حَفَظوا	ma-ḥafaẓūš	مَحَفَظوش	perfect
ána	áḥfaẓ	أَحْفَظ	ma-ḥfáẓš	مَحْفَظْش	imperfect
íḥna	níḥfaẓ	نِحْفَظ	ma-niḥfáẓš	مَنِحْفَظْش	imperfect
ínta	tíḥfaẓ	تِحْفَظ	ma-tiḥfáẓš	مَتِحْفَظْش	imperfect
ínti	tiḥfáẓi	تِحْفَظي	ma-tiḥfaẓīš	مَتِحْفَظيش	imperfect
íntu	tiḥfáẓu	تِحْفَظوا	ma-tiḥfaẓūš	مَتِحْفَظوش	imperfect
húwwa	yíḥfaẓ	يِحْفَظ	ma-yiḥfáẓš	مَيِحْفَظْش	imperfect
híyya	tíḥfaẓ	تِحْفَظ	ma-tiḥfáẓš	مَتِحْفَظْش	imperfect
húmma	yiḥfáẓu	يِحْفَظوا	ma-yiḥfaẓūš	مَيِحْفَظوش	imperfect
ána	báḥfaẓ	بَحْفَظ	ma-baḥfáẓš	مَبَحْفَظْش	bi-imperfect
íḥna	biníḥfaẓ	بِنِحْفَظ	ma-bniḥfáẓš	مَبْنِحْفَظْش	bi-imperfect
ínta	bitíḥfaẓ	بِتِحْفَظ	ma-btiḥfáẓš	مَبْتِحْفَظْش	bi-imperfect
ínti	bitiḥfáẓi	بِتِحْفَظي	ma-btiḥfaẓīš	مَبْتِحْفَظيش	bi-imperfect
íntu	bitiḥfáẓu	بِتِحْفَظوا	ma-btiḥfaẓūš	مَبْتِحْفَظوش	bi-imperfect
húwwa	biyíḥfaẓ	بِيِحْفَظ	ma-byiḥfáẓš	مَبْيِحْفَظْش	bi-imperfect
híyya	bitíḥfaẓ	بِتِحْفَظ	ma-btiḥfáẓš	مَبْتِحْفَظْش	bi-imperfect
húmma	biyiḥfáẓu	بِيِحْفَظوا	ma-byiḥfaẓūš	مَبْيِحْفَظوش	bi-imperfect
ána	háḥfaẓ	هَحْفَظ	miš háḥfaẓ	مِش هَحْفَظ	future
íḥna	haníḥfaẓ	هَنِحْفَظ	miš haníḥfaẓ	مِش هَنِحْفَظ	future
ínta	hatíḥfaẓ	هَتِحْفَظ	miš hatíḥfaẓ	مِش هَتِحْفَظ	future
ínti	hatiḥfáẓi	هَتِحْفَظي	miš hatiḥfáẓi	مِش هَتِحْفَظي	future
íntu	hatiḥfáẓu	هَتِحْفَظوا	miš hatiḥfáẓu	مِش هَتِحْفَظوا	future
húwwa	hayíḥfaẓ	هَيِحْفَظ	miš hayíḥfaẓ	مِش هَيِحْفَظ	future
híyya	hatíḥfaẓ	هَتِحْفَظ	miš hatíḥfaẓ	مِش هَتِحْفَظ	future
húmma	hayiḥfáẓu	هَيِحْفَظوا	miš hayiḥfáẓu	مِش هَيِحْفَظوا	future
ínta	íḥfaẓ	اِحْفَظ	ma-tiḥfáẓš	مَتِحْفَظْش	imperative
ínti	iḥfáẓi	اِحْفَظي	ma-tiḥfaẓīš	مَتِحْفَظيش	imperative
íntu	iḥfáẓu	اِحْفَظوا	ma-tiḥfaẓūš	مَتِحْفَظوش	imperative

	active		passive		
masculine	ḥāfiẓ	حافِظ	maḥfūẓ	مَحْفوظ	participles
feminine	ḥáfẓa	حافْظَة	maḥfūẓa	مَحْفوظَة	participles
plural	ḥafẓīn	حافْظين	maḥfuẓīn	مَحْفوظين	participles

verbal noun: ḥifẓ حِفْظ

①

حفظْت دوْرك في المسْرحية؟

ḫafáẓtᵊ dōrak fi -lmasraḫíyya?

Did you memorize your role [lines] in the play?

②

خلّي شعْبان يِحْفظْلك المِلفّات دي في الأرْشيف.

xálli ša3bān yiḫfáẓlak ilmilaffāt di fi -lʔaršīf.

Let Sha'ban save these files for you in the archive.

③

العِلب دي نَوْعِيِّتْها مُمْتازة. بِتِحْفظ الأكْل مُدّة طَويلة.

il3ílab di naw3iyyítha mumtāza. bitíḫfaẓ ilʔáklᵊ múdda ṭawīla.

These containers are of excellent quality. They keep food for a long time.

④

اِمْتِحان الرِّياضة بُكْره. هحْفظ جدْوَل الضّرْب.

imtiḫān irriyāḍa búkra. háḫfaẓ gádwal iḍḍárb.

My math exam is tomorrow. I'll memorize the multiplication table.

⑤

اِحْفظوا صِحِّةْ وِلادْكو و اِبْعدوهُم عن الأكْل غيْر الصِّحّي.

iḫfáẓu ṣíḫḫit wiládku w ib3adūhum 3an ilʔáklᵊ ɣēr iṣṣíḫḫi.

Keep your kids healthy by keeping them away from unhealthy food.

⑥

أنا محفظْتِش السّورة اللي عليّا لِسّه. هقْعُد أحْفظْها.

ána ma-ḫafáẓtiš issūra -lli 3aláyya líssa. háʔ3ud aḫfáẓha.

I haven't memorized the Surah [Quranic chapter] that I still have to study. I'll study it now.

❖ [1s1] **to keep, save; to memorize**

- Compare with حافِظ *ḫāfiẓ*. (➲ 76)

➲ 24.5

87 to obtain ɦáʔʔaʔ حقق

verbal noun: taɦʔīʔ تحقيق

	affirmative		negative		
ána	ɦaʔʔáʔt	حَقَّقْت	ma-ɦaʔʔáʔtiš	مَحَقَّقْتِش	perfect
íɦna	ɦaʔʔáʔna	حَقَّقْنا	ma-ɦaʔʔaʔnāš	مَحَقَّقْناش	
ínta	ɦaʔʔáʔt	حَقَّقْت	ma-ɦaʔʔáʔtiš	مَحَقَّقْتِش	
ínti	ɦaʔʔáʔti	حَقَّقْتي	ma-ɦaʔʔaʔtīš	مَحَقَّقْتيش	
íntu	ɦaʔʔáʔtu	حَقَّقْتوا	ma-ɦaʔʔaʔtūš	مَحَقَّقْتوش	
húwwa	ɦáʔʔaʔ	حَقَّق	ma-ɦaʔʔáʔš	مَحَقَّقْش	
híyya	ɦaʔʔáʔit	حَقَّقِت	ma-ɦaʔʔaʔítš	مَحَقَّقِتْش	
húmma	ɦaʔʔáʔu	حَقَّقوا	ma-ɦaʔʔaʔūš	مَحَقَّقوش	
ána	aɦáʔʔaʔ	أَحَقَّق	ma-ɦaʔʔáʔš	مَحَقَّقْش	imperfect
íɦna	niɦáʔʔaʔ	نِحَقَّق	ma-nɦaʔʔáʔš	مَنْحَقَّقْش	
ínta	tiɦáʔʔaʔ	تِحَقَّق	ma-tɦaʔʔáʔš	مَتْحَقَّقْش	
ínti	tiɦaʔʔáʔi	تِحَقَّقي	ma-tɦaʔʔaʔīš	مَتْحَقَّقيش	
íntu	tiɦaʔʔáʔu	تِحَقَّقوا	ma-tɦaʔʔaʔūš	مَتْحَقَّقوش	
húwwa	yiɦáʔʔaʔ	يِحَقَّق	ma-yɦaʔʔáʔš	مَيْحَقَّقْش	
híyya	tiɦáʔʔaʔ	تِحَقَّق	ma-tɦaʔʔáʔš	مَتْحَقَّقْش	
húmma	yiɦaʔʔáʔu	يِحَقَّقوا	ma-yɦaʔʔaʔūš	مَيْحَقَّقوش	
ána	baɦáʔʔaʔ	بَحَقَّق	ma-baɦaʔʔáʔš	مَبَحَقَّقْش	bi-imperfect
íɦna	binɦáʔʔaʔ	بِنْحَقَّق	ma-binɦaʔʔáʔš	مَبِنْحَقَّقْش	
ínta	bitɦáʔʔaʔ	بِتْحَقَّق	ma-bitɦaʔʔáʔš	مَبِتْحَقَّقْش	
ínti	bitɦaʔʔáʔi	بِتْحَقَّقي	ma-bitɦaʔʔaʔīš	مَبِتْحَقَّقيش	
íntu	bitɦaʔʔáʔu	بِتْحَقَّقوا	ma-bitɦaʔʔaʔūš	مَبِتْحَقَّقوش	
húwwa	biyɦáʔʔaʔ	بِيْحَقَّق	ma-biyɦaʔʔáʔš	مَبِيْحَقَّقْش	
híyya	bitɦáʔʔaʔ	بِتْحَقَّق	ma-bitɦaʔʔáʔš	مَبِتْحَقَّقْش	
húmma	biyɦaʔʔáʔu	بِيْحَقَّقوا	ma-biyɦaʔʔaʔūš	مَبِيْحَقَّقوش	
ána	haɦáʔʔaʔ	هَحَقَّق	miš haɦáʔʔaʔ	مِش هَحَقَّق	future
íɦna	hanɦáʔʔaʔ	هَنْحَقَّق	miš hanɦáʔʔaʔ	مِش هَنْحَقَّق	
ínta	hatɦáʔʔaʔ	هَتْحَقَّق	miš hatɦáʔʔaʔ	مِش هَتْحَقَّق	
ínti	hatɦaʔʔáʔi	هَتْحَقَّقي	miš hatɦaʔʔáʔi	مِش هَتْحَقَّقي	
íntu	hatɦaʔʔáʔu	هَتْحَقَّقوا	miš hatɦaʔʔáʔu	مِش هَتْحَقَّقوا	
húwwa	hayɦáʔʔaʔ	هَيْحَقَّق	miš hayɦáʔʔaʔ	مِش هَيْحَقَّق	
híyya	hatɦáʔʔaʔ	هَتْحَقَّق	miš hatɦáʔʔaʔ	مِش هَتْحَقَّق	
húmma	hayɦaʔʔáʔu	هَيْحَقَّقوا	miš hayɦaʔʔáʔu	مِش هَيْحَقَّقوا	
ínta	ɦáʔʔaʔ	حَقَّق	ma-tɦaʔʔáʔš	مَتْحَقَّقْش	imperative
ínti	ɦaʔʔáʔi	حَقَّقي	ma-tɦaʔʔaʔīš	مَتْحَقَّقيش	
íntu	ɦaʔʔáʔu	حَقَّقوا	ma-tɦaʔʔaʔūš	مَتْحَقَّقوش	

	active		passive		
masculine	miɦáʔʔaʔ	مِحَقَّق	mitɦáʔʔaʔ	مِتْحَقَّق	participles
feminine	miɦaʔʔáʔa	مِحَقَّقَة	mitɦaʔʔáʔa	مِتْحَقَّقَة	
plural	miɦaʔʔaʔīn	مِحَقَّقين	mitɦaʔʔaʔīn	مِتْحَقَّقين	

①

خِلال الخمس سِنين اللي فاتوا، محقّقْتِش أيّ إنْجاز مُهِمّ في حَياتي.

xilāl ilxámas sinīn ílli fātu, ma-ɧaʔʔáʔtiš ayyᵊ ʔingāz<i> </i>muhímmᵊ fi ɧayāti.

I haven't accomplished any important
goal in the last five years of my life.

②

حاوِل تِحقّق حِلْمك مهْما واجِهْت صُعوبات.

ɧāwil tiɧáʔʔaʔ ɧílmak máhma wagíhtᵊ ṣu3ubāt.

Try to achieve your dream even
if you face difficulties.

③

مِراتي بِتْحقّق معايا كُلّ يوْم لمّا أرْجع البيْت، كُنْت فيْن و معَ مين و عملْتوا أيْه. زهّقِتْني.

mirāti bitɧáʔʔaʔ ma3āya kullᵊ yōm lámm- árga3 ilbēt, kuntᵊ fēn wi má3a mīn wi 3amáltu ʔē. zahhaʔitni.

My wife interrogates me every time I get home. "Where were you?
And with whom? What did you do?" I'm fed up.

④

هَيْحقّقوا معاه النّهارْده و يِمْكِن يِحْبِسوه على ذِمّةْ التّحْقيق.

hayɧaʔʔáʔu ma3ā -nnahárda wi yímkin yiɧbisū 3ála zímmit ittaɧʔīʔ.

He will be investigated today, and he may be
locked up dependent on the investigation.

⑤

حقّقوا أحْلامْكو. هتْحِسّوا بِالفخْر بعْديْن.

ɧaʔʔáʔu ʔaɧlámku. hatɧíssu bi-lfaxrᵊ ba3dēn.

Achieve your dreams. You'll
be proud later.

❖ [2s2] **to accomplish, achieve; to interrogate, investigate**

➲ 28.4

88 to control ḫákam 

	affirmative		negative		
ána	ḫakámt	حَكَمْت	ma-ḫakámtiš	مَحَكَمْتِش	perfect
íḫna	ḫakámna	حَكَمْنا	ma-ḫakamnāš	مَحَكَمْناش	
ínta	ḫakámt	حَكَمْت	ma-ḫakámtiš	مَحَكَمْتِش	
ínti	ḫakámti	حَكَمْتي	ma-ḫakamtīš	مَحَكَمْتيش	
íntu	ḫakámtu	حَكَمْتوا	ma-ḫakamtūš	مَحَكَمْتوش	
húwwa	ḫákam	حَكَم	ma-ḫakámš	مَحَكَمْش	
híyya	ḫákamit	حَكَمِت	ma-ḫakamítš	مَحَكَمِتْش	
húmma	ḫákamu	حَكَموا	ma-ḫakamūš	مَحَكَموش	
ána	áḫkum	أَحْكُم	ma-ḫkúmš	مَحْكُمْش	imperfect
íḫna	núḫkum	نُحْكُم	ma-nuḫkúmš	مَنُحْكُمْش	
ínta	túḫkum	تُحْكُم	ma-tuḫkúmš	مَتُحْكُمْش	
ínti	tuḫkúmi	تُحْكُمي	ma-tuḫkumīš	مَتُحْكُميش	
íntu	tuḫkúmu	تُحْكُموا	ma-tuḫkumūš	مَتُحْكُموش	
húwwa	yúḫkum	يُحْكُم	ma-yuḫkúmš	مَيُحْكُمْش	
híyya	túḫkum	تُحْكُم	ma-tuḫkúmš	مَتُحْكُمْش	
húmma	yuḫkúmu	يُحْكُموا	ma-yuḫkumūš	مَيُحْكُموش	
ána	báḫkum	بَحْكُم	ma-baḫkúmš	مَبَحْكُمْش	bi-imperfect
íḫna	binúḫkum	بِنُحْكُم	ma-bnuḫkúmš	مَبْنُحْكُمْش	
ínta	bitúḫkum	بِتُحْكُم	ma-btuḫkúmš	مَبْتُحْكُمْش	
ínti	bituḫkúmi	بِتُحْكُمي	ma-btuḫkumīš	مَبْتُحْكُميش	
íntu	bituḫkúmu	بِتُحْكُموا	ma-btuḫkumūš	مَبْتُحْكُموش	
húwwa	biyúḫkum	بِيُحْكُم	ma-byuḫkúmš	مَبْيُحْكُمْش	
híyya	bitúḫkum	بِتُحْكُم	ma-btuḫkúmš	مَبْتُحْكُمْش	
húmma	biyuḫkúmu	بِيُحْكُموا	ma-byuḫkumūš	مَبْيُحْكُموش	
ána	háḫkum	هَحْكُم	miš háḫkum	مِش هَحْكُم	future
íḫna	hanúḫkum	هَنُحْكُم	miš hanúḫkum	مِش هَنُحْكُم	
ínta	hatúḫkum	هَتُحْكُم	miš hatúḫkum	مِش هَتُحْكُم	
ínti	hatuḫkúmi	هَتُحْكُمي	miš hatuḫkúmi	مِش هَتُحْكُمي	
íntu	hatuḫkúmu	هَتُحْكُموا	miš hatuḫkúmu	مِش هَتُحْكُموا	
húwwa	hayúḫkum	هَيُحْكُم	miš hayúḫkum	مِش هَيُحْكُم	
híyya	hatúḫkum	هَتُحْكُم	miš hatúḫkum	مِش هَتُحْكُم	
húmma	hayuḫkúmu	هَيُحْكُموا	miš hayuḫkúmu	مِش هَيُحْكُموا	
ínta	úḫkum	أُحْكُم	ma-tuḫkúmš	مَتُحْكُمْش	imperative
ínti	uḫkúmi	أُحْكُمي	ma-tuḫkumīš	مَتُحْكُميش	
íntu	uḫkúmu	أُحْكُموا	ma-tuḫkumūš	مَتُحْكُموش	

	active		passive		
masculine	ḫākim	حاكِم	maḫkūm	مَحْكوم	participles
feminine	ḫákma	حاكْمَة	maḫkūma	مَحْكومَة	
plural	ḫakmīn	حاكْمين	maḫkumīn	مَحْكومين	

verbal nouns: ḫakm حَكْم - ḫukm حُكْم

①

مُبارك حكم مصْر حَوالي ٣٠ سنة.

mubārak ɧákam maṣrᵊ ɧawāli talatīn sána.

Mubarak ruled Egypt for about 30 years.

②

مُصْطفى لِسّه هَيِسْتأْنِف بعْد ما القاضي يُحْكُم في قضِيِّتُه.

muṣṭáfa líssa hayistáʔnif ba3dᵊ ma -lʔāḍi yúɧkum fi ʔaḍiyyítu.

Mostafa will appeal after the judge rules in his case.

③

مبحْكُمْش على شخْص مِن أوِّل لحْظة. لازِم أتْعامِل معاه مُدّة عشان أعْرفُه.

ma-baɧkúmšᵊ 3ála šaxṣᵊ min áwwil láɧẓa. lāzim at3āmil ma3ā múdda 3ašān a3ráfu.

I don't judge a person at first sight. I need to interact
with them for a while to get to know them.

④

الرّئيس الجِديد هَيُحْكُم لِمُدِّةْ أرْبع سِنين.

irraʔīs ilgidīd hayúɧkum li-múddit árba3 sinīn.

The new president will govern for a term of four years.

⑤

اُحْكُم ما بينّا إنْتَ. إحْنا خلاص وِصِلْنا لِاخِرْنا في النِّقاش.

úɧkum ma bínna ʔínta. íɧna xalāṣ wiṣílna li-axírna fi -nniʔāš.

Judge between us. We have reached
a dead-end in this argument.

⑥

ماما حاكْمة علينْا نِنضّف البيْت كُلُّه قبْل ما نِنْزِل.

māma ɧákma 3alēna ninádḍaf ilbēt kúllu ʔablᵊ ma nínzil.

Mom has insisted that we clean the
whole house before we go out.

❖ [1s3] **to control; to rule**

- This verb, like other verbs of the [1s3] and [1s6] patterns, can optionally take ـُ *u* instead of ـِ *i* in the personal prefixes of the imperfect (including the bi-imperfect and future) and imperative. For example, يُحْكُم *yúɧkum* can also be pronounced يِحْكُم *yíɧkum*. These vowels are interchangeable, but the tables reflect the preferences of the speakers on the MP3s.

➲ 143.4

89 to tell ḫáka حَكَى

verbal nouns: ḫaky حكْي - ḫikāya حِكايَة

		affirmative		negative	
perfect					
ána	ḫakēt	حَكيْت	ma-ḫakítš	مَحَكيتْش
íḫna	ḫakēna	حَكيْنا	ma-ḫakināš	مَحَكيناش
ínta	ḫakēt	حَكيْت	ma-ḫakítš	مَحَكيتْش
ínti	ḫakēti	حَكيْتي	ma-ḫakitīš	مَحَكيتيش
íntu	ḫakētu	حَكيْتوا	ma-ḫakitūš	مَحَكيتوش
húwwa	ḫáka	حَكَى	ma-ḫakāš	مَحَكاش
híyya	ḫákit	حَكِت	ma-ḫakítš	مَحَكِتْش
húmma	ḫáku	حَكوا	ma-ḫakūš	مَحَكوش
imperfect					
ána	áḫki	أحْكي	ma-ḫkīš	مَحْكيش
íḫna	níḫki	نِحْكي	ma-niḫkīš	مَنِحْكيش
ínta	tíḫki	تِحْكي	ma-tiḫkīš	مَتِحْكيش
ínti	tíḫki	تِحْكي	ma-tiḫkīš	مَتِحْكيش
íntu	tíḫku	تِحْكوا	ma-tiḫkūš	مَتِحْكوش
húwwa	yíḫki	يِحْكي	ma-yiḫkīš	مَيِحْكيش
híyya	tíḫki	تِحْكي	ma-tiḫkīš	مَتِحْكيش
húmma	yíḫku	يِحْكوا	ma-yiḫkūš	مَيِحْكوش
bi-imperfect					
ána	báḫki	بَحْكي	ma-baḫkīš	مَبَحْكيش
íḫna	biníḫki	بِنِحْكي	ma-bniḫkīš	مَبْنِحْكيش
ínta	bitíḫki	بِتِحْكي	ma-btiḫkīš	مَبْتِحْكيش
ínti	bitíḫki	بِتِحْكي	ma-btiḫkīš	مَبْتِحْكيش
íntu	bitíḫku	بِتِحْكوا	ma-btiḫkūš	مَبْتِحْكوش
húwwa	biyíḫki	بِيِحْكي	ma-byiḫkīš	مَبْيِحْكيش
híyya	bitíḫki	بِتِحْكي	ma-btiḫkīš	مَبْتِحْكيش
húmma	biyíḫku	بِيِحْكوا	ma-byiḫkūš	مَبْيِحْكوش
future					
ána	háḫki	هَحْكي	miš háḫki	مِش هَحْكي
íḫna	haníḫki	هَنِحْكي	miš haníḫki	مِش هَنِحْكي
ínta	hatíḫki	هَتِحْكي	miš hatíḫki	مِش هَتِحْكي
ínti	hatíḫki	هَتِحْكي	miš hatíḫki	مِش هَتِحْكي
íntu	hatíḫku	هَتِحْكوا	miš hatíḫku	مِش هَتِحْكوا
húwwa	hayíḫki	هَيِحْكي	miš hayíḫki	مِش هَيِحْكي
híyya	hatíḫki	هَتِحْكي	miš hatíḫki	مِش هَتِحْكي
húmma	hayíḫku	هَيِحْكوا	miš hayíḫku	مِش هَيِحْكوا
imperative					
ínta	íḫki	اِحْكي	ma-tiḫkīš	مَتِحْكيش
ínti	íḫki	اِحْكي	ma-tiḫkīš	مَتِحْكيش
íntu	íḫku	اِحْكوا	ma-tiḫkūš	مَتِحْكوش

participles	active		passive	
masculine	ḫāki	حاكي	máḫki	مَحْكي
feminine	ḫákya	حاكْيَة	maḫkíyya	مَحْكِيَّة
plural	ḫakyīn	حاكْيين	maḫkiyīn	مَحْكِيين

①

محكيتْليش ، عملْت أيْه في المُقابْلة؟

ma-ḫakitlīš, 3amált^ə ʔē fi -lmuʔábla?

You didn't tell me yet; what did you do in the interview?

②

مِراتي قرّرِت تِحْكي لِلوِلاد حِكايِةْ قبْل النّوْم كُلّ يوْم.

mirāti qarrárit tíḫki li-lwilād ḫikāyit ʔabl innōm kull^ə yōm.

My wife decided to tell our kids a story every day at bedtime.

③

شَيْماء صاحْبِتي كُلّ يوْم بِتِحْكيلي مشاكِلْها معَ جوزْها، لمّا عقّدِتْني مِن الجَواز.

šaymāʔ ṣaḫbíti kull^ə yōm bitiḫkīli mašakílha má3a gúzha, lámma 3aʔʔadítni min ilgawāz.

Every day my friend Shaimaa tells me about her trouble with her husband, to the point that she's given me a complex about marriage.

④

حمْزة هَيِحْكيلْنا عمل أيْه في الرِّحْلة.

ḫámza hayiḫkílna 3ámal ʔē fi -rríḫla.

Hamza will tell us what he did on the trip.

⑤

اِحْكيلُه ، إحْكيلُه اللي حصلّك هِناك عشان يِسْمع كلامي لمّا أقولُّه مَيْروحْش.

iḫkīlu, iḫkīlu -lli ḫaṣállak hindruk 3ašān yísma3 kalāmi lámma ʔaʔúllu ma-yrúḫš.

Tell him, tell him what happened there, so he'll listen when I tell him not to go.

⑥

أُخْتي لِسّه حاكْيالي قِصّة مُؤْلِمة، مِأثّرة فِيّا أوي.

úxti líssa ḫakyāli qíṣṣa muʔlíma, miʔassára fíyya ʔáwi.

My sister just told me a painful story, which really affected me.

❖ [1d2] **to tell, recount**

➲ 193.3, 196.4

90 to shave ḥálaʔ حَلَق

		affirmative		negative	
perfect	ána	ḥaláʔt	حَلَقْت	ma-ḥaláʔtiš	مَحَلَقْتِش
	íḥna	ḥaláʔna	حَلَقْنا	ma-ḥalaʔnāš	مَحَلَقْناش
	ínta	ḥaláʔt	حَلَقْت	ma-ḥaláʔtiš	مَحَلَقْتِش
	ínti	ḥaláʔti	حَلَقْتي	ma-ḥalaʔtīš	مَحَلَقْتيش
	íntu	ḥaláʔtu	حَلَقْتوا	ma-ḥalaʔtūš	مَحَلَقْتوش
	húwwa	ḥálaʔ	حَلَق	ma-ḥaláʔš	مَحَلَقْش
	híyya	ḥálaʔit	حَلَقِت	ma-ḥalaʔítš	مَحَلَقِتْش
	húmma	ḥálaʔu	حَلَقوا	ma-ḥalaʔūš	مَحَلَقوش
imperfect	ána	áḥlaʔ	أَحْلَق	ma-ḥláʔš	مَحْلَقْش
	íḥna	níḥlaʔ	نِحْلَق	ma-niḥláʔš	مَنِحْلَقْش
	ínta	tíḥlaʔ	تِحْلَق	ma-tiḥláʔš	مَتِحْلَقْش
	ínti	tiḥláʔi	تِحْلَقي	ma-tiḥlaʔīš	مَتِحْلَقيش
	íntu	tiḥláʔu	تِحْلَقوا	ma-tiḥlaʔūš	مَتِحْلَقوش
	húwwa	yíḥlaʔ	يِحْلَق	ma-yiḥláʔš	مَيِحْلَقْش
	híyya	tíḥlaʔ	تِحْلَق	ma-tiḥláʔš	مَتِحْلَقْش
	húmma	yiḥláʔu	يِحْلَقوا	ma-yiḥlaʔūš	مَيِحْلَقوش
bi-imperfect	ána	báḥlaʔ	بَحْلَق	ma-baḥláʔš	مَبَحْلَقْش
	íḥna	biníḥlaʔ	بِنِحْلَق	ma-bniḥláʔš	مَبْنِحْلَقْش
	ínta	bitíḥlaʔ	بِتِحْلَق	ma-btiḥláʔš	مَبْتِحْلَقْش
	ínti	bitiḥláʔi	بِتِحْلَقي	ma-btiḥlaʔīš	مَبْتِحْلَقيش
	íntu	bitiḥláʔu	بِتِحْلَقوا	ma-btiḥlaʔūš	مَبْتِحْلَقوش
	húwwa	biyíḥlaʔ	بِيِحْلَق	ma-byiḥláʔš	مَبْيِحْلَقْش
	híyya	bitíḥlaʔ	بِتِحْلَق	ma-btiḥláʔš	مَبْتِحْلَقْش
	húmma	biyiḥláʔu	بِيِحْلَقوا	ma-byiḥlaʔūš	مَبْيِحْلَقوش
future	ána	háḥlaʔ	هَحْلَق	miš háḥlaʔ	مِش هَحْلَق
	íḥna	haníḥlaʔ	هَنِحْلَق	miš haníḥlaʔ	مِش هَنِحْلَق
	ínta	hatíḥlaʔ	هَتِحْلَق	miš hatíḥlaʔ	مِش هَتِحْلَق
	ínti	hatiḥláʔi	هَتِحْلَقي	miš hatiḥláʔi	مِش هَتِحْلَقي
	íntu	hatiḥláʔu	هَتِحْلَقوا	miš hatiḥláʔu	مِش هَتِحْلَقوا
	húwwa	hayíḥlaʔ	هَيِحْلَق	miš hayíḥlaʔ	مِش هَيِحْلَق
	híyya	hatíḥlaʔ	هَتِحْلَق	miš hatíḥlaʔ	مِش هَتِحْلَق
	húmma	hayiḥláʔu	هَيِحْلَقوا	miš hayiḥláʔu	مِش هَيِحْلَقوا
imperative	ínta	íḥlaʔ	اِحْلَق	ma-tiḥláʔš	مَتِحْلَقْش
	ínti	iḥláʔi	اِحْلَقي	ma-tiḥlaʔīš	مَتِحْلَقيش
	íntu	iḥláʔu	اِحْلَقوا	ma-tiḥlaʔūš	مَتِحْلَقوش

		active		passive	
participles	masculine	ḥāliʔ	حالِق	maḥlūʔ	مَحْلوق
	feminine	ḥálʔa	حالْقَة	maḥlūʔa	مَحْلوقَة
	plural	ḥalʔīn	حالْقين	maḥluʔīn	مَحْلوقين

verbal nouns: ḥalʔ حَلْق - ḥilāʔa حِلاقَة

①

حلقْت إمْبارِح قبْل زحْمِةْ العيد.

ḫaláʔt imbāriḫ ʔablᵊ záḫmit il3īd.

I had my hair cut yesterday before the holiday rush.

②

شادي مبْيِحْلقْش شعْرُه بقالُه ٦ شْهور. عامِل سْتايْل جِديد.

šādi ma-byiḫláʔšᵊ šá3ru baʔālu sittᵊ šhūr. 3āmilᵊ stāyl gidīd.

Shady hasn't cut his hair for six months. He's sporting a new style.

③

هحْلق شهْري زيرو لَوْ جِبْت اِمْتِياز السّنة دي.

háḫlaʔ šáhri zīru law gibt imtiyāz issanādi.

I'll shave my head if I get an A this year.

④

اِحْلقْلُه حلْقة قْصيّرة. أنا معنْديش وِلاد تِسبْسِب شعْرها.

iḫláʔlu ḫálʔa ʔuṣayyára. ána ma-3andīš wilād tisábsib ša3ráha.

Give him a short haircut. No son of mine grows his hair out.

⑤

أ: **إنْتَ حالِق زلبطّة ليْه؟**

ب: **تضامُناً معَ مرْضى السّرطان.**

A: *ínta ḫāliʔ zalabátṭa lē?*

B: *taḍámunan má3a márḍa -ssaraṭān.*

A: Why did you shave your head bald?

B: In solidarity with cancer patients.

❖ [1s1] **to shave; to get a hair cut**

➲ 78.8

91 to dream ḫílim حِلِم

verbal noun: ḫilm حِلْم

perfect

	affirmative		negative	
ána	ḫilímt	حِلِمْت	ma-ḫlímtiš	مَحْلِمْتِش
íḫna	ḫilímna	حِلِمْنا	ma-ḫlimnāš	مَحْلِمْناش
ínta	ḫilímt	حِلِمْت	ma-ḫlímtiš	مَحْلِمْتِش
ínti	ḫilímti	حِلِمْتي	ma-ḫlimtīš	مَحْلِمْتيش
íntu	ḫilímtu	حِلِمْتوا	ma-ḫlimtūš	مَحْلِمْتوش
húwwa	ḫílim	حِلِم	ma-ḫlímš	مَحْلِمْش
híyya	ḫílmit	حِلْمِت	ma-ḫilmítš	مَحِلْمِتْش
húmma	ḫílmu	حِلْموا	ma-ḫilmūš	مَحِلْموش

imperfect

	affirmative		negative	
ána	áḫlam	أحْلَم	ma-ḫlámš	مَحْلَمْش
íḫna	níḫlam	نِحْلَم	ma-niḫlámš	مَنِحْلَمْش
ínta	tíḫlam	تِحْلَم	ma-tiḫlámš	مَتِحْلَمْش
ínti	tiḫlámi	تِحْلَمي	ma-tiḫlamīš	مَتِحْلَميش
íntu	tiḫlámu	تِحْلَموا	ma-tiḫlamūš	مَتِحْلَموش
húwwa	yíḫlam	يِحْلَم	ma-yiḫlámš	مَيِحْلَمْش
híyya	tíḫlam	تِحْلَم	ma-tiḫlámš	مَتِحْلَمْش
húmma	yiḫlámu	يِحْلَموا	ma-yiḫlamūš	مَيِحْلَموش

bi-imperfect

	affirmative		negative	
ána	báḫlam	بَحْلَم	ma-baḫlámš	مَبَحْلَمْش
íḫna	biníḫlam	بِنِحْلَم	ma-bniḫlámš	مَبْنِحْلَمْش
ínta	bitíḫlam	بِتِحْلَم	ma-btiḫlámš	مَبْتِحْلَمْش
ínti	bitiḫlámi	بِتِحْلَمي	ma-btiḫlamīš	مَبْتِحْلَميش
íntu	bitiḫlámu	بِتِحْلَموا	ma-btiḫlamūš	مَبْتِحْلَموش
húwwa	biyíḫlam	بِيِحْلَم	ma-byiḫlámš	مَبْيِحْلَمْش
híyya	bitíḫlam	بِتِحْلَم	ma-btiḫlámš	مَبْتِحْلَمْش
húmma	biyiḫlámu	بِيِحْلَموا	ma-byiḫlamūš	مَبْيِحْلَموش

future

	affirmative		negative	
ána	háḫlam	هَحْلَم	miš háḫlam	مِش هَحْلَم
íḫna	haníḫlam	هَنِحْلَم	miš haníḫlam	مِش هَنِحْلَم
ínta	hatíḫlam	هَتِحْلَم	miš hatíḫlam	مِش هَتِحْلَم
ínti	hatiḫlámi	هَتِحْلَمي	miš hatiḫlámi	مِش هَتِحْلَمي
íntu	hatiḫlámu	هَتِحْلَموا	miš hatiḫlámu	مِش هَتِحْلَموا
húwwa	hayíḫlam	هَيِحْلَم	miš hayíḫlam	مِش هَيِحْلَم
híyya	hatíḫlam	هَتِحْلَم	miš hatíḫlam	مِش هَتِحْلَم
húmma	hayiḫlámu	هَيِحْلَموا	miš hayiḫlámu	مِش هَيِحْلَموا

imperative

	affirmative		negative	
ínta	íḫlam	اِحْلَم	ma-tiḫlámš	مَتِحْلَمْش
ínti	iḫlámi	اِحْلَمي	ma-tiḫlamīš	مَتِحْلَميش
íntu	iḫlámu	اِحْلَموا	ma-tiḫlamūš	مَتِحْلَموش

participles

	active		passive	
masculine	ḫālim	حالِم	–	–
feminine	ḫálma	حالْمَة	–	–
plural	ḫalmīn	حالْمين	–	–

①

حِلِمْت إمْبارِح إنِّنا في الشّقّة القديمة.

ḥilímt imbāriḥ innína fi -ššáʔʔa -lʔadīma.

Last night, I had a dream that
we were in the old apartment.

②

الجعان يِحْلم بِسوق العيْش.

ilga3ān yíḥlam bi-sūʔ il3ēš.

A hungry man dreams of
the bread market. (proverb)

③

قولّي بِتِحْلم بِايْه، أقولّك هتِبْقى أيْه.

ʔúlli bitíḥlam bi-ʔē, aʔúllak hatíbʔa ʔē.

Tell me what you dream of, and
I'll tell you what you'll become.

④

هحْلم بِيوْم أشوف فيه السّلام مالي العالم.

háḥlam bi-yōm ašūf fī -ssalām māli -l3ālam.

I'll dream of the day when
peace is all over the world.

⑤

اِحْلم و عيش في حِلْمك بِكُلّ تفاصيله، هَيِتْحقّق.

íḥlam wi 3īš fi ḥílmak bi-kúllᵊ tafaṣīlu, hayitḥáʔʔaʔ.

Dream and live your dream in all
its details, and it'll come true.

⑥

أنا مبحْلمْش. عَ الأقلّ، أنا عُمْري ما بقْدر أفْتِكِر أحْلامي.

ána ma-baḥlámš. 3a -lʔaʔáll, ána 3úmri ma báʔdar aftíkir aḥlāmi.

I don't dream. At least, I can never
remember my dreams.

❖ [1s4] **to dream** (**about, of** بِـ *bi-*)

92 to take *xad* خد

	affirmative		negative		
ána	*xadt / axádt*	خَدْت / أخَدْت	*ma-xádtiš*	مَخَدْتِش	**perfect**
íḫna	*xádna / axádna*	خَدْنا / أخَدْنا	*ma-xadnāš*	مَخَدْناش	
ínta	*xadt / axádt*	خَدْت / أخَدْت	*ma-xádtiš*	مَخَدْتِش	
ínti	*xádti / axádti*	خَدْتي / أخَدْتي	*ma-xadtīš*	مَخَدْتيش	
íntu	*xádtu / axádtu*	خَدْتوا / أخَدْتوا	*ma-xadtūš*	مَخَدْتوش	
húwwa	*xad / áxad*	خَد / أخَد	*ma-xádš*	مَخَدْش	
híyya	*xádit / áxadit*	خَدِت / أخَدِت	*ma-xadítš*	مَخَدِتْش	
húmma	*xádu / áxadu*	خَدوا / أخَدوا	*ma-xadūš*	مَخَدوش	
ána	*āxud*	أخُد	*ma-xúdš*	ماخُدْش	**imperfect**
íḫna	*nāxud*	ناخُد	*ma-naxúdš*	مَناخُدْش	
ínta	*tāxud*	تاخُد	*ma-taxúdš*	مَتاخُدْش	
ínti	*táxdi*	تاخْدي	*ma-taxdīš*	مَتاخْديش	
íntu	*táxdu*	تاخْدوا	*ma-taxdūš*	مَتاخْدوش	
húwwa	*yāxud*	ياخُد	*ma-yaxúdš*	مَياخُدْش	
híyya	*tāxud*	تاخُد	*ma-taxúdš*	مَتاخُدْش	
húmma	*yáxdu*	ياخْدوا	*ma-yaxdūš*	مَياخْدوش	
ána	*bāxud*	باخُد	*ma-baxúdš*	مَباخُدْش	**bi-imperfect**
íḫna	*bināxud*	بِناخُد	*ma-bnaxúdš*	مَبْناخُدْش	
ínta	*bitāxud*	بِتاخُد	*ma-btaxúdš*	مَبْتاخُدْش	
ínti	*bitáxdi*	بِتاخْدي	*ma-btaxdīš*	مَبْتاخْديش	
íntu	*bitáxdu*	بِتاخْدوا	*ma-btaxdūš*	مَبْتاخْدوش	
húwwa	*biyāxud*	بِياخُد	*ma-byaxúdš*	مَبْياخُدْش	
híyya	*bitāxud*	بِتاخُد	*ma-btaxúdš*	مَبْتاخُدْش	
húmma	*biyáxdu*	بِياخْدوا	*ma-byaxdūš*	مَبْياخْدوش	
ána	*hāxud*	هاخُد	*miš hāxud*	مِش هاخُد	**future**
íḫna	*hanāxud*	هَناخُد	*miš hanāxud*	مِش هَناخُد	
ínta	*hatāxud*	هَتاخُد	*miš hatāxud*	مِش هَتاخُد	
ínti	*hatáxdi*	هَتاخْدي	*miš hatáxdi*	مِش هَتاخْدي	
íntu	*hatáxdu*	هَتاخْدوا	*miš hatáxdu*	مِش هَتاخْدوا	
húwwa	*hayāxud*	هَياخُد	*miš hayāxud*	مِش هَياخُد	
híyya	*hatāxud*	هَتاخُد	*miš hatāxud*	مِش هَتاخُد	
húmma	*hayáxdu*	هَياخْدوا	*miš hayáxdu*	مِش هَياخْدوا	
ínta	*xud*	خُد	*ma-taxúdš*	مَتاخُدْش	**imperative**
ínti	*xúdi*	خُدي	*ma-taxdīš*	مَتاخْديش	
íntu	*xúdu*	خُدوا	*ma-taxdūš*	مَتاخْدوش	

	active		passive		
masculine	*wāxid*	واخِد	*mittāxid*	مِتّاخِد	**participles**
feminine	*wáxda*	واخْدَة	*mittáxda*	مِتّاخْدَة	
plural	*waxdīn*	واخْدين	*mittaxdīn*	مِتّاخْدين	

verbal nouns: *axd* أخْد - *axadān* أخَدان

①

أوِّل ما الخِناقة ابْتدِت، كريم خد ديْله في سْنانُه و جِري.

áwwil ma -lxināʔa -btádit, karīm xad dēlu fi snānu wi gíri.

As soon as the fight began, Karim hightailed it out of there [lit. took his tail in his teeth and ran].

②	③
جوْزي كُلّ ما يِرجع مِ السّفر ياخُد دوْر برْد. *gōzi kullᵊ ma yírga3 mi -ssáfar yāxud dōr bard.* Every time my husband comes back from traveling, he catches a cold.	بِتاخُد الدّوا في معادُه وَلّا لأ؟ *bitāxud iddáwa fi mi3ādu wálla laʔ?* Do you take your medicine on time or not?

④

مبحِبِّش السّهر. أنا نُصّ ساعة و هاخُد بعْضي و أمْشي.

ma-baħíbbiš issáhar. ána nuṣṣᵊ sā3a wi hāxud bá3ḍi w ámši.

I don't like to stay up late. I'll go in half an hour.

⑤

خُدوا بالْكو مِن وِلادْكو في أيّ مكان. بسْمع عن حالات خطْف كْتير.

xúdu bálku min wiládku fi ʔayyᵊ makān. básma3 3an ħalāt xaṭfᵊ ktīr.

Keep an eye on your kids everywhere. I hear about a lot of kidnappings.

⑥

واخِد بالك إنّ الدُّكْتور كُلّ مُحاضْرة بِيسْألك؟ واضِح إنّك الطّالِب المُفضّل عنْدُه.

wāxid bālak inn idduktūr kullᵊ muħáḍra yisʔálak? wāḍiħ ínnak iṭṭālib ilmufáḍḍal 3ándu.

Do you notice that the professor calls on you each lecture? It seems you're his favorite student.

⑦

أيْه ده؟ إنْتو كُلُّكو خدْتوا آيْس كْريم و أنا مخدْتِش. إشْمِعْنى؟

ʔē da? íntu kullúku xádtu ʔāys krīm w ána ma-xádtiš. išmí3na?

What's this? You all got ice cream, but I didn't. What's up with that?

⑧

خُد حذرك مِن الرّاجِل ده. شكْلُه عايِز يِنْصُب عليْك و ياخُد فِلوسك.

xud ħázarak min irrāgil da. šáklu 3āyiz yúnṣub 3alēk wi yāxud filūsak.

Watch out for that guy. It seems he wants to con you and take your money.

⑨	⑩
خُد تِليفوْنك و إنْتَ نازِل. *xud tilifōnak w ínta nāzil.* Take your phone with you when you're going out.	متاخْديش مِن العِنب ده. طعْمُه مِش حِلْو. *ma-taxdīš min il3ínab da. ṭá3mu miš ħilw.* Don't take any of these grapes. They're not sweet.

❖ [i3] **to take**

- This verb is used in many idiomatic expressions that may not translate as 'take'. (➲ 92.1, 92.2, 92.4, 92.5, 92.6, 92.8)
- The affirmative perfect forms have two variations, with or without an initial ا *a*.

➲ 27.6, 31.5, 48.2, 73.10, 75.7, 98.6, 102.1, 114.5, 141.4, 178.6, 201.5, 208.6, 216.1, 238.6, 240.1, 244.1

93 to serve xádam خدم

	affirmative		negative		
ána	xadámt	خَدَمْت	ma-xadámtiš	مَخَدَمْتِش	perfect
íḥna	xadámna	خَدَمْنا	ma-xadamnāš	مَخَدَمْناش	
ínta	xadámt	خَدَمْت	ma-xadámtiš	مَخَدَمْتِش	
ínti	xadámti	خَدَمْتي	ma-xadamtīš	مَخَدَمْتيش	
íntu	xadámtu	خَدَمْتوا	ma-xadamtūš	مَخَدَمْتوش	
húwwa	xádam	خَدَم	ma-xadámš	مَخَدَمْش	
híyya	xádamit	خَدَمِت	ma-xadamítš	مَخَدَمِتْش	
húmma	xádamu	خَدَموا	ma-xadamūš	مَخَدَموش	
ána	áxdim	أخْدِم	ma-xdímš	مَخْدِمْش	imperfect
íḥna	níxdim	نِخْدِم	ma-nixdímš	مَنِخْدِمْش	
ínta	tíxdim	تِخْدِم	ma-tixdímš	مَتِخْدِمْش	
ínti	tixdími	تِخْدِمي	ma-tixdimīš	مَتِخْدِميش	
íntu	tixdímu	تِخْدِموا	ma-tixdimūš	مَتِخْدِموش	
húwwa	yíxdim	يِخْدِم	ma-yixdímš	مَيِخْدِمْش	
híyya	tíxdim	تِخْدِم	ma-tixdímš	مَتِخْدِمْش	
húmma	yixdímu	يِخْدِموا	ma-yixdimūš	مَيِخْدِموش	
ána	báxdim	بَخْدِم	ma-baxdímš	مَبَخْدِمْش	bi-imperfect
íḥna	biníxdim	بِنِخْدِم	ma-bnixdímš	مَبْنِخْدِمْش	
ínta	bitíxdim	بِتِخْدِم	ma-btixdímš	مَبْتِخْدِمْش	
ínti	bitixdími	بِتِخْدِمي	ma-btixdimīš	مَبْتِخْدِميش	
íntu	bitixdímu	بِتِخْدِموا	ma-btixdimūš	مَبْتِخْدِموش	
húwwa	biyíxdim	بِيِخْدِم	ma-byixdímš	مَبْيِخْدِمْش	
híyya	bitíxdim	بِتِخْدِم	ma-btixdímš	مَبْتِخْدِمْش	
húmma	biyixdímu	بِيِخْدِموا	ma-byixdimūš	مَبْيِخْدِموش	
ána	háxdim	هَخْدِم	miš háxdim	مِش هَخْدِم	future
íḥna	haníxdim	هَنِخْدِم	miš haníxdim	مِش هَنِخْدِم	
ínta	hatíxdim	هَتِخْدِم	miš hatíxdim	مِش هَتِخْدِم	
ínti	hatixdími	هَتِخْدِمي	miš hatixdími	مِش هَتِخْدِمي	
íntu	hatixdímu	هَتِخْدِموا	miš hatixdímu	مِش هَتِخْدِموا	
húwwa	hayíxdim	هَيِخْدِم	miš hayíxdim	مِش هَيِخْدِم	
híyya	hatíxdim	هَتِخْدِم	miš hatíxdim	مِش هَتِخْدِم	
húmma	hayixdímu	هَيِخْدِموا	miš hayixdímu	مِش هَيِخْدِموا	
ínta	íxdim	اِخْدِم	ma-tixdímš	مَتِخْدِمْش	imperative
ínti	ixdími	اِخْدِمي	ma-tixdimīš	مَتِخْدِميش	
íntu	ixdímu	اِخْدِموا	ma-tixdimūš	مَتِخْدِموش	

	active		passive		
masculine	xādim	خادِم	maxdūm	مَخْدوم	participles
feminine	xádma	خادْمَة	maxdūma	مَخْدومَة	
plural	xadmīn	خادْمين	maxdumīn	مَخْدومين	

verbal noun: xídma خِدْمَة

①

أنا خدمْت في الوِزارة ٣٠ سنة.

ána xadámtᵊ fi -lwizāra talatīn sána.

I worked in this ministry [government department] for 30 years.

②

بحِبّ أخْدِم النّاس. بِيِدّي لْحَياتي معْنى.

baḫíbb áxdim innās. biyíddi l-ḫayāti má3na.

I like serving people. It gives my life purpose.

③

بِنْت خالْتي عنْدها واحْدة بْتِخْدِمْها . مِريحاها جِدّاً.

bintᵊ xálti 3andáha wáḫda btixdímha. miriḫāha gíddan.

My niece has a servant [lit. one who helps her]. She really makes her life easier.

④

روح الفُنْدُق اللي قُلْتِلك عليْه. هِناك هَيِخْدِموك خِدْمة ٥ نُجوم.

rūḫ ilfúndu? ílli ?ultílak 3alē. hināk hayixdimūk xídma xámas nugūm.

Go to the hotel I told you about. They will give you five-star service.

⑤

اِخْدِم أهْلك لمّا يِكْبروا زيّ ما طول عُمْرُهم بِيِخْدِموك.

íxdim áhlak lámma yikbáru, zayyᵊ ma ṭūl 3umrúhum biyixdimūk.

Serve your parents when they get old, just as they served you all their lives.

⑥

المطْعم ده مُحْترم. خادْمين الأكْل كْوَيِّس أوي.

ilmáṭ3am da muḫtáram. xadmīn il?áklᵊ kwáyyis áwi.

This a highly regarded restaurant. They serve very good food.

⑦

الرّاجِل ده بِتاع مصْلحْتُه. مبْيِخْدِمْش حدّ بْبلاش.

irrāgil dah bitā3 maṣláḫtu. ma-byixdímšᵊ ḫaddᵊ b-balāš.

This guy just thinks of himself. He doesn't help anyone for free.

❖ [1s2] **to serve; to work; to help**

94 to exit xárag خرج

	affirmative		negative		
ána	xarágt	خَرَجْت	ma-xarágtiš	مَخَرَجْتِش	perfect
íḥna	xarágna	خَرَجْنا	ma-xaragnāš	مَخَرَجْناش	
ínta	xarágt	خَرَجْت	ma-xarágtiš	مَخَرَجْتِش	
ínti	xarágti	خَرَجْتي	ma-xaragtīš	مَخَرَجْتيش	
íntu	xarágtu	خَرَجْتوا	ma-xaragtūš	مَخَرَجْتوش	
húwwa	xárag	خَرَج	ma-xarágš	مَخَرَجْش	
híyya	xáragit	خَرَجِت	ma-xaragítš	مَخَرَجِتْش	
húmma	xáragu	خَرَجوا	ma-xaragūš	مَخَرَجوش	

ána	áxrug	أخْرُج	ma-xrúgš	مَخْرُجْش	imperfect
íḥna	núxrug	نُخْرُج	ma-nuxrúgš	مَنُخْرُجْش	
ínta	túxrug	تُخْرُج	ma-tuxrúgš	مَتُخْرُجْش	
ínti	tuxrúgi	تُخْرُجي	ma-tuxrugīš	مَتُخْرُجيش	
íntu	tuxrúgu	تُخْرُجوا	ma-tuxrugūš	مَتُخْرُجوش	
húwwa	yúxrug	يُخْرُج	ma-yuxrúgš	مَيُخْرُجْش	
híyya	túxrug	تُخْرُج	ma-tuxrúgš	مَتُخْرُجْش	
húmma	yuxrúgu	يُخْرُجوا	ma-yuxrugūš	مَيُخْرُجوش	

ána	báxrug	بَخْرُج	ma-baxrúgš	مَبَخْرُجْش	bi-imperfect
íḥna	binúxrug	بِنُخْرُج	ma-bnuxrúgš	مَبْنُخْرُجْش	
ínta	bitúxrug	بِتُخْرُج	ma-btuxrúgš	مَبْتُخْرُجْش	
ínti	bituxrúgi	بِتُخْرُجي	ma-btuxrugīš	مَبْتُخْرُجيش	
íntu	bituxrúgu	بِتُخْرُجوا	ma-btuxrugūš	مَبْتُخْرُجوش	
húwwa	biyúxrug	بِيُخْرُج	ma-byuxrúgš	مَبْيُخْرُجْش	
híyya	bitúxrug	بِتُخْرُج	ma-btuxrúgš	مَبْتُخْرُجْش	
húmma	biyuxrúgu	بِيُخْرُجوا	ma-byuxrugūš	مَبْيُخْرُجوش	

ána	háxrug	هَخْرُج	miš háxrug	مِش هَخْرُج	future
íḥna	hanúxrug	هَنُخْرُج	miš hanúxrug	مِش هَنُخْرُج	
ínta	hatúxrug	هَتُخْرُج	miš hatúxrug	مِش هَتُخْرُج	
ínti	hatuxrúgi	هَتُخْرُجي	miš hatuxrúgi	مِش هَتُخْرُجي	
íntu	hatuxrúgu	هَتُخْرُجوا	miš hatuxrúgu	مِش هَتُخْرُجوا	
húwwa	hayúxrug	هَيُخْرُج	miš hayúxrug	مِش هَيُخْرُج	
híyya	hatúxrug	هَتُخْرُج	miš hatúxrug	مِش هَتُخْرُج	
húmma	hayuxrúgu	هَيُخْرُجوا	miš hayuxrúgu	مِش هَيُخْرُجوا	

ínta	úxrug	أُخْرُج	ma-tuxrúgš	مَتُخْرُجْش	imperative
ínti	uxrúgi	أُخْرُجي	ma-tuxrugīš	مَتُخْرُجيش	
íntu	uxrúgu	أُخْرُجوا	ma-tuxrugūš	مَتُخْرُجوش	

	active		passive		
masculine	xārig	خارِج	–	–	participles
feminine	xárga	خارْجَة	–	–	
plural	xargīn	خارْجين	–	–	

verbal noun: *xurūg* خُروج

①

خرجْت أنا و أصْحابي إمْبارِح خُروجة حِلْوَة.

xarágt ána w aṣḫābi imbāriḫ xurūga ḫílwa.

I went out yesterday on a nice
outing with my friends.

②

لمّا تُخْرُج ، متِنْساش مفاتيحك عشان أنا كمان خارْجة.

lámma túxrug, ma-tinsāš mafatīḫak 3ašān ána kamān xárga.

When you go out, don't forget your
keys, because I'm going out too.

③

مبْيُخْرُجوش طول الأُسْبوع و بْيِسْتنّوا الجُمْعة، باباهُم يِخرّجْهُم شُوَيّة.

ma-byuxrugūš ṭūl ilʔisbū3 wi byistánnu -lgúm3a, babāhum yixarrághum šuwáyya.

They don't go out all the week waiting for their
father to take them out at the weekend.

④

لَوْ متْتبعْتِش قَواعِد اللِّعْب، هتُخْرُج مِ الملْعب.

law ma-ttabá3tiš qawā3id illí3b, hatúxrug mi -lmál3ab.

If you don't follow the play rules,
you'll have to leave the playground.

⑤

أُخْرُجي و شوفي الدُّنْيا. بلاش قعْدِةْ البيْت على طول كِده.

uxrúgi w šūfi -ddúnya. balāš ʔá3dit ilbēt 3ála ṭūl kída.

Get out and see the world. Enough
with staying at home all the time.

⑥

و أنا خارِج دايْماً إبْني يِشْبط فِيّا و عايِزْني أخْدُه معايا.

w ána xārig dáyman íbni yíšbaṭ fíyya wi 3ayízni ʔáxdu ma3āya.

My son always clings onto me when I'm going
out. He wants me to take him with me.

❖ [1s3] **to exit, go out**

- This verb, like other verbs of the [1s3] and [1s6] patterns, can optionally take ـُ *u* instead of ـِ *i* in the personal prefixes of the imperfect (including the bi-imperfect and future) and imperative. For example, يُخْرُج *yúxrug* can also be pronounced يِخْرُج *yíxrug*. These vowels are interchangeable, but the tables reflect the preferences of the speakers on the MP3s.

➲ 40.1, 105.2, 130.4, 193.6, 197.1, 236.5, 258.1

95 to lose *xísir* خِسِر

	affirmative		negative		
ána	*xisírt*	خِسِرْت	*ma-xsírtiš*	مَخْسِرْتِش	**perfect**
íḫna	*xisírna*	خِسِرْنا	*ma-xsirnāš*	مَخْسِرْناش	
ínta	*xisírt*	خِسِرْت	*ma-xsírtiš*	مَخْسِرْتِش	
ínti	*xisírti*	خِسِرْتي	*ma-xsirtīš*	مَخْسِرْتيش	
íntu	*xisírtu*	خِسِرْتوا	*ma-xsirtūš*	مَخْسِرْتوش	
húwwa	*xísir*	خِسِر	*ma-xsírš*	مَخْسِرْش	
híyya	*xísrit*	خِسْرِت	*ma-xisrítš*	مَخِسْرِتْش	
húmma	*xísru*	خِسْروا	*ma-xisrūš*	مَخِسْروش	
ána	*áxsar*	أَخْسَر	*ma-xsárš*	مَخْسَرْش	**imperfect**
íḫna	*níxsar*	نِخْسَر	*ma-nixsárš*	مَنِخْسَرْش	
ínta	*tíxsar*	تِخْسَر	*ma-tixsárš*	مَتِخْسَرْش	
ínti	*tixsári*	تِخْسَري	*ma-tixsarīš*	مَتِخْسَريش	
íntu	*tixsáru*	تِخْسَروا	*ma-tixsarūš*	مَتِخْسَروش	
húwwa	*yíxsar*	يِخْسَر	*ma-yixsárš*	مَيِخْسَرْش	
híyya	*tíxsar*	تِخْسَر	*ma-tixsárš*	مَتِخْسَرْش	
húmma	*yixsáru*	يِخْسَروا	*ma-yixsarūš*	مَيِخْسَروش	
ána	*báxsar*	بَخْسَر	*ma-baxsárš*	مَبَخْسَرْش	**bi-imperfect**
íḫna	*biníxsar*	بِنِخْسَر	*ma-bnixsárš*	مَبْنِخْسَرْش	
ínta	*bitíxsar*	بِتِخْسَر	*ma-btixsárš*	مَبْتِخْسَرْش	
ínti	*bitixsári*	بِتِخْسَري	*ma-btixsarīš*	مَبْتِخْسَريش	
íntu	*bitixsáru*	بِتِخْسَروا	*ma-btixsarūš*	مَبْتِخْسَروش	
húwwa	*biyíxsar*	بِيِخْسَر	*ma-byixsárš*	مَبْيِخْسَرْش	
híyya	*bitíxsar*	بِتِخْسَر	*ma-btixsárš*	مَبْتِخْسَرْش	
húmma	*biyixsáru*	بِيِخْسَروا	*ma-byixsarūš*	مَبْيِخْسَروش	
ána	*háxsar*	هَخْسَر	*miš háxsar*	مِش هَخْسَر	**future**
íḫna	*haníxsar*	هَنِخْسَر	*miš haníxsar*	مِش هَنِخْسَر	
ínta	*hatíxsar*	هَتِخْسَر	*miš hatíxsar*	مِش هَتِخْسَر	
ínti	*hatixsári*	هَتِخْسَري	*miš hatixsári*	مِش هَتِخْسَري	
íntu	*hatixsáru*	هَتِخْسَروا	*miš hatixsáru*	مِش هَتِخْسَروا	
húwwa	*hayíxsar*	هَيِخْسَر	*miš hayíxsar*	مِش هَيِخْسَر	
híyya	*hatíxsar*	هَتِخْسَر	*miš hatíxsar*	مِش هَتِخْسَر	
húmma	*hayixsáru*	هَيِخْسَروا	*miš hayixsáru*	مِش هَيِخْسَروا	
ínta	*íxsar*	اِخْسَر	*ma-tixsárš*	مَتِخْسَرْش	**imperative**
ínti	*ixsári*	اِخْسَري	*ma-tixsarīš*	مَتِخْسَريش	
íntu	*ixsáru*	اِخْسَروا	*ma-tixsarūš*	مَتِخْسَروش	

	active		passive		
masculine	*xāsir / xasrān*	خاسِر / خَسْران	–	–	**participles**
feminine	*xásra / xasrāna*	خاسْرَة / خَسْرانَة	–	–	
plural	*xasrīn / xasrānīn*	خاسْرين / خَسْرانين	–	–	

verbal noun: *xusāra* خُسارَة

①

خِسِرْت كْتير لمّا مجيتْش معانا النّدْوَة. كانِت حاجة مُمْتِعة.

xisírtᵊ ktīr lámma ma-gítšᵊ ma3āna -nnádwa. kānit ḥāga mumtí3a.

You lost out big time when you didn't come with us to the seminar. It was exciting.

②

خايِف أدْخُل المشْروع ده، أخْسر فيه اللي وَرايا و اللي قُدّامي.

xāyif ádxul ilmašrū3 da, áxsar fī ílli warāya w ílli ʔuddāmi.

I'm afraid if I get into that project, that I'll lose everything [all my funds].

③

الدُّنْيا حرّ و الأكْل بيِخْسر برّه التّلاجة.

iddúnya ḥarrᵊ w ilʔáklᵊ biyíxsar bárra -ttalāga.

It's hot, and food spoils out of the fridge.

④

لَوْ مركِّزْتوش أوي الفترْة الجايّة، هنِخْسر المُسابْقة.

law ma-rakkiztūš ʔáwi -lfátra -lgáyya, haníxsar ilmusábʔa.

If you're not completely focused for a while, we're going to lose the competition.

⑤

اِخْسر وَزْنك الزّايِد بِالرِّياضة.

íxsar wáznak izzāyid bi-rriyāḍa.

Lose your extra weight by [playing] sports.

⑥

مخِسْروش وَلا ماتْش الموسِم ده.

ma-xisrūš wála matš ilmūsim da.

They haven't lost a single [soccer] match this season.

❖ [1s4] **to lose; to spoil**

➲ 195.2

96 to enter xašš خشّ ١س

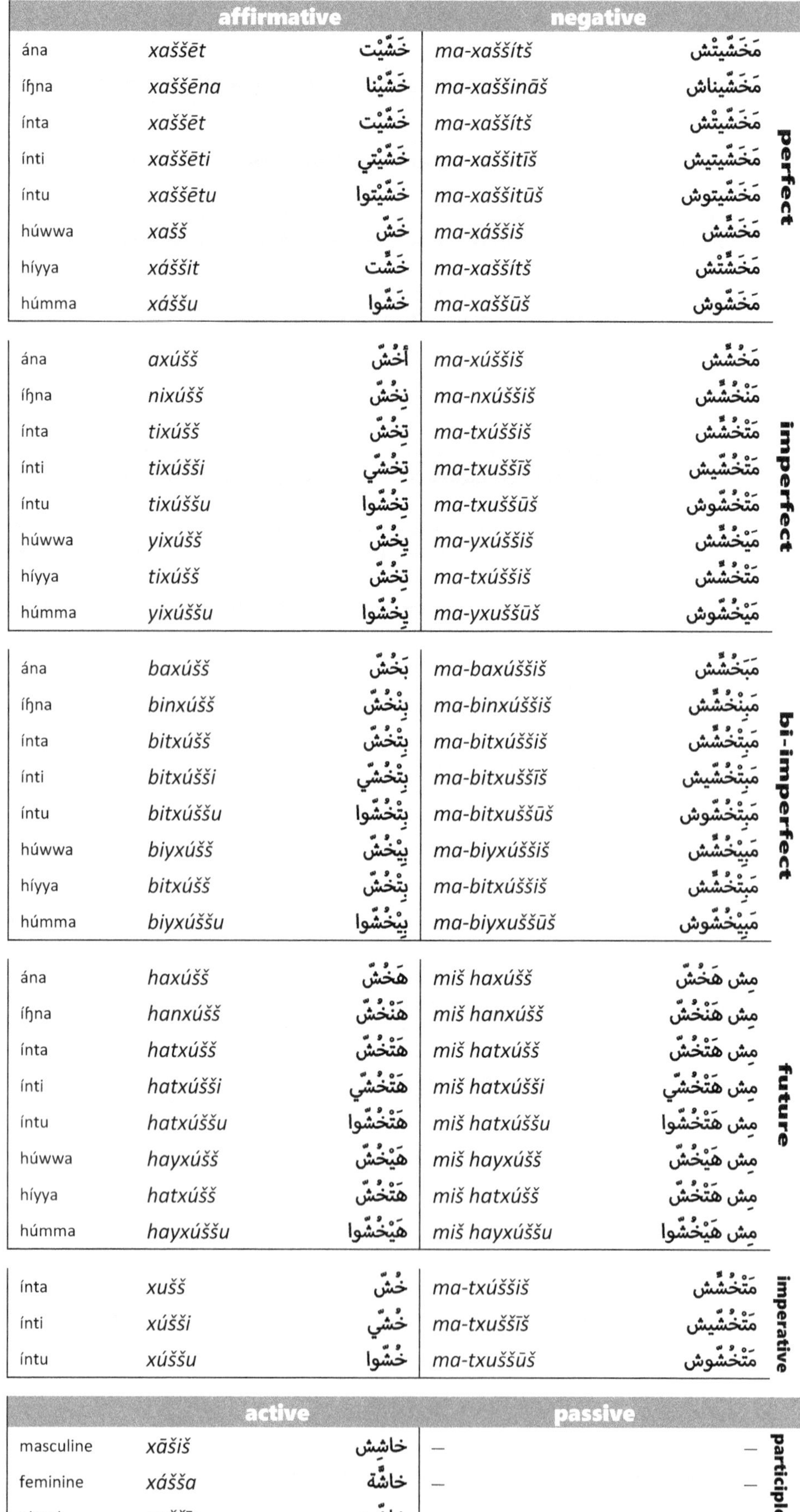

	affirmative		negative		
ána	xaššēt	خَشّيْت	ma-xaššítš	مَخَشّيْتْش	perfect
íḥna	xaššēna	خَشّيْنا	ma-xaššinā̆š	مَخَشّيناش	
ínta	xaššēt	خَشّيْت	ma-xaššítš	مَخَشّيْتْش	
ínti	xaššēti	خَشّيْتي	ma-xaššitīš	مَخَشّيتيش	
íntu	xaššētu	خَشّيْتوا	ma-xaššitūš	مَخَشّيتوش	
húwwa	xašš	خَشّ	ma-xáššiš	مَخَشّش	
híyya	xáššit	خَشّت	ma-xaššítš	مَخَشّتْش	
húmma	xáššu	خَشّوا	ma-xaššūš	مَخَشّوش	
ána	axúšš	أَخُشّ	ma-xúššiš	مَخُشّش	imperfect
íḥna	nixúšš	نِخُشّ	ma-nxúššiš	مَنْخُشّش	
ínta	tixúšš	تِخُشّ	ma-txúššiš	مَتْخُشّش	
ínti	tixúšši	تِخُشّي	ma-txuššīš	مَتْخُشّيش	
íntu	tixúššu	تِخُشّوا	ma-txuššūš	مَتْخُشّوش	
húwwa	yixúšš	يِخُشّ	ma-yxúššiš	مَيْخُشّش	
híyya	tixúšš	تِخُشّ	ma-txúššiš	مَتْخُشّش	
húmma	yixúššu	يِخُشّوا	ma-yxuššūš	مَيْخُشّوش	
ána	baxúšš	بَخُشّ	ma-baxúššiš	مَبَخُشّش	bi-imperfect
íḥna	binxúšš	بِنْخُشّ	ma-binxúššiš	مَبِنْخُشّش	
ínta	bitxúšš	بِتْخُشّ	ma-bitxúššiš	مَبِتْخُشّش	
ínti	bitxúšši	بِتْخُشّي	ma-bitxuššīš	مَبِتْخُشّيش	
íntu	bitxúššu	بِتْخُشّوا	ma-bitxuššūš	مَبِتْخُشّوش	
húwwa	biyxúšš	بِيْخُشّ	ma-biyxúššiš	مَبِيْخُشّش	
híyya	bitxúšš	بِتْخُشّ	ma-bitxúššiš	مَبِتْخُشّش	
húmma	biyxúššu	بِيْخُشّوا	ma-biyxuššūš	مَبِيْخُشّوش	
ána	haxúšš	هَخُشّ	miš haxúšš	مِش هَخُشّ	future
íḥna	hanxúšš	هَنْخُشّ	miš hanxúšš	مِش هَنْخُشّ	
ínta	hatxúšš	هَتْخُشّ	miš hatxúšš	مِش هَتْخُشّ	
ínti	hatxúšši	هَتْخُشّي	miš hatxúšši	مِش هَتْخُشّي	
íntu	hatxúššu	هَتْخُشّوا	miš hatxúššu	مِش هَتْخُشّوا	
húwwa	hayxúšš	هَيْخُشّ	miš hayxúšš	مِش هَيْخُشّ	
híyya	hatxúšš	هَتْخُشّ	miš hatxúšš	مِش هَتْخُشّ	
húmma	hayxúššu	هَيْخُشّوا	miš hayxúššu	مِش هَيْخُشّوا	
ínta	xušš	خُشّ	ma-txúššiš	مَتْخُشّش	imperative
ínti	xúšši	خُشّي	ma-txuššīš	مَتْخُشّيش	
íntu	xúššu	خُشّوا	ma-txuššūš	مَتْخُشّوش	

	active		passive		
masculine	xāšiš	خاشِش	—	—	participles
feminine	xášša	خاشّة	—	—	
plural	xaššīn	خاشّين	—	—	

verbal noun: xašš خشّ

①

مخشّيتيش تِلْبِسي لِحدّ دِلْوَقْتي. هنِتْأخّر عَ المعاد.

ma-xaššitīš tilbísi l-ḥádd^ə dilwáʔti. hanitʔáxxar 3a -lmi3ād.

You still haven't gotten dressed.
We're going to be late.

②

اِوْعى تْخُشّ المحلّ ده. أسْعارُه غالْيَة و حاجْتُه وِحْشة.

íw3a txúšš ilmaḥáll^ə da. as3āru ɣálya wi ḥágtu wíḥša.

Don't go to this shop. The prices
are high, and the stuff is ugly.

③

أحْلى حاجة فيك إنّك بِتْخُشّ في المَوْضوع على طول.

áḥla ḥāga fīk ínnak bitxúšš^ə fi -lmawḍū3 3ála ṭūl.

What I like about you [lit. the best thing about you]
is that you get straight to the point.

④

إنْتَ هتْخُشّ الاِمْتِحان وَلّا ناوي تْأجِّلُه؟

ínta hatxúšš ilʔimtiḥān wálla nāwi tʔaggílu?

Are you going to take the exam, or do
you intend to reschedule it?

⑤

خُشّ يا وَلد ذاكِر!

xušš^ə ya wálad zākir!

Go study, boy!

❖ [1g2] **to enter, go in**

97 to plan xáṭṭaṭ خطّط 13

	affirmative		negative		
ána	*xaṭṭáṭt*	خَطّطْت	*ma-xaṭṭáṭtiš*	مَخَطّطْتِش	perfect
íḥna	*xaṭṭáṭna*	خَطّطْنا	*ma-xaṭṭaṭnāš*	مَخَطّطْناش	
ínta	*xaṭṭáṭt*	خَطّطْت	*ma-xaṭṭáṭtiš*	مَخَطّطْتِش	
ínti	*xaṭṭáṭti*	خَطّطْتي	*ma-xaṭṭaṭtīš*	مَخَطّطْتيش	
íntu	*xaṭṭáṭtu*	خَطّطْتوا	*ma-xaṭṭaṭtūš*	مَخَطّطْتوش	
húwwa	*xáṭṭaṭ*	خَطّط	*ma-xaṭṭáṭš*	مَخَطّطْش	
híyya	*xaṭṭáṭit*	خَطّطِت	*ma-xaṭṭaṭítš*	مَخَطّطِتْش	
húmma	*xaṭṭáṭu*	خَطّطوا	*ma-xaṭṭaṭūš*	مَخَطّطوش	
ána	*axáṭṭaṭ*	أخَطّط	*ma-xaṭṭáṭš*	مَخَطّطْش	imperfect
íḥna	*nixáṭṭaṭ*	نِخَطّط	*ma-nxaṭṭáṭš*	مَنْخَطّطْش	
ínta	*tixáṭṭaṭ*	تِخَطّط	*ma-txaṭṭáṭš*	مَتْخَطّطْش	
ínti	*tixaṭṭáṭi*	تِخَطّطي	*ma-txaṭṭaṭīš*	مَتْخَطّطيش	
íntu	*tixaṭṭáṭu*	تِخَطّطوا	*ma-txaṭṭaṭūš*	مَتْخَطّطوش	
húwwa	*yixáṭṭaṭ*	يِخَطّط	*ma-yxaṭṭáṭš*	مَيْخَطّطْش	
híyya	*tixáṭṭaṭ*	تِخَطّط	*ma-txaṭṭáṭš*	مَتْخَطّطْش	
húmma	*yixaṭṭáṭu*	يِخَطّطوا	*ma-yxaṭṭaṭūš*	مَيْخَطّطوش	
ána	*baxáṭṭaṭ*	بَخَطّط	*ma-baxaṭṭáṭš*	مَبَخَطّطْش	bi-imperfect
íḥna	*binxáṭṭaṭ*	بِنْخَطّط	*ma-binxaṭṭáṭš*	مَبِنْخَطّطْش	
ínta	*bitxáṭṭaṭ*	بِتْخَطّط	*ma-bitxaṭṭáṭš*	مَبِتْخَطّطْش	
ínti	*bitxaṭṭáṭi*	بِتْخَطّطي	*ma-bitxaṭṭaṭīš*	مَبِتْخَطّطيش	
íntu	*bitxaṭṭáṭu*	بِتْخَطّطوا	*ma-bitxaṭṭaṭūš*	مَبِتْخَطّطوش	
húwwa	*biyxáṭṭaṭ*	بِيْخَطّط	*ma-biyxaṭṭáṭš*	مَبِيْخَطّطْش	
híyya	*bitxáṭṭaṭ*	بِتْخَطّط	*ma-bitxaṭṭáṭš*	مَبِتْخَطّطْش	
húmma	*biyxaṭṭáṭu*	بِيْخَطّطوا	*ma-biyxaṭṭaṭūš*	مَبِيْخَطّطوش	
ána	*haxáṭṭaṭ*	هَخَطّط	*miš haxáṭṭaṭ*	مِش هَخَطّط	future
íḥna	*hanxáṭṭaṭ*	هَنْخَطّط	*miš hanxáṭṭaṭ*	مِش هَنْخَطّط	
ínta	*hatxáṭṭaṭ*	هَتْخَطّط	*miš hatxáṭṭaṭ*	مِش هَتْخَطّط	
ínti	*hatxaṭṭáṭi*	هَتْخَطّطي	*miš hatxaṭṭáṭi*	مِش هَتْخَطّطي	
íntu	*hatxaṭṭáṭu*	هَتْخَطّطوا	*miš hatxaṭṭáṭu*	مِش هَتْخَطّطوا	
húwwa	*hayxáṭṭaṭ*	هَيْخَطّط	*miš hayxáṭṭaṭ*	مِش هَيْخَطّط	
híyya	*hatxáṭṭaṭ*	هَتْخَطّط	*miš hatxáṭṭaṭ*	مِش هَتْخَطّط	
húmma	*hayxaṭṭáṭu*	هَيْخَطّطوا	*miš hayxaṭṭáṭu*	مِش هَيْخَطّطوا	
ínta	*xáṭṭaṭ*	خَطّط	*ma-txaṭṭáṭš*	مَتْخَطّطْش	imperative
ínti	*xaṭṭáṭi*	خَطّطي	*ma-txaṭṭaṭīš*	مَتْخَطّطيش	
íntu	*xaṭṭáṭu*	خَطّطوا	*ma-txaṭṭaṭūš*	مَتْخَطّطوش	

	active		passive		
masculine	*mixáṭṭaṭ*	مِخَطّط	*mitxáṭṭaṭ*	مِتْخَطّط	participles
feminine	*mixaṭṭáṭa*	مِخَطّطة	*mitxaṭṭáṭa*	مِتْخَطّطة	
plural	*mixaṭṭaṭīn*	مِخَطّطين	*mitxaṭṭaṭīn*	مِتْخَطّطين	

verbal noun: *taxṭīṭ* تخْطيط

①

عِصام خطّط لِلرِّحْلة دي مِن سنتيْن. دايْماً بِيْخطّط لِقُدّام.

3iṣām xáṭṭaṭ li-rríḫla di min sanatēn. dáyman biyxáṭṭaṭ li-ʔuddām.

Essam made plans for this trip two
years ago. He always plans ahead.

②

كُلّ ما أحاوِل أخطّط لِمُسْتقْبلى، ألاقي الظُّروف بِتيجي عكْس خِططي.

kullᵊ m- aḫāwil axáṭṭaṭ li-mustaʔbáli, alāʔi -ẓẓurūf bitīgi 3aksᵊ xíṭaṭi.

Every time I try to plan for my future,
events interrupt my plans.

③

في الشِّرْكة القديمة كانوا مبِيْخطّطوش لِحاجة. عشان كِده الشِّرْكة فلِّسِت و قفلِت.

fi -ššírka -lʔadīma kānu ma-biyxaṭṭaṭūš li-ḫāga. 3ašān kída -ššírka fallísit wi ʔáfalit.

In the old company, they never planned for anything.
That's why it went bankrupt and closed.

④

هَيْخطّطوا المدينة الجِديدة بْشكْل دائِري و هَيْخلّلوا الخدمات في المركْز.

hayxaṭṭáṭu -lmadīna -lgidīda b-šáklᵊ daʔíri wi hayxallílu -lxadamāt fi -lmárkaz.

They'll plan the new city to be circular, with amenities
[banks, post offices, stores, etc.] in the center.

⑤

خطّطوا لْحَياتْكو بعْد الجَواز عشان تحدِّيّات الجَواز كِتيرة.

xaṭṭáṭu l-ḫayátku ba3d ilgawāz 3ašān taḫaddiyyāt ilgawāz kitīra.

Plan for your life after marriage, as the
challenges of marriage are many.

⑥

محْمود مِخطّط لِمُسْتقْبلُه المِهني بِدِقّة و مِش سايِب حاجة لِلصُّدْفة.

maḫmūd mixáṭṭaṭ li-mustaʔbálu -lmíhani bi-díqqa wi miš sāyib ḫāga li-ṣṣúdfa.

Mahmoud has planned for the future of his career
carefully, not leaving anything to chance.

❖ [2s2] **to plan; to draw lines**

98 to be finished xíliṣ خلص

	affirmative		negative		
ána	xilíṣt	خِلِصْت	ma-xlíṣtiš	مَخْلِصْتِش	perfect
íḫna	xilíṣna	خِلِصْنا	ma-xliṣnāš	مَخْلِصْناش	
ínta	xilíṣt	خِلِصْت	ma-xlíṣtiš	مَخْلِصْتِش	
ínti	xilíṣti	خِلِصْتي	ma-xliṣtīš	مَخْلِصْتيش	
íntu	xilíṣtu	خِلِصْتوا	ma-xliṣtūš	مَخْلِصْتوش	
húwwa	xíliṣ	خِلِص	ma-xlíṣš	مَخْلِصْش	
híyya	xílṣit	خِلْصِت	ma-xilṣítš	مَخِلْصِتْش	
húmma	xílṣu	خِلْصوا	ma-xilṣūš	مَخِلْصوش	
ána	áxlaṣ	أَخْلَص	ma-xláṣš	مَخْلَصْش	imperfect
íḫna	níxlaṣ	نِخْلَص	ma-nixláṣš	مَنِخْلَصْش	
ínta	tíxlaṣ	تِخْلَص	ma-tixláṣš	مَتِخْلَصْش	
ínti	tixláṣi	تِخْلَصي	ma-tixlaṣīš	مَتِخْلَصيش	
íntu	tixláṣu	تِخْلَصوا	ma-tixlaṣūš	مَتِخْلَصوش	
húwwa	yíxlaṣ	يِخْلَص	ma-yixláṣš	مَيِخْلَصْش	
híyya	tíxlaṣ	تِخْلَص	ma-tixláṣš	مَتِخْلَصْش	
húmma	yixláṣu	يِخْلَصوا	ma-yixlaṣūš	مَيِخْلَصوش	
ána	báxlaṣ	بَخْلَص	ma-baxláṣš	مَبَخْلَصْش	bi-imperfect
íḫna	biníxlaṣ	بِنِخْلَص	ma-bnixláṣš	مَبْنِخْلَصْش	
ínta	bitíxlaṣ	بِتِخْلَص	ma-btixláṣš	مَبْتِخْلَصْش	
ínti	bitixláṣi	بِتِخْلَصي	ma-btixlaṣīš	مَبْتِخْلَصيش	
íntu	bitixláṣu	بِتِخْلَصوا	ma-btixlaṣūš	مَبْتِخْلَصوش	
húwwa	biyíxlaṣ	بِيِخْلَص	ma-byixláṣš	مَبْيِخْلَصْش	
híyya	bitíxlaṣ	بِتِخْلَص	ma-btixláṣš	مَبْتِخْلَصْش	
húmma	biyixláṣu	بِيِخْلَصوا	ma-byixlaṣūš	مَبْيِخْلَصوش	
ána	háxlaṣ	هَخْلَص	miš háxlaṣ	مِش هَخْلَص	future
íḫna	haníxlaṣ	هَنِخْلَص	miš haníxlaṣ	مِش هَنِخْلَص	
ínta	hatíxlaṣ	هَتِخْلَص	miš hatíxlaṣ	مِش هَتِخْلَص	
ínti	hatixláṣi	هَتِخْلَصي	miš hatixláṣi	مِش هَتِخْلَصي	
íntu	hatixláṣu	هَتِخْلَصوا	miš hatixláṣu	مِش هَتِخْلَصوا	
húwwa	hayíxlaṣ	هَيِخْلَص	miš hayíxlaṣ	مِش هَيِخْلَص	
híyya	hatíxlaṣ	هَتِخْلَص	miš hatíxlaṣ	مِش هَتِخْلَص	
húmma	hayixláṣu	هَيِخْلَصوا	miš hayixláṣu	مِش هَيِخْلَصوا	
ínta	íxlaṣ	اِخْلَص	ma-tixláṣš	مَتِخْلَصْش	imperative
ínti	ixláṣi	اِخْلَصي	ma-tixlaṣīš	مَتِخْلَصيش	
íntu	ixláṣu	اِخْلَصوا	ma-tixlaṣūš	مَتِخْلَصوش	

	active		passive		
masculine	xāliṣ / xalṣān	خالِص / خَلْصان	–	–	participles
feminine	xálṣa / xalṣāna	خالْصَة / خَلْصانَة	–	–	
plural	xalṣīn / xalṣānīn	خالْصين / خَلْصانين	–		

verbal noun: خَلَصان xalaṣān

①

المُحاضْرة خِلْصِت و إحْنا برْضُه مِش فاهْمين حاجة.

ilmuḫáḍra xílṣit w íḫna bárḍu miš fahmīn ḫāga.

The lecture ended without us having understood anything.

②

لمّا يِخْلص الفيلْم المُمِلّ ده اِبْقى صحّيني.

lámma yíxlaṣ ilfílm ilmumíllᵊ da, íbʔa ṣaḫḫīni.

Wake me up when this boring movie ends.

③

مُش عارِف أعْمِل أيْه. المُذاكْرة مبْتِخْلصْش.

muš 3ārif á3mil ʔē. ilmuzákra ma-btixláṣš.

I don't know what to do. The studying never ends.

④

إحْنا مُش هَنِخْلَص مِ المَوْضوع ده بقى؟ أنا زِهِقْت.

íḫna muš haníxlaṣ mi -lmawḍū3 da báʔa? ána zihíʔt.

Aren't we going to put an end to this issue? I'm fed up.

⑤

صاحْبك ده غدّار. اِخْلص مِنُّه بْسُرْعة قبْل ما يِأْذيك.

ṣáḫbak da ɣaddār. íxlaṣ mínnu b-súr3a ʔablᵊ ma yiʔzīk.

That friend of yours is untrustworthy. Get rid of him fast before he hurts you.

⑥

أنا خلْصان مِ الحرّ. عايِز أخُد دُشّ و أنام.

ána xalṣān mi -lḫarr. 3āyiz āxud duššᵊ w anām.

I'm exhausted by the heat. I want to take a shower and go to bed.

❖ [1s4] **to finish, end; to put an end to** (مِن *min*)**; to get rid of** (مِن *min*)**; to be exhausted** (**by** مِن *min*)

➲ 13.3, 54.5, 56.1, 187.7

99 to finish xállaṣ خلّص 13

	affirmative		negative		
ána	xalláṣt	خَلّصْت	ma-xalláṣtiš	مَخَلّصْتِش	perfect
íḫna	xalláṣna	خَلّصْنا	ma-xallaṣnāš	مَخَلّصْناش	
ínta	xalláṣt	خَلّصْت	ma-xalláṣtiš	مَخَلّصْتِش	
ínti	xalláṣti	خَلّصْتي	ma-xallaṣtīš	مَخَلّصْتيش	
íntu	xalláṣtu	خَلّصْتوا	ma-xallaṣtūš	مَخَلّصْتوش	
húwwa	xállaṣ	خَلّص	ma-xalláṣš	مَخَلّصْش	
híyya	xalláṣit	خَلّصِت	ma-xallaṣítš	مَخَلّصِتْش	
húmma	xalláṣu	خَلّصوا	ma-xallaṣūš	مَخَلّصوش	
ána	axállaṣ	أخَلّص	ma-xalláṣš	مَخَلّصْش	imperfect
íḫna	nixállaṣ	نِخَلّص	ma-nxalláṣš	مَنْخَلّصْش	
ínta	tixállaṣ	تِخَلّص	ma-txalláṣš	مَتْخَلّصْش	
ínti	tixalláṣi	تِخَلّصي	ma-txallaṣīš	مَتْخَلّصيش	
íntu	tixalláṣu	تِخَلّصوا	ma-txallaṣūš	مَتْخَلّصوش	
húwwa	yixállaṣ	يِخَلّص	ma-yxalláṣš	مَيْخَلّصْش	
híyya	tixállaṣ	تِخَلّص	ma-txalláṣš	مَتْخَلّصْش	
húmma	yixalláṣu	يِخَلّصوا	ma-yxallaṣūš	مَيْخَلّصوش	
ána	baxállaṣ	بَخَلّص	ma-baxalláṣš	مَبَخَلّصْش	bi-imperfect
íḫna	binxállaṣ	بِنْخَلّص	ma-binxalláṣš	مَبِنْخَلّصْش	
ínta	bitxállaṣ	بِتْخَلّص	ma-bitxalláṣš	مَبِتْخَلّصْش	
ínti	bitxalláṣi	بِتْخَلّصي	ma-bitxallaṣīš	مَبِتْخَلّصيش	
íntu	bitxalláṣu	بِتْخَلّصوا	ma-bitxallaṣūš	مَبِتْخَلّصوش	
húwwa	biyxállaṣ	بِيْخَلّص	ma-biyxalláṣš	مَبِيْخَلّصْش	
híyya	bitxállaṣ	بِتْخَلّص	ma-bitxalláṣš	مَبِتْخَلّصْش	
húmma	biyxalláṣu	بِيْخَلّصوا	ma-biyxallaṣūš	مَبِيْخَلّصوش	
ána	haxállaṣ	هَخَلّص	miš haxállaṣ	مِش هَخَلّص	future
íḫna	hanxállaṣ	هَنْخَلّص	miš hanxállaṣ	مِش هَنْخَلّص	
ínta	hatxállaṣ	هَتْخَلّص	miš hatxállaṣ	مِش هَتْخَلّص	
ínti	hatxalláṣi	هَتْخَلّصي	miš hatxalláṣi	مِش هَتْخَلّصي	
íntu	hatxalláṣu	هَتْخَلّصوا	miš hatxalláṣu	مِش هَتْخَلّصوا	
húwwa	hayxállaṣ	هَيْخَلّص	miš hayxállaṣ	مِش هَيْخَلّص	
híyya	hatxállaṣ	هَتْخَلّص	miš hatxállaṣ	مِش هَتْخَلّص	
húmma	hayxalláṣu	هَيْخَلّصوا	miš hayxalláṣu	مِش هَيْخَلّصوا	
ínta	xállaṣ	خَلّص	ma-txalláṣš	مَتْخَلّصْش	imperative
ínti	xalláṣi	خَلّصي	ma-txallaṣīš	مَتْخَلّصيش	
íntu	xalláṣu	خَلّصوا	ma-txallaṣūš	مَتْخَلّصوش	

	active		passive		
masculine	mixállaṣ	مِخَلّص	mitxállaṣ	مِتْخَلّص	participles
feminine	mixalláṣa	مِخَلّصَة	mitxalláṣa	مِتْخَلّصَة	
plural	mixallaṣīn	مِخَلّصين	mitxallaṣīn	مِتْخَلّصين	

verbal noun: *taxlīṣ* تَخْليص

①

مكُنْتِش خلّصْت تنْضيف لمّا الضُّيوف خبطوا.

ma-kúntiš xalláṣtᵊ tanḍīf lámma -ḍḍuyūf xábaṭu.

I wasn't finished cleaning yet when the guests arrived [lit. knocked].

②

إبْني دايْماً بِيخلّص مصْروفُه على شِرا العربِيّات. بِيْحِبّها أوي.

íbni dáyman yixállaṣ maṣrūfu 3ála šíra -l3arabiyyāt. biyḫibbáha ʔáwi.

My son always spends all his money on buying cars. He really likes them.

③

مازِن بِيْخلّص شُغْل السّاعة ٥. هعدّي عليْه و نُخْرُج شُوَيّة.

māzin biyxállaṣ šuɣl issā3a xámsa. ha3áddi 3alē wi núxrug šuwáyya.

Mazen finishes work at five. I'll go by so we can go out for a bit.

④

طلّع اللي في جيْبك كُلُّه مِن سُكات وَ إلّا هخلّص عليْك!

ṭálla3 ílli fi gēbak kúllu min sukāt wa ʔílla haxállaṣ 3alēk!

Take everything out of your pockets, or I'll kill you!

⑤

متُسْكُتْش عَ اللي عملُه فيك. خلّص تارك مِنُّه.

ma-tuskútšᵊ 3a -lli 3ámalu fīk. xállaṣ tārak mínnu.

Don't let go of what he did to you. Get revenge on him.

⑥

أنا مْخلّص لِبْس أهُه و مِسْتنّيكي.

ána mxállaṣ libs áhu w mistannīki.

Okay, I've finished getting dressed now, and I'm waiting for you.

⑦

متْخلّصوش المحْشي. أنا لِسّه مكلْتِش.

ma-txallaṣūš ilmáḫši. ána líssa ma-káltiš.

Don't finish off the stuffed vegetables. I haven't had any yet.

❖ [2s2] **to finish; to use up, exhaust**

➲ 9.4, 31.4, 35.6, 40.5, 66.1, 75.3, 77.4, 104.3, 152.4, 172.4, 187.6, 195.3, 205.4, 228.2, 236.4, 239.4

100 to cause xálla خلّى ١٣

verbal noun: *taxliyya* تخلية

		affirmative		negative		
ána	*xallēt*	خلّيت	*ma-xallítš*	مخلّيتش	perfect
íḥna	*xallēna*	خلّينا	*ma-xallināš*	مخلّيناش	
ínta	*xallēt*	خلّيت	*ma-xallítš*	مخلّيتش	
ínti	*xallēti*	خلّيتي	*ma-xallitīš*	مخلّيتيش	
íntu	*xallētu*	خلّيتوا	*ma-xallitūš*	مخلّيتوش	
húwwa	*xálla*	خلّى	*ma-xallāš*	مخلّاش	
híyya	*xállit*	خلّت	*ma-xallítš*	مخلّتش	
húmma	*xállu*	خلّوا	*ma-xallūš*	مخلّوش	
ána	*axálli*	أخلّي	*ma-xallīš*	مخلّيش	imperfect
íḥna	*nixálli*	نخلّي	*ma-nxallīš*	منخلّيش	
ínta	*tixálli*	تخلّي	*ma-txallīš*	متخلّيش	
ínti	*tixálli*	تخلّي	*ma-txallīš*	متخلّيش	
íntu	*tixállu*	تخلّوا	*ma-txallūš*	متخلّوش	
húwwa	*yixálli*	يخلّي	*ma-yxallīš*	ميخلّيش	
híyya	*tixálli*	تخلّي	*ma-txallīš*	متخلّيش	
húmma	*yixállu*	يخلّوا	*ma-yxallūš*	ميخلّوش	
ána	*baxálli*	بخلّي	*ma-baxallīš*	مبخلّيش	bi-imperfect
íḥna	*binxálli*	بنخلّي	*ma-binxallīš*	مبنخلّيش	
ínta	*bitxálli*	بتخلّي	*ma-bitxallīš*	مبتخلّيش	
ínti	*bitxálli*	بتخلّي	*ma-bitxallīš*	مبتخلّيش	
íntu	*bitxállu*	بتخلّوا	*ma-bitxallūš*	مبتخلّوش	
húwwa	*biyxálli*	بيخلّي	*ma-biyxallīš*	مبيخلّيش	
híyya	*bitxálli*	بتخلّي	*ma-bitxallīš*	مبتخلّيش	
húmma	*biyxállu*	بيخلّوا	*ma-biyxallūš*	مبيخلّوش	
ána	*haxálli*	هخلّي	*miš haxálli*	مش هخلّي	future
íḥna	*hanxálli*	هنخلّي	*miš hanxálli*	مش هنخلّي	
ínta	*hatxálli*	هتخلّي	*miš hatxálli*	مش هتخلّي	
ínti	*hatxálli*	هتخلّي	*miš hatxálli*	مش هتخلّي	
íntu	*hatxállu*	هتخلّوا	*miš hatxállu*	مش هتخلّوا	
húwwa	*hayxálli*	هيخلّي	*miš hayxálli*	مش هيخلّي	
híyya	*hatxálli*	هتخلّي	*miš hatxálli*	مش هتخلّي	
húmma	*hayxállu*	هيخلّوا	*miš hayxállu*	مش هيخلّوا	
ínta	*xálli*	خلّي	*ma-txallīš*	متخلّيش	imperative
ínti	*xálli*	خلّي	*ma-txallīš*	متخلّيش	
íntu	*xállu*	خلّوا	*ma-txallūš*	متخلّوش	

		active		passive		
masculine	*mixálli*	مخلّي	–	–	participles
feminine	*mixallíyya*	مخلّية	–	–	
plural	*mixalliyīn*	مخلّيين	–	–	

①

إمْبارِح أحْمد خلّاني قاعِد بتْفرّج على فيلْم رُعْب و قام طافي النّور.

imbāriḥ áḥmad xallāni ʔā3id batfárrag 3āla filmᵊ ru3b, wi ʔām ṭāfi -nnūr.

Yesterday Ahmed found me watching a horror movie, so he went and turned off the lights on me!

②

بفضَّل أخلّي وِلادي يِلْعبوا بِدون قُيود. ده بِيْساعِدْهُم عَ الاِكْتِشاف.

bafáḍḍal axálli wilādi yil3ábu bidūn quyūd. da biysa3ídhum 3a -lʔiktišāf.

I prefer to let my kids play freely. It helps them explore.

③

عبْدُه بِيْخلّي بِنْتُه تْروح مُعسْكرات الجامْعة. هُوَّ بِيَثِق فيها.

3ábdu biyxálli bíntu trūḥ mu3askarāt ilgám3a. húwwa biyásiq fīha.

Abdo lets his daughter go on university camping trips. He trusts her.

④

هخلّيك تِروح الرِّحْلة لَوْ وَعدْتِني إنّك تِتْصرّف بِمسْئولية.

haxallīk tirūḥ irríḥla law wa3adtíni ínnak titṣárraf bi-masʔulíyya.

I'll let you go on the trip if you promise you'll behave responsibly.

⑤

خلّيك محْضر خيرْ. إحْنا بِنْحاوِل نِحِلّ المُشْكِلة.

xallīk máḥḍar xēr. íḥna binḥāwil niḥíll ilmuškíla.

Be a good witness. We are trying to solve this problem.

⑥

جوزْها مِش مِخلّيها مِحْتاجة حاجة.

gúzha miš mixallīha miḥtāga ḥāga.

Her husband doesn't leave her in need of anything.

⑦

خلّي بالك مِن الشُّنط. متْخلّيهُمْش يْغيبوا عن عيْنك لحْظة.

xálli bālak min iššúnaṭ. ma-txallīhumšᵊ yɣību 3an 3ēnak láḥẓa.

Pay attention to the luggage. Don't take your eyes off it.

⑧

خلّونا نِتْحرّك دِلْوَقْتي على طول. مُمْكِن نِلْحقْهُم.

xallūna nitḥárrak dilwáʔti 3ála ṭūl. múmkin nilḥáʔhum.

Let's get going right away. We may catch them in time.

⑨

اِتْفرّجْت مِن يوْميْن على فيلْم هِنْدي خلّاني أعيّط طول اللّيْل.

itfarrágtᵊ min yumēn 3ála filmᵊ híndi xallāni ʔa3áyyaṭ ṭūl illēl.

Two days ago, I watched an Indian movie that made me cry all night long.

❖ [2d] **to cause, make, let; to leave**

- This verb is usually followed by an object and then an imperfect verb or adjective.

➲ 1.6, 4.3, 13.3, 84.5, 86.2, 125.6, 137.2, 187.4, 193.2, 213.2, 214.2

101 to guess *xámmin* خمّن

verbal noun: *taxmīn* تخمين

perfect

	affirmative		negative	
ána	*xammínt*	خمّنت	*ma-xammíntiš*	مخمّنتش
íḥna	*xammínna*	خمّنّا	*ma-xamminnāš*	مخمّنّاش
ínta	*xammínt*	خمّنت	*ma-xammíntiš*	مخمّنتش
ínti	*xammínti*	خمّنتي	*ma-xammintīš*	مخمّنتيش
íntu	*xammíntu*	خمّنتوا	*ma-xammintūš*	مخمّنتوش
húwwa	*xámmin*	خمّن	*ma-xammínš*	مخمّنش
híyya	*xammínit*	خمّنت	*ma-xamminítš*	مخمّنتش
húmma	*xammínu*	خمّنوا	*ma-xamminūš*	مخمّنوش

imperfect

	affirmative		negative	
ána	*axámmin*	أخمّن	*ma-xammínš*	مخمّنش
íḥna	*nixámmin*	نخمّن	*ma-nxammínš*	منخمّنش
ínta	*tixámmin*	تخمّن	*ma-txammínš*	متخمّنش
ínti	*tixammíni*	تخمّني	*ma-txamminīš*	متخمّنيش
íntu	*tixammínu*	تخمّنوا	*ma-txamminūš*	متخمّنوش
húwwa	*yixámmin*	يخمّن	*ma-yxammínš*	ميخمّنش
híyya	*tixámmin*	تخمّن	*ma-txammínš*	متخمّنش
húmma	*yixammínu*	يخمّنوا	*ma-yxamminūš*	ميخمّنوش

bi-imperfect

	affirmative		negative	
ána	*baxámmin*	بخمّن	*ma-baxammínš*	مبخمّنش
íḥna	*binxámmin*	بنخمّن	*ma-binxammínš*	مبنخمّنش
ínta	*bitxámmin*	بتخمّن	*ma-bitxammínš*	مبتخمّنش
ínti	*bitxammíni*	بتخمّني	*ma-bitxamminīš*	مبتخمّنيش
íntu	*bitxammínu*	بتخمّنوا	*ma-bitxamminūš*	مبتخمّنوش
húwwa	*biyxámmin*	بيخمّن	*ma-biyxammínš*	مبيخمّنش
híyya	*bitxámmin*	بتخمّن	*ma-bitxammínš*	مبتخمّنش
húmma	*biyxammínu*	بيخمّنوا	*ma-biyxamminūš*	مبيخمّنوش

future

	affirmative		negative	
ána	*haxámmin*	هخمّن	*miš haxámmin*	مش هخمّن
íḥna	*hanxámmin*	هنخمّن	*miš hanxámmin*	مش هنخمّن
ínta	*hatxámmin*	هتخمّن	*miš hatxámmin*	مش هتخمّن
ínti	*hatxammíni*	هتخمّني	*miš hatxammíni*	مش هتخمّني
íntu	*hatxammínu*	هتخمّنوا	*miš hatxammínu*	مش هتخمّنوا
húwwa	*hayxámmin*	هيخمّن	*miš hayxámmin*	مش هيخمّن
híyya	*hatxámmin*	هتخمّن	*miš hatxámmin*	مش هتخمّن
húmma	*hayxammínu*	هيخمّنوا	*miš hayxammínu*	مش هيخمّنوا

imperative

	affirmative		negative	
ínta	*xámmin*	خمّن	*ma-txammínš*	متخمّنش
ínti	*xammíni*	خمّني	*ma-txamminīš*	متخمّنيش
íntu	*xammínu*	خمّنوا	*ma-txamminūš*	متخمّنوش

participles

	active		passive	
masculine	*mixámmin*	مخمّن	*mitxámmin*	متخمّن
feminine	*mixammína*	مخمّنة	*mitxammína*	متخمّنة
plural	*mixamminīn*	مخمّنين	*mitxamminīn*	متخمّنين

①

إمْبارِح كِسِبْت في مُسابْقة. خمِّنْت الأجابة و طِلْعِت صحّ.

imbāriḫ kisíbtᵊ fi musábʔa. xammínt ilʔagāba wi ṭíl3it ṣaḫḫ.

Yesterday I won a contest. I guessed the answer, and it was the right one.

②

نشْوى بِتْحِبّ الألْغاز البوليسية. و تُقْعُد تِخمِّن مين المُجْرِم.

nášwa bitḫíbb ilʔalɣāz ilbulisíyya. wi túʔ3ud tixámmin mīn ilmúgrim.

Nashwa likes detective mysteries, and she keeps guessing who the culprit is.

③

إنْتَ كُلّ ما بِتْخمِّن حاجة بِتِطْلع غلط. أرْجوك دوّر على المعْلومة و بطّل تخْمين.

ínta kullᵊ ma bitxámmin ḫāga bitíṭla3 ɣálaṭ. argūk, dáwwar 3ála -lma3lūma wi báṭṭal taxmīn.

Each time you guess something, it turns out to be wrong. Please search for the information and stop guessing.

④

إنْتو هتْخمِّنوا الأجابة الصّحيحة و ليكو جايْزة.

íntu hatxammínu -lʔagāba -ṣṣaḫīḫa wi līku gáyza.

You'll guess the right answer, and then you'll get the prize.

⑤

خمِّن مين جِهْ مِن السّفر إمْبارِح ؟ كوني و هاني جُم مِن سُويسْرا.

xámmin mīn gih min issáfar imbāriḫ ? kūni wi hāni gum min suwísra.

Guess who arrived yesterday! Conny and Hany came from Switzerland.

⑥

إنْتَ مخمِّنْتِش لِسّه مين اللي هَيْغنّي في الحفْلة بُكْره؟

ínta ma-xammíntiš líssa mīn ílli hayɣánni fi -lḫáfla búkra?

Haven't you guessed yet who's going to sing at the party tomorrow?

❖ [2s1] **to guess**

102 to defend *dāfi3* دافع

	affirmative		negative		
ána	*dafí3t*	دافِعْت	*ma-dafí3tiš*	مَدافِعْتِش	**perfect**
íḫna	*dafí3na*	دافِعْنا	*ma-dafi3nāš*	مَدافِعْناش	
ínta	*dafí3t*	دافِعْت	*ma-dafí3tiš*	مَدافِعْتِش	
ínti	*dafí3ti*	دافِعْتي	*ma-dafi3tīš*	مَدافِعْتيش	
íntu	*dafí3tu*	دافِعْتوا	*ma-dafi3tūš*	مَدافِعْتوش	
húwwa	*dāfi3*	دافع	*ma-dafí3š*	مَدافِعْش	
híyya	*dáf3it*	دافْعِت	*ma-daf3ítš*	مَدافْعِتْش	
húmma	*dáf3u*	دافْعوا	*ma-daf3ūš*	مَدافْعوش	
ána	*adāfi3*	أدافع	*ma-dafí3š*	مَدافِعْش	**imperfect**
íḫna	*nidāfi3*	نِدافع	*ma-ndafí3š*	مَنْدافِعْش	
ínta	*tidāfi3*	تِدافع	*ma-tdafí3š*	مَتْدافِعْش	
ínti	*tidáf3i*	تِدافْعي	*ma-tdaf3īš*	مَتْدافْعيش	
íntu	*tidáf3u*	تِدافْعوا	*ma-tdaf3ūš*	مَتْدافْعوش	
húwwa	*yidāfi3*	يِدافع	*ma-ydafí3š*	مَيْدافِعْش	
híyya	*tidāfi3*	تِدافع	*ma-tdafí3š*	مَتْدافِعْش	
húmma	*yidáf3u*	يِدافْعوا	*ma-ydaf3ūš*	مَيْدافْعوش	
ána	*badāfi3*	بَدافع	*ma-badafí3š*	مَبَدافِعْش	**bi-imperfect**
íḫna	*bindāfi3*	بِنْدافع	*ma-bindafí3š*	مَبِنْدافِعْش	
ínta	*bitdāfi3*	بِتْدافع	*ma-bitdafí3š*	مَبِتْدافِعْش	
ínti	*bitdáf3i*	بِتْدافْعي	*ma-bitdaf3īš*	مَبِتْدافْعيش	
íntu	*bitdáf3u*	بِتْدافْعوا	*ma-bitdaf3ūš*	مَبِتْدافْعوش	
húwwa	*biydāfi3*	بِيْدافع	*ma-biydafí3š*	مَبِيْدافِعْش	
híyya	*bitdāfi3*	بِتْدافع	*ma-bitdafí3š*	مَبِتْدافِعْش	
húmma	*biydáf3u*	بِيْدافْعوا	*ma-biydaf3ūš*	مَبِيْدافْعوش	
ána	*hadāfi3*	هَدافع	*miš hadāfi3*	مِش هَدافع	**future**
íḫna	*handāfi3*	هَنْدافع	*miš handāfi3*	مِش هَنْدافع	
ínta	*hatdāfi3*	هَتْدافع	*miš hatdāfi3*	مِش هَتْدافع	
ínti	*hatdáf3i*	هَتْدافْعي	*miš hatdáf3i*	مِش هَتْدافْعي	
íntu	*hatdáf3u*	هَتْدافْعوا	*miš hatdáf3u*	مِش هَتْدافْعوا	
húwwa	*haydāfi3*	هَيْدافع	*miš haydāfi3*	مِش هَيْدافع	
híyya	*hatdāfi3*	هَتْدافع	*miš hatdāfi3*	مِش هَتْدافع	
húmma	*haydáf3u*	هَيْدافْعوا	*miš haydáf3u*	مِش هَيْدافْعوا	
ínta	*dāfi3*	دافع	*ma-tdafí3š*	مَتْدافِعْش	**imperative**
ínti	*dáf3i*	دافْعي	*ma-tdaf3īš*	مَتْدافْعيش	
íntu	*dáf3u*	دافْعوا	*ma-tdaf3ūš*	مَتْدافْعوش	

	active		passive		
masculine	*midāfi3*	مِدافع	*mitdāfi3*	مِتْدافع	**participles**
feminine	*midáf3a*	مِدافْعَة	*mitdáf3a*	مِتْدافْعَة	
plural	*midaf3īn*	مِدافْعين	*mitdaf3īn*	مِتْدافْعين	

verbal noun: *difā3* دِفاع - *mudáf3a* مُدافْعَة

①

المُحامي مدافِعْش كْوَيِّس في القضية و المتّهم خد مُؤبّد.

ilmuɦāmi ma-dafíʕš kwáyyis fi -lʔaɖíyya w ilmuttáham xad muʔábbad.

The lawyer didn't put up a good defense during the trial, so the accused got a life sentence.

②

الرّاجِل ده مُهِمِّتُه يْدافِع عن الغلابة.

irrāgil da muhimmítu ydāfiʕ ʕan ilɣalāba.

This man's duty is to defend the poor.

③

لِلْاسف المُحامي ده مبْيِدافِعْش في قضايا سِياسية.

li-lʔásaf ilmuɦāmi da ma-byidafíʕš fi ʔaɖāya siyasíyya.

Unfortunately, this lawyer doesn't represent [lit. defend] in political cases.

④

رأْفت هَيْدافِع عن سلْمى لِحدّ آخِر لحْظة.

ráʔfat haydāfiʕ ʕan sálma li-ɦadd ʔāxir láɦʐa.

Raafat will defend Salma to the very end.

⑤

متْدافِعْش عنُّه و إنْتَ مُتأكِّد إنُّه غلْطان.

ma-tdafíʕš ʕánnu w ínta mutaʔákkid ínnu ɣalʈān.

Don't defend him when you know he's guilty.

⑥

أ: **إنْتَ هتِشْتِرك في تمْرينات كونْج فو؟**

ب: **أه، عايِز أعْرف أدافِع عن نفْسي في الخِناقات.**

A: *ínta hatištírik fi tamrināt kung fu?*

B: *ā, ʕāyiz áʕraf adāfiʕ ʕan náfsi fi -lxinaʔāt.*

A: Are you going to sign up for kung fu?

B: Yes, I want to be able to defend myself in fights.

❖ [3s] **to defend** (عن *ʕan*)

103 to enter dáxal دَخَل

verbal noun: duxūl دُخول

	affirmative		negative		
ána	daxált	دَخَلْت	ma-daxáltiš	مَدَخَلْتِش	perfect
íḫna	daxálna	دَخَلْنا	ma-daxalnāš	مَدَخَلْناش	
ínta	daxált	دَخَلْت	ma-daxáltiš	مَدَخَلْتِش	
ínti	daxálti	دَخَلْتي	ma-daxaltīš	مَدَخَلْتيش	
íntu	daxáltu	دَخَلْتوا	ma-daxaltūš	مَدَخَلْتوش	
húwwa	dáxal	دَخَل	ma-daxálš	مَدَخَلْش	
híyya	dáxalit	دَخَلِت	ma-daxalítš	مَدَخَلِتْش	
húmma	dáxalu	دَخَلْوا	ma-daxalūš	مَدَخَلْوش	
ána	ádxul	أَدْخُل	ma-dxúlš	مَدْخُلْش	imperfect
íḫna	nídxul	نِدْخُل	ma-nidxúlš	مَنِدْخُلْش	
ínta	tídxul	تِدْخُل	ma-tidxúlš	مَتِدْخُلْش	
ínti	tidxúli	تِدْخُلي	ma-tidxulīš	مَتِدْخُليش	
íntu	tidxúlu	تِدْخُلوا	ma-tidxulūš	مَتِدْخُلوش	
húwwa	yídxul	يِدْخُل	ma-yidxúlš	مَيِدْخُلْش	
híyya	tídxul	تِدْخُل	ma-tidxúlš	مَتِدْخُلْش	
húmma	yidxúlu	يِدْخُلوا	ma-yidxulūš	مَيِدْخُلوش	
ána	bádxul	بَدْخُل	ma-badxúlš	مَبَدْخُلْش	bi-imperfect
íḫna	binídxul	بِنِدْخُل	ma-bnidxúlš	مَبْنِدْخُلْش	
ínta	bitídxul	بِتِدْخُل	ma-btidxúlš	مَبْتِدْخُلْش	
ínti	bitidxúli	بِتِدْخُلي	ma-btidxulīš	مَبْتِدْخُليش	
íntu	bitidxúlu	بِتِدْخُلوا	ma-btidxulūš	مَبْتِدْخُلوش	
húwwa	biyídxul	بِيِدْخُل	ma-byidxúlš	مَبْيِدْخُلْش	
híyya	bitídxul	بِتِدْخُل	ma-btidxúlš	مَبْتِدْخُلْش	
húmma	biyidxúlu	بِيِدْخُلوا	ma-byidxulūš	مَبْيِدْخُلوش	
ána	hádxul	هَدْخُل	miš hádxul	مِش هَدْخُل	future
íḫna	hanídxul	هَنِدْخُل	miš hanídxul	مِش هَنِدْخُل	
ínta	hatídxul	هَتِدْخُل	miš hatídxul	مِش هَتِدْخُل	
ínti	hatidxúli	هَتِدْخُلي	miš hatidxúli	مِش هَتِدْخُلي	
íntu	hatidxúlu	هَتِدْخُلوا	miš hatidxúlu	مِش هَتِدْخُلوا	
húwwa	hayídxul	هَيِدْخُل	miš hayídxul	مِش هَيِدْخُل	
híyya	hatídxul	هَتِدْخُل	miš hatídxul	مِش هَتِدْخُل	
húmma	hayidxúlu	هَيِدْخُلوا	miš hayidxúlu	مِش هَيِدْخُلوا	
ínta	ídxul	اِدْخُل	ma-tidxúlš	مَتِدْخُلْش	imperative
ínti	idxúli	اِدْخُلي	ma-tidxulīš	مَتِدْخُليش	
íntu	idxúlu	اِدْخُلوا	ma-tidxulūš	مَتِدْخُلوش	

	active		passive		
masculine	dāxil	داخِل	madxūl	مَدْخول	participles
feminine	dáxla	داخْلَة	madxūla	مَدْخولَة	
plural	daxlīn	داخْلين	madxulīn	مَدْخولين	

①

دخلْنا الفيلْم ده قبْل كِده، بسّ مُمْكِن أدْخُلُه تاني عشر مرّات.

daxálna -lfilmᵊ da ʔablᵊ kída, bassᵊ múmkin adxúlu tāni 3ášar marrāt.

We've gone to this movie before, but I could go see it [lit. enter it] again ten times.

②

بصْحى بدْري عشان أدْخُل الحمّام أوِّل واحِد.

báṣḫa bádri 3ašān ádxul ilḫammām áwwil wāḫid.

I wake up early, so I can get into the bathroom first.

③

الشّابّ ده كُلّ مرّة بِيدْخُل المُحاضْرة مِتْأخّر و الدُّكْتور يِطْرُدُه.

iššábbᵊ da kullᵊ márra biyídxul ilmuḫáḍra mitʔáxxar w idduktūr yiṭrúdu.

This guy always comes to class late, and so the professor throws him out.

④

لمّا تِوْصل هتِدْخُل مِن تاني باب و تِسْأل على أُسْتاذ سمير.

lámma tíwṣal hatídxul min tāni bāb wi tísʔal 3ála ʔustāz samīr.

When you arrive, go through the second door and ask for Mr. Sameer.

⑤

اِدْخُل في المَوْضوع مِن غيرْ مُقدِّمات. أنا معنْديش وَقْت.

ídxul fi -lmawḍū3 min ɣēr muqaddimāt. ána ma-3andīš waʔt.

Get straight to the matter without the lead-ins. I don't have time.

⑥

و أنا داخِل الكافيْه اِتْكعْبِلْت في السِّلِّم و كُلّ اللي قاعْدين اِتْفرّجوا عليّا.

w ána dāxil ilkafēh itka3bíltᵊ fi -ssíllim wi kull ílli ʔa3dīn itfarrágu 3aláyya.

When entering the café, I tripped on the stairs, and everyone sitting there looked at me.

⑦

مدخلْناش النّدْوَة. مكانْش فيه مكان.

ma-daxalnāš innádwa. ma-kánšᵊ fī makān.

We didn't get into the seminar. There was no room.

❖ [1s3] **to enter, go in**

- This verb, like other verbs of the [1s3] and [1s6] patterns, can optionally take ـُ *u* instead of ـِ *i* in the personal prefixes of the imperfect (including the bi-imperfect and future) and imperative. For example, يِدْخُل *yídxul* can also be pronounced يُدْخُل *yúdxul.* These vowels are interchangeable, but the tables reflect the preferences of the speakers on the MP3s.

➲ 11.2, 20.2, 64.3, 70.3, 95.2, 103.6, 135.5, 141.2, 187.1, 195.5, 213.1, 214.1, 214.4, 215.4, 219.1, 221.2, 222.2, 224.2, 231.6, 236.2

104 to put in dáxxal دخّل ١ 13

	affirmative		negative		
ána	daxxált	دَخّلْت	ma-daxxáltiš	مَدَخّلْتِش	perfect
íḫna	daxxálna	دَخّلْنا	ma-daxxalnāš	مَدَخّلْناش	
ínta	daxxált	دَخّلْت	ma-daxxáltiš	مَدَخّلْتِش	
ínti	daxxálti	دَخّلْتي	ma-daxxaltīš	مَدَخّلْتيش	
íntu	daxxáltu	دَخّلْتوا	ma-daxxaltūš	مَدَخّلْتوش	
húwwa	dáxxal	دَخّل	ma-daxxálš	مَدَخّلْش	
híyya	daxxálit	دَخّلِت	ma-daxxalítš	مَدَخّلِتْش	
húmma	daxxálu	دَخّلوا	ma-daxxalūš	مَدَخّلوش	
ána	adáxxal	أدَخّل	ma-daxxálš	مَدَخّلْش	imperfect
íḫna	nidáxxal	نِدَخّل	ma-ndaxxálš	مَنْدَخّلْش	
ínta	tidáxxal	تِدَخّل	ma-tdaxxálš	مَتْدَخّلْش	
ínti	tidaxxáli	تِدَخّلي	ma-tdaxxalīš	مَتْدَخّليش	
íntu	tidaxxálu	تِدَخّلوا	ma-tdaxxalūš	مَتْدَخّلوش	
húwwa	yidáxxal	يِدَخّل	ma-ydaxxálš	مَيْدَخّلْش	
híyya	tidáxxal	تِدَخّل	ma-tdaxxálš	مَتْدَخّلْش	
húmma	yidaxxálu	يِدَخّلوا	ma-ydaxxalūš	مَيْدَخّلوش	
ána	badáxxal	بَدَخّل	ma-badaxxálš	مَبَدَخّلْش	bi-imperfect
íḫna	bindáxxal	بِنْدَخّل	ma-bindaxxálš	مَبِنْدَخّلْش	
ínta	bitdáxxal	بِتْدَخّل	ma-bitdaxxálš	مَبِتْدَخّلْش	
ínti	bitdaxxáli	بِتْدَخّلي	ma-bitdaxxalīš	مَبِتْدَخّليش	
íntu	bitdaxxálu	بِتْدَخّلوا	ma-bitdaxxalūš	مَبِتْدَخّلوش	
húwwa	biydáxxal	بِيْدَخّل	ma-biydaxxálš	مَبِيْدَخّلْش	
híyya	bitdáxxal	بِتْدَخّل	ma-bitdaxxálš	مَبِتْدَخّلْش	
húmma	biydaxxálu	بِيْدَخّلوا	ma-biydaxxalūš	مَبِيْدَخّلوش	
ána	hadáxxal	هَدَخّل	miš hadáxxal	مِش هَدَخّل	future
íḫna	handáxxal	هَنْدَخّل	miš handáxxal	مِش هَنْدَخّل	
ínta	hatdáxxal	هَتْدَخّل	miš hatdáxxal	مِش هَتْدَخّل	
ínti	hatdaxxáli	هَتْدَخّلي	miš hatdaxxáli	مِش هَتْدَخّلي	
íntu	hatdaxxálu	هَتْدَخّلوا	miš hatdaxxálu	مِش هَتْدَخّلوا	
húwwa	haydáxxal	هَيْدَخّل	miš haydáxxal	مِش هَيْدَخّل	
híyya	hatdáxxal	هَتْدَخّل	miš hatdáxxal	مِش هَتْدَخّل	
húmma	haydaxxálu	هَيْدَخّلوا	miš haydaxxálu	مِش هَيْدَخّلوا	
ínta	dáxxal	دَخّل	ma-tdaxxálš	مَتْدَخّلْش	imperative
ínti	daxxáli	دَخّلي	ma-tdaxxalīš	مَتْدَخّليش	
íntu	daxxálu	دَخّلوا	ma-tdaxxalūš	مَتْدَخّلوش	

	active		passive		
masculine	midáxxal	مِدَخّل	mitdáxxal	مِتْدَخّل	participles
feminine	midaxxála	مِدَخّلَة	mitdaxxála	مِتْدَخّلَة	
plural	midaxxalīn	مِدَخّلين	mitdaxxalīn	مِتْدَخّلين	

verbal noun: tadxīl تَدْخيل

①

الوَلد الصُّغيرّ دخّل إيدُه في عيْني و أنا بلاعْبُه.

ilwálad iṣṣuɣáyyar dáxxal īdu f 3ēni w ána balá3bu.

The little boy put his hand in my eye
while I was playing with him.

②

في الحضانة بِنْفضّل نِدخّل الأوْلاد مِن الجِنينة وَقْت الضُّهْر.

fi -lħaḍāna binfáḍḍal nidáxxal ilʔaulād min ilginīna waʔt iḍḍúhr.

At the preschool, we prefer to bring the kids in at noon.

③

بِيْدخّل البَيانات مِن إمْبارِح، و لِسّه مخلّصْش.

biydáxxal ilbayanāt min imbāriħ, wi líssa ma-xalláṣš.

He's been entering data since yesterday,
and he still hasn't finished.

④

مِش هَيْدخّلوكو الأوبْرا بِاللِّبْس ده أكيد.

miš haydaxxalūku -lʔúbra bi-llíbsᵊ da ʔakīd.

Of course, they won't let you in the
opera house in those outfits.

⑤

دخّل إيدك مِن الشِّبّاك عشان متِتْعوّرْش.

dáxxal īdak min iššibbāk 3ašān ma-tit3awwárš.

Bring your hand in from the [car]
window, so you don't get hurt.

⑥

أوِّل ما المطرة أبْتدِت، قُمْت مْدخّلة الغسيل مِن برّه بِسُرْعة.

áwwil ma -lmáṭara -btádit, ʔumtᵊ mdaxxála -lɣasīl min bárra bi-súr3a.

When it started to rain, I quickly went
to get the laundry from outside.

❖ [2s2] **to put in, insert; to cause to enter, take in, bring in**

➲ 118.4

105 to smoke dáxxan دَخَّن 1 13

verbal noun: tadxīn تدخين

	affirmative		negative		
ána	daxxánt	دَخَّنْت	ma-daxxántiš	مَدَخَّنْتِش	perfect
íḥna	daxxánna	دَخَّنّا	ma-daxxannāš	مَدَخَّنّاش	
ínta	daxxánt	دَخَّنْت	ma-daxxántiš	مَدَخَّنْتِش	
ínti	daxxánti	دَخَّنْتي	ma-daxxantīš	مَدَخَّنْتيش	
íntu	daxxántu	دَخَّنْتوا	ma-daxxantūš	مَدَخَّنْتوش	
húwwa	dáxxan	دَخَّن	ma-daxxánš	مَدَخَّنْش	
híyya	daxxánit	دَخَّنِت	ma-daxxanítš	مَدَخَّنِتْش	
húmma	daxxánu	دَخَّنوا	ma-daxxanūš	مَدَخَّنوش	
ána	adáxxan	أدَخَّن	ma-daxxánš	مَدَخَّنْش	imperfect
íḥna	nidáxxan	نِدَخَّن	ma-ndaxxánš	مَنْدَخَّنْش	
ínta	tidáxxan	تدَخَّن	ma-tdaxxánš	مَتْدَخَّنْش	
ínti	tidaxxáni	تدَخَّني	ma-tdaxxanīš	مَتْدَخَّنيش	
íntu	tidaxxánu	تدَخَّنوا	ma-tdaxxanūš	مَتْدَخَّنوش	
húwwa	yidáxxan	يِدَخَّن	ma-ydaxxánš	مَيْدَخَّنْش	
híyya	tidáxxan	تدَخَّن	ma-tdaxxánš	مَتْدَخَّنْش	
húmma	yidaxxánu	يِدَخَّنوا	ma-ydaxxanūš	مَيْدَخَّنوش	
ána	badáxxan	بَدَخَّن	ma-badaxxánš	مَبَدَخَّنْش	bi-imperfect
íḥna	bindáxxan	بِنْدَخَّن	ma-bindaxxánš	مَبِنْدَخَّنْش	
ínta	bitdáxxan	بِتْدَخَّن	ma-bitdaxxánš	مَبِتْدَخَّنْش	
ínti	bitdaxxáni	بِتْدَخَّني	ma-bitdaxxanīš	مَبِتْدَخَّنيش	
íntu	bitdaxxánu	بِتْدَخَّنوا	ma-bitdaxxanūš	مَبِتْدَخَّنوش	
húwwa	biydáxxan	بِيْدَخَّن	ma-biydaxxánš	مَبِيْدَخَّنْش	
híyya	bitdáxxan	بِتْدَخَّن	ma-bitdaxxánš	مَبِتْدَخَّنْش	
húmma	biydaxxánu	بِيْدَخَّنوا	ma-biydaxxanūš	مَبِيْدَخَّنوش	
ána	hadáxxan	هَدَخَّن	miš hadáxxan	مِش هَدَخَّن	future
íḥna	handáxxan	هَنْدَخَّن	miš handáxxan	مِش هَنْدَخَّن	
ínta	hatdáxxan	هَتْدَخَّن	miš hatdáxxan	مِش هَتْدَخَّن	
ínti	hatdaxxáni	هَتْدَخَّني	miš hatdaxxáni	مِش هَتْدَخَّني	
íntu	hatdaxxánu	هَتْدَخَّنوا	miš hatdaxxánu	مِش هَتْدَخَّنوا	
húwwa	haydáxxan	هَيْدَخَّن	miš haydáxxan	مِش هَيْدَخَّن	
híyya	hatdáxxan	هَتْدَخَّن	miš hatdáxxan	مِش هَتْدَخَّن	
húmma	haydaxxánu	هَيْدَخَّنوا	miš haydaxxánu	مِش هَيْدَخَّنوا	
ínta	dáxxan	دَخَّن	ma-tdaxxánš	مَتْدَخَّنْش	imperative
ínti	daxxáni	دَخَّني	ma-tdaxxanīš	مَتْدَخَّنيش	
íntu	daxxánu	دَخَّنوا	ma-tdaxxanūš	مَتْدَخَّنوش	

	active		passive		
masculine	midáxxan	مِدَخَّن	mitdáxxan	مِتْدَخَّن	participles
feminine	midaxxána	مِدَخَّنَة	mitdaxxána	مِتْدَخَّنَة	
plural	midaxxanīn	مِدَخَّنين	mitdaxxanīn	مِتْدَخَّنين	

①

دخّنْت مِن و أنا عنْدي عشر سِنين.

daxxánt^ə min w ána 3ándi 3ášar sinīn.

I started smoking at the age of ten.

②

لمّا تْعوز تِدخّن أُخْرُج برّه عشان هِنا ممْنوع التّدْخين.

lámma t3ūz tidáxxan úxrug bárra 3ašān hína mamnū3 ittadxīn.

If you want to smoke, go outside.
There's no smoking allowed here.

③

أنا بدخّن في قعْدِةْ الصُّحاب بسّ، مِش على طول.

ána badáxxan fi ʔá3dit iṣṣuḫāb bass, miš 3ála ṭūl.

I just smoke when I get together
with friends, not all the time.

④

عُمْري ما هدخّن . التّدْخين كان السّبب في موْت أبويا.

3úmri ma hadáxxan. ittadxīn kān issábab fi mōt abūya.

I'll never smoke. Smoking is what killed my father.

⑤

متْدخّنْش مهْما أصْحابك زنّوا عليْك. هُمّا مِش هَيِنْقِذوك لمّا صِحِّتك تِضيع.

ma-tdaxxánš^ə máhma ʔaṣḫābak zánnu 3alēk. húmma miš hayinʔizūk lámma ṣiḫḫítak tiḍī3.

Don't smoke no matter how much your friends pressure you.
They won't save you when your health goes.

❖ [2s2] **to smoke**

➲ 58.1, 264.1

106 to chat dárdiš دَرْدِش

verbal noun: dardáša دَرْدَشَة

perfect

	affirmative		negative	
ána	dardíšt	دَرْدِشْت	ma-dardíštiš	مَدَرْدِشْتِش
íḫna	dardíšna	دَرْدِشْنا	ma-dardišnāš	مَدَرْدِشْناش
ínta	dardíšt	دَرْدِشْت	ma-dardíštiš	مَدَرْدِشْتِش
ínti	dardíšti	دَرْدِشْتي	ma-dardištīš	مَدَرْدِشْتيش
íntu	dardíštu	دَرْدِشْتوا	ma-dardištūš	مَدَرْدِشْتوش
húwwa	dárdiš	دَرْدِش	ma-dardíšš	مَدَرْدِشّ
híyya	dardíšit	دَرْدِشِت	ma-dardišítš	مَدَرْدِشِتْش
húmma	dardíšu	دَرْدِشوا	ma-dardišūš	مَدَرْدِشوش

imperfect

	affirmative		negative	
ána	adárdiš	أدَرْدِش	ma-dardíšš	مَدَرْدِشّ
íḫna	nidárdiš	نِدَرْدِش	ma-ndardíšš	مَنْدَرْدِشّ
ínta	tidárdiš	تِدَرْدِش	ma-tdardíšš	مَتْدَرْدِشّ
ínti	tidardíši	تِدَرْدِشي	ma-tdardišīš	مَتْدَرْدِشيش
íntu	tidardíšu	تِدَرْدِشوا	ma-tdardišūš	مَتْدَرْدِشوش
húwwa	yidárdiš	يِدَرْدِش	ma-ydardíšš	مَيْدَرْدِشّ
híyya	tidárdiš	تِدَرْدِش	ma-tdardíšš	مَتْدَرْدِشّ
húmma	yidardíšu	يِدَرْدِشوا	ma-ydardišūš	مَيْدَرْدِشوش

bi-imperfect

	affirmative		negative	
ána	badárdiš	بَدَرْدِش	ma-badardíšš	مَبَدَرْدِشّ
íḫna	bindárdiš	بِنْدَرْدِش	ma-bindardíšš	مَبِنْدَرْدِشّ
ínta	bitdárdiš	بِتْدَرْدِش	ma-bitdardíšš	مَبِتْدَرْدِشّ
ínti	bitdardíši	بِتْدَرْدِشي	ma-bitdardišīš	مَبِتْدَرْدِشيش
íntu	bitdardíšu	بِتْدَرْدِشوا	ma-bitdardišūš	مَبِتْدَرْدِشوش
húwwa	biydárdiš	بِيْدَرْدِش	ma-biydardíšš	مَبِيْدَرْدِشّ
híyya	bitdárdiš	بِتْدَرْدِش	ma-bitdardíšš	مَبِتْدَرْدِشّ
húmma	biydardíšu	بِيْدَرْدِشوا	ma-biydardišūš	مَبِيْدَرْدِشوش

future

	affirmative		negative	
ána	hadárdiš	هَدَرْدِش	miš hadárdiš	مِش هَدَرْدِش
íḫna	handárdiš	هَنْدَرْدِش	miš handárdiš	مِش هَنْدَرْدِش
ínta	hatdárdiš	هَتْدَرْدِش	miš hatdárdiš	مِش هَتْدَرْدِش
ínti	hatdardíši	هَتْدَرْدِشي	miš hatdardíši	مِش هَتْدَرْدِشي
íntu	hatdardíšu	هَتْدَرْدِشوا	miš hatdardíšu	مِش هَتْدَرْدِشوا
húwwa	haydárdiš	هَيْدَرْدِش	miš haydárdiš	مِش هَيْدَرْدِش
híyya	hatdárdiš	هَتْدَرْدِش	miš hatdárdiš	مِش هَتْدَرْدِش
húmma	haydardíšu	هَيْدَرْدِشوا	miš haydardíšu	مِش هَيْدَرْدِشوا

imperative

	affirmative		negative	
ínta	dárdiš	دَرْدِش	ma-tdardíšš	مَتْدَرْدِشّ
ínti	dardíši	دَرْدِشي	ma-tdardišīš	مَتْدَرْدِشيش
íntu	dardíšu	دَرْدِشوا	ma-tdardišūš	مَتْدَرْدِشوش

participles

	active		passive	
masculine	midárdiš	مِدَرْدِش	mitdárdiš	مِتْدَرْدِش
feminine	midardíša	مِدَرْدِشَة	mitdardíša	مِتْدَرْدِشَة
plural	midardišīn	مِدَرْدِشين	mitdardišīn	مِتْدَرْدِشين

①

أنا و صاحْباتي اتْجمّعْنا أخيراً و درْدِشْنا كْتير أوي.

ána wi ṣaḫbāti -tgammá3na ʔaxīran wi dardíšna ktīr áwi.

My friends and I finally got together and chatted a lot.

②

اِتْعرّفْت إمْبارِح على بِنْت حِلْوَة و قعدْنا نْدرْدِش لِلصُّبْح.

it3arráft imbāriḫ 3ála bintᵊ ḫílwa wi ʔa3ádna ndárdiš li-ṣṣubḫ.

Yesterday I met a beautiful girl, and we chatted the night away.

③

سلْمى بِتْدرْدِش معَ أيّ حدّ بِسْهولة شْديدة. عنْدها كارِزْما.

sálma bitdárdiš má3a ʔayyᵊ ḫaddᵊ bi-shūla šdīda. 3andáha karízma.

Salma chats with anyone easily. She's charismatic [lit. has charisma].

④

لمّا مُعاذ يِصْحى هدرْدِش معاه في المَوْضوع ده.

lámma mu3āz yíṣḫa hadárdiš ma3ā fi -lmawḍū3 da.

When Moaaz wakes up, I'll chat with him about that issue.

⑤

نصيحْتي لِايّ زوجيْن: درْدِشوا معَ بعْض في مَواضيع ظريفة، مِش بسّ مشاكِل الحَياة.

naṣíḫti li-ayyᵊ zugēn: dardíšu má3a ba3ḍᵊ fi mawaḍī3 ẓarīfa, muš bassᵊ mašākil ilḫayāʔ.

My advice for married couples: Chat about nice topics, not just the problems of life.

⑥

أيْه الصّدْفة دي! إحْنا لِسّه مِدرْدِشين في المَوْضوع ده الصُّبْح.

ʔē -ṣṣúdfa di! íḫna líssa midardišīn fi -lmawḍū3 da -ṣṣúbḫ.

What a coincidence! We were just chatting about that this morning.

⑦

شوف قعدْنا قدّ أيْه و برْضُه مدرْدِشْناش كِفايَة.

šūf ʔa3ádna ʔaddᵊ ʔē wi bárḍu ma-dardišnāš kifāya.

Look how long we stayed, but we didn't finish chatting yet.

❖ [11s1] **to chat, talk**

107 to study dáras دَرَس

	affirmative		negative		
ána	darást	دَرَسْت	ma-darástiš	مَدَرَسْتِش	perfect
íḩna	darásna	دَرَسْنا	ma-darasnāš	مَدَرَسْناش	
ínta	darást	دَرَسْت	ma-darástiš	مَدَرَسْتِش	
ínti	darásti	دَرَسْتي	ma-darastīš	مَدَرَسْتيش	
íntu	darástu	دَرَسْتوا	ma-darastūš	مَدَرَسْتوش	
húwwa	dáras	دَرَس	ma-daráss̆	مَدَرَسْش	
híyya	dárasit	دَرَسِت	ma-darasítš	مَدَرَسِتْش	
húmma	dárasu	دَرَسوا	ma-darasūš	مَدَرَسوش	
ána	ádris	أدْرِس	ma-dríss̆	مَدْرِسْش	imperfect
íḩna	nídris	نِدْرِس	ma-nidríss̆	مَنِدْرِسْش	
ínta	tídris	تِدْرِس	ma-tidríss̆	مَتِدْرِسْش	
ínti	tidrísi	تِدْرِسي	ma-tidrisīš	مَتِدْرِسيش	
íntu	tidrísu	تِدْرِسوا	ma-tidrisūš	مَتِدْرِسوش	
húwwa	yídris	يِدْرِس	ma-yidríss̆	مَيِدْرِسْش	
híyya	tídris	تِدْرِس	ma-tidríss̆	مَتِدْرِسْش	
húmma	yidrísu	يِدْرِسوا	ma-yidrisūš	مَيِدْرِسوش	
ána	bádris	بَدْرِس	ma-badríss̆	مَبَدْرِسْش	bi-imperfect
íḩna	binídris	بِنِدْرِس	ma-bnidríss̆	مَبْنِدْرِسْش	
ínta	bitídris	بِتِدْرِس	ma-btidríss̆	مَبْتِدْرِسْش	
ínti	bitidrísi	بِتِدْرِسي	ma-btidrisīš	مَبْتِدْرِسيش	
íntu	bitidrísu	بِتِدْرِسوا	ma-btidrisūš	مَبْتِدْرِسوش	
húwwa	biyídris	بِيِدْرِس	ma-byidríss̆	مَبْيِدْرِسْش	
híyya	bitídris	بِتِدْرِس	ma-btidríss̆	مَبْتِدْرِسْش	
húmma	biyidrísu	بِيِدْرِسوا	ma-byidrisūš	مَبْيِدْرِسوش	
ána	hádris	هَدْرِس	miš hádris	مِش هَدْرِس	future
íḩna	hanídris	هَنِدْرِس	miš hanídris	مِش هَنِدْرِس	
ínta	hatídris	هَتِدْرِس	miš hatídris	مِش هَتِدْرِس	
ínti	hatidrísi	هَتِدْرِسي	miš hatidrísi	مِش هَتِدْرِسي	
íntu	hatidrísu	هَتِدْرِسوا	miš hatidrísu	مِش هَتِدْرِسوا	
húwwa	hayídris	هَيِدْرِس	miš hayídris	مِش هَيِدْرِس	
híyya	hatídris	هَتِدْرِس	miš hatídris	مِش هَتِدْرِس	
húmma	hayidrísu	هَيِدْرِسوا	miš hayidrísu	مِش هَيِدْرِسوا	
ínta	ídris	اِدْرِس	ma-tidríss̆	مَتِدْرِسْش	imperative
ínti	idrísi	اِدْرِسي	ma-tidrisīš	مَتِدْرِسيش	
íntu	idrísu	اِدْرِسوا	ma-tidrisūš	مَتِدْرِسوش	

	active		passive		
masculine	dāris	دارِس	madrūs	مَدْروس	participles
feminine	dársa	دارْسَة	madrūsa	مَدْروسَة	
plural	darsīn	دارْسين	madrusīn	مَدْروسين	

verbal nouns: *dirāsa* دِراسَة - *dars* دَرْس

①

فاطْمة درسِت هنْدسة في جامْعِةْ القاهِرة.

fáṭma dárasit handása fi gám3it ilqāhíra.

Fatma studied engineering
at Cairo University.

②

نِفْسي أدْرِس في مجال الترّْبية.

nífsi ʔádris fi magāl ittarbíyya.

I want to study in the
field of education.

③

الوِلاد بيِدْرِسوا معانا بْطريقة تفاعُلية بْتِعْجِبْهُم أوي.

ilwilād biyidrísu ma3āna b-ṭarīʔa tafa3ulíyya bti3gíbhum áwi.

Children learn with us in an interactive
way, which they like a lot.

④

هدْرِس فرنْساوي عشان عايِز أسافِر باريس في الأجازة.

hádris faransāwi 3ašān 3āyiz asāfir parīs fi -lʔagāza.

I'm going to study French because I want
to travel to Paris during the vacation.

⑤

إدْرِسوا في المجال اللي بِتْحِبّوة عشان تِقْدروا تِبْدعوا فيه.

idrísu fi -lmagāl ílli bitḥibbū 3ašān tiʔdáru tibdá3u fī.

Study the field that you like
so you can innovate in it.

⑥

شريف دارِس فُنون جميلة. مُمْكِن يِساعِدْكو في اِخْتِيار الألْوان.

šarīf dāris funūn gamīla. múmkin yisa3ídku fi -xtiyār ilʔalwān.

Sherif studied fine arts. He may
help you choose the colors.

⑦

مدرسْتِش أبداً نِجارة و ما زِلْت نِفْسي أتْعلِّمْها.

ma-darástiš ábadan nigāra wi ma zilt^{ə} nífsi ʔat3allímha.

I've never learned carpentry,
and I still want to learn it.

❖ [1s2] **to study, learn**

➲ 65.3, 194.3, 208.2, 208.6

108 to teach dárris دَرَّس

	affirmative		negative		
ána	darríst	دَرَّسْت	ma-darrístiš	مَدَرَّسْتِش	perfect
íḥna	darrísna	دَرَّسْنا	ma-darrisnāš	مَدَرَّسْناش	
ínta	darríst	دَرَّسْت	ma-darrístiš	مَدَرَّسْتِش	
ínti	darrísti	دَرَّسْتي	ma-darristīš	مَدَرَّسْتيش	
íntu	darrístu	دَرَّسْتوا	ma-darristūš	مَدَرَّسْتوش	
húwwa	dárris	دَرَّس	ma-darríss	مَدَرَّسْش	
híyya	darrísit	دَرِّسِت	ma-darrisítš	مَدَرِّسِتْش	
húmma	darrísu	دَرِّسوا	ma-darrisūš	مَدَرِّسوش	
ána	adárris	أدَرِّس	ma-darrísš	مَدَرِّسْش	imperfect
íḥna	nidárris	نِدَرِّس	ma-ndarrísš	مَنْدَرِّسْش	
ínta	tidárris	تِدَرِّس	ma-tdarrísš	مَتْدَرِّسْش	
ínti	tidarrísi	تِدَرِّسي	ma-tdarrisīš	مَتْدَرِّسيش	
íntu	tidarrísu	تِدَرِّسوا	ma-tdarrisūš	مَتْدَرِّسوش	
húwwa	yidárris	يِدَرِّس	ma-ydarrísš	مَيْدَرِّسْش	
híyya	tidárris	تِدَرِّس	ma-tdarrísš	مَتْدَرِّسْش	
húmma	yidarrísu	يِدَرِّسوا	ma-ydarrisūš	مَيْدَرِّسوش	
ána	badárris	بَدَرِّس	ma-badarrísš	مَبَدَرِّسْش	bi-imperfect
íḥna	bindárris	بِنْدَرِّس	ma-bindarrísš	مَبِنْدَرِّسْش	
ínta	bitdárris	بِتْدَرِّس	ma-bitdarrísš	مَبِتْدَرِّسْش	
ínti	bitdarrísi	بِتْدَرِّسي	ma-bitdarrisīš	مَبِتْدَرِّسيش	
íntu	bitdarrísu	بِتْدَرِّسوا	ma-bitdarrisūš	مَبِتْدَرِّسوش	
húwwa	biydárris	بِيْدَرِّس	ma-biydarrísš	مَبِيْدَرِّسْش	
híyya	bitdárris	بِتْدَرِّس	ma-bitdarrísš	مَبِتْدَرِّسْش	
húmma	biydarrísu	بِيْدَرِّسوا	ma-biydarrisūš	مَبِيْدَرِّسوش	
ána	hadárris	هَدَرِّس	miš hadárris	مِش هَدَرِّس	future
íḥna	handárris	هَنْدَرِّس	miš handárris	مِش هَنْدَرِّس	
ínta	hatdárris	هَتْدَرِّس	miš hatdárris	مِش هَتْدَرِّس	
ínti	hatdarrísi	هَتْدَرِّسي	miš hatdarrísi	مِش هَتْدَرِّسي	
íntu	hatdarrísu	هَتْدَرِّسوا	miš hatdarrísu	مِش هَتْدَرِّسوا	
húwwa	haydárris	هَيْدَرِّس	miš haydárris	مِش هَيْدَرِّس	
híyya	hatdárris	هَتْدَرِّس	miš hatdárris	مِش هَتْدَرِّس	
húmma	haydarrísu	هَيْدَرِّسوا	miš haydarrísu	مِش هَيْدَرِّسوا	
ínta	dárris	دَرِّس	ma-tdarrísš	مَتْدَرِّسْش	imperative
ínti	darrísi	دَرِّسي	ma-tdarrisīš	مَتْدَرِّسيش	
íntu	darrísu	دَرِّسوا	ma-tdarrisūš	مَتْدَرِّسوش	

	active		passive		
masculine	midárris	مِدَرِّس	mitdárris	مِتْدَرِّس	participles
feminine	midarrísa	مِدَرِّسَة	mitdarrísa	مِتْدَرِّسَة	
plural	midarrisīn	مِدَرِّسين	mitdarrisīn	مِتْدَرِّسين	

verbal noun: tadrīs تَدْريس

①

دُكْتورة سُهيرْ درّسِتْلي في الجامْعة.

duktūra suhēr darrisítli fi -lgám3a.

Dr. Soheir taught me in college.

②

هل مُمْكِن أدرِّس عنْدُكو ماث؟

hal múmkin adárris 3andúku māṯ?

May I teach math here?

③

في مدْرسِةْ وِلادي بِيْدرِّسوا اللُّغة التّانْية مِن تمْهيدي.

fi madrásit wilādi biydarrísu -llúɣa -ttaníyya min tamhīdi.

In my kids' school, they teach them a
second language starting in preschool.

④

هَيْدرِّسولْنا السّنة دي مادّة إسْمها إنْسانِيّات.

haydarrisúlna -ssanādi mádda ʔismáha ʔinsaniyyāt.

This year, they'll teach us a
subject called humanities.

⑤

درِّسوا لِلأطْفال بِشغف عشان تِحافْظوا على الفُضول اللي جُوّاهُم.

darrísu li-lʔaṭfāl bí-šáɣaf 3ašān tiḫáfẓu 3ála -lfuḍūl ílli guwwāhum.

Teach your children passionately in order to
maintain the curiosity inside them.

⑥

بابا اللي مِدرِّسْلي جُغْرافْيا. هُوَّ بِيْحِبّها أوي و حبِّبْني فيها.

bāba -lli midarrísli guɣráfya. húwwa biyḫibbáha ʔáwi wi ḫabbíbni fīha.

It was my dad who taught me geography.
He loves it, and he made me love it, too.

⑦

مبِيْدرِّسوش لِلوِلاد أشْغال يَدَوية كِفايَة في المدْرسة.

ma-biydarrisūš li-lwilād ašɣāl yadawíyya kifāya fi -lmadrása.

They don't teach kids arts and
crafts enough at school.

❖ [2s1] **to teach** (something) (**to** لِ *li-*)

- This verb is synonymous with علِّم *3állim.* (➲ 49.5, 116.2, 144.2, 174.2)

109 to pay dáfa3 دَفَع

		affirmative		negative	
perfect	ána	dafá3t	دَفَعْت	ma-dafá3tiš	مَدَفَعْتِش
	íḫna	dafá3na	دَفَعْنا	ma-dafa3nāš	مَدَفَعْناش
	ínta	dafá3t	دَفَعْت	ma-dafá3tiš	مَدَفَعْتِش
	ínti	dafá3ti	دَفَعْتي	ma-dafa3tīš	مَدَفَعْتيش
	íntu	dafá3tu	دَفَعْتوا	ma-dafa3tūš	مَدَفَعْتوش
	húwwa	dáfa3	دَفَع	ma-dafá3š	مَدَفَعْش
	híyya	dáfa3it	دَفَعِت	ma-dafa3ítš	مَدَفَعِتْش
	húmma	dáfa3u	دَفَعوا	ma-dafa3ūš	مَدَفَعوش
imperfect	ána	ádfa3	أَدْفَع	ma-dfá3š	مَدْفَعْش
	íḫna	nídfa3	نِدْفَع	ma-nidfá3š	مَنِدْفَعْش
	ínta	tídfa3	تِدْفَع	ma-tidfá3š	مَتِدْفَعْش
	ínti	tidfá3i	تِدْفَعي	ma-tidfa3īš	مَتِدْفَعيش
	íntu	tidfá3u	تِدْفَعوا	ma-tidfa3ūš	مَتِدْفَعوش
	húwwa	yídfa3	يِدْفَع	ma-yidfá3š	مَيِدْفَعْش
	híyya	tídfa3	تِدْفَع	ma-tidfá3š	مَتِدْفَعْش
	húmma	yidfá3u	يِدْفَعوا	ma-yidfa3ūš	مَيِدْفَعوش
bi-imperfect	ána	bádfa3	بَدْفَع	ma-badfá3š	مَبَدْفَعْش
	íḫna	binídfa3	بِنِدْفَع	ma-bnidfá3š	مَبْنِدْفَعْش
	ínta	bitídfa3	بِتِدْفَع	ma-btidfá3š	مَبْتِدْفَعْش
	ínti	bitidfá3i	بِتِدْفَعي	ma-btidfa3īš	مَبْتِدْفَعيش
	íntu	bitidfá3u	بِتِدْفَعوا	ma-btidfa3ūš	مَبْتِدْفَعوش
	húwwa	biyídfa3	بِيِدْفَع	ma-byidfá3š	مَبْيِدْفَعْش
	híyya	bitídfa3	بِتِدْفَع	ma-btidfá3š	مَبْتِدْفَعْش
	húmma	biyidfá3u	بِيِدْفَعوا	ma-byidfa3ūš	مَبْيِدْفَعوش
future	ána	hádfa3	هَدْفَع	miš hádfa3	مِش هَدْفَع
	íḫna	hanídfa3	هَنِدْفَع	miš hanídfa3	مِش هَنِدْفَع
	ínta	hatídfa3	هَتِدْفَع	miš hatídfa3	مِش هَتِدْفَع
	ínti	hatidfá3i	هَتِدْفَعي	miš hatidfá3i	مِش هَتِدْفَعي
	íntu	hatidfá3u	هَتِدْفَعوا	miš hatidfá3u	مِش هَتِدْفَعوا
	húwwa	hayídfa3	هَيِدْفَع	miš hayídfa3	مِش هَيِدْفَع
	híyya	hatídfa3	هَتِدْفَع	miš hatídfa3	مِش هَتِدْفَع
	húmma	hayidfá3u	هَيِدْفَعوا	miš hayidfá3u	مِش هَيِدْفَعوا
imperative	ínta	ídfa3	اِدْفَع	ma-tidfá3š	مَتِدْفَعْش
	ínti	idfá3i	اِدْفَعي	ma-tidfa3īš	مَتِدْفَعيش
	íntu	idfá3u	اِدْفَعوا	ma-tidfa3ūš	مَتِدْفَعوش

		active		passive	
participles	masculine	dāfi3	دافِع	madfū3	مَدْفوع
	feminine	dáf3a	دافْعَة	madfū3a	مَدْفوعَة
	plural	daf3īn	دافْعين	madfu3īn	مَدْفوعين

verbal noun: daf3 دفْع

①

دفعْت في العُزومة دي كُلّها ١٠٠ جِنيْهْ بسّ.

dafá3tᵊ fi -l3uzūma di kulláha mīt ginēh bass.

I only paid 100 pounds for this whole dinner party.

②

مُمْكِن أدْفع بِالفيزا؟

múmkin ádfa3 bi-lvīza?

Can I pay with Visa?

③

بدْفع لِابْني في الأجازة أكْتر مِن الدِّراسة. المُعسْكرات و الأنْشِطة الصّيْفي مُكلِّفة.

bádfa3 li-íbni fi -lʔagāza ʔáktar min iddirāsa. ilmu3askarāt w ilʔanšíṭa -ṣṣēfi mukallífa.

I spend more on my son in the [summer] vacation than [I do] for his school. The summer camps and activities are so expensive.

④

شُروق و خطيبْها اِتّفقوا هُوَّ هَيِدْفع مصاريف الفرح كُلّها.

šurūʔ wi xaṭíbha -ttáfaʔu húwwa hayídfa3 maṣarīf ilfáraḥ kulláha.

Shorouk and her fiancé agreed that he'd pay for all the wedding expenses.

⑤

اِدْفع دِلْوَقْتي المُقدّم و قسّط الباقي على سنتينْ.

ídfa3 dilwáʔti -lmuʔáddam wi ʔássaṭ ilbāʔi 3ála sanatēn.

Pay a deposit now, then pay in installments for two years.

⑥

أنا لِسّه دافِع فاتورْةْ الكهْربا. إزّاي جت فاتورة جْديدة؟

ána líssa dāfi3 fatúrt ilkahrába. izzāy gat fatūra gdīda?

I've just paid the electricity bill. How come we received a new one?

⑦

متِدْفعوش حاجة. إحْنا عازْمينْكو.

ma-tidfa3ūš ḥāga. íḥna 3azmínku.

Don't pay anything. It's on us.

❖ [1s1] **to pay**

➲ 39.1, 45.1, 109.6, 169.3

110 to spill dálaʔ دَلَق

verbal noun: dalʔ دَلْق

		affirmative			negative	
perfect	ána	daláʔt	دَلَقْت		ma-daláʔtiš	مَدَلَقْتِش
	íḫna	daláʔna	دَلَقْنا		ma-dalaʔnāš	مَدَلَقْناش
	ínta	daláʔt	دَلَقْت		ma-daláʔtiš	مَدَلَقْتِش
	ínti	daláʔti	دَلَقْتي		ma-dalaʔtīš	مَدَلَقْتيش
	íntu	daláʔtu	دَلَقْتوا		ma-dalaʔtūš	مَدَلَقْتوش
	húwwa	dálaʔ	دَلَق		ma-daláʔš	مَدَلَقْش
	híyya	dálaʔit	دَلَقِت		ma-dalaʔítš	مَدَلَقِتْش
	húmma	dálaʔu	دَلَقوا		ma-dalaʔūš	مَدَلَقوش
imperfect	ána	ádluʔ	أَدْلُق		ma-dlúʔš	مَدْلُقْش
	íḫna	nídluʔ	نِدْلُق		ma-nidlúʔš	مَنِدْلُقْش
	ínta	tídluʔ	تِدْلُق		ma-tidlúʔš	مَتِدْلُقْش
	ínti	tidlúʔi	تِدْلُقي		ma-tidluʔīš	مَتِدْلُقيش
	íntu	tidlúʔu	تِدْلُقوا		ma-tidluʔūš	مَتِدْلُقوش
	húwwa	yídluʔ	يِدْلُق		ma-yidlúʔš	مَيِدْلُقْش
	híyya	tídluʔ	تِدْلُق		ma-tidlúʔš	مَتِدْلُقْش
	húmma	yidlúʔu	يِدْلُقوا		ma-yidluʔūš	مَيِدْلُقوش
bi-imperfect	ána	bádluʔ	بَدْلُق		ma-badlúʔš	مَبَدْلُقْش
	íḫna	binídluʔ	بِنِدْلُق		ma-bnidlúʔš	مَبْنِدْلُقْش
	ínta	bitídluʔ	بِتِدْلُق		ma-btidlúʔš	مَبْتِدْلُقْش
	ínti	bitidlúʔi	بِتِدْلُقي		ma-btidluʔīš	مَبْتِدْلُقيش
	íntu	bitidlúʔu	بِتِدْلُقوا		ma-btidluʔūš	مَبْتِدْلُقوش
	húwwa	biyídluʔ	بِيِدْلُق		ma-byidlúʔš	مَبْيِدْلُقْش
	híyya	bitídluʔ	بِتِدْلُق		ma-btidlúʔš	مَبْتِدْلُقْش
	húmma	biyidlúʔu	بِيِدْلُقوا		ma-byidluʔūš	مَبْيِدْلُقوش
future	ána	hádluʔ	هَدْلُق		miš hádluʔ	مِش هَدْلُق
	íḫna	hanídluʔ	هَنِدْلُق		miš hanídluʔ	مِش هَنِدْلُق
	ínta	hatídluʔ	هَتِدْلُق		miš hatídluʔ	مِش هَتِدْلُق
	ínti	hatidlúʔi	هَتِدْلُقي		miš hatidlúʔi	مِش هَتِدْلُقي
	íntu	hatidlúʔu	هَتِدْلُقوا		miš hatidlúʔu	مِش هَتِدْلُقوا
	húwwa	hayídluʔ	هَيِدْلُق		miš hayídluʔ	مِش هَيِدْلُق
	híyya	hatídluʔ	هَتِدْلُق		miš hatídluʔ	مِش هَتِدْلُق
	húmma	hayidlúʔu	هَيِدْلُقوا		miš hayidlúʔu	مِش هَيِدْلُقوا
imperative	ínta	ídluʔ	اِدْلُق		ma-tidlúʔš	مَتِدْلُقْش
	ínti	idlúʔi	اِدْلُقي		ma-tidluʔīš	مَتِدْلُقيش
	íntu	idlúʔu	اِدْلُقوا		ma-tidluʔūš	مَتِدْلُقوش

		active			passive	
participles	masculine	dāliʔ	دالِق		madlūʔ	مَدْلوق
	feminine	dálʔa	دالْقَة		madlūʔa	مَدْلوقَة
	plural	dalʔīn	دالْقين		madluʔīn	مَدْلوقين

①

الوَلد دلق على نفْسُه الميّة.

ilwálad dála? 3ála náfsu -lmáyya.

The boy spilled the water on himself.

②

بِنْتي كُلّ ما بِتِمْسِك كُبّايَة تِدْلُقْها في الأرْض.

bínti kullᵊ ma bitímsik kubbāya tidlú?ha fi -l?arḍ.

When my daughter holds a glass, she always spills it on the floor.

③

بِالرّاحة و إنْتَ بِتْصُبّ. هتِدْلُق العصير في الأرْض.

bi-rrāḫa w ínta bitṣúbb. hatídlu? il3aṣīr fi -l?arḍ.

Be careful pouring juice, or you'll spill it on the floor.

④

متِدْلُقْش الميّة في الأرْض. معاناش غيرْها.

ma-tidlú?š ilmáyya fi -l?arḍ. ma-3anāš ɣírha.

Don't pour the water out. We don't have anymore.

⑤

إنْتي هتِدْلُقي نفْسِك عليْه؟ خلاص مِش عايْزِك، اِنْسيه.

ínti hatidlú?i náfsik 3alē? xalāṣ miš 3áyzik, insī.

Are you going to chase him? If he doesn't want you, forget him.

❖ [1s3] **to spill; to pour**

- This verb, like other verbs of the [1s3] and [1s6] patterns, can optionally take ـُ *u* instead of ـِ *i* in the personal prefixes of the imperfect (including the bi-imperfect and future) and imperative. For example, يِدْلُق *yídlu?* can also be pronounced يُدْلُق *yúdlu?*. These vowels are interchangeable, but the tables reflect the preferences of the speakers on the MP3s.

111 to turn dáwwar دوّر 1-13

verbal nouns: tadwīr تدوير - dawarān دوران

perfect

	affirmative		negative	
ána	dawwárt	دَوَّرْت	ma-dawwártiš	مَدَوَّرْتِش
íḥna	dawwárna	دَوَّرْنا	ma-dawwarnāš	مَدَوَّرْناش
ínta	dawwárt	دَوَّرْت	ma-dawwártiš	مَدَوَّرْتِش
ínti	dawwárti	دَوَّرْتي	ma-dawwartīš	مَدَوَّرْتيش
íntu	dawwártu	دَوَّرْتوا	ma-dawwartūš	مَدَوَّرْتوش
húwwa	dáwwar	دَوَّر	ma-dawwárš	مَدَوَّرْش
híyya	dawwárit	دَوَّرِت	ma-dawwarítš	مَدَوَّرِتْش
húmma	dawwáru	دَوَّروا	ma-dawwarūš	مَدَوَّروش

imperfect

	affirmative		negative	
ána	adáwwar	أدَوَّر	ma-dawwárš	مَدَوَّرْش
íḥna	nidáwwar	نِدَوَّر	ma-ndawwárš	مَنْدَوَّرْش
ínta	tidáwwar	تِدَوَّر	ma-tdawwárš	مَتْدَوَّرْش
ínti	tidawwári	تِدَوَّري	ma-tdawwarīš	مَتْدَوَّريش
íntu	tidawwáru	تِدَوَّروا	ma-tdawwarūš	مَتْدَوَّروش
húwwa	yidáwwar	يِدَوَّر	ma-ydawwárš	مَيْدَوَّرْش
híyya	tidáwwar	تِدَوَّر	ma-tdawwárš	مَتْدَوَّرْش
húmma	yidawwáru	يِدَوَّروا	ma-ydawwarūš	مَيْدَوَّروش

bi-imperfect

	affirmative		negative	
ána	badáwwar	بَدَوَّر	ma-badawwárš	مَبَدَوَّرْش
íḥna	bindáwwar	بِنْدَوَّر	ma-bindawwárš	مَبِنْدَوَّرْش
ínta	bitdáwwar	بِتْدَوَّر	ma-bitdawwárš	مَبِتْدَوَّرْش
ínti	bitdawwári	بِتْدَوَّري	ma-bitdawwarīš	مَبِتْدَوَّريش
íntu	bitdawwáru	بِتْدَوَّروا	ma-bitdawwarūš	مَبِتْدَوَّروش
húwwa	biydáwwar	بِيْدَوَّر	ma-biydawwárš	مَبِيْدَوَّرْش
híyya	bitdáwwar	بِتْدَوَّر	ma-bitdawwárš	مَبِتْدَوَّرْش
húmma	biydawwáru	بِيْدَوَّروا	ma-biydawwarūš	مَبِيْدَوَّروش

future

	affirmative		negative	
ána	hadáwwar	هَدَوَّر	miš hadáwwar	مِش هَدَوَّر
íḥna	handáwwar	هَنْدَوَّر	miš handáwwar	مِش هَنْدَوَّر
ínta	hatdáwwar	هَتْدَوَّر	miš hatdáwwar	مِش هَتْدَوَّر
ínti	hatdawwári	هَتْدَوَّري	miš hatdawwári	مِش هَتْدَوَّري
íntu	hatdawwáru	هَتْدَوَّروا	miš hatdawwáru	مِش هَتْدَوَّروا
húwwa	haydáwwar	هَيْدَوَّر	miš haydáwwar	مِش هَيْدَوَّر
híyya	hatdáwwar	هَتْدَوَّر	miš hatdáwwar	مِش هَتْدَوَّر
húmma	haydawwáru	هَيْدَوَّروا	miš haydawwáru	مِش هَيْدَوَّروا

imperative

	affirmative		negative	
ínta	dáwwar	دَوَّر	ma-tdawwárš	مَتْدَوَّرْش
ínti	dawwári	دَوَّري	ma-tdawwarīš	مَتْدَوَّريش
íntu	dawwáru	دَوَّروا	ma-tdawwarūš	مَتْدَوَّروش

participles

	active		passive	
masculine	midáwwar	مِدَوَّر	mitdáwwar	مِتْدَوَّر
feminine	midawwára	مِدَوَّرَة	mitdawwára	مِتْدَوَّرَة
plural	midawwarīn	مِدَوَّرين	mitdawwarīn	مِتْدَوَّرين

①

لمّا شُفْت الرّاجِل جايّ ناحْيِتى، دوّرْت العربية و جْريت.

lámma šuft irrāgil gayyᵊ naḫyíti, dawwárt il3arabíyya wi grīt.

When I saw the man coming towards me,
I started the car and sped away.

②

لمّا أدوّر المتُور، اِسْمع صوْتُه و قولّي كُوَيِّس وَلّا أيْه.

lámm- adáwwar ilmutūr, ísma3 ṣōtu wi ʔúlli kuwáyyis wálla ʔē.

When I turn on the engine, listen to its
noise and tell me if it's okay or not.

③

نُهى بِتْدوّر على راجِل يِحِبّها بْجدّ، مِش يِكون طمْعان في فْلوسْها.

núha bitdáwwar 3ála rāgil yiḫibbáha b-gadd, miš yikūn ṭam3ān fi flúsha.

Noha is looking for a man who loves
her and isn't after her money.

④

أ: **معاكي فكّة؟**

ب: **هدوّرْلك في الشّنْطة.**

A: *ma3āki fákka?*
B: *hadawwárlak fi -ššánṭa.*

A: Do you have any change?
B: I'll look in my purse.

⑤

دوّر عَ أصْحابك القُدام. دوْل كِنْز مَيِتْعوّضْش.

dáwwar 3ála ʔaṣḫābak ilʔudām. dōl kinzᵊ ma-yit3awwáḍš.

Look for your old friends. They are
an irreplaceable treasure.

⑥

إنْتي لقيتيها هِنا إزّاي؟ ده أنا لِسّه مْدوّرة هِنا و ملقيتْهاش.

ínti laʔitīha hína -zzāy? d- ána líssa mdawwára hína wi ma-laʔithāš.

How did you find it here? I was just
looking here and couldn't find it.

⑦

دوّرْت في البلكوْنة. لِسّه مدوّرْتِش في الأُوَض.

dawwártᵊ fi -lbalakōna. líssa ma-dawwártiš fi -lʔúwaḍ.

I searched on the balcony, but I haven't
looked in the rooms yet.

❖ [2s2] **to turn; to search** (**for** على *3ála*)

➲ 2.10, 13.2, 58.3, 101.3, 231.9, 254.1

112 to study *zākir* ذاكِر

	affirmative		negative		
ána	*zakírt*	ذاكِرْت	*ma-zakírtiš*	مَذاكِرْتِش	perfect
íḫna	*zakírna*	ذاكِرْنا	*ma-zakirnāš*	مَذاكِرْناش	
ínta	*zakírt*	ذاكِرْت	*ma-zakírtiš*	مَذاكِرْتِش	
ínti	*zakírti*	ذاكِرْتي	*ma-zakirtīš*	مَذاكِرْتيش	
íntu	*zakírtu*	ذاكِرْتوا	*ma-zakirtūš*	مَذاكِرْتوش	
húwwa	*zākir*	ذاكِر	*ma-zakírš*	مَذاكِرْش	
híyya	*zákrit*	ذاكْرِت	*ma-zakrítš*	مَذاكْرِتْش	
húmma	*zákru*	ذاكْروا	*ma-zakrūš*	مَذاكْروش	
ána	*azākir*	أذاكِر	*ma-zakírš*	مَذاكِرْش	imperfect
íḫna	*nizākir*	نِذاكِر	*ma-nzakírš*	مَنْذاكِرْش	
ínta	*tizākir*	تِذاكِر	*ma-tzakírš*	مَتْذاكِرْش	
ínti	*tizákri*	تِذاكْري	*ma-tzakrīš*	مَتْذاكْريش	
íntu	*tizákru*	تِذاكْروا	*ma-tzakrūš*	مَتْذاكْروش	
húwwa	*yizākir*	يِذاكِر	*ma-yzakírš*	مَيْذاكِرْش	
híyya	*tizākir*	تِذاكِر	*ma-tzakírš*	مَتْذاكِرْش	
húmma	*yizákru*	يِذاكْروا	*ma-yzakrūš*	مَيْذاكْروش	
ána	*bazākir*	بَذاكِر	*ma-bazakírš*	مَبَذاكِرْش	bi-imperfect
íḫna	*binzākir*	بِنْذاكِر	*ma-binzakírš*	مَبِنْذاكِرْش	
ínta	*bitzākir*	بِتْذاكِر	*ma-bitzakírš*	مَبِتْذاكِرْش	
ínti	*bitzákri*	بِتْذاكْري	*ma-bitzakrīš*	مَبِتْذاكْريش	
íntu	*bitzákru*	بِتْذاكْروا	*ma-bitzakrūš*	مَبِتْذاكْروش	
húwwa	*biyzākir*	بِيْذاكِر	*ma-biyzakírš*	مَبِيْذاكِرْش	
híyya	*bitzākir*	بِتْذاكِر	*ma-bitzakírš*	مَبِتْذاكِرْش	
húmma	*biyzákru*	بِيْذاكْروا	*ma-biyzakrūš*	مَبِيْذاكْروش	
ána	*hazākir*	هَذاكِر	*miš hazākir*	مِش هَذاكِر	future
íḫna	*hanzākir*	هَنْذاكِر	*miš hanzākir*	مِش هَنْذاكِر	
ínta	*hatzākir*	هَتْذاكِر	*miš hatzākir*	مِش هَتْذاكِر	
ínti	*hatzákri*	هَتْذاكْري	*miš hatzákri*	مِش هَتْذاكْري	
íntu	*hatzákru*	هَتْذاكْروا	*miš hatzákru*	مِش هَتْذاكْروا	
húwwa	*hayzākir*	هَيْذاكِر	*miš hayzākir*	مِش هَيْذاكِر	
híyya	*hatzākir*	هَتْذاكِر	*miš hatzākir*	مِش هَتْذاكِر	
húmma	*hayzákru*	هَيْذاكْروا	*miš hayzákru*	مِش هَيْذاكْروا	
ínta	*zākir*	ذاكِر	*ma-tzakírš*	مَتْذاكِرْش	imperative
ínti	*zákri*	ذاكْري	*ma-tzakrīš*	مَتْذاكْريش	
íntu	*zákru*	ذاكْروا	*ma-tzakrūš*	مَتْذاكْروش	

	active		passive		
masculine	*mizākir*	مِذاكِر	*mitzākir*	مِتْذاكِر	participles
feminine	*mizákra*	مِذاكْرَة	*mitzákra*	مِتْذاكْرَة	
plural	*mizakrīn*	مِذاكْرين	*mitzakrīn*	مِتْذاكْرين	

verbal noun: *muzákra* مُذاكْرَة

①

مذاكِرْتِش لِحدّ دِلْوَقْتي و بُكْره الاِمْتِحان.

mazakírtiš li-ħaddᵊ dilwáʔti wi búkra -lʔimtiħān.

I still haven't studied, and
the exam is tomorrow.

②

مها بِتْحِبّ تْذاكِر مِ الفجْر لِحدّ السّاعة ٧.

máha bitħíbbᵊ tzākir mi -lfágrᵊ li-ħadd issā3a sáb3a.

Maha likes to study from dawn until 7 a.m.

③

إسْراء مبِتْذاكِرْش خالِص. كِده هتْضيّع السّنة.

isrāʔ ma-bitzakíršᵊ xāliṣ. kída hatḍáyya3 issána.

Israa isn't studying at all. She's
going to fail this year.

④

محمّد هَيْذاكِر إنْجليزي و يِمْتِحِن في الجامْعة الأمْريكية.

maħámmad hayzākir ingilīzi wi yimtíħin fi -lgám3a -lʔamrikíyya.

Mohamed will study English and take exams [to get into]
A.U.C [the American University in Cairo].

⑤

ذاكْروا الفصْل الأخير كُوَيِّس.

zákru -lfaṣl ilʔaxīr kuwáyyis.

Study the last
chapter carefully.

❖ [3s] **to study**

- This verb and درس *dáras* both translate 'study', but with a difference in meaning. ذاكِر *zākir* means 'apply oneself to study', as in sitting with books, reviewing for a test, doing homework, etc. درس *dáras* means 'learn', as in being enrolled in a course, going to college, etc.

➲ 11.5, 40.5, 44.2, 52.4, 56.6, 96.5, 98.3, 136.3, 155.5, 170.1, 197.5, 213.1

113 to go rāḫ راح

	affirmative		negative		
ána	ruḫt	رُحْت	ma-rúḫtiš	مَرُحْتِش	**perfect**
íḫna	rúḫna	رُحْنا	ma-ruḫnāš	مَرُحْناش	
ínta	ruḫt	رُحْت	ma-rúḫtiš	مَرُحْتِش	
ínti	rúḫti	رُحْتي	ma-ruḫtīš	مَرُحْتيش	
íntu	rúḫtu	رُحْتوا	ma-ruḫtūš	مَرُحْتوش	
húwwa	rāḫ	راح	ma-ráḫš	مَراحْش	
híyya	rāḫit	راحِت	ma-raḫítš	مَراحْتِش	
húmma	rāḫu	راحوا	ma-raḫūš	مَراحوش	
ána	arūḫ	أروح	ma-rúḫš	مَروحْش	**imperfect**
íḫna	nirūḫ	نِروح	ma-nrúḫš	مَنْروحْش	
ínta	tirūḫ	تِروح	ma-trúḫš	مَتْروحْش	
ínti	tirūḫi	تِروحي	ma-truḫīš	مَتْروحيش	
íntu	tirūḫu	تِروحوا	ma-truḫūš	مَتْروحوش	
húwwa	yirūḫ	يِروح	ma-yrúḫš	مَيْروحْش	
híyya	tirūḫ	تِروح	ma-trúḫš	مَتْروحْش	
húmma	yirūḫu	يِروحوا	ma-yruḫūš	مَيْروحوش	
ána	barūḫ	بَروح	ma-barúḫš	مَبَروحْش	**bi-imperfect**
íḫna	binrūḫ	بِنْروح	ma-binrúḫš	مَبِنْروحْش	
ínta	bitrūḫ	بِتْروح	ma-bitrúḫš	مَبِتْروحْش	
ínti	bitrūḫi	بِتْروحي	ma-bitruḫīš	مَبِتْروحيش	
íntu	bitrūḫu	بِتْروحوا	ma-bitruḫūš	مَبِتْروحوش	
húwwa	biyrūḫ	بِيْروح	ma-biyrúḫš	مَبِيْروحْش	
híyya	bitrūḫ	بِتْروح	ma-bitrúḫš	مَبِتْروحْش	
húmma	biyrūḫu	بِيْروحوا	ma-biyruḫūš	مَبِيْروحوش	
ána	harūḫ	هَروح	miš harūḫ	مِش هَروح	**future**
íḫna	hanrūḫ	هَنْروح	miš hanrūḫ	مِش هَنْروح	
ínta	hatrūḫ	هَتْروح	miš hatrūḫ	مِش هَتْروح	
ínti	hatrūḫi	هَتْروحي	miš hatrūḫi	مِش هَتْروحي	
íntu	hatrūḫu	هَتْروحوا	miš hatrūḫu	مِش هَتْروحوا	
húwwa	hayrūḫ	هَيْروح	miš hayrūḫ	مِش هَيْروح	
híyya	hatrūḫ	هَتْروح	miš hatrūḫ	مِش هَتْروح	
húmma	hayrūḫu	هَيْروحوا	miš hayrūḫu	مِش هَيْروحوا	
ínta	rūḫ	روح	ma-trúḫš	مَتْروحْش	**imperative**
ínti	rūḫi	روحي	ma-truḫīš	مَتْروحيش	
íntu	rūḫu	روحوا	ma-truḫūš	مَتْروحوش	

	active		passive		
masculine	rāyiḫ	رايِح	mitrāḫ	مِتْراح	**participles**
feminine	ráyḫa	رايْحَة	mitrāḫa	مِتْراحَة	
plural	rayḫīn	رايْحين	mitraḫīn	مِتْراحين	

verbal nouns: rūḫa روحة - mirwāḫ مرواح

①	②
صاحْبِتي راحِت تايْلانْد في شهْر العسل.	بحِبّ أروح الجيم بِانْتِظام.
ṣaḩbíti rāḩit tāyland^ə f šahr il3ásal.	*baḩíbb arūḩ ilžīm bi-ntiẓām.*
My friend went to Thailand for her honeymoon.	I like going to the gym regularly.

③
جوْزي بِيْروح شُغْله مِن سِتّة و نُصّ الصُّبْح و بِيِرجع عَ المغْرب هلْكان.
gōzi biyrūḩ šúɣlu min sítta wi nuṣṣ iṣṣúbḩ, wi biyírga3 3a -lmáɣrab halkān.
My husband goes to work at 6:30 a.m. and gets home exhausted around sunset.

④
أخويا و أصْحابُه هَيْروحوا السّاحِل إسْبوع.
axūya w aṣḩābu hayrūḩu -ssāḩil isbū3.
My brother and his friends are going to the north coast for a week.

⑤
روحوا ناموا دِلْوَقْتي و بُكْره يِحِلّها حلّال.
rūḩu nāmu dilwáʔti wi búkra yiḩilláha ḩallāl.
Go to sleep now, and tomorrow God will help solve your problem.

⑥
أنا رايْحة الفرح ده معَ إنيّ تعْبانة، بسّ عشان صاحْبِتي متْزعلْش.
ána ráyḩa -lfáraḩ da má3a ʔínni ta3bāna, bass^ə 3ašān ṣaḩbíti ma-tzi3álš.
I'm going to this wedding even though I'm tired, just so my friend doesn't get upset.

⑦
اِشْتغلْت مِن البيْت بدل روحِة المكْتب.
ištaɣált^ə min ilbēt bádal rūḩit ilmáktab.
I worked from home instead of going into the office.

⑧
مرُحْتِش الهرم وَلا مرّة رغْم إنيّ ساكِن جنْبُه.
ma-rúḩtiš ilháram wála márra raɣm ínni sākin gámbu.
I've never once visited the pyramids, even though I live next to them.

⑨
المِشْوار ده مِتْراح كام مرّة لْحدّ دِلْوَقْتي؟
ilmišwār da mitrāḩ kam márra l-ḩadd^ə dilwáʔti?
How many times has that errand been run so far?

❖ [1h1] **to go (to)**

- This verb is transitive, unlike the English verb 'go', which requires the preposition 'to'.
- Although the vowel of the first and second persons of the perfect tense is a short *u,* it is common to see it written with و, also: روحْت *ruḩt* 'I went, etc.

➲ 2.6, 10.4, 20.5, 30.3, 31.4, 31.5, 36.1, 42.2, 46.2, 46.4, 58.4, 68.6, 72.4, 73.3 73.4, 73.5, 82.1, 89.5, 93.4, 100.3, 100.4, 113.8, 156.2, 169.4, 175.1, 176.4, 193.4, 194.1, 200.3, 228.6, 241.1, 241.2, 244.2, 259.2

114 to go back *rígi3* رجع

perfect

	affirmative		negative	
ána	*rigí3t*	رِجِعْت	*ma-rgí3tiš*	مَرْجِعْتِش
íḫna	*rigí3na*	رِجِعْنا	*ma-rgi3nāš*	مَرْجِعْناش
ínta	*rigí3t*	رِجِعْت	*ma-rgí3tiš*	مَرْجِعْتِش
ínti	*rigí3ti*	رِجِعْتي	*ma-rgi3tīš*	مَرْجِعْتيش
íntu	*rigí3tu*	رِجِعْتوا	*ma-rgi3tūš*	مَرْجِعْتوش
húwwa	*rígi3*	رِجِع	*ma-rgí3š*	مَرْجِعْش
híyya	*ríg3it*	رِجْعِت	*ma-rig3ítš*	مَرِجْعِتْش
húmma	*ríg3u*	رِجْعوا	*ma-rig3ūš*	مَرِجْعوش

imperfect

	affirmative		negative	
ána	*árga3*	أَرْجَع	*ma-rgá3š*	مَرْجَعْش
íḫna	*nírga3*	نِرْجَع	*ma-nirgá3š*	مَنِرْجَعْش
ínta	*tírga3*	تِرْجَع	*ma-tirgá3š*	مَتِرْجَعْش
ínti	*tirgá3i*	تِرْجَعي	*ma-tirga3īš*	مَتِرْجَعيش
íntu	*tirgá3u*	تِرْجَعوا	*ma-tirga3ūš*	مَتِرْجَعوش
húwwa	*yírga3*	يِرْجَع	*ma-yirgá3š*	مَيِرْجَعْش
híyya	*tírga3*	تِرْجَع	*ma-tirgá3š*	مَتِرْجَعْش
húmma	*yirgá3u*	يِرْجَعوا	*ma-yirga3ūš*	مَيِرْجَعوش

bi-imperfect

	affirmative		negative	
ána	*bárga3*	بَرْجَع	*ma-bargá3š*	مَبَرْجَعْش
íḫna	*binírga3*	بِنِرْجَع	*ma-bnirgá3š*	مَبْنِرْجَعْش
ínta	*bitírga3*	بِتِرْجَع	*ma-btirgá3š*	مَبْتِرْجَعْش
ínti	*bitirgá3i*	بِتِرْجَعي	*ma-btirga3īš*	مَبْتِرْجَعيش
íntu	*bitirgá3u*	بِتِرْجَعوا	*ma-btirga3ūš*	مَبْتِرْجَعوش
húwwa	*biyírga3*	بِيِرْجَع	*ma-byirgá3š*	مَبْيِرْجَعْش
híyya	*bitírga3*	بِتِرْجَع	*ma-btirgá3š*	مَبْتِرْجَعْش
húmma	*biyirgá3u*	بِيِرْجَعوا	*ma-byirga3ūš*	مَبْيِرْجَعوش

future

	affirmative		negative	
ána	*hárga3*	هَرْجَع	*miš hárga3*	مِش هَرْجَع
íḫna	*hanírga3*	هَنِرْجَع	*miš hanírga3*	مِش هَنِرْجَع
ínta	*hatírga3*	هَتِرْجَع	*miš hatírga3*	مِش هَتِرْجَع
ínti	*hatirgá3i*	هَتِرْجَعي	*miš hatirgá3i*	مِش هَتِرْجَعي
íntu	*hatirgá3u*	هَتِرْجَعوا	*miš hatirgá3u*	مِش هَتِرْجَعوا
húwwa	*hayírga3*	هَيِرْجَع	*miš hayírga3*	مِش هَيِرْجَع
híyya	*hatírga3*	هَتِرْجَع	*miš hatírga3*	مِش هَتِرْجَع
húmma	*hayirgá3u*	هَيِرْجَعوا	*miš hayirgá3u*	مِش هَيِرْجَعوا

imperative

	affirmative		negative	
ínta	*írga3*	اِرْجَع	*ma-tirgá3š*	مَتِرْجَعْش
ínti	*irgá3i*	اِرْجَعي	*ma-tirga3īš*	مَتِرْجَعيش
íntu	*irgá3u*	اِرْجَعوا	*ma-tirga3ūš*	مَتِرْجَعوش

participles

	active		passive	
masculine	*rāgi3*	راجِع	–	–
feminine	*rág3a*	راجْعَة	–	–
plural	*rag3īn*	راجْعين	–	–

verbal noun: *rugū3* رُجوع

①

أحْمد رِجِع لِهاجر لمّا عِرِف قيمِتْها في حَياتُه.

áђmad rígi3 li-hāgar lámma 3írif ʔimítha f ђayātu.

Ahmed went back to Hagar when he realized her value in his life.

②

لمّا بابا يِرجع مِ الشُّغْل، كلِّميه في المَوْضوع ده.

lámma bāba yírga3 mi -ššuɣl, kallimī fi -lmawḍū3 da.

When your dad comes home from work, talk to him about that matter.

③

كُلّ ما أقول هظبّط وَزْنى، برْجع لِلرّمْرمة تاني.

kullᵊ m- aʔūl haẓábbaṭ wázni, bárga3 li-rramráma tāni.

Every time I decide to watch my weight, I go back to snacking.

④

هرْجع شُغْلي في ديسِمْبِر.

hárga3 šúɣli f disímbir.

I'll be back to work in December.

⑤

متِرجعْش لِلمُخدّرات أبداً بعْد ما خدْت قرار تِنْقِذ نفْسك مِنْها.

ma-tirgá3šᵊ li-lmuxaddarāt abadan bá3dᵊ ma xadtᵊ qarār tínqiz náfsak mínha.

Never go back to drugs after deciding to rescue yourself from them.

⑥

أمير لِسّه مرجِعْش لْحدّ دِلْوَقْتي. أنا قلْقانة.

amīr líssa ma-rigí3šᵊ l-ђaddᵊ dilwáʔti. ána ʔalʔāna.

Amir hasn't come back yet. I'm worried.

⑦

إيّاك تِرجع تِصاحِب الشِّلّة دي تاني. هُمّا اللي بِيْجُرّوك لِلغلط.

iyyāk tírga3 tiṣāђib iššílla di tāni. húmma -lli biygurrūk li-lɣálaṭ.

Don't ever go back to associating with that group of friends. They're a bad influence on you.

❖ [1s4] **to go back, return (to** لِ *li-*)

- This verb can be used literally (to go back to a location), or figuratively (to a situation or habit). (➲ 114.1, 114.3, 114.5)
- It can be followed by a verbal noun (➲ 114.3) or imperfect verb (➲ 114.7).

➲ 7.2, 19.7, 23.5, 36.7, 58.3, 63.4, 66.6, 87.3, 92.2, 113.3, 127.1, 156.2, 202.4, 210.2, 228.4, 230.1, 243.1

115 to take back rágga3 رجّع 13

verbal noun: targī3 ترجيع

	affirmative		negative		
ána	raggá3t	رَجَّعْت	ma-raggá3tiš	مَرَجَّعْتِش	perfect
íḫna	raggá3na	رَجَّعْنا	ma-ragga3nāš	مَرَجَّعْناش	
ínta	raggá3t	رَجَّعْت	ma-raggá3tiš	مَرَجَّعْتِش	
ínti	raggá3ti	رَجَّعْتي	ma-ragga3tīš	مَرَجَّعْتيش	
íntu	raggá3tu	رَجَّعْتوا	ma-ragga3tūš	مَرَجَّعْتوش	
húwwa	rágga3	رَجَّع	ma-raggá3š	مَرَجَّعْش	
híyya	raggá3it	رَجَّعِت	ma-ragga3ítš	مَرَجَّعِتْش	
húmma	raggá3u	رَجَّعوا	ma-ragga3ūš	مَرَجَّعوش	
ána	arágga3	أرَجَّع	ma-raggá3š	مَرَجَّعْش	imperfect
íḫna	nirágga3	نِرَجَّع	ma-nraggá3š	مَنرُجَّعْش	
ínta	tirágga3	تِرَجَّع	ma-traggá3š	مَترُجَّعْش	
ínti	tiraggá3i	تِرَجَّعي	ma-tragga3īš	مَترُجَّعيش	
íntu	tiraggá3u	تِرَجَّعوا	ma-tragga3ūš	مَترُجَّعوش	
húwwa	yirágga3	يِرَجَّع	ma-yraggá3š	مَيرْجَّعْش	
híyya	tirágga3	تِرَجَّع	ma-traggá3š	مَترُجَّعْش	
húmma	yiraggá3u	يِرَجَّعوا	ma-yragga3ūš	مَيرْجَّعوش	
ána	barágga3	بَرَجَّع	ma-baraggá3š	مَبَرَجَّعْش	bi-imperfect
íḫna	binrágga3	بِنرُجَّع	ma-binraggá3š	مَبِنرُجَّعْش	
ínta	bitrágga3	بِترُجَّع	ma-bitraggá3š	مَبِترُجَّعْش	
ínti	bitraggá3i	بِترُجَّعي	ma-bitragga3īš	مَبِترُجَّعيش	
íntu	bitraggá3u	بِترُجَّعوا	ma-bitragga3ūš	مَبِترُجَّعوش	
húwwa	biyrágga3	بِيرْجَّع	ma-biyraggá3š	مَبِيرْجَّعْش	
híyya	bitrágga3	بِترُجَّع	ma-bitraggá3š	مَبِترُجَّعْش	
húmma	biyraggá3u	بِيرْجَّعوا	ma-biyragga3ūš	مَبِيرْجَّعوش	
ána	harágga3	هَرَجَّع	miš harágga3	مِش هَرَجَّع	future
íḫna	hanrágga3	هَنرُجَّع	miš hanrágga3	مِش هَنرُجَّع	
ínta	hatrágga3	هَترُجَّع	miš hatrágga3	مِش هَترُجَّع	
ínti	hatraggá3i	هَترُجَّعي	miš hatraggá3i	مِش هَترُجَّعي	
íntu	hatraggá3u	هَترُجَّعوا	miš hatraggá3u	مِش هَترُجَّعوا	
húwwa	hayrágga3	هَيرْجَّع	miš hayrágga3	مِش هَيرْجَّع	
híyya	hatrágga3	هَترُجَّع	miš hatrágga3	مِش هَترُجَّع	
húmma	hayraggá3u	هَيرْجَّعوا	miš hayraggá3u	مِش هَيرْجَّعوا	
ínta	rágga3	رَجَّع	ma-traggá3š	مَترُجَّعْش	imperative
ínti	raggá3i	رَجَّعي	ma-tragga3īš	مَترُجَّعيش	
íntu	raggá3u	رَجَّعوا	ma-tragga3ūš	مَترُجَّعوش	

	active		passive		
masculine	mirágga3	مِرَجَّع	mitrágga3	مِترُجَّع	participles
feminine	miraggá3a	مِرَجَّعَة	mitraggá3a	مِترُجَّعَة	
plural	miragga3īn	مِرَجَّعين	mitragga3īn	مِترُجَّعين	

①

إمْبارِح إشْتريْت جِبْنة و رجّعْتها النّهارْده عشان لقيتْها بايْظة.

imbāriḫ ištarēt gíbna wi ragga3táha -nnahárda 3ašān laʔítha báyẓa.

Yesterday I bought some cheese, but I returned it today because it was bad.

②

أنا مِتْأكِّدة إنّ منار ناوْيَة تِـرجّعْلي الفِلوس بِتاعْتي.

ána mutaʔakkída ʔinnᵊ manār náwya traggá3li -lfilūs bitá3ti.

I'm sure Manar intends to pay me back.

③

الوَلد بيِرْجّع مِن الصُّبْح. مِش عارْفة مالُه.

ilwálad biyrágga3 min iṣṣúbḫ. miš 3árfa mālu.

The boy has been vomiting since morning. I don't know what's wrong with him.

④

شذى هترْجّع إبْنها مدْرسْتُه القديمة عشان كان مبْسوط فيها.

šáza hatrágga3 ibnáha madrástu -lʔadīma, 3ašān kān mabsūṭ fīha.

Shaza will take her son back to his old school because he was happy there.

⑤

مِش عاجِبْني التّرْتيب الجِديد. رجّعوا كُلّ حاجة مكانْها.

muš 3agíbni -ttartīb ilgidīd. raggá3u kullᵊ ḫāga makánha.

I don't like the new arrangement. Put everything back in its place.

⑥

مترْجّعيش الفُسْتان الأزْرق. ده حِلْو أوي عليْكي.

ma-tragga3īš ilfustān ilʔázraʔ. da ḫilw ʔáwi 3alēki.

Don't return the blue dress. It looks so beautiful on you.

❖ [2s2] **to take back, give back, return** (something) (**to** لِ *li-*); **to vomit**

116 to reply *radd* رَدّ

	affirmative		negative		
ána	*raddēt*	رَدّيت	*ma-raddítš*	مَرَدّيتْش	**perfect**
íḫna	*raddēna*	رَدّينا	*ma-raddināš*	مَرَدّيناش	
ínta	*raddēt*	رَدّيت	*ma-raddítš*	مَرَدّيتْش	
ínti	*raddēti*	رَدّيتي	*ma-radditīš*	مَرَدّيتيش	
íntu	*raddētu*	رَدّيتوا	*ma-radditūš*	مَرَدّيتوش	
húwwa	*radd*	رَدّ	*ma-ráddiš*	مَرَدّش	
híyya	*ráddit*	رَدِّت	*ma-raddítš*	مَرَدِّتْش	
húmma	*ráddu*	رَدّوا	*ma-raddūš*	مَرَدّوش	
ána	*arúdd*	أَرُدّ	*ma-rúddiš*	مَرُدّش	**imperfect**
íḫna	*nirúdd*	نِرُدّ	*ma-nrúddiš*	مَنْرُدّش	
ínta	*tirúdd*	تِرُدّ	*ma-trúddiš*	مَتْرُدّش	
ínti	*tirúddi*	تِرُدّي	*ma-truddīš*	مَتْرُدّيش	
íntu	*tirúddu*	تِرُدّوا	*ma-truddūš*	مَتْرُدّوش	
húwwa	*yirúdd*	يِرُدّ	*ma-yrúddiš*	مَيْرُدّش	
híyya	*tirúdd*	تِرُدّ	*ma-trúddiš*	مَتْرُدّش	
húmma	*yirúddu*	يِرُدّوا	*ma-yruddūš*	مَيْرُدّوش	
ána	*barúdd*	بَرُدّ	*ma-barúddiš*	مَبَرُدّش	**bi-imperfect**
íḫna	*binrúdd*	بِنْرُدّ	*ma-binrúddiš*	مَبِنْرُدّش	
ínta	*bitrúdd*	بِتْرُدّ	*ma-bitrúddiš*	مَبِتْرُدّش	
ínti	*bitrúddi*	بِتْرُدّي	*ma-bitruddīš*	مَبِتْرُدّيش	
íntu	*bitrúddu*	بِتْرُدّوا	*ma-bitruddūš*	مَبِتْرُدّوش	
húwwa	*biyrúdd*	بِيْرُدّ	*ma-biyrúddiš*	مَبِيْرُدّش	
híyya	*bitrúdd*	بِتْرُدّ	*ma-bitrúddiš*	مَبِتْرُدّش	
húmma	*biyrúddu*	بِيْرُدّوا	*ma-biyruddūš*	مَبِيْرُدّوش	
ána	*harúdd*	هَرُدّ	*miš harúdd*	مِش هَرُدّ	**future**
íḫna	*hanrúdd*	هَنْرُدّ	*miš hanrúdd*	مِش هَنْرُدّ	
ínta	*hatrúdd*	هَتْرُدّ	*miš hatrúdd*	مِش هَتْرُدّ	
ínti	*hatrúddi*	هَتْرُدّي	*miš hatrúddi*	مِش هَتْرُدّي	
íntu	*hatrúddu*	هَتْرُدّوا	*miš hatrúddu*	مِش هَتْرُدّوا	
húwwa	*hayrúdd*	هَيْرُدّ	*miš hayrúdd*	مِش هَيْرُدّ	
híyya	*hatrúdd*	هَتْرُدّ	*miš hatrúdd*	مِش هَتْرُدّ	
húmma	*hayrúddu*	هَيْرُدّوا	*miš hayrúddu*	مِش هَيْرُدّوا	
ínta	*rudd*	رُدّ	*ma-trúddiš*	مَتْرُدّش	**imperative**
ínti	*rúddi*	رُدّي	*ma-truddīš*	مَتْرُدّيش	
íntu	*rúddu*	رُدّوا	*ma-truddūš*	مَتْرُدّوش	

	active		passive		
masculine	*rādid*	رادِد	*mardūd*	مَرْدود	**participles**
feminine	*rádda*	رادّة	*mardūda*	مَرْدودَة	
plural	*raddīn*	رادّين	*mardudīn*	مَرْدودين	

verbal noun: *radd* رَدّ

①

لمّا عُمر سأل على الجامْعة المفْتوحة ردّوا قالولُه إنّها اتْقفلِت.

lámma 3úmar sáʔal 3ála -lgám3a -lmaftūḫa ráddu ʔalūlu ʔinnáha -tʔáfalit.

When Omar asked about the open university,
they told him it had closed.

②

سيِّد بِيْعلِّم وِلادُه دايْماً يِـردّوا على النّاس بِادب.

sáyyid biy3állim wilādu dáyman yirúddu 3ála -nnās bi-ádab.

Sayed teaches his children to reply politely to people.

③

اللي بِيْسألْني عن سِنّى، برُدّ عليْه بِالحقيقة. مِش بعْمِل زيّ السِّتّات عادةً.

ílli biysaʔálni 3an sínni, barúddᵊ 3alē bi-lḫaʔīʔa. miš bá3mil zayy issittāt 3ādatan.

When I'm asked about my age, I reply truthfully,
not like women usually do.

④

هنْرُدّ عليْك خِلال يوْميْن مِن اِسْتِقْبال سُؤالك.

hanrúddᵊ 3alēk xilāl yumēn min istiʔbāl suʔālak.

We'll reply within two days of
receiving your query.

⑤

رُدّ على التِّليفوْن بِسُرْعة، و قولّي مين.

ruddᵊ 3ála -ttilifōn bi-súr3a, wi ʔúlli mīn.

Answer the phone quickly
and tell me who's calling.

⑥

مبرُدِّش على النِّمر الغريبة عشان بتْضايِق مِن المُعاكْسات.

ma-barúddiš 3ála -nnímar ilɣarība 3ašān batḍāyiʔ min ilmu3aksāt.

I don't answer unfamiliar numbers.
I get annoyed by the disturbances.

❖ [1g2] **to reply to, answer** (على *3ála*)

- Compare with جاوِب *gāwib*. (➲ 69)

➲ 2.2, 21.2, 59.5, 166.2, 167.10, 195.4

117 to draw rásam رَسَم

	affirmative		negative		
ána	rasámt	رَسَمْت	ma-rasámtiš	مَرَسَمْتِش	perfect
íḫna	rasámna	رَسَمْنا	ma-rasamnāš	مَرَسَمْناش	
ínta	rasámt	رَسَمْت	ma-rasámtiš	مَرَسَمْتِش	
ínti	rasámti	رَسَمْتي	ma-rasamtīš	مَرَسَمْتيش	
íntu	rasámtu	رَسَمْتوا	ma-rasamtūš	مَرَسَمْتوش	
húwwa	rásam	رَسَم	ma-rasámš	مَرَسَمْش	
híyya	rásamit	رَسَمِت	ma-rasamítš	مَرَسَمِتْش	
húmma	rásamu	رَسَموا	ma-rasamūš	مَرَسَموش	
ána	ársim	أَرْسِم	ma-rsímš	مَرْسِمْش	imperfect
íḫna	nírsim	نِرْسِم	ma-nirsímš	مَنِرْسِمْش	
ínta	tírsim	تِـرسِم	ma-tirsímš	مَتِـرسِمْش	
ínti	tirsími	تِـرسِمي	ma-tirsimīš	مَتِـرسِميش	
íntu	tirsímu	تِـرسِموا	ma-tirsimūš	مَتِـرسِموش	
húwwa	yírsim	يِـرسِم	ma-yirsímš	مَيِـرسِمْش	
híyya	tírsim	تِـرسِم	ma-tirsímš	مَتِـرسِمْش	
húmma	yirsímu	يِـرسِموا	ma-yirsimūš	مَيِـرسِموش	
ána	bársim	بَرْسِم	ma-barsímš	مَبَرْسِمْش	bi-imperfect
íḫna	binírsim	بِنِرْسِم	ma-bnirsímš	مَبْنِرْسِمْش	
ínta	bitírsim	بِتِـرسِم	ma-btirsímš	مَبْتِـرسِمْش	
ínti	bitirsími	بِتِـرسِمي	ma-btirsimīš	مَبْتِـرسِميش	
íntu	bitirsímu	بِتِـرسِموا	ma-btirsimūš	مَبْتِـرسِموش	
húwwa	biyírsim	بِيِـرسِم	ma-byirsímš	مَبْيِـرسِمْش	
híyya	bitírsim	بِتِـرسِم	ma-btirsímš	مَبْتِـرسِمْش	
húmma	biyirsímu	بِيِـرسِموا	ma-byirsimūš	مَبْيِـرسِموش	
ána	hársim	هَرْسِم	miš hársim	مِش هَرْسِم	future
íḫna	hanírsim	هَنِرْسِم	miš hanírsim	مِش هَنِرْسِم	
ínta	hatírsim	هَتِـرسِم	miš hatírsim	مِش هَتِـرسِم	
ínti	hatirsími	هَتِـرسِمي	miš hatirsími	مِش هَتِـرسِمي	
íntu	hatirsímu	هَتِـرسِموا	miš hatirsímu	مِش هَتِـرسِموا	
húwwa	hayírsim	هَيِـرسِم	miš hayírsim	مِش هَيِـرسِم	
híyya	hatírsim	هَتِـرسِم	miš hatírsim	مِش هَتِـرسِم	
húmma	hayirsímu	هَيِـرسِموا	miš hayirsímu	مِش هَيِـرسِموا	
ínta	írsim	اِرْسِم	ma-tirsímš	مَتِـرسِمْش	imperative
ínti	irsími	اِرْسِمي	ma-tirsimīš	مَتِـرسِميش	
íntu	irsímu	اِرْسِموا	ma-tirsimūš	مَتِـرسِموش	

	active		passive		
masculine	rāsim	راسِم	marsūm	مَرْسوم	participles
feminine	rásma	راسْمَة	marsūma	مَرْسومَة	
plural	rasmīn	راسْمين	marsumīn	مَرْسومين	

verbal noun: *rasm* رَسْم

①

شيريهان رسمِت أوِّل رسْمة و باعِتْها و هِيَّ عنْدها ٦ سْنين.

širihān rásamit áwwil rásma wi ba3ítha wi híyya 3andáha sitt[ə] snīn.

Sherihan drew her first drawing and sold it at age six.

②

بحِبّ أرْسِم أوي.

baĥíbb ársim áwi.

I like drawing so much

③

عبود بيِرسِم بِالأُوتوكاد بِاحْتِراف.

3abūd biyírsim bi-lʔutukād bi-ĥtirāf.

Abod draws professionally
with AutoCad.

④

هرْسِمْلك خطّ مْقطّع و إنْتَ أمْشي عليْه.

harsímlak xaṭṭ[ə] miʔáṭṭa3 w ínt- ímši 3alē.

I'll draw you a dashed line,
and you'll trace it.

⑤

اِرْسِم على كْبير مِن دِلْوَقْتى، حسِّن اللُّغة عشان تِسافِر برّه.

írsim 3ála kbīr min dilwáʔti, ĥássin illúɣa 3ašān tisāfir bárra.

Plan big. Start improving your language to travel abroad.

⑥

مرسمْتِش عَ الأوتوكاد بقالي فترْة.

ma-rasámtiš 3a -lʔutukād baʔāli fátra.

I haven't drawn on AutoCad
for a long time.

❖ [1s2] **to draw; to plan**

➲ 39.6, 52.1, 193.1, 231.8

118 to be satisfied *ríḍi* رِضي

	affirmative		negative		
ána	*riḍīt*	رِضيت	*ma-rḍítš*	مَرْضيتْش	**perfect**
íḫna	*riḍīna*	رِضينا	*ma-rḍināš*	مَرْضيناش	
ínta	*riḍīt*	رِضيت	*ma-rḍítš*	مَرْضيتْش	
ínti	*riḍīti*	رِضيتي	*ma-rḍitīš*	مَرْضيتيش	
íntu	*riḍītu*	رِضيتوا	*ma-rḍitūš*	مَرْضيتوش	
húwwa	*ríḍi*	رِضي	*ma-rḍīš*	مَرْضيش	
híyya	*nísyit*	رِضْيِت	*ma-riḍyítš*	مَرِضْيِتْش	
húmma	*nísyu*	رِضْيوا	*ma-riḍyūš*	مَرِضْيوش	
ána	*árḍa*	أرْضَى	*ma-rḍāš*	مَرْضاش	**imperfect**
íḫna	*nírḍa*	نِرْضَى	*ma-nirḍāš*	مَنِرْضاش	
ínta	*tírḍa*	تِـرضَى	*ma-tirḍāš*	مَتِـرضاش	
ínti	*tírḍi*	تِـرضي	*ma-tirḍīš*	مَتِـرضيش	
íntu	*tírḍu*	تِـرضوا	*ma-tirḍūš*	مَتِـرضوش	
húwwa	*yírḍa*	يِـرضَى	*ma-yirḍāš*	مَيِـرضاش	
híyya	*tírḍa*	تِـرضَى	*ma-tirḍāš*	مَتِـرضاش	
húmma	*yírḍu*	يِـرضوا	*ma-yirḍūš*	مَيِـرضوش	
ána	*bárḍa*	بَرْضَى	*ma-barḍāš*	مَبرّضاش	**bi-imperfect**
íḫna	*binírḍa*	بِنِرْضَى	*ma-bnirḍāš*	مَبْنِرْضاش	
ínta	*bitírḍa*	بِتِـرضَى	*ma-btirḍāš*	مَبْتِـرضاش	
ínti	*bitírḍi*	بِتِـرضي	*ma-btirḍīš*	مَبْتِـرضيش	
íntu	*bitírḍu*	بِتِـرضوا	*ma-btirḍūš*	مَبْتِـرضوش	
húwwa	*biyírḍa*	بِيِـرضَى	*ma-byirḍāš*	مَبْيِـرضاش	
híyya	*bitírḍa*	بِتِـرضَى	*ma-btirḍāš*	مَبْتِـرضاش	
húmma	*biyírḍu*	بِيِـرضوا	*ma-byirḍūš*	مَبْيِـرضوش	
ána	*hárḍa*	هَرْضَى	*miš hárḍa*	مِش هَرْضَى	**future**
íḫna	*hanírḍa*	هَنِرْضَى	*miš hanírḍa*	مِش هَنِرْضَى	
ínta	*hatírḍa*	هَتِـرضَى	*miš hatírḍa*	مِش هَتِـرضَى	
ínti	*hatírḍi*	هَتِـرضي	*miš hatírḍi*	مِش هَتِـرضي	
íntu	*hatírḍu*	هَتِـرضوا	*miš hatírḍu*	مِش هَتِـرضوا	
húwwa	*hayírḍa*	هَيِـرضَى	*miš hayírḍa*	مِش هَيِـرضَى	
híyya	*hatírḍa*	هَتِـرضَى	*miš hatírḍa*	مِش هَتِـرضَى	
húmma	*hayírḍu*	هَيِـرضوا	*miš hayírḍu*	مِش هَيِـرضوا	
ínta	*írḍa*	اِرْضَى	*ma-tirḍāš*	مَتِـرضاش	**imperative**
ínti	*írḍi*	اِرْضي	*ma-tirḍīš*	مَتِـرضيش	
íntu	*írḍu*	اِرْضوا	*ma-tirḍūš*	مَتِـرضوش	

	active		passive		
masculine	*rāḍi*	راضي	*márḍi*	مَرْضي	**participles**
feminine	*ráḍya*	راضْيَة	*marḍíyya*	مَرْضِيَّة	
plural	*raḍyīn*	راضْيين	*marḍiyīn*	مَرْضِيين	

verbal noun: *ríḍa* رِضَى

①

رِضينا بِالهمّ و الهمّ مِش راضي بينا.

riḍīna bi-lhámmᵊ w ilhámmᵊ miš rāḍi bīna.

We've accepted badness, but badness doesn't accept us. (a common saying)

②

نادِر و نُهى بِيْحاوْلوا يِقْنِعوا باباها يِـرضى بْجَوازْهُم.

nādir wi núha biyḥáwlu yiqní3u babāha yírḍa b-gawázhum.

Nader and Noha are trying to convince her father to accept their marriage.

③

عمّ سمير راجِل بسيط بِيِـرضى بْأيّ حاجة.

3ammᵊ samīr rāgil basīṭ biyírḍa b-ayyᵊ ḥāga.

Uncle Sameer is an easy-going guy who's happy with anything.

④

إتْحايْلوا على الحارِس شُوَيّة. هَيِـرضي يْدخّلْكو.

itḥáylu 3ála -lḥāris šuwáyya. hayírḍa ydaxxálku.

Keep pleading with the guard. He'll let you in.

⑤

اِرْضي يابْني بِاللي ربِّنا قسمْهولك. ربِّنا هَيدّيك أكْتر.

írḍi ya -bni bi-lli rabbína ʔasamhūlak. rabbína hayiddīk áktar.

Son, be happy with what God has given you, and he'll give you more.

⑥

سِهام مرضِتْش تِشْرب شيشة معَ صاحْباتْها.

sihām ma-raḍítšᵊ tíšrab šīša má3a ṣaḥbátha.

Seham refused to smoke shisha with her friends.

❖ [1d4] **to accept, be satisfied (with)** (بِـ *bi-*)

- Notice that the negative can be translated as 'refuse'. (➲ 118.6)

119 to chat *ráɣa* رَغَى

	affirmative		negative		
ána	*raɣēt*	رَغيْت	*ma-raɣítš*	مَرَغيْتْش	**perfect**
íḫna	*raɣēna*	رَغيْنا	*ma-raɣināš*	مَرَغيناش	
ínta	*raɣēt*	رَغيْت	*ma-raɣítš*	مَرَغيْتْش	
ínti	*raɣēti*	رَغيْتي	*ma-raɣitīš*	مَرَغيتيش	
íntu	*raɣētu*	رَغيْتوا	*ma-raɣitūš*	مَرَغيتوش	
húwwa	*ráɣa*	رَغَى	*ma-raɣāš*	مَرَغاش	
híyya	*ráɣit*	رَغِت	*ma-raɣítš*	مَرَغِتْش	
húmma	*ráɣu*	رَغوا	*ma-raɣūš*	مَرَغوش	
ána	*árɣi*	أرْغي	*ma-rɣīš*	مَرْغيش	**imperfect**
íḫna	*nírɣi*	نِرْغي	*ma-nirɣīš*	مَنِرْغيش	
ínta	*tírɣi*	تِرغي	*ma-tirɣīš*	مَتِرغيش	
ínti	*tírɣi*	تِرغي	*ma-tirɣīš*	مَتِرغيش	
íntu	*tírɣu*	تِرغوا	*ma-tirɣūš*	مَتِرغوش	
húwwa	*yírɣi*	يِرغي	*ma-yirɣīš*	مَيِرغيش	
híyya	*tírɣi*	تِرغي	*ma-tirɣīš*	مَتِرغيش	
húmma	*yírɣu*	يِرغوا	*ma-yirɣūš*	مَيِرغوش	
ána	*bárɣi*	بَرْغي	*ma-barɣīš*	مَبَرْغيش	**bi-imperfect**
íḫna	*binírɣi*	بِنِرْغي	*ma-bnirɣīš*	مَبْنِرْغيش	
ínta	*bitírɣi*	بِتِرغي	*ma-btirɣīš*	مَبْتِرغيش	
ínti	*bitírɣi*	بِتِرغي	*ma-btirɣīš*	مَبْتِرغيش	
íntu	*bitírɣu*	بِتِرغوا	*ma-btirɣūš*	مَبْتِرغوش	
húwwa	*biyírɣi*	بِيِرغي	*ma-byirɣīš*	مَبْيِرغيش	
híyya	*bitírɣi*	بِتِرغي	*ma-btirɣīš*	مَبْتِرغيش	
húmma	*biyírɣu*	بِيِرغوا	*ma-byirɣūš*	مَبْيِرغوش	
ána	*hárɣi*	هَرْغي	*miš hárɣi*	مِش هَرْغي	**future**
íḫna	*hanírɣi*	هَنِرْغي	*miš hanírɣi*	مِش هَنِرْغي	
ínta	*hatírɣi*	هَتِرغي	*miš hatírɣi*	مِش هَتِرغي	
ínti	*hatírɣi*	هَتِرغي	*miš hatírɣi*	مِش هَتِرغي	
íntu	*hatírɣu*	هَتِرغوا	*miš hatírɣu*	مِش هَتِرغوا	
húwwa	*hayírɣi*	هَيِرغي	*miš hayírɣi*	مِش هَيِرغي	
híyya	*hatírɣi*	هَتِرغي	*miš hatírɣi*	مِش هَتِرغي	
húmma	*hayírɣu*	هَيِرغوا	*miš hayírɣu*	مِش هَيِرغوا	
ínta	*írɣi*	اِرْغي	*ma-tirɣīš*	مَتِرغيش	**imperative**
ínti	*írɣi*	اِرْغي	*ma-tirɣīš*	مَتِرغيش	
íntu	*írɣu*	اِرْغوا	*ma-tirɣūš*	مَتِرغوش	

	active		passive		
masculine	*rāɣi*	راغي	*márɣi*	مَرْغي	**participles**
feminine	*ráɣya*	راغْيَة	–	–	
plural	*raɣyīn*	راغْيين	–	–	

verbal noun: *raɣy* رَغْي

①

الصُّبْح اِتّصلِت بيّا مِنّة و رغِت معايا ساعة.

iṣṣúbḥ ittáṣalit bíyya mínna wi ráɣit ma3āya sā3a.

Menna called me this morning and talked with me for an hour.

②

أنا صاحْيَة. مين عايِز يِـرغي؟

ána ṣáḥya. mīn 3āyiz yírɣi?

I'm awake. Who wants to chat?

③

بِتِـرغي في التِّليفوْن كُلّ ده معَ مين؟

bitírɣi fi -ttilifōn kullᵊ da má3a mīn?

Who were you talking with all that time on the phone?

④

لَوْ اِتّصلْتي بْشوشو دِلْوَقْتي هتِـرغي معاكي لِلصُّبْح.

law ittaṣálti b-šūšu dilwáʔti hatírɣi ma3āki li-ṣṣubḥ.

If you call Shosho now, she'll chat with you until morning.

⑤

متِـرغيش كِتير. عايِز أيْه؟

ma-tirɣīš kitīr. 3āyiz ʔē?

Don't talk too much. What exactly do you want?

⑥

القِصّة دي مرْغي فيها كْتير.

ilqíṣṣa di márɣi fīha ktīr.

This story has been discussed a lot.

❖ [1d2] **to chat, talk (with** معَ *má3a;* **about** في *fi*)

- As this verb requires a preposition, the passive participle is invariable. (➲ 119.6)

➲ 264.3

120 to refuse ráfaḍ رَفَض

	affirmative		negative		
ána	rafáḍt	رَفَضْت	ma-rafáḍtiš	مَرَفَضْتِش	perfect
íḫna	rafáḍna	رَفَضْنا	ma-rafaḍnāš	مَرَفَضْناش	
ínta	rafáḍt	رَفَضْت	ma-rafáḍtiš	مَرَفَضْتِش	
ínti	rafáḍti	رَفَضْتي	ma-rafaḍtīš	مَرَفَضْتيش	
íntu	rafáḍtu	رَفَضْتوا	ma-rafaḍtūš	مَرَفَضْتوش	
húwwa	ráfaḍ	رَفَض	ma-rafáḍš	مَرَفَضْش	
híyya	ráfaḍit	رَفَضِت	ma-rafaḍítš	مَرَفَضِتْش	
húmma	ráfaḍu	رَفَضوا	ma-rafaḍūš	مَرَفَضوش	
ána	árfuḍ	أرْفُض	ma-rfúḍš	مَرْفُضْش	imperfect
íḫna	núrfuḍ	نُرْفُض	ma-nurfúḍš	مَنُرْفُضْش	
ínta	túrfuḍ	تُرْفُض	ma-turfúḍš	مَتُرْفُضْش	
ínti	turfúḍi	تُرْفُضي	ma-turfuḍīš	مَتُرْفُضيش	
íntu	turfúḍu	تُرْفُضوا	ma-turfuḍūš	مَتُرْفُضوش	
húwwa	yúrfuḍ	يُرْفُض	ma-yurfúḍš	مَيُرْفُضْش	
híyya	túrfuḍ	تُرْفُض	ma-turfúḍš	مَتُرْفُضْش	
húmma	yurfúḍu	يُرْفُضوا	ma-yurfuḍūš	مَيُرْفُضوش	
ána	bárfuḍ	بَرْفُض	ma-barfúḍš	مَبَرْفُضْش	bi-imperfect
íḫna	binúrfuḍ	بِنُرْفُض	ma-bnurfúḍš	مَبْنُرْفُضْش	
ínta	bitúrfuḍ	بِتُرْفُض	ma-bturfúḍš	مَبْتُرْفُضْش	
ínti	biturfúḍi	بِتُرْفُضي	ma-bturfuḍīš	مَبْتُرْفُضيش	
íntu	biturfúḍu	بِتُرْفُضوا	ma-bturfuḍūš	مَبْتُرْفُضوش	
húwwa	biyúrfuḍ	بِيُرْفُض	ma-byurfúḍš	مَبْيُرْفُضْش	
híyya	bitúrfuḍ	بِتُرْفُض	ma-bturfúḍš	مَبْتُرْفُضْش	
húmma	biyurfúḍu	بِيُرْفُضوا	ma-byurfuḍūš	مَبْيُرْفُضوش	
ána	hárfuḍ	هَرْفُض	miš hárfuḍ	مِش هَرْفُض	future
íḫna	hanúrfuḍ	هَنُرْفُض	miš hanúrfuḍ	مِش هَنُرْفُض	
ínta	hatúrfuḍ	هَتُرْفُض	miš hatúrfuḍ	مِش هَتُرْفُض	
ínti	haturfúḍi	هَتُرْفُضي	miš haturfúḍi	مِش هَتُرْفُضي	
íntu	haturfúḍu	هَتُرْفُضوا	miš haturfúḍu	مِش هَتُرْفُضوا	
húwwa	hayúrfuḍ	هَيُرْفُض	miš hayúrfuḍ	مِش هَيُرْفُض	
híyya	hatúrfuḍ	هَتُرْفُض	miš hatúrfuḍ	مِش هَتُرْفُض	
húmma	hayurfúḍu	هَيُرْفُضوا	miš hayurfúḍu	مِش هَيُرْفُضوا	
ínta	írfuḍ	اِرْفُض	ma-turfúḍš	مَتُرْفُضْش	imperative
ínti	irfúḍi	اِرْفُضي	ma-turfuḍīš	مَتُرْفُضيش	
íntu	irfúḍu	اِرْفُضوا	ma-turfuḍūš	مَتُرْفُضوش	

	active		passive		
masculine	rāfiḍ	رافِض	marfūḍ	مَرْفوض	participles
feminine	ráfḍa	رافْضَة	marfūḍa	مَرْفوضَة	
plural	rafḍīn	رافْضين	marfuḍīn	مَرْفوضين	

verbal noun: rafḍ رَفْض

①

سلْمى رفضِت تِقْلع الحِجاب عشان تِشارِك في البُطولة.

sálma ráfaḍit tíʔla3 ilḥigāb 3ašān tišārik fi -lbuṭūla.

Salma refused to take off her hijab to participate in the championship.

②

بِنْتي عمّالة تُرْفُض العِرْسان، بسّ المرّة دي جايِبْلها واحِد مَيترْفِضْش.

bínti 3ammāla túrfuḍ il3irsān, bass ilmárra di gayibláha wāḥid ma-yitrifíḍš.

My daughter keeps rejecting [potential] husbands, but this time I brought her someone who can't be refused.

③

إبْني بِيرْفُض ياكُل خُضار. مِش عارْفة أعْمِلُّه أيْه.

íbni biyúrfuḍ yākul xuḍār. miš 3árfa ʔa3míllu ʔē.

My son refuses to eat vegetables. I don't know what to do with him.

④

شَيْماء مِش هترْفُض تُقْعُد في البيْت لَوْ جوزْها طلب مِنْها كِده.

šaymāʔ miš hatúrfuḍ túʔ3ud fi -lbēt law gúzha ṭálab mínha kída.

Shaimaa won't refuse to stay at home if her husband asks her to.

⑤

اِرْفُضي أيّ نوْع مِن التّمْييز بيْنك و بيْن زمايْلك.

irfúḍi ʔayyᵊ nō3 min ittamyīz bēnak wi bēn zamáylak.

Reject any kind of favoritism between you and your colleagues.

⑥

أخيراً ميريهان مرفضْتِش العريس اللي اتْقدِّمْلها.

axīran mirihān ma-rafáḍtiš il3arīs ílli -tʔaddimláha.

In the end, Merehan didn't refuse the suitor who proposed to her.

❖ [1s3] **to refuse, reject**

- This verb can be followed by an imperfect verb.
- The last word in 120.2 is the passive اِتْفرض *itfáraḍ*, يِتْفِرِض *yitfíriḍ*.
- This verb, like other verbs of the [1s3] and [1s6] patterns, can optionally take ـُ *u* instead of ـِ *i* in the personal prefixes of the imperfect (including the bi-imperfect and future) and imperative. For example, يُرْفُض *yúrfuḍ* can also be pronounced يِرفُض *yírfuḍ*. These vowels are interchangeable, but the tables reflect the preferences of the speakers on the MP3s.

➲ 51.6

121 to lift *ráfa3* رَفَع

	affirmative		negative		
ána	*rafá3t*	رَفَعْت	*ma-rafá3tiš*	مَرَفَعْتِش	**perfect**
íḥna	*rafá3na*	رَفَعْنا	*ma-rafa3nāš*	مَرَفَعْناش	
ínta	*rafá3t*	رَفَعْت	*ma-rafá3tiš*	مَرَفَعْتِش	
ínti	*rafá3ti*	رَفَعْتي	*ma-rafa3tīš*	مَرَفَعْتيش	
íntu	*rafá3tu*	رَفَعْتوا	*ma-rafa3tūš*	مَرَفَعْتوش	
húwwa	*ráfa3*	رَفَع	*ma-rafá3š*	مَرَفَعْش	
híyya	*ráfa3it*	رَفَعِت	*ma-rafa3ítš*	مَرَفَعِتْش	
húmma	*ráfa3u*	رَفَعوا	*ma-rafa3ūš*	مَرَفَعوش	
ána	*árfa3*	أَرْفَع	*ma-rfá3š*	مَرْفَعْش	**imperfect**
íḥna	*nírfa3*	نِرْفَع	*ma-nirfá3š*	مَنِرْفَعْش	
ínta	*tírfa3*	تِرفَع	*ma-tirfá3š*	مَتِرفَعْش	
ínti	*tirfá3i*	تِرفَعي	*ma-tirfa3īš*	مَتِرفَعيش	
íntu	*tirfá3u*	تِرفَعوا	*ma-tirfa3ūš*	مَتِرفَعوش	
húwwa	*yírfa3*	يِرفَع	*ma-yirfá3š*	مَيِرفَعْش	
híyya	*tírfa3*	تِرفَع	*ma-tirfá3š*	مَتِرفَعْش	
húmma	*yirfá3u*	يِرفَعوا	*ma-yirfa3ūš*	مَيِرفَعوش	
ána	*bárfa3*	بَرْفَع	*ma-barfá3š*	مَبَرْفَعْش	**bi-imperfect**
íḥna	*binírfa3*	بِنِرْفَع	*ma-bnirfá3š*	مَبْنِرْفَعْش	
ínta	*bitírfa3*	بِتِرفَع	*ma-btirfá3š*	مَبْتِرفَعْش	
ínti	*bitirfá3i*	بِتِرفَعي	*ma-btirfa3īš*	مَبْتِرفَعيش	
íntu	*bitirfá3u*	بِتِرفَعوا	*ma-btirfa3ūš*	مَبْتِرفَعوش	
húwwa	*biyírfa3*	بِيِرفَع	*ma-byirfá3š*	مَبْيِرفَعْش	
híyya	*bitírfa3*	بِتِرفَع	*ma-btirfá3š*	مَبْتِرفَعْش	
húmma	*biyirfá3u*	بِيِرفَعوا	*ma-byirfa3ūš*	مَبْيِرفَعوش	
ána	*hárfa3*	هَرْفَع	*miš hárfa3*	مِش هَرْفَع	**future**
íḥna	*hanírfa3*	هَنِرْفَع	*miš hanírfa3*	مِش هَنِرْفَع	
ínta	*hatírfa3*	هَتِرفَع	*miš hatírfa3*	مِش هَتِرفَع	
ínti	*hatirfá3i*	هَتِرفَعي	*miš hatirfá3i*	مِش هَتِرفَعي	
íntu	*hatirfá3u*	هَتِرفَعوا	*miš hatirfá3u*	مِش هَتِرفَعوا	
húwwa	*hayírfa3*	هَيِرفَع	*miš hayírfa3*	مِش هَيِرفَع	
híyya	*hatírfa3*	هَتِرفَع	*miš hatírfa3*	مِش هَتِرفَع	
húmma	*hayirfá3u*	هَيِرفَعوا	*miš hayirfá3u*	مِش هَيِرفَعوا	
ínta	*írfa3*	اِرْفَع	*ma-tirfá3š*	مَتِرفَعْش	**imperative**
ínti	*irfá3i*	اِرْفَعي	*ma-tirfa3īš*	مَتِرفَعيش	
íntu	*irfá3u*	اِرْفَعوا	*ma-tirfa3ūš*	مَتِرفَعوش	

	active		passive		
masculine	*rāfi3*	رافِع	*marfū3*	مَرْفوع	**participles**
feminine	*ráf3a*	رافْعَة	*marfū3a*	مَرْفوعَة	
plural	*raf3īn*	رافْعين	*marfu3īn*	مَرْفوعين	

verbal noun: *raf3* رَفْع

①

رفعْت السِّرير لِوَحْدي و كِتْفي وَجعْني.

rafá3t issirīr li-wáħdi wi kítfi wagá3ni.

I lifted up the bed by myself,
and my shoulder hurt me.

②

الوَلد ده شاطِر. كُلّ ما أسْأل سُؤال يِـرفع إيدُه.

ilwálad da šāṭir. kullᵊ m- ásʔal suʔāl yírfa3 īdu.

This boy is clever. Every time I ask
a question, he raises his hand.

③

هُدى بْتِـرفع اللِّعب فوْق الدّولاب أيّام الاِمْتِحانات.

húda bitráfa3 illí3ab fōʔ iddulāb ayyām ilʔimtiħanāt.

Hoda puts the toys up in the
cupboard during exam time.

④

التُّجّار هَيِـرفعوا الأسْعار في أغُسْطُس.

ittuggār hayirfá3u -lʔas3ār fi ʔaɣúsṭus.

The vendors will raise the prices in August.

⑤

اِرْفع راسك فوْق و اِعْتزّ بِنفْسك دايْماً.

írfa3 rāsak fōʔ w i3tázzᵊ bi-náfsak dáyman.

Always keep your head up
and be proud of yourself.

⑥

مرفعْتِش إيدك ليْه عشان تِجاوِب؟

ma-rafá3tiš īdak lē 3ašān tigāwib?

Why didn't you raise your hand
to answer the question?

❖ [1s1] **to lift, raise**

➲ 35.5

122 to dance ráʔaṣ رَقَص

	affirmative		negative		
ána	raʔáṣt	رَقَصْت	ma-raʔáṣtiš	مَرَقَصْتِش	perfect
íḥna	raʔáṣna	رَقَصْنا	ma-raʔaṣnāš	مَرَقَصْناش	
ínta	raʔáṣt	رَقَصْت	ma-raʔáṣtiš	مَرَقَصْتِش	
ínti	raʔáṣti	رَقَصْتي	ma-raʔaṣtīš	مَرَقَصْتيش	
íntu	raʔáṣtu	رَقَصْتوا	ma-raʔaṣtūš	مَرَقَصْتوش	
húwwa	ráʔaṣ	رَقَص	ma-raʔáṣš	مَرَقَصْش	
híyya	ráʔaṣit	رَقَصِت	ma-raʔaṣítš	مَرَقَصِتْش	
húmma	ráʔaṣu	رَقَصوا	ma-raʔaṣūš	مَرَقَصوش	
ána	árʔuṣ	أَرْقُص	ma-rʔúṣš	مَرْقُصْش	imperfect
íḥna	núrʔuṣ	نُرْقُص	ma-nurʔúṣš	مَنُرْقُصْش	
ínta	túrʔuṣ	تُرْقُص	ma-turʔúṣš	مَتُرْقُصْش	
ínti	turʔúṣi	تُرْقُصي	ma-turʔuṣīš	مَتُرْقُصيش	
íntu	turʔúṣu	تُرْقُصوا	ma-turʔuṣūš	مَتُرْقُصوش	
húwwa	yúrʔuṣ	يُرْقُص	ma-yurʔúṣš	مَيُرْقُصْش	
híyya	túrʔuṣ	تُرْقُص	ma-turʔúṣš	مَتُرْقُصْش	
húmma	yurʔúṣu	يُرْقُصوا	ma-yurʔuṣūš	مَيُرْقُصوش	
ána	bárʔuṣ	بَرْقُص	ma-barʔúṣš	مَبَرْقُصْش	bi-imperfect
íḥna	binúrʔuṣ	بِنُرْقُص	ma-bnurʔúṣš	مَبْنُرْقُصْش	
ínta	bitúrʔuṣ	بِتُرْقُص	ma-bturʔúṣš	مَبْتُرْقُصْش	
ínti	biturʔúṣi	بِتُرْقُصي	ma-bturʔuṣīš	مَبْتُرْقُصيش	
íntu	biturʔúṣu	بِتُرْقُصوا	ma-bturʔuṣūš	مَبْتُرْقُصوش	
húwwa	biyúrʔuṣ	بِيُرْقُص	ma-byurʔúṣš	مَبْيُرْقُصْش	
híyya	bitúrʔuṣ	بِتُرْقُص	ma-bturʔúṣš	مَبْتُرْقُصْش	
húmma	biyurʔúṣu	بِيُرْقُصوا	ma-byurʔuṣūš	مَبْيُرْقُصوش	
ána	hárʔuṣ	هَرْقُص	miš hárʔuṣ	مِش هَرْقُص	future
íḥna	hanúrʔuṣ	هَنُرْقُص	miš hanúrʔuṣ	مِش هَنُرْقُص	
ínta	hatúrʔuṣ	هَتُرْقُص	miš hatúrʔuṣ	مِش هَتُرْقُص	
ínti	haturʔúṣi	هَتُرْقُصي	miš haturʔúṣi	مِش هَتُرْقُصي	
íntu	haturʔúṣu	هَتُرْقُصوا	miš haturʔúṣu	مِش هَتُرْقُصوا	
húwwa	hayúrʔuṣ	هَيُرْقُص	miš hayúrʔuṣ	مِش هَيُرْقُص	
híyya	hatúrʔuṣ	هَتُرْقُص	miš hatúrʔuṣ	مِش هَتُرْقُص	
húmma	hayurʔúṣu	هَيُرْقُصوا	miš hayurʔúṣu	مِش هَيُرْقُصوا	
ínta	írʔuṣ	أُرْقُص	ma-turʔúṣš	مَتُرْقُصْش	imperative
ínti	irʔúṣi	أُرْقُصي	ma-turʔuṣīš	مَتُرْقُصيش	
íntu	irʔúṣu	أُرْقُصوا	ma-turʔuṣūš	مَتُرْقُصوش	

	active		passive		
masculine	rāʔiṣ	راقِص	–	–	participles
feminine	ráʔṣa	راقْصَة	–	–	
plural	raʔṣīn	راقْصين	–	–	

verbal noun: raʔṣ رَقْص

①

الشّباب رقصوا في الفرح رقْص.

iššabāb ráʔaṣu fi -lfáraḥ raʔṣ.

The guys danced a lot at the wedding.

②

إبْني دايْماً يُرْقُص لمّا يِسْمع أيّ مزّيكا.

íbni dáyman yúrʔuṣ lámma yísma3 ayyᵊ mazzīka.

My son always dances when he hears any music.

③

قلْبي بِيرُقُص مِ الفرْحة و إحْنا معَ بعْض.

ʔálbi biyúrʔuṣ mi -lfárḥa w íḥna má3a ba3ḍ.

My heart dances happily when we're together.

④

سَوْسن مِش هترُقُص في فرحْها. مِش بِتْحِبّ كِده.

sáwsan miš hatúrʔuṣ fi faráḥha. miš bitḥíbbᵊ kída.

Sawsan will not dance at her wedding. She doesn't like that.

⑤

أُرْقُصي عشان تِخِسّي.

urʔúṣi 3ašān tixíssi.

Dance to lose weight.

⑥

شاهِنْدة مرقصِتْش في الفرح. اِتْكسفِت مِن النّاس.

šahínda ma-raʔaṣítšᵊ fi -lfáraḥ. itkásafit min innās.

Shahinda didn't dance at the wedding. She was too embarrassed.

⑦

الرّقْصة دي مرْقوصة وِحِش أوي.

irráʔṣa di marʔūṣa wíḥiš áwi.

This dance was performed [lit. danced] badly.

❖ [1s3] **to dance**

- This verb, like other verbs of the [1s3] and [1s6] patterns, can optionally take ـُ *u* instead of ـِ *i* in the personal prefixes of the imperfect (including the bi-imperfect and future) and imperative. For example, يُرْقُص *yúrʔuṣ* can also be pronounced يِرقُص *yírʔuṣ*. These vowels are interchangeable, but the tables reflect the preferences of the speakers on the MP3s.

➲ 84.3

123 to ride *ríkib* رِكِب

verbal noun: *rukūb* رُكوب

	affirmative		negative		
ána	*rikíbt*	رِكِبْت	*ma-rkíbtiš*	مَرْكِبْتِش	**perfect**
íḫna	*rikíbna*	رِكِبْنا	*ma-rkibnāš*	مَرْكِبْناش	
ínta	*rikíbt*	رِكِبْت	*ma-rkíbtiš*	مَرْكِبْتِش	
ínti	*rikíbti*	رِكِبْتي	*ma-rkibtīš*	مَرْكِبْتيش	
íntu	*rikíbtu*	رِكِبْتوا	*ma-rkibtūš*	مَرْكِبْتوش	
húwwa	*ríkib*	رِكِب	*ma-rkíbš*	مَرْكِبْش	
híyya	*ríkbit*	رِكْبِت	*ma-rikbítš*	مَرِكْبِتْش	
húmma	*ríkbu*	رِكْبوا	*ma-rikbūš*	مَرِكْبوش	
ána	*árkab*	أَرْكَب	*ma-rkábš*	مَرْكَبْش	**imperfect**
íḫna	*nírkab*	نِرْكَب	*ma-nirkábš*	مَنِرْكَبْش	
ínta	*tírkab*	تِرْكَب	*ma-tirkábš*	مَتِرْكَبْش	
ínti	*tirkábi*	تِرْكَبي	*ma-tirkabīš*	مَتِرْكَبيش	
íntu	*tirkábu*	تِرْكَبوا	*ma-tirkabūš*	مَتِرْكَبوش	
húwwa	*yírkab*	يِرْكَب	*ma-yirkábš*	مَيِرْكَبْش	
híyya	*tírkab*	تِرْكَب	*ma-tirkábš*	مَتِرْكَبْش	
húmma	*yirkábu*	يِرْكَبوا	*ma-yirkabūš*	مَيِرْكَبوش	
ána	*bárkab*	بَرْكَب	*ma-barkábš*	مَبَرْكَبْش	**bi-imperfect**
íḫna	*binírkab*	بِنِرْكَب	*ma-bnirkábš*	مَبْنِرْكَبْش	
ínta	*bitírkab*	بِتِرْكَب	*ma-btirkábš*	مَبْتِرْكَبْش	
ínti	*bitirkábi*	بِتِرْكَبي	*ma-btirkabīš*	مَبْتِرْكَبيش	
íntu	*bitirkábu*	بِتِرْكَبوا	*ma-btirkabūš*	مَبْتِرْكَبوش	
húwwa	*biyírkab*	بِيِرْكَب	*ma-byirkábš*	مَبْيِرْكَبْش	
híyya	*bitírkab*	بِتِرْكَب	*ma-btirkábš*	مَبْتِرْكَبْش	
húmma	*biyirkábu*	بِيِرْكَبوا	*ma-byirkabūš*	مَبْيِرْكَبوش	
ána	*hárkab*	هَرْكَب	*miš hárkab*	مِش هَرْكَب	**future**
íḫna	*hanírkab*	هَنِرْكَب	*miš hanírkab*	مِش هَنِرْكَب	
ínta	*hatírkab*	هَتِرْكَب	*miš hatírkab*	مِش هَتِرْكَب	
ínti	*hatirkábi*	هَتِرْكَبي	*miš hatirkábi*	مِش هَتِرْكَبي	
íntu	*hatirkábu*	هَتِرْكَبوا	*miš hatirkábu*	مِش هَتِرْكَبوا	
húwwa	*hayírkab*	هَيِرْكَب	*miš hayírkab*	مِش هَيِرْكَب	
híyya	*hatírkab*	هَتِرْكَب	*miš hatírkab*	مِش هَتِرْكَب	
húmma	*hayirkábu*	هَيِرْكَبوا	*miš hayirkábu*	مِش هَيِرْكَبوا	
ínta	*írkab*	اِرْكَب	*ma-tirkábš*	مَتِرْكَبْش	**imperative**
ínti	*irkábi*	اِرْكَبي	*ma-tirkabīš*	مَتِرْكَبيش	
íntu	*irkábu*	اِرْكَبوا	*ma-tirkabūš*	مَتِرْكَبوش	

	active		passive		
masculine	*rākib*	راكِب	*markūb*	مَرْكوب	**participles**
feminine	*rákba*	راكْبَة	*markūba*	مَرْكوبَة	
plural	*rakbīn*	راكْبين	*markubīn*	مَرْكوبين	

①

رِكِبْت الأُتوبيس. وَصّلْني لْحدّ باب البيْت.

rikíbt ilʔutubīs. waṣṣálni l-ђaddᵊ bāb ilbēt.

I took the bus, and it dropped me off on the doorstep.

②

بحِبّ أرْكب المُواصْلات العامّة رغْم إنّ عنْدي عربية.

baђíbb árkab ilmuwaṣlāt il3ámma raɣm innᵊ 3ándi 3arabíyya.

I like riding public transportation though I have a car.

③

سُمَيَّة بْتِركب مرْسيدِس.

sumáyya btírkab marsīdis.

Somaya has a Mercedes.

④

هتِركبوا مِن هِنا المِتْرو لْحدّ آخِر الخطّ.

hatirkábu min hína -lmítru l-ђaddᵊ ʔāxir ilxáṭṭ.

You'll take the subway from here to the end of its line.

⑤

اِرْكبي أوبر أحْسنْلِك.

irkábi ūbar aђsánlik.

It's better for you to take Uber.

⑥

الجَوّ كان حرّ أوي إمْبارِح، فا مرْكِبْش العجلة و رِكِب بِدالْها أُتوبيس.

ilgáwwᵊ kān ђarrᵊ ʔáwi imbāriђ, fa ma-rkíbš il3ágala wi ríkib badálha ʔutubīs.

It was so hot yesterday, so he didn't ride his bike. Instead, he took the bus.

⑦

مرْكِبْناش طَيّارِتْنا عشان اِتْأخّرْنا في الوُصول.

ma-rkibnāš ṭayyarítna 3ašān itʔaxxárna fi -lwuṣūl.

We didn't catch our flight. We arrived too late.

❖ [1s4] **to ride, take** (transportation)

124 to give a ride to rákkib ركّب

verbal nouns: tarkīb تّركيب - rukūb ركوب

	affirmative		negative		
ána	rakkíbt	ركّبت	ma-rakkíbtiš	مركّبتش	perfect
íḥna	rakkíbna	ركّبنا	ma-rakkibnāš	مركّبناش	
ínta	rakkíbt	ركّبت	ma-rakkíbtiš	مركّبتش	
ínti	rakkíbti	ركّبتي	ma-rakkibtīš	مركّبتيش	
íntu	rakkíbtu	ركّبتوا	ma-rakkibtūš	مركّبتوش	
húwwa	rákkib	ركّب	ma-rakkíbš	مركّبش	
híyya	rakkíbit	ركّبت	ma-rakkibítš	مركّبتش	
húmma	rakkíbu	ركّبوا	ma-rakkibūš	مركّبوش	
ána	arákkib	أركّب	ma-rakkíbš	مركّبش	imperfect
íḥna	nirákkib	نركّب	ma-nrakkíbš	منركّبش	
ínta	tirákkib	تركّب	ma-trakkíbš	متركّبش	
ínti	tirakkíbi	تركّبي	ma-trakkibīš	متركّبيش	
íntu	tirakkíbu	تركّبوا	ma-trakkibūš	متركّبوش	
húwwa	yirákkib	يركّب	ma-yrakkíbš	ميركّبش	
híyya	tirákkib	تركّب	ma-trakkíbš	متركّبش	
húmma	yirakkíbu	يركّبوا	ma-yrakkibūš	ميركّبوش	
ána	barákkib	بركّب	ma-barakkíbš	مبركّبش	bi-imperfect
íḥna	binrákkib	بنركّب	ma-binrakkíbš	مبنركّبش	
ínta	bitrákkib	بتركّب	ma-bitrakkíbš	مبتركّبش	
ínti	bitrakkíbi	بتركّبي	ma-bitrakkibīš	مبتركّبيش	
íntu	bitrakkíbu	بتركّبوا	ma-bitrakkibūš	مبتركّبوش	
húwwa	biyrákkib	بيركّب	ma-biyrakkíbš	مبيركّبش	
híyya	bitrákkib	بتركّب	ma-bitrakkíbš	مبتركّبش	
húmma	biyrakkíbu	بيركّبوا	ma-biyrakkibūš	مبيركّبوش	
ána	harákkib	هركّب	miš harákkib	مش هركّب	future
íḥna	hanrákkib	هنركّب	miš hanrákkib	مش هنركّب	
ínta	hatrákkib	هتركّب	miš hatrákkib	مش هتركّب	
ínti	hatrakkíbi	هتركّبي	miš hatrakkíbi	مش هتركّبي	
íntu	hatrakkíbu	هتركّبوا	miš hatrakkíbu	مش هتركّبوا	
húwwa	hayrákkib	هيركّب	miš hayrákkib	مش هيركّب	
híyya	hatrákkib	هتركّب	miš hatrákkib	مش هتركّب	
húmma	hayrakkíbu	هيركّبوا	miš hayrakkíbu	مش هيركّبوا	
ínta	rákkib	ركّب	ma-trakkíbš	متركّبش	imperative
ínti	rakkíbi	ركّبي	ma-trakkibīš	متركّبيش	
íntu	rakkíbu	ركّبوا	ma-trakkibūš	متركّبوش	

	active		passive		
masculine	mirákkib	مركّب	mitrákkib	متركّب	participles
feminine	mirakkíba	مركّبة	mitrakkíba	متركّبة	
plural	mirakkibīn	مركّبين	mitrakkibīn	متركّبين	

①

رَكِّبْت مرّة معايا سِتّ كْبيرة. طِلْعِت جارْتي و أنا مكُنْتِش أعْرفْها.

rakkíbtᵊ márra ma3āya sittᵊ kbīra. ṭíl3it gárti w ána ma-kúntiš a3ráfha.

Once I gave an old woman a ride. It turned out that she's my neighbor, but I didn't know her before.

②

سمر مبْتِعْرفْش تْركِّب أمْبوبِةْ البوتاجاز.

sámar ma-bti3ráfšᵊ trákkib ambūbit ilbutagāz.

Samar can't fix the propane gas tank.

③

إسْماعيل بِيْركِّب معاه أيّ حدّ في السِّكّة.

isma3īl biyrákkib ma3ā ʔayyᵊ ḥaddᵊ fi -ssíkka.

Ismael gives rides to anyone on his way.

④

هَيْركِّبولْكو عدّاد ميّة إمْتى؟

hayrakkibúlku 3addād máyya ʔímta?

When are they going to install the water meter for you?

⑤

مترْكِّبيش رُموش. بِيِبْقى شكْلِك مُرْعِب.

ma-trakkibīš rumūš. biyíbʔa šáklik múr3ib.

Don't put on lashes. They make you look scary.

❖ [2s1] **to give a ride to; to install; to repair, fix**

125 to throw *ráma* رَمَى

	affirmative		negative		
ána	ramēt	رَمَيْت	ma-ramítš	مَرَميْتْش	perfect
íḥna	ramēna	رَمَيْنا	ma-raminā̃š	مَرَميناش	
ínta	ramēt	رَمَيْت	ma-ramítš	مَرَميْتْش	
ínti	ramēti	رَمَيْتي	ma-ramitīš	مَرَميتيش	
íntu	ramētu	رَمَيْتوا	ma-ramitūš	مَرَميتوش	
húwwa	ráma	رَمَى	ma-ramāš	مَرَماش	
híyya	rámit	رَمِت	ma-ramítš	مَرَمِتْش	
húmma	rámu	رَموا	ma-ramūš	مَرَموش	

ána	ármi	أَرْمي	ma-rmīš	مَرْميش	imperfect
íḥna	nírmi	نِرْمي	ma-nirmīš	مَنِرْميش	
ínta	tírmi	تِرمي	ma-tirmīš	مَتِرميش	
ínti	tírmi	تِرمي	ma-tirmīš	مَتِرميش	
íntu	tírmu	تِرموا	ma-tirmūš	مَتِرموش	
húwwa	yírmi	يِرمي	ma-yirmīš	مَيِرميش	
híyya	tírmi	تِرمي	ma-tirmīš	مَتِرميش	
húmma	yírmu	يِرموا	ma-yirmūš	مَيِرموش	

ána	bármi	بَرْمي	ma-barmīš	مَبَرْميش	bi-imperfect
íḥna	binírmi	بِنِرْمي	ma-bnirmīš	مَبْنِرْميش	
ínta	bitírmi	بِتِرمي	ma-btirmīš	مَبْتِرميش	
ínti	bitírmi	بِتِرمي	ma-btirmīš	مَبْتِرميش	
íntu	bitírmu	بِتِرموا	ma-btirmūš	مَبْتِرموش	
húwwa	biyírmi	بِيِرمي	ma-byirmīš	مَبْيِرميش	
híyya	bitírmi	بِتِرمي	ma-btirmīš	مَبْتِرميش	
húmma	biyírmu	بِيِرموا	ma-byirmūš	مَبْيِرموش	

ána	hármi	هَرْمي	miš hármi	مِش هَرْمي	future
íḥna	hanírmi	هَنِرْمي	miš hanírmi	مِش هَنِرْمي	
ínta	hatírmi	هَتِرمي	miš hatírmi	مِش هَتِرمي	
ínti	hatírmi	هَتِرمي	miš hatírmi	مِش هَتِرمي	
íntu	hatírmu	هَتِرموا	miš hatírmu	مِش هَتِرموا	
húwwa	hayírmi	هَيِرمي	miš hayírmi	مِش هَيِرمي	
híyya	hatírmi	هَتِرمي	miš hatírmi	مِش هَتِرمي	
húmma	hayírmu	هَيِرموا	miš hayírmu	مِش هَيِرموا	

ínta	írmi	اِرْمي	ma-tirmīš	مَتِرميش	imperative
ínti	írmi	اِرْمي	ma-tirmīš	مَتِرميش	
íntu	írmu	اِرْموا	ma-tirmūš	مَتِرموش	

	active		passive		
masculine	rāmi	رامي	mármi	مَرْمي	participles
feminine	rámya	رامْيَة	marmíyya	مَرْمِيَّة	
plural	ramyīn	رامْيين	marmiyīn	مَرْميين	

verbal noun: *ramy* رَمْى

①

أحْمد رمى الكوْرة عالي، علّقِت فوْق الشّجرة.

áḫmad ráma -lkōra 3āli, 3allá?it fō? iššágara.

Ahmed threw the ball so high
it got stuck up in the tree.

②

لمّا تِـرمي الكوْرة ركِّز أوي على السّلّة.

lámma tírmi -lkūra rákkiz ?áwi 3ála -ssálla.

When you throw the [basket]ball,
focus on the basket.

③

الرّاجِل ده بْيِـرمي مِن شِبّاك عربيتُه. أيْه القرف ده!

irrāgil da byírmi min šibbāk 3arabītu. ?ē -l?áraf da!

That man is tossing things out of his
car window. How disgusting!

④

مين عليْه الدّوْر؟ مين هَيِـرمي ؟

mīn 3alē -ddōr? mīn hayírmi?

Whose turn is it? Who's
throwing [the dice]?

⑤

اِرْمي حُمولك على اللّه. قادِر يِحِلّها كُلّها.

írmi ḫumūlak 3ála -llāh. ?ādir yiḫilláha kulláha.

Throw your problems to Allah. He's
capable of solving them all.

⑥

متِـرميش الحاجات دي. مُمْكِن نِخلّيها في التّلاجة.

ma-tirmīš ilḫagāt di. múmkin nixallīha fi -ttalāga.

Don't throw those away. We
can keep them in the fridge.

❖ [1d2] **to throw, toss, cast**

➲ 21.3, 80.5

126 to go home ráwwaḫ رَوَّح 1-3

	affirmative		negative		
ána	rawwáḫt	رَوَّحْت	ma-rawwáḫtiš	مَرَوَّحْتِش	perfect
íḫna	rawwáḫna	رَوَّحْنا	ma-rawwaḫnāš	مَرَوَّحْناش	
ínta	rawwáḫt	رَوَّحْت	ma-rawwáḫtiš	مَرَوَّحْتِش	
ínti	rawwáḫti	رَوَّحْتي	ma-rawwaḫtīš	مَرَوَّحْتيش	
íntu	rawwáḫtu	رَوَّحْتوا	ma-rawwaḫtūš	مَرَوَّحْتوش	
húwwa	ráwwaḫ	رَوَّح	ma-rawwáḫš	مَرَوَّحْش	
híyya	rawwáḫit	رَوَّحِت	ma-rawwaḫítš	مَرَوَّحِتْش	
húmma	rawwáḫu	رَوَّحوا	ma-rawwaḫūš	مَرَوَّحوش	
ána	aráwwaḫ	أرَوَّح	ma-rawwáḫš	مَرَوَّحْش	imperfect
íḫna	niráwwaḫ	نِرَوَّح	ma-nrawwáḫš	مَنْرَوَّحْش	
ínta	tiráwwaḫ	تِرَوَّح	ma-trawwáḫš	مَتْرَوَّحْش	
ínti	tirawwáḫi	تِرَوَّحي	ma-trawwaḫīš	مَتْرَوَّحيش	
íntu	tirawwáḫu	تِرَوَّحوا	ma-trawwaḫūš	مَتْرَوَّحوش	
húwwa	yiráwwaḫ	يِرَوَّح	ma-yrawwáḫš	مَيْرَوَّحْش	
híyya	tiráwwaḫ	تِرَوَّح	ma-trawwáḫš	مَتْرَوَّحْش	
húmma	yirawwáḫu	يِرَوَّحوا	ma-yrawwaḫūš	مَيْرَوَّحوش	
ána	baráwwaḫ	بَرَوَّح	ma-barawwáḫš	مَبَرَوَّحْش	bi-imperfect
íḫna	binráwwaḫ	بِنْرَوَّح	ma-binrawwáḫš	مَبِنْرَوَّحْش	
ínta	bitráwwaḫ	بِتْرَوَّح	ma-bitrawwáḫš	مَبِتْرَوَّحْش	
ínti	bitrawwáḫi	بِتْرَوَّحي	ma-bitrawwaḫīš	مَبِتْرَوَّحيش	
íntu	bitrawwáḫu	بِتْرَوَّحوا	ma-bitrawwaḫūš	مَبِتْرَوَّحوش	
húwwa	biyráwwaḫ	بِيْرَوَّح	ma-biyrawwáḫš	مَبِيْرَوَّحْش	
híyya	bitráwwaḫ	بِتْرَوَّح	ma-bitrawwáḫš	مَبِتْرَوَّحْش	
húmma	biyrawwáḫu	بِيْرَوَّحوا	ma-biyrawwaḫūš	مَبِيْرَوَّحوش	
ána	haráwwaḫ	هَرَوَّح	miš haráwwaḫ	مِش هَرَوَّح	future
íḫna	hanráwwaḫ	هَنْرَوَّح	miš hanráwwaḫ	مِش هَنْرَوَّح	
ínta	hatráwwaḫ	هَتْرَوَّح	miš hatráwwaḫ	مِش هَتْرَوَّح	
ínti	hatrawwáḫi	هَتْرَوَّحي	miš hatrawwáḫi	مِش هَتْرَوَّحي	
íntu	hatrawwáḫu	هَتْرَوَّحوا	miš hatrawwáḫu	مِش هَتْرَوَّحوا	
húwwa	hayráwwaḫ	هَيْرَوَّح	miš hayráwwaḫ	مِش هَيْرَوَّح	
híyya	hatráwwaḫ	هَتْرَوَّح	miš hatráwwaḫ	مِش هَتْرَوَّح	
húmma	hayrawwáḫu	هَيْرَوَّحوا	miš hayrawwáḫu	مِش هَيْرَوَّحوا	
ínta	ráwwaḫ	رَوَّح	ma-trawwáḫš	مَتْرَوَّحْش	imperative
ínti	rawwáḫi	رَوَّحي	ma-trawwaḫīš	مَتْرَوَّحيش	
íntu	rawwáḫu	رَوَّحوا	ma-trawwaḫūš	مَتْرَوَّحوش	

	active		passive		
masculine	miráwwaḫ	مِرَوَّح	—	—	participles
feminine	mirawwáḫa	مِرَوَّحَة	—	—	
plural	mirawwaḫīn	مِرَوَّحين	—	—	

verbal noun: mirwāḫ مِرْواح

①

إنْتَ لِسّه مروّحْتِش ؟ روّح يَلّا، الشُّغْل مَوْجود بُكْره.

ínta líssa ma-rawwáħtiš? ráwwaħ yálla, iššúɣlᵊ mawgūd búkra.

Haven't you gone home yet? Go, the work will still be here tomorrow.

②

جميل نِزِل يِـروّح مرْوَة و راجِع.

gamīl nízil yiráwwaħ márwa wi rāgi3.

Gameel went to take Marwa home and then will come back.

③

المُوَظّفين هِنا بِيْروّحوا عَ السّاعة ٤.

ilmuwaẓẓafīn hína biyrawwáħu 3a -ssā3a -rbá3a.

The employees here go home at four o'clock.

④

إحْنا هنرْوّح البيْت إمْتى؟ أنا تِعِبْت.

íħna hanráwwaħ ilbēt ímta? ána ti3íbt.

When are we going home? I'm tired.

⑤

مترْوّحوش دِلْوَقْتي. اِسْتنّوا لمّا المطرة تِهْدي.

ma-trawwaħūš dilwáʔti. istánnu lámma -lmáṭara tíhda.

Don't go now. Wait until the rain lets up.

❖ [2s2] **to go home; to take** (someone) **home**

➲ 171.8, 187.3, 222.9, 264.7

127 to tidy up ráwwaʔ روّق

verbal nouns: tarwīʔ ترويق - rawaʔān روقان

	affirmative		negative		
ána	rawwáʔt	روّقت	ma-rawwáʔtiš	مروّقتش	perfect
íḥna	rawwáʔna	روّقنا	ma-rawwaʔnāš	مروّقناش	
ínta	rawwáʔt	روّقت	ma-rawwáʔtiš	مروّقتش	
ínti	rawwáʔti	روّقتي	ma-rawwaʔtīš	مروّقتيش	
íntu	rawwáʔtu	روّقتوا	ma-rawwaʔtūš	مروّقتوش	
húwwa	ráwwaʔ	روّق	ma-rawwáʔš	مروّقش	
híyya	rawwáʔit	روّقت	ma-rawwaʔítš	مروّقتش	
húmma	rawwáʔu	روّقوا	ma-rawwaʔūš	مروّقوش	

ána	aráwwaʔ	أروّق	ma-rawwáʔš	مروّقش	imperfect
íḥna	niráwwaʔ	نروّق	ma-nrawwáʔš	منروّقش	
ínta	tiráwwaʔ	تروّق	ma-trawwáʔš	متروّقش	
ínti	tirawwáʔi	تروّقي	ma-trawwaʔīš	متروّقيش	
íntu	tirawwáʔu	تروّقوا	ma-trawwaʔūš	متروّقوش	
húwwa	yiráwwaʔ	يروّق	ma-yrawwáʔš	ميروّقش	
híyya	tiráwwaʔ	تروّق	ma-trawwáʔš	متروّقش	
húmma	yirawwáʔu	يروّقوا	ma-yrawwaʔūš	ميروّقوش	

ána	baráwwaʔ	بروّق	ma-barawwáʔš	مبروّقش	bi-imperfect
íḥna	binráwwaʔ	بنروّق	ma-binrawwáʔš	مبنروّقش	
ínta	bitráwwaʔ	بتروّق	ma-bitrawwáʔš	مبتروّقش	
ínti	bitrawwáʔi	بتروّقي	ma-bitrawwaʔīš	مبتروّقيش	
íntu	bitrawwáʔu	بتروّقوا	ma-bitrawwaʔūš	مبتروّقوش	
húwwa	biyráwwaʔ	بيروّق	ma-biyrawwáʔš	مبيروّقش	
híyya	bitráwwaʔ	بتروّق	ma-bitrawwáʔš	مبتروّقش	
húmma	biyrawwáʔu	بيروّقوا	ma-biyrawwaʔūš	مبيروّقوش	

ána	haráwwaʔ	هروّق	miš haráwwaʔ	مش هروّق	future
íḥna	hanráwwaʔ	هنروّق	miš hanráwwaʔ	مش هنروّق	
ínta	hatráwwaʔ	هتروّق	miš hatráwwaʔ	مش هتروّق	
ínti	hatrawwáʔi	هتروّقي	miš hatrawwáʔi	مش هتروّقي	
íntu	hatrawwáʔu	هتروّقوا	miš hatrawwáʔu	مش هتروّقوا	
húwwa	hayráwwaʔ	هيروّق	miš hayráwwaʔ	مش هيروّق	
híyya	hatráwwaʔ	هتروّق	miš hatráwwaʔ	مش هتروّق	
húmma	hayrawwáʔu	هيروّقوا	miš hayrawwáʔu	مش هيروّقوا	

ínta	ráwwaʔ	روّق	ma-trawwáʔš	متروّقش	imperative
ínti	rawwáʔi	روّقي	ma-trawwaʔīš	متروّقيش	
íntu	rawwáʔu	روّقوا	ma-trawwaʔūš	متروّقوش	

	active		passive		
masculine	miráwwaʔ	مروّق	mitráwwaʔ	متروّق	participles
feminine	mirawwáʔa	مروّقة	mitrawwáʔa	متروّقة	
plural	mirawwaʔīn	مروّقين	mitrawwaʔīn	متروّقين	

①

لمّا رْجِعْت البيْت لقيْت الوِلاد روّقوا الشّقّة.

lámma rgí3t ilbēt laʔēt ilwilād rawwáʔu -ššáʔʔa.

When I came back, I found that the boys had tidied up the apartment.

②

أنا عايْزك تِـروّق كِده و تِسْتمْتِع بِالاجازة.

ána 3áyzak tiráwwaʔ kída wi tistámti3 bi-lʔagāza.

I want you to relax and enjoy the vacation.

③

أنا مِش فاهْمة مبِنرْوّقْش المكْتب ده ليْه. إحْنا كِده مِش عارْفين نِشْتغل.

ána miš fáhma ma-binrawwáʔš ilmáktab da lē. íḫna kída miš 3arfīn ništáɣal.

I don't know why we aren't organizing this office. We can't work like this.

④

اِشْرب حبّةْ القهْوَة دي. هترْوّق.

íšrab ḫábbit ilʔáhwa di. hatráwwaʔ.

Drink some of this coffee. You'll feel better.

⑤

روّق كِده و إبْسِطْها يا عمّ.

ráwwaʔ kída w ibsíṭha ya 3amm.

Relax and take it easy, man.

❖ [2s2] **to tidy up, organize; to relax, feel at ease**

128 to increase *zād* زاد

verbal noun: *ziyāda* زِيادة

	affirmative		negative		
ána	*zidt*	زِدْت	*ma-zídtiš*	مَزِدْتِش	perfect
íḥna	*zídna*	زِدْنا	*ma-zidnāš*	مَزِدْناش	
ínta	*zidt*	زِدْت	*ma-zídtiš*	مَزِدْتِش	
ínti	*zídti*	زِدْتي	*ma-zidtīš*	مَزِدْتيش	
íntu	*zídtu*	زِدْتوا	*ma-zidtūš*	مَزِدْتوش	
húwwa	*zād*	زاد	*ma-zádš*	مَزادْش	
híyya	*zādit*	زادِت	*ma-zadítš*	مَزادِتْش	
húmma	*zādu*	زادوا	*ma-zadūš*	مَزادوش	
ána	*azīd*	أزيد	*ma-zídš*	مَزيدْش	imperfect
íḥna	*nizīd*	نِزيد	*ma-nzídš*	مَنْزيدْش	
ínta	*tizīd*	تِزيد	*ma-tzídš*	مَتْزيدْش	
ínti	*tizīdi*	تِزيدي	*ma-tzidīš*	مَتْزيديش	
íntu	*tizīdu*	تِزيدوا	*ma-tzidūš*	مَتْزيدوش	
húwwa	*yizīd*	يِزيد	*ma-yzídš*	مَيْزيدْش	
híyya	*tizīd*	تِزيد	*ma-tzídš*	مَتْزيدْش	
húmma	*yizīdu*	يِزيدوا	*ma-yzidūš*	مَيْزيدوش	
ána	*bazīd*	بَزيد	*ma-bazídš*	مَبَزيدْش	bi-imperfect
íḥna	*binzīd*	بِنْزيد	*ma-binzídš*	مَبِنْزيدِش	
ínta	*bitzīd*	بِتْزيد	*ma-bitzídš*	مَبِتْزيدِش	
ínti	*bitzīdi*	بِتْزيدي	*ma-bitzidīš*	مَبِتْزيديش	
íntu	*bitzīdu*	بِتْزيدوا	*ma-bitzidūš*	مَبِتْزيدوش	
húwwa	*biyzīd*	بِيْزيد	*ma-biyzídš*	مَبِيْزيدِش	
híyya	*bitzīd*	بِتْزيد	*ma-bitzídš*	مَبِتْزيدِش	
húmma	*biyzīdu*	بِيْزيدوا	*ma-biyzidūš*	مَبِيْزيدوش	
ána	*hazīd*	هَزيد	*miš hazīd*	مِش هَزيد	future
íḥna	*hanzīd*	هَنْزيد	*miš hanzīd*	مِش هَنْزيد	
ínta	*hatzīd*	هَتْزيد	*miš hatzīd*	مِش هَتْزيد	
ínti	*hatzīdi*	هَتْزيدي	*miš hatzīdi*	مِش هَتْزيدي	
íntu	*hatzīdu*	هَتْزيدوا	*miš hatzīdu*	مِش هَتْزيدوا	
húwwa	*hayzīd*	هَيْزيد	*miš hayzīd*	مِش هَيْزيد	
híyya	*hatzīd*	هَتْزيد	*miš hatzīd*	مِش هَتْزيد	
húmma	*hayzīdu*	هَيْزيدوا	*miš hayzīdu*	مِش هَيْزيدوا	
ínta	*zīd*	زيد	*ma-tzídš*	مَتْزيدْش	imperative
ínti	*zīdi*	زيدي	*ma-tzidīš*	مَتْزيديش	
íntu	*zīdu*	زيدوا	*ma-tzidūš*	مَتْزيدوش	

	active		passive		
masculine	*zāyid*	زايِد	–	–	participles
feminine	*záyda*	زايْدَة	–	–	
plural	*zaydīn*	زايْدين	–	–	

①

وَزْني زاد جِدّاً الفترْة اللي فاتِت.

wázni zād gíddan ilfátra -lli fātit.

My weight has increased so much lately.

②

أيْه الجمال ده؟ ربِّنا يْزيد و يْبارِك.

ʔēh ilgamāl da? rabbína yzīd wi ybārik.

What beauty is this? May God give you more and bless you.

③

كُلّ يوْم الأسْعار بِتْزيد، و بعْديْن؟

kullᵊ yōm ilʔas3ār bitzīd, wi ba3dēn?

Every day the prices go up, and then what?

④

وَزْنِك مِش هَيْزيد طالما بْتاكْلي صحّ.

wáznik miš hayzīd ṭaláma btákli ṣaḥḥ.

Your weight won't increase as long as you eat right.

⑤

زيد جُرْعِةْ الحنان في بيْتك، هتْلاقي الكُلّ سعيد.

zīd gúr3it ilḥanān fi bētak, hatlāʔi -lkullᵊ sa3īd.

Increase the portion of kindness in your home, and you'll find everyone happy.

⑥

الحمْدُ لِلّه، مصاريف الرِّحْلة مزادِتْش عن إمْكانِيّاتْنا.

ilḥámdu l-llāh, maṣarīf irríḥla ma-zaditšᵊ 3an imkaniyyátna.

Thank God the travel expenses didn't exceed our budget.

❖ [1h2] **to increase, go up; to exceed** (عن *3an*)

129 to visit *zār* زار

verbal noun: *ziyāra* زيارة

	affirmative		negative		
ána	*zurt*	زُرْت	*ma-zúrtiš*	مَزُرْتِش	**perfect**
íḫna	*zúrna*	زُرْنا	*ma-zurnāš*	مَزُرْناش	
ínta	*zurt*	زُرْت	*ma-zúrtiš*	مَزُرْتِش	
ínti	*zúrti*	زُرْتي	*ma-zurtīš*	مَزُرْتيش	
íntu	*zúrtu*	زُرْتوا	*ma-zurtūš*	مَزُرْتوش	
húwwa	*zār*	زار	*ma-zárš*	مَزارْش	
híyya	*zārit*	زارِت	*ma-zarítš*	مَزارِتْش	
húmma	*zāru*	زاروا	*ma-zarūš*	مَزاروش	
ána	*azūr*	أزور	*ma-zúrš*	مَزورْش	**imperfect**
íḫna	*nizūr*	نِزور	*ma-nzúrš*	مَنْزورْش	
ínta	*tizūr*	تِزور	*ma-tzúrš*	مَتْزورْش	
ínti	*tizūri*	تِزوري	*ma-tzurīš*	مَتْزوريش	
íntu	*tizūru*	تِزوروا	*ma-tzurūš*	مَتْزوروش	
húwwa	*yizūr*	يِزور	*ma-yzúrš*	مَيْزورْش	
híyya	*tizūr*	تِزور	*ma-tzúrš*	مَتْزورْش	
húmma	*yizūru*	يِزوروا	*ma-yzurūš*	مَيْزوروش	
ána	*bazūr*	بَزور	*ma-bazúrš*	مَبَزورْش	**bi-imperfect**
íḫna	*binzūr*	بِنْزور	*ma-binzúrš*	مَبِنْزورْش	
ínta	*bitzūr*	بِتْزور	*ma-bitzúrš*	مَبِتْزورْش	
ínti	*bitzūri*	بِتْزوري	*ma-bitzurīš*	مَبِتْزوريش	
íntu	*bitzūru*	بِتْزوروا	*ma-bitzurūš*	مَبِتْزوروش	
húwwa	*biyzūr*	بِيْزور	*ma-biyzúrš*	مَبِيْزورْش	
híyya	*bitzūr*	بِتْزور	*ma-bitzúrš*	مَبِتْزورْش	
húmma	*biyzūru*	بِيْزوروا	*ma-biyzurūš*	مَبِيْزوروش	
ána	*hazūr*	هَزور	*miš hazūr*	مِش هَزور	**future**
íḫna	*hanzūr*	هَنْزور	*miš hanzūr*	مِش هَنْزور	
ínta	*hatzūr*	هَتْزور	*miš hatzūr*	مِش هَتْزور	
ínti	*hatzūri*	هَتْزوري	*miš hatzūri*	مِش هَتْزوري	
íntu	*hatzūru*	هَتْزوروا	*miš hatzūru*	مِش هَتْزوروا	
húwwa	*hayzūr*	هَيْزور	*miš hayzūr*	مِش هَيْزور	
híyya	*hatzūr*	هَتْزور	*miš hatzūr*	مِش هَتْزور	
húmma	*hayzūru*	هَيْزوروا	*miš hayzūru*	مِش هَيْزوروا	
ínta	*zūr*	زور	*ma-tzúrš*	مَتْزورْش	**imperative**
ínti	*zūri*	زوري	*ma-tzurīš*	مَتْزوريش	
íntu	*zūru*	زوروا	*ma-tzurūš*	مَتْزوروش	

	active		passive		
masculine	*zāyir*	زايِر	*mitzār*	مِتْزار	**participles**
feminine	*záyra*	زايْرَة	*mitzāra*	مِتْزارَة	
plural	*zayrīn*	زايْرين	*mitzarīn*	مِتْزارين	

①

أنا زُرْت أسْوان مرِّتيْن و نِفْسي أزورْها تاني.

ána zurtᵊ ʔaswān marritēn wi nífsi ʔazúrha tāni.

I've visited Aswan twice and hope to visit it again.

②

مايْسة نِفْسها تْزور إيطالْيا.

máysa nifsáha tzūr iṭálya.

Maysa hopes to visit Italy.

③

رِحاب بِتْزور حماتْها كُلّ جُمْعة.

riħāb bitzūr ħamátha kullᵊ gúm3a.

Rehab visits her mother-in-law every Friday.

④

مُنير هَيْزور أخوه في أمْريكا الصّيْف الجايّ.

munīr hayzūr axūh f amrīka -ṣṣēf ilgáyy.

Mounir will visit his brother in America next summer.

⑤

زور قرايْبك. العيْلة الكِبيرة حاجة جميلة.

zūr ʔaráybak. il3ēla -lkibīra ħāga gamīla.

Visit your relatives. A big family is a blessing.

⑥

يابْني، إنْتَ مزُرْتِنيش بقالك تلات شُهور. مبَوْحشكْش؟

ya -bni, ínta ma-zurtinīš baʔālak tálat šuhūr. ma-bawħašákš?

You haven't visited me for three months, son. Don't you miss me?

❖ [1h1] **to visit**

➲ 78.1

130 to get annoyed zí3il زِعِل

	affirmative		negative		
ána	zi3ílt	زِعِلْت	ma-z3íltiš	مَزْعِلْتِش	perfect
íḫna	zi3ílna	زِعِلْنا	ma-z3ilnāš	مَزْعِلْناش	
ínta	zi3ílt	زِعِلْت	ma-z3íltiš	مَزْعِلْتِش	
ínti	zi3ílti	زِعِلْتي	ma-z3iltīš	مَزْعِلْتيش	
íntu	zi3íltu	زِعِلْتوا	ma-z3iltūš	مَزْعِلْتوش	
húwwa	zí3il	زِعِل	ma-z3ílš	مَزْعِلْش	
híyya	zí3lit	زِعْلِت	ma-zi3lítš	مَزِعْلِتْش	
húmma	zí3lu	زِعْلوا	ma-zi3lūš	مَزِعْلوش	
ána	áz3al	أزْعَل	ma-z3álš	مَزْعَلْش	imperfect
íḫna	níz3al	نِزْعَل	ma-niz3álš	مَنِزْعَلْش	
ínta	tíz3al	تِزْعَل	ma-tiz3álš	مَتِزْعَلْش	
ínti	tiz3áli	تِزْعَلي	ma-tiz3alīš	مَتِزْعَليش	
íntu	tiz3álu	تِزْعَلوا	ma-tiz3alūš	مَتِزْعَلوش	
húwwa	yíz3al	يِزْعَل	ma-yiz3álš	مَيِزْعَلْش	
híyya	tíz3al	تِزْعَل	ma-tiz3álš	مَتِزْعَلْش	
húmma	yiz3álu	يِزْعَلوا	ma-yiz3alūš	مَيِزْعَلوش	
ána	báz3al	بَزْعَل	ma-baz3álš	مَبَزْعَلْش	bi-imperfect
íḫna	biníz3al	بِنِزْعَل	ma-bniz3álš	مَبْنِزْعَلْش	
ínta	bitíz3al	بِتِزْعَل	ma-btiz3álš	مَبْتِزْعَلْش	
ínti	bitiz3áli	بِتِزْعَلي	ma-btiz3alīš	مَبْتِزْعَليش	
íntu	bitiz3álu	بِتِزْعَلوا	ma-btiz3alūš	مَبْتِزْعَلوش	
húwwa	biyíz3al	بِيِزْعَل	ma-byiz3álš	مَبْيِزْعَلْش	
híyya	bitíz3al	بِتِزْعَل	ma-btiz3álš	مَبْتِزْعَلْش	
húmma	biyiz3álu	بِيِزْعَلوا	ma-byiz3alūš	مَبْيِزْعَلوش	
ána	ház3al	هَزْعَل	miš ház3al	مِش هَزْعَل	future
íḫna	haníz3al	هَنِزْعَل	miš haníz3al	مِش هَنِزْعَل	
ínta	hatíz3al	هَتِزْعَل	miš hatíz3al	مِش هَتِزْعَل	
ínti	hatiz3áli	هَتِزْعَلي	miš hatiz3áli	مِش هَتِزْعَلي	
íntu	hatiz3álu	هَتِزْعَلوا	miš hatiz3álu	مِش هَتِزْعَلوا	
húwwa	hayíz3al	هَيِزْعَل	miš hayíz3al	مِش هَيِزْعَل	
híyya	hatíz3al	هَتِزْعَل	miš hatíz3al	مِش هَتِزْعَل	
húmma	hayiz3álu	هَيِزْعَلوا	miš hayiz3álu	مِش هَيِزْعَلوا	
ínta	íz3al	اِزْعَل	ma-tiz3álš	مَتِزْعَلْش	imperative
ínti	iz3áli	اِزْعَلي	ma-tiz3alīš	مَتِزْعَليش	
íntu	iz3álu	اِزْعَلوا	ma-tiz3alūš	مَتِزْعَلوش	

	active		passive		
masculine	za3lān	زَعْلان	–	–	participles
feminine	za3lāna	زَعْلانَة	–	–	
plural	za3lānīn	زَعْلانين	–	–	

verbal noun: *zá3al* زَعَل

①
زِعِلْت أوي مِن نفْسي لمّا غْلِطْت الغلْطة الغبية دي.
zi3ílt ʔáwi min náfsi lámma ɣlíṭt -lɣálṭa -lɣabíyya di.
I got mad at myself when I
made that stupid mistake.

②
محمّد مِش راضي يِتْجوِّز عشان خايِف أُمُّه تِزْعل.
maḫámmad miš rāḍi yitgáwwiz 3ašān xāyif úmmu tíz3al.
Mohamed won't get married because
he's afraid his mom will get upset.

③
نُهى دايْماً بِتْسامِح و مِش بِتِزْعل مِن حدّ.
núha dáyman bitsāmiḫ wi miš bitíz3al min ḫadd.
Noha is very forgiving and never
gets angry at anyone.

④
عيسى هَيِزْعل لَوْ عِرِف إنَّك خرجْت مِن غيْر إذْنُه.
3īsa hayíz3al law 3írif ínnak xarágtᵊ min ɣēr íznu.
Easa will get angry if he finds out that
you went out without his permission.

⑤
متِزْعلْش مِن طِفْل. عُمْرُهُم ما بِيُقْصُدوا يِزعّلونا.
ma-tiz3álšᵊ min ṭifl. 3umrúhum ma biyuʔṣúdu yiza33alūna.
Never get angry at a child. They never
intend to upset us.

❖ [1s4] **to become annoyed/angry/upset**

➲ 15.3, 25.1, 113.6, 211.8

131 to push zaʔʔ زقّ

	affirmative		negative		
ána	zaʔʔēt	زقّيت	ma-zaʔʔítš	مزقّيتش	perfect
íḩna	zaʔʔēna	زقّينا	ma-zaʔʔināš	مزقّيناش	
ínta	zaʔʔēt	زقّيت	ma-zaʔʔítš	مزقّيتش	
ínti	zaʔʔēti	زقّيتي	ma-zaʔʔitīš	مزقّيتيش	
íntu	zaʔʔētu	زقّيتوا	ma-zaʔʔitūš	مزقّيتوش	
húwwa	zaʔʔ	زقّ	ma-záʔʔiš	مزقّش	
híyya	záʔʔit	زقّت	ma-zaʔʔítš	مزقّتش	
húmma	záʔʔu	زقّوا	ma-zaʔʔūš	مزقّوش	
ána	azúʔʔ	أزُقّ	ma-zúʔʔiš	مزُقّش	imperfect
íḩna	nizúʔʔ	نِزُقّ	ma-nzúʔʔiš	منْزُقّش	
ínta	tizúʔʔ	تِزُقّ	ma-tzúʔʔiš	متْزُقّش	
ínti	tizúʔʔi	تِزُقّي	ma-tzuʔʔīš	متْزُقّيش	
íntu	tizúʔʔu	تِزُقّوا	ma-tzuʔʔūš	متْزُقّوش	
húwwa	yizúʔʔ	يِزُقّ	ma-yzúʔʔiš	ميْزُقّش	
híyya	tizúʔʔ	تِزُقّ	ma-tzúʔʔiš	متْزُقّش	
húmma	yizúʔʔu	يِزُقّوا	ma-yzuʔʔūš	ميْزُقّوش	
ána	bazúʔʔ	بزُقّ	ma-bazúʔʔiš	مبزُقّش	bi-imperfect
íḩna	binzúʔʔ	بِنْزُقّ	ma-binzúʔʔiš	مبِنْزُقّش	
ínta	bitzúʔʔ	بِتْزُقّ	ma-bitzúʔʔiš	مبِتْزُقّش	
ínti	bitzúʔʔi	بِتْزُقّي	ma-bitzuʔʔīš	مبِتْزُقّيش	
íntu	bitzúʔʔu	بِتْزُقّوا	ma-bitzuʔʔūš	مبِتْزُقّوش	
húwwa	biyzúʔʔ	بِيْزُقّ	ma-biyzúʔʔiš	مبِيْزُقّش	
híyya	bitzúʔʔ	بِتْزُقّ	ma-bitzúʔʔiš	مبِتْزُقّش	
húmma	biyzúʔʔu	بِيْزُقّوا	ma-biyzuʔʔūš	مبِيْزُقّوش	
ána	hazúʔʔ	هزُقّ	miš hazúʔʔ	مِش هزُقّ	future
íḩna	hanzúʔʔ	هنْزُقّ	miš hanzúʔʔ	مِش هنْزُقّ	
ínta	hatzúʔʔ	هتْزُقّ	miš hatzúʔʔ	مِش هتْزُقّ	
ínti	hatzúʔʔi	هتْزُقّي	miš hatzúʔʔi	مِش هتْزُقّي	
íntu	hatzúʔʔu	هتْزُقّوا	miš hatzúʔʔu	مِش هتْزُقّوا	
húwwa	hayzúʔʔ	هيْزُقّ	miš hayzúʔʔ	مِش هيْزُقّ	
híyya	hatzúʔʔ	هتْزُقّ	miš hatzúʔʔ	مِش هتْزُقّ	
húmma	hayzúʔʔu	هيْزُقّوا	miš hayzúʔʔu	مِش هيْزُقّوا	
ínta	zuʔʔ	زُقّ	ma-tzúʔʔiš	متْزُقّش	imperative
ínti	zúʔʔi	زُقّي	ma-tzuʔʔīš	متْزُقّيش	
íntu	zúʔʔu	زُقّوا	ma-tzuʔʔūš	متْزُقّوش	

	active		passive		
masculine	zāʔiʔ	زاقِق	mazʔūʔ	مزْقوق	participles
feminine	záʔʔa	زاقّة	mazʔūʔa	مزْقوقة	
plural	zaʔʔīn	زاقّين	mazʔuʔīn	مزْقوقين	

verbal noun: zaʔʔ زقّ

①

مزقِّتْش الدّولاب لِوَحْدي عشان تِقيل أوي.

ma-zaʔʔítš iddulāb li-wáħdi 3ašān tiʔīl áwi.

I didn't push the wardrobe alone
because it's so heavy.

②

قوليلُه يْبطّل يِزُقّ أخوه.

ʔulīlu ybáṭṭal yizúʔʔ axū.

Tell him to stop pushing
his brother.

③

بِتْزُقّي ليْه؟ ما كُلِّنا واقْفين في الطّابور.

bitzúʔʔi lē? ma kullína waʔfīn fi -ṭṭabūr.

Why are you pushing? We're
all waiting in line.

④

هقول واحِد اِتْنينْ تلاتة، هنْزُقّ مرّة واحْدة.

haʔūl wāħid itnēn talāta, hanzúʔʔᵊ márra wáħda.

I'll say one, two, three, and
we'll push all together.

⑤

زُقّ معايا العربية مِن فضْلك.

zuʔʔᵊ ma3āya -l3arabíyya, min fáḍlak.

Please, push the car with me.

❖ [1g2] **to push**

132 to add *záwwid* زَوِّد

verbal noun: *tazwīd* تزويد

	affirmative		negative		
ána	zawwídt	زَوِّدْت	ma-zawwídtiš	مَزَوِّدْتِش	perfect
íḥna	zawwídna	زَوِّدْنا	ma-zawwidnāš	مَزَوِّدْناش	
ínta	zawwídt	زَوِّدْت	ma-zawwídtiš	مَزَوِّدْتِش	
ínti	zawwídti	زَوِّدْتي	ma-zawwidtīš	مَزَوِّدْتيش	
íntu	zawwídtu	زَوِّدْتوا	ma-zawwidtūš	مَزَوِّدْتوش	
húwwa	záwwid	زَوِّد	ma-zawwídš	مَزَوِّدْش	
híyya	zawwídit	زَوِّدِت	ma-zawwidítš	مَزَوِّدِتْش	
húmma	zawwídu	زَوِّدوا	ma-zawwidūš	مَزَوِّدوش	
ána	azáwwid	أَزَوِّد	ma-zawwídš	مَزَوِّدْش	imperfect
íḥna	nizáwwid	نِزَوِّد	ma-nzawwídš	مَنْزَوِّدْش	
ínta	tizáwwid	تِزَوِّد	ma-tzawwídš	مَتْزَوِّدْش	
ínti	tizawwídi	تِزَوِّدي	ma-tzawwidīš	مَتْزَوِّديش	
íntu	tizawwídu	تِزَوِّدوا	ma-tzawwidūš	مَتْزَوِّدوش	
húwwa	yizáwwid	يِزَوِّد	ma-yzawwídš	مَيْزَوِّدْش	
híyya	tizáwwid	تِزَوِّد	ma-tzawwídš	مَتْزَوِّدْش	
húmma	yizawwídu	يِزَوِّدوا	ma-yzawwidūš	مَيْزَوِّدوش	
ána	bazáwwid	بَزَوِّد	ma-bazawwídš	مَبَزَوِّدْش	bi-imperfect
íḥna	binzáwwid	بِنْزَوِّد	ma-binzawwídš	مَبِنْزَوِّدْش	
ínta	bitzáwwid	بِتْزَوِّد	ma-bitzawwídš	مَبِتْزَوِّدْش	
ínti	bitzawwídi	بِتْزَوِّدي	ma-bitzawwidīš	مَبِتْزَوِّديش	
íntu	bitzawwídu	بِتْزَوِّدوا	ma-bitzawwidūš	مَبِتْزَوِّدوش	
húwwa	biyzáwwid	بِيْزَوِّد	ma-biyzawwídš	مَبِيْزَوِّدْش	
híyya	bitzáwwid	بِتْزَوِّد	ma-bitzawwídš	مَبِتْزَوِّدْش	
húmma	biyzawwídu	بِيْزَوِّدوا	ma-biyzawwidūš	مَبِيْزَوِّدوش	
ána	hazáwwid	هَزَوِّد	miš hazáwwid	مِش هَزَوِّد	future
íḥna	hanzáwwid	هَنْزَوِّد	miš hanzáwwid	مِش هَنْزَوِّد	
ínta	hatzáwwid	هَتْزَوِّد	miš hatzáwwid	مِش هَتْزَوِّد	
ínti	hatzawwídi	هَتْزَوِّدي	miš hatzawwídi	مِش هَتْزَوِّدي	
íntu	hatzawwídu	هَتْزَوِّدوا	miš hatzawwídu	مِش هَتْزَوِّدوا	
húwwa	hayzáwwid	هَيْزَوِّد	miš hayzáwwid	مِش هَيْزَوِّد	
híyya	hatzáwwid	هَتْزَوِّد	miš hatzáwwid	مِش هَتْزَوِّد	
húmma	hayzawwídu	هَيْزَوِّدوا	miš hayzawwídu	مِش هَيْزَوِّدوا	
ínta	záwwid	زَوِّد	ma-tzawwídš	مَتْزَوِّدْش	imperative
ínti	zawwídi	زَوِّدي	ma-tzawwidīš	مَتْزَوِّديش	
íntu	zawwídu	زَوِّدوا	ma-tzawwidūš	مَتْزَوِّدوش	

	active		passive		
masculine	mizáwwid	مِزَوِّد	mitzáwwid	مِتْزَوِّد	participles
feminine	mizawwída	مِزَوِّدَة	mitzawwída	مِتْزَوِّدَة	
plural	mizawwidīn	مِزَوِّدين	mitzawwidīn	مِتْزَوِّدين	

①

أَيْمن زوِّد بنْزين قبْل ما يِطْلع الرِّحْلة.

áyman záwwid banzīn ʔablᵊ ma yíṭla3 irríɦla.

Ayman put more gas in his car
before he started the trip.

②

لمّا حدّ يْزوِّد معاكي في الكلام، اِمْشي و سيبيه.

lámma ɦaddᵊ yzáwwid ma3āki fi -lkalām, ímši wi sibī.

If someone starts to talk to you
impolitely, leave him and go.

③

الحُكومة بِتْزوِّد المُرتّبات كُلّ أوِّل سنة مالية.

ilɦukūma bitzáwwid ilmurattabāt kullᵊ ʔáwwil sána malíyya.

The government raises the salaries
at the beginning of every fiscal year.

④

هنْزوِّد ٨ على ١٣، يِطْلع النّاتج كام؟

hanzáwwid tamánya 3ála talattāšar,
yíṭla3 innātig kām?

If we add 8 to 13, what do we get?

⑤

زوِّد فُرصك في النّجاح بِتنْمِيِّتك لِنفْسك بِاسْتِمْرار.

záwwid fúraṣak fi -nnagāɦ bi-tanmiyyítak li-náfsak bi-stimrār.

Increase your chances for success by
continually improving yourself.

⑥

اِسْكُت أحْسن. متْزوِّدْش الطّين بلّة.

ískut áɦsan. ma-tzawwídš iṭṭīn bálla.

You'd best just stop talking.
Don't make things worse.
[lit. Don't add water to the mud.]

❖ [2s1] **to add; to increase**

➲ 83.4

133 to decorate záwwaʔ زَوَّق

	affirmative		negative		
ána	zawwáʔt	زَوَّقْت	ma-zawwáʔtiš	مَزَوَّقْتِش	perfect
íḫna	zawwáʔna	زَوَّقْنا	ma-zawwaʔnāš	مَزَوَّقْناش	
ínta	zawwáʔt	زَوَّقْت	ma-zawwáʔtiš	مَزَوَّقْتِش	
ínti	zawwáʔti	زَوَّقْتي	ma-zawwaʔtīš	مَزَوَّقْتيش	
íntu	zawwáʔtu	زَوَّقْتوا	ma-zawwaʔtūš	مَزَوَّقْتوش	
húwwa	záwwaʔ	زَوَّق	ma-zawwáʔš	مَزَوَّقْش	
híyya	zawwáʔit	زَوَّقِت	ma-zawwaʔítš	مَزَوَّقِتْش	
húmma	zawwáʔu	زَوَّقوا	ma-zawwaʔūš	مَزَوَّقوش	
ána	azáwwaʔ	أزَوَّق	ma-zawwáʔš	مَزَوَّقْش	imperfect
íḫna	nizáwwaʔ	نِزَوَّق	ma-nzawwáʔš	مَنْزَوَّقْش	
ínta	tizáwwaʔ	تِزَوَّق	ma-tzawwáʔš	مَتْزَوَّقْش	
ínti	tizawwáʔi	تِزَوَّقي	ma-tzawwaʔīš	مَتْزَوَّقيش	
íntu	tizawwáʔu	تِزَوَّقوا	ma-tzawwaʔūš	مَتْزَوَّقوش	
húwwa	yizáwwaʔ	يِزَوَّق	ma-yzawwáʔš	مَيْزَوَّقْش	
híyya	tizáwwaʔ	تِزَوَّق	ma-tzawwáʔš	مَتْزَوَّقْش	
húmma	yizawwáʔu	يِزَوَّقوا	ma-yzawwaʔūš	مَيْزَوَّقوش	
ána	bazáwwaʔ	بَزَوَّق	ma-bazawwáʔš	مَبَزَوَّقْش	bi-imperfect
íḫna	binzáwwaʔ	بِنْزَوَّق	ma-binzawwáʔš	مَبِنْزَوَّقْش	
ínta	bitzáwwaʔ	بِتْزَوَّق	ma-bitzawwáʔš	مَبِتْزَوَّقْش	
ínti	bitzawwáʔi	بِتْزَوَّقي	ma-bitzawwaʔīš	مَبِتْزَوَّقيش	
íntu	bitzawwáʔu	بِتْزَوَّقوا	ma-bitzawwaʔūš	مَبِتْزَوَّقوش	
húwwa	biyzáwwaʔ	بِيْزَوَّق	ma-biyzawwáʔš	مَبِيْزَوَّقْش	
híyya	bitzáwwaʔ	بِتْزَوَّق	ma-bitzawwáʔš	مَبِتْزَوَّقْش	
húmma	biyzawwáʔu	بِيْزَوَّقوا	ma-biyzawwaʔūš	مَبِيْزَوَّقوش	
ána	hazáwwaʔ	هَزَوَّق	miš hazáwwaʔ	مِش هَزَوَّق	future
íḫna	hanzáwwaʔ	هَنْزَوَّق	miš hanzáwwaʔ	مِش هَنْزَوَّق	
ínta	hatzáwwaʔ	هَتْزَوَّق	miš hatzáwwaʔ	مِش هَتْزَوَّق	
ínti	hatzawwáʔi	هَتْزَوَّقي	miš hatzawwáʔi	مِش هَتْزَوَّقي	
íntu	hatzawwáʔu	هَتْزَوَّقوا	miš hatzawwáʔu	مِش هَتْزَوَّقوا	
húwwa	hayzáwwaʔ	هَيْزَوَّق	miš hayzáwwaʔ	مِش هَيْزَوَّق	
híyya	hatzáwwaʔ	هَتْزَوَّق	miš hatzáwwaʔ	مِش هَتْزَوَّق	
húmma	hayzawwáʔu	هَيْزَوَّقوا	miš hayzawwáʔu	مِش هَيْزَوَّقوا	
ínta	záwwaʔ	زَوَّق	ma-tzawwáʔš	مَتْزَوَّقْش	imperative
ínti	zawwáʔi	زَوَّقي	ma-tzawwaʔīš	مَتْزَوَّقيش	
íntu	zawwáʔu	زَوَّقوا	ma-tzawwaʔūš	مَتْزَوَّقوش	

	active		passive		
masculine	mizáwwaʔ	مِزَوَّق	mitzáwwaʔ	مِتْزَوَّق	participles
feminine	mizawwáʔa	مِزَوَّقة	mitzawwáʔa	مِتْزَوَّقة	
plural	mizawwaʔīn	مِزَوَّقين	mitzawwaʔīn	مِتْزَوَّقين	

verbal noun: tazwīʔ تَزْويق

①

جوري عملِت تورْتة و زوّقِتْها حِلْو أوي.

žūri 3ámalit túrta wi zawwaʔítha ḫilw áwi.

Jory made a cake and decorated it nicely.

②

شَيْماء بِتْحِبّ أوي تْزوّق التّورت.

šaymāʔ bitḫíbbᵊ ʔáwi tzáwwaʔ ittúrat.

Shaimaa likes decorating cakes so much.

③

هِبة بِتْزوّق كُلّ حاجة و أيّ حاجة بِاللّوْن الأحْمر.

híba bitzáwwaʔ kullᵊ ḫāga w ayyᵊ ḫāga bi-llōn ilʔáḫmar.

Heba decorates each and every thing with red.

④

اِتّفقْنا معَ ماكْيِيرة هتْزوّق العروسة.

ittafáʔna má3a makyīra hatzáwwaʔ il3arūsa.

We made a deal with a makeup artist to do the bride's makeup.

⑤

متْزوّقوش القاعة. الحفْلة خلاص اِتْلغِت.

ma-tzawwaʔūš ilqā3a. ilḫáfla xalāṣ itláɣit.

Don't decorate the hall. The party has been canceled.

❖ [2s2] **to decorate, adorn**

134 to ask sáʔal سَأَل

	affirmative		negative		
ána	saʔált	سَألْت	ma-saʔáltiš	مَسَألْتِش	perfect
íḥna	saʔálna	سَألْنا	ma-saʔalnāš	مَسَألْناش	
ínta	saʔált	سَألْت	ma-saʔáltiš	مَسَألْتِش	
ínti	saʔálti	سَألْتي	ma-saʔaltīš	مَسَألْتيش	
íntu	saʔáltu	سَألْتوا	ma-saʔaltūš	مَسَألْتوش	
húwwa	sáʔal	سَأل	ma-saʔálš	مَسَألْش	
híyya	sáʔalit	سَألِت	ma-saʔalítš	مَسَألِتْش	
húmma	sáʔalu	سَألوا	ma-saʔalūš	مَسَألوش	
ána	ásʔal	أسْأل	ma-sʔálš	مَسْألْش	imperfect
íḥna	nísʔal	نِسْأل	ma-nisʔálš	مَنِسْألْش	
ínta	tísʔal	تِسْأل	ma-tisʔálš	مَتِسْألْش	
ínti	tisʔáli	تِسْألي	ma-tisʔalīš	مَتِسْأليش	
íntu	tisʔálu	تِسْألوا	ma-tisʔalūš	مَتِسْألوش	
húwwa	yísʔal	يِسْأل	ma-yisʔálš	مَيِسْألْش	
híyya	tísʔal	تِسْأل	ma-tisʔálš	مَتِسْألْش	
húmma	yisʔálu	يِسْألوا	ma-yisʔalūš	مَيِسْألوش	
ána	básʔal	بَسْأل	ma-basʔálš	مَبَسْألْش	bi-imperfect
íḥna	binísʔal	بِنِسْأل	ma-bnisʔálš	مَبْنِسْألْش	
ínta	bitísʔal	بِتِسْأل	ma-btisʔálš	مَبْتِسْألْش	
ínti	bitisʔáli	بِتِسْألي	ma-btisʔalīš	مَبْتِسْأليش	
íntu	bitisʔálu	بِتِسْألوا	ma-btisʔalūš	مَبْتِسْألوش	
húwwa	biyísʔal	بِيِسْأل	ma-byisʔálš	مَبْيِسْألْش	
híyya	bitísʔal	بِتِسْأل	ma-btisʔálš	مَبْتِسْألْش	
húmma	biyisʔálu	بِيِسْألوا	ma-byisʔalūš	مَبْيِسْألوش	
ána	hásʔal	هَسْأل	miš hásʔal	مِش هَسْأل	future
íḥna	hanísʔal	هَنِسْأل	miš hanísʔal	مِش هَنِسْأل	
ínta	hatísʔal	هَتِسْأل	miš hatísʔal	مِش هَتِسْأل	
ínti	hatisʔáli	هَتِسْألي	miš hatisʔáli	مِش هَتِسْألي	
íntu	hatisʔálu	هَتِسْألوا	miš hatisʔálu	مِش هَتِسْألوا	
húwwa	hayísʔal	هَيِسْأل	miš hayísʔal	مِش هَيِسْأل	
híyya	hatísʔal	هَتِسْأل	miš hatísʔal	مِش هَتِسْأل	
húmma	hayisʔálu	هَيِسْألوا	miš hayisʔálu	مِش هَيِسْألوا	
ínta	ísʔal	اِسْأل	ma-tisʔálš	مَتِسْألْش	imperative
ínti	isʔáli	اِسْألي	ma-tisʔalīš	مَتِسْأليش	
íntu	isʔálu	اِسْألوا	ma-tisʔalūš	مَتِسْألوش	

	active		passive		
masculine	sāʔil	سائِل	masʔūl	مَسْؤول	participles
feminine	sáʔla	سائْلَة	masʔūla	مَسْؤولَة	
plural	saʔlīn	سائْلين	masʔulīn	مَسْؤولين	

verbal nouns: suʔāl سُؤال - suʔlān سُؤْلان

①

سألْتِلِك على البِلوزة اللي عاجْباكي. طِلْعِت مِش مقاسِك.

saʔaltílik 3ála -lbilūza -lli 3agbāki. ṭíl3it miš maʔāsik.

I asked about the blouse that you like for you, but it wasn't your size.

②

إبْني دايْماً يِسْألْني أسْئِلة معْرفْش أجاوِب عليْها.

íbni dáyman yisʔálni ʔasʔíla ma-3ráfš agāwib 3alēha.

My son always asks me questions that I can't answer.

③

محْمود بِيِسْأل على جِدِّتْه بِاسْتِمرار.

maḥmūd biyísʔal 3ála giddítu bi-stimarār.

Mahmoud continuously asks about his grandmother.

④

مُخْتار هَيِسْأل على أسْعار الفُنْدُق عشان يِحْجِز.

muxtār hayísʔal 3ála ʔas3ār ilfúnduʔ 3ašān yíḥgiz.

Mokhtar will ask about the hotel's prices to make a reservation.

⑤

اِسْألوا بعْض في كُلّ التّفاصيل قبْل الجَواز.

isʔálu ba3ḍ^{ə} f kull ittafaṣīl ʔabl ilgawāz.

Ask each other about every detail before you get married.

⑥

مِرات زكرِيّا دي مُؤدّبة أوي. مبِتِسْألْش أبداً في حاجة متْخُصّهاش.

mirāt zakaríyya di muʔaddába ʔáwi. ma-bitisʔálš ábadan fi ḥāga ma-txuṣṣahāš.

Zakaria's wife is a very decent woman. She never asks about things that aren't any of her business.

❖ [1s1] **to ask** (**about** على *3ála*)

➲ 50.1, 52.7, 92.6, 103.4, 116.1, 116.3, 121.2, 197.5

135 to leave *sāb* ساب

	affirmative		negative		
ána	*sibt*	سِبْت	*ma-síbtiš*	مَسِبْتِش	perfect
íḥna	*síbna*	سِبْنا	*ma-sibnāš*	مَسِبْناش	
ínta	*sibt*	سِبْت	*ma-síbtiš*	مَسِبْتِش	
ínti	*síbti*	سِبْتي	*ma-sibtīš*	مَسِبْتيش	
íntu	*síbtu*	سِبْتوا	*ma-sibtūš*	مَسِبْتوش	
húwwa	*sāb*	ساب	*ma-sábš*	مَسابْش	
híyya	*sābit*	سابِت	*ma-sabítš*	مَسابِتْش	
húmma	*sābu*	سابوا	*ma-sabūš*	مَسابوش	
ána	*asīb*	أسيب	*ma-síbš*	مَسيبْش	imperfect
íḥna	*nisīb*	نِسيب	*ma-nsíbš*	مَنْسيبْش	
ínta	*tisīb*	تِسيب	*ma-tsíbš*	مَتْسيبْش	
ínti	*tisībi*	تِسيبي	*ma-tsibīš*	مَتْسيبيش	
íntu	*tisību*	تِسيبوا	*ma-tsibūš*	مَتْسيبوش	
húwwa	*yisīb*	يِسيب	*ma-ysíbš*	مَيْسيبْش	
híyya	*tisīb*	تِسيب	*ma-tsíbš*	مَتْسيبْش	
húmma	*yisību*	يِسيبوا	*ma-ysibūš*	مَيْسيبوش	
ána	*basīb*	بَسيب	*ma-basíbš*	مَبَسيبْش	bi-imperfect
íḥna	*binsīb*	بِنْسيب	*ma-binsíbš*	مَبِنْسيبْش	
ínta	*bitsīb*	بِتْسيب	*ma-bitsíbš*	مَبِتْسيبْش	
ínti	*bitsībi*	بِتْسيبي	*ma-bitsibīš*	مَبِتْسيبيش	
íntu	*bitsību*	بِتْسيبوا	*ma-bitsibūš*	مَبِتْسيبوش	
húwwa	*biysīb*	بِيْسيب	*ma-biysíbš*	مَبِيْسيبْش	
híyya	*bitsīb*	بِتْسيب	*ma-bitsíbš*	مَبِتْسيبْش	
húmma	*biysību*	بِيْسيبوا	*ma-biysibūš*	مَبِيْسيبوش	
ána	*hasīb*	هَسيب	*miš hasīb*	مِش هَسيب	future
íḥna	*hansīb*	هَنْسيب	*miš hansīb*	مِش هَنْسيب	
ínta	*hatsīb*	هَتْسيب	*miš hatsīb*	مِش هَتْسيب	
ínti	*hatsībi*	هَتْسيبي	*miš hatsībi*	مِش هَتْسيبي	
íntu	*hatsību*	هَتْسيبوا	*miš hatsību*	مِش هَتْسيبوا	
húwwa	*haysīb*	هَيْسيب	*miš haysīb*	مِش هَيْسيب	
híyya	*hatsīb*	هَتْسيب	*miš hatsīb*	مِش هَتْسيب	
húmma	*haysību*	هَيْسيبوا	*miš haysību*	مِش هَيْسيبوا	
ínta	*sīb*	سيب	*ma-tsíbš*	مَتْسيبْش	imperative
ínti	*sībi*	سيبي	*ma-tsibīš*	مَتْسيبيش	
íntu	*sību*	سيبوا	*ma-tsibūš*	مَتْسيبوش	

	active		passive		
masculine	*sāyib*	سايِب	*mitsāb*	مِتْساب	participles
feminine	*sáyba*	سايْبَة	*mitsāba*	مِتْسابَة	
plural	*saybīn*	سايْبين	*mitsabīn*	مِتْسابين	

verbal noun: *sayabān* سَيَبان

①

أريج شافِت الكلْب، رُكبْها سابِت.

arīž šāfit ilkálb, rukábha sābit.

When Areej saw the dog, her knees started to tremble.

②

ياسِر لمّا بِيتْعب بِيُطْلُب مِنْهُم يِسيبوه لْوَحْدُه شْوَيّة.

yāsir lámma biyít3ab biyúṭlub mínhum yisibū l-wáḥdu šwáyya.

When Yasser gets tired, he asks them to leave him alone for a while.

③

حلا بِتْسيب تِليفونْها في البيْت و هِيَّ نازْلة الجيم.

ḥála bitsīb tilifúnha fi -lbēt wi híyya názla -lžīm.

Hala leaves her phone at home when she goes to the gym.

④

مِش هسيبك تِتْجوِّزي الحَيوان ده أبداً.

miš hasībak titgawwízi -lḥaywān da ʔábadan.

I'll never let you marry that animal.

⑤

سيبي اللي في إيدِك و ادْخُلي نامي شْوَيّة.

sībi -lli f īdik w idxúli nāmi šwáyya.

Put down what you're doing and go get some sleep.

⑥

جِدّي مسابْش قرْيِتُه مِن سِنين.

gíddi ma-sábšᵊ qaryítu min sinīn.

My grandfather hasn't left his village in years.

❖ [1h2] **to leave; to let, allow**

- This verb can be followed by an object and then an imperfect verb or adjective.
- Compare with خلّى *xálla.* (➲ 100)

➲ 7.5, 37.1, 53.5, 72.5, 74.6, 161.4, 174.5, 181.5, 189.8, 232.3, 245.1

136 to help *sā3id* ساعِد

verbal noun: *musá3da* مُساعْدة

	affirmative		negative		
ána	*sa3ídt*	ساعِدْت	*ma-sa3ídtiš*	مَساعِدْتِش	**perfect**
íḫna	*sa3ídna*	ساعِدْنا	*ma-sa3idnāš*	مَساعِدْناش	
ínta	*sa3ídt*	ساعِدْت	*ma-sa3ídtiš*	مَساعِدْتِش	
ínti	*sa3ídti*	ساعِدْتي	*ma-sa3idtīš*	مَساعِدْتيش	
íntu	*sa3ídtu*	ساعِدْتوا	*ma-sa3idtūš*	مَساعِدْتوش	
húwwa	*sā3id*	ساعِد	*ma-sa3ídš*	مَساعِدْش	
híyya	*sá3dit*	ساعْدِت	*ma-sa3dítš*	مَساعْدِتْش	
húmma	*sá3du*	ساعْدوا	*ma-sa3dūš*	مَساعْدوش	

	affirmative		negative		
ána	*asā3id*	أساعِد	*ma-sa3ídš*	مَساعِدْش	**imperfect**
íḫna	*nisā3id*	نِساعِد	*ma-nsa3ídš*	مَنْساعِدْش	
ínta	*tisā3id*	تِساعِد	*ma-tsa3ídš*	مَتْساعِدْش	
ínti	*tisá3di*	تِساعْدي	*ma-tsa3dīš*	مَتْساعْديش	
íntu	*tisá3du*	تِساعْدوا	*ma-tsa3dūš*	مَتْساعْدوش	
húwwa	*yisā3id*	يِساعِد	*ma-ysa3ídš*	مَيْساعِدْش	
híyya	*tisā3id*	تِساعِد	*ma-tsa3ídš*	مَتْساعِدْش	
húmma	*yisá3du*	يِساعْدوا	*ma-ysa3dūš*	مَيْساعْدوش	

	affirmative		negative		
ána	*basā3id*	بَساعِد	*ma-basa3ídš*	مَبَساعِدْش	**bi-imperfect**
íḫna	*binsā3id*	بِنْساعِد	*ma-binsa3ídš*	مَبِنْساعِدْش	
ínta	*bitsā3id*	بِتْساعِد	*ma-bitsa3ídš*	مَبِتْساعِدْش	
ínti	*bitsá3di*	بِتْساعْدي	*ma-bitsa3dīš*	مَبِتْساعْديش	
íntu	*bitsá3du*	بِتْساعْدوا	*ma-bitsa3dūš*	مَبِتْساعْدوش	
húwwa	*biysā3id*	بِيْساعِد	*ma-biysa3ídš*	مَبِيْساعِدْش	
híyya	*bitsā3id*	بِتْساعِد	*ma-bitsa3ídš*	مَبِتْساعِدْش	
húmma	*biysá3du*	بِيْساعْدوا	*ma-biysa3dūš*	مَبِيْساعْدوش	

	affirmative		negative		
ána	*hasā3id*	هَساعِد	*miš hasā3id*	مِش هَساعِد	**future**
íḫna	*hansā3id*	هَنْساعِد	*miš hansā3id*	مِش هَنْساعِد	
ínta	*hatsā3id*	هَتْساعِد	*miš hatsā3id*	مِش هَتْساعِد	
ínti	*hatsá3di*	هَتْساعْدي	*miš hatsá3di*	مِش هَتْساعْدي	
íntu	*hatsá3du*	هَتْساعْدوا	*miš hatsá3du*	مِش هَتْساعْدوا	
húwwa	*haysā3id*	هَيْساعِد	*miš haysā3id*	مِش هَيْساعِد	
híyya	*hatsā3id*	هَتْساعِد	*miš hatsā3id*	مِش هَتْساعِد	
húmma	*haysá3du*	هَيْساعْدوا	*miš haysá3du*	مِش هَيْساعْدوا	

	affirmative		negative		
ínta	*sā3id*	ساعِد	*ma-tsa3ídš*	مَتْساعِدْش	**imperative**
ínti	*sá3di*	ساعْدي	*ma-tsa3dīš*	مَتْساعْديش	
íntu	*sá3du*	ساعْدوا	*ma-tsa3dūš*	مَتْساعْدوش	

	active		passive		
masculine	*misā3id*	مِساعِد	*mitsā3id*	مِتْساعِد	**participles**
feminine	*misá3da*	مِساعْدَة	*mitsá3da*	مِتْساعْدَة	
plural	*misa3dīn*	مِساعْدين	*mitsa3dīn*	مِتْساعْدين	

①

الكِتاب ده ساعِدْني كْتير في فهْم المسائِل الصّعْبة.

ilkitāb da sa3ídni ktīr fi fahm ilmasāʔil iṣṣá3ba.

This book helped me a lot to understand complex equations.

②

مُهيْب بِيْحِبّ يْساعِد النّاس دايْماً.

muhēb biyḫibbᵊ ysā3id innās dáyman.

Moheb always likes to help people.

③

أنا و زمايْلي بِنْساعِد بعْض في المُذاكْرة.

ána wi zamáyli binsā3id ba3ḍᵊ fi -lmuzákra.

My classmates and I help each other study.

④

الدَّوا ده هَيْساعْدك تِنام.

iddáwa da haysa3ídak tinām.

This medicine will help you sleep.

⑤

ساعِدْني أغيرّ كاوِتْش العربية لَوْ سمحْت.

sa3ídni ʔaɣáyyar kawitš il3arabíyya law samáḫt.

Help me change the car tire, please.

⑥

متْساعِدْش شحّات في الشّارِع. دوْل كُلُّهُم نصّابين.

ma-tsā3idšᵊ šaḫḫāt fi -ššāri3. dōl kullúhum naṣṣabīn.

Don't help street beggars. They're all frauds.

❖ [3s] **to help** (someone **with** في *fi*)

- This verb is transitive, taking a direct object noun or pronoun. (➲ 136.6)
- It can also be followed by an object and then an imperfect verb (➲ 136.2, 136.4, 136.5) or في *fi* with a verbal noun (➲ 136.1, 136.3).

➲ 19.3, 37.2, 66.3, 82.4, 100.2, 107.6, 171.1, 199.5, 258.2

137 to travel *sāfir* سافِر

verbal noun: *sáfar* سَفَر

	affirmative		negative		
ána	*safírt*	سافِرْت	*ma-safírtiš*	مَسافِرْتِش	perfect
íḥna	*safírna*	سافِرْنا	*ma-safirnāš*	مَسافِرْناش	
ínta	*safírt*	سافِرْت	*ma-safírtiš*	مَسافِرْتِش	
ínti	*safírti*	سافِرْتي	*ma-safirtīš*	مَسافِرْتيش	
íntu	*safírtu*	سافِرْتوا	*ma-safirtūš*	مَسافِرْتوش	
húwwa	*sāfir*	سافِر	*ma-safírš*	مَسافِرْش	
híyya	*sáfrit*	سافْرِت	*ma-safrítš*	مَسافْرِتْش	
húmma	*sáfru*	سافْروا	*ma-safrūš*	مَسافْروش	
ána	*asāfir*	أسافِر	*ma-safírš*	مَسافِرْش	imperfect
íḥna	*nisāfir*	نِسافِر	*ma-nsafírš*	مَنْسافِرْش	
ínta	*tisāfir*	تِسافِر	*ma-tsafírš*	مَتْسافِرْش	
ínti	*tisáfri*	تِسافْري	*ma-tsafrīš*	مَتْسافْريش	
íntu	*tisáfru*	تِسافْروا	*ma-tsafrūš*	مَتْسافْروش	
húwwa	*yisāfir*	يِسافِر	*ma-ysafírš*	مَيْسافِرْش	
híyya	*tisāfir*	تِسافِر	*ma-tsafírš*	مَتْسافِرْش	
húmma	*yisáfru*	يِسافْروا	*ma-ysafrūš*	مَيْسافْروش	
ána	*basāfir*	بَسافِر	*ma-basafírš*	مَبَسافِرْش	bi-imperfect
íḥna	*binsāfir*	بِنْسافِر	*ma-binsafírš*	مَبِنْسافِرْش	
ínta	*bitsāfir*	بِتْسافِر	*ma-bitsafírš*	مَبِتْسافِرْش	
ínti	*bitsáfri*	بِتْسافْري	*ma-bitsafrīš*	مَبِتْسافْريش	
íntu	*bitsáfru*	بِتْسافْروا	*ma-bitsafrūš*	مَبِتْسافْروش	
húwwa	*biysāfir*	بِيْسافِر	*ma-biysafírš*	مَبِيْسافِرْش	
híyya	*bitsāfir*	بِتْسافِر	*ma-bitsafírš*	مَبِتْسافِرْش	
húmma	*biysáfru*	بِيْسافْروا	*ma-biysafrūš*	مَبِيْسافْروش	
ána	*hasāfir*	هَسافِر	*miš hasāfir*	مِش هَسافِر	future
íḥna	*hansāfir*	هَنْسافِر	*miš hansāfir*	مِش هَنْسافِر	
ínta	*hatsāfir*	هَتْسافِر	*miš hatsāfir*	مِش هَتْسافِر	
ínti	*hatsáfri*	هَتْسافْري	*miš hatsáfri*	مِش هَتْسافْري	
íntu	*hatsáfru*	هَتْسافْروا	*miš hatsáfru*	مِش هَتْسافْروا	
húwwa	*haysāfir*	هَيْسافِر	*miš haysāfir*	مِش هَيْسافِر	
híyya	*hatsāfir*	هَتْسافِر	*miš hatsāfir*	مِش هَتْسافِر	
húmma	*haysáfru*	هَيْسافْروا	*miš haysáfru*	مِش هَيْسافْروا	
ínta	*sāfir*	سافِر	*ma-tsafírš*	مَتْسافِرْش	imperative
ínti	*sáfri*	سافْري	*ma-tsafrīš*	مَتْسافْريش	
íntu	*sáfru*	سافْروا	*ma-tsafrūš*	مَتْسافْروش	

	active		passive		
masculine	*misāfir*	مِسافِر	–	–	participles
feminine	*misáfra*	مِسافْرَة	–	–	
plural	*misafrīn*	مِسافْرين	–	–	

①

مَيْسرة سافْرِت بلاد كِتير و لِسّه.

maysára sáfrit balād kitīr wi líssa.

Maysara has traveled to many countries,
but there are still many others [to see].

②

لمّا تْسافِر خلّي معاك خريطة لِلمكان اللي إنْتَ رايْحُه.

lámma tsāfir xálli ma3āk xarīṭa li-lmakān ílli -nta ráyḥu.

When you travel, have a map of
the place you're going to visit.

③

بسافِر كِتير و شنْطِتي دايْماً جاهْزة.

basāfir kitīr wi šanṭíti dáyman gáhza.

I travel a lot, so my bag
is always ready.

④

مُعْتزّ هَيْسافِر شرْم إسْبوع.

mu3tázzᵊ haysāfir šarm isbū3.

Moataz will travel to Sharm
[el-Sheikh] for a week.

⑤

سافْروا كْتير. السّفر مُتْعة و فايْدة.

sáfru ktīr. issáfar mút3a w fáyda.

Travel a lot. Traveling is
fun and beneficial.

⑥

مبسافِرْش السّودان في أغُسْطُس. الجَوّ هِناك بِيِبْقى صعْب أوي.

ma-basafírš issudān f ayústus. ilgáwwᵊ hinák biyíbʔa ṣa3b áwi.

I never travel to Sudan in August. The
weather there is so difficult.

❖ [3s] **to travel; to live abroad**

➲ 11.1, 16.4, 53.6, 61.5, 70.5, 107.4, 117.5, 142.2, 186.5, 194.1, 194.3, 228.7, 257.2

138 to drive *sāʔ* ساق

	affirmative		negative		
ána	*suʔt*	سُقْت	*ma-súʔtiš*	مَسُقْتِش	**perfect**
íḫna	*súʔna*	سُقْنا	*ma-suʔnāš*	مَسُقْناش	
ínta	*suʔt*	سُقْت	*ma-súʔtiš*	مَسُقْتِش	
ínti	*súʔti*	سُقْتي	*ma-suʔtīš*	مَسُقْتيش	
íntu	*súʔtu*	سُقْتوا	*ma-suʔtūš*	مَسُقْتوش	
húwwa	*sāʔ*	ساق	*ma-sáʔš*	مَساقْش	
híyya	*sāʔit*	ساقِت	*ma-saʔítš*	مَساقِتْش	
húmma	*sāʔu*	ساقوا	*ma-saʔūš*	مَساقوش	
ána	*asūʔ*	أسوق	*ma-súʔš*	مَسوقْش	**imperfect**
íḫna	*nisūʔ*	نِسوق	*ma-nsúʔš*	مَنْسوقْش	
ínta	*tisūʔ*	تِسوق	*ma-tsúʔš*	مَتْسوقْش	
ínti	*tisūʔi*	تِسوقي	*ma-tsuʔīš*	مَتْسوقيش	
íntu	*tisūʔu*	تِسوقوا	*ma-tsuʔūš*	مَتْسوقوش	
húwwa	*yisūʔ*	يِسوق	*ma-ysúʔš*	مَيْسوقْش	
híyya	*tisūʔ*	تِسوق	*ma-tsúʔš*	مَتْسوقْش	
húmma	*yisūʔu*	يِسوقوا	*ma-ysuʔūš*	مَيْسوقوش	
ána	*basūʔ*	بَسوق	*ma-basúʔš*	مَبَسوقْش	**bi-imperfect**
íḫna	*binsūʔ*	بِنْسوق	*ma-binsúʔš*	مَبِنْسوقْش	
ínta	*bitsūʔ*	بِتْسوق	*ma-bitsúʔš*	مَبِتْسوقْش	
ínti	*bitsūʔi*	بِتْسوقي	*ma-bitsuʔīš*	مَبِتْسوقيش	
íntu	*bitsūʔu*	بِتْسوقوا	*ma-bitsuʔūš*	مَبِتْسوقوش	
húwwa	*biysūʔ*	بِيْسوق	*ma-biysúʔš*	مَبِيْسوقْش	
híyya	*bitsūʔ*	بِتْسوق	*ma-bitsúʔš*	مَبِتْسوقْش	
húmma	*biysūʔu*	بِيْسوقوا	*ma-biysuʔūš*	مَبِيْسوقوش	
ána	*hasūʔ*	هَسوق	*miš hasūʔ*	مِش هَسوق	**future**
íḫna	*hansūʔ*	هَنْسوق	*miš hansūʔ*	مِش هَنْسوق	
ínta	*hatsūʔ*	هَتْسوق	*miš hatsūʔ*	مِش هَتْسوق	
ínti	*hatsūʔi*	هَتْسوقي	*miš hatsūʔi*	مِش هَتْسوقي	
íntu	*hatsūʔu*	هَتْسوقوا	*miš hatsūʔu*	مِش هَتْسوقوا	
húwwa	*haysūʔ*	هَيْسوق	*miš haysūʔ*	مِش هَيْسوق	
híyya	*hatsūʔ*	هَتْسوق	*miš hatsūʔ*	مِش هَتْسوق	
húmma	*haysūʔu*	هَيْسوقوا	*miš haysūʔu*	مِش هَيْسوقوا	
ínta	*sūʔ*	سوق	*ma-tsúʔš*	مَتسوقْش	**imperative**
ínti	*sūʔi*	سوقي	*ma-tsuʔīš*	مَتسوقيش	
íntu	*sūʔu*	سوقوا	*ma-tsuʔūš*	مَتسوقوش	

	active		passive		
masculine	*sāyiʔ*	سايِق	*mitsāʔ*	مِتْساق	**participles**
feminine	*sáyʔa*	سايْقَة	*mitsāʔa*	مِتْساقَة	
plural	*sayʔīn*	سايْقين	*mitsaʔīn*	مِتْساقين	

verbal noun: *siwwāʔa* سِواقة

①

آدم ساق ٧ ساعات و هُوَّ راجِع مِ الغرْدقة.

ādam sāʔ sába3 sa3āt wi húwwa rāgi3 mi -lɣardáʔa.

Adam drove for seven hours coming
back from Hurghada.

②

أخويا نِفْسُه يِسوق عربِيِّةْ سبق.

axūya nífsu yisūʔ 3arabíyyit sábaʔ.

My brother wishes he
drove a race car.

③

دالْيا كُلّ يوْم بِتْسوق مسافات طَويلة لمّا ضهْرها وَجعْها.

dálya kull[ə] yōm bitsūʔ masafāt ṭawīla lámma ḍahráha wagá3ha.

Dalia drives such long distances every day
that her back has started to hurt.

④

لمْيا مِش هتْسوق تاني بعْد الحادْثة بْتاعِتْها.

lámya miš hatsūʔ tāni ba3d ilḥádsa bta3ítha.

Lamia will not drive again
after her accident.

⑤

سوق بِهُدوء. المُهِمّ تِوْصل سليم.

sūʔ bi-hudūʔ. ilmuhímm[ə] tíwṣal salīm.

Drive slowly. It's important
to arrive safely.

⑥

إحْنا سْكِتْنالك مرّة. متْسوقْش فيها بقى.

íḥna skitnālak márra. ma-tsuʔš fīha báʔa.

We let one mistake you made
pass. Don't repeat it.

❖ [1h1] **to drive; to persist** (**in** في *fi*)

➲ 2.2

139 to steal sáraʔ سَرَق

verbal noun: sírʔa سِرْقة

perfect

	affirmative		negative	
ána	saráʔt	سَرَقْت	ma-saráʔtiš	مَسَرَقْتِش
íḫna	saráʔna	سَرَقْنا	ma-saraʔnāš	مَسَرَقْناش
ínta	saráʔt	سَرَقْت	ma-saráʔtiš	مَسَرَقْتِش
ínti	saráʔti	سَرَقْتي	ma-saraʔtīš	مَسَرَقْتيش
íntu	saráʔtu	سَرَقْتوا	ma-saraʔtūš	مَسَرَقْتوش
húwwa	sáraʔ	سَرَق	ma-saráʔš	مَسَرَقْش
híyya	sáraʔit	سَرَقِت	ma-saraʔítš	مَسَرَقِتْش
húmma	sáraʔu	سَرَقوا	ma-saraʔūš	مَسَرَقوش

imperfect

	affirmative		negative	
ána	ásraʔ	أسْرَق	ma-sráʔš	مَسْرَقْش
íḫna	nísraʔ	نِسْرَق	ma-nisráʔš	مَنِسْرَقْش
ínta	tísraʔ	تِسْرَق	ma-tisráʔš	مَتِسْرَقْش
ínti	tisráʔi	تِسْرَقي	ma-tisraʔīš	مَتِسْرَقيش
íntu	tisráʔu	تِسْرَقوا	ma-tisraʔūš	مَتِسْرَقوش
húwwa	yísraʔ	يِسْرَق	ma-yisráʔš	مَيِسْرَقْش
híyya	tísraʔ	تِسْرَق	ma-tisráʔš	مَتِسْرَقْش
húmma	yisráʔu	يِسْرَقوا	ma-yisraʔūš	مَيِسْرَقوش

bi-imperfect

	affirmative		negative	
ána	básraʔ	بَسْرَق	ma-basráʔš	مَبَسْرَقْش
íḫna	binísraʔ	بِنِسْرَق	ma-bnisráʔš	مَبْنِسْرَقْش
ínta	bitísraʔ	بِتِسْرَق	ma-btisráʔš	مَبْتِسْرَقْش
ínti	bitisráʔi	بِتِسْرَقي	ma-btisraʔīš	مَبْتِسْرَقيش
íntu	bitisráʔu	بِتِسْرَقوا	ma-btisraʔūš	مَبْتِسْرَقوش
húwwa	biyísraʔ	بِيِسْرَق	ma-byisráʔš	مَبْيِسْرَقْش
híyya	bitísraʔ	بِتِسْرَق	ma-btisráʔš	مَبْتِسْرَقْش
húmma	biyisráʔu	بِيِسْرَقوا	ma-byisraʔūš	مَبْيِسْرَقوش

future

	affirmative		negative	
ána	hásraʔ	هَسْرَق	miš hásraʔ	مِش هَسْرَق
íḫna	hanísraʔ	هَنِسْرَق	miš hanísraʔ	مِش هَنِسْرَق
ínta	hatísraʔ	هَتِسْرَق	miš hatísraʔ	مِش هَتِسْرَق
ínti	hatisráʔi	هَتِسْرَقي	miš hatisráʔi	مِش هَتِسْرَقي
íntu	hatisráʔu	هَتِسْرَقوا	miš hatisráʔu	مِش هَتِسْرَقوا
húwwa	hayísraʔ	هَيِسْرَق	miš hayísraʔ	مِش هَيِسْرَق
híyya	hatísraʔ	هَتِسْرَق	miš hatísraʔ	مِش هَتِسْرَق
húmma	hayisráʔu	هَيِسْرَقوا	miš hayisráʔu	مِش هَيِسْرَقوا

imperative

	affirmative		negative	
ínta	ísraʔ	اِسْرَق	ma-tisráʔš	مَتِسْرَقْش
ínti	isráʔi	اِسْرَقي	ma-tisraʔīš	مَتِسْرَقيش
íntu	isráʔu	اِسْرَقوا	ma-tisraʔūš	مَتِسْرَقوش

participles

	active		passive	
masculine	sāriʔ	سارِق	masrūʔ	مَسْروق
feminine	sárʔa	سارْقة	masrūʔa	مَسْروقة
plural	sarʔīn	سارْقين	masruʔīn	مَسْروقين

①

البِنْت دي سرقِت قلْبي مِن أوِّل لحْظة.

ilbíntᵊ di sáraʔit ʔálbi min áwwil láħẓa.

That girl stole my heart from the first moment.

②

يَعْني أيْه حدّ يِسْرق العربية في عِزّ الضُّهْر. ده شيْء غريب جِدّاً.

yá3ni ʔē ħaddᵊ yísraʔ il3arabíyya fi 3izz iḍḍúhr. da šēʔ ɣarīb gíddan.

How could someone steal the car in the middle of the day? That's really strange.

③

فيه عِصابة بْتِسْرق شُنط السِّتّات على موتوسيكْل.

fī 3iṣāba btísraʔ šúnaṭ issittāt 3ála mutusíkl.

There's a gang stealing women's purses on motorcycle.

④

هَيِسْرقوا أيْه تاني؟ ما خلاص شطّبوا كُلّ اللي في الشّقّة.

hayisráʔu ʔē tāni? ma xalāṣ, šaṭṭábu kull ílli fi -ššáʔʔa.

What else would they steal? They already took everything from the apartment.

⑤

سِمِعْت الخبر؟ إمْبارِح تلاتة سرقوا البنْك.

simí3t ilxábar? imbāriħ talāta sáraʔu -lbank.

Did you hear? Yesterday three people robbed the bank.

⑥

متْبُصّوليش كِده. أنا مسرقْتِش حاجة.

ma-tbuṣṣulīš kída. ána ma-saráʔtiš ħāga.

Don't look at me like that. I didn't take anything.

⑦

تامِر بِيِسْرق كُلّ يوْم فِلوس مِن محْفظِةْ أبوه.

tāmir biyísraʔ kullᵊ yōm filūs min maħfáẓit abū.

Tamer steals money from his father's wallet daily.

⑧

هنِسْرق الڤيلّا إمْتى يا ريِّس؟

hanísraʔ ilvílla ʔímta ya ráyyis?

When shall we rob the villa, boss?

⑨

متِسْرقيش قلْبي و تِهْربي. أنا عايْزك معايا طول العُمْر.

ma-tisraʔīš ʔálbi w tihrábi. ána 3áyzak ma3āya ṭūl il3úmr.

Don't steal my heart and run away. I need you with me for life.

❖ [1s1] **to steal; to rob**

- This verb can translate 'steal', the object being the thing stolen.
- It can also translate 'rob', the object being the person or place something was stolen from. (➲ 139.5, 139.8)
- This verb can be used metaphorically. (➲ 139.1, 139.9)

➲ 176.7, 203.1, 217.6

140 to live síkin سِكِن

		affirmative		negative		
ána	sikínt	سِكِنْت	ma-skíntiš	مَسْكِنْتِش	perfect
íḥna	sikínna	سِكِنّا	ma-skinnāš	مَسْكِنّاش	
ínta	sikínt	سِكِنْت	ma-skíntiš	مَسْكِنْتِش	
ínti	sikínti	سِكِنْتي	ma-skintīš	مَسْكِنْتيش	
íntu	sikíntu	سِكِنْتوا	ma-skintūš	مَسْكِنْتوش	
húwwa	síkin	سِكِن	ma-skínš	مَسْكِنْش	
híyya	síknit	سِكْنِت	ma-siknítš	مَسِكْنِتْش	
húmma	síknu	سِكْنوا	ma-siknūš	مَسِكْنوش	
ána	áskun	أَسْكُن	ma-skúnš	مَسْكُنْش	imperfect
íḥna	nískun	نِسْكُن	ma-niskúnš	مَنِسْكُنْش	
ínta	tískun	تِسْكُن	ma-tiskúnš	مَتِسْكُنْش	
ínti	tiskúni	تِسْكُني	ma-tiskunīš	مَتِسْكُنيش	
íntu	tiskúnu	تِسْكُنوا	ma-tiskunūš	مَتِسْكُنوش	
húwwa	yískun	يِسْكُن	ma-yiskúnš	مَيِسْكُنْش	
híyya	tískun	تِسْكُن	ma-tiskúnš	مَتِسْكُنْش	
húmma	yiskúnu	يِسْكُنوا	ma-yiskunūš	مَيِسْكُنوش	
ána	báskun	بَسْكُن	ma-baskúnš	مَبَسْكُنْش	bi-imperfect
íḥna	biniskun	بِنِسْكُن	ma-bniskúnš	مَبْنِسْكُنْش	
ínta	bitískun	بِتِسْكُن	ma-btiskúnš	مَبْتِسْكُنْش	
ínti	bitiskúni	بِتِسْكُني	ma-btiskunīš	مَبْتِسْكُنيش	
íntu	bitiskúnu	بِتِسْكُنوا	ma-btiskunūš	مَبْتِسْكُنوش	
húwwa	biyískun	بِيِسْكُن	ma-byiskúnš	مَبْيِسْكُنْش	
híyya	bitískun	بِتِسْكُن	ma-btiskúnš	مَبْتِسْكُنْش	
húmma	biyiskúnu	بِيِسْكُنوا	ma-byiskunūš	مَبْيِسْكُنوش	
ána	háskun	هَسْكُن	miš háskun	مِش هَسْكُن	future
íḥna	haniskun	هَنِسْكُن	miš haniskun	مِش هَنِسْكُن	
ínta	hatískun	هَتِسْكُن	miš hatískun	مِش هَتِسْكُن	
ínti	hatiskúni	هَتِسْكُني	miš hatiskúni	مِش هَتِسْكُني	
íntu	hatiskúnu	هَتِسْكُنوا	miš hatiskúnu	مِش هَتِسْكُنوا	
húwwa	hayískun	هَيِسْكُن	miš hayískun	مِش هَيِسْكُن	
híyya	hatískun	هَتِسْكُن	miš hatískun	مِش هَتِسْكُن	
húmma	hayiskúnu	هَيِسْكُنوا	miš hayiskúnu	مِش هَيِسْكُنوا	
ínta	ískun	اِسْكُن	ma-tiskúnš	مَتِسْكُنْش	imperative
ínti	iskúni	اِسْكُني	ma-tiskunīš	مَتِسْكُنيش	
íntu	iskúnu	اِسْكُنوا	ma-tiskunūš	مَتِسْكُنوش	

		active		passive		
masculine	sākin	ساكِن	maskūn	مَسْكون	participles
feminine	sákna	ساكْنَة	maskūna	مَسْكونَة	
plural	saknīn	ساكْنين	maskunīn	مَسْكونين	

verbal noun: sakan سَكَن

①

أنا سْكِنْت في الشّقّة دي مِن يوْم ما اتْجوِّزْت.

ána skíntᵊ fi -ššáʔʔa di min yōm ma -tgawwízt.

I've lived in this apartment since the day I got married.

②

غَيْداء نِفْسها تِسْكُن في الزّمالِك.

ɣaydāʔ nifsáha tískun fi -zzamālik.

Ghaida wishes she lived in Zamalek.

③

الشّباب عادةً بِيِسْكُنوا في المناطِق الجِديدة.

iššabāb 3ādatan biyiskúnu fi -lmanāṭiʔ ilgidīda.

Young people tend to live in the suburbs.

④

لمّا ربِّنا يِفْتح علیْنا هسْكُن في ڤيلّا بِحمّام سِباحة.

lámma rabbína yíftaḫ 3alēna háskun fi vílla bi-ḫammām sibāḫa.

When we get rich, I'll live in a villa with a swimming pool.

⑤

اِسْكُنوا قُريِّب مِن أهاليكو. أحْلى حاجة لمِّةْ العيْلة.

iskúnu ʔuráyyib min ahalīku. áḫla ḫāga lámmit il3ēla.

Live close to your parents. Getting together is the best thing.

⑥

أنا مسْكِنْتِش في وِسْط البلد قبْل كِده، بسّ مُتأكِّد إنّها تجْرِبة مُخْتلِفة.

ána ma-skíntiš fi wisṭ ilbálad ʔablᵊ kída, bassᵊ mutaʔákkid innáha tagríba muxtálifa.

I haven't lived downtown before, but I'm sure it's a unique experience.

❖ [1s6] **to live, reside**

- Compare with عاش *3āš*. (➲ 172)
- The passive participle مسْكون *maskūn* means 'haunted'. (➲ 7.6)
- This verb, like other verbs of the [1s3] and [1s6] patterns, can optionally take ـُ *u* instead of ـِ *i* in the personal prefixes of the imperfect (including the bi-imperfect and future) and imperative. For example, يِسْكُن *yískun* can also be pronounced يُسْكُن *yúskun*. These vowels are interchangeable, but the tables reflect the preferences of the speakers on the MP3s.

➲ 34.1, 60.4

141 to greet sállim سَلِّم

	affirmative		negative		
ána	sallímt	سَلِّمْت	ma-sallímtiš	مَسَلِّمْتِش	perfect
íḫna	sallímna	سَلِّمْنا	ma-sallimnāš	مَسَلِّمْناش	
ínta	sallímt	سَلِّمْت	ma-sallímtiš	مَسَلِّمْتِش	
ínti	sallímti	سَلِّمْتي	ma-sallimtīš	مَسَلِّمْتيش	
íntu	sallímtu	سَلِّمْتوا	ma-sallimtūš	مَسَلِّمْتوش	
húwwa	sállim	سَلِّم	ma-sallímš	مَسَلِّمْش	
híyya	sallímit	سَلِّمِت	ma-sallimítš	مَسَلِّمِتْش	
húmma	sallímu	سَلِّموا	ma-sallimūš	مَسَلِّموش	

	affirmative		negative		
ána	asállim	أَسَلِّم	ma-sallímš	مَسَلِّمْش	imperfect
íḫna	nisállim	نِسَلِّم	ma-nsallímš	مَنْسَلِّمْش	
ínta	tisállim	تِسَلِّم	ma-tsallímš	مَتْسَلِّمْش	
ínti	tisallími	تِسَلِّمي	ma-tsallimīš	مَتْسَلِّميش	
íntu	tisallímu	تِسَلِّموا	ma-tsallimūš	مَتْسَلِّموش	
húwwa	yisállim	يِسَلِّم	ma-ysallímš	مَيْسَلِّمْش	
híyya	tisállim	تِسَلِّم	ma-tsallímš	مَتْسَلِّمْش	
húmma	yisallímu	يِسَلِّموا	ma-ysallimūš	مَيْسَلِّموش	

	affirmative		negative		
ána	basállim	بَسَلِّم	ma-basallímš	مَبَسَلِّمْش	bi-imperfect
íḫna	binsállim	بِنْسَلِّم	ma-binsallímš	مَبِنْسَلِّمْش	
ínta	bitsállim	بِتْسَلِّم	ma-bitsallímš	مَبِتْسَلِّمْش	
ínti	bitsallími	بِتْسَلِّمي	ma-bitsallimīš	مَبِتْسَلِّميش	
íntu	bitsallímu	بِتْسَلِّموا	ma-bitsallimūš	مَبِتْسَلِّموش	
húwwa	biysállim	بِيْسَلِّم	ma-biysallímš	مَبِيْسَلِّمْش	
híyya	bitsállim	بِتْسَلِّم	ma-bitsallímš	مَبِتْسَلِّمْش	
húmma	biysallímu	بِيْسَلِّموا	ma-biysallimūš	مَبِيْسَلِّموش	

	affirmative		negative		
ána	hasállim	هَسَلِّم	miš hasállim	مِش هَسَلِّم	future
íḫna	hansállim	هَنْسَلِّم	miš hansállim	مِش هَنْسَلِّم	
ínta	hatsállim	هَتْسَلِّم	miš hatsállim	مِش هَتْسَلِّم	
ínti	hatsallími	هَتْسَلِّمي	miš hatsallími	مِش هَتْسَلِّمي	
íntu	hatsallímu	هَتْسَلِّموا	miš hatsallímu	مِش هَتْسَلِّموا	
húwwa	haysállim	هَيْسَلِّم	miš haysállim	مِش هَيْسَلِّم	
híyya	hatsállim	هَتْسَلِّم	miš hatsállim	مِش هَتْسَلِّم	
húmma	haysallímu	هَيْسَلِّموا	miš haysallímu	مِش هَيْسَلِّموا	

	affirmative		negative		
ínta	sállim	سَلِّم	ma-tsallímš	مَتْسَلِّمْش	imperative
ínti	sallími	سَلِّمي	ma-tsallimīš	مَتْسَلِّميش	
íntu	sallímu	سَلِّموا	ma-tsallimūš	مَتْسَلِّموش	

	active		passive		
masculine	misállim	مِسَلِّم	mitsállim	مِتْسَلِّم	participles
feminine	misallíma	مِسَلِّمة	mitsallíma	مِتْسَلِّمة	
plural	misallimīn	مِسَلِّمين	mitsallimīn	مِتْسَلِّمين	

verbal nouns: *taslīm* تَسْليم - *salām* سَلام

①

الحمْدُ لِلّه، إمْبارِح سلِّمْنا المشْروع في المعاد.

ilḫámdu li-llāh, imbāriḫ sallímna -lmašrū3 fi -lmi3ād.

Thank God, yesterday we turned in the project on time.

②

إيهاب يِسلِّم على الكُلّ لمّا يِدْخُل المكْتب.

ihāb yisállim 3āla -lkullᵊ lámma yídxul ilmáktab.

Ehab greets everybody when he arrives at the office.

③

المطْعم ده بِيْسلِّم الأكْل دايْماً سُخْن. مُمْتازين!

ilmáṭ3am da biysállim ilʔáklᵊ dáyman suxn. mumtazīn!

That restaurant always delivers food hot. They're great!

④

هسلِّم الشُّغْل ده و أخُد فترْةْ راحة إسْبوعينْ.

hasállim iššúɣlᵊ da w āxud fátrit rāḫa ʔisbu3ēn.

I'll hand over this job; then I'll take a break for two weeks.

⑤

أ: سلِّميلي على ماما.

ب: اللّه يِسلِّمِك.

A: *sallimīli 3āla māma.*

B: *allá ysallímik.*

A: Give my regards to mom.

B: Okay, I will.

⑥

مسلِّمْتِش على عمّك ليْه؟

ma-sallímtiš 3āla 3ámmak lē?

Why didn't you greet your uncle?

❖ [2s1] **to hand over, turn in; to deliver; to greet, say hi to** (على *3ála*)

- The verbal noun تسْليم *taslīm* means 'handing over', 'delivering'. سلام *salām* means 'greeting'.

➲ 147.2, 175.6

142 to allow sámaħ سَمَح

	affirmative		negative		
ána	samáħt	سَمَحْت	ma-samáħtiš	مَسَمَحْتِش	perfect
íħna	samáħna	سَمَحْنا	ma-samaħnāš	مَسَمَحْناش	
ínta	samáħt	سَمَحْت	ma-samáħtiš	مَسَمَحْتِش	
ínti	samáħti	سَمَحْتي	ma-samaħtīš	مَسَمَحْتيش	
íntu	samáħtu	سَمَحْتوا	ma-samaħtūš	مَسَمَحْتوش	
húwwa	sámaħ	سَمَح	ma-samáħš	مَسَمَحْش	
híyya	sámaħit	سَمَحِت	ma-samaħítš	مَسَمَحِتْش	
húmma	sámaħu	سَمَحوا	ma-samaħūš	مَسَمَحوش	
ána	ásmaħ	أَسْمَح	ma-smáħš	مَسْمَحْش	imperfect
íħna	nísmaħ	نِسْمَح	ma-nismáħš	مَنِسْمَحْش	
ínta	tísmaħ	تِسْمَح	ma-tismáħš	مَتِسْمَحْش	
ínti	tismáħi	تِسْمَحي	ma-tismaħīš	مَتِسْمَحيش	
íntu	tismáħu	تِسْمَحوا	ma-tismaħūš	مَتِسْمَحوش	
húwwa	yísmaħ	يِسْمَح	ma-yismáħš	مَيِسْمَحْش	
híyya	tísmaħ	تِسْمَح	ma-tismáħš	مَتِسْمَحْش	
húmma	yismáħu	يِسْمَحوا	ma-yismaħūš	مَيِسْمَحوش	
ána	básmaħ	بَسْمَح	ma-basmáħš	مَبَسْمَحْش	bi-imperfect
íħna	binísmaħ	بِنِسْمَح	ma-bnismáħš	مَبْنِسْمَحْش	
ínta	bitísmaħ	بِتِسْمَح	ma-btismáħš	مَبْتِسْمَحْش	
ínti	bitismáħi	بِتِسْمَحي	ma-btismaħīš	مَبْتِسْمَحيش	
íntu	bitismáħu	بِتِسْمَحوا	ma-btismaħūš	مَبْتِسْمَحوش	
húwwa	biyísmaħ	بِيِسْمَح	ma-byismáħš	مَبْيِسْمَحْش	
híyya	bitísmaħ	بِتِسْمَح	ma-btismáħš	مَبْتِسْمَحْش	
húmma	biyismáħu	بِيِسْمَحوا	ma-byismaħūš	مَبْيِسْمَحوش	
ána	hásmaħ	هَسْمَح	miš hásmaħ	مِش هَسْمَح	future
íħna	hanísmaħ	هَنِسْمَح	miš hanísmaħ	مِش هَنِسْمَح	
ínta	hatísmaħ	هَتِسْمَح	miš hatísmaħ	مِش هَتِسْمَح	
ínti	hatismáħi	هَتِسْمَحي	miš hatismáħi	مِش هَتِسْمَحي	
íntu	hatismáħu	هَتِسْمَحوا	miš hatismáħu	مِش هَتِسْمَحوا	
húwwa	hayísmaħ	هَيِسْمَح	miš hayísmaħ	مِش هَيِسْمَح	
híyya	hatísmaħ	هَتِسْمَح	miš hatísmaħ	مِش هَتِسْمَح	
húmma	hayismáħu	هَيِسْمَحوا	miš hayismáħu	مِش هَيِسْمَحوا	
ínta	ísmaħ	اِسْمَح	ma-tismáħš	مَتِسْمَحْش	imperative
ínti	ismáħi	اِسْمَحي	ma-tismaħīš	مَتِسْمَحيش	
íntu	ismáħu	اِسْمَحوا	ma-tismaħūš	مَتِسْمَحوش	

	active		passive		
masculine	sāmiħ	سامِح	masmūħ	مَسْموح	participles
feminine	sámħa	سامْحَة	masmūħa	مَسْموحَة	
plural	samħīn	سامْحين	masmuħīn	مَسْموحين	

verbal noun: samāħ سَماح

①

إنْتَ إزّاي سمحْت بْحاجة زيّ كِده؟

ínta -zzāy samáɧtᵊ b-ɧāga zayyᵊ kída?

How could you allow something like this?

②

مُفيد مِش مُمْكِن يِسْمح لِبِنْتُه تْسافِر لوَحْدها.

mufīd miš múmkin yísmaɧ li-bíntu tsāfir li-waɧdáha.

Mofeed would never allow his daughter to travel alone.

③

صفاء بْتِسْمح لِوِلادْها يْجرّبوا كُلّ حاجة.

ṣafāʔ bitísmaɧ li-wiládha ygarrábu kullᵊ ɧāga.

Safaa gives her kids the chance to try everything

④

مِش هسْمحْلك تِدمّر مُسْتقْبلي.

miš hasmáɧlak tidámmar mustaʔbáli.

I won't let you destroy my future.

⑤

لَوْ سمحْت ناوِلْني الكوبّايَة دي.

law samáɧtᵊ nawílni -lkubbāya di.

Please, hand me that glass.

⑥

متِسْمحْش لْحدّ يْهينك أبداً.

ma-tismáɧšᵊ l-ɧaddᵊ yhīnak ábadan.

Don't let anyone insult you.

❖ [1s1] **to allow, let**

- This verb takes an indirect object, which is the person who is given permission.
- The thing which is allowed can be noun with the prepositional prefix بِـ *bi-* (➲ 142.1).
- It can also be followed by an imperfect verb, translating 'allow __ to (do)...'.
- Compare with أتاح *ʔatāɧ*. (➲ 5)
- The expression لَوْ سمحْت *law samáɧt*, literally 'if you allow', translates 'please'.

➲ 1.5, 136.5, 166.4

143 to hear símí3 سمع

	affirmative		negative		
ána	simí3t	سِمِعْت	ma-smí3tiš	مَسْمِعْتِش	perfect
íḫna	simí3na	سِمِعْنا	ma-smi3nāš	مَسْمِعْناش	
ínta	simí3t	سِمِعْت	ma-smí3tiš	مَسْمِعْتِش	
ínti	simí3ti	سِمِعْتي	ma-smi3tīš	مَسْمِعْتيش	
íntu	simí3tu	سِمِعْتوا	ma-smi3tūš	مَسْمِعْتوش	
húwwa	sími3	سِمِع	ma-smí3š	مَسْمِعْش	
híyya	sím3it	سِمْعِت	ma-sim3ítš	مَسِمْعِتْش	
húmma	sím3u	سِمْعوا	ma-sim3ūš	مَسِمْعوش	
ána	ásma3	أَسْمَع	ma-smá3š	مَسْمَعْش	imperfect
íḫna	nísma3	نِسْمَع	ma-nismá3š	مَنِسْمَعْش	
ínta	tísma3	تِسْمَع	ma-tismá3š	مَتِسْمَعْش	
ínti	tismá3i	تِسْمَعي	ma-tisma3īš	مَتِسْمَعيش	
íntu	tismá3u	تِسْمَعوا	ma-tisma3ūš	مَتِسْمَعوش	
húwwa	yísma3	يِسْمَع	ma-yismá3š	مَيِسْمَعْش	
híyya	tísma3	تِسْمَع	ma-tismá3š	مَتِسْمَعْش	
húmma	yismá3u	يِسْمَعوا	ma-yisma3ūš	مَيِسْمَعوش	
ána	básma3	بَسْمَع	ma-basmá3š	مَبَسْمَعْش	bi-imperfect
íḫna	binísma3	بِنِسْمَع	ma-bnismá3š	مَبْنِسْمَعْش	
ínta	bitísma3	بِتِسْمَع	ma-btismá3š	مَبْتِسْمَعْش	
ínti	bitismá3i	بِتِسْمَعي	ma-btisma3īš	مَبْتِسْمَعيش	
íntu	bitismá3u	بِتِسْمَعوا	ma-btisma3ūš	مَبْتِسْمَعوش	
húwwa	biyísma3	بِيِسْمَع	ma-byismá3š	مَبْيِسْمَعْش	
híyya	bitísma3	بِتِسْمَع	ma-btismá3š	مَبْتِسْمَعْش	
húmma	biyismá3u	بِيِسْمَعوا	ma-byisma3ūš	مَبْيِسْمَعوش	
ána	hásma3	هَسْمَع	miš hásma3	مِش هَسْمَع	future
íḫna	hanísma3	هَنِسْمَع	miš hanísma3	مِش هَنِسْمَع	
ínta	hatísma3	هَتِسْمَع	miš hatísma3	مِش هَتِسْمَع	
ínti	hatismá3i	هَتِسْمَعي	miš hatismá3i	مِش هَتِسْمَعي	
íntu	hatismá3u	هَتِسْمَعوا	miš hatismá3u	مِش هَتِسْمَعوا	
húwwa	hayísma3	هَيِسْمَع	miš hayísma3	مِش هَيِسْمَع	
híyya	hatísma3	هَتِسْمَع	miš hatísma3	مِش هَتِسْمَع	
húmma	hayismá3u	هَيِسْمَعوا	miš hayismá3u	مِش هَيِسْمَعوا	
ínta	ísma3	اِسْمَع	ma-tismá3š	مَتِسْمَعْش	imperative
ínti	ismá3i	اِسْمَعي	ma-tisma3īš	مَتِسْمَعيش	
íntu	ismá3u	اِسْمَعوا	ma-tisma3ūš	مَتِسْمَعوش	

	active		passive		
masculine	sāmi3	سامِع	masmū3	مَسْموع	participles
feminine	sám3a	سامْعَة	masmū3a	مَسْموعَة	
plural	sam3īn	سامْعين	masmu3īn	مَسْموعين	

verbal nouns: sáma3 سَمَع - samā3 سَماع

①

داليا سِمْعِت إمْبارِح مارْسيل خليفة، و طايْرة مِن الفرح.

dálya sím3it imbāriɧ marsīl xalīfa, wi ţáyra min ilfáraɧ.

Dalia listened to Marcel Khalife yesterday and was over the moon.

②

أخويا بِيْحِبّ يِسْمع فيْروز.

axūya biyɧibbᵊ yísma3 fayrūz.

My brother likes listening to Fairouz.

③

تامِر بِيِسْمع كلام أبوه في كُلّ حاجة.

tāmir biyísma3 kalām abū f kullᵊ ɧāga.

Tamer obeys his father in everything.

④

هسْمع اللي هَيْقولوه الاِتْنيْن و بعْديْن هحْكُم.

hásma3 ílli hayʔulū -lʔitnēn wi ba3dēn háɧkum.

I'll listen to both of them; then I'll make a judgment.

⑤

اِسْمعْني أرْجوك. أنا بحِسّ إنّي بكلِّم نفْسي.

ismá3ni ʔargūk. ána baɧíss ínni bakállim náfsi.

Please listen to me. I feel like I'm talking to myself.

⑥

ساعات بسْمع أصْوات غريبة بِاللّيْل.

sa3āt básma3 aşwāt ɣarība bi-llēl.

Sometimes I hear strange noises at night.

⑦

أ: **سِمِعْت الصّوْت ده؟**

ب: **لأ، مسْمِعْتِش حاجة.**

A: *simí3t işşōt da?*

B: *laʔ, ma-smí3tiš ɧāga.*

A: Did you hear that?

B: No, I didn't hear anything.

⑧

بقْدر أسْمع الوِلاد بِيِلْعبوا برّه و أنا في المطْبخ.

báʔdar ásma3 ilwilād biyil3ábu bárra w ána fi -lmáţbax.

From the kitchen, I can hear the children playing outside.

❖ [1s4] **to listen to; to hear**

➲ 5.1, 23.4, 57.1, 65.6, 70.2, 71.5, 89.5, 92.5, 111.2, 122.2, 139.5, 177.6, 246.5

144 to name *sámma* سمّى

	affirmative		negative		
ána	*sammēt*	سَمّيْت	*ma-sammítš*	مَسَمّيْتْش	perfect
íḥna	*sammēna*	سَمّيْنا	*ma-samminā̈š*	مَسَمّيناش	
ínta	*sammēt*	سَمّيْت	*ma-sammítš*	مَسَمّيْتْش	
ínti	*sammēti*	سَمّيْتي	*ma-sammitīš*	مَسَمّيتيش	
íntu	*sammētu*	سَمّيْتوا	*ma-sammitūš*	مَسَمّيتوش	
húwwa	*sámma*	سَمّى	*ma-sammāš*	مَسَمّاش	
híyya	*sámmit*	سَمّت	*ma-sammítš*	مَسَمّتْش	
húmma	*sámmu*	سَمّوا	*ma-sammūš*	مَسَمّوش	
ána	*asámmi*	أسَمّي	*ma-sammīš*	مَسَمّيش	imperfect
íḥna	*nisámmi*	نِسَمّي	*ma-nsammīš*	مَنْسَمّيش	
ínta	*tisámmi*	تِسَمّي	*ma-tsammīš*	مَتْسَمّيش	
ínti	*tisámmi*	تِسَمّي	*ma-tsammīš*	مَتْسَمّيش	
íntu	*tisámmu*	تِسَمّوا	*ma-tsammūš*	مَتْسَمّوش	
húwwa	*yisámmi*	يِسَمّي	*ma-ysammīš*	مَيْسَمّيش	
híyya	*tisámmi*	تِسَمّي	*ma-tsammīš*	مَتْسَمّيش	
húmma	*yisámmu*	يِسَمّوا	*ma-ysammūš*	مَيْسَمّوش	
ána	*basámmi*	بَسَمّي	*ma-basammīš*	مَبَسَمّيش	bi-imperfect
íḥna	*binsámmi*	بِنْسَمّي	*ma-binsammīš*	مَبِنْسَمّيش	
ínta	*bitsámmi*	بِتْسَمّي	*ma-bitsammīš*	مَبِتْسَمّيش	
ínti	*bitsámmi*	بِتْسَمّي	*ma-bitsammīš*	مَبِتْسَمّيش	
íntu	*bitsámmu*	بِتْسَمّوا	*ma-bitsammūš*	مَبِتْسَمّوش	
húwwa	*biysámmi*	بِيْسَمّي	*ma-biysammīš*	مَبِيْسَمّيش	
híyya	*bitsámmi*	بِتْسَمّي	*ma-bitsammīš*	مَبِتْسَمّيش	
húmma	*biysámmu*	بِيْسَمّوا	*ma-biysammūš*	مَبِيْسَمّوش	
ána	*hasámmi*	هَسَمّي	*miš hasámmi*	مِش هَسَمّي	future
íḥna	*hansámmi*	هَنْسَمّي	*miš hansámmi*	مِش هَنْسَمّي	
ínta	*hatsámmi*	هَتْسَمّي	*miš hatsámmi*	مِش هَتْسَمّي	
ínti	*hatsámmi*	هَتْسَمّي	*miš hatsámmi*	مِش هَتْسَمّي	
íntu	*hatsámmu*	هَتْسَمّوا	*miš hatsámmu*	مِش هَتْسَمّوا	
húwwa	*haysámmi*	هَيْسَمّي	*miš haysámmi*	مِش هَيْسَمّي	
híyya	*hatsámmi*	هَتْسَمّي	*miš hatsámmi*	مِش هَتْسَمّي	
húmma	*haysámmu*	هَيْسَمّوا	*miš haysámmu*	مِش هَيْسَمّوا	
ínta	*sámmi*	سَمّي	*ma-tsammīš*	مَتْسَمّيش	imperative
ínti	*sámmi*	سَمّي	*ma-tsammīš*	مَتْسَمّيش	
íntu	*sámmu*	سَمّوا	*ma-tsammūš*	مَتْسَمّوش	

	active		passive		
masculine	*misámmi*	مِسَمّي	*mitsámmi*	مِتْسَمّي	participles
feminine	*misammíyya*	مِسَمّيّة	*mitsammíyya*	مِتْسَمّيّة	
plural	*misammiyīn*	مِسَمّيين	*mitsammiyīn*	مِتْسَمّيين	

verbal noun: *tasmíyya* تَسْمية

①

سمّيْتوا الوَلد أيْه؟

sammētu -lwálad ʔē?

What did you name the boy?

②

بعلِّم إبْني يِسمّي قبْل ما ياكُل.

ba3állim íbni yisámmi ʔablᵊ ma yākul.

I teach my son to say God's name before he eats.

③

فيه ناس اليومينْ دوْل بِيْسمّوا وِلادْهُم أسامي غريبة.

fī nās ilyumēn dōl biysámmu wiládhum asāmi ɣarība.

Nowadays, some people name their
kids very strange names.

④

مَيادة هتْسمّي بِنْتها شاكيرا.

mayāda hatsámmi bintáha šakīra.

Mayada will name her girl Shakira.

⑤

سمّي قبْل أيّ حاجة هتِعْمِلْها عشان ربِّنا يبارِكْلك فيها.

sámmi ʔabl ayyᵊ ɦāga hati3mílha 3ašān rabbína yibaríklak fīha.

Say the name of God before anything you're
going to do, so God may put his blessings in it.

⑥

مسمّيتوش الوَلد على إسْم جِدُّه ليْه؟

ma-sammitūš ilwálad 3ála ʔismᵊ gíddu lē?

Why didn't you name the
boy after his grandfather?

❖ [2d] **to name, call; to say the basmala (bismallah)**

- This verb is ditransitive, taking two objects. The first is the person (or thing) referred to, and the second is the name given to that person (or thing). (➲ 144.1, 144.3, 144.4, 144.6)
- The phrase بِسْمِ اللهِ الرَّحْمٰنِ الرَّحِيْمِ *bi-smi -llāhi -rraɦmāni -rraɦīm*[i], known as the basmala or bismallah, is commonly uttered by Muslims when beginning a task, especially before eating. (➲ 114.2, 114.5)

➲ 208.4

145 to support sánad سَنَد

verbal nouns: sand سَنْد - musánda مُسانْدة

	affirmative		negative		
ána	sanádt	سَنَدْت	ma-sanádtiš	مَسَنَدْتِش	perfect
íḥna	sanádna	سَنَدْنا	ma-sanadnāš	مَسَنَدْناش	
ínta	sanádt	سَنَدْت	ma-sanádtiš	مَسَنَدْتِش	
ínti	sanádti	سَنَدْتي	ma-sanadtīš	مَسَنَدْتيش	
íntu	sanádtu	سَنَدْتوا	ma-sanadtūš	مَسَنَدْتوش	
húwwa	sánad	سَنَد	ma-sanádš	مَسَنَدْش	
híyya	sánadit	سَنَدِت	ma-sanadítš	مَسَنَدِتْش	
húmma	sánadu	سَنَدوا	ma-sanadūš	مَسَنَدوش	
ána	ásnid	أَسْنِد	ma-snídš	مَسْنِدْش	imperfect
íḥna	nísnid	نِسْنِد	ma-nisnídš	مَنِسْنِدْش	
ínta	tísnid	تِسْنِد	ma-tisnídš	مَتِسْنِدْش	
ínti	tisnídi	تِسْنِدي	ma-tisnidīš	مَتِسْنِديش	
íntu	tisnídu	تِسْنِدوا	ma-tisnidūš	مَتِسْنِدوش	
húwwa	yísnid	يِسْنِد	ma-yisnídš	مَيِسْنِدْش	
híyya	tísnid	تِسْنِد	ma-tisnídš	مَتِسْنِدْش	
húmma	yisnídu	يِسْنِدوا	ma-yisnidūš	مَيِسْنِدوش	
ána	básnid	بَسْنِد	ma-basnídš	مَبَسْنِدْش	bi-imperfect
íḥna	binísnid	بِنِسْنِد	ma-bnisnídš	مَبْنِسْنِدْش	
ínta	bitísnid	بِتِسْنِد	ma-btisnídš	مَبْتِسْنِدْش	
ínti	bitisnídi	بِتِسْنِدي	ma-btisnidīš	مَبْتِسْنِديش	
íntu	bitisnídu	بِتِسْنِدوا	ma-btisnidūš	مَبْتِسْنِدوش	
húwwa	biyísnid	بِيِسْنِد	ma-byisnídš	مَبْيِسْنِدْش	
híyya	bitísnid	بِتِسْنِد	ma-btisnídš	مَبْتِسْنِدْش	
húmma	biyisnídu	بِيِسْنِدوا	ma-byisnidūš	مَبْيِسْنِدوش	
ána	hásnid	هَسْنِد	miš hásnid	مِش هَسْنِد	future
íḥna	hanísnid	هَنِسْنِد	miš hanísnid	مِش هَنِسْنِد	
ínta	hatísnid	هَتِسْنِد	miš hatísnid	مِش هَتِسْنِد	
ínti	hatisnídi	هَتِسْنِدي	miš hatisnídi	مِش هَتِسْنِدي	
íntu	hatisnídu	هَتِسْنِدوا	miš hatisnídu	مِش هَتِسْنِدوا	
húwwa	hayísnid	هَيِسْنِد	miš hayísnid	مِش هَيِسْنِد	
híyya	hatísnid	هَتِسْنِد	miš hatísnid	مِش هَتِسْنِد	
húmma	hayisnídu	هَيِسْنِدوا	miš hayisnídu	مِش هَيِسْنِدوا	
ínta	ísnid	اِسْنِد	ma-tisnídš	مَتِسْنِدْش	imperative
ínti	isnídi	اِسْنِدي	ma-tisnidīš	مَتِسْنِديش	
íntu	isnídu	اِسْنِدوا	ma-tisnidūš	مَتِسْنِدوش	

	active		passive		
masculine	sānid	سانِد	masnūd	مَسْنود	participles
feminine	sánda	سانْدَة	masnūda	مَسْنودَة	
plural	sandīn	سانْدين	masnudīn	مَسْنودين	

①

السِّتّ سندِت عليّا عشان أعدّيها الشّارِع.

issítt^ə sánadit 3aláyya 3ašān a3addīha -ššāri3.

The woman leaned on me so I could help her cross the road.

②

أنا مِحْتاجة حدّ يِسْنِدْني بعْد ما كْبِرت.

ána miђtāga ђadd^ə yisnídni ba3d^ə ma kbirt.

I need someone to support me when I'm old.

③

و إنْتو لزْمِتْكو أيْه في حَياتي. محدِّش فيكو حتّى بْيِسْنِدْني لمّا بقع.

w íntu lazmítku ʔē fi ђayāti. ma-ђáddiš fīku ђátta byisnídni lámma báʔa3.

What use are you in my life? Not a single one of you is even there for me when I'm down.

④

أنا همْسِك مِن هِنا و إنْتَ هتِسْنِد مِ النّاحْيَة التّانْيَة.

Ána hámsik min hína w ínta hatísnid mi -nnáђya -ttánya.

I'll hold [it] from here, and you support [it] from the other side.

⑤

متِسْنِدوش . سيبُه يْجرّب يِمْشي لْوَحْدُه.

ma-tisnidūš. sību ygárrab yímši l-wáђdu.

Don't support him. Let him try to walk by himself.

⑥

اِسْنِدي ضهْرِك هِنا و إنْتي بِتِعْمِلي التّمْرين ده.

isnídi ḍáhrik hína w ínti biti3míli -ttamrīn da.

Lean your back here when doing this exercise.

❖ [1s2] **to support; to lean** (**on** على *3ála*)

146 to stay up late *síhir* سِهِر

verbal noun: *sáhar* سَهَر

	affirmative		negative		
ána	*sihírt*	سِهِرْت	*ma-shírtiš*	مَسْهِرْتِش	perfect
íḫna	*sihírna*	سِهِرْنا	*ma-shirnāš*	مَسْهِرْناش	
ínta	*sihírt*	سِهِرْت	*ma-shírtiš*	مَسْهِرْتِش	
ínti	*sihírti*	سِهِرْتي	*ma-shirtīš*	مَسْهِرْتيش	
íntu	*sihírtu*	سِهِرْتوا	*ma-shirtūš*	مَسْهِرْتوش	
húwwa	*síhir*	سِهِر	*ma-shírš*	مَسْهِرْش	
híyya	*síhrit*	سِهْرِت	*ma-sihrítš*	مَسِهْرِتْش	
húmma	*síhru*	سِهْروا	*ma-sihrūš*	مَسِهْروش	
ána	*áshar*	أسْهَر	*ma-shárš*	مَسْهَرْش	imperfect
íḫna	*níshar*	نِسْهَر	*ma-nishárš*	مَنِسْهَرْش	
ínta	*tíshar*	تِسْهَر	*ma-tishárš*	مَتِسْهَرْش	
ínti	*tishári*	تِسْهَري	*ma-tisharīš*	مَتِسْهَريش	
íntu	*tisháru*	تِسْهَروا	*ma-tisharūš*	مَتِسْهَروش	
húwwa	*yíshar*	يِسْهَر	*ma-yishárš*	مَيِسْهَرْش	
híyya	*tíshar*	تِسْهَر	*ma-tishárš*	مَتِسْهَرْش	
húmma	*yisháru*	يِسْهَروا	*ma-yisharūš*	مَيِسْهَروش	
ána	*báshar*	بَسْهَر	*ma-bashárš*	مَبَسْهَرْش	bi-imperfect
íḫna	*biníshar*	بِنِسْهَر	*ma-bnishárš*	مَبْنِسْهَرْش	
ínta	*bitíshar*	بِتِسْهَر	*ma-btishárš*	مَبْتِسْهَرْش	
ínti	*bitishári*	بِتِسْهَري	*ma-btisharīš*	مَبْتِسْهَريش	
íntu	*bitisháru*	بِتِسْهَروا	*ma-btisharūš*	مَبْتِسْهَروش	
húwwa	*biyíshar*	بِيِسْهَر	*ma-byishárš*	مَبْيِسْهَرْش	
híyya	*bitíshar*	بِتِسْهَر	*ma-btishárš*	مَبْتِسْهَرْش	
húmma	*biyisháru*	بِيِسْهَروا	*ma-byisharūš*	مَبْيِسْهَروش	
ána	*háshar*	هَسْهَر	*miš háshar*	مِش هَسْهَر	future
íḫna	*haníshar*	هَنِسْهَر	*miš haníshar*	مِش هَنِسْهَر	
ínta	*hatíshar*	هَتِسْهَر	*miš hatíshar*	مِش هَتِسْهَر	
ínti	*hatishári*	هَتِسْهَري	*miš hatishári*	مِش هَتِسْهَري	
íntu	*hatisháru*	هَتِسْهَروا	*miš hatisháru*	مِش هَتِسْهَروا	
húwwa	*hayíshar*	هَيِسْهَر	*miš hayíshar*	مِش هَيِسْهَر	
híyya	*hatíshar*	هَتِسْهَر	*miš hatíshar*	مِش هَتِسْهَر	
húmma	*hayisháru*	هَيِسْهَروا	*miš hayisháru*	مِش هَيِسْهَروا	
ínta	*íshar*	اِسْهَر	*ma-tishárš*	مَتِسْهَرْش	imperative
ínti	*ishári*	اِسْهَري	*ma-tisharīš*	مَتِسْهَريش	
íntu	*isháru*	اِسْهَروا	*ma-tisharūš*	مَتِسْهَروش	

	active		passive		
masculine	*sahrān*	سَهْران	–	–	participles
feminine	*sahrāna*	سَهْرانَة	–	–	
plural	*sahranīn*	سَهْرانين	–	–	

①

لمّا سْهِرْنا جُعْنا، أَصْلِنا مِتْعشِّيين مِن بدْري.

lámma shírna gú3na, aṣlína mit3aššiyīn min bádri.

When we stayed up late, we got hungry because we'd had dinner so early.

②

الحارِس عنْدِنا كُلّ يوْم يِسْهر لِلصُّبْح قُدّام العِمارة.

ilḫāris 3andína kull[ə] yōm yíshar li-ṣṣubḫ[ə] ʔuddām il3imāra.

The security guard stays up all night every night in front of our building.

③

في الصّيْف بِنِسْهر عشان الجَوّ بِاللّيْل حِلْو.

fi -ṣṣēf biníshar 3ašān ilgáww[ə] bi-llēl ḫilw.

In the summer, we stay up late because the weather is nice in the evening.

④

هتِسْهر فيْن النّهارْده؟

hatíshar fēn innahárda?

Where are you going to be out tonight?

⑤

متِسْهرْش ليْلةْ الاِمْتِحان عشان تِركِّز الصُّبْح.

ma-tishárš[ə] lēlit ilʔimtiḫān 3ašān tirákkiz iṣṣúbḫ.

Don't stay up late the night before the exam, so you can focus in the morning.

❖ [1s4] **to stay up late, stay up all night**

➲ 92.4, 155.5

147 to see šāf شاف

verbal nouns: šawafān شَوَفان - šōf شوف

	affirmative		negative		
ána	šuft	شُفْت	ma-šúftiš	مَشُفْتِش	perfect
íḥna	šúfna	شُفْنا	ma-šufnāš	مَشُفْناش	
ínta	šuft	شُفْت	ma-šúftiš	مَشُفْتِش	
ínti	šúfti	شُفْتي	ma-šuftīš	مَشُفْتيش	
íntu	šúftu	شُفْتوا	ma-šuftūš	مَشُفْتوش	
húwwa	šāf	شاف	ma-šáfš	مَشافْش	
híyya	šāfit	شافِت	ma-šafítš	مَشافِتْش	
húmma	šāfu	شافوا	ma-šafūš	مَشافوش	
ána	ašūf	أشوف	ma-šúfš	مَشوفْش	imperfect
íḥna	nišūf	نِشوف	ma-nšúfš	مَنْشوفْش	
ínta	tišūf	تِشوف	ma-tšúfš	مَتْشوفْش	
ínti	tišūfi	تِشوفي	ma-tšufīš	مَتْشوفيش	
íntu	tišūfu	تِشوفوا	ma-tšufūš	مَتْشوفوش	
húwwa	yišūf	يِشوف	ma-yšúfš	مَيْشوفْش	
híyya	tišūf	تِشوف	ma-tšúfš	مَتْشوفْش	
húmma	yišūfu	يِشوفوا	ma-yšufūš	مَيْشوفوش	
ána	bašūf	بَشوف	ma-bašúfš	مَبَشوفْش	bi-imperfect
íḥna	binšūf	بِنْشوف	ma-binšúfš	مَبِنْشوفْش	
ínta	bitšūf	بِتْشوف	ma-bitšúfš	مَبِتْشوفْش	
ínti	bitšūfi	بِتْشوفي	ma-bitšufīš	مَبِتْشوفيش	
íntu	bitšūfu	بِتْشوفوا	ma-bitšufūš	مَبِتْشوفوش	
húwwa	biyšūf	بِيْشوف	ma-biyšúfš	مَبِيْشوفْش	
híyya	bitšūf	بِتْشوف	ma-bitšúfš	مَبِتْشوفْش	
húmma	biyšūfu	بِيْشوفوا	ma-biyšufūš	مَبِيْشوفوش	
ána	hašūf	هَشوف	miš hašūf	مِش هَشوف	future
íḥna	hanšūf	هَنْشوف	miš hanšūf	مِش هَنْشوف	
ínta	hatšūf	هَتْشوف	miš hatšūf	مِش هَتْشوف	
ínti	hatšūfi	هَتْشوفي	miš hatšūfi	مِش هَتْشوفي	
íntu	hatšūfu	هَتْشوفوا	miš hatšūfu	مِش هَتْشوفوا	
húwwa	hayšūf	هَيْشوف	miš hayšūf	مِش هَيْشوف	
híyya	hatšūf	هَتْشوف	miš hatšūf	مِش هَتْشوف	
húmma	hayšūfu	هَيْشوفوا	miš hayšūfu	مِش هَيْشوفوا	
ínta	šūf	شوف	ma-tšúfš	مَتْشوفْش	imperative
ínti	šūfi	شوفي	ma-tšufīš	مَتْشوفيش	
íntu	šūfu	شوفوا	ma-tšufūš	مَتْشوفوش	

	active		passive		
masculine	šāyif	شايِف	mitšāf	مِتْشاف	participles
feminine	šáyfa	شايْفَة	mitšāfa	مِتْشافَة	
plural	šayfīn	شايْفين	mitšafīn	مِتْشافين	

①

أنا شُفْت الفيلْم ده ٥ مرّات و مُسْتعِدّة أشوفُه تاني.

ána šuft ilfílmᵊ da xámas marrāt wi musta3ídda ʔašūfu tāni.

I've seen that movie five times,
and I'm ready to see it again.

②

لمّا تْشوف ناجي بلّغْه سلامي.

lámma tšūf nāgi balláɣu salāmi.

When you see Nagi, say
hi to him for me.

③

أبو الوِلاد بِيْشوفْهُم مرّتيْن في الإسْبوع بعْد الطّلاق.

ábu -lwilād biyšúfhum marritēn fi -lʔisbū3 ba3d iṭṭalāʔ.

After the divorce, the children's father
sees them twice a week.

④

ماهيتاب هتْشوف أبوها لِأوّل مرّة بُكْره.

mahitāb hatšūf abūha li-áwwil márra búkra.

Mahitab will see her father for
the first time tomorrow.

⑤

شوفي نفْسك يا بِنْتي و بطّلي تْضيّعي مجْهودك كُلُّه على النّاس.

šūfi náfsak ya bínti wi baṭṭáli tḍayyá3i maghūdak kúllu 3ála -nnās.

Just take care of yourself, dear, and stop
spending all your energy on others.

⑥

لِسّه مشُفْتيليش عروسة؟

líssa ma-šuftilīš 3arūsa?

Haven't you found me a
nice girl to marry yet?

❖ [1h1] **to see**

- While this verb usually translates 'see', it can be used idiomatically to mean 'look after' or 'find'. (➲ 147.5, 147.6)
- Although the vowel of the first and second persons of the perfect tense is a short *u,* it is common to see it written with و, also: شوفْت *šuft* 'I saw', etc.

➲ 4.3, 4.4, 21.4, 23.3, 24.3, 29.2, 57.6, 70.2, 71.3, 72.4, 80.6, 81.5, 83.5, 91.4, 94.5, 106.7, 135.1, 149.2, 153.1, 153.4, 157.6, 162.4, 164.3, 175.7, 190.6, 204.1, 204.5, 228.7, 231.11, 241.5

148 to carry *šāl* شال

	affirmative		negative		
ána	*šilt*	شِلْت	*ma-šíltiš*	مَشِلْتِش	perfect
íḫna	*šílna*	شِلْنا	*ma-šilnāš*	مَشِلْناش	
ínta	*šilt*	شِلْت	*ma-šíltiš*	مَشِلْتِش	
ínti	*šílti*	شِلْتي	*ma-šiltīš*	مَشِلْتيش	
íntu	*šíltu*	شِلْتوا	*ma-šiltūš*	مَشِلْتوش	
húwwa	*šāl*	شال	*ma-šálš*	مَشالْش	
híyya	*šālit*	شالِت	*ma-šalítš*	مَشالِتْش	
húmma	*šālu*	شالوا	*ma-šalūš*	مَشالوش	
ána	*ašīl*	أشيل	*ma-šílš*	مَشيلْش	imperfect
íḫna	*nišīl*	نِشيل	*ma-nšílš*	مَنْشيلْش	
ínta	*tišīl*	تِشيل	*ma-tšílš*	مَتْشيلْش	
ínti	*tišīli*	تِشيلي	*ma-tšilīš*	مَتْشيليش	
íntu	*tišīlu*	تِشيلوا	*ma-tšilūš*	مَتْشيلوش	
húwwa	*yišīl*	يِشيل	*ma-yšílš*	مَيْشيلْش	
híyya	*tišīl*	تِشيل	*ma-tšílš*	مَتْشيلْش	
húmma	*yišīlu*	يِشيلوا	*ma-yšilūš*	مَيْشيلوش	
ána	*bašīl*	بَشيل	*ma-bašílš*	مَبَشيلْش	bi-imperfect
íḫna	*binšīl*	بِنْشيل	*ma-binšílš*	مَبِنْشيلْش	
ínta	*bitšīl*	بِتْشيل	*ma-bitšílš*	مَبِتْشيلْش	
ínti	*bitšīli*	بِتْشيلي	*ma-bitšilīš*	مَبِتْشيليش	
íntu	*bitšīlu*	بِتْشيلوا	*ma-bitšilūš*	مَبِتْشيلوش	
húwwa	*biyšīl*	بِيْشيل	*ma-biyšílš*	مَبِيْشيلْش	
híyya	*bitšīl*	بِتْشيل	*ma-bitšílš*	مَبِتْشيلْش	
húmma	*biyšīlu*	بِيْشيلوا	*ma-biyšilūš*	مَبِيْشيلوش	
ána	*hašīl*	هَشيل	*miš hašīl*	مِش هَشيل	future
íḫna	*hanšīl*	هَنْشيل	*miš hanšīl*	مِش هَنْشيل	
ínta	*hatšīl*	هَتْشيل	*miš hatšīl*	مِش هَتْشيل	
ínti	*hatšīli*	هَتْشيلي	*miš hatšīli*	مِش هَتْشيلي	
íntu	*hatšīlu*	هَتْشيلوا	*miš hatšīlu*	مِش هَتْشيلوا	
húwwa	*hayšīl*	هَيْشيل	*miš hayšīl*	مِش هَيْشيل	
híyya	*hatšīl*	هَتْشيل	*miš hatšīl*	مِش هَتْشيل	
húmma	*hayšīlu*	هَيْشيلوا	*miš hayšīlu*	مِش هَيْشيلوا	
ínta	*šīl*	شيل	*ma-tšílš*	مَتْشيلْش	imperative
ínti	*šīli*	شيلي	*ma-tšilīš*	مَتْشيليش	
íntu	*šīlu*	شيلوا	*ma-tšilūš*	مَتْشيلوش	

	active		passive		
masculine	*šāyil*	شايِل	*mitšāl*	مِتْشال	participles
feminine	*šáyla*	شايْلَة	*mitšāla*	مِتْشالَة	
plural	*šaylīn*	شايْلين	*mitšalīn*	مِتْشالين	

verbal noun: *šēl* شَيْل

①

رامي شال مادّتين التِـرم ده.

rāmi šāl madditēn ittírmᵊ da.

Rami failed two classes this term.

②

ألْفت دايماً تِشيل إبْنها في حمّالة على ضهْرها.

úlfat dáyman tišīl ibnáha fi ḫammāla 3ála ḍahráha.

Olfat always carries her son
in a carrier on her back.

③

الزّبال مبيْشيلْش الزِّبالة بقالُه كام يوْم. المنْظر بقى صعْب.

izzabāl ma-biyšilš izzibāla baʔālu kām yōm. ilmánẓar báʔa ṣa3b.

The garbageman hasn't collected [lit. removed] the
garbage for many days. The view is getting bad.

④

إنْتَ مِش هتْشيل البِنْت دي مِن دِماغك بقى؟ دي خلاص فرحْها بُكْره.

ínta miš hatšīl ilbíntᵊ di min dimāɣak báʔaʔ di xalāṣ faráḫha búkra.

Won't you forget that girl? Her wedding is tomorrow.

⑤

شيل الوَرق مِن عَ الترّابيْزة عشان أحُطّ الأكْل.

šīl ilwáraʔ min 3a -ttarabēza 3ašān aḫúṭṭ ilʔákl.

Get those papers off the table,
so I can put out the food.

⑥

متْشيليش حاجة يا ماما عشان ضهْرِك.

ma-tšilīš ḫāga ya māma 3ašān ḍáhrik.

Don't carry anything, mom.
[You'll hurt] your back.

❖ [1h2] **to carry; to remove (from** مِن *min*)**; to fail**

➲ 25.2, 71.4, 172.3, 187.9

149 to indicate šāwir شاوِر

verbal noun: mušáwra مُشاوْرَة

	affirmative		negative		
ána	šawírt	شاوِرْت	ma-šawírtiš	مَشاوِرْتِش	perfect
íḥna	šawírna	شاوِرْنا	ma-šawirnāš	مَشاوِرْناش	
ínta	šawírt	شاوِرْت	ma-šawírtiš	مَشاوِرْتِش	
ínti	šawírti	شاوِرْتي	ma-šawirtīš	مَشاوِرْتيش	
íntu	šawírtu	شاوِرْتوا	ma-šawirtūš	مَشاوِرْتوش	
húwwa	šāwir	شاوِر	ma-šawírš	مَشاوِرْش	
híyya	šáwrit	شاوْرِت	ma-šawrítš	مَشاوْرِتْش	
húmma	šáwru	شاوْروا	ma-šawrūš	مَشاوْروش	
ána	ašāwir	أشاوِر	ma-šawírš	مَشاوِرْش	imperfect
íḥna	nišāwir	نِشاوِر	ma-nšawírš	مَنْشاوِرْش	
ínta	tišāwir	تِشاوِر	ma-tšawírš	مَتْشاوِرْش	
ínti	tišáwri	تِشاوْري	ma-tšawrīš	مَتْشاوْريش	
íntu	tišáwru	تِشاوْروا	ma-tšawrūš	مَتْشاوْروش	
húwwa	yišāwir	يِشاوِر	ma-yšawírš	مَيْشاوِرْش	
híyya	tišāwir	تِشاوِر	ma-tšawírš	مَتْشاوِرْش	
húmma	yišáwru	يِشاوْروا	ma-yšawrūš	مَيْشاوْروش	
ána	bašāwir	بَشاوِر	ma-bašawírš	مَبَشاوِرْش	bi-imperfect
íḥna	binšāwir	بِنْشاوِر	ma-binšawírš	مَبِنْشاوِرْش	
ínta	bitšāwir	بِتْشاوِر	ma-bitšawírš	مَبِتْشاوِرْش	
ínti	bitšáwri	بِتْشاوْري	ma-bitšawrīš	مَبِتْشاوْريش	
íntu	bitšáwru	بِتْشاوْروا	ma-bitšawrūš	مَبِتْشاوْروش	
húwwa	biyšāwir	بِيْشاوِر	ma-biyšawírš	مَبِيْشاوِرْش	
híyya	bitšāwir	بِتْشاوِر	ma-bitšawírš	مَبِتْشاوِرْش	
húmma	biyšáwru	بِيْشاوْروا	ma-biyšawrūš	مَبِيْشاوْروش	
ána	hašāwir	هَشاوِر	miš hašāwir	مِش هَشاوِر	future
íḥna	hanšāwir	هَنْشاوِر	miš hanšāwir	مِش هَنْشاوِر	
ínta	hatšāwir	هَتْشاوِر	miš hatšāwir	مِش هَتْشاوِر	
ínti	hatšáwri	هَتْشاوْري	miš hatšáwri	مِش هَتْشاوْري	
íntu	hatšáwru	هَتْشاوْروا	miš hatšáwru	مِش هَتْشاوْروا	
húwwa	hayšāwir	هَيْشاوِر	miš hayšāwir	مِش هَيْشاوِر	
híyya	hatšāwir	هَتْشاوِر	miš hatšāwir	مِش هَتْشاوِر	
húmma	hayšáwru	هَيْشاوْروا	miš hayšáwru	مِش هَيْشاوْروا	
ínta	šāwir	شاوِر	ma-tšawírš	مَتْشاوِرْش	imperative
ínti	šáwri	شاوْري	ma-tšawrīš	مَتْشاوْريش	
íntu	šáwru	شاوْروا	ma-tšawrūš	مَتْشاوْروش	

	active		passive		
masculine	mišāwir	مِشاوِر	mitšāwir	مِتْشاوِر	participles
feminine	mišáwra	مِشاوْرَة	mitšáwra	مِتْشاوْرَة	
plural	mišawrīn	مِشاوْرين	mitšawrīn	مِتْشاوْرين	

①

أحْمد شاوِرْلي على المحلّ اللي عامِل تخْفيضات.

áɦmad šawírli 3ála -lmaɦáll ílli 3āmil taxfiḍāt.

Ahmed pointed out to me the shop that is having sales.

②

إبْني لمّا بِيْشوف حُصان في الشّارِع لازِم يِشاوِر عليْه.

íbni lámma biyšūf ɦuṣān fi -ššāri3 lāzim yišāwir 3alē.

When my son sees a horse in the street, he always points at it.

③

مبِتْشاوْروش بعْض ليْه قبْل ما تاخْدوا القرار؟

ma-bitšawrūš ba3ḍᵊ lē ʔablᵊ ma táxdu -lqarār?

Why don't you consult with each other before making the decision?

④

هَيُقف قُدّامِك سِتّ مُشْتبهين و إنْتي هتْشاوْري عَ اللي شُفْتيه.

háyuʔaf ʔuddāmik sittᵊ muštabahīn w ínti hatšáwri 3a -lli šuftī.

Six suspects will stand in front of you, and you'll point at the one you saw.

⑤

متْشاوِرْش كِده عَ النّاس. مَيْصحّْش.

ma-tšawíršᵊ kída 3a -nnās. ma-yṣáɦɦiš.

Don't point at people like that. It's not polite.

❖ [3s] **to point (at** على *3ála*)**; to consult with**

➲ 263.4

150 to attach šábak شَبَك

	affirmative		negative		
ána	šabákt	شَبَكْت	ma-šabáktiš	مَشَبَكْتِش	perfect
íḫna	šabákna	شَبَكْنا	ma-šabaknāš	مَشَبَكْناش	
ínta	šabákt	شَبَكْت	ma-šabáktiš	مَشَبَكْتِش	
ínti	šabákti	شَبَكْتي	ma-šabaktīš	مَشَبَكْتيش	
íntu	šabáktu	شَبَكْتوا	ma-šabaktūš	مَشَبَكْتوش	
húwwa	šábak	شَبَك	ma-šabákš	مَشَبَكْش	
híyya	šábakit	شَبَكِت	ma-šabakítš	مَشَبَكِتْش	
húmma	šábaku	شَبَكوا	ma-šabakūš	مَشَبَكوش	
ána	ášbuk	أشْبُك	ma-šbúkš	مَشْبُكْش	imperfect
íḫna	núšbuk	نُشْبُك	ma-nušbúkš	مَنُشْبُكْش	
ínta	túšbuk	تُشْبُك	ma-tušbúkš	مَتُشْبُكْش	
ínti	tušbúki	تُشْبُكي	ma-tušbukīš	مَتُشْبُكيش	
íntu	tušbúku	تُشْبُكوا	ma-tušbukūš	مَتُشْبُكوش	
húwwa	yúšbuk	يُشْبُك	ma-yušbúkš	مَيُشْبُكْش	
híyya	túšbuk	تُشْبُك	ma-tušbúkš	مَتُشْبُكْش	
húmma	yušbúku	يُشْبُكوا	ma-yušbukūš	مَيُشْبُكوش	
ána	bášbuk	بَشْبُك	ma-bašbúkš	مَبَشْبُكْش	bi-imperfect
íḫna	binúšbuk	بِنُشْبُك	ma-bnušbúkš	مَبْنُشْبُكْش	
ínta	bitúšbuk	بِتُشْبُك	ma-btušbúkš	مَبْتُشْبُكْش	
ínti	bitušbúki	بِتُشْبُكي	ma-btušbukīš	مَبْتُشْبُكيش	
íntu	bitušbúku	بِتُشْبُكوا	ma-btušbukūš	مَبْتُشْبُكوش	
húwwa	biyúšbuk	بِيُشْبُك	ma-byušbúkš	مَبْيُشْبُكْش	
híyya	bitúšbuk	بِتُشْبُك	ma-btušbúkš	مَبْتُشْبُكْش	
húmma	biyušbúku	بِيُشْبُكوا	ma-byušbukūš	مَبْيُشْبُكوش	
ána	hášbuk	هَشْبُك	miš hášbuk	مِش هَشْبُك	future
íḫna	hanúšbuk	هَنُشْبُك	miš hanúšbuk	مِش هَنُشْبُك	
ínta	hatúšbuk	هَتُشْبُك	miš hatúšbuk	مِش هَتُشْبُك	
ínti	hatišbúki	هَتُشْبُكي	miš hatušbúki	مِش هَتُشْبُكي	
íntu	hatišbúku	هَتُشْبُكوا	miš hatušbúku	مِش هَتُشْبُكوا	
húwwa	hayúšbuk	هَيُشْبُك	miš hayúšbuk	مِش هَيُشْبُك	
híyya	hatúšbuk	هَتُشْبُك	miš hatúšbuk	مِش هَتُشْبُك	
húmma	hayušbúku	هَيُشْبُكوا	miš hayušbúku	مِش هَيُشْبُكوا	
ínta	úšbuk	أُشْبُك	ma-tušbúkš	مَتُشْبُكْش	imperative
ínti	ušbúki	أُشْبُكي	ma-tušbukīš	مَتُشْبُكيش	
íntu	ušbúku	أُشْبُكوا	ma-tušbukūš	مَتُشْبُكوش	

	active		passive		
masculine	šābik	شابِك	mašbūk	مَشْبوك	participles
feminine	šábka	شابْكَة	mašbūka	مَشْبوكَة	
plural	šabkīn	شابْكين	mašbukīn	مَشْبوكين	

verbal noun: šábk شَبْك

①

الوَلد شبك خيْط في العربية بْتاعْته و مِشي يْجُرّها.

ilwálad šábak xēṭ fi -l3arabíyya btá3tu wi míši ygurráha.

The boy attached a wire to his car and pulled it.

②

لازِم تِشْبُكي الغسيل بِمشابِك لَيُقع مِن عَ الحبْل.

lāzim tišbúki -lɣasīl bi-mašābik la-yúʔa3 min 3a -lḥabl.

You should clip the laundry with pins,
or else it'll fall off the [clothes] line.

③

مبْتِشْبُكيش شعْرِك بِتوكة ليْه؟

ma-btišbukīš šá3rak bi-tōka lē?

Why don't you pin your
hair up with a clip?

④

وَنيس هَيُشْبُك النّهارْده، و عامْلين حفْلة في بيْت العروسة.

wanīs hayúšbuk innahárda, wi 3amlīn ḥáfla f bēt il3arūsa.

Wanees is getting engaged today. They're
throwing a party at his fiancée's house.

⑤

متِشْبُكْش نفْسك في الموْضوع ده.

ma-tišbúkšᵊ náfsak fi -lmawḍū3 da.

Don't involve yourself in that issue.

❖ [1s3] **to attach**

- This verb can be used metaphorically, translating 'get engaged' (➲ 150.4) or 'involve oneself' (➲ 150.5).
- This verb, like other verbs of the [1s3] and [1s6] patterns, can optionally take ـِ *i* instead of ـُ *u* in the personal prefixes of the imperfect (including the bi-imperfect and future) and imperative. For example, يُشْبُك *yúšbuk* can also be pronounced يِشْبُك *yíšbuk*. These vowels are interchangeable, and you can hear in the audio that the speaker uses both pronunciations.

151 to drink šírib شِرِب

	affirmative		negative		
ána	širíbt	شِرِبْت	ma-širíbtiš	مَشْرِبْتِش	perfect
íḥna	širíbna	شِرِبْنا	ma-širibnāš	مَشْرِبْناش	
ínta	širíbt	شِرِبْت	ma-širíbtiš	مَشْرِبْتِش	
ínti	širíbti	شِرِبْتي	ma-širibtīš	مَشْرِبْتيش	
íntu	širíbtu	شِرِبْتوا	ma-širibtūš	مَشْرِبْتوش	
húwwa	šírib	شِرِب	ma-šríbš	مَشْرِبْش	
híyya	šírbit	شِرْبِت	ma-širbítš	مَشِرْبِتْش	
húmma	šírbu	شِرْبوا	ma-širbūš	مَشِرْبوش	
ána	ášrab	أشْرَب	ma-šrábš	مَشْرَبْش	imperfect
íḥna	níšrab	نِشْرَب	ma-nišrábš	مَنِشْرَبْش	
ínta	tíšrab	تِشْرَب	ma-tišrábš	مَتِشْرَبْش	
ínti	tišrábi	تِشْرَبي	ma-tišrabīš	مَتِشْرَبيش	
íntu	tišrábu	تِشْرَبوا	ma-tišrabūš	مَتِشْرَبوش	
húwwa	yíšrab	يِشْرَب	ma-yišrábš	مَيِشْرَبْش	
híyya	tíšrab	تِشْرَب	ma-tišrábš	مَتِشْرَبْش	
húmma	yišrábu	يِشْرَبوا	ma-yišrabūš	مَيِشْرَبوش	
ána	bášrab	بَشْرَب	ma-bašrábš	مَبَشْرَبْش	bi-imperfect
íḥna	biníšrab	بِنِشْرَب	ma-bnišrábš	مَبْنِشْرَبْش	
ínta	bitíšrab	بِتِشْرَب	ma-btišrábš	مَبْتِشْرَبْش	
ínti	bitišrábi	بِتِشْرَبي	ma-btišrabīš	مَبْتِشْرَبيش	
íntu	bitišrábu	بِتِشْرَبوا	ma-btišrabūš	مَبْتِشْرَبوش	
húwwa	biyíšrab	بِيِشْرَب	ma-byišrábš	مَبْيِشْرَبْش	
híyya	bitíšrab	بِتِشْرَب	ma-btišrábš	مَبْتِشْرَبْش	
húmma	biyišrábu	بِيِشْرَبوا	ma-byišrabūš	مَبْيِشْرَبوش	
ána	hášrab	هَشْرَب	miš hášrab	مِش هَشْرَب	future
íḥna	haníšrab	هَنِشْرَب	miš haníšrab	مِش هَنِشْرَب	
ínta	hatíšrab	هَتِشْرَب	miš hatíšrab	مِش هَتِشْرَب	
ínti	hatišrábi	هَتِشْرَبي	miš hatišrábi	مِش هَتِشْرَبي	
íntu	hatišrábu	هَتِشْرَبوا	miš hatišrábu	مِش هَتِشْرَبوا	
húwwa	hayíšrab	هَيِشْرَب	miš hayíšrab	مِش هَيِشْرَب	
híyya	hatíšrab	هَتِشْرَب	miš hatíšrab	مِش هَتِشْرَب	
húmma	hayišrábu	هَيِشْرَبوا	miš hayišrábu	مِش هَيِشْرَبوا	
ínta	íšrab	اِشْرَب	ma-tišrábš	مَتِشْرَبْش	imperative
ínti	išrábi	اِشْرَبي	ma-tišrabīš	مَتِشْرَبيش	
íntu	išrábu	اِشْرَبوا	ma-tišrabūš	مَتِشْرَبوش	

	active		passive		
masculine	šārib	شارِب	mašrūb	مشْروب	participles
feminine	šárba	شارْبَة	mašrūba	مشْروبَة	
plural	šarbīn	شارْبين	mašrubīn	مشْروبين	

verbal noun: *šurb* شُرْب

①

سُعاد شِرْبِت الشّورْبة بسّ و مكلتْش.

su3ād šírbit iššúrba bassᵊ w ma-kalítš.

Soad only had the soup but didn't eat [anything else].

②

بحِبّ أشْرب عصير القصب بِجُنون.

baḥíbb ášrab 3aṣīr ilʔáṣab bi-gunūn.

I'm crazy about drinking sugarcane juice.

③

بابا بْيِشْرب سجايِر، بسّ أنا بدْعيلُه يْبطّل.

bāba byíšrab sagāyir, bass ána bad3īlu ybáṭṭal.

My dad smokes, but I pray for him to stop.

④

هتِشْرب معانا وَلّا مِش ناوي؟

hatíšrab ma3āna wálla miš nāwi?

Will you drink with us, or do you not want to?

⑤

إشْرب ٨ كُبّايات ميّة يومِيّاً.

íšrab táman kubbiyyāt máyya yumíyyan.

Drink eight glasses of water a day.

⑥

متِشْرِبْش الميّة ساقْعة أوي.

ma-tišrábš ilmáyya sáʔ3a ʔáwi.

Don't drink very cold water.

❖ [1s4] **to drink; to smoke**

- While in English we 'eat' soup, in Arabic one 'drinks' soup. (➲ 151.1)
- In Arabic, you can 'drink' a cigarette, shisha, etc. (➲ 151.3)
- This verb does not *imply* drinking alcohol, as the English verb 'drink' can. (➲ 151.4)

➲ 31.3, 71.4, 118.6, 127.4, 211.4, 215.6

152 to thank šákar شَكَر

verbal noun: šukr شُكْر

		affirmative		negative	
perfect	ána	šakárt	شَكَرْت	ma-šakártiš	مَشَكَرْتِش
	íḥna	šakárna	شَكَرْنا	ma-šakarnāš	مَشَكَرْناش
	ínta	šakárt	شَكَرْت	ma-šakártiš	مَشَكَرْتِش
	ínti	šakárti	شَكَرْتي	ma-šakartīš	مَشَكَرْتيش
	íntu	šakártu	شَكَرْتوا	ma-šakartūš	مَشَكَرْتوش
	húwwa	šákar	شَكَر	ma-šakárš	مَشَكَرْش
	híyya	šákarit	شَكَرِت	ma-šakarítš	مَشَكَرِتْش
	húmma	šákaru	شَكَرُوا	ma-šakarūš	مَشَكَرُوش
imperfect	ána	áškur	أشْكُر	ma-škúrš	مَشْكُرْش
	íḥna	núškur	نُشْكُر	ma-nuškúrš	مَنُشْكُرْش
	ínta	túškur	تُشْكُر	ma-tuškúrš	مَتُشْكُرْش
	ínti	tuškúri	تُشْكُري	ma-tuškurīš	مَتُشْكُريش
	íntu	tuškúru	تُشْكُروا	ma-tuškurūš	مَتُشْكُروش
	húwwa	yúškur	يُشْكُر	ma-yuškúrš	مَيُشْكُرْش
	híyya	túškur	تُشْكُر	ma-tuškúrš	مَتُشْكُرْش
	húmma	yuškúru	يُشْكُروا	ma-yuškurūš	مَيُشْكُروش
bi-imperfect	ána	báškur	بَشْكُر	ma-baškúrš	مَبَشْكُرْش
	íḥna	binúškur	بِنُشْكُر	ma-bnuškúrš	مَبْنُشْكُرْش
	ínta	bitúškur	بِتُشْكُر	ma-btuškúrš	مَبْتُشْكُرْش
	ínti	bituškúri	بِتُشْكُري	ma-btuškurīš	مَبْتُشْكُريش
	íntu	bituškúru	بِتُشْكُروا	ma-btuškurūš	مَبْتُشْكُروش
	húwwa	biyúškur	بِيُشْكُر	ma-byuškúrš	مَبْيُشْكُرْش
	híyya	bitúškur	بِتُشْكُر	ma-btuškúrš	مَبْتُشْكُرْش
	húmma	biyuškúru	بِيُشْكُروا	ma-byuškurūš	مَبْيُشْكُروش
future	ána	háškur	هَشْكُر	miš háškur	مِش هَشْكُر
	íḥna	hanúškur	هَنُشْكُر	miš hanúškur	مِش هَنُشْكُر
	ínta	hatúškur	هَتُشْكُر	miš hatúškur	مِش هَتُشْكُر
	ínti	hatuškúri	هَتُشْكُري	miš hatuškúri	مِش هَتُشْكُري
	íntu	hatuškúru	هَتُشْكُروا	miš hatuškúru	مِش هَتُشْكُروا
	húwwa	hayúškur	هَيُشْكُر	miš hayúškur	مِش هَيُشْكُر
	híyya	hatúškur	هَتُشْكُر	miš hatúškur	مِش هَتُشْكُر
	húmma	hayuškúru	هَيُشْكُروا	miš hayuškúru	مِش هَيُشْكُروا
imperative	ínta	íškur	اِشْكُر	ma-tuškúrš	مَتُشْكُرْش
	ínti	iškúri	اِشْكُري	ma-tuškurīš	مَتُشْكُريش
	íntu	iškúru	اِشْكُروا	ma-tuškurūš	مَتُشْكُروش

		active		passive	
participles	masculine	šākir	شاكِر	maškūr	مَشْكور
	feminine	šákra	شاكْرَة	maškūra	مَشْكورَة
	plural	šakrīn	شاكْرين	maškurīn	مَشْكورين

①

جيهان شكرِتْني جامِد لمّا وَصّلْتها.

žihān šakarítni gāmid lámma waṣṣaltáha.

Jehan thanked me wholeheartedly
for giving her a ride.

②

سامي مِش مِتْعوِّد يِشْكُر أيّ حدّ على أيّ حاجة.

sāmi miš mit3áwwid yíškur ayyᵊ ɧaddᵊ 3ála ʔayyᵊ ɧāga.

Sami isn't in the habit of thanking
anyone for anything.

③

أنا بشْكُرك على كُلّ لحْظة حِلْوَة في حَياتي.

ána baškúrak 3ála kullᵊ láɧza ɧílwa f ɧayāti.

I thank you for every beautiful
moment in my life.

④

لمّا يِخلّص الكورْس هنِشْكُر الدُّكْتور و نْجيبْله هدية.

lámma yxállaṣ ilkúrs, haníškur idduktūr wi ngíblu hadíyya.

When the course has ended, we'll thank
the professor and bring him a gift.

⑤

اِشْكُروا النّاس على الصّحّ زيّ ما بِتْعلّقوا عَ الغلط.

iškúru -nnās 3ála -ṣṣaɧɧᵊ zayyᵊ ma bit3allá?u 3a -lɣálaṭ.

Thank people for what's right, just as
you comment on the mistakes.

⑥

متِشْكُرْنيش . ده واجْبي.

ma-tiškurnīš. da wágbi.

Don't thank me.
It's my duty.

❖ [1s3] **to thank** (someone **for** على *3ála*)

- This verb, like other verbs of the [1s3] and [1s6] patterns, can optionally take ـُ *u* instead of ـِ *i* in the personal prefixes of the imperfect (including the bi-imperfect and future) and imperative. For example, يُشْكُر *yúškur* can also be pronounced يِشْكُر *yíškur.* These vowels are interchangeable, but the tables reflect the preferences of the speakers on the MP3s.

153 to gasp šáhaʔ شَهَق

	affirmative		negative		
ána	šaháʔt	شَهَقْت	ma-šaháʔtiš	مَشَهَقْتِش	perfect
íḫna	šaháʔna	شَهَقْنا	ma-šahaʔnāš	مَشَهَقْناش	
ínta	šaháʔt	شَهَقْت	ma-šaháʔtiš	مَشَهَقْتِش	
ínti	šaháʔti	شَهَقْتي	ma-šahaʔtīš	مَشَهَقْتيش	
íntu	šaháʔtu	شَهَقْتوا	ma-šahaʔtūš	مَشَهَقْتوش	
húwwa	šáhaʔ	شَهَق	ma-šaháʔš	مَشَهَقْش	
híyya	šáhaʔit	شَهَقِت	ma-šahaʔítš	مَشَهَقِتْش	
húmma	šáhaʔu	شَهَقوا	ma-šahaʔūš	مَشَهَقوش	
ána	ášhaʔ	أشْهَق	ma-šháʔš	مَشْهَقْش	imperfect
íḫna	níšhaʔ	نِشْهَق	ma-nišháʔš	مَنِشْهَقْش	
ínta	tíšhaʔ	تِشْهَق	ma-tišháʔš	مَتِشْهَقْش	
ínti	tišháʔi	تِشْهَقي	ma-tišhaʔīš	مَتِشْهَقيش	
íntu	tišháʔu	تِشْهَقوا	ma-tišhaʔūš	مَتِشْهَقوش	
húwwa	yíšhaʔ	يِشْهَق	ma-yišháʔš	مَيِشْهَقْش	
híyya	tíšhaʔ	تِشْهَق	ma-tišháʔš	مَتِشْهَقْش	
húmma	yišháʔu	يِشْهَقوا	ma-yišhaʔūš	مَيِشْهَقوش	
ána	bášhaʔ	بَشْهَق	ma-bašháʔš	مَبَشْهَقْش	bi-imperfect
íḫna	biníšhaʔ	بِنِشْهَق	ma-bnišháʔš	مَبْنِشْهَقْش	
ínta	bitíšhaʔ	بِتِشْهَق	ma-btišháʔš	مَبْتِشْهَقْش	
ínti	bitišháʔi	بِتِشْهَقي	ma-btišhaʔīš	مَبْتِشْهَقيش	
íntu	bitišháʔu	بِتِشْهَقوا	ma-btišhaʔūš	مَبْتِشْهَقوش	
húwwa	biyíšhaʔ	بِيِشْهَق	ma-byišháʔš	مَبْيِشْهَقْش	
híyya	bitíšhaʔ	بِتِشْهَق	ma-btišháʔš	مَبْتِشْهَقْش	
húmma	biyišháʔu	بِيِشْهَقوا	ma-byišhaʔūš	مَبْيِشْهَقوش	
ána	hášhaʔ	هَشْهَق	miš hášhaʔ	مِش هَشْهَق	future
íḫna	haníšhaʔ	هَنِشْهَق	miš haníšhaʔ	مِش هَنِشْهَق	
ínta	hatíšhaʔ	هَتِشْهَق	miš hatíšhaʔ	مِش هَتِشْهَق	
ínti	hatišháʔi	هَتِشْهَقي	miš hatišháʔi	مِش هَتِشْهَقي	
íntu	hatišháʔu	هَتِشْهَقوا	miš hatišháʔu	مِش هَتِشْهَقوا	
húwwa	hayíšhaʔ	هَيِشْهَق	miš hayíšhaʔ	مِش هَيِشْهَق	
híyya	hatíšhaʔ	هَتِشْهَق	miš hatíšhaʔ	مِش هَتِشْهَق	
húmma	hayišháʔu	هَيِشْهَقوا	miš hayišháʔu	مِش هَيِشْهَقوا	
ínta	íšhaʔ	اِشْهَق	ma-tišháʔš	مَتِشْهَقْش	imperative
ínti	išháʔi	اِشْهَقي	ma-tišhaʔīš	مَتِشْهَقيش	
íntu	išháʔu	اِشْهَقوا	ma-tišhaʔūš	مَتِشْهَقوش	

	active		passive		
masculine	—	—	—	—	participles
feminine	—	—	—	—	
plural	—	—	—	—	

verbal noun: šāhʔ شَهْق

①

السِّتّ لمّا شافِت إبْنها بْيُقع، شهقِت و صَوّتِت.

issítt^ə^ lámma šāfit ibnáha byúʔa3, šáhaʔit wi ṣawwátit.

When the woman saw her son fall,
she gasped and screamed.

②

جِدِّتي كانِت تِقوليّ: لازِم تِشْهقي قُدّام المُلوخية.

giddíti kānit tiʔúlli: lāzim tišháʔi ʔuddām ilmuluxíyya.

My grandma used to say, "You should gasp in
front of mulukhiyah [Jew's mallow]."

③

صوّرْناكي و إنْتي بِتِشْهقي مِ المُفاجْأة.

ṣawwarnāki w ínti bitišháʔi mi -lmufágʔa.

We took your photo right as
you gasped in surprise.

④

أُمّي لَوْ شافِتْني بعْمِل كِده، هتِشْهق و مِش بِعيد تُلْطُم.

úmmi law šafítni bá3mil kída, hatíšhaʔ wi miš bi3īd túlṭum.

If my mom sees me doing this,
she'll gasp or even slap me.

⑤

متِشْهقيش كِده، خضّيتيني!

ma-tišhaʔīš kída, xaḍḍitīni!

Don't gasp like that!
You startled me.

❖ [1s1] **to gasp** (in surprise or admiration)

- The active and passive participles are not used in practice.

154 to pour ṣabb صبّ

	affirmative		negative		
ána	ṣabbēt	صَبّيْت	ma-ṣabbítš	مَصَبّيْتْش	perfect
íḫna	ṣabbēna	صَبّيْنا	ma-ṣabbināš	مَصَبّيْناش	
ínta	ṣabbēt	صَبّيْت	ma-ṣabbítš	مَصَبّيْتْش	
ínti	ṣabbēti	صَبّيْتي	ma-ṣabbitīš	مَصَبّيْتيش	
íntu	ṣabbētu	صَبّيْتوا	ma-ṣabbitūš	مَصَبّيْتوش	
húwwa	ṣabb	صَبّ	ma-ṣábbiš	مَصَبِّش	
híyya	ṣábbit	صَبِّت	ma-ṣabbítš	مَصَبِّتْش	
húmma	ṣábbu	صَبّوا	ma-ṣabbūš	مَصَبّوش	
ána	aṣúbb	أَصُبّ	ma-ṣúbbiš	مَصُبِّش	imperfect
íḫna	niṣúbb	نِصُبّ	ma-nṣúbbiš	مَنْصُبِّش	
ínta	tiṣúbb	تِصُبّ	ma-tṣúbbiš	مَتْصُبِّش	
ínti	tiṣúbbi	تِصُبّي	ma-tṣubbīš	مَتْصُبّيش	
íntu	tiṣúbbu	تِصُبّوا	ma-tṣubbūš	مَتْصُبّوش	
húwwa	yiṣúbb	يِصُبّ	ma-yṣúbbiš	مَيْصُبِّش	
híyya	tiṣúbb	تِصُبّ	ma-tṣúbbiš	مَتْصُبِّش	
húmma	yiṣúbbu	يِصُبّوا	ma-yṣubbūš	مَيْصُبّوش	
ána	baṣúbb	بَصُبّ	ma-baṣúbbiš	مَبَصُبِّش	bi-imperfect
íḫna	binṣúbb	بِنْصُبّ	ma-binṣúbbiš	مَبِنْصُبِّش	
ínta	bitṣúbb	بِتْصُبّ	ma-bitṣúbbiš	مَبِتْصُبِّش	
ínti	bitṣúbbi	بِتْصُبّي	ma-bitṣubbīš	مَبِتْصُبّيش	
íntu	bitṣúbbu	بِتْصُبّوا	ma-bitṣubbūš	مَبِتْصُبّوش	
húwwa	biyṣúbb	بِيْصُبّ	ma-biyṣúbbiš	مَبِيْصُبِّش	
híyya	bitṣúbb	بِتْصُبّ	ma-bitṣúbbiš	مَبِتْصُبِّش	
húmma	biyṣúbbu	بِيْصُبّوا	ma-biyṣubbūš	مَبِيْصُبّوش	
ána	haṣúbb	هَصُبّ	miš haṣúbb	مِش هَصُبّ	future
íḫna	hanṣúbb	هَنْصُبّ	miš hanṣúbb	مِش هَنْصُبّ	
ínta	hatṣúbb	هَتْصُبّ	miš hatṣúbb	مِش هَتْصُبّ	
ínti	hatṣúbbi	هَتْصُبّي	miš hatṣúbbi	مِش هَتْصُبّي	
íntu	hatṣúbbu	هَتْصُبّوا	miš hatṣúbbu	مِش هَتْصُبّوا	
húwwa	hayṣúbb	هَيْصُبّ	miš hayṣúbb	مِش هَيْصُبّ	
híyya	hatṣúbb	هَتْصُبّ	miš hatṣúbb	مِش هَتْصُبّ	
húmma	hayṣúbbu	هَيْصُبّوا	miš hayṣúbbu	مِش هَيْصُبّوا	
ínta	ṣubb	صُبّ	ma-tṣúbbiš	مَتْصُبِّش	imperative
ínti	ṣúbbi	صُبّي	ma-tṣubbīš	مَتْصُبّيش	
íntu	ṣúbbu	صُبّوا	ma-tṣubbūš	مَتْصُبّوش	

	active		passive		
masculine	ṣābib	صابِب	maṣbūb	مَصْبوب	participles
feminine	ṣábba	صابّة	maṣbūba	مَصْبوبة	
plural	ṣabbīn	صابّين	maṣbubīn	مَصْبوبين	

verbal noun: ṣabb صَبّ

①

أنا مصبّيتْش العصير لِسّه.

ána ma-ṣabbítš il3aṣīr líssa.

I haven't poured the juice yet.

②

اِغْسِلي فناجيل عشان نِصُبّ فيهُم القهْوَة.

iɣsíli fanagīl 3ašān niṣúbbᵊ fīhum il?áhwa.

Wash some cups to pour the coffee in.

③

عَ القهْوَة بِيْصُبّوا الشّاي في كُبّايَة إسْمها خمْسينة.

3a -l?áhwa biyṣúbbu -ššāy fi kubbāya ?ismáha xamsīna.

In a traditional coffee shop, they pour tea in a glass called a khaseena [lit. a fifty].

④

هصُبّ حاجة ساقْعة. مين عايِز؟

haṣúbbᵊ ḫāga sá?3a. mīn 3āyiz?

I'm pouring some cold drinks. Who wants one?

⑤

متْصُبّيليش . أنا لِسّه شارِب.

ma-tṣubbilīš. ána líssa šārib.

Don't pour any for me. I just had something to drink.

❖ [1g2] **to pour**

- This verb is synonymous with كبّ *kabb* (➲ 215) and دلق *dála?* (➲ 110).

➲ 110.3

155 to wake up ṣíḫi صحي

		affirmative		negative	
perfect	ána	ṣiḫīt	صِحيت	ma-ṣḫítš	مَصْحيتْش
	íḫna	ṣiḫīna	صِحينا	ma-ṣḫināš	مَصْحيناش
	ínta	ṣiḫīt	صِحيت	ma-ṣḫítš	مَصْحيتْش
	ínti	ṣiḫīti	صِحيتي	ma-ṣḫitīš	مَصْحيتيش
	íntu	ṣiḫītu	صِحيتوا	ma-ṣḫitūš	مَصْحيتوش
	húwwa	ṣíḫi	صِحي	ma-ṣḫīš	مَصْحيش
	híyya	ṣíḫyit	صِحْيِت	ma-ṣiḫyítš	مَصِحْيِتْش
	húmma	ṣíḫyu	صِحْيوا	ma-ṣiḫyūš	مَصِحْيوش
imperfect	ána	áṣḫa	أَصْحَى	ma-ṣḫāš	مَصْحاش
	íḫna	níṣḫa	نِصْحَى	ma-niṣḫāš	مَنِصْحاش
	ínta	tíṣḫa	تِصْحَى	ma-tiṣḫāš	مَتِصْحاش
	ínti	tíṣḫi	تِصْحي	ma-tiṣḫīš	مَتِصْحيش
	íntu	tíṣḫu	تِصْحوا	ma-tiṣḫūš	مَتِصْحوش
	húwwa	yíṣḫa	يِصْحَى	ma-yiṣḫāš	مَيِصْحاش
	híyya	tíṣḫa	تِصْحَى	ma-tiṣḫāš	مَتِصْحاش
	húmma	yíṣḫu	يِصْحوا	ma-yiṣḫūš	مَيِصْحوش
bi-imperfect	ána	báṣḫa	بَصْحَى	ma-baṣḫāš	مَبَصْحاش
	íḫna	biníṣḫa	بِنِصْحَى	ma-bniṣḫāš	مَبْنِصْحاش
	ínta	bitíṣḫa	بِتِصْحَى	ma-btiṣḫāš	مَبْتِصْحاش
	ínti	bitíṣḫi	بِتِصْحي	ma-btiṣḫīš	مَبْتِصْحيش
	íntu	bitíṣḫu	بِتِصْحوا	ma-btiṣḫūš	مَبْتِصْحوش
	húwwa	biyíṣḫa	بِيِصْحَى	ma-byiṣḫāš	مَبْيِصْحاش
	híyya	bitíṣḫa	بِتِصْحَى	ma-btiṣḫāš	مَبْتِصْحاش
	húmma	biyíṣḫu	بِيِصْحوا	ma-byiṣḫūš	مَبْيِصْحوش
future	ána	háṣḫa	هَصْحَى	miš háṣḫa	مِش هَصْحَى
	íḫna	haníṣḫa	هَنِصْحَى	miš haníṣḫa	مِش هَنِصْحَى
	ínta	hatíṣḫa	هَتِصْحَى	miš hatíṣḫa	مِش هَتِصْحَى
	ínti	hatíṣḫi	هَتِصْحي	miš hatíṣḫi	مِش هَتِصْحي
	íntu	hatíṣḫu	هَتِصْحوا	miš hatíṣḫu	مِش هَتِصْحوا
	húwwa	hayíṣḫa	هَيِصْحَى	miš hayíṣḫa	مِش هَيِصْحَى
	híyya	hatíṣḫa	هَتِصْحَى	miš hatíṣḫa	مِش هَتِصْحَى
	húmma	hayíṣḫu	هَيِصْحوا	miš hayíṣḫu	مِش هَيِصْحوا
imperative	ínta	íṣḫa	اِصْحَى	ma-tiṣḫāš	مَتِصْحاش
	ínti	íṣḫi	اِصْحي	ma-tiṣḫīš	مَتِصْحيش
	íntu	íṣḫu	اِصْحوا	ma-tiṣḫūš	مَتِصْحوش

		active		passive	
participles	masculine	ṣāḫi	صاحي	–	–
	feminine	ṣáḫya	صاحْيَة	–	–
	plural	ṣaḫyīn	صاحْيين	–	–

verbal noun: ṣaḫayān صحَيان

①

المِنبّهْ مضربْش و صْحيت مِتْأخّرة.

ilminábbih ma-ḍarábšᵊ wi ṣḫīt mitʔaxxára.

My alarm didn't go off, so I woke up late.

②

الوَلد كُلّ شْوَيّة يِصْحى يْعيّط و يْصحّي كُلّ اللي في البيْت.

ilwálad kullᵊ šwáyya yíṣḫa y3áyyaṭ wi yṣáḫḫi kull ílli fi -lbēt.

The boy wakes up crying every so often and wakes up the whole house with him.

③

ماما مِتْعوِّدة بْتِصْحى بدْري حتّى يوْم الأجازة.

māma mit3awwida btíṣḫa bádri ḫátta yōm ilʔagāza.

My mom is used to waking up early, even on the weekend.

④

هنِصْحي السّاعة ٥ و نْكون في محطِّةْ القطر السّاعة ٦:٣٠ بِالظّبْط.

haníṣḫa -ssā3a xámsa wi nkūn fi maḫáṭṭit ilʔáṭar issā3a sitte w nuṣṣ bi-ẓẓábṭ.

We'll wake up at 5:00 and be at the train station at 6:30 sharp.

⑤

اِصْحي بدْري و كمِّل مُذاكْرة أحْسن مِن السّهر.

íṣḫa bádri wi kámmil muzákra ʔáḫsan min issáhar.

Wake up early and continue studying rather than staying up late at night.

⑥

لَوْ مصْحيتْلوش هَيِضْحك عليْك.

law ma-ṣḫitlūš hayídḫak 3alēk.

If you're not on your guard with him, he may deceive you.

❖ [1d4] **to wake up**

- This verb is intransitive. Compare with صحّى *ṣáḫḫa*. (➲ 156)

➲ 20.1, 54.1, 74.1, 103.2, 106.4, 203.1, 204.3

156 to rouse ṣáḫḫa صَحّى 1 13

	affirmative		negative		
ána	ṣaḫḫēt	صَحّيْت	ma-ṣaḫḫítš	مَصَحّيْتْش	perfect
íḫna	ṣaḫḫēna	صَحّيْنا	ma-ṣaḫḫināš	مَصَحّيناش	
ínta	ṣaḫḫēt	صَحّيْت	ma-ṣaḫḫítš	مَصَحّيْتْش	
ínti	ṣaḫḫēti	صَحّيْتي	ma-ṣaḫḫitīš	مَصَحّيتيش	
íntu	ṣaḫḫētu	صَحّيْتوا	ma-ṣaḫḫitūš	مَصَحّيتوش	
húwwa	ṣáḫḫa	صَحّى	ma-ṣaḫḫāš	مَصَحّاش	
híyya	ṣáḫḫit	صَحّت	ma-ṣaḫḫítš	مَصَحّتْش	
húmma	ṣáḫḫu	صَحّوا	ma-ṣaḫḫūš	مَصَحّوش	

ána	aṣáḫḫi	أصَحّي	ma-ṣaḫḫīš	مَصَحّيش	imperfect
íḫna	niṣáḫḫi	نِصَحّي	ma-nṣaḫḫīš	مَنْصَحّيش	
ínta	tiṣáḫḫi	تِصَحّي	ma-tṣaḫḫīš	مَتْصَحّيش	
ínti	tiṣáḫḫi	تِصَحّي	ma-tṣaḫḫīš	مَتْصَحّيش	
íntu	tiṣáḫḫu	تِصَحّوا	ma-tṣaḫḫūš	مَتْصَحّوش	
húwwa	yiṣáḫḫi	يِصَحّي	ma-yṣaḫḫīš	مَيْصَحّيش	
híyya	tiṣáḫḫi	تِصَحّي	ma-tṣaḫḫīš	مَتْصَحّيش	
húmma	yiṣáḫḫu	يِصَحّوا	ma-yṣaḫḫūš	مَيْصَحّوش	

ána	baṣáḫḫi	بَصَحّي	ma-baṣaḫḫīš	مَبَصَحّيش	bi-imperfect
íḫna	binṣáḫḫi	بِنْصَحّي	ma-binṣaḫḫīš	مَبِنْصَحّيش	
ínta	bitṣáḫḫi	بِتْصَحّي	ma-bitṣaḫḫīš	مَبِتْصَحّيش	
ínti	bitṣáḫḫi	بِتْصَحّي	ma-bitṣaḫḫīš	مَبِتْصَحّيش	
íntu	bitṣáḫḫu	بِتْصَحّوا	ma-bitṣaḫḫūš	مَبِتْصَحّوش	
húwwa	biyṣáḫḫi	بِيْصَحّي	ma-biyṣaḫḫīš	مَبِيْصَحّيش	
híyya	bitṣáḫḫi	بِتْصَحّي	ma-bitṣaḫḫīš	مَبِتْصَحّيش	
húmma	biyṣáḫḫu	بِيْصَحّوا	ma-biyṣaḫḫūš	مَبِيْصَحّوش	

ána	haṣáḫḫi	هَصَحّي	miš haṣáḫḫi	مِش هَصَحّي	future
íḫna	hanṣáḫḫi	هَنْصَحّي	miš hanṣáḫḫi	مِش هَنْصَحّي	
ínta	hatṣáḫḫi	هَتْصَحّي	miš hatṣáḫḫi	مِش هَتْصَحّي	
ínti	hatṣáḫḫi	هَتْصَحّي	miš hatṣáḫḫi	مِش هَتْصَحّي	
íntu	hatṣáḫḫu	هَتْصَحّوا	miš hatṣáḫḫu	مِش هَتْصَحّوا	
húwwa	hayṣáḫḫi	هَيْصَحّي	miš hayṣáḫḫi	مِش هَيْصَحّي	
híyya	hatṣáḫḫi	هَتْصَحّي	miš hatṣáḫḫi	مِش هَتْصَحّي	
húmma	hayṣáḫḫu	هَيْصَحّوا	miš hayṣáḫḫu	مِش هَيْصَحّوا	

ínta	ṣáḫḫi	صَحّي	ma-tṣaḫḫīš	مَتْصَحّيش	imperative
ínti	ṣáḫḫi	صَحّي	ma-tṣaḫḫīš	مَتْصَحّيش	
íntu	ṣáḫḫu	صَحّوا	ma-tṣaḫḫūš	مَتْصَحّوش	

	active		passive		
masculine	miṣáḫḫi	مِصَحّي	mitṣáḫḫi	مِتْصَحّي	participles
feminine	miṣaḫḫíyya	مِصَحّيّة	mitṣaḫḫíyya	مِتْصَحّيّة	
plural	miṣaḫḫiyīn	مِصَحّيين	mitṣaḫḫiyīn	مِتْصَحّيين	

verbal noun: taṣḫíyya تَصْحِيّة

①

حاوِلْت أصّحيك بسّ إنْتَ كُنْت في سابِع نوْمة.

ḫawílt aṣṣaḫīk bass ínta kuntᵊ f sābi3 nōma.

I tried to wake you up, but
you were in a deep sleep.

②

صحّيْت جوْزي و رُحْت أعْمِل الفِطار، رِجِعْت لقيْتُه نام تاني.

ṣaḫḫēt gōzi wi ruḫt á3mil ilfiṭār, rigí3tᵊ laʔētu nām tāni.

I woke my husband up and went to make breakfast
but came back to find him asleep again.

③

ماما كُلّ يوْم بِتْصحّينا حتّى و إحْنا كُبار.

māma kullᵊ yōm bitṣaḫḫīna ḫátta w íḫna kubār.

My mom wakes us up every day,
even though we're adults.

④

هنْصحّي العِيال دي إزّاي؟ دوْل في غَيْبوبة!

hanṣáḫḫi -l3iyāl di -zzāy? dōl fi ɣaybūba!

How shall we wake these kids
up? They're in a coma!

⑤

صحّيني كمان عشر دقايِق. وَرايا حاجات كِتير.

ṣaḫḫīni kamān 3ášar daʔāyiʔ. warāya ḫagāt kitīr.

Wake me up in ten minutes.
I have lots of things to do.

⑥

متْصحّونيش الصُّبْح. أنا أجازة بُكْره و عايِز أنام بِـراحْتي.

ma-tṣaḫḫunīš iṣṣúbḫ. ána ʔagāza búkra wi 3āyiz anām bi-ráḫti.

Don't wake me up in the morning. I'm off
tomorrow, and I want to sleep in.

❖ [2d] **to wake** (someone) **up**

- This verb is transitive. Compare with صِحي *ṣíḫi*. (➲ 155)

➲ 56.2, 98.2

157 to believe sáddaʔ صدّق [13]

	affirmative		negative		
ána	saddáʔt	صَدّقْت	ma-saddáʔtiš	مَصَدّقْتِش	perfect
íḥna	saddáʔna	صَدّقْنا	ma-saddaʔnāš	مَصَدّقْناش	
ínta	saddáʔt	صَدّقْت	ma-saddáʔtiš	مَصَدّقْتِش	
ínti	saddáʔti	صَدّقْتي	ma-saddaʔtīš	مَصَدّقْتيش	
íntu	saddáʔtu	صَدّقْتوا	ma-saddaʔtūš	مَصَدّقْتوش	
húwwa	sáddaʔ	صَدّق	ma-saddáʔš	مَصَدّقْش	
híyya	saddáʔit	صَدّقِت	ma-saddaʔítš	مَصَدّقِتْش	
húmma	saddáʔu	صَدّقوا	ma-saddaʔūš	مَصَدّقوش	
ána	asáddaʔ	أصَدّق	ma-saddáʔš	مَصَدّقْش	imperfect
íḥna	nisáddaʔ	نِصَدّق	ma-nsaddáʔš	مَنْصَدّقْش	
ínta	tisáddaʔ	تِصَدّق	ma-tsaddáʔš	مَتْصَدّقْش	
ínti	tisaddáʔi	تِصَدّقي	ma-tsaddaʔīš	مَتْصَدّقيش	
íntu	tisaddáʔu	تِصَدّقوا	ma-tsaddaʔūš	مَتْصَدّقوش	
húwwa	yisáddaʔ	يِصَدّق	ma-ysaddáʔš	مَيْصَدّقْش	
híyya	tisáddaʔ	تِصَدّق	ma-tsaddáʔš	مَتْصَدّقْش	
húmma	yisaddáʔu	يِصَدّقوا	ma-ysaddaʔūš	مَيْصَدّقوش	
ána	basáddaʔ	بَصَدّق	ma-basaddáʔš	مَبَصَدّقْش	bi-imperfect
íḥna	binsáddaʔ	بِنْصَدّق	ma-binsaddáʔš	مَبِنْصَدّقْش	
ínta	bitsáddaʔ	بِتْصَدّق	ma-bitsaddáʔš	مَبِتْصَدّقْش	
ínti	bitsaddáʔi	بِتْصَدّقي	ma-bitsaddaʔīš	مَبِتْصَدّقيش	
íntu	bitsaddáʔu	بِتْصَدّقوا	ma-bitsaddaʔūš	مَبِتْصَدّقوش	
húwwa	biysáddaʔ	بِيْصَدّق	ma-biysaddáʔš	مَبِيْصَدّقْش	
híyya	bitsáddaʔ	بِتْصَدّق	ma-bitsaddáʔš	مَبِتْصَدّقْش	
húmma	biysaddáʔu	بِيْصَدّقوا	ma-biysaddaʔūš	مَبِيْصَدّقوش	
ána	hasáddaʔ	هَصَدّق	miš hasáddaʔ	مِش هَصَدّق	future
íḥna	hansáddaʔ	هَنْصَدّق	miš hansáddaʔ	مِش هَنْصَدّق	
ínta	hatsáddaʔ	هَتْصَدّق	miš hatsáddaʔ	مِش هَتْصَدّق	
ínti	hatsaddáʔi	هَتْصَدّقي	miš hatsaddáʔi	مِش هَتْصَدّقي	
íntu	hatsaddáʔu	هَتْصَدّقوا	miš hatsaddáʔu	مِش هَتْصَدّقوا	
húwwa	haysáddaʔ	هَيْصَدّق	miš haysáddaʔ	مِش هَيْصَدّق	
híyya	hatsáddaʔ	هَتْصَدّق	miš hatsáddaʔ	مِش هَتْصَدّق	
húmma	haysaddáʔu	هَيْصَدّقوا	miš haysaddáʔu	مِش هَيْصَدّقوا	
ínta	sáddaʔ	صَدّق	ma-tsaddáʔš	مَتْصَدّقْش	imperative
ínti	saddáʔi	صَدّقي	ma-tsaddaʔīš	مَتْصَدّقيش	
íntu	saddáʔu	صَدّقوا	ma-tsaddaʔūš	مَتْصَدّقوش	

	active		passive		
masculine	misáddaʔ	مِصَدّق	mitsáddaʔ	مِتْصَدّق	participles
feminine	misaddáʔa	مِصَدّقة	mitsaddáʔa	مِتْصَدّقة	
plural	misaddaʔīn	مِصَدّقين	mitsaddaʔīn	مِتْصَدّقين	

verbal noun: *tasdīʔ* تَصْديق

①

أنا صدّقْتك و إنْتَ ضْحِكْت عليّا.

ána saddáʔtak w ínta dɦíktᵊ 3aláyya.

I believed you, but you lied to me.

②

اِوْعي تْصدّق الخبر ده. دي كِدْبِةْ إبْريل.

íw3i tsáddaʔ ilxábar da. di kídbit ibrīl.

Don't believe that. It's an
April Fool's day prank.

③

تُقى بِتْصدّق النّاس بِسْهولة.

túʔa bitsáddaʔ innās bi-shūla.

Toka believes people easily.

④

رغْم كُلّ الغلطات، النّاس هَيْصدّقوا إنّ ده لْمصْلحِتْهُم.

raɣmᵊ kull ilɣalaṭāt, innās haysaddáʔu ʔinnᵊ da l-maṣlaɦíthum.

Despite all the failures, people will believe
that it's for their own good.

⑤

صدّقيني لمّا أقولّك إنّك الحُبّ الوَحيد في حَياتي.

saddaʔīni, lámma ʔaʔúllik ínnik ilɦúbb ilwaɦīd fi ɦayāti.

Believe me when I tell you that
you're the only love in my life.

⑥

حورية مبِتْصدّقْش الرِّجالة خلاص بعْد اللي شافِتُه مِن طليقْها.

ɦuríyya ma-bitsaddáʔš irrigāla xalāṣ ba3d ílli šafítu min ṭalíʔha.

Horeya doesn't believe men anymore after
what she saw from her ex-husband.

❖ [2s2] **to believe, consider true**

- Notice that this verb is pronounced with a *s* sound (rather than the *ṣ* of Modern Standard Arabic). Nonetheless, most Egyptians write it using the conventional spelling with ص.

➲ 25.4

158 to repair ṣállaḥ صلّح

verbal nouns: taṣlīḥ تَصْليح - iṣlāḥ إِصْلاح

	affirmative		negative		
ána	ṣalláḥt	صَلَّحْت	ma-ṣalláḥtiš	مَصَلَّحْتِش	perfect
íḥna	ṣalláḥna	صَلَّحْنا	ma-ṣallaḥnāš	مَصَلَّحْناش	
ínta	ṣalláḥt	صَلَّحْت	ma-ṣalláḥtiš	مَصَلَّحْتِش	
ínti	ṣalláḥti	صَلَّحْتي	ma-ṣallaḥtīš	مَصَلَّحْتيش	
íntu	ṣalláḥtu	صَلَّحْتوا	ma-ṣallaḥtūš	مَصَلَّحْتوش	
húwwa	ṣállaḥ	صَلَّح	ma-ṣalláḥš	مَصَلَّحْش	
híyya	ṣalláḥit	صَلَّحِت	ma-ṣallaḥítš	مَصَلَّحِتْش	
húmma	ṣalláḥu	صَلَّحوا	ma-ṣallaḥūš	مَصَلَّحوش	
ána	aṣállaḥ	أَصَلَّح	ma-ṣalláḥš	مَصَلَّحْش	imperfect
íḥna	niṣállaḥ	نِصَلَّح	ma-nṣalláḥš	مَنْصَلَّحْش	
ínta	tiṣállaḥ	تِصَلَّح	ma-tṣalláḥš	مَتْصَلَّحْش	
ínti	tiṣalláḥi	تِصَلَّحي	ma-tṣallaḥīš	مَتْصَلَّحيش	
íntu	tiṣalláḥu	تِصَلَّحوا	ma-tṣallaḥūš	مَتْصَلَّحوش	
húwwa	yiṣállaḥ	يِصَلَّح	ma-yṣalláḥš	مَيْصَلَّحْش	
híyya	tiṣállaḥ	تِصَلَّح	ma-tṣalláḥš	مَتْصَلَّحْش	
húmma	yiṣalláḥu	يِصَلَّحوا	ma-yṣallaḥūš	مَيْصَلَّحوش	
ána	baṣállaḥ	بَصَلَّح	ma-baṣalláḥš	مَبَصَلَّحْش	bi-imperfect
íḥna	binṣállaḥ	بِنْصَلَّح	ma-binṣalláḥš	مَبِنْصَلَّحْش	
ínta	bitṣállaḥ	بِتْصَلَّح	ma-bitṣalláḥš	مَبِتْصَلَّحْش	
ínti	bitṣalláḥi	بِتْصَلَّحي	ma-bitṣallaḥīš	مَبِتْصَلَّحيش	
íntu	bitṣalláḥu	بِتْصَلَّحوا	ma-bitṣallaḥūš	مَبِتْصَلَّحوش	
húwwa	biyṣállaḥ	بِيْصَلَّح	ma-biyṣalláḥš	مَبِيْصَلَّحْش	
híyya	bitṣállaḥ	بِتْصَلَّح	ma-bitṣalláḥš	مَبِتْصَلَّحْش	
húmma	biyṣalláḥu	بِيْصَلَّحوا	ma-biyṣallaḥūš	مَبِيْصَلَّحوش	
ána	haṣállaḥ	هَصَلَّح	miš haṣállaḥ	مِش هَصَلَّح	future
íḥna	hanṣállaḥ	هَنْصَلَّح	miš hanṣállaḥ	مِش هَنْصَلَّح	
ínta	hatṣállaḥ	هَتْصَلَّح	miš hatṣállaḥ	مِش هَتْصَلَّح	
ínti	hatṣalláḥi	هَتْصَلَّحي	miš hatṣalláḥi	مِش هَتْصَلَّحي	
íntu	hatṣalláḥu	هَتْصَلَّحوا	miš hatṣalláḥu	مِش هَتْصَلَّحوا	
húwwa	hayṣállaḥ	هَيْصَلَّح	miš hayṣállaḥ	مِش هَيْصَلَّح	
híyya	hatṣállaḥ	هَتْصَلَّح	miš hatṣállaḥ	مِش هَتْصَلَّح	
húmma	hayṣalláḥu	هَيْصَلَّحوا	miš hayṣalláḥu	مِش هَيْصَلَّحوا	
ínta	ṣállaḥ	صَلَّح	ma-tṣalláḥš	مَتْصَلَّحْش	imperative
ínti	ṣalláḥi	صَلَّحي	ma-tṣallaḥīš	مَتْصَلَّحيش	
íntu	ṣalláḥu	صَلَّحوا	ma-tṣallaḥūš	مَتْصَلَّحوش	

	active		passive		
masculine	miṣállaḥ	مِصَلَّح	mitṣállaḥ	مِتْصَلَّح	participles
feminine	miṣalláḥa	مِصَلَّحَة	mitṣalláḥa	مِتْصَلَّحَة	
plural	miṣallaḥīn	مِصَلَّحين	mitṣallaḥīn	مِتْصَلَّحين	

①

أنا حاوِلْت أصلّح الجِهاز بِنفْسي و منفعْش.

ána ɧawílt aṣállaɧ ilgihāz bináfsi wi ma-nafá3š.

I tried to fix this machine by myself, but I couldn't.

②

أبويا بِيْحِبّ يِصلّح كُلّ حاجة بْإيدُه.

abūya biyɧibbᵊ yiṣállaɧ kullᵊ ɧāga b-ʔīdu.

My father likes to repair everything with his own hands.

③

مبِتْصلّحوش عربِيِّتْكو ليْه؟

ma-bitṣallaɧūš 3arabiyyítku lē?

Why don't you repair your car?

④

أمْجد هَيْصلّحْلي ساعْتي النّهارْده.

ámgad hayṣalláɧli sá3ti -nnahárda.

Amgad will repair my watch today.

⑤

صلّح علاقْتك بِوِلادك. هتِبْقوا كُلُّكو أسْعد.

ṣállaɧ 3aláʔtak bi-wilādak. hatíbʔu kullúku ʔás3ad.

Fix your relationship with your kids. You'll all be happier.

❖ [2s2] **to repair, fix**

159 to pray ṣálla صلّى 13

verbal noun: ṣála صَلاة

		affirmative		negative	
perfect	ána	ṣallēt	صَلّيْت	ma-ṣallítš	مَصَلّيْتْش
	íḥna	ṣallēna	صَلّيْنا	ma-ṣallināš	مَصَلّيناش
	ínta	ṣallēt	صَلّيْت	ma-ṣallítš	مَصَلّيْتْش
	ínti	ṣallēti	صَلّيْتي	ma-ṣallitīš	مَصَلّيتيش
	íntu	ṣallētu	صَلّيْتوا	ma-ṣallitūš	مَصَلّيتوش
	húwwa	ṣálla	صَلّى	ma-ṣallāš	مَصَلّاش
	híyya	ṣállit	صَلّت	ma-ṣallítš	مَصَلّتْش
	húmma	ṣállu	صَلّوا	ma-ṣallūš	مَصَلّوش
imperfect	ána	aṣálli	أصَلّي	ma-ṣallīš	مَصَلّيش
	íḥna	niṣálli	نِصَلّي	ma-nṣallīš	مَنْصَلّيش
	ínta	tiṣálli	تِصَلّي	ma-tṣallīš	مَتْصَلّيش
	ínti	tiṣálli	تِصَلّي	ma-tṣallīš	مَتْصَلّيش
	íntu	tiṣállu	تِصَلّوا	ma-tṣallūš	مَتْصَلّوش
	húwwa	yiṣálli	يِصَلّي	ma-yṣallīš	مَيْصَلّيش
	híyya	tiṣálli	تِصَلّي	ma-tṣallīš	مَتْصَلّيش
	húmma	yiṣállu	يِصَلّوا	ma-yṣallūš	مَيْصَلّوش
bi-imperfect	ána	baṣálli	بَصَلّي	ma-baṣallīš	مَبَصَلّيش
	íḥna	binṣálli	بِنْصَلّي	ma-binṣallīš	مَبِنْصَلّيش
	ínta	bitṣálli	بِتْصَلّي	ma-bitṣallīš	مَبِتْصَلّيش
	ínti	bitṣálli	بِتْصَلّي	ma-bitṣallīš	مَبِتْصَلّيش
	íntu	bitṣállu	بِتْصَلّوا	ma-bitṣallūš	مَبِتْصَلّوش
	húwwa	biyṣálli	بِيْصَلّي	ma-biyṣallīš	مَبِيْصَلّيش
	híyya	bitṣálli	بِتْصَلّي	ma-bitṣallīš	مَبِتْصَلّيش
	húmma	biyṣállu	بِيْصَلّوا	ma-biyṣallūš	مَبِيْصَلّوش
future	ána	haṣálli	هَصَلّي	miš haṣálli	مِش هَصَلّي
	íḥna	hanṣálli	هَنْصَلّي	miš hanṣálli	مِش هَنْصَلّي
	ínta	hatṣálli	هَتْصَلّي	miš hatṣálli	مِش هَتْصَلّي
	ínti	hatṣálli	هَتْصَلّي	miš hatṣálli	مِش هَتْصَلّي
	íntu	hatṣállu	هَتْصَلّوا	miš hatṣállu	مِش هَتْصَلّوا
	húwwa	hayṣálli	هَيْصَلّي	miš hayṣálli	مِش هَيْصَلّي
	híyya	hatṣálli	هَتْصَلّي	miš hatṣálli	مِش هَتْصَلّي
	húmma	hayṣállu	هَيْصَلّوا	miš hayṣállu	مِش هَيْصَلّوا
imperative	ínta	ṣálli	صَلّي	ma-tṣallīš	مَتْصَلّيش
	ínti	ṣálli	صَلّي	ma-tṣallīš	مَتْصَلّيش
	íntu	ṣállu	صَلّوا	ma-tṣallūš	مَتْصَلّوش

participles		active		passive	
	masculine	miṣálli	مِصَلّي	mitṣálli	مِتْصَلّي
	feminine	miṣallíyya	مِصَلّيَّة	mitṣallíyya	مِتْصَلّيَّة
	plural	miṣalliyīn	مِصَلّيين	mitṣalliyīn	مِتْصَلّيين

①

صلّيْنا الجُمْعة في الأزْهر.

ṣallēna -lgúm3a fi -lʔázhar.

We performed the Friday prayer at Al-Azhar [Mosque].

②

ماما في رمضان بِتْحِبّ تْصلّي التّراويح في المسْجِد.

māma f ramaḍān bitḥíbbᵊ tiṣálli -ttarawīḥ fi -lmásgid.

During Ramadan, my mom likes to pray Tarawih at the mosque.

③

أحْمد بِيْصلّي في المسْجِد اللي قُدّام بيْتُه.

áḥmad biyṣálli fi -lmásgid ílli ʔuddām bētu.

Ahmed prays at the mosque across from his house.

④

هصلّي و أنْزِل على طول.

haṣálli w ánzil 3ála ṭūl.

I'll pray and go out immediately after.

⑤

صلّي بِانْتِظام، هتْحِسّ بْلذِّةْ الصّلاة.

ṣálli bi-ntiẓām, hatḥíssᵊ b-lázzit iṣṣála.

Pray regularly, and you'll feel the pleasure of praying.

⑥

متْصلّيش مِن غيْري. أنا بتْوَضّى و جايّ.

ma-tṣallīš min ɣēri. ána batwáḍḍa w gayy.

Don't pray without me. I'll perform ablution and come.

❖ [2d] **to pray** (an Islamic ritual prayer)

- This verb refers to the ritual prayers performed five times a day by Muslims, as well as other ritual prayers such as Tarawih. For the more general meaning of 'pray (to God / for something)', use دعا *dá3a* (➲ 151.3).
- The verbal noun can be pronounced *ṣalā* or *ṣála*.

➲ 10.1, 159.6

160 to photograph ṣáwwar صوّر 1s

verbal noun: taṣwīr تصْوير

	affirmative		negative		
ána	ṣawwárt	صَوَّرْت	ma-ṣawwártiš	مَصَوَّرْتِش	perfect
íḥna	ṣawwárna	صَوَّرْنا	ma-ṣawwarnāš	مَصَوَّرْناش	
ínta	ṣawwárt	صَوَّرْت	ma-ṣawwártiš	مَصَوَّرْتِش	
ínti	ṣawwárti	صَوَّرْتي	ma-ṣawwartīš	مَصَوَّرْتيش	
íntu	ṣawwártu	صَوَّرْتوا	ma-ṣawwartūš	مَصَوَّرْتوش	
húwwa	ṣáwwar	صَوَّر	ma-ṣawwárš	مَصَوَّرْش	
híyya	ṣawwárit	صَوَّرِت	ma-ṣawwarítš	مَصَوَّرِتْش	
húmma	ṣawwáru	صَوَّروا	ma-ṣawwarūš	مَصَوَّروش	
ána	aṣáwwar	أصَوَّر	ma-ṣawwárš	مَصَوَّرْش	imperfect
íḥna	niṣáwwar	نِصَوَّر	ma-nṣawwárš	مَنْصَوَّرْش	
ínta	tiṣáwwar	تِصَوَّر	ma-tṣawwárš	مَتْصَوَّرْش	
ínti	tiṣawwári	تِصَوَّري	ma-tṣawwarīš	مَتْصَوَّريش	
íntu	tiṣawwáru	تِصَوَّروا	ma-tṣawwarūš	مَتْصَوَّروش	
húwwa	yiṣáwwar	يِصَوَّر	ma-yṣawwárš	مَيْصَوَّرْش	
híyya	tiṣáwwar	تِصَوَّر	ma-tṣawwárš	مَتْصَوَّرْش	
húmma	yiṣawwáru	يِصَوَّروا	ma-yṣawwarūš	مَيْصَوَّروش	
ána	baṣáwwar	بَصَوَّر	ma-baṣawwárš	مَبَصَوَّرْش	bi-imperfect
íḥna	binṣáwwar	بِنْصَوَّر	ma-binṣawwárš	مَبِنْصَوَّرْش	
ínta	bitṣáwwar	بِتْصَوَّر	ma-bitṣawwárš	مَبِتْصَوَّرْش	
ínti	bitṣawwári	بِتْصَوَّري	ma-bitṣawwarīš	مَبِتْصَوَّريش	
íntu	bitṣawwáru	بِتْصَوَّروا	ma-bitṣawwarūš	مَبِتْصَوَّروش	
húwwa	biyṣáwwar	بِيْصَوَّر	ma-biyṣawwárš	مَبِيْصَوَّرْش	
híyya	bitṣáwwar	بِتْصَوَّر	ma-bitṣawwárš	مَبِتْصَوَّرْش	
húmma	biyṣawwáru	بِيْصَوَّروا	ma-biyṣawwarūš	مَبِيْصَوَّروش	
ána	haṣáwwar	هَصَوَّر	miš haṣáwwar	مِش هَصَوَّر	future
íḥna	hanṣáwwar	هَنْصَوَّر	miš hanṣáwwar	مِش هَنْصَوَّر	
ínta	hatṣáwwar	هَتْصَوَّر	miš hatṣáwwar	مِش هَتْصَوَّر	
ínti	hatṣawwári	هَتْصَوَّري	miš hatṣawwári	مِش هَتْصَوَّري	
íntu	hatṣawwáru	هَتْصَوَّروا	miš hatṣawwáru	مِش هَتْصَوَّروا	
húwwa	hayṣáwwar	هَيْصَوَّر	miš hayṣáwwar	مِش هَيْصَوَّر	
híyya	hatṣáwwar	هَتْصَوَّر	miš hatṣáwwar	مِش هَتْصَوَّر	
húmma	hayṣawwáru	هَيْصَوَّروا	miš hayṣawwáru	مِش هَيْصَوَّروا	
ínta	ṣáwwar	صَوَّر	ma-tṣawwárš	مَتْصَوَّرْش	imperative
ínti	ṣawwári	صَوَّري	ma-tṣawwarīš	مَتْصَوَّريش	
íntu	ṣawwáru	صَوَّروا	ma-tṣawwarūš	مَتْصَوَّروش	

	active		passive		
masculine	miṣáwwar	مِصَوَّر	mitṣáwwar	مِتْصَوَّر	participles
feminine	miṣawwára	مِصَوَّرَة	mitṣawwára	مِتْصَوَّرَة	
plural	miṣawwarīn	مِصَوَّرين	mitṣawwarīn	مِتْصَوَّرين	

①

صوّرْنا صُوَر حِلْوَة أوي في رِحْلِتْنا الأخيرة.

ṣawwárna ṣúwar ḫílwa ʔáwi fi riḫlítna -lʔaxīra.

We took some really beautiful photos on our last trip.

②

بحِبّ جِدّاً أصوّر العِيال الصُّغيّرة.

baḫíbbᵊ gíddan aṣáwwar il3iyāl iṣṣuɣayyára.

I love taking photos of little children.

③

الوَلد ده بِيْصوّر حِلْو أوي. عايِز أحْضرْله معْرض.

ilwálad da biyṣáwwar ḫilwᵊ ʔáwi. 3āyiz aḫḍárlu má3raḍ.

This guy takes great pictures. I'd like to attend an exhibition of his.

④

مُنى هتْصوّر الوَرق و تْجيبْلِنا نُسْخة.

múna hatṣáwwar ilwáraʔ wi tgiblína núsxa.

Mona will photocopy the papers and bring us a copy.

⑤

صوّرْني صورة حِلْوَة أرْجوك.

ṣawwárni ṣūra ḫílwa, argūk.

Please take a nice picture of me.

⑥

عمْرو مصوّرْش وَلا صورة في الحفْلة.

3amrᵊ ma-ṣawwáršᵊ wála ṣūra fi -lḫáfla.

Amr didn't take any pictures at the party.

⑦

مِن فضْلك، مُمْكِن تِصوّرْنا؟

min fáḍlak, múmkin tiṣawwárna?

Excuse me, would you mind taking our picture?

❖ [2s2] **to photograph, take a picture (of); to photocopy**

- The object of this verb can be 'picture' (➲ 160.1) or the person/thing photographed (➲ 160.2). It can also take both kinds of objects, being used ditransitively (➲ 160.5).

➲ 153.3, 180.1

161 to go missing ḍā3 ضاع

	affirmative		negative		
ána	ḍi3t	ضِعْت	ma-ḍí3tiš	مَضِعْتِش	perfect
íḥna	ḍí3na	ضِعْنا	ma-ḍi3nāš	مَضِعْناش	
ínta	ḍi3t	ضِعْت	ma-ḍí3tiš	مَضِعْتِش	
ínti	ḍí3ti	ضِعْتي	ma-ḍi3tīš	مَضِعْتيش	
íntu	ḍí3tu	ضِعْتوا	ma-ḍi3tūš	مَضِعْتوش	
húwwa	ḍā3	ضاع	ma-ḍá3š	مَضاعْش	
híyya	ḍā3it	ضاعِت	ma-ḍa3ítš	مَضاعِتْش	
húmma	ḍā3u	ضاعوا	ma-ḍa3ūš	مَضاعوش	
ána	aḍī3	أضيع	ma-ḍí3š	مَضيعْش	imperfect
íḥna	niḍī3	نِضيع	ma-nḍí3š	مَنْضيعْش	
ínta	tiḍī3	تِضيع	ma-tḍí3š	مَتْضيعْش	
ínti	tiḍī3i	تِضيعي	ma-tḍi3īš	مَتْضيعيش	
íntu	tiḍī3u	تِضيعوا	ma-tḍi3ūš	مَتْضيعوش	
húwwa	yiḍī3	يِضيع	ma-yḍí3š	مَيْضيعْش	
híyya	tiḍī3	تِضيع	ma-tḍí3š	مَتْضيعْش	
húmma	yiḍī3u	يِضيعوا	ma-yḍi3ūš	مَيْضيعوش	
ána	baḍī3	بَضيع	ma-baḍí3š	مَبَضيعْش	bi-imperfect
íḥna	binḍī3	بِنْضيع	ma-binḍí3š	مَبِنْضيعْش	
ínta	bitḍī3	بِتْضيع	ma-bitḍí3š	مَبِتْضيعْش	
ínti	bitḍī3i	بِتْضيعي	ma-bitḍi3īš	مَبِتْضيعيش	
íntu	bitḍī3u	بِتْضيعوا	ma-bitḍi3ūš	مَبِتْضيعوش	
húwwa	biyḍī3	بِيْضيع	ma-biyḍí3š	مَبِيْضيعْش	
híyya	bitḍī3	بِتْضيع	ma-bitḍí3š	مَبِتْضيعْش	
húmma	biyḍī3u	بِيْضيعوا	ma-biyḍi3ūš	مَبِيْضيعوش	
ána	haḍī3	هَضيع	miš haḍī3	مِش هَضيع	future
íḥna	hanḍī3	هَنْضيع	miš hanḍī3	مِش هَنْضيع	
ínta	hatḍī3	هَتْضيع	miš hatḍī3	مِش هَتْضيع	
ínti	hatḍī3i	هَتْضيعي	miš hatḍī3i	مِش هَتْضيعي	
íntu	hatḍī3u	هَتْضيعوا	miš hatḍī3u	مِش هَتْضيعوا	
húwwa	hayḍī3	هَيْضيع	miš hayḍī3	مِش هَيْضيع	
híyya	hatḍī3	هَتْضيع	miš hatḍī3	مِش هَتْضيع	
húmma	hayḍī3u	هَيْضيعوا	miš hayḍī3u	مِش هَيْضيعوا	
ínta	ḍī3	ضيع	ma-tḍí3š	مَتْضيعْش	imperative
ínti	ḍī3i	ضيعي	ma-tḍi3īš	مَتْضيعيش	
íntu	ḍī3u	ضيعوا	ma-tḍi3ūš	مَتْضيعوش	

	active		passive		
masculine	ḍāyi3	ضايِع	–	–	participles
feminine	ḍáy3a	ضايْعَة	–	–	
plural	ḍay3īn	ضايْعين	–	–	

verbal nouns: ḍaya3ān ضَيَعان - ḍayā3 ضَياع

①

موبايْلي ضاع و ضاعِت معاه كُلّ نمِري و صُوَري.

mubáyli ḍā3 wi ḍā3it ma3ā kullᵊ nímari wi ṣúwari.

I lost my cell phone [lit. my cell phone went missing] yesterday, along with all my phone numbers and photos.

②

عنْدي دايْماً هاجِس إنّ إبْني مُمْكِن يِضيع مِنّي.

3ándi dáyman hāgis inn íbni múmkin yiḍī3 mínni.

I always have a concern that my son may get lost.

③

أسْماء كُلّ ما تْجيب قلم بِيْضيع مِنْها.

asmāʔ kullᵊ ma tgīb ʔálam biyḍī3 mínha.

Whenever Asmaa buys a pen, she loses it.

④

أرْجوك متْسيبْنيش. أنا هضيع مِن غيْرك.

argūk ma-tsibnīš. ána haḍī3 min ɣērak.

Please don't leave me. I'll be lost without you.

⑤

ركِّز في المُحاضْرة و متْضيعْش في النُّصّ.

rákkiz fi -lmuḥáḍra wi ma-tḍí3šᵊ fi -nnuṣṣ.

Pay attention to the lecture, and don't get lost halfway through.

❖ [1h2] **to become lost, go missing**

- Whereas in English, we would say A loses B, in Arabic B 'goes missing' from (مِن *min*) A. (➲ 161.3)
- Compare with تاه *tāh*. (➲ 64)
- Compare with the transitive verb ضيّع *ḍáyya3* 'lose, waste (time)'. (➲ 24.3, 112.3, 147.5, 231.10, 245.3)

➲ 105.5

162 to laugh díḫik ضِحِك

	affirmative		negative		
ána	diḫíkt	ضِحِكْت	ma-dḫíktiš	مَضْحِكْتِش	perfect
íḫna	diḫíkna	ضِحِكْنا	ma-dḫiknāš	مَضْحِكْناش	
ínta	diḫíkt	ضِحِكْت	ma-dḫíktiš	مَضْحِكْتِش	
ínti	diḫíkti	ضِحِكْتي	ma-dḫiktīš	مَضْحِكْتيش	
íntu	diḫíktu	ضِحِكْتوا	ma-dḫiktūš	مَضْحِكْتوش	
húwwa	díḫik	ضِحِك	ma-dḫíkš	مَضْحِكْش	
híyya	díḫkit	ضِحْكِت	ma-diḫkítš	مَضِحْكِتْش	
húmma	díḫku	ضِحْكوا	ma-diḫkūš	مَضِحْكوش	
ána	ádḫak	أَضْحَك	ma-dḫákš	مَضْحَكْش	imperfect
íḫna	nídḫak	نِضْحَك	ma-nidḫákš	مَنِضْحَكْش	
ínta	tídḫak	تِضْحَك	ma-tidḫákš	مَتِضْحَكْش	
ínti	tidḫáki	تِضْحَكي	ma-tidḫakīš	مَتِضْحَكيش	
íntu	tidḫáku	تِضْحَكوا	ma-tidḫakūš	مَتِضْحَكوش	
húwwa	yídḫak	يِضْحَك	ma-yidḫákš	مَيِضْحَكْش	
híyya	tídḫak	تِضْحَك	ma-tidḫákš	مَتِضْحَكْش	
húmma	yidḫáku	يِضْحَكوا	ma-yidḫakūš	مَيِضْحَكوش	
ána	bádḫak	بَضْحَك	ma-badḫákš	مَبَضْحَكْش	bi-imperfect
íḫna	binídḫak	بِنِضْحَك	ma-bnidḫákš	مَبْنِضْحَكْش	
ínta	bitídḫak	بِتِضْحَك	ma-btidḫákš	مَبْتِضْحَكْش	
ínti	bitidḫáki	بِتِضْحَكي	ma-btidḫakīš	مَبْتِضْحَكيش	
íntu	bitidḫáku	بِتِضْحَكوا	ma-btidḫakūš	مَبْتِضْحَكوش	
húwwa	biyídḫak	بِيِضْحَك	ma-byidḫákš	مَبْيِضْحَكْش	
híyya	bitídḫak	بِتِضْحَك	ma-btidḫákš	مَبْتِضْحَكْش	
húmma	biyidḫáku	بِيِضْحَكوا	ma-byidḫakūš	مَبْيِضْحَكوش	
ána	hádḫak	هَضْحَك	miš hádḫak	مِش هَضْحَك	future
íḫna	hanídḫak	هَنِضْحَك	miš hanídḫak	مِش هَنِضْحَك	
ínta	hatídḫak	هَتِضْحَك	miš hatídḫak	مِش هَتِضْحَك	
ínti	hatidḫáki	هَتِضْحَكي	miš hatidḫáki	مِش هَتِضْحَكي	
íntu	hatidḫáku	هَتِضْحَكوا	miš hatidḫáku	مِش هَتِضْحَكوا	
húwwa	hayídḫak	هَيِضْحَك	miš hayídḫak	مِش هَيِضْحَك	
híyya	hatídḫak	هَتِضْحَك	miš hatídḫak	مِش هَتِضْحَك	
húmma	hayidḫáku	هَيِضْحَكوا	miš hayidḫáku	مِش هَيِضْحَكوا	
ínta	ídḫak	اِضْحَك	ma-tidḫákš	مَتِضْحَكْش	imperative
ínti	idḫáki	اِضْحَكي	ma-tidḫakīš	مَتِضْحَكيش	
íntu	idḫáku	اِضْحَكوا	ma-tidḫakūš	مَتِضْحَكوش	

	active		passive		
masculine	dāḫik	ضاحِك	madḫūk	مَضْحوك	participles
feminine	dáḫka	ضاحْكَة			
plural	daḫkīn	ضاحْكين			

verbal noun: diḫk ضِحْك

①

لمّا أُمّي عِرْفِت إنيّ حامِل ضِحْكِت أوي مِن قلْبها.

lámma ʔúmmi 3írfit ínni ħāmil díħkit ʔáwi min ʔalbáha.

When my mom learned that I was pregnant, she laughed heartily.

②

الجْروب كُلُّه دايْماً يِضْحك على قفشات رامي.

ilgrūb kúllu dáyman yídħak 3ála ʔafašāt rāmi.

The whole group always laughs at Rami's wisecracks.

③

حمْزة بْيِضْحك لمّا بْيِلْعب معَ أخوه.

ħámza byídħak lámma byíl3ab má3a ʔaxū.

Hamza laughs when he plays with his brother.

④

لَوْ حدّ شافْكو بِالمنْظر ده هَيِضْحك عليْكو.

law ħaddᵊ šáfku bi-lmánẓar da hayídħak 3alēku.

If anyone sees you like that, they'll laugh at you.

⑤

اِضْحك مِن قلْبك كُلّ يوْم. هتْحافِظ على شبابك.

ídħak min ʔálbak kullᵊ yōm. hatħāfiẓ 3ála šabābak.

Laugh from your heart daily. You'll keep your youth.

⑥

قوليّ الحقيقة. متِضْحكْش عليّا.

ʔúlli -lħaʔīʔa. ma-tidħákšᵊ 3aláyya.

Tell me the truth. Don't lie to me.

❖ [1s4] **to laugh (at** على *3ála*)**; to deceive, cheat** (على *3ála*)

- Notice that this verb is pronounced with a *d* sound (rather than the *ḍ* of Modern Standard Arabic). Nonetheless, most Egyptians write it using the conventional spelling with ض.
- As this verb requires a preposition, the passive participle is invariable. For example, مضْحوك عليْها *madħūk 3alēha* '(she is being) laughed at'.
- Besides its common meaning 'laugh', this verb (when followed by the preposition على *3ála*) means 'deceive, cheat'. (➲ 162.6, 155.6, 157.1)

➲ 8.3, 155.6, 157.1, 164.3, 207.4

163 to hit ḍárab ضَرَب

verbal noun: ḍarb ضَرْب

	affirmative		negative		
ána	ḍarábt	ضَرَبْت	ma-ḍarábtiš	مَضَرَبْتِش	perfect
íḫna	ḍarábna	ضَرَبْنا	ma-ḍarabnāš	مَضَرَبْناش	
ínta	ḍarábt	ضَرَبْت	ma-ḍarábtiš	مَضَرَبْتِش	
ínti	ḍarábti	ضَرَبْتي	ma-ḍarabtīš	مَضَرَبْتيش	
íntu	ḍarábtu	ضَرَبْتوا	ma-ḍarabtūš	مَضَرَبْتوش	
húwwa	ḍárab	ضَرَب	ma-ḍarábš	مَضَرَبْش	
híyya	ḍárabit	ضَرَبِت	ma-ḍarabítš	مَضَرَبِتْش	
húmma	ḍárabu	ضَرَبوا	ma-ḍarabūš	مَضَرَبوش	
ána	áḍrab	أضْرَب	ma-ḍrábš	مَضْرَبْش	imperfect
íḫna	níḍrab	نِضْرَب	ma-niḍrábš	مَنِضْرَبْش	
ínta	tíḍrab	تِضْرَب	ma-tiḍrábš	مَتِضْرَبْش	
ínti	tiḍrábi	تِضْرَبي	ma-tiḍrabīš	مَتِضْرَبيش	
íntu	tiḍrábu	تِضْرَبوا	ma-tiḍrabūš	مَتِضْرَبوش	
húwwa	yíḍrab	يِضْرَب	ma-yiḍrábš	مَيِضْرَبْش	
híyya	tíḍrab	تِضْرَب	ma-tiḍrábš	مَتِضْرَبْش	
húmma	yiḍrábu	يِضْرَبوا	ma-yiḍrabūš	مَيِضْرَبوش	
ána	báḍrab	بَضْرَب	ma-baḍrábš	مَبَضْرَبْش	bi-imperfect
íḫna	biníḍrab	بِنِضْرَب	ma-bniḍrábš	مَبْنِضْرَبْش	
ínta	bitíḍrab	بِتِضْرَب	ma-btiḍrábš	مَبْتِضْرَبْش	
ínti	bitiḍrábi	بِتِضْرَبي	ma-btiḍrabīš	مَبْتِضْرَبيش	
íntu	bitiḍrábu	بِتِضْرَبوا	ma-btiḍrabūš	مَبْتِضْرَبوش	
húwwa	biyíḍrab	بِيِضْرَب	ma-byiḍrábš	مَبْيِضْرَبْش	
híyya	bitíḍrab	بِتِضْرَب	ma-btiḍrábš	مَبْتِضْرَبْش	
húmma	biyiḍrábu	بِيِضْرَبوا	ma-byiḍrabūš	مَبْيِضْرَبوش	
ána	háḍrab	هَضْرَب	miš háḍrab	مِش هَضْرَب	future
íḫna	haníḍrab	هَنِضْرَب	miš haníḍrab	مِش هَنِضْرَب	
ínta	hatíḍrab	هَتِضْرَب	miš hatíḍrab	مِش هَتِضْرَب	
ínti	hatiḍrábi	هَتِضْرَبي	miš hatiḍrábi	مِش هَتِضْرَبي	
íntu	hatiḍrábu	هَتِضْرَبوا	miš hatiḍrábu	مِش هَتِضْرَبوا	
húwwa	hayíḍrab	هَيِضْرَب	miš hayíḍrab	مِش هَيِضْرَب	
híyya	hatíḍrab	هَتِضْرَب	miš hatíḍrab	مِش هَتِضْرَب	
húmma	hayiḍrábu	هَيِضْرَبوا	miš hayiḍrábu	مِش هَيِضْرَبوا	
ínta	íḍrab	اِضْرَب	ma-tiḍrábš	مَتِضْرَبْش	imperative
ínti	iḍrábi	اِضْرَبي	ma-tiḍrabīš	مَتِضْرَبيش	
íntu	iḍrábu	اِضْرَبوا	ma-tiḍrabūš	مَتِضْرَبوش	

	active		passive		
masculine	ḍārib	ضارِب	maḍrūb	مضْروب	participles
feminine	ḍárba	ضارْبَة	maḍrūba	مضْروبَة	
plural	ḍarbīn	ضارْبين	maḍrubīn	مضْروبين	

①

ضربْني و بكى و سبقْني و اِشْتكى.

ḍarábni wi báka wi sabáʔni w ištáka.

He hit me and cried, and ran ahead of me to complain first. (a well-known saying)

②

الوِلاد دايْماً يِضْربوا بعْض في لِعْبُهُم.

ilwilād dáyman yiḍrábu ba3ḍᵊ f li-3búhum.

Boys always hit each other when they play.

③

رشْوان بِيِضْرب جامِد. محدِّش بِيِقْدر يِغْلبُه.

rašwān biyíḍrab gāmid. ma-ḥáddiš biyíʔdar yiɣlíbu.

Rashwan hits hard. No one can beat him.

④

الرّاجِل ده شكْلُه هَيِضْربْنا . إجْروا!

irrāgil da šáklu hayiḍrábna. ígru!

It looks like that man is going to hit us. Run!

⑤

متِضْربْش حدّ على وِشُّه. دي إهانة.

ma-tiḍrábšᵊ ḥaddᵊ 3ála wíššu. di ihāna.

Don't hit anyone in the face. That's an insult.

❖ [1s1] **to hit; to go off, fire; to multiply**

➲ 86.4, 155.1, 176.3

164 to fly *ṭār* طار

verbal noun: *ṭayarān* طيَران

	affirmative		negative		
ána	*ṭirt*	طِرْت	*ma-ṭírtiš*	مَطِرْتِش	perfect
íḥna	*ṭírna*	طِرْنا	*ma-ṭirnāš*	مَطِرْناش	
ínta	*ṭirt*	طِرْت	*ma-ṭírtiš*	مَطِرْتِش	
ínti	*ṭírti*	طِرْتي	*ma-ṭirtīš*	مَطِرْتيش	
íntu	*ṭírtu*	طِرْتوا	*ma-ṭirtūš*	مَطِرْتوش	
húwwa	*ṭār*	طار	*ma-ṭárš*	مَطارْش	
híyya	*ṭārit*	طارِت	*ma-ṭaritš*	مَطارِتْش	
húmma	*ṭāru*	طاروا	*ma-ṭarūš*	مَطاروش	
ána	*aṭīr*	أطير	*ma-ṭírš*	مَطيرْش	imperfect
íḥna	*niṭīr*	نِطير	*ma-nṭírš*	مَنْطيرْش	
ínta	*tiṭīr*	تِطير	*ma-tṭírš*	مَتْطيرْش	
ínti	*tiṭīri*	تِطيري	*ma-tṭirīš*	مَتْطيريش	
íntu	*tiṭīru*	تِطيروا	*ma-tṭirūš*	مَتْطيروش	
húwwa	*yiṭīr*	يِطير	*ma-yṭírš*	مَيْطيرْش	
híyya	*tiṭīr*	تِطير	*ma-tṭírš*	مَتْطيرْش	
húmma	*yiṭīru*	يِطيروا	*ma-yṭirūš*	مَيْطيروش	
ána	*baṭīr*	بَطير	*ma-baṭírš*	مَبَطيرْش	bi-imperfect
íḥna	*binṭīr*	بِنْطير	*ma-binṭírš*	مَبِنْطيرْش	
ínta	*bitṭīr*	بِتْطير	*ma-bitṭírš*	مَبِتْطيرْش	
ínti	*bitṭīri*	بِتْطيري	*ma-bitṭirīš*	مَبِتْطيريش	
íntu	*bitṭīru*	بِتْطيروا	*ma-bitṭirūš*	مَبِتْطيروش	
húwwa	*biyṭīr*	بِيْطير	*ma-biyṭírš*	مَبِيْطيرْش	
híyya	*bitṭīr*	بِتْطير	*ma-bitṭírš*	مَبِتْطيرْش	
húmma	*biyṭīru*	بِيْطيروا	*ma-biyṭirūš*	مَبِيْطيروش	
ána	*haṭīr*	هَطير	*miš haṭīr*	مِش هَطير	future
íḥna	*hanṭīr*	هَنْطير	*miš hanṭīr*	مِش هَنْطير	
ínta	*hatṭīr*	هَتْطير	*miš hatṭīr*	مِش هَتْطير	
ínti	*hatṭīri*	هَتْطيري	*miš hatṭīri*	مِش هَتْطيري	
íntu	*hatṭīru*	هَتْطيروا	*miš hatṭīru*	مِش هَتْطيروا	
húwwa	*hayṭīr*	هَيْطير	*miš hayṭīr*	مِش هَيْطير	
híyya	*hatṭīr*	هَتْطير	*miš hatṭīr*	مِش هَتْطير	
húmma	*hayṭīru*	هَيْطيروا	*miš hayṭīru*	مِش هَيْطيروا	
ínta	*ṭīr*	طير	*ma-tṭírš*	مَتْطيرْش	imperative
ínti	*ṭīri*	طيري	*ma-tṭirīš*	مَتْطيريش	
íntu	*ṭīru*	طيروا	*ma-tṭirūš*	مَتْطيروش	

	active		passive		
masculine	*ṭāyir*	طايِر	–	–	participles
feminine	*ṭáyra*	طايْرَة	–	–	
plural	*ṭayrīn*	طايْرين	–	–	

①

المُرتّب طار مِن أوِّل إسْبوع في الشّهْر.

ilmuráttab ṭār min áwwil isbū3 fi -ššáhr.

My paycheck was gone [flew away]
within the first week of the month

②

ماجِد حاوِل يِطير مِن البلكوْنة و هُوَّ صُغيرّ بسّ الحمْدُ لله لِحِقْتُه.

māgid ḥāwil yiṭīr min ilbalakōna wi húwwa ṣuɣáyyar bass ilḥámdu li-llāh liḥíʔtu.

Maged tried to fly off the balcony when he was
young, but thank God I caught him in time.

③

أنا بطير مِن الفرْحة لمّا بشوف حدّ مِن وِلادي بيِضْحك.

ána baṭīr min ilfárḥa lámma bašūf ḥaddᵊ min wilādi biyíḍḥak.

I feel so happy when I see one of my kids laughing.

④

أمْجد هَيْطير على دُبيّ بُكْره.

ámgad hayṭīr 3ála dubáyyᵊ búkra.

Amgad will fly to Dubai tomorrow.

⑤

الطُّيور في الشِّتا مبِتْطيرْش ناحْيِةْ الشّمال. بِتْطير ناحْيِةْ الجنوب.

iṭṭuyūr fi -ššíta ma-bitṭíršᵊ náḥyit iššamāl. bitṭīr náḥyit ilganūb.

Birds don't fly north in the winter. They fly south.

❖ [1h2] **to fly**

165 to cook ṭábax طَبَخ

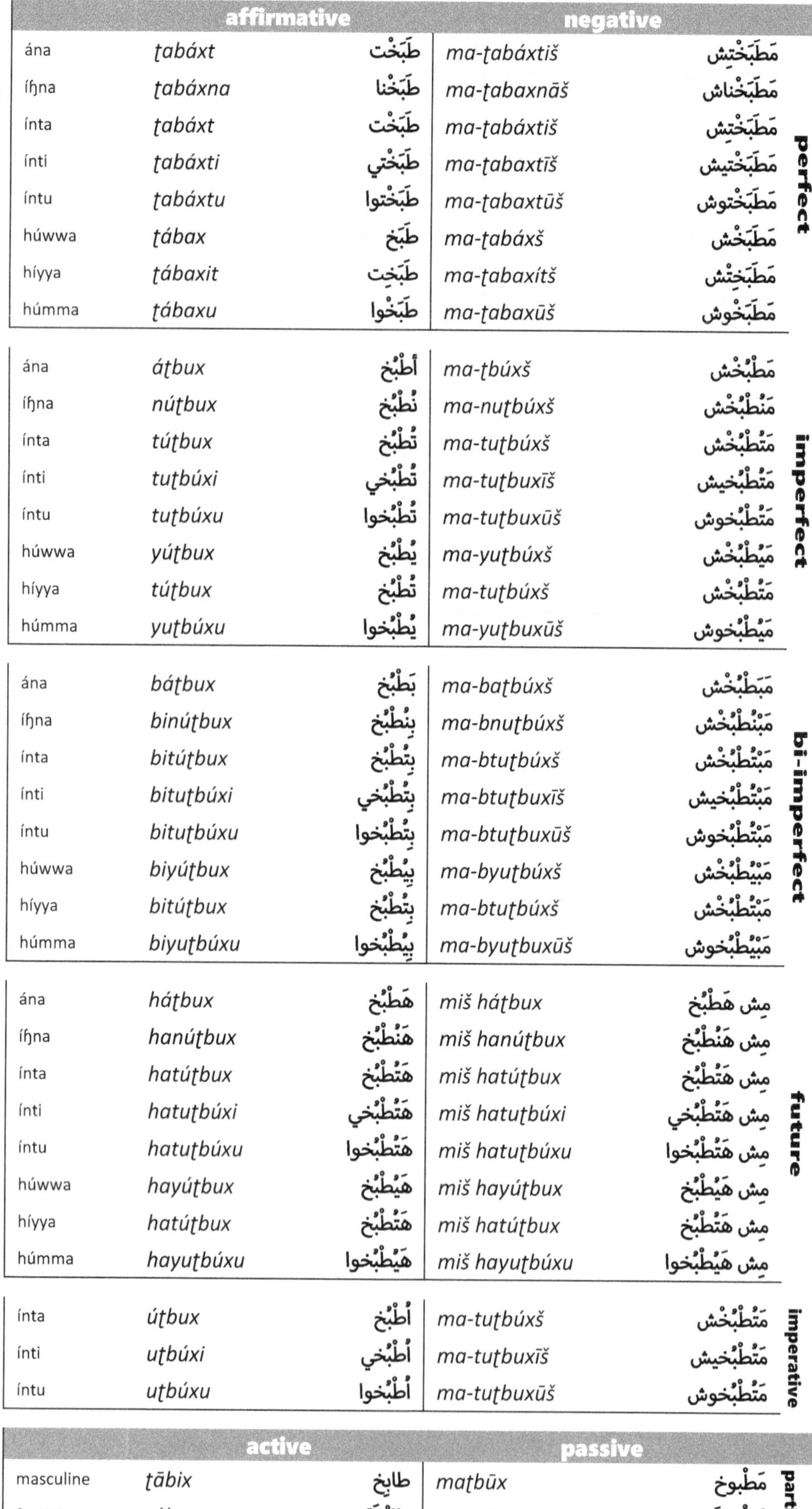

		affirmative		negative	
perfect	ána	ṭabáxt	طَبَخْت	ma-ṭabáxtiš	مَطَبَخْتِش
	íḥna	ṭabáxna	طَبَخْنا	ma-ṭabaxnāš	مَطَبَخْناش
	ínta	ṭabáxt	طَبَخْت	ma-ṭabáxtiš	مَطَبَخْتِش
	ínti	ṭabáxti	طَبَخْتي	ma-ṭabaxtīš	مَطَبَخْتيش
	íntu	ṭabáxtu	طَبَخْتوا	ma-ṭabaxtūš	مَطَبَخْتوش
	húwwa	ṭábax	طَبَخ	ma-ṭabáxš	مَطَبَخْش
	híyya	ṭábaxit	طَبَخِت	ma-ṭabaxítš	مَطَبَخِتْش
	húmma	ṭábaxu	طَبَخوا	ma-ṭabaxūš	مَطَبَخوش
imperfect	ána	áṭbux	أَطْبُخ	ma-ṭbúxš	مَطْبُخْش
	íḥna	núṭbux	نُطْبُخ	ma-nuṭbúxš	مَنُطْبُخْش
	ínta	túṭbux	تُطْبُخ	ma-tuṭbúxš	مَتُطْبُخْش
	ínti	tuṭbúxi	تُطْبُخي	ma-tuṭbuxīš	مَتُطْبُخيش
	íntu	tuṭbúxu	تُطْبُخوا	ma-tuṭbuxūš	مَتُطْبُخوش
	húwwa	yúṭbux	يُطْبُخ	ma-yuṭbúxš	مَيُطْبُخْش
	híyya	túṭbux	تُطْبُخ	ma-tuṭbúxš	مَتُطْبُخْش
	húmma	yuṭbúxu	يُطْبُخوا	ma-yuṭbuxūš	مَيُطْبُخوش
bi-imperfect	ána	báṭbux	بَطْبُخ	ma-baṭbúxš	مَبَطْبُخْش
	íḥna	binúṭbux	بِنُطْبُخ	ma-bnuṭbúxš	مَبْنُطْبُخْش
	ínta	bitúṭbux	بِتُطْبُخ	ma-btuṭbúxš	مَبْتُطْبُخْش
	ínti	bituṭbúxi	بِتُطْبُخي	ma-btuṭbuxīš	مَبْتُطْبُخيش
	íntu	bituṭbúxu	بِتُطْبُخوا	ma-btuṭbuxūš	مَبْتُطْبُخوش
	húwwa	biyúṭbux	بِيُطْبُخ	ma-byuṭbúxš	مَبْيُطْبُخْش
	híyya	bitúṭbux	بِتُطْبُخ	ma-btuṭbúxš	مَبْتُطْبُخْش
	húmma	biyuṭbúxu	بِيُطْبُخوا	ma-byuṭbuxūš	مَبْيُطْبُخوش
future	ána	háṭbux	هَطْبُخ	miš háṭbux	مِش هَطْبُخ
	íḥna	hanúṭbux	هَنُطْبُخ	miš hanúṭbux	مِش هَنُطْبُخ
	ínta	hatúṭbux	هَتُطْبُخ	miš hatúṭbux	مِش هَتُطْبُخ
	ínti	hatuṭbúxi	هَتُطْبُخي	miš hatuṭbúxi	مِش هَتُطْبُخي
	íntu	hatuṭbúxu	هَتُطْبُخوا	miš hatuṭbúxu	مِش هَتُطْبُخوا
	húwwa	hayúṭbux	هَيُطْبُخ	miš hayúṭbux	مِش هَيُطْبُخ
	híyya	hatúṭbux	هَتُطْبُخ	miš hatúṭbux	مِش هَتُطْبُخ
	húmma	hayuṭbúxu	هَيُطْبُخوا	miš hayuṭbúxu	مِش هَيُطْبُخوا
imperative	ínta	úṭbux	اُطْبُخ	ma-tuṭbúxš	مَتُطْبُخْش
	ínti	uṭbúxi	اُطْبُخي	ma-tuṭbuxīš	مَتُطْبُخيش
	íntu	uṭbúxu	اُطْبُخوا	ma-tuṭbuxūš	مَتُطْبُخوش

		active		passive	
participles	masculine	ṭābix	طابِخ	maṭbūx	مَطْبوخ
	feminine	ṭábxa	طابْخَة	maṭbūxa	مَطْبوخَة
	plural	ṭabxīn	طابْخين	maṭbuxīn	مَطْبوخين

verbal noun: ṭabx طَبْخ

①

مها إمْبارِح طبخِتْلِنا أكْل يِجنِّن.

máha -mbāriḫ ṭabaxitlína ʔaklᵊ yigánnin.

Yesterday, Maha cooked us great food.

②

بابا بِيْحِبّ يُطْبُخ و أكْله فِعْلاً حِلْو.

bāba biyḫibbᵊ yúṭbux w áklu fí3lan ḫilw.

My dad likes to cook, and he really makes good food.

③

حماتي بِتُطْبُخ كُلّ أكْلها بِالزِّبْدة.

ḫamāti btúṭbux kull akláha bi-zzíbda.

My mother-in-law cooks all her food with butter.

④

الشّيف هَيُطْبُخْلِنا النّهارْده أكْل أسْيَوي.

iššīf hayuṭbuxlína -nnahárda ʔaklᵊ ʔasyáwi.

The chef will cook us Asian food today.

⑤

أُطْبُخي يا جارْيَة. كلِّف يا سيدي.

uṭbúxi ya gárya. kállif ya sīdi.

Cook, girl. Pay for it, sir. (a proverb meaning 'the one who pays for something controls it.')

⑥

متُطْبُخيش النّهارْده. إحْنا معْزومين عنْد خالي.

ma-tuṭbuxīš innahárda. íḫna ma3zumīn 3andᵊ xāli.

Don't cook today. We've been invited to my uncle's.

❖ [1s3] **to cook**

- This verb, like other verbs of the [1s3] and [1s6] patterns, can optionally take ـُ *u* instead of ـِ *i* in the personal prefixes of the imperfect (including the bi-imperfect and future) and imperative. For example, يُطْبُخ *yúṭbux* can also be pronounced يِطْبُخ *yíṭbux*. These vowels are interchangeable, but the tables reflect the preferences of the speakers on the MP3s.

➲ 11.2, 20.6

166 to request ṭálab طلّب

	affirmative		negative		
ána	ṭalábt	طلّبْت	ma-ṭalábtiš	مَطلّبْتِش	perfect
íḥna	ṭalábna	طلّبْنا	ma-ṭalabnāš	مَطلّبْناش	
ínta	ṭalábt	طلّبْت	ma-ṭalábtiš	مَطلّبْتِش	
ínti	ṭalábti	طلّبْتي	ma-ṭalabtīš	مَطلّبْتيش	
íntu	ṭalábtu	طلّبْتوا	ma-ṭalabtūš	مَطلّبْتوش	
húwwa	ṭálab	طلّب	ma-ṭalábš	مَطلّبْش	
híyya	ṭálabit	طلّبِت	ma-ṭalabítš	مَطلّبِتْش	
húmma	ṭálabu	طلّبوا	ma-ṭalabūš	مَطلّبوش	
ána	áṭlub	أطْلُب	ma-ṭlúbš	مَطْلُبْش	imperfect
íḥna	núṭlub	نُطْلُب	ma-nuṭlúbš	مَنُطْلُبْش	
ínta	túṭlub	تُطْلُب	ma-tuṭlúbš	مَتُطْلُبْش	
ínti	tuṭlúbi	تُطْلُبي	ma-tuṭlubīš	مَتُطْلُبيش	
íntu	tuṭlúbu	تُطْلُبوا	ma-tuṭlubūš	مَتُطْلُبوش	
húwwa	yúṭlub	يُطْلُب	ma-yuṭlúbš	مَيُطْلُبْش	
híyya	túṭlub	تُطْلُب	ma-tuṭlúbš	مَتُطْلُبْش	
húmma	yuṭlúbu	يُطْلُبوا	ma-yuṭlubūš	مَيُطْلُبوش	
ána	báṭlub	بَطْلُب	ma-baṭlúbš	مَبَطْلُبْش	bi-imperfect
íḥna	binúṭlub	بِنُطْلُب	ma-bnuṭlúbš	مَبْنُطْلُبْش	
ínta	bitúṭlub	بِتُطْلُب	ma-btuṭlúbš	مَبْتُطْلُبْش	
ínti	bituṭlúbi	بِتُطْلُبي	ma-btuṭlubīš	مَبْتُطْلُبيش	
íntu	bituṭlúbu	بِتُطْلُبوا	ma-btuṭlubūš	مَبْتُطْلُبوش	
húwwa	biyúṭlub	بِيُطْلُب	ma-byuṭlúbš	مَبْيُطْلُبْش	
híyya	bitúṭlub	بِتُطْلُب	ma-btuṭlúbš	مَبْتُطْلُبْش	
húmma	biyuṭlúbu	بِيُطْلُبوا	ma-byuṭlubūš	مَبْيُطْلُبوش	
ána	háṭlub	هَطْلُب	miš háṭlub	مِش هَطْلُب	future
íḥna	hanúṭlub	هَنُطْلُب	miš hanúṭlub	مِش هَنُطْلُب	
ínta	hatúṭlub	هَتُطْلُب	miš hatúṭlub	مِش هَتُطْلُب	
ínti	hatuṭlúbi	هَتُطْلُبي	miš hatuṭlúbi	مِش هَتُطْلُبي	
íntu	hatuṭlúbu	هَتُطْلُبوا	miš hatuṭlúbu	مِش هَتُطْلُبوا	
húwwa	hayúṭlub	هَيُطْلُب	miš hayúṭlub	مِش هَيُطْلُب	
híyya	hatúṭlub	هَتُطْلُب	miš hatúṭlub	مِش هَتُطْلُب	
húmma	hayuṭlúbu	هَيُطْلُبوا	miš hayuṭlúbu	مِش هَيُطْلُبوا	
ínta	úṭlub	أُطْلُب	ma-tuṭlúbš	مَتُطْلُبْش	imperative
ínti	uṭlúbi	أُطْلُبي	ma-tuṭlubīš	مَتُطْلُبيش	
íntu	uṭlúbu	أُطْلُبوا	ma-tuṭlubūš	مَتُطْلُبوش	

	active		passive		
masculine	ṭālib	طالِب	maṭlūb	مَطْلوب	participles
feminine	ṭálba	طالْبَة	maṭlūba	مَطْلوبَة	
plural	ṭalbīn	طالْبين	maṭlubīn	مَطْلوبين	

verbal noun: ṭálab طلَب

①

أشْرف بِيْحِبّ شيرين و طلب إيدْها.

ášraf biyḥibbᵊ š(i)rīn wi ṭálab ídha.

Ashraf loves Sheren and asked
for her hand [in marriage].

②

بقالي ساعة بطْلُبك ، مبِترْدّيش. فيه أيْه؟

baʔāli sā3a baṭlúbak, ma-bitruddīš. fī ʔē?

I've been calling you for an hour, and you
don't answer. Is anything the matter?

③

هنُطْلُب ديلِفري. عايْزين تاكْلوا أيْه؟

hanúṭlub dilívari. 3ayzīn táklu ʔē?

We're going to call to have food delivered.
What would you like to eat?

④

اُطْلُبوا أيّ حاجة بِأدب و قولوا لَوْ سمحْت.

uṭlúbu ʔayyᵊ ḥāga bi-ádab wi ʔūlu law samáḥt.

Ask for anything politely by saying "please."

⑤

متُطْلُبوش مِن المطْعم ده تاني. أكْلُه دايْماً يِوْصل بارِد.

ma-tuṭlubūš min ilmáṭ3am da tāni. áklu dáyman yíwṣal bārid.

Don't order from that restaurant again.
The food is always delivered cold.

❖ [1s3] **to request, ask (for); to order**

- This verb, like other verbs of the [1s3] and [1s6] patterns, can optionally take ـُ *u* instead of ـِ *i* in the personal prefixes of the imperfect (including the bi-imperfect and future) and imperative. For example, يُطْلُب *yúṭlub* can also be pronounced يِطْلُب *yíṭlub*. These vowels are interchangeable, but the tables reflect the preferences of the speakers on the MP3s.

➲ 78.6, 120.4, 135.2

167 to ascend ṭíli3 طلع

	affirmative		negative		
ána	ṭíli3t	طِلِعْت	ma-ṭlí3tiš	مَطْلِعْتِش	perfect
íḥna	ṭíli3na	طِلِعْنا	ma-ṭli3nāš	مَطْلِعْناش	
ínta	ṭíli3t	طِلِعْت	ma-ṭlí3tiš	مَطْلِعْتِش	
ínti	ṭíli3ti	طِلِعْتي	ma-ṭli3tīš	مَطْلِعْتيش	
íntu	ṭíli3tu	طِلِعْتوا	ma-ṭli3tūš	مَطْلِعْتوش	
húwwa	ṭíli3	طِلِع	ma-ṭlí3š	مَطْلِعْش	
híyya	ṭíl3it	طِلْعِت	ma-ṭil3ítš	مَطِلْعِتْش	
húmma	ṭíl3u	طِلْعوا	ma-ṭil3ūš	مَطِلْعوش	
ána	áṭla3	أطْلَع	ma-ṭlá3š	مَطْلَعْش	imperfect
íḥna	níṭla3	نِطْلَع	ma-niṭlá3š	مَنِطْلَعْش	
ínta	tíṭla3	تِطْلَع	ma-tiṭlá3š	مَتِطْلَعْش	
ínti	tiṭlá3i	تِطْلَعي	ma-tiṭla3īš	مَتِطْلَعيش	
íntu	tiṭlá3u	تِطْلَعوا	ma-tiṭla3ūš	مَتِطْلَعوش	
húwwa	yíṭla3	يِطْلَع	ma-yiṭlá3š	مَيِطْلَعْش	
híyya	tíṭla3	تِطْلَع	ma-tiṭlá3š	مَتِطْلَعْش	
húmma	yiṭlá3u	يِطْلَعوا	ma-yiṭla3ūš	مَيِطْلَعوش	
ána	báṭla3	بَطْلَع	ma-baṭlá3š	مَبَطْلَعْش	bi-imperfect
íḥna	biníṭla3	بِنِطْلَع	ma-bniṭlá3š	مَبْنِطْلَعْش	
ínta	bitíṭla3	بِتِطْلَع	ma-btiṭlá3š	مَبْتِطْلَعْش	
ínti	bitiṭlá3i	بِتِطْلَعي	ma-btiṭla3īš	مَبْتِطْلَعيش	
íntu	bitiṭlá3u	بِتِطْلَعوا	ma-btiṭla3ūš	مَبْتِطْلَعوش	
húwwa	biyíṭla3	بِيِطْلَع	ma-byiṭlá3š	مَبْيِطْلَعْش	
híyya	bitíṭla3	بِتِطْلَع	ma-btiṭlá3š	مَبْتِطْلَعْش	
húmma	biyiṭlá3u	بِيِطْلَعوا	ma-byiṭla3ūš	مَبْيِطْلَعوش	
ána	háṭla3	هَطْلَع	miš háṭla3	مِش هَطْلَع	future
íḥna	haníṭla3	هَنِطْلَع	miš haníṭla3	مِش هَنِطْلَع	
ínta	hatíṭla3	هَتِطْلَع	miš hatíṭla3	مِش هَتِطْلَع	
ínti	hatiṭlá3i	هَتِطْلَعي	miš hatiṭlá3i	مِش هَتِطْلَعي	
íntu	hatiṭlá3u	هَتِطْلَعوا	miš hatiṭlá3u	مِش هَتِطْلَعوا	
húwwa	hayíṭla3	هَيِطْلَع	miš hayíṭla3	مِش هَيِطْلَع	
híyya	hatíṭla3	هَتِطْلَع	miš hatíṭla3	مِش هَتِطْلَع	
húmma	hayiṭlá3u	هَيِطْلَعوا	miš hayiṭlá3u	مِش هَيِطْلَعوا	
ínta	íṭla3	اِطْلَع	ma-tiṭlá3š	مَتِطْلَعْش	imperative
ínti	iṭlá3i	اِطْلَعي	ma-tiṭla3īš	مَتِطْلَعيش	
íntu	iṭlá3u	اِطْلَعوا	ma-tiṭla3ūš	مَتِطْلَعوش	

	active		passive		
masculine	ṭāli3	طالِع	maṭlū3	مَطْلوع	participles
feminine	ṭál3a	طالْعَة	maṭlū3a	مَطْلوعَة	
plural	ṭal3īn	طالْعين	maṭlu3īn	مَطْلوعين	

verbal noun: ṭulū3 طُلوع

①

الواحِد لمّا يِطْلع مِن هنْدسة بقوا يْقولولُه كفّارة.

ilwāḫid lámma yíṭla3 min handása báʔu yʔulūlu kafāra.

When you graduate from the engineering faculty, they tell you, "Welcome back!"

②

الشّجرة اللي قُدّامْنا بيِطْلع فيها وَرْد بُرْتُقاني في آخِر شهْر خمْسة.

iššágara -lli ʔuddámna biyíṭla3 fīha ward burtuʔāni fi ʔāxir šahrᵊ xámsa.

Orange flowers appear on the tree in front of us at the end of May.

③

أحْمد طِلِع رِحْلِةْ صيْد يوْميْن.

áḫmad ṭíli3 ríḫlit ṣēd yumēn.

Ahmed went on a two-day fishing trip.

④

خميس هتِطْلع طيّارْتُه السّاعة سِتّة.

xamīs hatíṭla3 ṭayyártu -ssā3a sítta.

Khames's plane will take off at 6:00.

⑤

اِطْلع مِن القالِب اللي النّاس بِتْحُطّك فيه. إعْمِل اللي بِتْحِبُّه.

íṭla3 min ilʔālib ílli -nnās bitḫúṭṭak fī. í3mil ílli bitḫíbbu.

Break out of the mold people put you in, and do what you love.

⑥

عارْفين البِنْت السّمْرا دي؟ مطِلْعِتْش مصْرية، دي مِن السّودان.

3arfīn ilbínt issámra di? ma-ṭil3ítšᵊ maṣríyya, di min issudān.

Do you know that dark-skinned girl? It turns out she isn't Egyptian; she's from Sudan.

⑦

ما شاء اللّه الوَلد طالِع حِتّة مِن أبوه.

ma šāʔ allāh, ilwálad ṭāli3 ḫitta min abū.

God bless him; the boy's the spitting image of his father.

⑧

الشّمْس طِلْعِت النّهارْده السّاعة خمْسة و نُصّ.

iššámsᵊ ṭíl3it innahárda -ssā3a xámsa wi nuṣṣ.

Sunrise was at 5:30 today.

⑨

عَويس بيِطْلع النّخْلة بْسُرْعة. هُوَّ مِتْعوِّد على كِده.

3awīs biyíṭli3 innáxla b-súr3a. húwwa mit3áwwid 3ála kída.

Eweas goes up the palm tree fast. He's used to that.

⑩

الوَلد طِلِع برّه المُحاضْرة لمّا ردّ على الدُّكْتور وِحِش.

ilwálad ṭíli3 bárra -lmuḫáḍra lámma raddᵊ 3ála -dduktūr wíḫiš.

The young man was kicked out of the lecture after he answered the professor rudely.

⑪

اِطْلِع هات الكيس اللي نْسيناه عَ السُّفْرة.

íṭli3 hāt ilkīs ílli nsinā 3a -ssúfra.

Go up and get the bag we forgot on the dining table.

❖ [1s4] **to ascend, go up, rise;** (plane) **to take off; to embark on** (a journey)**; to turn out (to be); to come out of** (مِن *min*)

➲ 14.1, 38.3, 72.1, 81.1, 101.1, 101.3, 124.1, 132.1, 132.4 134.1, 171.7, 203.2, 211.1, 211.3, 248.1

168 to issue ṭálla3 طلّع

verbal noun: taṭlī3 تطْليع

perfect

	affirmative		negative	
ána	ṭallá3t	طلّعْت	ma-ṭallá3tiš	مَطلّعْتِش
íḥna	ṭallá3na	طلّعْنا	ma-ṭalla3nāš	مَطلّعْناش
ínta	ṭallá3t	طلّعْت	ma-ṭallá3tiš	مَطلّعْتِش
ínti	ṭallá3ti	طلّعْتي	ma-ṭalla3tīš	مَطلّعْتيش
íntu	ṭallá3tu	طلّعْتوا	ma-ṭalla3tūš	مَطلّعْتوش
húwwa	ṭálla3	طلّع	ma-ṭallá3š	مَطلّعْش
híyya	ṭallá3it	طلّعِت	ma-ṭalla3ítš	مَطلّعِتْش
húmma	ṭallá3u	طلّعوا	ma-ṭalla3ūš	مَطلّعوش

imperfect

	affirmative		negative	
ána	aṭálla3	أطلّع	ma-ṭallá3š	مَطلّعْش
íḥna	niṭálla3	نِطلّع	ma-nṭallá3š	مَنْطلّعْش
ínta	tiṭálla3	تِطلّع	ma-tṭallá3š	مَتْطلّعْش
ínti	tiṭallá3i	تِطلّعي	ma-tṭalla3īš	مَتْطلّعيش
íntu	tiṭallá3u	تِطلّعوا	ma-tṭalla3ūš	مَتْطلّعوش
húwwa	yiṭálla3	يِطلّع	ma-yṭallá3š	مَيْطلّعْش
híyya	tiṭálla3	تِطلّع	ma-tṭallá3š	مَتْطلّعْش
húmma	yiṭallá3u	يِطلّعوا	ma-yṭalla3ūš	مَيْطلّعوش

bi-imperfect

	affirmative		negative	
ána	baṭálla3	بَطلّع	ma-baṭallá3š	مَبَطلّعْش
íḥna	binṭálla3	بِنْطلّع	ma-binṭallá3š	مَبِنْطلّعْش
ínta	bitṭálla3	بِتْطلّع	ma-bitṭallá3š	مَبِتْطلّعْش
ínti	bitṭallá3i	بِتْطلّعي	ma-bitṭalla3īš	مَبِتْطلّعيش
íntu	bitṭallá3u	بِتْطلّعوا	ma-bitṭalla3ūš	مَبِتْطلّعوش
húwwa	biyṭálla3	بِيْطلّع	ma-biyṭallá3š	مَبِيْطلّعْش
híyya	bitṭálla3	بِتْطلّع	ma-bitṭallá3š	مَبِتْطلّعْش
húmma	biyṭallá3u	بِيْطلّعوا	ma-biyṭalla3ūš	مَبِيْطلّعوش

future

	affirmative		negative	
ána	haṭálla3	هَطلّع	miš haṭálla3	مِش هَطلّع
íḥna	hanṭálla3	هَنْطلّع	miš hanṭálla3	مِش هَنْطلّع
ínta	hatṭálla3	هَتْطلّع	miš hatṭálla3	مِش هَتْطلّع
ínti	hatṭallá3i	هَتْطلّعي	miš hatṭallá3i	مِش هَتْطلّعي
íntu	hatṭallá3u	هَتْطلّعوا	miš hatṭallá3u	مِش هَتْطلّعوا
húwwa	hayṭálla3	هَيْطلّع	miš hayṭálla3	مِش هَيْطلّع
híyya	hatṭálla3	هَتْطلّع	miš hatṭálla3	مِش هَتْطلّع
húmma	hayṭallá3u	هَيْطلّعوا	miš hayṭallá3u	مِش هَيْطلّعوا

imperative

	affirmative		negative	
ínta	ṭálla3	طلّع	ma-tṭallá3š	مَتْطلّعْش
ínti	ṭallá3i	طلّعي	ma-tṭalla3īš	مَتْطلّعيش
íntu	ṭallá3u	طلّعوا	ma-tṭalla3ūš	مَتْطلّعوش

participles

	active		passive	
masculine	miṭálla3	مِطلّع	mitṭálla3	مِتْطلّع
feminine	miṭallá3a	مِطلّعَة	mitṭallá3a	مِتْطلّعَة
plural	miṭalla3īn	مِطلّعين	mitṭalla3īn	مِتْطلّعين

①

الوَلد طلّع معانا الحاجة و مِشي على طول. مسْتنّاش نِدّيلُه حاجة.

ilwálad ţálla3 ma3āna -lħāga w míši 3ála ţūl. ma-stannāš niddīlu ħāga.

The boy took the bags up with us and went away immediately. He didn't wait for us to give him a tip.

②

لمّا الزّرع بِتاعي يِطلّع ثمر، هعْزِمْكو تيجوا تْدوقوه.

lámma -zzára3 bitā3i yiţálla3 sámar, ha3zímku tīgu tduʔū.

When my [vegetable] plants start producing, I'll invite you over to taste them.

③

بيوت الشّباب بِتْطلّع رحلات حِلْوَة أوي.

biyūt iššabāb bitţálla3 raħalāt ħílwa ʔáwi.

Youth hostels make for very good trips.

④

المجلّة هتْطلّع العدد الجِديد كمان أُسْبوع.

ilmagálla hatţálla3 il3ádad ilgidīd kamān isbū3.

The magazine will publish the new issue in a week.

⑤

متْطلّعْش زهقك عليْنا. ما إحْنا برْضُه فينا اللي مْكفّينا.

ma-tţallá3š[ə] záhaʔak 3alēna. ma -ħna bárḑu fīna -lli mkaffīna.

If you're fed up, don't take it out on us. We're fed up, too.

❖ [2s2] **to take/bring up; to take out, remove; to produce, yield; to issue, publish**

➲ 99.4, 187.6

169 to repeat *3ād* عاد

verbal noun: *3ōda* عودة

	affirmative		negative		
ána	*3udt*	عُدْت	*ma-3údtiš*	مَعُدْتِش	**perfect**
íḥna	*3údna*	عُدْنا	*ma-3udnāš*	مَعُدْناش	
ínta	*3udt*	عُدْت	*ma-3údtiš*	مَعُدْتِش	
ínti	*3údti*	عُدْتي	*ma-3udtīš*	مَعُدْتيش	
íntu	*3údtu*	عُدْتوا	*ma-3udtūš*	مَعُدْتوش	
húwwa	*3ād*	عاد	*ma-3ádš*	مَعادْش	
híyya	*3ādit*	عادِت	*ma-3adítš*	مَعادِتْش	
húmma	*3ādu*	عادوا	*ma-3adūš*	مَعادوش	
ána	*a3ūd*	أعود	*ma-3údš*	مَعودْش	**imperfect**
íḥna	*ni3ūd*	نِعود	*ma-n3údš*	مَنْعودْش	
ínta	*ti3ūd*	تِعود	*ma-t3údš*	مَتْعودْش	
ínti	*ti3ūdi*	تِعودي	*ma-t3udīš*	مَتْعوديش	
íntu	*ti3ūdu*	تِعودوا	*ma-t3udūš*	مَتْعودوش	
húwwa	*yi3ūd*	يِعود	*ma-y3údš*	مَيْعودْش	
híyya	*ti3ūd*	تِعود	*ma-t3údš*	مَتْعودْش	
húmma	*yi3ūdu*	يِعودوا	*ma-y3udūš*	مَيْعودوش	
ána	*ba3ūd*	بَعود	*ma-ba3údš*	مَبَعودْش	**bi-imperfect**
íḥna	*bin3ūd*	بِنْعود	*ma-bin3údš*	مَبِنْعودْش	
ínta	*bit3ūd*	بِتْعود	*ma-bit3údš*	مَبِتْعودْش	
ínti	*bit3ūdi*	بِتْعودي	*ma-bit3udīš*	مَبِتْعوديش	
íntu	*bit3ūdu*	بِتْعودوا	*ma-bit3udūš*	مَبِتْعودوش	
húwwa	*biy3ūd*	بِيْعود	*ma-biy3údš*	مَبِيْعودْش	
híyya	*bit3ūd*	بِتْعود	*ma-bit3údš*	مَبِتْعودْش	
húmma	*biy3ūdu*	بِيْعودوا	*ma-biy3udūš*	مَبِيْعودوش	
ána	*ha3ūd*	هَعود	*miš ha3ūd*	مِش هَعود	**future**
íḥna	*han3ūd*	هَنْعود	*miš han3ūd*	مِش هَنْعود	
ínta	*hat3ūd*	هَتْعود	*miš hat3ūd*	مِش هَتْعود	
ínti	*hat3ūdi*	هَتْعودي	*miš hat3ūdi*	مِش هَتْعودي	
íntu	*hat3ūdu*	هَتْعودوا	*miš hat3ūdu*	مِش هَتْعودوا	
húwwa	*hay3ūd*	هَيْعود	*miš hay3ūd*	مِش هَيْعود	
híyya	*hat3ūd*	هَتْعود	*miš hat3ūd*	مِش هَتْعود	
húmma	*hay3ūdu*	هَيْعودوا	*miš hay3ūdu*	مِش هَيْعودوا	
ínta	*3ūd*	عود	*ma-t3údš*	مَتْعودْش	**imperative**
ínti	*3ūdi*	عودي	*ma-t3udīš*	مَتْعوديش	
íntu	*3ūdu*	عودوا	*ma-t3udūš*	مَتْعودوش	

	active		passive		
masculine	*3āyid*	عايِد	–	–	**participles**
feminine	*3áyda*	عايْدَة	–	–	
plural	*3aydīn*	عايْدين	–	–	

①

هُوَّ فِهِم غلْطِتُه و معادْش يِعْمِل كِده تاني.

húwwa fíhim ɣalṭítu wi ma-3ádšᵊ yí3mil kída tāni.

He understood his mistake and never made it again.

②

كُلّ سنة و إنْتو طيِّبين، ربِّنا يْعودُه عليْكو بْخيرْ.

kullᵊ sána w íntu ṭayyibīn, rabbína y3ūdu 3alēku b-xēr.

Happy holidays, and may God bring you happiness.

③

معادْش معايا فْلوس أدْفع إيجار الشقّة.

ma-3ádš ma3āya flūs ádfa3 igār iššáʔʔa.

I don't have any money left to pay rent.

④

شايْفين اللي بِيِجْرالْكو كُلّ ما تْروحوا. معُدْتوش تِروحوا المكان ده تاني.

šayfīn ílli biyigrálku kullᵊ ma trūḫu. ma-3udtūš tirūḫu -lmakān da tāni.

Do you see what happens to you each time you go there? Don't go to that place again.

⑤

النّاس معادِتْش تِتْكلِّم زيّ زمان. دِلْوَقْتي كُلُّه باصِص في جِهازُه و ساكِت.

innās ma-3adítšᵊ titkállim zayyᵊ zamān. dilwáʔti kúllu bāṣiṣ fi gihāzu wi sākit.

People don't talk like they used to. Now, everyone stares at their cell phone in silence.

⑥

واللهِ المشْروع ده عاد علیْنا بِالخيرْ.

wallāhi -lmašrū3 da 3ād 3alēna bi-lxēr.

Indeed, this project has brought us affirmative returns.

❖ [1h1] **to repeat; to affect** (على *3ála* **with** بِـ *bi-*), **bring** (**upon** على *3ála* something بِـ *bi-*)

- This verb followed by an imperfect verb means '__ again', but is more commonly used in the negative, translating 'not __ anymore', 'no longer __'. (➲ 169.1, 169.4, 169.5)

170 to do again *3ād* عاد

	affirmative		negative		
ána	*3idt*	عِدْت	*ma-3ídtiš*	مَعِدْتِش	perfect
íḥna	*3ídna*	عِدْنا	*ma-3idnāš*	مَعِدْناش	
ínta	*3idt*	عِدْت	*ma-3ídtiš*	مَعِدْتِش	
ínti	*3ídti*	عِدْتي	*ma-3idtīš*	مَعِدْتيش	
íntu	*3ídtu*	عِدْتوا	*ma-3idtūš*	مَعِدْتوش	
húwwa	*3ād*	عاد	*ma-3ádš*	مَعادْش	
híyya	*3ādit*	عادِت	*ma-3adítš*	مَعادِتْش	
húmma	*3ādu*	عادوا	*ma-3adūš*	مَعادوش	
ána	*a3īd*	أعيد	*ma-3ídš*	مَعيدْش	imperfect
íḥna	*ni3īd*	نِعيد	*ma-n3ídš*	مَنْعيدْش	
ínta	*ti3īd*	تِعيد	*ma-t3ídš*	مَتْعيدْش	
ínti	*ti3īdi*	تِعيدي	*ma-t3idīš*	مَتْعيديش	
íntu	*ti3īdu*	تِعيدوا	*ma-t3idūš*	مَتْعيدوش	
húwwa	*yi3īd*	يِعيد	*ma-y3ídš*	مَيْعيدْش	
híyya	*ti3īd*	تِعيد	*ma-t3ídš*	مَتْعيدْش	
húmma	*yi3īdu*	يِعيدوا	*ma-y3idūš*	مَيْعيدوش	
ána	*ba3īd*	بَعيد	*ma-ba3ídš*	مَبَعيدْش	bi-imperfect
íḥna	*bin3īd*	بِنْعيد	*ma-bin3ídš*	مَبِنْعيدْش	
ínta	*bit3īd*	بِتْعيد	*ma-bit3ídš*	مَبِتْعيدْش	
ínti	*bit3īdi*	بِتْعيدي	*ma-bit3idīš*	مَبِتْعيديش	
íntu	*bit3īdu*	بِتْعيدوا	*ma-bit3idūš*	مَبِتْعيدوش	
húwwa	*biy3īd*	بِيْعيد	*ma-biy3ídš*	مَبِيْعيدْش	
híyya	*bit3īd*	بِتْعيد	*ma-bit3ídš*	مَبِتْعيدْش	
húmma	*biy3īdu*	بِيْعيدوا	*ma-biy3idūš*	مَبِيْعيدوش	
ána	*ha3īd*	هَعيد	*miš ha3īd*	مِش هَعيد	future
íḥna	*han3īd*	هَنْعيد	*miš han3īd*	مِش هَنْعيد	
ínta	*hat3īd*	هَتْعيد	*miš hat3īd*	مِش هَتْعيد	
ínti	*hat3īdi*	هَتْعيدي	*miš hat3īdi*	مِش هَتْعيدي	
íntu	*hat3īdu*	هَتْعيدوا	*miš hat3īdu*	مِش هَتْعيدوا	
húwwa	*hay3īd*	هَيْعيد	*miš hay3īd*	مِش هَيْعيد	
híyya	*hat3īd*	هَتْعيد	*miš hat3īd*	مِش هَتْعيد	
húmma	*hay3īdu*	هَيْعيدوا	*miš hay3īdu*	مِش هَيْعيدوا	
ínta	*3īd*	عيد	*ma-t3ídš*	مَتْعيدْش	imperative
ínti	*3īdi*	عيدي	*ma-t3idīš*	مَتْعيديش	
íntu	*3īdu*	عيدوا	*ma-t3idūš*	مَتْعيدوش	

	active		passive		
masculine	*3āyid*	عايِد	*mit3ād*	مِتْعاد	participles
feminine	*3áyda*	عايْدَة	*mit3āda*	مِتْعادَة	
plural	*3aydīn*	عايْدين	*mit3adīn*	مِتْعادين	

verbal noun: *3iyāda* عِيادة

①

مها عادِت السّنة مرِّتيْن. هِيَّ دِماغْها مِش في المُذاكْرة.

máha 3ādit issána marritēn. híyya dimáɣha miš fi -lmuzákra.

Maha repeated this year twice.
She's not that into studying.

②

سامِر بيِْعيد كُلّ اللي بقولُّه. بيِتْرّيَق عليّا.

sāmir biy3īd kull ílli baʔúllu. biyittáryaʔ 3aláyya.

Samer repeats everything I say.
He's making fun of me.

③

عيدي النِّمْرة مِن فضْلِك عشان أكْتِبْها.

3īdi -nnímara min fáḍlik 3ašān aktíbha.

Please repeat the number,
so I can write it down.

④

مبحِبِّش أعيد الكلام. اللي أقولُه يِتْنفِّذ مِن أوِّل مرّة.

ma-baḫíbbiš a3īd ilkalām. íll- aʔūlu yitnáffiz min áwwil márra.

I don't like repeating myself. What I say should be done
the first time. [i.e. Do what I say the first time.]

❖ [1h2] **to repeat, do again; to repeat, say again**

➲ 13.4, 196.1

171 to want *3āz* عاز

	affirmative		negative		
ána	*3uzt*	عُزْت	*ma-3úztiš*	مَعُزْتِش	perfect
íḫna	*3úzna*	عُزْنا	*ma-3uznāš*	مَعُزْناش	
ínta	*3uzt*	عُزْت	*ma-3úztiš*	مَعُزْتِش	
ínti	*3úzti*	عُزْتي	*ma-3uztīš*	مَعُزْتيش	
íntu	*3úztu*	عُزْتوا	*ma-3uztūš*	مَعُزْتوش	
húwwa	*3āz*	عاز	*ma-3ázš*	مَعازْش	
híyya	*3āzit*	عازِت	*ma-3azítš*	مَعازِتْش	
húmma	*3āzu*	عازوا	*ma-3azūš*	مَعازوش	
ána	*a3ūz*	أعوز	*ma-3úzš*	مَعوزْش	imperfect
íḫna	*ni3ūz*	نِعوز	*ma-n3úzš*	مَنْعوزْش	
ínta	*ti3ūz*	تِعوز	*ma-t3úzš*	مَتْعوزْش	
ínti	*ti3ūzi*	تِعوزي	*ma-t3uzīš*	مَتْعوزيش	
íntu	*ti3ūzu*	تِعوزوا	*ma-t3uzūš*	مَتْعوزوش	
húwwa	*yi3ūz*	يِعوز	*ma-y3úzš*	مَيْعوزْش	
híyya	*ti3ūz*	تِعوز	*ma-t3úzš*	مَتْعوزْش	
húmma	*yi3ūzu*	يِعوزوا	*ma-y3uzūš*	مَيْعوزوش	
ána	*ba3ūz*	بَعوز	*ma-ba3úzš*	مَبَعوزْش	bi-imperfect
íḫna	*bin3ūz*	بِنْعوز	*ma-bin3úzš*	مَبِنْعوزْش	
ínta	*bit3ūz*	بِتْعوز	*ma-bit3úzš*	مَبِتْعوزْش	
ínti	*bit3ūzi*	بِتْعوزي	*ma-bit3uzīš*	مَبِتْعوزيش	
íntu	*bit3ūzu*	بِتْعوزوا	*ma-bit3uzūš*	مَبِتْعوزوش	
húwwa	*biy3ūz*	بِيْعوز	*ma-biy3úzš*	مَبِيْعوزْش	
híyya	*bit3ūz*	بِتْعوز	*ma-bit3úzš*	مَبِتْعوزْش	
húmma	*biy3ūzu*	بِيْعوزوا	*ma-biy3uzūš*	مَبِيْعوزوش	
ána	*ha3ūz*	هَعوز	*miš ha3ūz*	مِش هَعوز	future
íḫna	*han3ūz*	هَنْعوز	*miš han3ūz*	مِش هَنْعوز	
ínta	*hat3ūz*	هَتْعوز	*miš hat3ūz*	مِش هَتْعوز	
ínti	*hat3ūzi*	هَتْعوزي	*miš hat3ūzi*	مِش هَتْعوزي	
íntu	*hat3ūzu*	هَتْعوزوا	*miš hat3ūzu*	مِش هَتْعوزوا	
húwwa	*hay3ūz*	هَيْعوز	*miš hay3ūz*	مِش هَيْعوز	
híyya	*hat3ūz*	هَتْعوز	*miš hat3ūz*	مِش هَتْعوز	
húmma	*hay3ūzu*	هَيْعوزوا	*miš hay3ūzu*	مِش هَيْعوزوا	
ínta	*3ūz*	عوز	*ma-t3úzš*	مَتْعوزْش	imperative
ínti	*3ūzi*	عوزي	*ma-t3uzīš*	مَتْعوزيش	
íntu	*3ūzu*	عوزوا	*ma-t3uzūš*	مَتْعوزوش	

	active		passive		
masculine	*3āyiz / 3āwiz*	عايِز / عاوِز	*mit3āz*	مِتْعاز	participles
feminine	*3áyza / 3áwza*	عايْزَة / عاوْزَة	*mit3āza*	مِتْعازَة	
plural	*3ayzīn / 3awzīn*	عايْزين / عاوْزين	*mit3azīn*	مِتْعازين	

verbal nouns: *3ōz* عوز - *3awazān* عوزان

①

لمّا عُزْت مُساعْدة، لقيْت الكُلّ حَواليّا، واللهِ الدُّنْيا لِسّه بِخير.

lámma 3uzt^ə musá3da, laʔēt ilkúll^ə ɧawaláyya, wallāhi -ddúnya líssa bi-xēr.

When I needed help, everybody was there for me. Life is still good.

②

عايِز أفْهم إزّاي البنات بِيِسْتحْمِلوا المكْياج في الحرّ ده.

3āyiz áfham izzāy ilbanāt biyistaɧmílu -lmakyāž fi -lɧarr^ə da.

I want to understand how girls can bear [wearing] makeup in this heat.

③

رشا لمّا بْتِعوز حاجة بِتِتِّصِل بِالسّوبر مارْكِت يِبْعتْلها.

ráša lámma bt3ūz ɧāga bitittíṣil bi-ssūbar márkit yib3atláha.

When she needs something, Rasha calls the supermarket to have it delivered to her.

④	⑤
هتْعوزي أيْه تاني معاكي في الرِّحْلة؟	متْعوزوش حدّ مِش عايْزْكو.
hat3ūzi ʔē tāni ma3āki fi -rríɧla?	*ma-t3uzūš ɧadd^ə miš 3ayízku.*
What else will you need with you on the journey?	Don't want someone who doesn't want you.

⑥

الكِتاب؟ أنا مِش عايْزُه . ده هِيَّ اللي عايْزاه.

ilkitāb? ána miš 3áyzu. da híyya -lli 3ayzā.

The book? I didn't want it, but she wanted it.

⑦

طول عُمْري عايِز أطْلع الفضاء.

ṭūl 3úmri 3āyiz áṭla3 ilfaḍāʔ.

I've always wanted to travel to space.

⑧

أنا مُتأكِّد إنّها هتِبْقى عايْزة تِعدّي عَ المحلّ ده قبْل ما نْروّح.

ána mutaʔákkid innáha hatíbʔa 3áyza t3áddi 3a -lmaɧáll^ə da ʔabl^ə ma nráwwaɧ.

I'm sure she'll want to stop at that shop before going back home.

❖ [1h1] **to want; to need**

- As a perfect or imperfect verb, this verb can be followed by a noun, verbal noun, or imperfect verb, and usually translates as 'need'.
- It is most commonly used as an active participle followed by a noun (or pronoun) (➲171.1, 171.3, 171.5, 171.6) or imperfect verb (➲ 171.2, 171.8), and translates as 'want'.

➲ 3.5, 13.6, 19.6, 22.5, 28.4, 41.1, 41.4, 44.2, 55.4, 65.1, 72.3, 73.4, 83.5, 92.8, 94.6, 98.6, 102.6, 105.2, 107.4, 110.5, 119.2, 119.5, 127.2, 139.9. 154.4, 156.6, 160.3, 166.3, 172.2, 174.7, 177.6, 178.3, 181.5, 187.6, 187.7, 190.4, 195.3, 196.5, 203.2, 213.5, 219.2, 257.5

172 to live 3āš عاش

verbal noun: 3ēša عِيشة

	affirmative		negative		
ána	3išt	عِشْت	ma-3íštiš	مَعِشْتِش	perfect
íḥna	3íšna	عِشْنا	ma-3išnāš	مَعِشْناش	
ínta	3išt	عِشْت	ma-3íštiš	مَعِشْتِش	
ínti	3íšti	عِشْتي	ma-3ištīš	مَعِشْتيش	
íntu	3íštu	عِشْتوا	ma-3ištūš	مَعِشْتوش	
húwwa	3āš	عاش	ma-3ášš	مَعاشّ	
híyya	3āšit	عاشِت	ma-3ašítš	مَعاشِتْش	
húmma	3āšu	عاشوا	ma-3ašūš	مَعاشوش	

	affirmative		negative		
ána	a3īš	أعيش	ma-3íšš	مَعيشّ	imperfect
íḥna	ni3īš	نِعيش	ma-n3íšš	مَنْعيشّ	
ínta	ti3īš	تِعيش	ma-t3íšš	مَتْعيشّ	
ínti	ti3īši	تِعيشي	ma-t3išīš	مَتْعيشيش	
íntu	ti3īšu	تِعيشوا	ma-t3išūš	مَتْعيشوش	
húwwa	yi3īš	يِعيش	ma-y3íšš	مَيْعيشّ	
híyya	ti3īš	تِعيش	ma-t3íšš	مَتْعيشّ	
húmma	yi3īšu	يِعيشوا	ma-y3išūš	مَيْعيشوش	

	affirmative		negative		
ána	ba3īš	بَعيش	ma-ba3íšš	مَبَعيشّ	bi-imperfect
íḥna	bin3īš	بِنْعيش	ma-bin3íšš	مَبِنْعيشّ	
ínta	bit3īš	بِتْعيش	ma-bit3íšš	مَبِتْعيشّ	
ínti	bit3īši	بِتْعيشي	ma-bit3išīš	مَبِتْعيشيش	
íntu	bit3īšu	بِتْعيشوا	ma-bit3išūš	مَبِتْعيشوش	
húwwa	biy3īš	بِيْعيش	ma-biy3íšš	مَبِيْعيشّ	
híyya	bit3īš	بِتْعيش	ma-bit3íšš	مَبِتْعيشّ	
húmma	biy3īšu	بِيْعيشوا	ma-biy3išūš	مَبِيْعيشوش	

	affirmative		negative		
ána	ha3īš	هَعيش	miš ha3īš	مِش هَعيش	future
íḥna	han3īš	هَنْعيش	miš han3īš	مِش هَنْعيش	
ínta	hat3īš	هَتْعيش	miš hat3īš	مِش هَتْعيش	
ínti	hat3īši	هَتْعيشي	miš hat3īši	مِش هَتْعيشي	
íntu	hat3īšu	هَتْعيشوا	miš hat3īšu	مِش هَتْعيشوا	
húwwa	hay3īš	هَيْعيش	miš hay3īš	مِش هَيْعيش	
híyya	hat3īš	هَتْعيش	miš hat3īš	مِش هَتْعيش	
húmma	hay3īšu	هَيْعيشوا	miš hay3īšu	مِش هَيْعيشوا	

	affirmative		negative		
ínta	3īš	عيش	ma-t3íšš	مَتْعيشّ	imperative
ínti	3īši	عيشي	ma-t3išīš	مَتْعيشيش	
íntu	3īšu	عيشوا	ma-t3išūš	مَتْعيشوش	

	active		passive		
masculine	3āyiš	عايِش	mit3āš	مِتْعاش	participles
feminine	3áyša	عايْشَة	mit3āš	مِتْعاشَة	
plural	3ayšīn	عايْشين	mit3ašīn	مِتْعاشين	

①

أنا عِشْت في البيْت ده أكْتر مِن تلاتين سنة.

ána 3išt^ə fi -lbēt da ʔáktar min talatīn sána.

I lived in this house for more than thirty years.

②

بحِبّ أعيش على راحْتي. عشان كِده مُش عايِز أتجوِّز.

baḫíbb a3īš 3ála ráḫti. 3ašān kída muš 3āyiz atgáwwiz.

I like to live freely. That's why I don't want to marry.

③

أنا بعيش اليوْم بِيوْمُه. لا بشيل همّ إمْبارِح وَلا بفكّر في بُكْره.

ána ba3īš ilyōm bi-yōmu. la bašīl hamm imbāriḫ wála bafákkar fi búkra.

I live day by day. I do not carry worries from
yesterday, nor do I think about tomorrow.

④

مرام هتْعيش في لنْدن سنتيْن على ما تْخلّص دِراسِتْها هِناك.

marām hat3īš fi lándan sanatēn 3ála ma txállaṣ dirasítha hinā k.

Maram will live in London for two years
until she finishes her studies there.

⑤

عيشوا حَياتْكو بِالطّول و العرْض. إنْتو هتْعيشوا كام مرّة؟

3īšu ḫayátku bi-ṭṭūl w il3árḍ. íntu hat3īšu kām márra?

Live your life to the fullest. How many
lives do you get anyhow?

⑥

أنا عايِش في الجيزة طول عُمْري.

ána 3āyiš fi -lgīza ṭūl 3úmri.

I've lived in Giza my whole life.

⑦

أنا معِشْتِش برّه مصْر أبداً.

ána ma-3íštiš bárra maṣr ábadan.

I've never lived outside of Egypt.

❖ [1h2] **to live; to experience**

- This verb is usually intransitive and means 'live'.
- It can also be transitive when meaning 'experience'. (➲ 172.5)

➲ 10.6, 20.4, 20.6, 37.5, 91.5, 175.7, 172.1, 172.6, 172.7, 178.7

173 to swim 3ām عام

	affirmative		negative		
ána	3umt	عُمْت	ma-3úmtiš	مَعُمْتِش	perfect
íḫna	3úmna	عُمْنا	ma-3umnāš	مَعُمْناش	
ínta	3umt	عُمْت	ma-3úmtiš	مَعُمْتِش	
ínti	3úmti	عُمْتي	ma-3umtīš	مَعُمْتيش	
íntu	3úmtu	عُمْتوا	ma-3umtūš	مَعُمْتوش	
húwwa	3ām	عام	ma-3ámš	مَعامْش	
híyya	3āmit	عامِت	ma-3amítš	مَعامِتْش	
húmma	3āmu	عاموا	ma-3amūš	مَعاموش	

	affirmative		negative		
ána	a3ūm	أعوم	ma-3úmš	مَعومْش	imperfect
íḫna	ni3ūm	نِعوم	ma-n3úmš	مَنْعومْش	
ínta	ti3ūm	تِعوم	ma-t3úmš	مَتْعومْش	
ínti	ti3ūmi	تِعومي	ma-t3umīš	مَتْعوميش	
íntu	ti3ūmu	تِعوموا	ma-t3umūš	مَتْعوموش	
húwwa	yi3ūm	يِعوم	ma-y3úmš	مَيْعومْش	
híyya	ti3ūm	تِعوم	ma-t3úmš	مَتْعومْش	
húmma	yi3ūmu	يِعوموا	ma-y3umūš	مَيْعوموش	

	affirmative		negative		
ána	ba3ūm	بَعوم	ma-ba3úmš	مَبَعومْش	bi-imperfect
íḫna	bin3ūm	بِنْعوم	ma-bin3úmš	مَبِنْعومْش	
ínta	bit3ūm	بِتْعوم	ma-bit3úmš	مَبِتْعومْش	
ínti	bit3ūmi	بِتْعومي	ma-bit3umīš	مَبِتْعوميش	
íntu	bit3ūmu	بِتْعوموا	ma-bit3umūš	مَبِتْعوموش	
húwwa	biy3ūm	بِيْعوم	ma-biy3úmš	مَبِيْعومْش	
híyya	bit3ūm	بِتْعوم	ma-bit3úmš	مَبِتْعومْش	
húmma	biy3ūmu	بِيْعوموا	ma-biy3umūš	مَبِيْعوموش	

	affirmative		negative		
ána	ha3ūm	هَعوم	miš ha3ūm	مِش هَعوم	future
íḫna	han3ūm	هَنْعوم	miš han3ūm	مِش هَنْعوم	
ínta	hat3ūm	هَتْعوم	miš hat3ūm	مِش هَتْعوم	
ínti	hat3ūmi	هَتْعومي	miš hat3ūmi	مِش هَتْعومي	
íntu	hat3ūmu	هَتْعوموا	miš hat3ūmu	مِش هَتْعوموا	
húwwa	hay3ūm	هَيْعوم	miš hay3ūm	مِش هَيْعوم	
híyya	hat3ūm	هَتْعوم	miš hat3ūm	مِش هَتْعوم	
húmma	hay3ūmu	هَيْعوموا	miš hay3ūmu	مِش هَيْعوموا	

	affirmative		negative		
ínta	3ūm	عوم	ma-t3úmš	مَتْعومْش	imperative
ínti	3ūmi	عومي	ma-t3umīš	مَتْعوميش	
íntu	3ūmu	عوموا	ma-t3umūš	مَتْعوموش	

	active		passive		
masculine	3āyim	عايِم	–	–	participles
feminine	3áyma	عايْمَة	–	–	
plural	3aymīn	عايْمين	–	–	

verbal noun: 3ōm عوْم

①

البطّة اللي عالِجْنا جْناحْها نِزْلِت عامِت في البُحيرْة.

ilbátṭa -lli 3alígna gnáḫha nízlit 3āmit fi -lbuḫēra.

The duck, whose wing we fixed,
went to swim in the lake.

②

نِفْسي أعوم في المُحيط. ده حِلْم حَياتي.

nífsi ʔa3ūm fi -lmuḫīṭ. da ḫilmᵊ ḫayāti.

I wish to swim in the ocean.
That's my life dream.

③

سامْيَة بِتْعوم كُلّ يوْم نُصّ ساعة عشان تِحافِظ على لِياقِتْها.

sámya bit3ūm kullᵊ yōm nuṣṣᵊ sā3a 3ašān tiḫāfiẓ 3ála liyaqítha.

Samia swims half an hour every day to keep fit.

④

إنْتَ هتْعوم إزّاي و إنْتَ عيّان كِده؟

ínta hat3ūm izzāy w ínta 3ayyān kída?

How are you going to swim
if you're so sick?

⑤

لمّا تْحِسّوا بِالتّعب عوموا على ضهْركُو شْوَيّة.

lámma tḫíssu bi-ttá3ab 3ūmu 3ála ḍahrúku šwáyya.

If you feel tired, swim on your back for a while.

⑥

إحْنا عايْمين الصُّبْح ٣ ساعات، لمّا خلاص، مِش قادْرين نِتْحرّك.

íḫna 3aymīn iṣṣúbḫ tálat sa3āt, lámma xalāṣ, miš ʔadrīn nitḫárrak.

We swam for three hours this morning, and
now we can't move [i.e. we're exhausted].

⑦

متْعومْش دِلْوَقْتي. الموْج عالي أوي.

ma-t3úmšᵊ dilwáʔti. ilmōg 3āli ʔáwi.

Don't swim now. The waves
are too high.

❖ [1h1] **to swim**

174 to count 3add عدّ

	affirmative		negative		
ána	3addēt	عَدّيْت	ma-3addítš	مَعَدّيْتْش	perfect
íḫna	3addēna	عَدّيْنا	ma-3addināš	مَعَدّيناش	
ínta	3addēt	عَدّيْت	ma-3addítš	مَعَدّيْتْش	
ínti	3addēti	عَدّيْتي	ma-3additīš	مَعَدّيتيش	
íntu	3addētu	عَدّيْتوا	ma-3additūš	مَعَدّيتوش	
húwwa	3add	عَدّ	ma-3áddiš	مَعَدّش	
híyya	3áddit	عَدّت	ma-3addítš	مَعَدّتْش	
húmma	3áddu	عَدّوا	ma-3addūš	مَعَدّوش	
ána	a3ídd	أعِدّ	ma-3íddiš	مَعِدّش	imperfect
íḫna	ni3ídd	نعِدّ	ma-n3íddiš	مَنْعِدّش	
ínta	ti3ídd	تعِدّ	ma-t3íddiš	مَتْعِدّش	
ínti	ti3íddi	تِعِدّي	ma-t3iddīš	مَتْعِدّيش	
íntu	ti3íddu	تِعِدّوا	ma-t3iddūš	مَتْعِدّوش	
húwwa	yi3ídd	يِعِدّ	ma-y3íddiš	مَيْعِدّش	
híyya	ti3ídd	تعِدّ	ma-t3íddiš	مَتْعِدّش	
húmma	yi3íddu	يِعِدّوا	ma-y3iddūš	مَيْعِدّوش	
ána	ba3ídd	بَعِدّ	ma-ba3íddiš	مَبَعِدّش	bi-imperfect
íḫna	bin3ídd	بِنْعِدّ	ma-bin3íddiš	مَبِنْعِدّش	
ínta	bit3ídd	بِتْعِدّ	ma-bit3íddiš	مَبِتْعِدّش	
ínti	bit3íddi	بِتْعِدّي	ma-bit3iddīš	مَبِتْعِدّيش	
íntu	bit3íddu	بِتْعِدّوا	ma-bit3iddūš	مَبِتْعِدّوش	
húwwa	biy3ídd	بِيْعِدّ	ma-biy3íddiš	مَبِيْعِدّش	
híyya	bit3ídd	بِتْعِدّ	ma-bit3íddiš	مَبِتْعِدّش	
húmma	biy3íddu	بِيْعِدّوا	ma-biy3iddūš	مَبِيْعِدّوش	
ána	ha3ídd	هَعِدّ	miš ha3ídd	مِش هَعِدّ	future
íḫna	han3ídd	هَنْعِدّ	miš han3ídd	مِش هَنْعِدّ	
ínta	hat3ídd	هَتْعِدّ	miš hat3ídd	مِش هَتْعِدّ	
ínti	hat3íddi	هَتْعِدّي	miš hat3íddi	مِش هَتْعِدّي	
íntu	hat3íddu	هَتْعِدّوا	miš hat3íddu	مِش هَتْعِدّوا	
húwwa	hay3ídd	هَيْعِدّ	miš hay3ídd	مِش هَيْعِدّ	
híyya	hat3ídd	هَتْعِدّ	miš hat3ídd	مِش هَتْعِدّ	
húmma	hay3íddu	هَيْعِدّوا	miš hay3íddu	مِش هَيْعِدّوا	
ínta	3idd	عِدّ	ma-t3íddiš	مَتْعِدّش	imperative
ínti	3íddi	عِدّي	ma-t3iddīš	مَتْعِدّيش	
íntu	3íddu	عِدّوا	ma-t3iddūš	مَتْعِدّوش	

	active		passive		
masculine	3ādid	عادِد	ma3dūd	مَعْدود	participles
feminine	3ádda	عادّة	ma3dūda	مَعْدودَة	
plural	3addīn	عادّين	ma3dudīn	مَعْدودين	

verbal nouns: 3add عدّ - 3adadān عدَدان

①

المُوَظّف عدّ الفِلوس مرّتيْن قبْل ما يِسْتِلِمْها مِنّي.

ilmuwáẓẓaf 3add ilfilūs marritēn ʔablᵊ ma yistilímha mínni.

The employee counted the money twice
before he received it from me.

②

بفْضل أعِدّ معَ إبْني عشان أعلِّمُه الأرْقام.

báfḍal a3íddᵊ má3a ʔíbni 3ašān a3allímu -lʔarqām.

I keep counting with my son
to teach him numbers.

③

بعِدّ خِرْفان قدّ كِده قبْل ما أنام و برْضُه مِش بِييجيلي نوْم.

ba3íddᵊ xirfān addᵊ kída ʔablᵊ m- anām wi bárḍu miš biyigīli nōm.

I count so many sheep in bed, but I can't fall asleep.

④

الحكم هَيْعِدّ لْحدّ عشرة و بعْديْن يِعْلِن الفايِز.

ilḫákam hay3íddᵊ l-ḫaddᵊ 3ášara wi ba3dēn yí3lin ilfāyiz.

The arbiter will count to ten, and then
he'll announce the winner.

⑤

عِدّوا فْلوسْكو و اِتْأكِّدوا مِن حسابْكو قبْل ما تْسيبوا المحلّ.

3íddu flúsku w itʔakkídu min ḫasábku ʔablᵊ ma tsību -lmaḫáll.

Count your money and check your receipt
before you leave the shop.

⑥

أنا عادِد الحاجات دي قبْل ما أتْحرّك و مُتأكِّد إنّها كامْلة.

ána 3ādid ilḫagāt di ʔablᵊ m- atḫárrak wi mutaʔákkid innáha kámla.

I counted these things before I moved,
and I'm sure they're all there.

⑦

اللي عايْزين ياخْدوا الكورْس كْتير. متْعِدِّش.

ílli 3ayzīn yáxdu -lkursᵊ ktīr. ma-t3íddiš.

There are many people who want to attend
the course. Don't even bother counting.

❖ [1g3] **to count**

175 to cross 3ádda عَدّى

verbal noun: *ta3díyya* تَعْدِيَة

perfect

	affirmative		negative	
ána	3addēt	عَدّيْت	ma-3addítš	مَعَدّيْتْش
íḫna	3addēna	عَدّيْنا	ma-3addināš	مَعَدّيناش
ínta	3addēt	عَدّيْت	ma-3addítš	مَعَدّيْتْش
ínti	3addēti	عَدّيْتي	ma-3additīš	مَعَدّيتيش
íntu	3addētu	عَدّيْتوا	ma-3additūš	مَعَدّيتوش
húwwa	3ádda	عَدّى	ma-3addāš	مَعَدّاش
híyya	3áddit	عَدّت	ma-3addítš	مَعَدّتْش
húmma	3áddu	عَدّوا	ma-3addūš	مَعَدّوش

imperfect

	affirmative		negative	
ána	a3áddi	أَعَدّي	ma-3addīš	مَعَدّيش
íḫna	ni3áddi	نِعَدّي	ma-n3addīš	مَنْعَدّيش
ínta	ti3áddi	تِعَدّي	ma-t3addīš	مَتْعَدّيش
ínti	ti3áddi	تِعَدّي	ma-t3addīš	مَتْعَدّيش
íntu	ti3áddu	تِعَدّوا	ma-t3addūš	مَتْعَدّوش
húwwa	yi3áddi	يِعَدّي	ma-y3addīš	مَيْعَدّيش
híyya	ti3áddi	تِعَدّي	ma-t3addīš	مَتْعَدّيش
húmma	yi3áddu	يِعَدّوا	ma-y3addūš	مَيْعَدّوش

bi-imperfect

	affirmative		negative	
ána	ba3áddi	بَعَدّي	ma-ba3addīš	مَبَعَدّيش
íḫna	bin3áddi	بِنْعَدّي	ma-bin3addīš	مَبِنْعَدّيش
ínta	bit3áddi	بِتْعَدّي	ma-bit3addīš	مَبِتْعَدّيش
ínti	bit3áddi	بِتْعَدّي	ma-bit3addīš	مَبِتْعَدّيش
íntu	bit3áddu	بِتْعَدّوا	ma-bit3addūš	مَبِتْعَدّوش
húwwa	biy3áddi	بِيْعَدّي	ma-biy3addīš	مَبِيْعَدّيش
híyya	bit3áddi	بِتْعَدّي	ma-bit3addīš	مَبِتْعَدّيش
húmma	biy3áddu	بِيْعَدّوا	ma-biy3addūš	مَبِيْعَدّوش

future

	affirmative		negative	
ána	ha3áddi	هَعَدّي	miš ha3áddi	مِش هَعَدّي
íḫna	han3áddi	هَنْعَدّي	miš han3áddi	مِش هَنْعَدّي
ínta	hat3áddi	هَتْعَدّي	miš hat3áddi	مِش هَتْعَدّي
ínti	hat3áddi	هَتْعَدّي	miš hat3áddi	مِش هَتْعَدّي
íntu	hat3áddu	هَتْعَدّوا	miš hat3áddu	مِش هَتْعَدّوا
húwwa	hay3áddi	هَيْعَدّي	miš hay3áddi	مِش هَيْعَدّي
híyya	hat3áddi	هَتْعَدّي	miš hat3áddi	مِش هَتْعَدّي
húmma	hay3áddu	هَيْعَدّوا	miš hay3áddu	مِش هَيْعَدّوا

imperative

	affirmative		negative	
ínta	3áddi	عَدّي	ma-t3addīš	مَتْعَدّيش
ínti	3áddi	عَدّي	ma-t3addīš	مَتْعَدّيش
íntu	3áddu	عَدّوا	ma-t3addūš	مَتْعَدّوش

participles

	active		passive	
masculine	mi3áddi	مِعَدّي	mit3áddi	مِتْعَدّي
feminine	mi3addíyya	مِعَدّيَّة	mit3addíyya	مِتْعَدّيَّة
plural	mi3addiyīn	مِعَدّيين	mit3addiyīn	مِتْعَدّيين

①

خطيبي عدّى عليّا أمْبارِح بِاللّيْل و رُحْنا نِتْمشّى شْوَيّة.

xaṭību 3ádda 3aláyya -mbāriḫ bi-llēl wi rúḫna nitmášša šwáyya.

My fiancé came by yesterday evening
and took me for a walk.

②

لمّا تْعدّي الشّارِع، بُصّ يمْين و شْمال.

lámma t3áddi -ššāri3, buṣṣ[ə] ymīn wi šmāl.

Look left and right when you cross the street.

③

جارْنا بِيْعدّي عليْه حفيدُه كُلّ يوْم يِتْعشّى معاه.

gárna biy3áddi 3alē ḫafīdu kull[ə] yōm yit3ašša ma3ā.

Our neighbor's grandson goes over to
have dinner with him every day.

④

نِسْمة مِش هتْعدّي السّنة دي. هِيَّ مِش حابّة الدِّراسة دي أصْلاً.

nísma miš hat3áddi -ssanādi. híyya miš ḫábba -ddirāsa di ʔáṣlan.

Nesma won't pass this year. She hasn't liked
this field of study from the beginning.

⑤

عدّوا على أهاليكو بِاِسْتِمْرار. إنْتو أكيد بِتِوْحشوهُم.

3áddu 3ála ʔahalīku bi-stimrār. íntu ʔakīd bitiwḫašūhum.

Go by to see your parents often. They miss you for sure.

⑥

لقيْت نفْسي مِعدّية جنْبك، قُلْت أسلِّم.

laʔēt náfsi mi3addíyya gámbak, ʔult asállim.

I happened to be passing by, so I thought I'd say hi.

⑦

لمّا تْشوف حاجة مِش عاجْباك عدّيها ، عشان تِعْرف تِعيش بِسلام.

lámma tšūf ḫāga miš 3agbāk 3addīha, 3ašān tí3raf ti3īš bi-salām.

When you see something you don't like,
just let it go, so you can live in peace.

⑧

متْعِدّيش عليْنا. البيْت كُلُّه عيّان، هنْعدّيك.

ma-t3iddīš 3alēna. ilbēt kúllu 3ayyān, han3iddīk.

Don't come over. The whole house
is sick, and you'll catch it.

❖ [2d] **to cross; to let pass; to go by, come over (to visit)** (على *3ála*)

➲ 14.6, 73.1, 99.3, 145.1, 171.8, 200.1, 257.1

176 to know 3írif عِرِف

	affirmative		negative		
ána	3irift	عِرِفْت	ma-3riftiš	مَعْرِفْتِش	perfect
íḫna	3irífna	عِرِفْنا	ma-3rifnāš	مَعْرِفْناش	
ínta	3irift	عِرِفْت	ma-3ríftiš	مَعْرِفْتِش	
ínti	3irífti	عِرِفْتي	ma-3riftīš	مَعْرِفْتيش	
íntu	3iríftu	عِرِفْتوا	ma-3riftūš	مَعْرِفْتوش	
húwwa	3írif	عِرِف	ma-3rífš	مَعْرِفْش	
híyya	3írfit	عِرْفِت	ma-3irfítš	مَعِرْفِتْش	
húmma	3írfu	عِرْفوا	ma-3irfūš	مَعِرْفوش	
ána	á3raf	أعْرَف	ma-3ráfš	مَعْرَفْش	imperfect
íḫna	ní3raf	نِعْرَف	ma-ni3ráfš	مَنِعْرَفْش	
ínta	tí3raf	تِعْرَف	ma-ti3ráfš	مَتِعْرَفْش	
ínti	ti3ráfi	تِعْرَفي	ma-ti3rafīš	مَتِعْرَفيش	
íntu	ti3ráfu	تِعْرَفوا	ma-ti3rafūš	مَتِعْرَفوش	
húwwa	yí3raf	يِعْرَف	ma-yi3ráfš	مَيِعْرَفْش	
híyya	tí3raf	تِعْرَف	ma-ti3ráfš	مَتِعْرَفْش	
húmma	yi3ráfu	يِعْرَفوا	ma-yi3rafūš	مَيِعْرَفوش	
ána	bá3raf	بَعْرَف	ma-ba3ráfš	مَبَعْرَفْش	bi-imperfect
íḫna	biní3raf	بِنِعْرَف	ma-bni3ráfš	مَبْنِعْرَفْش	
ínta	bití3raf	بِتِعْرَف	ma-bti3ráfš	مَبْتِعْرَفْش	
ínti	biti3ráfi	بِتِعْرَفي	ma-bti3rafīš	مَبْتِعْرَفيش	
íntu	biti3ráfu	بِتِعْرَفوا	ma-bti3rafūš	مَبْتِعْرَفوش	
húwwa	biyí3raf	بِيِعْرَف	ma-byi3ráfš	مَبْيِعْرَفْش	
híyya	bití3raf	بِتِعْرَف	ma-bti3ráfš	مَبْتِعْرَفْش	
húmma	biyi3ráfu	بِيِعْرَفوا	ma-byi3rafūš	مَبْيِعْرَفوش	
ána	há3raf	هَعْرَف	miš há3raf	مِش هَعْرَف	future
íḫna	haní3raf	هَنِعْرَف	miš haní3raf	مِش هَنِعْرَف	
ínta	hatí3raf	هَتِعْرَف	miš hatí3raf	مِش هَتِعْرَف	
ínti	hati3ráfi	هَتِعْرَفي	miš hati3ráfi	مِش هَتِعْرَفي	
íntu	hati3ráfu	هَتِعْرَفوا	miš hati3ráfu	مِش هَتِعْرَفوا	
húwwa	hayí3raf	هَيِعْرَف	miš hayí3raf	مِش هَيِعْرَف	
híyya	hatí3raf	هَتِعْرَف	miš hatí3raf	مِش هَتِعْرَف	
húmma	hayi3ráfu	هَيِعْرَفوا	miš hayi3ráfu	مِش هَيِعْرَفوا	
ínta	í3raf	اِعْرَف	ma-ti3ráfš	مَتِعْرَفْش	imperative
ínti	i3ráfi	اِعْرَفي	ma-ti3rafīš	مَتِعْرَفيش	
íntu	i3ráfu	اِعْرَفوا	ma-ti3rafūš	مَتِعْرَفوش	

	active		passive		
masculine	3ārif	عارِف	ma3rūf	مَعْروف	participles
feminine	3árfa	عارْفَة	ma3rūfa	مَعْروفَة	
plural	3arfīn	عارْفين	ma3rufīn	مَعْروفين	

verbal noun: ma3rífa مَعْرِفة

①

أحْمد و مُنى عِرْفوا بعْض عن طريق أصْدِقائُهم.

áɦmad wi múna 3írfu ba3ḑᵊ 3an ţarī? aşdiqá?hum.

Ahmed and Mona met [lit. knew each other] through their friends.

②

لمّا تِعْرف إزّاي تِكلِّم حدّ كْبير، إبْقى تعالى كلِّمْني.

lámma tí3raf izzāy tikállim ɦaddᵊ kbīr, íb?a ta3āla kallímni.

Come talk to me when you learn how to talk with grown-ups.

③

إيهاب مِش بيِعْرف يِكلِّم بنات. بيِضْرب لخْمة و يِسْكُت.

ihāb miš biyí3raf yikállim banāt. biyíḑrab láxma wi yískut.

Ehab doesn't know how to talk to girls. He gets confused and shuts up.

④

هتِعْرفي تْروحي المِشْوار ده لِوَحْدِك وَلّا أجي معاكي؟

hati3ráfi trūɦi -lmišwār da li-wáɦdik wálla ?ági ma3āki?

Can you go on this trip by yourself, or shall I come with you?

⑤

اِعْرفوا مَواهِبْكو كُوَيِّس عشان تِنْجحوا في إخْتِيار مجال دِراسِتْكو.

i3ráfu mawahíbku kuwáyyis 3ašān tingáɦu fi ixtiyār magāl dirasítku.

Know your talents well to succeed in choosing your field of studies.

⑥

مبعْرِفْش أداري مضايْقِتي مِن حدّ.

ma-ba3ráfš adāri maḑáy?íti min ɦadd.

I can't hide it when I'm angry at someone.

⑦

بطّل تِسْرق مقالاتي. النّاس بقِت تِعْرف تميِّز أُسْلوبي.

báţţal tísra? maqalāti. innās bá?it tí3raf timáyyiz uslūbi.

Stop stealing my articles. People can recognize my style.

❖ [1s4] **to know; to be able to, know how to**

- This verb can be followed by an imperfect verb, meaning 'can', 'could', 'be able to'. (➲ 176.3, 176.4, 176.6, 176.7)

➲ 4.4, 12.4, 48.5, 51.3, 55.2, 56.6, 76.2, 81.3, 83.2, 98.3, 115.3, 120.3, 124.2, 127.3, 167.6, 175.7, 197.2, 199.3, 204.2, 204.4, 207.2, 208.2, 210.6, 235.5, 239.5, 243.5

177 to play 3ázaf عَزَف

perfect

	affirmative		negative	
ána	*3azáft*	عَزَفْت	*ma-3azáftiš*	مَعَزَفْتِش
íḥna	*3azáfna*	عَزَفْنا	*ma-3azafnāš*	مَعَزَفْناش
ínta	*3azáft*	عَزَفْت	*ma-3azáftiš*	مَعَزَفْتِش
ínti	*3azáfti*	عَزَفْتي	*ma-3azaftīš*	مَعَزَفْتيش
íntu	*3azáftu*	عَزَفْتوا	*ma-3azaftūš*	مَعَزَفْتوش
húwwa	*3ázaf*	عَزَف	*ma-3azáfš*	مَعَزَفْش
híyya	*3ázafit*	عَزَفِت	*ma-3azafítš*	مَعَزَفِتْش
húmma	*3ázafu*	عَزَفوا	*ma-3azafūš*	مَعَزَفوش

imperfect

	affirmative		negative	
ána	*á3zif*	أَعْزِف	*ma-3zífš*	مَعْزِفْش
íḥna	*ní3zif*	نِعْزِف	*ma-ni3zífš*	مَنِعْزِفْش
ínta	*tí3zif*	تِعْزِف	*ma-ti3zífš*	مَتِعْزِفْش
ínti	*ti3zífi*	تِعْزِفي	*ma-ti3zifīš*	مَتِعْزِفيش
íntu	*ti3zífu*	تِعْزِفوا	*ma-ti3zifūš*	مَتِعْزِفوش
húwwa	*yí3zif*	يِعْزِف	*ma-yi3zífš*	مَيِعْزِفْش
híyya	*tí3zif*	تِعْزِف	*ma-ti3zífš*	مَتِعْزِفْش
húmma	*yi3zífu*	يِعْزِفوا	*ma-yi3zifūš*	مَيِعْزِفوش

bi-imperfect

	affirmative		negative	
ána	*bá3zif*	بَعْزِف	*ma-ba3zífš*	مَبَعْزِفْش
íḥna	*biní3zif*	بِنِعْزِف	*ma-bni3zífš*	مَبْنِعْزِفْش
ínta	*bití3zif*	بِتِعْزِف	*ma-bti3zífš*	مَبْتِعْزِفْش
ínti	*biti3zífi*	بِتِعْزِفي	*ma-bti3zifīš*	مَبْتِعْزِفيش
íntu	*biti3zífu*	بِتِعْزِفوا	*ma-bti3zifūš*	مَبْتِعْزِفوش
húwwa	*biyí3zif*	بِيِعْزِف	*ma-byi3zífš*	مَبْيِعْزِفْش
híyya	*bití3zif*	بِتِعْزِف	*ma-bti3zífš*	مَبْتِعْزِفْش
húmma	*biyi3zífu*	بِيِعْزِفوا	*ma-byi3zifūš*	مَبْيِعْزِفوش

future

	affirmative		negative	
ána	*há3zif*	هَعْزِف	*miš há3zif*	مِش هَعْزِف
íḥna	*haní3zif*	هَنِعْزِف	*miš haní3zif*	مِش هَنِعْزِف
ínta	*hatí3zif*	هَتِعْزِف	*miš hatí3zif*	مِش هَتِعْزِف
ínti	*hati3zífi*	هَتِعْزِفي	*miš hati3zífi*	مِش هَتِعْزِفي
íntu	*hati3zífu*	هَتِعْزِفوا	*miš hati3zífu*	مِش هَتِعْزِفوا
húwwa	*hayí3zif*	هَيِعْزِف	*miš hayí3zif*	مِش هَيِعْزِف
híyya	*hatí3zif*	هَتِعْزِف	*miš hatí3zif*	مِش هَتِعْزِف
húmma	*hayi3zífu*	هَيِعْزِفوا	*miš hayi3zífu*	مِش هَيِعْزِفوا

imperative

	affirmative		negative	
ínta	*í3zif*	اِعْزِف	*ma-ti3zífš*	مَتِعْزِفْش
ínti	*i3zífi*	اِعْزِفي	*ma-ti3zifīš*	مَتِعْزِفيش
íntu	*i3zífu*	اِعْزِفوا	*ma-ti3zifūš*	مَتِعْزِفوش

participles

	active		passive	
masculine	*3āzif*	عازِف	*ma3zūf*	مَعْزوف
feminine	*3ázfa*	عازْفَة	*ma3zūfa*	مَعْزوفَة
plural	*3azfīn*	عازْفين	*ma3zufīn*	مَعْزوفين

verbal noun: *3azf* عَزْف

①

الفِرْقة إمْبارِح عزفِت شُوَيِّةْ موسيقى تُحْفة.

ilfírʔa -mbāriḫ 3ázafit šuwáyyit musīqa túḫfa.

The band played some great music yesterday.

②

حدّ مِن جيرانّا كُلّ يوْم يِعْزِف عَ الكمان في نفْس المعاد.

ḫaddᵊ min giránna kullᵊ yōm yí3zif 3a -lkamān fi nafs ilmi3ād.

One of our neighbors plays the violin every day at the same time.

③

هاجر بِتِعْزِف عَ الأورْج مِن و هِيَّ صْغيرّة.

hāgar bití3zif 3a -lʔurgᵊ min wi híyya ṣɣayyára.

Hagar has played the keyboard since she was young.

④

خالِد هَيِعْزِف مقْطوعة جميلة اللّيْلة دي.

xālid hayí3zif maqṭū3a gamīla -llilādi.

Khaled will play a beautiful melody tonight.

⑤

اِعْزِف عَ البِيانو. صَوابْعك دي صَوابِع بِيانيسْت.

í3zif 3a -lpiyānu. ṣawáb3ak di ṣawābi3 piyānist.

Play the piano. Those fingers of yours are a pianist's fingers.

⑥

متِعْزِفْش لحْن حزين. عايْزين نِسْمع حاجة مْفرْفِشة.

ma-ti3zífšᵊ laḫnᵊ ḫazīn. 3ayzīn nísma3 ḫāga mfarfíša.

Don't play a sad melody. We'd like to hear a happy one.

❖ [1s2] **to play** (music); **to play** (على *3ála* a musical instrument)

- Notice that this verb is transitive when the object is *not* a musical instrument (➲ 177.1, 177.4, 177.6), but takes the preposition على *3ála* when the object *is* a musical instrument (➲ 177.2, 177.3, 177.5).

178 to move 3ázzil عزّل

verbal nouns: 3izāl عزال - ta3zīl تعزيل

	affirmative		negative		
ána	3azzílt	عَزّلت	ma-3azzíltiš	مَعَزّلتش	perfect
íḥna	3azzílna	عَزّلنا	ma-3azzilnāš	مَعَزّلناش	
ínta	3azzílt	عَزّلت	ma-3azzíltiš	مَعَزّلتش	
ínti	3azzílti	عَزّلتي	ma-3azziltīš	مَعَزّلتيش	
íntu	3azzíltu	عَزّلتوا	ma-3azziltūš	مَعَزّلتوش	
húwwa	3ázzil	عَزّل	ma-3azzílš	مَعَزّلش	
híyya	3azzílit	عَزّلِت	ma-3azzilítš	مَعَزّلِتْش	
húmma	3azzílu	عَزّلوا	ma-3azzilūš	مَعَزّلوش	
ána	a3ázzil	أعَزّل	ma-3azzílš	مَعَزّلش	imperfect
íḥna	ni3ázzil	نِعَزّل	ma-n3azzílš	مَنْعَزّلش	
ínta	ti3ázzil	تِعَزّل	ma-t3azzílš	مَتْعَزّلش	
ínti	ti3azzíli	تِعَزّلي	ma-t3azzilīš	مَتْعَزّليش	
íntu	ti3azzílu	تِعَزّلوا	ma-t3azzilūš	مَتْعَزّلوش	
húwwa	yi3ázzil	يِعَزّل	ma-y3azzílš	مَيْعَزّلش	
híyya	ti3ázzil	تِعَزّل	ma-t3azzílš	مَتْعَزّلش	
húmma	yi3azzílu	يِعَزّلوا	ma-y3azzilūš	مَيْعَزّلوش	
ána	ba3ázzil	بَعَزّل	ma-ba3azzílš	مَبَعَزّلش	bi-imperfect
íḥna	bin3ázzil	بِنْعَزّل	ma-bin3azzílš	مَبِنْعَزّلش	
ínta	bit3ázzil	بِتْعَزّل	ma-bit3azzílš	مَبِتْعَزّلش	
ínti	bit3azzíli	بِتْعَزّلي	ma-bit3azzilīš	مَبِتْعَزّليش	
íntu	bit3azzílu	بِتْعَزّلوا	ma-bit3azzilūš	مَبِتْعَزّلوش	
húwwa	biy3ázzil	بِيْعَزّل	ma-biy3azzílš	مَبِيْعَزّلش	
híyya	bit3ázzil	بِتْعَزّل	ma-bit3azzílš	مَبِتْعَزّلش	
húmma	biy3azzílu	بِيْعَزّلوا	ma-biy3azzilūš	مَبِيْعَزّلوش	
ána	ha3ázzil	هَعَزّل	miš ha3ázzil	مِش هَعَزّل	future
íḥna	han3ázzil	هَنْعَزّل	miš han3ázzil	مِش هَنْعَزّل	
ínta	hat3ázzil	هَتْعَزّل	miš hat3ázzil	مِش هَتْعَزّل	
ínti	hat3azzíli	هَتْعَزّلي	miš hat3azzíli	مِش هَتْعَزّلي	
íntu	hat3azzílu	هَتْعَزّلوا	miš hat3azzílu	مِش هَتْعَزّلوا	
húwwa	hay3ázzil	هَيْعَزّل	miš hay3ázzil	مِش هَيْعَزّل	
híyya	hat3ázzil	هَتْعَزّل	miš hat3ázzil	مِش هَتْعَزّل	
húmma	hay3azzílu	هَيْعَزّلوا	miš hay3azzílu	مِش هَيْعَزّلوا	
ínta	3ázzil	عَزّل	ma-t3azzílš	مَتْعَزّلش	imperative
ínti	3azzíli	عَزّلي	ma-t3azzilīš	مَتْعَزّليش	
íntu	3azzílu	عَزّلوا	ma-t3azzilūš	مَتْعَزّلوش	

	active		passive		
masculine	mi3ázzil	مِعَزّل	mit3ázzil	مِتْعَزّل	participles
feminine	mi3azzíla	مِعَزّلة	mit3azzíla	مِتْعَزّلة	
plural	mi3azzilīn	مِعَزّلين	mit3azzilīn	مِتْعَزّلين	

①

عزِّلْنا الشّقّة دي مِن حَوالي ٣ سِنين.

3azzílna -ššá??a di min ḫawāli tálat sinīn.

We moved into this apartment nearly three years ago.

②

لمّا نْعزِّل مِن هِنا اِبْقى اِعْزِم النّاس في الشّقّة الجِديدة.

lámma n3ázzil min hína ?íb?a -3zim innās fi -ššá??a -lgidīda.

When we move, invite people to our new apartment.

③

بِنْعزِّل الأيّام دي و عنْدي مِلْيوْن حاجة عايْزة تِترْتِّب.

bin3ázzil il?ayyām di wi 3ándi milyōn ḫāga 3áyza titráttib.

We are moving these days, and I have a million things to arrange.

④

مِش هعزِّل مِن هِنا. البيْت ده فيه كُلّ ذِكْرَياتي.

miš ha3ázzil min hína. ilbēt da fī kull[ə] zakrayāti.

I'll never leave this house. It contains all my memories.

⑤

عزِّلوا بقى مِ الحِتّة دي. دي بقِت وِحْشة أوي.

3azzílu bá?a mi -lḫítta di. di bá?it wíḫša ?áwi.

Move away from this neighborhood. It's become so dirty.

⑥

لِسّه مِعزِّلين مِن أُسْبوعيْن، و يادوْب إبْتديْت أخُد عَ الشّقّة الجِديدة.

líssa mi3azzilīn min usbu3ēn, wi yadōb ibtadēt āxud 3a -ššá??a -lgidīda.

We just moved here a couple of weeks ago, and I've just started to get settled into the new apartment.

⑦

لأ، معزِّلْتِش . لِسّه عايِش في نفْس البيْت اللي كْبِرت فيه.

lā, ma-3azzíltiš. líssa 3āyiš fi nafs ilbēt ílli kbírt[ə] fī.

No, I haven't moved. I still live in the same house I grew up in.

❖ [2s1] **to move (to)**

- This verb means 'move' as in 'change residences'. Compare with حرّك *ḫárrak* (➲ 79) and اِتْحرّك *itḫárrak* (➲ 10).

179 to invite 3ázam عَزَم

verbal nouns: 3azm عَزْم - 3uzūma عُزومة

	affirmative		negative		
ána	3azámt	عَزَمْت	ma-3azámtiš	مَعَزَمْتِش	perfect
íḫna	3azámna	عَزَمْنا	ma-3azamnāš	مَعَزَمْناش	
ínta	3azámt	عَزَمْت	ma-3azámtiš	مَعَزَمْتِش	
ínti	3azámti	عَزَمْتي	ma-3azamtīš	مَعَزَمْتيش	
íntu	3azámtu	عَزَمْتوا	ma-3azamtūš	مَعَزَمْتوش	
húwwa	3ázam	عَزَم	ma-3azámš	مَعَزَمْش	
híyya	3ázamit	عَزَمِت	ma-3azamítš	مَعَزَمِتْش	
húmma	3ázamu	عَزَموا	ma-3azamūš	مَعَزَموش	
ána	á3zim	أَعْزِم	ma-3zímš	مَعْزِمْش	imperfect
íḫna	ní3zim	نِعْزِم	ma-ni3zímš	مَنِعْزِمْش	
ínta	tí3zim	تِعْزِم	ma-ti3zímš	مَتِعْزِمْش	
ínti	ti3zími	تِعْزِمي	ma-ti3zimīš	مَتِعْزِميش	
íntu	ti3zímu	تِعْزِموا	ma-ti3zimūš	مَتِعْزِموش	
húwwa	yí3zim	يِعْزِم	ma-yi3zímš	مَيِعْزِمْش	
híyya	tí3zim	تِعْزِم	ma-ti3zímš	مَتِعْزِمْش	
húmma	yi3zímu	يِعْزِموا	ma-yi3zimūš	مَيِعْزِموش	
ána	bá3zim	بَعْزِم	ma-ba3zímš	مَبَعْزِمْش	bi-imperfect
íḫna	biní3zim	بِنِعْزِم	ma-bni3zímš	مَبْنِعْزِمْش	
ínta	bití3zim	بِتِعْزِم	ma-bti3zímš	مَبْتِعْزِمْش	
ínti	biti3zími	بِتِعْزِمي	ma-bti3zimīš	مَبْتِعْزِميش	
íntu	biti3zímu	بِتِعْزِموا	ma-bti3zimūš	مَبْتِعْزِموش	
húwwa	biyí3zim	بِيِعْزِم	ma-byi3zímš	مَبْيِعْزِمْش	
híyya	bití3zim	بِتِعْزِم	ma-bti3zímš	مَبْتِعْزِمْش	
húmma	biyi3zímu	بِيِعْزِموا	ma-byi3zimūš	مَبْيِعْزِموش	
ána	há3zim	هَعْزِم	miš há3zim	مِش هَعْزِم	future
íḫna	haní3zim	هَنِعْزِم	miš haní3zim	مِش هَنِعْزِم	
ínta	hatí3zim	هَتِعْزِم	miš hatí3zim	مِش هَتِعْزِم	
ínti	hati3zími	هَتِعْزِمي	miš hati3zími	مِش هَتِعْزِمي	
íntu	hati3zímu	هَتِعْزِموا	miš hati3zímu	مِش هَتِعْزِموا	
húwwa	hayí3zim	هَيِعْزِم	miš hayí3zim	مِش هَيِعْزِم	
híyya	hatí3zim	هَتِعْزِم	miš hatí3zim	مِش هَتِعْزِم	
húmma	hayi3zímu	هَيِعْزِموا	miš hayi3zímu	مِش هَيِعْزِموا	
ínta	í3zim	اِعْزِم	ma-ti3zímš	مَتِعْزِمْش	imperative
ínti	i3zími	اِعْزِمي	ma-ti3zimīš	مَتِعْزِميش	
íntu	i3zímu	اِعْزِموا	ma-ti3zimūš	مَتِعْزِموش	

	active		passive		
masculine	3āzim	عازِم	ma3zūm	مَعْزوم	participles
feminine	3ázma	عازْمَة	ma3zūma	مَعْزومَة	
plural	3azmīn	عازْمين	ma3zumīn	مَعْزومين	

①

لمّا شريف قابِل سلْمى أوِّل مرّة، عزمْها تِحْضر معاه حفْلة بِاللّيْل.

lámma šarīf ʔābil sálma ʔáwwil márra, 3azámha tíɦḍar ma3ā ɦáfla bi-llēl.

When Sherif first met Salma, he invited her to attend an evening concert with him.

②

بحِبّ أعْزِم النّاس عنْدي. بحِبّ اللّمّة.

baɦíbb á3zim innās 3ándi. baɦíbb illámma.

I like inviting people to my place. I love gatherings.

③

إنْتَ مبِتِعْزِمْش بِقلْب. عُزومِةْ مراكْبية يَعْني.

ínta ma-biti3zímšᵊ bi-ʔálb. 3uzūmit marakbíyya yá3ni.

You're not making a genuine invitation. It's just empty talk.

④

إنْتو مِش هتِعْزِموا أهْل العروسة عنْدُكو وَلّا أيْه؟

íntu miš hati3zímu ʔahl il3arūsa 3andúku wálla ʔē?

Aren't you going to invite the bride's parents over?

⑤

اِعْزِم على عمّك ييجي معانا المصْيَف.

í3zim 3ála 3ámmak yīgi ma3āna -lmáṣyaf.

Invite your uncle to come with us to the beach.

⑥

مُنى دي بِنْت جدعة. لِسّه عازْمة المجْموعة كُلّها عَ الفِطار.

múna di bintᵊ gáda3a. líssa 3ázma -lmagmū3a kulláha 3a -lfiṭār.

Mona is such a generous girl. She just treated the whole group to breakfast.

❖ [1s2] **to invite; to treat** (someone **to** على *3ála*)

- This verb can be followed by an object then an imperfect verb, meaning 'invite (someone) to __'. (➲ 179.1, 179.5)
- It is usually transitive, but can be heard with the preposition على *3ála*, as well. (➲ 179.5)
- If you 'invite' someone, it is assumed you are treating (paying). (➲ 179.6)

➲ 22.7, 109.7, 168.2, 178.2, 179.6

180 to love 3íšiʔ عِشِق

	affirmative		negative		
ána	3išíʔt	عِشِقْت	ma-3šíʔtiš	مَعْشِقْتِش	perfect
íḫna	3išíʔna	عِشِقْنا	ma-3šiʔnāš	مَعْشِقْناش	
ínta	3išíʔt	عِشِقْت	ma-3šíʔtiš	مَعْشِقْتِش	
ínti	3išíʔti	عِشِقْتي	ma-3šiʔtīš	مَعْشِقْتيش	
íntu	3išíʔtu	عِشِقْتوا	ma-3šiʔtūš	مَعْشِقْتوش	
húwwa	3íšiʔ	عِشِق	ma-3šíʔš	مَعْشِقْش	
híyya	3íšʔit	عِشْقِت	ma-3išʔítš	مَعِشْقِتْش	
húmma	3íšʔu	عِشْقوا	ma-3išʔūš	مَعِشْقوش	
ána	á3šaʔ	أَعْشَق	ma-3šáʔš	مَعْشَقْش	imperfect
íḫna	ní3šaʔ	نِعْشَق	ma-ni3šáʔš	مَنِعْشَقْش	
ínta	tí3šaʔ	تِعْشَق	ma-ti3šáʔš	مَتِعْشَقْش	
ínti	ti3šáʔi	تِعْشَقي	ma-ti3šaʔīš	مَتِعْشَقيش	
íntu	ti3šáʔu	تِعْشَقوا	ma-ti3šaʔūš	مَتِعْشَقوش	
húwwa	yí3šaʔ	يِعْشَق	ma-yi3šáʔš	مَيِعْشَقْش	
híyya	tí3šaʔ	تِعْشَق	ma-ti3šáʔš	مَتِعْشَقْش	
húmma	yi3šáʔu	يِعْشَقوا	ma-yi3šaʔūš	مَيِعْشَقوش	
ána	bá3šaʔ	بَعْشَق	ma-ba3šáʔš	مَبَعْشَقْش	bi-imperfect
íḫna	biní3šaʔ	بِنِعْشَق	ma-bni3šáʔš	مَبْنِعْشَقْش	
ínta	bití3šaʔ	بِتِعْشَق	ma-bti3šáʔš	مَبْتِعْشَقْش	
ínti	biti3šáʔi	بِتِعْشَقي	ma-bti3šaʔīš	مَبْتِعْشَقيش	
íntu	biti3šáʔu	بِتِعْشَقوا	ma-bti3šaʔūš	مَبْتِعْشَقوش	
húwwa	biyí3šaʔ	بِيِعْشَق	ma-byi3šáʔš	مَبْيِعْشَقْش	
híyya	bití3šaʔ	بِتِعْشَق	ma-bti3šáʔš	مَبْتِعْشَقْش	
húmma	biyi3šáʔu	بِيِعْشَقوا	ma-byi3šaʔūš	مَبْيِعْشَقوش	
ána	há3šaʔ	هَعْشَق	miš há3šaʔ	مِش هَعْشَق	future
íḫna	haní3šaʔ	هَنِعْشَق	miš haní3šaʔ	مِش هَنِعْشَق	
ínta	hatí3šaʔ	هَتِعْشَق	miš hatí3šaʔ	مِش هَتِعْشَق	
ínti	hati3šáʔi	هَتِعْشَقي	miš hati3šáʔi	مِش هَتِعْشَقي	
íntu	hati3šáʔu	هَتِعْشَقوا	miš hati3šáʔu	مِش هَتِعْشَقوا	
húwwa	hayí3šaʔ	هَيِعْشَق	miš hayí3šaʔ	مِش هَيِعْشَق	
híyya	hatí3šaʔ	هَتِعْشَق	miš hatí3šaʔ	مِش هَتِعْشَق	
húmma	hayi3šáʔu	هَيِعْشَقوا	miš hayi3šáʔu	مِش هَيِعْشَقوا	
ínta	í3šaʔ	اِعْشَق	ma-ti3šáʔš	مَتِعْشَقْش	imperative
ínti	i3šáʔi	اِعْشَقي	ma-ti3šaʔīš	مَتِعْشَقيش	
íntu	i3šáʔu	اِعْشَقوا	ma-ti3šaʔūš	مَتِعْشَقوش	

	active		passive		
masculine	3āšiʔ	عاشِق	ma3šūʔ	مَعْشوق	participles
feminine	3ášʔa	عاشْقَة	ma3šūʔa	مَعْشوقَة	
plural	3ašʔīn	عاشْقين	ma3šuʔīn	مَعْشوقين	

verbal noun: 3íšʔ عِشْق

①

عِشِقْت التّصْوير الفوتوغْرافي مِن زمان. و حِلْمي أبْقى مُصوِّرة كْبيرة.

3iší?t ittaṣwīr ilfutuɣrāfi min zamān. wi ḫílmi ?áb?a muṣawwíra kbīra.

I've always loved photography. My dream is to become a famous photographer.

②

أنا احْترْت في السِّتّات. أعْشق البيْضا وَلّا السّمْرا، الذّكية وَلّا المرِحة؟

ána -ḫtártᵊ fi -ssittāt. á3ša? ilbēḍa wálla -ssámra, izzakíyya wálla -lmáriḫa?

I'm puzzled by women. Should I love blonds or brunettes, smart ones or funny ones?

③

أنا بعْشق البحْر، هِيَّ واحْدة مِن أجْمل أغاني نجاةْ.

ána bá3ša? ilbáḫr, híyya wáḫda min ágmal aɣāni nagāt.

I Love the Sea is one of the most beautiful songs by Nagat.

④

لَوْ خيرّوني مِلْيوْن مرّة، هعْشقِك إنْتي كُلّ مرّة.

law xayyarūni milyōn márra, ha3šá?ik ínti kullᵊ márra.

If I were to choose a million times, it would be you. I loved you every time.

⑤

المثل بِيْقول: إنّ عْشِقْت أعْشق قمر.

ilmásal biy?ūl: innᵊ 3ší?t á3ša? ?ámar.

A proverb says: Want to love? Love the moon.

⑥

أنا عاشِق كُلّ حِتّة في البلد دي.

ána 3āši? kullᵊ ḫítta fi -lbálad di.

I'm in love with every inch of this country.

⑦

محمّد معْشِقْش حدّ زيّ خديجة زوجْتُه الأولى.

maḫámmad ma-3ší?šᵊ ḫaddᵊ zayyᵊ xadīga zúgtu -l?ūla.

Mohamed never loved anyone like his first wife, Khadija.

❖ [1s4] **to love** (passionately)

- Compare with حبّ *ḫabb.* (➲ 78)

181 to do 3ámal عَمَل

	affirmative		negative		
ána	3amált	عَمَلْت	ma-3amáltiš	مَعَمَلْتِش	perfect
íḥna	3amálna	عَمَلْنا	ma-3amalnāš	مَعَمَلْناش	
ínta	3amált	عَمَلْت	ma-3amáltiš	مَعَمَلْتِش	
ínti	3amálti	عَمَلْتي	ma-3amaltīš	مَعَمَلْتيش	
íntu	3amáltu	عَمَلْتوا	ma-3amaltūš	مَعَمَلْتوش	
húwwa	3ámal	عَمَل	ma-3amálš	مَعَمَلْش	
híyya	3ámalit	عَمَلِت	ma-3amalítš	مَعَمَلِتْش	
húmma	3ámalu	عَمَلوا	ma-3amalūš	مَعَمَلوش	

	affirmative		negative		
ána	á3mil	أعْمِل	ma-3mílš	مَعْمِلْش	imperfect
íḥna	ní3mil	نِعْمِل	ma-ni3mílš	مَنِعْمِلْش	
ínta	tí3mil	تِعْمِل	ma-ti3mílš	مَتِعْمِلْش	
ínti	ti3míli	تِعْمِلي	ma-ti3milīš	مَتِعْمِليش	
íntu	ti3mílu	تِعْمِلوا	ma-ti3milūš	مَتِعْمِلوش	
húwwa	yí3mil	يِعْمِل	ma-yi3mílš	مَيِعْمِلْش	
híyya	tí3mil	تِعْمِل	ma-ti3mílš	مَتِعْمِلْش	
húmma	yi3mílu	يِعْمِلوا	ma-yi3milūš	مَيِعْمِلوش	

	affirmative		negative		
ána	bá3mil	بَعْمِل	ma-ba3mílš	مَبَعْمِلْش	bi-imperfect
íḥna	biní3mil	بِنِعْمِل	ma-bni3mílš	مَبْنِعْمِلْش	
ínta	bití3mil	بِتِعْمِل	ma-bti3mílš	مَبْتِعْمِلْش	
ínti	biti3míli	بِتِعْمِلي	ma-bti3milīš	مَبْتِعْمِليش	
íntu	biti3mílu	بِتِعْمِلوا	ma-bti3milūš	مَبْتِعْمِلوش	
húwwa	biyí3mil	بِيِعْمِل	ma-byi3mílš	مَبْيِعْمِلْش	
híyya	bití3mil	بِتِعْمِل	ma-bti3mílš	مَبْتِعْمِلْش	
húmma	biyi3mílu	بِيِعْمِلوا	ma-byi3milūš	مَبْيِعْمِلوش	

	affirmative		negative		
ána	há3mil	هَعْمِل	miš há3mil	مِش هَعْمِل	future
íḥna	haní3mil	هَنِعْمِل	miš haní3mil	مِش هَنِعْمِل	
ínta	hatí3mil	هَتِعْمِل	miš hatí3mil	مِش هَتِعْمِل	
ínti	hati3míli	هَتِعْمِلي	miš hati3míli	مِش هَتِعْمِلي	
íntu	hati3mílu	هَتِعْمِلوا	miš hati3mílu	مِش هَتِعْمِلوا	
húwwa	hayí3mil	هَيِعْمِل	miš hayí3mil	مِش هَيِعْمِل	
híyya	hatí3mil	هَتِعْمِل	miš hatí3mil	مِش هَتِعْمِل	
húmma	hayi3mílu	هَيِعْمِلوا	miš hayi3mílu	مِش هَيِعْمِلوا	

	affirmative		negative		
ínta	í3mil	اِعْمِل	ma-ti3mílš	مَتِعْمِلْش	imperative
ínti	i3míli	اِعْمِلي	ma-ti3milīš	مَتِعْمِليش	
íntu	i3mílu	اِعْمِلوا	ma-ti3milūš	مَتِعْمِلوش	

	active		passive		
masculine	3āmil	عامِل	ma3mūl	مَعْمول	participles
feminine	3ámla	عامْلَة	ma3mūla	مَعْمولَة	
plural	3amlīn	عامْلين	ma3mulīn	مَعْمولين	

verbal noun: 3amāyil عمايل - 3ámal عَمَل

①

عملْت إمْبارِح رُزّ بِلبن تُحْفة.

3amált imbāriḥ ruzzᵊ bi-lában túḥfa.

I made wonderful rice pudding yesterday.

②

عايْزة أعْمِل فرحي في أفْخم فُنْدُق في البلد.

3áyza ʔá3mil fáraḥi f áfxam fúnduʔ fi -lbálad.

I want my wedding to be in the most luxurious hotel in the country.

③

حازِم و هُوَّ صْغيرّ كان بِيِعْمِل حركات كوميدية أوي.

ḥāzim wi húwwa ṣɣáyyar kān biyí3mil ḥarakāt kumidíyya ʔáwi.

Hazem would do lots of funny things when he was young.

④

لمّا نوسة هتِنْجح، مامِتْها هتِعْمِلْها حفْلة كْبيرة.

lámma nūsa hatíngaḥ, mamítha hati3mílha ḥáfla kbīra.

When Nousa succeeds this year, her mother will have a big party for her.

⑤

اِعْمِل اللي عليْك و سيب النّتيجة على ربِّنا.

í3mil ílli 3alēk wi sīb innatīga 3ála rabbína.

Do what you have to, and leave the result to God.

⑥

شِهاب عامِل حِتِّةْ مُفاجْأة. خطيبْتُه هتِفْرح أكيد.

šihāb 3āmil ḥíttit mufágʔa. xaṭíbtu hatífraḥ akīd.

Shehab set up a great surprise. His fiancée is sure to be happy.

⑦

معملْتيش الواجِب ليْه؟

ma-3amaltīš ilwāgib lē?

Why didn't you do the homework?

❖ [1s2] **to do; to make**

➲ 12.4, 14.7, 19.6, 22.4, 33.2, 46.1, 46.7, 46.7, 47.3, 56.6, 61.5, 61.6, 62.2, 64.1, 67.2, 68.8, 69.5, 76.5, 85.5, 87.3, 89.1, 89.4, 90.2, 98.3, 99.5, 116.3, 120.3, 133.1, 144.5, 145.6, 149.1, 150.4, 153.4, 156.2, 167.5, 169.1, 181.6, 182.2, 191.1, 192.1, 205.2, 208.1, 210.3, 228.1, 232.1, 242.1, 245.2, 246.1, 250.1, 255.6, 259.4, 264.2

182 to weep 3áyyat عَيَّط

	affirmative		negative		
ána	3ayyáṭt	عَيَّطْت	ma-3ayyáṭtiš	مَعَيَّطْتِش	**perfect**
íḥna	3ayyáṭna	عَيَّطْنا	ma-3ayyaṭnāš	مَعَيَّطْناش	
ínta	3ayyáṭt	عَيَّطْت	ma-3ayyáṭtiš	مَعَيَّطْتِش	
ínti	3ayyáṭti	عَيَّطْتي	ma-3ayyaṭtīš	مَعَيَّطْتيش	
íntu	3ayyáṭtu	عَيَّطْتوا	ma-3ayyaṭtūš	مَعَيَّطْتوش	
húwwa	3áyyaṭ	عَيَّط	ma-3ayyáṭš	مَعَيَّطْش	
híyya	3ayyáṭit	عَيَّطِت	ma-3ayyaṭítš	مَعَيَّطِتْش	
húmma	3ayyáṭu	عَيَّطوا	ma-3ayyaṭūš	مَعَيَّطوش	
ána	a3áyyaṭ	أعَيَّط	ma-3ayyáṭš	مَعَيَّطْش	**imperfect**
íḥna	ni3áyyaṭ	نِعَيَّط	ma-n3ayyáṭš	مَنْعَيَّطْش	
ínta	ti3áyyaṭ	تِعَيَّط	ma-t3ayyáṭš	مَتْعَيَّطْش	
ínti	ti3ayyáṭi	تِعَيَّطي	ma-t3ayyaṭīš	مَتْعَيَّطيش	
íntu	ti3ayyáṭu	تِعَيَّطوا	ma-t3ayyaṭūš	مَتْعَيَّطوش	
húwwa	yi3áyyaṭ	يِعَيَّط	ma-y3ayyáṭš	مَيْعَيَّطْش	
híyya	ti3áyyaṭ	تِعَيَّط	ma-t3ayyáṭš	مَتْعَيَّطْش	
húmma	yi3ayyáṭu	يِعَيَّطوا	ma-y3ayyaṭūš	مَيْعَيَّطوش	
ána	ba3áyyaṭ	بَعَيَّط	ma-ba3ayyáṭš	مَبَعَيَّطْش	**bi-imperfect**
íḥna	bin3áyyaṭ	بِنْعَيَّط	ma-bin3ayyáṭš	مَبِنْعَيَّطْش	
ínta	bit3áyyaṭ	بِتْعَيَّط	ma-bit3ayyáṭš	مَبِتْعَيَّطْش	
ínti	bit3ayyáṭi	بِتْعَيَّطي	ma-bit3ayyaṭīš	مَبِتْعَيَّطيش	
íntu	bit3ayyáṭu	بِتْعَيَّطوا	ma-bit3ayyaṭūš	مَبِتْعَيَّطوش	
húwwa	biy3áyyaṭ	بِيْعَيَّط	ma-biy3ayyáṭš	مَبِيْعَيَّطْش	
híyya	bit3áyyaṭ	بِتْعَيَّط	ma-bit3ayyáṭš	مَبِتْعَيَّطْش	
húmma	biy3ayyáṭu	بِيْعَيَّطوا	ma-biy3ayyaṭūš	مَبِيْعَيَّطوش	
ána	ha3áyyaṭ	هَعَيَّط	miš ha3áyyaṭ	مِش هَعَيَّط	**future**
íḥna	han3áyyaṭ	هَنْعَيَّط	miš han3áyyaṭ	مِش هَنْعَيَّط	
ínta	hat3áyyaṭ	هَتْعَيَّط	miš hat3áyyaṭ	مِش هَتْعَيَّط	
ínti	hat3ayyáṭi	هَتْعَيَّطي	miš hat3ayyáṭi	مِش هَتْعَيَّطي	
íntu	hat3ayyáṭu	هَتْعَيَّطوا	miš hat3ayyáṭu	مِش هَتْعَيَّطوا	
húwwa	hay3áyyaṭ	هَيْعَيَّط	miš hay3áyyaṭ	مِش هَيْعَيَّط	
híyya	hat3áyyaṭ	هَتْعَيَّط	miš hat3áyyaṭ	مِش هَتْعَيَّط	
húmma	hay3ayyáṭu	هَيْعَيَّطوا	miš hay3ayyáṭu	مِش هَيْعَيَّطوا	
ínta	3áyyaṭ	عَيَّط	ma-t3ayyáṭš	مَتْعَيَّطْش	**imperative**
ínti	3ayyáṭi	عَيَّطي	ma-t3ayyaṭīš	مَتْعَيَّطيش	
íntu	3ayyáṭu	عَيَّطوا	ma-t3ayyaṭūš	مَتْعَيَّطوش	

	active		passive		
masculine	mi3áyyaṭ	مِعَيَّط	mit3áyyaṭ	مِتْعَيَّط	**participles**
feminine	mi3ayyáṭa	مِعَيَّطَة	–	–	
plural	mi3ayyaṭīn	مِعَيَّطين	–	–	

verbal noun: 3iyāṭ عِياط

①

عيّطْت كِتير قُدّام الفيلْم الهِنْدي إمْبارِح.

3ayyáṭtᵊ ktīr ʔuddām ilfílm ilhíndi -mbāriḥ.

I cried a lot while watching that Indian movie yesterday.

②

دايْماً أعيّط و أنا بعْمِل البصل.

dáyman a3áyyaṭ w ána bá3mil ilbáṣal.

I always cry while cutting onions.

③

أمينة دايْماً بِتْعيّط في الأفْراح.

amīna dáyman bit3áyyaṭ fi -lʔafrāḥ.

Amina always cries at weddings.

④

هِيَّ مُتَوَقّعة إنّ الحُقْنة هتِوْجعْها و هتْعيّط.

híyya mutawaqqá3a ʔinn ilḥúʔna hatiwgá3ha wi hat3áyyaṭ.

She's expecting the injection to hurt and that she'll cry.

⑤

عيّط لَوْ عايِز. العِياط مِش لِلبنات بسّ.

3áyyaṭ law 3āyiz. il3iyāṭ miš li-lbanāt bass.

Cry if you want. Crying isn't just for girls.

⑥

بحاوِل معيّطْش لمّا أتْضايِق بسّ مِش بعْرف أمْسك نفْسي.

baḥāwil ma-3ayyáṭšᵊ lámm- atḍāyiʔ bassᵊ miš bá3raf ámsak náfsi.

I try not to cry when I'm upset, but I can't help it.

❖ [2s2] **to weep, cry** (**over** على *3ála*)

- As this verb requires a preposition, the passive participle is invariable. For example, مِتْعيّط عليْها *mit3áyyaṭ 3alēha* '(she is being) cried over'. It is, however, very rarely used.

➲ 100.9, 155.2

183 to get sick 3íyi عيي

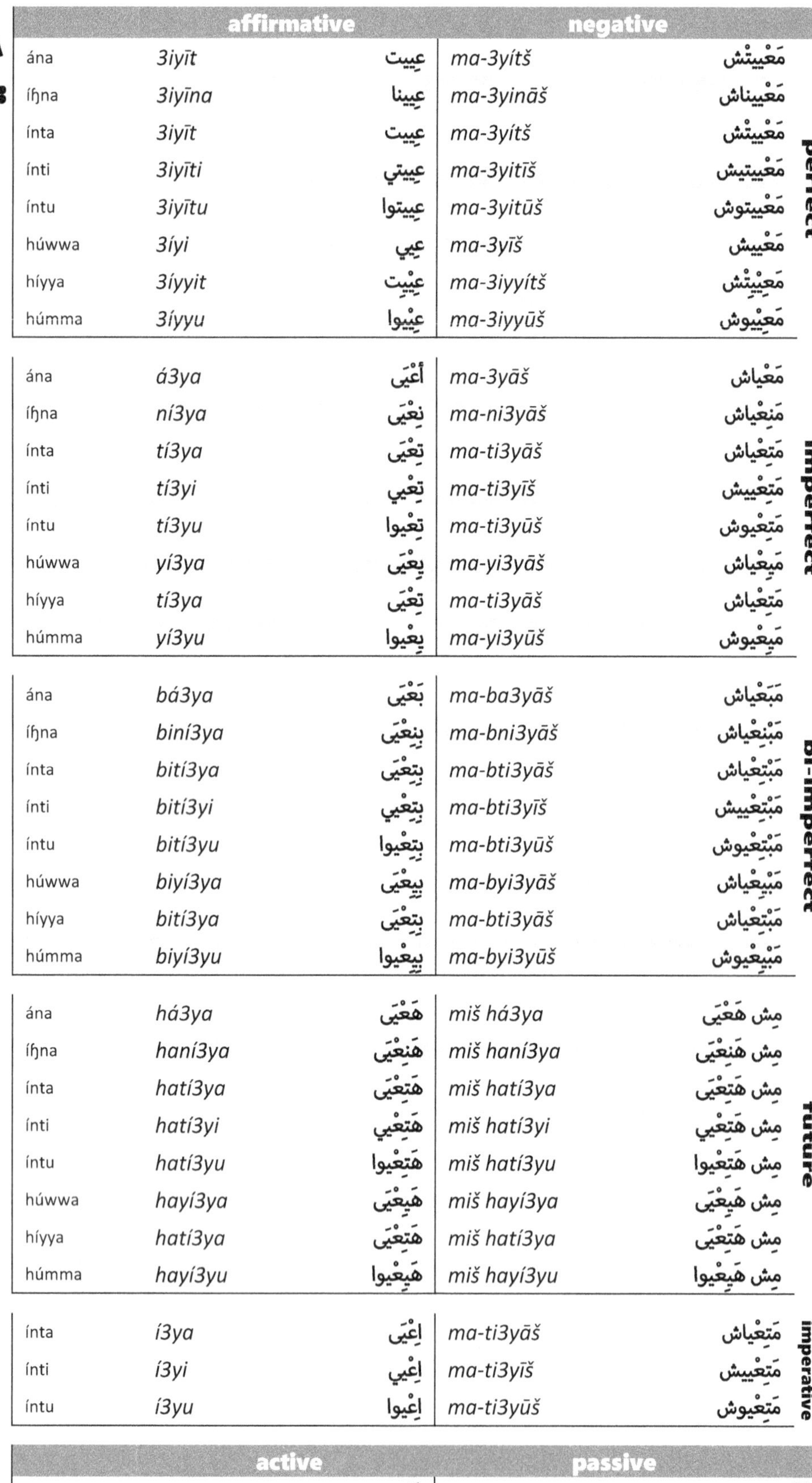

	affirmative		negative		
ána	3iyīt	عييت	ma-3yítš	معييتش	perfect
íḫna	3iyīna	عيينا	ma-3yināš	معييناش	
ínta	3iyīt	عييت	ma-3yítš	معييتش	
ínti	3iyīti	عييتي	ma-3yitīš	معييتيش	
íntu	3iyītu	عييتوا	ma-3yitūš	معييتوش	
húwwa	3íyi	عيي	ma-3yīš	معييش	
híyya	3íyyit	عيّيت	ma-3iyyítš	معيّيتش	
húmma	3íyyu	عيّوا	ma-3iyyūš	معيّوش	
ána	á3ya	أعيَى	ma-3yāš	معياش	imperfect
íḫna	ní3ya	نعيَى	ma-ni3yāš	منعياش	
ínta	tí3ya	تعيَى	ma-ti3yāš	متعياش	
ínti	tí3yi	تعيي	ma-ti3yīš	متعييش	
íntu	tí3yu	تعيوا	ma-ti3yūš	متعيوش	
húwwa	yí3ya	يعيَى	ma-yi3yāš	ميعياش	
híyya	tí3ya	تعيَى	ma-ti3yāš	متعياش	
húmma	yí3yu	يعيوا	ma-yi3yūš	ميعيوش	
ána	bá3ya	بعيَى	ma-ba3yāš	مبعياش	bi-imperfect
íḫna	biní3ya	بنعيَى	ma-bni3yāš	مبنعياش	
ínta	bití3ya	بتعيَى	ma-bti3yāš	مبتعياش	
ínti	bití3yi	بتعيي	ma-bti3yīš	مبتعييش	
íntu	bití3yu	بتعيوا	ma-bti3yūš	مبتعيوش	
húwwa	biyí3ya	بيعيَى	ma-byi3yāš	مبيعياش	
híyya	bití3ya	بتعيَى	ma-bti3yāš	مبتعياش	
húmma	biyí3yu	بيعيوا	ma-byi3yūš	مبيعيوش	
ána	há3ya	هعيَى	miš há3ya	مش هعيَى	future
íḫna	haní3ya	هنعيَى	miš haní3ya	مش هنعيَى	
ínta	hatí3ya	هتعيَى	miš hatí3ya	مش هتعيَى	
ínti	hatí3yi	هتعيي	miš hatí3yi	مش هتعيي	
íntu	hatí3yu	هتعيوا	miš hatí3yu	مش هتعيوا	
húwwa	hayí3ya	هيعيَى	miš hayí3ya	مش هيعيَى	
híyya	hatí3ya	هتعيَى	miš hatí3ya	مش هتعيَى	
húmma	hayí3yu	هيعيوا	miš hayí3yu	مش هيعيوا	
ínta	í3ya	اِعيَى	ma-ti3yāš	متعياش	imperative
ínti	í3yi	اِعيي	ma-ti3yīš	متعييش	
íntu	í3yu	اِعيوا	ma-ti3yūš	متعيوش	

	active		passive		
masculine	3ayyān	عيّان	–	–	participles
feminine	3ayyāna	عيّانة	–	–	
plural	3ayyanīn	عيّانين	–	–	

verbal noun: 3áya عيا

①

إبْني عِيي جامِد لمّا نام قُدّام التّكْييف.

íbni 3íyi gāmid lámma nām ʔuddām ittakyīf.

My son got sick when he slept
in front of the air conditioner.

②

أُمّي مناعِتْها ضعيفة و دايْماً تِعْيى.

úmmi mana3ítha ḍa3īfa wi dáyman tí3ya.

My mother's immune system is
weak. She always gets sick.

③

خالِتْها بْتِعْيي مِن أيّ تيّار هَوا.

xalítha btí3ya min ayyᵊ tayyār háwa.

Her aunt gets sick from
any air current.

④

اِلْعب رِياضة، مُش هتِعْيي.

íl3ab riyāḍa, muš hatí3ya.

Exercise, and you
won't get sick.

⑤

متِعْياش تاني أرْجوك. إنْتَ لِسّه قايِم مِ العَيا.

ma-ti3yāš tāni ʔaragūk. ínta líssa ʔāyim mi -l3áya.

Please, don't get sick again. You've
just gotten over being sick.

⑥

مبعْياش كِتير، بسّ لمّا بعْيى العَيا بِيْكون جامِد أوي.

ma-ba3yāš kitīr, bassᵊ lámma bá3ya, il3áya biykūn gāmid áwi.

I don't get sick often, but when
I do, it's pretty severe.

❖ [1d4] **to get sick, become ill**

➲ 214.2

184 to wash ɣásal غَسَل

	affirmative		negative		
ána	ɣasált	غَسَلْت	ma-ɣasáltiš	مَغَسَلْتِش	**perfect**
íḫna	ɣasálna	غَسَلْنا	ma-ɣasalnāš	مَغَسَلْناش	
ínta	ɣasált	غَسَلْت	ma-ɣasáltiš	مَغَسَلْتِش	
ínti	ɣasálti	غَسَلْتي	ma-ɣasaltīš	مَغَسَلْتيش	
íntu	ɣasáltu	غَسَلْتوا	ma-ɣasaltūš	مَغَسَلْتوش	
húwwa	ɣásal	غَسَل	ma-ɣasálš	مَغَسَلْش	
híyya	ɣásalit	غَسَلِت	ma-ɣasalítš	مَغَسَلِتْش	
húmma	ɣásalu	غَسَلوا	ma-ɣasalūš	مَغَسَلوش	
ána	áɣsil	أغْسِل	ma-ɣsílš	مَغْسِلْش	**imperfect**
íḫna	níɣsil	نِغْسِل	ma-niɣsílš	مَنِغْسِلْش	
ínta	tíɣsil	تِغْسِل	ma-tiɣsílš	مَتِغْسِلْش	
ínti	tiɣsíli	تِغْسِلي	ma-tiɣsilīš	مَتِغْسِليش	
íntu	tiɣsílu	تِغْسِلوا	ma-tiɣsilūš	مَتِغْسِلوش	
húwwa	yíɣsil	يِغْسِل	ma-yiɣsílš	مَيِغْسِلْش	
híyya	tíɣsil	تِغْسِل	ma-tiɣsílš	مَتِغْسِلْش	
húmma	yiɣsílu	يِغْسِلوا	ma-yiɣsilūš	مَيِغْسِلوش	
ána	báɣsil	بَغْسِل	ma-baɣsílš	مَبَغْسِلْش	**bi-imperfect**
íḫna	biníɣsil	بِنِغْسِل	ma-bniɣsílš	مَبْنِغْسِلْش	
ínta	bitíɣsil	بِتِغْسِل	ma-btiɣsílš	مَبْتِغْسِلْش	
ínti	bitiɣsíli	بِتِغْسِلي	ma-btiɣsilīš	مَبْتِغْسِليش	
íntu	bitiɣsílu	بِتِغْسِلوا	ma-btiɣsilūš	مَبْتِغْسِلوش	
húwwa	biyíɣsil	بِيِغْسِل	ma-byiɣsílš	مَبْيِغْسِلْش	
híyya	bitíɣsil	بِتِغْسِل	ma-btiɣsílš	مَبْتِغْسِلْش	
húmma	biyiɣsílu	بِيِغْسِلوا	ma-byiɣsilūš	مَبْيِغْسِلوش	
ána	háɣsil	هَغْسِل	miš háɣsil	مِش هَغْسِل	**future**
íḫna	haníɣsil	هَنِغْسِل	miš haníɣsil	مِش هَنِغْسِل	
ínta	hatíɣsil	هَتِغْسِل	miš hatíɣsil	مِش هَتِغْسِل	
ínti	hatiɣsíli	هَتِغْسِلي	miš hatiɣsíli	مِش هَتِغْسِلي	
íntu	hatiɣsílu	هَتِغْسِلوا	miš hatiɣsílu	مِش هَتِغْسِلوا	
húwwa	hayíɣsil	هَيِغْسِل	miš hayíɣsil	مِش هَيِغْسِل	
híyya	hatíɣsil	هَتِغْسِل	miš hatíɣsil	مِش هَتِغْسِل	
húmma	hayiɣsílu	هَيِغْسِلوا	miš hayiɣsílu	مِش هَيِغْسِلوا	
ínta	íɣsil	اِغْسِل	ma-tiɣsílš	مَتِغْسِلْش	**imperative**
ínti	iɣsíli	اِغْسِلي	ma-tiɣsilīš	مَتِغْسِليش	
íntu	iɣsílu	اِغْسِلوا	ma-tiɣsilūš	مَتِغْسِلوش	

	active		passive		
masculine	ɣāsil	غاسِل	maɣsūl	مَغْسول	**participles**
feminine	ɣásla	غاسْلَة	maɣsūla	مَغْسولَة	
plural	ɣaslīn	غاسْلين	maɣsulīn	مَغْسولين	

verbal nouns: ɣasīl غَسيل - ɣasl غَسْل

①

غسلْت سْنانك قبْل ما تْنام؟

ɣasált^ə snānak ʔabl^ə ma tnām?

Did you brush your teeth
before you went to bed?

②

لازِم تِغْسِل عربيتك. مِش نضيفة خالِص.

lāzim tíɣsil 3arabītak. miš naḍīfa xāliṣ.

You should wash your car.
It's not clean at all.

③

نادِر بيِغْسِل كِلى كُلّ أُسْبوع.

nādir biyíɣsil kíla kull^ə ʔusbū3.

Nader undergoes dialysis treatments
[lit. washes kidney] every week.

④

هتِغْسِلي شعْرِك وَلّا هتْقُصّية بسّ؟

hatiɣsíli šá3rik wálla hatʔuṣṣī bass?

(hairdresser:) Would you like your
hair washed or just cut?

⑤

اِغْسِلوا الهُدوم دي و بعْديْن اِغْسِلوا المَواعين.

aɣsílu -lhudūm di wi ba3dēn iɣsílu -lmawa3īn.

Do the laundry, then wash the dishes.

⑥

متِغْسِليش وِشِّك بِالصّابون ده. هَيْنشِّف بشْرِتِك.

ma-tiɣsilīš wíššik bi-ṣṣabūn da. haynáššif bašrátik.

Don't use this soap on your face.
It'll make your skin dry.

❖ [1s2] **to wash**

- This verb essentially means 'wash', but can translate numerous ways idiomatically in English. (➲ 184.1, 184.3, 184.5, 184.6)

➲ 154.2

185 to sing ɣánna غنّى

	affirmative		negative		
ána	ɣannēt	غنّيت	ma-ɣannítš	مغنّيتش	perfect
íḥna	ɣannēna	غنّينا	ma-ɣanninā́š	مغنّيناش	
ínta	ɣannēt	غنّيت	ma-ɣannítš	مغنّيتش	
ínti	ɣannēti	غنّيتي	ma-ɣannitī́š	مغنّيتيش	
íntu	ɣannētu	غنّيتوا	ma-ɣannitū́š	مغنّيتوش	
húwwa	ɣánna	غنّى	ma-ɣannā́š	مغنّاش	
híyya	ɣánnit	غنّت	ma-ɣannítš	مغنّتش	
húmma	ɣánnu	غنّوا	ma-ɣannū́š	مغنّوش	
ána	aɣánni	أغنّي	ma-ɣannī́š	مغنّيش	imperfect
íḥna	niɣánni	نغنّي	ma-nɣannī́š	منغنّيش	
ínta	tiɣánni	تغنّي	ma-tɣannī́š	متغنّيش	
ínti	tiɣánni	تغنّي	ma-tɣannī́š	متغنّيش	
íntu	tiɣánnu	تغنّوا	ma-tɣannū́š	متغنّوش	
húwwa	yiɣánni	يغنّي	ma-yɣannī́š	ميغنّيش	
híyya	tiɣánni	تغنّي	ma-tɣannī́š	متغنّيش	
húmma	yiɣánnu	يغنّوا	ma-yɣannū́š	ميغنّوش	
ána	baɣánni	بغنّي	ma-baɣannī́š	مبغنّيش	bi-imperfect
íḥna	binɣánni	بنغنّي	ma-binɣannī́š	مبنغنّيش	
ínta	bitɣánni	بتغنّي	ma-bitɣannī́š	مبتغنّيش	
ínti	bitɣánni	بتغنّي	ma-bitɣannī́š	مبتغنّيش	
íntu	bitɣánnu	بتغنّوا	ma-bitɣannū́š	مبتغنّوش	
húwwa	biyɣánni	بيغنّي	ma-biyɣannī́š	مبيغنّيش	
híyya	bitɣánni	بتغنّي	ma-bitɣannī́š	مبتغنّيش	
húmma	biyɣánnu	بيغنّوا	ma-biyɣannū́š	مبيغنّوش	
ána	haɣánni	هغنّي	miš haɣánni	مش هغنّي	future
íḥna	hanɣánni	هنغنّي	miš hanɣánni	مش هنغنّي	
ínta	hatɣánni	هتغنّي	miš hatɣánni	مش هتغنّي	
ínti	hatɣánni	هتغنّي	miš hatɣánni	مش هتغنّي	
íntu	hatɣánnu	هتغنّوا	miš hatɣánnu	مش هتغنّوا	
húwwa	hayɣánni	هيغنّي	miš hayɣánni	مش هيغنّي	
híyya	hatɣánni	هتغنّي	miš hatɣánni	مش هتغنّي	
húmma	hayɣánnu	هيغنّوا	miš hayɣánnu	مش هيغنّوا	
ínta	ɣánni	غنّي	ma-tɣannī́š	متغنّيش	imperative
ínti	ɣánni	غنّي	ma-tɣannī́š	متغنّيش	
íntu	ɣánnu	غنّوا	ma-tɣannū́š	متغنّوش	

	active		passive		
masculine	miɣánni	مغنّي	mitɣánni	متغنّي	participles
feminine	miɣanníyya	مغنّية	mitɣanníyya	متغنّية	
plural	miɣanniyīn	مغنّيين	mitɣanniyīn	متغنّيين	

verbal noun: ɣúna غنا

①

مُحمّد مُنير غنّى أغاني حِلْوَة كْتير.

maħámmad munīr ɣánna ʔaɣāni ħílwa ktīr.

Mohamed Mounir sang
many nice songs.

②

دينا بِتْحِبّ تْغنّي في الحمّام.

dīna bitħíbbᵊ tɣánni fi -lħammām.

Dina likes to sing
in the shower.

③

خالِد دايْماً بِيْغنّي في حفلات المدْرسة.

xālid dáyman biyɣánni fi ħafalāt ilmadrása.

Khaled always sings at school parties.

④

هغنّي النّهارْده في الحفْلة أُغْنية لِأُمّ كُلْثوم.

haɣánni -nnahárda fi -lħáfla ʔuɣníyya li-ummᵊ kulsūm.

I'll sing a song by Umm Kulthum
at the concert today.

⑤

متْغنّيش بِصوْت واطي. صوْتك جميل.

ma-tɣannīš bi-ṣōt wāṭi. ṣōtak gamīl.

Don't sing so quietly. You
have a beautiful voice.

❖ [2d] **to sing**

➲ 23.4, 235.2

186 to change *ɣáyyar* غَيَّر

verbal noun: *taɣyīr* تَغْيير

		affirmative		negative	
perfect	ána	ɣayyárt	غَيَّرْت	ma-ɣayyártiš	مَغَيَّرْتِش
	íḫna	ɣayyárna	غَيَّرْنا	ma-ɣayyarnāš	مَغَيَّرْناش
	ínta	ɣayyárt	غَيَّرْت	ma-ɣayyártiš	مَغَيَّرْتِش
	ínti	ɣayyárti	غَيَّرْتي	ma-ɣayyartīš	مَغَيَّرْتيش
	íntu	ɣayyártu	غَيَّرْتوا	ma-ɣayyartūš	مَغَيَّرْتوش
	húwwa	ɣáyyar	غَيَّر	ma-ɣayyárš	مَغَيَّرْش
	híyya	ɣayyárit	غَيَّرِت	ma-ɣayyarítš	مَغَيَّرِتْش
	húmma	ɣayyáru	غَيَّروا	ma-ɣayyarūš	مَغَيَّروش
imperfect	ána	aɣáyyar	أغَيَّر	ma-ɣayyárš	مَغَيَّرْش
	íḫna	niɣáyyar	نِغَيَّر	ma-nɣayyárš	مَنْغَيَّرْش
	ínta	tiɣáyyar	تِغَيَّر	ma-tɣayyárš	مَتْغَيَّرْش
	ínti	tiɣayyári	تِغَيَّري	ma-tɣayyarīš	مَتْغَيَّريش
	íntu	tiɣayyáru	تِغَيَّروا	ma-tɣayyarūš	مَتْغَيَّروش
	húwwa	yiɣáyyar	يِغَيَّر	ma-yɣayyárš	مَيْغَيَّرْش
	híyya	tiɣáyyar	تِغَيَّر	ma-tɣayyárš	مَتْغَيَّرْش
	húmma	yiɣayyáru	يِغَيَّروا	ma-yɣayyarūš	مَيْغَيَّروش
bi-imperfect	ána	baɣáyyar	بَغَيَّر	ma-baɣayyárš	مَبَغَيَّرْش
	íḫna	binɣáyyar	بِنْغَيَّر	ma-binɣayyárš	مَبِنْغَيَّرْش
	ínta	bitɣáyyar	بِتْغَيَّر	ma-bitɣayyárš	مَبِتْغَيَّرْش
	ínti	bitɣayyári	بِتْغَيَّري	ma-bitɣayyarīš	مَبِتْغَيَّريش
	íntu	bitɣayyáru	بِتْغَيَّروا	ma-bitɣayyarūš	مَبِتْغَيَّروش
	húwwa	biyɣáyyar	بِيْغَيَّر	ma-biyɣayyárš	مَبِيْغَيَّرْش
	híyya	bitɣáyyar	بِتْغَيَّر	ma-bitɣayyárš	مَبِتْغَيَّرْش
	húmma	biyɣayyáru	بِيْغَيَّروا	ma-biyɣayyarūš	مَبِيْغَيَّروش
future	ána	haɣáyyar	هَغَيَّر	miš haɣáyyar	مِش هَغَيَّر
	íḫna	hanɣáyyar	هَنْغَيَّر	miš hanɣáyyar	مِش هَنْغَيَّر
	ínta	hatɣáyyar	هَتْغَيَّر	miš hatɣáyyar	مِش هَتْغَيَّر
	ínti	hatɣayyári	هَتْغَيَّري	miš hatɣayyári	مِش هَتْغَيَّري
	íntu	hatɣayyáru	هَتْغَيَّروا	miš hatɣayyáru	مِش هَتْغَيَّروا
	húwwa	hayɣáyyar	هَيْغَيَّر	miš hayɣáyyar	مِش هَيْغَيَّر
	híyya	hatɣáyyar	هَتْغَيَّر	miš hatɣáyyar	مِش هَتْغَيَّر
	húmma	hayɣayyáru	هَيْغَيَّروا	miš hayɣayyáru	مِش هَيْغَيَّروا
imperative	ínta	ɣáyyar	غَيَّر	ma-tɣayyárš	مَتْغَيَّرْش
	ínti	ɣayyári	غَيَّري	ma-tɣayyarīš	مَتْغَيَّريش
	íntu	ɣayyáru	غَيَّروا	ma-tɣayyarūš	مَتْغَيَّروش

		active		passive	
participles	masculine	miɣáyyar	مِغَيَّر	mitɣáyyar	مِتْغَيَّر
	feminine	miɣayyára	مِغَيَّرَة	mitɣayyára	مِتْغَيَّرَة
	plural	miɣayyarīn	مِغَيَّرين	mitɣayyarīn	مِتْغَيَّرين

①

نُهى كانِت رافْضة الجَواز بسّ غيَّرِت رأْيها لمّا قابْلِت مازِن.

núha kānit ráfda -lgawāz bassᵊ ɣayyárit raʔyáha lámma ʔáblit māzin.

Noha refused to get married, but she changed her mind when she met Mazen.

②

مُمْكِن تِغيّر رأْيك في أيّ وَقْت و تِسْحب فِلوسك.

múmkin tiɣáyyar raʔīk fi ʔayyᵊ waʔt, wi tísḥab filūsak.

You may change your mind at any time and withdraw your money.

③

بِنْغيّر ديكور الشّقّة و كُلّ حاجة مقْلوبة.

binɣáyyar dikūr iššáʔʔa wi kullᵊ ḥāga maʔlūba.

We're redecorating [lit. changing the décor of] the apartment, and everything is in disarray.

④

هغيّر هُدومي و أنْزِلُّكو على طول.

haɣáyyar hudūmi w anzillúku 3ála ṭūl.

I'll change my clothes and come down to you immediately.

⑤

غيّر جَوّ، سافِر أيّ حِتّة، نفْسِيِّتك هتِتْحسِّن.

ɣáyyar gaww, sāfir ayyᵊ ḥítta, nafsiyyítak hatitḥássin.

Change places, travel somewhere, and your mood will be better.

⑥

بقالي مُدّة مغيّرْتِش فِلْتِر الزّيْت.

baʔāli múdda ma-ɣayyártiš filtir izzēt.

It's been a while since I changed the oil filter.

❖ [2s2] **to change**

- This is a transitive verb. The intransitive verb is اِتْغيّر *itɣáyyar*. (➲ 23)

➲ 58.3, 74.3, 136.5, 214.4

187 to pass *fāt* فات

	affirmative		negative		
ána	*futt*	فُتّ	*ma-fúttiš*	مَفُتِّش	perfect
íḫna	*fútna*	فُتْنا	*ma-futnāš*	مَفُتْناش	
ínta	*futt*	فُتّ	*ma-fúttiš*	مَفُتِّش	
ínti	*fútti*	فُتّي	*ma-futtīš*	مَفُتّيش	
íntu	*fúttu*	فُتّوا	*ma-futtūš*	مَفُتّوش	
húwwa	*fāt*	فات	*ma-fátš*	مَفاتْش	
híyya	*fātit*	فاتِت	*ma-fatítš*	مَفاتِتْش	
húmma	*fātu*	فاتوا	*ma-fatūš*	مَفاتوش	
ána	*afūt*	أفوت	*ma-fútš*	مَفوتْش	imperfect
íḫna	*nifūt*	نِفوت	*ma-nfútš*	مَنْفوتْش	
ínta	*tifūt*	تِفوت	*ma-tfútš*	مَتْفوتْش	
ínti	*tifūti*	تِفوتي	*ma-tfutīš*	مَتْفوتيش	
íntu	*tifūtu*	تِفوتوا	*ma-tfutūš*	مَتْفوتوش	
húwwa	*yifūt*	يِفوت	*ma-yfútš*	مَيْفوتْش	
híyya	*tifūt*	تِفوت	*ma-tfútš*	مَتْفوتْش	
húmma	*yifūtu*	يِفوتوا	*ma-yfutūš*	مَيْفوتوش	
ána	*bafūt*	بَفوت	*ma-bafútš*	مَبَفوتْش	bi-imperfect
íḫna	*binfūt*	بِنْفوت	*ma-binfútš*	مَبِنْفوتْش	
ínta	*bitfūt*	بِتْفوت	*ma-bitfútš*	مَبِتْفوتْش	
ínti	*bitfūti*	بِتْفوتي	*ma-bitfutīš*	مَبِتْفوتيش	
íntu	*bitfūtu*	بِتْفوتوا	*ma-bitfutūš*	مَبِتْفوتوش	
húwwa	*biyfūt*	بِيْفوت	*ma-biyfútš*	مَبِيْفوتْش	
híyya	*bitfūt*	بِتْفوت	*ma-bitfútš*	مَبِتْفوتْش	
húmma	*biyfūtu*	بِيْفوتوا	*ma-biyfutūš*	مَبِيْفوتوش	
ána	*hafūt*	هَفوت	*miš hafūt*	مِش هَفوت	future
íḫna	*hanfūt*	هَنْفوت	*miš hanfūt*	مِش هَنْفوت	
ínta	*hatfūt*	هَتْفوت	*miš hatfūt*	مِش هَتْفوت	
ínti	*hatfūti*	هَتْفوتي	*miš hatfūti*	مِش هَتْفوتي	
íntu	*hatfūtu*	هَتْفوتوا	*miš hatfūtu*	مِش هَتْفوتوا	
húwwa	*hayfūt*	هَيْفوت	*miš hayfūt*	مِش هَيْفوت	
híyya	*hatfūt*	هَتْفوت	*miš hatfūt*	مِش هَتْفوت	
húmma	*hayfūtu*	هَيْفوتوا	*miš hayfūtu*	مِش هَيْفوتوا	
ínta	*fūt*	فوت	*ma-tfútš*	مَتْفوتْش	imperative
ínti	*fūti*	فوتي	*ma-tfutīš*	مَتْفوتيش	
íntu	*fūtu*	فوتوا	*ma-tfutūš*	مَتْفوتوش	

	active		passive		
masculine	*fāyit*	فايِت	*mitfāt*	مِتْفات	participles
feminine	*fáyta*	فايْتَة	*mitfāta*	مِتْفاتَة	
plural	*faytīn*	فايْتين	*mitfatīn*	مِتْفاتين	

verbal nouns: *fōt* فوْت - *fawāt* فَوات - *fawatān* فَوَتان

①

اِدْخُلوا بْسُرْعة. مفاتْش كْتير مِن المُحاضْرة.

idxúlu b-súr3a. ma-fátšᵊ ktīr min ilmuħáḍra.

Enter quickly. The lecture's just begun. [lit. Not much of the lecture has passed.]

②

باص المدْرسة دايْماً يِفوت على حمْزة بدْري أوي.

bāṣ ilmadrása dáyman yifūt 3ála ħámza bádri ʔáwi.

The school bus always passes by Hamza's [house] so early.

③

سامِح بِيْفوت على بِنْته في التّدْريب و يْروّحوا معَ بعْض.

sāmiħ biyfūt 3ála bíntu fi -ttadrīb wi yrawwáħu má3a ba3ḍ.

Sameh drops by his daughter's training, and they return home together.

④

هفوت عليْك عَ السّاعة ٥. خلّيك جاهِز.

hafūt 3alēk 3a -ssā3a xámsa. xallīk gāhiz.

I'll come by around five. Be ready!

⑤

أحْمد اِتْأخّر و القطر فاته.

áħmad itʔáxxar w ilʔáṭar fātu.

Ahmed was late, and he missed his train.

⑥

أ: أنا عايِز أطلّع شهادة، مِن فضْلك.

ب: خلّصْنا يا أُسْتاذ. فوت عليْنا بُكْره.

A: *ána 3āyiz aṭálla3 šahāda, min fáḍlik.*

B: *xalláṣna ya ʔustāz. fūt 3alēna búkra.*

A: I want a certificate, please.

B: We're done [for today], sir. Come by tomorrow.

⑦

رُخْصِتي خلصانة مِ الشّهْر اللي فات. عايْزة أجدِّدْها.

ruxṣíti xalaṣāna mi -ššahr ílli fāt. 3áyz- agaddídha.

My license expired last month. I want to renew it.

⑧

أيْه اللي نيِّلْته ده! ده أنْتَ يوْمك مِش فايِت!

ʔē ílli nayyíltu da! da -nta yōmak miš fāyit!

What a mess you've made! You're going to have a long day!

⑨

اِنْسى بقى و متْشيلْش همّ. ده اللي فات مات.

ínsa báʔa w ma-tšílšᵊ hamm. da -lli fāt māt.

Forget your sorrows, and don't be troubled. What is done is done [lit. what has passed is dead].

❖ [1h1] **to pass (by** على *3ála*)**; to come by, drop by** (to visit) (على *3ála*)**; to miss***

- *Whereas in English you might miss your train, bus, plane, etc., in Arabic your train, bus, plane 'passes' you. Notice that, in this context, the verb takes a direct object. (➲ 187.5)
- The expression اللى فات *ílli fāt*, literally 'which has passed', translates 'last' with time expressions, such as 'last week', 'last month', etc. Following a feminine noun, it would be اللى فاتِت *ílli fātit*, for example, السّنه اللى فاتِت *issána -lli fātit* 'last year'. (➲ 128.1)

➲ 6.1, 63.7, 87.1, 128.1, 245.5

188 to win *fāz* فاز

	affirmative		negative		
ána	*fuzt*	فُزْت	*ma-fúztiš*	مَفُزْتش	**perfect**
íḫna	*fúzna*	فُزْنا	*ma-fuznāš*	مَفُزْناش	
ínta	*fuzt*	فُزْت	*ma-fúztiš*	مَفُزْتش	
ínti	*fúzti*	فُزْتي	*ma-fuztīš*	مَفُزْتيش	
íntu	*fúztu*	فُزْتوا	*ma-fuztūš*	مَفُزْتوش	
húwwa	*fāz*	فاز	*ma-fázš*	مَفازْش	
híyya	*fāzit*	فازِت	*ma-fazítš*	مَفازِتْش	
húmma	*fāzu*	فازوا	*ma-fazūš*	مَفازوش	
ána	*afūz*	أفوز	*ma-fúzš*	مَفوزْش	**imperfect**
íḫna	*nifūz*	نِفوز	*ma-nfúzš*	مَنْفوزْش	
ínta	*tifūz*	تِفوز	*ma-tfúzš*	مَتْفوزْش	
ínti	*tifūzi*	تِفوزي	*ma-tfuzīš*	مَتْفوزيش	
íntu	*tifūzu*	تِفوزوا	*ma-tfuzūš*	مَتْفوزوش	
húwwa	*yifūz*	يِفوز	*ma-yfúzš*	مَيْفوزْش	
híyya	*tifūz*	تِفوز	*ma-tfúzš*	مَتْفوزْش	
húmma	*yifūzu*	يِفوزوا	*ma-yfuzūš*	مَيْفوزوش	
ána	*bafūz*	بَفوز	*ma-bafúzš*	مَبَفوزْش	**bi-imperfect**
íḫna	*binfūz*	بِنْفوز	*ma-binfúzš*	مَبِنْفوزْش	
ínta	*bitfūz*	بِتْفوز	*ma-bitfúzš*	مَبِتْفوزْش	
ínti	*bitfūzi*	بِتْفوزي	*ma-bitfuzīš*	مَبِتْفوزيش	
íntu	*bitfūzu*	بِتْفوزوا	*ma-bitfuzūš*	مَبِتْفوزوش	
húwwa	*biyfūz*	بِيْفوز	*ma-biyfúzš*	مَبِيْفوزْش	
híyya	*bitfūz*	بِتْفوز	*ma-bitfúzš*	مَبِتْفوزْش	
húmma	*biyfūzu*	بِيْفوزوا	*ma-biyfuzūš*	مَبِيْفوزوش	
ána	*hafūz*	هَفوز	*miš hafūz*	مِش هَفوز	**future**
íḫna	*hanfūz*	هَنْفوز	*miš hanfūz*	مِش هَنْفوز	
ínta	*hatfūz*	هَتْفوز	*miš hatfūz*	مِش هَتْفوز	
ínti	*hatfūzi*	هَتْفوزي	*miš hatfūzi*	مِش هَتْفوزي	
íntu	*hatfūzu*	هَتْفوزوا	*miš hatfūzu*	مِش هَتْفوزوا	
húwwa	*hayfūz*	هَيْفوز	*miš hayfūz*	مِش هَيْفوز	
híyya	*hatfūz*	هَتْفوز	*miš hatfūz*	مِش هَتْفوز	
húmma	*hayfūzu*	هَيْفوزوا	*miš hayfūzu*	مِش هَيْفوزوا	
ínta	*fūz*	فوز	*ma-tfúzš*	مَتْفوزْش	**imperative**
ínti	*fūzi*	فوزي	*ma-tfuzīš*	مَتْفوزيش	
íntu	*fūzu*	فوزوا	*ma-tfuzūš*	مَتْفوزوش	

	active		passive		
masculine	*fāyiz*	فايِز	*mitfāz*	مِتْفاز	**participles**
feminine	*fáyza*	فايْزَة	–	–	
plural	*fayzīn*	فايْزين	–	–	

verbal nouns: *fōz* فوْز - *fawazān* فوَزان

①

حنان فازِت بِألْف جْنيْهْ في مُسابْقة.

ɧanān fāzit bi-alfᵊ gnēh fi musábʔa.

Hanan won a thousand pounds
in a competition.

②

حامِد دايْماً يِفوز في أيّ مُسابْقِةْ جرْي.

ɧāmid dáyman yifūz fi ʔayyᵊ musábʔit gary.

Hamed always wins any
running competition.

③

مبفوزْش أبداً في أيّ مُسابْقة.

ma-bafúzš ábadan fi ʔayyᵊ musábʔa.

I never win in any competition.

④

اللي هيِتْمرّن كُوَيِّس هَيْفوز.

ílli hayitmárran kuwáyyis hayfūz.

He who trains well will win.

⑤

فوز على مُنافِسيك بِالعزيمة القوّية و الجُهْد.

fūz 3ála munafisīk bi-l3azīma -lqawwíyya w ilgúhd.

Beat your competitors through strong
determination and effort.

❖ [1h1] **to win** (a prize, money) (بِـ *bi-*); **to win** (a game) (في *fi*); **to beat, win against** (على *3ála*)

- As this verb requires a preposition, the passive participle is invariable (always masculine). It is, however, very rarely used.
- Notice that this verb takes different prepositions, according to the context.

189 to open *fátaḥ* فتح

	affirmative		negative		
ána	*fatáḥt*	فَتَحْت	*ma-fatáḥtiš*	مَفَتَحْتِش	**perfect**
íḥna	*fatáḥna*	فَتَحْنا	*ma-fataḥnāš*	مَفَتَحْناش	
ínta	*fatáḥt*	فَتَحْت	*ma-fatáḥtiš*	مَفَتَحْتِش	
ínti	*fatáḥti*	فَتَحْتي	*ma-fataḥtīš*	مَفَتَحْتيش	
íntu	*fatáḥtu*	فَتَحْتوا	*ma-fataḥtūš*	مَفَتَحْتوش	
húwwa	*fátaḥ*	فَتَح	*ma-fatáḥš*	مَفَتَحْش	
híyya	*fátaḥit*	فَتَحِت	*ma-fataḥítš*	مَفَتَحِتْش	
húmma	*fátaḥu*	فَتَحوا	*ma-fataḥūš*	مَفَتَحوش	
ána	*áftaḥ*	أَفْتَح	*ma-ftáḥš*	مَفْتَحْش	**imperfect**
íḥna	*níftaḥ*	نِفْتَح	*ma-niftáḥš*	مَنِفْتَحْش	
ínta	*tíftaḥ*	تِفْتَح	*ma-tiftáḥš*	مَتِفْتَحْش	
ínti	*tiftáḥi*	تِفْتَحي	*ma-tiftaḥīš*	مَتِفْتَحيش	
íntu	*tiftáḥu*	تِفْتَحوا	*ma-tiftaḥūš*	مَتِفْتَحوش	
húwwa	*yíftaḥ*	يِفْتَح	*ma-yiftáḥš*	مَيِفْتَحْش	
híyya	*tíftaḥ*	تِفْتَح	*ma-tiftáḥš*	مَتِفْتَحْش	
húmma	*yiftáḥu*	يِفْتَحوا	*ma-yiftaḥūš*	مَيِفْتَحوش	
ána	*báftaḥ*	بَفْتَح	*ma-baftáḥš*	مَبَفْتَحْش	**bi-imperfect**
íḥna	*biníftaḥ*	بِنِفْتَح	*ma-bniftáḥš*	مَبْنِفْتَحْش	
ínta	*bitíftaḥ*	بِتِفْتَح	*ma-btiftáḥš*	مَبْتِفْتَحْش	
ínti	*bitiftáḥi*	بِتِفْتَحي	*ma-btiftaḥīš*	مَبْتِفْتَحيش	
íntu	*bitiftáḥu*	بِتِفْتَحوا	*ma-btiftaḥūš*	مَبْتِفْتَحوش	
húwwa	*biyíftaḥ*	بِيِفْتَح	*ma-byiftáḥš*	مَبْيِفْتَحْش	
híyya	*bitíftaḥ*	بِتِفْتَح	*ma-btiftáḥš*	مَبْتِفْتَحْش	
húmma	*biyiftáḥu*	بِيِفْتَحوا	*ma-byiftaḥūš*	مَبْيِفْتَحوش	
ána	*háftaḥ*	هَفْتَح	*miš háftaḥ*	مِش هَفْتَح	**future**
íḥna	*haníftaḥ*	هَنِفْتَح	*miš haníftaḥ*	مِش هَنِفْتَح	
ínta	*hatíftaḥ*	هَتِفْتَح	*miš hatíftaḥ*	مِش هَتِفْتَح	
ínti	*hatiftáḥi*	هَتِفْتَحي	*miš hatiftáḥi*	مِش هَتِفْتَحي	
íntu	*hatiftáḥu*	هَتِفْتَحوا	*miš hatiftáḥu*	مِش هَتِفْتَحوا	
húwwa	*hayíftaḥ*	هَيِفْتَح	*miš hayíftaḥ*	مِش هَيِفْتَح	
híyya	*hatíftaḥ*	هَتِفْتَح	*miš hatíftaḥ*	مِش هَتِفْتَح	
húmma	*hayiftáḥu*	هَيِفْتَحوا	*miš hayiftáḥu*	مِش هَيِفْتَحوا	
ínta	*íftaḥ*	اِفْتَح	*ma-tiftáḥš*	مَتِفْتَحْش	**imperative**
ínti	*iftáḥi*	اِفْتَحي	*ma-tiftaḥīš*	مَتِفْتَحيش	
íntu	*iftáḥu*	اِفْتَحوا	*ma-tiftaḥūš*	مَتِفْتَحوش	

	active		passive		
masculine	*fātiḥ*	فاتِح	*maftūḥ*	مَفْتوح	**participles**
feminine	*fátḥa*	فاتْحَة	*maftūḥa*	مَفْتوحَة	
plural	*fatḥīn*	فاتْحين	*maftuḥīn*	مَفْتوحين	

verbal nouns: *fatḥ* فَتْح - *fataḥān* فَتَحان

①
شعْبان فتح محلّ ملابِس في الدُّقّي.
ša3bān fátaḫ maḫállᵊ malābis fi -ddúʔʔi.
Sha'ban opened a dress shop in Dokki.

②
بحِبّ أفْتح الإيميْل بِتاعي كُلّ يوْم الصُّبْح.
baḫíbb áftaḫ ilʔīmēl bitā3i kullᵊ yōm iṣṣúbḫ.
I like to check [lit. open]
my email every morning.

③
أُخْتي بِتِفْتح النّور و أنا نايْمة دايْماً.
úxti bitíftaḫ innūr w ána náyma dáyman.
My sister always turns the lights
on while I'm sleeping.

④
لمّا تِوْصل، خبّط و أنا هفْتحْلك.
lámma tíwṣal, xábbaṭ w ána haftáḫlak.
When you arrive, knock,
and I'll open the door.

⑤
اِفْتحي يا رُؤى. أنا نجْلاء.
iftáḫi ya rúʔa. ána naglāʔ.
Open up, Roaa. It's me, Naglaa.

⑥
البنْك بْيِفْتح ٨ و بِيِقْفِل ٢.
ilbánkᵊ byíftaḫ tamánya w biyíʔfil itnēn.
The bank opens at eight and closes at two.

⑦
أنا نازْلة رُبْع ساعة و جايّة. متِفْتحيش لِأيّ حدّ.
ána názla rub3ᵊ sā3a wi gáyya. ma-tiftaḫīš li-ayyᵊ ḫadd.
I'm going out for 15 minutes. Don't
open [the door] for anyone.

⑧
متْسيبْش الشِّبّاك مفْتوح. اِقْفِلُه قبْل ما تْنام.
ma-tsíbš iššibbāk maftūḫ. iʔfílu ʔablᵊ ma tnām.
Don't leave the window open. Close
it before you go to sleep.

❖ [1s1] **to open; to turn on** (lights, etc.)

➲ 140.4, 231.4

190 to cancel *fárkiš* فَرْكِش

verbal noun: *farkáša* فَرْكَشَة

perfect

	affirmative		negative	
ána	*farkíšt*	فَرْكِشْت	*ma-farkíštiš*	مَفَرْكِشْتِش
íḫna	*farkíšna*	فَرْكِشْنا	*ma-farkišnāš*	مَفَرْكِشْناش
ínta	*farkíšt*	فَرْكِشْت	*ma-farkíštiš*	مَفَرْكِشْتِش
ínti	*farkíšti*	فَرْكِشْتي	*ma-farkištīš*	مَفَرْكِشْتيش
íntu	*farkíštu*	فَرْكِشْتوا	*ma-farkištūš*	مَفَرْكِشْتوش
húwwa	*fárkiš*	فَرْكِش	*ma-farkíšš*	مَفَرْكِشّ
híyya	*farkíšit*	فَرْكِشِت	*ma-farkišítš*	مَفَرْكِشِتْش
húmma	*farkíšu*	فَرْكِشوا	*ma-farkišūš*	مَفَرْكِشوش

imperfect

	affirmative		negative	
ána	*afárkiš*	أفَرْكِش	*ma-farkíšš*	مَفَرْكِشّ
íḫna	*nifárkiš*	نِفَرْكِش	*ma-nfarkíšš*	مَنْفَرْكِشّ
ínta	*tifárkiš*	تِفَرْكِش	*ma-tfarkíšš*	مَتْفَرْكِشّ
ínti	*tifarkíši*	تِفَرْكِشي	*ma-tfarkišīš*	مَتْفَرْكِشيش
íntu	*tifarkíšu*	تِفَرْكِشوا	*ma-tfarkišūš*	مَتْفَرْكِشوش
húwwa	*yifárkiš*	يِفَرْكِش	*ma-yfarkíšš*	مَيْفَرْكِشّ
híyya	*tifárkiš*	تِفَرْكِش	*ma-tfarkíšš*	مَتْفَرْكِشّ
húmma	*yifarkíšu*	يِفَرْكِشوا	*ma-yfarkišūš*	مَيْفَرْكِشوش

bi-imperfect

	affirmative		negative	
ána	*bafárkiš*	بَفَرْكِش	*ma-bafarkíšš*	مَبَفَرْكِشّ
íḫna	*binfárkiš*	بِنْفَرْكِش	*ma-binfarkíšš*	مَبِنْفَرْكِشّ
ínta	*bitfárkiš*	بِتْفَرْكِش	*ma-bitfarkíšš*	مَبِتْفَرْكِشّ
ínti	*bitfarkíši*	بِتْفَرْكِشي	*ma-bitfarkišīš*	مَبِتْفَرْكِشيش
íntu	*bitfarkíšu*	بِتْفَرْكِشوا	*ma-bitfarkišūš*	مَبِتْفَرْكِشوش
húwwa	*biyfárkiš*	بِيْفَرْكِش	*ma-biyfarkíšš*	مَبِيْفَرْكِشّ
híyya	*bitfárkiš*	بِتْفَرْكِش	*ma-bitfarkíšš*	مَبِتْفَرْكِشّ
húmma	*biyfarkíšu*	بِيْفَرْكِشوا	*ma-biyfarkišūš*	مَبِيْفَرْكِشوش

future

	affirmative		negative	
ána	*hafárkiš*	هَفَرْكِش	*miš hafárkiš*	مِش هَفَرْكِش
íḫna	*hanfárkiš*	هَنْفَرْكِش	*miš hanfárkiš*	مِش هَنْفَرْكِش
ínta	*hatfárkiš*	هَتْفَرْكِش	*miš hatfárkiš*	مِش هَتْفَرْكِش
ínti	*hatfarkíši*	هَتْفَرْكِشي	*miš hatfarkíši*	مِش هَتْفَرْكِشي
íntu	*hatfarkíšu*	هَتْفَرْكِشوا	*miš hatfarkíšu*	مِش هَتْفَرْكِشوا
húwwa	*hayfárkiš*	هَيْفَرْكِش	*miš hayfárkiš*	مِش هَيْفَرْكِش
híyya	*hatfárkiš*	هَتْفَرْكِش	*miš hatfárkiš*	مِش هَتْفَرْكِش
húmma	*hayfarkíšu*	هَيْفَرْكِشوا	*miš hayfarkíšu*	مِش هَيْفَرْكِشوا

imperative

	affirmative		negative	
ínta	*fárkiš*	فَرْكِش	*ma-tfarkíšš*	مَتْفَرْكِشّ
ínti	*farkíši*	فَرْكِشي	*ma-tfarkišīš*	مَتْفَرْكِشيش
íntu	*farkíšu*	فَرْكِشوا	*ma-tfarkišūš*	مَتْفَرْكِشوش

participles

	active		passive	
masculine	*mifárkiš*	مِفَرْكِش	*mitfárkiš*	مِتْفَرْكِش
feminine	*mifarkíša*	مِفَرْكِشَة	*mitfarkíša*	مِتْفَرْكِشَة
plural	*mifarkišīn*	مِفَرْكِشين	*mitfarkišīn*	مِتْفَرْكِشين

①

فرْكِشْنا الخُروجة لمّا لقيْنا أكْتر مِن نُصّ النّاس اِعْتذروا.

farkíšna -lxurūga lámma laʔēna ʔáktar min nuṣṣ innās i3tázaru.

We canceled the outing when more
than half of the people backed out.

②

محْمود كُلّ ما يِعْرف واحْدة يِفرْكِش معاها أوِّل ما تْجيب سيرْةْ الجَواز.

maḫmūd kull[ə] ma yí3raf wáḫda yifárkiš ma3āha ʔáwwil ma tgīb sirt ilgawāz.

Mahmoud breaks it off with any girl he knows
as soon as she brings up the topic of marriage.

③

فريدة بِتْفرْكِش لِعبْها كُلّ أرتِّبْها.

farīda bitfárkiš li3ábha kull[ə] m- arattíbha.

Every time I arrange Farida's toys,
she scatters them around again.

④

أنا هفرْكِش مُقابْلِةْ النّهارْده. مِش عايْزة أقابِل عِرْسان بِالطّريقة دي.

ána hafárkiš muʔáblit innahárda. miš 3áyza ʔaʔābil 3irsān bi-ṭṭarīʔa di.

I'll cancel today's interview. I don't want
to meet potential suitors that way.

⑤

فرْكِشي الخُطوبة دي قبْل ما الفاس تُقع في الرّاس.

farkíši -lxuṭūba di ʔabl[ə] ma -lfās túʔa3 fi -rrās.

Break off this engagement before it's too late.

⑥

متْفرْكِشوش المُقابْلة المرّة دي. أنا نِفْسي أشوفْكو بقى.

ma-tfarkišūš ilmuʔábla -lmarrādi. ána nífsi ʔašúfku báʔa.

Don't cancel the meeting this time. I want to see you.

❖ [11s1] **to cancel; to break off, end; to scatter**

191 to fail fíšil فِشِل

	affirmative		negative		
ána	fišílt	فِشِلْت	ma-fšíltiš	مَفْشِلْتِش	perfect
íḫna	fišílna	فِشِلْنا	ma-fšilnāš	مَفْشِلْناش	
ínta	fišílt	فِشِلْت	ma-fšíltiš	مَفْشِلْتِش	
ínti	fišílti	فِشِلْتي	ma-fšiltīš	مَفْشِلْتيش	
íntu	fišíltu	فِشِلْتوا	ma-fšiltūš	مَفْشِلْتوش	
húwwa	fíšil	فِشِل	ma-fšílš	مَفْشِلْش	
híyya	fíšlit	فِشْلِت	ma-fišlítš	مَفِشْلِتْش	
húmma	fíšlu	فِشْلوا	ma-fišlūš	مَفِشْلوش	
ána	áfšal	أَفْشَل	ma-fšálš	مَفْشَلْش	imperfect
íḫna	nífšal	نِفْشَل	ma-nifšálš	مَنِفْشَلْش	
ínta	tífšal	تِفْشَل	ma-tifšálš	مَتِفْشَلْش	
ínti	tifšáli	تِفْشَلي	ma-tifšalīš	مَتِفْشَليش	
íntu	tifšálu	تِفْشَلوا	ma-tifšalūš	مَتِفْشَلوش	
húwwa	yífšal	يِفْشَل	ma-yifšálš	مَيِفْشَلْش	
híyya	tífšal	تِفْشَل	ma-tifšálš	مَتِفْشَلْش	
húmma	yifšálu	يِفْشَلوا	ma-yifšalūš	مَيِفْشَلوش	
ána	báfšal	بَفْشَل	ma-bafšálš	مَبَفْشَلْش	bi-imperfect
íḫna	binífšal	بِنِفْشَل	ma-bnifšálš	مَبْنِفْشَلْش	
ínta	bitífšal	بِتِفْشَل	ma-btifšálš	مَبْتِفْشَلْش	
ínti	bitifšáli	بِتِفْشَلي	ma-btifšalīš	مَبْتِفْشَليش	
íntu	bitifšálu	بِتِفْشَلوا	ma-btifšalūš	مَبْتِفْشَلوش	
húwwa	biyífšal	بِيِفْشَل	ma-byifšálš	مَبْيِفْشَلْش	
híyya	bitífšal	بِتِفْشَل	ma-btifšálš	مَبْتِفْشَلْش	
húmma	biyifšálu	بِيِفْشَلوا	ma-byifšalūš	مَبْيِفْشَلوش	
ána	háfšal	هَفْشَل	miš háfšal	مِش هَفْشَل	future
íḫna	hanífšal	هَنِفْشَل	miš hanífšal	مِش هَنِفْشَل	
ínta	hatífšal	هَتِفْشَل	miš hatífšal	مِش هَتِفْشَل	
ínti	hatifšáli	هَتِفْشَلي	miš hatifšáli	مِش هَتِفْشَلي	
íntu	hatifšálu	هَتِفْشَلوا	miš hatifšálu	مِش هَتِفْشَلوا	
húwwa	hayífšal	هَيِفْشَل	miš hayífšal	مِش هَيِفْشَل	
híyya	hatífšal	هَتِفْشَل	miš hatífšal	مِش هَتِفْشَل	
húmma	hayifšálu	هَيِفْشَلوا	miš hayifšálu	مِش هَيِفْشَلوا	
ínta	ífšal	اِفْشَل	ma-tifšálš	مَتِفْشَلْش	imperative
ínti	ifšáli	اِفْشَلي	ma-tifšalīš	مَتِفْشَليش	
íntu	ifšálu	اِفْشَلوا	ma-tifšalūš	مَتِفْشَلوش	

	active		passive		
masculine	fāšil	فاشِل	–	–	participles
feminine	fášla	فاشْلَة	–	–	
plural	fašlīn	فاشْلين	–	–	

verbal noun: fášal فَشَل

①

مُعْتزّ عمل كذا مشْروع و فِشِل فيهُم.

mu3tázzᵊ 3ámal káza mašrū3 wi fíšil fīhum.

Moataz started many projects
but failed in them all.

②

مِن كُتْر ما أنا بكْرَه إنّي أفْشل مِش ببْدأ في الحاجات أصْلاً.

min kutrᵊ m- ána bákrah ínni ʔáfšal miš bábdaʔ fi -lħagāt áṣlan.

I hate failing so much that I don't start anything ever.

③

سليم عُمْرُه ما بِيِفْشل في اللِّعْبة دي. مُحْترِف.

salīm 3úmru ma biyífšal fi -llí3ba di. muħtárif.

Selim never fails in this game. He's a pro.

④

إنْتو هتِفْشلوا في حَياتْكو طول ما أنْتو بِالكسل و السِّلْبية دي.

íntu hatifšálu fi ħayátku ṭūl ma -ntu bi-lkásal w issilbíyya di.

You'll fail in life as long as you're so lazy and negative.

⑤

أرْجوك ركِّز في الاِمْتِحانات. متِفْشلْش السّنة دي عشان خاطْري.

argūk rákkiz fi -lʔimtiħanāt. ma-tifšálš issanādi 3ašān xáṭri.

(father to son:) Please, concentrate on your exams.
For my own sake, don't fail this year.

❖ [1s4] **to fail** (**in/at** في *fi*)

- This verb can also be فشل *fášal* [1s1].

➲ 60.1

192 to separate *fáṣal* فَصَل

	affirmative		negative		
ána	*faṣált*	فَصَلْت	*ma-faṣáltiš*	مَفَصَلْتِش	perfect
íḫna	*faṣálna*	فَصَلْنا	*ma-faṣalnāš*	مَفَصَلْناش	
ínta	*faṣált*	فَصَلْت	*ma-faṣáltiš*	مَفَصَلْتِش	
ínti	*faṣálti*	فَصَلْتي	*ma-faṣaltīš*	مَفَصَلْتيش	
íntu	*faṣáltu*	فَصَلْتوا	*ma-faṣaltūš*	مَفَصَلْتوش	
húwwa	*fáṣal*	فَصَل	*ma-faṣálš*	مَفَصَلْش	
híyya	*fáṣalit*	فَصَلِت	*ma-faṣalítš*	مَفَصَلِتْش	
húmma	*fáṣalu*	فَصَلوا	*ma-faṣalūš*	مَفَصَلوش	
ána	*áfṣil*	أَفْصِل	*ma-fṣílš*	مَفْصِلْش	imperfect
íḫna	*nífṣil*	نِفْصِل	*ma-nifṣílš*	مَنِفْصِلْش	
ínta	*tífṣil*	تِفْصِل	*ma-tifṣílš*	مَتِفْصِلْش	
ínti	*tifṣíli*	تِفْصِلي	*ma-tifṣilīš*	مَتِفْصِليش	
íntu	*tifṣílu*	تِفْصِلوا	*ma-tifṣilūš*	مَتِفْصِلوش	
húwwa	*yífṣil*	يِفْصِل	*ma-yifṣílš*	مَيِفْصِلْش	
híyya	*tífṣil*	تِفْصِل	*ma-tifṣílš*	مَتِفْصِلْش	
húmma	*yifṣílu*	يِفْصِلوا	*ma-yifṣilūš*	مَيِفْصِلوش	
ána	*báfṣil*	بَفْصِل	*ma-bafṣílš*	مَبَفْصِلْش	bi-imperfect
íḫna	*binífṣil*	بِنِفْصِل	*ma-bnifṣílš*	مَبْنِفْصِلْش	
ínta	*bitífṣil*	بِتِفْصِل	*ma-btifṣílš*	مَبْتِفْصِلْش	
ínti	*bitifṣíli*	بِتِفْصِلي	*ma-btifṣilīš*	مَبْتِفْصِليش	
íntu	*bitifṣílu*	بِتِفْصِلوا	*ma-btifṣilūš*	مَبْتِفْصِلوش	
húwwa	*biyífṣil*	بِيِفْصِل	*ma-byifṣílš*	مَبْيِفْصِلْش	
híyya	*bitífṣil*	بِتِفْصِل	*ma-btifṣílš*	مَبْتِفْصِلْش	
húmma	*biyifṣílu*	بِيِفْصِلوا	*ma-byifṣilūš*	مَبْيِفْصِلوش	
ána	*háfṣil*	هَفْصِل	*miš háfṣil*	مِش هَفْصِل	future
íḫna	*hanífṣil*	هَنِفْصِل	*miš hanífṣil*	مِش هَنِفْصِل	
ínta	*hatífṣil*	هَتِفْصِل	*miš hatífṣil*	مِش هَتِفْصِل	
ínti	*hatifṣíli*	هَتِفْصِلي	*miš hatifṣíli*	مِش هَتِفْصِلي	
íntu	*hatifṣílu*	هَتِفْصِلوا	*miš hatifṣílu*	مِش هَتِفْصِلوا	
húwwa	*hayífṣil*	هَيِفْصِل	*miš hayífṣil*	مِش هَيِفْصِل	
híyya	*hatífṣil*	هَتِفْصِل	*miš hatífṣil*	مِش هَتِفْصِل	
húmma	*hayifṣílu*	هَيِفْصِلوا	*miš hayifṣílu*	مِش هَيِفْصِلوا	
ínta	*ífṣil*	اِفْصِل	*ma-tifṣílš*	مَتِفْصِلْش	imperative
ínti	*ifṣíli*	اِفْصِلي	*ma-tifṣilīš*	مَتِفْصِليش	
íntu	*ifṣílu*	اِفْصِلوا	*ma-tifṣilūš*	مَتِفْصِلوش	

	active		passive		
masculine	*fāṣil*	فاصِل	*mafṣūl*	مَفْصول	participles
feminine	*fáṣla*	فاصْلَة	*mafṣūla*	مَفْصولَة	
plural	*faṣlīn*	فاصْلين	*mafṣulīn*	مَفْصولين	

verbal noun: *faṣl* فَصْل

①

فصلْنا المُتفوِّقين عن الطّلبة العادِيّين و هنِعْمِلْهُم بِـرنامِج خاصّ.

faṣálna -lmutafawwiqīn 3an iṭṭálaba -l3adiyyīn wi hani3mílhum birnāmig xaṣṣ.

We separated the excellent students from the ordinary ones, and we'll give them a special program.

②

بحاوِل أفْصِل مشاعْري عن عقْلي في الشُّغْل.

baḫāwil áfṣil mašá3ri 3an 3áʔli fi -ššuɣl.

I try to separate my emotions from my mind at work.

③

إنْتَ يابْني مبْتِفْصِلْش ؟! اِسْكُت و سيبْني أركِّز شُوَيّة.

ínta ya -bni ma-btifṣílš?! ískut wi síbni ʔarákkiz šuwáyya.

Don't you ever stop?! Shut up and let me concentrate for a while!

④

تِليفوْني هَيِفْصِل دِلْوَقْتي. معادْنا زيّ ما هُوَّ. سلام!

tilifōni hayífṣil dilwáʔti. mi3ádna zayyᵊ ma húwwa. salām!

My phone's battery is about to die [lit. separate] now. Our appointment is as it is. Bye!

⑤

اِفْصِل كُلّ لوْن لِوَحْدُه.

ífṣil kullᵊ lōn li-wáḫdu.

Separate each color.

❖ [1s2] **to separate**

193 to remain *fíḍil* فِضِل يِـ

		affirmative		negative		
ána	*fiḍílt*	فِضِلْت	*ma-fḍíltiš*	مَفْضِلْتِش	perfect
íḥna	*fiḍílna*	فِضِلْنا	*ma-fḍilnāš*	مَفْضِلْناش	
ínta	*fiḍílt*	فِضِلْت	*ma-fḍíltiš*	مَفْضِلْتِش	
ínti	*fiḍílti*	فِضِلْتي	*ma-fḍiltīš*	مَفْضِلْتيش	
íntu	*fiḍíltu*	فِضِلْتوا	*ma-fḍiltūš*	مَفْضِلْتوش	
húwwa	*fíḍil*	فِضِل	*ma-fḍílš*	مَفْضِلْش	
híyya	*fíḍlit*	فِضْلِت	*ma-fiḍlítš*	مَفِضْلِتْش	
húmma	*fíḍlu*	فِضْلوا	*ma-fiḍlūš*	مَفِضْلوش	
ána	*áfḍal*	أَفْضَل	*ma-fḍálš*	مَفْضَلْش	imperfect
íḥna	*nífḍal*	نِفْضَل	*ma-nifḍálš*	مَنِفْضَلْش	
ínta	*tífḍal*	تِفْضَل	*ma-tifḍálš*	مَتِفْضَلْش	
ínti	*tifḍáli*	تِفْضَلي	*ma-tifḍalīš*	مَتِفْضَليش	
íntu	*tifḍálu*	تِفْضَلوا	*ma-tifḍalūš*	مَتِفْضَلوش	
húwwa	*yífḍal*	يِفْضَل	*ma-yifḍálš*	مَيِفْضَلْش	
híyya	*tífḍal*	تِفْضَل	*ma-tifḍálš*	مَتِفْضَلْش	
húmma	*yifḍálu*	يِفْضَلوا	*ma-yifḍalūš*	مَيِفْضَلوش	
ána	*báfḍal*	بَفْضَل	*ma-bafḍálš*	مَبَفْضَلْش	bi-imperfect
íḥna	*binífḍal*	بِنِفْضَل	*ma-bnifḍálš*	مَبْنِفْضَلْش	
ínta	*bitífḍal*	بِتِفْضَل	*ma-btifḍálš*	مَبْتِفْضَلْش	
ínti	*bitifḍáli*	بِتِفْضَلي	*ma-btifḍalīš*	مَبْتِفْضَليش	
íntu	*bitifḍálu*	بِتِفْضَلوا	*ma-btifḍalūš*	مَبْتِفْضَلوش	
húwwa	*biyífḍal*	بِيِفْضَل	*ma-byifḍálš*	مَبْيِفْضَلْش	
híyya	*bitífḍal*	بِتِفْضَل	*ma-btifḍálš*	مَبْتِفْضَلْش	
húmma	*biyifḍálu*	بِيِفْضَلوا	*ma-byifḍalūš*	مَبْيِفْضَلوش	
ána	*háfḍal*	هَفْضَل	*miš háfḍal*	مِش هَفْضَل	future
íḥna	*hanífḍal*	هَنِفْضَل	*miš hanífḍal*	مِش هَنِفْضَل	
ínta	*hatífḍal*	هَتِفْضَل	*miš hatífḍal*	مِش هَتِفْضَل	
ínti	*hatifḍáli*	هَتِفْضَلي	*miš hatifḍáli*	مِش هَتِفْضَلي	
íntu	*hatifḍálu*	هَتِفْضَلوا	*miš hatifḍálu*	مِش هَتِفْضَلوا	
húwwa	*hayífḍal*	هَيِفْضَل	*miš hayífḍal*	مِش هَيِفْضَل	
híyya	*hatífḍal*	هَتِفْضَل	*miš hatífḍal*	مِش هَتِفْضَل	
húmma	*hayifḍálu*	هَيِفْضَلوا	*miš hayifḍálu*	مِش هَيِفْضَلوا	
ínta	*ífḍal*	اِفْضَل	*ma-tifḍálš*	مَتِفْضَلْش	imperative
ínti	*ifḍáli*	اِفْضَلي	*ma-tifḍalīš*	مَتِفْضَليش	
íntu	*ifḍálu*	اِفْضَلوا	*ma-tifḍalūš*	مَتِفْضَلوش	

		active		passive		
masculine	*fāḍil*	فاضِل	–	–	participles
feminine	*fáḍla*	فاضْلَة	–	–	
plural	*faḍlīn*	فاضْلين	–	–	

no verbal noun

①

فِضِلْت أحاوِل أتْعلِّم الرّسْم لِحدّ ما أتْقنْته.

fiḍílt aḫāwil at3állim irrásmᵊ li-ḫaddᵊ ma -tqántu.

I kept trying to learn to draw until I mastered it.

②

متْخلّيش إبْنك يِفْضل يِتْفرّج عَ التِّليفِزْيوْن مُدد طَويلة.

ma-txallīš íbnak yífḍal yitfárrag 3a -ttilifizyōn múdad ṭawīla.

Don't leave your child watching TV for long periods.

③

مِراتي بِتِفْضل تِحْكي لِلوِلاد قِصص لِحدّ ما يْناموا.

mirāti bitífḍal tíḫki li-lwilād qíṣaṣ li-ḫaddᵊ ma ynāmu.

My wife keeps telling the kids stories until they fall asleep.

④

إنْتَ هتِفْضل حزين على الشُّغْلانة اللي راحِت لِحدّ إمْتى؟

ínta hatífḍal ḫazīn 3ála -ššuɣlāna -lli rāḫit li-ḫadd ímta?

How long are you going to remain upset about the job that you lost?

⑤

متِفْضلْش ساكِت لِحدّ ما النّاس تاكُل حقّك.

ma-tifḍálšᵊ sākit li-ḫaddᵊ ma -nnās tākul ḫáʔʔak.

Don't remain silent until people take your rights away.

⑥

سماح خرجِت مِ الاِمْتِحان و كان لِسّه فاضِلّها ساعة مِ الوَقْت.

samāḫ xáragit mi -lʔimtiḫān wi kān líssa faḍilláha sā3a mi -lwaʔt.

When Samah finished the exam, there was still one hour remaining / we still had one hour left.

❖ [1s4] **to remain, stay; to continue, keep** (doing)

- This verb is usually followed by an imperfect verb.
- It can also be followed by an adjective. (➲ 193.4, 193.5)
- The masculine active participle can take an indirect object pronoun followed by a time expression to express how much time is remaining for someone. (➲ 193.6)

➲ 1.2, 25.4, 37.3, 56.5, 77.1, 174.2, 210.5, 216.2, 233.5

194 to prefer fáḍḍal فضّل ١٠ ١٣

verbal noun: tafḍīl تفضيل

perfect

	affirmative		negative	
ána	faḍḍált	فَضّلْت	ma-faḍḍáltiš	مَفَضّلْتِش
íḥna	faḍḍálna	فَضّلْنا	ma-faḍḍalnāš	مَفَضّلْناش
ínta	faḍḍált	فَضّلْت	ma-faḍḍáltiš	مَفَضّلْتِش
ínti	faḍḍálti	فَضّلْتي	ma-faḍḍaltīš	مَفَضّلْتيش
íntu	faḍḍáltu	فَضّلْتوا	ma-faḍḍaltūš	مَفَضّلْتوش
húwwa	fáḍḍal	فَضّل	ma-faḍḍálš	مَفَضّلْش
híyya	faḍḍálit	فَضّلِت	ma-faḍḍalítš	مَفَضّلِتْش
húmma	faḍḍálu	فَضّلوا	ma-faḍḍalūš	مَفَضّلوش

imperfect

	affirmative		negative	
ána	afáḍḍal	أفَضّل	ma-faḍḍálš	مَفَضّلْش
íḥna	nifáḍḍal	نِفَضّل	ma-nfaḍḍálš	مَنْفَضّلْش
ínta	tifáḍḍal	تِفَضّل	ma-tfaḍḍálš	مَتْفَضّلْش
ínti	tifaḍḍáli	تِفَضّلي	ma-tfaḍḍalīš	مَتْفَضّليش
íntu	tifaḍḍálu	تِفَضّلوا	ma-tfaḍḍalūš	مَتْفَضّلوش
húwwa	yifáḍḍal	يِفَضّل	ma-yfaḍḍálš	مَيْفَضّلْش
híyya	tifáḍḍal	تِفَضّل	ma-tfaḍḍálš	مَتْفَضّلْش
húmma	yifaḍḍálu	يِفَضّلوا	ma-yfaḍḍalūš	مَيْفَضّلوش

bi-imperfect

	affirmative		negative	
ána	bafáḍḍal	بَفَضّل	ma-bafaḍḍálš	مَبَفَضّلْش
íḥna	binfáḍḍal	بِنْفَضّل	ma-binfaḍḍálš	مَبِنْفَضّلْش
ínta	bitfáḍḍal	بِتْفَضّل	ma-bitfaḍḍálš	مَبِتْفَضّلْش
ínti	bitfaḍḍáli	بِتْفَضّلي	ma-bitfaḍḍalīš	مَبِتْفَضّليش
íntu	bitfaḍḍálu	بِتْفَضّلوا	ma-bitfaḍḍalūš	مَبِتْفَضّلوش
húwwa	biyfáḍḍal	بِيْفَضّل	ma-biyfaḍḍálš	مَبِيْفَضّلْش
híyya	bitfáḍḍal	بِتْفَضّل	ma-bitfaḍḍálš	مَبِتْفَضّلْش
húmma	biyfaḍḍálu	بِيْفَضّلوا	ma-biyfaḍḍalūš	مَبِيْفَضّلوش

future

	affirmative		negative	
ána	hafáḍḍal	هَفَضّل	miš hafáḍḍal	مِش هَفَضّل
íḥna	hanfáḍḍal	هَنْفَضّل	miš hanfáḍḍal	مِش هَنْفَضّل
ínta	hatfáḍḍal	هَتْفَضّل	miš hatfáḍḍal	مِش هَتْفَضّل
ínti	hatfaḍḍáli	هَتْفَضّلي	miš hatfaḍḍáli	مِش هَتْفَضّلي
íntu	hatfaḍḍálu	هَتْفَضّلوا	miš hatfaḍḍálu	مِش هَتْفَضّلوا
húwwa	hayfáḍḍal	هَيْفَضّل	miš hayfáḍḍal	مِش هَيْفَضّل
híyya	hatfáḍḍal	هَتْفَضّل	miš hatfáḍḍal	مِش هَتْفَضّل
húmma	hayfaḍḍálu	هَيْفَضّلوا	miš hayfaḍḍálu	مِش هَيْفَضّلوا

imperative

	affirmative		negative	
ínta	fáḍḍal	فَضّل	ma-tfaḍḍálš	مَتْفَضّلْش
ínti	faḍḍáli	فَضّلي	ma-tfaḍḍalīš	مَتْفَضّليش
íntu	faḍḍálu	فَضّلوا	ma-tfaḍḍalūš	مَتْفَضّلوش

participles

	active		passive	
masculine	mifáḍḍal	مِفَضّل	mufáḍḍal	مُفَضّل
feminine	mifaḍḍála	مِفَضّلة	mufaḍḍála	مُفَضّلة
plural	mifaḍḍalīn	مِفَضّلين	mufaḍḍalīn	مُفَضّلين

①

نادِر فضّل يِسافِر معَ أُسْرِتُه على إنُّه يِـروح معَ أصْحابُه.

nādir fáḍḍal yisāfir má3a ʔusrítu 3ála ʔínnu yirūḥ má3a ʔaṣḥābu.

Nader preferred traveling with his family over going with his friends.

②

أنا مفضّلْش الفُسْتان ده. لوْنُه فاقِع أوي.

ána ma-faḍḍálš ilfustān da. lōnu fāʔi3 áwi.

I don't care for this dress. It's too bright.

③

أُميْمة بِتْفضّل تِسافِر تِدْرِس برّه على إنّها تُقْعُد هِنا.

umēma bitfáḍḍal tisāfir tídris bárra 3ála -nnáha túʔ3ud hína.

Omaima would rather go abroad to study than stay here.

④

لَوْ خيّروني بينْ أنْواع اللُّحوم، هفضّل الضّاني.

law xayyarūni bēn anwā3 illuḥūm, hafáḍḍal iḍḍāni.

If they let me choose the kind of meat, I'd prefer lamb.

⑤

متْفضّلْش النّاس على بعْض بْشكْلُهُم. المُهِمّ الأخْلاق.

ma-tfaḍḍálš innās 3ála ba3ḍ^{a} b-šaklúhum. ilmuhímm ilʔaxlāʔ.

Don't give preference to people by their looks. Manners are the important thing.

❖ [2s2] **to prefer, favor**

- The passive participle can translate as 'favorite'. (➲ 92.6)
- The passive participle can also be متْفضّل *mitfáḍḍal*.

➲ 35.3, 81.2, 100.2, 104.2

195 to think fákkar فكّر 

	affirmative		negative		
ána	fakkárt	فَكَّرْت	ma-fakkártiš	مَفَكَّرْتِش	perfect
íḥna	fakkárna	فَكَّرْنا	ma-fakkarnāš	مَفَكَّرْناش	
ínta	fakkárt	فَكَّرْت	ma-fakkártiš	مَفَكَّرْتِش	
ínti	fakkárti	فَكَّرْتي	ma-fakkartīš	مَفَكَّرْتيش	
íntu	fakkártu	فَكَّرْتوا	ma-fakkartūš	مَفَكَّرْتوش	
húwwa	fákkar	فَكَّر	ma-fakkárš	مَفَكَّرْش	
híyya	fakkárit	فَكَّرِت	ma-fakkarítš	مَفَكَّرِتْش	
húmma	fakkáru	فَكَّروا	ma-fakkarūš	مَفَكَّروش	
ána	afákkar	أَفَكَّر	ma-fakkárš	مَفَكَّرْش	imperfect
íḥna	nifákkar	نِفَكَّر	ma-nfakkárš	مَنْفَكَّرْش	
ínta	tifákkar	تِفَكَّر	ma-tfakkárš	مَتْفَكَّرْش	
ínti	tifakkári	تِفَكَّري	ma-tfakkarīš	مَتْفَكَّريش	
íntu	tifakkáru	تِفَكَّروا	ma-tfakkarūš	مَتْفَكَّروش	
húwwa	yifákkar	يِفَكَّر	ma-yfakkárš	مَيْفَكَّرْش	
híyya	tifákkar	تِفَكَّر	ma-tfakkárš	مَتْفَكَّرْش	
húmma	yifakkáru	يِفَكَّروا	ma-yfakkarūš	مَيْفَكَّروش	
ána	bafákkar	بَفَكَّر	ma-bafakkárš	مَبَفَكَّرْش	bi-imperfect
íḥna	binfákkar	بِنْفَكَّر	ma-binfakkárš	مَبِنْفَكَّرْش	
ínta	bitfákkar	بِتْفَكَّر	ma-bitfakkárš	مَبِتْفَكَّرْش	
ínti	bitfakkári	بِتْفَكَّري	ma-bitfakkarīš	مَبِتْفَكَّريش	
íntu	bitfakkáru	بِتْفَكَّروا	ma-bitfakkarūš	مَبِتْفَكَّروش	
húwwa	biyfákkar	بِيْفَكَّر	ma-biyfakkárš	مَبِيْفَكَّرْش	
híyya	bitfákkar	بِتْفَكَّر	ma-bitfakkárš	مَبِتْفَكَّرْش	
húmma	biyfakkáru	بِيْفَكَّروا	ma-biyfakkarūš	مَبِيْفَكَّروش	
ána	hafákkar	هَفَكَّر	miš hafákkar	مِش هَفَكَّر	future
íḥna	hanfákkar	هَنْفَكَّر	miš hanfákkar	مِش هَنْفَكَّر	
ínta	hatfákkar	هَتْفَكَّر	miš hatfákkar	مِش هَتْفَكَّر	
ínti	hatfakkári	هَتْفَكَّري	miš hatfakkári	مِش هَتْفَكَّري	
íntu	hatfakkáru	هَتْفَكَّروا	miš hatfakkáru	مِش هَتْفَكَّروا	
húwwa	hayfákkar	هَيْفَكَّر	miš hayfákkar	مِش هَيْفَكَّر	
híyya	hatfákkar	هَتْفَكَّر	miš hatfákkar	مِش هَتْفَكَّر	
húmma	hayfakkáru	هَيْفَكَّروا	miš hayfakkáru	مِش هَيْفَكَّروا	
ínta	fákkar	فَكَّر	ma-tfakkárš	مَتْفَكَّرْش	imperative
ínti	fakkári	فَكَّري	ma-tfakkarīš	مَتْفَكَّريش	
íntu	fakkáru	فَكَّروا	ma-tfakkarūš	مَتْفَكَّروش	

	active		passive		
masculine	mifákkar	مِفَكَّر	mitfákkar	مِتْفَكَّر	participles
feminine	mifakkára	مِفَكَّرَة	mitfakkára	مِتْفَكَّرَة	
plural	mifakkarīn	مِفَكَّرين	mitfakkarīn	مِتْفَكَّرين	

verbal noun: *tafkīr* تَفْكير - *fikr* فِكْر

①

أنا فكّرْت أجيلّك إمْبارِح بسّ كِسِلْت.

ána fakkárt agíllak imbārih bassᵊ kisílt.

I thought about coming over [to your place] yesterday, but I couldn't be bothered.

②

المُحامي حاوِل يِفكّر في كُلّ الدِّفاعات بسّ واضِح إنّ القضية خسْرانة.

ilmuhāmi hāwil yifákkar fi kull iddifa3āt bassᵊ wādih inn ilʔadíyya xasrāna.

The lawyer tried to think of all the defenses, but it appears that it's a lost case.

③

سُنْدُس مبتْفكّرْش في الخِلْفة دِلْوَقْتي. عايْزة تْخلّص دِراسِتْها الأوِّل.

súndus ma-batfakkáršᵊ fi -lxílfa dilwáʔti. 3áyza txállas dirasítha -lʔáwwil.

Sondos isn't thinking of having a child now. She wants to finish her studies first.

④

هفكّر في عرْضك و أرُدّ عليْك بُكْره.

hafákkar fi 3árdak w arúddᵊ 3alēk búkra.

I'll think about your offer and get back to you tomorrow.

⑤

متْفكّريش تُدْخُلي هنْدسة. كُلّية صعْبة أوي لَوْ معنْدِكيش فيها هدف واضِح.

ma-tfakkarīš tudxúli handása. kullíyya sá3ba ʔáwi law ma-3andikīš fīha hádaf wādih.

Don't think of studying [in the department of] engineering. It's a tough place if you don't have a clear objective.

⑥

أُمّي دايْماً تِفكّرْني أخُد الجاكيتّ عشان الجَوّ هَيِبْرد.

úmmi dáyman tifakkárni ʔāxud ilžakíttᵊ 3ašān ilgáwwᵊ hayíbrad.

My mom always reminds me to take a jacket with me because it'll get cold.

⑦

متْفكّروش بِاليوْم ده. كُلّ ما يِفْتِكِر بِيِتْنكِّد.

ma-tfakkarūš bi-lyōm da. kullᵊ ma yiftíkir biyitnákkid.

Don't remind him of that day. He gets upset every time he remembers.

❖ [2s2] **to think** (**of/about** في *fi*); **to remind** (someone **of/about** بِـ *bi-*)

➲ 64.1, 172.3

196 to understand *fíhim* فِهِم

	affirmative		negative		
ána	*fihímt*	فِهِمْت	*ma-fhímtiš*	مَفْهِمْتِش	perfect
íḥna	*fihímna*	فِهِمْنا	*ma-fhimnāš*	مَفْهِمْناش	
ínta	*fihímt*	فِهِمْت	*ma-fhímtiš*	مَفْهِمْتِش	
ínti	*fihímti*	فِهِمْتي	*ma-fhimtīš*	مَفْهِمْتيش	
íntu	*fihímtu*	فِهِمْتوا	*ma-fhimtūš*	مَفْهِمْتوش	
húwwa	*fíhim*	فِهِم	*ma-fhímš*	مَفْهِمْش	
híyya	*fíhmit*	فِهْمِت	*ma-fihmítš*	مَفِهْمِتْش	
húmma	*fíhmu*	فِهْموا	*ma-fihmūš*	مَفِهْموش	
ána	*áfham*	أَفْهَم	*ma-fhámš*	مَفْهَمْش	imperfect
íḥna	*nífham*	نِفْهَم	*ma-nifhámš*	مَنِفْهَمْش	
ínta	*tífham*	تِفْهَم	*ma-tifhámš*	مَتِفْهَمْش	
ínti	*tifhámi*	تِفْهَمي	*ma-tifhamīš*	مَتِفْهَميش	
íntu	*tifhámu*	تِفْهَموا	*ma-tifhamūš*	مَتِفْهَموش	
húwwa	*yífham*	يِفْهَم	*ma-yifhámš*	مَيِفْهَمْش	
híyya	*tífham*	تِفْهَم	*ma-tifhámš*	مَتِفْهَمْش	
húmma	*yifhámu*	يِفْهَموا	*ma-yifhamūš*	مَيِفْهَموش	
ána	*báfham*	بَفْهَم	*ma-bafhámš*	مَبَفْهَمْش	bi-imperfect
íḥna	*binífham*	بِنِفْهَم	*ma-bnifhámš*	مَبْنِفْهَمْش	
ínta	*bitífham*	بِتِفْهَم	*ma-btifhámš*	مَبْتِفْهَمْش	
ínti	*bitifhámi*	بِتِفْهَمي	*ma-btifhamīš*	مَبْتِفْهَميش	
íntu	*bitifhámu*	بِتِفْهَموا	*ma-btifhamūš*	مَبْتِفْهَموش	
húwwa	*biyífham*	بِيِفْهَم	*ma-byifhámš*	مَبْيِفْهَمْش	
híyya	*bitífham*	بِتِفْهَم	*ma-btifhámš*	مَبْتِفْهَمْش	
húmma	*biyifhámu*	بِيِفْهَموا	*ma-byifhamūš*	مَبْيِفْهَموش	
ána	*háfham*	هَفْهَم	*miš háfham*	مِش هَفْهَم	future
íḥna	*hanífham*	هَنِفْهَم	*miš hanífham*	مِش هَنِفْهَم	
ínta	*hatífham*	هَتِفْهَم	*miš hatífham*	مِش هَتِفْهَم	
ínti	*hatifhámi*	هَتِفْهَمي	*miš hatifhámi*	مِش هَتِفْهَمي	
íntu	*hatifhámu*	هَتِفْهَموا	*miš hatifhámu*	مِش هَتِفْهَموا	
húwwa	*hayífham*	هَيِفْهَم	*miš hayífham*	مِش هَيِفْهَم	
híyya	*hatífham*	هَتِفْهَم	*miš hatífham*	مِش هَتِفْهَم	
húmma	*hayifhámu*	هَيِفْهَموا	*miš hayifhámu*	مِش هَيِفْهَموا	
ínta	*ífham*	اِفْهَم	*ma-tifhámš*	مَتِفْهَمْش	imperative
ínti	*ifhámi*	اِفْهَمي	*ma-tifhamīš*	مَتِفْهَميش	
íntu	*ifhámu*	اِفْهَموا	*ma-tifhamūš*	مَتِفْهَموش	

	active		passive		
masculine	*fāhim*	فاهِم	*mafhūm*	مَفْهوم	participles
feminine	*fáhma*	فاهْمَة	*mafhūma*	مَفْهومَة	
plural	*fahmīn*	فاهْمين	*mafhumīn*	مَفْهومين	

verbal noun: *fahm* فَهْم

①

شذا فِهْمِت الدّرْس بعْد ما المُدرِّس عاد تلات مرّات.

šáza fíhmit iddárs^ə ba3d^ə ma -lmudárris 3ād tálat marrāt.

Shatha understood the lesson after the teacher repeated it three times.

②

أنا مُش قادْرة أفْهم سبب مُضايْقْتك مِن كلامُه.

ána muš ʔádr- áfham sábab muḍáyʔtak min kalāmu.

I can't understand why what he said upset you.

③

المُدرِّس بيْقول إنّ شادي دايْماً مَبْيِفْهمْش في الفصْل.

ilmudárris biyʔūl inn^ə šādi dáyman ma-byifhámš^ə fi -lfaṣl.

The teacher says that Shady never understands in class.

④

هفهم المَوْضوع و أجي أحْكيلك.

háfham ilmawḍū3 w ági ʔaḫkīlak.

I'll figure out the issue and come tell you.

⑤

متِفْهمْش إني خايْفة مِنّك، أبداً. أنا بسّ مِش عايْزة أجرّحك.

ma-tifhámš ínni xáyfa mínnak, ábadan. ána bass^ə miš 3áyz- agarráḫak.

Don't think that I'm afraid of you. Not at all. It's just that I don't want to hurt you.

❖ [1s4] **to understand**

➲ 1.2, 26.3, 98.1, 127.3, 136.1, 169.1, 171.2, 228.1, 228.5

197 to explain *fáhhim* فهّم

١٠ ٣١

	affirmative		negative		
ána	*fahhímt*	فهّمْت	*ma-fahhímtiš*	مَفَهّمْتِش	perfect
íḥna	*fahhímna*	فهّمْنا	*ma-fahhimnāš*	مَفَهّمْناش	
ínta	*fahhímt*	فهّمْت	*ma-fahhímtiš*	مَفَهّمْتِش	
ínti	*fahhímti*	فهّمْتي	*ma-fahhimtīš*	مَفَهّمْتيش	
íntu	*fahhímtu*	فهّمْتوا	*ma-fahhimtūš*	مَفَهّمْتوش	
húwwa	*fáhhim*	فهّم	*ma-fahhímš*	مَفَهّمْش	
híyya	*fahhímit*	فهّمِت	*ma-fahhimítš*	مَفَهّمِتْش	
húmma	*fahhímu*	فهّموا	*ma-fahhimūš*	مَفَهّموش	
ána	*afáhhim*	أفهّم	*ma-fahhímš*	مَفَهّمْش	imperfect
íḥna	*nifáhhim*	نِفهّم	*ma-nfahhímš*	مَنْفهّمْش	
ínta	*tifáhhim*	تِفهّم	*ma-tfahhímš*	مَتْفهّمْش	
ínti	*tifahhími*	تِفهّمي	*ma-tfahhimīš*	مَتْفهّميش	
íntu	*tifahhímu*	تِفهّموا	*ma-tfahhimūš*	مَتْفهّموش	
húwwa	*yifáhhim*	يِفهّم	*ma-yfahhímš*	مَيْفهّمْش	
híyya	*tifáhhim*	تِفهّم	*ma-tfahhímš*	مَتْفهّمْش	
húmma	*yifahhímu*	يِفهّموا	*ma-yfahhimūš*	مَيْفهّموش	
ána	*bafáhhim*	بَفهّم	*ma-bafahhímš*	مَبَفهّمْش	bi-imperfect
íḥna	*binfáhhim*	بِنْفهّم	*ma-binfahhímš*	مَبِنْفهّمْش	
ínta	*bitfáhhim*	بِتْفهّم	*ma-bitfahhímš*	مَبِتْفهّمْش	
ínti	*bitfahhími*	بِتْفهّمي	*ma-bitfahhimīš*	مَبِتْفهّميش	
íntu	*bitfahhímu*	بِتْفهّموا	*ma-bitfahhimūš*	مَبِتْفهّموش	
húwwa	*biyfáhhim*	بِيْفهّم	*ma-biyfahhímš*	مَبِيْفهّمْش	
híyya	*bitfáhhim*	بِتْفهّم	*ma-bitfahhímš*	مَبِتْفهّمْش	
húmma	*biyfahhímu*	بِيْفهّموا	*ma-biyfahhimūš*	مَبِيْفهّموش	
ána	*hafáhhim*	هَفهّم	*miš hafáhhim*	مِش هَفهّم	future
íḥna	*hanfáhhim*	هَنْفهّم	*miš hanfáhhim*	مِش هَنْفهّم	
ínta	*hatfáhhim*	هَتْفهّم	*miš hatfáhhim*	مِش هَتْفهّم	
ínti	*hatfahhími*	هَتْفهّمي	*miš hatfahhími*	مِش هَتْفهّمي	
íntu	*hatfahhímu*	هَتْفهّموا	*miš hatfahhímu*	مِش هَتْفهّموا	
húwwa	*hayfáhhim*	هَيْفهّم	*miš hayfáhhim*	مِش هَيْفهّم	
híyya	*hatfáhhim*	هَتْفهّم	*miš hatfáhhim*	مِش هَتْفهّم	
húmma	*hayfahhímu*	هَيْفهّموا	*miš hayfahhímu*	مِش هَيْفهّموا	
ínta	*fáhhim*	فهّم	*ma-tfahhímš*	مَتْفهّمْش	imperative
ínti	*fahhími*	فهّمي	*ma-tfahhimīš*	مَتْفهّميش	
íntu	*fahhímu*	فهّموا	*ma-tfahhimūš*	مَتْفهّموش	

	active		passive		
masculine	*mifáhhim*	مِفهّم	*mitfáhhim*	مِتْفهّم	participles
feminine	*mifahhíma*	مِفهّمة	*mitfahhíma*	مِتْفهّمة	
plural	*mifahhimīn*	مِفهّمين	*mitfahhimīn*	مِتْفهّمين	

verbal noun: *tafhīm* تفهيم

①

فهِّمْني أزّاي تُخْرُج تِتْغدّى معَ السِّكِرْتيرْة لْوَحْدُكو؟ بِمُناسْبِةْ أيْه؟

fahhímni -zzāy túxrug tityáddaa má3a -ssikirtēra l-waḥdúku? bi-munásbit ʔē?

Explain to me how you would have lunch alone
with the secretary? Under what circumstances?

②

لَوْ مفهِّمْتيهاش المسْألة دي مُش هتِعْرف تِحِلّ في الاِمْتِحان.

law ma-fahhimtihāš ilmasʔála di muš hatí3raf tiḥillᵊ fi -lʔimtiḥān.

If you don't explain this equation to her, she
may not be able to get it on the exam.

③

بِيْفهِّمونا إنّ الخيرْ دايْماً بِيِنْتِصِر، بسّ دي مِش حقيقة.

biyfahhimūna ʔinn ilxēr dáyman biyintíṣir, bassᵊ di miš ḥaʔīʔa.

They tell us that good always
prevails, but it isn't true.

④

شُروق هتْفهِّمْكو الدّرْس ده و بعْديْن هنْحِلّ أمْثِلة معَ بعْض.

šurūʔ hatfahhímku -ddarsᵊ da wi ba3dēn hanḥíll amsíla má3a ba3ḍ.

Shorouk will explain this lesson to you. Then
we'll solve some examples together.

⑤

متْفِهِّمْنيش إنّك كُلّ ده كُنْت بِتْذاكِر معَ صاحْبك، لِإنُّه إتّصل مِن ساعة و سأل عليْك.

ma-tfihhimnīš ínnak kullᵊ da kuntᵊ bitzākir má3a ṣáḥbak, li-ínnu -ttáṣal min sā3a wi sáʔal 3alēk.

(father to son:) Don't tell me that you were studying with your friend all that
time, because he called asking for you an hour ago.

❖ [2s1] **to explain, make understand**

- This verb can be ditransitive, taking two objects. The first is the person, and the second is the thing being explained.

198 to meet ʔābil قابِل

	affirmative		negative		
ána	ʔabílt	قابِلْت	ma-ʔabíltiš	مَقابِلْتِش	perfect
íḥna	ʔabílna	قابِلْنا	ma-ʔabilnāš	مَقابِلْناش	
ínta	ʔabílt	قابِلْت	ma-ʔabíltiš	مَقابِلْتِش	
ínti	ʔabílti	قابِلْتي	ma-ʔabiltīš	مَقابِلْتيش	
íntu	ʔabíltu	قابِلْتوا	ma-ʔabiltūš	مَقابِلْتوش	
húwwa	ʔābil	قابِل	ma-ʔabílš	مَقابِلْش	
híyya	ʔáblit	قابْلِت	ma-ʔablítš	مَقابْلِتْش	
húmma	ʔáblu	قابْلوا	ma-ʔablūš	مَقابْلوش	
ána	aʔābil	أقابِل	ma-ʔabílš	مَقابِلْش	imperfect
íḥna	niʔābil	نِقابِل	ma-nʔabílš	مَنْقابِلْش	
ínta	tiʔābil	تِقابِل	ma-tʔabílš	مَتْقابِلْش	
ínti	tiʔábli	تِقابْلي	ma-tʔablīš	مَتْقابْليش	
íntu	tiʔáblu	تِقابْلوا	ma-tʔablūš	مَتْقابْلوش	
húwwa	yiʔābil	يِقابِل	ma-yʔabílš	مَيْقابِلْش	
híyya	tiʔābil	تِقابِل	ma-tʔabílš	مَتْقابِلْش	
húmma	yiʔáblu	يِقابْلوا	ma-yʔablūš	مَيْقابْلوش	
ána	baʔābil	بَقابِل	ma-baʔabílš	مَبَقابِلْش	bi-imperfect
íḥna	binʔābil	بِنْقابِل	ma-binʔabílš	مَبِنْقابِلْش	
ínta	bitʔābil	بِتْقابِل	ma-bitʔabílš	مَبِتْقابِلْش	
ínti	bitʔábli	بِتْقابْلي	ma-bitʔablīš	مَبِتْقابْليش	
íntu	bitʔáblu	بِتْقابْلوا	ma-bitʔablūš	مَبِتْقابْلوش	
húwwa	biyʔābil	بِيْقابِل	ma-biyʔabílš	مَبِيْقابِلْش	
híyya	bitʔābil	بِتْقابِل	ma-bitʔabílš	مَبِتْقابِلْش	
húmma	biyʔáblu	بِيْقابْلوا	ma-biyʔablūš	مَبِيْقابْلوش	
ána	haʔābil	هَقابِل	miš haʔābil	مِش هَقابِل	future
íḥna	hanʔābil	هَنْقابِل	miš hanʔābil	مِش هَنْقابِل	
ínta	hatʔābil	هَتْقابِل	miš hatʔābil	مِش هَتْقابِل	
ínti	hatʔábli	هَتْقابْلي	miš hatʔábli	مِش هَتْقابْلي	
íntu	hatʔáblu	هَتْقابْلوا	miš hatʔáblu	مِش هَتْقابْلوا	
húwwa	hayʔābil	هَيْقابِل	miš hayʔābil	مِش هَيْقابِل	
híyya	hatʔābil	هَتْقابِل	miš hatʔābil	مِش هَتْقابِل	
húmma	hayʔáblu	هَيْقابْلوا	miš hayʔáblu	مِش هَيْقابْلوا	
ínta	ʔābil	قابِل	ma-tʔabílš	مَتْقابِلْش	imperative
ínti	ʔábli	قابْلي	ma-tʔablīš	مَتْقابْليش	
íntu	ʔáblu	قابْلوا	ma-tʔablūš	مَتْقابْلوش	

	active		passive		
masculine	miʔābil	مِقابِل	mitʔābil	مِتْقابِل	participles
feminine	miʔábla	مِقابْلَة	mitʔábla	مِتْقابْلَة	
plural	miʔablīn	مِقابْلين	mitʔablīn	مِتْقابْلين	

verbal noun: *muʔábla* مُقابْلَة

①

إِنْتَ قابِلْت محمّد قبْل كِده؟

ínta ʔabílt[ə] maђámmad ʔabl[ə] kída?

Have you met Mohamed before?

②

زِياد نِفْسُه يْقابِل نانْسي عجْرم.

ziyād nífsu yʔābil nánsi 3ágram.

Zeyad wishes he could meet Nancy Ajram [the Lebanese singer].

③

أنا و بنات خيلاني مبْنِتْقابِلْش كْتير لِلأسف.

ána wi banāt xilāni ma-bnitʔabílš[ə] ktīr li-lʔásaf.

My cousins and I don't meet much, unfortunately.

④

هنِتْقابِل إمْتي؟ وَحشْتوني.

hanitʔābil ímta? waђaštūni?

When will we meet? I miss you guys.

⑤

متْقابِلْش أهْل العريس برّه. تعالى نْقابِلْهُم في البيْت.

ma-tʔabílš ahl il3arīs bárra. ta3āla nʔabílhum fi -lbēt.

Don't meet the [potential] groom's parents out [i.e. in a restaurant, etc.]. Let's have them over to meet.

⑥

قابِلْني عَ الناصْيَة كمان نُصّ ساعة.

ʔabílni 3a -nnáṣya kamān nuṣṣ[ə] sā3a.

Meet me at the corner in half an hour.

❖ [3s] **to meet**

- This verb can cover two meanings, as does the English 'meet': meet for the first time (become acquainted with) (➲ 198.1, 198.2, 198.5) and meet up with (as an arrangement) (➲ 198.3, 198.4, 198.6).

➲ 179.1, 186.1, 244.6

199 to lead qād قاد

	affirmative		negative		
ána	qudt	قُدْت	ma-qúdtiš	مَقُدْتِش	perfect
íḫna	qúdna	قُدْنا	ma-qudnāš	مَقُدْناش	
ínta	qudt	قُدْت	ma-qúdtiš	مَقُدْتِش	
ínti	qúdti	قُدْتي	ma-qudtīš	مَقُدْتيش	
íntu	qúdtu	قُدْتوا	ma-qudtūš	مَقُدْتوش	
húwwa	qād	قاد	ma-qádš	مَقادْش	
híyya	qādit	قادِت	ma-qadítš	مَقادِتْش	
húmma	qādu	قادوا	ma-qadūš	مَقادوش	
ána	aqūd	أقود	ma-qúdš	مَقودْش	imperfect
íḫna	niqūd	نِقود	ma-nqúdš	مَنْقودْش	
ínta	tiqūd	تِقود	ma-tqúdš	مَتْقودْش	
ínti	tiqūdi	تِقودي	ma-tqudīš	مَتْقوديش	
íntu	tiqūdu	تِقودوا	ma-tqudūš	مَتْقودوش	
húwwa	yiqūd	يِقود	ma-yqúdš	مَيْقودْش	
híyya	tiqūd	تِقود	ma-tqúdš	مَتْقودْش	
húmma	yiqūdu	يِقودوا	ma-yqudūš	مَيْقودوش	
ána	baqūd	بَقود	ma-baqúdš	مَبَقودْش	bi-imperfect
íḫna	binqūd	بِنْقود	ma-binqúdš	مَبِنْقودْش	
ínta	bitqūd	بِتْقود	ma-bitqúdš	مَبِتْقودْش	
ínti	bitqūdi	بِتْقودي	ma-bitqudīš	مَبِتْقوديش	
íntu	bitqūdu	بِتْقودوا	ma-bitqudūš	مَبِتْقودوش	
húwwa	biyqūd	بِيْقود	ma-biyqúdš	مَبِيْقودْش	
híyya	bitqūd	بِتْقود	ma-bitqúdš	مَبِتْقودْش	
húmma	biyqūdu	بِيْقودوا	ma-biyqudūš	مَبِيْقودوش	
ána	haqūd	هَقود	miš haqūd	مِش هَقود	future
íḫna	hanqūd	هَنْقود	miš hanqūd	مِش هَنْقود	
ínta	hatqūd	هَتْقود	miš hatqūd	مِش هَتْقود	
ínti	hatqūdi	هَتْقودي	miš hatqūdi	مِش هَتْقودي	
íntu	hatqūdu	هَتْقودوا	miš hatqūdu	مِش هَتْقودوا	
húwwa	hayqūd	هَيْقود	miš hayqūd	مِش هَيْقود	
híyya	hatqūd	هَتْقود	miš hatqūd	مِش هَتْقود	
húmma	hayqūdu	هَيْقودوا	miš hayqūdu	مِش هَيْقودوا	
ínta	qūd	قود	ma-tqúdš	مَتْقودْش	imperative
ínti	qūdi	قودي	ma-tqudīš	مَتْقوديش	
íntu	qūdu	قودوا	ma-tqudūš	مَتْقودوش	

	active		passive		
masculine	qāyid	قايِد	mitʔād	مِتْقاد	participles
feminine	qáyda	قايْدَة	mitʔāda	مِتْقادَة	
plural	qaydīn	قايْدين	mitʔadīn	مِتْقادين	

verbal noun: *qiyāda* قِيادة

①

المايِسْترو قاد الفِرْقة بِشكْل مُمْتاز.

ilmáystru qād ilfírʔa bi-šáklᵊ mumtāz.

The conductor conducted [lit. led]
the orchestra perfectly.

②

لمّا حاوِلْت أقود فريق الكشّافة، اِكْتشفْت إنّها مُهِمّة صعْبة.

lámma ħawílt aqūd farīʔ ilkaššāfa, iktašáft innáha muhímma ṣá3ba.

When I tried to lead the scout troop,
I discovered it's a difficult task.

③

أنا عارْفة إنّ معنْديش مهارِةْ القِيادة. عشان كِده مبقودْش فريقْنا أبداً.

ána 3árfa ʔinnᵊ ma-3andīš mahārit ilqiyāda. 3ašān kída ma-baqúdšᵊ faríʔna ʔábadan.

I know I don't have leadership skills. That's
why I don't ever lead our team.

④

المُدرِّسة حدِّدِت إنّ جنا هِيَّ اللي هتْقود الفِرْقة عَ المسْرح.

ilmudarrísa ħaddídit innᵊ žána híyya -lli hatqūd ilfírʔa 3a -lmásraħ.

The teacher chose Jana to lead the band in the theater.

⑤

متْقودْش فريقك بِالشّخْط و النّطْر. لازِم تِساعْدوا بعْض عشان تِنْجحوا كُلُّكو.

ma-tqúdšᵊ farīʔak bi-ššaxṭᵊ w innáṭr. lāzim tisá3du ba3ḍᵊ 3ašān tingáħu kullúku.

Don't lead your team by screaming and yelling.
You should help each other to succeed.

❖ [1h1] **to lead**

- Notice that ق is pronounced *q* in all forms except the passive participle, where it is pronounced *ʔ*.

200 to say ʔāl قال

verbal nouns: ʔōl قوْل - ʔiwāla قِوالة - ʔawalān قوَلان

	affirmative		negative		
ána	ʔult	قُلْت	ma-ʔúltiš	مَقُلْتِش	perfect
íḫna	ʔúlna	قُلْنا	ma-ʔulnāš	مَقُلْناش	
ínta	ʔult	قُلْت	ma-ʔúltiš	مَقُلْتِش	
ínti	ʔúlti	قُلْتي	ma-ʔultīš	مَقُلْتيش	
íntu	ʔúltu	قُلْتوا	ma-ʔultūš	مَقُلْتوش	
húwwa	ʔāl	قال	ma-ʔálš	مَقالْش	
híyya	ʔālit	قالِت	ma-ʔalítš	مَقالِتْش	
húmma	ʔālu	قالوا	ma-ʔalūš	مَقالوش	
ána	aʔūl	أقول	ma-ʔúlš	مَقولْش	imperfect
íḫna	niʔūl	نِقول	ma-nʔúlš	مَنْقولْش	
ínta	tiʔūl	تِقول	ma-tʔúlš	مَتْقولْش	
ínti	tiʔūli	تِقولي	ma-tʔulīš	مَتْقوليش	
íntu	tiʔūlu	تِقولوا	ma-tʔulūš	مَتْقولوش	
húwwa	yiʔūl	يِقول	ma-yʔúlš	مَيْقولْش	
híyya	tiʔūl	تِقول	ma-tʔúlš	مَتْقولْش	
húmma	yiʔūlu	يِقولوا	ma-yʔulūš	مَيْقولوش	
ána	baʔūl	بَقول	ma-baʔúlš	مَبَقولْش	bi-imperfect
íḫna	binʔūl	بِنْقول	ma-binʔúlš	مَبِنْقولْش	
ínta	bitʔūl	بِتْقول	ma-bitʔúlš	مَبِتْقولْش	
ínti	bitʔūli	بِتْقولي	ma-bitʔulīš	مَبِتْقوليش	
íntu	bitʔūlu	بِتْقولوا	ma-bitʔulūš	مَبِتْقولوش	
húwwa	biyʔūl	بِيْقول	ma-biyʔúlš	مَبِيْقولْش	
híyya	bitʔūl	بِتْقول	ma-bitʔúlš	مَبِتْقولْش	
húmma	biyʔūlu	بِيْقولوا	ma-biyʔulūš	مَبِيْقولوش	
ána	haʔūl	هَقول	miš haʔūl	مِش هَقول	future
íḫna	hanʔūl	هَنْقول	miš hanʔūl	مِش هَنْقول	
ínta	hatʔūl	هَتْقول	miš hatʔūl	مِش هَتْقول	
ínti	hatʔūli	هَتْقولي	miš hatʔūli	مِش هَتْقولي	
íntu	hatʔūlu	هَتْقولوا	miš hatʔūlu	مِش هَتْقولوا	
húwwa	hayʔūl	هَيْقول	miš hayʔūl	مِش هَيْقول	
híyya	hatʔūl	هَتْقول	miš hatʔūl	مِش هَتْقول	
húmma	hayʔūlu	هَيْقولوا	miš hayʔūlu	مِش هَيْقولوا	
ínta	ʔūl	قول	ma-tʔúlš	مَتْقولْش	imperative
ínti	ʔūli	قولي	ma-tʔulīš	مَتْقوليش	
íntu	ʔūlu	قولوا	ma-tʔulūš	مَتْقولوش	

	active		passive		
masculine	ʔāyil	قايِل	mitʔāl	مِتْقال	participles
feminine	ʔáyla	قايْلَة	mitʔāla	مِتْقالَة	
plural	ʔaylīn	قايْلين	mitʔalīn	مِتْقالين	

①

إنْتَ مقُلْتِش لِنعْمات تِعدّي علَيْنا؟

ínta ma-ʔúltiš li-na3māt ti3áddi 3alēna?

Didn't you tell Neamat to come by?

②

جِدّي كان دايْماً يِقول أُسْرِتْكو هِيَّ سنِدْكو.

gíddi kān dáyman yiʔūl usrítku híyya sanádku.

My grandfather always said, "Your family is your support."

③

بقولّك أيْه، ما تيجي نْروح السّيما.

baʔúllak ʔē, ma tīgi nrūḥ issīma.

Hey, let's go to the cinema.

④

عُمْري ما هقولّك سِرّ. إنْتَ مبْيِتْبلِّش في بُقّك فولة.

3úmri ma haʔúllak sirr. ínta ma-byitbálliš fi búʔʔak fūla.

I'll never tell you a secret. You can't keep your mouth closed.

⑤

وَدّينا الملاهي يا بابا، عشان خاطْري متْقولْش لأ.

waddīna -lmalāhi ya bāba, 3ašān xáṭri ma-tʔúlšᵊ laʔ.

Dad, take us to the amusement park. Please don't say no.

❖ [1h1] **to say (to), tell** (لِ *li-*)

- When the indirect object suffix لِ is added to a form of this verb ending in ل (lam), we have a double lam. Many Egyptians write a single lam (with an implied ّ (shadda)), as is done in this book: بِتْقولُّه *bitʔúllu* 'she tells him', while others write two lams: بِتْقولْله.

➲ 9.4, 12.3, 15.5, 21.5, 22.4, 27.5, 28.5, 36.4, 60.5, 66.2, 73.6, 73.8, 73.9, 77.4, 78.2, 89.5, 91.3, 93.4, 111.2, 114.3, 116.1, 116.5, 131.2, 131.4, 143.4, 153.2, 157.5, 162.6, 166.4, 167.1, 170.2, 170.4, 175.6, 180.5, 196.3, 200.1, 213.2, 255.2

201 to get up ʔām قام

verbal nouns: ʔōm قوْم - ʔawamān قَوَمان

	affirmative		negative		
ána	ʔumt	قُمْت	ma-ʔúmtiš	مَقُمْتِش	perfect
íḥna	ʔúmna	قُمْنا	ma-ʔumnāš	مَقُمْناش	
ínta	ʔumt	قُمْت	ma-ʔúmtiš	مَقُمْتِش	
ínti	ʔúmti	قُمْتي	ma-ʔumtīš	مَقُمْتيش	
íntu	ʔúmtu	قُمْتوا	ma-ʔumtūš	مَقُمْتوش	
húwwa	ʔām	قام	ma-ʔámš	مَقامْش	
híyya	ʔāmit	قامِت	ma-ʔamítš	مَقامِتْش	
húmma	ʔāmu	قاموا	ma-ʔamūš	مَقاموش	
ána	aʔūm	أقوم	ma-ʔúmš	مَقومْش	imperfect
íḥna	niʔūm	نِقوم	ma-nʔúmš	مَنْقومْش	
ínta	tiʔūm	تِقوم	ma-tʔúmš	مَتْقومْش	
ínti	tiʔūmi	تِقومي	ma-tʔumīš	مَتْقوميش	
íntu	tiʔūmu	تِقوموا	ma-tʔumūš	مَتْقوموش	
húwwa	yiʔūm	يِقوم	ma-yʔúmš	مَيْقومْش	
híyya	tiʔūm	تِقوم	ma-tʔúmš	مَتْقومْش	
húmma	yiʔūmu	يِقوموا	ma-yʔumūš	مَيْقوموش	
ána	baʔūm	بَقوم	ma-baʔúmš	مَبَقومْش	bi-imperfect
íḥna	binʔūm	بِنْقوم	ma-binʔúmš	مَبِنْقومْش	
ínta	bitʔūm	بِتْقوم	ma-bitʔúmš	مَبِتْقومْش	
ínti	bitʔūmi	بِتْقومي	ma-bitʔumīš	مَبِتْقوميش	
íntu	bitʔūmu	بِتْقوموا	ma-bitʔumūš	مَبِتْقوموش	
húwwa	biyʔūm	بِيْقوم	ma-biyʔúmš	مَبِيْقومْش	
híyya	bitʔūm	بِتْقوم	ma-bitʔúmš	مَبِتْقومْش	
húmma	biyʔūmu	بِيْقوموا	ma-biyʔumūš	مَبِيْقوموش	
ána	haʔūm	هَقوم	miš haʔūm	مِش هَقوم	future
íḥna	hanʔūm	هَنْقوم	miš hanʔūm	مِش هَنْقوم	
ínta	hatʔūm	هَتْقوم	miš hatʔūm	مِش هَتْقوم	
ínti	hatʔūmi	هَتْقومي	miš hatʔūmi	مِش هَتْقومي	
íntu	hatʔūmu	هَتْقوموا	miš hatʔūmu	مِش هَتْقوموا	
húwwa	hayʔūm	هَيْقوم	miš hayʔūm	مِش هَيْقوم	
híyya	hatʔūm	هَتْقوم	miš hatʔūm	مِش هَتْقوم	
húmma	hayʔūmu	هَيْقوموا	miš hayʔūmu	مِش هَيْقوموا	
ínta	ʔūm	قوم	ma-tʔúmš	مَتْقومْش	imperative
ínti	ʔūmi	قومي	ma-tʔumīš	مَتْقوميش	
íntu	ʔūmu	قوموا	ma-tʔumūš	مَتْقوموش	

	active		passive		
masculine	ʔāyim	قايِم	–	–	participles
feminine	ʔáyma	قايْمَة	–	–	
plural	ʔaymīn	قايْمين	–	–	

①

نُهى قامِت مِن القعْدة لمّا بدأ الشّباب يِهزّروا هِزار سخيف.

núha ʔāmit min ilʔá3da lámma báda? iššabāb yihazzáru hizār saxīf.

Noha left the gathering when the guys started getting nasty with the kidding around.

②

أماني مبِتْحِبِّش تِقوم بدْري. كُلّ يوْم تِتْأخّر عَ الشُّغْل.

amāni ma-bitḫíbbiš tiʔūm bádri. kullᵊ yōm titʔáxxar 3a -ššuɣl.

Amany doesn't like getting up early. She's always late for work.

③

أُمّي بِتْقوم الفجر كُلّ يوْم مِن سِنين.

úmmi bitʔūm ilfágar kullᵊ yōm min sinīn.

My mom has been getting up every day at dawn for years.

④

طيّارْتك مِش هتْقوم في مْعادْها. اِتْأجِّلِت ساعْتينْ.

ṭayyártak miš hatʔūm fi m3ádha. itʔaggílit sa3tēn.

Your plane won't take off on time. It's been delayed two hours.

⑤

قوم خُد دُشّ و نام شُوَيّة عشان جِسْمك يِرتاح.

ʔūm xud duššᵊ wi nām šuwáyya 3ašān gísmak yirtāḫ.

Go take a shower and sleep for a while, so your body can get some rest.

❖ [1h1] **to get up; to take off, leave** (**from** مِن *min*)

➲ 24.1, 25.5, 28.4, 100.1, 104.6, 230.1, 236.5

202 to accept ʔibil قبل

		affirmative		negative	
perfect	ána	ʔibílt	قِبِلْت	ma-ʔibíltiš	مَقِبِلْتِش
	íḫna	ʔibílna	قِبِلْنا	ma-ʔibilnāš	مَقِبِلْناش
	ínta	ʔibílt	قِبِلْت	ma-ʔibíltiš	مَقِبِلْتِش
	ínti	ʔibílti	قِبِلْتي	ma-ʔibiltīš	مَقِبِلْتيش
	íntu	ʔibíltu	قِبِلْتوا	ma-ʔibiltūš	مَقِبِلْتوش
	húwwa	ʔibil	قِبِل	ma-ʔibílš	مَقِبِلْش
	híyya	ʔiblit	قِبْلِت	ma-ʔiblítš	مَقِبْلِتْش
	húmma	ʔiblu	قِبْلوا	ma-ʔiblūš	مَقِبْلوش
imperfect	ána	áʔbal	أَقْبَل	ma-ʔbálš	مَقْبَلْش
	íḫna	níʔbal	نِقْبَل	ma-niʔbálš	مَنِقْبَلْش
	ínta	tíʔbal	تِقْبَل	ma-tiʔbálš	مَتِقْبَلْش
	ínti	tiʔbáli	تِقْبَلي	ma-tiʔbalīš	مَتِقْبَليش
	íntu	tiʔbálu	تِقْبَلوا	ma-tiʔbalūš	مَتِقْبَلوش
	húwwa	yíʔbal	يِقْبَل	ma-yiʔbálš	مَيِقْبَلْش
	híyya	tíʔbal	تِقْبَل	ma-tiʔbálš	مَتِقْبَلْش
	húmma	yiʔbálu	يِقْبَلوا	ma-yiʔbalūš	مَيِقْبَلوش
bi-imperfect	ána	báʔbal	بَقْبَل	ma-baʔbálš	مَبَقْبَلْش
	íḫna	biníʔbal	بِنِقْبَل	ma-bniʔbálš	مَبْنِقْبَلْش
	ínta	bitíʔbal	بِتِقْبَل	ma-btiʔbálš	مَبْتِقْبَلْش
	ínti	bitiʔbáli	بِتِقْبَلي	ma-btiʔbalīš	مَبْتِقْبَليش
	íntu	bitiʔbálu	بِتِقْبَلوا	ma-btiʔbalūš	مَبْتِقْبَلوش
	húwwa	biyíʔbal	بِيِقْبَل	ma-byiʔbálš	مَبْيِقْبَلْش
	híyya	bitíʔbal	بِتِقْبَل	ma-btiʔbálš	مَبْتِقْبَلْش
	húmma	biyiʔbálu	بِيِقْبَلوا	ma-byiʔbalūš	مَبْيِقْبَلوش
future	ána	háʔbal	هَقْبَل	miš háʔbal	مِش هَقْبَل
	íḫna	haníʔbal	هَنِقْبَل	miš haníʔbal	مِش هَنِقْبَل
	ínta	hatíʔbal	هَتِقْبَل	miš hatíʔbal	مِش هَتِقْبَل
	ínti	hatiʔbáli	هَتِقْبَلي	miš hatiʔbáli	مِش هَتِقْبَلي
	íntu	hatiʔbálu	هَتِقْبَلوا	miš hatiʔbálu	مِش هَتِقْبَلوا
	húwwa	hayíʔbal	هَيِقْبَل	miš hayíʔbal	مِش هَيِقْبَل
	híyya	hatíʔbal	هَتِقْبَل	miš hatíʔbal	مِش هَتِقْبَل
	húmma	hayiʔbálu	هَيِقْبَلوا	miš hayiʔbálu	مِش هَيِقْبَلوا
imperative	ínta	íʔbal	اِقْبَل	ma-tiʔbálš	مَتِقْبَلْش
	ínti	iʔbáli	اِقْبَلي	ma-tiʔbalīš	مَتِقْبَليش
	íntu	iʔbálu	اِقْبَلوا	ma-tiʔbalūš	مَتِقْبَلوش

participles		active		passive	
	masculine	ʔābil	قابِل	maʔbūl	مَقْبول
	feminine	ʔábla	قابْلَة	maʔbūla	مَقْبولَة
	plural	ʔablīn	قابْلين	maʔbulīn	مَقْبولين

verbal nouns: ʔabalān قَبَلان - ʔabūl قَبول - ʔubūl قُبول

①

أنا قِبِلْت أجي بسّ عشان ماما.

ána ʔibílt ági bassᵊ 3ašān māma.

I just agreed to come for mom's sake.

②

لمّا تِقْبل في الوَظيفة، لينا الحلاوَة.

lámma tíʔbal fi -lwaẓīfa, līna -lḫalāwa.

When you get [lit. are accepted into] the job, treat us to something nice.

③

جمْعِيِّةْ رِسالة بْتِقْبل التّبرُّعات العَيْنية و المادّية.

gam3íyyit risāla btíʔbal ittabarru3āt il3ayníyya w ilmaddíyya.

The Resala Foundation accepts physical and financial donations.

④

نُهى مِش هتِقْبل تِرجع لِنادِر. ده جرّحْها جامِد.

núha miš hatíʔbal tírga3 li-nādir. da garráḫha gāmid.

Noha isn't willing to go back to Nader. He's hurt her so much.

⑤

متِقْبليش بِالمُعامْلة دي أبداً. إعْلِني اِعْتِراضِك.

ma-tiʔbalīš bi-lmu3ámla di ʔábadan. i3líni i3tirāḍik.

Don't accept this way of treatment. Show your objection.

❖ [1s4] **to accept; to agree on; to be willing to; to be accepted into** (في *fi*)

- This verb can be followed by an imperfect verb. (➲ 202.1, 202.4)
- When meaning 'accept' or 'agree on', this verb is usually transitive (➲ 202.3), but can also take the the preposition بِـ *bi-* (➲ 202.5).

203 to kill ʔátal قتل

	affirmative		negative		
ána	ʔatált	قَتَلْت	ma-ʔatáltiš	مَقَتَلْتِش	perfect
íḥna	ʔatálna	قَتَلْنا	ma-ʔatalnāš	مَقَتَلْناش	
ínta	ʔatált	قَتَلْت	ma-ʔatáltiš	مَقَتَلْتِش	
ínti	ʔatálti	قَتَلْتي	ma-ʔataltīš	مَقَتَلْتيش	
íntu	ʔatáltu	قَتَلْتوا	ma-ʔataltūš	مَقَتَلْتوش	
húwwa	ʔátal	قَتَل	ma-ʔatálš	مَقَتَلْش	
híyya	ʔátalit	قَتَلِت	ma-ʔatalítš	مَقَتَلِتْش	
húmma	ʔátalu	قَتَلوا	ma-ʔatalūš	مَقَتَلوش	
ána	áʔtil	أَقْتِل	ma-ʔtílš	مَقْتِلْش	imperfect
íḥna	níʔtil	نِقْتِل	ma-niʔtílš	مَنِقْتِلْش	
ínta	tíʔtil	تِقْتِل	ma-tiʔtílš	مَتِقْتِلْش	
ínti	tiʔtíli	تِقْتِلي	ma-tiʔtilīš	مَتِقْتِليش	
íntu	tiʔtílu	تِقْتِلوا	ma-tiʔtilūš	مَتِقْتِلوش	
húwwa	yíʔtil	يِقْتِل	ma-yiʔtílš	مَيِقْتِلْش	
híyya	tíʔtil	تِقْتِل	ma-tiʔtílš	مَتِقْتِلْش	
húmma	yiʔtílu	يِقْتِلوا	ma-yiʔtilūš	مَيِقْتِلوش	
ána	báʔtil	بَقْتِل	ma-baʔtílš	مَبَقْتِلْش	bi-imperfect
íḥna	biníʔtil	بِنِقْتِل	ma-bniʔtílš	مَبْنِقْتِلْش	
ínta	bitíʔtil	بِتِقْتِل	ma-btiʔtílš	مَبْتِقْتِلْش	
ínti	bitiʔtíli	بِتِقْتِلي	ma-btiʔtilīš	مَبْتِقْتِليش	
íntu	bitiʔtílu	بِتِقْتِلوا	ma-btiʔtilūš	مَبْتِقْتِلوش	
húwwa	biyíʔtil	بِيِقْتِل	ma-byiʔtílš	مَبْيِقْتِلْش	
híyya	bitíʔtil	بِتِقْتِل	ma-btiʔtílš	مَبْتِقْتِلْش	
húmma	biyiʔtílu	بِيِقْتِلوا	ma-byiʔtilūš	مَبْيِقْتِلوش	
ána	háʔtil	هَقْتِل	miš háʔtil	مِش هَقْتِل	future
íḥna	haníʔtil	هَنِقْتِل	miš haníʔtil	مِش هَنِقْتِل	
ínta	hatíʔtil	هَتِقْتِل	miš hatíʔtil	مِش هَتِقْتِل	
ínti	hatiʔtíli	هَتِقْتِلي	miš hatiʔtíli	مِش هَتِقْتِلي	
íntu	hatiʔtílu	هَتِقْتِلوا	miš hatiʔtílu	مِش هَتِقْتِلوا	
húwwa	hayíʔtil	هَيِقْتِل	miš hayíʔtil	مِش هَيِقْتِل	
híyya	hatíʔtil	هَتِقْتِل	miš hatíʔtil	مِش هَتِقْتِل	
húmma	hayiʔtílu	هَيِقْتِلوا	miš hayiʔtílu	مِش هَيِقْتِلوا	
ínta	íʔtil	اِقْتِل	ma-tiʔtílš	مَتِقْتِلْش	imperative
ínti	iʔtíli	اِقْتِلي	ma-tiʔtilīš	مَتِقْتِليش	
íntu	iʔtílu	اِقْتِلوا	ma-tiʔtilūš	مَتِقْتِلوش	

	active		passive		
masculine	ʔātil	قاتِل	maʔtūl	مَقْتول	participles
feminine	ʔátla	قاتْلَة	maʔtūla	مَقْتولَة	
plural	ʔatlīn	قاتْلين	maʔtulīn	مَقْتولين	

verbal noun: ʔatl قَتْل

①

المُجْرِم قتل السِّتّ و وِلادْها عشان صِحْيوا و هُوَّ بِيِسْرق.

ilmúgrim ʔátal issítt^ə w wiládha 3ašān șíḫyu wi húwwa biyísraʔ.

The criminal killed the mother and her children because they woke up while he was robbing [them].

②

عايِز تِقْتِل المَلّل؟ تعالى نِطْلع سفاري.

3āyiz tíʔtil ilmállal? ta3āla níțla3 safāri.

Want to kill boredom? Let's go on a [desert] safari.

③

مبْتِقْتِلْش الدِّبّانة دي ليْه؟ دي زهّقِتْني.

ma-btiʔtílš iddibbāna di lē? di zahhaʔítni.

Why don't you kill that fly? It's bothering me.

④

أبويا هَيِقْتِلْني لَوْ عِرِف اللي حصل.

abūya hayiʔtílni law 3írif ílli ḫáșal.

My dad will kill me when he finds out what happened.

⑤

اِقْتِل الخوْف اللي جُوّاك و إنْطلق.

íʔtil ilxōf ílli guwwāk w ințálaq.

Kill the fear inside you and go.

❖ [1s2] **to kill**

- This verb, like its English translation 'kill', can be used metaphorically (➲ 203.2, 203.5) or in hyperbole (➲ 203.4).

204 to be able to ʔídir قِدِر

	affirmative		negative		
ána	ʔidírt	قِدِرْت	ma-ʔdírtiš	مَقْدِرْتِش	perfect
íḫna	ʔidírna	قِدِرْنا	ma-ʔdirnāš	مَقْدِرْناش	
ínta	ʔidírt	قِدِرْت	ma-ʔdírtiš	مَقْدِرْتِش	
ínti	ʔidírti	قِدِرْتي	ma-ʔdirtīš	مَقْدِرْتيش	
íntu	ʔidírtu	قِدِرْتوا	ma-ʔdirtūš	مَقْدِرْتوش	
húwwa	ʔídir	قِدِر	ma-ʔdírš	مَقْدِرْش	
híyya	ʔídrit	قِدْرِت	ma-ʔidrítš	مَقِدْرِتْش	
húmma	ʔídru	قِدْروا	ma-ʔidrūš	مَقِدْروش	
ána	áʔdar	أَقْدَر	ma-ʔdárš	مَقْدَرْش	imperfect
íḫna	níʔdar	نِقْدَر	ma-niʔdárš	مَنِقْدَرْش	
ínta	tíʔdar	تِقْدَر	ma-tiʔdárš	مَتِقْدَرْش	
ínti	tiʔdári	تِقْدَري	ma-tiʔdarīš	مَتِقْدَريش	
íntu	tiʔdáru	تِقْدَروا	ma-tiʔdarūš	مَتِقْدَروش	
húwwa	yíʔdar	يِقْدَر	ma-yiʔdárš	مَيِقْدَرْش	
híyya	tíʔdar	تِقْدَر	ma-tiʔdárš	مَتِقْدَرْش	
húmma	yiʔdáru	يِقْدَروا	ma-yiʔdarūš	مَيِقْدَروش	
ána	báʔdar	بَقْدَر	ma-baʔdárš	مَبَقْدَرْش	bi-imperfect
íḫna	biníʔdar	بِنِقْدَر	ma-bniʔdárš	مَبْنِقْدَرْش	
ínta	bitíʔdar	بِتِقْدَر	ma-btiʔdárš	مَبْتِقْدَرْش	
ínti	bitiʔdári	بِتِقْدَري	ma-btiʔdarīš	مَبْتِقْدَريش	
íntu	bitiʔdáru	بِتِقْدَروا	ma-btiʔdarūš	مَبْتِقْدَروش	
húwwa	biyíʔdar	بِيِقْدَر	ma-byiʔdárš	مَبْيِقْدَرْش	
híyya	bitíʔdar	بِتِقْدَر	ma-btiʔdárš	مَبْتِقْدَرْش	
húmma	biyiʔdáru	بِيِقْدَروا	ma-byiʔdarūš	مَبْيِقْدَروش	
ána	háʔdar	هَقْدَر	miš háʔdar	مِش هَقْدَر	future
íḫna	haníʔdar	هَنِقْدَر	miš haníʔdar	مِش هَنِقْدَر	
ínta	hatíʔdar	هَتِقْدَر	miš hatíʔdar	مِش هَتِقْدَر	
ínti	hatiʔdári	هَتِقْدَري	miš hatiʔdári	مِش هَتِقْدَري	
íntu	hatiʔdáru	هَتِقْدَروا	miš hatiʔdáru	مِش هَتِقْدَروا	
húwwa	hayíʔdar	هَيِقْدَر	miš hayíʔdar	مِش هَيِقْدَر	
híyya	hatíʔdar	هَتِقْدَر	miš hatíʔdar	مِش هَتِقْدَر	
húmma	hayiʔdáru	هَيِقْدَروا	miš hayiʔdáru	مِش هَيِقْدَروا	
ínta	íʔdar	اِقْدَر	ma-tiʔdárš	مَتِقْدَرْش	imperative
ínti	iʔdári	اِقْدَري	ma-tiʔdarīš	مَتِقْدَريش	
íntu	iʔdáru	اِقْدَروا	ma-tiʔdarūš	مَتِقْدَروش	

	active		passive		
masculine	ʔādir	قادِر	maʔdūr	مَقْدور	participles
feminine	ʔádra	قادْرَة	–	–	
plural	ʔadrīn	قادْرين	–	–	

verbal noun: ʔúdra قُدْرَة

①

أنا مقْدِرْتِش أشوف الخبر مِن كُتْر بشاعْتُه.

ána ma-ʔdírtiš ašūf ilxábar min kutrᵊ bašá3tu.

I couldn't watch the news because it was so horrible.

②

لازِم تِقْدر على المجْهود ده ، وَ إلّا مُش هتِعْرف تِحافِظ على مرْكزك.

lāzim tíʔdar 3ála -lmaghūd da , wa ʔílla muš hatí3raf tiђāfiẓ 3ála markázak.

You have to be able to make all that effort, or else you won't be able to maintain your position.

③

مبقْدرْش أصْحى بدْرى، حتّى و أنا نايْمة بدْري.

ma-baʔdárš áṣђa bádri, ђátta w ána náyma bádri.

I can't wake up early, even when I go to bed early.

④

صُبْحي هَيِقْدر يِجيب المرْكز الأوِّل. أنا عارِف إمْكانِيّاتُه.

ṣúbђi hayíʔdar yigīb ilmárkaz ilʔáwwil. ána 3ārif imkaniyyātu.

Sobhy will manage to get first place. I know his abilities.

⑤

متِقْدرْش تِمْنعْني أشوف وِلادي.

ma-tiʔdáršᵊ timná3ni ʔašūf wilādi.

You can't prohibit me from seeing my kids.

❖ [1s4] **to be able to; to manage, be able (to do), endure** (على *3ála*); **to master** (على *3ála*)

- This verb is most commonly used to mean 'can', 'could', 'be able to', and is followed by an imperfect verb. (➲ 204.1, 204.3, 204.4, 204.5)
- When followed by a noun (instead of an imperfect verb), it takes the preposition على *3ála*. (➲ 204.2)
- The passive participle is invariable (always masculine), for example, حاجة مقْدور عليْها *ђāga maʔdūr 3alēha* 'something manageable'

➲ 14.2, 20.3, 37.6, 41.2, 43.2, 47.1, 49.2, 60.2, 91.6, 107.5, 125.5, 143.8, 163.3, 173.6, 196.2, 222.6

205 to estimate ʔáddar قَدَّر 13

	affirmative		negative		
ána	ʔaddárt	قَدَّرْت	ma-ʔaddártiš	مَقَدَّرْتِش	perfect
íḥna	ʔaddárna	قَدَّرْنا	ma-ʔaddarnāš	مَقَدَّرْناش	
ínta	ʔaddárt	قَدَّرْت	ma-ʔaddártiš	مَقَدَّرْتِش	
ínti	ʔaddárti	قَدَّرْتي	ma-ʔaddartīš	مَقَدَّرْتيش	
íntu	ʔaddártu	قَدَّرْتوا	ma-ʔaddartūš	مَقَدَّرْتوش	
húwwa	ʔáddar	قَدَّر	ma-ʔaddárš	مَقَدَّرْش	
híyya	ʔaddárit	قَدَّرِت	ma-ʔaddarítš	مَقَدَّرِتْش	
húmma	ʔaddáru	قَدَّروا	ma-ʔaddarūš	مَقَدَّروش	
ána	aʔáddar	أقَدَّر	ma-ʔaddárš	مَقَدَّرْش	imperfect
íḥna	niʔáddar	نِقَدَّر	ma-nʔaddárš	مَنْقَدَّرْش	
ínta	tiʔáddar	تِقَدَّر	ma-tʔaddárš	مَتْقَدَّرْش	
ínti	tiʔaddári	تِقَدَّري	ma-tʔaddarīš	مَتْقَدَّريش	
íntu	tiʔaddáru	تِقَدَّروا	ma-tʔaddarūš	مَتْقَدَّروش	
húwwa	yiʔáddar	يِقَدَّر	ma-yʔaddárš	مَيْقَدَّرْش	
híyya	tiʔáddar	تِقَدَّر	ma-tʔaddárš	مَتْقَدَّرْش	
húmma	yiʔaddáru	يِقَدَّروا	ma-yʔaddarūš	مَيْقَدَّروش	
ána	baʔáddar	بَقَدَّر	ma-baʔaddárš	مَبَقَدَّرْش	bi-imperfect
íḥna	binʔáddar	بِنْقَدَّر	ma-binʔaddárš	مَبِنْقَدَّرْش	
ínta	bitʔáddar	بِتْقَدَّر	ma-bitʔaddárš	مَبِتْقَدَّرْش	
ínti	bitʔaddári	بِتْقَدَّري	ma-bitʔaddarīš	مَبِتْقَدَّريش	
íntu	bitʔaddáru	بِتْقَدَّروا	ma-bitʔaddarūš	مَبِتْقَدَّروش	
húwwa	biyʔáddar	بِيْقَدَّر	ma-biyʔaddárš	مَبِيْقَدَّرْش	
híyya	bitʔáddar	بِتْقَدَّر	ma-bitʔaddárš	مَبِتْقَدَّرْش	
húmma	biyʔaddáru	بِيْقَدَّروا	ma-biyʔaddarūš	مَبِيْقَدَّروش	
ána	haʔáddar	هَقَدَّر	miš haʔáddar	مِش هَقَدَّر	future
íḥna	hanʔáddar	هَنْقَدَّر	miš hanʔáddar	مِش هَنْقَدَّر	
ínta	hatʔáddar	هَتْقَدَّر	miš hatʔáddar	مِش هَتْقَدَّر	
ínti	hatʔaddári	هَتْقَدَّري	miš hatʔaddári	مِش هَتْقَدَّري	
íntu	hatʔaddáru	هَتْقَدَّروا	miš hatʔaddáru	مِش هَتْقَدَّروا	
húwwa	hayʔáddar	هَيْقَدَّر	miš hayʔáddar	مِش هَيْقَدَّر	
híyya	hatʔáddar	هَتْقَدَّر	miš hatʔáddar	مِش هَتْقَدَّر	
húmma	hayʔaddáru	هَيْقَدَّروا	miš hayʔaddáru	مِش هَيْقَدَّروا	
ínta	ʔáddar	قَدَّر	ma-tʔaddárš	مَتْقَدَّرْش	imperative
ínti	ʔaddári	قَدَّري	ma-tʔaddarīš	مَتْقَدَّريش	
íntu	ʔaddáru	قَدَّروا	ma-tʔaddarūš	مَتْقَدَّروش	

	active		passive		
masculine	miʔáddar	مِقَدَّر	mitʔáddar	مِتْقَدَّر	participles
feminine	miʔaddára	مِقَدَّرَة	mitʔaddára	مِتْقَدَّرَة	
plural	miʔaddarīn	مِقَدَّرين	mitʔaddarīn	مِتْقَدَّرين	

verbal noun: taʔdīr تقدير

①

يوسِف قدّر المسافة مِن هِنا لْهناك بِحَوالي ١٠ مِترْ.

yūsif ʔáddar ilmasāfa min hína l-hināk bi-ɦawāli ʔášara mitr.

Yousef estimated the distance from here to there to be approximately 10 meters.

②

آمال دايْماً تِقدّر اللي بيِعْمِلْها حاجة كْوَيِّسة.

amāl dáyman tiʔáddar ílli biyi3mílha ɦāga kwayyísa.

Amaal always appreciates those who do nice things for her.

③

حُسام مبِيْقدّرْش الوَقْت كوَيِّس.

ɦusām ma-biyʔaddárš ilwáʔtᵊ kwáyyis.

Hossam doesn't estimate time well.

④

ربِّنا هَيْقدّرْني و أخلّص في المعاد.

rabbína hayʔaddárni w axállaṣ fi -lmi3ād.

God will enable me to finish on time.

⑤

متْقدّرْش النّاس غلط. اِدّي كُلّ واحِد حقُّه.

ma-tʔaddárš innās ɣálaṭ. íddi kullᵊ wāɦid ɦáʔʔu.

Don't underestimate people. Give everyone a chance.

⑥

طب، قدّر حصل حاجة في السِّكّة. هتِتْصرّف إزّاي؟

ṭab, ʔáddar ɦáṣal ɦāga fi -ssíkka. hatitṣárraf izzāy?

Suppose something happens on the journey. What will you do then?

❖ [2s2] **to estimate; to appreciate; to enable; to suppose, imagine**

206 to present ʔáddim قدّم 2s1

verbal noun: *taʔdīm* تقديم

		affirmative		negative		
perfect	ána	*ʔaddímt*	قَدِّمْت	*ma-ʔaddímtiš*	مَقَدِّمْتِش
	íḥna	*ʔaddímna*	قَدِّمْنا	*ma-ʔaddimnāš*	مَقَدِّمْناش
	ínta	*ʔaddímt*	قَدِّمْت	*ma-ʔaddímtiš*	مَقَدِّمْتِش
	ínti	*ʔaddímti*	قَدِّمْتي	*ma-ʔaddimtīš*	مَقَدِّمْتيش
	íntu	*ʔaddímtu*	قَدِّمْتوا	*ma-ʔaddimtūš*	مَقَدِّمْتوش
	húwwa	*ʔáddim*	قَدِّم	*ma-ʔaddímš*	مَقَدِّمْش
	híyya	*ʔaddímit*	قَدِّمِت	*ma-ʔaddimítš*	مَقَدِّمِتْش
	húmma	*ʔaddímu*	قَدِّموا	*ma-ʔaddimūš*	مَقَدِّموش
imperfect	ána	*aʔáddim*	أقَدِّم	*ma-ʔaddímš*	مَقَدِّمْش
	íḥna	*niʔáddim*	نِقَدِّم	*ma-nʔaddímš*	مَنْقَدِّمْش
	ínta	*tiʔáddim*	تِقَدِّم	*ma-tʔaddímš*	مَتْقَدِّمْش
	ínti	*tiʔaddími*	تِقَدِّمي	*ma-tʔaddimīš*	مَتْقَدِّميش
	íntu	*tiʔaddímu*	تِقَدِّموا	*ma-tʔaddimūš*	مَتْقَدِّموش
	húwwa	*yiʔáddim*	يِقَدِّم	*ma-yʔaddímš*	مَيْقَدِّمْش
	híyya	*tiʔáddim*	تِقَدِّم	*ma-tʔaddímš*	مَتْقَدِّمْش
	húmma	*yiʔaddímu*	يِقَدِّموا	*ma-yʔaddimūš*	مَيْقَدِّموش
bi-imperfect	ána	*baʔáddim*	بَقَدِّم	*ma-baʔaddímš*	مَبَقَدِّمْش
	íḥna	*binʔáddim*	بِنْقَدِّم	*ma-binʔaddímš*	مَبِنْقَدِّمْش
	ínta	*bitʔáddim*	بِتْقَدِّم	*ma-bitʔaddímš*	مَبِتْقَدِّمْش
	ínti	*bitʔaddími*	بِتْقَدِّمي	*ma-bitʔaddimīš*	مَبِتْقَدِّميش
	íntu	*bitʔaddímu*	بِتْقَدِّموا	*ma-bitʔaddimūš*	مَبِتْقَدِّموش
	húwwa	*biyʔáddim*	بِيْقَدِّم	*ma-biyʔaddímš*	مَبِيْقَدِّمْش
	híyya	*bitʔáddim*	بِتْقَدِّم	*ma-bitʔaddímš*	مَبِتْقَدِّمْش
	húmma	*biyʔaddímu*	بِيْقَدِّموا	*ma-biyʔaddimūš*	مَبِيْقَدِّموش
future	ána	*haʔáddim*	هَقَدِّم	*miš haʔáddim*	مِش هَقَدِّم
	íḥna	*hanʔáddim*	هَنْقَدِّم	*miš hanʔáddim*	مِش هَنْقَدِّم
	ínta	*hatʔáddim*	هَتْقَدِّم	*miš hatʔáddim*	مِش هَتْقَدِّم
	ínti	*hatʔaddími*	هَتْقَدِّمي	*miš hatʔaddími*	مِش هَتْقَدِّمي
	íntu	*hatʔaddímu*	هَتْقَدِّموا	*miš hatʔaddímu*	مِش هَتْقَدِّموا
	húwwa	*hayʔáddim*	هَيْقَدِّم	*miš hayʔáddim*	مِش هَيْقَدِّم
	híyya	*hatʔáddim*	هَتْقَدِّم	*miš hatʔáddim*	مِش هَتْقَدِّم
	húmma	*hayʔaddímu*	هَيْقَدِّموا	*miš hayʔaddímu*	مِش هَيْقَدِّموا
imperative	ínta	*ʔáddim*	قَدِّم	*ma-tʔaddímš*	مَتْقَدِّمْش
	ínti	*ʔaddími*	قَدِّمي	*ma-tʔaddimīš*	مَتْقَدِّميش
	íntu	*ʔaddímu*	قَدِّموا	*ma-tʔaddimūš*	مَتْقَدِّموش

		active		passive	
participles	masculine	*miʔáddim*	مِقَدِّم	*mitʔáddim*	مِتْقَدِّم
	feminine	*miʔaddíma*	مِقَدِّمَة	*mitʔaddíma*	مِتْقَدِّمَة
	plural	*miʔaddimīn*	مِقَدِّمين	*mitʔaddimīn*	مِتْقَدِّمين

①

البيّاع قدِّمْلِنا عُروض لأ تُقاوَم.

ilbayyā3 ʔaddimlína 3urūḍ lā tuqāwam.

The salesman made us irresistible offers.

②

المطْعم ده دايْماً يِقدِّم الأكْل بْطريقة مُبْهِرة.

ilmáṭ3am da dáyman yiʔáddim ilʔákl^ə b-ṭarīʔa mubhíra.

This restaurant always serves food in a fancy way.

③

مرْوَة بِتْقدِّم بِـرنامِج هايِل في الأذاعة.

márwa bitʔáddim birnāmig hāyil fi -lʔazā3a.

Marwa presents a good program on the radio.

④

مِش هتْقدِّمْلِنا حاجة وَلّا أيْه؟

miš hatʔaddimlína ḥāga wálla ʔē?

Aren't you going to give us something to drink?

⑤

متْقدِّمْش في المِنْحة دي. إنْتَ أكْبر مِن السِّنّ المطْلوب.

ma-tʔaddímš^ə fi -lmínḥa di. ínta ʔákbar min issínn ilmaṭlūb.

Don't apply for this scholarship. You're over the age limit.

❖ [2s1] **to present** (something **to** لِـ *li-*)**; to offer, serve; to apply** (**for** في *fi*)**; to submit, turn in; to participate**

➲ 69.4, 227.2, 235.2, 240.2

207 to read ʔára قرا

	affirmative		negative		
ána	ʔarēt	قَرَيْت	ma-ʔarítš	مَقَرَيتْش	perfect
íḫna	ʔarēna	قَرَيْنا	ma-ʔarināš	مَقَريناش	
ínta	ʔarēt	قَرَيْت	ma-ʔarítš	مَقَرَيتْش	
ínti	ʔarēti	قَرَيْتي	ma-ʔaritīš	مَقَرَيتيش	
íntu	ʔarētu	قَرَيْتوا	ma-ʔaritūš	مَقَرَيتوش	
húwwa	ʔára	قَرا	ma-ʔarāš	مَقَراش	
híyya	ʔárit	قَرِت	ma-ʔarítš	مَقَرِتْش	
húmma	ʔáru	قَروا	ma-ʔarūš	مَقَروش	
ána	áʔra	أقْرا	ma-ʔrāš	مَقْراش	imperfect
íḫna	níʔra	نِقْرا	ma-niʔrāš	مَنِقْراش	
ínta	tíʔra	تِقْرا	ma-tiʔrāš	مَتِقْراش	
ínti	tíʔri	تِقْري	ma-tiʔrīš	مَتِقْريش	
íntu	tíʔru	تِقْروا	ma-tiʔrūš	مَتِقْروش	
húwwa	yíʔra	يِقْرا	ma-yiʔrāš	مَيِقْراش	
híyya	tíʔra	تِقْرا	ma-tiʔrāš	مَتِقْراش	
húmma	yíʔru	يِقْروا	ma-yiʔrūš	مَيِقْروش	
ána	báʔra	بَقْرَى	ma-baʔrāš	مَبَقْراش	bi-imperfect
íḫna	biníʔra	بِنِقْرَى	ma-bniʔrāš	مَبْنِقْراش	
ínta	bitíʔra	بِتِقْرَى	ma-btiʔrāš	مَبْتِقْراش	
ínti	bitíʔri	بِتِقْري	ma-btiʔrīš	مَبْتِقْريش	
íntu	bitíʔru	بِتِقْروا	ma-btiʔrūš	مَبْتِقْروش	
húwwa	biyíʔra	بِيِقْرَى	ma-byiʔrāš	مَبْيِقْراش	
híyya	bitíʔra	بِتِقْرَى	ma-btiʔrāš	مَبْتِقْراش	
húmma	biyíʔru	بِيِقْروا	ma-byiʔrūš	مَبْيِقْروش	
ána	háʔra	هَقْرَى	miš háʔra	مِش هَقْرَى	future
íḫna	haníʔra	هَنِقْرَى	miš haníʔra	مِش هَنِقْرَى	
ínta	hatíʔra	هَتِقْرَى	miš hatíʔra	مِش هَتِقْرَى	
ínti	hatíʔri	هَتِقْري	miš hatíʔri	مِش هَتِقْري	
íntu	hatíʔru	هَتِقْروا	miš hatíʔru	مِش هَتِقْروا	
húwwa	hayíʔra	هَيِقْرَى	miš hayíʔra	مِش هَيِقْرَى	
híyya	hatíʔra	هَتِقْرَى	miš hatíʔra	مِش هَتِقْرَى	
húmma	hayíʔru	هَيِقْروا	miš hayíʔru	مِش هَيِقْروا	
ínta	íʔra	اِقْرا	ma-tiʔrāš	مَتِقْراش	imperative
ínti	íʔri	اِقْري	ma-tiʔrīš	مَتِقْريش	
íntu	íʔru	اِقْروا	ma-tiʔrūš	مَتِقْروش	

	active		passive		
masculine	ʔāri	قاري	máʔri	مَقْري	participles
feminine	ʔárya	قارْيَة	maʔríyya	مَقْرِيَّة	
plural	ʔaryīn	قارْيين	maʔriyīn	مَقْرِيين	

verbal noun: ʔirāya قِرايَة

①

أنا مقريتْش الكِتاب لِسّه.

ána ma-ʔarítš ilkitāb líssa.

I haven't read the book yet.

②

إنْتَ بِتِعْرف تِقْرا عربي؟

ínta bití3raf tíʔra 3árabi?

Can you read Arabic?

③

ضُحى بْتِقْرا كُلّ ليْلة قبْل ما تْنام.

ḍúḫa btíʔra kullᵊ lēla ʔablᵊ ma tnām.

Doha reads every night
before going to sleep.

④

اِقْرا دي. تِضحّك أوي!!

íʔra di. tidáḫḫak áwi!!

Read this! It's so funny!!

⑤

هتِقْري أيْه الأُسْبوع اللي جايّ؟

hatíʔri ʔē -lʔisbū3 ílli gáyy?

What are you going
to read next week?

❖ [1d1] **to read**

- This verb is conjugated like other 1d1 verbs (➲), except that the final *a* is written ـا instead of ـى.

➲ 41.2, 43.3, 43.7, 209.3

208 to decide qárrar قرر ١٣

verbal noun: *taqrīr* تقرير - *qarār* قرار

perfect

	affirmative		negative	
ána	*qarrárt*	قرّرْت	*ma-qarrártiš*	مَقرّرْتش
íḫna	*qarrárna*	قرّرْنا	*ma-qarrarnāš*	مَقرّرْناش
ínta	*qarrárt*	قرّرْت	*ma-qarrártiš*	مَقرّرْتش
ínti	*qarrárti*	قرّرْتي	*ma-qarrartīš*	مَقرّرْتيش
íntu	*qarrártu*	قرّرْتوا	*ma-qarrartūš*	مَقرّرْتوش
húwwa	*qárrar*	قرّر	*ma-qarrárš*	مَقرّرْش
híyya	*qarrárit*	قرّرِت	*ma-qarrarítš*	مَقرّرِتْش
húmma	*qarráru*	قرّروا	*ma-qarrarūš*	مَقرّروش

imperfect

	affirmative		negative	
ána	*aqárrar*	أقرّر	*ma-qarrárš*	مَقرّرْش
íḫna	*niqárrar*	نِقرّر	*ma-nqarrárš*	مَنْقرّرْش
ínta	*tiqárrar*	تِقرّر	*ma-tqarrárš*	مَتْقرّرْش
ínti	*tiqarrári*	تِقرّري	*ma-tqarrarīš*	مَتْقرّريش
íntu	*tiqarráru*	تِقرّروا	*ma-tqarrarūš*	مَتْقرّروش
húwwa	*yiqárrar*	يِقرّر	*ma-yqarrárš*	مَيْقرّرْش
híyya	*tiqárrar*	تِقرّر	*ma-tqarrárš*	مَتْقرّرْش
húmma	*yiqarráru*	يِقرّروا	*ma-yqarrarūš*	مَيْقرّروش

bi-imperfect

	affirmative		negative	
ána	*baqárrar*	بقرّر	*ma-baqarrárš*	مَبقرّرْش
íḫna	*binqárrar*	بِنْقرّر	*ma-binqarrárš*	مَبِنْقرّرْش
ínta	*bitqárrar*	بِتْقرّر	*ma-bitqarrárš*	مَبِتْقرّرْش
ínti	*bitqarrári*	بِتْقرّري	*ma-bitqarrarīš*	مَبِتْقرّريش
íntu	*bitqarráru*	بِتْقرّروا	*ma-bitqarrarūš*	مَبِتْقرّروش
húwwa	*biyqárrar*	بِيْقرّر	*ma-biyqarrárš*	مَبِيْقرّرْش
híyya	*bitqárrar*	بِتْقرّر	*ma-bitqarrárš*	مَبِتْقرّرْش
húmma	*biyqarráru*	بِيْقرّروا	*ma-biyqarrarūš*	مَبِيْقرّروش

future

	affirmative		negative	
ána	*haqárrar*	هَقرّر	*miš haqárrar*	مِش هَقرّر
íḫna	*hanqárrar*	هَنْقرّر	*miš hanqárrar*	مِش هَنْقرّر
ínta	*hatqárrar*	هَتْقرّر	*miš hatqárrar*	مِش هَتْقرّر
ínti	*hatqarrári*	هَتْقرّري	*miš hatqarrári*	مِش هَتْقرّري
íntu	*hatqarráru*	هَتْقرّروا	*miš hatqarráru*	مِش هَتْقرّروا
húwwa	*hayqárrar*	هَيْقرّر	*miš hayqárrar*	مِش هَيْقرّر
híyya	*hatqárrar*	هَتْقرّر	*miš hatqárrar*	مِش هَتْقرّر
húmma	*hayqarráru*	هَيْقرّروا	*miš hayqarráru*	مِش هَيْقرّروا

imperative

	affirmative		negative	
ínta	*qárrar*	قرّر	*ma-tqarrárš*	مَتْقرّرْش
ínti	*qarrári*	قرّري	*ma-tqarrarīš*	مَتْقرّريش
íntu	*qarráru*	قرّروا	*ma-tqarrarūš*	مَتْقرّروش

participles

	active		passive	
masculine	*muqárrir*	مُقرّر	*mitqárrar*	مِتْقرّر
feminine	*muqarríra*	مُقرّرة	*mitqarrára*	مِتْقرّرة
plural	*muqarrirīn*	مُقرّرين	*mitqarrarīn*	مِتْقرّرين

①

أنا قرّرْت أعْمِل رِجيم مِن بُكْره.

ána qarrárt á3mil rigīm min búkra.

I decided to go on a diet
starting tomorrow.

②

سارة مِش عارْفة تْقرّر هتِدْرِس أيْه في الجامْعة.

sāra miš 3árfa tqárrar hatídris ʔē fi -lgám3a.

Sara can't decide what
to study in college.

③

برْتاح لمّا جوْزي بِيْقرّر يِغدّينا برّه.

bartāḥ lámma gōzi biyqárrar yiɣaddīna bárra.

I feel relaxed when my husband
decides to take us out for lunch.

④

هنْقرّر هنْسمّي البيبي أيْه بعْد الوِلادة.

hanqárrar hansammi -lbībi ʔē ba3d ilwilāda.

We'll decide what to name
the baby after he's born.

⑤

قرّر بِسُرْعة هتاكُل أيْه؟

qárrar bi-súr3a. hatākul ʔē?

Decide what you're
going to eat quickly.

⑥

متْقرّرْش دِلْوَقْتي. خُد وَقْتك و اِدْرِس الموْضوع كُوَيِّس.

ma-tqarrárš[ə] dilwáʔti. xud wáʔtak w ídris ilmawḍū3 kuwáyyis.

Don't decide now. Take your time
and study the issue well.

❖ [2s2] **to decide**

- This verb can be followed by an imperfect verb. (➲ 208.1, 208.3)

➲ 66.3, 89.2

209 to spend (time) ʔáḍḍa قضّى ١٣ 13

verbal noun: taʔḍíyya تقضية

	affirmative		negative		
ána	ʔaḍḍēt	قَضّيْت	ma-ʔaḍḍítš	مَقَضّيتْش	perfect
íḥna	ʔaḍḍēna	قَضّيْنا	ma-ʔaḍḍināš	مَقَضّيناش	
ínta	ʔaḍḍēt	قَضّيْت	ma-ʔaḍḍítš	مَقَضّيتْش	
ínti	ʔaḍḍēti	قَضّيْتي	ma-ʔaḍḍitīš	مَقَضّيتيش	
íntu	ʔaḍḍētu	قَضّيْتوا	ma-ʔaḍḍitūš	مَقَضّيتوش	
húwwa	ʔáḍḍa	قَضّى	ma-ʔaḍḍāš	مَقَضّاش	
híyya	ʔáḍḍit	قَضّت	ma-ʔaḍḍítš	مَقَضّتْش	
húmma	ʔáḍḍu	قَضّوا	ma-ʔaḍḍūš	مَقَضّوش	

	affirmative		negative		
ána	aʔáḍḍi	أقَضّي	ma-ʔaḍḍīš	مَقَضّيش	imperfect
íḥna	niʔáḍḍi	نِقَضّي	ma-nʔaḍḍīš	مَنْقَضّيش	
ínta	tiʔáḍḍi	تِقَضّي	ma-tʔaḍḍīš	مَتْقَضّيش	
ínti	tiʔáḍḍi	تِقَضّي	ma-tʔaḍḍīš	مَتْقَضّيش	
íntu	tiʔáḍḍu	تِقَضّوا	ma-tʔaḍḍūš	مَتْقَضّوش	
húwwa	yiʔáḍḍi	يِقَضّي	ma-yʔaḍḍīš	مَيْقَضّيش	
híyya	tiʔáḍḍi	تِقَضّي	ma-tʔaḍḍīš	مَتْقَضّيش	
húmma	yiʔáḍḍu	يِقَضّوا	ma-yʔaḍḍūš	مَيْقَضّوش	

	affirmative		negative		
ána	baʔáḍḍi	بَقَضّي	ma-baʔaḍḍīš	مَبَقَضّيش	bi-imperfect
íḥna	binʔáḍḍi	بِنْقَضّي	ma-binʔaḍḍīš	مَبِنْقَضّيش	
ínta	bitʔáḍḍi	بِتْقَضّي	ma-bitʔaḍḍīš	مَبِتْقَضّيش	
ínti	bitʔáḍḍi	بِتْقَضّي	ma-bitʔaḍḍīš	مَبِتْقَضّيش	
íntu	bitʔáḍḍu	بِتْقَضّوا	ma-bitʔaḍḍūš	مَبِتْقَضّوش	
húwwa	biyʔáḍḍi	بِيْقَضّي	ma-biyʔaḍḍīš	مَبِيْقَضّيش	
híyya	bitʔáḍḍi	بِتْقَضّي	ma-bitʔaḍḍīš	مَبِتْقَضّيش	
húmma	biyʔáḍḍu	بِيْقَضّوا	ma-biyʔaḍḍūš	مَبِيْقَضّوش	

	affirmative		negative		
ána	haʔáḍḍi	هَقَضّي	miš haʔáḍḍi	مِش هَقَضّي	future
íḥna	hanʔáḍḍi	هَنْقَضّي	miš hanʔáḍḍi	مِش هَنْقَضّي	
ínta	hatʔáḍḍi	هَتْقَضّي	miš hatʔáḍḍi	مِش هَتْقَضّي	
ínti	hatʔáḍḍi	هَتْقَضّي	miš hatʔáḍḍi	مِش هَتْقَضّي	
íntu	hatʔáḍḍu	هَتْقَضّوا	miš hatʔáḍḍu	مِش هَتْقَضّوا	
húwwa	hayʔáḍḍi	هَيْقَضّي	miš hayʔáḍḍi	مِش هَيْقَضّي	
híyya	hatʔáḍḍi	هَتْقَضّي	miš hatʔáḍḍi	مِش هَتْقَضّي	
húmma	hayʔáḍḍu	هَيْقَضّوا	miš hayʔáḍḍu	مِش هَيْقَضّوا	

	affirmative		negative		
ínta	ʔáḍḍi	قَضّي	ma-tʔaḍḍīš	مَتْقَضّيش	imperative
ínti	ʔáḍḍi	قَضّي	ma-tʔaḍḍīš	مَتْقَضّيش	
íntu	ʔáḍḍu	قَضّوا	ma-tʔaḍḍūš	مَتْقَضّوش	

	active		passive		
masculine	miʔáḍḍi	مِقَضّي	mitʔáḍḍi	مِتْقَضّي	participles
feminine	miʔaḍḍíyya	مِقَضّية	mitʔaḍḍíyya	مِتْقَضّية	
plural	miʔaḍḍiyīn	مِقَضّيين	mitʔaḍḍiyīn	مِتْقَضّيين	

①

قضّيْت نُصّ عُمْري بينْ البِلاد.

ʔaddēt nuṣṣᵊ 3úmri bēn ilbilād.

I spent half of my life living in different countries.

②

أكْتر حاجة بِيْحِبّها أخويا إنُّه يْقضّي وَقْتُه سايِق.

áktar ħāga biyħibbáha ʔaxūya ʔínnu yʔáddi wáʔtu sāyiʔ.

What my brother likes most is spending his time driving.

③

تامِر بِيْقضّي وَقْت فراغُه في القِراية.

tāmir biyʔáddi waʔtᵊ farāɣu fi -lʔirāya.

Tamer spends his spare time reading.

④

عمّتي هتْقضّي الصّيْف في مارينا.

3ammíti hatʔáddi -ṣṣēf fi marīna.

My aunt will spend the summer in Marina.

⑤

قضّي وَقْت أكْتر معَ أُمّك.

ʔáddi waʔt áktar má3a ʔúmmak.

Spend more time with your mother.

⑥

إنْتَ مْقضّي وَقْتك في أيْه في الأجازة؟

ínta mʔáddi wáʔtak fi ʔē fi -lʔagāza?

How did you spend your time on vacation?

⑦

مقضّيناش وَقْت كْبير في المصْيَف. كُنّا حاجْزين أرْبع أيّام بسّ.

ma-ʔaddināš waʔtᵊ kbīr fi -lmáṣyaf. kúnna ħagzīn árba3 tiyyām bass.

We didn't spend a lot of time at the summer resort. We just reserved it for four days.

❖ [2d] **to spend** (time) (**on** في *fi*)

- This verb is followed by the word وَقْت *waʔt* or another time expression (➲ 209.1, 209.4), and then a prepositional phrase (➲ 209.1, 209.4, 209.5, 209.7), active participle (➲ 209.2), or verbal noun (➲ 209.3).

210 to cut ʔáṭa3 قَطَع

	affirmative		negative		
ána	ʔaṭá3t	قَطَعْت	ma-ʔaṭá3tiš	مَقَطَعْتِش	perfect
íḥna	ʔaṭá3na	قَطَعْنا	ma-ʔaṭa3nāš	مَقَطَعْناش	
ínta	ʔaṭá3t	قَطَعْت	ma-ʔaṭá3tiš	مَقَطَعْتِش	
ínti	ʔaṭá3ti	قَطَعْتي	ma-ʔaṭa3tīš	مَقَطَعْتيش	
íntu	ʔaṭá3tu	قَطَعْتوا	ma-ʔaṭa3tūš	مَقَطَعْتوش	
húwwa	ʔáṭa3	قَطَع	ma-ʔaṭá3š	مَقَطَعْش	
híyya	ʔáṭa3it	قَطَعِت	ma-ʔaṭa3ítš	مَقَطَعِتْش	
húmma	ʔáṭa3u	قَطَعوا	ma-ʔaṭa3ūš	مَقَطَعوش	
ána	áʔṭa3	أَقْطَع	ma-ʔṭá3š	مَقْطَعْش	imperfect
íḥna	níʔṭa3	نِقْطَع	ma-niʔṭá3š	مَنِقْطَعْش	
ínta	tíʔṭa3	تِقْطَع	ma-tiʔṭá3š	مَتِقْطَعْش	
ínti	tiʔṭá3i	تِقْطَعي	ma-tiʔṭa3īš	مَتِقْطَعيش	
íntu	tiʔṭá3u	تِقْطَعوا	ma-tiʔṭa3ūš	مَتِقْطَعوش	
húwwa	yíʔṭa3	يِقْطَع	ma-yiʔṭá3š	مَيِقْطَعْش	
híyya	tíʔṭa3	تِقْطَع	ma-tiʔṭá3š	مَتِقْطَعْش	
húmma	yiʔṭá3u	يِقْطَعوا	ma-yiʔṭa3ūš	مَيِقْطَعوش	
ána	báʔṭa3	بَقْطَع	ma-baʔṭá3š	مَبَقْطَعْش	bi-imperfect
íḥna	biníʔṭa3	بِنِقْطَع	ma-bniʔṭá3š	مَبْنِقْطَعْش	
ínta	bitíʔṭa3	بِتِقْطَع	ma-btiʔṭá3š	مَبْتِقْطَعْش	
ínti	bitiʔṭá3i	بِتِقْطَعي	ma-btiʔṭa3īš	مَبْتِقْطَعيش	
íntu	bitiʔṭá3u	بِتِقْطَعوا	ma-btiʔṭa3ūš	مَبْتِقْطَعوش	
húwwa	biyíʔṭa3	بِيِقْطَع	ma-byiʔṭá3š	مَبْيِقْطَعْش	
híyya	bitíʔṭa3	بِتِقْطَع	ma-btiʔṭá3š	مَبْتِقْطَعْش	
húmma	biyiʔṭá3u	بِيِقْطَعوا	ma-byiʔṭa3ūš	مَبْيِقْطَعوش	
ána	háʔṭa3	هَقْطَع	miš háʔṭa3	مِش هَقْطَع	future
íḥna	haníʔṭa3	هَنِقْطَع	miš haníʔṭa3	مِش هَنِقْطَع	
ínta	hatíʔṭa3	هَتِقْطَع	miš hatíʔṭa3	مِش هَتِقْطَع	
ínti	hatiʔṭá3i	هَتِقْطَعي	miš hatiʔṭá3i	مِش هَتِقْطَعي	
íntu	hatiʔṭá3u	هَتِقْطَعوا	miš hatiʔṭá3u	مِش هَتِقْطَعوا	
húwwa	hayíʔṭa3	هَيِقْطَع	miš hayíʔṭa3	مِش هَيِقْطَع	
híyya	hatíʔṭa3	هَتِقْطَع	miš hatíʔṭa3	مِش هَتِقْطَع	
húmma	hayiʔṭá3u	هَيِقْطَعوا	miš hayiʔṭá3u	مِش هَيِقْطَعوا	
ínta	íʔṭa3	اِقْطَع	ma-tiʔṭá3š	مَتِقْطَعْش	imperative
ínti	iʔṭá3i	اِقْطَعي	ma-tiʔṭa3īš	مَتِقْطَعيش	
íntu	iʔṭá3u	اِقْطَعوا	ma-tiʔṭa3ūš	مَتِقْطَعوش	

	active		passive		
masculine	ʔāṭi3	قاطِع	maʔṭū3	مَقْطوع	participles
feminine	ʔáṭ3a	قاطْعَة	maʔṭū3a	مَقْطوعَة	
plural	ʔaṭ3īn	قاطْعين	maʔṭu3īn	مَقْطوعين	

verbal noun: ʔaṭ3 قَطْع

①

أنا قطعْت خمس تذاكِر لِحفْلِةْ بُكْره.

ána ʔaṭá3tᵊ xámas tazākir li-ḫáflit búkra.

I've bought five tickets for tomorrow's concert.

②

آدم إضْطرّ يِقْطع رِحْلِتُه و يِرجع لمّا عِرِف إنّ باباه تعْبان.

ādam iḍṭárrᵊ yíʔṭa3 riḫlítu wi yírga3 lámma 3írif innᵊ babā ta3bān.

Adam had to cut his trip short and come back when he learned that his father was sick.

③

الدُّكْتور بِيِقْطع كلامُه لمّا حدّ بِيِعْمِل دَوْشة.

idduktūr biyíʔṭa3 kalāmu lámma ḫaddᵊ biyí3mil dáwša.

The professor stops speaking whenever someone makes noise.

④

أسْفة، هقْطع كلامْكو، بسّ هُوَّ ده شارِع قصْر النّيل؟

ásfa, háʔṭa3 kalámku, bassᵊ húwwa da šāri3 ʔaṣr innīl?

(to people talking:) Sorry for interrupting, but is this Qasr al-Nil street?

⑤

الكابْتِن فِضِل يمرّن الوَلد تلات ساعات لمّا قطع نفسُه.

ilkábtin fíḍil yimárran ilwálad tálat sa3āt lámma ʔáṭa3 náfasu.

The coach kept training the boy for three hours until he was exhausted.

⑥

متِقْطعْش وُعود مِش هتِعْرف تِوَفّيها.

ma-tiʔṭá3šᵊ wu3ūd miš hatí3raf tiwaffīha.

Don't promise what you can't do.

⑦

اِقْطعي بِالرّاحة. السِّكينة دي حامْية أوي.

iʔṭá3i bi-rrāḫa. issikīna di ḫámya ʔáwi.

Cut slowly. That knife is really sharp.

❖ [1s1] **to cut; to buy** (tickets)

- This verb can be used literally (➲ 210.7), but is often used metaphorically in various idioms.

211 to sit ʔá3ad قَعَد

verbal nouns: ʔá3da قَعْدة - ʔu3ād قعاد

	affirmative		negative		
ána	ʔa3ádt	قَعَدْت	ma-ʔa3ádtiš	مَقَعَدْتِش	perfect
íḥna	ʔa3ádna	قَعَدْنا	ma-ʔa3adnāš	مَقَعَدْناش	
ínta	ʔa3ádt	قَعَدْت	ma-ʔa3ádtiš	مَقَعَدْتِش	
ínti	ʔa3ádti	قَعَدْتي	ma-ʔa3adtīš	مَقَعَدْتيش	
íntu	ʔa3ádtu	قَعَدْتوا	ma-ʔa3adtūš	مَقَعَدْتوش	
húwwa	ʔá3ad	قَعَد	ma-ʔa3ádš	مَقَعَدْش	
híyya	ʔá3adit	قَعَدِت	ma-ʔa3adítš	مَقَعَدِتْش	
húmma	ʔá3adu	قَعَدوا	ma-ʔa3adūš	مَقَعَدوش	
ána	áʔ3ud	أَقْعُد	ma-ʔ3údš	مَقْعُدْش	imperfect
íḥna	núʔ3ud	نُقْعُد	ma-nuʔ3údš	مَنُقْعُدْش	
ínta	túʔ3ud	تُقْعُد	ma-tuʔ3údš	مَتُقْعُدْش	
ínti	tuʔ3údi	تُقْعُدي	ma-tuʔ3udīš	مَتُقْعُديش	
íntu	tuʔ3údu	تُقْعُدوا	ma-tuʔ3udūš	مَتُقْعُدوش	
húwwa	yúʔ3ud	يُقْعُد	ma-yuʔ3údš	مَيُقْعُدْش	
híyya	túʔ3ud	تُقْعُد	ma-tuʔ3údš	مَتُقْعُدْش	
húmma	yuʔ3údu	يُقْعُدوا	ma-yuʔ3udūš	مَيُقْعُدوش	
ána	báʔ3ud	بَقْعُد	ma-baʔ3údš	مَبَقْعُدْش	bi-imperfect
íḥna	binúʔ3ud	بِنُقْعُد	ma-bnuʔ3údš	مَبْنُقْعُدْش	
ínta	bitúʔ3ud	بِتُقْعُد	ma-btuʔ3údš	مَبْتُقْعُدْش	
ínti	bituʔ3údi	بِتُقْعُدي	ma-btuʔ3udīš	مَبْتُقْعُديش	
íntu	bituʔ3údu	بِتُقْعُدوا	ma-btuʔ3udūš	مَبْتُقْعُدوش	
húwwa	biyúʔ3ud	بِيُقْعُد	ma-byuʔ3údš	مَبْيُقْعُدْش	
híyya	bitúʔ3ud	بِتُقْعُد	ma-btuʔ3údš	مَبْتُقْعُدْش	
húmma	biyuʔ3údu	بِيُقْعُدوا	ma-byuʔ3udūš	مَبْيُقْعُدوش	
ána	háʔ3ud	هَقْعُد	miš háʔ3ud	مِش هَقْعُد	future
íḥna	hanúʔ3ud	هَنُقْعُد	miš hanúʔ3ud	مِش هَنُقْعُد	
ínta	hatúʔ3ud	هَتُقْعُد	miš hatúʔ3ud	مِش هَتُقْعُد	
ínti	hatuʔ3údi	هَتُقْعُدي	miš hatuʔ3údi	مِش هَتُقْعُدي	
íntu	hatuʔ3údu	هَتُقْعُدوا	miš hatuʔ3údu	مِش هَتُقْعُدوا	
húwwa	hayúʔ3ud	هَيُقْعُد	miš hayúʔ3ud	مِش هَيُقْعُد	
híyya	hatúʔ3ud	هَتُقْعُد	miš hatúʔ3ud	مِش هَتُقْعُد	
húmma	hayuʔ3údu	هَيُقْعُدوا	miš hayuʔ3údu	مِش هَيُقْعُدوا	
ínta	úʔ3ud	أُقْعُد	ma-tuʔ3údš	مَتُقْعُدْش	imperative
ínti	uʔ3údi	أُقْعُدي	ma-tuʔ3udīš	مَتُقْعُديش	
íntu	uʔ3údu	أُقْعُدوا	ma-tuʔ3udūš	مَتُقْعُدوش	

	active		passive		
masculine	ʔā3id	قاعِد	maʔ3ūd	مَقْعود	participles
feminine	ʔá3da	قاعْدَة	–	–	
plural	ʔa3dīn	قاعْدين	–	–	

①

مُهند قعد عَ الكُرْسى، طِلِع مكْسور و وِقِع بيه.

múhanad ʔá3ad 3a -lkúrsi, ṭíli3 maksūr wi wíʔi3 bī.

Mohanad sat on the chair, but it was broken, and he fell down.

②

جوْزي بِيْحِبّ يُقْعُد عَ القهْوَة كُلّ خميس.

gōzi biyḥibbᵊ yúʔ3ud 3a -lʔáhwa kullᵊ xamīs.

Every Thursday, my husband likes to sit in the coffee shop.

③

قعدْنا عَ الكنبة عشان نِجرّبْها، طِلْعِت مُريحة أوي.

ʔa3ádna 3a -lkánaba 3ašān nigarrábha, ṭíl3it murīḥa ʔáwi.

We sat on the couch to try it out, and we found it so comfortable.

④

الضُّيوف مقعدوش كِتير. دوْل حتّى مشِرْبوش الشّاي.

iḍḍuyūf ma-ʔa3adūš kitīr. dōl ḥátta ma-širbūš iššāy.

The guests didn't stay long. They didn't even drink the tea.

⑤

تامِر قعد تِسِع سِنين في الكُلّية.

tāmir ʔá3ad tísi3 sinīn fi -lkullíyya.

Tamer spent nine years in college.

⑥

أنا قعدْت معاهُم عشان أصالِحْهُم و الحمْدُ لله نِجِحْت.

ána ʔa3ádtᵊ ma3āhum 3ašān aṣalíḥhum w ilḥámdu li-llāh nigíḥt.

I stayed to help them reconcile, and I succeeded, thank God.

⑦

أ: إنْتَ قاعِد قدّ أيْه في مصْر؟

ب: هقْعُد شهْر.

A: ínta ʔā3id add ʔē fi maṣr?

B: háʔ3ud šahr.

A: How long are you going to stay in Egypt?

B: I'm staying for a month.

⑧

مها لمّا بِتِزْعل بِتُقْعُد تاكُل.

máha lámma bitíz3al bitúʔ3ud tākul.

When Maha gets upset, she keeps eating.

⑨

مِن الصُّبْح قاعِد أتْكلِّم و إنْتَ وَلا إنْتَ هِنا.

min iṣṣúbḥᵊ ʔā3id atkállim w ínta wála ʔínta hína.

I've been talking all day long, and you're not listening.

❖ [1s3] **to sit; to remain, stay** (somewhere)**; to spend** (time)**; to continue, keep** (doing)

- This primary meaning of this verb is 'sit', but it can be synonymous with قضّى *ʔáḍḍa* (➲ 209).
- It can be followed by an imperfect verb to emphasis a continuous action. (➲ 211.8, 211.9)
- As this verb requires a preposition, the passive participle is invariable: مقْعود عليْه *maʔ3ūd 3alē* 'sat upon'.
- This verb, like other verbs of the [1s3] and [1s6] patterns, can optionally take ـُ *u* instead of ـِ *i* in the personal prefixes of the imperfect (including the bi-imperfect and future) and imperative. For example, يُقْعُد *yúʔ3ud* can also be pronounced يِقْعُد *yíʔ3ud*. These vowels are interchangeable, but the tables reflect the preferences of the speakers on the MP3s.

➲ 30.5, 65.2, 86.6, 94.5, 101.2, 106.2, 106.7, 120.4, 194.3, 216.2, 254.4

212 to close ʔáfal قفل

	affirmative		negative		
ána	ʔafált	قَفَلْت	ma-ʔafáltiš	مَقَفَلْتِش	perfect
íḫna	ʔafálna	قَفَلْنا	ma-ʔafalnāš	مَقَفَلْناش	
ínta	ʔafált	قَفَلْت	ma-ʔafáltiš	مَقَفَلْتِش	
ínti	ʔafálti	قَفَلْتي	ma-ʔafaltīš	مَقَفَلْتيش	
íntu	ʔafáltu	قَفَلْتوا	ma-ʔafaltūš	مَقَفَلْتوش	
húwwa	ʔáfal	قَفَل	ma-ʔafálš	مَقَفَلْش	
híyya	ʔáfalit	قَفَلِت	ma-ʔafalítš	مَقَفَلِتْش	
húmma	ʔáfalu	قَفَلوا	ma-ʔafalūš	مَقَفَلوش	
ána	áʔfil	أَقْفِل	ma-ʔfílš	مَقْفِلْش	imperfect
íḫna	níʔfil	نِقْفِل	ma-niʔfílš	مَنِقْفِلْش	
ínta	tíʔfil	تِقْفِل	ma-tiʔfílš	مَتِقْفِلْش	
ínti	tiʔfíli	تِقْفِلي	ma-tiʔfilīš	مَتِقْفِليش	
íntu	tiʔfílu	تِقْفِلوا	ma-tiʔfilūš	مَتِقْفِلوش	
húwwa	yíʔfil	يِقْفِل	ma-yiʔfílš	مَيِقْفِلْش	
híyya	tíʔfil	تِقْفِل	ma-tiʔfílš	مَتِقْفِلْش	
húmma	yiʔfílu	يِقْفِلوا	ma-yiʔfilūš	مَيِقْفِلوش	
ána	báʔfil	بَقْفِل	ma-baʔfílš	مَبَقْفِلْش	bi-imperfect
íḫna	biníʔfil	بِنِقْفِل	ma-bniʔfílš	مَبْنِقْفِلْش	
ínta	bitíʔfil	بِتِقْفِل	ma-btiʔfílš	مَبْتِقْفِلْش	
ínti	bitiʔfíli	بِتِقْفِلي	ma-btiʔfilīš	مَبْتِقْفِليش	
íntu	bitiʔfílu	بِتِقْفِلوا	ma-btiʔfilūš	مَبْتِقْفِلوش	
húwwa	biyíʔfil	بِيِقْفِل	ma-byiʔfílš	مَبْيِقْفِلْش	
híyya	bitíʔfil	بِتِقْفِل	ma-btiʔfílš	مَبْتِقْفِلْش	
húmma	biyiʔfílu	بِيِقْفِلوا	ma-byiʔfilūš	مَبْيِقْفِلوش	
ána	háʔfil	هَقْفِل	miš háʔfil	مِش هَقْفِل	future
íḫna	haníʔfil	هَنِقْفِل	miš haníʔfil	مِش هَنِقْفِل	
ínta	hatíʔfil	هَتِقْفِل	miš hatíʔfil	مِش هَتِقْفِل	
ínti	hatiʔfíli	هَتِقْفِلي	miš hatiʔfíli	مِش هَتِقْفِلي	
íntu	hatiʔfílu	هَتِقْفِلوا	miš hatiʔfílu	مِش هَتِقْفِلوا	
húwwa	hayíʔfil	هَيِقْفِل	miš hayíʔfil	مِش هَيِقْفِل	
híyya	hatíʔfil	هَتِقْفِل	miš hatíʔfil	مِش هَتِقْفِل	
húmma	hayiʔfílu	هَيِقْفِلوا	miš hayiʔfílu	مِش هَيِقْفِلوا	
ínta	íʔfil	اِقْفِل	ma-tiʔfílš	مَتِقْفِلْش	imperative
ínti	iʔfíli	اِقْفِلي	ma-tiʔfilīš	مَتِقْفِليش	
íntu	iʔfílu	اِقْفِلوا	ma-tiʔfilūš	مَتِقْفِلوش	

	active		passive		
masculine	ʔāfil	قافِل	maʔfūl	مَقْفول	participles
feminine	ʔáfla	قافْلَة	maʔfūla	مَقْفولَة	
plural	ʔaflīn	قافْلين	maʔfulīn	مَقْفولين	

verbal nouns: ʔafl قَفْل - ʔafalān قَفَلان

①

لمّا وْصِلْت المحلّ لقيْتُه قفل.

lámma wṣílt ilmaḥáll^ə laʔētu ʔáfal.

When I reached the shop,
I found it closed.

②

حمْزة قبْل ما يْنام لازِم يِقْفِل باب الشّقّة بِالمُفْتاح و القِفْل.

ḥámza ʔablᵊ ma ynām lāzim yíʔfil bāb iššáʔʔa bi-lmuftāḥ w ilʔífl.

Before he goes to sleep, Hamza locks the apartment door.

③

أُمْنية بِتِقْفِل حِساب الفيْسبوك بِتاعْها أيّام الاِمْتِحانات.

umníyya bitíʔfil ḥisāb ilfēsbūk bitá3ha ʔayyām ilʔimtiḥanāt.

During the exam period, Omnia
closes her Facebook account.

④

تعالي بْراحْتِك يافنْدِم. إحْنا مُش هنِقْفِل قبْل الفجْر.

ta3āli b-ráḥtik ya -fándim. íḥna muš haníʔfil ʔabl ilfágr.

Come at your leisure, ma'am.
We won't close until dawn.

⑤

اِقْفِلي السِّكّة في وِشُّه الحَيَوان ده.

iʔfíli -ssíkka fi wíššu -lḥayawān da.

Just hang up on that jerk.

❖ [1s2] **to close; to lock**

➲ 97.3, 189.6, 189.8

213 to finish up ʔáffil قفّل

		affirmative		negative		
perfect	ána	ʔaffílt	قفّلت	ma-ʔaffíltiš	مقفّلتش
	íḥna	ʔaffílna	قفّلنا	ma-ʔaffilnāš	مقفّلناش
	ínta	ʔaffílt	قفّلت	ma-ʔaffíltiš	مقفّلتش
	ínti	ʔaffílti	قفّلتي	ma-ʔaffiltīš	مقفّلتيش
	íntu	ʔaffíltu	قفّلتوا	ma-ʔaffiltūš	مقفّلتوش
	húwwa	ʔáffil	قفّل	ma-ʔaffílš	مقفّلش
	híyya	ʔaffílit	قفّلت	ma-ʔaffilítš	مقفّلتش
	húmma	ʔaffílu	قفّلوا	ma-ʔaffilūš	مقفّلوش
imperfect	ána	aʔáffil	أقفّل	ma-ʔaffílš	مقفّلش
	íḥna	niʔáffil	نقفّل	ma-nʔaffílš	منقفّلش
	ínta	tiʔáffil	تقفّل	ma-tʔaffílš	متقفّلش
	ínti	tiʔaffíli	تقفّلي	ma-tʔaffilīš	متقفّليش
	íntu	tiʔaffílu	تقفّلوا	ma-tʔaffilūš	متقفّلوش
	húwwa	yiʔáffil	يقفّل	ma-yʔaffílš	ميقفّلش
	híyya	tiʔáffil	تقفّل	ma-tʔaffílš	متقفّلش
	húmma	yiʔaffílu	يقفّلوا	ma-yʔaffilūš	ميقفّلوش
bi-imperfect	ána	baʔáffil	بقفّل	ma-baʔaffílš	مبقفّلش
	íḥna	binʔáffil	بنقفّل	ma-binʔaffílš	مبنقفّلش
	ínta	bitʔáffil	بتقفّل	ma-bitʔaffílš	مبتقفّلش
	ínti	bitʔaffíli	بتقفّلي	ma-bitʔaffilīš	مبتقفّليش
	íntu	bitʔaffílu	بتقفّلوا	ma-bitʔaffilūš	مبتقفّلوش
	húwwa	biyʔáffil	بيقفّل	ma-biyʔaffílš	مبيقفّلش
	híyya	bitʔáffil	بتقفّل	ma-bitʔaffílš	مبتقفّلش
	húmma	biyʔaffílu	بيقفّلوا	ma-biyʔaffilūš	مبيقفّلوش
future	ána	haʔáffil	هقفّل	miš haʔáffil	مش هقفّل
	íḥna	hanʔáffil	هنقفّل	miš hanʔáffil	مش هنقفّل
	ínta	hatʔáffil	هتقفّل	miš hatʔáffil	مش هتقفّل
	ínti	hatʔaffíli	هتقفّلي	miš hatʔaffíli	مش هتقفّلي
	íntu	hatʔaffílu	هتقفّلوا	miš hatʔaffílu	مش هتقفّلوا
	húwwa	hayʔáffil	هيقفّل	miš hayʔáffil	مش هيقفّل
	híyya	hatʔáffil	هتقفّل	miš hatʔáffil	مش هتقفّل
	húmma	hayʔaffílu	هيقفّلوا	miš hayʔaffílu	مش هيقفّلوا
imperative	ínta	ʔáffil	قفّل	ma-tʔaffílš	متقفّلش
	ínti	ʔaffíli	قفّلي	ma-tʔaffilīš	متقفّليش
	íntu	ʔaffílu	قفّلوا	ma-tʔaffilūš	متقفّلوش

		active		passive	
participles	masculine	miʔáffil	مقفّل	mitʔáffil	متقفّل
	feminine	miʔaffíla	مقفّلة	mitʔaffíla	متقفّلة
	plural	miʔaffilīn	مقفّلين	mitʔaffilīn	متقفّلين

verbal noun: taʔfīl تقفيل

①
نادِر كان مِذاكِر كُوَيِّس و دخل قفِّل الاِمْتِحان.

nādir kān mizākir kuwáyyis wi dáxal ʔáffil ilʔimtiħān.

Nader studied so well and answered
the exam completely right.

②
قولي لْيِحْيى مَيْقفِّلْش مُخُّه و خلِّيه يِتْعاوِن معانا أحْسن.

ʔúli l-yíħya ma-yʔaffílšᵊ múxxu wi xallī yt3āwin ma3āna ʔáħsan.

Tell Yahia not to be so close-minded and
make him cooperate with us better.

③
سُمَيَّة لمّا مبْيِعْجِبْهاش الأُسْلوب بِتْقفِّل في الكلام.

sumáyya lámma ma-byi3gibhāš ilʔuslūb bitʔáffil fi -lkalām.

When Somaya doesn't like the way someone is
talking to her, she wraps up the conversation.

④
مُعْتزّ هَيْقفِّل الرُّسومات النّهارْده و يِبْعتْهالك.

mu3tázzᵊ hayʔáffil irrusumāt innahárda wi yib3athālak.

Moataz will finish the drawings
today and send them to you.

⑤
متْقفِّليش الشّبابيك كُلّها. عايْزين تيّار هَوا.

ma-tʔaffilīš iššababīk kulláha. 3ayzīn tayyār háwa.

Don't close all the windows.
We need an air current.

❖ [2s1] **to close up/off; to close** (a number of things)**; to finish up**

- Compare with قفل *ʔáfal*. (➲ 212)

214 to undress ʔála3 قَلَع

verbal nouns: ʔal3 قَلْع - ʔala3ān قَلَعان

	affirmative		negative		
ána	ʔalá3t	قَلَعْت	ma-ʔalá3tiš	مَقَلَعْتِش	perfect
íḫna	ʔalá3na	قَلَعْنا	ma-ʔala3nāš	مَقَلَعْناش	
ínta	ʔalá3t	قَلَعْت	ma-ʔalá3tiš	مَقَلَعْتِش	
ínti	ʔalá3ti	قَلَعْتي	ma-ʔala3tīš	مَقَلَعْتيش	
íntu	ʔalá3tu	قَلَعْتوا	ma-ʔala3tūš	مَقَلَعْتوش	
húwwa	ʔála3	قَلَع	ma-ʔalá3š	مَقَلَعْش	
híyya	ʔála3it	قَلَعِت	ma-ʔala3ítš	مَقَلَعِتْش	
húmma	ʔála3u	قَلَعوا	ma-ʔala3ūš	مَقَلَعوش	
ána	áʔla3	أَقْلَع	ma-ʔlá3š	مَقْلَعْش	imperfect
íḫna	níʔla3	نِقْلَع	ma-niʔlá3š	مَنِقْلَعْش	
ínta	tíʔla3	تِقْلَع	ma-tiʔlá3š	مَتِقْلَعْش	
ínti	tiʔlá3i	تِقْلَعي	ma-tiʔla3īš	مَتِقْلَعيش	
íntu	tiʔlá3u	تِقْلَعوا	ma-tiʔla3ūš	مَتِقْلَعوش	
húwwa	yíʔla3	يِقْلَع	ma-yiʔlá3š	مَيِقْلَعْش	
híyya	tíʔla3	تِقْلَع	ma-tiʔlá3š	مَتِقْلَعْش	
húmma	yiʔlá3u	يِقْلَعوا	ma-yiʔla3ūš	مَيِقْلَعوش	
ána	báʔla3	بَقْلَع	ma-baʔlá3š	مَبَقْلَعْش	bi-imperfect
íḫna	biníʔla3	بِنِقْلَع	ma-bniʔlá3š	مَبْنِقْلَعْش	
ínta	bitíʔla3	بِتِقْلَع	ma-btiʔlá3š	مَبْتِقْلَعْش	
ínti	bitiʔlá3i	بِتِقْلَعي	ma-btiʔla3īš	مَبْتِقْلَعيش	
íntu	bitiʔlá3u	بِتِقْلَعوا	ma-btiʔla3ūš	مَبْتِقْلَعوش	
húwwa	biyíʔla3	بِيِقْلَع	ma-byiʔlá3š	مَبْيِقْلَعْش	
híyya	bitíʔla3	بِتِقْلَع	ma-btiʔlá3š	مَبْتِقْلَعْش	
húmma	biyiʔlá3u	بِيِقْلَعوا	ma-byiʔla3ūš	مَبْيِقْلَعوش	
ána	háʔla3	هَقْلَع	miš háʔla3	مِش هَقْلَع	future
íḫna	haníʔla3	هَنِقْلَع	miš haníʔla3	مِش هَنِقْلَع	
ínta	hatíʔla3	هَتِقْلَع	miš hatíʔla3	مِش هَتِقْلَع	
ínti	hatiʔlá3i	هَتِقْلَعي	miš hatiʔlá3i	مِش هَتِقْلَعي	
íntu	hatiʔlá3u	هَتِقْلَعوا	miš hatiʔlá3u	مِش هَتِقْلَعوا	
húwwa	hayíʔla3	هَيِقْلَع	miš hayíʔla3	مِش هَيِقْلَع	
híyya	hatíʔla3	هَتِقْلَع	miš hatíʔla3	مِش هَتِقْلَع	
húmma	hayiʔlá3u	هَيِقْلَعوا	miš hayiʔlá3u	مِش هَيِقْلَعوا	
ínta	íʔla3	اِقْلَع	ma-tiʔlá3š	مَتِقْلَعْش	imperative
ínti	iʔlá3i	اِقْلَعي	ma-tiʔla3īš	مَتِقْلَعيش	
íntu	iʔlá3u	اِقْلَعوا	ma-tiʔla3ūš	مَتِقْلَعوش	

	active		passive		
masculine	ʔāli3	قالِع	maʔlū3	مَقْلوع	participles
feminine	ʔál3a	قالْعَة	maʔlū3a	مَقْلوعَة	
plural	ʔal3īn	قالْعين	maʔlu3īn	مَقْلوعين	

①

الجَوّ حرّ أوي. أوِّل ما وْصِلْت البيْت، قلعْت هِدومي و دخلْت الدُّشّ.

ilgáwwᵊ ḥarrᵊ ʔáwi. áwwil ma wṣílt ilbēt, ʔalá3tᵊ hidūmi wi daxált iddúšš.

It's so hot. As soon as I got home, I got undressed and got in the shower.

②

خلّيه يِقْلع الهُدوم المبْلولة دي قبْل ما يِعْيى.

xallī yíʔla3 ilhudūm ilmablūla di ʔablᵊ ma yí3ya.

Take him to change out of these wet clothes before he catches a cold.

③

ماما دايْماً بِتِقْلع ساعِتْها و خَواتِمْها و تِنْساهُم.

māma dáyman bitíʔla3 sa3ítha wi xawatímha wi tinsāhum.

My mom always takes off her watch and rings, then forgets them.

④

إنْتَ هتِقْلع هِنا؟ اِدْخُل غيرّ في أوضْتك.

ínta hatíʔla3 hína? ídxul ɣáyyar fi úḍtak.

Are you getting undressed here? Go change in your room.

⑤

متِقْلعْش الجاكيتّ ده حتّى لَوْ المطر وِقِف. الجَوّ برْد جِدّاً.

ma-tiʔlá3š ilžakíttᵊ da ḥátta law ilmáṭar wíʔif. ilgáwwᵊ bardᵊ gíddan.

Don't take off that jacket even if the rain stops. It's too cold.

❖ [1s1] **to undress, get undressed; to take off**

➲ 120.1

215 to pour *kabb* كبّ

	affirmative		negative	
perfect				
ána	*kabbēt*	كبّيت	*ma-kabbítš*	مكبّيتش
íḫna	*kabbēna*	كبّينا	*ma-kabbināš*	مكبّيناش
ínta	*kabbēt*	كبّيت	*ma-kabbítš*	مكبّيتش
ínti	*kabbēti*	كبّيتي	*ma-kabbitīš*	مكبّيتيش
íntu	*kabbētu*	كبّيتوا	*ma-kabbitūš*	مكبّيتوش
húwwa	*kabb*	كبّ	*ma-kábbiš*	مكبّش
híyya	*kábbit*	كبّت	*ma-kabbítš*	مكبّتش
húmma	*kábbu*	كبّوا	*ma-kabbūš*	مكبّوش
imperfect				
ána	*akúbb*	أكُبّ	*ma-kúbbiš*	مكُبّش
íḫna	*nikúbb*	نِكُبّ	*ma-nkúbbiš*	مَنْكُبّش
ínta	*tikúbb*	تِكُبّ	*ma-tkúbbiš*	مَتْكُبّش
ínti	*tikúbbi*	تِكُبّي	*ma-tkubbīš*	مَتْكُبّيش
íntu	*tikúbbu*	تِكُبّوا	*ma-tkubbūš*	مَتْكُبّوش
húwwa	*yikúbb*	يِكُبّ	*ma-ykúbbiš*	مَيْكُبّش
híyya	*tikúbb*	تِكُبّ	*ma-tkúbbiš*	مَتْكُبّش
húmma	*yikúbbu*	يِكُبّوا	*ma-ykubbūš*	مَيْكُبّوش
bi-imperfect				
ána	*bakúbb*	بكُبّ	*ma-bakúbbiš*	مبكُبّش
íḫna	*binkúbb*	بِنْكُبّ	*ma-binkúbbiš*	مَبِنْكُبّش
ínta	*bitkúbb*	بِتْكُبّ	*ma-bitkúbbiš*	مَبِتْكُبّش
ínti	*bitkúbbi*	بِتْكُبّي	*ma-bitkubbīš*	مَبِتْكُبّيش
íntu	*bitkúbbu*	بِتْكُبّوا	*ma-bitkubbūš*	مَبِتْكُبّوش
húwwa	*biykúbb*	بِيْكُبّ	*ma-biykúbbiš*	مَبِيْكُبّش
híyya	*bitkúbb*	بِتْكُبّ	*ma-bitkúbbiš*	مَبِتْكُبّش
húmma	*biykúbbu*	بِيْكُبّوا	*ma-biykubbūš*	مَبِيْكُبّوش
future				
ána	*hakúbb*	هَكُبّ	*miš hakúbb*	مِش هَكُبّ
íḫna	*hankúbb*	هَنْكُبّ	*miš hankúbb*	مِش هَنْكُبّ
ínta	*hatkúbb*	هَتْكُبّ	*miš hatkúbb*	مِش هَتْكُبّ
ínti	*hatkúbbi*	هَتْكُبّي	*miš hatkúbbi*	مِش هَتْكُبّي
íntu	*hatkúbbu*	هَتْكُبّوا	*miš hatkúbbu*	مِش هَتْكُبّوا
húwwa	*haykúbb*	هَيْكُبّ	*miš haykúbb*	مِش هَيْكُبّ
híyya	*hatkúbb*	هَتْكُبّ	*miš hatkúbb*	مِش هَتْكُبّ
húmma	*haykúbbu*	هَيْكُبّوا	*miš haykúbbu*	مِش هَيْكُبّوا
imperative				
ínta	*kubb*	كُبّ	*ma-tkúbbiš*	مَتْكُبّش
ínti	*kúbbi*	كُبّي	*ma-tkubbīš*	مَتْكُبّيش
íntu	*kúbbu*	كُبّوا	*ma-tkubbūš*	مَتْكُبّوش

participles	active		passive	
masculine	*kābib*	كابِب	*makbūb*	مَكْبوب
feminine	*kábba*	كابّة	*makbūba*	مَكْبوبَة
plural	*kabbīn*	كابّين	*makbubīn*	مَكْبوبين

verbal noun: *kabb* كبّ

①

يابْني، بِالرّاحة! كبّيْت اللّبن في الأرْض.

ya -bni, bi-rrāḥa! kabbēt illában fi -lʔarḍ.

Be careful! You spilled milk on the floor.

②

بلاش تِكُبّ الشّاي في الكوبّايَة دي.

balāš tikúbb iššāy fi -lkubbāya di.

Don't pour tea in that glass.

③

بِتْكُبّ الميّة في الأرْض ليْه يا حبيبي؟

bitkúbb ilmáyya fi -lʔarḍᵊ lē ya ḥabībi?

(to a small child:) Why are you pouring water on the floor, honey?

④

إنْتَ أدْخُل ريّح و أنا هكُبّلك شُوَيّةْ عصير.

ínta -dxul ráyyaḥ w ána hakubbílak šuwáyyit 3aṣīr.

You go relax, and I'll pour you some juice.

⑤

متْكُبّيليش . أنا لِسّه شارِب.

ma-tkubbilīš. ána líssa šārib.

Don't pour any for me. I just had something to drink.

⑥

إبْني اِتْعلّم لمّا ييجي يِشْرب مَيْكُبّش في الأرْض.

íbni -t3állam lámma yīgi yíšrab ma-ykúbbiš fi -lʔarḍ.

My son learned not to spill on the floor when he drinks.

❖ [1g2] **to pour; to spill**

- This verb is synonymous with صبّ *ṣabb* (➲ 154) and دلق *dála?* (➲ 110).

216 to become big *kíbir* كِبِر

		affirmative		negative	
perfect	ána	*kibírt*	كِبِرت	*ma-kbírtiš*	مَكْبِرتِش
	íḫna	*kibírna*	كِبِرنا	*ma-kbirnāš*	مَكْبِرناش
	ínta	*kibírt*	كِبِرت	*ma-kbírtiš*	مَكْبِرتِش
	ínti	*kibírti*	كِبِرتي	*ma-kbirtīš*	مَكْبِرتيش
	íntu	*kibírtu*	كِبِرتوا	*ma-kbirtūš*	مَكْبِرتوش
	húwwa	*kíbir*	كِبِر	*ma-kbírš*	مَكْبِرش
	híyya	*kíbrit*	كِبْرِت	*ma-kibrítš*	مَكِبْرِتْش
	húmma	*kíbru*	كِبْروا	*ma-kibrūš*	مَكِبْروش
imperfect	ána	*ákbar*	أكْبَر	*ma-kbárš*	مَكْبَرْش
	íḫna	*níkbar*	نِكْبَر	*ma-nikbárš*	مَنِكْبَرْش
	ínta	*tíkbar*	تِكْبَر	*ma-tikbárš*	مَتِكْبَرْش
	ínti	*tikbári*	تِكْبَري	*ma-tikbarīš*	مَتِكْبَريش
	íntu	*tikbáru*	تِكْبَروا	*ma-tikbarūš*	مَتِكْبَروش
	húwwa	*yíkbar*	يِكْبَر	*ma-yikbárš*	مَيِكْبَرْش
	híyya	*tíkbar*	تِكْبَر	*ma-tikbárš*	مَتِكْبَرْش
	húmma	*yikbáru*	يِكْبَروا	*ma-yikbarūš*	مَيِكْبَروش
bi-imperfect	ána	*bákbar*	بَكْبَر	*ma-bakbárš*	مَبَكْبَرْش
	íḫna	*biníkbar*	بِنِكْبَر	*ma-bnikbárš*	مَبْنِكْبَرْش
	ínta	*bitíkbar*	بِتِكْبَر	*ma-btikbárš*	مَبْتِكْبَرْش
	ínti	*bitikbári*	بِتِكْبَري	*ma-btikbarīš*	مَبْتِكْبَريش
	íntu	*bitikbáru*	بِتِكْبَروا	*ma-btikbarūš*	مَبْتِكْبَروش
	húwwa	*biyíkbar*	بِيِكْبَر	*ma-byikbárš*	مَبْيِكْبَرْش
	híyya	*bitíkbar*	بِتِكْبَر	*ma-btikbárš*	مَبْتِكْبَرْش
	húmma	*biyikbáru*	بِيِكْبَروا	*ma-byikbarūš*	مَبْيِكْبَروش
future	ána	*hákbar*	هَكْبَر	*miš hákbar*	مِش هَكْبَر
	íḫna	*haníkbar*	هَنِكْبَر	*miš haníkbar*	مِش هَنِكْبَر
	ínta	*hatíkbar*	هَتِكْبَر	*miš hatíkbar*	مِش هَتِكْبَر
	ínti	*hatikbári*	هَتِكْبَري	*miš hatikbári*	مِش هَتِكْبَري
	íntu	*hatikbáru*	هَتِكْبَروا	*miš hatikbáru*	مِش هَتِكْبَروا
	húwwa	*hayíkbar*	هَيِكْبَر	*miš hayíkbar*	مِش هَيِكْبَر
	híyya	*hatíkbar*	هَتِكْبَر	*miš hatíkbar*	مِش هَتِكْبَر
	húmma	*hayikbáru*	هَيِكْبَروا	*miš hayikbáru*	مِش هَيِكْبَروا
imperative	ínta	*íkbar*	اِكْبَر	*ma-tikbárš*	مَتِكْبَرْش
	ínti	*ikbári*	اِكْبَري	*ma-tikbarīš*	مَتِكْبَريش
	íntu	*ikbáru*	اِكْبَروا	*ma-tikbarūš*	مَتِكْبَروش

		active		passive	
participles	masculine	*kabrān*	كَبْران	–	–
	feminine	*kabrāna*	كَبْرانَة	–	–
	plural	*kabranīn*	كَبْرانين	–	–

verbal nouns: *kubr* كُبْر – *kábar* كَبَر - *kibar* كِبَر

①

القاهِرة كِبْرِت أوي لِدرجِةْ إنّك مُمْكِن تاخُد تلات ساعات في مِشْوار.

ilqāhíra kíbrit ʔáwi li-dáragit ínnak múmkin tāxud tálat sa3āt fi mišwār.

Cairo has gotten so big that it could take
you three hours to get across it.

②

المُشْكِلة دي هتِفْضل تِكْبر لِحدّ ما تُقْعُدوا معَ بعْض و تِنْهوها.

ilmuškíla di hatífḍal tíkbar li-ḫaddᵊ ma tuʔ3údu má3a ba3ḍᵊ wi tinhūha.

The problem will keep growing until you both
sit down together and put an end to it.

③

متْغيرّتيش خالِص يا أمل. كإنِّك مبْتِكْبريش . قوليلْنا أيْه سِرّ الشّباب الدّائِم!

ma-tɣayyartīš xāliṣ ya ʔámal. ka-ínnik ma-btikbarīš. ʔulílna ʔē sirr iššabāb iddāʔim!

You haven't changed at all, Amal. It's as if you don't
age. Tell us the secret of everlasting youth!

④

متِسْتعْجِليش عَ الرّوج و الكعْب. هتِكْبري و هَيِبْقى نِفْسِك تِصْغري.

ma-tista3gilīš 3a -rrūž w ilká3b. hatikbári wi hayíbʔa nífsik tiṣɣári.

Don't be so eager to put on makeup and wear heels.
When you grow up, you'll wish you were younger.

⑤

اِكْبري بقى و بطّلي شُغْل العِيال ده.

ikbári báʔa w baṭṭáli šuɣl il3iyāl da.

Grow up and stop this childishness.

❖ [1s4] **to become big, grow; to grow up, age, get old**

➲ 70.5, 93.5, 145.2, 178.7, 223.5

217 to write *kátab* كَتَب

verbal noun: *kitāba* كِتابَة

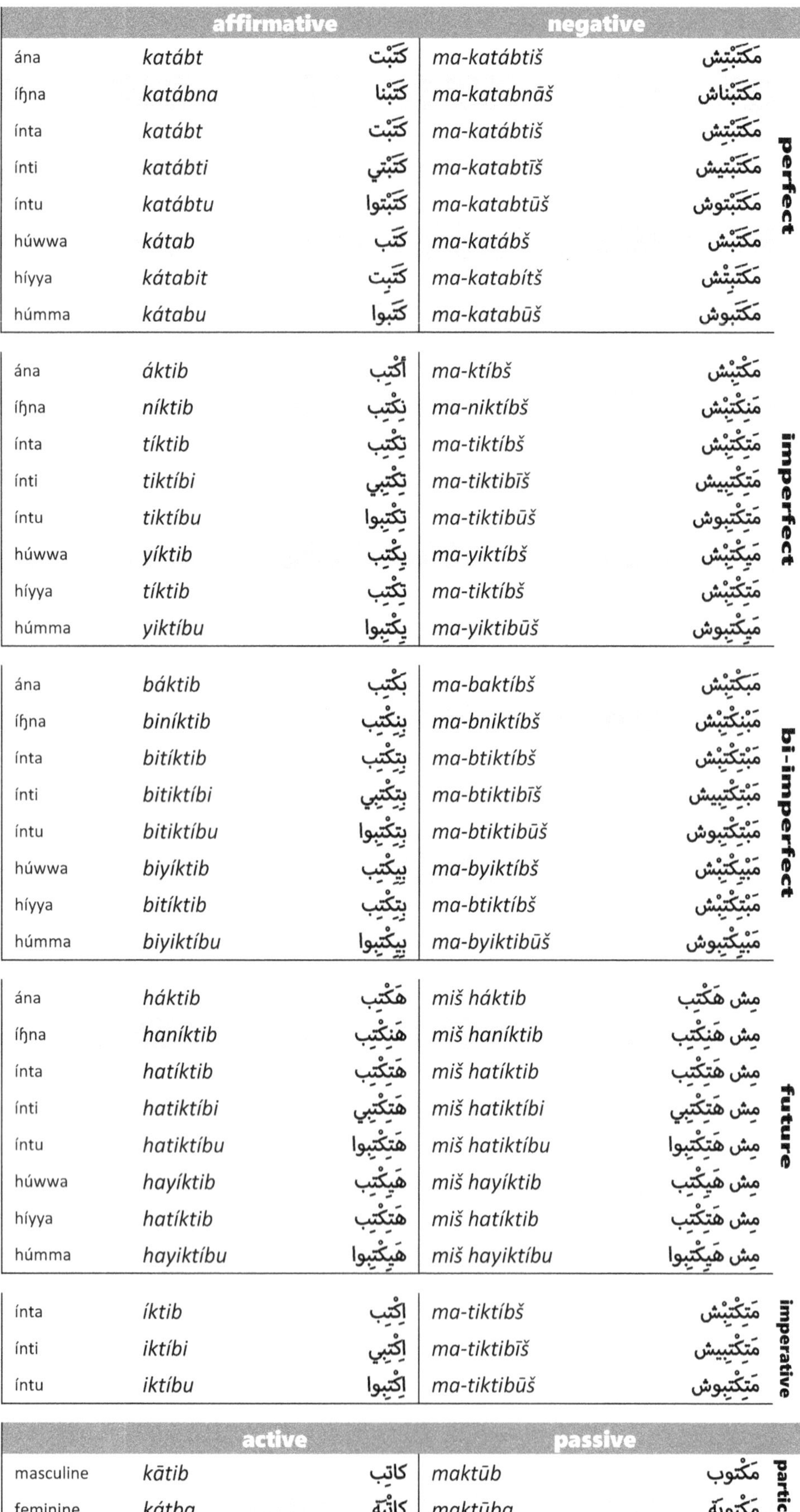

	affirmative		negative		
ána	*katábt*	كَتَبْت	*ma-katábtiš*	مَكَتَبْتِش	**perfect**
íḥna	*katábna*	كَتَبْنا	*ma-katabnāš*	مَكَتَبْناش	
ínta	*katábt*	كَتَبْت	*ma-katábtiš*	مَكَتَبْتِش	
ínti	*katábti*	كَتَبْتي	*ma-katabtīš*	مَكَتَبْتيش	
íntu	*katábtu*	كَتَبْتوا	*ma-katabtūš*	مَكَتَبْتوش	
húwwa	*kátab*	كَتَب	*ma-katábš*	مَكَتَبْش	
híyya	*kátabit*	كَتَبِت	*ma-katabítš*	مَكَتَبِتْش	
húmma	*kátabu*	كَتَبوا	*ma-katabūš*	مَكَتَبوش	
ána	*áktib*	أَكْتِب	*ma-ktíbš*	مَكْتِبْش	**imperfect**
íḥna	*níktib*	نِكْتِب	*ma-niktíbš*	مَنِكْتِبْش	
ínta	*tíktib*	تِكْتِب	*ma-tiktíbš*	مَتِكْتِبْش	
ínti	*tiktíbi*	تِكْتِبي	*ma-tiktibīš*	مَتِكْتِبيش	
íntu	*tiktíbu*	تِكْتِبوا	*ma-tiktibūš*	مَتِكْتِبوش	
húwwa	*yíktib*	يِكْتِب	*ma-yiktíbš*	مَيِكْتِبْش	
híyya	*tíktib*	تِكْتِب	*ma-tiktíbš*	مَتِكْتِبْش	
húmma	*yiktíbu*	يِكْتِبوا	*ma-yiktibūš*	مَيِكْتِبوش	
ána	*báktib*	بَكْتِب	*ma-baktíbš*	مَبَكْتِبْش	**bi-imperfect**
íḥna	*biníktib*	بِنِكْتِب	*ma-bniktíbš*	مَبْنِكْتِبْش	
ínta	*bitíktib*	بِتِكْتِب	*ma-btiktíbš*	مَبْتِكْتِبْش	
ínti	*bitiktíbi*	بِتِكْتِبي	*ma-btiktibīš*	مَبْتِكْتِبيش	
íntu	*bitiktíbu*	بِتِكْتِبوا	*ma-btiktibūš*	مَبْتِكْتِبوش	
húwwa	*biyíktib*	بِيِكْتِب	*ma-byiktíbš*	مَبْيِكْتِبْش	
híyya	*bitíktib*	بِتِكْتِب	*ma-btiktíbš*	مَبْتِكْتِبْش	
húmma	*biyiktíbu*	بِيِكْتِبوا	*ma-byiktibūš*	مَبْيِكْتِبوش	
ána	*háktib*	هَكْتِب	*miš háktib*	مِش هَكْتِب	**future**
íḥna	*haníktib*	هَنِكْتِب	*miš haníktib*	مِش هَنِكْتِب	
ínta	*hatíktib*	هَتِكْتِب	*miš hatíktib*	مِش هَتِكْتِب	
ínti	*hatiktíbi*	هَتِكْتِبي	*miš hatiktíbi*	مِش هَتِكْتِبي	
íntu	*hatiktíbu*	هَتِكْتِبوا	*miš hatiktíbu*	مِش هَتِكْتِبوا	
húwwa	*hayíktib*	هَيِكْتِب	*miš hayíktib*	مِش هَيِكْتِب	
híyya	*hatíktib*	هَتِكْتِب	*miš hatíktib*	مِش هَتِكْتِب	
húmma	*hayiktíbu*	هَيِكْتِبوا	*miš hayiktíbu*	مِش هَيِكْتِبوا	
ínta	*íktib*	اِكْتِب	*ma-tiktíbš*	مَتِكْتِبْش	**imperative**
ínti	*iktíbi*	اِكْتِبي	*ma-tiktibīš*	مَتِكْتِبيش	
íntu	*iktíbu*	اِكْتِبوا	*ma-tiktibūš*	مَتِكْتِبوش	

	active		passive		
masculine	*kātib*	كاتِب	*maktūb*	مَكْتوب	**participles**
feminine	*kátba*	كاتْبَة	*maktūba*	مَكْتوبَة	
plural	*katbīn*	كاتْبين	*maktubīn*	مَكْتوبين	

①

مَحْمود و إيناس كتبوا كِتابْهُم في مسْجِد جميل في الدُّقّي.

maɦmūd wi inās kátabu kitábhum fi másgid gamīl fi -ddúʔʔi.

Mahmoud and Enas signed their marriage documents in a beautiful mosque in Dokki.

②

شادي بِيْحِبّ يِكْتِب شِعْر.

šādi biyɦibbᵊ yíktib ši3r.

Shady likes writing poems.

③

مبْتِكْتِبْش ليْه. فيْن كُرّاسْتك؟

ma-btiktíbšᵊ lē. fēn kurrástak?

Why aren't you writing? Where is your notebook?

④

حضْرِتك هتِكْتِب إسْمك هِنا و تْوَقّع هِنا.

ɦaḍrítak hatíktib ísmak hína wi twáqqa3 hína.

Sir, you'll write your name here and sign here.

⑤

متِكْتِبْش كلام ملوش لُزْمة في السّي في بْتاعك.

ma-tiktíbšᵊ kalām ma-lūš lúzma fi -ssī-vī btā3ak.

Don't write unnecessary things on your CV [resumé].

⑥

اِكْتِب المراجِع اللي بِتِسْتخْدِمْها عشان متِسْرقْش مجْهود غيْرك.

íktib ilmarāgi3 ílli bitistaxdímha 3ašān ma-tisráʔšᵊ maghūd ɣērak.

Mention the references that you used, so you aren't stealing others' work.

❖ [1s2] **to write**

➲ 170.3, 225.4, 259.3

218 to lie *kídib* كدب

verbal noun: *kidb* كِدْب

perfect

	affirmative		negative	
ána	*kidíbt*	كِدِبْت	*ma-kdíbtiš*	مَكْدِبْتِش
íḥna	*kidíbna*	كِدِبْنا	*ma-kdibnāš*	مَكْدِبْناش
ínta	*kidíbt*	كِدِبْت	*ma-kdíbtiš*	مَكْدِبْتِش
ínti	*kidíbti*	كِدِبْتي	*ma-kdibtīš*	مَكْدِبْتيش
íntu	*kidíbtu*	كِدِبْتوا	*ma-kdibtūš*	مَكْدِبْتوش
húwwa	*kídib*	كِدِب	*ma-kdíbš*	مَكْدِبْش
híyya	*kídbit*	كِدْبِت	*ma-kidbítš*	مَكِدْبِتْش
húmma	*kídbu*	كِدْبوا	*ma-kidbūš*	مَكِدْبوش

imperfect

	affirmative		negative	
ána	*ákdib*	أَكْدِب	*ma-kdíbš*	مَكْدِبْش
íḥna	*níkdib*	نِكْدِب	*ma-nikdíbš*	مَنِكْدِبْش
ínta	*tíkdib*	تِكْدِب	*ma-tikdíbš*	مَتِكْدِبْش
ínti	*tikdíbi*	تِكْدِبي	*ma-tikdibīš*	مَتِكْدِبيش
íntu	*tikdíbu*	تِكْدِبوا	*ma-tikdibūš*	مَتِكْدِبوش
húwwa	*yíkdib*	يِكْدِب	*ma-yikdíbš*	مَيِكْدِبْش
híyya	*tíkdib*	تِكْدِب	*ma-tikdíbš*	مَتِكْدِبْش
húmma	*yikdíbu*	يِكْدِبوا	*ma-yikdibūš*	مَيِكْدِبوش

bi-imperfect

	affirmative		negative	
ána	*bákdib*	بَكْدِب	*ma-bakdíbš*	مَبَكْدِبْش
íḥna	*biníkdib*	بِنِكْدِب	*ma-bnikdíbš*	مَبْنِكْدِبْش
ínta	*bitíkdib*	بِتِكْدِب	*ma-btikdíbš*	مَبْتِكْدِبْش
ínti	*bitikdíbi*	بِتِكْدِبي	*ma-btikdibīš*	مَبْتِكْدِبيش
íntu	*bitikdíbu*	بِتِكْدِبوا	*ma-btikdibūš*	مَبْتِكْدِبوش
húwwa	*biyíkdib*	بِيِكْدِب	*ma-byikdíbš*	مَبْيِكْدِبْش
híyya	*bitíkdib*	بِتِكْدِب	*ma-btikdíbš*	مَبْتِكْدِبْش
húmma	*biyikdíbu*	بِيِكْدِبوا	*ma-byikdibūš*	مَبْيِكْدِبوش

future

	affirmative		negative	
ána	*hákdib*	هَكْدِب	*miš hákdib*	مِش هَكْدِب
íḥna	*haníkdib*	هَنِكْدِب	*miš haníkdib*	مِش هَنِكْدِب
ínta	*hatíkdib*	هَتِكْدِب	*miš hatíkdib*	مِش هَتِكْدِب
ínti	*hatikdíbi*	هَتِكْدِبي	*miš hatikdíbi*	مِش هَتِكْدِبي
íntu	*hatikdíbu*	هَتِكْدِبوا	*miš hatikdíbu*	مِش هَتِكْدِبوا
húwwa	*hayíkdib*	هَيِكْدِب	*miš hayíkdib*	مِش هَيِكْدِب
híyya	*hatíkdib*	هَتِكْدِب	*miš hatíkdib*	مِش هَتِكْدِب
húmma	*hayikdíbu*	هَيِكْدِبوا	*miš hayikdíbu*	مِش هَيِكْدِبوا

imperative

	affirmative		negative	
ínta	*íkdib*	اِكْدِب	*ma-tikdíbš*	مَتِكْدِبْش
ínti	*ikdíbi*	اِكْدِبي	*ma-tikdibīš*	مَتِكْدِبيش
íntu	*ikdíbu*	اِكْدِبوا	*ma-tikdibūš*	مَتِكْدِبوش

participles

	active		passive	
masculine	*kādib*	كادِب	*makdūb*	مَكْدوب
feminine	*kádba*	كادْبَة	–	–
plural	*kadbīn*	كادْبين	–	–

①

الوَلد كِدِب عشان مامْتُه مـتْعاقْبوش.

ilwálad kídib 3ašān mámtu ma-t3aqbūš.

The boy lied so he wouldn't be punished by his mother.

②

مودي مِتْعوِّد يِكْدِب عشان يِهْرب مِن أيّ مَوْقِف صعْب.

mūdi mit3áwwid yíkdib 3ašān yíhrab min ayyᵊ máwqif ṣa3b.

Mody tends to lie to get out of any difficult situation.

③

سُعاد مبْتِكْدِبْش وَلا بْتِتْكلِّم على حدّ.

su3ād ma-btikdíbšᵊ wála btitkállim 3ála ḥadd.

Soad doesn't tell lies or talk about anyone.

④

اِوْعى تْكون هتِكْدِب عليْهُم. دوْل مِسْتأمِّنينك.

íw3a tkūn hatíkdib 3alēhum. dōl misti?amminīnak.

Don't even think of lying to them. They trust you.

⑤

متِكْدِبْش أبداً مهْما كانِت الظُّروف.

ma-tikdíbš ábadan máhma kānit iẓẓurūf.

Don't ever tell a lie under any circumstances.

❖ [1s5] **to lie, tell a lie** (**to** على *3ála*)

- As this verb requires a preposition, the passive participle is invariable: النّاس مكْدوب عليْهُم *innās makdūb 3alēhum* 'the people (who were) lied to'.

➲ 7.2, 235.5

219 to pile up *káddis* كَدّس

	affirmative		negative		
ána	*kaddíst*	كَدّسْت	*ma-kaddístiš*	مَكَدّسْتِش	**perfect**
íḫna	*kaddísna*	كَدّسْنا	*ma-kaddisnāš*	مَكَدّسْناش	
ínta	*kaddíst*	كَدّسْت	*ma-kaddístiš*	مَكَدّسْتِش	
ínti	*kaddísti*	كَدّسْتي	*ma-kaddistīš*	مَكَدّسْتيش	
íntu	*kaddístu*	كَدّسْتوا	*ma-kaddistūš*	مَكَدّسْتوش	
húwwa	*káddis*	كَدّس	*ma-kaddísš*	مَكَدّسْش	
híyya	*kaddísit*	كَدّسِت	*ma-kaddisítš*	مَكَدّسِتْش	
húmma	*kaddísu*	كَدّسوا	*ma-kaddisūš*	مَكَدّسوش	
ána	*akáddis*	أكَدّس	*ma-kaddísš*	مَكَدّسْش	**imperfect**
íḫna	*nikáddis*	نِكَدّس	*ma-nkaddísš*	مَنْكَدّسْش	
ínta	*tikáddis*	تِكَدّس	*ma-tkaddísš*	مَتْكَدّسْش	
ínti	*tikaddísi*	تِكَدّسي	*ma-tkaddisīš*	مَتْكَدّسيش	
íntu	*tikaddísu*	تِكَدّسوا	*ma-tkaddisūš*	مَتْكَدّسوش	
húwwa	*yikáddis*	يِكَدّس	*ma-ykaddísš*	مَيْكَدّسْش	
híyya	*tikáddis*	تِكَدّس	*ma-tkaddísš*	مَتْكَدّسْش	
húmma	*yikaddísu*	يِكَدّسوا	*ma-ykaddisūš*	مَيْكَدّسوش	
ána	*bakáddis*	بَكَدّس	*ma-bakaddísš*	مَبَكَدّسْش	**bi-imperfect**
íḫna	*binkáddis*	بِنْكَدّس	*ma-binkaddísš*	مَبِنْكَدّسْش	
ínta	*bitkáddis*	بِتْكَدّس	*ma-bitkaddísš*	مَبِتْكَدّسْش	
ínti	*bitkaddísi*	بِتْكَدّسي	*ma-bitkaddisīš*	مَبِتْكَدّسيش	
íntu	*bitkaddísu*	بِتْكَدّسوا	*ma-bitkaddisūš*	مَبِتْكَدّسوش	
húwwa	*biykáddis*	بِيْكَدّس	*ma-biykaddísš*	مَبِيْكَدّسْش	
híyya	*bitkáddis*	بِتْكَدّس	*ma-bitkaddísš*	مَبِتْكَدّسْش	
húmma	*biykaddísu*	بِيْكَدّسوا	*ma-biykaddisūš*	مَبِيْكَدّسوش	
ána	*hakáddis*	هَكَدّس	*miš hakáddis*	مِش هَكَدّس	**future**
íḫna	*hankáddis*	هَنْكَدّس	*miš hankáddis*	مِش هَنْكَدّس	
ínta	*hatkáddis*	هَتْكَدّس	*miš hatkáddis*	مِش هَتْكَدّس	
ínti	*hatkaddísi*	هَتْكَدّسي	*miš hatkaddísi*	مِش هَتْكَدّسي	
íntu	*hatkaddísu*	هَتْكَدّسوا	*miš hatkaddísu*	مِش هَتْكَدّسوا	
húwwa	*haykáddis*	هَيْكَدّس	*miš haykáddis*	مِش هَيْكَدّس	
híyya	*hatkáddis*	هَتْكَدّس	*miš hatkáddis*	مِش هَتْكَدّس	
húmma	*haykaddísu*	هَيْكَدّسوا	*miš haykaddísu*	مِش هَيْكَدّسوا	
ínta	*káddis*	كَدّس	*ma-tkaddísš*	مَتْكَدّسْش	**imperative**
ínti	*kaddísi*	كَدّسي	*ma-tkaddisīš*	مَتْكَدّسيش	
íntu	*kaddísu*	كَدّسوا	*ma-tkaddisūš*	مَتْكَدّسوش	

	active		passive		
masculine	*mikáddis*	مِكَدّس	*mitkáddis*	مِتْكَدّس	**participles**
feminine	*mikaddísa*	مِكَدّسَة	*mitkaddísa*	مِتْكَدّسَة	
plural	*mikaddisīn*	مِكَدّسين	*mitkaddisīn*	مِتْكَدّسين	

verbal noun: *takdīs* تَكْديس

①

دخلْت المكْتب لقيتْهُم كدِّسوا كُلّ الوَرق على مكْتبي.

daxált ilmáktab laʔíthum kaddísu kull ilwára? 3ála maktábi.

I went into the office to find that they had piled all the paper on my desk.

②

عُمْر دايْماً يِكدِّس أيّ حاجة مِش عايِزْها فوْق الدّولاب.

3umrᵊ dáyman yikáddis ayyᵊ ɦāga miš 3ayízha fōʔ iddulāb.

Omar always piles up everything that he doesn't want on top of the wardrobe.

③

إنْتَ بِتْكدِّس الكُتُب كُلّ مرّة غلط، و بعْديْن تِبوظ و تِترْمي.

ínta bitkáddis ilkútub kullᵊ márra ɣálaṭ, wi ba3dēn tibūẓ wi titrími.

You always pile up the books badly, and then they're ruined and have to be thrown away.

④

الشّباب هَيْكدِّسوا الهُدوم هِنا و البنات هَيِفْرِزوها.

iššabāb haykaddísu -lhudūm hína w ilbanāt hayifrizūha.

The boys will pile up the clothes here, and the girls will sort them.

⑤

متْكدِّسْليش كُلّ حاجة كِده. أنضّف إزّاي دِلْوَقْتي؟

ma-tkaddislīš kullᵊ ɦāga kída. anáḍḍaf izzāy dilwáʔti?

Don't pile up everything for me like this. How am I supposed to clean it up now?

❖ [2s1] **to pile (up)**

220 to hate *kírih* كِرِه

perfect

	affirmative		negative	
ána	*kiríht*	كِرِهْت	*ma-kríhtiš*	مَكْرِهْتِش
íḥna	*kiríhna*	كِرِهْنا	*ma-krihnāš*	مَكْرِهْناش
ínta	*kiríht*	كِرِهْت	*ma-kríhtiš*	مَكْرِهْتِش
ínti	*kiríhti*	كِرِهْتي	*ma-krihtīš*	مَكْرِهْتيش
íntu	*kiríhtu*	كِرِهْتوا	*ma-krihtūš*	مَكْرِهْتوش
húwwa	*kírih*	كِرِه	*ma-kríhš*	مَكْرِهْش
híyya	*kírhit*	كِرْهِت	*ma-kirhítš*	مَكِرْهِتْش
húmma	*kírhu*	كِرْهوا	*ma-kirhūš*	مَكِرْهوش

imperfect

	affirmative		negative	
ána	*ákrah*	أَكْرَه	*ma-kráhš*	مَكْرَهْش
íḥna	*níkrah*	نِكْرَه	*ma-nikráhš*	مَنِكْرَهْش
ínta	*tíkrah*	تِكْرَه	*ma-tikráhš*	مَتِكْرَهْش
ínti	*tikráhi*	تِكْرَهي	*ma-tikrahīš*	مَتِكْرَهيش
íntu	*tikráhu*	تِكْرَهوا	*ma-tikrahūš*	مَتِكْرَهوش
húwwa	*yíkrah*	يِكْرَه	*ma-yikráhš*	مَيِكْرَهْش
híyya	*tíkrah*	تِكْرَه	*ma-tikráhš*	مَتِكْرَهْش
húmma	*yikráhu*	يِكْرَهوا	*ma-yikrahūš*	مَيِكْرَهوش

bi-imperfect

	affirmative		negative	
ána	*bákrah*	بَكْرَه	*ma-bakráhš*	مَبَكْرَهْش
íḥna	*biníkrah*	بِنِكْرَه	*ma-bnikráhš*	مَبْنِكْرَهْش
ínta	*bitíkrah*	بِتِكْرَه	*ma-btikráhš*	مَبْتِكْرَهْش
ínti	*bitikráhi*	بِتِكْرَهي	*ma-btikrahīš*	مَبْتِكْرَهيش
íntu	*bitikráhu*	بِتِكْرَهوا	*ma-btikrahūš*	مَبْتِكْرَهوش
húwwa	*biyíkrah*	بِيِكْرَه	*ma-byikráhš*	مَبْيِكْرَهْش
híyya	*bitíkrah*	بِتِكْرَه	*ma-btikráhš*	مَبْتِكْرَهْش
húmma	*biyikráhu*	بِيِكْرَهوا	*ma-byikrahūš*	مَبْيِكْرَهوش

future

	affirmative		negative	
ána	*hákrah*	هَكْرَه	*miš hákrah*	مِش هَكْرَه
íḥna	*haníkrah*	هَنِكْرَه	*miš haníkrah*	مِش هَنِكْرَه
ínta	*hatíkrah*	هَتِكْرَه	*miš hatíkrah*	مِش هَتِكْرَه
ínti	*hatikráhi*	هَتِكْرَهي	*miš hatikráhi*	مِش هَتِكْرَهي
íntu	*hatikráhu*	هَتِكْرَهوا	*miš hatikráhu*	مِش هَتِكْرَهوا
húwwa	*hayíkrah*	هَيِكْرَه	*miš hayíkrah*	مِش هَيِكْرَه
híyya	*hatíkrah*	هَتِكْرَه	*miš hatíkrah*	مِش هَتِكْرَه
húmma	*hayikráhu*	هَيِكْرَهوا	*miš hayikráhu*	مِش هَيِكْرَهوا

imperative

	affirmative		negative	
ínta	*íkrah*	اِكْرَه	*ma-tikráhš*	مَتِكْرَهْش
ínti	*ikráhi*	اِكْرَهي	*ma-tikrahīš*	مَتِكْرَهيش
íntu	*ikráhu*	اِكْرَهوا	*ma-tikrahūš*	مَتِكْرَهوش

participles

	active		passive	
masculine	*kārih*	كارِه	*makrūh*	مَكْروه
feminine	*kárha*	كارْهَة	*makrūha*	مَكْروهَة
plural	*karhīn*	كارْهين	*makruhīn*	مَكْروهين

verbal noun: *kurh* كُرْه

①

مها كِرْهِت الأكْل مِن ساعِةْ ما لقِت صُرْصار في طبقْها.

máha kírhit ilʔáklᵊ min sā3it ma láʔit ṣurṣār fi ṭabáʔha.

Maha has hated eating ever since she found a cockroach on her plate.

②

رغْم كُلّ عمايِلك، حاوِلْت أكْرهك ، معْرِفْتِش.

raɣmᵊ kullᵊ 3amáylak, ḫawílt akráhak, ma-3ríftiš.

Despite all you've done, I can't hate you.

③

ماما بِتِكْرَهْ ريحْةْ السّجايِر.

māma bitíkrah riḫt issagāyir.

My mom hates the smell of cigarettes.

④

أنا هكْرَهْ البيْت ده مِن كُتْر المصايِب اللي بْتِجْرالْنا فيه.

ána hákrah ilbēt da min kutr ilmaṣāyib ílli btigrálna fī.

I'll come to hate this house because of all the tragedies that befall us here.

⑤

متِكْرهيش أبوكي. إحْنا اِتْطلّقْنا صحيح، لكِن هُوَّ أبوكي و بِيْحِبِّك.

ma-tikrahīš abūki. íḫna -tṭalláʔna ṣaḫīḫ, lākin húwwa ʔabūki wi biyḫíbbik.

Don't hate your father. True, we got divorced, but he's still your father and loves you.

❖ [1s4] **to hate**

➲ 191.2

221 to win *kísib* كسب

	affirmative		negative		
ána	*kisíbt*	كِسِبْت	*ma-ksíbtis*	مَكْسِبْتِش	**perfect**
íḫna	*kisíbna*	كِسِبْنا	*ma-ksibnās*	مَكْسِبْناش	
ínta	*kisíbt*	كِسِبْت	*ma-ksíbtis*	مَكْسِبْتِش	
ínti	*kisíbti*	كِسِبْتي	*ma-ksibtīs*	مَكْسِبْتيش	
íntu	*kisíbtu*	كِسِبْتوا	*ma-ksibtūs*	مَكْسِبْتوش	
húwwa	*kísib*	كِسِب	*ma-ksíbs*	مَكْسِبْش	
híyya	*kísbit*	كِسْبِت	*ma-kisbíts*	مَكِسْبِتْش	
húmma	*kísbu*	كِسْبوا	*ma-kisbūs*	مَكِسْبوش	
ána	*áksab*	أكْسَب	*ma-ksábs*	مَكْسَبْش	**imperfect**
íḫna	*níksab*	نِكْسَب	*ma-niksábs*	مَنِكْسَبْش	
ínta	*tíksab*	تِكْسَب	*ma-tiksábs*	مَتِكْسَبْش	
ínti	*tiksábi*	تِكْسَبي	*ma-tiksabīs*	مَتِكْسَبيش	
íntu	*tiksábu*	تِكْسَبوا	*ma-tiksabūs*	مَتِكْسَبوش	
húwwa	*yíksab*	يِكْسَب	*ma-yiksábs*	مَيِكْسَبْش	
híyya	*tíksab*	تِكْسَب	*ma-tiksábs*	مَتِكْسَبْش	
húmma	*yiksábu*	يِكْسَبوا	*ma-yiksabūs*	مَيِكْسَبوش	
ána	*báksab*	بَكْسَب	*ma-baksábs*	مَبَكْسَبْش	**bi-imperfect**
íḫna	*biníksab*	بِنِكْسَب	*ma-bniksábs*	مَبْنِكْسَبْش	
ínta	*bitíksab*	بِتِكْسَب	*ma-btiksábs*	مَبْتِكْسَبْش	
ínti	*bitiksábi*	بِتِكْسَبي	*ma-btiksabīs*	مَبْتِكْسَبيش	
íntu	*bitiksábu*	بِتِكْسَبوا	*ma-btiksabūs*	مَبْتِكْسَبوش	
húwwa	*biyíksab*	بِيِكْسَب	*ma-byiksábs*	مَبْيِكْسَبْش	
híyya	*bitíksab*	بِتِكْسَب	*ma-btiksábs*	مَبْتِكْسَبْش	
húmma	*biyiksábu*	بِيِكْسَبوا	*ma-byiksabūs*	مَبْيِكْسَبوش	
ána	*háksab*	هَكْسَب	*mis háksab*	مِش هَكْسَب	**future**
íḫna	*haníksab*	هَنِكْسَب	*mis haníksab*	مِش هَنِكْسَب	
ínta	*hatíksab*	هَتِكْسَب	*mis hatíksab*	مِش هَتِكْسَب	
ínti	*hatiksábi*	هَتِكْسَبي	*mis hatiksábi*	مِش هَتِكْسَبي	
íntu	*hatiksábu*	هَتِكْسَبوا	*mis hatiksábu*	مِش هَتِكْسَبوا	
húwwa	*hayíksab*	هَيِكْسَب	*mis hayíksab*	مِش هَيِكْسَب	
híyya	*hatíksab*	هَتِكْسَب	*mis hatíksab*	مِش هَتِكْسَب	
húmma	*hayiksábu*	هَيِكْسَبوا	*mis hayiksábu*	مِش هَيِكْسَبوا	
ínta	*íksab*	اِكْسَب	*ma-tiksábs*	مَتِكْسَبْش	**imperative**
ínti	*iksábi*	اِكْسَبي	*ma-tiksabīs*	مَتِكْسَبيش	
íntu	*iksábu*	اِكْسَبوا	*ma-tiksabūs*	مَتِكْسَبوش	

	active		passive		
masculine	*kasbān*	كَسْبان	–	–	**participles**
feminine	*kasbāna*	كَسْبانَة	–	–	
plural	*kasbanīn*	كَسْبانين	–	–	

verbal noun: *kasb* كَسْب

①

هاني جاب مُحامي شاطِر و كِسِب القضية.

hāni gāb muḫāmi šāṭir wi kísib ilʔaḍíyya.

Hany got a good lawyer and won the case.

②

لازِم تِكْسبوا الماْتش ده عشان تُدْخُلوا التّصْفِيّات.

lāzim tiksábu -lmātšᵊ da 3ašān tidxúlu -ttaṣfiyyāt.

You should win this match to get into the finals.

③

ما شاء اللّه محْمود بِيِكْسب دهب مِ المحلّ بْتاعُه.

ma šāʔ allāh, maḫmūd biyíksab dáhab mi -lmaḫállᵊ btā3u.

God bless, Mahmoud makes
a good profit from his shop.

④

لَوْ إسْتمرّيْنا في التّدْريب بِالشّكْل ده، هنِكْسب البُطولة بِإذن اللّه.

law istamarrēna fi -ttadrīb bi-ššaklᵊ da, haníksab ilbuṭūla bi-ízn allāh.

If we continue training like this, we'll
win the championship, God willing.

⑤

اِكْسبي حماتِك عشان تِرتاحي في جَوازِك.

iksábi ḫamātik 3ašān tirtāḫi fi gawāzik.

In order to have a comfortable marriage,
win over your mother-in-law.

❖ [1s4] **to win**

- Although this is a transitive verb, the passive participle is not in common usage.

➲ 39.2, 101.1, 221.1

222 to break *kásar* كَسَر

	affirmative		negative		
ána	*kasárt*	كَسَرْت	*ma-kasártiš*	مَكَسَرْتِش	perfect
íḫna	*kasárna*	كَسَرْنا	*ma-kasarnāš*	مَكَسَرْناش	
ínta	*kasárt*	كَسَرْت	*ma-kasártiš*	مَكَسَرْتِش	
ínti	*kasárti*	كَسَرْتي	*ma-kasartīš*	مَكَسَرْتيش	
íntu	*kasártu*	كَسَرْتوا	*ma-kasartūš*	مَكَسَرْتوش	
húwwa	*kásar*	كَسَر	*ma-kasárš*	مَكَسَرْش	
híyya	*kásarit*	كَسَرِت	*ma-kasarítš*	مَكَسَرِتْش	
húmma	*kásaru*	كَسَروا	*ma-kasarūš*	مَكَسَروش	
ána	*áksar*	أكْسَر	*ma-ksárš*	مَكْسَرْش	imperfect
íḫna	*níksar*	نِكْسَر	*ma-niksárš*	مَنِكْسَرْش	
ínta	*tíksar*	تِكْسَر	*ma-tiksárš*	مَتِكْسَرْش	
ínti	*tiksári*	تِكْسَري	*ma-tiksarīš*	مَتِكْسَريش	
íntu	*tiksáru*	تِكْسَروا	*ma-tiksarūš*	مَتِكْسَروش	
húwwa	*yíksar*	يِكْسَر	*ma-yiksárš*	مَيِكْسَرْش	
híyya	*tíksar*	تِكْسَر	*ma-tiksárš*	مَتِكْسَرْش	
húmma	*yiksáru*	يِكْسَروا	*ma-yiksarūš*	مَيِكْسَروش	
ána	*báksar*	بَكْسَر	*ma-baksárš*	مَبَكْسَرْش	bi-imperfect
íḫna	*biníksar*	بِنِكْسَر	*ma-bniksárš*	مَبْنِكْسَرْش	
ínta	*bitíksar*	بِتِكْسَر	*ma-btiksárš*	مَبْتِكْسَرْش	
ínti	*bitiksári*	بِتِكْسَري	*ma-btiksarīš*	مَبْتِكْسَريش	
íntu	*bitiksáru*	بِتِكْسَروا	*ma-btiksarūš*	مَبْتِكْسَروش	
húwwa	*biyíksar*	بِيِكْسَر	*ma-byiksárš*	مَبْيِكْسَرْش	
híyya	*bitíksar*	بِتِكْسَر	*ma-btiksárš*	مَبْتِكْسَرْش	
húmma	*biyiksáru*	بِيِكْسَروا	*ma-byiksarūš*	مَبْيِكْسَروش	
ána	*háksar*	هَكْسَر	*miš háksar*	مِش هَكْسَر	future
íḫna	*haníksar*	هَنِكْسَر	*miš haníksar*	مِش هَنِكْسَر	
ínta	*hatíksar*	هَتِكْسَر	*miš hatíksar*	مِش هَتِكْسَر	
ínti	*hatiksári*	هَتِكْسَري	*miš hatiksári*	مِش هَتِكْسَري	
íntu	*hatiksáru*	هَتِكْسَروا	*miš hatiksáru*	مِش هَتِكْسَروا	
húwwa	*hayíksar*	هَيِكْسَر	*miš hayíksar*	مِش هَيِكْسَر	
híyya	*hatíksar*	هَتِكْسَر	*miš hatíksar*	مِش هَتِكْسَر	
húmma	*hayiksáru*	هَيِكْسَروا	*miš hayiksáru*	مِش هَيِكْسَروا	
ínta	*íksar*	اِكْسَر	*ma-tiksárš*	مَتِكْسَرْش	imperative
ínti	*iksári*	اِكْسَري	*ma-tiksarīš*	مَتِكْسَريش	
íntu	*iksáru*	اِكْسَروا	*ma-tiksarūš*	مَتِكْسَروش	

	active		passive		
masculine	*kāsir*	كاسِر	*maksūr*	مَكْسور	participles
feminine	*kásra*	كاسْرَة	*maksūra*	مَكْسورَة	
plural	*kasrīn*	كاسْرين	*maksurīn*	مَكْسورين	

verbal noun: *kasr* كَسْر

①

ماجْدة كسرِت دِراعْها و هِيَّ بْتِتْمرّن.

mágda kásarit dirá3ha wi híyya btitmárran.

Magda broke her arm broken while training.

②

سلْمان لازِم يِكْسر حاجة كُلّ ما يِدْخُل المطْبخ.

salmān lāzim yíksar ḥāga kullᵊ ma yídxul ilmáṭbax.

Every time Salman goes into the kitchen,
he breaks something.

③

إسْلام حريص جِدّاً على لِعبُه، مبْيِكْسرْش حاجة.

islām ḥarīṣ gíddan 3ála li3ábu , ma-byiksáršᵊ ḥāga.

Islam is very careful with his toys.
He never breaks any of them.

④

حاسِب هتِكْسر التِّليفِزْيوْن.

ḥāsib hatíksar ittilivizyōn.

Careful, or you'll break the TV.

⑤

متِكْسرْش عليّا يا إبْني آدم. اِمْشي في حارْتك.

ma-tiksáršᵊ 3aláyya ya ʔíbni ʔādam. ímši f ḥártak.

Stop crossing over the line,
turkey! Drive in your lane!

⑥

محدِّش يِقْدر يِكْسرْني . أنا معْرفْش الإحْباط.

ma-ḥáddiš yíʔdar yiksárni. ána ma-3ráfš ilʔiḥbāṭ.

No one can break me. I don't know
the meaning of despondence.

⑦

مُراد مبْيِكْسرْش إشارة أبداً.

murād ma-byiksárš išāra ʔábadan.

Murad never runs a red light.

⑧

متِكْسرْش بْخاطِر أهْلك أبداً.

ma-tiksáršᵊ b-xāṭir áhlak ábadan.

Don't ever break your parents' hearts.

⑨

ده أنا هكْسر دِماغك، بسّ لمّا نْروّح البيْت.

da ʔána háksar dimāɣak, bassᵊ lámma nráwwaḥ ilbēt.

(parent to child:) I'm going to have your hide
[lit. breakyour head] when we get back home.

❖ [1s1] **to break; to veer, swerve**

➲ 29.5, 261.1

223 to eat *kal* كَل

verbal noun: *akl* أكل

	affirmative		negative		
ána	*kalt / akált*	كَلْت / أكَلْت	*ma-káltiš*	مَكَلْتِش	**perfect**
íḥna	*kálna / akálna*	كَلْنا / أكَلْنا	*ma-kalnāš*	مَكَلْناش	
ínta	*kalt / akált*	كَلْت / أكَلْت	*ma-káltiš*	مَكَلْتِش	
ínti	*kálti / akálti*	كَلْتي / أكَلْتي	*ma-kaltīš*	مَكَلْتيش	
íntu	*káltu / akáltu*	كَلْتوا / أكَلْتوا	*ma-kaltūš*	مَكَلْتوش	
húwwa	*kal / ákal*	كَل / أكَل	*ma-kálš*	مَكَلْش	
híyya	*kálit / ákalit*	كَلِت / أكَلِت	*ma-kalítš*	مَكَلِتْش	
húmma	*kálu / ákalu*	كَلوا / أكَلوا	*ma-kalūš*	مَكَلوش	
ána	*ākul*	آكُل	*ma-kúlš*	ماكُلْش	**imperfect**
íḥna	*nākul*	ناكُل	*ma-nakúlš*	مَناكُلْش	
ínta	*tākul*	تاكُل	*ma-takúlš*	مَتاكُلْش	
ínti	*tákli*	تاكْلي	*ma-taklīš*	مَتاكْليش	
íntu	*táklu*	تاكْلوا	*ma-taklūš*	مَتاكْلوش	
húwwa	*yākul*	ياكُل	*ma-yakúlš*	مَياكُلْش	
híyya	*tākul*	تاكُل	*ma-takúlš*	مَتاكُلْش	
húmma	*yáklu*	ياكْلوا	*ma-yaklūš*	مَياكْلوش	
ána	*bākul*	باكُل	*ma-bakúlš*	مَباكُلْش	**bi-imperfect**
íḥna	*binākul*	بِناكُل	*ma-bnakúlš*	مَبْناكُلْش	
ínta	*bitākul*	بِتاكُل	*ma-btakúlš*	مَبْتاكُلْش	
ínti	*bitákli*	بِتاكْلي	*ma-btaklīš*	مَبْتاكْليش	
íntu	*bitáklu*	بِتاكْلوا	*ma-btaklūš*	مَبْتاكْلوش	
húwwa	*biyākul*	بِياكُل	*ma-byakúlš*	مَبْياكُلْش	
híyya	*bitākul*	بِتاكُل	*ma-btakúlš*	مَبْتاكُلْش	
húmma	*biyáklu*	بِياكْلوا	*ma-byaklūš*	مَبْياكْلوش	
ána	*hākul*	هاكُل	*miš hākul*	مِش هاكُل	**future**
íḥna	*hanākul*	هَناكُل	*miš hanākul*	مِش هَناكُل	
ínta	*hatākul*	هَتاكُل	*miš hatākul*	مِش هَتاكُل	
ínti	*hatákli*	هَتاكْلي	*miš hatákli*	مِش هَتاكْلي	
íntu	*hatáklu*	هَتاكْلوا	*miš hatáklu*	مِش هَتاكْلوا	
húwwa	*hayākul*	هَياكُل	*miš hayākul*	مِش هَياكُل	
híyya	*hatākul*	هَتاكُل	*miš hatākul*	مِش هَتاكُل	
húmma	*hayáklu*	هَياكْلوا	*miš hayáklu*	مِش هَياكْلوا	
ínta	*kul*	كُل	*ma-takúlš*	مَتاكُلْش	**imperative**
ínti	*kúli*	كُلي	*ma-taklīš*	مَتاكْليش	
íntu	*kúlu*	كُلوا	*ma-taklūš*	مَتاكْلوش	

	active		passive		
masculine	*wākil*	واكِل	*mittākil*	مِتّاكِل	**participles**
feminine	*wákla*	واكْلَة	*mittákla*	مِتّاكْلَة	
plural	*waklīn*	واكْلين	*mittaklīn*	مِتّاكْلين	

①

فرح أكلِت رِنْجة أخيراً.

fárah ákalit rínga ʔaxīran.

Farah finally ate ringa.

②

عشان تِخِسّى، لازِم متاكْليش دُهون و سُكّرِيّات كِتير.

3ašān tixíssi, lāzim ma-taklīš duhūn wi sukkariyyāt kitīr.

To lose weight, you need to not eat so much fat and sugar.

③

بِتاكْلي أيْه؟

bitákli ʔē?

What are you eating?

④

هناكُل النّهارْده مِسقّعة.

hanākul innahárda misaʔʔá3a.

We are having moussaka today.

⑤

متاكُلْش حقّ إخْواتك. لمّا يِكْبروا مِش هَيْسامْحوك.

ma-takúlšᵊ ħaʔʔ ixwātak. lámma yikbáru miš haysamħūk.

Don't take away your brothers' rights. They won't forgive you when they grow up.

❖ [i3] **to eat**

➲ 2.2, 19.2, 33.1, 99.7, 120.3, 128.4, 144.2, 151.1, 166.3, 193.5, 208.5, 211.8, 225.3

224 to talk kállim كلّم

	affirmative		negative		
ána	kallímt	كَلّمْت	ma-kallímtiš	مَكَلّمْتِش	perfect
íḫna	kallímna	كَلّمْنا	ma-kallimnāš	مَكَلّمْناش	
ínta	kallímt	كَلّمْت	ma-kallímtiš	مَكَلّمْتِش	
ínti	kallímti	كَلّمْتي	ma-kallimtīš	مَكَلّمْتيش	
íntu	kallímtu	كَلّمْتوا	ma-kallimtūš	مَكَلّمْتوش	
húwwa	kállim	كَلّم	ma-kallímš	مَكَلّمْش	
híyya	kallímit	كَلّمِت	ma-kallimítš	مَكَلّمِتْش	
húmma	kallímu	كَلّموا	ma-kallimūš	مَكَلّموش	
ána	akállim	أكَلّم	ma-kallímš	مَكَلّمْش	imperfect
íḫna	nikállim	نِكَلّم	ma-nkallímš	مَنْكَلّمْش	
ínta	tikállim	تِكَلّم	ma-tkallímš	مَتْكَلّمْش	
ínti	tikallími	تِكَلّمي	ma-tkallimīš	مَتْكَلّميش	
íntu	tikallímu	تِكَلّموا	ma-tkallimūš	مَتْكَلّموش	
húwwa	yikállim	يِكَلّم	ma-ykallímš	مَيْكَلّمْش	
híyya	tikállim	تِكَلّم	ma-tkallímš	مَتْكَلّمْش	
húmma	yikallímu	يِكَلّموا	ma-ykallimūš	مَيْكَلّموش	
ána	bakállim	بَكَلّم	ma-bakallímš	مَبَكَلّمْش	bi-imperfect
íḫna	binkállim	بِنْكَلّم	ma-binkallímš	مَبِنْكَلّمْش	
ínta	bitkállim	بِتْكَلّم	ma-bitkallímš	مَبِتْكَلّمْش	
ínti	bitkallími	بِتْكَلّمي	ma-bitkallimīš	مَبِتْكَلّميش	
íntu	bitkallímu	بِتْكَلّموا	ma-bitkallimūš	مَبِتْكَلّموش	
húwwa	biykállim	بِيْكَلّم	ma-biykallímš	مَبِيْكَلّمْش	
híyya	bitkállim	بِتْكَلّم	ma-bitkallímš	مَبِتْكَلّمْش	
húmma	biykallímu	بِيْكَلّموا	ma-biykallimūš	مَبِيْكَلّموش	
ána	hakállim	هَكَلّم	miš hakállim	مِش هَكَلّم	future
íḫna	hankállim	هَنْكَلّم	miš hankállim	مِش هَنْكَلّم	
ínta	hatkállim	هَتْكَلّم	miš hatkállim	مِش هَتْكَلّم	
ínti	hatkallími	هَتْكَلّمي	miš hatkallími	مِش هَتْكَلّمي	
íntu	hatkallímu	هَتْكَلّموا	miš hatkallímu	مِش هَتْكَلّموا	
húwwa	haykállim	هَيْكَلّم	miš haykállim	مِش هَيْكَلّم	
híyya	hatkállim	هَتْكَلّم	miš hatkállim	مِش هَتْكَلّم	
húmma	haykallímu	هَيْكَلّموا	miš haykallímu	مِش هَيْكَلّموا	
ínta	kállim	كَلّم	ma-tkallímš	مَتْكَلّمْش	imperative
ínti	kallími	كَلّمي	ma-tkallimīš	مَتْكَلّميش	
íntu	kallímu	كَلّموا	ma-tkallimūš	مَتْكَلّموش	

	active		passive		
masculine	mikállim	مِكَلّم	–	–	participles
feminine	mikallíma	مِكَلّمَة	–	–	
plural	mikallimīn	مِكَلّمين	–	–	

verbal noun: kalām كلام

①

كلِّمْت عمّك وَلّا لِسّه؟

kallímtᵊ 3ámmak wálla líssa?

Have you talked to your uncle yet?

②

أنا مِش مُشْترِك في النّادى، بسّ بدْخُل على طول مِن غيرْ مِكلِّم حدّ.

ána miš muštárik fi -nnādi, bassᵊ bádxul 3ála ţūl min ɣēr mikállim ɧadd.

I'm not a member of the club, so I always enter without talking to anyone.

③

لينا مبِتْكلِّمْش حدّ مِن ساعِةْ الحادْثة.

līna ma-bitkallímšᵊ ɧaddᵊ min sā3it ilɧádsa.

Lina doesn't speak to anyone ever since the accident.

④

سامِح هَيْكلِّم المحلّ عشان يِعْرف مَواعيد شُغْلُهْم.

sāmiɧ haykállim ilmaɧállᵊ 3ašān yí3raf mawa3īd šuɣlúhum.

Sameh will call the shop to find out their business hours.

⑤

متْكلِّمْنيش بِالطّريقة دي.

ma-tkallimnīš bi-ţţarīʔa di.

Don't talk to me that way.

❖ [2s1] **to talk (to); to call, phone**

- Notice that this verb is transitive, taking a direct object, whereas the English verb 'talk' requires the preposition 'to' or 'with'.
- Compare with اِتْكلِّم *itkállim.* (➲ 26)

➲ 15.2, 21.2, 52.6, 64.3, 83.5, 114.2, 143.5, 176.2, 176.3, 218.3, 228.5, 228.9

225 to finish kámmil كَمِّل

verbal noun: takmila تَكْمِلة

perfect

	affirmative		negative	
ána	kammílt	كَمِّلْت	ma-kammíltiš	مَكَمِّلْتِش
íḥna	kammílna	كَمِّلْنا	ma-kammilnāš	مَكَمِّلْناش
ínta	kammílt	كَمِّلْت	ma-kammíltiš	مَكَمِّلْتِش
ínti	kammílti	كَمِّلْتي	ma-kammiltīš	مَكَمِّلْتيش
íntu	kammíltu	كَمِّلْتوا	ma-kammiltūš	مَكَمِّلْتوش
húwwa	kámmil	كَمِّل	ma-kammílš	مَكَمِّلْش
híyya	kammílit	كَمِّلِت	ma-kammilítš	مَكَمِّلِتْش
húmma	kammílu	كَمِّلوا	ma-kammilūš	مَكَمِّلوش

imperfect

	affirmative		negative	
ána	akámmil	أكَمِّل	ma-kammílš	مَكَمِّلْش
íḥna	nikámmil	نِكَمِّل	ma-nkammílš	مَنْكَمِّلْش
ínta	tikámmil	تِكَمِّل	ma-tkammílš	مَتْكَمِّلْش
ínti	tikammíli	تِكَمِّلي	ma-tkammilīš	مَتْكَمِّليش
íntu	tikammílu	تِكَمِّلوا	ma-tkammilūš	مَتْكَمِّلوش
húwwa	yikámmil	يِكَمِّل	ma-ykammílš	مَيْكَمِّلْش
híyya	tikámmil	تِكَمِّل	ma-tkammílš	مَتْكَمِّلْش
húmma	yikammílu	يِكَمِّلوا	ma-ykammilūš	مَيْكَمِّلوش

bi-imperfect

	affirmative		negative	
ána	bakámmil	بَكَمِّل	ma-bakammílš	مَبَكَمِّلْش
íḥna	binkámmil	بِنْكَمِّل	ma-binkammílš	مَبِنْكَمِّلْش
ínta	bitkámmil	بِتْكَمِّل	ma-bitkammílš	مَبِتْكَمِّلْش
ínti	bitkammíli	بِتْكَمِّلي	ma-bitkammilīš	مَبِتْكَمِّليش
íntu	bitkammílu	بِتْكَمِّلوا	ma-bitkammilūš	مَبِتْكَمِّلوش
húwwa	biykámmil	بِيْكَمِّل	ma-biykammílš	مَبِيْكَمِّلْش
híyya	bitkámmil	بِتْكَمِّل	ma-bitkammílš	مَبِتْكَمِّلْش
húmma	biykammílu	بِيْكَمِّلوا	ma-biykammilūš	مَبِيْكَمِّلوش

future

	affirmative		negative	
ána	hakámmil	هَكَمِّل	miš hakámmil	مِش هَكَمِّل
íḥna	hankámmil	هَنْكَمِّل	miš hankámmil	مِش هَنْكَمِّل
ínta	hatkámmil	هَتْكَمِّل	miš hatkámmil	مِش هَتْكَمِّل
ínti	hatkammíli	هَتْكَمِّلي	miš hatkammíli	مِش هَتْكَمِّلي
íntu	hatkammílu	هَتْكَمِّلوا	miš hatkammílu	مِش هَتْكَمِّلوا
húwwa	haykámmil	هَيْكَمِّل	miš haykámmil	مِش هَيْكَمِّل
híyya	hatkámmil	هَتْكَمِّل	miš hatkámmil	مِش هَتْكَمِّل
húmma	haykammílu	هَيْكَمِّلوا	miš haykammílu	مِش هَيْكَمِّلوا

imperative

	affirmative		negative	
ínta	kámmil	كَمِّل	ma-tkammílš	مَتْكَمِّلْش
ínti	kammíli	كَمِّلي	ma-tkammilīš	مَتْكَمِّليش
íntu	kammílu	كَمِّلوا	ma-tkammilūš	مَتْكَمِّلوش

participles

	active		passive	
masculine	mikámmil	مِكَمِّل	mitkámmil	مِتْكَمِّل
feminine	mikammíla	مِكَمِّلة	mitkammíla	مِتْكَمِّلة
plural	mikammilīn	مِكَمِّلين	mitkammilīn	مِتْكَمِّلين

①

عُمْران مكمِّلْش دْراسْتُه لمّا باباه مات.

3umrān ma-kammílšᵊ drástu lámma babā māt.

Omran didn't continue his schooling after his father died.

②

وائِل لمّا بْيِبْدأ حاجة لازِم يِكمِّلْها لِلآخِر.

wāyil lámma byíbdaʔ ɧāga lāzim yikammílha li-lʔāxir.

When Wael starts something, he always finishes it.

③

أنا باكُل سنْدِوِتْش في الشُّغْل و بكمِّل أكْل في البيْت.

ána bākul sandiwítšᵊ fi -ššuɣlᵊ wi bakámmil áklᵊ fi -lbēt.

I have a sandwich at work, and then I continue eating [it] at home.

④

هتْكمِّل كِتابِةْ المقالة بْتاعْتك إمْتى؟

hatkámmil kitābit ilmaqāla btá3tak ímta?

When will you finish writing your article?

⑤

متْجيبْش السِّيرة دي تاني. متْكمِّلْش عليّا.

ma-tgíbš issīra di tāni. ma-tkammílšᵊ 3aláyya.

Don't bring up this issue again. Stop adding to my sorrows.

❖ [2s1] **to finish; to continue** (doing)

- This verb can be followed by a verbal noun. (➲ 225.3, 225.4)

➲ 13.2, 47.1, 66.2, 77.2, 155.5, 234.1

226 to wear *líbis* لِبِس

	affirmative		negative	
perfect				
ána	*libíst*	لِبِسْت	*ma-lbístiš*	مَلْبِسْتِش
íḫna	*libísna*	لِبِسْنا	*ma-lbisnāš*	مَلْبِسْناش
ínta	*libíst*	لِبِسْت	*ma-lbístiš*	مَلْبِسْتِش
ínti	*libísti*	لِبِسْتي	*ma-lbistīš*	مَلْبِسْتيش
íntu	*libístu*	لِبِسْتوا	*ma-lbistūš*	مَلْبِسْتوش
húwwa	*líbis*	لِبِس	*ma-lbísš*	مَلْبِسْش
híyya	*líbsit*	لِبْسِت	*ma-libsítš*	مَلِبْسِتْش
húmma	*líbsu*	لِبْسوا	*ma-libsūš*	مَلِبْسوش
imperfect				
ána	*álbis*	أَلْبِس	*ma-lbísš*	مَلْبِسْش
íḫna	*nílbis*	نِلْبِس	*ma-nilbísš*	مَنِلْبِسْش
ínta	*tílbis*	تِلْبِس	*ma-tilbísš*	مَتِلْبِسْش
ínti	*tilbísi*	تِلْبِسي	*ma-tilbisīš*	مَتِلْبِسيش
íntu	*tilbísu*	تِلْبِسوا	*ma-tilbisūš*	مَتِلْبِسوش
húwwa	*yílbis*	يِلْبِس	*ma-yilbísš*	مَيِلْبِسْش
híyya	*tílbis*	تِلْبِس	*ma-tilbísš*	مَتِلْبِسْش
húmma	*yilbísu*	يِلْبِسوا	*ma-yilbisūš*	مَيِلْبِسوش
bi-imperfect				
ána	*bálbis*	بَلْبِس	*ma-balbísš*	مَبَلْبِسْش
íḫna	*binílbis*	بِنِلْبِس	*ma-bnilbísš*	مَبْنِلْبِسْش
ínta	*bitílbis*	بِتِلْبِس	*ma-btilbísš*	مَبْتِلْبِسْش
ínti	*bitilbísi*	بِتِلْبِسي	*ma-btilbisīš*	مَبْتِلْبِسيش
íntu	*bitilbísu*	بِتِلْبِسوا	*ma-btilbisūš*	مَبْتِلْبِسوش
húwwa	*biyílbis*	بِيِلْبِس	*ma-byilbísš*	مَبْيِلْبِسْش
híyya	*bitílbis*	بِتِلْبِس	*ma-btilbísš*	مَبْتِلْبِسْش
húmma	*biyilbísu*	بِيِلْبِسوا	*ma-byilbisūš*	مَبْيِلْبِسوش
future				
ána	*hálbis*	هَلْبِس	*miš hálbis*	مِش هَلْبِس
íḫna	*hanílbis*	هَنِلْبِس	*miš hanílbis*	مِش هَنِلْبِس
ínta	*hatílbis*	هَتِلْبِس	*miš hatílbis*	مِش هَتِلْبِس
ínti	*hatilbísi*	هَتِلْبِسي	*miš hatilbísi*	مِش هَتِلْبِسي
íntu	*hatilbísu*	هَتِلْبِسوا	*miš hatilbísu*	مِش هَتِلْبِسوا
húwwa	*hayílbis*	هَيِلْبِس	*miš hayílbis*	مِش هَيِلْبِس
híyya	*hatílbis*	هَتِلْبِس	*miš hatílbis*	مِش هَتِلْبِس
húmma	*hayilbísu*	هَيِلْبِسوا	*miš hayilbísu*	مِش هَيِلْبِسوا
imperative				
ínta	*ílbis*	اِلْبِس	*ma-tilbísš*	مَتِلْبِسْش
ínti	*ilbísi*	اِلْبِسي	*ma-tilbisīš*	مَتِلْبِسيش
íntu	*ilbísu*	اِلْبِسوا	*ma-tilbisūš*	مَتِلْبِسوش

participles	active		passive	
masculine	*lābis*	لابِس	*malbūs*	مَلْبوس
feminine	*lábsa*	لابْسَة	*malbūsa*	مَلْبوسَة
plural	*labsīn*	لابْسين	*malbusīn*	مَلْبوسين

verbal noun: *libs* لِبْس

①

بهْجة لِبْسِت فُسْتان أحْمر. كان حِلْو أوي عليْها.

báhga líbsit fustān áḫmar. kān ḫilwᵊ ʔáwi 3alēha.

Bahga put on a red dress.
It was so beautiful on her.

②

شاهيناز بِتْحِبّ تِلْبِس فساتين فيها وَرْد.

šahināz bitḫíbbᵊ tílbis fasatīn fīha ward.

Shahinaz likes to wear
floral-print dresses.

③

نوسة بْتِلْبِس التّوْب السّوداني في المُناسبات.

nūsa btílbis ittōb issudāni fi -lmunasabāt.

Nosa wears a Sudanese dress
on special occasions.

④

اِنْتِبِهْ و إنْتَ سايِق وَ إلّا هتِلْبِس في اللي قُدّامك.

intíbih w ínta sāyiʔ wa ʔílla hatílbis fi -lli ʔuddāmak.

Concentrate while driving, or you'll
hit the car in front of you.

⑤

متِلْبِسْش كاجْوال و إنْتَ رايِح إنْتِرفْيو.

ma-tilbísšᵊ kāžuwal w ínta rāyiḫ intirvyu.

Don't dress casually when
you go for an interview.

⑥

هكون جاهْزة في عشر دقايِق. هسْتحمّى و ألْبِس على طول.

hakūn gáhza fi 3ášar daʔāyiʔ. hastaḫámma w álbis 3ála ṭūl.

I'll be ready in ten minutes. I'll take a
shower and get dressed right away.

❖ [1s5] **to wear; to put on; to get dressed; to hit, collide with**

➲ 75.3, 96.1, 99.6

227 to do on time líħiʔ لِحِق

verbal nouns: laħaʔān لَحَقان - laħʔ لَحْق - luħūʔ لُحوق

	affirmative		negative		
ána	liħíʔt	لِحِقْت	ma-lħíʔtiš	مَلْحِقْتِش	perfect
íħna	liħíʔna	لِحِقْنا	ma-lħiʔnāš	مَلْحِقْناش	
ínta	liħíʔt	لِحِقْت	ma-lħíʔtiš	مَلْحِقْتِش	
ínti	liħíʔti	لِحِقْتي	ma-lħiʔtīš	مَلْحِقْتيش	
íntu	liħíʔtu	لِحِقْتوا	ma-lħiʔtūš	مَلْحِقْتوش	
húwwa	líħiʔ	لِحِق	ma-lħíʔš	مَلْحِقْش	
híyya	líħʔit	لِحْقِت	ma-liħʔítš	مَلِحْقِتْش	
húmma	líħʔu	لِحْقوا	ma-liħʔūš	مَلِحْقوش	
ána	álħaʔ	أَلْحَق	ma-lħáʔš	مَلْحَقْش	imperfect
íħna	nílħaʔ	نِلْحَق	ma-nilħáʔš	مَنِلْحَقْش	
ínta	tílħaʔ	تِلْحَق	ma-tilħáʔš	مَتِلْحَقْش	
ínti	tilħáʔi	تِلْحَقي	ma-tilħaʔīš	مَتِلْحَقيش	
íntu	tilħáʔu	تِلْحَقوا	ma-tilħaʔūš	مَتِلْحَقوش	
húwwa	yílħaʔ	يِلْحَق	ma-yilħáʔš	مَيِلْحَقْش	
híyya	tílħaʔ	تِلْحَق	ma-tilħáʔš	مَتِلْحَقْش	
húmma	yilħáʔu	يِلْحَقوا	ma-yilħaʔūš	مَيِلْحَقوش	
ána	bálħaʔ	بَلْحَق	ma-balħáʔš	مَبَلْحَقْش	bi-imperfect
íħna	binílħaʔ	بِنِلْحَق	ma-bnilħáʔš	مَبْنِلْحَقْش	
ínta	bitílħaʔ	بِتِلْحَق	ma-btilħáʔš	مَبْتِلْحَقْش	
ínti	bitilħáʔi	بِتِلْحَقي	ma-btilħaʔīš	مَبْتِلْحَقيش	
íntu	bitilħáʔu	بِتِلْحَقوا	ma-btilħaʔūš	مَبْتِلْحَقوش	
húwwa	biyílħaʔ	بِيِلْحَق	ma-byilħáʔš	مَبْيِلْحَقْش	
híyya	bitílħaʔ	بِتِلْحَق	ma-btilħáʔš	مَبْتِلْحَقْش	
húmma	biyilħáʔu	بِيِلْحَقوا	ma-byilħaʔūš	مَبْيِلْحَقوش	
ána	hálħaʔ	هَلْحَق	miš hálħaʔ	مِش هَلْحَق	future
íħna	hanílħaʔ	هَنِلْحَق	miš hanílħaʔ	مِش هَنِلْحَق	
ínta	hatílħaʔ	هَتِلْحَق	miš hatílħaʔ	مِش هَتِلْحَق	
ínti	hatilħáʔi	هَتِلْحَقي	miš hatilħáʔi	مِش هَتِلْحَقي	
íntu	hatilħáʔu	هَتِلْحَقوا	miš hatilħáʔu	مِش هَتِلْحَقوا	
húwwa	hayílħaʔ	هَيِلْحَق	miš hayílħaʔ	مِش هَيِلْحَق	
híyya	hatílħaʔ	هَتِلْحَق	miš hatílħaʔ	مِش هَتِلْحَق	
húmma	hayilħáʔu	هَيِلْحَقوا	miš hayilħáʔu	مِش هَيِلْحَقوا	
ínta	ílħaʔ	اِلْحَق	ma-tilħáʔš	مَتِلْحَقْش	imperative
ínti	ilħáʔi	اِلْحَقي	ma-tilħaʔīš	مَتِلْحَقيش	
íntu	ilħáʔu	اِلْحَقوا	ma-tilħaʔūš	مَتِلْحَقوش	

	active		passive		
masculine	lāħiʔ	لاحِق	malħūʔ	مَلْحوق	participles
feminine	láħʔa	لاحْقَة	malħūʔa	مَلْحوقَة	
plural	laħʔīn	لاحْقين	malħuʔīn	مَلْحوقين	

①

ماهِر ملْحِقْش النّدْوَة مِن أوِّلْها.

māhir ma-lḫíʔš innádwa min awwílha.

Maher didn't make it on time for the beginning of the seminar.

②

أميرة لازِم تِلْحق تِقدِّم وَرقْها. بُكْره آخِر يوْم.

amīra lāzim tílḫaʔ tiʔáddim waráʔha. búkra āxir yōm.

Amira should submit her paper on time. Tomorrow is the deadline.

③

عنْدي شُغْل كْتير أوي . مبلْحقْش أبُصّ في المِرايَة.

3ándi šuɣlᵊ ktīr ʔáwi . ma-balḫáʔš abúṣṣᵊ fi -lmirāya.

I have lots of work to do. I don't have time to look at myself in the mirror.

④

اِسْبِقْني إنْتَ و أنا هلْحقك.

isbíʔni ínta w ána halḫáʔak.

You go first, and I'll catch up with you.

⑤

اِلْحق اِشْتِريلك شُوَيِّةْ لِبْس في الأوكازِيوْن.

ílḫaʔ ištirīlak šuwáyyit libsᵊ fi -lʔukaziyōn.

Hurry up and buy yourself some clothes on sale.

❖ [1s4] **to do on time, have time to; to catch up with; to hurry** (before it's too late)

- This verb can be followed by an imperfect verb.

➲ 15.1, 15.5, 22.4, 35.6, 64.4, 100.8, 164.2

228 to be necessary *lázam* لَزَم

	affirmative		negative		
ána	*lazámt*	لَزَمْت	*ma-lazámtiš*	مَلَزَمْتِش	perfect
íḫna	*lazámna*	لَزَمْنا	*ma-lazamnāš*	مَلَزَمْناش	
ínta	*lazámt*	لَزَمْت	*ma-lazamtiš*	مَلَزَمْتِش	
ínti	*lazámti*	لَزَمْتي	*ma-lazamtīš*	مَلَزَمْتيش	
íntu	*lazámtu*	لَزَمْتوا	*ma-lazamtūš*	مَلَزَمْتوش	
húwwa	*lázam*	لَزَم	*ma-lazámš*	مَلَزَمْش	
híyya	*lázamit*	لَزَمِت	*ma-lazamítš*	مَلَزَمِتْش	
húmma	*lázamu*	لَزَموا	*ma-lazamūš*	مَلَزَموش	
ána	*álzam*	أَلْزَم	*ma-lzámš*	مَلْزَمْش	imperfect
íḫna	*nílzam*	نِلْزَم	*ma-nilzámš*	مَنِلْزَمْش	
ínta	*tílzam*	تِلْزَم	*ma-tilzámš*	مَتِلْزَمْش	
ínti	*tilzámi*	تِلْزَمي	*ma-tilzamīš*	مَتِلْزَميش	
íntu	*tilzámu*	تِلْزَموا	*ma-tilzamūš*	مَتِلْزَموش	
húwwa	*yílzam*	يِلْزَم	*ma-yilzámš*	مَيِلْزَمْش	
híyya	*tílzam*	تِلْزَم	*ma-tilzámš*	مَتِلْزَمْش	
húmma	*yilzámu*	يِلْزَموا	*ma-yilzamūš*	مَيِلْزَموش	
ána	*bálzam*	بَلْزَم	*ma-balzámš*	مَبَلْزَمْش	bi-imperfect
íḫna	*binílzam*	بِنِلْزَم	*ma-bnilzámš*	مَبْنِلْزَمْش	
ínta	*bitílzam*	بِتِلْزَم	*ma-btilzámš*	مَبْتِلْزَمْش	
ínti	*bitilzámi*	بِتِلْزَمي	*ma-btilzamīš*	مَبْتِلْزَميش	
íntu	*bitilzámu*	بِتِلْزَموا	*ma-btilzamūš*	مَبْتِلْزَموش	
húwwa	*biyílzam*	بِيِلْزَم	*ma-byilzámš*	مَبْيِلْزَمْش	
híyya	*bitílzam*	بِتِلْزَم	*ma-btilzámš*	مَبْتِلْزَمْش	
húmma	*biyilzámu*	بِيِلْزَموا	*ma-byilzamūš*	مَبْيِلْزَموش	
ána	*hálzam*	هَلْزَم	*miš hálzam*	مِش هَلْزَم	future
íḫna	*hanílzam*	هَنِلْزَم	*miš hanílzam*	مِش هَنِلْزَم	
ínta	*hatílzam*	هَتِلْزَم	*miš hatílzam*	مِش هَتِلْزَم	
ínti	*hatilzámi*	هَتِلْزَمي	*miš hatilzámi*	مِش هَتِلْزَمي	
íntu	*hatilzámu*	هَتِلْزَموا	*miš hatilzámu*	مِش هَتِلْزَموا	
húwwa	*hayílzam*	هَيِلْزَم	*miš hayílzam*	مِش هَيِلْزَم	
híyya	*hatílzam*	هَتِلْزَم	*miš hatílzam*	مِش هَتِلْزَم	
húmma	*hayilzámu*	هَيِلْزَموا	*miš hayilzámu*	مِش هَيِلْزَموا	
ínta	*ílzam*	اِلْزَم	*ma-tilzámš*	مَتِلْزَمْش	imperative
ínti	*ilzámi*	اِلْزَمي	*ma-tilzamīš*	مَتِلْزَميش	
íntu	*ilzámu*	اِلْزَموا	*ma-tilzamūš*	مَتِلْزَموش	

	active		passive		
masculine	*lāzim*	لازِم	–	–	participles
feminine	*lázma*	لازْمَة	–	–	
plural	*lazmīn*	لازْمين	–	–	

verbal nouns: *lizūm* لِزوم - *luzūm* لُزوم

①

لزمْني ١٥ سنة عشان أفْهم أنا بحِبّ أيْه بِجدّ و نِفْسي أعْمِل أيْه في حَياتي.

lazámni xamastāšar sána 3ašān áfham ána baɦíbb ʔē bigádd[ə] wi nífsi ʔá3mil ʔē fi ɦayāti.

I needed 15 years to understand what I really like and what I want to do with my life.

②

إنْتَ يِلْزمك قدّ أيْه وَقْت عشان تِخلّص العربية؟

ínta yilzámak add[ə] ʔē waʔt[ə] 3ašān tixállaṣ il3arabíyya?

How long do you need to fix the car?

③

مبْيِلْزمكْش فْلوس و إنْتَ رايِح الرِّحْلة دي؟

ma-byilzamákš[ə] flūs w ínta rāyiɦ irríɦla di?

Don't you need money for that trip?

④

هَيِلْزمْها قدّ أيْه عشان تِـرجع تُقف على رِجْليْها؟

hayilzámha ʔadd ʔē 3ašān tírga3 túʔaf 3ála riglēha?

How long will she need to get back on her feet?

⑤

اِلْزم حُدودك و اِفْهم إنْتَ بِتْكلِّم مين.

ílzam ɦudūdak w ífham ínta bitkállim mīn.

Watch yourself [lit. keep to your limits] and remember who you're talking to.

⑥

إنْتَ كُنْت لازِم تِبلّغْني قبْل ما تْروح.

ínta kunt[ə] lāzim tiballáɣni ʔabl[ə] ma trūɦ.

You should have told me before you went.

⑦

أنا لازِم أشوفِك قبْل ما تْسافْري.

ána lāzim ašūfik ʔabl[ə] ma tsáfri.

I need to see you before you leave.

⑧

لازِم لمّا تِعْطس تِقول الحمْدُ لِلّه.

lāzim lámma tí3ṭas tiʔūl ilɦámdu li-llāh.

When you sneeze, you should say alhamdu -lillaah.

⑨

لازِم نُهى تْكلِّم مامِتْها النّهارْده ضروري.

lāzim núha tkállim mamítha -nnahárda ḍarūri.

Noha urgently needs to call her mom today.

⑩

اِلْزم حُدودك!

ílzam ɦudūdak!

Mind your own business!

❖ [1s1] **to be necessary (for); to need; to keep to, mind**

- This verb can be used in two ways to mean 'need'. Literally, it means 'be necessary for', so the subject and object of the verb are swapped in an English translation. In other words, بيِلْزمْنى *biyilzámni* (literally 'it is necessary for me) better translates 'I need it'. It can also take the form of an invariable (always masculine) active participle followed by an imperfect verb. (➲ 228.9)
- The active participle can be used in any of its three forms (masculine, feminine, or plural) when used as an adjective meaning 'necessary'.

➲ 4.2, 9.2, 20.2, 21.2, 23.2, 28.5, 29.2, 32.2, 47.2, 48.2, 63.2, 69.4, 72.4, 73.9, 74.2, 75.2, 75.6, 84.2, 88.3, 149.2, 150.2, 153.2, 184.2, 199.5, 204.2, 212.2, 221.2, 222.2, 223.2, 225.2, 227.2, 230.2, 236.2, 237.2, 239.2, 244.2, 251.2, 258.2, 264.2

229 to play *lí3ib* لِعِب

	affirmative		negative		
ána	*li3íbt*	لِعِبْت	*ma-l3íbtiš*	مَلْعِبْتِش	perfect
íḥna	*li3íbna*	لِعِبْنا	*ma-l3ibnāš*	مَلْعِبْناش	
ínta	*li3íbt*	لِعِبْت	*ma-l3íbtiš*	مَلْعِبْتِش	
ínti	*li3íbti*	لِعِبْتي	*ma-l3ibtīš*	مَلْعِبْتيش	
íntu	*li3íbtu*	لِعِبْتوا	*ma-l3ibtūš*	مَلْعِبْتوش	
húwwa	*lí3ib*	لِعِب	*ma-l3íbš*	مَلْعِبْش	
híyya	*lí3bit*	لِعْبِت	*ma-li3bítš*	مَلِعْبِتْش	
húmma	*lí3bu*	لِعْبوا	*ma-li3būš*	مَلِعْبوش	
ána	*ál3ab*	أَلْعَب	*ma-l3ábš*	مَلْعَبْش	imperfect
íḥna	*níl3ab*	نِلْعَب	*ma-nil3ábš*	مَنِلْعَبْش	
ínta	*tíl3ab*	تِلْعَب	*ma-til3ábš*	مَتِلْعَبْش	
ínti	*til3ábi*	تِلْعَبي	*ma-til3abīš*	مَتِلْعَبيش	
íntu	*til3ábu*	تِلْعَبوا	*ma-til3abūš*	مَتِلْعَبوش	
húwwa	*yíl3ab*	يِلْعَب	*ma-yil3ábš*	مَيِلْعَبْش	
híyya	*tíl3ab*	تِلْعَب	*ma-til3ábš*	مَتِلْعَبْش	
húmma	*yil3ábu*	يِلْعَبوا	*ma-yil3abūš*	مَيِلْعَبوش	
ána	*bál3ab*	بَلْعَب	*ma-bal3ábš*	مَبَلْعَبْش	bi-imperfect
íḥna	*biníl3ab*	بِنِلْعَب	*ma-bnil3ábš*	مَبْنِلْعَبْش	
ínta	*bitíl3ab*	بِتِلْعَب	*ma-btil3ábš*	مَبْتِلْعَبْش	
ínti	*bitil3ábi*	بِتِلْعَبي	*ma-btil3abīš*	مَبْتِلْعَبيش	
íntu	*bitil3ábu*	بِتِلْعَبوا	*ma-btil3abūš*	مَبْتِلْعَبوش	
húwwa	*biyíl3ab*	بِيِلْعَب	*ma-byil3ábš*	مَبْيِلْعَبْش	
híyya	*bitíl3ab*	بِتِلْعَب	*ma-btil3ábš*	مَبْتِلْعَبْش	
húmma	*biyil3ábu*	بِيِلْعَبوا	*ma-byil3abūš*	مَبْيِلْعَبوش	
ána	*hál3ab*	هَلْعَب	*miš hál3ab*	مِش هَلْعَب	future
íḥna	*haníl3ab*	هَنِلْعَب	*miš haníl3ab*	مِش هَنِلْعَب	
ínta	*hatíl3ab*	هَتِلْعَب	*miš hatíl3ab*	مِش هَتِلْعَب	
ínti	*hatil3ábi*	هَتِلْعَبي	*miš hatil3ábi*	مِش هَتِلْعَبي	
íntu	*hatil3ábu*	هَتِلْعَبوا	*miš hatil3ábu*	مِش هَتِلْعَبوا	
húwwa	*hayíl3ab*	هَيِلْعَب	*miš hayíl3ab*	مِش هَيِلْعَب	
híyya	*hatíl3ab*	هَتِلْعَب	*miš hatíl3ab*	مِش هَتِلْعَب	
húmma	*hayil3ábu*	هَيِلْعَبوا	*miš hayil3ábu*	مِش هَيِلْعَبوا	
ínta	*íl3ab*	اِلْعَب	*ma-til3ábš*	مَتِلْعَبْش	imperative
ínti	*il3ábi*	اِلْعَبي	*ma-til3abīš*	مَتِلْعَبيش	
íntu	*il3ábu*	اِلْعَبوا	*ma-til3abūš*	مَتِلْعَبوش	

	active		passive		
masculine	*lā3ib*	لاعِب	*mal3ūb*	مَلْعوب	participles
feminine	*lá3ba*	لاعْبَة	*mal3ūba*	مَلْعوبَة	
plural	*la3bīn*	لاعْبين	*mal3ubīn*	مَلْعوبين	

verbal noun: *li3b* لِعْب

①

لِعِبْنا إمْبارِح حِتّة ماتْش.

li3íbna -mbāriḥ ḥíttit matš.

We played a great soccer match yesterday.

②

سيبي شعْرِك مفْكوك. بحِبّ ألْعب فيه.

sībi šá3rik mafkūk. baḥíbb ál3ab fī.

Let your hair loose. I like playing with it.

③

بلْعب كوتْشينة أنا و رِحاب طول اللّيْل.

bál3ab kutšīna ʔána wi riḥāb ṭūl illēl.

Rehab and I play cards all night.

④

الوِلاد هَيِلْعبوا في الجِنيْنة.

ilwilād hayil3ábu fi -lginēna.

The kids will play in the yard.

⑤

متِلْعبْش في الحاجات دي يا وَلد.

ma-til3ábšᵊ fi -lḥagāt di ya wálad.

Don't play around with these things, kid.

❖ [1s4] **to play; to play around** (**with** في *fi*)

➲ 20.1, 48.4, 100.2, 143.8, 162.3, 163.2, 183.4, 232.3

230 to turn *laff* لفّ

	affirmative		negative		
ána	*laffēt*	لَفّيْت	*ma-laffítš*	مَلَفّيْتْش	perfect
íḥna	*laffēna*	لَفّيْنا	*ma-laffināš*	مَلَفّيناش	
ínta	*laffēt*	لَفّيْت	*ma-laffítš*	مَلَفّيْتْش	
ínti	*laffēti*	لَفّيْتي	*ma-laffitīš*	مَلَفّيتيش	
íntu	*laffētu*	لَفّيْتوا	*ma-laffitūš*	مَلَفّيتوش	
húwwa	*laff*	لَفّ	*ma-láffiš*	مَلَفّش	
híyya	*láffit*	لَفّت	*ma-laffítš*	مَلَفّتْش	
húmma	*láffu*	لَفّوا	*ma-laffūš*	مَلَفّوش	
ána	*alíff*	ألِفّ	*ma-líffiš*	مَلِفّش	imperfect
íḥna	*nilíff*	نِلِفّ	*ma-nlíffiš*	مَنْلِفّش	
ínta	*tilíff*	تِلِفّ	*ma-tlíffiš*	مَتْلِفّش	
ínti	*tilíffi*	تِلِفّي	*ma-tliffīš*	مَتْلِفّيش	
íntu	*tilíffu*	تِلِفّوا	*ma-tliffūš*	مَتْلِفّوش	
húwwa	*yilíff*	يِلِفّ	*ma-ylíffiš*	مَيْلِفّش	
híyya	*tilíff*	تِلِفّ	*ma-tlíffiš*	مَتْلِفّش	
húmma	*yilíffu*	يِلِفّوا	*ma-yliffūš*	مَيْلِفّوش	
ána	*balíff*	بَلِفّ	*ma-balíffiš*	مَبَلِفّش	bi-imperfect
íḥna	*binlíff*	بِنْلِفّ	*ma-binlíffiš*	مَبِنْلِفّش	
ínta	*bitlíff*	بِتْلِفّ	*ma-bitlíffiš*	مَبِتْلِفّش	
ínti	*bitlíffi*	بِتْلِفّي	*ma-bitliffīš*	مَبِتْلِفّيش	
íntu	*bitlíffu*	بِتْلِفّوا	*ma-bitliffūš*	مَبِتْلِفّوش	
húwwa	*biylíff*	بِيْلِفّ	*ma-biylíffiš*	مَبِيْلِفّش	
híyya	*bitlíff*	بِتْلِفّ	*ma-bitlíffiš*	مَبِتْلِفّش	
húmma	*biylíffu*	بِيْلِفّوا	*ma-biyliffūš*	مَبِيْلِفّوش	
ána	*halíff*	هَلِفّ	*miš halíff*	مِش هَلِفّ	future
íḥna	*hanlíff*	هَنْلِفّ	*miš hanlíff*	مِش هَنْلِفّ	
ínta	*hatlíff*	هَتْلِفّ	*miš hatlíff*	مِش هَتْلِفّ	
ínti	*hatlíffi*	هَتْلِفّي	*miš hatlíffi*	مِش هَتْلِفّي	
íntu	*hatlíffu*	هَتْلِفّوا	*miš hatlíffu*	مِش هَتْلِفّوا	
húwwa	*haylíff*	هَيْلِفّ	*miš haylíff*	مِش هَيْلِفّ	
híyya	*hatlíff*	هَتْلِفّ	*miš hatlíff*	مِش هَتْلِفّ	
húmma	*haylíffu*	هَيْلِفّوا	*miš haylíffu*	مِش هَيْلِفّوا	
ínta	*liff*	لِفّ	*ma-tlíffiš*	مَتْلِفّش	imperative
ínti	*líffi*	لِفّي	*ma-tliffīš*	مَتْلِفّيش	
íntu	*líffu*	لِفّوا	*ma-tliffūš*	مَتْلِفّوش	

	active		passive		
masculine	*lāfif*	لافِف	*malfūf*	مَلْفوف	participles
feminine	*láffa*	لافّة	*malfūfa*	مَلْفوفة	
plural	*laffīn*	لافّين	*malfufīn*	مَلْفوفين	

verbal noun: *laff* لَفّ - *lafafān* لفَفان

①

لقيْت نفْسي هتوهْ، قُمْت لفّيْت و رْجِعْت.

laʔēt náfsi hatūh, ʔumtᵊ laffēt wi rgi3t.

I was going to get lost, so I turned around and went back.

②

ماما لازِم تِلِفّ السّوق كُلُّه قبْل ما تِشْترِي.

māma lāzim tilíff issūʔ kúllu ʔablᵊ ma tištíri.

My mom must go around the whole market before she decides what to buy.

③

آية بِتْلِفّ الهدايا حِلْو أوي.

āya bitlíff ilhadāya ḥilwᵊ ʔáwi.

Aya wraps gifts nicely.

④

هتْلِفّ يمْين في شْمال هتْلاقي العِمارة قُدّامك.

hatlíffᵊ ymīn fi šmāl hatlāʔi -l3imāra ʔuddāmak.

You'll turn right, then left, and you'll find the building in front of you.

⑤

متْلِفِّش كِتير. طلبك عنْدِنا.

ma-tlíffiš kitīr. ṭálabak 3andína.

(shopkeeper to customer:) Don't search around. We have what you want.

❖ [1g3] **to turn; to wrap; to wander around, traverse**

231 to find *láʔa* لَقَى

	affirmative		negative		
ána	*laʔēt*	لَقيْت	*ma-laʔítš*	مَلَقيتْش	perfect
íḥna	*laʔēna*	لَقيْنا	*ma-laʔināš*	مَلَقيناش	
ínta	*laʔēt*	لَقيْت	*ma-laʔítš*	مَلَقيتْش	
ínti	*laʔēti*	لَقيْتي	*ma-laʔitīš*	مَلَقيتيش	
íntu	*laʔētu*	لَقيْتوا	*ma-laʔitūš*	مَلَقيتوش	
húwwa	*láʔa*	لَقَى	*ma-laʔāš*	مَلَقاش	
híyya	*láʔit*	لَقِت	*ma-laʔítš*	مَلَقِتْش	
húmma	*láʔu*	لَقوا	*ma-laʔūš*	مَلَقوش	
ána	*alāʔi*	ألاقي	*ma-laʔīš*	مَلاقيش	imperfect
íḥna	*nilāʔi*	نِلاقي	*ma-nlaʔīš*	مَنْلاقيش	
ínta	*tilāʔi*	تِلاقي	*ma-tlaʔīš*	مَتْلاقيش	
ínti	*tilāʔi*	تِلاقي	*ma-tlaʔīš*	مَتْلاقيش	
íntu	*tilāʔu*	تِلاقوا	*ma-tlaʔūš*	مَتْلاقوش	
húwwa	*yilāʔi*	يِلاقي	*ma-ylaʔīš*	مَيْلاقيش	
híyya	*tilāʔi*	تِلاقي	*ma-tlaʔīš*	مَتْلاقيش	
húmma	*yilāʔu*	يِلاقوا	*ma-ylaʔūš*	مَيْلاقوش	
ána	*balāʔi*	بَلاقي	*ma-balaʔīš*	مَبَلاقيش	bi-imperfect
íḥna	*binlāʔi*	بِنْلاقي	*ma-binlaʔīš*	مَبِنْلاقيش	
ínta	*bitlāʔi*	بِتْلاقي	*ma-bitlaʔīš*	مَبِتْلاقيش	
ínti	*bitlāʔi*	بِتْلاقي	*ma-bitlaʔīš*	مَبِتْلاقيش	
íntu	*bitlāʔu*	بِتْلاقوا	*ma-bitlaʔūš*	مَبِتْلاقوش	
húwwa	*biylāʔi*	بِيْلاقي	*ma-biylaʔīš*	مَبِيْلاقيش	
híyya	*bitlāʔi*	بِتْلاقي	*ma-bitlaʔīš*	مَبِتْلاقيش	
húmma	*biylāʔu*	بِيْلاقوا	*ma-biylaʔūš*	مَبِيْلاقوش	
ána	*halāʔi*	هَلاقي	*miš halāʔi*	مِش هَلاقي	future
íḥna	*hanlāʔi*	هَنْلاقي	*miš hanlāʔi*	مِش هَنْلاقي	
ínta	*hatlāʔi*	هَتْلاقي	*miš hatlāʔi*	مِش هَتْلاقي	
ínti	*hatlāʔi*	هَتْلاقي	*miš hatlāʔi*	مِش هَتْلاقي	
íntu	*hatlāʔu*	هَتْلاقوا	*miš hatlāʔu*	مِش هَتْلاقوا	
húwwa	*haylāʔi*	هَيْلاقي	*miš haylāʔi*	مِش هَيْلاقي	
híyya	*hatlāʔi*	هَتْلاقي	*miš hatlāʔi*	مِش هَتْلاقي	
húmma	*haylāʔu*	هَيْلاقوا	*miš haylāʔu*	مِش هَيْلاقوا	
ínta	*šūf*	شوف	*ma-tšúfš*	مَتْشوفْش	imperative
ínti	*šūfi*	شوفي	*ma-tšufīš*	مَتْشوفيش	
íntu	*šūfu*	شوفوا	*ma-tšufūš*	مَتْشوفوش	

	active		passive		
masculine	*lāʔi*	لاقي	–	–	participles
feminine	*láʔya*	لاقْيَة	–	–	
plural	*laʔyīn*	لاقْيين	–	–	

no verbal noun

①

الدِّمِرْداش لقي في هاجر فتاةْ أحْلامُه.

iddimirdāš láʔa f hāgar fatāt aḫlāmu.

Demerdash found in Hagar
the girl of his dreams.

②a

اِمْشي في الشّارِع ده طوّالي و إنْتَ تْلاقِي النّادي قُدّامك.

ímši fi -ššāri3 da ṭawwāli w ínta tlāʔi -nnādi ʔuddāmak.

Walk straight down this street, and
you'll find the club in front of you.

②b

اِمْشي في الشّارِع ده طوّالي و إنْتَ تِلْقى النّادي قُدّامك.

ímši fi -ššāri3 da ṭawwāli w ínta tílʔa -nnādi ʔuddāmak.

Walk straight down this street, and
you'll find the club in front of you.

③a

مُهاب بِيْلاقِي فْلوس في الأرْض علي طول.

muhāb biylāʔi flūs fi -lʔarḍᵊ 3áli ṭūl.

Mohab finds money on the ground all the time.

③b

مُهاب بِيِلْقي فِلوس في الأرْض علي طول.

muhāb biyílʔa filūs fi -lʔarḍᵊ 3áli ṭūl.

Mohab finds money on the ground all the time.

④a

اِفْتح الضّلْفة دي هتْلاقي الفِلْفِل.

íftaḫ iḍḍálfa di hatlāʔi -lfílfil.

Open this cupboard, and you'll find the pepper.

④b

اِفْتح الضّلْفة دي هِتِلْقي الفِلْفِل.

íftaḫ iḍḍálfa di hatílʔa -lfílfil.

Open this cupboard, and you'll find the pepper.

⑤a

حاوِل تِلاقيلي نضّارْتي. أنا كُنْت سايِبْها هِنا.

ḫāwil tilaʔīli naḍḍárti. ána kuntᵊ sayíbha hína.

Try to find my glasses for me. I left them here.

⑤b

حاوِل تِلْقالي نضّارْتي. أنا كُنْت سايِبْها هِنا.

ḫāwil tilʔāli naḍḍárti. ána kuntᵊ sayíbha hína.

Try to find my glasses for me. I left them here.

⑥

الدُّكْتور لقاني دخلْت المُحاضْرة مِتْأخّر، خرّجْني.

idduktūr laʔāni daxált ilmuḫáḍra mitʔáxxar, xarrágni.

When I entered the lecture late,
the professor told me to go out.

⑦a

ملاقيش عنْدك مُلوخية؟

ma-laʔīš 3ándak muluxíyya?

Do you have mulukhiyah [Jew's mallow]?
[lit. Don't I find at you[r shop] mulukhiyah?]

⑦b

ملْقاش عنْدك مُلوخية؟

ma-lʔāš 3ándak muluxíyya?

Do you have mulukhiyah [Jew's mallow]?
[lit. Don't I find at you[r shop] mulukhiyah?]

⑧a

تسْبيح بِتْلاقي نفْسها في الرّسْم.

tasbīḫ bitlāʔi nafsáha fi -rrasm.

Tasbeeh finds her passion in painting.

⑧b

تسْبيح بِتِلْقي نفْسها في الرّسْم.

tasbīḫ bitílʔa nafsáha fi -rrasm.

Tasbeeh finds her passion in painting.

⑨a

لَوْ بصّيْت كُوَيِّس هتْلاقي اللي بِتْدوّر عليْه.

law baṣṣēt kuwáyyis hatlāʔi -lli bitdáwwar 3alē.

If you look carefully, you'll find
what you're looking for.

⑨b

لَوْ بصّيْت كُوَيِّس هتِلْقي اللي بِتْدوّر عليْه.

law baṣṣēt kuwáyyis hatílʔa -lli bitdáwwar 3alē.

If you look carefully, you'll find
what you're looking for.

⑩a

متْلاقيش أبداً حدّ ناجِح بِيْضيّع وَقْتُه.

ma-tlaʔīš ábadan ḫaddᵊ nāgiḫ biyḍáyya3 wáʔtu.

You'll never meet a successful person who wastes his time.

⑩b

متِلْقاش أبداً حدّ ناجِح بِيْضيّع وَقْتُه.

ma-tilʔāš ábadan ḫaddᵊ nāgiḫ biyḍáyya3 wáʔtu.

You'll never meet a successful person who wastes his time.

⑪

شوفْلي فينْ مفاتيحي. مِش لاقيها.

šúfli fēn mafatīḫi. miš laʔīha.

Find me my keys. I can't find them.

❖ [i4] **to find; to meet**

- This verb was originally two separate verbs: ⓐ لاقى *lāʔa* (يِلاقي *yilāʔi*) and ⓑ لقى *láʔa* (يِلْقى *yílʔa*). However, in everyday usage, they have overlapped somewhat. (An alternate perfect form is لِقي *líʔi.)*
- The perfect forms are taken from ⓑ and are always pronounced with a short *a.* Some Egyptians may write first and second person forms of the perfect tense with ا (alif) (taken from ⓐ), although this is a moot point in pronunciation, as the alif appears in an unstressed syllable, thus pronounced as a short *a:* لاقيْت/لقيْت *laʔēt* 'I found'.
- * ⓐ is much more commonly used for non-perfect tenses and is shown in the table for this verb. However, you may hear some speakers use non-perfect forms built on ⓑ. Both variations are given in the examples above, marked with [a] and [b].
- This verb does not have imperative forms. Instead, imperatives are borrowed from other verbs. When meaning 'find', use شوف *šūf* (➲ 231.11), and for 'meet', use قابِل *ʔābil* (➲ 198.6).
- The active participle in common. It is formed from ⓑ, as shown in the table. (➲ 19.2)
- This verb has no passive participle or verbal noun in common usage.
- The audio starts with the perfect followed by both variations of the imperfect: لقى / يِلاقي / يِلْقى *láʔa / yilāʔi / yílʔa*

➲ 8.1, 57.1, 80.5, 111.6, 115.1, 127.1, 156.2, 171.1, 175.6, 190.1, 212.1, 219.1, 230.1, 255.1, 255.3

232 to collect *lamm* لَمّ

	affirmative		negative		
ána	*lammēt*	لَمّيْت	*ma-lammítš*	مَلَمّيْتْش	**perfect**
íḫna	*lammēna*	لَمّيْنا	*ma-lamminā̌š*	مَلَمّيناش	
ínta	*lammēt*	لَمّيْت	*ma-lammítš*	مَلَمّيْتْش	
ínti	*lammēti*	لَمّيْتي	*ma-lammitīš*	مَلَمّيتيش	
íntu	*lammētu*	لَمّيْتوا	*ma-lammitūš*	مَلَمّيتوش	
húwwa	*lamm*	لَمّ	*ma-lámmiš*	مَلَمّش	
híyya	*lámmit*	لَمّت	*ma-lammítš*	مَلَمّتْش	
húmma	*lámmu*	لَمّوا	*ma-lammūš*	مَلَمّوش	
ána	*alímm*	ألِمّ	*ma-límmiš*	مَلِمّش	**imperfect**
íḫna	*nilímm*	نِلِمّ	*ma-nlímmiš*	مَنْلِمّش	
ínta	*tilímm*	تِلِمّ	*ma-tlímmiš*	مَتْلِمّش	
ínti	*tilímmi*	تِلِمّي	*ma-tlimmīš*	مَتْلِمّيش	
íntu	*tilímmu*	تِلِمّوا	*ma-tlimmūš*	مَتْلِمّوش	
húwwa	*yilímm*	يِلِمّ	*ma-ylímmiš*	مَيْلِمّش	
híyya	*tilímm*	تِلِمّ	*ma-tlímmiš*	مَتْلِمّش	
húmma	*yilímmu*	يِلِمّوا	*ma-ylimmūš*	مَيْلِمّوش	
ána	*balímm*	بَلِمّ	*ma-balímmiš*	مَبَلِمّش	**bi-imperfect**
íḫna	*binlímm*	بِنْلِمّ	*ma-binlímmiš*	مَبِنْلِمّش	
ínta	*bitlímm*	بِتْلِمّ	*ma-bitlímmiš*	مَبِتْلِمّش	
ínti	*bitlímmi*	بِتْلِمّي	*ma-bitlimmīš*	مَبِتْلِمّيش	
íntu	*bitlímmu*	بِتْلِمّوا	*ma-bitlimmūš*	مَبِتْلِمّوش	
húwwa	*biylímm*	بِيْلِمّ	*ma-biylímmiš*	مَبِيْلِمّش	
híyya	*bitlímm*	بِتْلِمّ	*ma-bitlímmiš*	مَبِتْلِمّش	
húmma	*biylímmu*	بِيْلِمّوا	*ma-biylimmūš*	مَبِيْلِمّوش	
ána	*halímm*	هَلِمّ	*miš halímm*	مِش هَلِمّ	**future**
íḫna	*hanlímm*	هَنْلِمّ	*miš hanlímm*	مِش هَنْلِمّ	
ínta	*hatlímm*	هَتْلِمّ	*miš hatlímm*	مِش هَتْلِمّ	
ínti	*hatlímmi*	هَتْلِمّي	*miš hatlímmi*	مِش هَتْلِمّي	
íntu	*hatlímmu*	هَتْلِمّوا	*miš hatlímmu*	مِش هَتْلِمّوا	
húwwa	*haylímm*	هَيْلِمّ	*miš haylímm*	مِش هَيْلِمّ	
híyya	*hatlímm*	هَتْلِمّ	*miš hatlímm*	مِش هَتْلِمّ	
húmma	*haylímmu*	هَيْلِمّوا	*miš haylímmu*	مِش هَيْلِمّوا	
ínta	*limm*	لِمّ	*ma-tlímmiš*	مَتْلِمّش	**imperative**
ínti	*límmi*	لِمّي	*ma-tlimmīš*	مَتْلِمّيش	
íntu	*límmu*	لِمّوا	*ma-tlimmūš*	مَتْلِمّوش	

	active		passive		
masculine	*lāmim*	لامِم	*malmūm*	مَلْموم	**participles**
feminine	*lámma*	لامّة	*malmūma*	مَلْمومَة	
plural	*lammīn*	لامّين	*malmumīn*	مَلْمومين	

verbal noun: *lamm* لَمّ

①

عملْنا حفْلِةْ جمْع التّبرُّعات، و لمّينا مبْلغ كِبير.

3amálna ḫáflit gam3 ittabarru3āt, wi lammēna máblay kibīr.

We had a fundraising party and raised
[lit. collected] a large amount of money.

②

نِسيم كُلّ سنة يِلِمّ المنْهج قبْل الاِمْتِحان بِيومينْ و يِنْجح بِتقْدير.

nisīm kullᵊ sána yilímm ilmánhag ʔabl ilʔimtiḫān bi-yumēn wi yíngaḫ bi-taʔdīr.

Every year, Neseem crams [lit. collects the whole curriculum]
two days before the exam and gets high scores.

③

الوِلاد مبِيْلِمّوش بعْد ما يِلْعبوا و بِيْسيبولي الدُّنْيا فَوْضي.

ilwilād ma-biylimmūš ba3dᵊ ma yil3ábu wi biysibūli -ddúnya fáwḍa.

The kids don't clean up after playing.
They leave the place in chaos for me.

④

هلِمّ أوْراقي و أمْشي حالاً.

halímm awrāʔi w ámši ḫālan.

I'll collect my papers
and go now.

⑤

لِمّ نفْسك بدل ما ألِمّك.

limmᵊ náfsak bádal ma -límmak.

Behave [lit. collect yourself]
before I force you to.

❖ [1g3] **to collect, gather, pick up**

➲ 44.2

233 to die *māt* مات

perfect

	affirmative		negative	
ána	*mutt*	مُتّ	*ma-múttiš*	مَمُتّش
íḥna	*mútna*	مُتْنا	*ma-mutnāš*	مَمُتْناش
ínta	*mutt*	مُتّ	*ma-múttiš*	مَمُتّش
ínti	*mútti*	مُتّي	*ma-muttīš*	مَمُتّيش
íntu	*múttu*	مُتّوا	*ma-muttūš*	مَمُتّوش
húwwa	*māt*	مات	*ma-mátš*	مَماتْش
híyya	*mātit*	ماتِت	*ma-matítš*	مَماتِتْش
húmma	*mātu*	ماتوا	*ma-matūš*	مَماتوش

imperfect

	affirmative		negative	
ána	*amūt*	أموت	*ma-mútš*	مَموتْش
íḥna	*nimūt*	نِموت	*ma-nmútš*	مَنْموتْش
ínta	*timūt*	تِموت	*ma-tmútš*	مَتْموتْش
ínti	*timūti*	تِموتي	*ma-tmutīš*	مَتْموتيش
íntu	*timūtu*	تِموتوا	*ma-tmutūš*	مَتْموتوش
húwwa	*yimūt*	يِموت	*ma-ymútš*	مَيْموتْش
híyya	*timūt*	تِموت	*ma-tmútš*	مَتْموتْش
húmma	*yimūtu*	يِموتوا	*ma-ymutūš*	مَيْموتوش

bi-imperfect

	affirmative		negative	
ána	*bamūt*	بَموت	*ma-bamútš*	مَبَموتْش
íḥna	*binmūt*	بِنْموت	*ma-binmútš*	مَبِنْموتْش
ínta	*bitmūt*	بِتْموت	*ma-bitmútš*	مَبِتْموتْش
ínti	*bitmūti*	بِتْموتي	*ma-bitmutīš*	مَبِتْموتيش
íntu	*bitmūtu*	بِتْموتوا	*ma-bitmutūš*	مَبِتْموتوش
húwwa	*biymūt*	بِيْموت	*ma-biymútš*	مَبِيْموتْش
híyya	*bitmūt*	بِتْموت	*ma-bitmútš*	مَبِتْموتْش
húmma	*biymūtu*	بِيْموتوا	*ma-biymutūš*	مَبِيْموتوش

future

	affirmative		negative	
ána	*hamūt*	هَموت	*miš hamūt*	مِش هَموت
íḥna	*hanmūt*	هَنْموت	*miš hanmūt*	مِش هَنْموت
ínta	*hatmūt*	هَتْموت	*miš hatmūt*	مِش هَتْموت
ínti	*hatmūti*	هَتْموتي	*miš hatmūti*	مِش هَتْموتي
íntu	*hatmūtu*	هَتْموتوا	*miš hatmūtu*	مِش هَتْموتوا
húwwa	*haymūt*	هَيْموت	*miš haymūt*	مِش هَيْموت
híyya	*hatmūt*	هَتْموت	*miš hatmūt*	مِش هَتْموت
húmma	*haymūtu*	هَيْموتوا	*miš haymūtu*	مِش هَيْموتوا

imperative

	affirmative		negative	
ínta	*mūt*	موت	*ma-tmútš*	مَتْموتْش
ínti	*mūti*	موتي	*ma-tmutīš*	مَتْموتيش
íntu	*mūtu*	موتوا	*ma-tmutūš*	مَتْموتوش

participles

	active		passive	
masculine	*māyit*	مايِت	—	—
feminine	*máyta*	مايْتَة	—	—
plural	*maytīn*	مايْتين	—	—

verbal noun: *mōt* موْت

①

سُهى أبوها مات مِن قبْل ما تِتْوِلِد.

súha ʔabūha māt min ʔablᵊ ma titwílid.

Soha's father died before she was born.

②

عمّ أحْمد مُمْكِن يموت لَوْ عِرِف إنّ إبْنُه مات.

3amm áħmad múmkin yimūt law 3írif inn íbnu māt.

Uncle Ahmed might die if he knew that his son has died.

③

بموت في الحلَوِيّات.

bamūt fi -lħalawiyyāt.

I like [lit. I die for] sweets so much.

④

الدّكاتْرة بِيْقولوا مينا هَيْموت خِلال شهْريْن.

iddakátra biyʔūlu mīna haymūt xilāl šahrēn.

Doctors say that Mina will die within a couple of months.

⑤

متْموتْش دِلْوَقْتي. إنْتَ وَعدْتِني نِفْضل معَ بعْض طول العُمْر.

ma-tmútšᵊ dilwáʔti. ínta wa3adtíni nífḍal má3a ba3ḍᵊ ṭūl il3úmr.

Don't die now. You promised me we'd be together forever.

❖ [1h1] **to die**

➲ 13.6, 49.1, 105.4, 187.9, 225.1

234 to practice māris مارِس

verbal noun: *mumársa* مُمارْسة

	affirmative		negative		
ána	*maríst*	مارِسْت	*ma-marístiš*	مَمارِسْتِش	**perfect**
íḫna	*marísna*	مارِسْنا	*ma-marisnāš*	مَمارِسْناش	
ínta	*maríst*	مارِسْت	*ma-marístiš*	مَمارِسْتِش	
ínti	*marísti*	مارِسْتي	*ma-maristīš*	مَمارِسْتيش	
íntu	*marístu*	مارِسْتوا	*ma-maristūš*	مَمارِسْتوش	
húwwa	*māris*	مارِس	*ma-marísš*	مَمارِسْش	
híyya	*mársit*	مارْسِت	*ma-marsítš*	مَمارْسِتْش	
húmma	*mársu*	مارْسوا	*ma-marsūš*	مَمارْسوش	
ána	*amāris*	أمارِس	*ma-marísš*	مَمارِسْش	**imperfect**
íḫna	*nimāris*	نِمارِس	*ma-nmarísš*	مَنْمارِسْش	
ínta	*timāris*	تِمارِس	*ma-tmarísš*	مَتْمارِسْش	
ínti	*timársi*	تِمارْسي	*ma-tmarsīš*	مَتْمارْسيش	
íntu	*timársu*	تِمارْسوا	*ma-tmarsūš*	مَتْمارْسوش	
húwwa	*yimāris*	يِمارِس	*ma-ymarísš*	مَيْمارِسْش	
híyya	*timāris*	تِمارِس	*ma-tmarísš*	مَتْمارِسْش	
húmma	*yimársu*	يِمارْسوا	*ma-ymarsūš*	مَيْمارْسوش	
ána	*bamāris*	بَمارِس	*ma-bamarísš*	مَبَمارِسْش	**bi-imperfect**
íḫna	*binmāris*	بِنْمارِس	*ma-binmarísš*	مَبِنْمارِسْش	
ínta	*bitmāris*	بِتْمارِس	*ma-bitmarísš*	مَبِتْمارِسْش	
ínti	*bitmársi*	بِتْمارْسي	*ma-bitmarsīš*	مَبِتْمارْسيش	
íntu	*bitmársu*	بِتْمارْسوا	*ma-bitmarsūš*	مَبِتْمارْسوش	
húwwa	*biymāris*	بِيْمارِس	*ma-biymarísš*	مَبِيْمارِسْش	
híyya	*bitmāris*	بِتْمارِس	*ma-bitmarísš*	مَبِتْمارِسْش	
húmma	*biymársu*	بِيْمارْسوا	*ma-biymarsūš*	مَبِيْمارْسوش	
ána	*hamāris*	هَمارِس	*miš hamāris*	مِش هَمارِس	**future**
íḫna	*hanmāris*	هَنْمارِس	*miš hanmāris*	مِش هَنْمارِس	
ínta	*hatmāris*	هَتْمارِس	*miš hatmāris*	مِش هَتْمارِس	
ínti	*hatmársi*	هَتْمارْسي	*miš hatmársi*	مِش هَتْمارْسي	
íntu	*hatmársu*	هَتْمارْسوا	*miš hatmársu*	مِش هَتْمارْسوا	
húwwa	*haymāris*	هَيْمارِس	*miš haymāris*	مِش هَيْمارِس	
híyya	*hatmāris*	هَتْمارِس	*miš hatmāris*	مِش هَتْمارِس	
húmma	*haymársu*	هَيْمارْسوا	*miš haymársu*	مِش هَيْمارْسوا	
ínta	*māris*	مارِس	*ma-tmarísš*	مَتْمارِسْش	**imperative**
ínti	*mársi*	مارْسي	*ma-tmarsīš*	مَتْمارْسيش	
íntu	*mársu*	مارْسوا	*ma-tmarsūš*	مَتْمارْسوش	

	active		passive		
masculine	*mimāris*	مِمارِس	*mitmāris*	مِتْمارِس	**participles**
feminine	*mimársa*	مِمارْسَة	*mitmársa*	مِتْمارْسَة	
plural	*mimarsīn*	مِمارْسين	*mitmarsīn*	مِتْمارْسين	

①

عمْرو مارِس لِعب كِتير بسّ مكمِّلْش في وَلا واحْدة.

3amrᵊ māris lí3ab kitīr bassᵊ ma-kammílšᵊ f wálla wáћda.

Amr used to do lots of sports, but he didn't keep up any of them.

②

نِفْسي أمارِس السِّباحة بِاِنْتِظام.

nífsi ʔamāris issibāћa bi-ntiẓām.

I hope to practice swimming regularly.

③

حمّاد بِيْمارِس التّجْديف مِن زمان.

ћammād biymāris ittagdīf min zamān.

Hamad has been doing rowing for a long time.

④

هَيْمارْسوا عليْك كُلّ أنْواع الضّغْط عشان تِعْتِرف.

haymársu 3alēk kullᵊ ʔanwā3 iḍḍáɣṭᵊ 3ašān ti3tírif.

They'll put all kinds of pressure on you to confess.

⑤

متْمارِسْش رِياضة عنيفة لِحدّ ما رِجْلك تِخِفّ.

ma-tmarísšᵊ riyāḍa 3anīfa li-ћáddᵊ ma ríglak tixíff.

Don't practice hard training until your leg is totally healed.

❖ [3s] **to practice, do** (sports, etc.)

➲ 5.2, 5.5

235 to represent mássil مَثِّل

verbal noun: tamsīl تَمْسيل

	affirmative		negative		
ána	massílt	مَثِّلْت	ma-massíltiš	مَمَثِّلْتِش	perfect
íḥna	massílna	مَثِّلْنا	ma-massilnāš	مَمَثِّلْناش	
ínta	massílt	مَثِّلْت	ma-massíltiš	مَمَثِّلْتِش	
ínti	massílti	مَثِّلْتي	ma-massiltīš	مَمَثِّلْتيش	
íntu	massíltu	مَثِّلْتوا	ma-massiltūš	مَمَثِّلْتوش	
húwwa	mássil	مَثِّل	ma-massílš	مَمَثِّلْش	
híyya	massílit	مَثِّلِت	ma-massilítš	مَمَثِّلِتْش	
húmma	massílu	مَثِّلوا	ma-massilūš	مَمَثِّلوش	
ána	amássil	أمَثِّل	ma-massílš	مَمَثِّلْش	imperfect
íḥna	nimássil	نِمَثِّل	ma-nmassílš	مَنْمَثِّلْش	
ínta	timássil	تِمَثِّل	ma-tmassílš	مَتْمَثِّلْش	
ínti	timassíli	تِمَثِّلي	ma-tmassilīš	مَتْمَثِّليش	
íntu	timassílu	تِمَثِّلوا	ma-tmassilūš	مَتْمَثِّلوش	
húwwa	yimássil	يِمَثِّل	ma-ymassílš	مَيْمَثِّلْش	
híyya	timássil	تِمَثِّل	ma-tmassílš	مَتْمَثِّلْش	
húmma	yimassílu	يِمَثِّلوا	ma-ymassilūš	مَيْمَثِّلوش	
ána	bamássil	بَمَثِّل	ma-bamassílš	مَبَمَثِّلْش	bi-imperfect
íḥna	binmássil	بِنْمَثِّل	ma-binmassílš	مَبِنْمَثِّلْش	
ínta	bitmássil	بِتْمَثِّل	ma-bitmassílš	مَبِتْمَثِّلْش	
ínti	bitmassíli	بِتْمَثِّلي	ma-bitmassilīš	مَبِتْمَثِّليش	
íntu	bitmassílu	بِتْمَثِّلوا	ma-bitmassilūš	مَبِتْمَثِّلوش	
húwwa	biymássil	بِيْمَثِّل	ma-biymassílš	مَبِيْمَثِّلْش	
híyya	bitmássil	بِتْمَثِّل	ma-bitmassílš	مَبِتْمَثِّلْش	
húmma	biymassílu	بِيْمَثِّلوا	ma-biymassilūš	مَبِيْمَثِّلوش	
ána	hamássil	هَمَثِّل	miš hamássil	مِش هَمَثِّل	future
íḥna	hanmássil	هَنْمَثِّل	miš hanmássil	مِش هَنْمَثِّل	
ínta	hatmássil	هَتْمَثِّل	miš hatmássil	مِش هَتْمَثِّل	
ínti	hatmassíli	هَتْمَثِّلي	miš hatmassíli	مِش هَتْمَثِّلي	
íntu	hatmassílu	هَتْمَثِّلوا	miš hatmassílu	مِش هَتْمَثِّلوا	
húwwa	haymássil	هَيْمَثِّل	miš haymássil	مِش هَيْمَثِّل	
híyya	hatmássil	هَتْمَثِّل	miš hatmássil	مِش هَتْمَثِّل	
húmma	haymassílu	هَيْمَثِّلوا	miš haymassílu	مِش هَيْمَثِّلوا	
ínta	mássil	مَثِّل	ma-tmassílš	مَتْمَثِّلْش	imperative
ínti	massíli	مَثِّلي	ma-tmassilīš	مَتْمَثِّليش	
íntu	massílu	مَثِّلوا	ma-tmassilūš	مَتْمَثِّلوش	

	active		passive		
masculine	mimássil	مِمَثِّل	mitmássil	مِتْمَثِّل	participles
feminine	mimassíla	مِمَثِّلَة	mitmassíla	مِتْمَثِّلَة	
plural	mimassilīn	مِمَثِّلين	mitmassilīn	مِتْمَثِّلين	

①

رشْوان مثِّل مصْر تمْثيل مُشرّف في الأولِمْبِياد.

rašwān mássil maṣrᵊ tamsīl mušárraf fi -lʔulimbiyād.

Rashwan represented Egypt
honorably in the Olympics.

②

أُمْنية بِتْحِبّ تمْثِّل و تْغنّي. هتْقدِّم في بِرنامِج مَواهِب.

umníyya bitḥíbbᵊ tmássil wi tɣánni. hatʔáddim fi birnāmig mawāhib.

Omnia likes to act and sing. She'll
participate in a talent show.

③

بِيْقولوا إنّ اللّوْن الأصْفر في الوَرْد بِيْمثِّل الغيرة.

biyʔūlu ʔinn illōn ilʔáṣfar fi -lwárd biymássil ilɣīra.

They say that the color yellow in
flowers represents jealousy.

④

هَيْمثِّلوا مُسلْسل جِديد عن حَياةْ أحْمد شَوْقي.

haymassílu musálsal gidīd 3an ḥayāt áḥmad šáwʔi.

They're going to do a new series
about the life of Ahmed Shawqi.

⑤

متْمثِّليش عليّا. أنا عارِف إنِّك بِتِكْدِبي.

ma-tmassílīš 3aláyya. ána 3ārif ínnik bitikdíbi.

Don't put on an act.
I know you're lying.

❖ [2s1] **to represent; to act, perform; to depict, portray**

236 to wipe másaħ مَسَح

verbal nouns: masħ مَسْح - masaħān مَسَحان

	affirmative		negative		
ána	masáħt	مَسَحْت	ma-masáħtiš	مَمَسَحْتِش	perfect
íħna	masáħna	مَسَحْنا	ma-masaħnāš	مَمَسَحْناش	
ínta	masáħt	مَسَحْت	ma-masáħtiš	مَمَسَحْتِش	
ínti	masáħti	مَسَحْتي	ma-masaħtīš	مَمَسَحْتيش	
íntu	masáħtu	مَسَحْتوا	ma-masaħtūš	مَمَسَحْتوش	
húwwa	másaħ	مَسَح	ma-masáħš	مَمَسَحْش	
híyya	másaħit	مَسَحِت	ma-masaħítš	مَمَسَحِتْش	
húmma	másaħu	مَسَحوا	ma-masaħūš	مَمَسَحوش	
ána	ámsaħ	أَمْسَح	ma-msáħš	مَمْسَحْش	imperfect
íħna	nímsaħ	نِمْسَح	ma-nimsáħš	مَنِمْسَحْش	
ínta	tímsaħ	تِمْسَح	ma-timsáħš	مَتِمْسَحْش	
ínti	timsáħi	تِمْسَحي	ma-timsaħīš	مَتِمْسَحيش	
íntu	timsáħu	تِمْسَحوا	ma-timsaħūš	مَتِمْسَحوش	
húwwa	yímsaħ	يِمْسَح	ma-yimsáħš	مَيِمْسَحْش	
híyya	tímsaħ	تِمْسَح	ma-timsáħš	مَتِمْسَحْش	
húmma	yimsáħu	يِمْسَحوا	ma-yimsaħūš	مَيِمْسَحوش	
ána	bámsaħ	بَمْسَح	ma-bamsáħš	مَبَمْسَحْش	bi-imperfect
íħna	binímsaħ	بِنِمْسَح	ma-bnimsáħš	مَبْنِمْسَحْش	
ínta	bitímsaħ	بِتِمْسَح	ma-btimsáħš	مَبْتِمْسَحْش	
ínti	bitimsáħi	بِتِمْسَحي	ma-btimsaħīš	مَبْتِمْسَحيش	
íntu	bitimsáħu	بِتِمْسَحوا	ma-btimsaħūš	مَبْتِمْسَحوش	
húwwa	biyímsaħ	بِيِمْسَح	ma-byimsáħš	مَبْيِمْسَحْش	
híyya	bitímsaħ	بِتِمْسَح	ma-btimsáħš	مَبْتِمْسَحْش	
húmma	biyimsáħu	بِيِمْسَحوا	ma-byimsaħūš	مَبْيِمْسَحوش	
ána	hámsaħ	هَمْسَح	miš hámsaħ	مِش هَمْسَح	future
íħna	hanímsaħ	هَنِمْسَح	miš hanímsaħ	مِش هَنِمْسَح	
ínta	hatímsaħ	هَتِمْسَح	miš hatímsaħ	مِش هَتِمْسَح	
ínti	hatimsáħi	هَتِمْسَحي	miš hatimsáħi	مِش هَتِمْسَحي	
íntu	hatimsáħu	هَتِمْسَحوا	miš hatimsáħu	مِش هَتِمْسَحوا	
húwwa	hayímsaħ	هَيِمْسَح	miš hayímsaħ	مِش هَيِمْسَح	
híyya	hatímsaħ	هَتِمْسَح	miš hatímsaħ	مِش هَتِمْسَح	
húmma	hayimsáħu	هَيِمْسَحوا	miš hayimsáħu	مِش هَيِمْسَحوا	
ínta	ímsaħ	اِمْسَح	ma-timsáħš	مَتِمْسَحْش	imperative
ínti	imsáħi	اِمْسَحي	ma-timsaħīš	مَتِمْسَحيش	
íntu	imsáħu	اِمْسَحوا	ma-timsaħūš	مَتِمْسَحوش	

	active		passive		
masculine	māsiħ	ماسِح	mamsūħ	مَمْسوح	participles
feminine	másħa	ماسْحَة	mamsūħa	مَمْسوحَة	
plural	masħīn	ماسْحين	mamsuħīn	مَمْسوحين	

①

مسحْت كُلّ حاجة مِن على جِهازي قبْل ما أوَدِّيه الصِّيانة.

masáḫtᵊ kullᵊ ḫāga min 3ála gihāzi ʔablᵊ m- awaddī -ṣṣiyāna.

I deleted everything from my phone before I sent it to the maintenance center.

②

لازِم نِمْسح السّبّورة قبْل ما الميس تُدْخُل.

lāzim nímsaḫ issabbūra ʔablᵊ ma -lmīs tídxul.

We should erase the board before the teacher comes in.

③

مبْتِمْسحْش إيدك في منْديل ليْه؟

ma-btimsáḫš īdak fi mandīl lē?

Why don't you wipe your hand with a napkin?

④

أُمّ أحْمد هتِمْسح الأرْض و تِبْقى خلّصِت.

umm áḫmad hatímsaḫ ilʔárḍᵊ wi tíbʔa xalláṣit.

Om Ahmed will mop the floor, and then she's finished.

⑤

اِمْسحي دْموعِك و قومي نُخْرُج شُوَيّة.

imsáḫi dmū3ik wi ʔūmi núxrug šuwáyya.

Wipe your tears, and let's go out.

❖ [1s1] **to wipe; to mop; to erase**

237 to catch mísik مسك

verbal nouns: mask مَسْك - masakān مَسَكان

	affirmative		negative		
ána	misíkt	مِسِكْت	ma-msíktiš	مَمْسِكْتِش	perfect
íḥna	misíkna	مِسِكْنا	ma-msiknāš	مَمْسِكْناش	
ínta	misíkt	مِسِكْت	ma-msíktiš	مَمْسِكْتِش	
ínti	misíkti	مِسِكْتي	ma-msiktīš	مَمْسِكْتيش	
íntu	misíktu	مِسِكْتوا	ma-msiktūš	مَمْسِكْتوش	
húwwa	mísik	مِسِك	ma-msíkš	مَمْسِكْش	
híyya	mískit	مِسْكِت	ma-miskítš	مَمِسْكِتْش	
húmma	mísku	مِسْكوا	ma-miskūš	مَمِسْكوش	
ána	ámsik	أَمْسِك	ma-msíkš	مَمْسِكْش	imperfect
íḥna	nímsik	نِمْسِك	ma-nimsíkš	مَنِمْسِكْش	
ínta	tímsik	تِمْسِك	ma-timsíkš	مَتِمْسِكْش	
ínti	timsíki	تِمْسِكي	ma-timsikīš	مَتِمْسِكيش	
íntu	timsíku	تِمْسِكوا	ma-timsikūš	مَتِمْسِكوش	
húwwa	yímsik	يِمْسِك	ma-yimsíkš	مَيِمْسِكْش	
híyya	tímsik	تِمْسِك	ma-timsíkš	مَتِمْسِكْش	
húmma	yimsíku	يِمْسِكوا	ma-yimsikūš	مَيِمْسِكوش	
ána	bámsik	بَمْسِك	ma-bamsíkš	مَبَمْسِكْش	bi-imperfect
íḥna	binímsik	بِنِمْسِك	ma-bnimsíkš	مَبْنِمْسِكْش	
ínta	bitímsik	بِتِمْسِك	ma-btimsíkš	مَبْتِمْسِكْش	
ínti	bitimsíki	بِتِمْسِكي	ma-btimsikīš	مَبْتِمْسِكيش	
íntu	bitimsíku	بِتِمْسِكوا	ma-btimsikūš	مَبْتِمْسِكوش	
húwwa	biyímsik	بِيِمْسِك	ma-byimsíkš	مَبْيِمْسِكْش	
híyya	bitímsik	بِتِمْسِك	ma-btimsíkš	مَبْتِمْسِكْش	
húmma	biyimsíku	بِيِمْسِكوا	ma-byimsikūš	مَبْيِمْسِكوش	
ána	hámsik	هَمْسِك	miš hámsik	مِش هَمْسِك	future
íḥna	hanímsik	هَنِمْسِك	miš hanímsik	مِش هَنِمْسِك	
ínta	hatímsik	هَتِمْسِك	miš hatímsik	مِش هَتِمْسِك	
ínti	hatimsíki	هَتِمْسِكي	miš hatimsíki	مِش هَتِمْسِكي	
íntu	hatimsíku	هَتِمْسِكوا	miš hatimsíku	مِش هَتِمْسِكوا	
húwwa	hayímsik	هَيِمْسِك	miš hayímsik	مِش هَيِمْسِك	
híyya	hatímsik	هَتِمْسِك	miš hatímsik	مِش هَتِمْسِك	
húmma	hayimsíku	هَيِمْسِكوا	miš hayimsíku	مِش هَيِمْسِكوا	
ínta	ímsik	اِمْسِك	ma-timsíkš	مَتِمْسِكْش	imperative
ínti	imsíki	اِمْسِكي	ma-timsikīš	مَتِمْسِكيش	
íntu	imsíku	اِمْسِكوا	ma-timsikūš	مَتِمْسِكوش	

	active		passive		
masculine	māsik	ماسِك	mamsūk	مَمْسوك	participles
feminine	máska	ماسْكَة	mamsūka	مَمْسوكَة	
plural	maskīn	ماسْكين	mamsukīn	مَمْسوكين	

①

هَيْثم مِسِك إيد هِبة و هُمّا بِيْعدّوا الشّارِع.

háysam mísik īd híba wi húmma biy3áddu -ššāri3.

Haitham held Heba's hand while they crossed the road.

②

لازِم تمِْسك أعْصابك شُوَيّة. العصبية هتأْذيك.

lāzim tímsak a3ṣābak šuwáyya. il3aṣabíyya hatiʔzīk.

You should watch [lit. hold] your temper. Getting upset isn't good for you.

③

إنْتي بْتِمْسِكي إزّاي الحِلل و هِيَّ سُخْنة كِده؟

ínti btimsíki izzāy ilħílal wi híyya súxna kída?

How do you hold the pots when they're so hot?

④

محْمود هَيِمْسِك فرْع الشِّرْكة في القاهِرة.

maħmūd hayímsik far3 iššírka fi -lqāhíra.

Mahmoud will manage the company's branch in Cairo.

⑤

سيبي الوَلد بِـراحْتُه. متِمْسِكيلوش عَ الواحْدة.

sībi -lwálad bi-ráħtu. ma-timsikilūš 3a -lwáħda.

Leave the boy alone. Don't harp on him for every little thing.

❖ [1s5] **to catch; to hold; to nag, harp on** (لِ *li-* **about** على *3ála*)

➲ 110.2, 145.4, 182.6

238 to walk míši مشي

verbal noun: mašy مَشْي - mašayān مَشَيان

	affirmative		negative		
ána	mišít	مِشيت	ma-mšítš	مَمْشيتْش	perfect
íḥna	mišína	مِشينا	ma-mšináš	مَمْشيناش	
ínta	mišít	مِشيت	ma-mšítš	مَمْشيتْش	
ínti	mišíti	مِشيتي	ma-mšitíš	مَمْشيتيش	
íntu	mišítu	مِشيتوا	ma-mšitúš	مَمْشيتوش	
húwwa	míši	مِشي	ma-mšíš	مَمْشيش	
híyya	míšyit	مِشْيِت	ma-mišyítš	مَمِشْيِتْش	
húmma	míšyu	مِشْيوا	ma-mišyúš	مَمِشْيوش	
ána	ámši	أَمْشي	ma-mšíš	مَمْشيش	imperfect
íḥna	nímši	نِمْشي	ma-nimšíš	مَنِمْشيش	
ínta	tímši	تِمْشي	ma-timšíš	مَتِمْشيش	
ínti	tímši	تِمْشي	ma-timšíš	مَتِمْشيش	
íntu	tímšu	تِمْشوا	ma-timšúš	مَتِمْشوش	
húwwa	yímši	يِمْشي	ma-yimšíš	مَيِمْشيش	
híyya	tímši	تِمْشي	ma-timšíš	مَتِمْشيش	
húmma	yímšu	يِمْشوا	ma-yimšúš	مَيِمْشوش	
ána	bámši	بَمْشي	ma-bamšíš	مَبَمْشيش	bi-imperfect
íḥna	binímši	بِنِمْشي	ma-bnimšíš	مَبْنِمْشيش	
ínta	bitímši	بِتِمْشي	ma-btimšíš	مَبْتِمْشيش	
ínti	bitímši	بِتِمْشي	ma-btimšíš	مَبْتِمْشيش	
íntu	bitímšu	بِتِمْشوا	ma-btimšúš	مَبْتِمْشوش	
húwwa	biyímši	بِيِمْشي	ma-byimšíš	مَبْيِمْشيش	
híyya	bitímši	بِتِمْشي	ma-btimšíš	مَبْتِمْشيش	
húmma	biyímšu	بِيِمْشوا	ma-byimšúš	مَبْيِمْشوش	
ána	hámši	هَمْشي	miš hámši	مِش هَمْشي	future
íḥna	hanímši	هَنِمْشي	miš hanímši	مِش هَنِمْشي	
ínta	hatímši	هَتِمْشي	miš hatímši	مِش هَتِمْشي	
ínti	hatímši	هَتِمْشي	miš hatímši	مِش هَتِمْشي	
íntu	hatímšu	هَتِمْشوا	miš hatímšu	مِش هَتِمْشوا	
húwwa	hayímši	هَيِمْشي	miš hayímši	مِش هَيِمْشي	
híyya	hatímši	هَتِمْشي	miš hatímši	مِش هَتِمْشي	
húmma	hayímšu	هَيِمْشوا	miš hayímšu	مِش هَيِمْشوا	
ínta	ímši	اِمْشي	ma-timšíš	مَتِمْشيش	imperative
ínti	ímši	اِمْشي	ma-timšíš	مَتِمْشيش	
íntu	ímšu	اِمْشوا	ma-timšúš	مَتِمْشوش	

	active		passive		
masculine	máši	ماشي	–	–	participles
feminine	mášya	ماشْيَة	–	–	
plural	mašyín	ماشْيين	–	–	

①

بهاء مِشي كِتير أوي عشان يِلاقي مكنِةْ سحْب فْلوس.

bahāʔ míši kitīr ʔáwi 3ašān yilāʔi mákanit saḫbᵊ flūs.

Bahaa walked a lot to find an ATM.

②

حاوْلي تمْشي كُلّ يوْم نُصّ ساعة.

ḫáwli tímši kullᵊ yōm nuṣṣᵊ sā3a.

Try to walk half an hour a day.

③

سُعاد بِتِمْشي مِن بيتْها لِشُغْلها.

su3ād bitímši min bítha li-šuɣláha.

Soad walks from home to work.

④

النّاس هتِمْشي في الماراثوْن ده ٥ كيلو.

innās hatímši fi -lmarasōn da xámsa kīlu.

People will do five kilometers in this race.

⑤

متِمْشيش قبْل ما تِتْعشّى معانا.

ma-timšīš ʔablᵊ ma tit3áššu ma3āna.

Don't go until you have dinner with us.

⑥

الرّاجِل خد إزازْتيْن بيبْسي و مِشي.

irrāgil xad izaztēn bíbsi wi míši.

The man took two bottles
of Pepsi and left.

❖ [1d5] **to walk; to go; to leave, go away**

➲ 53.7, 56.3, 73.3, 77.1, 92.4, 117.4, 132.2, 145.5, 150.1, 168.1, 222.5, 232.4

239 to sign máḍa مَضَى

	affirmative		negative		
ána	maḍēt	مَضيْت	ma-maḍítš	مَمَضيتْش	perfect
íḫna	maḍēna	مَضيْنا	ma-maḍināš	مَمَضيناش	
ínta	maḍēt	مَضيْت	ma-maḍítš	مَمَضيتْش	
ínti	maḍēti	مَضيْتي	ma-maḍitīš	مَمَضيتيش	
íntu	maḍētu	مَضيْتوا	ma-maḍitūš	مَمَضيتوش	
húwwa	máḍa	مَضَى	ma-maḍāš	مَمَضاش	
híyya	máḍit	مَضِت	ma-maḍítš	مَمَضِتْش	
húmma	máḍu	مَضوا	ma-maḍūš	مَمَضوش	

ána	ámḍi	أمْضي	ma-mḍīš	مَمْضيش	imperfect
íḫna	nímḍi	نِمْضي	ma-nimḍīš	مَنِمْضيش	
ínta	tímḍi	تِمْضي	ma-timḍīš	مَتِمْضيش	
ínti	tímḍi	تِمْضي	ma-timḍīš	مَتِمْضيش	
íntu	tímḍu	تِمْضوا	ma-timḍūš	مَتِمْضوش	
húwwa	yímḍi	يِمْضي	ma-yimḍīš	مَيِمْضيش	
híyya	tímḍi	تِمْضي	ma-timḍīš	مَتِمْضيش	
húmma	yímḍu	يِمْضوا	ma-yimḍūš	مَيِمْضوش	

ána	bámḍi	بَمْضي	ma-bamḍīš	مَبَمْضيش	bi-imperfect
íḫna	binímḍi	بِنِمْضي	ma-bnimḍīš	مَبْنِمْضيش	
ínta	bitímḍi	بِتِمْضي	ma-btimḍīš	مَبْتِمْضيش	
ínti	bitímḍi	بِتِمْضي	ma-btimḍīš	مَبْتِمْضيش	
íntu	bitímḍu	بِتِمْضوا	ma-btimḍūš	مَبْتِمْضوش	
húwwa	biyímḍi	بِيِمْضي	ma-byimḍīš	مَبْيِمْضيش	
híyya	bitímḍi	بِتِمْضي	ma-btimḍīš	مَبْتِمْضيش	
húmma	biyímḍu	بِيِمْضوا	ma-byimḍūš	مَبْيِمْضوش	

ána	hámḍi	هَمْضي	miš hámḍi	مِش هَمْضي	future
íḫna	hanímḍi	هَنِمْضي	miš hanímḍi	مِش هَنِمْضي	
ínta	hatímḍi	هَتِمْضي	miš hatímḍi	مِش هَتِمْضي	
ínti	hatímḍi	هَتِمْضي	miš hatímḍi	مِش هَتِمْضي	
íntu	hatímḍu	هَتِمْضوا	miš hatímḍu	مِش هَتِمْضوا	
húwwa	hayímḍi	هَيِمْضي	miš hayímḍi	مِش هَيِمْضي	
híyya	hatímḍi	هَتِمْضي	miš hatímḍi	مِش هَتِمْضي	
húmma	hayímḍu	هَيِمْضوا	miš hayímḍu	مِش هَيِمْضوا	

ínta	ímḍi	اِمْضي	ma-timḍīš	مَتِمْضيش	imperative
ínti	ímḍi	اِمْضي	ma-timḍīš	مَتِمْضيش	
íntu	ímḍu	اِمْضوا	ma-timḍūš	مَتِمْضوش	

	active		passive		
masculine	māḍi	ماضي	mámḍi	مَمْضي	participles
feminine	máḍya	ماضْيَة	mamḍíyya	مَمْضِيَّة	
plural	maḍyīn	ماضْيين	mamḍiyīn	مَمْضِيين	

verbal noun: ímḍa اِمْضا

①

إنْتَ مضيْت على باسْبورك وَلّا لِسّه؟

ínta maḍēt 3ála paspōrak wálla líssa?

Have you signed your passport yet?

②

لازِم محمّد يِمْضي العقْد بْنفْسُه.

lāzim maḥámmad yímḍi -l3aʔdᵊ b-náfsu.

Mohamed should sign the contract personally.

③

شِرْكِةْ الإدارة هِيَّ اللي بِتْراجِع و تِمْضي مُسْتخْلصات المقاوِل.

šírkit ilʔidāra híyya -lli bitrāgi3 wi tímḍi mustaxlaṣāt ilmaʔāwil.

The PMC (project management company) revises and signs the contractor's invoices.

④

كُلّ واحِد لمّا يْخلّص، هَيِمْضي في آخِر الوَرقة.

kullᵊ wāḥid lámma yxállaṣ, hayímḍi f āxir ilwáraʔa.

When you finish, you'll sign at the bottom of the paper.

⑤

متِمْضيش على وَرقة إنْتَ مِش عارِف مُحْتَواها.

ma-timḍīš 3ála wáraʔa ʔínta miš 3ārif muḥtawāha.

Don't sign a paper without knowing its contents.

❖ [1d2] **to sign**

- This verb is synonymous with وَقّع *wáqqa3.* (➲ 217.4)

240 to fill *mála* مَلَى

	affirmative		negative		
ána	*malēt*	مَليْت	*ma-malítš*	مَمَليتْش	**perfect**
íḫna	*malēna*	مَليْنا	*ma-malināš*	مَمَليناش	
ínta	*malēt*	مَليْت	*ma-malítš*	مَمَليتْش	
ínti	*malēti*	مَليْتي	*ma-malitīš*	مَمَليتيش	
íntu	*malētu*	مَليْتوا	*ma-malitūš*	مَمَليتوش	
húwwa	*mála*	مَلَى	*ma-malāš*	مَمَلاش	
híyya	*málit*	مَلِت	*ma-malítš*	مَمَلِتْش	
húmma	*málu*	مَلوا	*ma-malūš*	مَمَلوش	
ána	*ámla*	أمْلَى	*ma-mlāš*	مَمْلاش	**imperfect**
íḫna	*nímla*	نِمْلَى	*ma-nimlāš*	مَنِمْلاش	
ínta	*tímla*	تِمْلَى	*ma-timlāš*	مَتِمْلاش	
ínti	*tímli*	تِمْلي	*ma-timlīš*	مَتِمْليش	
íntu	*tímlu*	تِمْلوا	*ma-timlūš*	مَتِمْلوش	
húwwa	*yímla*	يِمْلَى	*ma-yimlāš*	مَيِمْلاش	
híyya	*tímla*	تِمْلَى	*ma-timlāš*	مَتِمْلاش	
húmma	*yímlu*	يِمْلوا	*ma-yimlūš*	مَيِمْلوش	
ána	*bámla*	بَمْلَى	*ma-bamlāš*	مَبَمْلاش	**bi-imperfect**
íḫna	*binímla*	بِنِمْلَى	*ma-bnimlāš*	مَبْنِمْلاش	
ínta	*bitímla*	بِتِمْلَى	*ma-btimlāš*	مَبْتِمْلاش	
ínti	*bitímli*	بِتِمْلي	*ma-btimlīš*	مَبْتِمْليش	
íntu	*bitímlu*	بِتِمْلوا	*ma-btimlūš*	مَبْتِمْلوش	
húwwa	*biyímla*	بِيِمْلَى	*ma-byimlāš*	مَبْيِمْلاش	
híyya	*bitímla*	بِتِمْلَى	*ma-btimlāš*	مَبْتِمْلاش	
húmma	*biyímlu*	بِيِمْلوا	*ma-byimlūš*	مَبْيِمْلوش	
ána	*hámla*	هَمْلَى	*miš hámla*	مِش هَمْلَى	**future**
íḫna	*hanímla*	هَنِمْلَى	*miš hanímla*	مِش هَنِمْلَى	
ínta	*hatímla*	هَتِمْلَى	*miš hatímla*	مِش هَتِمْلَى	
ínti	*hatímli*	هَتِمْلي	*miš hatímli*	مِش هَتِمْلي	
íntu	*hatímlu*	هَتِمْلوا	*miš hatímlu*	مِش هَتِمْلوا	
húwwa	*hayímla*	هَيِمْلَى	*miš hayímla*	مِش هَيِمْلَى	
híyya	*hatímla*	هَتِمْلَى	*miš hatímla*	مِش هَتِمْلَى	
húmma	*hayímlu*	هَيِمْلوا	*miš hayímlu*	مِش هَيِمْلوا	
ínta	*ímla*	اِمْلَى	*ma-timlāš*	مَتِمْلاش	**imperative**
ínti	*ímli*	اِمْلي	*ma-timlīš*	مَتِمْليش	
íntu	*ímlu*	اِمْلوا	*ma-timlūš*	مَتِمْلوش	

	active		passive		
masculine	*māli*	مالي	*mámli*	مَمْلي	**participles**
feminine	*málya*	مالْيَة	*mamlíyya*	مَمْلِيَّة	
plural	*malyīn*	مالْيين	*mamliyīn*	مَمْلِيين	

verbal nouns: *maly* مَلْي - *malw* مَلْو

①

الوِلاد خدوا العيدية و نِزْلوا ملوا شنْطِةْ حلَويّات.

ilwilād xádu -l3idíyya wi nízlu málu šánţit ḫalawiyyāt.

The kids took their holiday money
and bought a bag full of candy.

②

حاوْلي تمِْلي البَيانات المطْلوبة و تْقدِّميها قبْل السّاعة ٥.

ḫáwli tímli -lbayanāt ilmaţlūba wi tʔaddimīha ʔabl issā3a xámsa.

Try to fill in the required information
and submit it before five o'clock.

③

الإنْسان مبْيِمْلاش عيْنُه إلّا التُّراب.

ilʔinsān ma-byimlāš 3ēnu ʔílla -tturāb.

Nothing fills a person's eyes except dust. [i.e.
Humans are always so greedy.] (proverb)

④

حلا هتِمْلي الأزايِز عشان ناخُدْهُم معانا.

ḫála hatímla -lʔazāyiz 3ašān naxúdhum ma3āna.

Hala will fill the bottles for
us to take with us.

⑤

متِمْلاش بُقّك كِده. عيْب.

ma-timlāš búʔʔak kída. 3ēb.

Don't put so much in your
mouth. That's not proper.

❖ [1d1] **to fill; to fill in/out** (a form)

241 to forbid *mána3* مَنَع

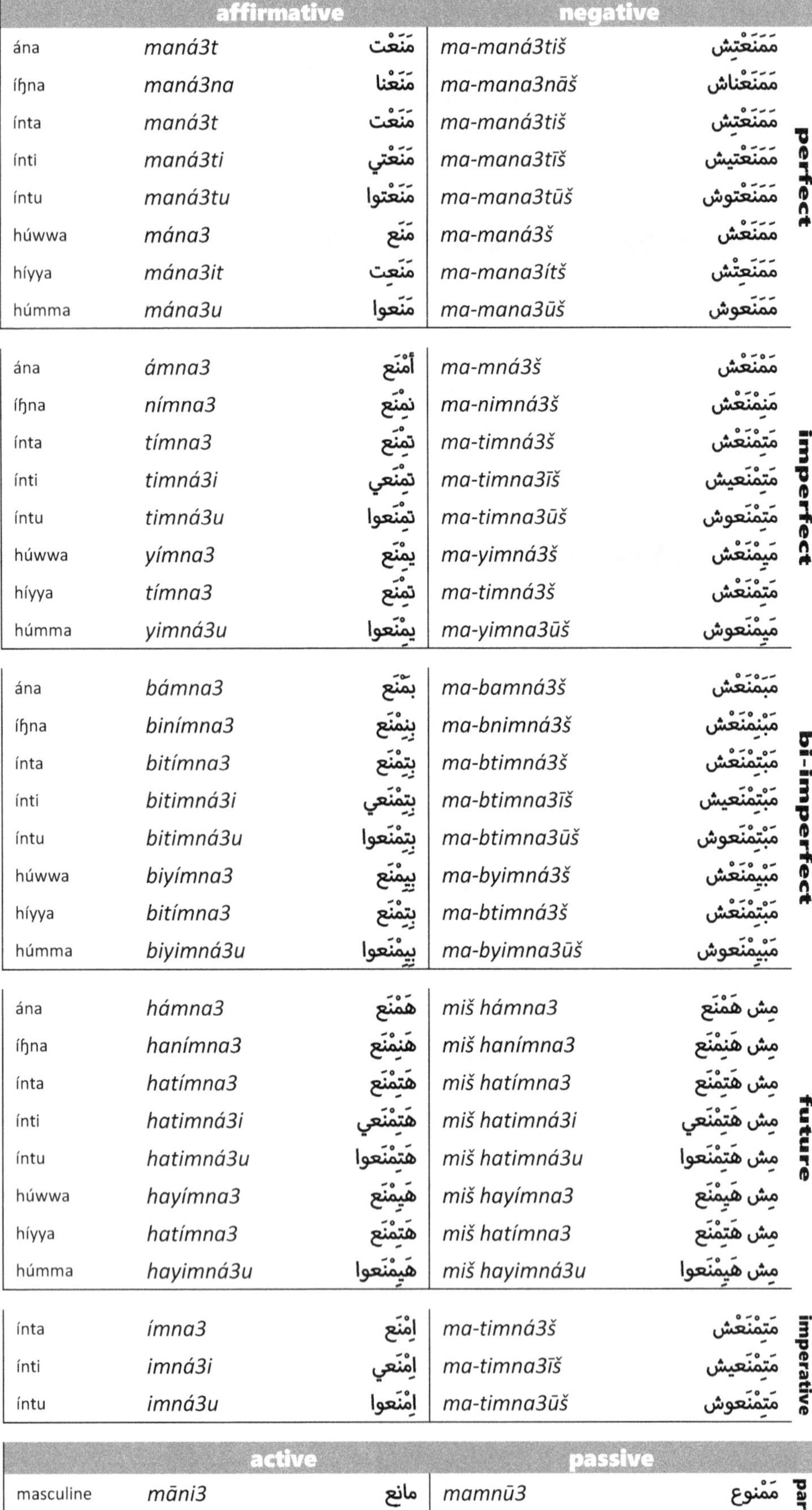

		affirmative		negative		
ána	*manáǝt*	مَنَعْت	*ma-manáǝtiš*	مَمَنَعْتِش	**perfect**
íḥna	*manáǝna*	مَنَعْنا	*ma-manaǝnāš*	مَمَنَعْناش	
ínta	*manáǝt*	مَنَعْت	*ma-manáǝtiš*	مَمَنَعْتِش	
ínti	*manáǝti*	مَنَعْتي	*ma-manaǝtīš*	مَمَنَعْتيش	
íntu	*manáǝtu*	مَنَعْتوا	*ma-manaǝtūš*	مَمَنَعْتوش	
húwwa	*mánaǝ*	مَنَع	*ma-manáǝš*	مَمَنَعْش	
híyya	*mánaǝit*	مَنَعِت	*ma-manaǝítš*	مَمَنَعِتْش	
húmma	*mánaǝu*	مَنَعوا	*ma-manaǝūš*	مَمَنَعوش	
ána	*ámnaǝ*	أَمْنَع	*ma-mnáǝš*	مَمْنَعْش	**imperfect**
íḥna	*nímnaǝ*	نِمْنَع	*ma-nimnáǝš*	مَنِمْنَعْش	
ínta	*tímnaǝ*	تِمْنَع	*ma-timnáǝš*	مَتِمْنَعْش	
ínti	*timnáǝi*	تِمْنَعي	*ma-timnaǝīš*	مَتِمْنَعيش	
íntu	*timnáǝu*	تِمْنَعوا	*ma-timnaǝūš*	مَتِمْنَعوش	
húwwa	*yímnaǝ*	يِمْنَع	*ma-yimnáǝš*	مَيِمْنَعْش	
híyya	*tímnaǝ*	تِمْنَع	*ma-timnáǝš*	مَتِمْنَعْش	
húmma	*yimnáǝu*	يِمْنَعوا	*ma-yimnaǝūš*	مَيِمْنَعوش	
ána	*bámnaǝ*	بَمْنَع	*ma-bamnáǝš*	مَبَمْنَعْش	**bi-imperfect**
íḥna	*binímnaǝ*	بِنِمْنَع	*ma-bnimnáǝš*	مَبْنِمْنَعْش	
ínta	*bitímnaǝ*	بِتِمْنَع	*ma-btimnáǝš*	مَبْتِمْنَعْش	
ínti	*bitimnáǝi*	بِتِمْنَعي	*ma-btimnaǝīš*	مَبْتِمْنَعيش	
íntu	*bitimnáǝu*	بِتِمْنَعوا	*ma-btimnaǝūš*	مَبْتِمْنَعوش	
húwwa	*biyímnaǝ*	بِيِمْنَع	*ma-byimnáǝš*	مَبْيِمْنَعْش	
híyya	*bitímnaǝ*	بِتِمْنَع	*ma-btimnáǝš*	مَبْتِمْنَعْش	
húmma	*biyimnáǝu*	بِيِمْنَعوا	*ma-byimnaǝūš*	مَبْيِمْنَعوش	
ána	*hámnaǝ*	هَمْنَع	*miš hámnaǝ*	مِش هَمْنَع	**future**
íḥna	*hanímnaǝ*	هَنِمْنَع	*miš hanímnaǝ*	مِش هَنِمْنَع	
ínta	*hatímnaǝ*	هَتِمْنَع	*miš hatímnaǝ*	مِش هَتِمْنَع	
ínti	*hatimnáǝi*	هَتِمْنَعي	*miš hatimnáǝi*	مِش هَتِمْنَعي	
íntu	*hatimnáǝu*	هَتِمْنَعوا	*miš hatimnáǝu*	مِش هَتِمْنَعوا	
húwwa	*hayímnaǝ*	هَيِمْنَع	*miš hayímnaǝ*	مِش هَيِمْنَع	
híyya	*hatímnaǝ*	هَتِمْنَع	*miš hatímnaǝ*	مِش هَتِمْنَع	
húmma	*hayimnáǝu*	هَيِمْنَعوا	*miš hayimnáǝu*	مِش هَيِمْنَعوا	
ínta	*ímnaǝ*	اِمْنَع	*ma-timnáǝš*	مَتِمْنَعْش	**imperative**
ínti	*imnáǝi*	اِمْنَعي	*ma-timnaǝīš*	مَتِمْنَعيش	
íntu	*imnáǝu*	اِمْنَعوا	*ma-timnaǝūš*	مَتِمْنَعوش	

	active		passive		
masculine	*māniǝ*	مانِع	*mamnūǝ*	مَمْنوع	**participles**
feminine	*mánǝa*	مانْعَة	*mamnūǝa*	مَمْنوعَة	
plural	*manǝīn*	مانْعين	*mamnuǝīn*	مَمْنوعين	

verbal nouns: *manǝ* مَنْع - *manaǝān* مَنَعان

①

مرْيَم منعِت إبْنها يْروح رِحْلِةْ المدْرسة عشان خافِت عليْه يْتوهْ.

máryam mána3it ibnáha yrūḫ ríḫlit ilmadrása 3ašān xāfit 3alē ytūh.

Mariam didn't let her son go on the school trip
because she was afraid that he would get lost.

②

إنْتَ ليْه تمِْنع البِنْت تْروح الحفْلة؟

ínta lē tímna3 ilbíntᵊ trūḫ ilḫáfla?

Why aren't you allowing the
girl to attend the party?

③

منال بِتِمْنع وِلادْها ياكْلوا مِ الشّارِع.

manāl bitímna3 wiládha yáklu mi -ššāri3.

Manal forbids her children from eating
street food [i.e. unhealthy fast food].

④

المُدير هَيِمْنع التّأْخير بعْد ٩ و نُصّ.

ilmudīr hayímna3 itta?xīr ba3d tís3a w nuṣṣ.

The manager will forbid
arriving later than 9:30.

⑤

متِمْنعيش الوِلاد يِشوفوا أبوهُم.

ma-timna3īš ilwilād yišūfu ?abūhum.

Don't forbid the kids from
seeing their father.

❖ [1s1] **to forbid** (someone **from**)

- This verb is followed by an object and then an imperfect verb or verbal noun.

➲ 204.5

242 to call out *nāda* نادَى

verbal noun: *minadíyya* مِنَدْيَة

	affirmative		negative		
ána	*nadēt*	نادِيْت	*ma-nadítš*	مَناديتْش	**perfect**
íḫna	*nadēna*	نادِيْنا	*ma-nadināš*	مَنادِيناش	
ínta	*nadēt*	نادِيْت	*ma-nadítš*	مَناديتْش	
ínti	*nadēti*	نادِيْتي	*ma-naditīš*	مَناديتيش	
íntu	*nadētu*	نادِيْتوا	*ma-naditūš*	مَناديتوش	
húwwa	*nāda*	نادَى	*ma-nadāš*	مَناداش	
híyya	*nādit*	نادِت	*ma-nadítš*	مَنادِتْش	
húmma	*nādu*	نادوا	*ma-nadūš*	مَنادوش	
ána	*anādi*	أنادي	*ma-nadīš*	مَناديش	**imperfect**
íḫna	*ninādi*	نِنادي	*ma-nnadīš*	مَنْناديش	
ínta	*tinādi*	تِنادي	*ma-tnadīš*	مَتْناديش	
ínti	*tinādi*	تِنادي	*ma-tnadīš*	مَتْناديش	
íntu	*tinādu*	تِنادوا	*ma-tnadūš*	مَتْنادوش	
húwwa	*yinādi*	يِنادي	*ma-ynadīš*	مَيْناديش	
híyya	*tinādi*	تِنادي	*ma-tnadīš*	مَتْناديش	
húmma	*yinādu*	يِنادوا	*ma-ynadūš*	مَيْنادوش	
ána	*banādi*	بَنادي	*ma-banadīš*	مَبَناديش	**bi-imperfect**
íḫna	*binnādi*	بِنْنادي	*ma-binnadīš*	مَبِنْناديش	
ínta	*bitnādi*	بِتْنادي	*ma-bitnadīš*	مَبِتْناديش	
ínti	*bitnādi*	بِتْنادي	*ma-bitnadīš*	مَبِتْناديش	
íntu	*bitnādu*	بِتْنادوا	*ma-bitnadūš*	مَبِتْنادوش	
húwwa	*biynādi*	بِيْنادي	*ma-biynadīš*	مَبِيْناديش	
híyya	*bitnādi*	بِتْنادي	*ma-bitnadīš*	مَبِتْناديش	
húmma	*biynādu*	بِيْنادوا	*ma-biynadūš*	مَبِيْنادوش	
ána	*hanādi*	هَنادي	*miš hanādi*	مِش هَنادي	**future**
íḫna	*hannādi*	هَنْنادي	*miš hannādi*	مِش هَنْنادي	
ínta	*hatnādi*	هَتْنادي	*miš hatnādi*	مِش هَتْنادي	
ínti	*hatnādi*	هَتْنادي	*miš hatnādi*	مِش هَتْنادي	
íntu	*hatnādu*	هَتْنادوا	*miš hatnādu*	مِش هَتْنادوا	
húwwa	*haynādi*	هَيْنادي	*miš haynādi*	مِش هَيْنادي	
híyya	*hatnādi*	هَتْنادي	*miš hatnādi*	مِش هَتْنادي	
húmma	*haynādu*	هَيْنادوا	*miš haynādu*	مِش هَيْنادوا	
ínta	*nādi*	نادي	*ma-tnadīš*	مَتْناديش	**imperative**
ínti	*nādi*	نادي	*ma-tnadīš*	مَتْناديش	
íntu	*nādu*	نادوا	*ma-tnadūš*	مَتْنادوش	

	active		passive		
masculine	*minādi*	مِنادي	*mitnādi*	مِتْنادي	**participles**
feminine	*minadíyya*	مِنادْيَة	*mitnadíyya*	مِتْنادْيَة	
plural	*minadiyīn*	مِنادِيين	*mitnadiyīn*	مِتْنادِيين	

①

المُدرِّب لمّا نادي على إسْمي، اِتْوَتّرْت و معْرِفْتِش أعْمِل وَلا حركة.

ilmudárrib lámma nāda 3ála ʔísmi, itwattárt[ə] w ma-3ríftiš á3mil wála ɦáraka.

When the coach called my name, I got nervous, and I couldn't make any move.

②

بطّل تِنادي عليّا بِصوْت عالي كِده.

báṭṭal tinādi 3aláyya b-ṣōt 3āli kída.

Stop calling me so loudly.

③

البيّاع بيْنادي عَ الطّماطِم بِصوْت حِلْو أوي.

ilbayyā3 biynādi 3a -ṭṭamāṭim bi-ṣōt ɦilw áwi.

The vendor calls out "Tomatoes!" in a very nice voice.

④

الميس هتْنادي عليْك دِلْوَقْتي.

ilmīs hatnādi 3alēk dilwáʔti.

The teacher will call on you now.

⑤

متْناديش عليْهُم. مِش هَيِصْحوا.

ma-tnadīš 3alēhum. miš hayíṣɦu.

Don't call for them. They won't wake up.

❖ [3d] **to call** (**for/on** على *3ála*)

- This verb is synonymous with ندَه *nádah.* (➲ 246)

243 to sleep nām نام

verbal noun: nōm نوْم

perfect

	affirmative		negative	
ána	nimt	نمْت	ma-nímtiš	مَنمْتش
íḫna	nímna	نمْنا	ma-nimnāš	مَنمْناش
ínta	nimt	نمْت	ma-nímtiš	مَنمْتش
ínti	nímti	نمْتي	ma-nimtīš	مَنمْتيش
íntu	nímtu	نمْتوا	ma-nimtūš	مَنمْتوش
húwwa	nām	نام	ma-námš	مَنامْش
híyya	nāmit	نامِت	ma-namítš	مَنامِتْش
húmma	nāmu	ناموا	ma-namūš	مَناموش

imperfect

	affirmative		negative	
ána	anām	أنام	ma-námš	مَنامْش
íḫna	ninām	نِنام	ma-nnámš	مَنْنامْش
ínta	tinām	تِنام	ma-tnámš	مَتْنامْش
ínti	tināmi	تِنامي	ma-tnamīš	مَتْناميش
íntu	tināmu	تِناموا	ma-tnamūš	مَتْناموش
húwwa	yinām	يِنام	ma-ynámš	مَيْنامْش
híyya	tinām	تِنام	ma-tnámš	مَتْنامْش
húmma	yināmu	يِناموا	ma-ynamūš	مَيْناموش

bi-imperfect

	affirmative		negative	
ána	banām	بَنام	ma-banámš	مَبَنامْش
íḫna	binnām	بِنْنام	ma-binnámš	مَبِنْنامْش
ínta	bitnām	بِتْنام	ma-bitnámš	مَبِتْنامْش
ínti	bitnāmi	بِتْنامي	ma-bitnamīš	مَبِتْناميش
íntu	bitnāmu	بِتْناموا	ma-bitnamūš	مَبِتْناموش
húwwa	biynām	بِيْنام	ma-biynámš	مَبِيْنامْش
híyya	bitnām	بِتْنام	ma-bitnámš	مَبِتْنامْش
húmma	biynāmu	بِيْناموا	ma-biynamūš	مَبِيْناموش

future

	affirmative		negative	
ána	hanām	هَنام	miš hanām	مِش هَنام
íḫna	hannām	هَنْنام	miš hannām	مِش هَنْنام
ínta	hatnām	هَتْنام	miš hatnām	مِش هَتْنام
ínti	hatnāmi	هَتْنامي	miš hatnāmi	مِش هَتْنامي
íntu	hatnāmu	هَتْناموا	miš hatnāmu	مِش هَتْناموا
húwwa	haynām	هَيْنام	miš haynām	مِش هَيْنام
híyya	hatnām	هَتْنام	miš hatnām	مِش هَتْنام
húmma	haynāmu	هَيْناموا	miš haynāmu	مِش هَيْناموا

imperative

	affirmative		negative	
ínta	nām	نام	ma-tnámš	مَتْنامْش
ínti	nāmi	نامي	ma-tnamīš	مَتْناميش
íntu	nāmu	ناموا	ma-tnamūš	مَتْناموش

participles

	active		passive	
masculine	nāyim	نايِم	mitnām	مِتْنام
feminine	náyma	نايْمَة	mitnāma	مِتْنامَة
plural	naymīn	نايْمين	mitnamīn	مِتْنامين

①

رِجِعْنا مِن السّفر تعْبانين و نمِنْا طول اليوْم.

rigí3na min issáfar ta3banīn wi nímna ṭūl ilyōm.

We got back from traveling tired, and we slept all day.

②

بابا بِيْشخّر لمّا يْنام.

bāba biyšáxxar lámma ynām.

Daddy snores when he's asleep.

③

أحْمد بِيْنام مِن ١٠ لـ٦.

áḥmad biynām min 3ášara li-sítta.

Ahmed sleeps from 10 to 6.

④

هتْنامي إمْتى؟

hatnāmi ímta?

When are you going to bed?

⑤

متْنامْش دِلْوَقْتي عشان تِعْرف تِنام بِاللّيْل.

ma-tnámšᵊ dilwáʔti 3ašān tí3raf tinām bi-llēl.

Don't sleep now so that you'll be able to get to sleep tonight.

❖ [1h3] **to sleep; to go to bed**

➲ 20.5, 98.6, 113.5, 136.4, 156.2, 156.6, 174.3, 183.1, 184.1, 189.8, 193.3, 201.5, 207.3, 212.2, 243.1

244 to succeed nígiḫ نجح

	affirmative		negative		
ána	nigíḫt	نِجِحْت	ma-ngíḫtiš	مَنْجِحْتِش	perfect
íḫna	nigíḫna	نِجِحْنا	ma-ngiḫnāš	مَنْجِحْناش	
ínta	nigíḫt	نِجِحْت	ma-ngíḫtiš	مَنْجِحْتِش	
ínti	nigíḫti	نِجِحْتي	ma-ngiḫtīš	مَنْجِحْتيش	
íntu	nigíḫtu	نِجِحْتوا	ma-ngiḫtūš	مَنْجِحْتوش	
húwwa	nígiḫ	نِجِح	ma-ngíḫš	مَنْجِحْش	
híyya	nígḫit	نِجْحِت	ma-nigḫítš	مَنِجْحِتْش	
húmma	nígḫu	نِجْحوا	ma-nigḫūš	مَنِجْحوش	
ána	ángaḫ	أَنْجَح	ma-ngáḫš	مَنْجَحْش	imperfect
íḫna	níngaḫ	نِنْجَح	ma-ningáḫš	مَنِنْجَحْش	
ínta	tíngaḫ	تِنْجَح	ma-tingáḫš	مَتِنْجَحْش	
ínti	tingáḫi	تِنْجَحي	ma-tingaḫīš	مَتِنْجَحيش	
íntu	tingáḫu	تِنْجَحوا	ma-tingaḫūš	مَتِنْجَحوش	
húwwa	yíngaḫ	يِنْجَح	ma-yingáḫš	مَيِنْجَحْش	
híyya	tíngaḫ	تِنْجَح	ma-tingáḫš	مَتِنْجَحْش	
húmma	yingáḫu	يِنْجَحوا	ma-yingaḫūš	مَيِنْجَحوش	
ána	bángaḫ	بَنْجَح	ma-bangáḫš	مَبَنْجَحْش	bi-imperfect
íḫna	biníngaḫ	بِنِنْجَح	ma-bningáḫš	مَبِنِنْجَحْش	
ínta	bitíngaḫ	بِتِنْجَح	ma-btingáḫš	مَبْتِنْجَحْش	
ínti	bitingáḫi	بِتِنْجَحي	ma-btingaḫīš	مَبْتِنْجَحيش	
íntu	bitingáḫu	بِتِنْجَحوا	ma-btingaḫūš	مَبْتِنْجَحوش	
húwwa	biyíngaḫ	بِيِنْجَح	ma-byingáḫš	مَبْيِنْجَحْش	
híyya	bitíngaḫ	بِتِنْجَح	ma-btingáḫš	مَبْتِنْجَحْش	
húmma	biyingáḫu	بِيِنْجَحوا	ma-byingaḫūš	مَبْيِنْجَحوش	
ána	hángaḫ	هَنْجَح	miš hángaḫ	مِش هَنْجَح	future
íḫna	haníngaḫ	هَنِنْجَح	miš haníngaḫ	مِش هَنِنْجَح	
ínta	hatíngaḫ	هَتِنْجَح	miš hatíngaḫ	مِش هَتِنْجَح	
ínti	hatingáḫi	هَتِنْجَحي	miš hatingáḫi	مِش هَتِنْجَحي	
íntu	hatingáḫu	هَتِنْجَحوا	miš hatingáḫu	مِش هَتِنْجَحوا	
húwwa	hayíngaḫ	هَيِنْجَح	miš hayíngaḫ	مِش هَيِنْجَح	
híyya	hatíngaḫ	هَتِنْجَح	miš hatíngaḫ	مِش هَتِنْجَح	
húmma	hayingáḫu	هَيِنْجَحوا	miš hayingáḫu	مِش هَيِنْجَحوا	
ínta	íngaḫ	اِنْجَح	ma-tingáḫš	مَتِنْجَحْش	imperative
ínti	ingáḫi	اِنْجَحي	ma-tingaḫīš	مَتِنْجَحيش	
íntu	ingáḫu	اِنْجَحوا	ma-tingaḫūš	مَتِنْجَحوش	

	active		passive		
masculine	nāgiḫ	ناجِح	–	–	participles
feminine	nágḫa	ناجْحَة	–	–	
plural	nagḫīn	ناجْحين	–	–	

verbal noun: nagāḫ نَجاح

①

حنان نِجْحِت إنّها تِقْنع بابا ياخُد الدَّوا.

ḫanān nigḫit innáha tíqna3 bāba yāxud iddáwa.

Hanan succeeded in convincing dad to take his medicine.

②

لازِم تِنْجح السّنة دي وَ إلّا هترْوح عليْك المِنْحة.

lāzim tíngaḫ issanādi wa ʔílla hatrūḫ 3alēk ilmínḫa.

You must succeed this year, or you'll lose the scholarship.

③

أخويا الصُّغير بيِنْجح كُلّ سنة بِالعافْيَة.

axūya -ṣṣuɣáyyar biyíngaḫ kullᵊ sána bi-l3áfya.

My little brother just barely passes [his classes] every year.

④

التّجْرِبة هتِنْجح المرّة دي بِإذْن اللّه.

ittagríba hatíngaḫ ilmarrādi bi-zn allāh.

The experiment will be successful this time, God willing.

⑤

متِنْجحْش بِالغِشّ. إبْذِل مجْهود عشان تِحِسّ بْطعْم النّجاح.

ma-tingáḫšᵊ bi-lɣišš. íbzil maghūd 3ašān tiḫíssᵊ b-ṭá3m innagāḫ.

Don't cheat to succeed. Make an effort in order to taste success.

⑥

اِبْقى قابِلْني لَوْ نِجِحْت السّنة دي.

íbʔa ʔabílni law nigíḫt issanādi.

There's no way you'll succeed this year.

❖ [1s4] **to succeed, be successful**

➲ 17.4, 34.2, 176.5, 181.4, 199.5, 211.6, 232.2

245 to regret *nídim* نِدِم

verbal noun: *nádam* نَدَم

	affirmative		negative		
ána	*nidímt*	نِدِمْت	*ma-ndímtiš*	مَنْدِمْتِش	perfect
íḫna	*nidímna*	نِدِمْنا	*ma-ndimnāš*	مَنْدِمْناش	
ínta	*nidímt*	نِدِمْت	*ma-ndímtiš*	مَنْدِمْتِش	
ínti	*nidímti*	نِدِمْتي	*ma-ndimtīš*	مَنْدِمْتيش	
íntu	*nidímtu*	نِدِمْتوا	*ma-ndimtūš*	مَنْدِمْتوش	
húwwa	*nídim*	نِدِم	*ma-ndímš*	مَنْدِمْش	
híyya	*nídmit*	نِدْمِت	*ma-nidmítš*	مَنِدْمِتْش	
húmma	*nídmu*	نِدْموا	*ma-nidmūš*	مَنِدْموش	
ána	*ándam*	أَنْدَم	*ma-ndámš*	مَنْدَمْش	imperfect
íḫna	*níndam*	نِنْدَم	*ma-nindámš*	مَنِنْدَمْش	
ínta	*tíndam*	تِنْدَم	*ma-tindámš*	مَتِنْدَمْش	
ínti	*tindámi*	تِنْدَمي	*ma-tindamīš*	مَتِنْدَميش	
íntu	*tindámu*	تِنْدَموا	*ma-tindamūš*	مَتِنْدَموش	
húwwa	*yíndam*	يِنْدَم	*ma-yindámš*	مَيِنْدَمْش	
híyya	*tíndam*	تِنْدَم	*ma-tindámš*	مَتِنْدَمْش	
húmma	*yindámu*	يِنْدَموا	*ma-yindamūš*	مَيِنْدَموش	
ána	*bándam*	بَنْدَم	*ma-bandámš*	مَبَنْدَمْش	bi-imperfect
íḫna	*biníndam*	بِنِنْدَم	*ma-bnindámš*	مَبْنِنْدَمْش	
ínta	*bitíndam*	بِتِنْدَم	*ma-btindámš*	مَبْتِنْدَمْش	
ínti	*bitindámi*	بِتِنْدَمي	*ma-btindamīš*	مَبْتِنْدَميش	
íntu	*bitindámu*	بِتِنْدَموا	*ma-btindamūš*	مَبْتِنْدَموش	
húwwa	*biyíndam*	بِيِنْدَم	*ma-byindámš*	مَبْيِنْدَمْش	
híyya	*bitíndam*	بِتِنْدَم	*ma-btindámš*	مَبْتِنْدَمْش	
húmma	*biyindámu*	بِيِنْدَموا	*ma-byindamūš*	مَبْيِنْدَموش	
ána	*hándam*	هَنْدَم	*miš hándam*	مِش هَنْدَم	future
íḫna	*haníndam*	هَنِنْدَم	*miš haníndam*	مِش هَنِنْدَم	
ínta	*hatíndam*	هَتِنْدَم	*miš hatíndam*	مِش هَتِنْدَم	
ínti	*hatindámi*	هَتِنْدَمي	*miš hatindámi*	مِش هَتِنْدَمي	
íntu	*hatindámu*	هَتِنْدَموا	*miš hatindámu*	مِش هَتِنْدَموا	
húwwa	*hayíndam*	هَيِنْدَم	*miš hayíndam*	مِش هَيِنْدَم	
híyya	*hatíndam*	هَتِنْدَم	*miš hatíndam*	مِش هَتِنْدَم	
húmma	*hayindámu*	هَيِنْدَموا	*miš hayindámu*	مِش هَيِنْدَموا	
ínta	*índam*	اِنْدَم	*ma-tindámš*	مَتِنْدَمْش	imperative
ínti	*indámi*	اِنْدَمي	*ma-tindamīš*	مَتِنْدَميش	
íntu	*indámu*	اِنْدَموا	*ma-tindamūš*	مَتِنْدَموش	

	active		passive		
masculine	*nādim / nadmān*	نادِم / نَدْمان	–	–	participles
feminine	*nádma / nadmāna*	نادْمَة / نَدْمانَة	–	–	
plural	*nadmīn / nadmanīn*	نادْمين / نَدْمانين	–	–	

①

عُمْري ما نْدِمْت على حاجة قدّ ما نْدِمْت إني سِبْت جوْزي.

3úmri ma ndímtᵊ 3ála ḫāga ʔaddᵊ ma ndímt ínni sibtᵊ gōzi.

I've never regretted anything as much as I do leaving my husband.

②

سيرين مُسْتحيل تِنْدم على حاجة عملِتْها.

sirīn mustaḫīl tíndam 3ála ḫāga 3amalítha.

Seren never regrets things she's done.

③

يُسْرا بْتِنْدم على الوَقْت اللي ضيّعِتُه معَ المُغفّل ده.

yúsra btíndam 3ála -lwaʔt ílli ḍayyá3itu má3a -lmuɣáffal da.

Yousra is regretting the time she wasted with that idiot.

④

مِشيْل هَيِنْدم على تصرُّفاتُه دي قُريِّب.

mišēl hayíndam 3ála taṣarrufātu di ʔuráyyib.

Michel will soon regret these actions.

⑤

متِنْدمْش على حاجة فاتِت. اِتْعلِّم مِنْها و اِتْحرّك.

ma-tindámšᵊ 3ála ḫāga fātit. it3állim mínha w itḫárrak.

Don't regret the past. Learn from it and move on.

❖ [1s4] **to regret** (على *3ála*)

➲ 19.7, 43.5, 70.5

246 to call out nádah نَدَه

perfect

	affirmative		negative	
ána	nadáht	نَدَهْت	ma-nadáhtiš	مَنَدَهْتِش
íḫna	nadáhna	نَدَهْنا	ma-nadahnāš	مَنَدَهْناش
ínta	nadáht	نَدَهْت	ma-nadáhtiš	مَنَدَهْتِش
ínti	nadáhti	نَدَهْتي	ma-nadahtīš	مَنَدَهْتيش
íntu	nadáhtu	نَدَهْتوا	ma-nadahtūš	مَنَدَهْتوش
húwwa	nádah	نَدَه	ma-nadáhš	مَنَدَهْش
híyya	nádahit	نَدَهِت	ma-nadahítš	مَنَدَهِتْش
húmma	nádahu	نَدَهوا	ma-nadahūš	مَنَدَهوش

imperfect

	affirmative		negative	
ána	ándah	أَنْدَه	ma-ndáhš	مَنْدَهْش
íḫna	níndah	نِنْدَه	ma-nindáhš	مَنِنْدَهْش
ínta	tíndah	تِنْدَه	ma-tindáhš	مَتِنْدَهْش
ínti	tindáhi	تِنْدَهي	ma-tindahīš	مَتِنْدَهيش
íntu	tindáhu	تِنْدَهوا	ma-tindahūš	مَتِنْدَهوش
húwwa	yíndah	يِنْدَه	ma-yindáhš	مَيِنْدَهْش
híyya	tíndah	تِنْدَه	ma-tindáhš	مَتِنْدَهْش
húmma	yindáhu	يِنْدَهوا	ma-yindahūš	مَيِنْدَهوش

bi-imperfect

	affirmative		negative	
ána	bándah	بَنْدَه	ma-bandáhš	مَبَنْدَهْش
íḫna	biníndah	بِنِنْدَه	ma-bnindáhš	مَبْنِنْدَهْش
ínta	bitíndah	بِتِنْدَه	ma-btindáhš	مَبْتِنْدَهْش
ínti	bitindáhi	بِتِنْدَهي	ma-btindahīš	مَبْتِنْدَهيش
íntu	bitindáhu	بِتِنْدَهوا	ma-btindahūš	مَبْتِنْدَهوش
húwwa	biyíndah	بِيِنْدَه	ma-byindáhš	مَبْيِنْدَهْش
híyya	bitíndah	بِتِنْدَه	ma-btindáhš	مَبْتِنْدَهْش
húmma	biyindáhu	بِيِنْدَهوا	ma-byindahūš	مَبْيِنْدَهوش

future

	affirmative		negative	
ána	hándah	هَنْدَه	miš hándah	مِش هَنْدَه
íḫna	haníndah	هَنِنْدَه	miš haníndah	مِش هَنِنْدَه
ínta	hatíndah	هَتِنْدَه	miš hatíndah	مِش هَتِنْدَه
ínti	hatindáhi	هَتِنْدَهي	miš hatindáhi	مِش هَتِنْدَهي
íntu	hatindáhu	هَتِنْدَهوا	miš hatindáhu	مِش هَتِنْدَهوا
húwwa	hayíndah	هَيِنْدَه	miš hayíndah	مِش هَيِنْدَه
híyya	hatíndah	هَتِنْدَه	miš hatíndah	مِش هَتِنْدَه
húmma	hayindáhu	هَيِنْدَهوا	miš hayindáhu	مِش هَيِنْدَهوا

imperative

	affirmative		negative	
ínta	índah	اِنْدَه	ma-tindáhš	مَتِنْدَهْش
ínti	indáhi	اِنْدَهي	ma-tindahīš	مَتِنْدَهيش
íntu	indáhu	اِنْدَهوا	ma-tindahūš	مَتِنْدَهوش

participles

	active		passive	
masculine	nādih	نادِه	mandūh	مَنْدوه
feminine	nádha	نادْهَة	mandūha	مَنْدوهَة
plural	nadhīn	نادْهين	manduhīn	مَنْدوهين

verbal noun: *nadh* نَدْه

①

المُدرِّب لمّا ندَهْ على إسْمى، اِتْوَتّرْت و معْرِفْتِش أعْمِل وَلا حركة.

ilmudárrib lámma nádah 3ála ʔísmi, itwattártᵊ w ma-3ríftiš á3mil wála ɦáraka.

When the coach called my name, I got nervous, and I couldn't move.

②

بطّل تِنْدَهْ عليّا بْصوْت عالي كِده.

báṭṭal tíndah 3aláyya b-ṣōt 3āli kída.

Stop calling me so loudly.

③

الوَلد بيِنْدَهْ على أخوه كُلّ شْوَيّة.

ilwálad biyíndah 3ála ʔaxū kullᵊ šwáyya.

The boy calls out to his brother every so often.

④

الميس هتِنْدَهْ عليّا بعْديك.

ilmīs hatíndah 3aláyya ba3dīk.

The teacher will call my name after yours.

⑤

متِنْدهْش عليْهُم. مِش هَيِسْمعوك.

ma-tindáhšᵊ 3alēhum. miš hayisma3ūk.

Don't call for them. They won't hear you.

❖ [1s1] **to call** (**for/on** على *3ála*)

- This verb is synonymous with نادى *nāda.* (➲ 242)

247 to make nervous *nárfiz* نَرْفِز

verbal noun: *narfáza* نَرْفَزَة

perfect

	affirmative		negative	
ána	*narfízt*	نَرْفِزْت	*ma-narfíztiš*	مَنرْفِزْتِش
íḫna	*narfízna*	نَرْفِزْنا	*ma-narfiznāš*	مَنرْفِزْناش
ínta	*narfízt*	نَرْفِزْت	*ma-narfíztiš*	مَنرْفِزْتِش
ínti	*narfízti*	نَرْفِزْتي	*ma-narfiztīš*	مَنرْفِزْتيش
íntu	*narfíztu*	نَرْفِزْتوا	*ma-narfiztūš*	مَنرْفِزْتوش
húwwa	*nárfiz*	نَرْفِز	*ma-narfízš*	مَنرْفِزْش
híyya	*narfízit*	نَرْفِزِت	*ma-narfizítš*	مَنرْفِزِتْش
húmma	*narfízu*	نَرْفِزوا	*ma-narfizūš*	مَنرْفِزوش

imperfect

	affirmative		negative	
ána	*anárfiz*	أَنَرْفِز	*ma-narfízš*	مَنرْفِزْش
íḫna	*ninárfiz*	نِنَرْفِز	*ma-nnarfízš*	مَنّرْفِزْش
ínta	*tinárfiz*	تِنَرْفِز	*ma-tnarfízš*	مَتْنرْفِزْش
ínti	*tinarfízi*	تِنَرْفِزي	*ma-tnarfizīš*	مَتْنرْفِزيش
íntu	*tinarfízu*	تِنَرْفِزوا	*ma-tnarfizūš*	مَتْنرْفِزوش
húwwa	*yinárfiz*	يِنَرْفِز	*ma-ynarfízš*	مَيْنرْفِزْش
híyya	*tinárfiz*	تِنَرْفِز	*ma-tnarfízš*	مَتْنرْفِزْش
húmma	*yinarfízu*	يِنَرْفِزوا	*ma-ynarfizūš*	مَيْنرْفِزوش

bi-imperfect

	affirmative		negative	
ána	*banárfiz*	بَنَرْفِز	*ma-banarfízš*	مَبَنرْفِزْش
íḫna	*binnárfiz*	بِنْنَرْفِز	*ma-binnarfízš*	مَبِنْنرْفِزْش
ínta	*bitnárfiz*	بِتْنَرْفِز	*ma-bitnarfízš*	مَبِتْنرْفِزْش
ínti	*bitnarfízi*	بِتْنَرْفِزي	*ma-bitnarfizīš*	مَبِتْنرْفِزيش
íntu	*bitnarfízu*	بِتْنَرْفِزوا	*ma-bitnarfizūš*	مَبِتْنرْفِزوش
húwwa	*biynárfiz*	بِيْنَرْفِز	*ma-biynarfízš*	مَبِيْنرْفِزْش
híyya	*bitnárfiz*	بِتْنَرْفِز	*ma-bitnarfízš*	مَبِتْنرْفِزْش
húmma	*biynarfízu*	بِيْنَرْفِزوا	*ma-biynarfizūš*	مَبِيْنرْفِزوش

future

	affirmative		negative	
ána	*hanárfiz*	هَنَرْفِز	*miš hanárfiz*	مِش هَنَرْفِز
íḫna	*hannárfiz*	هَنّنَرْفِز	*miš hannárfiz*	مِش هَنّنَرْفِز
ínta	*hatnárfiz*	هَتْنَرْفِز	*miš hatnárfiz*	مِش هَتْنَرْفِز
ínti	*hatnarfízi*	هَتْنَرْفِزي	*miš hatnarfízi*	مِش هَتْنَرْفِزي
íntu	*hatnarfízu*	هَتْنَرْفِزوا	*miš hatnarfízu*	مِش هَتْنَرْفِزوا
húwwa	*haynárfiz*	هَيْنَرْفِز	*miš haynárfiz*	مِش هَيْنَرْفِز
híyya	*hatnárfiz*	هَتْنَرْفِز	*miš hatnárfiz*	مِش هَتْنَرْفِز
húmma	*haynarfízu*	هَيْنَرْفِزوا	*miš haynarfízu*	مِش هَيْنَرْفِزوا

imperative

	affirmative		negative	
ínta	*nárfiz*	نَرْفِز	*ma-tnarfízš*	مَتْنرْفِزْش
ínti	*narfízi*	نَرْفِزي	*ma-tnarfizīš*	مَتْنرْفِزيش
íntu	*narfízu*	نَرْفِزوا	*ma-tnarfizūš*	مَتْنرْفِزوش

participles

	active		passive	
masculine	*minárfiz*	مِنَرْفِز	*mitnárfiz*	مِتْنَرْفِز
feminine	*minarfíza*	مِنَرْفِزَة	*mitnarfíza*	مِتْنَرْفِزَة
plural	*minarfizīn*	مِنَرْفِزين	*mitnarfizīn*	مِتْنَرْفِزين

①

البيّاع اِتْكلِّم بِسخافة لْحدّ ما نرْفِزْني.

ilbayyā3 itkállim bi-saxāfa l-ḩaddᵊ ma narfízni.

The salesman spoke ludicrously until he made me mad.

②

كُلّ يوْم الوِلاد بِنرْفِزوني عَ الصُّبْح.

kullᵊ yōm ilwilād yinarfizūni 3a -ṣṣubḩ.

Every morning, the boys get on my nerves.

③

كلامك ده مبِيْنرْفِزْنيش ، وَفّرْه لْنفْسك.

kalāmak da ma-biynarfiznīš, waffáru l-náfsak.

Your words don't make me mad, so keep them to yourself.

④

السِّواقة في مصْر متْناسِبْش مامْتك. هتْنرْفِزْها و تِتْعِبْها.

issiwāʔa f maṣr, ma-tnasíbšᵊ mámtak. hatnarfízha wi tit3íbha.

Driving in Egypt isn't suitable for your mom. It'll make her nervous and tired.

⑤

متْنرْفِزْنيش أكْتر مِن كِده. هتْعلّيلي الضّغْط.

ma-tnarfiznīš áktar min kída. hat3allīli -ḑḑaɣţ.

Don't aggravate me further. You'll increase my blood pressure.

❖ [11s1] **to make nervous; to aggravate, anger, get on one's nerves**

248 to descend *nízil* نِزِل

verbal noun: *nuzūl* نزول

perfect

	affirmative		negative	
ána	*nizílt*	نِزِلْت	*ma-nzíltiš*	مَنْزِلْتِش
íḥna	*nizílna*	نِزِلْنا	*ma-nzilnāš*	مَنْزِلْناش
ínta	*nizílt*	نِزِلْت	*ma-nzíltiš*	مَنْزِلْتِش
ínti	*nizílti*	نِزِلْتي	*ma-nziltīš*	مَنْزِلْتيش
íntu	*nizíltu*	نِزِلْتوا	*ma-nziltūš*	مَنْزِلْتوش
húwwa	*nízil*	نِزِل	*ma-nzílš*	مَنْزِلْش
híyya	*nízlit*	نِزْلِت	*ma-nizlítš*	مَنِزْلِتْش
húmma	*nízlu*	نِزْلوا	*ma-nizlūš*	مَنِزْلوش

imperfect

	affirmative		negative	
ána	*ánzil*	أنْزِل	*ma-nzílš*	مَنْزِلْش
íḥna	*nínzil*	نِنْزِل	*ma-ninzílš*	مَنِنْزِلْش
ínta	*tínzil*	تِنْزِل	*ma-tinzílš*	مَتِنْزِلْش
ínti	*tinzíli*	تِنْزِلي	*ma-tinzilīš*	مَتِنْزِليش
íntu	*tinzílu*	تِنْزِلوا	*ma-tinzilūš*	مَتِنْزِلوش
húwwa	*yínzil*	يِنْزِل	*ma-yinzílš*	مَيِنْزِلْش
híyya	*tínzil*	تِنْزِل	*ma-tinzílš*	مَتِنْزِلْش
húmma	*yinzílu*	يِنْزِلوا	*ma-yinzilūš*	مَيِنْزِلوش

bi-imperfect

	affirmative		negative	
ána	*bánzil*	بَنْزِل	*ma-banzílš*	مَبَنْزِلْش
íḥna	*binínzil*	بِنِنْزِل	*ma-bninzílš*	مَبْنِنْزِلْش
ínta	*bitínzil*	بِتِنْزِل	*ma-btinzílš*	مَبْتِنْزِلْش
ínti	*bitinzíli*	بِتِنْزِلي	*ma-btinzilīš*	مَبْتِنْزِليش
íntu	*bitinzílu*	بِتِنْزِلوا	*ma-btinzilūš*	مَبْتِنْزِلوش
húwwa	*biyínzil*	بِيِنْزِل	*ma-byinzílš*	مَبْيِنْزِلْش
híyya	*bitínzil*	بِتِنْزِل	*ma-btinzílš*	مَبْتِنْزِلْش
húmma	*biyinzílu*	بِيِنْزِلوا	*ma-byinzilūš*	مَبْيِنْزِلوش

future

	affirmative		negative	
ána	*hánzil*	هَنْزِل	*miš hánzil*	مِش هَنْزِل
íḥna	*hanínzil*	هَنِنْزِل	*miš hanínzil*	مِش هَنِنْزِل
ínta	*hatínzil*	هَتِنْزِل	*miš hatínzil*	مِش هَتِنْزِل
ínti	*hatinzíli*	هَتِنْزِلي	*miš hatinzíli*	مِش هَتِنْزِلي
íntu	*hatinzílu*	هَتِنْزِلوا	*miš hatinzílu*	مِش هَتِنْزِلوا
húwwa	*hayínzil*	هَيِنْزِل	*miš hayínzil*	مِش هَيِنْزِل
híyya	*hatínzil*	هَتِنْزِل	*miš hatínzil*	مِش هَتِنْزِل
húmma	*hayinzílu*	هَيِنْزِلوا	*miš hayinzílu*	مِش هَيِنْزِلوا

imperative

	affirmative		negative	
ínta	*ínzil*	اِنْزِل	*ma-tinzílš*	مَتِنْزِلْش
ínti	*inzíli*	اِنْزِلي	*ma-tinzilīš*	مَتِنْزِليش
íntu	*inzílu*	اِنْزِلوا	*ma-tinzilūš*	مَتِنْزِلوش

participles

	active		passive	
masculine	*nāzil*	نازِل	–	–
feminine	*názla*	نازْلَة	–	–
plural	*nazlīn*	نازْلين	–	–

①

أَنْدْرو طِلِع اِتْغدّى و نِزِل على طول.

ándru ţíli3 ityádda w nízil 3ála ţūl.

Andrew arrived, had lunch, then went out immediately after.

②

إنْتَ ناوي تِنْزِل إمْتى؟

ínta nāwi tínzil ímta?

When are you going to come out?

③

بِتِنْزِلي الجيم السّاعة كام؟

bitinzíli -lžīm issā3a kām?

When do you go to the gym?

④

هتِنْزِلوا البحْر وَلّا لأ؟

hatinzílu -lbaħrᵊ wálla la??

Are you going to the sea [i.e. beach] or not?

⑤

متِنْزِلْش في الحرّ ده يا بابا.

ma-tinzílšᵊ fi -lħarrᵊ da ya bāba.

Don't go out in this hot weather, dad.

❖ [1s5] **to descend; to go out, leave the house; to be released, be published**

➲ 22.5, 42.1, 48.1, 50.3, 55.1, 57.5, 74.1, 74.6, 88.6, 126.2, 159.4, 173.1, 186.4, 240.1, 251.1

249 to take down *názzil* نزّل

		affirmative		negative		
ána	*nazzílt*	نزّلت	*ma-nazzíltiš*	منزّلتش	perfect
íḥna	*nazzílna*	نزّلنا	*ma-nazzilnāš*	منزّلناش	
ínta	*nazzílt*	نزّلت	*ma-nazzíltiš*	منزّلتش	
ínti	*nazzílti*	نزّلتي	*ma-nazziltīš*	منزّلتيش	
íntu	*nazzíltu*	نزّلتوا	*ma-nazziltūš*	منزّلتوش	
húwwa	*názzil*	نزّل	*ma-nazzílš*	منزّلش	
híyya	*nazzílit*	نزّلت	*ma-nazzilítš*	منزّلتش	
húmma	*nazzílu*	نزّلوا	*ma-nazzilūš*	منزّلوش	
ána	*anázzil*	أنزّل	*ma-nazzílš*	منزّلش	imperfect
íḥna	*ninázzil*	ننزّل	*ma-nnazzílš*	مننزّلش	
ínta	*tinázzil*	تنزّل	*ma-tnazzílš*	متنزّلش	
ínti	*tinazzíli*	تنزّلي	*ma-tnazzilīš*	متنزّليش	
íntu	*tinazzílu*	تنزّلوا	*ma-tnazzilūš*	متنزّلوش	
húwwa	*yinázzil*	ينزّل	*ma-ynazzílš*	مينزّلش	
híyya	*tinázzil*	تنزّل	*ma-tnazzílš*	متنزّلش	
húmma	*yinazzílu*	ينزّلوا	*ma-ynazzilūš*	مينزّلوش	
ána	*banázzil*	بنزّل	*ma-banazzílš*	مبنزّلش	bi-imperfect
íḥna	*binnázzil*	بننزّل	*ma-binnazzílš*	مبننزّلش	
ínta	*bitnázzil*	بتنزّل	*ma-bitnazzílš*	مبتنزّلش	
ínti	*bitnazzíli*	بتنزّلي	*ma-bitnazzilīš*	مبتنزّليش	
íntu	*bitnazzílu*	بتنزّلوا	*ma-bitnazzilūš*	مبتنزّلوش	
húwwa	*biynázzil*	بينزّل	*ma-biynazzílš*	مبينزّلش	
híyya	*bitnázzil*	بتنزّل	*ma-bitnazzílš*	مبتنزّلش	
húmma	*biynazzílu*	بينزّلوا	*ma-biynazzilūš*	مبينزّلوش	
ána	*hanázzil*	هنزّل	*miš hanázzil*	مش هنزّل	future
íḥna	*hannázzil*	هننزّل	*miš hannázzil*	مش هننزّل	
ínta	*hatnázzil*	هتنزّل	*miš hatnázzil*	مش هتنزّل	
ínti	*hatnazzíli*	هتنزّلي	*miš hatnazzíli*	مش هتنزّلي	
íntu	*hatnazzílu*	هتنزّلوا	*miš hatnazzílu*	مش هتنزّلوا	
húwwa	*haynázzil*	هينزّل	*miš haynázzil*	مش هينزّل	
híyya	*hatnázzil*	هتنزّل	*miš hatnázzil*	مش هتنزّل	
húmma	*haynazzílu*	هينزّلوا	*miš haynazzílu*	مش هينزّلوا	
ínta	*názzil*	نزّل	*ma-tnazzílš*	متنزّلش	imperative
ínti	*nazzíli*	نزّلي	*ma-tnazzilīš*	متنزّليش	
íntu	*nazzílu*	نزّلوا	*ma-tnazzilūš*	متنزّلوش	

	active		passive		
masculine	*minázzil*	منزّل	*mitnázzil*	متنزّل	participles
feminine	*minazzíla*	منزّلة	*mitnazzíla*	متنزّلة	
plural	*minazzilīn*	منزّلين	*mitnazzilīn*	متنزّلين	

verbal noun: *tanzīl* تنزيل

①

أخوك منزِّلْش الكلْب ليْه؟ ده دوْره النّهارْده.

axūk ma-nazzílš ilkálbᵊ lē? da dōru -nnahárda.

Why didn't your brother take the dog out? It's his turn today.

②

مِحْتاجة حدّ يْنزِّل الكراتين دي معايا.

miḫtāga ḫaddᵊ ynázzil ilkaratīn di ma3āya.

I need someone to take those boxes downstairs with me.

③

بنزِّل حِتّةْ فيلْم. هَيِعْجبك أوي.

banázzil ḫíttit film. hayi3gábak áwi.

I'm downloading an amazing movie. You'll like it.

④

مِن فضْلك، إنْتو هتْنزِّلوا التّشْكيلة الشِّتَوي إمْتى؟

min fáḍlak, íntu hatnazzílu -ttaškīla -ššítawi ímta?

Excuse me, when will you put out the winter collection?

⑤

متْنزِّلوش حاجة إلّا أمّا العربية تِوْصل.

ma-tnazzilūš ḫāga ʔílla ʔámma -l3arabíyya tíwṣal.

Don't take these things down until the truck arrives.

❖ [2s1] **to take down, take downstairs; to take out** (of the house)**; to release, publish**

➲ 15.7

250 to forget *nísi* نسي

	affirmative		negative		
ána	*nisīt*	نِسيت	*ma-nsítš*	مَنْسيتْش	**perfect**
íḥna	*nisīna*	نِسينا	*ma-nsināš*	مَنْسيناش	
ínta	*nisīt*	نِسيت	*ma-nsítš*	مَنْسيتْش	
ínti	*nisīti*	نِسيتي	*ma-nsitīš*	مَنْسيتيش	
íntu	*nisītu*	نِسيتوا	*ma-nsitūš*	مَنْسيتوش	
húwwa	*nísi*	نِسي	*ma-nsīš*	مَنْسيش	
híyya	*nísyit*	نِسْيِت	*ma-nisyítš*	مَنِسْيِتْش	
húmma	*nísyu*	نِسْيوا	*ma-nisyūš*	مَنِسْيوش	
ána	*ánsa*	أنْسَى	*ma-nsāš*	مَنْساش	**imperfect**
íḥna	*nínsa*	نِنْسَى	*ma-ninsāš*	مَنِنْساش	
ínta	*tínsa*	تِنْسَى	*ma-tinsāš*	مَتِنْساش	
ínti	*tínsi*	تِنْسي	*ma-tinsīš*	مَتِنْسيش	
íntu	*tínsu*	تِنْسوا	*ma-tinsūš*	مَتِنْسوش	
húwwa	*yínsa*	يِنْسَى	*ma-yinsāš*	مَيِنْساش	
híyya	*tínsa*	تِنْسَى	*ma-tinsāš*	مَتِنْساش	
húmma	*yínsu*	يِنْسوا	*ma-yinsūš*	مَيِنْسوش	
ána	*bánsa*	بَنْسَى	*ma-bansāš*	مَبَنْساش	**bi-imperfect**
íḥna	*binínsa*	بِنِنْسَى	*ma-bninsāš*	مَبْنِنْساش	
ínta	*bitínsa*	بِتِنْسَى	*ma-btinsāš*	مَبْتِنْساش	
ínti	*bitínsi*	بِتِنْسي	*ma-btinsīš*	مَبْتِنْسيش	
íntu	*bitínsu*	بِتِنْسوا	*ma-btinsūš*	مَبْتِنْسوش	
húwwa	*biyínsa*	بِيِنْسَى	*ma-byinsāš*	مَبْيِنْساش	
híyya	*bitínsa*	بِتِنْسَى	*ma-btinsāš*	مَبْتِنْساش	
húmma	*biyínsu*	بِيِنْسوا	*ma-byinsūš*	مَبْيِنْسوش	
ána	*hánsa*	هَنْسَى	*miš hánsa*	مِش هَنْسَى	**future**
íḥna	*hanínsa*	هَنِنْسَى	*miš hanínsa*	مِش هَنِنْسَى	
ínta	*hatínsa*	هَتِنْسَى	*miš hatínsa*	مِش هَتِنْسَى	
ínti	*hatínsi*	هَتِنْسي	*miš hatínsi*	مِش هَتِنْسي	
íntu	*hatínsu*	هَتِنْسوا	*miš hatínsu*	مِش هَتِنْسوا	
húwwa	*hayínsa*	هَيِنْسَى	*miš hayínsa*	مِش هَيِنْسَى	
híyya	*hatínsa*	هَتِنْسَى	*miš hatínsa*	مِش هَتِنْسَى	
húmma	*hayínsu*	هَيِنْسوا	*miš hayínsu*	مِش هَيِنْسوا	
ínta	*ínsa*	اِنْسَى	*ma-tinsāš*	مَتِنْساش	**imperative**
ínti	*ínsi*	اِنْسي	*ma-tinsīš*	مَتِنْسيش	
íntu	*ínsu*	اِنْسوا	*ma-tinsūš*	مَتِنْسوش	

	active		passive		
masculine	*nāsi*	ناسي	*mánsi*	مَنْسي	**participles**
feminine	*násya*	ناسْيَة	*mansíyya*	مَنْسِيَّة	
plural	*nasyīn*	ناسْيين	*mansiyīn*	مَنْسِيين	

verbal noun: *nisyān* نِسْيان

①

أنا منْسيتْش عيد ميلادك بسّ كُنْت عامِلّك مُفاجْأة.

ána ma-nsítš[ə] 3īd milādak bass[ə] kunt[ə] 3amíllak mufágʔa.

I didn't forget your birthday. I was making a surprise for you.

②

حاوِل تِنْسى المَوْضوع ده و بطّل تِنكِّد على نفْسك.

ḫāwil tínsa -lmawḍū3 da wi báṭṭal tinákkid 3ála náfsak.

Try to forget that issue and stop making yourself miserable.

③

أنا بقيْت بنْسى جامِد أوي.

ána baʔēt bánsa gāmid áwi.

I've started to forget so much.

④

إنْتَ مِش هتِنْسي المَوْضوع ده بقى؟

ínta miš hatínsa -lmawḍū3 da báʔa?

Won't you just drop it? [i.e. stop bringing up the issue]

⑤

متِنْساش تِجيب هدية لِمْراتك النّهارْده.

ma-tinsāš tigīb hadíyya li-mrātak innahárda.

Don't forget to bring a present to your wife today.

❖ [1d4] **to forget**

- This verb can be followed by an imperfect verb. (➲ 250.5)

➲ 110.5, 167.11, 187.9

251 to clean náḍḍaf نضّف

verbal noun: tanḍīf تنضيف

perfect

	affirmative		negative	
ána	naḍḍáft	نَضَّفْت	ma-naḍḍáftiš	مَنَضَّفْتِش
íḫna	naḍḍáfna	نَضَّفْنا	ma-naḍḍafnāš	مَنَضَّفْناش
ínta	naḍḍáft	نَضَّفْت	ma-naḍḍáftiš	مَنَضَّفْتِش
ínti	naḍḍáfti	نَضَّفْتي	ma-naḍḍaftīš	مَنَضَّفْتيش
íntu	naḍḍáftu	نَضَّفْتوا	ma-naḍḍaftūš	مَنَضَّفْتوش
húwwa	náḍḍaf	نَضَّف	ma-naḍḍáfš	مَنَضَّفْش
híyya	naḍḍáfit	نَضَّفِت	ma-naḍḍafítš	مَنَضَّفِتْش
húmma	naḍḍáfu	نَضَّفوا	ma-naḍḍafūš	مَنَضَّفوش

imperfect

	affirmative		negative	
ána	anáḍḍaf	أنَضّف	ma-naḍḍáfš	مَنَضَّفْش
íḫna	nináḍḍaf	نِنَضّف	ma-nnaḍḍáfš	مَنْنَضَّفْش
ínta	tináḍḍaf	تِنَضّف	ma-tnaḍḍáfš	مَتْنَضَّفْش
ínti	tinaḍḍáfi	تِنَضّفي	ma-tnaḍḍafīš	مَتْنَضّفيش
íntu	tinaḍḍáfu	تِنَضّفوا	ma-tnaḍḍafūš	مَتْنَضّفوش
húwwa	yináḍḍaf	يِنَضّف	ma-ynaḍḍáfš	مَيْنَضَّفْش
híyya	tináḍḍaf	تِنَضّف	ma-tnaḍḍáfš	مَتْنَضَّفْش
húmma	yinaḍḍáfu	يِنَضّفوا	ma-ynaḍḍafūš	مَيْنَضّفوش

bi-imperfect

	affirmative		negative	
ána	banáḍḍaf	بَنَضّف	ma-banaḍḍáfš	مَبَنَضَّفْش
íḫna	binnáḍḍaf	بِنْنَضّف	ma-binnaḍḍáfš	مَبِنْنَضَّفْش
ínta	bitnáḍḍaf	بِتْنَضّف	ma-bitnaḍḍáfš	مَبِتْنَضَّفْش
ínti	bitnaḍḍáfi	بِتْنَضّفي	ma-bitnaḍḍafīš	مَبِتْنَضّفيش
íntu	bitnaḍḍáfu	بِتْنَضّفوا	ma-bitnaḍḍafūš	مَبِتْنَضّفوش
húwwa	biynáḍḍaf	بِيْنَضّف	ma-biynaḍḍáfš	مَبِيْنَضَّفْش
híyya	bitnáḍḍaf	بِتْنَضّف	ma-bitnaḍḍáfš	مَبِتْنَضَّفْش
húmma	biynaḍḍáfu	بِيْنَضّفوا	ma-biynaḍḍafūš	مَبِيْنَضّفوش

future

	affirmative		negative	
ána	hanáḍḍaf	هَنَضّف	miš hanáḍḍaf	مِش هَنَضّف
íḫna	hannáḍḍaf	هَنْنَضّف	miš hannáḍḍaf	مِش هَنْنَضّف
ínta	hatnáḍḍaf	هَتْنَضّف	miš hatnáḍḍaf	مِش هَتْنَضّف
ínti	hatnaḍḍáfi	هَتْنَضّفي	miš hatnaḍḍáfi	مِش هَتْنَضّفي
íntu	hatnaḍḍáfu	هَتْنَضّفوا	miš hatnaḍḍáfu	مِش هَتْنَضّفوا
húwwa	haynáḍḍaf	هَيْنَضّف	miš haynáḍḍaf	مِش هَيْنَضّف
híyya	hatnáḍḍaf	هَتْنَضّف	miš hatnáḍḍaf	مِش هَتْنَضّف
húmma	haynaḍḍáfu	هَيْنَضّفوا	miš haynaḍḍáfu	مِش هَيْنَضّفوا

imperative

	affirmative		negative	
ínta	náḍḍaf	نَضّف	ma-tnaḍḍáfš	مَتْنَضَّفْش
ínti	naḍḍáfi	نَضّفي	ma-tnaḍḍafīš	مَتْنَضّفيش
íntu	naḍḍáfu	نَضّفوا	ma-tnaḍḍafūš	مَتْنَضّفوش

participles

	active		passive	
masculine	mináḍḍaf	مِنَضّف	mitnáḍḍaf	مِتْنَضّف
feminine	minaḍḍáfa	مِنَضّفَة	mitnaḍḍáfa	مِتْنَضّفَة
plural	minaḍḍafīn	مِنَضّفين	mitnaḍḍafīn	مِتْنَضّفين

①

منضّفْتوش البيْت قبْل ما تِنْزِلوا ليْه يا هَوانِم؟

ma-naḍḍaftūš ilbēt ʔablᵊ ma tinzílu lē ya hawānim?

Why didn't you clean the house
before going out, princesses?

②

البنات عنْدي لازِم يِنضّفوا البيْت كُلّ يوْم.

ilbanāt 3ándi lāzim yinaḍḍáfu -lbēt kullᵊ yōm.

My girls have to clean the house every day.

③

مبِتْنضّفْش أوضْتك ليْه؟

ma-bitnaḍḍáfš úḍtak lē?

Why don't you clean your room?

④

أمينة هتْنضّفْلي المطْبخ و الحمّام.

amīna hatnaḍḍáfli -lmáṭbax w ilḩammām.

Amena will clean the kitchen
and bathroom for me.

⑤

نضّفوا الشّارِع! ليْه سايْبينُه كِده؟

naḍḍáfu -ššāri3! lē saybīnu kída?

Clean the street. Why have
you left it like this?

❖ [2s2] **to clean**

- This verb can also be spelled with ظ, as in Modern Standard Arabic, although the pronunciation is always with *ḍ*.

➲ 88.6, 99.1, 219.5

252 to jump *natt* نَطّ

verbal noun: *natt* نَطّ

	affirmative		negative		
ána	naṭṭēt	نَطّيْت	ma-naṭṭítš	مَنَطّيْتْش	**perfect**
íḫna	naṭṭēna	نَطّيْنا	ma-naṭṭināš	مَنَطّيْناش	
ínta	naṭṭēt	نَطّيْت	ma-naṭṭítš	مَنَطّيْتْش	
ínti	naṭṭēti	نَطّيْتي	ma-naṭṭitīš	مَنَطّيْتيش	
íntu	naṭṭētu	نَطّيْتوا	ma-naṭṭitūš	مَنَطّيْتوش	
húwwa	naṭṭ	نَطّ	ma-náṭṭiš	مَنَطّش	
híyya	náṭṭit	نَطّت	ma-naṭṭítš	مَنَطّتْش	
húmma	náṭṭu	نَطّوا	ma-naṭṭūš	مَنَطّوش	

ána	anúṭṭ	أنُطّ	ma-núṭṭiš	مَنُطّش	**imperfect**
íḫna	ninúṭṭ	نِنُطّ	ma-nnúṭṭiš	مَنْنُطّش	
ínta	tinúṭṭ	تِنُطّ	ma-tnúṭṭiš	مَتْنُطّش	
ínti	tinúṭṭi	تِنُطّي	ma-tnuṭṭīš	مَتْنُطّيش	
íntu	tinúṭṭu	تِنُطّوا	ma-tnuṭṭūš	مَتْنُطّوش	
húwwa	yinúṭṭ	يِنُطّ	ma-ynúṭṭiš	مَيْنُطّش	
híyya	tinúṭṭ	تِنُطّ	ma-tnúṭṭiš	مَتْنُطّش	
húmma	yinúṭṭu	يِنُطّوا	ma-ynuṭṭūš	مَيْنُطّوش	

ána	banúṭṭ	بَنُطّ	ma-banúṭṭiš	مَبَنُطّش	**bi-imperfect**
íḫna	binnúṭṭ	بِنْنُطّ	ma-binnúṭṭiš	مَبِنْنُطّش	
ínta	bitnúṭṭ	بِتْنُطّ	ma-bitnúṭṭiš	مَبِتْنُطّش	
ínti	bitnúṭṭi	بِتْنُطّي	ma-bitnuṭṭīš	مَبِتْنُطّيش	
íntu	bitnúṭṭu	بِتْنُطّوا	ma-bitnuṭṭūš	مَبِتْنُطّوش	
húwwa	biynúṭṭ	بِيْنُطّ	ma-biynúṭṭiš	مَبِيْنُطّش	
híyya	bitnúṭṭ	بِتْنُطّ	ma-bitnúṭṭiš	مَبِتْنُطّش	
húmma	biynúṭṭu	بِيْنُطّوا	ma-biynuṭṭūš	مَبِيْنُطّوش	

ána	hanúṭṭ	هَنُطّ	miš hanúṭṭ	مِش هَنُطّ	**future**
íḫna	hannúṭṭ	هَنْنُطّ	miš hannúṭṭ	مِش هَنْنُطّ	
ínta	hatnúṭṭ	هَتْنُطّ	miš hatnúṭṭ	مِش هَتْنُطّ	
ínti	hatnúṭṭi	هَتْنُطّي	miš hatnúṭṭi	مِش هَتْنُطّي	
íntu	hatnúṭṭu	هَتْنُطّوا	miš hatnúṭṭu	مِش هَتْنُطّوا	
húwwa	haynúṭṭ	هَيْنُطّ	miš haynúṭṭ	مِش هَيْنُطّ	
híyya	hatnúṭṭ	هَتْنُطّ	miš hatnúṭṭ	مِش هَتْنُطّ	
húmma	haynúṭṭu	هَيْنُطّوا	miš haynúṭṭu	مِش هَيْنُطّوا	

ínta	nuṭṭ	نُطّ	ma-tnúṭṭiš	مَتْنُطّش	**imperative**
ínti	núṭṭi	نُطّي	ma-tnuṭṭīš	مَتْنُطّيش	
íntu	núṭṭu	نُطّوا	ma-tnuṭṭūš	مَتْنُطّوش	

	active		passive		
masculine	nāṭiṭ	ناطط	manṭūṭ	مَنْطوط	**participles**
feminine	náṭṭa	ناطّة	manṭūṭa	مَنْطوطة	
plural	naṭṭīn	ناطّين	manṭuṭīn	مَنْطوطين	

①

القُطّة نطِّت مِن الدّوْر الخامِس، رِجْلها اتْكسرِت.

il?úṭṭa náṭṭit min iddōr ilxāmis, rigláha -tkásarit.

The cat jumped from the fifth floor and broke its leg.

②

اِوْعى تْنُطّ مِن عَ المُرْجيْحة.

íw3a tnúṭṭᵊ min 3a -lmurgēḫa.

Don't jump off the swing!

③

العِيال بِتْنُطّ مِن على المدْرسة.

il3iyāl bitnúṭṭᵊ min 3ála -lmadrása.

The kids jump from the school fence.

④

مُهند هَيْنُطّ في الميّة مِن على أرْتِفاع ١٠ مِترْ.

múhanad haynúṭṭᵊ fi -lmáyya min 3ála -rtifā3 3ášara mitr.

Mohanad will jump in the water from 10 meters high.

⑤

متْنُطّش على أُخْتك! هتْعوّرْها.

ma-tnúṭṭiš 3ála ?úxtak! hat3awwárha.

Don't jump on your sister! You'll hurt her.

❖ [1g2] **to jump**

253 to organize *náẓẓam* نَظَّم

verbal noun: *tanẓīm* تّنْظيم - *niẓām* نِظام

	affirmative		negative		
ána	*naẓẓámt*	نَظَّمْت	*ma-naẓẓámtiš*	مَنَظَّمْتِش	**perfect**
íḥna	*naẓẓámna*	نَظَّمْنا	*ma-naẓẓamnāš*	مَنَظَّمْناش	
ínta	*naẓẓámt*	نَظَّمْت	*ma-naẓẓámtiš*	مَنَظَّمْتِش	
ínti	*naẓẓámti*	نَظَّمْتي	*ma-naẓẓamtīš*	مَنَظَّمْتيش	
íntu	*naẓẓámtu*	نَظَّمْتوا	*ma-naẓẓamtūš*	مَنَظَّمْتوش	
húwwa	*náẓẓam*	نَظَّم	*ma-naẓẓámš*	مَنَظَّمْش	
híyya	*naẓẓámit*	نَظَّمِت	*ma-naẓẓamítš*	مَنَظَّمِتْش	
húmma	*naẓẓámu*	نَظَّموا	*ma-naẓẓamūš*	مَنَظَّموش	
ána	*anáẓẓam*	أنَظَّم	*ma-naẓẓámš*	مَنَظَّمْش	**imperfect**
íḥna	*ninázzam*	نِنَظَّم	*ma-nnaẓẓámš*	مَنْنَظَّمْش	
ínta	*tináẓẓam*	تِنَظَّم	*ma-tnaẓẓámš*	مَتْنَظَّمْش	
ínti	*tinaẓẓámi*	تِنَظَّمي	*ma-tnaẓẓamīš*	مَتْنَظَّميش	
íntu	*tinaẓẓámu*	تِنَظَّموا	*ma-tnaẓẓamūš*	مَتْنَظَّموش	
húwwa	*yináẓẓam*	يِنَظَّم	*ma-ynaẓẓámš*	مَيْنَظَّمْش	
híyya	*tináẓẓam*	تِنَظَّم	*ma-tnaẓẓámš*	مَتْنَظَّمْش	
húmma	*yinaẓẓámu*	يِنَظَّموا	*ma-ynaẓẓamūš*	مَيْنَظَّموش	
ána	*banáẓẓam*	بَنَظَّم	*ma-banaẓẓámš*	مَبَنَظَّمْش	**bi-imperfect**
íḥna	*binnáẓẓam*	بِنْنَظَّم	*ma-binnaẓẓámš*	مَبِنْنَظَّمْش	
ínta	*bitnáẓẓam*	بِتْنَظَّم	*ma-bitnaẓẓámš*	مَبِتْنَظَّمْش	
ínti	*bitnaẓẓámi*	بِتْنَظَّمي	*ma-bitnaẓẓamīš*	مَبِتْنَظَّميش	
íntu	*bitnaẓẓámu*	بِتْنَظَّموا	*ma-bitnaẓẓamūš*	مَبِتْنَظَّموش	
húwwa	*biynáẓẓam*	بِيْنَظَّم	*ma-biynaẓẓámš*	مَبِيْنَظَّمْش	
híyya	*bitnáẓẓam*	بِتْنَظَّم	*ma-bitnaẓẓámš*	مَبِتْنَظَّمْش	
húmma	*biynaẓẓámu*	بِيْنَظَّموا	*ma-biynaẓẓamūš*	مَبِيْنَظَّموش	
ána	*hanáẓẓam*	هَنَظَّم	*miš hanáẓẓam*	مِش هَنَظَّم	**future**
íḥna	*hannáẓẓam*	هَنْنَظَّم	*miš hannáẓẓam*	مِش هَنْنَظَّم	
ínta	*hatnáẓẓam*	هَتْنَظَّم	*miš hatnáẓẓam*	مِش هَتْنَظَّم	
ínti	*hatnaẓẓámi*	هَتْنَظَّمي	*miš hatnaẓẓámi*	مِش هَتْنَظَّمي	
íntu	*hatnaẓẓámu*	هَتْنَظَّموا	*miš hatnaẓẓámu*	مِش هَتْنَظَّموا	
húwwa	*haynáẓẓam*	هَيْنَظَّم	*miš haynáẓẓam*	مِش هَيْنَظَّم	
híyya	*hatnáẓẓam*	هَتْنَظَّم	*miš hatnáẓẓam*	مِش هَتْنَظَّم	
húmma	*haynaẓẓámu*	هَيْنَظَّموا	*miš haynaẓẓámu*	مِش هَيْنَظَّموا	
ínta	*náẓẓam*	نَظَّم	*ma-tnaẓẓámš*	مَتْنَظَّمْش	**imperative**
ínti	*naẓẓámi*	نَظَّمي	*ma-tnaẓẓamīš*	مَتْنَظَّميش	
íntu	*naẓẓámu*	نَظَّموا	*ma-tnaẓẓamūš*	مَتْنَظَّموش	

	active		passive		
masculine	*mináẓẓam*	مِنَظَّم	*mitnáẓẓam*	مِتْنَظَّم	**participles**
feminine	*minaẓẓáma*	مِنَظَّمَة	*mitnaẓẓáma*	مِتْنَظَّمَة	
plural	*minaẓẓamīn*	مِنَظَّمين	*mitnaẓẓamīn*	مِتْنَظَّمين	

①

هارون نظّم حفْلِةْ التّخرُّج بِاحْتِراف.

harūn náẓẓam ḫáflit ittaxárrug bi-ḫtirāf.

Haron organized the graduation party professionally.

②

عهْد بِتْحِبّ أوي تْنظّم مكْتبْها.

3ahdᵊ bitḫíbb ʔáwi tnáẓẓam maktábha.

Ahd really likes to keep her desk organized.

③

خليل مبِيْنظّمْش حاجْتُه أبداً.

xalīl ma-biynaẓẓámšᵊ ḫágtu ʔábadan.

Khalil doesn't ever keep his stuff organized.

④

هنظّم أفْكاري و أكْتِبْها و بعْديْن هعْرِضْها عليْكو.

hanáẓẓam afkāri w aktíbha wi ba3dēn ha3ríḍha 3alēku.

I'll organize my thoughts, write them down, then present them to you.

⑤

نظّم أوْضْتك، و متْقولّيش الفُنون جُنون.

náẓẓam úḍtak, wi ma-tʔullīš ilfunūn gunūn.

Organize your room, and don't tell me "art is chaos."

❖ [2s2] **to organize, arrange**

254 to dishevel náǎkiš نَعْكِش

	affirmative		negative		
ána	na3kíšt	نَعْكِشْت	ma-na3kíštiš	مَنَعْكِشْتِش	perfect
íḫna	na3kíšna	نَعْكِشْنا	ma-na3kišnāš	مَنَعْكِشْناش	
ínta	na3kíšt	نَعْكِشْت	ma-na3kíštiš	مَنَعْكِشْتِش	
ínti	na3kíšti	نَعْكِشْتي	ma-na3kištīš	مَنَعْكِشْتيش	
íntu	na3kíštu	نَعْكِشْتوا	ma-na3kištūš	مَنَعْكِشْتوش	
húwwa	ná3kiš	نَعْكِش	ma-na3kíšš	مَنَعْكِشّ	
híyya	na3kíšit	نَعْكِشِت	ma-na3kišítš	مَنَعْكِشِتْش	
húmma	na3kíšu	نَعْكِشوا	ma-na3kišūš	مَنَعْكِشوش	
ána	aná3kiš	أنَعْكِش	ma-na3kíšš	مَنَعْكِشّ	imperfect
íḫna	niná3kiš	نْنَعْكِش	ma-nna3kíšš	مَنْنَعْكِشّ	
ínta	tiná3kiš	تْنَعْكِش	ma-tna3kíšš	مَتْنَعْكِشّ	
ínti	tina3kíši	تْنَعْكِشي	ma-tna3kišīš	مَتْنَعْكِشيش	
íntu	tina3kíšu	تْنَعْكِشوا	ma-tna3kišūš	مَتْنَعْكِشوش	
húwwa	yiná3kiš	يْنَعْكِش	ma-yna3kíšš	مَيْنَعْكِشّ	
híyya	tiná3kiš	تْنَعْكِش	ma-tna3kíšš	مَتْنَعْكِشّ	
húmma	yina3kíšu	يْنَعْكِشوا	ma-yna3kišūš	مَيْنَعْكِشوش	
ána	baná3kiš	بَنَعْكِش	ma-bana3kíšš	مَبَنَعْكِشّ	bi-imperfect
íḫna	binná3kiš	بِنْنَعْكِش	ma-binna3kíšš	مَبِنْنَعْكِشّ	
ínta	bitná3kiš	بِتْنَعْكِش	ma-bitna3kíšš	مَبِتْنَعْكِشّ	
ínti	bitna3kíši	بِتْنَعْكِشي	ma-bitna3kišīš	مَبِتْنَعْكِشيش	
íntu	bitna3kíšu	بِتْنَعْكِشوا	ma-bitna3kišūš	مَبِتْنَعْكِشوش	
húwwa	biyná3kiš	بِيْنَعْكِش	ma-biyna3kíšš	مَبِيْنَعْكِشّ	
híyya	bitná3kiš	بِتْنَعْكِش	ma-bitna3kíšš	مَبِتْنَعْكِشّ	
húmma	biyna3kíšu	بِيْنَعْكِشوا	ma-biyna3kišūš	مَبِيْنَعْكِشوش	
ána	haná3kiš	هَنَعْكِش	miš haná3kiš	مِش هَنَعْكِش	future
íḫna	hanná3kiš	هَنْنَعْكِش	miš hanná3kiš	مِش هَنْنَعْكِش	
ínta	hatná3kiš	هَتْنَعْكِش	miš hatná3kiš	مِش هَتْنَعْكِش	
ínti	hatna3kíši	هَتْنَعْكِشي	miš hatna3kíši	مِش هَتْنَعْكِشي	
íntu	hatna3kíšu	هَتْنَعْكِشوا	miš hatna3kíšu	مِش هَتْنَعْكِشوا	
húwwa	hayná3kiš	هَيْنَعْكِش	miš hayná3kiš	مِش هَيْنَعْكِش	
híyya	hatná3kiš	هَتْنَعْكِش	miš hatná3kiš	مِش هَتْنَعْكِش	
húmma	hayna3kíšu	هَيْنَعْكِشوا	miš hayna3kíšu	مِش هَيْنَعْكِشوا	
ínta	ná3kiš	نَعْكِش	ma-tna3kíšš	مَتْنَعْكِشّ	imperative
ínti	na3kíši	نَعْكِشي	ma-tna3kišīš	مَتْنَعْكِشيش	
íntu	na3kíšu	نَعْكِشوا	ma-tna3kišūš	مَتْنَعْكِشوش	

	active		passive		
masculine	miná3kiš	مِنَعْكِش	mitná3kiš	مِتْنَعْكِش	participles
feminine	mina3kíša	مِنَعْكِشَة	mitna3kíša	مِتْنَعْكِشَة	
plural	mina3kišīn	مِنَعْكِشين	mitna3kišīn	مِتْنَعْكِشين	

verbal noun: *na3káša* نَعْكَشَة

①

داليا نعْكِشِت أوضِتْها و هِيَّ بِتْدوّر على فرْدِةْ الجزْمة.

dálya na3kíšit uḍítha wi híyya bitdáwwar 3ála fárdit ilgázma.

Dalia messed up her room while looking for her shoe.

②

حدّ يْقول لِجْريْني مَيْنعْكِشّ شعْرُه كِده.

ḫaddᵊ yʔūl li-grēni ma-ynáʒkišš šá3ru kída.

Somebody should tell Greiny not to mess up his hair like that.

③

هالة بِتْحِبّ النِّظام. مبِتْنعْكِشّ مكْتبْها أبداً.

hāla bitḫíbb inniẓām. ma-bitna3kíššᵊ maktábha ʔábadan.

Hala loves order. She never messes up her desk.

④

إنْتي هتْنعْكِشي شعْرِك بعْد ما قعدْت ساعة أضْفُرُه؟

ínti hatna3kíši šá3rik ba3dᵊ ma ʔa3ádtᵊ sā3a ʔaḍfúru?

Are you going to mess up your hair after I spent an hour braiding it?

⑤

متْنعْكِشْليش حاجْتي يا زِفْت!

ma-tna3kišlīš ḫágti ya zift!

Don't mess up my stuff, jerk.

❖ [11s1] **to dishevel, mess up**

255 to mess up nákaš نَكَش

	affirmative		negative		
ána	nakášt	نَكَشْت	ma-nakáštiš	مَنَكَشْتِش	perfect
íḫna	nakášna	نَكَشْنا	ma-nakašnāš	مَنَكَشْناش	
ínta	nakášt	نَكَشْت	ma-nakáštiš	مَنَكَشْتِش	
ínti	nakášti	نَكَشْتي	ma-nakaštīš	مَنَكَشْتيش	
íntu	nakáštu	نَكَشْتوا	ma-nakaštūš	مَنَكَشْتوش	
húwwa	nákaš	نَكَش	ma-nakášš	مَنَكَشّ	
híyya	nákašit	نَكَشِت	ma-nakašítš	مَنَكَشِتْش	
húmma	nákašu	نَكَشوا	ma-nakašūš	مَنَكَشوش	
ána	ánkuš	أَنْكُش	ma-nkúšš	مَنْكُشّ	imperfect
íḫna	núnkuš	نُنْكُش	ma-nunkúšš	مَنُنْكُشّ	
ínta	túnkuš	تُنْكُش	ma-tunkúšš	مَتُنْكُشّ	
ínti	tunkúši	تُنْكُشي	ma-tunkušīš	مَتُنْكُشيش	
íntu	tunkúšu	تُنْكُشوا	ma-tunkušūš	مَتُنْكُشوش	
húwwa	yúnkuš	يُنْكُش	ma-yunkúšš	مَيُنْكُشّ	
híyya	túnkuš	تُنْكُش	ma-tunkúšš	مَتُنْكُشّ	
húmma	yunkúšu	يُنْكُشوا	ma-yunkušūš	مَيُنْكُشوش	
ána	bánkuš	بَنْكُش	ma-bankúšš	مَبَنْكُشّ	bi-imperfect
íḫna	binúnkuš	بِنُنْكُش	ma-bnunkúšš	مَبْنُنْكُشّ	
ínta	bitúnkuš	بِتُنْكُش	ma-btunkúšš	مَبْتُنْكُشّ	
ínti	bitunkúši	بِتُنْكُشي	ma-btunkušīš	مَبْتُنْكُشيش	
íntu	bitunkúšu	بِتُنْكُشوا	ma-btunkušūš	مَبْتُنْكُشوش	
húwwa	biyúnkuš	بِيُنْكُش	ma-byunkúšš	مَبْيُنْكُشّ	
híyya	bitúnkuš	بِتُنْكُش	ma-btunkúšš	مَبْتُنْكُشّ	
húmma	biyunkúšu	بِيُنْكُشوا	ma-byunkušūš	مَبْيُنْكُشوش	
ána	hánkuš	هَنْكُش	miš hánkuš	مِش هَنْكُش	future
íḫna	hanúnkuš	هَنُنْكُش	miš hanúnkuš	مِش هَنُنْكُش	
ínta	hatúnkuš	هَتُنْكُش	miš hatúnkuš	مِش هَتُنْكُش	
ínti	hatunkúši	هَتُنْكُشي	miš hatunkúši	مِش هَتُنْكُشي	
íntu	hatunkúšu	هَتُنْكُشوا	miš hatunkúšu	مِش هَتُنْكُشوا	
húwwa	hayúnkuš	هَيُنْكُش	miš hayúnkuš	مِش هَيُنْكُش	
híyya	hatúnkuš	هَتُنْكُش	miš hatúnkuš	مِش هَتُنْكُش	
húmma	hayunkúšu	هَيُنْكُشوا	miš hayunkúšu	مِش هَيُنْكُشوا	
ínta	únkuš	أُنْكُش	ma-tunkúšš	مَتُنْكُشّ	imperative
ínti	unkúši	أُنْكُشي	ma-tunkušīš	مَتُنْكُشيش	
íntu	unkúšu	أُنْكُشوا	ma-tunkušūš	مَتُنْكُشوش	

	active		passive		
masculine	nākiš	ناكِش	mankūš	مَنْكوش	participles
feminine	nákša	ناكْشَة	mankūša	مَنْكوشَة	
plural	nakšīn	ناكْشين	mankušīn	مَنْكوشين	

verbal noun: nakš نَكْش

①

كُلّ ما أسرَّح لِلبِنْت ألاقيها نكشِت شعْرها.

kullᵊ m- asárrah li-lbint alaʔīha nákašit ša3ráha.

Each time I comb the girl's hair, she messes it up.

②

هُدى بِتْحِبّ تُنْكُش شعْرها، قال أيْه موْضة.

húda bitḥíbbᵊ túnkuš ša3ráha, ʔāl ʔē mōḍa.

Hoda likes to mess up her hair as a style.

③

سُهيْلة بْتُنْكُشْني لمّا بِتْلاقيني مِتْضايْقة.

suhēla btunkúšni lámma bitlaʔīni mitḍāyʔa.

Sohaila makes me laugh when she finds me upset.

④

متِنْكُشيش شعْرك كِده.

ma-tinkušīš šá3rak kída.

Don't mess up your hair like this.

⑤

مين اللي نكش الوَرق ده؟ أنا لِسّه مْرتِّبُه.

mīn ílli nákaš ilwáraʔ da? ána líssa mrattíbu.

Who messed up the papers? I had just tidied them up.

⑥

إنْتَ ليْه بْتُنْكُش في مَواضيع تِعْمِلّك مشاكِل؟

ínta lē btúnkuš fi mawaḍī3 ti3míllak mašākil?

Why do you mess with issues that will bring you trouble?

❖ [1s3] **to mess up, dishevel; to mess with** (في *fi*)

- This verb, like other verbs of the [1s3] and [1s6] patterns, can optionally take ـُ *u* instead of ـِ *i* in the personal prefixes of the imperfect (including the bi-imperfect and future) and imperative. For example, يُنْكُش *yúnkuš* can also be pronounced يِنْكُش *yínkuš*. These vowels are interchangeable, but the tables reflect the preferences of the speakers on the MP3s.

256 to agree wāfiʔ وافِق

	affirmative		negative		
ána	wafíʔt	وافِقْت	ma-wafíʔtiš	مَوافِقْتِش	**perfect**
íḫna	wafíʔna	وافِقْنا	ma-wafiʔnāš	مَوافِقْناش	
ínta	wafíʔt	وافِقْت	ma-wafíʔtiš	مَوافِقْتِش	
ínti	wafíʔti	وافِقْتي	ma-wafiʔtīš	مَوافِقْتيش	
íntu	wafíʔtu	وافِقْتوا	ma-wafiʔtūš	مَوافِقْتوش	
húwwa	wāfiʔ	وافِق	ma-wafíʔš	مَوافِقْش	
híyya	wáfʔit	وافْقِت	ma-wafʔítš	مَوافْقِتْش	
húmma	wáfʔu	وافْقوا	ma-wafʔūš	مَوافْقوش	
ána	awāfiʔ	أوافِق	ma-wafíʔš	مَوافِقْش	**imperfect**
íḫna	niwāfiʔ	نِوافِق	ma-nwafíʔš	مَنْوافِقْش	
ínta	tiwāfiʔ	تِوافِق	ma-twafíʔš	مَتْوافِقْش	
ínti	tiwáfʔi	تِوافْقي	ma-twafʔīš	مَتْوافْقيش	
íntu	tiwáfʔu	تِوافْقوا	ma-twafʔūš	مَتْوافْقوش	
húwwa	yiwāfiʔ	يِوافِق	ma-ywafíʔš	مَيْوافِقْش	
híyya	tiwāfiʔ	تِوافِق	ma-twafíʔš	مَتْوافِقْش	
húmma	yiwáfʔu	يِوافْقوا	ma-ywafʔūš	مَيْوافْقوش	
ána	bawāfiʔ	بَوافِق	ma-bawafíʔš	مَبَوافِقْش	**bi-imperfect**
íḫna	binwāfiʔ	بِنْوافِق	ma-binwafíʔš	مَبِنْوافِقْش	
ínta	bitwāfiʔ	بِتْوافِق	ma-bitwafíʔš	مَبِتْوافِقْش	
ínti	bitwáfʔi	بِتْوافْقي	ma-bitwafʔīš	مَبِتْوافْقيش	
íntu	bitwáfʔu	بِتْوافْقوا	ma-bitwafʔūš	مَبِتْوافْقوش	
húwwa	biywāfiʔ	بِيْوافِق	ma-biywafíʔš	مَبِيْوافِقْش	
híyya	bitwāfiʔ	بِتْوافِق	ma-bitwafíʔš	مَبِتْوافِقْش	
húmma	biywáfʔu	بِيْوافْقوا	ma-biywafʔūš	مَبِيْوافْقوش	
ána	hawāfiʔ	هَوافِق	miš hawāfiʔ	مِش هَوافِق	**future**
íḫna	hanwāfiʔ	هَنْوافِق	miš hanwāfiʔ	مِش هَنْوافِق	
ínta	hatwāfiʔ	هَتْوافِق	miš hatwāfiʔ	مِش هَتْوافِق	
ínti	hatwáfʔi	هَتْوافْقي	miš hatwáfʔi	مِش هَتْوافْقي	
íntu	hatwáfʔu	هَتْوافْقوا	miš hatwáfʔu	مِش هَتْوافْقوا	
húwwa	haywāfiʔ	هَيْوافِق	miš haywāfiʔ	مِش هَيْوافِق	
híyya	hatwāfiʔ	هَتْوافِق	miš hatwāfiʔ	مِش هَتْوافِق	
húmma	haywáfʔu	هَيْوافْقوا	miš haywáfʔu	مِش هَيْوافْقوا	
ínta	wāfiʔ	وافِق	ma-twafíʔš	مَتْوافِقْش	**imperative**
ínti	wáfʔi	وافْقي	ma-twafʔīš	مَتْوافْقيش	
íntu	wáfʔu	وافْقوا	ma-twafʔūš	مَتْوافْقوش	

	active		passive		
masculine	miwāfiʔ	مِوافِق	mitwāfiʔ	مِتْوافِق	**participles**
feminine	miwáfʔa	مِوافْقَة	mitwáfʔa	مِتْوافْقَة	
plural	miwafʔīn	مِوافْقين	mitwafʔīn	مِتْوافْقين	

verbal nouns: muwáfʔa مُوافْقَة - miwáfʔa مِوافْقَة

①

وافِقْت أتْجوِّز سعيد عشان حنين أوي معايا.

wafíʔt atgáwwiz sa3īd 3ašān ḥanīn ʔáwi ma3āya.

I agreed to marry Saed because he's so kind to me.

②

إمْتى تْوافْقي بقى و نْهِجّ مِن هِنا؟

ímta twáfʔi báʔa wi nhigg° min hína?

When will you agree to emigrate from here?

③

الجامْعة بِتْوافِق عَ المِنح لِلطّلبة المُتفوِّقين بسّ.

ilgám3a bitwāfiʔ 3á -lmínaḥ li-ṭṭálaba -lmutafawwiqīn bass.

The university only grants scholarships for excellent students.

④

يا ترى هَيْوافْقولي عَ المِنْحة إمْتى؟

ya tára haywafʔūli 3a -lmínḥa ʔímta?

I wonder when they'll grant my scholarship.

⑤

متْوافِقْش على شيْء ضِدّ مبادْئَك أبداً.

ma-twafíʔš 3ála šēʔ ḍidd° mabádʔak ábadan.

Don't ever accept something against your principles.

⑥

الخميس الجايّ هَيْوافِق عيد ميلاد نودي.

ilxamīs ilgáyy° haywāfiʔ 3īd milād nūdi.

Next Thursday is Nody's birthday.

❖ [3s] **to agree on/to; to grant; to correspond to**

- This verb can be followed by an imperfect verb.
- It can be used with information such as dates to mean 'correspond to'. (➲ 156.6)

➲ 7.4

257 to be missed wáɦaš وَحَش

	affirmative		negative		
ána	waɦášt	وَحَشْت	ma-waɦáštiš	مَوَحَشْتِش	perfect
íɦna	waɦášna	وَحَشْنا	ma-waɦašnāš	مَوَحَشْناش	
ínta	waɦášt	وَحَشْت	ma-waɦáštiš	مَوَحَشْتِش	
ínti	waɦášti	وَحَشْتي	ma-waɦaštīš	مَوَحَشْتيش	
íntu	waɦáštu	وَحَشْتوا	ma-waɦaštūš	مَوَحَشْتوش	
húwwa	wáɦaš	وَحَش	ma-waɦášš	مَوَحَشّ	
híyya	wáɦašit	وَحَشِت	ma-waɦašítš	مَوَحَشِتْش	
húmma	wáɦašu	وَحَشوا	ma-waɦašūš	مَوَحَشوش	
ána	áwɦaš	أَوْحَش	ma-wɦášš	مَوْحَشّ	imperfect
íɦna	níwɦaš	نِوْحَش	ma-niwɦášš	مَنِوْحَشّ	
ínta	tíwɦaš	تِوْحَش	ma-tiwɦášš	مَتِوْحَشّ	
ínti	tiwɦáši	تِوْحَشي	ma-tiwɦašīš	مَتِوْحَشيش	
íntu	tiwɦášu	تِوْحَشوا	ma-tiwɦašūš	مَتِوْحَشوش	
húwwa	yíwɦaš	يِوْحَش	ma-yiwɦášš	مَيِوْحَشّ	
híyya	tíwɦaš	تِوْحَش	ma-tiwɦášš	مَتِوْحَشّ	
húmma	yiwɦášu	يِوْحَشوا	ma-yiwɦašūš	مَيِوْحَشوش	
ána	báwɦaš	بَوْحَش	ma-bawɦášš	مَبَوْحَشّ	bi-imperfect
íɦna	biníwɦaš	بِنِوْحَش	ma-bniwɦášš	مَبْنِوْحَشّ	
ínta	bitíwɦaš	بِتِوْحَش	ma-btiwɦášš	مَبْتِوْحَشّ	
ínti	bitiwɦáši	بِتِوْحَشي	ma-btiwɦašīš	مَبْتِوْحَشيش	
íntu	bitiwɦášu	بِتِوْحَشوا	ma-btiwɦašūš	مَبْتِوْحَشوش	
húwwa	biyíwɦaš	بِيِوْحَش	ma-byiwɦášš	مَبْيِوْحَشّ	
híyya	bitíwɦaš	بِتِوْحَش	ma-btiwɦášš	مَبْتِوْحَشّ	
húmma	biyiwɦášu	بِيِوْحَشوا	ma-byiwɦašūš	مَبْيِوْحَشوش	
ána	háwɦaš	هَوْحَش	miš háwɦaš	مِش هَوْحَش	future
íɦna	haníwɦaš	هَنِوْحَش	miš haníwɦaš	مِش هَنِوْحَش	
ínta	hatíwɦaš	هَتِوْحَش	miš hatíwɦaš	مِش هَتِوْحَش	
ínti	hatiwɦáši	هَتِوْحَشي	miš hatiwɦáši	مِش هَتِوْحَشي	
íntu	hatiwɦášu	هَتِوْحَشوا	miš hatiwɦášu	مِش هَتِوْحَشوا	
húwwa	hayíwɦaš	هَيِوْحَش	miš hayíwɦaš	مِش هَيِوْحَش	
híyya	hatíwɦaš	هَتِوْحَش	miš hatíwɦaš	مِش هَتِوْحَش	
húmma	hayiwɦášu	هَيِوْحَشوا	miš hayiwɦášu	مِش هَيِوْحَشوا	
ínta	íwɦaš	اِوْحَش	ma-tiwɦášš	مَتِوْحَشّ	imperative
ínti	iwɦáši	اِوْحَشي	ma-tiwɦašīš	مَتِوْحَشيش	
íntu	iwɦášu	اِوْحَشوا	ma-tiwɦašūš	مَتِوْحَشوش	

	active		passive		
masculine	wāɦiš	واحِش	–	–	participles
feminine	wáɦša	واحْشَة	–	–	
plural	waɦšīn	واحْشين	–	–	

verbal noun: wáɦša وَحْشَة

①

هعدّي عليْكو النّهارْده. إنْتو واحْشينْني أوي.

ha3áddi 3alēku -nnahárda. íntu waɧšínni ʔáwi.

I'll come by your place today. I miss you a lot.

②

أهي اللّمّة دي أكْتر حاجة مُمْكِن تِوْحشْنا لمّا نْسافِر.

ahí -llámma di ʔáktar ɧāga múmkin tiwɧášna lámma nsāfir.

Getting together like this is probably what
we'll miss most when we're away.

③

و مين مبْتِوْحشوش مصْر في الغُرْبة؟

wi mīn ma-btiwɧašūš maṣrᵊ fi -lɣúrba?

Who doesn't miss Egypt while abroad?

④

هتِوْحشوني أوي. متْطولوش المرّة دي.

hatiwɧašūni ʔáwi. ma-tṭulūš ilmarrādi.

I'll miss you guys so much.
Don't stay away for long.

⑤

متِوْحشْنيش . أنا مِش عايْزاك تاني.

ma-tiwɧašnīš. ána miš 3ayzāk tāni.

I don't miss you. I don't
want you anymore.

❖ [1s1] **to be missed (by)**

- This subject and object of this verb are swapped when translated with the English verb 'miss'.

➲ 129.6, 175.5, 198.4

258 to take wádda ودّى

verbal noun: *tawdíyya* تودْية

	affirmative		negative		
ána	waddēt	ودّيت	ma-waddítš	مَودّيتْش	**perfect**
íḫna	waddēna	ودّينا	ma-waddināš	مَودّيناش	
ínta	waddēt	ودّيت	ma-waddítš	مَودّيتْش	
ínti	waddēti	ودّيتي	ma-wadditīš	مَودّيتيش	
íntu	waddētu	ودّيتوا	ma-wadditūš	مَودّيتوش	
húwwa	wádda	ودّى	ma-waddāš	مَودّاش	
híyya	wáddit	ودّت	ma-waddítš	مَودّتْش	
húmma	wáddu	ودّوا	ma-waddūš	مَودّوش	
ána	awáddi	أودّي	ma-waddīš	مَودّيش	**imperfect**
íḫna	niwáddi	نِودّي	ma-nwaddīš	مَنْودّيش	
ínta	tiwáddi	تِودّي	ma-twaddīš	مَتْودّيش	
ínti	tiwáddi	تِودّي	ma-twaddīš	مَتْودّيش	
íntu	tiwáddu	تِودّوا	ma-twaddūš	مَتْودّوش	
húwwa	yiwáddi	يِودّي	ma-ywaddīš	مَيْودّيش	
híyya	tiwáddi	تِودّي	ma-twaddīš	مَتْودّيش	
húmma	yiwáddu	يِودّوا	ma-ywaddūš	مَيْودّوش	
ána	bawáddi	بَودّي	ma-bawaddīš	مَبَودّيش	**bi-imperfect**
íḫna	binwáddi	بِنْودّي	ma-binwaddīš	مَبِنْودّيش	
ínta	bitwáddi	بِتْودّي	ma-bitwaddīš	مَبِتْودّيش	
ínti	bitwáddi	بِتْودّي	ma-bitwaddīš	مَبِتْودّيش	
íntu	bitwáddu	بِتْودّوا	ma-bitwaddūš	مَبِتْودّوش	
húwwa	biywáddi	بِيْودّي	ma-biywaddīš	مَبِيْودّيش	
híyya	bitwáddi	بِتْودّي	ma-bitwaddīš	مَبِتْودّيش	
húmma	biywáddu	بِيْودّوا	ma-biywaddūš	مَبِيْودّوش	
ána	hawáddi	هَودّي	miš hawáddi	مِش هَودّي	**future**
íḫna	hanwáddi	هَنْودّي	miš hanwáddi	مِش هَنْودّي	
ínta	hatwáddi	هَتْودّي	miš hatwáddi	مِش هَتْودّي	
ínti	hatwáddi	هَتْودّي	miš hatwáddi	مِش هَتْودّي	
íntu	hatwáddu	هَتْودّوا	miš hatwáddu	مِش هَتْودّوا	
húwwa	haywáddi	هَيْودّي	miš haywáddi	مِش هَيْودّي	
híyya	hatwáddi	هَتْودّي	miš hatwáddi	مِش هَتْودّي	
húmma	haywáddu	هَيْودّوا	miš haywáddu	مِش هَيْودّوا	
ínta	wáddi	ودّي	ma-twaddīš	مَتْودّيش	**imperative**
ínti	wáddi	ودّي	ma-twaddīš	مَتْودّيش	
íntu	wáddu	ودّوا	ma-twaddūš	مَتْودّوش	

	active		passive		
masculine	miwáddi	مِودّي	mitwáddi	مِتْودّي	**participles**
feminine	miwaddíyya	مِودّية	mitwaddíyya	مِتْودّية	
plural	miwaddiyīn	مِودّيين	mitwaddiyīn	مِتْودّيين	

①

وَدّيْنا الوِلاد عنْد ماما و خرجْت أنا و جوْزي معَ بعْض.

waddēna -lwilād 3andᵊ māma wi xarágt ána wi gōzi má3a ba3ḍ.

We took the kids over to my mom's, and I went out with my husband.

②

لازِم تِوَدّي الوَلد حضانة عشان تِساعْدُه يِتْطوّر.

lāzim tiwáddi -lwálad ħaḍāna 3ašān tisá3du yittáwwar.

You should take the boy to a preschool to help him develop.

③

جوْزي بِيْوَدّي الوِلاد المدْرسة قبْل شُغْلُه.

gōzi biywáddi -lwilād ilmadrása ʔablᵊ šúɣlu.

My husband drives the kids to school before [going to] work.

④

هتْوَدّي الهُدوم المغْسلة إمْتى؟

hatwáddi -lhudūm ilmaɣsála ʔímta?

When are you going to drop off the clothes at the laundry shop?

⑤

متْوَدّيش أهْلك دار مُسِنّين. كانوا هُمّا بعتوك ملْجأ.

ma-twaddīš áhlak dār musinnīn. kānu húmma ba3atūk málgaʔ.

Don't put your parents in an old people's home. They could have put you in an orphanage!

❖ [2d] **to take; to send**

➲ 43.2, 200.5, 236.1

259 to show wárra ورّى

verbal noun: tawríyya تورْيَة

	affirmative		negative		
ána	warrēt	ورّيْت	ma-warrítš	مَورّيتْش	perfect
íḫna	warrēna	ورّيْنا	ma-warrināš	مَورّيناش	
ínta	warrēt	ورّيْت	ma-warrítš	مَورّيتْش	
ínti	warrēti	ورّيْتي	ma-warritīš	مَورّيتيش	
íntu	warrētu	ورّيْتوا	ma-warritūš	مَورّيتوش	
húwwa	wárra	ورّى	ma-warrāš	مَورّاش	
híyya	wárrit	ورّت	ma-warrítš	مَورّتْش	
húmma	wárru	ورّوا	ma-warrūš	مَورّوش	
ána	awárri	أورّي	ma-warrīš	مَورّيش	imperfect
íḫna	niwárri	نِورّي	ma-nwarrīš	مَنْورّيش	
ínta	tiwárri	تِورّي	ma-twarrīš	مَتْورّيش	
ínti	tiwárri	تِورّي	ma-twarrīš	مَتْورّيش	
íntu	tiwárru	تِورّوا	ma-twarrūš	مَتْورّوش	
húwwa	yiwárri	يِورّي	ma-ywarrīš	مَيْورّيش	
híyya	tiwárri	تِورّي	ma-twarrīš	مَتْورّيش	
húmma	yiwárru	يِورّوا	ma-ywarrūš	مَيْورّوش	
ána	bawárri	بَورّي	ma-bawarrīš	مَبورّيش	bi-imperfect
íḫna	binwárri	بِنْورّي	ma-binwarrīš	مَبِنْورّيش	
ínta	bitwárri	بِتْورّي	ma-bitwarrīš	مَبِتْورّيش	
ínti	bitwárri	بِتْورّي	ma-bitwarrīš	مَبِتْورّيش	
íntu	bitwárru	بِتْورّوا	ma-bitwarrūš	مَبِتْورّوش	
húwwa	biywárri	بِيْورّي	ma-biywarrīš	مَبِيْورّيش	
híyya	bitwárri	بِتْورّي	ma-bitwarrīš	مَبِتْورّيش	
húmma	biywárru	بِيْورّوا	ma-biywarrūš	مَبِيْورّوش	
ána	hawárri	هَورّي	miš hawárri	مِش هَورّي	future
íḫna	hanwárri	هَنْورّي	miš hanwárri	مِش هَنْورّي	
ínta	hatwárri	هَتْورّي	miš hatwárri	مِش هَتْورّي	
ínti	hatwárri	هَتْورّي	miš hatwárri	مِش هَتْورّي	
íntu	hatwárru	هَتْورّوا	miš hatwárru	مِش هَتْورّوا	
húwwa	haywárri	هَيْورّي	miš haywárri	مِش هَيْورّي	
híyya	hatwárri	هَتْورّي	miš hatwárri	مِش هَتْورّي	
húmma	haywárru	هَيْورّوا	miš haywárru	مِش هَيْورّوا	
ínta	wárri	ورّي	ma-twarrīš	مَتْورّيش	imperative
ínti	wárri	ورّي	ma-twarrīš	مَتْورّيش	
íntu	wárru	ورّوا	ma-twarrūš	مَتْورّوش	

	active		passive		
masculine	miwárri	مِورّي	mitwárri	مِتْورّي	participles
feminine	miwarríyya	مِورّية	mitwarríyya	مِتْورّية	
plural	miwarriyīn	مِورّيين	mitwarriyīn	مِتْورّيين	

①

الأُسْتاذ وَرّانا فيلْم مُشوِّق عن الدَّيْناصورات.

il?ustāz warrāna filmᵊ mušáwwiq 3an iddaynaṣurāt.

The teacher showed us an interesting movie about dinosaurs.

②

لمّا بِنْروح لِجِدِّتي بِتْحِبّ تْوَرّينا صْوَرْها القديمة.

lámma binrūḫ li-giddíti bitḫíbbᵊ twarrīna ṣwárha -l?adīma.

When we go to my grandma's, she likes to show us her old photos.

③

نِهاد بِتِكْتِب شِعْر و مبِتْوَرّيهوليش أبداً.

nihād bitíktib ši3rᵊ wi ma-bitwarrihulīš ábadan.

Nehad writes poems but never shows them to me.

④

في الاِمْتِحان هَيْوَرّوك نموذَج و مطْلوب مِنّك تِعْمِل زيُّه.

fi -l?imtiḫān haywarrūk namūzag wi maṭlūb mínnak tí3mil záyyu.

On the exam, they'll show you a model, and you should make one like it.

⑤

متْوَرّيش العريس الفُسْتان لِحدّ يوْم الفرح.

ma-twarrīš il3arīs ilfustān li-ḫaddᵊ yōm ilfárah.

Don't show the groom the dress until the wedding day.

❖ [2d] **to show**

- This verb is ditransitive, taking two direct objects.

260 to arrive wíṣil وِصِل

	affirmative		negative	
perfect				
ána	*wiṣílt*	وِصِلْت	*ma-wṣíltiš*	مَوْصِلْتِش
íḫna	*wiṣílna*	وِصِلْنا	*ma-wṣilnāš*	مَوْصِلْناش
ínta	*wiṣílt*	وِصِلْت	*ma-wṣíltiš*	مَوْصِلْتِش
ínti	*wiṣílti*	وِصِلْتي	*ma-wṣiltīš*	مَوْصِلْتيش
íntu	*wiṣíltu*	وِصِلْتوا	*ma-wṣiltūš*	مَوْصِلْتوش
húwwa	*wíṣil*	وِصِل	*ma-wṣílš*	مَوْصِلْش
híyya	*wíṣlit*	وِصْلِت	*ma-wiṣlítš*	مَوِصْلِتْش
húmma	*wíṣlu*	وِصْلوا	*ma-wiṣlūš*	مَوِصْلوش
imperfect				
ána	*áwṣal*	أوْصَل	*ma-wṣálš*	مَوْصَلْش
íḫna	*níwṣal*	نِوْصَل	*ma-niwṣálš*	مَنِوْصَلْش
ínta	*tíwṣal*	تِوْصَل	*ma-tiwṣálš*	مَتِوْصَلْش
ínti	*tiwṣáli*	تِوْصَلي	*ma-tiwṣalīš*	مَتِوْصَليش
íntu	*tiwṣálu*	تِوْصَلوا	*ma-tiwṣalūš*	مَتِوْصَلوش
húwwa	*yíwṣal*	يِوْصَل	*ma-yiwṣálš*	مَيِوْصَلْش
híyya	*tíwṣal*	تِوْصَل	*ma-tiwṣálš*	مَتِوْصَلْش
húmma	*yiwṣálu*	يِوْصَلوا	*ma-yiwṣalūš*	مَيِوْصَلوش
bi-imperfect				
ána	*báwṣal*	بَوْصَل	*ma-bawṣálš*	مَبَوْصَلْش
íḫna	*biníwṣal*	بِنِوْصَل	*ma-bniwṣálš*	مَبْنِوْصَلْش
ínta	*bitíwṣal*	بِتِوْصَل	*ma-btiwṣálš*	مَبْتِوْصَلْش
ínti	*bitiwṣáli*	بِتِوْصَلي	*ma-btiwṣalīš*	مَبْتِوْصَليش
íntu	*bitiwṣálu*	بِتِوْصَلوا	*ma-btiwṣalūš*	مَبْتِوْصَلوش
húwwa	*biyíwṣal*	بِيِوْصَل	*ma-byiwṣálš*	مَبْيِوْصَلْش
híyya	*bitíwṣal*	بِتِوْصَل	*ma-btiwṣálš*	مَبْتِوْصَلْش
húmma	*biyiwṣálu*	بِيِوْصَلوا	*ma-byiwṣalūš*	مَبْيِوْصَلوش
future				
ána	*háwṣal*	هَوْصَل	*miš háwṣal*	مِش هَوْصَل
íḫna	*haníwṣal*	هَنِوْصَل	*miš haníwṣal*	مِش هَنِوْصَل
ínta	*hatíwṣal*	هَتِوْصَل	*miš hatíwṣal*	مِش هَتِوْصَل
ínti	*hatiwṣáli*	هَتِوْصَلي	*miš hatiwṣáli*	مِش هَتِوْصَلي
íntu	*hatiwṣálu*	هَتِوْصَلوا	*miš hatiwṣálu*	مِش هَتِوْصَلوا
húwwa	*hayíwṣal*	هَيِوْصَل	*miš hayíwṣal*	مِش هَيِوْصَل
híyya	*hatíwṣal*	هَتِوْصَل	*miš hatíwṣal*	مِش هَتِوْصَل
húmma	*hayiwṣálu*	هَيِوْصَلوا	*miš hayiwṣálu*	مِش هَيِوْصَلوا
imperative				
ínta	*íwṣal*	اِوْصَل	*ma-tiwṣálš*	مَتِوْصَلْش
ínti	*iwṣáli*	اِوْصَلي	*ma-tiwṣalīš*	مَتِوْصَليش
íntu	*iwṣálu*	اِوْصَلوا	*ma-tiwṣalūš*	مَتِوْصَلوش

participles	active		passive	
masculine	*wāṣil*	واصِل	–	–
feminine	*wáṣla*	واصْلَة	–	–
plural	*waṣlīn*	واصْلين	–	–

verbal noun: *wuṣūl* وُصول

①

العروسة وِصْلِت مِتْأَخَّرة ساعْتينْ.

il3arūsa wíṣlit mitʔaxxára sa3tēn.

The bride arrived two hours late.

②

ناجي دايْماً يِوْصل بدْري عن معادُه.

nāgi dáyman yíwṣal bádri 3an mi3ādu.

Nagy always arrives early.

③

مبْتِوْصلْش في معادك ليْه أبداً؟

ma-btiwṣálšᵊ f mi3ādak lē ábadan?

Why don't you ever arrive on time?

④

هتِوْصلوا إمْتى؟ إحْنا مِسْتنِّيين بقالْنا كْتير.

hatiwṣálu ʔímta? íḥna mistanniyīn baʔálna ktīr.

When will you arrive? We've been waiting for so long.

⑤

اِوْصل لِحدّ جارِتْنا و إدّيها الطّبق ده.

íwṣal li-ḥaddᵊ garítna w iddīha -ṭṭábaʔ da.

Go to our neighbor and give her this plate.

❖ [1s4] **to arrive**

- This perfect of this verb can also, but less commonly, be وَصَل *wáṣal,* as heard in 76.1.

➲ 3.3, 10.1, 12.5, 57.4, 76.1, 81.4, 88.5, 103.4, 138.5, 166.5, 189.4, 212.1, 214.1, 249.5

261 to deliver wáṣṣal وصّل 13 1

verbal noun: tawṣīl توْصيل

perfect

	affirmative		negative	
ána	waṣṣált	وَصّلْت	ma-waṣṣáltiš	مَوَصّلْتِش
íḥna	waṣṣálna	وَصّلْنا	ma-waṣṣalnāš	مَوَصّلْناش
ínta	waṣṣált	وَصّلْت	ma-waṣṣáltiš	مَوَصّلْتِش
ínti	waṣṣálti	وَصّلْتي	ma-waṣṣaltīš	مَوَصّلْتيش
íntu	waṣṣáltu	وَصّلْتوا	ma-waṣṣaltūš	مَوَصّلْتوش
húwwa	wáṣṣal	وَصّل	ma-waṣṣálš	مَوَصّلْش
híyya	waṣṣálit	وَصّلِت	ma-waṣṣalítš	مَوَصّلِتْش
húmma	waṣṣálu	وَصّلوا	ma-waṣṣalūš	مَوَصّلوش

imperfect

	affirmative		negative	
ána	awáṣṣal	أوَصّل	ma-waṣṣálš	مَوَصّلْش
íḥna	niwáṣṣal	نِوَصّل	ma-nwaṣṣálš	مَنْوَصّلْش
ínta	tiwáṣṣal	تِوَصّل	ma-twaṣṣálš	مَتْوَصّلْش
ínti	tiwaṣṣáli	تِوَصّلي	ma-twaṣṣalīš	مَتْوَصّليش
íntu	tiwaṣṣálu	تِوَصّلوا	ma-twaṣṣalūš	مَتْوَصّلوش
húwwa	yiwáṣṣal	يِوَصّل	ma-ywaṣṣálš	مَيْوَصّلْش
híyya	tiwáṣṣal	تِوَصّل	ma-twaṣṣálš	مَتْوَصّلْش
húmma	yiwaṣṣálu	يِوَصّلوا	ma-ywaṣṣalūš	مَيْوَصّلوش

bi-imperfect

	affirmative		negative	
ána	bawáṣṣal	بَوَصّل	ma-bawaṣṣálš	مَبَوَصّلْش
íḥna	binwáṣṣal	بِنْوَصّل	ma-binwaṣṣálš	مَبِنْوَصّلْش
ínta	bitwáṣṣal	بِتْوَصّل	ma-bitwaṣṣálš	مَبِتْوَصّلْش
ínti	bitwaṣṣáli	بِتْوَصّلي	ma-bitwaṣṣalīš	مَبِتْوَصّليش
íntu	bitwaṣṣálu	بِتْوَصّلوا	ma-bitwaṣṣalūš	مَبِتْوَصّلوش
húwwa	biywáṣṣal	بِيْوَصّل	ma-biywaṣṣálš	مَبِيْوَصّلْش
híyya	bitwáṣṣal	بِتْوَصّل	ma-bitwaṣṣálš	مَبِتْوَصّلْش
húmma	biywaṣṣálu	بِيْوَصّلوا	ma-biywaṣṣalūš	مَبِيْوَصّلوش

future

	affirmative		negative	
ána	hawáṣṣal	هَوَصّل	miš hawáṣṣal	مِش هَوَصّل
íḥna	hanwáṣṣal	هَنْوَصّل	miš hanwáṣṣal	مِش هَنْوَصّل
ínta	hatwáṣṣal	هَتْوَصّل	miš hatwáṣṣal	مِش هَتْوَصّل
ínti	hatwaṣṣáli	هَتْوَصّلي	miš hatwaṣṣáli	مِش هَتْوَصّلي
íntu	hatwaṣṣálu	هَتْوَصّلوا	miš hatwaṣṣálu	مِش هَتْوَصّلوا
húwwa	haywáṣṣal	هَيْوَصّل	miš haywáṣṣal	مِش هَيْوَصّل
híyya	hatwáṣṣal	هَتْوَصّل	miš hatwáṣṣal	مِش هَتْوَصّل
húmma	haywaṣṣálu	هَيْوَصّلوا	miš haywaṣṣálu	مِش هَيْوَصّلوا

imperative

	affirmative		negative	
ínta	wáṣṣal	وَصّل	ma-twaṣṣálš	مَتْوَصّلْش
ínti	waṣṣáli	وَصّلي	ma-twaṣṣalīš	مَتْوَصّليش
íntu	waṣṣálu	وَصّلوا	ma-twaṣṣalūš	مَتْوَصّلوش

participles

	active		passive	
masculine	miwáṣṣal	مِوَصّل	mitwáṣṣal	مِتْوَصّل
feminine	miwaṣṣála	مِوَصّلَة	mitwaṣṣála	مِتْوَصّلَة
plural	miwaṣṣalīn	مِوَصّلين	mitwaṣṣalīn	مِتْوَصّلين

①

الوَلد وَصّلّنا البيْض نُصُّه مْكسّر.

ilwálad waṣṣallína -lbēḍ núṣṣu mkássar.

When the boy delivered the eggs to us, half of them were broken.

②

المحلّ ده دايْماً يِوَصّل الطّلبات بِسُرْعة.

ilmaḫállᵊ da dáyman yiwáṣṣal iṭṭalabāt bi-súr3a.

This market always delivers things fast.

③

بِتْوَصّلوا الوِلاد البيْت السّاعة كام؟

bitwaṣṣálu -lwilād ilbēt issā3a kām?

What time do you drive the kids home?

④

هتْوَصّلْني في سِكّتك بِسُرْعة.

hatwaṣṣálni f sikkítak bi-súr3a.

Quickly drop me off on your way.

⑤

متْوَصّلْش الوِلاد المدْرسة مِتْأخّر.

ma-twaṣṣálš ilwilād ilmadrása mitʔáxxar.

Don't drop the kids off late for school.

⑥

الشّاشة مِش راضْيَة تِشْتغل عشان إنْتَ مَوَصّلْتهاش بِالكهْربا.

iššāša miš ráḍya tištáɣal 3ašān ínta ma-waṣṣaltahāš bi-lkahrába.

The monitor won't work because you haven't connected it to power.

⑦

إبْني الصُّغيرّ حاوِل يِوَصّل النُّقط بِبعْضها بسّ معْرفْش.

íbni -ṣṣuɣáyyar ḫāwil yiwáṣṣal innúʔaṭ bi-ba3ḍáha bassᵊ ma-3rífš.

My little son tried to connect the dots, but he couldn't.

❖ [2s2] **to deliver; to drop off; to connect**

- This verb can be ditransitive, taking two direct objects. The first object can be the person or thing delivered while the second object is the destination (➲ 261.3, 261.5), or the first object can be the person something is delivered to while the second is the thing delivered (➲ 261.1).

➲ 123.1, 152.1

262 to fall wiʔiʔ3 وِقِع

	affirmative		negative		
ána	wiʔí3t	وِقِعْت	ma-wʔí3tiš	مَوْقِعْتِش	perfect
íḥna	wiʔí3na	وِقِعْنا	ma-wʔi3nāš	مَوْقِعْناش	
ínta	wiʔí3t	وِقِعْت	ma-wʔí3tiš	مَوْقِعْتِش	
ínti	wiʔí3ti	وِقِعْتي	ma-wʔi3tīš	مَوْقِعْتيش	
íntu	wiʔí3tu	وِقِعْتوا	ma-wʔi3tūš	مَوْقِعْتوش	
húwwa	wíʔi3	وِقِع	ma-wʔí3š	مَوْقِعْش	
híyya	wíʔ3it	وِقْعِت	ma-wiʔ3ítš	مَوِقْعِتْش	
húmma	wíʔ3u	وِقْعوا	ma-wiʔ3ūš	مَوِقْعوش	
ána	áʔa3	أَقَع	ma-ʔá3š	مَقَعْش	imperfect
íḥna	núʔa3	نُقَع	ma-nuʔá3š	مَنُقَعْش	
ínta	túʔa3	تُقَع	ma-tuʔá3š	مَتُقَعْش	
ínti	túʔa3i	تُقَعي	ma-tuʔa3īš	مَتُقَعيش	
íntu	túʔa3u	تُقَعوا	ma-tuʔa3ūš	مَتُقَعوش	
húwwa	yúʔa3	يُقَع	ma-yuʔá3š	مَيُقَعْش	
híyya	túʔa3	تُقَع	ma-tuʔá3š	مَتُقَعْش	
húmma	yúʔa3u	يُقَعوا	ma-yuʔa3ūš	مَيُقَعوش	
ána	báʔa3	بَقَع	ma-baʔá3š	مَبَقَعْش	bi-imperfect
íḥna	binúʔa3	بِنُقَع	ma-bnuʔá3š	مَبْنُقَعْش	
ínta	bitúʔa3	بِتُقَع	ma-btuʔá3š	مَبْتُقَعْش	
ínti	bitúʔa3i	بِتُقَعي	ma-btuʔa3īš	مَبْتُقَعيش	
íntu	bitúʔa3u	بِتُقَعوا	ma-btuʔa3ūš	مَبْتُقَعوش	
húwwa	biyúʔa3	بِيُقَع	ma-byuʔá3š	مَبْيُقَعْش	
híyya	bitúʔa3	بِتُقَع	ma-btuʔá3š	مَبْتُقَعْش	
húmma	biyúʔa3u	بِيُقَعوا	ma-byuʔa3ūš	مَبْيُقَعوش	
ána	háʔa3	هَقَع	miš háʔa3	مِش هَقَع	future
íḥna	hanúʔa3	هَنُقَع	miš hanúʔa3	مِش هَنُقَع	
ínta	hatúʔa3	هَتُقَع	miš hatúʔa3	مِش هَتُقَع	
ínti	hatúʔa3i	هَتُقَعي	miš hatúʔa3i	مِش هَتُقَعي	
íntu	hatúʔa3u	هَتُقَعوا	miš hatúʔa3u	مِش هَتُقَعوا	
húwwa	hayúʔa3	هَيُقَع	miš hayúʔa3	مِش هَيُقَع	
híyya	hatúʔa3	هَتُقَع	miš hatúʔa3	مِش هَتُقَع	
húmma	hayúʔa3u	هَيُقَعوا	miš hayúʔa3u	مِش هَيُقَعوا	
ínta	úʔa3	أُقَع	ma-tuʔá3š	مَتُقَعْش	imperative
ínti	úʔa3i	أُقَعي	ma-tuʔa3īš	مَتُقَعيش	
íntu	úʔa3u	أُقَعوا	ma-tuʔa3ūš	مَتُقَعوش	

	active		passive		
masculine	wāʔi3	واقِع	mawʔū3	مَوْقوع	participles
feminine	wáʔ3a	واقْعَة	mawʔū3a	مَوْقوعَة	
plural	waʔ3īn	واقْعين	mawʔu3īn	مَوْقوعين	

verbal noun: wuʔū3 وُقوع

①

أيْمن وِقِع في حُبّ أميرة مِن أوِّل نظْرة.

áyman wíʔi3 fi ħubb amīra min áwwil náẓra.

Ayman fell in love with
Amira at first sight.

②

حاسْبي تِتْكعْبِلي بْفُسْتانِك الطّويل ده. تُقعي عَ المسْرح.

ħásbi titka3bíli b-fustānik iṭṭawīl da. túʔa3i 3a -lmásraħ.

Be careful not to trip on your long dress.
You might fall in the theater.

③

بُصّ، الشّجرة دي بْيُقع مِنْها توت.

buṣṣ, iššágara di byúʔa3 mínha tūt.

Look, mulberries are falling
from this tree.

④

اِوْعى الوَلد هَيُقع مِن عَ الشّجرة.

íw3a -lwálad hayúʔa3 min 3a -ššágara.

Watch out, or the boy will
fall out of the tree.

⑤

متُقعْش في نفْس الغلْطة مرِّتيْن.

ma-tuʔá3š^ə f nafs ilɣálṭa marritēn.

Don't make [lit. fall into] the
same mistake twice.

❖ [i5] **to fall**

- The ُ *u* of the imperfect personal prefixes does not elide, as an exception to the rules of vowel elision. (➲ *Pronunciaiton: Sound Changes: Vowel Elision* p. vi)

➲ 51.1, 145.3, 150.2, 153.1, 164.7, 190.5, 211.1, 262.2, 262.5

263 to stand wíʔif وِقِف

	affirmative		negative		
ána	wiʔíft	وِقِفْت	ma-wʔíftiš	مَوْقِفْتِش	perfect
íḥna	wiʔífna	وِقِفْنا	ma-wʔifnāš	مَوْقِفْناش	
ínta	wiʔíft	وِقِفْت	ma-wʔíftiš	مَوْقِفْتِش	
ínti	wiʔífti	وِقِفْتي	ma-wʔiftīš	مَوْقِفْتيش	
íntu	wiʔíftu	وِقِفْتوا	ma-wʔiftūš	مَوْقِفْتوش	
húwwa	wíʔif	وِقِف	ma-wʔífš	مَوْقِفْش	
híyya	wíʔfit	وِقْفِت	ma-wiʔfítš	مَوِقْفِتْش	
húmma	wíʔfu	وِقْفوا	ma-wiʔfūš	مَوِقْفوش	
ána	áʔaf	أقَف	ma-ʔáfš	مَقَفْش	imperfect
íḥna	núʔaf	نُقَف	ma-nuʔáfš	مَنْقَفْش	
ínta	túʔaf	تُقَف	ma-tuʔáfš	مَتْقَفْش	
ínti	túʔafi	تُقَفي	ma-tuʔafīš	مَتْقَفيش	
íntu	túʔafu	تُقَفوا	ma-tuʔafūš	مَتْقَفوش	
húwwa	yúʔaf	يُقَف	ma-yuʔáfš	مَيْقَفْش	
híyya	túʔaf	تُقَف	ma-tuʔáfš	مَتْقَفْش	
húmma	yúʔafu	يُقَفوا	ma-yuʔafūš	مَيْقَفوش	
ána	báʔaf	بَقَف	ma-baʔáfš	مَبَقَفْش	bi-imperfect
íḥna	binúʔaf	بِنُقَف	ma-bnuʔáfš	مَبْنُقَفْش	
ínta	bitúʔaf	بِتُقَف	ma-btuʔáfš	مَبْتُقَفْش	
ínti	bitúʔafi	بِتُقَفي	ma-btuʔafīš	مَبْتُقَفيش	
íntu	bitúʔafu	بِتُقَفوا	ma-btuʔafūš	مَبْتُقَفوش	
húwwa	biyúʔaf	بِيُقَف	ma-byuʔáfš	مَبْيُقَفْش	
híyya	bitúʔaf	بِتُقَف	ma-btuʔáfš	مَبْتُقَفْش	
húmma	biyúʔafu	بِيُقَفوا	ma-byuʔafūš	مَبْيُقَفوش	
ána	háʔaf	هَقَف	miš háʔaf	مِش هَقَف	future
íḥna	hanúʔaf	هَنُقَف	miš hanúʔaf	مِش هَنُقَف	
ínta	hatúʔaf	هَتُقَف	miš hatúʔaf	مِش هَتُقَف	
ínti	hatúʔafi	هَتُقَفي	miš hatúʔafi	مِش هَتُقَفي	
íntu	hatúʔafu	هَتُقَفوا	miš hatúʔafu	مِش هَتُقَفوا	
húwwa	hayúʔaf	هَيُقَف	miš hayúʔaf	مِش هَيُقَف	
híyya	hatúʔaf	هَتُقَف	miš hatúʔaf	مِش هَتُقَف	
húmma	hayúʔafu	هَيُقَفوا	miš hayúʔafu	مِش هَيُقَفوا	
ínta	úʔaf	أُقَف	ma-tuʔáfš	مَتْقَفْش	imperative
ínti	úʔafi	أُقَفي	ma-tuʔafīš	مَتْقَفيش	
íntu	úʔafu	أُقَفوا	ma-tuʔafūš	مَتْقَفوش	

	active		passive		
masculine	wāʔif	واقِف	—	—	participles
feminine	wáʔfa	واقْفَة	—	—	
plural	waʔfīn	واقْفين	—	—	

verbal noun: wuʔūf وُقوف

①

مُصْطفى وِقِف في طابور العيْش ساعة.

muṣṭáfa wíʔif fi ṭabūr il3ēš sā3a.

Mostafa stood in line for an hour to buy bread.

②

أخويا دايْماً يُقف صفّ تاني بْعربِيّتُه.

axūya dáyman yúʔaf ṣaffᵊ tāni b-3arabītu.

My brother always parks his car in the second row.

③

نائِل لمّا بْيِبْقى مِسْتعْجِل، مبْيُقفْش في الطّريق لِايّ سبب.

nāʔil lámma byíbʔa mistá3gil, ma-byuʔáfšᵊ f -ṭṭarīʔ li-ayyᵊ sábab.

When Nael is in a hurry, he never stops for any reason on his way.

④

أوِّل ما تْشاوِرْلي هقف.

áwwil ma tšawírli háʔaf.

Once you wave to me, I'll stop.

⑤

متُقفْش هِنا مِن فضْلك.

ma-tuʔáfšᵊ hína min fáḍlak.

Please don't stand here.

❖ [i5] **to stand; to stop**

- This verb is intransitive. Compare with the transitive وَقّف *wáʔʔaf*. (➲ 264)

➲ 36.5, 73.1, 131.3, 149.5, 214.5, 228.4, 263.5

264 to stop wáʔʔaf وقّف 13

verbal noun: tawʔīf توقيف

	affirmative		negative		
ána	waʔʔáft	وَقّفْت	ma-waʔʔáftiš	مَوَقّفْتِش	perfect
íḥna	waʔʔáfna	وَقّفْنا	ma-waʔʔafnāš	مَوَقّفْناش	
ínta	waʔʔáft	وَقّفْت	ma-waʔʔáftiš	مَوَقّفْتِش	
ínti	waʔʔáfti	وَقّفْتي	ma-waʔʔaftīš	مَوَقّفْتيش	
íntu	waʔʔáftu	وَقّفْتوا	ma-waʔʔaftūš	مَوَقّفْتوش	
húwwa	wáʔʔaf	وَقّف	ma-waʔʔáfš	مَوَقّفْش	
híyya	waʔʔáfit	وَقّفِت	ma-waʔʔafítš	مَوَقّفِتْش	
húmma	waʔʔáfu	وَقّفوا	ma-waʔʔafūš	مَوَقّفوش	
ána	awáʔʔaf	أوَقّف	ma-waʔʔáfš	مَوَقّفْش	imperfect
íḥna	niwáʔʔaf	نِوَقّف	ma-nwaʔʔáfš	مَنْوَقّفْش	
ínta	tiwáʔʔaf	تِوَقّف	ma-twaʔʔáfš	مَتْوَقّفْش	
ínti	tiwaʔʔáfi	تِوَقّفي	ma-twaʔʔafīš	مَتْوَقّفيش	
íntu	tiwaʔʔáfu	تِوَقّفوا	ma-twaʔʔafūš	مَتْوَقّفوش	
húwwa	yiwáʔʔaf	يِوَقّف	ma-ywaʔʔáfš	مَيْوَقّفْش	
híyya	tiwáʔʔaf	تِوَقّف	ma-twaʔʔáfš	مَتْوَقّفْش	
húmma	yiwaʔʔáfu	يِوَقّفوا	ma-ywaʔʔafūš	مَيْوَقّفوش	
ána	bawáʔʔaf	بَوَقّف	ma-bawaʔʔáfš	مَبَوَقّفْش	bi-imperfect
íḥna	binwáʔʔaf	بِنْوَقّف	ma-binwaʔʔáfš	مَبِنْوَقّفْش	
ínta	bitwáʔʔaf	بِتْوَقّف	ma-bitwaʔʔáfš	مَبِتْوَقّفْش	
ínti	bitwaʔʔáfi	بِتْوَقّفي	ma-bitwaʔʔafīš	مَبِتْوَقّفيش	
íntu	bitwaʔʔáfu	بِتْوَقّفوا	ma-bitwaʔʔafūš	مَبِتْوَقّفوش	
húwwa	biywáʔʔaf	بِيْوَقّف	ma-biywaʔʔáfš	مَبِيْوَقّفْش	
híyya	bitwáʔʔaf	بِتْوَقّف	ma-bitwaʔʔáfš	مَبِتْوَقّفْش	
húmma	biywaʔʔáfu	بِيْوَقّفوا	ma-biywaʔʔafūš	مَبِيْوَقّفوش	
ána	hawáʔʔaf	هَوَقّف	miš hawáʔʔaf	مِش هَوَقّف	future
íḥna	hanwáʔʔaf	هَنْوَقّف	miš hanwáʔʔaf	مِش هَنْوَقّف	
ínta	hatwáʔʔaf	هَتْوَقّف	miš hatwáʔʔaf	مِش هَتْوَقّف	
ínti	hatwaʔʔáfi	هَتْوَقّفي	miš hatwaʔʔáfi	مِش هَتْوَقّفي	
íntu	hatwaʔʔáfu	هَتْوَقّفوا	miš hatwaʔʔáfu	مِش هَتْوَقّفوا	
húwwa	haywáʔʔaf	هَيْوَقّف	miš haywáʔʔaf	مِش هَيْوَقّف	
híyya	hatwáʔʔaf	هَتْوَقّف	miš hatwáʔʔaf	مِش هَتْوَقّف	
húmma	haywaʔʔáfu	هَيْوَقّفوا	miš haywaʔʔáfu	مِش هَيْوَقّفوا	
ínta	wáʔʔaf	وَقّف	ma-twaʔʔáfš	مَتْوَقّفْش	imperative
ínti	waʔʔáfi	وَقّفي	ma-twaʔʔafīš	مَتْوَقّفيش	
íntu	waʔʔáfu	وَقّفوا	ma-twaʔʔafūš	مَتْوَقّفوش	

	active		passive		
masculine	miwáʔʔaf	مِوَقّف	mitwáʔʔaf	مِتْوَقّف	participles
feminine	miwaʔʔáfa	مِوَقّفة	mitwaʔʔáfa	مِتْوَقّفة	
plural	miwaʔʔafīn	مِوَقّفين	mitwaʔʔafīn	مِتْوَقّفين	

①

حُسام وَقّف تدْخين لمّا الدُّكْتور حذّرُه.

ḫusām wáʔʔaf tadxīn lámma -dduktūr ḫazzáru.

Hossam stopped smoking when
the doctor warned him.

②

ماهي لازِم تِوَقّف الفيْسْبوك شُوَيّة. دي مبْتِعْمِلْش حاجة تانْيَة في حَياتْها.

māhi lāzim tiwáʔʔaf ilfēsbūk šuwáyya. di ma-bti3mílšᵊ ḫāga tánya f ḫayátha.

Mahy should lay off Facebook for a while.
She doesn't do anything else in her life.

③

غدير مبِتْوَقّفْش رغْي طول النّهار.

ɣadīr ma-bitwaʔʔáfšᵊ raɣyᵊ ṭūl innahār.

Ghader doesn't stop talking all day.

④

هُمّا هَيْوَقّفوا الصّوْت المُزْعِج ده إمْتى؟

húmma haywaʔʔáfu -ṣṣōt ilmúz3ig da ʔímta?

When will they stop making
that annoying noise?

⑤

متْوَقّفْش سعْي وَرا حِلْمك.

ma-twaʔʔáfšᵊ sa3yᵊ wára ḫílmak.

Don't stop chasing your dream.

⑥

وقّفْت العربية في آخِر لحْظة عشان مخبطْش القُطّة.

waʔʔáft il3arabíyya fi ʔāxir láḫẓa 3ašān ma-xbáṭš ilʔúṭṭa.

I stopped the car just in time not to hit the cat.

⑦

وَقّفْلِنا تاكْسي عشان نِروّح.

waʔʔaflína táksi 3ašān niráwwaḫ.

Hail a taxi for us to get home.

❖ [2s2] **to stop** (something)

- This verb is transitive. Compare with the intransitive وِقِف *wíʔif*. (➲ 263)
- It can be followed by a verbal noun. (➲ 264.1, 264.3, 264.5)

INDEX

You can look up verbs by their English translations using references to their TABLE numbers. For example, T-264 refers to table 264 (on p. 532).

CPSIA information can be obtained
at www.ICGtesting.com
Printed in the USA
BVHW010500300921
617778BV00009B/43

9 780985 816094